ASIA AND THE PACIFIC

A HANDBOOK

Volume 2

HANDBOOKS TO THE MODERN WORLD

HANDBOOKS TO THE MODERN WORLD

ASIA AND THE PACIFIC

Volume 2

Edited by

ROBERT H. TAYLOR

Facts On File

New York • Oxford

ASIA AND THE PACIFIC
Copyright © 1991 by Facts On File Publications

Facts On File, Inc.   Facts On File Limited
460 Park Avenue South   or   Collins Street
New York NY 10016   Oxford OX4 1XJ
USA   United Kingdom

British CIP data available on request from Facts On File.

Facts On File books are available at special discounts when purchased in bulk quantities for businesses, associations, institutions or sales promotion. Please contact the Special Sales Department of our New York office at 212/683-2244 (dial 800/322-8755 except in NY, AK or HI).

Library of Congress Cataloging-in-Publication Data
Asia and the Pacific / edited by Robert H. Taylor.
       p.   cm. — (Handbooks to the modern world)
     Includes bibliographical references.
     1. Asia.   2. Australasia.   3. Islands of the Pacific.   I. Taylor,
Robert H., 1943–   II. Series: Handbooks to the modern world
(Facts on File, Inc.)
DS5.A79 1990
950—dc20   89-23376
     ISBN 0-8160-1826-x (Vol. I)   CIP
     ISBN 0-8160-1827-8 (Vol. II)
     ISBN 0-8160-1622-4 (set)

Composition by Maple-Vail Book Manufacturing Group
Manufactured by Maple-Vail Book Manufacturing Group
Printed in the United States of America

10 9 8 7 6 5 4 3 2 1

This book is printed on acid-free paper.

CONTRIBUTORS

SHIRIN AKINER is lecturer in Central Asian studies at the School of Oriental and African Studies, University of London. Her publications include *Islamic Peoples of the Soviet Union* (1986). She has traveled widely in Soviet Central Asia and western China, and has been a consultant on many films and broadcasts on these regions.

BARBARA WATSON ANDAYA received her doctorate in history from Cornell University and has held positions at the University of Malaya and the Australian National University. She is now senior tutor in the department of history at Auckland University, New Zealand. Her major publications include *Perak, the Abode of Grace: A Study of an Eighteenth Century Malay State* (1979) and *A History of Malaysia* (with Leonard Y. Andaya, 1982).

LEONARD Y. ANDAYA is associate professor of history and director of the Centre for Asian Studies at the University of Auckland, New Zealand. He has taught at the University of Malaya and has been a research fellow in the department of Pacific and Southeast Asian history at the Australian National University. His publications include *The Kingdom of Johor 1641–1728* (1975), *The Heritage of Arung Palakka: A History of South Sulawesi (Celebes) in the Seventeenth Century* (1981) and *A History of Malaysia* (with Barbara Watson Andaya, 1982).

ROBERT F. ASH is lecturer in economics at the School of Oriental and African Studies, University of London, where he is also chairman of the Contemporary China Institute. He has published widely on Chinese agriculture and economy.

HUGH D. R. BAKER is reader in modern Chinese at the University of London, where he teaches Mandarin and Cantonese as well as Chinese social institutions. He has carried out anthropological fieldwork in Hong Kong and China. Publications include *A Chinese Lineage Village: Sheung Shui* (1968), *Ancestral Images: A Hong Kong Album*, 3 vols. (1979–81), *New Peace County: A Chinese Gazetteer of the Hong Kong Region* (with Peter Y. L. Ng, 1983) and *The Overseas Chinese* (1987).

SANJOY BANERJEE is a lecturer in the international relations program at San Francisco State University. He received his doctorate from Yale University in international relations in 1982 and is the author of *Dominant Classes and the State in Development: Theory and the Case of India* (1984). In addition, he has contributed articles to the *International Studies Quarterly* and the *Journal of Conflict Resolution*.

CRAIG BAXTER, professor of the politics and history of Asia at Juniata College, Huntingdon, Pennsylvania, was a U.S. Foreign Service officer from 1956 to 1980 and served in several posts in South Asia, including Dhaka. Among his books are *Bangladesh: A New Nation in an Old Setting* (1984) and *A Historical Dictionary of*

Bangladesh (with Syedur Rahman, forthcoming). He has also written extensively on Pakistan and India.

JAMES R. BRANDON is professor in the department of drama and theater, University of Hawaii, Manoa. His major publications include *Traditional Asian Plays* (1972), *Kabuki: Five Classic Plays* (1975) and *Chushingura: Studies in Kabuki and the Puppet Theater* (1982). Brandon was founding editor of the *Asian Theatre Journal*.

IAN BROWN is lecturer in economic history with reference to Southeast Asia at the School of Oriental and African Studies, University of London. He is the author of *The Elite and the Economy in Siam, c. 1890–1920* (1988) and is editor of and contributor to *The Economics of Africa and Asia in the later-War Depression* (1989).

RICHARD BURGHART was educated at Williams College and the University of London. He has taught at the London School of Economics and the School of Oriental and African Studies, University of London. His present post is at Heidelberg University. He has published widely on Bhutan and Nepal, and has edited works on Hinduism in Great Britain and on Indian religions.

LARRY L. BURMEISTER is assistant professor of sociology at the University of Kentucky and a specialist in international development. His recent publications include *Research, Realpolitik and Development in Korea: The State and the Green Revolution,* and articles in *Pacific Focus, Economic Development* and *Cultural Change.*

TERENCE J. BYRES, founder-editor of the *Journal of Peasant Studies,* is senior lecturer in economics at the School of Oriental and African Studies, University of London. He has written extensively on the Indian economy, especially the agrarian question. Among his works are contributions to *Sharecropping and Sharecroppers* (1983) and *Feudalism and Non-European Societies* (1985).

CHAN HENG CHEE is former head of the department of political science at the National University of Singapore, and is at present director of the Institute of Policy Studies, Singapore. Dr. Chan is the author of many books and articles, including *Singapore: The Politics of Survival, 1965–1967* (1971) and *The Dynamics of One Party Dominance: The PAP at the Grassroots* (1976).

DAVID CHANDLER is research director of Southeast Asian studies at Monash University, Melbourne. Educated at Harvard, Yale and Michigan, he served in the U.S. Foreign Service in Cambodia in the early 1960s. He is the author of numerous publications, including *A History of Cambodia* (1983) and *The Tragedy of Cambodian History* (forthcoming).

EDWARD K. Y. CHEN is director of Asian studies, University of Hong Kong, has held visiting professorships at Yale, Oxford, the East-West Center in Hawaii and the University of California at Davis. He is the author of *Hyper-Growth in Asian Economies* (1979) and *Multinational Corporations: Technology and Employment* (1983).

YANGSUN CHOU is a graduate of National Taiwan University and a doctoral candidate in the department of political science, Columbia University. He is the author and editor of numerous books and articles in Chinese, and teaches political science at National Taiwan University.

STEPHEN P. COHEN, professor of political science in Asian studies at the University of Illinois, has worked on the policy planning staff of the U.S. Department of State (1985–87). He is the author or editor of five books, including *The Pakistan Army* and *The Security of South Asia*. He is cofounder of the Program in Arms Control, Disarmament and International Security at the University of Illinois.

ELISABETH CROLL, a fellow at the School of Oriental and African Studies, University of London, is an anthropologist who has spent over a decade engaged in research on the People's Republic of China. She is the author of numerous books on China, including *Feminism and Socialism in China*, *The Politics of Marriage in Contemporary China*, *The Family Rice Bowl: Food and the Domestic Economy in China*, and *Chinese Women since Mao*. She has undertaken several studies and consultancies for the United Nations and other agencies.

BRUCE CUMINGS is professor of East Asian history at the University of Chicago and the author of the two-volume study *The Origins of the Korean War* (1981, 1989) as well as *Industrial Behemoth: The Northeast Asian Political Economy in the 20th Century* (forthcoming). He visited North Korea twice in 1987 with a Thames Television documentary film team.

CHRISTOPHER FINDLAY received his doctorate in economics from the Australian National University, where he subsequently did research on East Asia in the Research School of Pacific Studies. In 1984 he joined the economics department of the University of Adelaide, where he is a visiting senior lecturer. He is also a research associate of the Australia-Japan Research Centre at the Australian National University. Findlay's major publications include *The Political Economy of Manufacturing Protection: Experiences of ASEAN and Australia* (jointly edited with Ross Garnaut, 1986).

DON M. FLOURNOY is associate professor in the school of telecommunications at Ohio University, where he served as dean of University College for 10 years. Educated at Southern Methodist University, University of Texas, Boston University and the University of London, Flournoy has worked as a consultant to the ministries of Education, Information and Science, and Technologies of Indonesia; and he has conducted research on corporate video and the new technologies of telecommunication, especially satellite communications in development.

HARUHIRO FUKUI is a professor in the department of political science, University of California, Santa Barbara. He studied at Tokyo University and received his doctorate from the Australian National University. Fukui's publications include *Party in Power: The Japanese Liberal-Democrats and Policy-Making* (coauthor, 1970), *Managing an Alliance: The Politics of U.S.-Japanese Relations* (1976), *The Textile Wrangle: Conflict in Japanese-American Relations, 1969–1971* (1979) and *Japan and the New Ocean Regime* (1985). He also edited *Political Parties of Asia and the Pacific* (1985) and *Japan and the World* (1988).

SUMIT GANGULY is an assistant professor of political science at Hunter College of the City University of New York. He is the author of *The Origins of War in South Asia: The Indo-Pakistani Conflicts since 1947* (1986) and is at present working on a book that seeks to reassess the origins of the Sino-Indian border war of 1962.

ANTHONY GOLDSTONE is editor for the Far East and Australasia at the Economist Intelligence Unit in London.

SHARON HOFFMAN, who holds a master's degree in public policy from Carnegie-Mellon University, is a research fellow with the Energy Program at the East-West Center in Honolulu, where she supervises research on the Australian and Philippine energy programs as well as the Ocean Thermal Energy Conversion project. She was previously a research fellow at Harvard University and has worked as a consultant for several governments and oil companies. Her publications include *World Synthetic Fuels Production: A Realistic Assessment* (with David T. Isaak, 1983) and *Deregulating Australia's Oil: The Implications for Global and Regional Markets* (with Fereidun Fesharaki, 1987).

CHRISTOPHER HOWE is professor of the economics of Asia at the School of Oriental and African Studies, University of London. He has written widely on the economies of China and Japan.

COLIN A. HUGHES is a graduate of Columbia University and the London School of Economics. He has written extensively about Australian government and politics, and elections in particular. He is professor of government at the University of Queensland and has been professorial fellow in political science at the Institute of Advanced Studies at the Australian National University (1975–84). In 1984–88 he was electoral commissioner of Australia.

GRAHAM HUTCHINGS, a journalist and historian, is China specialist with the London *Daily Telegraph*. He has written on the Republican period in Chinese history for the *China Quarterly,* and has taught modern Chinese history at Hatfield Polytechnic and the City Literary Institute, London.

CHRISTINE INGLIS is senior lecturer in the department of social and policy studies at the University of Sydney. She has conducted research on a variety of educational topics, including ethnic relations in Australia, Southeast Asia and the Pacific, and their relevance to education and economics.

TAKASHI INOGUCHI is associate professor of political science at the University of Tokyo. He received a doctorate at the Massachusetts Institute of Technology, and has worked at Sophia University in Japan, the Graduate Institute of International Studies in Geneva, Harvard University and the Australian National University. Inoguchi has published 10 books in Japanese and in English, his most recent being *State and Societies* (in Japanese) and Vol. 2 of *The Political Economy of Japan: The Changing International Context,* of which he was coeditor (1988). He has also served on the editorial boards of such publications as the *Journal of Japanese Studies* and *International Studies Quarterly.*

GEORGE JOFFE is consulting editor for the Middle East and North Africa for The Economist publications; research associate, Centre of Near and Middle East Studies, School of Oriental and African Studies, University of London; and the author of the articles "Islam in Africa" and "The Maghreb, or Western Arab World: Algeria, Morocco and Tunisia" in companion volumes of the Handbooks to the Modern World series.

GAVIN W. JONES is professorial fellow in the department of demography of the Research School of Social Sciences at the Australian National University. He has worked with the Population Council in New York City, and has spent 10 years working with universities and planning agencies in Indonesia, Malaysia, Thailand and Sri Lanka. Dr. Jones has published several books and many articles on population and development issues in Indonesia, Malaysia and Asia generally, as well as on educational planning and population mobility.

AUDREY KAHIN was educated at Nottingham University and Cornell University. She is the editor of Cornell's journal *Indonesia*, as well as of many other publications of the Cornell Southeast Asia Program. Dr. Kahin is the author of articles on the Indonesian revolution, Minangkabau society and the nationalist movement. She has edited *Regional Dynamics of the Indonesian Revolution* (1985), coedited *Interpreting Indonesian Politics* (1982) and translated *Prisoners of Kota Cane* (1986).

FAITH KEENAN, graduate of Columbia University's School of International Affairs, has worked for the Intergovernmental Committee for Migration at the Philippine Refugee Processing Center (1983) and has covered Indochina and Thailand as a reporter for United Press International's Bangkok bureau (1985). She has traveled extensively in Indoichina and has written several articles for Hearst Newspapers on Vietnam, Cambodia and Laos. She is a contributor to *Indochina Issues*, a publication of the Indochina Project in Washington, D.C., and is currently a reporter in the New York bureau of Hearst Newspapers.

SIR EDMUND LEACH, F.B.A. (1910–89), was provost of King's College (1966–79), university reader in social anthropology (1957–72) and professor of social anthropology (1972–78) at the University of Cambridge. He was in Myanmar and eastern India during World War II, combining military service with anthropological research. He later did fieldwork in Sarawak and Sri Lanka, and published extensively on the Asia and Pacific region. After taking a first degree from Cambridge in engineering, he received a doctorate in social anthropology from the London School of Economics in 1946.

LEE POH PING received his doctorate from Cornell University in government and teaches in the faculty of economics, University of Malaya, Kuala Lumpur. Dr. Lee has published on the economic and political evolution of Southeast Asia, and on the region's relations with Japan and other extraregional powers.

JOHN A. LENT, who studied in Norway, Mexico, Japan and India, received his doctorate from the University of Iowa. He was a Fulbright Scholar in the Philippines and first coordinator of the pioneering mass communications program in Malaysia, at Universiti Sains Malaysia. He also pioneered in the study of international communications, especially Third World mass media. Lent is a professor at Temple University, Philadelphia, and the founder-director of Third World Media Associates.

R. A. LONGMIRE is editor of *Asian Affairs*, the journal of the Royal Society for Asian Affairs, London. Formerly with the British Foreign Office Research Department as a specialist on Soviet and Southeast Asian affairs, his latest publication is *A Historical Survey of Soviet Relations with South-East Asia* (1988).

ERHARD LOUVEN, holder of a doctorate in economics, was until 1981 research fellow in the department of East Asian sciences at Ruhr University Bochum. He is at present senior research fellow at the Institute for Asian Studies, Hamburg. His major works include *Technologietransfer und angepasste Technologien* (1982) and *Perspektiven der Wirtschaftsreform in China* (1987).

JAMES MANOR is professorial fellow and director of research at the Institute of Development Studies, University of Sussex. He has taught at Yale, Harvard and Leicester universities, and since 1980 has edited the *Journal of Commonwealth and Comparative Politics*. His most recent book is *The Excellent Utopian: Bandaranaike and Ceylon* (forthcoming).

THOMAS W. MARETZKI is professor of medical anthropology at the University of Hawaii, Manoa. He has done research on health-related topics in Southeast Asia and in Hawaii and has served as a consultant to government and private agencies in these regions.

BRUCE MATTHEWS is the C. B. Lumsden professor of comparative religion at Acadia University, Nova Scotia. He is the author of *Craving and Salvation: A Study of Buddhist Soteriology* (1983) and numerous articles on religio-cultural and communal problems in South and Southeast Asia.

F. A. MEDIANSKY holds degrees in government from universities in the United States and Australia. He is associate professor and head of the School of Political Science at the University of New South Wales. He has written widely on Pacific security issues and has coedited a major reader on Australian foreign policy.

JUDITH NAGATA was educated at University College, London, and the University of Illinois. She is professor of anthropology at York University, Toronto, where she is conducting research on Southeast Asian immigrants. Dr. Nagata is the author of *Malaysian Mosaic: Perspectives on a Poly-Ethnic Society* (1979) and *The Reflowering of Malaysian Islam: Modern Religious Radicals and Their Roots* (1984), and has also edited *Pluralism in Malaysia: Myth or Reality?* (1975).

ANDREW J. NATHAN, a member of the department of political science at Columbia University, is author of *Chinese Democracy* (1985), coauthor of *Human Rights in Contemporary China* (1986) and coeditor of *Popular Culture in Late Imperial China* (1985).

WILLIAM NESTER received his doctorate in political science from the University of California, Santa Barbara. He teaches politics at St. John's University, New York City. He has done research on marine policy issues in the South Pacific and is the author of two forthcoming books: *Japan's Growing Power over East Asia and the World Economy: Ends and Means*; and *Japan's Modern Political Economy: Continuities, Changes, Challenges*.

URMILA PHADNIS is professor of South Asian studies at Jawaharlal Nehru University, New Delhi. She has written extensively on the politics of South Asia, including *Toward Integration of Indian States* (1968), *Sri Lanka* (1972), *Religion and Politics in Sri Lanka* (1976) and *Maldives: Winds of Change in an Atoll State* (with Indira Malani, 1985).

JONATHAN D. POLLACK is head of the political science department of The RAND Corporation, Santa Monica, California. He has published widely on U.S.-Chinese relations, Sino-Soviet affairs, Chinese strategic and technological development, and East Asian security. His recent writings include *Reluctant Warrior: China in the Korean War* (1989) and *Planning for China's Defense: Military R&D in Transition* (1989).

DAVID C. POTTER is senior lecturer in government in the social sciences faculty of the Open University, Great Britain. He is editor of the *Journal of Commonwealth and Comparative Politics*. His research has focused on India's bureaucracy, and his publications include *Government in Rural India* (1964), *Lords, Peasants and Politics* (1974), *The Practice of Comparative Politics* (coeditor, 1978), *Society and the Social Sciences* (coeditor, 1981) and *India's Public Administrators, 1919–1983* (1986).

J. MOHAN RAO, who holds a doctorate in economics from Harvard University, is an assistant professor of economics at Boston University. He has written several articles on the theory of economic development, agrarian relations, agricultural policy and Indian economic history. He has been a consultant to the Food and Agriculture Organization and the World Institute of Development Economics Research.

LINDA K. RICHTER is associate professor of political science at Kansas State University, where she teaches public administration and policy. She is an associate editor of *Annals of Tourism Research,* and the author of two books and many articles on tourism policy. Her most recent volume is *The Politics of Tourism in Asia: A Comparative Policy Perspective* (1989).

WILLIAM L. RICHTER is head of the department of political science at Kansas State University. He has conducted research in India and Pakistan, and has published numerous articles on the South Asian region in such publications as *Asian Survey, Journal of Asian Studies, Pacific Affairs* and *Current History.*

HANS CHRISTOPH RIEGER is research fellow at the South Asia Institute, Heidelberg University. Since 1987 he has been an adviser and visiting fellow of the ASEAN Economic Research Unit of the Institute of Southeast Asian Studies, Singapore, and the representative of the Konrad Adenauer Foundation in Singapore.

ANTHONY ROWLEY was for seven years business editor of the *Far Eastern Economic Review,* and was based in Hong Kong, from where he traveled extensively to study capital market development. He has written for *The Times* of London and has published two books: *Asian Stockmarkets: The Inside Story* and *The Barons of European Industry.* He is at present international finance editor of the *Far Eastern Economic Review* and is based in London.

IRINA RYBACEK is a freelance editor and writer. Since 1980 she has worked on various projects for Scribner's reference department, and she has also edited and written articles for *Worldmark Encyclopedia of the Nations, Lands and Peoples, Academic American Encyclopedia* and *Funk & Wagnalls New Encyclopedia.*

E. F. SCHUMACHER (1911–   ), was born in Bonn and emigrated to England in 1937. He was educated at the universities of Bonn and Berlin, Oxford (as a Rhodes Scholar) and Columbia University. After several years in business, farming and journalism, he joined the British Control Commission for Germany in 1946 as economic adviser. In 1950 he became economic adviser of the National Coal Board, London, and in 1963 director of statistics. In 1955 he was posted to the United Nations as economic adviser to the government of the Union of Burma; and in 1962 he was invited by the government of India to advise the Indian Planning Commission on problems of Indian development policy. Schumacher, who traveled widely in Europe, the United States and Asia, published many articles and several books on economic and philosophical subjects, of which the best known is *Small Is Beautiful: A Study of Economics as if People Mattered* (1973).

HENRY G. SCHWARZ teaches courses on Mongolian history, society and culture, as well as on modern Chinese history at the Center for East Asian Studies of Western Washington University, Bellingham. Over the past 14 years he has spent much time at the Central Nationalities Institute in Beijing and in the border areas of northern China, particularly Inner Mongolia. He has also been a delegate to several conferences of the International Congress of Mongolists in Ulaanbaatar. Professor Schwarz is the director of the Mongolian Summer Program for U.S. students studying Mongolian at Inner Mongolia University.

GERALD SEGAL is editor of the *Pacific Review* and lecturer in politics at the University of Bristol. His publications include *The Great Power Triangle* (1982) and *A Guide to the World Today* (1987); he also edited *The Soviet Union in East Asia* (1984) and *Sino-Soviet Relations after Mao* (1987).

BHABANI SEN GUPTA received his doctorate in comparative politics and international relations from the City University of New York and is research professor at New Delhi's Centre for Policy Research. He has also taught at Jawaharlal Nehru University and at Columbia University. Sen Gupta's numerous articles and 15 books include *The Fulcrum of Asia: Relations among China, India, Pakistan and the USSR* (1968), *Communism in Indian Politics* (1972) and *The Gorbachev Factor in World Politics* (1988).

PHILIP STOTT, a tropical ecologist specializing in Asia, is head of the department of geography and former chairman of the Centre of South East Asian Studies at the School of Oriental and African Studies, University of London. His most recent research has dealt with fire and forestry in Thailand. He is editor of the *Journal of Biogeography* and is a member of the editorial advisory board of *Progress in Physical Geography*. Mr. Stott has written, in addition to other publications, *Historical Plant Geography* (1981), a basic text in the field.

ULF SUNDHAUSSEN has degrees from the Free University, Berlin, and Monash University, Melbourne. He has taught at the University of Papua New Guinea and is now senior lecturer in government at the University of Queensland. He is the author of *The Road to Power: Indonesian Military Politics 1945–1967* and coauthor of *Abdul Haris Nasution: A Political Biography,* and he has written many articles on the military in politics.

DAVID TAYLOR is lecturer in politics with reference to South Asia, and chairman of the Centre of South Asian Studies at the School of Oriental and African Studies, University of London. His field of specialization is the politics of India and Pakistan. He has coedited several volumes, including *Political Identity in South Asia*

(1978) and *Changing South Asia* (1984), and has written numerous articles on India and Pakistan.

ROBERT H. TAYLOR is professor of politics and head of the department of economic and political studies at the School of Oriental and African Studies, University of London. He has taught at the University of Sydney and at Wilberforce University in Ohio. His publications include *The State in Burma* (1987) and he was a contributor to *In Search of Southeast Asia: A Modern History* (edited by David Joel Steinberg, rev. ed. 1987).

M. J. C. TEMPLETON was a New Zealand Foreign Service officer from 1946 to 1984. He served as New Zealand's permanent representative to the United Nations from 1973 to 1978; as leader of the New Zealand delegation to the Law of the Sea Conference, 1978–84; and as deputy secretary of foreign affairs, 1978–84. He was then appointed as the first director of the Institute of Policy Studies at the Victoria University of Wellington, a position he held until 1986. He now coordinates a program of historical research on aspects of the development and conduct of New Zealand's foreign policy.

MARINA THORBORG, an economist who has spent over a decade in research on the People's Republic of China and on Asia, is a fellow at the Center for East and Southeast Asian Studies at the University of Copenhagen. She received her doctorate from the University of Uppsala and has published widely on the subject of women in China and elsewhere in Asia.

CHIEN-CHUNG TSAO is a doctoral candidate in the School of Communication Art and Theater at Temple University, Philadelphia. He holds a master's degree in communication from Western Illinois University (1983). Before he came from Taiwan to the United States, Tsao served as a magazine editor and television producer. He has written several articles in the field of international communications. At present he is an instructor in the department of radio-TV-film at Temple and serves as a research associate for the Third World Media Associates.

WILLIAM S. TURLEY received his doctorate at the University of Washington and is professor of political science at Southern Illinois University. In addition to *The Second Indochina War,* he has written numerous articles and edited volumes on Vietnamese communism and on the third Indochina war. In 1982–84 he was a visiting professor at Chulalongkorn University, Bangkok, under the auspices of the Fulbright Program and the John F. Kennedy Foundation of Thailand.

ANDREW TURTON is senior lecturer in anthropology and chairman of the Centre of South East Asian Studies at the School of Oriental and African Studies, University of London. He has conducted extensive fieldwork in Thailand. His numerous publications include *Production, Power and Participation in Rural Thailand: Experiences of Poor Farmers' Groups* (1987). Turton has also been involved as a consultant in Thailand for various U.N. agencies.

WILFRIDO V. VILLACORTA, who studied at the University of the Philippines and the Catholic University of America, is vice-president of De La Salle University in Manila, where he is also professor of international relations. He is the author of many articles on Philippine politics and affairs, and has been a member of the

Philippines Council for Foreign Relations as well as of the drafting commission of the 1987 Philippine constitution.

ANDREW G. WALDER is professor of sociology at Harvard University. He is the author of *Chang Ch'un-ch'iao and Shanghai's January Revolution* and *Communist Neo-Traditionalism: World and Authority in Chinese Industry*. The latter won the Joseph Levenson prize of the Association of Asian Studies.

MARTIN E. WEINSTEIN holds the Japan chair and is the director of the Japan Program at the Center for Strategic and International Studies in Washington, D.C., while on leave from the University of Illinois. He previously worked at Columbia University, the Brookings Institution and the U.S. Embassy in Tokyo. His numerous publications include *Northeast Asian Security after Vietnam* (1982) and *The Making of Japan's Future Leaders: Portraits of an International Elite*.

JO ANN WHITE, a writer and editor specializing in Third World affairs, holds a master's degree in international relations from New York University. She was managing editor of *Lands and Peoples* and senior social studies editor of *The New Book of Knowledge* and *Academic American Encyclopedia*. Other projects have included work for *Merit Students Encyclopedia, Americana Annual, Worldmark Encyclopedia of the Nations* and *The World and its Peoples*. She is also the author of *Impact: Asian Views of the West and African Views of the West*.

ROBERT WIHTOL, a native of Finland, holds a master's degree from the University of Helsinki and a doctorate from Oxford University. He worked for the International Labor Organization for five years in Asia before taking his present position at the ILO headquarters in Geneva. He is the author of *The Asian Development Bank and Rural Development: Policy and Practice*.

ALAN WOOD is lecturer in Russian history at the University of Lancaster, convenor of the British Universities Siberian Studies Seminar and editor of its journal *SIBIRICA*. Among his most recent publications are *Siberia: Problems and Prospects for Regional Development* (1987), *The Origins of the Russian Revolution 1861–1917* (1987) and *The Development of Siberia: People and Resources* (1989).

M. E. YAPP is professor of the modern history of Western Asia at the School of Oriental and African Studies, University of London. He has studied Afghan history for many years, and in addition to his *Strategies of British India* (1980) has published several articles on the subject. His most recent book is *The Making of the Modern Near East* (1987).

JOSEPH J. ZASLOFF is professor of political science at the University of Pittsburgh. He holds a doctorate in international relations from the Graduate Institute of International Studies at the University of Geneva, and has served as visiting professor at the universities of Saigon, the Philippines and Nice. His most recent publication is *Apprentice Revolutionaries: The Communist Movement in Laos, 1930–1985* (with MacAlister Brown, 1985); and he edited *Postwar Indochina: Old Enemies and New Allies* (1988).

CONTENTS

CONTENTS

xvii

CONTENTS

MAPS

PART TWO

HISTORY

ASIA AND THE PACIFIC SINCE 1945: A FILIPINO PERSPECTIVE

WILFRIDO V. VILLACORTA

LIVING in a country only recently extricated from dictatorship and still struggling to free itself from foreign domination, how would a Filipino look at the dramatic events that have unfolded in Asia since World War II? Several trends have dominated Asian politics in the postwar period; the strength of nationalist sentiments in response to the Western powers' attempts at recolonization; the liberalization of Communist states; and, more recently, the waging of democratic revolutions against authoritarianism.

The momentum that the different nationalist struggles gained during World War II intensified the desire of Asians to be free from the yoke of colonialism. The colonial powers tried to preempt the liberation of the conquered nations that, they claimed, were not prepared for democracy and independence. They also argued that ethnic differences among the different colonized peoples would lead to unequal and undemocratic representation in the envisioned independent nations. Whenever such excuses proved insufficient, the Communists were a ready scapegoat for denying independence.[1]

But the will of the Asian peoples triumphed. As Dutch historian Jan Romein has written, "This century has shown that capitalism and Western rule are not eternal."[2]

In July 1946 the Philippines became one of the first countries granted political independence after World War II. Sovereignty has remained an important issue for Filipinos, as the United States continues to exert pressure on Philippine domestic affairs, particularly in the political and economic spheres. A glaring example was the Bell Trade Act of 1945 that the first postwar Philippine administration had to pass in order to receive war damage payments from the U.S. Congress. Among other provisions, the act granted U.S. citizens and corporations the right to exploit the natural

---

[1] D. G. E. Hall, *A History of South-East Asia* (London: Macmillan, 1964), 784–819.
[2] Jan Romein, *The Asian Century: A History of Modern Nationalism in Asia* (Berkeley and Los Angeles: University of California Press, 1962), 27.

resources of the Philippines.[3] The United States also maintains two of its largest overseas military bases in the Philippines: Clark Air Force Base and Subic Bay Naval Base.

THE UNIQUE PHILIPPINE HERITAGE

Filipinos take pride in a long nationalist tradition, one of the oldest in Asia. Resistance to foreign rule began as early as 1521 when King Lapu-lapu slew the Portuguese navigator Ferdinand Magellan. The first anticolonial revolution in Asia erupted in the Philippines in 1896 against Spanish colonial rule. In 1898 Asia's first republic was proclaimed by the Filipino revolutionary movement. But the new republic was short-lived as expansionist U.S. forces invaded the Philippines and imposed a new colonial rule. Filipinos resisted U.S. control in a war of resistance that began in 1898 and extended through the 1930s. During World War II Filipinos staged a fierce anti-Japanese underground movement that played a major role in the liberation of the country. The defeat of Japan signaled the return of American rule for a brief period of time. In all, more than 40 years of U.S. control in the Philippines resulted in the deliberate maintenance of a local elite that supported American designs in the country.[4]

SURGE OF NATIONALIST MOVEMENTS

Filipinos could identify with the nationalist aspirations of other Asians, which reached their peak during World War II but which were thwarted by Allied occupation forces. The rivalry between the United States and the Soviet Union was decisive in determining the fates of countries under their influence.

In December 1945 Korea was divided into northern and southern occupation zones supervised by the two superpowers.[5] Vietnam, which had been controlled by France, was another victim of superpower maneuverings. In September 1945 a republic under Ho Chi Minh was proclaimed. However, the British forces occupying the southern part of the country rearmed the French and helped the former colonial power regain power. Vietnamese forces, led by the Vietminh, resisted. Peace negotiations led to the division of the country in 1954.[6]

In Burma (now Myanmar) nationalist leaders were not satisfied with self-government within the British Commonwealth. But the threat of a Communist revolution convinced the British to yield control over the country; in January 1948 the Union of Burma was proclaimed.[7] Indonesian independence was proclaimed in August 1945. British occupation forces were or-

---

[3] Teodoro Agoncillo and Oscar Alfonso, *History of the Filipino People* (Quezon City: Malaya Books, 1971), 503–04.
[4] Nathaniel Peffer, *The Far East: A Modern History* (Ann Arbor: University of Michigan Press, 1968), 455–64.
[5] *Ibid.*, pp. 465–76.
[6] Hall, *A History of South-East Asia*, pp. 799–804.
[7] *Ibid.*, pp. 792–96.

dered to disarm the Japanese and protect Dutch settlers. However, they had to request the cooperation of the Sukarno government. Attempts by foreign forces to reassert Dutch authority were resisted by the new republic; negotiations for a compromise solution failed. In November 1949 an agreement was reached, with the assistance of the United Nations; a month later the new nation was formally established.[8]

Nationalist ferment also swept South Asia. Soon after self-rule was granted to India and Pakistan in August 1947, riots between Hindus and Muslims erupted.[9] Jawaharlal Nehru, admired in India and the Third World, took the democratic road in solving India's immense political and economic problems. As a staunch advocate of nonalignment, Nehru pushed for a more prominent role for newly independent countries in international politics.

When Ayub Khan seized power in Pakistan in 1958, he opted for the authoritarian way.[10] He claimed that Western democracy could not work in societies plagued by widespread poverty and illiteracy. Filipinos, then enjoying a liberal democratic form of rule, viewed the Pakistani experiment from a distance. But in 1972 authoritarianism had become a painful reality for them.

TEMPEST IN EAST ASIA

In 1947 the Truman Doctrine proclaimed support for governments threatened by Communist attack. When the occupation forces withdrew in 1949, the governments of North Korea and South Korea each claimed sovereignty over the entire peninsula. The following year, North Korea, claiming an attack from the South, sent troops across the 38th parallel.[11] In October 1949 the Western world was shocked by the victory of Chinese Communist forces led by Mao Zedong. By December the nationalist forces, under Chiang Kai-shek, had formed a separate government in Taiwan.[12] Mao's victory and the rise to power of a Communist government in the world's biggest nation intensified the cold war in Asia. This major development provided a "yellow peril" dimension to anti-Communist propaganda in the Philippines and other Southeast Asian countries with sizeable overseas Chinese populations.

The United States, determined to contain the advance of communism in Asia, launched an all-out military operation in defense of South Korea. The Filipino delegates to the United Nations were directed by their government to support the U.S. position on the Korean issue. A Philippine expeditionary force under the auspices of the United Nations was also sent to Korea.

As the Korean War raged, Japan was pulled into the security network of the Western powers. Japan became a procurement center for U.N. forces

[8]*Ibid.,* pp. 804–09; Romein, *The Asian Century,* pp. 363–65.
[9]T. Walter Wallbank, *A Short History of India and Pakistan* (New York: New American Library, 1965), 148–246.
[10]*Ibid.,* pp. 319–21.
[11]Peffer, *The Far East,* pp. 455–64.
[12]*Ibid.,* pp. 443–54.

in Korea where billions of dollars worth of goods were bought. This opportunity provided a significant impetus for Japan's economic recovery. The Korean War impressed on the Japanese the need to make their nation capable of defending itself. A security pact concluded with the United States in 1952 gave the Americans the right to maintain land, sea and air forces in Japan.[13] Japan's Self-Defense Force gradually assumed responsibility for the country's defense. But the prospect of a rearmed Japan worried Southeast Asian nations, including the Philippines.

DECOLONIZATION AND RECOLONIZATION

From 1954 to 1959 other countries joined the Philippines, Burma and Indonesia as independent nations in the region. The 1954 Geneva Conference granted full independence to Laos and Cambodia. Malaya was given its independence in 1957, and Singapore in 1959.[14]

In 1954 the United States, France and Great Britain initiated the Southeast Asian Collective Defense Treaty. The treaty—which was signed in Manila by the three Western powers, Australia, New Zealand, Pakistan, Thailand and the Philippines—created the Southeast Asian Treaty Organization.[15]

In April 1955, 30 leaders of newly independent nations of Asia, Africa and Latin America met in Bandung and formed the Non-Aligned Movement. The new movement served as forum where the problems and ideas of the leaders of underdeveloped countries could be heard. The Non-Aligned Movement, with prominent leaders such as Nehru of India, Sukarno of Indonesia and Nasser of Egypt, eventually became an influential bloc of countries in the U. N. General Assembly.[16]

The vulnerability of Western powers in the face of popular nationalist movements was once more demonstrated by the defeat of the French by Vietnamese forces at Dien Bien Phu in 1953. The United States took over France's role as protector of South Vietnam in 1954, plunging into what became America's most humiliating military defeat. The dogged resistance of the Vietnamese to foreign domination compelled the U.S. government to escalate the war and to pour in more military and economic aid to the South Vietnamese regime. But no amount of support could prevent the downfall of a government plagued by corruption and ineptitude, and a military organization marked by inefficiency and severe demoralization.[17]

[13] J. Kennedy, *Asian Nationalism in the Twentieth Century* (London: Macmillan, 1968), 24.
[14] Fred von der Mehden, *South-East Asia, 1930–1970: The Legacy of Colonialism and Nationalism* (London: Thames and Hudson, 1974), pp. 56–59.
[15] Alejandro Fernandez, *The Philippines and the United States: The Forging of New Relations* (Quezon City: NSDB-UP Integrated Research Program, 1977), 333–39.
[16] Hall, *A History of South-East Asia*, pp. 825–27; Romein, *The Asian Century*, pp. 389–90.
[17] Barbara Tuchman, *The March of Folly: From Troy to Vietnam* (New York: Alfred A. Knopf, 1984), 283–310.

THE TUMULTUOUS SIXTIES

In 1962 the government of U Nu in Burma was overthrown by General Ne Win, who ushered in a period of economic stagnation and isolationism. On the other hand, Japan joined the ranks of industrialized nations, and what was once a feared militarist power was now an Asian economic giant.

In the mid-1960s the Philippines and Indonesia became embroiled in a controversy over the proposed Federation of Malaysia, which was to be composed of Malaya, Singapore and the British colonies of Sabah and Sarawak. Indonesia labeled the federation a neocolonialist scheme. The Philippines also opposed the proposal on account of its own claim to Sabah. Philippine President Diosdado Macapagal tried to defuse the situation by proposing the formation of the Maphilindo Confederation, composed of Malaysia, the Philippines and Indonesia, all sharing a common Malay-based culture. Despite the support given the Maphilindo concept by Indonesian President Sukarno and Malayan Prime Minister Tungku Abdul Rahman, the Federation of Malaysia was established in 1963.[18] Singapore left the federation in 1965 after a disagreement over the ethnic configuration of the federation's political system. In September 1965, Sukarno was ousted by a military coup led by General Suharto.

These problems notwithstanding, regional stability was improved with the formation of the Association of Southeast Asian Nations (ASEAN) in 1967. The organization is committed to regional growth and stability. Member-countries have chosen to avoid controversial political issues that would only divide them.

Communal riots erupted in Malaysia in 1969, exposing the fundamental weaknesses of its multiracial society. The tumult led to the implementation of a policy that sought to correct the imbalance in wealth distribution by giving more opportunities to the ethnic Malays.[19] Conflicts also flared up in South Asia and East Asia. Incursions by Chinese forces into northern India in 1962 led to hostilities between the two countries.[20] This, in turn, resulted in a loose alliance between China and Pakistan. Meanwhile, China sent military assistance to the North Vietnamese and Vietcong forces. The United States tried to halt the flow of supplies and manpower into South Vietnam by bombing the North. Mao's Cultural Revolution of the late 1960s was supposedly meant to preserve and advance the Chinese Communist revolution. But the excesses of the campaign created deep impressions among Asians, particularly those in search of appropriate systems for their own societies.

[18] Bernard Gordon, *The Dimensions of Conflict in Southeast Asia* (Englewood Cliffs, New Jersey: Prentice-Hall, 1966), 9–40, 68–119.
[19] See Simon Barraclough, "Communalism and Confusion: Towards a Clarification of Terms in the Study of Malaysian Politics," in *Readings in Malaysian Politics,* ed. Bruce Gale (Selangor: Pelanduk Publications, 1986), 268–81.
[20] Wallbank, *Short History of India and Pakistan,* pp. 321–25.

THE CONFRONTATIONAL SEVENTIES

The 1970s were marked by military conflicts and political upheavals that fundamentally transformed power relations in Asia. The wars in the Middle East had a direct effect on the economic and political stability of the oil-dependent countries of Asia. Among the most severely affected was the Philippines, where a Muslim secessionist uprising in the south was exacerbated by support from Arab countries. The Arab oil embargo enabled Muslims to appreciate the power a united Islamic world could wield over industrialized nations. The Vietnam War, meanwhile, served as a stimulus for active political involvement: student protests erupted around the world, including many Asian countries. In the Philippines, President Ferdinand Marcos used urban unrest and insurgency as a reason to declare martial rule in 1972. In Thailand a student uprising led to the overthrow of the military government in 1973.[21]

The Vietnam War, which ended in 1975, created a lasting impact on American society. But it also raised disturbing questions for Asian societies—such as: Does one country have the right to thwart another country's nationalist movement just because it has been "adulterated" by Marxist ideas? Can a foreign power reverse the tide of nationalism and continually back a client government? How effective is waging total war against determined revolutionaries? Barbara Tuchman has summarized the folly of the United States in Vietnam as "the absence of reflective thought about the nature of what we are doing, about effectiveness in relation to the object sought, about balance of possible gain as against loss and against harm both to the ally and to the United States."[22]

In Asian countries such as the Philippines that had fallen under dictatorial rule, the plight of Zulfikar Ali Bhutto in Pakistan was of serious interest. Bhutto, another charismatic and populist leader, assumed the presidency in 1971. He vowed to improve relations with Arab countries, he redistributed land to peasants and he nationalized some basic industries. Bhutto began steps toward Pakistan's withdrawal from the Central Treaty Organization military alliance and entry into the Non-aligned Movement. His independent-mindedness made him the target of a destabilization campaign. In 1977 he was overthrown in a coup led by General Mohammed Zia ul-Haq. A campaign to discredit Bhutto followed and led to his execution.

In 1976 Mao died and the Cultural Revolution came to an end. A new leadership implemented steps toward the modernization of China, introducing reforms such as the granting of bonuses to workers and the restoration of university entrance examinations.[23] The sweeping changes that took place disillusioned many adherents of Mao's thought and led to ideo-

---

[21] Likhit Dhiravegin, *Thai Politics: Selected Aspects of Development and Change* (Bangkok: Tri-Sciences Publishing House, 1985), 278–93.
[22] Tuchman, *The March of Folly*, p. 376.
[23] Immanuel C. Y. Hsu, *China Without Mao: A Search for a New Order* (Oxford: Oxford University Press, 1982), 29–55.

logical reexaminations by other Asian communist parties. Likewise, these changes were reminders of the fallibility of revered leaders and the transience of their power, however great their contributions might be.

In Cambodia the horrors of the Pol Pot regime, which came to power in 1975 demonstrated the tragedy that could result from the dogmatic application of an ideology. Pol Pot wanted an immediate change to a classless, communist society without going through the rigors of a socialist transition. His persecution of intellectuals and his terrorist approach to national discipline brought untold suffering and death to countless Cambodians. In 1978, Vietnam invaded Cambodia and overthrew the Pol Pot regime. The following year border hostilities broke out between China and Vietnam.

The latter part of the 1970s witnessed the rise of Asia's newly industrialized countries, namely Singapore, South Korea, Taiwan and Hong Kong. The record of these countries has made Filipinos more cognizant of the fact that they have been lagging behind, considering that until 1977 the Philippine economy had been one of the healthiest in the region.

RECKONING IN THE EIGHTIES

The major events of the 1980s were, in general, results of the turmoil of the preceding decade. Refugees from Vietnam, the boat people, sought a new future in neighboring Asian countries or in the West. Mostly of Chinese origin and of upper- or middle-class backgrounds, many of these refugees drowned at sea or were murdered by pirates. They were welcomed and nursed by Filipino villagers when they came, even though they were sometimes turned away, robbed or stoned in other countries.

Two other issues gained prominence in the Philippine media: the religious unrest in India and the revival of Japan as a military power in the Pacific. The Sikh revolt had an impact on informed Filipinos because of the continuing unrest in the Muslim-dominated provinces in the southern part of the Philippines. In June 1984, Indian Prime Minister Indira Gandhi ordered troops to storm the Golden Temple of Amristar and expel thousands of Sikh activists who had used it as a base. The attack left hundreds dead. In October two of her own guards, both Sikhs, assassinated Gandhi. Japan, under pressure from the United States to share the cost of defending the Pacific, boosted its military expenditures and expanded its already advanced defense capability. Most analysts believed the remilitarization of Japan inevitable. But such a prospect also caused apprehension among ASEAN countries that feared Japan's growing influence in the Asia-Pacific region.[24]

DEMOCRATIC REVOLUTIONS AND SOCIALIST LIBERALIZATION

More recent events in Asia have vindicated the cause of freedom and human rights. The 1986 People Power uprising in the Philippines has served as a

[24] See Wilfrido Villacorta and Romeo Bautista, "Political and Economic Aspects of Philippine-Japanese Trade," in *ASEAN-Japan Relations: Trade and Development,* ed. Narongchai Akranasee (Singapore: Institute of Southeast Asian Studies, 1982).

model for other Asian countries under authoritarian rule, particularly South Korea, Burma and Pakistan, where popular movements are seeking or have successfully sought the overthrow of militarist rule. The Philippine experience has shown that no dictator is invulnerable, and that a people united and determined can make the difference—and not guns or the instrumentalities of the state.

Another development closely watched by the Filipino public is the opening up of Communist societies, such as those of the Soviet Union, China and Vietnam. Communism has always evoked fear for Filipinos educated under the American system. Typically, their initial reaction would be that the withdrawal of Soviet troops from Afghanistan and Vietnamese troops from Cambodia is a sign of capitulation to U.S. pressures. They would also have the impression that the liberalization of the economies of China and Vietnam is a surrender to capitalism. But they soon realize, however, that when these countries offer liberal terms to foreign investors and begin to provide incentives to their workers, it is because they already have confidence that mechanisms for preventing economic exploitation are securely in place. In other words, these countries can now afford to be innovative because their societies are no longer as susceptible to foreign domination and exploitation as neighboring non-Communist countries are. In any event, the entente that the capitalist powers are developing with Communist countries is a welcome situation for Filipinos in that it now accords "respectability" to better relations with these countries.

HOMECOMING AT LAST

The resurgence of Asia—the reassertion of the identity of Asian peoples and the fruition of their capabilities—has come about since World War II. Faced with the demands of postwar rehabilitation and continuing domination by the United States, Filipinos have taken time to appreciate the potentials of their Asian environment. In the early years following independence, governmental policies were premised on the identicality of Philippine and American interests. There is now, however, greater awareness, even among the political elite, of the importance of a less-dependent economy and military. The examples of neighboring nations that have succeeded in liberating themselves from the shackles of foreign domination have created an impact on the consciousness of more and more Filipinos. They are beginning to regard U.S. military bases less as means for warding off external threats and more as staging grounds for intervention to advance American military and economic interests.

More sectors in the Philippines are calling for an independent foreign policy that offers peace and friendship to all nations. There has developed widespread consciousness of the need for a new international economic order and for greater identification with equally beleaguered Third World countries whose growth is stunted by heavy external debts and the stranglehold of foreign hegemonial interests. Given the fundamental nature of power, however, it is a fact that no affluent country readily gives up its privileges or prerogatives. The growing realization that the best way to

escape exploitation is by not remaining poor has given a visible determination and confidence to Filipinos to be once more a progressive and respectable nation. In the mid-1960s the Philippines had the second fastest growing economy in Asia. As the Asia-Pacific region becomes the center of economic growth in the 21st century, prospects for the Philippines to play an important role in the region are bright. As long as foreign powers do not interfere in domestic affairs, the Filipino people will assume their rightful place in Asia and the world.

FURTHER READING

Chawla, Sudershan, ed. *Changing Patterns of Security and Stability in Asia.* New York: Praeger, 1980.

Ebinger, Charles. *Great Power Rivalry in the Far East: The Politics of Energy.* Washington, D.C.: Center for Strategic and International Studies, 1977.

Ellison, Herbert J., ed. *Japan and the Pacific Quadrille: The Major Powers in East Asia.* Boulder, Colorado: Westview Press, 1987.

Girling, John L. *America and the Third World: Revolution and Intervention.* London: Routledge and Kegan Paul, 1980.

Grinter, Lawrence, and Kihl, Young Whan, eds. *East Asia Conflict Zones: Prospects for Regional Stability and Deescalation.* Basingstoke, Hampshire: Macmillan, 1987.

Gurtov, Melvin. *The United States against the Third World: Antinationalism and Intervention.* New York: Praeger, 1974.

Gustov, Martin, and Maghroori, Ray. *Roots of Failure: United States Policy and the Third World.* Westport, Connecticut: Greenwood Press, 1984.

Hart, Thomas G. *Sino-Soviet Relations: Reexamining the Prospects for Normalisation.* Aldershot, Hampshire: Gower, 1987.

Hosmer, Stephen, and Wolfe, Thomas. *Soviet Policy and Practice Toward Third World Conflicts.* Lexington, Massachusetts: Lexington Books, 1983.

Jorgensen-Dahl, Arnfinn. *Regional Organisation and Order in Southeast Asia.* Basingstoke, Hampshire: Macmillan, 1982.

Karnow, Stanley. *In Our Image: America's Empire in the Philippines.* New York: Random House, 1989.

Schurmann, Franz. *The Logic of World Power: An Inquiry into the Origins, Currents, and Contradictions of World Politics.* New York: Pantheon, 1974.

Sigur, Gaston Joseph, and Kim, Young C., eds. *Japanese and United States Policy in Asia.* New York: Praeger, 1982.

Tien, Hung-mao, ed. *Mainland China, Taiwan, and United States Policy.* Cambridge, Massachusetts: Oelgeschlagher, Gunn and Hain, 1983.

ASIA AND THE PACIFIC SINCE 1945: AN INDIAN PERSPECTIVE

BHABANI SEN GUPTA

MANY currents of joy and pain, hope, and frustration, light and shadow have mingled to shape the nations that since the late 1940s have emerged as sovereign states from the wombs of Europe's globe-straddling empires. These crosscurrents have helped to mold the heart and soul of each of these nations. The course of their relatively young lives bears the imprint of three global processes of our times—decolonization, revolution and intervention. These processes have been working in the ambience of the cold war from which few of the new nations have been able to keep a safe distance. The growth and development of these nations have to be seen in the context of global trends and processes. Only then can the distinctiveness of the larger nations be identified and the evolution of their self-images as well as their perceptions of the world be traced.

The Indian subcontinent occupies a distinctive place in the history of these new nations because it is here that decolonization began. The subcontinent was carved into two mutually hostile sovereign neighbors, India and Pakistan. For more than 40 years each has been the pathological preoccupation of the other. India, however, has earned several distinctions of its own. It is the giant of South Asia as well as the world's largest democracy and the most stable one of the developing world. Through slow but steady and largely self-reliant growth, India now compels the world's attention with its size and vast population; its military, economic and technological strength; and its proved ability to make nuclear bombs, which it has declined to do unless compelled to.

In any narrative or analytical account of Asia and the Pacific, however, India has to be seen in comparison with its larger and relatively unfriendly neighbor, China. Each following in its own model, India and China have grown into major powers. China shows the promise of becoming a global power at the end of the century. India flutters its impatient wings to break out of its regional binds where it is seen by its neighbors as the hegemonic power. However, the Indian and Chinese national experiences have been vastly different. China's four wars since mid-century have been fought with

880

the United States, the Soviet Union, India and Vietnam. Two of China's four opponents are socialist powers, the third is a leader of nonalignment and the fourth, the United States, is the world's strongest military and economic power. India's four wars have been fought with only two states, both neighbors—three with Pakistan, one with China. China has changed its worldview six times and its strategic posture three times—from a security alliance treaty with the Soviet Union to an unwritten security compact with the United States and then to a partnership with the Third World and an independent position somewhere between the two superpowers. India, by contrast, has remained petulantly perched on the stabler and more comfortable heights of nonalignment, flaunting a treaty of peace and friendship with the Soviet Union. Its worldview has remained as steady and durable as its political personality. Seen from India, the world, and especially the Asia-Pacific region, has changed but slowly over a long period of time. Seen from China, the world has changed abruptly and fundamentally several times.

NEHRU'S WORLDVIEW: PAN-ASIAN VISIONS

Independent India's founders, men of stature and vision, were aware that the nation that they had undertaken to build had been gravely crippled by the partition. It was not the India for whose liberation they had fought the British for 40 years. As if to dismiss any injury to India's born-again stature resulting from the partition, master builder Jawaharlal Nehru immediately linked Indian independence to a much larger historical process: the liberation of Asia from colonialism; and the evolution of resurgent Asia as a building block of a new world order based on universal equality and justice among nations regardless of size, resources, geography and the color of their people's skin. Midnight's prodigal son, then, looked at the world dreaming of the manifest destiny of an awakened Asia of which it was a frontline standard-bearer. "We stand on the razor's edge of the present," declared Nehru in a speech to the Indian Constituent Assembly, which was writing the constitution of a modern democracy in a traditional agrarian country of many languages and diverse cultures. At midnight of "the day appointed by history" Nehru's voice acquired intimations of a new beginning in human affairs: "It is a fateful moment for us in India, for all Asia and for the world. A new star rises, the star of freedom in the East, a new hope comes into being, a vision long cherished materializes. May that star never set and that hope never be betrayed."

Nehru's worldview had evolved step by step since the 1920s, and it shaped the perspective of two successive generations in India; it formed the cognitive balance of India's mainstream perceptions of the world. "In developing our foreign policy, we shall naturally first cultivate friendly relations with the countries of the East which have so much in common with us," mused Nehru as far back as 1927, two years before the Indian National Congress formulated its demand for "complete independence" from British rule. "The world problem is ultimately one of imperialism—the finance-imperialism of the present day," he added. Fascism was in Nehru's eyes an important aspect of the problem of imperialism, while the Soviet Union represented "a new order fundamentally opposed to that of imperialism." The Indian National Congress was, in Nehru's view in those years, a popular front against British imperialism; opposing it were the domestic feudal and other reactionary forces allied with colonial rule. He likened the polarization in India to the antifascist and fascist groupings in Europe, thereby linking the Indian freedom struggle to the global conflict between fascism and democracy.

Brick by brick Nehru built the left-of-center image of the Indian National Congress, not without resistance from some of his powerful colleagues and comrades, including, at times, Mahatma Gandhi. In the 1940s, during World War II, Gandhi, Nehru and their followers supported the Allies against Nazi tyranny, and logically demanded immediate independence so that the Indian people might willingly join that struggle. When the British refused, Gandhi organized the Quit India movement as the final battle for freedom. At the war's end the complex process of negotiation began, turning on the question of whether decolonization would leave India undivided or split into India and Pakistan. Partition was agreed upon by the British, the Indian National Congress and the Muslim League. Even as independence loomed on the horizon, Nehru convened the Asian Relations Conference in New Delhi, to which were invited delegates from what is now regarded as the Asia-Pacific region, including Soviet Central Asia. Addressing that conference, Nehru projected a pan-Asian vision that was at once romantic, visionary, evocative and utopian. "All countries of Asia have to meet together on an equal footing in a common task and endeavour. It is fitting that India should play her part in this new phase of Asian development. Apart from the fact that India herself is emerging into freedom and independence, she is the natural centre and focal point of the many forces at work in Asia. Geography is a compelling factor, and geographically she is so situated as to be the meeting point of West and North and East and South-East Asia."

INDEPENDENT FOREIGN POLICY

On August 15, 1947, Nehru became independent India's first prime minister—with an unsullied idealistic vision of a resurgent Asia where free nations would collectively plow antiimperialist democratic furrows on uncharted fields of international relations; build their political economies on their own chosen models; and work with the rest of the world without being tied to either of the two great powers. Nehru realized that the crux of a nation's independence lay in its foreign policy. What did independence consist of, he asked in a 1949 speech, and hastened to supply the answer: "It consists fundamentally and basically of foreign relations. That is the test of independence. All else is local autonomy." Nehru and his colleagues, with the solid support of the nation, formulated a foreign policy of independence of the two rival blocs and gave it the name of nonalignment. It was not a policy of neutrality or passivism. "When freedom is menaced or injustice threatened or where aggression takes place, we cannot and shall not be neutral." For India and most of the new nations of the erstwhile empires, freedom, injustice and aggression had meanings quite different from those used by the West. For Nehru and his generation of Asian leaders, the threat to freedom, justice and peace came basically from imperialism and neocolonialism. For the West and its allies in Asia, it came from Soviet and Chinese communism. Even now, when imperialism of the classical mold has all but vanished and the images of the Communist powers are tarnished in Asian eyes, these concepts that determine the balance of social and political forces in the world do not carry the same meaning for the developing countries as they do for the developed nations of the West.

BEGINNING OF NONALIGNMENT

India's worldview was formulated between 1951 and 1961, partly with Nehru's vision of a deeply divided world—which was shared by the majority of the elites—and partly as a result of India's interaction with a rapidly changing world. In 1947 Nehru, like many other world leaders, did not expect the Chinese Communists led by Mao Zedong to defeat the Nationalists in a matter of two years. Nehru also patiently waited for Stalin's perception of India to change, paying little heed to the torrent of abuse hurled at him and at India by Soviet media in the first years of independence. When Moscow began to smile on India in recognition of the Indian role in the Korean armistice, Nehru took the bold step toward conceptualizing a foreign policy of nonalignment. He needed a benign Soviet Union to distance India from Britain and the United States, the two powers to which India had been largely linked since independence. But the Communist victory in China was an entirely different matter: it brought a resurgent revolutionary nation to India's border in the Himalaya, threatening the privileges India had "inherited" from the British in Tibet, Nepal, Sikkim and Bhutan. Indian leaders had little knowledge of the doctrines and applications of Mao's Marxism-Leninism, although Nehru was probably the first world statesman to detect the inherent and inevitable clash of interests between the Soviet Union and China. The two countries, however, forged a security treaty in 1950 and Mao, unlike Nehru, decided, after a debate at the highest levels of the Chinese Communist party, to "lean on one side" since there was "no third road." This compelled a readjustment of India's security concerns. In his first exercise in realpolitik, Nehru unilaterally brought Nepal within India's security orbit; abandoned postcolonial "rights" in Tibet and vaguely recognized China's sovereignty over that Himalayan nation; streamlined India's "special relationship" with Bhutan; and reduced Sikkim to a small principality of limited autonomy in internal affairs.

Nehru's trip to China in 1954 had been made possible by the role India played at the Geneva Conference on Indochina earlier that year, and the visit to India by Chinese Prime Minister Zhou Enlai immediately thereafter. Nehru knew that India and China were different worlds unto themselves. "I have come to this great country of China, which is itself a little world, from another great country, which is also a little world of its own," he told his hosts. For him, both countries were going through revolutionary changes even though the two revolutions "differed in their content, symbolizing the new spirit of Asia and the new vitality which is finding expression in the countries of Asia." He hailed the five principles of peaceful coexistence that China and India had already crafted for a treaty on Tibet. Sovereignty, independence, equality, nonaggression and noninterference lent new substance to the concept of nonalignment. Drawing strength from the freshly minted "brotherly relations" with China, and encouraged by the signals that were coming from Moscow, Nehru in 1954–55 turned down U.S. approaches for Indian participation in a chain of security treaties to contain Sino-Soviet communism. He announced the decision to build in India "a socialist pattern of society." Yet over the next three decades Indian society clearly developed along capitalist lines under the regulating guidance of the state, which remained committed to economic independence, self-reliance and a large if no longer predominant public sector. Nehru was also less ambiguous about nonalignment's antiimperialist thrust: "We believe that each country has not only the right to freedom, but also to decide its own policy and way of life. Only thus can true freedom flourish and a people grow according to its own genius. We believe, therefore, in nonaggression and noninterference by one country in the affairs of another, and the growth of tolerance between them and the capacity for peaceful coexistence."

India's friendship with China culminated at the Bandung conference of Asian and African nations in 1955. Here, Nehru projected an ambitious but short-lived Indian role as reconciler of the diverse revolutions of Asia and Africa into one great tide of enlightened, independent, antiimperialist nationalism. The threat to peace and stability, in Nehru's view, came from nuclear weapons, from the cold war and its military alliances, and from imperialism's reluctance to complete the process of political decolonization and surrender economic power. He took great care, however, not to pit the newly independent countries against the West, but he was equally firm in his rejection of the United States policy of encirclement of China and the Soviet Union through military alliances.

RAPPROCHEMENT WITH MOSCOW

Nehru might not have deliberately built India's short-lived brotherly relations with China to compel the Soviet Union's friendliness with India. But this could not have been far from his strategic thinking. Even in 1954 he was aware of Sino-Indian differences over large areas of territory in the Himalaya, where India meets China across a 1,864-mile/3,000-km. undefined, undemarcated frontier. He had raised the matter with Zhou in 1954, only to be told that the Chinese government had had no time to address itself to the India-China border issue. As noted, Nehru had intimations as early as 1951 of potential and actual tensions between the Soviet Union and China. He did not consider it accidental that Moscow should begin to reveal its own policy of friendship for India in 1953. A series of friendly actions and gestures led to Nehru's remarkable 10-day visit to the Soviet

Union in 1955—remarkable because he traveled to several industrial and agricultural centers, delivered the gospel of Gandhi to a vast audience in Moscow and was treated to an unprecedented welcome. The joint statement issued on the talks between Nehru and General Secretary Nikita Krushchev—the drafting of which was left largely to the Indian team—precluded either country's participation in any coalition or action directed against the other. This was a mutual commitment of far-reaching strategic import. It was a vast improvement on the Sino-Indian agreement of 1954, which, apart from crafting the five principles, did not commit India and China to any concrete strategic mutuality. The statement also laid the foundation of the Indo-Soviet Treaty of Peace and Friendship that was concluded in 1971.

In the mid-1950s, however, the Soviet Union, China and India deftly maintained the facade of the unity and friendship of the three great Eurasian powers. Nehru, having been to Beijing before his state visit to Moscow, met Zhou once again in New Delhi within a few days of his return from the Soviet Union. Khrushchev and Prime Minister Bulganin went to Beijing a few days before their visit to India. This 1955 trip inaugurated the foundations of Indo-Soviet friendship, the most positive and least strained bilateral relationship that has flourished in the world since World War II.[1] Since this visit there has been no turning back, by either power, on progressive expansion of friendly ties.

The Khrushchev-Bulganin visit led to political, strategic and developmental cooperation between the Soviet Union and India on an ever-widening front. Soviet leaders committed themselves to support India's position on the disputed state of Jammu and Kashmir (Pakistan's claim to it had the backing of Britain and the United States), and the Portuguese colony of Goa on India's western coast. The Soviet Union agreed to help India build a heavy-industry base, which Nehru regarded as indispensable for economic independence. In the years that followed the Soviets supported the course and direction of India's political and social development, debating in their scholarly institutions if India was in a position to skip the capitalist path of development. They agreed that India was indeed traversing the socialist path, although not the scientific socialism of the Marxist-Leninist brand—until, in the early 1980s, scholars determined that India had actually embarked on capitalist development outside the international capitalist system while maintaining large-scale linkages with the Soviet bloc. Chinese leaders, for their part, closely monitored the progress of Indo-Soviet friendship. In the mid-1950s Zhou cautiously refused to endorse the Indian stand on Kashmir. China did not support the Pakistani claim either, but began to cultivate Pakistan's friendship to counter Moscow's growing

---

[1] Even the Anglo-U.S. friendship, often described as the strongest bilateral relationship in the world, came under considerable strain during the Suez crisis of 1956–57. The Indo-Soviet friendship has not come under any serious strain. The Soviets have for all practical purposes recognized South Asia as India's sphere of influence. They have, in recent years, supported the Indian peacekeeping intervention in Sri Lanka (this has been supported by the United States too) and an Indian role in Afghanistan following the Geneva agreement of April 14, 1988.

friendship with India. In 1959 India and China were locked in a bitter controversy over Tibet. The Chinese had already dated India's deviation from "progressive policies" as early as 1956. That was the year of the 20th Congress of the Communist party of the Soviet Union (CPSU), marking the Soviet Union's de-Stalinization drive. It was also the year when the Soviets began an appraisal of India in the light of the 20th Congress's political thesis and arrived at several favorable conclusions. One was that India was entitled to the status of great power by virtue of its size, resources and independent foreign policy; another conclusion recognized that "under certain conditions" nonalignment could serve as one of the "principal means of strengthening general security." For Maoist China, 1956 was the year when the CPSU embraced "revisionism" and deviated from the true path of Marxism-Leninism.

THREE DOMINANT FACTORS

In India's first formative decade or so, the country's perceptions of the world, and more specifically of the Asia-Pacific region, were almost completely determined by its relations with Pakistan, the Soviet Union and China. Until 1951 India's external relationships, strategic as well as economic, had been necessarily confined mostly to Great Britain and the United States. Nehru, however, developed a sharp antipathy to the United States, which in his view came into Asia after World War II largely as protector of the residual interests of the erstwhile colonial European powers: the Netherlands in Indonesia; France in Indochina; Portugal in Goa; and Britain in Malaysia, Singapore, the Arab/Persian Gulf and the Indian Ocean.[2]

The containment strategy of the United States was, in Indian perceptions, simultaneously aimed at securing three objectives in Asia and Africa: first, to regulate the process of decolonization; second, to safeguard the residual political and considerable economic interests of the colonial powers in their former colonies, even as the United States gradually took over those interests, especially in the Arab/Persian Gulf and the Middle East; and third, to lock as many of the newly independent countries as possible into the United States containment strategy. As soon as Nehru formulated the conceptual and operational frame of his foreign policy of nonalignment, a distance grew between India and those countries of Asia that chose to be linked strategically with the West. Thus, in the early 1950s India's sympathies lay with the nationalist upsurgence in Iran and its leader, Muhammad Mossadeq, while the young shah, dethroned by the nationalist rising and rethroned by the Central Intelligence Agency, was seen as an American vassal. Pakistan's military pact with the United States also widened the division between the two neighbors.

The Southeast Asia Treaty Organization (SEATO) and Baghdad pacts were condemned as extending the cold war to nearly all of Asia, and their members as willing or reluctant dependents of the United States. At Bandung, Nehru openly differed with delegates from countries such as Iraq

---

[2] See Robert Tower's article in *Atlantic Monthly,* September 1983.

and the Philippines, but his hand was strengthened when Nasser of Egypt and Sukarno of Indonesia embraced nonalignment. During the Suez crisis India played a prominent role in support of Egypt and, at the same time, as a bridge between London, Washington and Cairo. Not until S. W. R. D. Bandaranaike gained political power in Sri Lanka and brought the island republic into the expanding group of nonaligned nations did India's relations with its neighbor take off. In 1950 Nehru helped King Mahendra of Nepal get himself out of the grip of the ruling feudal-military clan and encouraged him to set up a constitutional monarchy. The process was dissolved by his son, King Birendra, in 1958 and the monarchy was fully restored. However, Nehru had already brought Nepal within India's security orbit by a treaty of friendship in 1950. Years later Birendra, without prior consultation with India, declared Nepal to be a "zone of peace" and had this strategic concept written into the constitution. The Indian government avoided discussing the matter with the royal government of Nepal, while Indian commentators saw the move as an attempt on Nepal's part to invalidate the original 1950 treaty. Additionally, in Indian perceptions, the ANZUS treaty was a mere extension of SEATO, and Malaysia's defense links with Britain, Australia and New Zealand deprived it of Indian sympathies during Sukarno's unsuccessful confrontation over the expanded federation.

BORDER WAR WITH CHINA

The border war with China in 1962 ended India's age of innocence. The crisis began building in 1958–59. The root cause was Chinese determination to bring the regions of Xinjiang and Tibet under communist control, which, despite a cautious pace of reform, sparked protests. It is noteworthy that China's problems with the Soviet Union and India stemmed from the relatively "soft" regions of the vast Chinese nation—Manchuria, Xinjiang and Tibet. Unrest in Tibet ignited dormant desires among groups of Indians for a presence on the "roof of the world." In his own mind Nehru knew the folly of getting involved in Tibet and was not indifferent to Zhou's offer of a trade-off between the McMahon Line as India's border with China in the eastern sector and Aksai Chin, in Ladakh, falling within the Chinese claim line. But Nehru was compelled to take a hard line in the face of an aroused parliament and an outraged public, while the Chinese regarded with deep suspicion and grave misgivings Indian hospitality for the Dalai Lama who was granted asylum. It became clear in 1959 that the Chinese view of India and of Nehru was vastly different from that of the Soviets.

At first, the Chinese differentiated between the "reactionary" Indians and "progressive" ones but as the border crisis intensified, they attacked Nehru himself as a vacillator between the two strata of the Indian bourgeoisie.[3]

[3] "More on Nehru's Philosophy in the Light of the Sino-Indian Boundary Question," *Peking Review* (November 2, 1962). This is the only comprehensive thesis on India formulated in China and printed in an authoritative Chinese journal since

At the same time, they moved strategically closer to Pakistan. In 1959 President Ayub Khan of Pakistan had proposed to Nehru joint defense of the subcontinent against Chinese aggression.[4] Turned down by Nehru, Ayub approached Beijing for a peaceful settlement of Pakistan's northern border with China. The agreement provoked a strong Indian protest. Zhou had announced as far back as 1956, during the Beijing visit of the then prime minister of Pakistan, H. S. Suhrawardy, that "although Pakistan was a member of SEATO, since its government and people had expressed friend-liness for China, there was no reason why China could not be friendly with Pakistan."[5] In the 1960s Pakistan made it clear that it shared U.S. percep-tions of a threat from the Soviet Union, but not from China. Washington too appeared to adopt a flexible policy about Pakistan's growing entente with the Chinese. It was reported that in 1963 the United States tried to use Pakistan as a bridge to Beijing. In the early 1960s the United States winked at several accords between Pakistan and China, of relatively small political-strategic substance; they included the border agreement that an-gered India. But when it came to the possibility of Pakistan concluding a defense pact with China, the United States intervened strongly and pre-vented progress in that direction.[6]

MOSCOW'S INDIA TILT

Between 1959 and 1962 the Soviet Union gradually abandoned its Chinese brothers for Indian friends. Soviet and Chinese leaders took considerable pains to persuade each other of the validity and wisdom of their respective India policies. Neither could count much success. The Cuban missile crisis brought the Sino-Soviet schism into the open.[7] Faced with Chinese military intervention into what is now the state of Arunachal Pradesh, Nehru ap-pealed for military help to the United States, Britain and the Soviet Union. Each responded immediately with urgently needed matériel. The Soviets made the first commitment to transfer MiG fighters to India, initiating a military supply relationship that continued to grow until the Soviet Union

the revolution of 1949. In July 1984, the author, on a visit to Beijing, asked a "responsible person" in the Chinese ministry of external affairs whether any other political thesis on India had been written. The reply was that a new thesis was under preparation. It was not published until the summer of 1988. Those who are interested in the debate between Moscow, Beijing and Delhi in 1959–62 may see Bhabani Sen Gupta, *The Fulcrum of Asia: Relations among China, India, Pakistan and the USSR* (New York: Pegasus, 1968), reprinted in 1988 in India with a new introduction (New Delhi: Konarak Publishers), ch.4–5 and notes.

[4] Nehru's instant reaction was "Defense against whom?". Nehru could not imagine the possibility of joint India-Pakistan defense against China. For him, Pakistan, with its security linkages with the United States, was a greater enemy than Com-munist China.

[5] See Gupta, *Fulcrum of Asia*, pp. 133–34.

[6] Ibid.

[7] For details, see ibid., ch. 4, notes, pp. 350–51; also, *The Hindu* (October 29, 1962); *Pravda* (November 7, 1962); and *The Hindu* (November 7, 1962).

became the steady supplier of 70 percent of India's imported military hardware. It made solid and enduring contributions to India's emergence in the 1980s as a significant military power, with elements of a blue-water navy and a sizable indigenous arms industry able to manufacture fighters and bombers, design its own tanks and build its own aircraft carriers with foreign collaboration.

THE WAR OF 1965

With the death of Nehru, and even in his last two years, little remained of India's utopian pan-Asian visions, of its perceptions of a resurgent Asia riding the crest of a new epoch in history. India discovered to its dismay that not many of the nonaligned countries shared its perception of China as an aggressive, expansionist power, and few were willing to take India's side against its Communist neighbor.

The next prime minister, Lal Bahadur Shastri, had a brief tenure in office (June 1964–January 1966). It was a lean period for India, extending to the first four years of the prime ministership of Indira Gandhi. Shastri's two years as prime minister proved to be traumatic for India. In 1964 China became a nuclear power, at once setting off a debate in India on whether India too should not quickly make its own nuclear bomb.[8] In the arms race with China, India seemed to have fallen farther behind. Vast resources were rapidly diverted to the building of military strength after the Indian debacle in the border war with China. This inevitably strained the country's limited development investments. In 1965 a Pakistani bid to seize Kashmir led to the first full-scale India-Pakistan war along the entire northwestern border. Neither belligerent won and therefore each claimed victory. The war was marked by three major external factors. First, the United States cut off economic and military assistance to both Pakistan and India, a diplomatic action that accelerated the Indian economic crisis of the late 1960s and led many Pakistanis to regard the United States as an unreliable patron. Second, the Chinese, with a view to coming to Pakistan's help, served an "ultimatum" on the Indian government demanding the immediate dismantling of "hundreds of illegal structures" allegedly built by Indian troops on Chinese territory along the northeastern border, or else face dire consequences.[9] The third and most important factor was Soviet mediation between India and Pakistan. In accordance with the agreement, India returned to Pakistan the relatively small patches of territory it had seized in the war, and the two agreed to coexist peacefully.[10] The agree-

[8] Bhabani Sen Gupta, "India and Disarmament," in B. R. Nanda, ed., *India's Foreign Policy: The Nehru Years* (New Delhi; Vikas Publishing House, 1976).
[9] For the text of the Chinese note, see *Peking Review* (September 24, 1965); also, Sen Gupta, *Fulcrum of Asia,* pp. 212–18. The BBC special correspondent who visited the border reported that "the Chinese certainly seem to be preparing for an attack." BBC Newsreel, September 20, 1965.
[10] The Tashkent Declaration, signed on January 10, 1965, was a tenuous compromise between the main positions of India and Pakistan. The two countries "reaffirmed their pledge, in conformity with the [U.N.] Charter, not to resort to force

ment created a major controversy in Pakistan; it was opposed by Zulfikar Ali Bhutto, who resigned from Ayub's cabinet. Ayub, who had been misled by advisers to exaggerate the fighting ability of Pakistani soldiers and underrate that of the Indians, left office in 1969 amid widespread protests throughout Pakistan. He then handed over power to the army chief of staff, General Yahya Khan.

ADVENT OF INDIRA GANDHI

Shastri died of a heart attack within hours of concluding peace agreements with Pakistan. His death, plus the great unpopularity of the accord in Pakistan, made it more acceptable to Indians than it otherwise might have been. However, the Soviet Union emerged as conflict manager in the subcontinent, and, after a brief attempt to build a "balanced" relationship with India and Pakistan, it again leaned clearly toward India.

The next prime minister was Indira Gandhi, who made her first state visit to Moscow. Her first three years in office proved to be politically and economically bleak. The country faced its first famine since independence (and the last to date): India's dependence on American grain became palpably humiliating when President Lyndon Johnson slowed down shipments to punish Gandhi for her mild criticism of U.S. escalation of the war against North Vietnam. The rupee was devalued against the wishes of the Congress party bosses. In the elections of 1967–68 the party lost the entire Hindi-speaking north and much of the northeast, and Gandhi's prime ministership was sustained in parliament by the support of the Communists.[11] However, after her break with the old guard of the party, Gandhi formed her own Congress party in 1969 with an evocative battle cry—"Abolish poverty"—and won a handsome victory. The Congress order was restored at the national level. It took two more years, and the emergence of Bangladesh in what used to be East Pakistan, to restore fully the political hegemony of Gandhi's party throughout the country.

Although Gandhi had learned her lessons in politics and diplomacy from her father, she had none of Nehru's idealistic visions of India's role in world affairs, or of Asian resurgence as a great new political force. What mattered most for her was India's security and national interest, of which territory and prestige were integral parts. She was "matter-of-fact and non-ideological," according to one study of her foreign policy.[12] She attached as much

but to resolve their disputes peacefully." For Pakistan's negative popular reaction, see *The Times,* London, March 7, 1966.

[11] The united Communist party of India (CPI) broke up into two factions in 1964 under the impact of the Sino-Soviet schism and the India-China border war. The Communist party of India (Marxist) (CPI-M) was branded as pro-China, while the CPI remained committed to the CPSU line. However, in 1969, the two Communist parties, despite their many differences, supported Gandhi in the lower house of parliament, and joined a United Front ministry in West Bengal, of which the CPI-M was the largest constituent.

[12] Surjit Mansingh, *India's Search for Power: Indira Gandhi's Foreign Policy 1966–1982* (New Delhi: Sage Publications, 1984), p. 26.

importance as did Nehru, however, to the Indian brand of socialism and to the fast-growing public sector, which, even in the first years of her rule, was officially elevated to the "commanding heights" of the mixed economy. Her pragmatism was "allied to a grasp for the tangible attributes of power—including military power." [13] The 16 years of her prime ministership—broken by two years of non-Congress rule—generated considerable internal controversy. She created dissension by declaring a national emergency in 1975, and in the 1980s, in the last three and one-half years of her rule, she was embroiled in serious, bloody conflicts in Assam and Punjab. In the end, she was assassinated by Sikh members of her personal guard in late 1984. She had, however, built up a solid national consensus. After the Indian victory over the Pakistani army in Bangladesh in 1971, Indians saw their country as the leading power in South Asia, and so did most of the outside world. [14]

EMERGENCE OF BANGLADESH

In order to make war on the Pakistani army in East Pakistan on behalf of the explicit request of the newly born republic of Bangladesh, Indira Gandhi needed the Soviet Union to neutralize Pakistan's two great external patrons, the United States and China. [15] At first Gandhi mounted a massive diplomatic initiative to persuade a host of governments, especially those of the United States and Britain, of the just cause she had determined to support and promote. When this failed she went to Moscow. In 1971 the 20-year Indo-Soviet Treaty of Peace and Friendship was concluded, with an explicit mutual security commitment. [16] Armed with a firm promise of Soviet political, diplomatic and military support, Gandhi sent the Indian armed forces into Bangladesh. Pakistan then declared war on India. Little fighting took place along the northwestern frontier of India, and the Pakistani army in Bangladesh surrendered in two weeks. The republic of Bangladesh was ceremoniously inaugurated in Dhaka, and Indira Gandhi became the popular war heroine of India. This time, the Chinese served no ultimatum on India, even though they sharply condemned Indian "aggression." The United States dispatched a nuclear aircraft carrier to the Bay of Bengal to warn India against extending the war to West Pakistan and/or Kashmir. [17] But by that time Gandhi had declared a unilateral cease-fire. In a few months she released the 93,000 Pakistani war prisoners the Indian army had taken into custody in Bangladesh, and signed the Simla agreement with Zulfikar Ali Bhutto, who had taken over from the military as

[13] Ibid.

[14] Bhabani Sen Gupta, "Foreign Policy: Quest for Power," in M.K. Mankekar, ed., *Indira Gandhi: An Appraisal* (New Delhi; Avinabh Publishers, 1986).

[15] For comprehensive documentation of the Bangladesh crisis, see *Bangladesh Documents*, Vols. I and II (New Delhi: Government of India, 1972).

[16] See Clause 9 of the treaty; for text, see appendix to Mansingh, *India's Search for Power*, note 12.

[17] Henry Kissinger, *White House Years* (Boston: Little, Brown & Company, 1979), ch. XXI.

Pakistan's leader immediately after the Pakistani army's defeat in Bangladesh. The agreement bound the two neighbors to resolve the Kashmir dispute only through peaceful means, and pledged them to promote normal economic, trade and cultural relations.[18]

In 1974 India exploded a "peaceful" nuclear device in Rajasthan. Despite Indian protestations, the world saw it as a demonstration of India's ability, if not its will, to make nuclear weapons. With the Rajasthan explosion, India did not become the world's sixth nuclear power, but, as Fred C. Ikle, then director of the U.S. Arms Control and Disarmament Agency, remarked in 1975, it did emerge as "number one among a great many countries" to come up with nuclear power aspirations. Earlier Gandhi had silenced public demand for a "quick bomb" with the announcement of a 10-year plan to build an ambitious nuclear-energy infrastructure, which could be converted at the appropriate time, if necessary, into a credible weapons program. Between 1974 and 1988 India's nuclear infrastructure progressed impressively, despite several setbacks and attempts by a number of countries, including the United States, Canada and the Soviet Union, to make it very difficult for India to acquire weapons-grade nuclear fuel. Pakistan's parallel progress toward a similar if necessarily smaller capability in the 1980s pushed South Asia to the threshold of proliferation. India was in no mood to cooperate with Pakistani efforts to deter proliferation. Indira Gandhi and, after her, Rajiv Gandhi remained committed to the atom's peaceful application to India's development, but both made it clear—the son more stridently than the mother—that if Pakistan made the bomb, India would not lag behind.[19]

In the 1980s Indian strategists linked the country's nuclear capability to China's nuclear power. It appeared that Rajiv Gandhi was steadfastly laying out the infrastructure of credible weapons capability, with India's own satellite, missile and carrier programs, so that if the nuclear option were actually taken, India would not fall far behind China as a nuclear power. The country was, in any case, far ahead of Pakistan. In reality India's nuclear program and its nuclear aspirations were status-oriented rather than a response to perceived security threats from nuclear China or near-nuclear Pakistan. Therein lies the main dilemma of any Indian prime minister, including Rajiv Gandhi. The capability-yes weapons-no policy does not violate India's traditional opposition to nuclear weapons; moreover, it confers on India a certain stature in the world community.

NARROW HORIZONS

Through the 1970s India's foreign policy remained more or less confined to the South Asian region and to interactions with the Soviet Union, the United States and China. From 1962 on, China and Pakistan dominated

[18] For text of Simla agreement, see appendix to Mansingh, *India's Search for Power.*
[19] There is a sizable literature on India's nuclear program. For a good overview, see Leonard S. Spector, *Nuclear Proliferation Today* (New York: Vintage Books, 1984).

India's strategic thinking and defense policies. Friendship with the Soviet Union continued to grow, but relations with the United States seesawed because of Washington's military relationship with Pakistan and its perception of India as a friend or ally, and sometimes a stooge, of the Soviet Union.

India's perceptions of countries in the Asia-Pacific region were determined mostly by three factors: the country's security relations with the United States, its attitude toward China and its position in the nonaligned movement. Thus, Nehru broke with Sukarno when the latter drew close to China and away from the Soviet Union; the Indonesian leader's concept of the "newly emergent forces" made no impression on the Indian mind. Indians had a more benign view of Malaysia partly because of the existence of a strong Tamil community in that country and partly because of anti-Chinese sentiment in Malaysia as a result of Chinese support for communist insurgency in its territory. However, Malaysia's security ties with Britain and Australia and the pro-U.S. attitudes of its ruling elites stood as barriers to cordiality between New Delhi and Kuala Lumpur. Indians watched Japan's gradual economic recovery and its steady emergence as an economic power; but until the end of the 1970s they were put off by their image of Japan as a security-bound ally of the United States and therefore not a fruitful target of political rapprochement. South Korea and Singapore aroused similar feelings.

Nevertheless, between the late 1960s and mid-1970s, Indira Gandhi tried to expand the horizon of India's foreign relations. She visited Indonesia and Australia in 1968 and Japan in 1973. But the visits did not produce tangible political or economic results. As described in the most comprehensive study of Indira Gandhi's foreign policy;

> The attitude of the Indian Foreign Office [to Japan till the 1970s] can be summed up in an oft-heard aphorism, 'Japan may be an economic giant, but it is a political pigmy.' Japan was uncomfortable with India's assertiveness in international councils on behalf of nationalism in the Third World. India was disappointed with Japan's firm identification with the United States. At the political-security level, the two governments were unable to bridge their separate perceptions, especially of China and the Soviet Union, with anything more than platitudes. On the level of economic relations, the advance country–developing country syndrome was much in evidence. . . .[20]

It was only in the north-south, south-south forums, and also the General Agreement on Tariffs and Trade, that India found limited cooperation with Asia-Pacific countries possible. But here too India stood apart from the so-called newly industrializing countries of East and Southeast Asia—South Korea, Taiwan, Hong Kong and Singapore. These export-oriented models of growth seemed to Indians to be essentially dependency models, since the prosperity of these small, enterprising nations rested on the predominantly Japanese and/or American orientation of their economies.

[20] Mansingh, *India's Search for Power.*

THE INDIAN OCEAN

In the latter half of the 1960s India began to develop an awareness of the Indian Ocean, from which a strategic concept stemmed in the next 10 or 12 years. In the words of K. Subrahmanyan, the most vocal Indian strategic thinker, "The Indian Ocean can . . . justifiably be called the ocean of non-alignment and of the developing nations." The concept of the Indian Ocean as a zone of peace was, according to Subrahmanyan, "a logical extension of non-alignment."[21] India protested to Britain when the latter transferred to the United States the island of Diego Garcia for the purpose of building a naval base, and protested to the United States when the naval base was started.

From the late 1960s through the 1970s India held the United States primarily responsible for militarizing the Indian Ocean; the Soviet naval presence was seen as a restrained response to the larger American penetration. However, by 1979 Indian ardor for the peace-zone concept had diminished, while a new conservative, pro-Western government in Sri Lanka was no more than symbolically committed to it.[22]

In India itself subtle but meaningful attitudinal changes took place after 1979. The concept of the Indian Ocean as a zone of peace was discussed often, including before parliament. Official spokespersons in and out of parliament said that the government was closely monitoring the naval movements of the United States and the Soviet Union. On most occasions, however, official statements now referred to "great power presence" or "superpower presence" in the Indian Ocean rather than naming the United States. Similarly, Indian delegates at the United Nations strongly criticized the "negativism of certain countries, however powerful" regarding the zone of peace, but the United States was hardly identified specifically. Nor did the Indian government take major diplomatic initiatives to mobilize support for the zone. Perhaps it was sobered by the chilly response to whatever low-level diplomatic moves it might have made from time to time. Indira Gandhi, who returned to power in early 1980 after two years in the political wilderness, conceded that no Indian initiative would "affect the confrontation of bigger powers who wanted to play out their rivalries away from their shores." Confessing helplessness, she added, "We cannot match the strength of the major powers, but we are trying to maintain defense preparedness. . . . Much as we would like to think it does, international opinion does not have any effect on the big powers." Gandhi evidently had in mind the new cold war that had broken out in 1979 between the superpowers, following the collapse of the pro-U.S. regime of the shah of Iran

---

[21] K. Subrahmanyan, "Indian Ocean as a Zone of Peace," in A. N. Kakkar, et al., *Indian Ocean: Proceedings of an International Seminar* (Allahabad: New Book House, 1987).

[22] Indians welcomed the dialogue that took place in the 1970s between the United States and the Soviet Union about naval arms control in the Indian Ocean, and regretted the talks' indefinite suspension in 1979 following the Soviet military intervention in Afghanistan.

and the Soviet military intervention in Afghanistan to protect a wobbling Marxist government.

AFGHANISTAN AND CAMBODIA

Under Indira Gandhi's direction, the Indian government did not condemn the Soviet intervention in Afghanistan; indeed, at international forums it even defended the Soviet position. In bilateral exchanges, however, Gandhi showed her disapproval and urged Moscow to pull out its troops as soon as possible. At the same time India kept an accusing finger pointed to other interventions—by the United States, China, Saudi Arabia and Egypt, who supplied generous quantities of arms to the Afghan rebels. She held Pakistan responsible for bringing the cold war to South Asia by acting as a frontline nation opposing Soviet expansionism.[23] For two years, India was seen in the West and in much of Asia as blandly pro-Soviet, a perception that was reinforced when Gandhi recognized the Heng Samrin government installed in Cambodia by Vietnam after the Vietnamese military intervention had driven out the widely abhorred Pol Pot regime.

In taking both actions, which were more unpopular abroad than at home, Gandhi was motivated only by India's national interests as she saw them. No other power would have given India half the benefits it derived from the long-standing friendship with the Soviet Union. Besides, yielding Afghanistan to the rebellious Mujahideen, who were led by Islamic fundamentalists and who were under Pakistan's protection, would have meant the installation of a fundamentalist, pro-Pakistan government in Afghanistan, and this would have been detrimental to India's domestic stability. It would also upset the balance of power in South Asia. In Southeast Asia, a united, strong Vietnam leading the three Indochinese states was regarded by Gandhi as a reliable barrier to Chinese expansionism. Neither issue, therefore, divided the Indian political parties, and both issues had the support of the foreign policy community.

Gandhi, however, moved fast to wrest whatever advantage she could from the Soviet predicament in Afghanistan. She got from Moscow a very favorable arms-supply deal. Extended after Rajiv Gandhi came to power, it now runs to the end of the century. In 1982–83 Indira Gandhi improved bilateral relations with the United States, separating them from the many multilateral issues over which the two nations were hard put to find areas

[23] In 1980–81 Indira Gandhi took more than one initiative to persuade Gen. Zia ul-Haq of Pakistan to work with India rather than with the United States to secure withdrawal of Soviet troops from Afghanistan. The Pakistani president rejected the Indian initiatives. See Bhabani Sen Gupta, *The Afghan Syndrome: How to Live with Soviet Power* (New Delhi: Vikas Publishing House, 1981). In May 1988 Prime Minister Rajiv Gandhi took an unsuccessful initiative to persuade Pakistan to work with India, the Kabul regime and the Afghan Mujahideen to create a government in Afghanistan—after the withdrawal of Soviet troops—that would be acceptable to most Afghan people. Pakistan refused to give India a role in post-Geneva political settlement in Afghanistan.

of agreement.[24] She had started taking small but not insignificant steps toward improving relations with China even in 1976, during the period of national emergency. After her return to power in 1980, she hastened the process. Three major international events in India between 1980 and 1983—the conference of the heads of Commonwealth countries, the conference of foreign ministers of nonaligned countries and the seventh nonaligned summit—enabled India to recapture some of its former international prominence.

In South Asia, Pakistan's prominent role in supporting the Mujahideen's war of resistance in Afghanistan as well as the flow of high-tech American arms to Islamabad created serious tensions between the two neighbors for the first time since 1972. India was able to run the arms race with generous help from the Soviet Union. Gandhi kept the pressure on Pakistan. At the same time she offered Pakistan a treaty of peace and friendship even as she rejected Pakistan's offer to India of a no-war pact. For the first time, India and Pakistan carried on an extended strategic-political dialogue. Although it produced nothing positive, the establishment of a joint India-Pakistan commission gave the relationship an institutional frame of limited cooperation for the first time.

Among the many contradictory consequences of the Soviet intervention in Afghanistan, perhaps the most significant was the belated creation of a regional cooperation organization of seven South Asian nations. The concept originated with the then president of Bangladesh, Ziaur Rahman, who sent a proposal to the South Asian governments in 1981, when relations between Pakistan and Afghanistan were tense. Both countries' first reaction to the proposal was suspicion and skepticism. In less than two years, however, the idea took root and the decision was made to create the South Asian Regional Cooperation group, later renamed South Asian Association for Regional Cooperation (SAARC), with a low-level, consensus-oriented cooperation program. The organization was inaugurated at a meeting of foreign ministers in New Delhi. It was agreed that there would be an annual summit of heads of government and an annual meeting of foreign ministers to prepare for the summit. This created an extraordinarily high political profile for a regional cooperation body built on a modest programmatic foundation.[25] Three successive summits, in Dhaka, New Delhi and Kathmandu, dramatically highlighted the wide gaps between South Asian desires for bilateral and multilateral cooperation, and the barriers to cooperation created by intransigent realities and hard negative perceptions. Nevertheless, each summit proved to be a crisis-defusing occasion, not as a result of multilateral accords but through bilateral talks. The summit

---

[24] President Reagan responded to the Indian initiative warmly after his cordial meeting with Gandhi at Cancun.

[25] There is a growing literature on SAARC and on South Asian regional cooperation. See Bhabani Sen Gupta, ed., *Regional Cooperation for Development in South Asia,* Vols. I and II, (New Delhi: South Asia Publishers, for Centre for Policy Research, 1985); Pran Chopra, ed., *Future of South Asia* (New Delhi: Macmillan, for Centre for Policy Research, 1986).

became an effective and highly useful forum for communication and informal diplomatic and political exchanges in a region marked by a surfeit of conflicts, and also for the airing of the different visions of South Asian political figures.[26]

By the time Gandhi was killed, the world image of India as a Soviet "stooge" had virtually disappeared, first in the United States and then in Western Europe, Japan, China and the Association of Southeast Asian Nations (ASEAN) members. Gandhi herself paid her second visit to Japan in 1983. Indians began to develop an awareness of the emergent importance of the Pacific Basin in the world economy. The decision to diversify arms procurement brought to India, in 1980 and thereafter, presidents, prime ministers and monarchs from Western Europe. Substantial deals were struck with France, Britain, West Germany, Sweden and Switzerland. Then came the Japanese, first tentatively, and then rapidly, with greater and firmer intent to do business; in a few years, they captured almost the entire collaborative effort offered by India in the automotive field. Finally, trade delegations began to come from South Korea, Singapore and Malaysia.

EXPANDING FRONTIERS

Rajiv Gandhi, who became prime minister in his own right after decisively winning the parliamentary election of December 1984, has carried these linkages forward. Keeping to the track laid out by his mother, he has significantly expanded bilateral economic and trade relations with the United States and, going a bold step further, has inaugurated a delicate relationship of transfer of high-tech defense and dual-purpose technologies. The prime minister, who has been diligently courted by the Americans, is seen in the United States as a modernizing technocrat, more accepting of Western models of growth and development than were his mother and grandfather, less ideologically committed to the Indian brand of socialism and the public sector. Rajiv Gandhi visited Washington in the summer of 1985 after a successful visit to Moscow earlier in May. He went to Jakarta, Wellington and Bangkok, twice to Hanoi in three years, and paid a welcome visit to Tokyo in 1988. Indian diplomacy was deployed to work for a settlement of the Cambodian issue, and was partly instrumental in bringing together the opposing factions.

In 1988 Gandhi prepared the ground for the first visit of an Indian prime minister to China since 1954. Also by 1988, Japan emerged as the largest donor of foreign aid to India. A couple of years earlier, South Koreans built a modern international airport in Delhi named after Indira Gandhi. Visiting India in 1988 was the Singapore prime minister, Lee Kuan Yew, carrying a large portfolio of collaboration proposals. India, for both

---

[26] In their speeches to the plenary sessions of the summits, South Asian heads of government air their visions about regional cooperation. They do this knowing well that SAARC's programmatic foundation is very modest, that it is barred by its charter from going into controversial issues and that all its decisions have to be made by consensus.

economic and diplomatic reasons, was now buying rice and palm oil from Thailand and Indonesia, and tin and rubber from Malaysia. Conferences were being held in New Delhi and Singapore on the possibilities of India-ASEAN economic cooperation, while chambers of commerce began to play an active role in exploring trade opportunities. None of these developments eroded India's friendly intercourse with the Soviet Union, which took on new life after Mikhail Gorbachev became general secretary of the CPSU in 1985. After Rajiv Gandhi's May 1985 visit to Moscow, Gorbachev paid a state visit to New Delhi in November 1986. The prime minister made two more short visits to Moscow in 1985 and 1987. In July 1988 the president of India, R. Venkataraman, paid an official visit to the Soviet Union, and Gorbachev paid his second visit to New Delhi in November. An India festival in the Soviet Union and a Soviet festival in India proved to be equally popular events.

ASIA-PACIFIC VISIONS

It would not be an exaggeration to say that Gorbachev planted the Asia-Pacific region firmly in the Indian imagination with his Vladivostok speech of July 1986. Indians had begun to realize the pivotal position the Pacific Basin had acquired in world economic affairs even at the beginning of the 1980s, with Japan's emergence as an economic superpower and a contender for global technological leadership. The relative economic decline of the United States, its heavy trade and budget deficits, and its spiraling foreign and national debts rendered it more vulnerable than before to changes in the world's fiscal and economic weather. The newly industrialized countries of East and Southeast Asia were no longer looked down upon by Indians but cultivated as mutually beneficial sources of collaboration. However, it required Gorbachev's Vladivostok speech to convince the Indian elite that Japan was emerging as an independent economic giant despite its security relations with the United States, and that China's independent foreign policy—based on nonalignment with the two superpowers but cooperation with both—was a stable phenomenon in world politics. Indeed, far more than the Sino-U.S. entente of the 1970s, Gorbachev's open recognition of China as a world power with whom the Soviets were ready to resolve their border dispute largely to Beijing's satisfaction, and with whose leader, Deng Xiaoping, Gorbachev openly sought a summit meeting, convinced the Indians that China was truly edging toward world power status by the end of the century. Indians did not buy Gorbachev's concept of Asian security on the European Helsinki model, but they were more open to it than they had been to the Brezhnev plan for collective Asian security. They reacted positively to the Gorbachev plan because it embraced all Asian powers as well as the United States, and all Asian regional organizations, including ASEAN and SAARC, and also because it had no possibility of taking shape in the foreseeable future.

In 1987, with Gorbachev's blessing and the assistance of the external affairs ministry, an Institute of Asia-Pacific Studies was set up in New Delhi with former Foreign Secretary Maharaj Krishna Rasgotra as director.

It held well-attended national and international meetings.[27] The organizers of the institute and its scholarly and journalistic adherents held perceptions of the Asia-Pacific region that were not fully shared by the mainstream elite, but neither were they rejected as partisan. Most Indians had consciously or unconsciously adopted a common measure to judge the importance and relevance of other nations, namely, the particular nation's independence of the United States. Japan earned Indian respect not so much because of its towering economic power as for its efforts to assert its independent political and strategic personality. China deserved a new Indian look because it had broken away from its strategic alliance with the United States and adopted an independent position. The ASEAN group drew Indian attention because its members were finding it difficult to keep in step with the American line in view of protectionist tendencies and chronic trade deficits in the United States. In India's view, the Pacific region was emerging into extraordinary importance because it was finally edging out of the American security and economic orbit. Indians did not wish to see the American order replaced by a Soviet order. However, they wanted the Soviet Union to be accepted as an Asian-European power since three-fourths of its territory is in Asia, and because Siberia, with its vast untapped natural resources, holds the key to the Soviet Union's future growth and development. In short, Indians preferred a multipolar world to a bipolar one, with several centers of power rather than merely two. For India, welcome events signaling the coming of a truly pluralistic world, in terms of political and economic power, were the emergence of Western European nations as independent centers of power; a certain amount of decoupling of Western Europe from the United States; Western Europe's economic and infrastructural integration, each little step taken to further its political integration; and the cooperative bridges built between Western and Eastern Europe and between the European Community and the Council for Mutual Economic Assistance. Indian analysts saw in the Pacific region a stable balance of four major powers—the United States, the Soviet Union, Japan and China—with regional balances emerging in Southeast Asia, South Asia and the Arab/Persian Gulf.

In 1985–86 Indian policy- and opinion-makers debated more intensely than ever before what should be the pattern of Sino-Indian relations in the context of approaching normalization of relations between the Soviet Union and China. Four broad conclusions were reached. First, normalization of Moscow-Beijing relations would not hurt India; it would, on the contrary, help India normalize its own relations with China. Even with normalization, a process that was bound to be slow, the Soviet Union and China would not return to their relationship of the 1950s, and India would continue to enjoy its special position in Moscow's foreign policy. Second, improvement of relations with China should no longer be hostage to a reso-

[27] K. P. Misra, et al., eds., *Southern Asia-Pacific Perceptions and Strategies;* V. D. Chopra, et al., eds., *Asia-Pacific Economic Potential and Prospects;* M. Rasgotra, et al., eds., *Southern Asia-Pacific: A Region in Turbulence* (all three New Delhi: Continental Publishing House, on behalf of International Institute for Southern Asia Pacific Studies).

lution of the border dispute; the two issues should be separated and handled at different levels. Third, the border issue could be settled only on the basis of give and take, over a fairly long period of time; diplomacy should be deployed toward that end. Finally, the talks between India and China should be raised to the political level. Indian officials told several visiting delegations from China that the bilateral relationship should be improved despite disagreement on the border question. Visits were made to Beijing by two cabinet ministers as well as delegations of the two Indian Communist parties and the Congress party. In 1988 the chief minister of the Marxist-led state government of West Bengal, Jyoti Basu, who is regarded in India as an elder statesman, went to China with a message from the prime minister. The cumulative result of all these positive developments was the decision of Rajiv Gandhi to visit China in 1988.

BEYOND SOUTH ASIA

Beginning with an idealistic view of Asia, based on its ancient civilization and its strivings and struggles for liberation from imperialist domination, Indian perceptions of international politics—and particularly of the drift and scale of Asian affairs—settled in the 1970s around its own national interests as viewed by its elected rulers. A parliamentary democracy is often more open to the impact of external events and ideas than an authoritarian political system. The first generation of India's rulers decided to adopt an eclectic model of development. The Indian state was born under the joint impact of three traumas. Partition created its generic conflict with Pakistan. Decolonization released its long-arrested visions and energies and brought the distant past within the grasp of a dream-laden future. And the cold war threw a shadow on India's own image of independence and cautioned against getting involved in the cleavage of a polarized world. The significance of the Indian experiment is that for some 40 years it has developed as an open political society. It has drawn upon the wisdom and follies of the capitalist West and the socialist East. Through a continuing process of trial and error, slippage and success, it has created a state that demands world attention on its own merit, finding over 90 percent of development resources within its own frontiers. However the West may have reacted to specific thrusts of India's foreign policy actions, however unpalatable India's pro-Soviet stance may have been to Western political taste, India has never believed that it has acted on Moscow's behalf under duress. The congruence of Indian and Soviet world perceptions and foreign-policy actions is traced by Indians to a natural rather than contrived unity of mind and vision.

Two final observations: It will be noticed by students of Indian foreign policy that throughout this period Indians made many real efforts on their own to comprehend international forces and their complex interactions, creating original concepts such as nonalignment and generating with China the five principles of peaceful coexistence, often responding with an open mind to positive ideas and moves originating in the West as well as in the

900

Soviet Union, but at the same time clinging stubbornly to their own foreign-policy thinking, however correct or mistaken it may have been.

The result has been satisfying and disappointing at the same time. It is satisfying to the extent that India has grown into a stable democracy whose independence and sovereignty have not been questioned even when its specific foreign-policy actions have been criticized; and also to the extent that it has saved itself from disruptive social or political convulsions, though not from a normal load of conflicts and tensions, and in the process has developed a firm stake in orderly, incremental change, in evolution rather than revolution, in a radical center rather than radical left or right, in continuities rather than abrupt traumatic change. The result is disappointing in that India has remained what may be called a provincial power, laboring, not without success, to have its primacy in South Asia recognized by the world community, assertive within the region to the extent of generating hegemonic fears in the minds of its weaker neighbors, fighting wars with them and intervening in their internal affairs with a self-fulfilling impulse of enlightened national and regional interests. India has not yet been able to graduate to global power like its larger neighbor, China, and to operate at the center of international politics rather than at its periphery. But that is where India's attention is now directed. Rajiv Gandhi's awareness of the advent of the 21st century, his readiness to modernize the Indian economy with a liberal policy of technology imports, his opening to the United States and Japan, and his efforts to plant on the minds of the nations of Europe and Asia the image of an India that has arrived are all components of the quest for a larger role. To play this role, India is now assembling a navy; developing its own space, missile and nuclear capabilities; and streamlining its large (120-million-strong) middle-class base of society. India's weaknesses, however, still stem from the miserable poverty of nearly 40 percent of its population—over 300 million men, women and children—and from the growing dichotomy between the relatively affluent, numbering 120 million, and the huge deprived human mass of over 600 million.

FURTHER READING

Achuthan, Nisha Sahai. *Soviet Arms Transfers in South Asia, 1955–1981,* New Delhi: Lancer International, 1988.

Appadorai, A., and Rajan, M.S. *India's Foreign Policy and Relations.* New Delhi: South Asian Publishers, 1985.

Crunden, Robert M., ed. *Traffic of Ideas Between India and America.* Delhi: Chanakya Publications, 1985.

Kakkar, A.N., et al. eds. *Indian Ocean.* Allahabad: India, New Book House, 1987.

Kamath, P.M., ed. *Indo-US Relations: Dynamics of Change.* New Delhi: South Asian Publishers, 1987.

Kaushik, Devendra. *Perspectives on Security in the Indian Ocean.* New Delhi: Allied Publishers, 1987.

Mansingh, Surjit. *India's Search for Power: Indira Gandhi's Foreign Policy, 1966–1982.* New Delhi and Beverly Hills, California: Sage Publications, 1984.

Nanda, B.R., ed. *Indian Foreign Policy: The Nehru Years.* New Delhi: Asia Publishing House, 1976.

Rajan, M.S., et al., eds. *The Non-Aligned and the United Nations.* New Delhi: South Asian Publishers, 1987.

Sen Gupta, Bhabani. *The Afghan Syndrome: How to Live with Soviet Power.* New Delhi: Vikas, 1982.

————, ed. *Regional Cooperation and Development in South Asia.* 2 vols. New Delhi: South Asian Publishers, 1986.

————. *South Asian Perspectives.* New Delhi: B.R. Publishing, 1988.

Spector, Leonard S. *The New Nuclear Nations.* New York: Vintage Books, 1985.

————. *Nuclear Proliferation Today.* Vintage Books, 1984.

Subrahmanyan, K., and Singh, Jasjit, eds. *Scarcity without Nuclear Weapons: Indo-Soviet Dialogue.* New Delhi: Lancer International, 1986.

Thomas, Raju G.C. *Indian Security Policy.* Princeton, New Jersey: Princeton University Press, 1986.

ASIA AND THE PACIFIC SINCE 1945: A JAPANESE PERSPECTIVE

TAKASHI INOGUCHI

LOOKED at from the vantage point of the late 1980s, the history of the countries of the Asia-Pacific region evokes two major images: One is that of war devastation and struggles for national development; the other is that of decolonization overshadowed by the cold war and the emergence of the region during a slow decline of what may be called "Pax Americana." The Asia-Pacific region has experienced polar extremes—from devastation to development, from humiliation to self-confidence—in a period of little more than 40 years since World War II. What is most striking about this region is the tenacity and vigor with which its peoples rebound from adversity.

WAR AND DEVASTATION

War has been a recurrent theme in the history of the Asia-Pacific region.[1] In China alone more than 10 million people were killed during the war with the Japanese in the years 1937–45, and about 20 million were killed during the political turmoil of the Chinese Cultural Revolution of 1966–76.[2] One can give no less awesome figures for the Korean War and the Vietnam War, as well as for the suppression of Communists in Indonesia after 1965 and the massacre in Cambodia between 1975 and 1979. It is not an exaggeration to say that the Asia-Pacific region has been one of the most conflict ridden during the 20th century.

The colonization drives of the Western powers, and later of Japan, swept across the region in the 19th and 20th centuries. Colonization left few countries unscathed.[3] China was half colonized, with Hong Kong and Ma-

[1] For useful overviews of the history of Asia and the Pacific, see, inter alia, John K. Fairbank et al., *East Asia: The Modern Transformation* (Boston: Houghton Mifflin, 1965); David Joel Steinberg et al., *In Search of Southeast Asia* (Honolulu: University of Hawaii Press, 1987).

[2] These figures are cited as the Chinese official view in *Yomiuri Shimbun*, 16 October 1981.

[3] See, inter alia, Fairbank et al., *East Asia;* Steinberg et al., *Southeast Asia;* Lloyd

cao, Taiwan, Manchuria and Mongolia, Tibet and Sinkiang coming under the direct control or "spheres of influence" of the colonial powers. Korea was colonized by Japan; Vietnam, Laos and Cambodia by France; and Burma (now Myanmar) and Malaya by Great Britain. Indonesia was colonized by the Netherlands; the Philippines first by Spain and later by the United States; and various islands in the Pacific by France, Britain, Germany, Japan, and the United States.

Colonization had three ·major consequences. First, it robbed people of self-confidence. At the same time, it planted the seeds of a deep sense of national pride, which was to manifest itself dramatically in the movement for independence. Second, it integrated the economy with that of the colonial powers. The incorporation of colonial economies with the world economy dramatically increased production and population. This effect is sometimes called the "modernizing" influence. At the same time, it skewed and distorted the local economy in many ways, subsequently slowing down self-sustained economic development. Third, it bred war among the colonial powers themselves. The consequences were devastating. So humiliated were those elites who sided with the colonial powers that their political foundation became tenuous and their subsequent political development was detoured. Most directly, war made it plain that the destinies of the colonized were at the mercy of the colonial powers and that the only alternative was national independence. With the region a battlefield for colonial powers and economic mobilization for war making life more miserable, it appeared foolhardy for local elites to cooperate with these powers. Thus, in many ways, World War II prepared the ground for most of the countries of Asia and the Pacific to start anew in its aftermath.

There was virtually no place that was unaffected by war. Throughout China, war permeated the lives of ordinary people for more than eight years. Korea and Manchuria were transformed into a base of military production for the Japanese war machine. Taiwan became the supply base of food for the Japanese.[4] The Philippines was a battlefield between the Japanese and the Americans. So, too, were many Pacific islands. The forced export of food from Vietnam brought about acute food shortages, which gave momentum to the Communists to assume the leadership in peasant-led uprisings. Burma was a battlefield between the Japanese and the British, as were Malaya and Singapore, and Indonesia was a battlefield between the Japanese and the Dutch.

When the war was finally over, virtually no one could predict what would happen. For instance, as late as the mid-1950s an American mission made a recommendation that the scheme for bullet trains between Tokyo and Osaka was unrealistic. It was only about a dozen years later that this "unrealistic" plan was realized. This presaged the rapid recovery and steady

G. Reynolds, *Economic Development in the Third World, 1850–1980* (New Haven: Yale University Press, 1985); W. H. Morris-Jones and Georges Fisher, eds., *Decolonization and After: The British and French Experience* (London: Frank Cass, 1980).
[4] Ramon H. Myers and Mark P. Peattie, eds., *The Japanese Colonial Empire, 1895–1945* (Princeton, New Jersey: Princeton University Press, 1984).

development of Japan, and later the region as a whole. Also, in 1945 it was unthinkable that Communist countries would go to war with each other.[5] As late as the early 1960s, when the Sino-Soviet ideological conflict came to the surface, many people refused to admit that the two countries were really at odds with each other. Yet war was waged in 1969 between China and the Soviet Union, and in 1979 between Cambodia and Vietnam and between China and Vietnam. These wars underlined the fluidity of power realignments in the region. Furthermore, it was inconceivable that South Korea would propose to the United States that it should have independent military command, which was precisely the case in 1987 during the talks between the then ruling party chairman Roh Tae Woo and U.S. President Ronald Reagan. This seems to signify the growing self-confidence of South Korea and perhaps the region as a whole in the late 1980s. Thus, the rapidity and steadiness of economic recovery and development, the fluidity and uncertainty of power configuration, and the growing self-confidence seem to capture the basic tone of the history of the Asia-Pacific region since 1945.

The Asia-Pacific region has achieved a great deal since 1945. However, it was accomplished despite almost insurmountable adversities and achieved at incalculable cost.

DECOLONIZATION AND THE COLD WAR

The impact of World War II on the peoples of the Asia-Pacific region was twofold. First, it set them free from colonial powers to chart their own course—but at their own risk. Second, it introduced a new dimension of international politics to the newly emerging countries of the region. Decolonization in the aftermath of war forced people to organize themselves and to manage their own politics and economics. Prior to independence, the influence of world economic and political forces was through the filter of the colonial powers. After independence, the newly independent countries had to cope with these forces directly. One of the most important new forces was that of the cold war between the United States and the Soviet Union, the two major victors of World War II.[6]

The process of decolonization took a number of years. Roughly by the end of the 1950s most countries had achieved independence, with some exceptions such as Singapore, Brunei, Hong Kong, Papua New Guinea and many in the Pacific. The Asia-Pacific countries were able to accelerate their independence due to war. Especially important in this respect were the humiliation of colonial powers at the hands of the Japanese and the dominance of the U.S. liberating spirit after World War II. There are important exceptions, however. Formerly British Brunei became independent only in 1985, while British Hong Kong is destined to return to Chinese sover-

[5] Benedict O. Anderson, *Imagined Communities: Reflections on the Origin and Spread of Nationalism* (London: Verso, 1983).
[6] John Lewis Gaddis, *Strategies of Containment: A Critical Appraisal of Postwar American National Security Policy* (New York: Oxford University Press, 1982).

eignty in 1997. French New Caledonia, among others in the Pacific, has been refused independence. From north to south in this region, the situation is as follows.

First, China was independent but full sovereignty was restored to a number of former colonies including Manchuria and Taiwan.[7] Civil war between the Communists and the Nationalists erupted soon after World War II. The victory of the Communists was followed half a year later by the outbreak of the Korean War, which was to bring China into the conflict. Thus China was engaged in a succession of wars before and after its revolution—1937–45, 1946–49 and 1950–53. The adversities that confronted the Chinese Communists during these years, especially in 1949–50, made it natural for them to "lean to one side," that of the Soviet Union. The Sino-Soviet alliance of 1950 had enormous consequences for the Chinese Communists, affecting the way they have run their government and economy ever since. It also contributed to the polarization of international politics in the region. Although the alliance lasted 30 years, at least in form, its spirit virtually evaporated 10 years after the conclusion of the treaty. One of the Chinese complaints was the manner in which the Soviet Union, reminiscent of colonial powers, dealt with China on such matters as the utilization of manufacturing and mining facilities, ports and railways in China's northeastern region, which had been a Japanese colony. Taiwan had been controlled by the Nationalists since 1945, but its fate changed by their defeat on the mainland in 1949. From then on Taiwan became overwhelmingly dependent on the protection offered by the United States. It is ironic that the Nationalists, whose cause célèbre was the redemption of sovereignty and national pride lost since the late 19th century, became so tightly subordinated to the will and whim of the United States. It must be noted, however, that Mao Zedong appreciated Chiang Kai-shek's refusal to allow foreign armies on the soil of Taiwan. China, while waiting for the return of Hong Kong, along with Macao has been trying to "unite" with Taiwan under the "one country–two systems" idea.

Second, Korea was divided in 1945 by the United States and the Soviet Union in terms of their respective spheres of influence.[8] The division was further given institutional basis in 1948 when the Republic of Korea in the south and the Democratic People's Republic of Korea in the north were established under the aegis of their patrons. Like China and Taiwan, South and North Korea were placed in an ironic situation, in which vehemently nationalistic regimes were subordinated largely to the logic of the two major powers. Even before the advent of the Japanese defeat, Korean nationalists and Communists alike had been fighting to achieve independence and power. Their efforts continued after 1945. The Communists were especially active in South Korea, as the postwar economic, social and political con-

---

[7] See, inter alia, Jonathan Spence, *The Gate of Heavenly Peace: The Chinese and Their Revolution, 1895–1980* (New York: Viking Press, 1981).
[8] Bruce Cumings, *The Origins of the Korean War* (Princeton, New Jersey: Princeton University Press, 1981); Peter Lowe, *The Origins of the Korean War* (London: Longman, 1986).

ditions there were conducive to rebellion and revolution. Local rebellions erupted intermittently, and the Communists in the north and the south saw them as a golden opportunity, especially when the United States hinted that it would not defend South Korea against the Communists' onslaught—which in fact took place later that year. The Korean War that ensued reinforced the cold war structure in the region as China stood on the side of the North Koreans in opposition to the American-led forces allied with the South Koreans.

The consequence of the Korean war on both Koreas was immense. After decolonization the fate of both Koreas was tightly linked to their neighboring powers, the United States, the Soviet Union and China. Because of the cold war, the course of Korea's development since then has been constrained. Even after these neighboring powers reached accord and accommodation with each other, both Koreas continued to find it difficult to do what both Germanys did after the 1961 construction of the Berlin Wall.

Third, Japan was incorporated into the cold war structure, relinquishing the status of a vanquished and occupied power.[9] The outbreak of the Korean War precipitated the conclusion of the peace treaty between Japan and the Allied powers (except the Soviet Union) and the U.S.-Japanese security treaty. The United States reversed its policy of punishing Japan to one of creating a strong Japan—sans military power—in order to cope with Communist threats in the Asia-Pacific region. An exception to Japan's independence was Okinawa. The Ryukyu Islands, which accommodate large U.S. military bases, were kept outside the control of Japan, an arrangement that lasted until 1972. Since then the U.S. bases in Japan, including those in Okinawa, have been indispensable to the United States. The U.S. forces in Japan since the end of the Vietnam War have been the largest in the entire region.

In the late 1940s and early 1950s the United States concluded security treaties whereby the U.S. unilateral security umbrella was accorded to such countries as the Philippines, South Korea, Taiwan, South Vietnam and Thailand, thus forming the U.S.-led cold war blockade against communism in the Asia-Pacific region.[10] Taiwan, however, did not allow U.S. forces to be stationed there. Furthermore, in the wake of the rapprochement between the United States and China, in 1971, relations with the United States underwent a qualitative change. Yet the U.S. commitment to deter China from "repatriating" Taiwan militarily has kept Taiwan where it is. With the United States having downgraded its China connection in its dealings with the Soviet Union around 1981–82, Taiwan has considerably revived its U.S. ties. South Vietnam was liberated by North Vietnam in 1975; subsequently, Vietnam has allowed the Soviet Union to make use of air bases and naval facilities. In part to counter these moves, the United

[9] Robert Ward and Yoshikazu Sakamoto, eds., *The Democratization of Japan* (Honolulu: University of Hawaii Press, 1986).
[10] See Gaddis, *Strategies of Containment;* Bruce Cumings, ed., *Child of Conflict: The Korean-American Relationship, 1943–1953* (Berkeley: University of California Press, 1988).

States has been strengthening its maritime strategy in the Asia-Pacific region. Thailand relinquished the U.S. bases in 1975 in response to widespread demands. An antimilitary protest and democratization movement in that year proclaimed itself vehemently against the stationing of the U.S. bases there. In the 1980s, however, Thai-U.S. military cooperation was greatly enhanced as the United States saw the need to strengthen Thai defense capability against Soviet-aided Vietnam. For years the Philippines has been negotiating the terms of retaining U.S. bases. But the intensified activities of the New People's Army, the Philippine Communist party's military wing, apparently prompted the United States to encourage the anti-Marcos forces to take power in February 1986. The Aquino government is no less insistent on getting better terms vis-à-vis the U.S. bases. Irrespective of the bargains between the Philippines and the United States on the U.S. bases, the New People's Army has been increasing its strength steadily, with the future of the Subic Bay and Clark air bases somewhat uncertain. In South Korea the demand for an independent military command reflects the growing nationalism and self-confidence of the South Koreans.

All this does not mean that Japan alone lacks groups opposed to the stationing of the U.S. forces on domestic soil. There have been, and are, such forces in Japan. But it is clear that Japan has been the consistent and reliable core of the U.S.-led cold war alignment in the Asia-Pacific region. It should be mentioned, however, that other allies have been more directly involved in cold war–related conflicts, and have thus shouldered more burdens and made greater sacrifices than Japan. South Korea fought one of the largest-scale conventional wars since 1945; even now its vigilance has not been lost concerning North Korea. Taiwan has retained until recently a watchful posture toward China, spending enormous sums for military preparedness. South Vietnam collapsed after having fought a war of attrition for so many years. Thailand has long been a frontline state while Vietnam, Cambodia and Laos were engaged in a war against communism, and since 1975 it has been a neighboring state to Communist Cambodia under the Khmer Rouge and later the pro-Vietnamese Heng Samrin government. The Philippines has been in intermittent confrontation with communist forces for years.

The crux of the problem is that the process of decolonization and the incorporation into the cold war structure of these newly independent countries coincided, and thus the task of nation building and development was made more complex. This combination had both positive and negative effects from the viewpoint of the newly independent countries. Positively, they could obtain economic assistance in large amounts at a time when resource scarcity posed a serious constraint on their nation-building task. In a similar vein, they could rely on the generosity and largesse of the United States in terms of their access to the U.S. market, while maintaining their own protectionism. Also, they could arm themselves against external Communist foes and domestic antagonists, Communist or otherwise. Without foreign backing many of them, unable to cope with vast demands from the masses below, could not have consolidated their political-economic-military foundations in the relatively short span of time after independence.[11] Negatively, the fact that these newly independent nations were allied with foreign powers made them appear as pawns in many ways, thus sometimes undermining the very basis of their legitimacy. That was exactly the fate the government of South Vietnam faced. Also, the facile dependence on foreign aid tended to weaken self-reliant efforts at widening and consolidating their power bases. That has been the tendency of the government of the Philippines for years, from the time of Roxas and Magsaysay through Marcos and Aquino. In other words, all the counties in the Asia-Pacific region had to cope with the long and difficult transition from colonialism and occupation to independence and national development in the shadow of the cold war structure, which sometimes took on the character of neocolonialism, in both its capitalist and communist variants.[12]

It has already been mentioned that China felt it was unjustifiably subjected to the demands and pressures of the Soviet Union during the decade of their alliance. North Korea perhaps felt that these two Communist brothers were not sufficiently supportive of North Korea at the critical time of the fledgling revolutionary state in 1950–53. Similarly, it felt that they were not generous enough thereafter in the difficult process of socialist construction on the ruins of devastation, which was to lead North Korea to develop its overtly nationalistic autarkic strategy of *juche*. North Vietnam apparently felt that the two big brothers did not appreciate the commitment and sacrifice of a fledgling revolutionary movement-cum-front-line state in the world Communist movement. The feeling of resentment was intense, especially when North Vietnam was forced by them to come to terms with South Vietnam, France and the United States in the form of imposed geographical division in 1954, and when it was not fully supported by them in its execution of the war of liberation in 1965–75.[13] Like the newly independent countries of the non-Communist world, the Communist counterparts experienced the very difficult process of revolutionary struggle and socialist construction at almost the same time. The cold war environment worked both positively and negatively for them. Positively, they could justify their revolutionary struggle and socialist construction in terms of the expansion and consolidation of national liberation and world socialism, thus obtaining support from the Soviet Union and China. Negatively, the alignment with the Communist bloc has tended to invite intervention from the big brothers, which is deemed unjustifiable in light of the spirit of world socialism.

In other countries that are more remote from the cold war frontiers— countries such as Indonesia, Malaysia, Singapore and Papua New Guinea—

---

[11] See Frederic Deyo, ed., *The Political Economy of the New Asian Industrialism* (Ithaca, New York: Cornell University Press, 1986).

[12] On the Philippine political economy, see Gary Hawes, *The Philippine State and the Marcos Regime: The Politics of Export* (Ithaca, New York: Cornell University Press, 1986).

[13] William J. Duiker, *The Communist Road to Power in Vietnam* (Boulder, Colorado: Westview Press, 1981).

the road to independence took somewhat different paths. Indonesia had to fight an independence war against the Dutch, becoming independent in 1949, but its drive was further directed at Portuguese Timor (now Indonesian Timor), Western Borneo (now eastern Malaysia) and western New Guinea (now Indonesian Irian Jaya). Indonesia's incorporation of Timor and western New Guinea is sometimes viewed as a new colonialism. Malaya was plagued by the Communist insurrection led largely by ethnic Chinese Communists, and had to wait until the threat subsided in the late 1950s. Papua New Guinea won independence from Australia in 1975, while western New Guinea was incorporated into Indonesia by plebiscite in 1969.

Despite the difficulties of decolonization and the constraints posed by cold war developments, the Asia-Pacific countries have in fact grown much more steadily than many expected. They have shown remarkable tenacity and vigor in pursuing their goals of power and plenty. Even though feeble and desolate in the aftermath of war and independence, they pursued their struggle for national development.

STRUGGLES FOR NATIONAL DEVELOPMENT

It has been seen thus far that, placed in the broader context of decolonization and the cold war, the newly independent countries in the Asia-Pacific region had to cope with many complex problems in the international arena. Vulnerable to the penetration of international forces, they were exceedingly fragile in terms of their domestic foundation. These countries were not sufficiently able to monopolize allegiance from the populace, since they were still competing with many social forces that remained resistant to centralized control. National identity was not strong enough to cement the societies as nations. Thus, these countries were too often unable to create sufficiently robust infrastructures for taxation and administration of popular public policies. The ability of these countries to penetrate society was shallow at best, and too often was dependent on the protection and largesse of the major powers.

First, the problem of national identity was difficult to resolve in many newly emerging countries, largely because, under colonialism, a sense of being a part of a distinctive and proud nation was curtailed and budding nationalism was repressed. In many islands in Indonesia it was difficult, first, to conceive that one was an Indonesian when one did not understand the national language and when state officials were not normally present. It was ironic that the war of independence against the Dutch, as well as the confrontation with major and neighboring powers, and territorial expansion into Timor and western New Guinea, was one of the most instrumental forces to enhance national identity, along with the diffusion of the national standard language. External confrontation and expansion were the primary forces fostering nationalism.

The colonial legacy of arbitrary political division and a deliberate policy of playing one ethnic group against another made this problem all the more difficult for the newly emerging countries to resolve. In Malaya, the Malays, Chinese and Indians were the three largest ethnic groups, with a fairly clear division of labor maintained by the British colonialists. The Malays worked in the countryside, the Chinese in commerce, and the Indians in mining and on plantations. The Malay predominance in politics after independence further forced the other ethnic groups to work in commercial activities. National identity was slow to develop among them when the preferential policy was adopted by the Malay-dominated government. Ethnic antagonism was difficult to hide and sometimes manifested itself in violent forms.[14]

Even where national identity did not pose a grave problem, the government was not able to enjoy wide acceptance of its legitimacy. Similarly, the rule of the government was not perceived as working for public purposes. South Vietnam was a good example. In Vietnam independence was not realized in the 1945 settlement. France came back shortly after the end of World War II, and war ensued between the Communists and the anti-Communists. The latter were backed by France and subsequently by the United States. The Geneva agreement of 1954 temporarily stopped the colonial-civil war, but the step-up of civil war in 1960 led to large-scale U.S. intervention by 1964. The 1973 armistice agreement was followed by the 1975 liberation of South Vietnam. During the period 1945–75 the government was unable to enjoy strong support from the populace. The Communist challenge reinforced the persistence of personalistic authoritarianism and overdependence on foreign powers. Political participation was severely circumscribed by governmental authoritarianism, which in turn fundamentally limited government penetration into society. Shallow rule gave rise to difficulties of taxation, poverty of public policy and dependence on external forces.

South Korea has shown another contrasting example. National liberation came in 1945, but the ensuing occupation by Soviet and American forces in the north and south, respectively, led to the formation of two republics with different ideological foundations. The sporadic civil war between Communists and anti-Communists became an international war between the countries, backed by foreign powers in 1950 under the shadow of the cold war. After the armistice agreement of 1953 South Korea was plagued by the problem of legitimacy. Its authoritarian government was not so different from that in South Vietnam. But the democratic overthrow of the government in 1960 and the military coup of 1961 significantly changed its orientation.

By the mid-1960s South Korea had embarked on the ambitious task of economic development with the help of four factors. One was the government's orientation, often called "developmental authoritarianism," whereby freedom and democracy are kept at a minimum for the sake of economic development.[15] In other words, wealth must be accumulated before people

---

[14] For Malaysian politics, see Karl von Vorys, *Democracy Without Consensus: Communalism and Political Stability in Malaysia* (London: Oxford University Press, 1976).
[15] For the economic development of South Korea, see Kwang Suk Kim and Michael

oil crisis hit every country hard, the Asia-Pacific region was particularly affected since most of those countries were not rich in energy resources. But contrary to the expectation of some pessimists, the NICs began to flourish in the post–oil crisis period. They were able to make full use of their comparative advantage as latecomers with low wages, long working hours, fast technological catch-up, intensive capital utilization and good developmental planning. Thus, by the late 1970s, when the NICs joined the redoubtable Japan, which among the industrialized countries was least harmed by the oil crises, the emergence of the Asia-Pacific region was visible and tangible.[19] Third, the international alignment pattern was steadily changing the way in which many political leaders looked at the region. The cold war division began to erode. In 1969 China and the Soviet Union clashed on their common borders. In 1971 the United States and China normalized diplomatic relations. In 1973 the United States and North Vietnam negotiated an armistice agreement. In 1975 Vietnam was unified. In 1978 Japan and China concluded a treaty of peace and friendship. In 1979 the Sino-Soviet treaty of peace and mutual assistance was automatically terminated. Also in 1979 Vietnam occupied Cambodia and China invaded Vietnam, two incidents involving Communist neighbors. These developments complicated, or at least blurred, the image of the traditional cold war antagonism between the Communist and the anti-communist blocs in the Asia-Pacific region. The picture of Pacific dynamism has become more salient. Though political uncertainties continue, economic vigor has become the foremost feature of the region.[20]

The emergence of the Asia-Pacific region was further consolidated by two movements in the 1980s: One was the increasing integration of the regional economy with the U.S. economy; the other was the tighter strategic integration with the United States of Japan, South Korea and the Philippines, and to a lesser extent Thailand, Taiwan, China and Australia. Economic integration between the U.S. economy and the Asia-Pacific economies has kept a steady pace, with the U.S. trade pattern shifting from the Atlantic to the Pacific in the late 1970s. But the trend broadened in the 1980s. Manufacturing patterns have become truly cross-Pacific, with capital, technology, resources and labor factors all flowing freely across national borders. Trade has thrived, with Japan-United States activity annually registering the largest transoceanic volume and the NICs-United States commerce steadily catching up. International monetary interdependence became extraordinary in the 1980s. The acceleration of capital movements between the United States and Japan in particular was enormous. The economic management of both countries would have been difficult to conceive without fuller coordination between them. Despite often insurmountable problems, the reality of inexorable economic interdependence and penetra-

[19] Deyo, *Political Economy of the New Asian Industrialism.*

[20] Takashi Inoguchi, *Tadanori to ikkoku hanei shugi o koete* (Beyond Free Ride and One-Country-Prosperity) (Tokyo: Toyo keizai shimposha, 1987); Takashi Inoguchi and Daniel I. Okimoto, eds., *The Political Economy of Japan,* Vol II: *The Changing International Context* (Stanford, California: Stanford University Press, 1988).

tion resides there. All in all, the phrase "the Pacific economy" has come to take on an authentic character. Not only Japan and the United States but also the NICs and the ASEAN countries have begun to do more business with each other. Pacific dynamism has also attracted the attention of Communist neighbors, including China, the Soviet Union, Vietnam and North Korea, encouraging economic reforms and the opening to the West.

Strategic integration among the Asia-Pacific countries and the United States has gone forward significantly. The vigorous military buildup of the United States, unprecedented in peacetime, has permeated the northwestern Pacific region. The U.S. maritime strategy, with forward defense and horizontal escalation concepts, has been applied to the region to a considerable degree. Enhanced deterrence efforts along the Asia-Pacific corridor have solidified with an increase in the number of submarine-launched ballistic and cruise missiles. Especially important is U.S.-Japanese defense cooperation, which has deepened with the latter's participation in the U.S. Strategic Defense Initiative program. The U.S. defense umbrella has been very tight vis-à-vis South Korea, Japan and the Philippines; defense cooperation with Thailand and Taiwan has also been strong, although there are no security treaties with the United States. The U.S. defense arrangements with China and Australia, especially the one allowing installation of high-technology equipment for intelligence in the midst of desert areas, are indispensable to the U.S. international security network, given their geographical location. Despite the steps toward complete abolition of land-based intermediate-range nuclear missiles, agreed on in 1987 between the United States and the Soviet Union, competition between the two countries in the northwestern Pacific has intensified.[21]

The emergence and achievement of the Asia-Pacific region merit special attention. In addition to having suffered from colonialism, imperial rivalries and the cold war, many of the region's countries, especially those regarded as dynamic cores, do not enjoy bounteous natural resources. However, as Elvin Jones argues in his book *The European Miracle* this smaller endowment of resources, along with the hardships of disease, hunger and war, may exert a strong drive for power and plenty.[22]

ALTERNATIVE FUTURE SCENARIOS

The history of Asia and the Pacific in the minds of most Japanese has until recently been confined to East and Southeast Asia. South Asia was regarded as relatively unimportant for a number of reasons, including the different trajectories of its history; the absence of international, extraregional war in this area; and its lower rates of growth and lower degree of involvement in world trade. South Asia had attracted Japanese attention mainly for the following reasons: (1) the Japanese role of encouraging nationalists in Burma

[21] Takashi Inoguchi, "Trade, Technology and Security: Implications for East Asia and the West," *Adelphi Papers,* no. 218 (Spring 1987): 39–55.
[22] E. L. Jones, *The European Miracle: Environment, Economies and Geopolitics in the History of Europe and Asia* (Cambridge: Cambridge University Press, 1981).

and India toward independence during World War II; (2) Judge Pal's position in the Far Eastern Tribunal of World War II; (3) Jawaharlal Nehru's role in the nonalignment movement; (4) regional wars among India, Pakistan, China, Sri Lanka and Bangladesh; and (5) Soviet intervention in Afghanistan. It was only in the 1980s that South Asia came to occupy a more than negligible place in the minds of many Japanese. First, the Soviet intervention in Afghanistan brought a sense of strategic need to help the region cope with its difficulties. Second, economic development has expanded noticeably in the region. The fact that many countries neighboring Japan—most notably South Korea, Taiwan, Singapore, Thailand and Malaysia—can no longer supply low-wage manufacturing bases has been pushing Japan to farther peripheral areas, such as the Philippines, China and South Asia. Japan is now the number-one donor of official development assistance to most South Asian countries, including India, Pakistan and Bangladesh. The significance of South Asia has become apparent. In less than a decade it will be covered in any Japanese-written history of the Asia-Pacific region in full depth.

How has the Japanese elite perceived the place of Japan in Asia and the Pacific in the decades since 1945? In that year Japanese self-confidence was completely lost. Japan was discredited in Asia and the Pacific and had no role whatsoever in the region. All efforts were directed at recovery and reconstruction under the benevolent umbrella of the United States. In 1955 the accelerating recovery of their country encouraged the Japanese to announce the end of the postwar era in a white paper of the Economic Planning Agency. Also, Japanese war reparations were under way to a number of East and Southeast Asian countries. With the departure of the occupation forces, the armistice agreement in the Korean peninsula and the inauguration of rapid economic development, Japan's role in Asia and the Pacific was motivated by the combination of the debt of history and economic opportunities in such forms as reparations, foreign aid and export markets.

By 1965 the Japanese elite recovered its self-confidence significantly as Japan's profile expanded in the region. Most noteworthy were increased economic transactions with South Korea and Taiwan. These two former colonies revived their close economic ties with Japan. Also important was Japan's role in the implementation of the U.S. war in Vietnam, a role that was primarily economic, however, as it was during the Korean War. In 1975 Japan and other countries in the region were coping with the oil crisis and the collapse of South Vietnam. Determined to achieve what they called economic security, including assured energy supply when the United States no longer seemed to provide as solid a security umbrella, the Japanese elite started to talk about the Asia-Pacific region in a determined manner. In 1985 Japan's role was redefined as that of a good member of the Western alliance when President Reagan and Prime Minister Nakasone coordinated their policies against the Soviet threat. Japan's role was a supporting one, making up for the reduced role played by the United States in the region—hence the enhanced official development assistance and the enlarged defense perimeter of the Japanese Self-Defense Forces in the western Pacific. Yet the debt of history was felt by the Japanese elite, as the history-textbook controversies and others with South Korea and China demonstrated in the 1980s. At the same time their improved profile in the world has given most Japanese self-confidence and a sense of national pride.

Japan's role in the region is primarily conceived as economic but with increasing security components as well. The Japanese elite have come to acquire a sense of mission through representing the interests and concerns of the regional countries in international forums such as the Organization for Economic Cooperation and Development (OECD) and the Western summits. They have also moved to forge and/or promote regional institutions such as the Pacific Economic Cooperation Council and the Asian Development Bank. This is indicative of their concern for shaping and sharing the benefits of the Pacific dynamism encompassing northern Mexico, the Pacific areas of the United States and Canada, East and South Asia and the South Pacific, as North America and Western Europe appear to be moving toward the formation of regional protectionist blocs. The Japanese defined their role in this respect as shaping a Pacific economic community in an open multilateral form, which would create a zone of prosperity with free trade, and rolling back the protectionist and regionalist trends that might accelerate in other parts of the world.

As to the alternative futures now being articulated by the Japanese elite, the question is: In which direction will the Asia-Pacific region go? Considering the differing way in which the world—and this region—will be organized, there seem to be four major possibilities at the beginning of the 21st century.[23] They are what have been called: (1) Pax Americana Phase II; (2) Pax Ameripponica; (3) Pax Consortis; and (4) Pax Nipponica. Although the focus in this article is on the two leading protagonists in the region, the United States and Japan, the following images should convey the alternatives for the Asia-Pacific region.

Pax Americana Phase II: This image of the future is that of the United States retaining its leading position, making full use of the advantage of being the creator of institutions of post–World War II order and security, after somehow riding out the current difficulties into the 1990s. It is an America experienced in forging the "balanced," or globalist, view of the Western alliance, and deftly prodding and cajoling allies into an enlightened joint action. Japan's roles in Pax Americana Phase II would not be significantly different from those it now plays.[24] Essentially, they would be economic in nature, the bulk of global security roles being shouldered by the United States. Even if Japan-United States security cooperation is accelerated, this basic division is unlikely to change. Similarly, if Japan increases its security-related assistance to some Third World countries such as Pakistan, Turkey, Papua New Guinea and Honduras, the security leadership of the

---

[23] The following is adapted from Takashi Inoguchi, "Japan's Global Roles in a Multipolar World," paper prepared for presentation at the Council on Foreign Relations, New York, May 18, 1988.
[24] Takashi Inoguchi, "Japan's Images and Options: Not a Challenger, But a Supporter," *Journal of Japanese Studies* 12, no. 1 (Winter 1986): 95–119.

United States will remain strong. Needless to say, there are those who argue that Japan will in due course start to exert influence by accumulating credit to the United States and recipient countries. Japan's regional roles will be heavily economic. More concretely, Japan will become the vital core of the Pacific growth crescent encompassing three areas: (1) northern Mexico and the Pacific areas of the United States and Canada; (2) Japan; and (3) the NICs, coastal China, the ASEAN countries, and Australia and New Zealand. The incorporation of the second and third economic groups into the extended U.S. economic role would link the United States with the Asia-Pacific economies in a more balanced manner.

Pax Ameripponica: This image of the future focuses on the increasingly steady development and integration of what Robert Gilpin calls the *"nichibei* [Japanese-U.S.] economy".[25] That is to say, the economies of Japan and the United States will have become one integrated economy of a sort. Since the major external activities of Japan and the United States are found in the Asia-Pacific region, this image is sometimes called the Pax Pacifica.

Japan's role in this Pax Ameripponica, primarily economic, are not fundamentally different from those envisaged in Pax Americana Phase II. However, as economic power almost inevitably becomes military power Japan would not likely constitute the historic exception to this rule. But the form in which Japan's economic power would translate into military power needs close attention. The techno-economic-strategic cooperation and integration between the United States and Japan could become formidable and of the largest scale in history. The strategic integration of many countries in the region may make it hard to accommodate the Soviet Union within an invigorated structure of U.S.-Japanese dominance, thus consigning it to a far less important status than it has now.

Pax Consortis: The third image portrays a future world of many consortia in which the major protagonists are busily forging coalitions to effectuate policy adjustments and agreements among themselves and no single actor is allowed to dominate the rest.[26] The thrust of this image rests on the pluralistic nature of policy adjustments among interested parties. This is a good contrast to the first image of Pax Americana Phase II, which subtly conveys the desirability or necessity—or even hoped for inevitability—of the "administrative guidance" by, or "moral leadership" of, the primus inter pares—that is, the United States. This third image will be favored by many actors in the Asia-Pacific region because of their resentment of America's arrogant behavior, especially when it only grudgingly admits its relative decline.

Japan's roles in the Pax Consortis are essentially two. With the strategic nuclear arsenals increasingly nullified either by the de facto U.S.-Soviet détente process or by a technological breakthrough, Japan's role would be primarily one of quiet economic diplomacy through forging coalitions and

[25] Gilpin, *Political Economy of International Relations.*
[26] Kuniko Inoguchi, *Posuto-haken Sisutemu to Nihon no sentaku* (The Emerging Post-hegemonic System: Choices for Japan) (Tokyo: Chikuma shobo, 1987).

918

shaping policy adjustments among peers. Its secondary role would be to help create a world spared of the need for military solutions. That would include, if possible, the diffusion of an antinuclear defensive system to all the countries, and the extension of massive economic aid tied to cease-fires or peace agreements between belligerents. Japan's primary regional role therein would be that of coordinator-promoter of interests of the Asia-Pacific countries, which have not been fully represented either in the U.S. system or in economic institutions of industrialized countries such as the OECD. It is remarkable that despite the fact that Japan, Taiwan and South Korea have accumulated most of the world's trade surpluses, not one has been adequately represented in world economic institutions. Japan's secondary regional role would be that of moderator, especially in security areas, and might involve relations between South Korea and China or neutral peacekeeping forces in Cambodia and Afghanistan.

Pax Nipponica: This is the world in which Japanese economic power reigns supreme. This image has been most vigorously propagated by those Americans who are concerned about the visible contrast between the relative loss of technological and manufacturing competitiveness of the United States and the concomitant gain of Japan in those terms.[27] As in Pax Consortis at its most effective, strategic nuclear arsenals must be eliminated or the antinuclear defense system perfected before the advent of Pax Nipponica. Without the nullification of nuclear weapons, Japan's leading role in security areas would be minimized, hence the difficulty of a true Pax Nipponica being realized. In this image, Japan's regional roles would coincide with its global roles, as its preeminent position would enable it to assume paramount importance in the Asia-Pacific region as well.

The above scenarios do not exhaust all possible alternatives. However, one common theme can be discerned: the increasing centrality of the region in world economic-political development—a view strongly shared by the Japanese elite. In their view, the future of the Asia-Pacific region—and indeed the rest of the world as well—seems to rest to a considerable extent on how the peoples of the area manage this centrality. The challenge is immense, both exciting and risky. But the balance and moderation that will be acquired gradually as economic maturity advances and permeates the region will make the transition to a new future smoother and more manageable.

FURTHER READING

Cady, John F. *The History of Post-war Southeast Asia.* Athens: Ohio University Press, 1974.
Cumings, Bruce. *The Origins of the Korean War.* Princeton, New Jersey: Princeton University Press, 1981.
Fairbank, John King. *The Great Chinese Revolution, 1800–1985.* New York: Harper & Row, 1986.

[27] Ronald Morse, "Japan's Drive to Pre-eminence," *Foreign Policy,* no. 69 (Winter 1987–88): 3–21.

Frost, Ellen L. *For Richer, For Poorer: The New U.S.-Japan Relationship.* New York: Council on Foreign Relations, 1987.

Gaddis, John Lewis. *The Long Peace: Inquiries into the History of the Cold War.* New York: Oxford University Press, 1987.

Hofheinz, Roy, and Calder, Kent E. *The East Asia Edge.* New York: Basic Books, 1982.

Inoguchi, Takashi, and Okimoto, Daniel I., eds. *The Political Economy of Japan.* Vol. 2: *The Changing International Context.* Stanford, California: Stanford University Press, 1988.

Iriye, Akira. *The Cold War in Asia.* Englewood Cliffs, New Jersey: Prentice-Hall, 1974.

Steinberg, David Joel, ed. *In Search of Southeast Asia: A Modern History.* 2nd ed. Sydney: Allen & Unwin, 1987.

Thorne, Christopher. *The Issue of War: States, Societies, and the Far Eastern Conflict of 1941–1945.* London: Hamish Hamilton, 1985.

ASIA AND THE PACIFIC SINCE 1945: A MALAYSIAN PERSPECTIVE

LEE POH PING

INTRODUCTION

SOUTHEAST Asia has always interested outside powers. Its wealth of natural resources and its strategic location between the two Asian giants India and China have, among other factors, attracted the interest of foreign nations, particularly Western ones, many with predatory intent. Indeed, it can be argued that the dominant theme in Southeast Asian history since the Portuguese conquest of Melaka in 1511 to the advent of World War II has been one of responding to this Western intrusion. Historians may argue about the depth of the Western impact on indigenous Southeast Asian societies or indeed if Southeast Asia might ultimately evolve its own response to the Western challenge rather than develop characteristics found in other societies that have had to cope with industrial development. None suggest that the Western factor can be ignored.

The foreign challenge has remained undiminished even after World War II. But where the prewar impact had come primarily from Europeans and where the nature of the domination was more clearly classical colonialism, the postwar impact has been more complex. It emanates from the United States, the Soviet Union, China and Japan, but these four big powers may not necessarily have an underlying common purpose. The prewar Europeans had theirs in the maintenance of European domination, however much they differed in the perceptions of their national interests and the policies adopted to pursue them. In the 1950s, for example, the United States could be described as a status quo power while the Soviet Union and China professed revolutionary aims. Nor is the nature of the impact the same. This refers not only to the United States and the Soviet Union being militarily stronger in Southeast Asia than China and Japan, but also that their impact lies in different areas. Some powers such as Japan, for example, are strong primarily in the economic field and much less so in the military arena, while others such as the Soviet Union are militarily strong but possess little or no economic influence in Southeast Asia.

921

IMPACT OF WORLD WAR II

There is no doubt that the initial Japanese defeat of the European colonial powers in Southeast Asia profoundly changed Southeast Asian perceptions of the European powers. Where previously the Europeans had been perceived as superior beings and militarily invincible, the rapid march of imperial Japanese forces in Southeast Asia caused the scales to fall from Southeast Asian eyes. This advance culminated in the fall of Singapore in February 1942 (Winston Churchill called it Britain's greatest military disaster), made official by the surrender of the British to Japanese Gen. Tomoyuki Yamashita. Southeast Asians had never seen anything like this before—the only other example of an Asian nation defeating a European one militarily was the Japanese defeat of Czarist Russia in 1905. This time the Japanese conquerors, in order to destroy the white man's prestige, deliberately humiliated the former European masters by forcing them to perform menial tasks in front of Southeast Asians. This convinced many Southeast Asians that the Europeans were no longer invincible, and that they could achieve independence themselves from their European rulers.

In addition the Japanese brought into the center of the political arena many rural-based groups that had either been dormant or excluded from the European-dominated political process. Examples of these were Islamic groups in Indonesia and non-English-educated Malay nationalist groups in Malaysia. The Japanese also helped create military structures and trained officers who in the postwar period came to dominate the political systems of many Southeast Asia countries, notably in Indonesia and Burma (now Myanmar). President Suharto came from one of these Japanese-created military units, and Ne Win was one of 30 comrades trained by the Japanese during the war.

RETURN OF THE EUROPEAN COLONIAL POWERS

Many of the European colonial powers did not believe that their days were over in Southeast Asia after the war. While the circumstances had changed drastically, the Europeans, particularly the French and the Dutch, tried to wrest back their former colonies. France, humiliated by the German conquest and shamed by the establishment of the collaborationist Vichy government, hoped to regain as much of its former glory as possible by recolonizing Indochina. As for the Dutch, the possession of the Indonesian islands was their major means of participating on the world stage. It was, however, a somewhat different situation for the British.

Southeast Asian colonies such as Burma and Malaya were not the main focus of British efforts after the war. These efforts were directed at India. Thus, when the decision was made to leave India, the granting of independence to Burma and Malaya did not create traumatic agonies concerning the loss of imperial splendor. Moreover, in the case of Burma an enlightened act of statesmanship by the supreme commander of Allied forces in Southeast Asia, Lord Louis Mountbatten—recognizing Aung San, leader of the Burmese nationalist, Anti-Fascist People's Freedom League—paved the way for a more peaceful decolonization.

Whatever the case, the European powers had to contend with nationalist forces better armed and organized than before. Southeast Asian nationalists fighting for their freedom knew that they were part of a worldwide battle against colonialism and that time was on their side. The Dutch and the French learned this eventually but not without cost. In response to the demands of independence by Indonesian nationalists led by Sukarno and Muhammad Hatta, the Dutch resorted to force. Those Indonesians who resisted were suppressed by military means. This did not prove successful, and the Dutch finally yielded. In 1949 Sukarno was declared the president of the independent republic of Indonesia.

The Vietnamese struggle against the French took longer. At the time of the defeat of the Japanese, the Vietnamese nationalist movement had developed and had come under the Communist leadership of Ho Chi Minh. Unlike what happened in Burma, Mountbatten, who headed the temporary Allied military administration in Vietnam, did not deal with the Vietnamese. Instead he freed and rearmed French soldiers imprisoned by the Japanese in Indochina. Thus, it was difficult for the French government in Paris to come to terms with Ho Chi Minh—not that it really wanted to. In 1946 the French shelled the port of Haiphong, and the Vietminh retaliated by launching an insurrection.

The French became bogged down in a war with the Vietminh that lasted until 1954. France's military might proved of no avail against an enemy engaged in guerrilla warfare and supported by most of the Vietnamese population. This protracted war had its denouement in the battle of Dien Bien Phu, more a conventional battle than a big guerrilla skirmish. But by 1954 the Vietminh had become armed and organized sufficiently to take on the French and to defeat them.

The significance of Dien Bien Phu in Southeast Asian history is enormous. It shoved that an Asian power weaker in industrial might could, by the adoption of a revolutionary strategy, including guerrilla warfare and grass-roots political mobilization, defeat a foreign industrial power of far greater military strength. (The initial Japanese defeat of the Allies in Southeast Asia had been one of an Asian industrial power against Western industrial powers.) The example of Dien Bien Phu has thus given hope to many developing countries that if they were to organize themselves like the Vietnamese did they could defeat any occupying power. By the same token, an industrial power, with an intent to embark in an imperialistic adventure leading to occupation, has had to consider the potentially prohibitive political and military costs involved in the subjugation of an alien population.

ERA OF U.S. DOMINANCE

The American experience in Vietnam
The United States was not unaware of the significance of Dien Bien Phu, but it believed it differed from France in that it was not a colonial power. The United States stood for the spread of democracy and anticommunism,

ideals it presumed were acceptable to the majority of the Vietnamese and other Indochinese people. Moreover, France was, militarily speaking, a second-rate power while the United States was the superpower par excellence. Armed with immense firepower from arsenals filled with the latest technological gadgets, Americans would surely be a match for people in yellow pajamas!

Thus, after the French withdrew in 1954 under the provisions of a bilateral agreement with the Vietminh, the United States proceeded to create the nation of South Vietnam, south of the 17th parallel, as a bulwark against the Communist-dominated north, despite the fact that the agreement explicitly stated that the 17th parallel was only a military demarcation line and not to be construed as a political one.

There has been much talk of American restraint in the military prosecution of the Vietnam War. This is certainly true of nuclear weapons; none were used. It may also be true to some extent with respect to the use of conventional weapons. Nevertheless, a historian cannot but be impressed by the sheer magnitude of the military means that were employed. The total number of bombs dropped in the Vietnam War by the United States exceeded the total number of bombs dropped in World War II. At the height of the war the total number of American soldiers was about half a million. If 1 million South Vietnamese soldiers (the total number of South Vietnamese troops existing at the same time) were to be added, the combined total of people actually in uniform was one and one-half million. Given a population then of about 16 million South Vietnamese, the ratio of soldiers to civilians was about one to 12. Compare this to World War II, where at the height of the Nazi occupation of Europe the ratio was one German soldier to 90 Europeans. Moreover, the amount of money involved was no less staggering. At the war's height the United States was spending about $30 billion yearly to wage the war. Deployment of such immense firepower was not notably successful in destroying the North Vietnamese and Vietcong military capacity to fight back.

Nor was there success in establishing a credible political base to fight the Communists. In the beginning the United States apparently stood a chance of doing so by backing Ngo Dinh Diem, a Vietnamese mandarin figure with anticolonial credentials. But Diem's narrowing of his political base to South Vietnam's Catholic population, among other things, destroyed his political credibility and usefulness. He and his family were toppled by South Vietnamese officers encouraged by the Americans. One general after another took over, but with no more political success than Diem had.

The response of the Vietnamese Communists to the U.S. involvement was to employ, as they did against the French, guerrilla warfare. This time they were better prepared militarily. They had control of North Vietnam, though heavily bombed, and they had a standing North Vietnamese army, which complemented the Vietcong guerrilla forces in the south. They were also given military supplies by the Soviets and the Chinese, who were immune from U.S. attack. But the decisive fight was in the political arena.

The Vietnamese Communists offered a social and economic program that appealed to a majority of the South Vietnamese, particularly the peasantry, who were tired of exploitative landlords and a parasitic middle class. The Communists also succeeded in wrapping themselves up in the flag of Vietnamese nationalism and branding the government of South Vietnam the stooges of American imperialism. The communist strategy on the one hand was aimed at destroying the political basis of U.S. involvement in Vietnam and on the other calculated to influence American public opinion. The 1968 Tet offensive, for example, by its demonstration of Vietcong strength in the cities despite devastating military losses, was designed to enlighten the American public to their government's deception in announcing that the Communists were being beaten. After a series of negotiations between Henry Kissinger and Le Duc Tho, a fragile peace was established in 1973. But it was to be shattered in 1975 when South Vietnamese troops turned tail as the North Vietnamese army began to advance in the south. Just before the Communists reached Saigon, President Nguyen Van Thieu fled, as did the American ambassador. The latter's departure with the American flag symbolized for many an end of an era in Southeast Asia for the United States.

Southeast Asian responses to the Vietnam War
But where there was little or no sympathy among Southeast Asians for the French in Indochina, it was not necessarily the case with respect to the Americans. No doubt many Southeast Asians had felt somewhat uneasy at the U.S. lack of a sense of proportion (so much firepower aimed at such a small country), but they had not been unsympathetic to American aims, at least not in Malaysia, Singapore, the Philippines, Thailand and Indonesia after Sukarno. These were staunchly anti-Communist nations, and U.S. planes involved in Vietnam had flown from bases in Thailand and the Philippines. If the Southeast Asians had been worried it was because they believed American methods were proving ineffectual and even counterproductive in attaining the goal of a non-Communist South Vietnam; they were not worried about the goal itself.

Leaders such as Lee Kuan Yew of Singapore have contended that the U.S. involvement in Vietnam gave the non-Communist countries of Southeast Asia time to develop their political and economic systems to a stage where the requisite resilience had been achieved to counter internal Communist subversion, which presumably would have been given new life if the neighboring countries of Indochina had turned Communist. Had the United States not resisted for such a long time and Indochina fallen to communism much earlier, their task of developing such resilience would have been immensely more difficult.

By the time of the heavy U.S. involvement in Vietnam, all the other Southeast Asian countries (except Brunei) had achieved independence and were reasonably confident that their grip on their own governments would not be greatly threatened by external powers. If anything, they feared domestic subversion. Thus, there was no instinctive sympathy such as that for the Vietnamese against the colonial French. Also, American aims in Southeast Asia were primarily of a political and security nature. The United

States was in Vietnam not so much to dominate Southeast Asia, as the European colonial powers had done, but because of a worldwide strategy of containing communism. To achieve such goals, bases were maintained in the Philippines and for a time in Thailand while anti-Communist security pacts such as the Southeast Asia Treaty Organization were formed. To the non-Communist countries, particularly those now members of the Association of Southeast Asian Nations (ASEAN), the American burden was not especially onerous. There was no real American economic or bureaucratic exploitation. In fact Americans absorbed more manufactured goods from the ASEAN countries than either the European countries or Japan. The various Southeast Asian governments may have had to operate within the political parameters set by the United States, often influenced by the exigencies of U.S. global security concerns, but they were able to live with that. At least, they believed, better the Americans than the Russians, Chinese or Japanese. Finally, Southeast Asia was primarily interested in improving its standard of living. This meant the region wanted to emphasize economic growth and development, and this could only come about through economic links with the advanced Western industrial nations and Japan. The communist model had not been notably successful in this regard, and not much could be gained from economic links with the Soviet Union and China.

It is perhaps one of the greatest ironies in postwar Southeast Asian history that at the hour of the Vietnamese triumph against the mightiest power in the world, events would unfold that would not vindicate the triumph but rather work against it. One would have thought that with such a brilliant demonstration of revolutionary strategy, other Southeast Asian countries would have gone the Vietnamese way. But the reverse has happened. Southeast Asia, particularly the ASEAN countries, has instead resolved to work collectively and to strengthen its capacity to resist communism internally. And what is even more astonishing, the dominoes have fallen backwards. Vietnamese and Cambodian Communists have gone to war resulting in a Vietnamese occupation of Cambodia, and there have been sporadic hostilities between Vietnam and China.

AIMS OF OTHER ASIAN POWERS

Although Vietnam had been the primary object of American energies in Southeast Asia in the era before 1975, the United States was nevertheless the dominant power in the region in almost every sense of the word. Neither China nor the Soviet Union could match the military might the United States had deployed in the area. Neither power had troops in Southeast Asia, although the Soviets could have deployed a sizeable number had they wanted to. Also, the United States then had the strongest economy in the world, while Japanese economic influence in the area was nothing like it has become. Ideologically, the United States could match the communism of the Soviet Union and China not so much with an American concept of democracy but by consumerism, a far more powerful doctrine such as could only be brought about by the economic development in which the United States then excelled.

China

It has been argued that one of the Chinese aims in Southeast Asia from the mid-1950s to the mid-1970s had been revolutionary in the sense of encouraging the establishment of Communist regimes there. To this end the Chinese encouraged and aided local Communist parties to overthrow non-Communist governments. An example of this, frequently cited at least by the Indonesian government, was the attempted coup by the Indonesian Communist party in 1965 when six generals were killed. It must be said, however, that not all scholars agree that China was behind the coup. Another Chinese aim was to establish itself as a big power in Southeast Asia with all the influence and prerogatives that go along with such a status. The U.S. policy of containment of China was thus seen as the major impediment toward this. It amounted to a denial of the amour propre of China. Chinese aggressive behavior arose in response to such American denial.

A far more compelling argument, however, is that China at this period was primarily obsessed with its own national security. China was threatened from almost all sides. On its northern border China faced a hostile Soviet Union far superior in military capability. In the southwest there was a border problem with India that resulted in a limited war in 1962. In the east U.S. troops stationed in Japan and South Korea were part of the means used to encircle China. Also, there was Taiwan, whose avowed aim was reunification with the mainland under an anti-Communist government. Then of course there was the United States in Vietnam. The Chinese could not help but interpret that the presence of half a million U.S. troops in Vietnam might lead to a possible attack on China. Chinese hostility toward the United States should be seen within this context. This hostility lessened, however, when President Lyndon Johnson made the decision to withdraw U.S. forces from Vietnam and convinced the Chinese that this was a signal that the United States no longer had the will to contain China. It was not surprising, then, that the focus of China's attention immediately began to shift elsewhere, particularly to the Soviet Union in the north. In addition, China then developed a frame of mind receptive to American overtures that resulted in Kissinger's visit in 1971.

Many Southeast Asians, however, did not see China's behavior as resulting from its security concerns. Apart from the underlying fear of some Southeast Asians that the Chinese might at a future date bring their military might to bear on them, the main reasons for their suspicion of China pertained to two factors: Southeast Asians of Chinese descent (the overseas Chinese), and the Communist parties found within Southeast Asia.

To many Southeast Asians the Chinese in their midst posed as a potential fifth column for mainland China. This fear is exemplified, according to some, by the insurrection of the Malayan Communist party, the bulk of whom were of Chinese descent, in 1948. Despite whatever pronouncements and actions the Chinese government had taken to divest itself of the overseas Chinese, many Southeast Asians still contend that the Chinese government was not consistent. Some cite the example of Maoists during the Cultural Revolution, instigating local Chinese in Burma (now Myanmar) to involve themselves in Burmese politics when the government of China had already conceded that the Chinese in Burma were either Burmese citizens or if not should respect the laws and customs of Burma. To be sure, the Southeast Asian attitude on this subject has been greatly influenced by the degree of assimilation of the overseas Chinese in the various countries. In this respect, Thailand, which has the best record of integration, has had fewer suspicions of Chinese intentions than Indonesia where the degree of integration has been considerably less.

Nor were many Southeast Asians impressed by the distinction made by the Chinese government between state-to-state relations and party-to-party relations as far as Southeast Asian Communist parties were concerned. Beijing claimed that the political, military or moral support it gave Southeast Asian Communist parties had nothing to do with the diplomatic relations the government of China had with the governments of Southeast Asia. Many Southeast Asians saw this as a specious distinction, especially in that the Communist party controlled the government in China.

The Soviet Union

It has been argued that one of the motivations behind Soviet policy toward Southeast Asia had been strategic, that the Soviet Union needed the Strait of Malacca for its naval vessels to move from European Russia to the Soviet Far East. But this view stretches things quite a bit. A more likely explanation of Soviet Southeast Asian involvement is related to the Soviet Union's ideological confrontation with the United States in the early stages of the cold war. The Soviets sought to keep the Third World, of which Southeast Asia was a part, either on their side or neutral. The rationale shifted with the advent of the Chinese-Soviet conflict in 1960 when both countries contended for influence, particularly among the various national Communist parties. In this battle China had the upper hand mostly, with the biggest Southeast Asian Communist party, the Indonesian Communist party, as an ally. One of the few Soviet successes occurred in the early 1960s when the Soviet Union had quite good relations with Sukarno's Indonesia and even supplied Indonesia with arms. But Sukarno rejected the Soviets when he turned to China as a partner to lead the newly emerging forces of the world against the old established forces, which presumably included the Soviet Union. Indonesia's pro-Chinese policy was abandoned after Sukarno's overthrow by Suharto. But Suharto did not become more enthusiastic toward the Soviets.

Southeast Asians have not felt particularly warm toward the Soviet Union because of its policy of encouraging revolution during a more militant period. The fact that the Soviet Union was a superpower also heightened apprehensions among those Southeast Asians ever wary of superpower domination. Moreover, there was not much the Soviets could offer in terms of technology, aid and investment on the scale of the United States and Japan.

Japan

Japanese relations with Southeast Asia were governed by three considerations: supply of the necessary raw material; a market for their value-added manufactured goods; and that the Strait of Malacca should not fall into hostile hands choking off oil from the Arab/Persian Gulf. The Japanese were particularly dependent on Southeast Asia through the 1960s because Japan had been stripped of its colonies of Taiwan, Manchuria and Korea after the war. To achieve these three objectives, Japan resorted to a policy of *seikei bunri,* or the separation of economics from politics. The Japanese concentrated essentially on economic relations with Southeast Asia, while relying on U.S. foreign policy objectives in the region they totally agreed with and needed. This policy has proved spectacularly successful. From a war-devastated country whose economic interests and assets in Southeast Asia were all but reduced to nothing, Japan had become by 1975 one of the leading investing and trading nations in the region. But this success was not achieved without resentment from Southeast Asians, as exemplified by the violent demonstrations in January 1974 while the Japanese prime minister, Kakuei Tanaka, was visiting Southeast Asia. Demonstrations were also particularly intense in Thailand and Indonesia.

Underlying Southeast Asians sentiments were memories of the cruelties of the Japanese occupation during World War II. But there were more substantive reasons. One was the Southeast Asian dislike of the economic practices of the Japanese, which they regarded as unenlightened and feared could be turned into a classical colonial pattern. They noted that the Japanese invested very little in those intermediary industries that added some value to the raw materials exported. There was also a feeling that Japan, while developing into a considerable economic power, was not giving much in return to Southeast Asia either in the form of aid or in economic policies that could further regional development.

MULTIPOLAR SCENARIO SINCE 1975

The U.S. defeat in Vietnam in 1975 did not completely destroy American power in Southeast Asia. Rather, the United States changed from being the dominant actor to being one of the major, possibly still preeminent, actors on the Southeast Asian stage. In fact this change had been presaged in President Richard Nixon's Guam Doctrine of 1969, delivered at a time of increasing American weariness with the Vietnam War. The thrust of the doctrine was that the United States would no longer commit combat troops in Asia. Asians would have to fight the battles themselves. At the time not much concern was generated by the doctrine among non-Communist Southeast Asian nations, which were at any rate coming to the view that they had to fend for themselves. But the actual U.S. withdrawal in 1975 was another matter. It jolted these countries, particularly the ASEAN group, into the realization that there might possibly be a complete U.S. strategic withdrawal with the additional possibility of hostile superpowers replacing the Americans. The ASEAN countries thus resolved that they had to work together or else they might hang separately. This new spirit was manifested at the first meeting of ASEAN heads of state in Bali in 1976.

ASEAN

The Association of Southeast Asian Nations, formed in 1967 and consisting of Indonesia, Thailand, the Philippines, Malaysia and Singapore (Brunei joined later), was at first not taken seriously. ASEAN was considered by many as an organization long on rhetoric but rather short on concrete achievement. Bali gave it a new spirit.

First, this new ASEAN spirit helped greatly in ameliorating many of the tensions the ASEAN countries had with one another. There was the case of the Philippine claim to Sabah. Sometime just before Sabah joined Malaysia in 1963, the Philippine government claimed the territory. Filipinos justified their claim on the grounds that the sultan of the Sulu Islands had only leased, not ceded, Sabah to the British. As the British were now about to give it up, the Philippines should have the right to take it back. The Malaysian government rejected the Philippine claim as baseless. Moreover, the people of Sabah, according to the Malaysian government, after being surveyed by reputable international groups, had indicated that they wanted to belong to Malaysia. The Sabah problem was more or less resolved in 1977 when Philippines President Ferdinand Marcos visited Kuala Lumpur to attend the second ASEAN heads of states meeting and unilaterally announced the dropping of the Philippine claim to Sabah. This was seen as an important gesture toward ASEAN solidarity. Similarly, the Bali spirit reduced much of the tension between Malaysia and Singapore, brought about by the latter's withdrawal from Malaysia in 1965. There were mutual recriminations following the break, but the fact that the two countries still had many things in common, including their memberships in ASEAN, improved relations greatly.

Second, the ASEAN countries decided to work closely in the diplomatic area. They began to establish dialogues with advanced countries as a group rather than individually. Thus there was an ASEAN-Japan dialogue, an ASEAN-U.S. dialogue and so forth. But one of their most impressive achievements was their common front in the face of the Vietnamese invasion and occupation of Cambodia beginning in December 1978. Despite purported differences of opinion about which country constituted the real long-term threat to Southeast Asia (Indonesia and Malaysia believed it to be China, whereas Thailand and Singapore thought it was the Soviet Union acting through its proxy, Vietnam), they managed to overcome these differences by deferring to the ASEAN country most affected, Thailand. As a front-line nation Thailand managed to forge an ASEAN consensus for the condemnation of Vietnam for the violation of the principle of territorial integrity and for creating a situation that would involve the superpowers in Southeast Asia.

But ASEAN has not seen fit to engage in a pact of collective security. In the first place, the countries believe their existing arrangements are working satisfactorily. Malaysia has cooperated militarily with Indonesia and Thailand on the borders they share. These countries, particularly Malaysia, face the problem of domestic insurgents crossing over the borders when pursued. Such cooperation has made it difficult for insurgents to seek sanctuary across the border. The Philippines has a mutual security pact with the United States, while Singapore and Malaysia share with Britain, Australia and New Zealand another defense pact. Moreover, the ASEAN countries have not wished to indicate to Vietnam that ASEAN is necessarily hostile to it, such as might be the case if a collective pact were formed. In addition, a security arrangement would tarnish ASEAN's image as a group devoted to peaceful economic cooperation. There has also been much talk of building national resilience, which means not only the creation of national capacity to face external attack but also domestic threats. To this end there has been much stress on economic development premised on the assumption that such growth will bring about greater political unity. The ASEAN group firmly integrates member economies into the international capitalist economy, and if there have been policies instituted for achieving economic equity (such as in the case of Malaysia), these have not been at the expense of economic growth.

Japan

One of the greatest pressures created by the U.S. withdrawal was on the Japanese to take a far more active role in Southeast Asia. It had become clear to the Americans that while they were spending their substance in Vietnam in order to maintain the market-oriented non-Communist order in the region, the biggest beneficiary of this arrangement was Japan. The Japanese had profited economically but had done very little in the American view, beyond symbolic statements of support to stop the Communist tide. Thus the notion of a Japanese free ride came into vogue.

The inability to resist this pressure forced the Japanese to abandon slowly their policy separating economics from politics. While it had yet to work out an explicit political role in Southeast Asia for itself, Japan nevertheless became more forthcoming in terms of aid offers to countries in the region, and more willing to undertake economic policies that could aid ASEAN's industrial development. In the diplomatic arena Japan became more sympathetic to ASEAN; when Vietnam invaded Cambodia, the Japanese fully supported ASEAN diplomatic initiatives in the conflict.

Another development of great consequence occurred in Japan. By the 1970s and 1980s Japan had developed from a primarily regional economic power in the 1950s and 1960s, vitally in need of Southeast Asia, into a global economic power. This meant that Japan had become less dependent on Southeast Asia for trade and raw materials. Southeast Asia in fact needed to trade more with Japan than Japan with the region. With the increasing miniaturization of the world economy (and hence a lesser need for traditional raw materials) and the oversupply of many raw materials (allowing for Japan to diversify away from Southeast Asia), Southeast Asia could no longer effectively use the threat of a cutoff of raw materials to pressure Japan.

By the 1970s Southeast Asia, particularly the non-Communist countries of ASEAN, had for a variety of reasons become increasingly receptive to

931

working with Japan economically. The memories of the occupation were fading as a new generation of Southeast Asians who knew little of the war began taking over, while the older generation allowed time and economic necessity to temper any lingering hatreds. Second, there was little or no alternative. Given the fact that ASEAN needed an advanced country as a market and as a source of aid, investment and technology, Japan with its superpower economic status and proximity to the area increasingly fitted the bill. The European countries had more or less withdrawn from Southeast Asia, while the United States was showing declining enthusiasm to lead in the field. The twin deficits of budget and trade the United States was beginning to experience increased this weariness.

Third, the fascination with Japan as a model was caused no doubt by the spectacular rebuilding of its postwar economy. This was manifested in the official policies of two ASEAN countries, Malaysia and Singapore. Malaysia maintained a "Look East Policy," while Singapore had a "Learn from Japan" campaign. Singapore saw a basic similarity with Japan in that both were very poor in natural resources and thus heavily dependent on their human resources. Singapore believed it could replicate Japan's successes. Malaysia on the other hand hoped to emulate the work ethic and social discipline of the Japanese, qualities that were in rather short supply in Malaysia. To this end Malaysia introduced the concept of "Malaysia Incorporated" after the fashion of "Japan Incorporated." This concept was meant to encourage a harmony of objectives between government and the private sector as well as between management and labor to stimulate hard work by Malaysians.

On the other hand it was clear ASEAN did not want Japan to pursue an independent military role in South Asia, a possibility not too remote given the changed geopolitical situation, the disproportion between Japan's economic strength and political and military influence, and U.S. pressure on Japan to spend more on defense. Japanese warships and Japanese troops in the ASEAN area could ignite memories, fading though they might be, of the cruelties of World War II. There was also no great confidence that a heavily rearmed Japan would not encourage the return of right-wing nationalism or militarism in Japan that might propel it to embark on imperialistic adventures. There was also simply the fact of the sheer strength of the Japanese economy. If only one percent of Japan's GNP were devoted to military expenditure, the figure for 1988–89, given the revaluation of the yen, would be about U.S. $30 billion. This would make Japan's military budget the third largest in the world, exceeded only by those of the United States and the Soviet Union. An independent actor with such might would unsettle, if not change, the status quo in Southeast Asia. ASEAN already had difficulty accommodating the present strategic equation without having to cope with new changes. ASEAN was quite content to have Japan tied to the United States in its current mutual security pact.

The United States

Since the Guam Doctrine the United States had begun to emphasize economic relations with Southeast Asia. This attitude began to figure more importantly after 1975 and by the 1980s, at a time of declining American competitiveness (as manifested in the U.S. trade and budget deficits), economic issues such as trade had come to dominate U.S. relations with the region.

The United States had become increasingly hard-nosed in its dealings with Southeast Asia. It had for long time been a vast consumer market sucking in all manner of imports from overseas, including many from East Asia and Southeast Asia. Faced with the prospects of job losses due to such foreign imports, many American industries had begun clamoring for protection. Such protectionist pressure had grown stronger, particularly in the U.S. Congress; protectionist bills were introduced and passed. One particular piece of legislation, the Jenkins bill, designed to restrict textile imports, would have hit many Southeast Asian exporters, particularly Indonesia, very hard. To fend off protectionist pressure, the administration of President Ronald Reagan took certain steps that had adverse effects on Southeast Asian countries. One was the removal of Singapore from the list of developing countries enjoying the general system of privileges. This arrangement had allowed exports of goods to the United States with little or no tariffs; Singapore was now regarded as having "graduated" from the developing countries. Another was a federal subsidy to American rice farmers that enabled them to sell rice in the international market at market rates. (The administration would pay American farmers the difference between the cost of their production and the market price, which was lower.) This affected the interests of a million Thai rice farmers. Also, the administration, under the concept of intellectual property rights, pressured several Southeast Asian countries to stop the pirating and counterfeiting of American-made goods.

There was less discordance on the diplomatic front where the United States, over an issue such as the Cambodian conflict, was quite happy to follow ASEAN initiatives. The strategic situation had become increasingly vexed with negotiations concerning U.S. bases in the Philippines, considered integral to the military position of the United States in Southeast Asia and indeed in the Asia-Pacific region. The U.S. lease for the bases would end in 1991, and American desire for renewal had to be seen in the context of increasing Philippine nationalism and Philippine demands for substantially higher rent.

Southeast Asians perceived American pressure on the economic front as unjustified. They did not believe their exports to the United States contributed in any substantial way to the American trade deficit that, if not a result of declining American competitiveness, was caused by Japanese exports. They thus saw themselves as victims of the bilateral U.S.-Japanese trade conflict. Moreover Singapore claimed that there was an informal understanding with the United States that in exchange for its passing a law for the protection of intellectual property rights, the U.S. government would not remove Singapore from the general system of privileges. So too with the Thais, who believed that the Americans had been rather insensitive to their plight and to the possibility that such tough American action played into the hands of the Soviet Union.

933

Concerning the Philippine bases, private ASEAN opinion was clear. It was entirely in favor of U.S. bases there and extremely worried about the implications of a U.S. military withdrawal. But except for Singapore the member countries felt they could not publicly take a position supporting the United States, on the grounds that many of the countries were also members of the nonaligned movement and hence could not publicly support the establishment of foreign military bases. Moreover, this was essentially a bilateral U.S.-Philippine issue, and one of the tenets of ASEAN was noninterference in the sovereign rights of any ASEAN member.

The Soviet Union
The Soviet Union made a strategic gain when it drew the Vietnamese to its side following Vietnam's invasion of Cambodia. To protect themselves from Chinese retaliation (the defeated Khmer Rouge government of Cambodia was an ally of China), the Vietnamese went along with the Soviet Union, which also gave them financial aid. In return the Soviets were given the use of the bases Americans had built during the Vietnam War, the biggest of which was at Cam Ranh Bay. An important strategic foothold in Southeast Asia was thus achieved. The Soviets justified their presence by comparing it to the U.S. bases in the Philippines. The United States rejected the notion of the comparability of the bases.

But the Soviets made no headway in non-Communist Southeast Asia, particularly with the ASEAN members, until Mikhail Gorbachev's speech in Vladivostok in July 1986. At that time Gorbachev showed a very friendly face to Asia, offering among other things, concessions on the border with China, the withdrawal of Soviet troops from Afghanistan and a willingness to contribute to the Asia-Pacific economy. ASEAN, however, continued to hold the initiative in dealings with the Soviet Union, and countries such as Thailand and Singapore viewed the Soviets as the long-term enemy in Southeast Asia. The ASEAN group determined to regard as a test of Soviet sincerity whether it would persuade the Vietnamese to withdraw from Cambodia.

China
China after the death of Mao Zedong had begun to turn increasingly to solving its internal problems. Conscious of the country's appalling economic backwardness, not only when compared with advanced Western nations and Japan but even with culturally akin entities such as South Korea, Taiwan and Hong Kong, the new Chinese leadership under Deng Xiaoping decided to embark on a policy of modernization in agriculture, industry, defense and technology. But in Southeast Asia, China had become embroiled in the Indochina conflict because of its support of the Khmer Rouge. This involvement, while not directly threatening the internal modernization plan, would not help it either. The Chinese were drawn into a limited war with Vietnam in 1979 in order to teach the Vietnamese a lesson for daring to invade a Chinese ally. The Chinese did not perform impressively from a military standpoint, and decided instead to withdraw their troops and embark on the more successful strategy of isolating Vietnam. In this

they found common cause with the ASEAN countries and the United States. But some countries in the ASEAN group were uneasy with this shift in policy, and believed a strong Vietnam could instead be a buffer against a possibly expansionist China. Such reservations were submerged by the need for a common ASEAN front. On the other hand, the view that ASEAN could cash in economically on China's modernization program began to gain more adherents. China was already a growing market for ASEAN commodities and industrial goods.

SOUTHEAST ASIA AND THE FUTURE

If the geopolitical situation became more complex after 1975, it is nevertheless becoming clear that by the 1990s the challenge Southeast Asia faces will be increasingly economic in nature. One should not, however, underestimate the continuing role of political ideology or religious doctrine, but these pertain more to the domestic arena. As far as the big powers are concerned, there is a trend toward détente. The perestroika of Gorbachev and the modernization plans of Deng suggest that the Soviet Union and China will devote more of their energies to their own economic development, leaving less time for foreign adventures. Nor should one ignore the possibility of military clashes. There are the examples of Vietnam's invasion of Cambodia and border skirmishes between Thailand and Laos. But these are among ASEAN nation. The big powers themselves are unlikely to commit their own troops. The United States has the bitter experience of Vietnam, while the Soviet Union has had its Afghanistan lesson. The Chinese may think twice before they take on Vietnam again. (This does not rule out Chinese use of force in matters relating to territorial claims such as clashes with Vietnam over the disputed Spratly Islands.)

But it is problems of protectionism in the advanced nations, possible trading blocs, competition for investment and reduced demand for commodities—all vitally affecting Southeast Asia—that will dominate the agenda of the international relations of the region. Two developments should be considered. They are the decreasing demand for commodities and the increasing automation of the world economy.

Since 1984 there has been a drastic drop in the demand for the commodities produced by Southeast Asia. One consequence of this has been the creation of a severe recession in the ASEAN economies. At one stage countries such as Singapore and Malaysia had their high economic growth rates reduced to almost zero. Indeed it was suggested that this drop was a greater threat to the national security of the ASEAN countries than traditional ones like military invasion or Communist subversion. It is likely that this growth rate drop is part of a trend due to the miniaturization of the world economy. Moreover, there had been overproduction of commodities by many developing countries, brought about by false estimates of world demand and supply.

As for automation, it has been argued that a new industrial society is in the process of formation, one that will significantly alter the structure of the world economy. Based essentially on computers and microelectronics, this new order will change the relationship between labor and the means of production: the proportion of workers involved in planning and development will increase compared to those manually engaged in production. Such a development would profoundly alter the comparative advantages of nations and the international division of labor. This would mean that Southeast Asia, host to many industries relocated by either Japan or the West because of high labor costs, would find these industries drying up because labor costs would no longer be a crucial factor in Japan or the West.

Does this bode ill for Southeast Asia? It could in the long run if Southeast Asia does not make the necessary adjustments, but the argument can be stretched too far. For example, it is reported that robots and computers have taken over many of the functions of humans in manufacturing, but exactly in what functions and in what ways they affect labor costs has not been adequately spelled out. Human labor is still needed. In addition, the differential in the wage rate may be so great in some cases (for example, the average wage for labor in Japan is about 10 times the average wage in Thailand) that manufacturers could be quite easily influenced by this to postpone further computerization and robotization. In the Japanese case, this change has been further affected by the revaluation of the yen that put a tremendous strain on the Japanese economy, particularly small and medium industries. Unable to cope with the increased labor costs, many of these industries have rushed to invest in South Korea, Taiwan and suitable ASEAN countries.

Finally, the ASEAN countries have no choice but to take the path of industrialization. They will have to look among themselves for necessary markets, thus stimulating genuine economic cooperation. And for the markets of advanced countries, they will probably look toward Japan. For in an era of increasing protectionism in the West, Japan might oblige by taking some of these new responsibilities. At least that is the hope.

FURTHER READING

Barnett, A., Doak. *Communist China and Asia; Challenge to American Policy.* New York: Harper Brothers, 1960.

Colbert, Evelyn. *Southeast Asia in International Politics, 1941–1956.* Ithaca, New York: Cornell University Press, 1977.

Fitzgerald, Stephen, *China and the Overseas Chinese: A Study of Peking's Changing Policy, 1949–1970.* Cambridge: Cambridge University Press, 1972.

Hellmann, Don. *Japan and East Asia: The New International Order.* New York: Praeger, 1972.

Hinton, Harold. *Communist China in World Politics.* London: Macmillan, 1966.

Kahin, George, and Lewis, John, eds. *The United States in Vietnam.* New York: Dell, 1967.

Kosai, Yutaka, and Murakami, Yasusuke, eds. *Japan in the Global Community: Its Role and Contribution on the Eve of the 21st Century.* Tokyo: University of Tokyo Press, 1986.

McCoy, Alfred, ed. *Southeast Asia under Japanese Occupation.* New Haven, Connecticut: Yale University Press, 1980.

Nishihara, Masashi. *The Japanese and Sukarno's Indonesia: Tokyo-Jakarta Relations, 1951–1966.* Honolulu: University of Hawaii Press, 1976.

Vogel, Ezra. *Japan As Number One: Lessons for America.* Cambridge, Massachusetts: Harvard University Press, 1979.

Wang, Gungwu. *China and the World Since 1949: The Impact of Independence, Modernity and Revolution.* London and New York: Macmillan, 1977.

ASIA AND THE PACIFIC SINCE 1945: A U.S. PERSPECTIVE

BRUCE CUMINGS

INTRODUCTION

THE U.S. position in East Asia today was defined by the resolution of World War II and the subsequent conflict in Korea. The postwar settlement emphasized the revival of the one industrial nation in the region, Japan, and its predictable pump-priming effects on regional development. The Korean War shifted the emphasis toward bipolar security concerns, while placing decisive limits on American military and political expansion in East Asia. The rigidity thus induced froze American policy for the next quarter-century (1950–75) in a fruitless business of either containing or rolling back the putative expansionism of the Communist states. The palpable failures of the Korean and Vietnam Wars then induced another decade of wound-licking, recriminations and blanketed nostalgia of the cold war certainties of the 1950s.

The United States is now in the Reagan-Bush period of détente with the Soviet Union, broadening economic ties with China, a deepening economic crisis with Japan and, with the global decline of regional conflict, perhaps even trade with and recognition of the pariah states of the previous period, Vietnam and North Korea. What is striking is the rapidity with which the heretofore impermeable barriers of East-West conflict seem to disappear, allowing the nation to bring into focus another reality: the rise to economic power of Japan, South Korea, Taiwan, Singapore and other Asian nations. This newer reality is still dimly perceived in the United States, yet paradoxically it was the underpinning of the American internationalist structure four decades ago.

Japan was the centerpiece of American policy in the late 1940s, and today it is—or ought to be—the centerpiece of American concern in Asia: for there is the historical anomaly of the most dynamic economy in the world having no commensurate political or military clout, a condition that is unlikely to persist for long. Robert Scalapino has remarked: "Since U.S.-Japan relations rest fundamentally upon economic interdependence and

938

strategic dependence, they [sic] will survive current and future storms."[1] This bland formula and rosy prediction nonetheless discloses, perhaps inadvertently, the essence of the relationship: economic interdependence (cum rivalry) and security dependency. The prediction only makes sense if the statement is altered to read, stipulating that economic interdependence and strategic dependence continue, the relationship "will survive current and future storms."

U.S. HEGEMONY IN EARLY POSTWAR ASIA

The United States became the hegemonic power in northeastern Asia by virtue of its victory over and unilateral occupation of Japan, and a resulting unilateral American sway in the entire Pacific. In the early postwar period American hegemony meant the elaboration of a "grand area" within which nations oriented themselves toward Washington rather than Moscow; it meant the demarcation of outer limits in economics, politics and international security relationships, the transgression of which carried grave risks for any nonhegemonic nation. It is these outer limits that came to define the greater field of national security strategy. A hierarchy of economic and political preferences with the ideal goals of free trade, open systems and liberal democracy enmeshed a variety of nations, including effective neomercantile nations and authoritarian systems (for example, Japan and South Korea, respectively). The United States used methods for dealing with the included nations that ranged from classic negotiations and trade-offs (in regard to nations sharing American assumptions or approximating American levels of political and economic development) to wars and interventions in the periphery or Third World, thus to assure continuing orientation toward Washington.

The success and longevity of this system grew out of the unprecedented power of the United States amid a prostrate world, and its pursuit of classic internationalist, free-trade policies for getting the world economy moving again, combined with a sleight of hand by which power politics came in the side door, as the underpinning of the system. The very breadth of this international system—its nonterritoriality, its universalism and its open systems (within the grand area)—made for a style of hegemony that was more open than previous types of imperialism to competition from below. Indeed, it may eventually be concluded that this was its undoing. That is, this form of hegemony establishes a hierarchy of nations, but not one that is frozen; it is open to rising talent from below, and gives leverage and room for maneuver to dependencies.[2]

[1] Robert A. Scalapino, "Asia's Future," *Foreign Affairs* (Fall 1987): 106.
[2] For an elaboration of this conception, see Bruce Cumings, "The Origins and Development of the Northeast Asian Political Economy," *International Organization* (Winter 1984): 1–40; also Cumings, "Power and Plenty in Northeast Asia," *World Policy Journal* (Winter 1987–88): 79–106.

In the formative stages of such a hegemonic system, military and strategic considerations will be paramount, as the lines are drawn that mark the outer limits and the included space. But over time the system matures, and indeed a definition of a mature hegemonic system is an ongoing, daily *automaticity* of interaction and mutually reinforcing orientation, which will come not through military force but through complex, ongoing, mostly economic relations. One argument, therefore, is that this internationalist system has matured, and that relationships between the member-states are evolving, but that no fundamental change has occurred. This is not the realm that Robert Keohane has denoted "after hegemony,"[3] but one illustrating the dailiness of interaction characteristic of systemic maturity (not senescence).

This form of hegemony fused security and economic considerations so inextricably that the United States has never been sure whether economic competition from its allies is good or bad for grand-area security: Should the Japanese stoke their industries or spend more on defense? Furthermore, national economic decisions often cannot be understood apart from regional security relationships. For example, Japan's provision of the large amount of funds for South Korea's first integrated steel mill in 1969, and of some U.S.$4 billion in loans and credits to Seoul in 1983, was justified by reference to South Korea's integral role in the defense of Japan. The latter amount was about 10 percent of South Korea's outstanding debt, and was essentially a trade-off for Japan's inability to make sharp increases in defense spending at home. The point is that to grasp the essentials of the northeastern Asian system, one must understand how security structures interact with economic and political structures.

This system also had to account for the antisystem: the Soviet Union and its allies. Security in northeastern Asia meant manning the fault lines of the cold war that bisected Korea and then arced south through the Sea of Japan and Taiwan Straits to the shifting perimeters of Southeast Asia. But if anti-Sovietism were all this hegemonic system was about, its specific features could never be fully grasped; nor could one imagine the systematic erosion of these ostensibly formidable cold war barriers by the automaticity of the mature system's economic interaction: for example, the billions of dollars in informal trade now going on among China, Taiwan and South Korea, in spite of the absence of political relations and the continued potential for military conflict.

The 1940s settlement in northeastern Asia[4]

In the 1930s Japan withdrew from the world system and pursued, with its colonies, a self-reliant, go-it-alone path to development that resulted in aggressions devasting for the subject peoples, but that also generated re-

---

[3] Robert Keohane, *After Hegemony* (Princeton, N.J.: Princeton University Press, 1986).
[4] The following sketch is drawn from, and documented at length in, Bruce Cumings, *Origins of the Korean War*, Vol. 2 (Princeton, N.J.: Princeton University Press, 1989).

markably high industrial growth rates that changed the face of northeastern Asia. This was interpreted in the West mainly in strategic terms, as the basis for further militarist expansion—power and not plenty. But it was clearly both. In this decade what might be called the "natural economy" of the region was created; although it was not natural, its rational division of labor and set of possibilities have skewed East Asian development ever since. Heavy industries were built in Manchuria and northern Korea; southern Korea's textile industry began to boom; Taiwan produced sugar at rates second only to Cuba, and had a highly developed agrarian economy by 1945.

After Japan's defeat, it took less than two years before the imperatives of this political economy reasserted themselves. As thinking about a revived Japan evolved in 1947–50, two problems emerged: First, how could Japan's vital but second-rate status (vis-à-vis the United States) be assured; second, how could a prewar political economy that got raw materials and labor from the Asian periphery survive in the postwar world without a hinterland?

If Dean Acheson was the architect of American global policy in this period, George Kennan was the engineer. The core of Kennan's containment vision was a neat theory of industrial structure. Whereas Acheson shaped the grand area into which marched a bloc of American world-competitive industrial corporations, Kennan had a realpolitik conception of national industry: An advanced industrial base was essential to war making capacity and great-power status. The United States had four such bases and they had one, and things should be kept that way; this was the parsimonious little idea behind containment.[5] That is, containment meant defending the United States, Britain, Western Europe and Japan, but not worrying about every brushfire war or revolution in the preindustrial underbelly. Kennan also reversed the classic imagery of the Chinese emperors: Asia was for him the barbarian periphery of a high civilization that radiated outward from Western Europe. The first drop down was in Eastern Europe, the next was in Russia—most of whose vices were Oriental—and when one reached China and its little brother, Korea, one truly scraped the barrel of civilization and found mostly barbarism. Japan was the exception in Asia, not because of its "petite" culture, but because it had an industrial base.

These concise views remained firmly fixed in Kennan's mind, giving his policy recommendations a curious prescience founded in anachronism. Thus, on the China issue he arrived at the right conclusions for the wrong reasons: The United States should not intervene in the Chinese civil war because China was incontinent, and how could you have containment with incontinence? China was "a country with a marvelous capacity for corrupting not only itself but all those who have to do with it"; "you can help any government but one which does not know how to govern." The day would come when those Chinese who now revile American "imperialism" would "long bitterly" for it return. In the meantime, the West should keep out.

[5] John Lewis Gaddis, *Strategies of Containment: A Critical Appraisal of Postwar American National Security Policy* (New York: Oxford University Press, 1982).

His opposition to the Vietnam War drew upon the same wellsprings, although few at the time understood this.[6]

If Acheson wanted Japan revived as an industrial power of the second rank and posted as an engine of world-economy accumulation, Kennan wanted it restored as a regional power of the second rank, hamstrung by the hegemonic power but free to dominate its historic territory. Acheson and other internationalists had a world-economy conception of how Korea and other places in the Asian hinterland could be hinged to the revival of Japan and to the growth of world plenty; Kennan agreed with that, but also wanted the Japanese back on the mainland to butt against the Soviets, thus establishing a balance of power like that at the turn of the century, and saving the needless spillage of American blood and money.

Kennan also did not shrink before etching out Japan's presumed need for an economic hinterland. In October 1949 he referred to "a terrible dilemma" for American policy:

> You have the terrific problem of how then the Japanese are going to get along unless they reopen some sort of Empire toward the South. Clearly we have got . . . to achieve opening up of trade possibilities, commercial possibilities for Japan on a scale very far greater than anything Japan knew before. It is a formidable task. On the other hand, it seems to me absolutely inevitable that we must keep completely the maritime and air controls as a means . . . of keeping control of the situation with respect to [the] Japanese in all eventualities . . . [it is] all the more imperative that we retain the ability to control their situation by controlling the overseas sources of supply and the naval power and air power without which it cannot become again aggressive.

As if the listener might mistake his intent, he went on:

> If we really in the Western world could work out controls, I suppose, adept enough and foolproof enough and cleverly enough exercised really to have power over what Japan imports in the way of oil and such other things as she has got to get from overseas, we would have veto power on what she does need in the military and industrial field.[7]

It was a masterful performance, this, elaborating in detail what Japan-lobby figure Harry Kern meant when he once said of the U.S.-Japanese relationship, " 'remote control' is best."[8] It all resembled a type of liberal or hegemonic protectorate, capturing in the fundaments Japan's position in the American realm in the Pacific ever since.

Japan has had political independence since 1952, generally democratic and stable politics at home, and extraordinarily rapid economic growth rates. Yet Japan is remarkably dependent upon the United States for its security and its essential resources, mainly oil and food, and also for its access to advanced-country markets. The United States has maintained a light hold on the Japanese jugular, so to speak, possessing but never in-

---

[6]"China," February 1948, George Kennan Papers, box 23, Princeton University Library.

[7]George Kennan Papers, October 1949.

[8]Harry Kern, "American Policy toward Japan," 1948, a privately circulated paper, in Pratt Papers, Naval War College, box 2.

voking a capacity to squeeze Japan economically and dominate it militarily. The strong economy but weak defense of Japan was a great virtue when it helped fuel the postwar economic boom and when the United States could easily pay defense costs in the 1950s and 1960s. By the 1970s the obvious virtues had begun to look like vices, with Japan devastating American home industries and the United States increasingly unable to pay for its far-flung commitments.

The structure of U.S.-Japanese relations has remained essentially the same since 1950. The United States provides security, shapes the flow of resources to Japan (the growing role of the U.S. Navy in the Arab/Persian Gulf, where Japan gets 60 percent of its oil, is the best contemporary example), and hopes that Japan will manufacture those products no longer produced efficiently by American industries (textiles, autos, steel). The economic basis of the relationship is imbedded in theories of comparative advantage and the product cycle: Japan moves from textiles and light-assembly industries in the 1950s; to cars and steel in the 1960s and 1970s; to electronics, computers and "knowledge" industries in the 1980s. Although this international division of labor has been opposed in the United States by declining industries and protectionist interests, it has had the support of internationalists and free traders, and of those industries that compete well in the world markets. The model has been replicated in a somewhat different form and at a lower level in the product cycle in Taiwan, South Korea, Singapore and Hong Kong.

At the global level, American internationalists pursued a revival and flourishing of the world economy: for example, the Marshall Plan for European recovery. Japan was to be the engine of growth in the Asian region, shorn of military and political power and reintegrated into a potent industrial position in the world economy, but one of the second rank. American planners thought that this necessitated a hinterland providing raw materials, labor and markets. Therefore, as Michael Schaller has so aptly discussed, Acheson and others developed a "great crescent" strategy as the underpinning to the containment strategy, linking an offshore island defense with a Japanese hinterland. The hinterland would include Japan's former colonies, to the extent that they were available, but above all it would encompass Southeast Asia and Indochina.[9]

The economic (and even theoretical) conception for this policy may be seen in draft papers leading up to National Security Council (NSC) document No. 48, adopted at the end of 1949. It embodied a design for an Asian grand area, a regional hierarchy of core, semiperipheral and peripheral economies in the broader world system. A revived industrial core in Japan came first; keeping South Korea, Taiwan and Southeast Asia (including especially Indochina) in the world market system came next; then there was the question of what else might be brought in if conditions permitted. China was one of those potential economies, in spite of its successful communist revolution.

[9] Michael Schaller, *The American Occupation of Japan: The Origins of the Cold War in Asia* (New York: Oxford University Press, 1985).

The core thinking for the whole of the new policy appeared first in an August 1949 draft, entitled "Asia, Economic Section."[10] It began by saying that American economic policy should be "measured against principles." What were the principles? First: "The economic life of the modern world is geared to expansion." This required "the establishment of conditions favorable to the export of technology and capital and to a liberal trade policy throughout the world." Second principle: "Reciprocal exchange and mutual advantage." Third principle: "Production and trade which truly reflect comparative advantage." Fourth principle: Opposition to "general industrialization." That is, Asian countries do, indeed, possess "special resources" and the like, "but none of them alone has adequate resources as a base for general industrialization." India, China and Japan merely "approximate that condition." "General industrialization" in individual countries "could be achieved only at a high cost as a result of sacrificing production in fields of comparative advantage." Fifth principle: Certain parts of the world, such as Southeast Asia (but also parts of South America and Africa), are "natural sources of supply of strategic commodities and other basic materials," giving the United States "a special opportunity for leverage" as a "large and very welcome customer." Sixth principle: "In trade with countries under Soviet control or domination, the above principles are not applicable." The United States must instead find means of "exerting economic pressure" on such countries (the germ of subsequent embargoes against Soviet-aligned economies).

The paper went on to mention that Japan had received 80 percent of its coal from northern and northeastern China, and from northern Korea; that Japan's economy, to be viable, must quickly realize "an enlargement of foreign trade"; that Japan should also revive steel production—but only to a level of four million tons or so, for domestic market needs; that Japan should revive merchant shipping (but only to Asian countries); and that Japan should find its markets in Asia. Japan, too, was unfit for comprehensive, world-class industrialization.

An October 1949 draft paper elaborated on the virtues of a triangular, hierarchical structure, which

> would involve the export from the US to Japan of such commodities as cotton, wheat, coal and possibly specialized industrial machinery; the export from Japan of such items as low-cost agricultural and transportation equipment, textiles, and shipping services to Southeast Asia; and the export from the latter of tin, manganese, rubber, hard fibers, and possibly lead and zinc to the US.

Anticipating nationalist objections in the grand manner of the 19th-century Rothschilds, the paper went on to remark:

> The complexity of international trade makes it well to bear in mind that such ephemeral matters as national pride and ambition can inhibit or prevent the necessary degree of international cooperation, or the development of a favorable atmosphere and conditions to promote economic expansion.[11]

[10] In Cumings, *Origins of the Korean War,* Vol. 2.
[11] Ibid.

Southeast Asia was to be a pivot for both the Japanese and the Western European economies, each having important sources of raw materials and markets, such that the revival of industry in northeastern Asia dovetailed with revival in Europe. Japan, however, was in the region of unilateral American dominance, whereas Southeast Asia had been held exclusively by the European imperial powers. The reentry of Japan would thus benefit the United States and draw down the competing European empires, while allowing the United States an entry into previously off-limits markets—"for its own convenience," as the Central Intelligence Agency (CIA) nicely put it. The French and Dutch were happy, the Germans were uninvolved, but the British resisted both the Japanese revival and its linkage to Southeast Asia.

The irony, of course, is that Japan never really developed markets or intimate core-periphery linkages in Southeast Asia. The Korean War gave the critical boost to its economy, and thereafter Japan succeeded in penetrating the American and other Western markets. But the logic of an Asian hinterland persisted through the Korean War; it is remarkable to see how vexed the Eisenhower administration still was with "the restoration of Japan's lost colonial empire." [12]

With the complete routing of the Chinese Nationalists on the mainland predictable by late 1948 and accomplished by the summer of 1949, American policy toward China could be conceived simply. As Dean Rusk once put it, "Our first choice in respect to Peiping [sic] was that it fall . . . our second choice was that, if it didn't fall, it could somehow be separated from Moscow." George Kennan supplied the geopolitical rationale for the second choice. The Soviet Union, he argued, had an enormous internal market yet to be developed, and its links to East Asia were stretched thin and rather primitive; he did not think the Soviets could give the Chinese what they needed, or "do much in the way of inter-twining its economy with that of China." He recalled a meeting with Joseph Stalin, where the latter had said "If anybody is going to give anything to the Far East, I think it's you." [13]

Acheson thought that the China policy of the United States should avoid arousing elemental forces of Chinese nationalism, while using the charms and enticements of the market to bring China out of isolation and render it dependent on the West and Japan. For Acheson and Kennan, China in

[12] At the 139th meeting of the NSC, April 8, 1953, "The President expressed the belief that there was no future for Japan unless access were provided for it to the markets and raw materials of Manchuria and North China." Secretary of Treasury Humphrey wanted the United States to be "aggressive" in providing Japan and West Germany with a secure position where they could "thrive, and have scope for their virile populations. In some respects, it seemed to him, we had licked the two wrong nations in the last war," Whereupon, "Mr. Cutler [Special Assistant to the President] inquired whether the Council wished to go further than this and adopt a policy which would look to the restoration of Japan's lost colonial empire." Eisenhower said no, probably not. (Eisenhower Papers [Whitman file], National Security Council Series, box 4, Eisenhower Library, Abilene, Kansas.)

[13] In Cumings, *Origins of The Korean War*, Vol. 2.

the 1940s was little more than an agrarian political economy with a modern fringe stitched along its coast and in Manchuria by the imperial powers; it could not industrialize on its own resources. The Soviet Union, however, was the biggest self-sufficient political economy in the world next to the United States, and was the one nation since Japan to show itself capable of general industrialization on its own. The feasibility of enmeshing China was thus much greater.

State Department internationalists tended to agree with British policy, that is, to maintain diplomatic recognition of a China gone communist, to continue trade, to avoid military skirmishes, and to hope that at a later point China would turn to the West in search of its superior technology, financial resources and expertise. Chinese industrialization "will require foreign capital, foreign capital goods, and foreign technical assistance," the British said, and will be "almost entirely dependent on non-Communist sources for supplies of rubber, oil, and fertilizers." American Far East chief Walton Butterworth agreed, and emphasized the uses of oil to American policy in rendering China tractable, given U.S. dominance over the world oil regime; he and others in the State Department also wanted to continue Sino-Japanese trade for similar reasons. This policy was thwarted by American domestic politics and destroyed by the Korean War, but it came back 30 years later, with energy resources again used in search of outer limits on Chinese action.[14]

Taiwan was a buzzing, irritating fly in this ointment. Without the bizarre influence of the China issue and the China lobby in American politics, Acheson might have got his way, and a flourishing Sino-American relationship might not have had to wait the passage of a quarter-century—to wait for Richard Nixon to pick up Acheson's policy from the dustbin of history. As it happened, however, Acheson became the flypaper for a horde of Republican and right-wing horse flies, something that might well defeat the grandest architect.

South Korea occupied a contingent position in this architecture. Was it "little China" or "little Japan"? If it were a little China, its first president, Syngman Rhee, just another Chiang Kai-shek, the economy corrupted and inviable, and were North Korea an authentic revolutionary nationalist challenge linked to China, then South Korea would just be another domino. If it were a little Japan, however, with effective anti-Communist leadership, a growing economy with the necessary links to Japan and the United States, and North Korea was a "little Russia," a mere extension of Soviet power, the whole picture changed: It might be a place to reverse the tide of Communist expansion.

The Communist threat in Asia
The great antagonist to the free-trade grand area was socialist control of the Eurasian land mass, stretching "from Berlin to Canton, from Mur-

[14]"Review of the World Situation," April 20, 1949, NSC file, box 206, CIA, Truman Library Independence, Missouri; *Foreign Relations of the United States,* 1949, Vol. IX, pp. 826–42, draft of NSC41, Feb. 28, 1949, and U.K. Embassy to U.S. State Dept., April 5, 1949.

mansk to Tirhana," in a 1950s formulation. The feasible and practical remedy was therefore to draw lines of containment around its periphery, revive the industrial economies of Western Europe and Japan, link up the underdeveloped hinterlands, and seek to split the Soviets and the Chinese.

The Korean War was in essence an attempt to break the emerging East Asian system. The authors, or breakers, were the North Koreans, not Stalin. This assertion cannot be proved here, but it flows first from the nature of the North Korean regime, and second from the evidence on its motives in 1950.[15] North Korea is and has been a form of neomercantilist socialism—national socialism, if the term were still possible to use. Its Marxist aberration is to reinterpret class struggle as a species of national struggle: national assertion as the means to wealth and power. It takes the nation-state as the primary unit of conflict, rather than class. It is the supreme example in the postcolonial developing world of conscious withdrawal from the capitalist world system. Few countries have a more unfortunate geopolitical position, jammed cheek-by-jowl against two socialist giants, with an always tense confrontation with the United States and South Korea. Today, as in 1950, North Korea is the main antagonist of the East Asian grand area, or what is now called the Pacific Rim community.

In the late 1940s North Korea watched as its old enemy, Japan, revived. The one motive for war that stands out in the evidence in early 1950 is North Korea's growing concern with the revival of Japan, and especially its economic and military relations with South Korea. The formative maturation of Kim Il-sung and his followers occurred in the struggle against Japanese imperialism. In spite of their incessant denunciations of American imperialism, the North Koreans have always seen it as a disease of the skin; Japanese imperialism has been a disease of the heart (to borrow Chiang Kai-shek's metaphor).

Perhaps the most interesting North Korean commentary on Acheson's grand design in 1950 came in articles linking U.S. policy to those at the turn of the century, when Theodore Roosevelt blessed Japanese control of Korea. One author said the United States, while preaching "science and democracy" to Asians, had simply followed on the heels of the European imperialists in China, and had justified Japanese imperialism. Here the author quoted Roosevelt on the presumed "perils of propinquity," causing Japan to find its natural sphere of influence in its near reaches, Korea and Manchuria. The United States supported the Nationalists' Nanking government in 1927–37, while simultaneously supplying Japan with war matériel right up to the months before Pearl Harbor; the Americans then warred on Japan to weaken it, so the United States could substitute for Japan as Asia's leading imperialist. After the war, the United States hoped that China would become its great Asian ally, and thus sent huge amounts of aid to the Nationalists. Now, with Chiang's regime in ruins, it had turned to Japan.[16] It was a sophisticated argument.

---

[15] See Cumings, *Origins of the Korean War*, Vol. 2.
[16] Kang Chol-su, "U.S. Imperialism Is the Enemy of the Chinese People," *Nodong sinmun* [Worker's News], March 10, 1950.

The Korean War beclouded the Achesonian conception of power and plenty. The North Korean assault and subsequent Chinese intervention seemed to confirm all the worst fear of "cold warriors," and thus skewed global conflict toward bipolarism and the reinforcement of containment bulwarks; the iron and bamboo curtains that divided the world also fell across people's minds, inducing a rigidity nowhere better exemplified than in the thought and policies of John Foster Dulles. Most of the NSC records of the Eisenhower administration are now available to scholars, and it is remarkable to see how the geographic fault lines of the bipolar conflict consumed the attentions of Dulles and other high policymakers. They were capable of devoting nearly exclusive attention to nondescript islands off the China coast, such as Quemoy and Matsu. The Kennedy administration began with a flourish of new thinking about America's role in the world, only to be drawn into overwhelming concern with a little island named Cuba. What is truly amazing, however, is the degree to which the entire foreign policy apparatus of the Johnson administration devoted itself to a small country named Vietnam, with a fervor that from today's vantage point can only seem fantastic.

The cold war security structure similarly influenced the other side. For decades Andrei Gromyko structured Soviet foreign policy to guard against the revanche of Germany and Japan, resulting in a fixation on yet more tiny islands, the windswept ones just north of Japan that have stood in the way of Soviet-Japan relations, and that exemplify the rigidity of the Soviet approach to Asia up to the Gorbachev era. From 1950 well into the 1980s, both superpowers diverted their attentions toward security structures and expenditures, neglecting the centrality of economic and technological progress to world position. The result was that when these fixations began to end in the most recent period, both superpowers awoke to find themselves outclassed economically by Japan and Western Europe.

At the same time, the Korean War served to place distinct outer limits on American expansionism. To the extent that this was a "limited war," it was the Chinese who limited it when they intervened in late 1950 and then fought for two years to get a settlement roughly at the place where the war first started. It can be said that China also limited the Vietnam War, in that Lyndon Johnson and his advisers always worried that an invasion of North Vietnam (on the model of North Korea) would bring China into the war. China viewed both conflicts as proxy wars mounted against their old tributary states, with the real issue being the Chinese revolution.[17]

Without belaboring these points, what this article has sought to demonstrate is both the hegemonic conception that underpinned the northeastern Asian system, and a brief argument on the reasons for the major attempt to break it—the North Korean assault in June 1950. Acheson and Kennan had drawn tentative lines in the late 1940s, demarking the area of

---

[17] See, for example, George McT. Kahin, *Intervention* (New York: Knopf, 1986); also Richard Drinnon, *Facing West: The Metaphysics of Indian-Hating and Empire Building* (Minneapolis: University of Minnesota Press, 1980), 402–13.

free trade more than the area of containment, and hoping that the bamboo curtain would prove permeable to the charms and wiles of the market. Economic concerns were dominant. The Korean War hardened the outer limits into seemingly impermeable bulwarks of national security; power politics was dominant for the next two decades. But as time has passed, the imperatives of economic exchange have systematically eroded the edifice of security.

The strategic lines of the new northeastern Asian political economy brought the peculiar nature of American hegemony to the fore. The United States retrieved South Korea and Taiwan from oblivion in 1950, but invoking the threat of oblivion to keep them in line in later years was unthinkable. The United States kept Japan on a food, oil and security dependency, yet to squeeze Japan at this fundamental level would be disastrous. In other words, outer limits are not enough to bring recalcitrant allies to heel; the outer limits can be invoked only in crises. Furthermore, within those outer limits a dependent but strong state obtains leverage over the American "weak state," weak in the sense of competing centers of power and economic interest that can be played off against one another. Thus, the postwar settlement simultaneously gave Japan, South Korea and Taiwan dependency and autonomous capability.

When the Korean War ended, both Taiwan and South Korea had absurdly swollen military machines—about 600,000 soldiers in each army, ranking among the highest military/civilian ratios in the world. Both were also authoritarian states with large security and intelligence bureaucracies. These big militaries served as a perimeter defense for the hegemonic grand area, and their formidable policing agencies quieted labor and the left. These same peripheral militaries processed millions of young men and women in their formative years, imbuing virtues of discipline, hard work, basic literacy and the like, making a strong but mostly unappreciated contribution to the economic development of Taiwan and South Korea.

In Japan, South Korea and Taiwan, the post-Korean War settlement bequeathed states that were strong in relation to their own economies or peoples, but weak laterally. That is, they were penetrated by various agencies of the hegemonic power—military, political, economic and intelligence agencies. The best example of lateral penetration is perennial American operational control of the South Korean military. Since 1945, in only one year has the United States not had such control in South Korea, and that was the year that war came (1949–50). A better-known and more important lateral penetration is American control of nuclear weapons on Japanese and South Korean soil. The United States still places some 50,000 troops and 118 military facilities on Japanese soil, creating a historically unique situation in which the hegemonic power provides basic security for the rising power (although the role of the British navy in policing the Atlantic might be a vague precedent).

For Japan the legacy of the postwar settlement was to make its success highly contingent on a continued relationship with the United States, one in which Japan was far from an equal. Japan got autonomy in terms of economic development, dependency in terms of power or security. It has therefore gained rapidly on the United States in economic competition, but is ever vulnerable to the invocation of extra-economic levers to keep it in line. Japan may be a "core" state in Wallersteinian terms, if its economy, the enormous influence of its banks or its advanced technology is considered. But it still does not dispose of plenty and power. This will obtain as long as Japan does not provide for its own defense. Furthermore, the Japanese state does not at this time have the domestic autonomy to raise a strong defense—which would require entering the nuclear arms race—nor does it have the autonomy to break with the United States. Japan is still somewhere in between a dependency and a great power.

THE 1970S TRANSITION: NIXONIAN CHANGES

Richard Nixon's strategy in regard to East Asia, briefly put, was to revive the Achesonian position on China and South Korea, and to invoke for the first time the levers of power implicit in the settlement with Japan. The Nixon period was literally pivotal, being both continuous with previous policy and skewing policy toward the use of heretofore unmentionable means against American allies: especially the invocation of the outer limits of hegemony. The best example is Nixon's New Economic Policy, announced on V-J Day, 1971. For Japan this was the so-called Nixon *shokku* (shock). Nixon also reaped the rewards of the splitting of Moscow and Beijing, a split Acheson had projected. And Nixon laid the foundations for the economic enmeshment of China with the United States and the world economy. Franz Schurmann argued that for Nixon and other conservatives:

> Peaceful coexistence could be meaningful only if Russia and China agreed to join the world market system. If they did, the conservatives foresaw that conservatizing forces would set in in both countries. The more these militantly revolutionary countries were involved in world trade, the more their barbaric regimes would be civilized under the weight of international responsibility.[18]

This is true, but these might as well be Acheson's words, so close were Nixon and Henry Kissinger to Acheson's viewpoint.

On Korea, it is well to remember that Acheson's original, pre-Korean War policy was troop withdrawal with containment; South Korea was to occupy the same position as Greece and Turkey: military aid and advice, yes, but no American troops on the ground. Since the demobilization in 1953, Nixon was the only president successfully to withdraw a division of troops from South Korea. One would suspect that this withdrawal had the ultimate goal of substituting Japan for the United States as South Korea's security guarantor (i.e., Kennan's original policy).

Nixon did not so much change the rules of the game as issue reminders that the rules had powerful levers that could be invoked against Japan. A sense of unease and foreboding has marked Japanese-American interactions ever since. This can be sensed in the following simple statement by one

[18] Franz Schurmann, *The Logic of World Power* (New York: Pantheon, 1974), 52.

Japanese commentator: "When Japan is weak and small, the United States is kind and generous . . . and when Japan becomes big and strong, the United States gets annoyed and resorts to Japan-bashing."[19]

Nixon's engineer was not Kennan, but Treasury Secretary John Connally. His stock-in-trade was nasty comments about Japan ("Don't they remember who won the war?"). In 1979, during a failed campaign for the presidency, Connally was the first to invoke the rhetoric of American nationalism that is now commonplace, thanks to presidential candidates such as Michael Dukakis and others. If Japan did not abide by "fair trade," well, then, "they could just sit in their Toyotas in Yokohama and watch their color TVs and leave us alone"—so said Connally. For internationalists like Zbigniew Brzezinski and David Rockefeller (and their brainchild, the Trilateral Commission), after the Nixon *shokku* the problem was how to shape the articulation of the new Japan with the world economy—so that what Brzezinski called the "fragile blossom" did not turn into Tokyo Rose.

Because of Japan's structural dependence, it is subject not just to kicks in the shins but blows to the solar plexus. The 1970s made clear that while the United States may be dependent on foreign oil, its relative vulnerability is so much less than Japan's (or Western Europe's for that matter) that it can benefit from allied adversity. Many Japanese still believe the quadrupling of oil prices was abetted by Nixon and Kissinger, thus to change the terms of trade to the American favor.

Japan's preference is for the United States to be the hegemon, to provide the single world authority that guarantees the larger structure within which Japan exists and competes. But this should be done as it was until 1971, with Japan's growth understood to be salutary for the whole system, not detrimental to it. In other words, the United States should look after the whole, and let Japan look after the parts. The problem of the present, of course, is that the United States can no longer look after the whole.

INDIAN SUMMER IN THE 1980S

When Ronald Reagan was nominated in 1980, delegates to the Republican convention poured forth their insistent belief that "We're Number One." Reagan pledged to "make America great again." From that point to his "ride off into the sunset" in 1989, his speeches were marked with the theme of a lost but recoverable past, even as that past recedes and America's problems deepen. The faint sense of anachronism one gets while watching Japanese or South Korean auto workers scurry about an assembly line is matched by the musty symbolism of a bygone era wafting through Reagan's words.

To the extent that the Reagan administration had an Asian policy, the essential idea was to place Japan first and link the rest of the region to that assumption and that connection. Judging Japan to be preeminent as a regional power because of its industrial prowess, the conception merged se-

[19] Shibusawa Masahide, *Japan and the Asian Pacific Region* (London: Croom Helm for the Royal Institute of International Affairs, 1984), 163.

curity and development, pushing and prodding Japan toward filling out its economic capability with commensurate (or at least modestly appropriate) military power. Simultaneously the policy sought to enhance Japan's dependence on American high technology, most of it defense-related. Defense Secretary Caspar Weinberger—who stayed in office for years and departed only at that moment when Reagan seemed to opt for Nixonian détente—was the author of the Japan-first tendency, and pushed it from the time of the first Reagan inauguration.[20]

Ever since Franklin Roosevelt was in office, a critical question for Americans has been which power, Japan or China, should be the centerpiece of America's Asian policy. The leitmotiv for Reagan's Japan-first strategy was the Soviet development of a blue-ocean navy and the emergence of a powerful Pacific fleet, something begun in the 1960s but highly visible (if almost always exaggerated) by the late 1970s. Furthermore, the Carter Doctrine had drawn off American naval strength to the Indian Ocean and Arab/Persian Gulf, leaving the North Pacific with a reduced contingent of carriers and other ships. This was another strategic reason for a buildup in the environs of Japan.

Almost as soon as he took office, Weinberger began drawing up his five-year (1984–88) "Defense Guidance," which some later called "a revolution in military doctrine."[21] Whether it was that or not, various authors were certainly correct to focus on the plan's naval emphasis—or what some called the "Lehman Doctrine," after the brash secretary of the navy, John F. Lehman, Jr. The basis for a projected $200 billion, 600-ship navy, the doctrine had a strategic conception of the United States rather like that of Japan: The United States was akin to "an island nation," "vitally dependent on access to the sealanes for trade in peacetime and for reinforcement of allies in time of war." In 1981 Weinberger said that American dependence on such access was so great that "we must be able to defeat any military adversary who threatens such access.' Michael Klare found the most significant innovation in the new naval policy to be "the concept of sending battle groups into 'high-threat' waters adjacent to the USSR in order to strike key Soviet facilities and to divert Soviet strength from the Central Front in Europe."[22]

Meanwhile, Americans seemed transfixed in the 1980s by the paradox of claiming to have launched Japanese and Korean development, while wincing at the successes of these "offspring" in undermining American industries. Lionel Olmer, Commerce Department under secretary for foreign trade, argued that the United States had transferred $10 billion in advanced technology to Japan since 1950 in "the biggest fire sale in history"—but Japan

---

[20] See Chuma Kiyofuku, "What Price the Defense of Japan," *Japan Quarterly* 34, no. 3 (July-September 1987): 251–58; the author cited Weinberger's continuous pressure to increase defense spending and commitments, and noted how U.S. and Japanese defense hawks worked together in the 1980s.
[21] Michael Klare, "The Reagan Doctrine," *Inquiry* (March-April 1984): 18–22.
[22] *Ibid.*

had not reciprocated.[23] What these Americans forgot, of course, is precisely the Acheson-Kennan conception that deemed the revival of Japanese industry—requiring this transfer of technology—essential to the grand area and the containment doctrine in East Asia. As has been seen, this "free ride" had a powerful corollary in making Japan dependent on the United States, giving the United States remarkable leverage over a competing economic giant.

In January 1983 Prime Minister Yasuhiro Nakasone visited Washington, where he compared the Japanese archipelago to "an unsinkable aircraft carrier putting up a tremendous bulwark of defense," and also agreed to transfer the package of loans and credits, totaling about $4 billion, to South Korea—viewed by the Reagan administration as a contribution to South Korean, and therefore Japanese, security. Nakasone's defense minister, Yoshio Sakarauchi, stated at the same time that peace and security in South Korea was "vital" to Japan, and acknowledged that the United States and Japan were jointly studying mutual responses to "contingencies in the Far East area extending outside Japan."

Before Nakasone came into office, Weinberger had called on Japan to develop the capacity to defend "the airspace and the sealanes up to a thousand miles from [Japan's] shoreline," something Japan committed itself to in 1981. Japan has also begun to participate in American naval exercises in the Pacific, such as the RIMPAC exercises off Hawaii. A new domestically produced cruise missile, the SSM-1, is credited by some as giving Japan the capability to destroy Soviet surface ships in adjacent waters.[24]

Until recently the Soviets kept up a steady drumbeat of attacks on American "collusion" with reviving Japanese militarism. The shooting down of the Korean Airlines jet in September 1983, of course, greatly intensified security concerns for both powers in the region near Japan, while demonstrating the degree of American-Japanese cooperation in intelligence gathering. In July 1986, however, Mikhail Gorbachev gave an important speech on Soviet East Asian policy in Vladivostok, which called attention to U.S.-Japanese cooperation in military exercises and the like, but also signaled a willingness to warm up relations with Japan, and end the Soviet fixation, begun by Stalin and sustained for decades by Gromyko, with a revanchist Japan.

Although this shift has not yet borne fruit, it would not be surprising if Gorbachev's supple diplomacy in other regions eventually attains success in East Asia as well. By the late 1980s the Soviets and the Chinese appeared on the verge of a summit meeting. The 1988 Olympics in Seoul led to enhanced trade between South Korea, the Soviet Union, China and Hungary. Furthermore, the INF agreement and the Reagan-Gorbachev summits in Washington and New York severely undercut a prime rationale for pressing Japan on security issues: the Soviet threat in general, and the

---

[23] *Business Week* (March 14, 1983).
[24] John J. O'Connell, "Strategic Implications of the Japanese SSM-1 Cruise Missile," *Journal of Northeast Asian Studies* 6, no. 2 (Summer 1987): 53–66.

positioning of SS20 missiles in the Soviet Far East in particular, which are now being dismantled. This may provide an important opening for the Soviet Union and for Japan to defuse defense-spending pressures from Washington that they both have reasons to resist.

Washington's policy in the 1980s had another goal besides that of pushing and prodding Japan toward greater regional security efforts. A cover article in *Business Week* in 1983 argued that "if the Pentagon had its way, Japan would shoulder responsibility for bottling up the entire Soviet Pacific fleet within the Sea of Japan." But Washington's real goal, according to the article, was "to offer Japan a limited range of weapons, making Tokyo dependent on the U.S. for most of its military needs"; tying Japan to American military programs would in turn give the United States access to advanced Japanese technology in semiconductors, fiber optics, robotics and ceramics. A key Defense Department official remarked that as for the United States, it did not intend to give Japan access "to any of our high technology."[25]

It is clear that Reagan-era planning continued the structure of the "reverse course" settlement—Japanese industry or rearmament was to grow, yes, but as a boon to American interests, not necessarily to Japanese interests, and only to the point where it would not threaten American positions. Although it is problematic whether technological dependencies can be sustained in computer hardware, where Japan is rivaling the United States in building supercomputers so essential to high-technology defense, Japan still lags far behind in the necessary software and in systems engineering. Most of the software Japan uses for its air and sea defense and its electronic warfare systems comes from the United States. The United States may be a declining economic power, but it still does know how to do some things—like hemorrhage money into defense systems. The "Star Wars" program is the best example, of course, and is among other things a cloak for a state-led program to develop supercomputers and the requisite software—"industrial policy," national security style.

Japan seemed unlikely to hold still for the Reagan administration's attempts to maintain technological dependencies, and it was by no means fully compliant with American wishes. Japan decided in January 1987 to breach the famed one percent of GNP figure for defense expenditures; a small incremental move, it was nonetheless a symbolic leap forward. Its capacity to implement airspace and sealane defenses around Japan is at least a decade off, however, and likely to proceed more slowly now that Nakasone is no longer prime minister.

The Japanese public is still hostile to a big defense buildup, in spite of reports of rising Japanese nationalism.[26] Even mild revisions of textbook accounts of Japan's prewar aggression in Asia have prompted frothy outrage at home and in neighboring countries. It may be that planners in the

---

[25] "Rearming Japan," *Business Week* (March 14, 1983).

[26] An *Asahi Shimbun* poll in March 1987 showed that only 15 percent of the Japanese approved lifting the one percent GNP limit on defense spending, and 61 percent were opposed. See Chuma Kiyofuku, "What Price the Defense of Japan."

economic ministries were happy to see the revisions and the predictable response, which they can then point to as reasons to go slow on defense spending.

The other great issue between the United States and Japan in the 1980s was economic conflict. This expressed itself in continuous pressure throughout the decade for Japan to continue opening its markets to American goods, to adopt policies to stimulate the Japanese economy and to sit still while U.S. central bankers, Paul Volcker and his successor Alan Greenspan, seek through the policies of the Federal Reserve to pass onto Japan and other nations the costs of American economic infirmity. The latter effort has induced a sort of bankers' *shokku,* as one book after another appears claiming that American bankers, or Jews, or both, are involved in a conspiracy to keep Japan in its place.[27] A more substantive response came from Haruo Maekawa, former governor of the Bank of Japan, who issued a report in March 1986 calling for serious structural reform in the Japanese economy; the Foreign Ministry endorsed this in its "Blue Book" in July, and called for a "second opening of the country," analogous to the Meiji Restoration. But little of significance has followed that unprecedented statement. The recent world glut in food stocks, especially American stocks, has also led to attempts by the United States to get Japan and South Korea to buy more American grains, fostering resentment in the agrarian sector that also feeds residual nationalism.

The great problem of the 1980s was that the power-political elements of the postwar settlement came increasingly to be used against Japan, as the American capacity for producing economic growth and for invoking the old dependencies declined. The original conception was that military and political means would be used to fashion the limits of the grand area, but would give way to a glue provided by manifold economic relationships. But with Japan—and increasingly South Korea and Taiwan—besting America in economic competition, the United States seemed reduced to mimicking previous empires in decline, flexing political and military muscles to get its way economically.

It was not at all clear, in other words, that American pressures in the 1980s significantly advanced American goals, let alone those of a more mature U.S.-Japanese relationship. Were Japan rapidly to fulfill this agenda and become a regional military power, who would benefit? It could not be done without giving unwonted reinforcement to the Japanese right and to stirring Japanese nationalism, which would in turn stimulate even more anti-Japanese sentiment in the United States. The older American generation, in particular, still mistrusted the exercise of Japanese power by independent Japanese—as witnessed by a particularly virulent article written by Theodore White, and by Henry Kissinger's warning on the consequences of arming Japan.[28]

[27] See, for example, *If You Can Understand the Jews You'll Be Able to Understand the Japanese* (Tokyo, 1986).
[28] Theodore White, *New York Times Magazine,* 28 July 1985; also Henry Kissinger in the *Washington Post,* 29 January 1987. For a perceptive essay on these tensions,

More important, by emphasizing the security elements of U.S.-Japanese relations—trying to get them to follow the American path—it was likely that the American economic decline vis-à-vis Japan would only have been hastened. Americans might better have adopted a position of openness, if not humility, toward the lessons of Japanese industrial success—that is, follow their path of investing in wealth rather than weapons.

CHINA: THE ACHESONIAN LINEAGE

The Reagan administration curiously reversed the China-policy sequence of the Carter administration. Under Jimmy Carter, the Sino-American relationship deteriorated in the first year, and then was followed by a significant period of policy parallelism between the United States and China; under Reagan, a first year of continuity and parallelism was followed by two years of degeneration. The latter shift came so suddenly that within a year of the inauguration the deputy foreign minister of China said that "relations are facing a crisis."

Most significant in the scuttling of the Brzezinski-Haig "China card" was Weinberger's policy. His Defense Guidance said much about Japan, but little about China. Its forward policy of "global reach" implied a strong role for the navy and for highly mobile missile forces, but not much of a role for China, a country with little or no navy, an obsolescent air force, almost no capacity for high-technology weaponry and an antique missile arsenal—not to mention its doubtful reliability against non-Soviet but nonetheless insurgent forces (e.g., North Korea).[29]

Weinberger visited China in 1983, seeking to enlist China in "strategic cooperation." The Chinese seemed far more reticent than in the halcyon days of Carter and Brzezinski. They were happy, however, with Weinberger for lifting restrictions on certain types of advanced technology exports. Weinberger's visit in 1986 was more fruitful, as the Chinese finally agreed to permit U.S. warships to make a port visit—to Qingdao, just across the Yellow Sea from Korea. (The visit merely underlined the prominence of Weinberger's naval strategy.)

Sino-American relations warmed markedly in the summer of 1983, and have since proceeded without further talk of "crisis." However, whereas the Carter administration pursued both a strategic and economic basis for the relationship, the Reagan administration pursued the second but not the first. American global strategy no longer depends on the China card. The combination of a new war plan based on control of sealanes, maneuverable forward postures and high-technology war fighting capability, and a domestic Republican coalition biased toward anti-Communist stalwarts like Taiwan (and anticommunism everywhere), put China in a secondary posi-

see John Dower, "Psychological Aspects of Contemporary U.S.-Japan Relations," *Kokusai Mondai* [International Problems] (March-April 1988).

[29] For a well-informed discussion of Beijing's recent policies, see Hao Yu-fan, "China and the Korean Peninsula: A Chinese View," *Asian Survey* 27, no. 8 (August 1987): 862–84.

tion to Japan, if not completely on the back burner. But the *economic* logic of influencing and supporting changes in the outward orientation of the Chinese economy continued uninterrupted.

This economic rationale for the Sino-American relationship was articulated nicely by Acheson-ventriloquist Richard Nixon in 1982, when he argued that the more the United States engaged China "in an intricate network of commercial relations, the more we increase its stake in peace"—not to mention make a lot of money.[30] This enmeshment, in good hegemonic fashion, has placed special emphasis on American help with China's energy needs. Indeed, one American official remarked that "the real strategic cooperation between our two countries is not military, it's in energy."[31]

Throughout the 1970s and 1980s the United States sought to shape China's economic and strategic policies, with far greater success than most analysts have suggested. It is a commonplace to observe that China developed the strategic policy the United States wanted it to have: opposition to "hegemonism" (the Soviet Union) but not to imperialism (the United States). But China also adopted in part the economic strategy that the United States—or world agencies dominated by the United States, such as the World Bank—wanted it to have.

The critical shift for China came in late 1978, when perennial heavy-industry-first policies gave way to ones emphasizing light industry, exports, limited play for market forces and the like. The economic logic of the Sino-American relationship had many parallels with the case of Japan, parallels perceived as such by U.S. and Chinese leaders. As with Japan, security and economic issues mingled. For China, the essential point was to minimize defense costs by forging an informal alliance with Washington, and to maximize economic benefits by opening its doors to foreign capital, corporations and technology. In both defense relations and energy, the United States encouraged China to take a long-term path that would entail continuing, if subtle, defense, resource and high-technology dependency. And precisely because such investments and relations were for the long term, and because China could not realize the foreign exchange from oil exports that it had hoped to in the late 1970s, a different exporting strategy was essential: light-industry exports such as textiles and consumer electronics. This strategy would also enmesh China in the world economy's division of labor.

PICKLES IN THE MIDDLE: KOREA AND VIETNAM

In 1950 the Korean War shattered the Acheson-Kennan plans for East Asia (temporarily at least), hardened strategic lines, and greatly skewed American policy toward harsh anticommunism and military solutions. In the late 1980s the Korean peninsula remained the most volatile flashpoint in north-

[30] *New York Times,* 19 August 1982.
[31] *Far Eastern Economic Review,* April 21, 1983.

eastern Asia—both for reasons of international politics, and because of the percolating crisis in South Korean politics and North Korean economics.

The Korean peninsula remains a cold war island in a post-cold war sea. For a North Korean leadership that cut its teeth fighting Japanese imperialism in the 1930s, the heightened nationalism and bold commitments of the Nakasone years must have been very worrisome. In April 1984 Kim Il-sung chose an interview with Tass correspondents to drum on the theme of revived Japanese militarism and American imperialism, in that order. China's deepening involvement with the United States, Japan and South Korea ("informal" trade between China and South Korea was more than $1 billion in 1985–86, $2 billion in 1987) also causes concern, and has pushed the North back toward the Soviets for the first time in a generation.

As in 1950, North Korea retains a capacity to disrupt, if not to break, the northeastern Asian system. But today, for the first time, it faces dire pressures from its Communist allies to loosen up or even demobilize its Stalinist economic policies of self-reliance, priority to heavy industry and production for the home market. Most of all, the pressures come from socialist countries interested in trading with South Korea. When Hungary decided at the time of the 1988 Olympics to open diplomatic relations with Seoul, Pyongyang let out a howl of protest.[32] North Korea is between the devil and the deep blue sea: if it throws its doors open, it will threaten the central leadership (witness Yugoslavia's problems in late 1988) and require it to acknowledge the relative failure of its autarkic economic strategy. If it keeps the doors shut it will, in Deng Xiaoping's phrase, "crawl along at a snail's pace" behind its capitalist industrializing rivals in the Pacific Basin, and end up like Romania. And neither Yugoslavia nor Romania are models to emulate today.

Vietnam is in a similar but even less advantageous position than North Korea. Its industrial base is tiny in contrast to that of North Korea, and therefore its ability to pursue self-reliant withdrawal and general industrialization is similarly circumscribed. Meanwhile, it has much less capacity to feed its own people, whereas North Korea has been self-sufficient in food for a generation, Vietnam has pockets of starvation and more general malnutrition. For the past several years, as Alexander Woodside and other scholars have pointed out, Vietnam's leaders have searched for a way out of their dilemma of underdevelopment.

Vietnam's case is both poignant and revelatory of the main thrust of this essay: After a 30-year war fought with unprecedented tenacity, Vietnam succeeded in pushing back the tide of American expansion. But just as it did so, in 1975, a Pacific era dawned in which the name of the game was economic, not military, prowess. In other words, the internationalist vision won out just as the expansionist impulse lost out.

South Korea nearly lost out in the military blitz of 1950, yet survived to become the star performer among the East Asian "gang-of-four." No one who knew South Korea during the war can believe that a strange dialectic, a mysterious pattern of reversal and advance, is not at work here.

[32] Korean Central News Agency, 17 October 1988.

Yet without the Korean War, South Korea would much sooner have joined what is now called the Pacific Basin economy as a major exporter. It is another example of internationalist prescience. Yet South Korea today may cause the greatest problem for American strategy in the region, because the internationalists had little to say about politics, and South Korea has always rejected the liberal model of politics that one associates with internationalism.

The extraordinary volatility of South Korean politics is expressed in a pattern of seeming stasis punctuated by devastating eruptions (the "student revolution" that overthrew Rhee in 1960, the Kwangju rebellion in 1980, the bubbling crisis that erupted in June 1987). Why should a country of South Korea's economic wealth have such a pattern? Why should a nation that was retrieved from oblivion by the United States have so many young people who hate America? There is no easy answer to these questions, but by far the most neglected cause, if not the only cause, is the structure of South Korean-American security relations.

An American general still has residual command of the world's sixth largest army. The authoritarian institutions of the South Korean state resulted from American midwifery—the police and the army in the 1940s (both Park Chung Hee and his 1979 assassin, the director of central intelligence, graduated from officers' school under the American occupation), the South Korean CIA in 1961—and the state remains laterally penetrated by various American agencies. The Reagan administration, in particular, both enhanced the security apparatus more than any president since Eisenhower and pressured the South Koreans on economic issues more than any president including Nixon. American troop levels were about 45,000 at the end of the 1980s, compared to 40,000 in 1980; throughout the Reagan period massive military exercises involving as many as 200,000 South Korean and American troops were held in the early spring. Strong American pressures were brought against South Korea to open its markets to agricultural and service-industry products, and to revalue its currency upward to draw down exports to the American market.

In other words, Reagan invoked against South Korea what Nixon invoked against Japan: the hidden rules of power in the American relationship with northeastern Asia. What he got in return was a profound reassertion of South Korean nationalism, causing a temporary unity between the ferocious South Korean right and the developing South Korean left, united on nothing but their patriotism and independence.

CONCLUSION: THE ROAD AHEAD IN A NEW ERA

In the 1940s and 1950s U.S. military and political power etched the boundaries of the East Asian system, but slowly the element of power receded to the background as economic interchange increased—a definition of a mature hegemonic system. But the heyday of system maturity was remarkably brief; all too quickly economic competition between the United States and Japan revived, all too soon American planners looked askance at the unintended consequences of their own handiwork and returned to the levers of power inherent in the relationship.

Japan was the linchpin of strategy in the late 1940s, and remains so today. But Japan's economic prowess came too soon for the system's health, from the standpoint of American interests; the growth of Japan's heavy industries was too closely hinged to the decline of American steel, automobiles and electronics. Thus, from 1971 onward, but especially in the 1980s, the power-political elements of the system were invoked, just as the American capacity for producing wealth and for managing the old power dependencies receded. American policy is now all too reminiscent of previous empires in decline, using political and military means to get its way economically—and failing.

A new Japanese prime minister, Noboru Takeshita, quietly sought to distance Japan from the bold commitments of the Nakasone years by reviving the "good neighbor" policy of showering aid on distant Southeast Asian countries, rather than bolstering the security of near neighbors like South Korea. His goal, it seemed, was to maximize the economic possibilities of the mature northeastern Asian regional system, and soft-pedal the elements of power and security. Throughout the 1980s China, also, called for a peaceful environment for its modernization goals. Gorbachev's Soviet Union, too, signaled its intent to participate in the Pacific Rim economic colossus. Hanging in the balance was the future direction of U.S. policy in the region.

In his essay "Asia and the Pacific since 1945: A Japanese Perspective," in this Handbook, Takashi Inoguchi has discussed a fascinating set of alternatives for the United States-Japan relationship in the future, and there seems no reason to add to his presentation. It would appear that the challenge for the United States will be to join this competition on the tough field of economic prowess, the production of plenty, rather than seek to deploy yet more military force and play on receding dependencies to get its way, through the exercise of its residual power. This will ultimately require that the problem be brought home, that Americans stop spending money on the far-flung and anachronistic commitments of empire, and renew their commitment to a dynamic American economy. This will probably not happen until a crisis brings home to the American people the full dimensions of their dilemma.

The world of the 1990s, it now seems, will be a virgin terrain in which one after another of the seeming certainties of the postwar settlement 40 years ago will come unstuck. The Soviet Union will refuse to play the role of enemy, let alone "evil empire." Japan is not going to sit still for dependence on American military might. China will have an interest in beneficial relations with all its neighbors, including the Soviet Union, which will disorder local problems such as the Korean conflict and global considerations such as American anti-Communist strategy. Vietnam and North Korea will be faced with joining a world that the Achesons rather than the Ho Chi Minhs and Kim Il-sungs created. South Korea and the Philippines will have difficulty in creating a stable politics out of unprecedented change and continued stagnation, respectively.

For all of these countries except Japan, the recent extraordinary changes, or those likely to remain in prospect, represent choices born of crisis. For China it was the crisis of the Cultural Revolution and Mao Zedong's failed attempt at a third path between the superpowers. For the Soviet Union, Vietnam and, increasingly, North Korea, it was the crisis of a socialist system that could win wars against expansionism but had no long-standing and effective answer to the dynamics of capitalist internationalism, and increasingly had little to offer its own people beyond a more-or-less adequate welfare standard.

The American people, however, do not yet understand the challenges that face them. In a sense, the internationalist vision has won; it has demonstrated the superior ability of capitalism to deliver goods and services and enhance people's livelihood. But that does not mean that the American people have won. Capitalism, as Joseph Schumpeter told us in 1942, moves forward in waves of creation and destruction. The dynamism of the Pacific Basin has its ineluctable counterpart in lost jobs, hollowed out industrial cities and a declining middle class in America. The internationalists, as has been seen, were not just exporters of goods, but of capital equipment and technology to make goods. The latter have now been married to a region accustomed to the rigors of hard work, educational prowess, and strong cultural and national pride. This marriage now presages a fundamental shift in the world economy. But all this has little to do with the rhetoric of renewal, nostalgia and a recaptured American dream with which Americans coasted through the Reagan era. Instead, the United States confronts a new century, unlikely to be an American century.

FURTHER READING

Blum, Robert M. *Drawing the Line: The Origin of the American Containment Policy in East Asia.* New York: Norton, 1982.

Borden, William S. *The Pacific Alliance: United States Foreign Economic Policy and Japanese Trade Recovery, 1947–1955.* Madison: University of Wisconsin Press, 1984.

Calleo, David P. *The Imperious Economy.* Cambridge, Massachusetts: Harvard University Press, 1982.

Cumings, Bruce. *Origins of the Korean War.* 2 vols. Princeton, New Jersey: Princeton University Press, 1981, 1989.

Dower, John W. *Empire and Aftermath: Yoshida Shigeru and the Japanese Experience, 1878–1954.* Cambridge, Massachusetts: Council on East Asian Studies, 1979.

Gayn, Mark J. *Japan Diary.* New York: W. Sloane Associates, 1948.

Halliday, Jon. *A Political History of Japanese Capitalism.* New York: Pantheon, 1975.

Kahin, George McT. *Intervention: How America Became Involved in Vietnam.* New York: Knopf, 1986.

Nagai, Yonosuke, and Iriye, Akira, eds. *The Origins of the Cold War in Asia.* Tokyo: University of Tokyo Press, 1977.

Rotter, Andrew J. *The Path to Vietnam: Origins of the American Commitment to Southeast Asia.* Ithaca, New York: Cornell University Press, 1987.

Stueck, William Whitney. *The Road to Confrontation: American Policy Toward China and Korea, 1947–1950.* Chapel Hill: University of North Carolina Press, 1981.

Tsou, Tang. *America's Failure in China, 1941–1950.* 2 vols. Chicago: University of Chicago Press, 1963.

PART THREE

POLITICAL AFFAIRS

ASIAN POLITICAL LEADERSHIP

STEPHEN P. COHEN

INTRODUCTION

THE terms leadership and Asia independently resonate in popular and academic culture. Their juxtaposition in this essay produces a rich variety of examples. Different types of regimes and the strategies by which Asia's leaders exercise power as well as the underlying social, economic and political trends that affect leadership and regime patterns in Asia will be considered. Before moving to these tasks, however, it is necessary to devote a few words to the meaning of both leadership and Asia.

Theories of leadership
In accordance with Robert C. Tucker's[1] view leadership is not merely the pursuit of power through various skills nor a surface manifestation of deeper currents and trends, but consists of three distinct activities: The first is *diagnosis.* How does a leader define or perceive the chief issues and problems facing a political community? An inspired leader may detect such problems before others are aware of them. That leader may have undergone certain experiences that increase sensitivity toward such problems, or may be able to articulate social and political problems in a new way. Second, how do leaders *prescribe* a course of action (policy) to deal with the problems facing a political community? Other individuals or groups in a society may have identified the problem but a successful or innovative leader is one who suggests a viable way of coping with or eliminating it. Third, how do leaders *mobilize* resources in such a way as to implement their policies? How do they organize their followers, gather and concentrate other resources, and sustain these efforts as long as necessary?

Political leaders thus blend diagnosis, policy recommendation and implementation. These tasks interact and interpenetrate. A single leader may or may not possess the skills (or opportunity) to exercise all three aspects of leadership. Indeed, the problems facing any nation change over time, as do available resources, thus making the task of leadership more difficult.

[1] See his *Politics as Leadership* (Columbia: University of Missouri Press, 1981) and James MacGregor Burns, *Leadership* (New York: Harper and Row, 1978).

965

For example, in most of Asia the dominant issue of political discourse forty years ago—decolonization—has vanished, to be replaced by a number of social, political and economic challenges whose very identification may require different leadership skills, and whose resolution may be far more difficult for contemporary leaders than the task of decolonization was for their predecessors. In some Asian nations even these goals seem distant: leaders expend most of their energy merely trying to seize or retain power; they have little time left for substantive policy. In short, leadership is made manifest in the complex interaction between leaders of a state, followers and the problems and issues that confront them. Seeking power or being powerful is in itself not leadership, although power is an essential component of leadership.

Asia: A continent of regions

The concept of Asia has had a peculiar history. As several scholars have noted the term is purely Western in origin: it was coined by the Greeks in reference to the Persians.[2] At the popular level there are persistent images of oriental despots and opulent cruelty on one hand and sainted holy men leading their people to spiritual and political salvation on the other. Such films as *The Last Emperor* and *Gandhi,* while less misleading than most, perpetuate some of these stereotypes. Ironically, these stereotypes are offered not only to Western viewers but to mass audiences in Taipei, Beijing, Bombay, Bangkok and Tokyo. Indeed some Asians are learning about one another through the eyes of Western filmmakers. At the official level stereotypes also abound: among academics there is some disagreement concerning the concept of Asia as a cultural or historical entity. Harold Isaacs has documented official American images of Asia, and anyone with extensive contact with Indian, Chinese, Japanese or other Asian officials will be able to match Isaacs' stories of misperception with regional examples. An example of this stereotyping is the mid-level Chinese official who, upon the conclusion of a long discussion, characterized New Delhi's diplomats as "inscrutable."[3]

At the very least it should be remembered that Asia is a continent of many cultures, consisting of at least three distinct regions—East Asia, Southeast Asia and South Asia. In these regions there is considerable diversity as well as considerable contact with areas no one would call Asia. The concept of Asia is an artificial construct—at times the construct may be useful and harmless, but occasionally it may mislead.

[2] See John Steadman, *The Myth of Asia* (New York: Simon and Schuster, 1969) and Arnold Toynbee, " 'Asia' and 'Europe': Facts and Fantasies," in *A Study of History,* abr. ed., vol. 2 (New York: Oxford University Press, 1957), 238–40. For a different perspective, which argues for the unity of an "Asian" or "Oriental" culture and its fundamental difference from the "West" and an "Occidental" way, see Joseph Campbell, *The Mask of God: Oriental Mythology* (New York: Viking Press, 1962).

[3] Harold Isaacs, *Scratches on Our Mind,* 1958, reprinted as *Images of Asia: American Views of China and India* (New York: Harper and Row, 1972).

LEADERS, NATIONS AND INSTITUTIONS

Asia is a continent of highly diverse nations. In some areas (notably South Asia) the central tasks facing the national leadership are the consolidation of state power, the development of national loyalties (in the face of widespread separatist movements), the elimination of extreme poverty and gross economic inequalities, and the protection of the nation from a variety of external threats. In much of East Asia national consolidation has already taken place: there are few separatist threats, external alliances have brought regional stability, and leaders have focused their energies on sustaining economic growth of a very high order.

There are also significant differences in nation types in each of Asia's regions. There are giant multiethnic states in East Asia (China), South Asia (India) and Southeast Asia (Indonesia). South Asia and Southeast Asia each contain ministates (Bhutan and Maldives in South Asia, Brunei and Singapore in Southeast Asia). East Asia contains the continent's most powerful and advanced economic power (Japan), but in terms of overall capacity China, India, South Korea and Taiwan are also important.

Finally, different Asian nations have evolved different arrangements to concentrate, distribute and contain power on one hand and to fulfil popular expectations concerning the symbolic expression of the nation on the other.

Leaders and nations: Who governs?
Every country must make provisions for what Walter Bagehot refers to as the "dignified" and "efficient" functions of government. The former refers to the symbolic role of national leadership (concentrated in the crown in constitutional monarchies), the latter to the practical day-to-day task of government (located in the prime minister in most countries). The United States is rare in combining both functions (head of state and head of government) in the office of the presidency, and only the Philippines and Maldives share this practice.

In most noncommunist Asian nations the symbolic and the political roles are divided between a royal family (or a figurehead president) and an elected prime minister. Royal heads of state are found in Thailand (where military officers and civilian politicians compete for the prime ministership, with the monarchy providing a degree of stability during periods of political turmoil), Japan and Malaysia. Weak presidents perform this task in Singapore and India. However, in Brunei and the Himalayan kingdoms of Nepal and Bhutan real power is held by the monarch. Since the 1970s (especially in South Asia) there has been a significant movement away from the traditional British model of a strong prime minister and a weak president toward the French pattern of a strong president and a weak prime minister. Sri Lanka and Bangladesh both now have such systems, and the model has been widely debated in India.

Noncommunist Burma (now Myanmar) and Taiwan share one feature with communist China, North Korea, Mongolia, Vietnam, Laos and Cambodia. In each nation the leader of the ruling party holds effective national power. However, different countries have made different arrangements. In

Burma until his 1988 retirement the head of the socialist party, ex-general Ne Win, ruled through a figurehead president, but in Taiwan the head of the Kuomintang (KMT) also serves as president. This pattern is found in North Korea, where the head of the communist party, Kim Il-sung, has been president since 1946, and in Mongolia, where the party head is also head of state. The Vietnamese have their own arrangement—the head of the party is chairman of the state council (effectively head of the government); in Laos the party head is prime minister; but in China the head of the party's politburo holds no government post at all.

Military regimes have also evolved in very different ways. In Pakistan the head of the army, General Zia ul-Haq, assumed the office of president without relinquishing his army post. In Bangladesh and Indonesia presidents H. M. Ershad and Suharto left their military posts; as president and head of state, however, each retains technical command over the military (and, in practice, retains close ties with it as well).

Clearly, there is no Asian pattern of central political leadership. Asian nations have borrowed from European and American models and from one another in an eclectic fashion. Further, where there is a regional pattern—in South Asia where power is increasingly concentrated in the presidency—it is in response to increasing political disorder. In India, where the prime ministership has been retained, the prime minister's office has been expanded enormously and the office has acquired a symbolic status that far overshadows the nominal head of state, the president.

Political institutionalization

Besides the economic, social and cultural factors that influence the kind and quality of political leadership in each Asian nation and besides the formal institutional arrangements each has evolved, there is a more purely political variable at work: each nation's degree of political institutionalization. Asian countries differ significantly in the degree to which they have evolved routine patterns and structures concerning the sharing, distribution and transfer of power as well as the basic economic, social and ideological issues that concern these societies.[4] Some have fully developed political parties, interest groups, bureaucracies, mass media and political analysts. Others lack all of these features, and decisions are handled by a small core of bureaucrats, politicians or soldiers. The communist countries usually have a sophisticated party apparatus that regulates its own affairs and supervises those of the state bureaucracy. However, both communist and non-communist Asian nations are susceptible to the rise of a charismatic leader who appears to transcend conventional rules and norms, thus setting the stage for a severe leadership transition crisis.

Political institutionalization is not necessarily correlated with economic development. India, in particular, has very highly developed political institutions and a high ratio of citizen political participation. Pakistan, on

[4] For a comprehensive survey, see Robert A. Scalapino, Seizaburo Sato and Josuf Wanandi, eds., *Asian Political Institutionalization* (Berkeley, California: Institute of East Asian Studies, 1986).

968

the other hand, has a weaker tradition of political participation, its political parties are still fragmented, and the government bureaucracy and military have by default emerged as significant political forces. Personality itself is a critical political variable. The death of Mohammed Ali Jinnah shortly after Pakistan's creation and the assassination of his successor, Liaquat Ali Khan, adversely affected political stability, while the long stewardship of Jawaharlal Nehru in India helped that country remain a relatively stable democracy. Similarly in East Asia and Southeast Asia the long intellectual and political dominance of Mao Zedong, Ho Chi Minh and Kim Il-sung helped the Chinese, Vietnamese and North Korean communist parties conduct insurgency, wage civil war and, ultimately, consolidate political power.

LEADERS AND REGIMES IN ASIA

The ensuing division of Asian leaders into ten major (often overlapping) categories is somewhat arbitrary. This approach derives from a consideration of broad historical, social, cultural and political factors. These categories may be grouped as follows: (1) the varying impact of Western colonialism upon the nations of Asia, in which some states were deeply and permanently influenced by Western patterns and models, others less so and a few hardly at all (*traditional* and *colonial-like* leaders); (2) the different postcolonial political responses to the problems of nation building ranging from the accommodative to the radical (*democratic* and *revolutionary* leaders); (3) the subsequent (or simultaneous) attempts by the military or communist party to govern, the former often after a breakdown of civilian rule, the latter often as a result of victory in a civil war (*armed bureaucratic* and communist leaders); (4) the more recent successes of traditional leaders seeking national leadership on the grounds that they can combine the best of the old with the best of the new (*revitalist* leaders); (5) idiosyncratic patterns where leaders stake claims on the grounds that they have special insights into contemporary international economic affairs (*econocratic* leaders) or that they personally transcend party, nation, people and ideology (*charismatic* leaders); and finally (6) the type that represents the obverse of every positive claim to rule: *destructive* leaders whose avarice and savagery become their own perverse justification.

Traditional leadership
In at least two Asian nations, Nepal in South Asia and Brunei in Southeast Asia, the central objective of the present leadership is the preservation of a political structure essentially rooted in traditional precolonial patterns. The politics of these nations is characterized by adaptation to the modern world without transformation by it. Their leaders seek to preserve the spiritual and social cores of their societies, and to retain as much of their monarchical traditions as possible, both as ends in themselves and as means to retain popular support.

Although their economic status puts them at the opposite ends of the world's GNP scale, Nepal and Brunei are both governed by royal families that trace their origins back to the Middle Ages in Nepal and the 15th

969

century in Brunei. Although both had come under British rule (Brunei was a protectorate until 1984), both royal families managed to regain power—in Nepal in the face of strong pressure to democratize from neighboring India; in Brunei in the face of strong pressure to merge with adjacent Malaysia. In both states the monarchy is the central political institution. Nepal's reigning King Birendra is in his mid-30s. He was educated at Harvard and Tokyo universities, and is linked by family and marriage to many Nepali officials and army leaders. The sultan of Brunei, Haji Hassanal Bolkiah, is in his mid-40s. He is the 29th in his line and has ruled for over 20 years.

Nepal's leadership has cautiously supported economic development even though the country is among the poorest nations in the world: over 60 percent of the more than 18 million inhabitants live below South Asia's poverty line. Brunei's leadership, with vast resources at its command (per capita income is estimated at over US $17,500 and national reserves are thought to be about $20 billion) can literally afford to satisfy almost every material whim of the country's 227,000 people.

While Nepal and Brunei seem to be anomalies, tradition-driven political leaders are frequently encountered at the subnational level in each of Asia's regions. In East Asia there is the special case of the bifurcated Tibetan elite. Before incorporation by China, Tibet's leadership traditions were rooted in orthodox Tantric Buddhism. Today, both Chinese Tibetans and the Tibetan diaspora (led by the Dalai Lama) have been transformed—the first group through domination by the Han Chinese, the second by widespread contacts in Asia and various Western countries.

Elsewhere in Asia—especially in South Asia and Southeast Asia—successive colonial occupations did not penetrate very deeply and left behind powerful and cohesive ethnic, linguistic, religious and subregional groups that view the world through traditional lenses. Traditional leader-follower patterns thrive in much of India, Pakistan, Burma, Thailand (where a monarch still reigns), Indonesia, Malaysia and elsewhere. In these states membership in a former ruling family still carries a great deal of political weight at the local level. However, as these traditional ruling families and elites enter the political process they are themselves transformed. This is especially true in a democracy such as India where the image of a former maharaja campaigning by elephant for a seat in a state assembly nicely sums up the melding of the old and the new into something that is not quite either.[5] Traditional images and symbols are often borrowed by a new class of politicians, more skillful (or perhaps less restrained) in mass politics than former ruling families.

Colonial-like leadership

The first generation of independent Asian leaders were in many ways larger than life. Compared with most of their successors, Mao Zedong, Jawaharlal

[5] See Lloyd Rudolph and Susanne Rudolph, *The Modernity of Tradition* (Chicago: University of Chicago Press, 1967), for a careful discussion of the way in which traditional societies have adapted to modern political idioms.

Nehru, Mahatma Gandhi, U Nu, Achmed Sukarno, Ho Chi Minh, Syngman Rhee and Mohammed Ali Jinnah seem like giants. Most members of this generation of "founding fathers" engaged in extended political struggles against both the colonial power and competing national movements. Their twin goal was to achieve national independence while developing the process of nation building. Often they had to utilize the sometimes untrustworthy instruments of state power left behind by the colonial rulers. Many of these leaders, educated in the colonial country's universities, shared certain values and interests of the ruling power. Indeed, egalitarian doctrines taught in London or Paris usually became the basis for revolutionary movements in the colonies. At various stages in their careers such leaders as Jinnah, Nehru, Gandhi, Norodom Sihanouk and Lee Kuan Yew were indistinguishable from their British and French counterparts. Today, only few Asian nations are governed by leaders who epitomize the style and aspirations of former colonial powers. Those who remain do so not because they represent the interests of the former rulers, but because they have internalized some of these values and believe that it is necessary to continue the process of guided social change begun in the colonial era.

The most vivid example of this colonial remnant is the senior Singapore leadership. Until the late 1980s it consisted of the triumvirate of Prime Minister Lee Kuan Yew (the world's longest-serving democratically elected leader), S. Rajaratnam (Singapore's first foreign minister and chief ideologist for the People's Action party) and C.V. Devan Nair (now out of favor but formerly Singapore's figurehead president). All three were British-educated and deeply influenced both by British practices and classical Western philosophy. For Lee and the other ethnic Chinese, there were important parallels between the didactic state advocated by Plato and Confucian doctrine. Lee regards the nation as a teacher and a molder of men, and believes that such practices are compatible with democratic and egalitarian theory. His efforts at reform and civic education exceed those of the British in colonial Malaya, and have brought ridicule upon the city-state for being excessively boring and clean, and have created an opposition movement. Lee has governed through Singapore's only mass political party, the People's Action party, since 1959. In addition he has relied on a skilled Chinese-dominated bureaucracy and the ideological assistance of Rajaratnam (who is also an articulate spokesman for Singapore on the world stage).[6] The Singapore leadership knows that it is something of an anachronism, but it has explicitly trained a successor leadership that combines a Western orientation with concessions to Chinese traditions and the demands of a multiracial society (75 percent Chinese, 15 percent Malay and 10 percent Indian). But, like the British, these leaders have not neglected the roots of power: Singapore maintains a small but tough military establishment, and Lee's son, Brigadier General Lee Hsien Loong, is regarded as an eventual successor.

[6] For a brief biography as well as selections from his writings and speeches, see Chan Heng Chee and Obaid ul Haq, S. Rajaratnam: The Prophetic and the Political (Singapore: Graham Brash, 1987).

Democratic leadership

Asian anticolonial movements took many paths. All claimed to be based upon principles of equality and justice; very few actually went far in that direction. The ones that did are found primarily in South Asia where strong democratic movements exist in almost every nation and where two states, India and Sri Lanka, have maintained nearly unbroken democratic patterns since 1947.

Jawaharlal Nehru served as India's prime minister from 1947 to his death in 1964. He was born of a patrician Brahmin family and educated at Harrow and Cambridge. His father, Motilal Nehru, was a noted lawyer; his daughter, Indira Gandhi, also became prime minister, and his grandson, Rajiv Gandhi, has been prime minister since Indira Gandhi's assassination in 1984. The Nehru/Gandhi family has been called a dynasty by some critics but all three leaders have been more or less committed to fundamental democratic norms, although even her supporters acknowledge that Indira Gandhi did much to destroy democratic procedures in India and in the Congress party.

Jawaharlal Nehru could have ruled as an autocrat, but he saw the importance of spreading democratic principles throughout Indian politics.[7] For Nehru the social and political problems which beset India could best be solved by democratic means. He and many of his generation were influenced by Mahatma Gandhi's principal teaching that ends and means are identical; one cannot take economic or political shortcuts by resorting to coercion and violence. Nehru firmly believed—and continually stated—that political and economic change will occur when people are peacefully mobilized, when many voices are heard and when issues are publicly debated. By their words and by numerous examples Nehru, Mahatma Gandhi, J. P. Narayan, Morarji Desai and other Indian politicians taught the succeeding generation the utility as well as the moral value of democratic politics.

Paradoxically, Indira Gandhi severely weakened the very democracy her father had cultivated by declaring a national emergency in 1975 and by manipulating the ruling Congress party—in both cases to save her own political career. Rajiv Gandhi entered politics in 1984 in the wake of his mother's death. His initial appeal was as a member of the Nehru/Gandhi dynasty, but he soon became known as a technocrat. With one eye on the newly industrialized countries (NICs)—South Korea, Taiwan and Singapore—of East Asia and Southeast Asia, he has promised change and reform. But there are many signs that Rajiv Gandhi takes democratic values and practices as seriously as his mother.

India is not alone in having a political leadership strongly committed to democracy. Sri Lanka has maintained a democracy for over 40 years, first veering to the left under Sirimavo Bandaranaike and then to the right under J. R. Jayewardene. Despite sharp ideological disagreement, both leaders have been united in the face of extremist and separatist movements.

[7] For the authoritative family biography, see S. Gopal, *Jawaharlal Nehru*, 3 vols. (Cambridge, Massachusetts: Harvard University Press, 1975, 1982, 1984).

Jayewardene presided over a change in the Sri Lankan constitution that gave the country a presidential system still well within democratic norms.

Elsewhere in South Asia democratic leaders have emerged but have not survived. A fledgling democratic movement was crushed in Nepal. Democratically elected leaders in Pakistan (Zulfikar Ali Bhutto) and in Bangladesh (Mujibur Rahman) used rough tactics to suppress political opposition, and were both violently deposed. Bhutto was arrested, tried, and eventually executed in 1979; Mujibur was assassinated in a military coup in 1975. In both countries, close relatives have picked up the threads: Mujibur's daughter, Hasina Wajed, heads her father's Awami League and Bhutto's daughter, Benazir, became prime minister when her father's Pakistan People's party won the election following the death of strongman Mohammed Zia ul-Haq in 1988. Both women, however, are regarded warily by the military and other politicians.

In East Asia there are a number of democratic movements whose leaders remain on the edge of political power. In South Korea a strong democratic opposition group (the New Korea Democratic party), whose main factions are led by Kim Dae Jung and Kim Young Sam, is trying to extract further concessions from the country's fast-retreating military leaders and the ruling Democratic Justice party. Despite Kim Dae Jung's appeal and foreign support, the South Korean armed forces remain suspicious of his views on North Korea and his soft foreign policy line.[8] The election of Roh Tae Woo, handpicked candidate of the Democratic Justice party, to the presidency in 1987 was largely due to a split in the opposition. Despite some claims of fraud, the election was fair and democratic traditions were upheld.

The bland leadership of Japan's long-ruling Liberal Democratic party (LDP) is certainly democratic, but its outstanding feature seems to be the way in which it has managed Japan's economic policy, not its acceptance of political democracy. A more threatened and problematic democratic leadership is to be found in the Philippines. As in Japan, democracy was part of the legacy of American occupation, but the Philippines lacked the industrial resources of Japan and, more important, never underwent the kind of social change (especially land reform) that the United States imposed on Japan. Thus, the most widely known democratic leader in Southeast Asia, Corazon Aquino, faces a multilayered challenge. Not only was she inexperienced in practical politics when she returned home, but she was closely associated with the United States, a country about which Filipinos have ambivalent feelings. Added to this is a weak party structure, a high level of corruption (exacerbated, but not created, during the kleptocratic rule of Ferdinand Marcos) and a low sense of civic duty and patriotism. Thus the future of democracy in the Philippines—with or without Aquino—is uncertain.

Finally there is the interesting case of Taiwan. Long governed by the authoritarian KMT, democratic leaders are slowly emerging, in this case

[8] See Dae-Sook Suh and Chae-Jin Lee, *Political Leadership in Korea* (Seattle: University of Washington Press, 1976).

from *within* the ruling party, not as an external challenge to it. Taiwan's political elite has undergone an important generational change in recent years. With the death in 1988 of President Chiang Ching-kuo (who succeeded his father, Chiang Kai-shek, 10 years earlier), the KMT's leadership passed to Lee Teng-hui, the first Taiwan-born leader of the country. Lee epitomizes the econocrats, discussed in greater detail below. A Japanese- and U.S.-educated agricultural expert, he and most of his colleagues are more interested in economic prosperity than in conquering the mainland. Further, the threat from China has receded, as has the KMT's fear of a native Taiwanese separatist movement. With a freer press, the promise of direct election of the president, and even party competition, Taiwan may soon be added to the list of Asia's democracies.

Revolutionary leadership
Many Asian leaders advocated revolution against colonial rule. Today, with nearly all foreign colonial powers gone from Asia, the theme is repeated at the subnational level in the context of separatist movements. Sikhs, Nagas and Mizos call for a "revolution" against the government of India; Tamils do the same in Sri Lanka, as do Moros in the Philippines and Tibetans in China. However, it is now rare to encounter a leader who seeks a revolution against his *own* society, tearing down not only what the colonial power had erected, but what remains of the traditional social and political structure. True or double revolutionaries were more common in the 1940s and 1950s. Theorists and leaders such as Mao Zedong, Mahatma Gandhi, Ho Chi Minh and Subhas Chandra Bose sought two revolutions: the first to free their people from foreign rule, the second to free them from the past. Two archetypes will be considered here: Gandhi and Mao. Gandhi was killed by an assassin in 1948 and Mao died in 1976, but the lives of both men continue to exert a profound influence on Asian and global politics.

Gandhi's impact was enormous because he excelled in all dimensions of leadership.[9] He defined India's political and social problems in terms that were appealing to both traditional groups and the Westernized middle and upper classes. Gandhi taught his followers that India was a proud and ancient society. Colonialism had ruined that society, but India had made itself vulnerable to imperialism. The policies necessary to remove the British and to reform Indian society were to be found in India's own traditions, not in those of the West. Indians, he claimed, should not try to become like the colonial power, but should return to traditional practices and beliefs. This meant purging Indian society of excrescences such as untouchability. In addition Gandhi was a superb organizer—his political talents were honed early in South Africa. He was able to mobilize India's masses as well as the educated Westernized class created by British rule.

Gandhi's influence in India and elsewhere has been pervasive. Although he could be authoritarian in dealing with colleagues, Gandhi's tolerance set the tone for contemporary Indian politics. His advocacy of nonviolent social

[9] For a standard collection, see Louis Fisher, *The Essential Gandhi* (New York: Vintage Books, 1962).

change has had a profound impact on politics in Africa, Latin America and the Middle East as well as on the civil rights movement in the United States. Although contemporary Indian Gandhians have little formal influence, Gandhian thought permeates Indian politics, contributing a degree of civility and restraint in an otherwise tumultuous society.

This notion of restraint and civility was regarded by Mao as a weakness.[10] Mao shared with Gandhi a belief that traditional society had decayed, in this case making China vulnerable to foreign exploitation. But Mao was contemptuous of traditional society and sought to purge and supplant it. Mao had received a substantial but incomplete classical Chinese education, and saw no solution to China's problems within that tradition. Instead, he turned to revolutionary communism and Lenin's emphasis on the importance of armed power. To this he added the importance of struggle for its own sake as a purifying force. Mao never wavered from his belief in the virtue of revolution. Concerned that a new generation of Chinese had lost their ideals and grown soft, he introduced the Cultural Revolution in 1966 as a massive experiment conducted on 800 million people.

By force of example and with direct Chinese support, Mao's revolution influenced hundreds of millions elsewhere in Asia and the world. In most cases Maoist movements flourished briefly and then collapsed under the weight of government opposition, fights with other communist groups or sheer irrelevance. The idea of armed revolution still survives in many subnational movements in Asia and some of these groups call themselves Maoists. But few hold Mao's distinctive view of a revolution against society, not merely colonial oppression. The Khmer Rouge is the significant exception.

Armed bureaucratic leadership

Except for the communist nations (China, Vietnam and North Korea) and the stronger democracies (India and Sri Lanka) very few postcolonial Asian countries have been able to sustain civilian rule. By the 1950s a wave of coups had swept through the region, and at various times Pakistan, Burma, South Korea, Thailand, South Vietnam and Indonesia were governed by the generals; in many other nations the military has been an important force behind the scenes.

The common theme of Asia's first generation of armed bureaucrats (Ayub Khan of Pakistan, Ne Win of Burma, Suharto of Indonesia and Park Chung Hee of South Korea) was that their nations needed order and discipline to ensure political and territorial integrity. Without such order economic development would be impossible. They saw the introduction of a diluted form of martial law as a necessary corrective for the indiscipline and chaos of their societies. In most instances (especially when there were legitimate defense concerns) the armed forces kept out of direct administration but in Burma, under General Ne Win, the military plunged deeply into administration. Indonesia is another exception because its armed forces, having participated in the anticolonial revolution, developed the doctrine of *dwi-*

[10] For an excellent biography, see Ross Terrill, *Mao* (New York: Harper and Row, 1980).

fungsi ("two functions") which justified a political as well as a military role. This doctrine is undergoing reconsideration as the military turns Indonesia over to civilian technocrats. Significantly, both the Burmese and Indonesian armies were partly trained by the Japanese during World War II, and the South Korean military had a Japanese tradition as well.

Asia's remaining military leaders face three problems. First, involvement in politics can harm the integrity of the armed forces. There is an incompatibility between the spirit of compromise and adjustment required for politics and the spirit of discipline and obedience demanded by the military profession. Second, armies which stay in politics tend to become corrupt, and thereby wind up alienating a large portion of the population. This can lead to a disastrous loss of faith in the military or successive coups with junior officers intolerant of the corruption of senior officers. Yahya Khan's incompetence in losing East Pakistan in 1971 led to his removal by fellow officers and the temporary restoration of civilian rule. Finally, it has become increasingly clear—especially in East Asia and Southeast Asia—that soldiers cannot manage complex modern economies, and that military rule retards economic development. This is a factor in civilian-military politics in South Korea and Indonesia, and may underlie the public discontent with military influence in Burma. The trend in Asia has been away from military rule, but officers have found it easier to seize power than to leave it. The decision to intervene was usually taken amid great political turmoil and was often welcomed by the public. The decision to withdraw from politics involves considerable risk and uncertainty.

No nation and no military leader sums up this dilemma as clearly as Pakistan's Zia. Zia was appointed chief of staff of the Pakistan army by Zulfikar Ali Bhutto. After months of increasing political and social turmoil, senior Pakistani army officers arrested Bhutto, had him tried, and executed him. Zia governed Pakistan as "chief martial law administrator" and then as president, but he retained command of the army.

Zia had originally been selected by Bhutto as army chief because he was thought to be a professional officer with no political ambitions. Zia's background was modest: he came from a middle class Punjabi family, joined the British Indian Army at the end of World War II and slowly worked his way up the army hierarchy. Zia was sincere in his early pronouncements that he wanted to turn power back to the civilians as soon as possible. What changed his mind was contact with Pakistan's politicians who were held in low repute by military officers. Zia was also concerned about overly ambitious fellow generals, some of whom wanted to supplant him and rule the country themselves.[11]

Until his death in an airplane crash in 1988, Zia ruled Pakistan for eleven years, longer than any other Pakistani leaders. He held on to power by a mixture of shrewd politics, retention of his army post, surprisingly skillful use of radio and television, good advisors, and a degree of luck (the 1979 Soviet invasion of Afghanistan revived Pakistan's strategic impor-

[11] I have surveyed army politics and ideology in *The Pakistan Army* (Berkeley: University of California Press, 1984).

tance). No Pakistani politician—not even Bhutto's articulate daughter, Benazir—was able to outmaneuver him. Indeed, Pakistan's elitist and largely upper class politicians derided Zia's lack of polish and underestimated him from the beginning. They failed to note that he was representative of Pakistan's officer corps, now a thoroughly middle class bureaucracy.

Zia provided Pakistan with over a decade of forceful order and a degree of economic prosperity; he allowed some expansion of human rights such as political freedom; and he kept the military largely free of corruption and day-to-day involvement in politics. But Zia and his army colleagues were unable to find the kind of politicians they would trust to assume complete power. After eleven years of sometimes heavy-handed, but mostly benevolent paternalism, Pakistan seemed not much closer to full-fledged democracy than it was in 1977. After Zia's death the national elections brought Benazir Bhutto to power democratically, but Pakistan's acceptance of democratic norms still remains to be tested.

Communist leadership

Five Asian countries—China, North Korea, Vietnam, Cambodia and Laos—are ruled by communist parties and may be considered as a group.[12] All are variants of the basic Soviet model in which the party embodies the revolutionary process and the state is subordinated to the party. In these nations regulation of entry into the party, control of the party apparatus and the party's direction of state policy are all critical political decisions. The communist systems also have to manage the transition from one generation to another and—in some cases—from one outstanding figure to another. Increasingly, they have had to adapt their countries to international economic realities, especially in East Asia and Southeast Asia where South Korea, Taiwan, Japan, Singapore, Thailand and even Malaysia are pulling ahead of their communist neighbors.

The leadership of North Korea is exceptional, even by Asian communist standards. Kim Il-sung holds a transcendent, almost godlike position in North Korea where he has been president since 1948. He dominates both party (the Korean Workers party) and government, and, in the way of historic Korean rulers, has set the stage for his son, Kim Jong-il, to succeed him. No other ruling Asian communist party maintains a personality cult. With the death of Ho Chi Minh, the rather anonymous Vietnamese party leadership is overwhelmed with problems of national unification, the occupation of Cambodia, and a declining economy. Although Mao was virtually deified during the Cultural Revolution his image and books are hard to find in China today. The Communist party in China has embarked upon a vast program of economic modernization, and has carefully played down personality as an instrument of rule. Indeed, the party abolished the position of party chairman in 1982. The venerable Deng Xiaoping holds the nominal title of head of the party advisory commission.

[12] Robert Scalapino surveys several of these in "Legitimacy and Institutionalization in Asian Socialist societies," in Scalapino, Sato, and Wanandi, *Asian Political Institutionalization.*

Both the popularity of the communist party and respect for state institutions plummeted after the Cultural Revolution, and the post-Mao leadership has systematically set out to revive both without losing political control. The Chinese have experimented widely with increased responsibility for regional party and government leaders, who in turn are encouraged to respond to popular demands for increased political freedom and economic opportunity. In many ways (especially in economic matters) the party anticipated recent changes in Soviet policy, and it is likely that the Chinese and the Soviet examples will affect communist leaders elsewhere in Asia. As in other communist countries, the reform minded Chinese leadership is in a race with itself. With the new emphasis on economic development the party leadership has adopted a more conciliatory foreign policy and has made startling concessions to foreign investors. But there are powerful groups in the party and other Chinese institutions who regard recent policies as a betrayal of the communist legacy. Even well-informed outsiders only glimpse these factional disputes intermittently. Thus, policy changes in China, Vietnam, and other Communist countries often come as a surprise to outsiders even though they may be the result of extensive inner party debate.

Revitalist leadership
The battle against colonialism was generally led by Asian leaders who were strongly influenced by values and strategies learned in the West itself. They sought to establish modern nations, in the process drawing together disparate ethnic, religious and linguistic groups. While centralizing, nationalist and generally secular leaders held sway in India, Indonesia, Malaysia, Sri Lanka, the Philippines, Bangladesh, Afghanistan, and, for much of its history, Pakistan, each of these nations has seen the rise of significant revitalist movements—groups that wish to revive their religion and/or their ethnic identity by either creating a separate state or by transforming an existing state and society.

The outstanding example is Iran's Ayatollah Ruhollah Khomeini, the model for South Asia's least effective but best known revitalist leader, Sant Bhindranwale. Born in a middle class Punjabi family, Bhindranwale preached against the lax ways of the Sikhs, arguing that they were being morally corrupted by their "Hinduization." He and his supporters argued that Sikhism owed more to Islam than to Hinduism, and deserved at least an autonomous province within India. This was a thinly disguised fiction; they really wanted Khalistan—land of the pure—a separate Sikh nation. Bhindranwale died when the Indian army occupied Amritsar's Golden Temple in 1984, but the movement continues. In turn, it has provided a model for some of India's Hindus and Muslims who have created their own revitalist leadership (also directly influenced by the Iranian example).

Important revitalist leaders thrive elsewhere in Asia. In Sri Lanka a revitalist Buddhist movement has challenged several secular governments. In Japan the Soka Gakkai has attracted popular support. And in the Philippines a separatist, revitalist Islamic movement continues to battle the government for control over several southern islands. All of these movements are indigenous, although some have received significant outside assistance (certainly the Sikhs from Pakistan and the overseas Sikh community, and the Filipino Muslims from Libya and perhaps Iran). Many have been influenced by the Iranian example; to that extent, the late 1980s contraction of Iran's revolution may have important consequences for revitalism in Asia.

Econocratic leadership

During the colonial era many Asian countries were run by bureaucracies staffed both by colonials and natives. These bureaucracies have, at times, been supplanted (although never replaced) by political parties, by the military, and by dominant or charismatic leaders. In recent years, however, there has been a resurgence of civilian bureaucrats and experts, especially in East Asia and Southeast Asia, as the importance of managing national economies becomes greater. This has produced a generation of economically-oriented bureaucrats or econocrats who are skilled managers of fiscal policies. The prototypical econocratic leadership is in Japan. A high percentage of Japanese politicians have had previous bureaucratic or business experience. Many in the elite leadership, especially in the dominant LDP, followed the same career path: a prestigious education (especially at Tokyo University), service in an economic or trade ministry, and lateral movement to the LDP. Typically, these Japanese econocrats have close personal ties to the upper levels of Japan's major corporations. "Japan, Inc.," as some critics have dubbed it, is really a close working relationship between private and public managers. This relationship, coupled to a prudent diplomacy and a very low level of defense spending, has enabled resource-poor Japan to emerge as a global economic power.

The Japanese pattern has been influential elsewhere in Asia. It has been copied to some degree by Singapore, South Korea and Taiwan (all of which were at times occupied by Japan, the latter two for extended periods). These nations as well as Thailand, Indonesia and Malaysia (three other candidates for NIC status) have also been able to observe Japanese management style at first hand because each has received heavy Japanese investment. In each of these countries a new generation of economic planners and managers is becoming increasingly powerful. Unlike the Japanese, these econocrats tend to have received some higher education abroad, and fewer of them have had government (as opposed to corporate or academic) experience. As a class they tend to be bland. Yet these are individuals who can talk with confidence to international lending institutions, to multinational corporations, and to other financial experts. They are less interested in ideology than in growth and competitiveness; they see their countries as mini-Japans searching for regional and international economic niches that will allow the transformation of their people from backward peasants to modern industrial producers.

It is important to remember that the technocrats and econocrats are no substitute for coherent political institutions. They may excel at economic and managerial politics, but different and broader skills are necessary to meet the diverse demands that occur in any society. In Japan, the quintessential econocratic state, political order rests upon a complex LDP factional structure whose roots penetrate the country at local and prefectural levels.

This is not the case in many of the NICs or in Burma and Pakistan where bureaucrats and technocrats have just come to power; it will be interesting to see whether such men can hold on to power and perform the expected economic miracle.

If the true NICs (South Korea, Taiwan and Singapore) are successful, then the gap between Asia's rich and poor nations will continue to grow. The NICs are located in East Asia and Southeast Asia; there is none in South Asia. Pakistan lacks the human resources needed for economic modernization (although it is just beginning to move into middle income status). Sri Lanka was a candidate for rapid economic change until the Tamil-Sinhalese conflict erupted in 1983. India has developed its own class of econocrats (encouraged strongly by Rajiv Gandhi), and segments of the Indian economy have witnessed dramatic changes, but India is also burdened by massive poverty, chronic capital shortages and an increasing, rather than decreasing, defense burden.

Charismatic leadership

Asia's first generation of leaders included towering, dramatic figures. Even in cases where there was an efficient and powerful independence movement or party (such as the Indian National Congress, the Viet Minh in Vietnam or the Chinese Communist party) it was often useful to focus attention on a single leader to mobilize mass participation. And, in states where no such party existed, a single, charismatic figure was essential—as in Sukarno's Indonesia or Rhee's South Korea.

In recent years there has been a significant revival of charismatic leadership in Asia, especially in South Asia. Personality cults grew up around Indira Gandhi and Zulfikar Ali Bhutto, with journalists, scholars and press agents vying with one another to produce panegyrics of their leaders. Indira Gandhi and her political advisors believed in the 1960s that this treatment was necessary in order to circumvent the established Congress party leadership; by the 1970s and 1980s Gandhi (like Bhutto in Pakistan) probably regarded the personality cult as a necessary component of governance.

The emergence of mass popular cultures in several Asian countries has provided new political openings at the subnational level, and has brought to Asia a kind of leader found elsewhere—the synthetic charismatic hero. Not unlike their American counterparts, a number of Asian motion picture personalities have entered politics, capitalizing on their film personae to attract voters. Film stars have become chief ministers in the Indian states of Andhra Pradesh and Tamil Nadu and are politically influential in several others. In some cases voters have found it hard to separate fictional film heroes from real politicians.

It is likely that this process will continue in South Asia and Southeast Asia. Popular figures who can tap deeply held traditional beliefs about leadership have a remarkable advantage when they turn to politics. Their chief problem is institutionalizing this popularity since by its very nature charisma—especially the synthetic variety possessed by the film or sports star—is not easily transferred. In Tamil Nadu the late chief minister's wife and mistress—both former film stars themselves—contested for his political mantle.

Simultaneously, established political figures increasingly borrow tactics and techniques from those skilled in mass media. By the time of her death Indira Gandhi had learned how to reach a huge Indian audience through television and direct contact; her son Rajiv is learning rapidly, assisted by India's most popular film star. Even Pakistan's stolid President Zia mastered television in his final years. As new communications technologies penetrate the countryside and urban slums of the least developed nations of Asia new paths will open for leaders and the public alike. Those publics now have access to foreign sources of information. During the 1988 Burmese riots the British Broadcasting Corporation's Burmese-language transmission could be clearly heard in the streets of Rangoon, coming from dozens of radios tuned to the same frequency. These sources also portray a world of change and apparent progress, another factor in the popular Burmese uprising against a government that had retarded Burmese economic growth. Defying official censors, video and audio tapes now circulate widely among dissident and opposition groups in many Asian countries, competing with official television and radio programs for the attention of largely illiterate audiences. Increasingly, the talents and skills necessary to produce and distribute such material will be pitted against the talents of those who control older forms of mass media. If the European and American patterns are relevant, the net loser would seem to be the traditional political parties that have based their strength on a complex network of contacts on the local level and authoritarian parties that have controlled the mass media.

Destructive leadership

Asia has had its share of corrupt leaders who have robbed and stolen from the nation for their personal benefit, for the benefit of their supporters or even for a ruling class. Despite their ideological or political pretensions they have been in politics for the money. The Marcoses were neither the first nor will they be the last of Asia's kleptocrats, and less spectacular examples can be found in many Asian countries. What are rarer, but of more terrible significance, are those leaders who occasionally come to power in the grip of a visionary megalomania. Such leaders appear regularly in history: Adolph Hitler and Idi Amin come to mind.[13] In Southeast Asia there is the example of Pol Pot, the mysterious leader of Cambodia's Khmer Rouge. Pol Pot is a European-trained communist radical whose apocalyptic remaking of Cambodia between 1976 and 1979 resulted in the killing of over a million Cambodians. Driven less by ideology than by a pathological chauvinism, the Khmer Rouge awaits the moment Vietnam withdraws completely from Cambodia. Pol Pot's publicists acknowledge that the Khmer Rouge has "made mistakes," but its leadership remains intact, including the regional commander, Ta Mok, dubbed "Pol Pot's Himmler" by Prince Sihanouk.

[13] For a profound study, see Elias Canetti, *Crowds and Power* (New York: Seabury Press, 1978).

No other contemporary Asian leader or political party approaches Pol Pot and the Khmer Rouge in sheer ferocity, although the post-1949 consolidation of the Chinese revolution and the rampage of China's Red Guards led to atrocities on a vast scale—and may have been inspirations for the Khmer Rouge. The only other recent group that seemed capable of such destruction was the Tamil Tigers of Sri Lanka, headed by the fugitive Vellupillai Prabakaran. Comparing himself to Napoleon and requiring his followers to carry cyanide death capsules, Prabakaran masterminded a number of massacres of unarmed Sri Lankan citizens at bus stations and religious shrines. Once supported by the Indian intelligence services, he has been since 1987 the subject of a manhunt by Indian and Sri Lankan forces; his movement is in disarray but not destroyed.

ASIAN LEADERSHIP AND THE FUTURE

Four trends seem to be discernible in Asian politics. They concern the survival and expansion of democracy, the dead-end nature of political ability in military dictatorships, the perils of uncertainty in communist countries and the uneven impact of external events on national political orders.

The expansion of democracy
Asia is a freer and more open region than it was in the 1970s. While military-dominated governments hang on in Burma, Bangladesh and Indonesia, none is truly vicious. Several of the communist countries (most notably China) have permitted a greater degree of autonomous political activity. East Asia's Confucian autocracies, Taiwan and South Korea, are slowly transforming themselves into more open nations.

Although this trend could reverse, democratization (or at least a greater degree of political and economic openness) is increasingly seen as useful by political leaders almost everywhere in Asia (except the orthodox Vietnamese and the pathological Khmer Rouge). Most leaderships are becoming cognizant of the fact that an oppressed population cannot compete in an international economy. And perhaps more important, they know that they cannot hide for long the facts of their economic stagnation and political deprivation from populations that now have direct access (via radio, television, enhanced travel opportunities, and the widespread illicit traffic in tape cassettes) to the wider world.

If a leadership anywhere in Asia has second thoughts about democracy it is in the multiethnic states. India and Sri Lanka in South Asia, and the Philippines in Southeast Asia have separatist and terrorist movements that have further complicated the already daunting task of economic development. We are likely to see the continued expansion of political freedom and political participation in Asia. This may be accompanied by increased national violence in parts of some Asian countries (even the democracies), but the trend toward more coherent political institutions, buttressed by substantial economic development, seems well under way in much of East Asia and Southeast Asia.

Dead-end regimes

Still, half of Asia's military regimes are not likely to break the cycle of intervention—unstable civilian rule—mass disorder—intervention. There is a standoff between the military and a fragmented political community in Burma and Bangladesh. Pakistan has only recently (1988) broken this trend. Their military cannot civilianize itself; the civilians cannot force the military to yield power. The presence of soldiers and students on the streets is a sure indication of the absence of institutions to perform the most basic political functions.

The case of South Korea seems to indicate the minimal conditions for the withdrawal of a military regime from power. A combination of extraordinary economic prosperity, an improvement in the international security environment and unusual international interest (brought on by the 1988 Seoul Olympics) may have together made a difference. One is less optimistic about Bangladesh and Burma. Pakistan has real prospects of slow but steady movement to a more open and democratic political order if it can maintain the political process under constitutional guidelines in the post-Zia period.

From Lenin to Marx?

Communist parties whose basic precepts are Leninist know how to retain power and to conduct war, but little else. Asia's communist nations are surrounded by neighbors that have made enormous economic strides while effectively protecting their borders and maintaining internal order. Led by the Chinese, who are now joined by the Soviet Union, these communists are reconsidering the fundamental assumptions of their systems as they conduct a series of daring political and economic experiments. The smaller Communist nations of Asia find change threatening, and Asia's other communist parties (such as those in India) fiercely debate the challenges to Leninism and even Marxism that flow from Beijing and Moscow.

It would be risky to predict the outcome of these debates, but it would be foolish to believe that the Leninist temperament—the ruthless desire to control, direct and dominate—will not persist. Communist parties may evolve and change, but totalitarianism will thrive in societies that are undergoing extreme social and economic change. Those who have joined the communists in the past will seek outlets elsewhere if necessary. In some Asian countries this has taken and will increasingly take the form of ethnic or religious revitalism. And in those nations where communism fails, it may be supplanted by parochial movements which lack even communism's residual link to a broader humanitarian tradition.

The regional and subregional environment

Finally, the international and regional environment of the nations of Asia affects domestic politics in some countries more than in others. There is a modest irony in the fact that for many Asian nations the greatest impediments to political order come from their Asian neighbors. Clearly, the countries of South Asia will remain under greater external pressure than those in East Asia or even Southeast Asia. Southeast Asia has achieved a strategic stalemate with Vietnam and its client states (Laos and Cambodia) on one side and the members of the Association of Southeast Asian Nations (Thailand, Indonesia, Malaysia, the Philippines, Singapore and Brunei) on the other. This stalemate has been further stabilized by the collaborative actions of major external powers (the United States, China and Japan) that together counterbalance Soviet influence in Vietnam. East Asia has long since reached a degree of regional stability with the continuation of an American presence and a receding threat from the Soviet Union and China. Japan's rise as a military power is still many years away.

In South Asia there is a very different picture. Here, because of the complex ethnic and social composition of most South Asian countries as well as their relative poverty, one cannot tell where the process of nation building ends and that of foreign policy begins. Pakistan, Bangladesh, Nepal and Sri Lanka all have important (and sometimes dissident) ethnic groups that spill over into India. Pakistan also has large Baluchi and Pathan populations that have close ties with fellow tribals in Iran and Afghanistan. Pakistan's domestic political order was profoundly disturbed by the war in Afghanistan, although, paradoxically, the increased foreign assistance that resulted from the war enabled the military regime to liberalize; the withdrawal of the Soviets in 1989 may lead to a reassertion of military power.

South Asia is also linked to the neighboring region of the Persian Gulf.[14] The two regions are connected by a flow of skilled and unskilled workers from South Asia to the Gulf, by Pakistan's military ties to various Gulf states, by India's expanding naval power, and by the perception of both Indian and Pakistani strategists that the Middle East and the Gulf region are made closer by their own military competition. This was further complicated in 1988 when China—a strong supporter of Pakistan—delivered medium range ballistic missiles to Saudi Arabia. If present trends continue South Asia is likely to become increasingly militarized and linked to Gulf and Middle Eastern issues. India's expanding navy will make it a factor there as well as in Southeast Asia. Nuclear capability by India and Pakistan would affect strategic calculations in Riyadh, Tehran and Beijing as well as in Seoul, Jakarta and Taipei. Such weapons transcend any region of Asia—they transcend Asia itself—and will provide a vexing and, by and large, unnecessary challenge to the next generation of Asia's leaders.

FURTHER READING

Pye, Lucian W. *Asian Power and Politics: The Cultural Dimensions of Authority*. Cambridge, Massachusetts: Belknap Press, 1985.
Scalapino, Robert A., Sato, Seizaburo, and Wanandi, Josuf, eds. *Asian Political Institutionalization*. Berkeley, California: Institute of East Asian Studies, 1986.
Wriggins, W. Howard, *The Ruler's Imperative: Strategies for Political Survival in Asia and Africa*. (New York: Columbia University Press, 1969.
Periodicals: Far Eastern Economic Review. Hong Kong. Monthly.

[14] For two excellent surveys, see Mohammed Ayoob, ed., *Regional Security in the Third World* (London: Croom Helm, 1986), and Barry Buzan and Gowher Rizvi, *South Asian Insecurity and the Great Powers* (New York: St. Martin's Press, 1986).

India Today. New Delhi. Monthly.
Asian Affairs. Quarterly.
Asian Survey. Quarterly.
Pacific Affairs. Quarterly.

THE MILITARY IN POLITICS

ULF SUNDHAUSSEN

THERE are few comparative studies of the role of the military in Asian and Pacific politics. Only two books[1] and a couple of articles[2] claim to analyze civilian-military relations in the entire continent. There are, however, some specialized books on the military in Southeast Asia.[3] The armies of Asia have for a variety of reasons staged coups, or have chosen to stay out of politics; coups have been successful or abortive; military regimes have achieved impressive goals, or have failed to do so; and military regime leaders have returned their armies to the barracks, or have hung on to power. Yet, there are similarities in these circumstances, as shall be seen. Limitations of space prohibit dealing with all the military establishments of Asia and the Pacific in detail. Rather, an attempt will be made to provide a comparative overview of some of the problems involved in military intervention in Asia. This review will focus on the Indian subcontinent, Southeast Asia, East Asia, and the Pacific islands but will omit Australia and New Zealand because their respective military establishments are among the least interventionist armed forces in the world.

METHODOLOGY

Diehard liberals see military intervention essentially as a willful, illegal, and thus objectionable interruption of civilian politics leading to the oppression of Western democratic values. Similarly, Marxists traditionally

---

[1] See H. Z. Schiffrin, ed., *Military and State in Modern Asia* (Jerusalem: Academic Press, 1976), and E. A. Olsen and S. Jurika, eds., *The Armed Forces in Contemporary Asian Societies* (Boulder, Colorado: Westview Press, 1986). Both books are the results of conferences, and are basically collections of papers without a strong, shared theoretical framework.

[2] See, for instance, C. I. Eugene Kim, "Asian Military Regimes: Political Systems and Styles," in *Civil-Military Relations, Regional Perspectives,* ed. M. Janowitz (Beverly Hills, California and London: Sage, 1981).

[3] See J. S. Hoadley, *Soldiers and Politics in Southeast Asia* (Cambridge, Massachusetts: Schenkman, 1975), and Zakaria Haji Ahmad and H. Crouch, eds., *Military-Civilian Relations in South-East Asia* (Singapore: Oxford University Press, 1985).

obsessed with the dangers of Bonapartism expose the military as the oppressor of particularly the working class. Both schools of thought, for good measure, denounce military interventionists as the running dogs or puppets of the sinister Central Intelligence Agency (CIA) whenever such a connection can plausibly be made.[4] The concern with oppression is certainly a noble sentiment, but rarely do sentiments help in understanding causes. The often unfounded allegations of the CIA masterminding Third World coups, however, are regarded at least partially as a relic of Orientalism, an ethnocentric and essentially racist concept discriminating against nonwhites. In that particular context, black, brown, or yellow soldiers are regarded as without political ideas and convictions of their own and can be bought by the highest bidder.

For those unfamiliar with studies of civilian-military relationships a brief summary may be necessary. In the early 1960s Professor M. Janowitz and other sociologists at the University of Chicago began studies of the role of the military in the Third World. Two questions were posed:

> First, what characteristics of the military establishment of a new nation facilitate its involvement in domestic politics? Second, what are the capacities of the military to supply effective political leadership for a new nation striving for rapid economic development and social modernization?[5]

Obviously, answering these questions is only part of the process. In many countries where the military has the capacity to intervene—the means to stage a coup—it has not done so.[6] This provoked a political scientist from Harvard University, Professor S.P. Huntington, to argue that

> [T]he effort to answer the question, "What characteristics of the military establishment of a new nation facilitate its involvement in domestic politics?" is misdirected because the most important causes of military intervention in politics are not military but political and reflect not the social and organizational characteristics of the military establishment but the political and institutional structure of the society. Military explanations do not explain military interventions. The reason for this is simply that military interventions are only one specific manifestation of a broader phenomenon in underdeveloped societies: the general politicization of social forces and institutions. . . . Society as a whole is out-of-joint, not just the military.[7]

The ensuing, drawn out argument between the two schools of thought, on whether military intervention should solely or primarily be explained

---

[4] Occasionally the evidence advanced is somewhere between the comical and the absurd. In the case of the first Fiji coup in May 1987 it was alleged that the soldiers who occupied the parliament must have been U.S. black marines because of "[T]heir gait, Fijian soldiers just don't walk like that." See Max Watts, "Fiji Coup: Was Parliament Stormed by a U.S. Marine Squad?," in *The Beacon*, (Melbourne Unitarian Peace Memorial Church, November 1987): 5.

[5] M. Janowitz, *Military Institutions and Coercion in the Developing Nations* (Chicago: University of Chicago Press, 1977), 77.

[6] The military overthrew the civilian government of Togo when it had no more than 250 men under arms.

[7] S. P. Huntington, *Political Order in Changing Societies* (New Haven, Connecticut and London: Yale University Press, 1968), 194.

by factors internal to the military or by the failure of the political system, is really unnecessary. In 1962 Oxford University Professor S.E. Finer had postulated that for a coup to succeed two factors are required: the disposition within the military to intervene and the opportunity to do so. If only the disposition exists but no opportunity, the result will be an abortive coup; if the reverse, a temporary military caretaker government may be installed,[8] or the military may become the junior partner in an authoritarian government under civilian leadership. The latter was the case in Achmed Sukarno's Guided Democracy in Indonesia and the martial law administration of Ferdinand Marcos in the Philippines.

Finer has also categorized the different levels of intervention, and has related them to political systems or cultures in which they are likely to occur. In "mature political cultures" (i.e., so-called Anglo-Saxon societies), the military only exercises influence within the prescribed constitutional boundaries. In "developed political cultures" (i.e., many socialist countries), all kinds of illegal pressures may be brought to bear on civilian governments and even coup attempts are possible but all are bound to fail. The concern of this study is with "low and minimal political cultures" (i.e., most of the Third World), in which civilian governments may be displaced and substituted with more amenable civilian regimes, or be supplanted by military regimes.

Finer's classifications hinge on the concept of legitimacy; Huntington's "levels of institutionalization" depend on systemic failure. Both appear to be constructive approaches. But one must look more closely at Finer's concept of legitimacy for the purpose of categorizing the levels of political culture:

> The level of political culture is high when (1) the "political formula," i.e. the belief or emotion by virtue of which the rulers claim the moral right to govern and to be obeyed, is generally accepted. Or, to say this in another way, where (2) the complex of civil procedures and organs which jointly constitute the political system are recognized as authoritative, i.e., as duty-worthy, by a wide consensus. Or, again in other words, where (3) public involvement in and attachment to these civil institutions is strong and widespread. . . . We must ask. . . . Is the public proportionately large and well-mobilized into private associations? . . . [Do] we find cohesive churches, industrial associations and firms, labor unions, and political parties?[9]

If each statement can stand as a compact definition of legitimacy, then we are looking at a concept of universal applicability; if, however, the three statements are only different formulations of the same idea—and this is what the actual wording suggests—then we are facing an ethnocentric interpretation of what constitutes legitimacy. Evidently, "cohesive churches, industrial associations and firms, labor unions, and political parties" are, if they are working properly, the hallmarks of social and political organization in Western democracies which, not surprisingly, are at the top of the

[8] See S. E. Finer, *The Man on Horseback: The Role of the Military in Politics,* 2nd ed. (Harmondsworth: Penguin, 1976), 74f.
[9] Ibid., p. 78.

ladder as "mature political cultures," while developing countries which almost by definition do not—or only inadequately—feature such institutions, finish at the bottom of the heap as "low and minimal political cultures." Yet, in traditional societies, as well as in large sections of transitional societies on the way to modernity, there are many firm patterns of social and political relationships which (if we were to employ the first statement only) would qualify these societies for a high degree of legitimacy. In other words, by equating legitimacy with Western democracy we largely predetermine the outcome of our research about developing countries generally, and Asian nations in particular.

What, then, is required is an investigation of the concept of legitimacy in the context of the political thought and the particular culture of the societies under investigation. Professor L.W. Pye in his study of the cultural dimension of authority and legitimacy in Asia points out that while Westerners accord a high degree of legitimacy to a political system that provides a high degree of participation, exactly the opposite may be true of political traditions of Asia: "Making decisions means taking risks, while security lies in having no choices to make".[10] To accept authority, civilian or military, is thus "not inherently bad but rather is an accepted key to finding personal security".[11] The point needs to be made that order, security, tranquility, and consensus are highly valued political commodities in Asia, and legitimacy accrues to any kind of regime which can supply them. Thus democratic rule may not be in itself a highly desirable feature, particularly if it exhibits instability and insecurity. On the other hand, authoritarian systems of government, including military regimes, may gain legitimacy simply by imposing order.

This is not merely an esoteric argument about the differences between Eastern and Western perceptions of legitimacy and its inherent values. With legitimacy having very real ramifications for the character and endurance of political systems it is of paramount importance for our comprehension of military intervention in politics, the conduct of military regimes, and the retreat of the military from positions of political supremacy, to understand and accept that Asian perceptions of legitimacy may be completely different from those widely accepted in Western cultures.

But to analyze Asian politics purely in the terms of its traditional cultural norms would also be inadequate. Asia is involved in a process of rapid transition from tradition to modernity, particularly with economic successes surpassing those of other developing regions in the world. There is still a long way to go, especially regarding political modernization, and it is impossible at this stage to predict whether Asian societies will proceed along the same paths that Western nations have traveled or, given their particular political traditions, develop more sophisticated political systems of their own. What can be said is that Asia is caught in the upheavals and uncertainties of rapid change, and that the military, as part of the modern-

---

[10] L. W. Pye, *Asian Power and Politics, The Cultural Dimensions of Authority,* (Cambridge, Massachusetts: Harvard University Press, 1985), 1.
[11] Ibid. p. x.

izing elites, plays an integral part in determining direction for this transition and in finding solutions to surfacing problems.

MILITARY INTERVENTION

In Asia the military often, but not always, enters the political stage forcefully by way of a coup d'état.[12] It overthrows civilian governments because, obviously, it is disposed to intervention and, often less obviously, because there is amply opportunity for doing so. The relative importance of factors endogenous (disposition) or exogenous (opportunity) to the military for the occurrence of coups is of less importance here. Suffice it to say that at least as far as Asia is concerned, systemic failure appears to create the will to usurp government responsibility even among military officers who by the nature of their training and/or their personal values are initially disinclined to intervene in politics.

The disposition to intervene

In Asia, central authority has been traditionally recognized as essential because only the state is able to carry out large-scale public works, such as flood control and irrigation projects or the construction of large places of worship. Even on the village level, for example, rice cultivation requires communal efforts to maintain interconnected irrigated fields. The results of such environmental and organizational circumstances were authoritarian regimes supported by concepts of power based on cultural variations of divine kingship. In these societies demands for political participation were limited, at best, to local, often collective, self-government. The rulers were powerful, but were also bound by obligations of good personal conduct and benevolence toward their subjects lest they incur the wrath of cosmic powers. As long as they were seen to enjoy a "Mandate of Heaven" they were eminently legitimate; under these circumstances it was difficult and extremely dangerous to challenge their authority.

In such societies the military owed its allegiance to the ruler, not to the state or society. Its function was as much the maintenance of internal security as it was external defense. By and large, military leaders and officers were disinclined to challenge the rulers. The fear of taking on more than just mortal rulers was certainly part of it. But also military men were either part of the ruling classes—the *kshatriya* in India or the *samurai* in Japan—or they had little social prestige—as in China where they were ranked, with traders and prostitutes, below peasants—so that even if they had been

---

[12] There are exceptions to acquiring political power by the application of force or the threat thereof. For the details of General Ne Win being "invited" by the incumbent prime minister to form a caretaker government in Burma in 1958, see R. H. Taylor, "Burma," in Zakaria Haji Ahmad and H. Crouch, *Military-Civilian Relations,* pp. 30 ff. Alternatively, the military may be invited to become the junior partner in a coalition run by a civilian president, as was the case in Sukarno's Guided Democracy. See U. Sundhaussen, *The Road to Power: Indonesian Military Politics 1945–1967* (Kuala Lumpur: Oxford University Press, 1982), 122–194.

successful in overthrowing the emperor they faced immediate legitimacy crises of their own.

The colonial interlude did not last long enough to erode completely traditional value systems; it only destroyed formal power structures. Countries which escaped colonialism often had only modified traditional power structures. Thus the 20th century, and particularly the post-World War II era, saw the emergence of a great number of Asian states whose constitutions, military establishments, and economic structures, appeared to be modern but whose political and social relationships and value systems were still largely influenced by traditional norms.

The problem of the military in the postcolonial era has been to find its place in the new political environment. Many military officers were trained at Sandhurst, St. Cyr, Breda or West Point, and were imbued with the professional military ethos of Western democracies, which includes the principle of civilian supremacy over the military, but their home countries were neither Western nor really democratic. With traditional loyalty patterns directed to divine rulers removed, the military had to find a new focus for its allegiance. And while traditional values were still partly in vogue new ideologies, particularly nationalism, modernization, and homegrown varieties of socialism, started to supersede older value systems. Not surprisingly, the military, like most groups and institutions in the countries of postcolonial Asia and the Pacific, became disoriented, unsure of its direction and functions, and in search of its appropriate role.

Almost inevitably, the military came to define its interests and acted upon them when possible and appropriate. There are five broadly categorized interests which motivate officers; the disposition to intervene usually stems from more than just one kind of interest. First, there is personal interest which leads particular officers to assume political power in pursuit of self-aggrandizement. Many, but by no means all, Chinese warlords were motivated primarily by self-interest.[13]

A second kind of interest contributing to the disposition of the military to intervene in politics is corporate interest. Soldiers may be grossly underpaid and undersupplied, and promotion or terms of service so bad, that they mutiny. For instance, at the end of the Sukarno era Indonesian soldiers as well as officers had great difficulties surviving for one week on their monthly salaries. (The monthly salary of a full colonel amounted to approximately US$16.) This kind of situation obviously breeds intense discontent and the desire to create an economic structure that is capable of sustaining the livelihood of state employees.

Third, officers may act in defense of the interests of that class from which they derive or to which they desire to belong. The problem with class analysis regarding the Third World is that until very recently few people identified with class divisions in society and it may, therefore, be less than appropriate to categorize Asians along class lines when their actions are determined by motivations other than class consciousness. Another problem

[13] See H. Z. Schiffrin, "Military and Politics in China: Is the Warlord Model Pertinent?" in Schiffrin, *Military and State,* p. 116.

is that the middle class—that class which is supposed to be in the forefront of demolishing authoritarian and traditional systems of government—is defined narrowly in Western studies as a trading and manufacturing class. A middle class defined in this way either hardly exists in Asia and Africa or is made up of nonindigenous entrepreneurs. Only if a middle class is defined not in terms of property ownership but more in terms of educational standards, is the notion of class analysis of any value. Officers do belong to a relatively well-educated middle class, and their usual drive for modernization may to some extent be viewed as the pursuit of the interests of this kind of middle class.

Fourth, soldiers may easily identify with ethnic or regional interests. They may side with majorities in suppressing minorities, or sections of the officer corps may take up the grievances of ethnic minorities and initiate regional revolts. The result is often civil war or prolonged guerrilla wars rather than outright coups. But employing the military for internal security tasks is potentially dangerous. Officers resent doing police work. More important, they begin to realize that the cause of this situation is the failure of politicians to settle crises by political means, and that the only way of bringing guerrilla and antiguerrilla warfare to an end is by nonmilitary, "winning-the-hearts-and-minds" kinds of actions. But employing such means puts the military right in the middle of politics.[14] Many civil and guerrilla wars have been fought and are still being fought in Asia, with the result of involving the military in politics. Probably the best example is Burma (now Myanmar) which has experienced civil war without interruption from the moment of achieving independence from Britain in 1947 to the present.

The final category is national interest or, rather, what the military considers to be the national interest. The officers' view of what is good for the country may be radically different from the perceptions of ruling civilian elites. The sense of professionalism soldiers acquire while attending cadet schools and advanced courses in the West is really a two-edged sword. Only if civilian elites behave professionally as well, that is, like Western governments, will the officers in the long run be prepared to recognize their political supremacy. But if civilian governments do not provide good government—if, for instance, legislators concentrate single-mindedly on toppling cabinets rather than providing legislation—then the military will have no difficulty in seeing itself as the savior of the nation from inefficient, rapacious civilian politicians and, "in the interest of the nation," will remove governing civilian elites from power. These officers will believe that given their educational standards they have skills to offer that are in short supply in society and, moreover, that they have the drive and the discipline—even the vision—to put these skills to good use. Or they may have visions of national grandeur not readily shared by civilian elites who are removed from power. This happened in Japan in the 1930s, paving the way for the Pacific war.

[14] See A. H. Nasution, *Fundamentals of Guerrilla Warfare* (London: Pall Mall Press, 1965).

The opportunity to intervene
In Finer's low political cultures, legitimacy is fluid, and "easily impugned by the military" in its quest to overthrow constituted government. In minimal political cultures the military does not "require the assistance or even the blessing of civilian institutions or forces to acquire and maintain . . . power." [15] This has never been true for 20th-century Asia except under the most extraordinary circumstances, although the situation has occurred more regularly in Africa. The military usually seeks public support, or at least tolerance, from important and/or large sections of the community whenever it embarks upon such severe intervention in politics.

Admittedly, the military can always carry out coups by itself, but it cannot maintain itself in power without external support. The military can try, for a while, to resort to the tactics of a foreign occupation army and bank on respect for authority, but if it has to govern by terror and indiscriminate oppression the damage to its self-image as savior of the nation, and thus its unity and sense of purpose, will be incalculable. Rather, coups have occurred when legitimacy (defined within the boundary of the culture concerned) has broken down already, when society as a whole is "out-of-joint," and important sections of it are ready to consider or tolerate alternative forms of government.

There are, evidently, many reasons why the consensus in society that any particular government ought to have the legitimate right to rule breaks down or diminishes significantly. Three main causes for such a breakdown can be isolated although, more often than not, they are interrelated.

One cause is ethnicity. In fact, most Asian states are pluralistic societies along racial, tribal, religious, linguistic, regional, and/or cultural lines. Their boundaries were determined long ago by colonial offices in London, Paris, The Hague, and other imperialist capitals, without regard to the wishes of the governed peoples. Ethnic groups unwilling to be incorporated in a state in which their culture would presumably be denigrated and their interests ignored have often taken up arms against colonial governments out of a probably exaggerated fear of extermination. Thus for many countries in the immediate postcolonial era the primary task has been to secure territorial integrity against secessionist movements, usually by military means.

The military may sometimes function as an integrative force in societies riven by ethnic conflict, acting as the proverbial school of the nation. For instance in Papua New Guinea where the population of just over three million is divided among over 700 distinct tribes, recruitment in the Papua New Guinea Defence Force is spread evenly among all provinces, accompanied by a drive to develop new loyalty patterns directed at the army which has become a sort of "super tribe" in its own right. [16] But just as often the military may be a force exacerbating ethnic conflict, especially if it is ethnically imbalanced. Ethnic imbalance in the military may be the

---

[15] Finer, *Man on Horseback,* pp. 103 and 118.
[16] For a discussion of intra-army tribalism and ethnic integration in the Pacific Islands Regiment, see Harry Bell, "Goodbye to all That?" *New Guinea and Australia, the Pacific and Southeast Asia* 2, no. 2 (June 1967).

aftereffect of the practice of colonial administrations to recruit indigenous soldiers from so-called "martial races," and to balance potential political threats from large ethnic groups by raising colonial armies from usually more backward minorities and "hill tribes." Nationalist governments may reverse this policy and create armies from loyal majorities which will be keen to crack down on dissident minorities.

For instance, the national army of Indonesia was recruited largely from ethnic Javanese while soldiers from particular minorities were fighting on the side of the Dutch when they tried to re-establish their control over the archipelago after the Japanese occupation during World War II. Smouldering discontent with Jakarta among the minorities of the outer islands erupted in 1958 leading to the creation of a countergovernment in Sumatra. It was the heavily Javanese-staffed air force that precluded any political solution by unilaterally deciding to raid rebel-held cities,[17] thus starting a civil war.

But the most outstanding and clear-cut example of military intervention in politics for ethnic reasons has been the two coups in Fiji in 1987. Similar to Malaysia which inherited from British rule huge Chinese and Indian minorities which soon came to dominate the Malaysian economy, Fiji at the time of independence in 1970 faced an immigrant Indian community which controlled practically all commercial activities and actually outnumbered the indigenous people. The implicit consensus between the two communities was—as it had been established on the Malay peninsula a decade and a half earlier—that the immigrant community would more or less control the economy while the indigenous people would run the government, a consensus institutionalized in Fiji's complicated 1970 constitution and electoral system which denied Indians easy access to political power. The test of the delicate arrangements came in the 1977 elections when the Indian-dominated National Federation party gained 26 seats in parliament while the ethnic Fijian-dominated Alliance party under Ratu Sir Kamisese Mara finished with 24 seats, two seats went to independents. Yet the governor-general denied Indians the right to form a government, and new elections were called.[18] Ten years later, Indians, following the general election of April 1987, again challenged this consensus by forming a coalition with a Fijian splinter group, the Labour party. Timoci Bavadra, an ethnic Fijian, was made prime minister, but this did not stem fear of extinction sentiments among native Fijians. Thus, in May 1987, the overwhelmingly ethnic Fijian-staffed army toppled the Bavadra government in a bloodless coup but left negotiations for a solution to the crisis in the hands of civilian politicians. When these negotiations failed to produce ironclad safeguards for the political supremacy of ethnic Fijians the army intervened again in September. It returned to the barracks in November on the understanding that the top Fijian politicians would form a government and develop new constitutional guarantees against further attempts by Indians to gain political power.

[17] See Sundhaussen, *Road to Power,* p. 108.
[18] See R. Alley, "Political Shake-Up in Fiji," *The Round Table,* 67, no. 267 (July 1977).

A second major cause for the breakdown of consensus in society, providing the opportunity for the military to intervene, is economic mismanagement. In Asia, however, the economic motive for military coups is rare. Asian societies, by and large, have taken up economic development with great zeal; the only outstanding exceptions have been Burma and, at particular times, Indonesia as well as the communist countries. In communist countries socioeconomic experiments falling short of achieving marked increases in the general standard of living have not triggered military intervention since the military is solidly indoctrinated and controlled by political commissars, and the officer corps is part of the ruling elite spared the economic hardships caused by the political philosophy of leaders such as Mao Zedong, Ho Chi Minh, Kim Il-sung, and Pol Pot. Burma's dismal economic record is equally shared by civilian and military regimes, and appeared until the demonstrations of 1988 to be of no great concern to any major section of Burmese society. Indonesia is the major Asian example of how economic mismanagement can lead directly to the overthrow of an essentially civilian regime.

In 1957 President Achmed Sukarno established a more authoritarian system of government called Guided Democracy. His guided economy accompanying the new polity focused primarily on international issues. In his fight against neocolonialism, colonialism, and imperialism, Sukarno started a semiwar against the Dutch over the possession of western New Guinea and, when this conflict was resolved in Indonesia's favor, he launched into a confrontation with Malaysia, claiming that there was an imperialist plot to surround progressive, revolutionary Indonesia. The repercussions of this policy on the domestic economy were devastating. Because almost 80 percent of Indonesia's revenue went to war and defense, the infrastructure collapsed from lack of maintenance; the expropriation of foreign property led to a nosedive in exports. Real income declined drastically, making Indonesia one of the first developing countries unable to service its foreign debts. By the end of Sukarno's rule the inflation rate passed the 600 percent per year mark, and budgetary planning had ceased altogether.

The army had no sympathy for these policies. As a group of freedom fighters that had fought the Dutch even when the civilian government had given itself up in 1948, it was committed to the ideals which had once led them to volunteer for military service. Under the leadership of Abdul Nasution, longtime army chief-of-staff and later minister of defense, the military had developed its own distinctive ideological platform. It gave priority to feeding the starving masses over fighting external wars, a commitment it considered that the independence movement had undertaken when it promised in 1945 a just and prosperous society. Moreover, by continually fighting internal insurrections the military had become aware that the socioeconomic causes of the uprisings could not simply be overcome by military means but had to be rectified by sound social and economic policies.[19] Nasution consistently opposed putting the liberation of western New Guinea

---

[19] See Ulf Sundhaussen, *Social Policy Aspects in Defence and Security Planning in Indonesia, 1947–1977* (Townsville: South East Asian Studies, James Cook University, 1980).

above the need for economic rehabilitation and, as a consequence, lost command of the army. But other army officers took up his cause and prevented the anti-Malaysia confrontation from developing into a full-scale war.

In 1965 the prevailing power constellation changed dramatically. In October a group of dissident army and air force officers with the help of communist and leftist nationalists kidnapped and killed army commander A. Yani and five of his closest colleagues; Nasution narrowly escaped the same fate.[20] When Sukarno rejected a demand by surviving generals that all involved in the coup attempt be brought to justice, the army under its new strongman, T.N.J. Suharto, and noncommunist civilians took the law into their own hands. The communists, Sukarno's most trusted allies and widely regarded as having masterminded the coup attempt, were killed by the hundreds of thousands.

This action weakened the absolute power Sukarno had been used to wielding, but the destruction of his principal ally did not cost him the presidency since the army was not disposed to toppling him. The military and other critics of presidential policies had become bold enough to demand that the costly confrontation against Malaysia be stopped and that the rehabilitation of the economy be given top priority. Only when Sukarno refused to make adjustments to his policies was impeachment contemplated. Sukarno was relieved of office in March 1967 by strictly constitutional means.

But by far the most common cause for systemic failure in Asia that provides the opportunity for the military to intervene is political mismanagement. The varieties of political mismanagement are almost endless. Single traditional rulers or ruling elites may lose legitimacy because they attempt to modernize too fast and before they have sufficiently educated the more conservative masses. This was the mistake King Amanullah of Afghanistan made in the 1920s before he was swept aside by a tribal army, a mistake repeated by leftist activists and legislators before General Mohammad Daud, himself a more moderate reformer, seized power in 1953, only to be forced from office for the very same reasons ten years later.[21] Conversely, a ruler may lose legitimacy because he modernizes too slowly. The 1932 revolution in Thailand staged by army and navy officers as well as higher civil servants ended several centuries of absolute monarchy[22] and set the country on an unsteady course toward constitutional government.

President Ngo Dinh Diem lost legitimacy in the eyes of the majority of South Vietnamese when he began to rely increasingly on fellow Catholics for political support in an essentially Buddhist society; a number of spectacular self-immolations by Buddhist monks gave this widening rift political momentum. This loss of legitimacy sufficiently alarmed the United

---

[20] See C. L. M. Penders and Ulf Sundhaussen, *Abdul Haris Nasution: A Political Biography* (St Lucia: University of Queensland Press, 1985), 153ff.

[21] See L. Dupree, *Afghanistan* (Princeton, New Jersey: Princeton University Press, 1980), 449–558.

[22] Chai-Anan Samudavanija and Suchit Bunbongkarn, "Thailand," in Zakaria Haji Ahmad and H. Crouch, *Military-Civilian Relations,* p. 79.

States which was financing Diem's war against the Viet Cong so that it tacitly backed a coup by army and air force officers in 1963.[23]

In neighboring Cambodia Prince Norodom Sihanouk was deposed as head of state in March 1970 because his neutral foreign policy had become increasingly pro-North Vietnam and anti-United States. This as well as economic mismanagement mostly based on Sihanouk's vision of socialism, his personal corruption, and his perceived disinclination to perform his official duties created enough alienation among the urban elites of Phnom Penh that, under the leadership of the prime minister, General Lon Nol, they moved to repudiate one after another of Sihanouk's policies. In the end, parliament removed Sihanouk from office. Strictly speaking, this was not a coup since, as in the case of Indonesia, the constitutional rules about replacing a head of state were followed.[24] But the action had the effect of a coup because it led to the establishment of a military regime under Lon Nol. As in the toppling of Diem, the United States gave tacit approval for the change in Cambodian government.

In the above instances of the military toppling civilian-authoritarian governments it may be argued that a military coup is almost the only way of affecting a change of government. The other, less likely possibility is a revolution. But the same is true regarding Asian democracies. It is rare that the governing elite is changed in Asian democracies by way of a general election: polities are constructed and electoral laws manipulated in such a way that opposition parties stand no realistic change of gaining office by the ballot box. The conduct of civilian politicians is often highly questionable, and provides the ready opportunity for the military to step in. Politicians, in pursuit of personal or at best sectional interests, often create parties without any ideological platforms. Not surprisingly, such legislators fail to grasp the responsibilities they have to create democratic rule, develop policies, and provide laws for the nation as a whole.

Pakistan's politicians implemented none of these three goals. Prime Minister Liaquat Ali Khan declared in 1950 that the formation of opposition parties was "against the best interests of Pakistan," and subsequent governments cheated the Bengali majority of East Pakistan from gaining a majority in parliament, a policy which ultimately led to the violent secession of the eastern portion of the country and the establishment of Bangladesh. It took legislators nine years to produce a constitution; during the 31 months this constitution remained in force, before the military finally took over in 1958, Pakistan experienced four coalition governments, each without programs or policies.[25] "Pakistan was very much like Hobbes' state of nature where every political or provincial group fought against every other group."[26]

[23] See Hoadley, *Soldiers and Politics,* pp. 75ff.
[24] See Ibid., pp. 135–140.
[25] See C. G. P. Rakisits, *National Integration in Pakistan: The Role of Religion, Ethnicity, and the External Environment* (Ph.D. dissertation, University of Queensland, 1986), 55–60.
[26] Hasan Askari Rizvi, *The Military and Politics in Pakistan* (Lahore: Progressive Publ., 1974), 89ff.

The record of Indonesian politicians during the era of parliamentary government is no less disgraceful. In less than 12 years, between November 1945 and March 1957, fifteen cabinets fell; 11 were toppled in parliamentary politicking, usually by intracoalition cabal. The politicians were so keen to hang on to their spoils that the first general election was held only in 1955, and only after the army, of all groups, had demanded in a show of force that such elections be held. A constituent assembly elected in the same year bickered indecisively for four years while the parliamentary system collapsed and Sukarno ruled by martial law. In the end, the 1945 constitution was repromulgated for lack of a better or, really, any input into the constitutional crisis by the legislators.

Thai legislators may serve as a third example of civilian politicians failing to live up to the leadership roles they had claimed for themselves. Thai political parties are notorious for their lack of political platforms, serving primarily as vehicles for the private ambitions of their patrons. Typically, the Pramoj brothers, Seni and Kukrit, set up different political parties and fought each other rather than making a concerted effort to establish a parliamentary tradition or code of conduct, with the almost inevitable result that the military continued to intervene in politics and functioned as the center of political power.

The list of shortsighted and selfish politicians damaging prospects of civilian rule and providing the military with opportunities to intervene, could easily be extended. One probably could try to explain this conduct by civilian politicians with the observation that these Asian nations are young and their political cultures radically different and inconducive to parliamentary government. It may be equally argued, however, that it is precisely because Asian political traditions are so vastly different that the failure of the civilian politicians is so much graver. It is not simply a matter of those legislators failing to do their duty according to modern (i.e., democratic) norms; they are also offending traditional norms. In communal societies authority has to exist and rest with someone regarded as possessing legitimacy. But politicians' reckless jockeying for personal power and riches only fills traditional people with distrust and disdain for the legislators and the institutions they claim to represent. More important, communal societies pride themselves in their traditional ways of conflict resolution by various forms of deliberation leading to consensus. But in the freely elected parliaments of Asia consensus—or even a sense of common purpose—has been a very rare commodity.

Failed by both modern Western democratic institutions and traditional consensus politics, the peoples of Asia in the 1960s and 1970s had little choice but to accept or tolerate more authoritarian forms of government. Military regimes, once they came to power, have enjoyed at least initially a not inconsiderable amount of legitimacy in society at large.

MILITARY RULE

Once the military has occupied center stage of the political arena the question arises, how do they perform as rulers? But any attempt to reach a relatively correct evaluation is hampered by two factors. One problem is the blatantly antimilitary bias of a large variety of scholars who are most reluctant to grant any credit to military regimes. The second problem is methodological. In order to establish the achievements or failures of military regimes they would have to be compared with civilian regimes. Cross-national, usually quantitative comparisons between civilian and military regimes at any one time or over larger periods[27] may produce more or less correct data, but they leave out one important consideration which is difficult to quantify, namely the fact that military regimes do not emerge under normal circumstances but are the result of crisis situations. In other words, military regimes usually start with huge disadvantages. A more enlightening approach might be to consider government within one country, investigating how military regimes compare with preceding or succeeding civilian regimes.

Socioeconomic performance
In the wake of a series of military takeovers in 1958 which at least for the time being effectively sank the hopes the West had held for democracy in the new nations of Asia and Africa, observers began to take heart from the fact that the new kind of rulers might not be such bad choices after all. Replacing messy, and often leftist, civilian polities, military rule was regarded as "practicable and apparently stable,"[28] and the armed forces as "agents of modernization."[29] According to this view, officers in presidential palaces first of all create order, the prerequisite for economic growth, development, and foreign investment, and then initiate industrialization, the panacea of all economic woes of underdeveloped countries.

A different view is stated by Professor E.A. Nordlinger who argues that military regimes outperform civilians only in the least modernized developing countries; for the great majority of Third World military regimes "rapid economic growth is not a common phenomenon, and sustained growth is decidedly uncommon." Military rulers are "not generally motivated to adopt progressive socioeconomic policies," and if they make economic decisions these "are primarily affected by their corporate interests,"[30] that is, the wish to increase the defense budget.

A third approach comes from R.D. McKinley and A.S. Cohen, who question the utility of measuring civilian and military regimes in terms of

---

[27] See, for instance, R. D. McKinley and A. S. Cohen, "A Comparative Analysis of the Political and Economic Performance of Military and Civilian Regimes," *Comparative Politics* 8, no. 1 (October 1975), and R. N. Tannahill, "The Performance of Military and Civilian Governments in South America, 1948–1967," *Journal of Political and Military Sociology* 4, no. 2 (Fall 1976).
[28] E. Shils, "The Military in the Political Development of the New States," in *The Role of the Military in Underdeveloped Countries,* ed. J. J. Johnson (Princeton, New Jersey: Princeton University Press, 1962), 9.
[29] L. W. Pye, "Armies in the Process of Political Modernization," in Johnson, *Role of the Military,* pp. 80–89.
[30] See E. A. Nordlinger, *Soldiers in Politics, Military Coups and Governments* (Englewood Cliffs, New Jersey: Prentice-Hall, 1977), 137, 170, 171.

economic development since this continues to be an ill-defined concept. In addition, they suggest that military regimes are as diverse and different from one another as are civilian regimes and that "while some military regimes are quite clearly distinct, as indeed are some civilian regimes, a sizeable proportion of military and civilian regimes are indistinguishable in terms of performance."[31]

The actual facts of the Asian scene support the third approach. Certainly, there are military regimes which in terms of their economic performance must be considered high-flyers. The four "Asian Tigers," the newly industrializing countries of East and Southeast Asia, consist of one independent city-state in a prime geographical location (Singapore), a British crown colony which functions also as entrepôt for China (Hong Kong), and two military-backed regimes (South Korea and Taiwan). As clients of the United States both South Korea and Taiwan enjoy large amounts of foreign aid and easy access to American markets; they also feel obliged to maintain huge military establishments to counter real or perceived threats of invasion from North Korea and China, respectively. Nevertheless, both countries have virtually no raw materials but have achieved and sustained fantastic growth rates in GNP and per capita income over the last three decades, turning backward agricultural countries with insufficient arable land into export-oriented, industrialized nations with sizeable stakes in world trade.

At the opposite end of the spectrum is Burma, until recently governed by General Ne Win, that in terms of economic growth is clearly an underperformer. But the pursuit of ever-increasing growth rates, so important to capitalist economies, was not the primary goal of the general who professed a specifically Burmese kind of socialism. According to the manifesto of the Burma Revolutionary Council in 1962, "Socialist economy does not serve the narrow self-interest of a group, an organization, a class, or a party, but plans its economy with the sole aim of giving maximum satisfaction to material, spiritual and cultural needs of the whole nation."[32] Thus the "Burmese Way to Socialism is the Programme of Beatitudes for the society in the Union of Burma."[33] It ought to be pointed out, however, that even in terms of the regime's proclaimed goals, all has not been well in Burma's economy. In fact, it is beset by shortages in essential goods leading to a thriving black market.

Other military regimes in Asia do not stand out in any cross-national comparison with civilian regimes. They may, however, have achieved outstanding successes when compared with preceding civilian regimes. This is most decidedly the case in Indonesia which under Suharto has begun a process of export-oriented industrialization, has achieved self-sufficiency in

[31] McKinley and Cohen, "Analysis of Military and Civilian Regimes," p. 23.
[32] "The Burmese Way to Socialism," in *Burma's Foreign Policy*, W. C. Johnstone (Cambridge, Massachusetts: Harvard University Press, 1963), Appendix IV, p. 314.
[33] Maung Maung, *Burma and General Ne Win* (Bombay: Asia Publishing House, 1969), 317.

food, and, moreover, has drastically improved the standard of living of its vast population.

Nordlinger's sweeping statement that economic decisions by military regimes are "primarily affected by their corporate interest" should not be allowed to stand unchallenged. Globally speaking Latin America, the continent most prone to military intervention, has also been the region "with the lowest military expenditure as a ratio of GNP."[34] But military takeovers may also directly result in a reduction in military spending. This happened in an austere way in Indonesia in 1967[35] when the defense budget was slashed in half by Suharto in order to redirect scarce state funds toward the rehabilitation of the country's economy. In regard to Southeast Asia generally, it has been observed "that the countries in which the military has the largest political role (Thailand and Indonesia) are the ones in which defence spending has grown more slowly than the ASEAN average."[36] Military spending also declined in Pakistan during the regime of Ayub Khan.[37]

This, of course, is not always the norm. Military spending may increase after a coup, particularly with regard to salaries. Soldiers, like other state employees, often have had their incomes eroded to such an extent that they had become unable to support their families, and the choice for the government simply has been to risk a barracks revolt in the military, and increased corruption and absenteeism in the civil service, or provide salaries on which state employees, civil and military, can subsist.

By and large it can be argued that military regimes have adopted more pragmatic and less ideological and utopian formulas for economic policies. Usually lacking sufficient economic expertise, military rulers enlist technocrats to devise their economic policies,[38] confining themselves to providing the power base required to enforce initially unpopular austerity measures, and to guaranteeing the continuation of economic growth policies.

Political performance

Military regimes are popularly equated with oppression. Obviously, they are not democratic and, thus, do not represent the best of all political options (according to Western liberal standards). While there have, indeed, been very brutal and distasteful military regimes like those of Idi Amin in

[34] H. A. Dietz and K. Schmitt, "Militarization in Latin America: For What? And Why," *Inter-American Economic Affairs* 28, no. 1 (Summer 1984): 60.
[35] See U. Sundhaussen, "The New Order of General Soeharto," *Internationales Asienforum* 4 (1973): 54.
[36] D. B. H. Denoon, "Defence Spending in ASEAN: An Overview," in *Defence Spending in Southeast Asia,* ed. Chin Kin Wah (Singapore: Institute of Southeast Asian Studies, 1987), 49.
[37] See Rizvi, *Military and Politics in Pakistan,* p. 162.
[38] See, for instance, J. J. MacDougall, "The Technocratic Model of Modernization: The Case of Indonesia's New Order," *Asian Survey* 16, no. 12 (December 1976), and L. D. Stifel, "Technocrats and Modernization in Thailand," *Asian Survey* 16 no. 12 (December 1976).

Uganda and Jean-Bédel Bokassa in the Central Africa Republic, even the worst military regimes do not match the murderous brutality exhibited by civilian regimes such as Hitler's Nazi Germany or Pol Pot's Cambodia.

As an organization that functions only if the principles of discipline and hierarchy are strictly observed, the military is naturally inclined toward order. Politics—the art of bargaining and compromise—contravenes soldiers' inclinations, particularly when politics becomes disorderly with political strikes, rioting in the streets, and people taking up arms in pursuit of idiosyncratic goals. Armed forces, like all organized groups, have corporate interests. But also like other organized groups, the military has ideas and ideals as well which influence its actions. When military officers are in political control of a country they are as likely as civilian politicians to pursue their ideological preferences.

As observed already, military regimes can be very different in several ways. Paradoxically, in heterogeneous Asia military regimes have followed a roughly similar pattern of behavior. And among them are neither the most brutal and notorious nor the most radical and populist military regimes,[39] unlike those which have emerged in Latin America, the Middle East, or sub-Saharan Africa. Moreover, unlike in other regions, successful coups in Asia are usually headed by senior officers,[40] and lead to prolonged military rule[41] rather than short-term intervention.

Military regimes in Asia consider economic injustice and maladministration primary causes for unrest in society at large, and economic progress the way to contain it. On the other hand, they are aware that economic progress depends on political stability. Thus their immediate objective is usually to enforce internal peace, even if this requires harsh measures against groups both on the left and the right of the political spectrum that threaten the territorial integrity of the country or the basic consensus necessary to operate a polity. Often society is temporarily depoliticized, with radical groups banned or even eliminated, political parties, trade unions, and professional organizations emasculated, and freedom of the press curtailed while

[39] The exception here is the short-lived regime of Konge Le, who assumed power in Laos in a coup in August 1960. For details, see G. C. Gunn, "Laos," in Zakaria Haji Ahmad and H. Crouch, *Military-Civilian Relations,* pp. 212–14.

[40] The exception in this case is, again, Kong Le who was only a captain in the Laotian paratroops corps. See Zakaria Haji Ahmad and H. Crouch, *Military-Civilian Relations.* Coups led by junior officers fail in Asian countries. See, for instance, the story of the 1962 conspiracy in Ceylon, detailed in D. L. Horowitz, *Coup Theories and Officers' Motives: Sri Lanka in Comparative Perspective* (Princeton, New Jersey: Princeton University Press, 1980) and for the upheaval created by futile revolts of junior officers and ranks in the Bangladeshi armed forces, see Zillur R. Khan, "Politicization of the Bangladesh Military: A Response to Perceived Shortcomings of Civilian Government," *Asian Survey* 21, no. 5 (May 1981).

[41] The regime of Kong Le, as well as another regime resulting from the December 1959 intervention by Gen. Phoumi Nosavan in Laos, lasted only for very brief periods. A military "caretaker" government was formed in Burma in late 1958, which undertook to return power to the civilians within six months and, indeed, did so with a delay of twelve months. See Taylor, "Burma," pp. 28–34.

long-term economic plans are initiated, consensus-building policies introduced, and political institutions gradually restructured. The basic strategy is to enforce a prolonged period of political stability in which society is confined to adopting new values and accepting the need for middle-of-the-road policies.

Particular strategies vary from country to country. In Pakistan where civilian politics had been severely hampered by the lack of consensus among the various ethnic and religious groups, Field Marshal Ayub Khan set out to construct a viable political system by way of gradually building a five-tier democratic order called Basic Democracy, that would be simple to understand, would allow participation by all citizens initially confined to levels they were able to comprehend, and would produce stable government. Ayub Khan has been described as coming "close to filling the role of a Solon or Lycurgus or 'Great Legislator' on the Platonic or Rousseauian model."[42]

This kind of praise has so far eluded Suharto whose regime has developed the concept of the Floating Mass by which—except for short periods of campaigning before general elections—party politics is kept out of village life. The countryside had lost its traditional tranquility with the first national elections in 1955 and had been the major killing grounds for the anticommunist massacres ten years later. While assuring by various means that the government always has a huge majority in the legislative assembly two other parties are not only tolerated but subsidized to save them from oblivion. The practice of legislating not by majority vote but by deliberation until consensus is reached gives minority parties, in theory at least, something close to veto power.[43] At the same time, consensus is built by large-scale indoctrination campaigns that confine all organizations to adhering to *Pancasila,* the state ideology proclaimed in 1945 which, on the surface, appears to be noncontroversial,[44] but which in the interpretation of the current regime discriminates against communists, Islamic fundamentalists, advocates of divisive political liberalism, and secessionists. The ultimate aim is to establish *Pancasila* Democracy, a political system based on the traditional Indonesian ideals of consensus and consultation, and disfranchising all extremists.

Ne Win sought to build consensus and institutions suitable to Burmese conditions by developing a state ideology which attempted to wed the principles of socialism to the basic tenets of Buddhism, with a single-party system to implement its ideals. The Thai revolution of 1958 which brought

---

[42] Huntington, *Political Order,* p. 251. For a more detailed but brief explanation of the working of Basic Democracy, see Ibid, pp. 250–255. A more sceptical view of Basic Democracy, and the reasons for its demise, is provided in Rakisits, *National Integration in Pakistan,* pp. 61–74.

[43] For the forms and degrees of democracy operating in Indonesia, see U. Sundhaussen, "Indonesia: Encounters with Democracy," in *Democracy in Developing Countries,* vol. 3: *Asia,* ed. L. Diamond et al. (Boulder, Colorado: Lynne Rienner Publ., forthcoming).

[44] The *Pancasila,* or Five Pillars, consist of: Nationalism, International Cooperation, Popular Sovereignty, Social Justice and Belief in One God.

Field Marshal Sarit Thanarat to power was equally motivated by the need to build consensus. In a National Day speech in June 1959 Sarit pointed out:

> If you recall the condition of the country prior to the revolution you will observe clearly that there were severe divisions, intrigues . . . and the desire to destroy each other. . . . Therefore, the revolution's first plan is to . . . rebuild national solidarity. . . . Because of this, I have relied upon the principle of *Samakhitham* [solidarity] as the first principle of the task of the revolution.[45]

Both the Sarit regime and, at least initially, the revolutionary council led by Sarit's successor, Thanom Kittikachorn, professed to be committed to establishing democratic government in Thailand, but "a Thai way of democracy." Moreover, the prestige of the monarch, eclipsed since the 1932 revolution, was restored by Sarit to some of its former glory as yet another means of consensus building.

Most military regimes have attempted to secure a minimum degree of national solidarity, often by identifying external or internal enemies, or by promoting economic development as the prerequisite of political modernization. Some set out to rediscover traditional political and social norms while remaining client regimes of the West. Taiwan and South Korea have embraced capitalist values, but in tradition-marked frameworks.

Even when not formally in a position of power, the military may be the last resort in order to prevent the disintegration of society. When Mao Zedong's proletarian Cultural Revolution degenerated into utter chaos he had to call on the People's Liberation Army to restore a semblance of order, and for years after the Chinese military remained in control of much of China's administrative, legislative, and political structures, not because it was inclined to intervene but because the collapse of civil authority left it no choice but to step in.[46]

But few military regimes have succeeded in or made substantial progress toward their initial goals. None of the particular forms of democracy they have designed has been lastingly implemented, and the political institutions they have created have yet to stand the test of time. Some can claim that a higher degree of national consensus exists after years of military rule, but others cannot. Corruption, which usually serves as one of the justifications for military coups, has affected military regimes as well, the more so the longer they last. Often military rulers apply more oppressive force than is required for attaining their aims. But this is not peculiar to military regimes. It may be argued that military elites have governed in much the same way as civilian elites have exercised political control. The basic differ-

---

[45] Quoted in Thak Chaloemtiarana, *Thailand, The Politics of Despotic Paternalism* (Bangkok: The Social Science Association of Thailand, 1979), 156.

[46] PLA officers, being part of the overall ruling elite, have not been tempted to seize political control despite periods of extreme provocation by civilian leaders. See, for instance, A. P. L. Liu, "The 'Gang of Four' and the Chinese People's Liberation Army," *Asian Survey* 19, no. 9 (September 1979).

ence between presidents in uniform and those in mufti is that the former inherited crisis situations that the latter had created or allowed to develop.

RETREAT TO THE BARRACKS

Military regimes can last for a long time—in fact, for several decades—but at some point they have to leave center stage of the political arena. The dilemma they all face sooner or later has little to do with levels of performance. If they perform badly, that is, fail to achieve the goals they set out to accomplish, they lose the legitimacy they initially may have enjoyed. Obviously, if failure is the justification for toppling civilian regimes it makes no sense to maintain indefinitely military regimes that do not do substantially better. Military rulers very often realize that trying to stay on will only bring, at best, disgrace to themselves and the armed forces, and, at worst, intraservice dissent and riots in the streets. The best example is Pakistan's Ayub Khan who, after he failed to rally support in society and the military for his plans to introduce democracy, quietly abdicated. On the other hand, if military regimes perform well, solving the crises which had served as both reasons and justifications for their initial intervention, they have, for all practical purposes, worked themselves out of the job. Certainly in the eyes of urban civilian elites, without whose at least tacit support most military regimes would be unable to govern, the right thing to do for the military rulers is to hand power over civilian politicians, administrators, and technocrats. So, no matter how military regimes perform, there will come the time when they have to consider the problem of eroding legitimacy.

The options
According to Huntington, military regimes have to grapple with two problems regarding their future: should they retain power or should they return it to civilian politicians; should they expand popular participation in the decision-making processes of the country or should they restrict it. Theoretically, these two notions allow for four options:

> *Retain* power, and *Restrict* participation;
> *Retain* power, and *Expand* participation;
> *Return* power, and *Restrict* participation; and
> *Return* power, and *Expand* participation[47]

If the appropriate option is not selected when choices have to be made the result is likely to be an impasse. The impasse regime is either toppled by another faction within the armed forces, by civilian revolutionaries and students, or it will have to abandon office in a quick and undignified way.

The question, then, is what is—from the regime's point of view—the appropriate choice. This will partly depend on what kind of regime it has perceived itself to be, and whether it intervened only to rectify a particular problem and then retreat to the barracks as soon as possible, or whether it

---

[47] See Huntington, *Political Order,* pp. 233–237.

1005

intended to bring about fundamental changes requiring prolonged intervention. But what choice to make is not solely the prerogative of the soldiers. Just as their entry on to the political stage had been largely determined by the political environment (the opportunity to intervene), so their exit is dependent on forces outside the military. Pressures on the regime to quit the presidential palace from both inside and outside the country may be so strong that returning power to civilians may, indeed, appear to be the most appropriate step to take. On the other hand, political circumstances may not really be conducive to such a choice. One of the most important preconditions for a withdrawal which needs to be considered is whether civilian elites capable and willing to assume political responsibility are in fact available. Making the wrong choice by not evaluating carefully enough both the reasons for withdrawal and the preconditions to do so, may create disastrous consequences. For instance, a military regime which decides to retain power and restrict participation in a rapidly modernizing society will ultimately find itself in the impasse situation; alternatively, a regime which has given up power too readily without the required preconditions being met may find itself involved in another takeover bid before long.

The options applied

The record of recivilianization by military regimes in Asia is checkered at best. Practically all options have been tried—sometimes appropriately, sometimes not—and impasses have often occurred.

The regime of Nguyen Van Thieu in South Vietnam collapsed under the combination of three factors: the onslaught of the North Vietnamese army and the Viet Cong as well as the panic this caused among the leaders in Saigon, the abandonment of Thieu by his patron, the United States, and, probably most important, the marked erosion of legitimacy of the rulers in Saigon in the eyes of the majority of the South Vietnamese population. Similarly, an impasse affected the Lon Nol military regime in Cambodia. Lon Nol only enjoyed a measure of support among the urban elites in the capital. When he toppled Sihanouk, who continued to enjoy the adoration of the rural population, the Khmer Rouge had no difficulty in mustering enough support for the violent overthrow of the American-backed regime in Phnom Penh. In 1973 the corrupt and ineffective Thai military regime found itself confronted by a rising tide of student unrest. When regime leaders attempted to smash the student uprising by force the king took the unprecedented step of intervening directly on the students' behalf. Deserted by the Bangkok garrison command, the regime leaders had no choice but to go into exile. In the end, none of these regimes found themselves in a position where they could make the right decisions to maintain themselves in office, or to make any deals with their respective opponents. Possibly the most dramatic demise of a military regime was that of Japan in 1945, leading to the total defeat of an entire nation and causing lasting public resentment against strong-arm forces and particularly any involvement of the military in political affairs.

But where regimes have been left to consider the best course of action, all available options have been tried. The least popular option in Asia, and probably the most difficult choice to sustain, is that of retaining power and restricting participation. Burma comes closest to this situation. The single party allowed to operate had been firmly under the control of the military, and no other group had been allowed any significant input into the processes of decision making. Paradoxically, it was Ne Win who returned power to the civilians two years after his 1958 takeover. He led the army back to the barracks without reserving any special powers for the military. But since the 1988 resignation and retirement of Ne Win, and the subsequent popular clamor for reform and democratization of Burmese society, a repressive military government has been in charge.

The only other example of this kind of choice being made in Asia occurred in Pakistan. After Ayub Khan's Basic Democracy had foundered his successor, General Yahya Khan, held free elections with the aim of bringing unrestrained, Western democracy to the country. But elections are not necessarily the panacea to deep-rooted problems. As it turned out Zulfikar Ali Bhutto and his West Pakistan-based People's party were unwilling to accept that the East Pakistan-based Awami League had clearly won the elections; nor apparently was Sheikh Mujib, the Awami leader, willing or able to contain secession sentiment in the East. The results of this election were civil war and the emergence of Bangladesh.

But, clearly, the majority of Asian military regimes have chosen a middle way between the extremes of completely liberalizing politics and hanging on to power by any means. At the more restrictive, authoritarian end of this middle way is Indonesia's vigorously propagated *Pancasila* Democracy which provides important rights for minorities but still has to be considered a close-knit polity in which one man, General Suharto, calls all the shots and the military is more or less confined to obedience and essentially supportive roles. But the so-called 1945 generation of officers who have been the main pillar of the regime are reaching retirement. The problem of handing power to a younger generation has, in fact, been discussed for more than a decade but whether, when, what kind, and which amount of change is to come about is still anybody's guess.

Varieties of the retain-and-expand option are presently being tested in other countries too. In Thailand, after 50 years of revolutions, military coups, and countercoups, as well as intermittent civilian regimes, the political landscape seems stable. Political parties are developing, from little more than personal cliques to platform parties standing for some kinds of principles. The military, still clearly the most important political force in the country, tolerates elections and the expression of political ideas as long as legislators are willing to elect a retired general as prime minister. Coups by particular military factions have been attempted in the late 1980s but have consistently failed to gain support. If legislators behave prudently and responsibly the probability is that military coups will have become a feature of the past.

In both Pakistan and Bangladesh the military has greatly expanded or allowed popular participation. In Pakistan before the 1988 death of General Zia ul-Haq, a civilian prime minister worked with a parliament whose members were compelled to campaign as individuals rather than under party banners. The most important powers belonged to Zia. Elections in late 1988 brought a civilian government to power headed by Benazir Bhutto, daughter of the former (and executed) prime minister. General H. M. Ershad has offered a deal similar to that of Zia for Bangladesh. The problem in both countries is that political parties are heavily ideologized and splintered, and the chances of workable coalitions emerging in completely unregulated elections, are slim. In any case, the fact that Bhutto is both prime minister and a woman, and that the three major parties in both countries are led by women, may bode ill for nations founded to preserve Islamic society on the Indian subcontinent.

The return-and-restrict option was chosen in Taiwan when the leadership of the Kuomintang (KMT) party became civilianized in the 1970s. Moreover, the indigenous Taiwanese have been given more scope inside the party and in the government by the refugees from the mainland who control politics in Taipei. Since 1987 opposition parties have been officially allowed provided they do not agitate against the One China policy that is still the political platform of the KMT or propagate communist ideas. With the death of reform-minded President Chiang Ching-kuo in 1988 the presidency passed to an indigenous Taiwanese, Lee Teng-hui. These political concessions had become an inevitable necessity after decades of Taiwan's being developed by the KMT into an entrepreneurial middle-class society. But the military still holds certain reserve powers as well as important positions in both the KMT and government bureaucracy.

In Fiji, Colonel Sitiveni Rabuka never made a serious effort to govern by himself; he only formed a cabinet after there was no one willing to fill the role of ruler. But as soon as Fijian politicians made themselves available again Rabuka returned power to civilians provided they restricted participation in such a way that the Indian majority would never be able to seize the government.

Probably the most curious case of military disengagement from government responsibility in Asia has occurred in South Korea. After persistent student riots during 1987 the regime was forced to make substantial concessions culminating in the provision for a free presidential election. Retired General Roh Tae Woo, the regime's candidate, was handpicked by incumbent President Chun Doo Hwan. He would have been swept aside by antigovernment sentiment if the opposition forces could have remained united. But the two main opposition leaders chose to put their personal ambitions above all else and campaigned against each other, leaving Roh to take the presidency with 36 percent of the vote. Thus, it seems that the regime's leaders had left it to the electorate to decide whether the military was to retain power or not. But there had been unsubstantiated reports that sections in the military would launch another coup if Roh were not elected. Given the way civilian politicians conducted themselves in the campaign, and the violence displayed by their respective followers, military leaders no doubt wondered if South Korea was indeed ready to embrace democratic government.

Reintervention by the military is always a distinct possibility; it becomes a probability where military regimes have allowed the emergence of an open, democratic system of government while neither the civilian elites nor the electorate at large are willing and ready to uphold such a system and adopt the minimum consensus required for operating it. Such a preparedness is not evident yet in most Asian nations. Under the existing cross-pressures, on one hand, to recivilianize and, on the other hand, to retain power as long as societies are ill-prepared to abide by the norms of democratic life, military regimes in Asia are highly likely to prefer a middle solution somewhere along the lines of the retain-and-expand option or, at best, a form of the return-and-restrict option.[48]

CONCLUSION

The basic theme of this essay has been that military intervention in politics in Asia and the Pacific is not principally due to intramilitary dynamics but has to be seen in the wider context of the political environment, the social values, the process of rapid change sweeping the continent, and the dislocation of norms and role perceptions so typical of societies in transition from traditional values and structures to modern ones. In this process the military plays an important function: it steps in when civilian leaders lose control over this process, lose sight of what their duties ought to be, and, ultimately, lose legitimacy or the authority to rule.

But the ordinary military leader is not necessarily a better ruler than the average civilian politician kicked out of office. What he brings to the job, particularly in Asia, is an inclination for order as well as the means to enforce this inclination. As far as Asia is concerned, the military ruler is a moderate modernizer, emphasizing orderly and pragmatic change. Asian military leaders abhor political emotionalism and any form of radicalism, and there is virtually not one among them with the charismatic qualities of a Kemal Atatürk, a Juan Perón, a Gamal Abdel Nasser, or a Jerry Rawlings. While some of the Asian military regimes have outstanding economic successes to their credit, their political programs, always subordinated to economic progress, have by and large not stood the test of time, or perhaps have not yet matured. Their political visions are more often than not limited by their preference for order and their resulting inability to cater to different political structures when economic and social change requires flexibility.

In the end, even clearly successful military regimes face legitimacy problems. The very policies of modernization they themselves have generated create demands for change and more popular participation that appear to be best accommodated by abrupt or, better, gradual abdication from power. Again, the political environment is of utmost importance, especially regarding the question of whether the clamoring for more open government is matched by the availability of civilian politicians of the quality and ideo-

[48] For a more detailed argument, see U. Sundhaussen, "The Durability of Military Regimes in South-East Asia," in Zakaria Haji Ahmad and H. Crouch, *Military-Civilian Relations,* pp. 269–86.

logical inclinations acceptable to the military. The empirical data at hand so far suggests that this has been rarely the case.

Essentially, military rule in Asia should be seen as a holding operation, admittedly with small gains made here and there, but not marked by any great political innovations. Only under the most unusual circumstances is the military more qualified and more inclined to provide a political vision of consequence. But military rule in societies in which the civilians have lost the legitimacy to rule can contain—rather than solve—conflict, and enforce a period of political calm in which new values and a higher sense of national consensus may emerge. Given the character of conflict in Asia arising primarily from the persistence of primordial loyalties or deriving from problems associated with rapid change, as well as the intensity of conflict, it would not be too presumptuous to predict that Asian military establishments will play political roles for some time to come.

FURTHER READING

Clapham, C, and Philip, G., eds., *The Political Dilemmas of Military Regimes.* London: Croom Helm, 1985.

Diamond, L., Linz, J., and Lipset, S.M., eds., *Democracy in Developing Countries.* Vol. 3 (Asia). Boulder, Colorado: Lynne Rienner, 1988.

Finer, S.E. *The Man on Horseback: The Role of the Military in Politics.* 2nd ed., Harmondsworth, Middlesex: Penguin 1976.

Huntington, S.P. *Political Order in Changing Societies.* New Haven, Connecticut: Yale University Press, 1968.

Janowitz, M., ed., *Civil-Military Relations: Regional Perspectives.* Beverly Hills, California, and London: Sage, 1981.

Nordlinger, E.A. *Soldiers in Politics: Military Coups and Governments.* Englewood Cliffs, New Jersey: Prentice-Hall, 1977.

Olsen, E.A., and Jurika, S., eds. *The Armed Forces in Contemporary Asian Societies.* Boulder, Colorado: Westview Press, 1986.

Pye, L.W. *Asian Power and Politics: The Cultural Dimensions of Authority.* Cambridge, Massachusetts: Harvard University Press, 1985.

Sundhaussen, U. *The Road to Power: Indonesian Military Politics, 1945–1967.* Kuala Lumpur and London: Oxford University Press, 1982.

Zakaria, Haji Ahmad, and Crouch, H., eds. *Military-Civilian Relations in South-East Asia.* Singapore and London: Oxford University Press, 1985.

BUREAUCRACY

DAVID C. POTTER

Writings on bureaucracy in Asia and the Pacific are uneven: single country studies abound but comparative analyses are virtually unknown. One approach asks questions about improving the effectiveness of a particular bureaucracy, usually examining its internal working broadly in terms of Max Weber's model. It is normally assumed that the closer the bureaucracy approximates the model, the more effective it tends to be. Another approach assesses the power of a specific bureaucracy in relation to the particular political regime. Studies of China or North Korea, for example, suggest that the bureaucracy is penetrated and controlled quite firmly by the ruling communist party; bureaucracies in Indonesia or Pakistan, however, seem to be less closely watched by the military; whereas bureaucracies in Japan or Australia appear to have considerable autonomy vis-à-vis the competitive party system. But in all, Asian bureaucracies probably have had more power in society than bureaucracies in other regions of the world. In this essay the internal working of Asian bureaucracies as well as their relative power within different types of political regime will be discussed.

WEBER'S MODEL AND ASIAN REALITY

Max Weber identified four main features of large-scale, modern bureaucracies.[1] First, such organizations are characterized by hierarchy: each official has a definite role within a hierarchical division of labor and is answerable to a superior. Second, there is continuity: the roles that make up the organization provide full-time salaried occupations for incumbents, with career structures offering prospects of advancement. Third, there is impersonality: the work of the organization is conducted according to prescribed rules without favoritism, and a written record is kept. Finally, there is expertise: officials are selected according to merit, trained for their positions and control access to information stored in files. Weber was careful to distinguish between a bureaucracy with these four features and the governing body that employs it. The function of the governing body is to give broad direction to the bureaucracy regarding its policies and rules, including de-

---

[1] The summary of Weber's model in this section leans heavily on D. Betham, *Bureaucracy* (Milton Keynes: Open University Press, 1987).

cisions as to how necessary funds for its activities are to be obtained. In contrast to bureaucratic officials, members of the governing body are typically elected and may work only part time. Their responsibility is outward to shareholders, an electorate, a party membership or some other group.

Weber's bureaucratic model identified the most general features common to bureaucracies in all sectors of modern society, whether devoted to the pursuit of private profit or public interest. Students of public administration, however, have not fully accepted this universal conception. They have argued that there are noticeable differences between bureaucratic administration in public and nonpublic spheres. Even though public bureaucracies may be hierarchical, continuous, impersonal and expert, they still have a quite different orientation and mode of operation due to their location in the public arena. For example, the work is carried out subject in principle to public scrutiny and public accountability. This encourages the impersonal application of rules when dealing with the public and the recording of such transactions on files. (The red tape that ensues is widely regarded as a feature peculiar to a public bureaucracy.) By contrast, businessmen in private can more legitimately bend rules, exercise individual initiative and resort to informal (unwritten) understandings in pursuit of profit. Another reason is that the tasks of a public bureaucracy are uniquely various because of the complexity of social life and the individuality of citizens. In consequence, there are many types of organization in a public bureaucracy, and no single criterion of efficiency (such as profit) can be used to assess performance. This conception of "the public" helps to create an important idea found only in pubic bureaucracies: that of public service, of administration for the public.

The term bureaucracy, as used throughout the world today, combines Weberian and public administration perspectives. It normally refers to the civil (rather than the military) side of the state apparatus. Bureaucracies, then, can be defined formally as complex and large-scale ensembles of hierarchical, continuous, impersonal and expert organizations working for public purposes defined by the government or political leadership to which the ensemble is collectively accountable.

This bureaucratic model amounts to an ideal type. Few if any bureaucracies in Asia (or elsewhere) fit it closely. What may look like hierarchies are frequently "facades for pyramids of informal, but enduring, patron-client groupings."[2] Impersonal application of the rules "for the public" is confounded by widespread bribery and corruption. Expertise is frequently lacking due to inadequate training. The norm of public accountability can be merely a euphemism for secret shenanigans in private designed to mislead the public. Indeed, some Asian nations appear to depart so fundamentally from the model that it seems misleading to refer to them as even having bureaucracies.

Take a specific example. D. Emmerson interviewed a bureau chief in one of the smaller government departments in Indonesia in 1969. This official

[2]L. Pye, *Asian Power and Politics: The Cultural Dimensions of Authority* (Cambridge, Massachusetts: Harvard University Press, 1985), 27.

reflected on his activities in the multiparty regime of the late 1950s and early 1960s:

> A became Minister in 195-. He and I had been in the same political party, so he brought me in as head of personnel. A rival political party had been making inroads into the ministry, and he wanted to replace them with people from our party. I was given—secretly, of course—the duty of ousting their people from the ministry and bringing our people in. I did this. [Then, he said, in self-defense:] But I always saw that at least the quality of our man wasn't less than the fellow he was to replace. And, anyway, in those days everyone was trying to put people from his own group into government offices. . . . Later, when B came in as a minister, the first person he fired was me. Even though we'd worked together years earlier. He called me into his office and apologized, but he fired me. He said it was the wish of the masses. I knew which masses he meant [that is, B's party]. So I left. I went back to A [who meanwhile had become a minister without portfolio] and asked for help. He got me a job, but there was nothing to do; they just added my name to a payroll. I would go to the office and sit around, reading the paper or chatting, before going home again. And the next day the same. For two years.[3]

The picture described by this Asian bureaucrat departs substantially from all four of Weber's features of bureaucratic organization. Hierarchy? At one point he spent two years in a government organization receiving a salary and doing nothing because there was nothing to do; the formal hierarchy hid the reality of a government department that was primarily a repository for political supporters. Continuity? Bureaucratic tenure for this individual and others like him was short and uncertain; duration of employment was determined by the shifting fortunes of ministers. Impersonality in applying the rules? The illustration does not bear directly on this Weberian principle, but personal loyalties were clearly more important than prescribed well-established rules in the relationships described. Expertise and the merit principle of selection? In this organization, selection was governed first by political loyalty, then by expertise.

The example, however, is misleading as an overall description of Indonesian bureaucracy for two reasons. First, the man was a top-level bureaucrat in that department and his experience would rarely be repeated at lower levels of such organizations. Incoming ministers in such regimes in Asia have frequently tried to restaff their offices several ranks deep with people they can trust—a type of spoils system not uncommon elsewhere. Such political penetration of higher levels may have impeded the growth of institutional and career-centered loyalties lower down, but it did not wholly compromise the existence more generally in the organization of hierarchy, continuity, impersonality and expertise. Second, the example relates only to one period in Indonesia's history. The bureaucracy was depoliticized in the late 1960s following the start of the New Order under Suharto in 1965. The bureaucratic reforms that accompanied that change of regime

[3] D. Emmerson, "The Bureaucracy in Political Context: Weakness in Strength," in K. Jackson and L. Pye, eds. *Political Power and Communications in Indonesia,* (Berkeley: University of California Press, 1978), 94.

eliminated the practice of periodic political penetrations that had occurred previously. By the 1980s the bureaucracy had moved closer to the Weberian model, although there were still many distinctively Indonesian characteristics and overtones.

For example, there was continuity. Work in the civil service was exceptionally secure in Indonesian society. Dismissal was very unusual, and pensions were provided. These features helped to give the Indonesian bureaucracy, one of the largest groups in the labor force, quite a high status in an economically underdeveloped society. They also helped to justify the low starting pay. A distinctly Indonesian feature helped to compensate. Indonesian civil servants augmented their inadequate salaries through a complex system of special payments at all levels for their services. One common method, linked to the massive flow of development funding under the New Order, was to accumulate honoraria from association with a number of projects. Such payments were acceptable as part of normal bureaucratic life in Indonesia as long as they were kept within reasonable bounds. This unusual system had a profound affect on work rates and the incentives that shaped them.

There was also impersonality in the sense that formal rules existed that affected bureaucratic performance. But there is no doubt that informal relationships and linkages were of central importance to bureaucratic decision making and implementation in Indonesian society. Family connections, ethnic loyalty, religion and educational background counted for much.

There was also some expertise in the Indonesian bureaucracy resulting from selection by merit and the provision of training programs. Particularly noticeable were increasing numbers of highly skilled technocrats who had been trained in the United States or elsewhere abroad and had returned to influential positions in the economic and technical ministries and in national planning organizations. The new technocrats ran up against an older bureaucratic tradition carried by the majority of civil servants for whom individuality and personal initiative were discounted, and where any expertise obtained from limited training in one government department served them throughout their careers because movement among departments was minimal.

The further the workings of Indonesia's bureaucracy are plumbed, the more one is made made aware of the extent to which its formal Weberian structure is modified by a wide range of complex personal relationships and culturally specific norms of behavior. A detailed description of another Asian bureaucracy would reveal different organizational arrangements and different normative codes of behavior. The more one reads these country specific studies of Asian bureaucracy, the more one is struck by detailed differences.

But are there also broad similarities? The Indonesian bureaucracy approximates what is normally defined as the bureaucratic model; other Asian bureaucracies also tend to have noticeable elements of hierarchy, continuity, impersonal rules and expertise. Beyond that definitional similarity, however, there has also been a tendency throughout much of Asia to see certain problems of bureaucracy in broadly similar terms. This essay will focus on five such problems. Two are personnel problems—lack of commitment and inadequate skills. One is a problem in the relationship between bureaucrats and the public—the problem of corruption. The other two are structural problems related to political control over the bureaucracy and bureaucratic power in society. Although these problems are found throughout Asia and the Pacific, they tend to be defined somewhat differently in more developed countries such as Australia, New Zealand, Japan, South Korea, Taiwan, Singapore and Hong Kong than in more underdeveloped countries such as Afghanistan, India, Bangladesh, Burma (now Myanmar), Cambodia, Laos, Vietnam, Mongolia and China.

INADEQUATE SKILLS

Less developed countries in Asia have been preoccupied with the shortage of skilled personnel; more developed countries recognize that trained and expert personnel are essential and must continue to be reproduced. One of the factors that helps to explain the rapid industrial development in South Korea, Taiwan, Singapore and Hong Kong, for example, is the large investment that has been made in educating and training the workforce, including those in the public sector. The consequence is that the level of expertise throughout such bureaucracies is quite high, and national leaderships are committed to sustaining and improving it. The same cannot be said so confidently of less developed Asian countries. In these countries one certainly finds bureaucracies with skilled administrative elites, with generalists who advise on policy (including successors to previous colonial administrative elites) and highly trained technocrats who tend to congregate in economic and planning departments. But lower down in these bureaucracies there are armies of officials who, having once been recipients of rather perfunctory training programs, remain relatively unskilled throughout their careers (although not without a certain expertise based largely on experience). The prominence given to inadequate skills as an administrative problem in such countries is easily seen in commissions reports that note the need for administrative reform and that continually stress the importance of improved training programs.

The personnel problem of inadequate skills has also been a central preoccupation in communist nations such as China, North Korea and Vietnam. The problem arises initially from a special dilemma faced by such regimes. This is the so-called contradiction between "expert" and "red". The party needs a bureaucracy containing skilled and expert officials, but initially at least most such people have bourgeois backgrounds, having been trained in Western (capitalist) universities or in indigenous institutions patterned after them. The party also needs a bureaucracy that is politically reliable. Shortages of skilled "red experts" are particularly evident at higher levels of these bureaucracies.

In China the handling of this contradiction has tended to follow a cyclical pattern.[4] When economic development strategies encountered difficul-

[4] H. Harding, *Organizing China: the Problem of Bureaucracy, 1949–1976* (Stanford, California: Stanford University Press, 1981), 348–50.

ties in 1956 and 1960–1961, more effort was made to recruit and use experts; and when the experts were judged to have demonstrated their political unreliability as in 1957–1958 and 1967–1976, power tended to move back to reliable "reds." More recently, such stark contrasts between "red" generalists and "white" specialists has begun to blur. During Deng Xiaoping's "Second Chinese Revolution" in the 1980s ("a little capitalism isn't necessarily a bad thing"), skilled specialists in the bureaucracy were again in the ascendency. There were references to the "coming of age of a talented, self-confident young technocratic elite" and Deng's "yuppie corps." At the Thirteenth Congress of the communist party in 1987, General Secretary Zhao Ziyang underlined the importance of "a civil service system based on merit" and announced that "there would be a division between political civil servants, who hold their jobs for specified periods, and professionals, who gain permanent jobs by passing competitive examinations."[5]

Concerted efforts were being made in most countries in the 1980s to ease the problem of lack of expertise. More money was budgeted for training programs. Two particular previous problems had been inadequate resources and overstretched training staff insufficiently remunerated. The general strategies varied depending to some extent on the spread and character of the educational system in the country. In Malaysia, for example, the emphasis was on preservice training, whereas in the Philippines, where educational services were probably more widespread, greater effort was directed at in-service training. A continuing problem was that in most Asian countries attempts to improve bureaucratic expertise were poorly articulated in relation to personnel planning and development. In many cases, for example, training was not linked to promotion. On the other hand, the content of training programs was becoming more realistic. Even bureaucrats whose careers would keep them mainly at the center were required to learn something of conditions in the rural areas—a welcome development.

LACK OF COMMITMENT

The other principal personnel problem in many Asian bureaucracies has been lack of commitment to the goals of the organization. This has several aspects. One is the phenomenon, reported extensively, of bureaucratic officials motivated more by self-interest than by organizational goals. This is frequently referred to as the bureaucratic value of personalism (which can lead to nepotism). Personalism is the belief that personal relationships and family (or kin) loyalties should be the basis for bureaucratic behavior. If there is a conflict between advancing one's personal or group interest and advancing the work of the formal organization, the former takes precedence. A related phenomenon is that of ministers or other political leaders using bureaucratic departments as parking lots (with payrolls) for political

[5] R. Baum, "China in 1985: The Greening of the Revolution," *Asian Survey* 26; no. 1 (January 1986): 31, 35; S. Rosen, "China in 1987," *Asian Survey* 28, no. 1 (January 1988): 43.

supporters. The case of minister A and minister B in Indonesia in the late 1950s, cited above, is one example. Similar examples of personalism can be found in many Asian countries. In Thailand, bureaucrats have tended to be ego oriented rather than task oriented, and "the Thai bureaucrat . . . views his position as his personal possession that can be used to advance his and his clique's interests."[6]

Personalism and nepotism were also apparently the organizing principles in the bureaucracy of Afghanistan in the period before the change in regime in 1978. Recruitment was by individual ministers and vacancies were not publicly advertised. The ministry's employing officer was not supposed to employ any relatives under his direct control, but in actuality family connections were essential for obtaining civil service positions. L. Dupree has described how the rural power elite sent a "second line of power" to Kabul "as a first line of defence":

the second line of power, after setting up shop in Kabul, began to build its power base with horizontal links to the government, in addition to the regional vertical tribal kin links. The men of the second line were able to feed brothers, sons, cousins and other relatives into the government bureaucracy, thus strengthening their position in a single generation.[7]

In this way, the Afghan bureaucracy was infiltrated "by people whose first allegiance lay in regional, tribal or kinships links."

Another aspect of lack of commitment to the goals of the organization relates to the allegation frequently expressed in the Asian context that bureaucracies are naturally conservative whereas many political leaderships in Asia espouse policies emanating from at least mildly socialist ideologies. Because of this disjuncture, it is argued that bureaucracies pose a problem because they are not committed to the policy goals of the government to which they are responsible. In India, for example, Congress party leaders in 1969 called for a civil service more committed to their program. Jagjivan Ram, in his presidential address to the Bombay session of the All-India Congress Committee, declared that "the so-called neutral administrative machinery is a hindrance, not a help" and "is hardly relevant to Indian conditions." Gandhi also called for greater bureaucratic commitment; Chandra Shekhar, Mohan Dharia and others, in an important policy note of the party, said that

the present bureaucracy under the orthodox and conservative leadership of the ICS [Indian Civil Service] with its upper-class prejudices can hardly be expected to meet the requirements of social and economic change along socialist

[6]J. Mosel, "Thai Administrative Behavior," in *Toward the Comparative Study of Public Administration,* ed. W. Siffin (Bloomington: Indiana University Press, 1957), 321; C. Samudavenija, "The Bureaucracy," in *Government and Politics of Thailand,* ed. S. Xuto (Singapore: Oxford University Press, 1987), 92.
[7]B. Male, *Revolutionary Afghanistan* (London: Croom Helm, 1982), 95; L. Dupree, *Afghanistan Continues the Experiment in Democracy,* American Universities Field Staff Reports, South Asia Series, XV, no. 3 (July 1971), 8.

lines. The creation of an administrative cadre *committed* to national objectives and responsive to our social needs is an urgent necessity.[8]

These remarks were hotly debated within the bureaucracy, the argument turning on the desirability or otherwise of a neutral civil service in a parliamentary democracy. Gandhi was even forced to clarify what she had meant by commitment. But the general problem, even if exaggerated by politicians at the time, was a real one. In political regimes ruled by communist parties this problem of lack of (ideological) commitment is perhaps even more serious. Mao Zedong, for example, periodically complained that Chinese bureaucratic officials were more than just conservative, they were revisonist.

It is difficult in most Asian countries to obtain reliable information on the political attitudes of civil servants. It is likely that many hold more conservative views than politicians and this almost certainly contributes to the personnel problem of lack of commitment to organizational goals set by political leadership, although the extent to which it does is not known. It is not in principle impossible for conservative bureaucracies to perform well for socialist governments.

CORRUPTION

Bureaucratic corruption, in the sense of misuse of public office for personal gain, is apparently rampant in many less developed countries in Asia. No decision is made or action taken for a member of the public, indeed nothing happens at all, unless files move from desk to desk. And no files move unless money changes hands—it's called *baksheesh* in South Asia. The rates differ depending on the level in the bureaucracy at which it is handled, the importance of the file, how fast an outcome is needed, and what the traffic will bear. If a peasant needs a file to move across a number of desks, the overall costs involved can be crippling. The picture presented borders on caricature if it is meant to apply to all of Asia. Not only does the extent of corruption differ from one Asian country to another; it varies also among different types of government departments. For example, there is likely to be more corruption surrounding the activities of tax collectors, customs officers, officials on investment boards and employees of public utilities. There is likely to be less corruption in animal husbandry departments, education inspectorates and archeological surveys. These differences are reflected in distinctions made in India between "wet" posts (from which rupees pour) and "dry" posts.

It is, understandably, difficult to obtain reliable, systematic evidence measuring actual levels of corruption. In consequence, studies tend to be full of brief references to the problem of bureaucratic corruption, couched in terms of rather general assessments (or condemnations) relating to a single bureaucracy, based on a few unusual illustrations. One of the most

[8] The quotes on this incident are cited in D. Potter, *India's Political Administrators, 1919–1983* (Oxford: Clarendon Press, 1986), 155–56.

interesting examples is in a summary of events in China in 1986. The reader is informed in passing that in January of that year there was a crackdown on corruption by high-level officials in the bureaucracy, popularly known as "tiger beating in the year of the tiger"; by March, it seems, the tiger hunt had cooled, very few having been caught.[9]

References to bureaucratic corruption can be found in studies of all Asian countries. They are most frequent and prominent for some of the less developed, noncommunist regimes such as Bangladesh, India, Thailand and Indonesia; less frequent perhaps for communist regimes; least frequent for more highly developed countries such as Australia, New Zealand and Japan. The question is not whether corruption exists. A more fruitful question, although a difficult one to answer, is whether corruption poses a major problem for bureaucratic performance. Certain bureaucratic practices in an Asian country, formally defined as corrupt by Western standards, may be part of normal social relations, and deeply embedded in the culture. For civil servants to refuse to countenance any such practices in dealings with the public, even on a nominal scale, may actually be counterproductive. Engaging in such practices may in fact be a requisite for organizational effectiveness. One may even argue that increasing levels of corruption do not necessarily pose problems for bureaucratic effectiveness if organizational achievements multiply at equivalent or faster rates.

Clearly there are limits. All Asian governments make efforts to control corruption. In doing so, it is normally accepted that corruption is likely to thrive under two circumstances: first, opportunity is present because monitoring is ineffectual and penalties are weak; second, motivation is high because salaries are inadequate. The importance of the first circumstance is suggested by the apparently lower levels of bureaucratic corruption in communist regimes; one important reason is that party and other monitors stay very close to the bureaucracy at all levels and penalties for dishonest practices can be severe. The importance of the second is suggested by what appears to be the existence of more widespread problems of corruption in poorer countries where bureaucratic salaries are low. It was observed above that in Indonesia bureaucratic salaries are so inadequate that the widespread practice of engaging in sideline activities and enlarging one's income by charging fees for project work is considered legitimate as long as it is kept within reasonable bounds. Similar practices are reported in Thailand. In Cambodia, one of the world's poorest countries, salaried employees in the bureaucracy receive very low wages; a government report in 1987 noted that 78 percent of state employees' families practiced sideline occupations.[10] Such activities are not identified as corrupt, and indeed may well not be by any definition, but the possibilities in such circumstances are there. The situation seems to have been similar in Laos in 1986 where civil servants were regularly accused of corruption. It was complicated by the

[9] S. Rosen, "China in 1986," *Asian Survey* 27, no. 1 (January 1987): 36.
[10] Cited in N. Chanda, "Cambodia in 1987," *Asian Survey* 28, no. 1 (January 1988): 109.

fact that the government employees there were paid only about 10 percent of their inadequate salaries in cash, the rest in the form of coupons for use in the government store.

Civil service salaries in Afghanistan up to 1978 (although comparatively high in Afghan terms) had not kept pace with inflation and had in fact declined in real terms by 50 percent since the late 1960s. There were fringe benefits, such as being able to buy essential goods at subsidized prices from cooperatives, but these benefits could not make up for the decline in real income. The result was "a high incidence of corruption—*baksheesh* payments for a whole variety of permits, licences and other documents." A vested interest grew up in developing unnecessarily complicated bureaucratic procedures: "at one stage it was necessary to apply to seventeen or eighteen offices for a licence to trade, with "efficiency charges" imposed by each." The general result in terms of bureaucratic relations with the public is summarized as follows: "Apart from the administrative inefficiency involved, this practice resulted in poor relationships between civil servants and members of the public who had to deal with the bureaucracy."[11]

It is worth noting that there is no necessary connection between low salaries and corruption. In Myanmar, for example, the salaries of bureaucrats failed to keep pace with inflation but references to corruption were rare in General Ne Win's regime from 1962 to 1988. This may be due to the lack of information about Myanmar's bureaucracy since the 1960s. It may also be a result of very tough sentences imposed (and widely publicized) in those cases where persons have been found guilty of corrupt practices.

Bureaucratic corruption is a problem because it can lead to adverse political, economic and social consequences. Politically, any regime that is regarded over time as corrupt begins to find its political legitimacy slipping away. No regime wants that. Administratively, there can be unfortunate side effects: conscientious and idealistic civil servants already in government service, or recently recruited to the bureaucracy, find it hard to maintain their dedication if blatant corruption is going on around them. Overall performance eventually begins to be affected. There are also perhaps more general costs: "Corruption may tend to destroy some of a new nation's greatest potential assets, the enthusiasm, idealism, and sympathy of its youth and students. In the event that the idealism and enthusiasm of the younger generation turns to cynicism, not only political stability but long-run economic development efforts are bound to be affected."[12]

POLITICAL CONTROL

Political control of the bureaucracy is a major problem throughout Asia. The problem is differently conceived in different types of political regimes. A

[11]Quotations in this paragraph are from Male, *Revolutionary Afghanistan,* pp. 95–96.

[12]T. Smith, *Corruption, Tradition and Change* (1971), 36, cited in B. Glassburner, "Indonesia's New Economic Policy and Its Social-Political Implications," in *Political Power and Communications,* eds. Jackson and Pye, p. 164.

typology of Asian political regimes is therefore needed before the problem can be discussed. There have been a number of attempts to classify political regimes and their bureaucracies.[13] A simple typology for Asia contains three main types: (1) communist party mobilization regimes; (2) those regimes where the military, or a civilian party controlled by the military, is the dominant political force; (3) competitive or semicompetitive polyarchal regimes. No regime in Asia is a pure example of any of these types. In categorizing any particular one, qualifications have to be made and special circumstances identified and elaborated.

Figure 1 locates the main Asian and Pacific countries roughly within such a typology as of 1987–1988. It shows these countries tending to cluster around the three types of regimes identified above. The clustering is tightest around the pole of communist party mobilization regimes. It is less tight around the pole of competitive or semicompetitive polyarchal regimes. The clustering is comparatively loose around the military or civilian party military pole. If one were to move the typology through time, from 1950 to the mid-1980s, the countries clustered around the pole on the bottom left of the figure would be found to be the busiest.

A regime where the armed forces or a military-controlled civilian party is dominant usually originates as a consequence of a coup d'état; officers in the armed forces then place their own people in key posts at various levels in the bureaucracy. The military initially provides the political leadership in the regime to which the bureaucracy is accountable. Later, military leaders either sponsor a political party or eventually, as civilians, lead one themselves. Whatever the precise mixture of military and civilian party, it is characteristic of such regimes that power centers in society other than the military and its party are not allowed to develop.

Normally military officers set out with some élan, following the coup that brings them to power, to bring the bureaucracy under their direction and control. In this, however, they are not usually very successful once the regime settles down. Bureaucracies in military regimes appear to be much less effectively controlled than bureaucracies controlled by a dominant communist party. Such bureaucracies, although having considerable autonomy, are still subject finally to military direction. In Pakistan, for example, "even when the military is in the barracks, they have exerted a veto power on the political system," although they "have remained exceedingly dependent on the civilian bureaucracy for all phases of the policy process."[14] In the 1980s, President (General) Mohammed Zia ul-Haq set about trying to increase his

[13] For example, F. Heady, *Public Administration: A Comparative Perspective,* 3rd ed. (New York: Marcel Dekker, 1984); J. Coleman, "Conclusion," in *The Politics of the Developing Areas,* eds. G. Almond and J. Coleman (Princeton, New Jersey: Princeton University Press, 1960), 532–76; F. Riggs, ed., *Frontiers of Developmental Movement Regimes* (Durham, North Carolina: Duke University Press, 1970), 486–537; M. Fainsod, "Bureaucracy and Modernization: The Russian and Soviet Case," in *Bureaucracy and Political Development,* ed. J. LaPalombara (Princeton, New Jersey: Princeton University Press, 1963), esp. 234–39.
[14] C. Kennedy, *Bureaucracy in Pakistan* (Karachi: Oxford University Press, 1987), 4.

Figure 1
A TYPOLOGY OF 27 ASIAN POLITICAL REGIMES, 1987–88

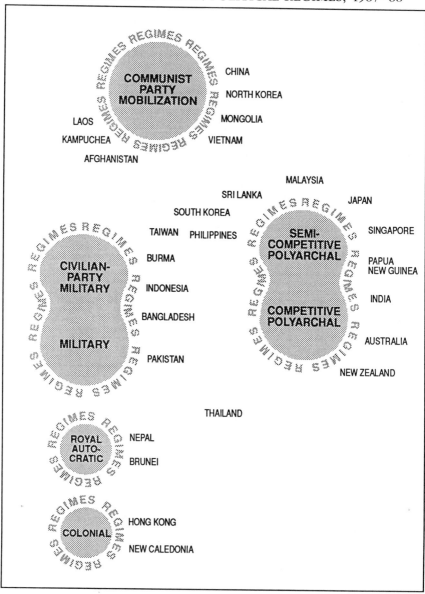

control over this bureaucracy: up to 10 percent of the senior positions in the civil service were reserved for military personnel and the high-powered selection committee that was set up to recruit and assign them was chaired by Zia.

The military regime in Bangladesh has also struggled with the problem of bureaucratic control. The cause of the coup by Lieutenant General H. M. Ershad and his colleagues in 1982 was widespread allegations of bureaucratic corruption and incompetence. Hence administrative reform committees chaired by military officers went to work almost immediately. Their recommendations were aimed at streamlining the bureaucracy to improve effectiveness, allowing greater popular participation in administration at local levels and subjecting the bureaucracy to tighter political (military) control. By 1987, with the military back in the barracks, the government was beginning again to rely increasingly on the bureaucracy in the central secretariat and elsewhere. For example, bureaucratic reforms had called for a reduction in the number of ministries and the number of bureaucrats. Initially this happened, but by 1987 the number of ministries had nearly doubled, frozen bureaucratic posts were unfrozen, bureaucratic empire building and interservice rivalries were again reported to be rampant, and rules and guidelines formulated and interpreted by civil servants were proliferating (a sure sign of increasing bureaucratic power). The Bangladesh example suggests that public bureaucracies in military-dominated regimes can become very powerful after such regimes settle down and in the absence of other countervailing forces such as competitive political parties.

There are, however, instances of civilian-party military regimes that apparently do retain close control over the bureaucracy. This seems to have been the case in Burma.[15] When the government of Prime Minister U Nu and his Union party was ousted by General Ne Win's military revolutionary council in 1962, there was only a short pause before the Burma Socialist Program party (BSPP) was formed charting an ideological path "between capitalism and communism." At first, only members of the revolutionary council were members. To control the bureaucracy, security and administrative committees were formed at various levels within the nation to ensure that central directions were followed. Each committee was chaired by a soldier and composed of local military commanders, police and civil bureaucrats from the relevant level of administration. After 10 years it appeared that the bureaucracy was becoming less amenable to control, thus following the familiar pattern. But then came sweeping administrative changes in 1972 emphasizing that the revolutionary council and the BSPP were still very much in command. The colonial-style secretariats were abolished; ministers henceforth were able to communicate directly with experts in subordinate government departments rather than having to go through an elite generalist permanent secretary. Equally stunning was the abolition of the colonial-style district administration. Security and administrative committees were henceforth organized on the basis of states, divisions and

---

[15] The following summary relies on R. Taylor, *The State in Burma* (London: Hurst & Co., 1987).

townships. In 1974 the committees became people's councils under a new constitution, with BSPP and other representatives taking part in their activities vis-à-vis the bureaucracy. Control of the bureaucracy appears to have remained firm until the 1988 retirement of Ne Win. Burma, however, is an unusual case, closer in this respect to the situation in party mobilization regimes.

Most military regimes tend to be politically unstable as they grapple with the twin problems of bureaucratic control and political legitimacy. The two are frequently in conflict. If military control of the bureaucracy is tightened, then political legitimacy among the civilian population can slip away; if the military retires to barracks and lets civilian representatives try to build up the legitimacy of the regime, then bureaucratic control is loosened. This dialectic governs the tendency of military regimes to oscillate between tighter military and looser civilian types of political leaderships. The dominant trend in Asia has been for such regimes, following military coups, to move in a civilian direction and then, in some cases, to drift toward the semicompetitive polyarchal pole (see Figure 1). South Korea and the Philippines had probably moved farthest along this trajectory by 1988. In South Korea a new president was elected in 1987 by popular vote for the first time in 26 years. There was also widespread recognition among the South Korean elite that to sustain the economic miracle would require further civilianizing of the government and enhancing of the autonomy of the bureaucracy. The military, however, is still a powerful political force in the system, ready to intervene at any time.

A communist party mobilization regime, by contrast, tends to have a totalitarian dimension in the sense that it seeks to encompass the entire society in its embrace. Strong leaderships attempt through the party and bureaucracy to mobilize the entire society for the purposes of nation building and social reconstruction in accordance with socialist ideology. Figure 1 shows that the main examples of such regimes are China, North Korea, Mongolia and Vietnam. Laos, Cambodia and Afghanistan also belonged in this category in the mid-1980s, although in these countries the situation was complicated by the presence of foreign troops providing support for the regimes (Soviet troops in Afghanistan, Vietnamese troops in Laos and Cambodia).

Bureaucracies in communist regimes tend on the whole to be controlled quite firmly by the ruling party apparatus. This is so despite the fact that Asian communist leaders regularly draw attention to problems of bureaucratic control. In 1987, for example, the new general secretary of the communist party in Vietnam, Nguyen Van Linh, went out of his way to denounce the top-heavy, overstaffed bureaucracy in Hanoi and bureaucratic inefficiency generally. In Mongolia, in an address to the People's Revolutionary party congress in 1986 in Ulaanbaatar, General Secretary Jambyn Batmonh declared: "It is important to wage a determined struggle against bureaucracy, formalism, and routine, narrow views."[16] There are numerous

[16]Cited in J. H. Esterline, "Vietnam in 1987: Steps towards Rejuvenation," *Asian*

other examples from communist regimes in Asia. It seems that all modern political regimes, including communist ones, "cannot get along without bureaucracies, and it also seems to be practically impossible to get along with them." [17]

How have Chinese communists handled this bureaucratic dilemma? [18] The record of bureaucratic responsiveness to direction from higher levels was "remarkably good" between 1949 and 1976, although there were occasions during that period when maintaining bureaucratic control was a problem for Chinese leaders. Indeed, the problem of bureaucracy was considered so serious during the Cultural Revolution (1966–1968) that some Chinese leaders "proposed the complete destruction of the bureaucracy and its replacement by a much more participatory and less hierarchical form" in keeping with the writings of Marx, Engels and Lenin. Internal rectification campaigns have also occurred from time to time. Mobilization of the masses to serve as bureaucratic monitors has been attempted, especially during the Cultural Revolution and the Hundred Flowers period (1956–1957) when it was proposed that the people's congresses be given greater power to direct the state bureaucracy. The Chinese also experimented with bureaucratic rationalization: "rules and regulations were promulgated, a complex network of bureaucratic auditing and monitoring agencies was established, career lines were systematized, and specialized bureaucratic agencies were allowed to proliferate." These moves were then followed later by "attempts to control the excess of bureaucracy," for example staff reduction, decentralization measures, partial recentralization and simplification of bureaucratic structures.

Although bureaucratic responsiveness to political control has been described as "remarkably good," there have been occasions when the Chinese bureaucracy did not respond well to central directions. A review of those occasions during the period when bureaucratic control became a particular problem suggests that it flourished under three sets of circumstances. First, there were problems when policy directions were vague. On several occasions central leaders called for a retreat from the unrealistic policies of a preceding campaign, but failed to give clear guidelines on how far the retreat should go; the response of lower-level bureaucrats was understandably sluggish. In such cases, control was restored when central guidelines were clearly enunciated and disciplinary measures announced for those who flouted them. Second, problems of control developed when there were serious divisions over policy at the top. For example, "the sluggish response of the bureaucracy to Mao's policy initiations in the early 1960s and to the leftists' revolutionary great debates in the early 1970s stemmed from offi-

Survey 28, no. 1 (January 1988): 86–94, and in W. P. Heaton, "Mongolia in 1986," *Asian Survey* 27, no. 1 (January 1987): 79.
[17] G. A. Almond and G. B. Powell, *Comparative Politics: System, Process, and Policy,* 2nd ed. (Boston), 226–67.
[18] Harding, *Organizing China.* The following summary as well as the quotations in this paragraph and the next are taken from this study.

cials' realization that the central leadership was not united behind these programmes, and that it would be relatively safe to ignore unpopular directives or to implement them in an unenthusiastic manner. Third, bureaucratic resistance to control became a problem in China (as elsewhere) when programs clearly threatened to cost officials their staff, their comfort, their status and even their jobs. Such opposition was overcome, however, when political leaders showed clearly that they were united behind the program and that definite results were expected from its implementation.

The post-Mao reforms that took place between 1978 and the mid-1980s affecting state, economy and society slowly changed the character of the Chinese bureaucracy. By 1986, as noted above, it was becoming clear that a more professional, specialist bureaucracy was being established. Such bureaucracies tend to require and acquire more autonomy from the political leadership. By 1988 the Chinese bureaucracy had become both a more powerful independent force within the Chinese state and a correspondingly more difficult institution for the political leadership to control.

Competitive or semicompetitive polyarchal regimes are quite different from communist mobilization regimes. There are many legitimate power centers in society (business organizations, trade unions and other interest groups) in addition to political leaderships formed through a system of competitive parties and regular elections. Australia and New Zealand are the two examples of such competitive polyarchal regimes of the sort found in Western Europe and North America. More common in Asia are what can be called semicompetitive polyarchal regimes where there are regular elections but one dominant party normally continues to form the government, the bureaucracy tends to be fairly cozy with the dominant party and its ideology, and the polyarchal feature is less pronounced because trade unions and other interest groups tend to be fairly closely controlled or monitored by the dominant party and bureaucracy. Figure 1 shows that the main examples in Asia are Japan, Malaysia, Singapore, Sri Lanka and India. India's federal system is perhaps a hybrid case in that the country's national politics tend toward the semicompetitive, while the individual states tend toward the competitive.

Bureaucracies in such regimes tend to be responsive to the political or policy agenda of the party (or parties) that have the support of the electorate. However, they also have considerable autonomy in relation to the government of the day, their actions being shaped by what they perceive as an underlying political consensus usually expressed in a constitution and accompanying legal arrangements and interpretations. Such bureaucracies are found in the competitive polyarchal regimes of Australia and New Zealand. The bureaucracies in Australia, for example, are normally responsive to the policy agenda of the government as expressed in legislation in the national and state parliaments. Although these parliaments approve legislation affecting the bureaucracy, including budgets, there is little doubt that the major instruments of administrative control are the national and state cabinets. The cabinet is, in Walter Bagehot's words, "a hyphen which joins, a buckle which fastens politics and administration." In Australia the cabinet's overall control has certainly been effective as long as its parliamentary majority has been maintained. At the same time, detailed political control is probably more pronounced in the states than in the country as a whole, and more effective in a small state such as Tasmania than in large and populous ones such as New South Wales and Victoria. One reason is that state ministers tend to be more closely involved with their departments because state parliaments sit less often than the national one in Canberra.

Bureaucracy in semicompetitive polyarchal regimes can also be, broadly speaking, both relatively autonomous and responsive to cabinets accountable to national legislatures. There are in addition notable differences in regular relationships between politicians and bureaucrats. In Japan, for example, the relationship has been in some ways unique. Government bureaucrats and political leaders in the dominant Liberal Democratic party (LDP) have been closely interlocked with one another since the late 1940s, both in fact and in the popular consciousness. There is also little dispute about which of these two is the more senior and influential. In Japan, it has been said, "the politicians reign and the bureaucrats rule"; the LDP has been "commonly regarded as largely an extension of the civil service." [19] Japan has always had an especially strong administrative branch ever since its Prussian-inspired constitution of 1889. Japan's military expansion, economic development and involvement in war in the first half of the 20th century resulted in the bureaucracy becoming accustomed to leadership. The impact of the United States occupation on the bureaucracy was considerably less than on other areas of the state and society. Such historical factors help to demonstrate why the Japanese bureaucracy has been a dominant influence in the postwar political regime. Another factor is regular recruitment to the civil service of the ablest graduates of an elitist educational system, thereby reinforcing the bureaucracy's influence and status. Also important has been the practice known as *amakudari* (descent from heaven), whereby senior civil servants normally retire early to enter politics or private firms—a practice that has resulted in many of the leading politicians of the ruling LDP being former civil servants. These practices help to explain why, in Japan, there has been comparatively little attention given to political control of the bureaucracy as a problem. The political tradition in Japan legitimizes the position of the bureaucracy within the state as a powerful and responsible body representing the national interest. However, the Japanese buuracracy is not completely autonomous. Behind it, so to speak, sits the Japanese cabinet responsible to the Diet with at least formal political control.

There was not the same cozy intermingling in the other semicompetitive polyarchal regimes of Malaysia, Sri Lanka and India. All three experienced British colonial rule through the mid-20th century, and when independence came, new political leaders retained colonial bureaucracies virtually intact. Colonial bureaucrats were used to ruling without much interference

[19] C. Johnson, *MITI and the Japanese Miracle* (Stanford, California: Stanford University Press, 1982), 316; J. Stockwin, *Japan: Divided Politics in a Growth Economy*, 2nd ed. (London: Weidenfeld and Nicolson, 1982), 149.

from politicians, and so in the early years of these semicompetitive regimes relations between inexperienced politicians and seasoned bureaucrats were not particularly easy. Invasions of bureaucratic autonomy were common. Such conflicts were comparatively mild in Malaysia. First, hardly any indigenous officers had entered the administrative elite prior to World War II and when the British left the new political elite did not feel threatened by the administrators because they were also new. Second, "many Malay nationalist leaders came from the civil service and, whether they left the civil service to enter politics or stayed on in it, they were very much part of the same group."[20] Such conflicts were more intense in India and Sri Lanka because indigenous officers were firmly entrenched in the administrative elites at the time of independence. Political struggles between these two sides were much in evidence while this generation of civil servants worked its way through the system. The governor of the Indian state of Bihar in 1962–1967, for example, remarked candidly in an account of his experience there that he "never felt that either the ministers or the officers seriously addressed themselves to economic and social problems," so preoccupied were they with their political struggle, with each other.[21] In Sri Lanka in early 1960s, an elite civil servant reportedly told a member of parliament that the reason for the shortage of water buffaloes in the country at that time was that "the buffaloes are now in Parliament."[22]

By the 1980s, the bureaucrats in these Indian, Malaysian and Sri Lankan regimes were probably more amenable to political direction and control. In India the bureaucracies at the center and in the states had never been out of control anyway. There was the law and the constitution. There was the power of the central and state cabinet that could and did make decisions regarding senior bureaucratic appointments. Ministers at the heads of government departments had the power to transfer bureaucrats, a very important sanction that normally ensured bureaucratic compliance. Even members of the celebrated, elite Indian Administrative Service were transferred with amazing speed—one complained that an administrative officer "is always a bird of passage . . . a gypsy," and "the whirl or merry (misery)-go-round of transfers goes on continuously."[23] Bureaucratic organizations also had to account for their behavior to parliamentary or legislative assembly committees and other external agents (e.g., ombudsman, comptroller and Auditor General), and these devices kept bureaucrats on their toes. Political and other constraints on India's responsible and relatively autonomous bureaucracy were still in operation in the 1980s. For example, the transfer market was still very brisk. A majority of the entire Indian Administrative Service was still unable to hold an elite post such as district

[20] M. Puthucheary, "The Administrative Elite," in *Government and Politics of Malaysia,* ed. Zakaria Haji Ahmad (Singapore: Oxford University Press, 1987), 95.
[21] M. A. Ayyangar, "Administration of a State as Seen by a Governor," *Management Perspective* (Delhi) 7 (April–June 1969): 38.
[22] Ceylon, House of Representatives, *Parliamentary Debates* vol. 48 (Sept. 10, 1962), col. 2738.
[23] Cited in D. Potter, "IAS Mobility Patterns," *Indian Journal of Public Administration* 33, no. 4 (Oct.–Dec. 1987): 845–56.

collector or secretariat officer or manager of a public enterprise for more than 12 months on average before being moved on. One other factor is worth mentioning. By the mid-1980s all bureaucrats employed by the central government had spent their entire working lives operating in a political context dominated by the Congress party (except for the brief Janata party interlude of 1977–1979). It is hardly surprising that attitude surveys of them suggested that they broadly subscribed to the ideology of the dominant party—a characteristic phenomenon in semicompetitive polyarchal regimes that have been in existence for some time.

Although the term bureaucratic state has been widely used in describing Asian bureaucracies, it is not used in this essay because it is useless for comparative analyses. All nations have bureaucracies and in no nation does the bureaucracy rule in the absence of political control by others. Regimes which would come closest to being bureaucratic states are the two remaining types in Figure 1: royal autocratic regimes and colonial regimes. In the former the bureaucracy is certainly the dominant political institution, although it is still subject ultimately to the political leadership of the royal court, as in Nepal and Brunei. As for the bureaucracy in colonies such as Hong Kong and New Caledonia, the governor is appointed in London or Paris and he then chooses his top officials who enjoy ministerial as well as bureaucratic status. The situation of any particular colony, of course, has never been quite that simple; it was, for example, commonly said in the mid-1980s that Hong Kong "genuflects to London but prays to Beijing."

BUREAUCRATIC POWER

Finally, there is the problem of the power of the bureaucracy in Asian societies. The first thing to say is that the problem is not one that relates exclusively to the bureaucracy. Asian bureaucracies are inextricably part of, and controlled more or less by, the political regimes in which they are located. When a political leadership decides on a course of action, it is principally the bureaucracy that translates that decision into a series of interventions in society. Even though the political and the bureaucratic may be said to be inseparable in this sense, it is the bureaucracy that is by far the most visible manifestation of the state's day-to-day relations with society or the public. Because of this high visibility, it is appropriate to focus on the problem of bureaucratic power while bearing the essential political context in mind.

Broadly speaking, bureaucratic power in society is more noticeable in Asia than elsewhere. The typology of the main Asian countries in Figure 1 shows 18 out of 27 are either communist party mobilization regimes, colonies, royal autocracies or regimes where the military is dominant either on its own or through a political party of its own creation. Such regimes are not polyarchic, that is, countervailing power centers in society other than the state are not allowed to develop in importance, and if they threaten to, they are crushed. The bureaucracy is thus the only significant instrument of power in such regimes. This poses a problem because unchecked bureaucratic power in society can become arrogant and brutal, and social life in such regimes can be, and frequently is, marked by state violence and human suffering.

Even in those comparatively few Asian regimes (9 out of 27) where polyarchy and political competition are present, at least to some extent, the bureaucratic presence in society is exceptional when compared to competitive polyarchal regimes elsewhere. The tough policing of Asian cities in such regimes is common. In Sri Lanka, for example, the usual pattern has been "armed security forces on street corners, security checks at government buildings, arrests and detentions of those suspected of subversive political activities, and extralegal operations carried out by security forces out of uniform."[24] Sri Lanka has been one of Asia's less authoritarian regimes; policing methods in most regimes have been even more direct in areas where the state's writ applies. On the whole, Asian peoples, particularly those of a more lively disposition, know their police bureaucracies only too well.

Turning from the law and order side of state activity in society to the role of the state in the economy, it is worth noting that most Asian countries have either command or planned economies. Such economies are controlled, more or less, by the bureaucracy. What is remarkable is that such bureaucratic control has also been a prominent feature of Asia's most advanced capitalist country—Japan. Japan's economic miracle has owed much to administrative guidance, that is the authority of the officials in the various ministries "to issue directions (*shiji*), request (*yōbō*), warnings (*keikoku*), suggestions (*kankoku*), and encouragements (*kansho*) to enterprises or clients within a particular ministry's jurisdiction."[25] Penalties for noncompliance have never been specified, but since such guidance has been normally couched in the national interest few objections have been possible. The Japanese press likes to cite the case of a bank executive who called on the ministry of finance to protest that his bank could not absorb the full quota of government bonds assigned to it by administrative guidance. A banking bureau official replied, "So you think your bank can survive even after Japan collapses? Go back and tell your president exactly what I said."[26] Even in Japan the scope and penetration of the bureaucracy in the economy has been noteworthy in contrast to the general Western practice of macro and micro interventions by the state taking much less interventionist forms.

Administrative guidance has also been central to the exceptional growth patterns in the newly industrializing countries of South Korea, Taiwan and Singapore. Bureaucratic intervention has been integral to the South Korean miracle:

> A firm that does not respond as expected to particular incentives may find that its tax returns are subject to careful examination, or that its application for bank credit is studiously ignored, or that its outstanding bank loans are not renewed. If incentive procedures do not work, government agencies show

[24] B. Pfaffenberger, "Sri Lanka in 1987," *Asian Survey* 28, no. 2 (February 1988): 147.

[25] Johnson, *MITI*, p. 265.

[26] *Mainishi Daily News*, 8 January 1976, cited in Johnson, *MITI*, pp. 266–67.

no hesitation in resorting to command backed by compulsion. In general, it does not take a Korean firm long to learn that it will "get along" best by "going along." Obviously, such a system of implementation requires not only cooperation among the various government agencies that administer compliance procedures but continuous consultation between firms and public officials.[27]

Such administrative guidance and command of the economy has been broadly the norm throughout Asia although Hong Kong is a clear exception.

Asia, then, stands out as marked by rather authoritarian regimes and heavy bureaucratic controls exercised in relation to the economy and the social order. Why? The question of bureaucratic power has been addressed from broadly two theoretical traditions in the West—Weberian and Marxist. Weberians explain bureaucratic power essentially in terms of its technical rationality and specialist expertise as well as its increasing necessity in society due to the increasing complexities of modern life. Marxists, by contrast, situate bureaucracy and the state within the class divisions and conflicts of industrial societies, and explain changes in their power in terms of the intensity of class conflict and the extent to which the bureaucracy must intervene to regulate the conflict and control the labor force so that the dominant class can continue to extract the surplus from the workers and make a profit. Neither theory, as it stands, is really useful for explaining the power of Asian bureaucracies. Indeed, a full explanation based on comparative analyses of Asian societies does not at present exist. A general explanation covering all Asian bureaucracies is unlikely to be very satisfactory. Each country has had a different political and economic history affecting the power of its bureaucracy. Nevertheless, there are three broad factors that would figure in any more detailed explanations: Asian colonialisms, Asian wars, and global pressures and ideologies.

Much of Asia experienced colonial bureaucratic rule subject only to general metropolitan control, and such bureaucracies were used to exercising power locally without much interference from others. Japanese colonialism in Korea and Taiwan was perhaps particularly aggressive in this regard. Most of these bureaucracies survived largely intact after independence. Even the Japanese bureaucracy was little disturbed by defeat in war and the United States occupation. It seems clear that an experienced, postcolonial bureaucracy in a nonpolyarchal, excolonial society tends to have more power in that society than a bureaucracy that has had a different historical experience. Also, it was widely believed during the colonial period that economic development in Asia had been blocked by the colonial presence; new Asian leaders naturally demanded rapid economic development to correct the colonial exploitations of the past. This was true even in Asian countries that were not colonies such as China. Planned development required greater effort by the state and in consequence bureaucracies grew in size and im-

---

[27] E. Mason et al., *The Economic and Social Modernization of the Republic of Korea* (Cambridge, Massachusetts: Harvard University Press, 1980), 255. Cf. more generally, F. Deyo. ed., *The Political Economy of the New Asian Industrialism* (Ithaca, New York: Cornell University Press, 1987).

portance after independence. These trends probably increased bureaucratic power in society.

For most of the latter part of the 20th century Asia has been the most violent region in the world. It seems there have always been wars and revolutions somewhere in Asia—China, Korea, Malaysia, Vietnam, Cambodia, the Philippines, Indonesia, India, Pakistan, Sri Lanka, Afghanistan. Violent conflicts can have profound social and political consequences, including a tendency to strengthen state bureaucracies. The consequences of World War II in Asia illustrate the point. For one thing, the war undermined the legitimacy of colonial rule. Over much of Asia European colonialists either fled or were captured and humiliated, even though the colonial bureaucracies remained and worked for the Japanese overlords. Sjahrir in Indonesia remarked that as a consequence of the war, "all layers of society came to see the past in another light. If these barbarians [the Japanese] had been able to replace the old colonial authority, why had that authority been necessary at all?"[28] The war enhanced the political importance of the military. It also habituated many people to violence as a way of life. The war transformed the size and shape of economies, calling into being new industries, enlarging existing ones and moving people from the countryside to towns. An aggressive, dominant class of industrialists and other economic leaders was strengthened with the assistance of the state although there was no corresponding increase in the strength of organized labor. State leaderships beefed up their bureaucracies to cope with these class and other conflicts. The war also altered patterns of ownership and control. Governments became much more heavily involved in the direction, planning and control of the economy as part of the war effort. Bureaucracies swelled in size where settled governments, still functioned. These and other consequences of World War II were the breeding ground for authoritarian political tendencies and powerful bureaucracies.

Finally, changes in the power of Asian bureaucracies can also be explained with reference to the effects of global processes. For example, in the mid-1980s the reformist thrust of *glasnost* (openness) and *perestroika* (reconstruction) in the Soviet Union was beginning to hit the Asian communist world. Changes in the character of communist regimes and the bureaucracies' roles in them were increasingly affected by these ideological shifts, as mentioned above in the case of China. As for the noncommunist Asian nations, many of them appeared by the mid-1980s to be substantially entangled in the economic constraints of the global capitalist system. Bureaucracies and their modes of operation were likewise affected by these constraints. This seemed particularly the case for South Korea, Taiwan, Singapore and Hong Kong, whose bureaucracies appeared slimmer, more expert and more autonomous. Perhaps the power of Asian bureaucracies in general may begin to reduce in the future. In short, it is becoming increasingly difficult to understand the changing character of any single Asian bureaucracy without reference to wider Asian and global concerns.

[28] Cited in C. Thorne, *The Far Eastern War: States and Societies 1941–45* (London: Unwin Paperbacks, 1986), 301.

FURTHER READING

Braibanti, Ralph J. D., ed. *Asian Bureaucratic Systems Emergent from the British Imperial Tradition.* Durham, North Carolina: Duke University Press, 1966.

Harding, H. *Organizing China: The Problem of Bureaucracy, 1949–1976.* Stanford, California: Stanford University Press, 1981.

Johnson, Chalmers A. *MITI and the Japanese Miracle: The Growth of Industrial Policy, 1925–1975* Stanford, California: Stanford University Press, 1982.

Potter, David C. *India's Political Administrators, 1919–1983.* Oxford: Clarendon Press; New York: Oxford University Press, 1986.

Raksasataya, A. and Siedentopf, H., eds. *Asian Civil Services: Developments and Trends.* Kuala Lumpur: Asian and Pacific Development and Administration Centre, 1980.

Weidner, F., ed. *Development Administration in Asia.* Durham, North Carolina: Duke University Press, 1970.

POLITICAL PARTIES

HARUHIRO FUKUI

A sprawling domain straddling the equator along the western edge of the Pacific Ocean, Asia and the Pacific islands have 150 organizations, commonly recognized as political parties, in 27 of the 36 independent polities that currently exist in the area.[1] If we regard each of the several stable coalitions of parties as a de facto single party, there are still about 125 parties to account for. It is impossible to discuss each of these parties individually in a short article such as this. Fortunately, they can be divided into several distinctive categories by the type of party system to which they belong.

Political parties can be defined and party systems classified in a number of ways, but the definition and classification proposed by Giovanni Sartori serve our purposes as well as any other. A political party is, according to Sartori, "any political group that presents at elections, and is capable of placing through elections, candidates for public office."[2] His classification of party systems consists of seven types: One-party, hegemonic party, predominant party, two-party, moderate pluralism, polarized pluralism and atomized.[3] Of these seven types, all but the last two are found in Asia and the Pacific islands.

---

[1] The 36 polities include two in China (the People's Republic of China and Taiwan) and two in Cambodia (Democratic Cambodia and the People's Republic of Kampuchea), as well as two in Korea (the Democratic People's Republic of Korea and the Republic of Korea). Nine of them, however, do not have an unambiguously identifiable party at the present time, as we shall see later. The 15 nonindependent territories in the area are excluded from our discussion: Hong Kong, Macao, Spratly and Paracel Islands, Micronesia (Trust Territory of the Pacific Islands), American Samoa, Guam, Wake Island, Pitcairn Island, New Caledonia, French Polynesia, Wallis and Futuna, Cook Islands, Niue, Tokelau and Norfolk Island. None of these territories currently has a bona fide political party.

[2] Giovanni Sartori, *Parties and Party Systems: A Framework for Analysis* (Cambridge, England: Cambridge University Press, 1976), p. 64. For a sample of alternative definitions, see p. 62.

[3] Ibid., pp. 125–28. Sartori explains the differences between a hegemonic party and a predominant party system and between a moderate pluralism and a polarized pluralism system as follows: In a hegemonic party system, "[O]ther parties are permitted to exist, but as second class, licensed parties; for they are not permitted to compete with the hegemonic party in antagonistic terms and on an equal basis."

TYPOLOGY OF PARTY SYSTEMS

Five states in the area currently have a one-party system. These are Mongolia, Cambodia, Laos, Burma (now Myanmar) and Afghanistan. All five are located in mainland Asia; four of them are under self-proclaimed Marxist and one (Burma) under pseudo-socialist rule. In this area, as in other parts of the world, a one-party system thus embodies or mimics the classic Leninist ideal of a vanguard proletarian party.

Only one of the five one-party systems, however, appears to be stable. Mongolia has been continuously and exclusively ruled by the Mongolian People's Revolutionary party since the founding of the republic in 1924, and there are no visible signs of an imminent collapse of the regime.[4] Afghanistan and Cambodia, on the other hand, have both suffered from chronic political instability since independence—achieved, respectively, in 1919 and 1954—and during the last decade from a state of civil war triggered in both cases by an armed foreign intervention.

Throughout the decade of Soviet military presence, the government in Kabul, installed by the Soviets and sustained by the one-party rule of the People's Democratic Party of Afghanistan, has met persistent and increasingly effective resistance by nearly a dozen guerrilla groups.[5] Now that the Soviet troops have left the country, the regime faces an uncertain future. The state of the government in Phnom Penh, installed by the Vietnamese a decade ago and since maintained by the one-party rule of the Kampuchean People's Revolutionary party (KPRP), has been almost identical. It has been subjected to determined and devastating challenges by a rival government, Democratic Kampuchea, based on a coalition of three opposition groups and their guerrilla units.[6] A substantial Vietnamese military presence has so far averted the collapse of the KPRP government, but the departure of the Vietnamese troops—scheduled to be completed by 1990—

A predominant party system, on the other hand, is a variant of a pluralist party system in which "[p]arties other than the major one not only are permitted to exist, but do exist as legal and legitimate—if not necessarily effective—competitors of the predominant party." A moderate pluralism system is "characterized by (i) a relatively small ideological distance among its relevant parties, (ii) a bipolar coalition configuration, and (iii) centripetal competition." A polarized pluralism system, on the other hand, is characterized by "the presence of relevant *anti-system parties,*" which amounts to saying that there is a large ideological distance among its relevant parties, "the existence of *bilateral oppositions,*" which leads to multipolar competition, and "the center placement of one party . . . or of a group of parties," which discourages centripetal competition. See pp. 132–35, 179, 195, 230.

[4] Arthur S. Banks, ed., *Political Handbook of the World 1987: Governments and Intergovernmental Organizations as of March 15, 1987* (Binghamton, N.Y.: State University of New York/CSA Publications, 1987), pp. 392–94.

[5] Ibid., pp. 3–5, 312–16; Kyodo tsushinsha, *Sekai nenkan '88* [World Yearbook, 1988] (Tokyo: Kyodo tsushinsha, 1988), pp. 238–39; Tonan ajiya chosakai [Southeast Asia Research Association], *Tonan ajiya yoran: 1988–ban* [Southeast Asia Handbook, 1988 ed.] (Tokyo: Tonan ajiya chosakai, 1988), p. 15/4.

[6] Kyodo tsushinsha, pp. 210–11; Tonan ajiya chosakai, pp. 3/3–3/5; Banks, pp. 312–16.

raises distinct prospects of a merger of the two rival regimes, if not a replacement of the People's Republic by the Democratic Republic, and an inevitable collapse of the one-party system.

The one-party rule by the Burma Socialist Program party has also met recurrent armed as well as verbal challenges from a host of Marxist and ethnic insurgent groups since its inception in 1962, and vastly more widespread and determined opposition in 1988.[7] The survival of the Burmese system is thus now as much in doubt as that of both Afghanistan and Cambodia. Nor has the durability of the similar regime in Vientiane based on the Lao People's Revolutionary party (LPRP) been proven. While this regime does not currently face as well organized and effective an opposition as those in Afghanistan, Cambodia and Burma do, the long-promised National Assembly election is yet to be called, a fact that suggests the LPRP's failure to date to build a solid nationwide base of support.[8]

A hegemonic party system is also found in five polities in the area: North Korea, China, Taiwan, Vietnam and Indonesia. Of these five, three are self-professed Marxist regimes, while the other two (Taiwan and Indonesia) are right wing, authoritarian regimes. The first three are located in Northeast Asia and the last two in Southeast Asia. In practice, all of them are nearly indistinguishable from the one-party systems mentioned above, except that the hegemonic parties tolerate the existence of a few other, though practically powerless, minor parties.

Compared to most one-party systems, the hegemonic party systems appear considerably more stable, thanks partly to the greater cohesiveness and sophistication of their ruling elites, partly to the greater economic and military capabilities of their states that discourage foreign interventions and partly to the presence of legal, even if nominal, opposition. In the two noncommunist hegemonic party systems, Taiwan and Indonesia, there is limited, but more than purely nominal, electoral competition between the ruling parties, the Nationalist party (Kuomintang) and the Golkar (Gologan Karya), respectively, and the opposition parties, Taiwan's Democratic Progressive party and Indonesia's United Development party (Partia Persatuan Pembangunan) and Indonesian Democratic party (Partai Demokrasi Indonesia).[9]

In the three Marxist regimes, the legal opposition is more purely symbolic and this makes these regimes more closely resemble the one-party systems. Even a purely symbolic opposition, however, must help a hegemonic party regime maintain a regular channel of communications with, keep tabs on and occasionally co-opt disaffected and potentially hostile and subversive groups, such as intellectuals. One or another of such roles seems to be played by the North Korean Democratic party and the Chondokyo Young Friends' party for the Korean Workers' party;[10] the China Demo-

---

[7] Banks, pp. 84–86.
[8] Kyodo tsushinsha, pp. 207–208; Banks, pp. 336–38.
[9] Kyodo tsushinsha, pp. 176–77, 198.
[10] Haruhiro Fukui, ed., *Political Parties of Asia and the Pacific* (Westport, Conn.: Greenwood Press, 1985), vol. I, pp. 651–53.

cratic League, the China Democratic National Construction Association, the Revolutionary Committee of the Kuomintang, for the Chinese Communist party;[11] and the Vietnam Socialist party and the Democratic party for the Vietnamese Communist party.[12]

More common than either one-party or hegemonic party systems in this area are predominant party systems. Nine states—Singapore, Malaysia, Philippines, India, Pakistan, Sri Lanka, Bangladesh, Japan and Vanuatu—currently have such systems. As this list indicates, they are widely scattered over the whole area: three in Southeast Asia, four in South Asia and one each in Northeast Asia and in the Pacific. Within each system, the predominant party currently controls substantially more than one half the seats in the national legislature or, in the case of a bicameral parliament, in the popularly elected and usually more powerful lower house.

Of the nine systems of this type found in this area, Singapore's under the People's Action party rule, Malaysia's under the National Front's, India's under the Indian National Congress-Indira's and Japan's under the Liberal Democratic party's are the most stable, with their (and their immediate antecedents') more or less continuous predominance stretching back for more than three decades and, in the INC-I's case, for more than a century.

Singapore's People's Action party had totally monopolized parliamentary seats until 1981, when for the first time it conceded a seat to the opposition Workers' party in a by-election.[13] In 1984, the PAP lost another seat to the Singapore Democratic party, thus retaining 77, or 97 percent, of the 79 seats. Since its founding in 1974, Malaysia's National Front has won in parliamentary elections as consistently and nearly as overwhelmingly as Singapore's PAP. In the most recent House of Representatives election held in 1986, the NF won 84 percent of the 177 seats.[14] The Indian National Congress-I lost one lower-house (Lok Sabha) election to the newly founded Janata party in 1977, but regained its predominant position in the next lower-house election in 1980.[15] It has since maintained that position and currently controls about three-quarters of the 544 lower-house seats. Japan's Liberal Democratic party has not lost a single national Diet election since it was founded in 1955 and it currently controls about 59 percent of the 512 seats in the House of Representatives.[16]

Among the other predominant party systems in the area, the United National party rule in Sri Lanka dates back to 1977.[17] Its future, however, is increasingly in doubt in the face of the mounting communal tension and violence between the Sinhalese majority and the Tamil minority. In the case of Bangladesh, it is almost perverse to call its present system a pre-

---

[11] Ibid., vol. II, pp. 1112.
[12] Ibid., vol. II, pp. 1112–13, 1179–80.
[13] Ibid., vol. II, p. 983; Banks, p. 520; Tonan ajiya chosakai, p. 6/4.
[14] Fukui, vol. II, pp. 752–54; Banks, pp. 370–72; Tonan ajiya chosakai, p. 5/9.
[15] Fukui, vol. I, p. 335; Tonan ajiya chosakai, pp. 11/5–11/6; Banks, p. 260.
[16] Fukui, vol. I, pp. 554–56.
[17] Ibid., vol. II, pp. 1048–55; Tonan ajiya chosakai, p. 10/3.

dominant party system, or any other kind of party system for that matter, in the absence, albeit temporary, of an elected parliamentary institution. General Hussain Mohammed Ershad, who has rules the country since 1982, first as chief martial law administrator and then as president (since 1983), declared a state of emergency in November 1987, and disbanded the national parliament.[18]

The parliamentary election called in 1986 was boycotted by the coalition of seven opposition parties, the Bangladesh National party, making its results highly problematical as a measure of the true strength of any party. Among the parties that participated in the controversial election, the ruling National party (Jatiyo Dal)—a four-party coalition of the People's party (Jana Dal), the United People's party, the Democratic party and the Bangladesh Muslim League—won 153, or 51 percent, of the 300 elected seats in the national parliament. Of the remaining 147 seats, the Awami League took the lion's share of 76, followed by Jama'at-i-Islam with 10 and 8 others with 5 or fewer seats each. As a result of subsequent realignments, the National party's strength was raised to 208, or 63 percent of the 330 seats, including 30 reserved for women representatives.[19] The 1988 parliamentary election was also boycotted by the opposition and the National party won 83 percent of the seats. In appearance alone, Bangladesh thus has a pseudo-predominant party system at the present time, but the circumstances of the last two general elections and, more importantly, the suspension of the parliament itself make it nearly meaningless to place it in any category of party system.

Pakistan's case is even more problematical. While the Pakistan Muslim League (PML), the present party nominally in power, finds its roots in the All India Muslim League, formed in 1906, and a few other extant parties date back to the 1940s, Pakistan has been under the rule of military and marshal law regimes for the greater part of its history since its independence in 1947.[20] Most recently, since the end of 1985, the country has been free from marshal law and political parties free from legal ban. Under the circumstances, a vaguely predominant party pattern has emerged in the competition between the PML and an opposition coalition, the Movement for the Restoration of Democracy, led by the Pakistan People's party.[21] Apparently genuine party pluralism followed legislative elections held in 1988, which resulted in the appointment of Benazir Bhutto as prime minister.

The Philippine Democratic party-People's Power Movement coalition, known as the PDP-Laban, is too young to be considered a well-established predominant party. It was founded in 1983 as an opposition coalition and became the country's predominant parliamentary party only in the 1987

[18] Banks, pp. 45–46; Kyodo tsushinsha, pp. 234–35; Tonan ajiya chosakai, p. 14/1.
[19] Banks, pp. 47–48.
[20] Fukui, vol. II, pp. 877–79; Tonan ajiya chosakai, p. 13/1; Banks, pp. 443–45.
[21] Banks, pp. 446–47.

general election.[22] Vanuatu's is also a problematic case for similar reasons. The country's history of electoral politics is very short, Vanuatu having been independent only since 1980. Moreover, while the ruling Vanuaaku Pati won 57 percent of the 46 parliamentary seats in the 1987 election, its share of the vote fell below 50 percent for the first time.[23] With the steady rise in the popularity of the opposition Union of Moderate Parties, the case looks increasingly like a two-party rather than a predominant party system.

There are four Westminster-style two-party systems in the area. Australia and New Zealand have the oldest and most stable systems of this type. In both, a well-entrenched labor party—the Australian Labor party (ALP) was founded in the 1890s and the New Zealand Labour party (NZLP) in 1916—and its rival—a coalition of the Liberal and National parties in Australia and the New Zealand National party—have dominated nearly every parliamentary election and alternated in power.[24] At present, the ALP controls about 58 percent of seats in the lower house of the bicameral federal parliament and the NZLP about 60 percent of seats in the unicameral House of Representatives.

In the two much younger and smaller Pacific island states, the two-party pattern is only emergent and far from stable. In both, the uncertainty caused by the recency of their independence and the youth of their party systems is compounded by the highly parochial and personal nature of politics. The history of Western Samoa's system is short; the Human Rights Protection Party, which won about two-thirds of the 47 seats in the unicameral Legislative Assembly in 1985, was formed in 1979, while its rival, and the only other party in the country, the Christian Democratic party, did not exist until 1985.[25]

Fiji has a longer history of party politics. For 17 years there was a predominant party system under the rule of the Fijian-based Alliance party. This ended in 1987 when a coalition of the Indian-based National Federation party and the newly formed Fiji Labour party won about 54 percent of the 52 lower-house seats in a general election.[26] Moreover, the election of the first Indian prime minister led to two bloodless coups d'état, renunciation of the constitutional ties to the British crown and de facto restoration of Fijian supremacy. Amidst the turmoil, the fledgling two-party system may have been replaced by a de facto one-party, if not no-party, system.

Four examples of party pluralism are found in the area, two in countries with a long history of military government and periodic coups d'état, the Republic of Korea and Thailand, and two in young Pacific island countries, Papua New Guinea and the Solomon Islands. In South Korea, a predominant party pattern had prevailed until the 1988 election for the 299-member unicameral National Assembly when the ruling Democratic Justice party

---

[22] Ibid., p. 449; Tonan ajiya chosakai, p. 8/8.
[23] Kyodo tsushinsha, p. 270; Banks, p. 652.
[24] Fukui, vol. I, pp. 21–24, vol. II, pp. 847–49.
[25] Ibid., vol. II, p. 1198; Banks, p. 668.
[26] Banks, p. 190; Kyodo tsushinsha, p. 268.

(DJP) failed to win a majority of seats, while two or three major opposition parties made a strong showing.[27] The DJP won 42 percent of the 299 seats, followed by the Party for Peace and Democracy with 23 percent, the Reunification Democratic party with 20 percent and the New Democratic Republican party with 12 percent.

In Thailand, a pluralist pattern has been gradually taking shape since about 1980 and now appears to be somewhat more stable than in South Korea. In the 1986 election for the 347-member House of Representatives, a dozen legal parties, differentiated more by the personalities of their leaders than by ideology or policy, competed.[28] The Democrat, Thai Nation, Social action and People's parties won, respectively, about 29 percent, 18 percent, 15 percent and 4 percent, or a total of 67 percent, of the total and formed the new ruling coalition. The remainder of the legal parties, that is, with the exception of the illegal Communist party of Thailand, automatically formed a parliamentary opposition.

Since the late 1960s, electoral politics in Papua New Guinea have been characterized by competition and alternation in power between a series of coalitions led by Pangu Pati and rival coalitions led, formerly, by the People's Progress party and, currently, by the People's Democratic Movement.[29] In the 1987 general election, the anti-Pangu coalition won about 51 percent of the 109 seats in the unicameral House of Representatives.[30] The system may be thus regarded as two-party, rather than pluralist, but, unlike Malaysia's National Front, the rival coalitions that form at the time of election in Papua New Guinea are strictly temporary and their memberships are extremely loose and shifting. For this reason, it makes sense to count each individual party within each temporary and precarious coalition as an independent party unit. Since the 1987 election, a six-party anti-Pangu ruling coalition led by the People's Democratic Movement has been in power.

The Solomon Islands has evolved a loose three-party pattern since 1973 when the first parliamentary election was held in the island country.[31] In the most recent (1984) election, however, it was replaced by a more diffuse pattern, with the Solomon Islands United party winning 13 of the 38 seats, the People's Alliance party 12, independents 7, My Land (Solomon Agu Sogufenua) 4 and the National Democratic party 1, with 1 seat left unfilled.

In seven of the nine remaining states in the area, including Cambodia, no parliamentary party exists at the present time. In the Kingdom of Nepal, parties have been banned by royal decree since 1960, and members of the 140-seat National Assembly (Rashtriya Panchayat) are all independents, at least nominally.[32] In the nearby Kingdom of Bhutan, no legal party has

---

[27] Fukui, vol. I, pp. 663–64; Banks, pp. 331–32.
[28] Banks, p. 585; Tonan ajiya chosakai, p. 4/5.
[29] Fukui, vol. II, pp. 940–42.
[30] Banks, pp. 456–57.
[31] Fukui, vol. II, pp. 999–1000; Banks, pp. 522–23.
[32] Banks, p. 411; Tonan ajiya chosakai, p. 12/3. But see also Narayan Khadka,

ever been formed—an illegal Bhutan National Congress is based in northeastern India—and the 151 National Assembly seats are all filled with appointed members, 12 representing religious (Lamaist) groups, 34 government agencies and the remaining 105 the "people."[33] In the Sultanate of Brunei, where several parties have been organized since the early 1960s, the 21 members of the Legislative Council are also all appointed, and even this nonelective body has been suspended since 1984.[34] In the fourth monarchical state in the area, the Kingdom of Tonga, one-half of the 18 Legislative Assembly seats are filled with nobles and the other half with elected "representatives of the people."[35] No political party is involved in either case.

The Republic of Maldives has a partially elected 48-member Citizens' Assembly (Majlis). Eight of them are appointed by the president of the republic and the remainder are elected by all adult citizens.[36] No political party exists, however. The three island mini-states in the Pacific—Kiribati, Nauru and Tuvalu—all have elective legislatures, with 39, 18 and 12 seats, respectively.[37] Kiribati and Nauru have one organized party each, called, respectively, the Christian Democratic party and the Democratic Party of Nauru, while members of Nauru's parliament have formed two fairly durable rival factions since the 1986 election.

COMMONALITIES AND VARIATIONS WITHIN EACH SYSTEM

Some parties in each of the several types of party systems found in Asia and Pacific islands share at least one important characteristic. In all one-party systems, for example, one party monopolizes legitimacy and power and constitutes government by itself. In all hegemonic party systems, the ruling party permits another party or parties to exist and cooperate, but not to compete, with it. There are, however, also considerable differences among parties in different states.

Parties in similar positions in one-party systems in the area are all self-consciously revolutionary, populist and ideologically puritanical. Those in Mongolia, Cambodia and Laos officially call themselves "people's revolutionary" parties and the one in Afghanistan "people's democratic" party. Burma's non-Marxist Burma Socialist Program party is direct heir to the group of military officers who engineered the 1962 coup d'état and then called themselves the Revolutionary Council.

While the ruling parties in these one-party systems do not permit the existence of any other parties, three of them have built and maintain under their strict control a mass-based front organization which acts as their eyes

"Crisis in Nepal's Partyless Panchayat System: The Case for More Democracy," *Pacific Affairs* 59, no. 3 (Fall 1986), 429–54.
[33] Banks, p. 62; Fukui, vol. I, p. 91.
[34] Fukui, vol. I, pp. 94–95.
[35] Banks, p. 589.
[36] Ibid., p. 374.
[37] Ibid., pp. 322, 409, 603.

and ears to monitor and mobilize public opinion in support of the regime and its policy. The Kampuchean People's Revolutionary party thus has its Kampuchean United Front for National Salvation, the Lao People's Revolutionary party its Lao Front for National Reconstruction and the People's Democratic Party of Afghanistan its National Front.[38] The Mongolian People's Revolutionary party and the Burma Socialist Program party have so far managed without the aid of such an organization to keep tabs on the pulse of society, but only at an increasingly visible cost, especially in Burma's case.

The ruling parties in the four communist one-party systems in the area were all born in polities under either direct foreign rule or indirect but strong foreign influence. They came into being either in reaction against or in response to such foreign physical or psychological presence, and that, in a sense, provided their raison d'être. The oldest among them, the Mongolian People's Revolutionary party, was formed in 1921 when the country was simultaneously under formal Chinese rule and informal but powerful Soviet influence.[39] It was not until January 1946, that the Chinese rule was officially removed, while the Soviet influence has not only continued but has steadily increased over the years.

The Kampuchean People's Revolutionary party was originally organized as a section of the Vietnamese-dominated Indochinese Communist party in the wake of World War II when the country, along with Vietnam and Laos, remained under French rule.[40] Subsequently, the party established dominance over rival political forces during a protracted civil war, which lasted until 1975, and in which American and Vietnamese forces extensively intervened. The Lao People's Revolutionary party emerged from the same source as its Cambodian counterpart in the mid-1950s, following the formal termination of French rule, and also built its power base throughout the country during a subsequent civil war in which American and Thai armed forces were extensively involved.[41]

By contrast, the People's Democratic Party of Afghanistan (PDPA) was founded in 1965 in the absence of direct and visible foreign intervention but in the shadow of formidable Soviet political and military presence across the border and, in fact, with implicit Soviet support.[42] In 1978, the party engineered a coup d'état, in collaboration with a group of pro-Soviet army officers, against General Mohammad Daud's increasingly pro-Western government. The next year, Soviet forces invaded and occupied Afghanistan, a move that has apparently failed to help the PDPA consolidate its rule. The withdrawal of Soviet troops in the face of determined opposition by several guerrilla groups, left the PDPA's future, and that of Afghanistan uncertain.[43]

[38] Ibid., pp. 5, 316, 337; Tonan ajiya chosakai, pp. 2/6–2/7, 3/9, 15/3–15/4.
[39] Fukui, vol. II, pp. 791–93.
[40] Ibid., vol. I, pp. 634–35; Tonan ajiya chosakai, p. 3/7.
[41] Fukui, vol. II, pp. 691–95; Tonan ajiya chosakai, p. 2/5.
[42] Fukui, vol. I, pp. 16–17.
[43] William Maley, "Political Legitimation in Contemporary Afghanistan," *Asian Survey* 27, no. 6 (June 1987), 705–25.

The only noncommunist one-party system in the area, the Burma Socialist Program party, and the country it rules now face political instability and uncertainty nearly as great as Afghanistan's. Unlike the four communist parties mentioned above, the BSPP was formed in 1962 in a country not subject to either direct foreign intervention or significant foreign influence.[44] Neither was available as a justification for its creation or perpetuation and the party was to succeed or fail on its own merit. The chronic failure of economic policies and the resulting deterioration of living conditions throughout the country have bred a host of opposition groups, mostly associated either with the Burma Communist party or with the coalition of several ethnic minority organizations, the National Democratic Front, both of which have dramatically escalated their antigovernment activities in the last few years. The Burma Socialist Program party's one-party rule thus appears as precarious as that of the People's Democratic party in Afghanistan.

Even greater variations are found among parties in parallel positions in the five hegemonic party systems in the area. Similar to some of those in the one-party systems, three of the five hegemonic parties were born in reaction to foreign rule or dominance. The Chinese Communist party was established in 1921 in the aftermath of a widespread nationalist outburst against Japanese imperialism known as the May Fourth Movement.[45] The Chinese Nationalist party, known more commonly as Kuomintang, is even older, having its roots in a small nationalist group organized by Sun Yat-sen in Hawaii toward the end of the 19th century.[46] If the CCP became an embodiment and vehicle of peasant nationalism, the KMT spoke for and mobilized nationalism among China's fledgling urban bourgeoisie.[47] Likewise, the Vietnamese Communist party was founded in 1930, originally in Hong Kong, to organize and lead an Indochina-wide movement for national liberation against French colonial rule.[48] All these three parties won a hegemonic position in their respective country only through victory in a protracted and extremely costly civil war.

By comparison, the Korean Workers' party and Indonesia's Golkar somewhat resemble the People's Democratic Party of Afghanistan and the Burma Socialist Program party, respectively. The former was organized in North Korea in 1945, after Japanese surrender, with support and protection provided by the Soviet Union.[49] This is a case of a communist party planted as a hegemonic party from the beginning in a country already freed from colonial rule. Golkar was originally set up in 1958 as a substitute for real

[44] Fukui, vol. I, pp. 122–25.
[45] Ibid., pp. 182–86.
[46] Ibid., pp. 214–15.
[47] Chalmers Johnson, *Peasant Nationalism and Communist Power: The Emergence of Revolutionary China* (Stanford: Stanford University Press, 1962); Paul K. T. Shih, ed., *Nationalist China during the Sino-Japanese War, 1937–1945* (New York: Exposition Press, 1977).
[48] Tonan ajiya chosakai, p. 1/7.
[49] Robert A. Scalapino and Chong-sik Lee, *Communism in Korea*, 2 vols. (Berkeley: University of California Press, 1972); Dae-Sook Suh, *The Korean Communist Movement, 1918–1948* (Princeton, N.J.: Princeton University Press, 1967).

political parties upon President Sukarno's initiative, and it was subsequently developed and used by Sukarno's successor, General Suharto, for similar purposes.[50] It is a case of an anticommunist hegemonic party originally created by an opportunistically procommunist civilian dictator and then perpetuated by an anticommunist military dictator.

Unlike those in one-party systems, all of the five hegemonic party systems permit the survival and, in some cases creation, of largely powerless and nominal opposition parties. As pointed out earlier, in the People's Republic of China eight such parties, referred to as "democratic parties and groups," have maintained their token existence since the prerevolutionary days. These are the China Association for the Promotion of Democracy, the China Democratic League, the China Democratic National Construction Association, the China Zhigongdang, the Chinese Peasants and Workers Democratic party, the Jiusan Society, the Revolutionary Committee of the Kuomintang and the Taiwan Democratic Self-Government League. Taiwan also has two older, though virtually inactive, parties, the Chinese Youth party and the Democratic Socialist party, and two newer ones, the Democratic Progress party and the Labor party.[51]

Their counterparts in Vietnam, the Vietnamese Democratic party and the Vietnamese Socialist party, date back, respectively, to 1944 and 1946. During the first (1946–54) and second (1959–75) Vietnam wars, both were affiliated, first, with the Viet Minh and Lien Viet united fronts and, later, with the Vietnam Fatherland Front.[52] Since the fall of Saigon in 1975, they have remained the Vietnamese Communist party's noncommunist but loyal partners. Indonesia's Golkar also tolerates the survival of two other parties, or rather coalitions of parties, the United Development party (Partai Persatuan Pembangunan) and the Indonesian Democratic party (Partai Demokrasi Indonesia). Both were formed in 1973 through the merger of all existing Muslim and non-Muslim parties, respectively, under the so-called "simplification" program.[53] They continue to seek and win modest shares of seats in Indonesia's partially elected pseudo-parliament, the People's Representation Council (Dewan Perwakilan Rakyat).

All the five hegemonic party systems were once dominated by strong and charismatic leaders: Mao Zedong, Chiang Kai-shek, Kim Il-sung, Ho Chi Minh and Suharto. Mao, Chiang and Ho have passed away and been succeeded by leaders far less powerful and charismatic who have moved away, to varying degrees, from their predecessors' highly personal, ideological and rigid styles of rule. The new leaders in these three systems have all begun to loosen government control of the economy and, to a much more limited extent, of society and politics. Indonesia's Suharto and North Korea's Kim remain in power and in their rigidly authoritarian postures, but their deaths are likely to lead to developments similar to those in the other three countries.

[50] Fukui, vol. I, pp. 392–96.
[51] Banks, p. 121.
[52] Fukui, vol. II, pp. 1168–69, 1180; Tonan ajiya chosakai, p. 1/10.
[53] Fukui, vol. I, p. 383; Tonan ajiya chosakai, p. 7/6.

Parties in the predominant party systems are still more diverse than those in either one-party or hegemonic party systems. Of the three such parties that exist now in Southeast Asia, Singapore's People's Action party looks almost like a hegemonic party, having virtually monopolized all seats in the parliament.[54] Moreover, it maintains nearly as tight party discipline under an extremely strong leader as a ruling party in either a one-party or a hegemonic party system. In the most recent parliamentary election, held in 1984, it won 77 of the 79 seats, yielding one each to the Workers' party and the Singapore Democratic party. It is nonetheless a predominant, rather than a hegemonic, party since it wins as spectacularly in essentially free and competitive elections held at regular intervals.

In terms of electoral strength alone, Malaysia's National Front comes close to Singapore's PAP, having won 84 percent of the 177 parliamentary seats in the 1986 elections.[55] There are, however, some important differences between the two parties. While the PAP is a single party, the NF is a 13-party coalition dominated by the United Malays National Organization (UMNO), which alone won more than half of the NF seats in the 1986 elections. The UMNO is thus clearly the senior partner in the coalition, but the coalition is run and maintained by a collegial leadership group, rather than a single individual leader.

Behind the organizational difference between the PAP and the NF lie two polities with fundamentally different demographic and social structures. The PAP is a Chinese party in a country in which Chinese account for 76 percent, Malays 15 percent and Indians and Pakistanis 7 percent of the total population, while Malaysia is a country in which Malays comprise 46 percent, Chinese 32 percent, non-Malay tribal population 12 percent, and Indians and Pakistanis 8 percent.[56] Given the multiracial character of its population and its history of racial conflicts, most notably in the wake of the 1969 parliamentary elections, an interracial coalition is a logical, and probably the only, option available to Malaysia, if it is to maintain the level of political stability and the pace of economic and social development it has maintained in recent years. The NF has so far endured to a remarkable degree the tensions and stresses inherent in this type of coalition.

The Philippine Democratic Party-Laban coalition, which was formed before and won over 70 percent of the 250 congressional seats in the 1987 election, is a much looser one whose durability is yet to be tested.[57] The coalition consists of three erstwhile anti-Marcos groups: the People's Power Movement (Lakas ng Bayan), founded in 1978 by the late Benigno Aquino and Lorenzo Tañada, the Pilipino Democratic party and the United Nationalist Democratic Organization, the last two founded in 1982. Legal opposition by the former Marcos machine, the New Society Movement (Kilusan Bagong Lipunan) and the rumps of two older parties, the Nacion-

---

[54] Fukui, vol. II, pp. 972–73; Banks, p. 520.
[55] Fukui, pp. 752–54; Banks, p. 372; Tonan ajiya chosakai, p. 5/9.
[56] Kyodo tsushinsha, pp. 212, 215.
[57] Banks, p. 470; Tonan ajiya chosakai, pp. 8/3–8/4; *The Strait Times*, May 14, 1987.

alista party of 1907 and the Liberal party of 1946, is badly divided and ineffectual, as the results of the 1987 congressional elections proved. Nor do challenges from illegal radical groups, notably the Communist Party of the Philippines and the Moro National Liberation Front, pose immediate peril to Aquino's government. The system, however, faces a far more serious threat from the continuing disaffection, mainly over economic issues, both among army ranks and urban and rural masses.

Parties in the three predominant party systems in South Asia are just as diverse. The Indian National Congress-Indira is one of the oldest political parties in Asia and has continuously dominated India's federal-level politics both before and after independence, except for a brief three-and-a-half-year period in the late 1970s. Led now by the late Indira Gandhi's son, Rajiv Gandhi, INC-I faces no major threat to its predominance from the divided and ineffectual parliamentary opposition. The Janata party that defeated the INC-I in 1977, now has only a dozen Lok Sabha seats and is overshadowed by both Telugu Desam, led by the popular film star Nandamuri Taraki Ram, which controls about 30 seats, and the Communist Party of India-Marxist with about 20 seats.[58] The remainder of the lower house seats are divided among several other minor parties: the Communist Party of India, the Tamil-based All India Dravidian Progressive Federation, the Assam People's Council (Assam Gana Parishad), the Punjab-based Shiromaki Akali Dal and so forth.

The INC-I's popularity, however, has been on the wane at the state and local levels. In the latest series of state legislative elections, the INC-I has suffered major defeats in several states, such as Mizoram, West Bengal, Kerala and Haryana.[59] Clearly, center-local and intercommunal relations—what may be called a Punjab syndrome—pose the most serious danger to the survival of the INC-I's continuing predominance.[60]

Sri Lanka's United National party is much younger and much less predominant than the INC-I. Founded in 1946, the party has been in power longer than any other party in the country, but not as continuously as the INC-I. At the present time, it controls 83 percent of the 168 parliamentary seats, dwarfing its parliamentary opposition—made up of the Sri Lanka Freedom party, and the Communist Party of Sri Lanka—even more than the INC-I.[61] Meanwhile, however, violent extraparliamentary opposition by radical Tamil organizations, notably the Liberation Tigers of Tamil Eelam and its associated groups, has drastically escalated in the last few years and threatens the survival of the Sinhalese-dominated predominant party system.

[58] Banks, p. 267; Tonan ajiya chosakai, p. 11/3.
[59] Kyodo tsushinsha, pp. 228–29.
[60] Gurharpal Singh, "Understanding the 'Punjab Problem,' " *Asian Survey* 27, no. 12 (December 1987), 1268–77; T. R. Sharma, "Defusion and Accommodation: The Contending Strategies of the Congress Party and the Akali Dal in Punjab," *Pacific Affairs* 59, no. 4 (Winter 1986–87), 634–54. See also the four articles under the general title of "Politics in Punjab," *Pacific Affairs* 6, no. 1 (Spring 1987).
[61] Banks, p. 554; Tonan ajiya chosakai, p. 10/2.

Notwithstanding the number of salient differences mentioned above, most of the predominant party systems in Asia and the Pacific islands do share at least one important characteristic: factionalization. Just as a predominant party system is more tolerant of interparty diversity and competition than either a one-party system or a hegemonic party system, individual parties in a predominant party system tend to be more tolerant of intraparty diversity and competition. Moreover, by and large, a predominant party is a catchall party that embraces, or attempts to embrace, wide-ranging interests without imposing the degree of discipline and conformity upon them that a ruling party in a one-party or hegemonic party system tends to impose. The result is a proclivity toward decentralization of power and intraparty disputation that often takes the form of factionalism.

Even Singapore's PAP, which now stands out for its degree of party unity and discipline, once experienced severe factional strife between the so-called radicals and moderates during the first decade of its life, leading to the radicals' departure from the party in 1961.[62] The party has since remained united under Lee Kuan Yew's austere leadership, at least superficially, as have its largely powerless opposition, the Worker's party and the Singapore Democratic party.

Malaysia's NF suffered in the late 1970s a defection by a member party, Partai Islam, and conflict over control of the Chinese vote between two predominantly Chinese members—the Malaysian People's Movement (Gerakan Rakyat Malaysia) and the Malaysian Chinese Association.[63] Like Singapore's PAP, the NF has since managed to maintain a facade of unity to a remarkable extent. The state of factionalism in Malaysia's opposition parties is hard to gauge, but one of the most important among them, the Pan-Malaysian Islamic party, has been known as a faction-ridden party.[64] The other major opposition party, the Democratic Action party, which is an offshoot of Singapore's PAP, appears to have been relatively free from serious factional contention.

By comparison, the factional groups among parliamentary members of Japan's LDP are so entrenched and influential that each looks like an independent party and the LDP a coalition of several independent parties.[65] Ever since the party was founded in 1955, balancing the interests of several competing factions has been a primary consideration in the appointment not only of all important party officials but also of cabinet ministers and chairmen of Diet committees under the LDP's control. At the present time, five such factions, each led by one of the most influential party leaders, make up the LDP's parliamentary contingent. In a Diet election, LDP candidates run as representatives of an intraparty faction as well as of the party and compete as vigorously with each other as with opposition party

---

[62] Fukui, vol. II, pp. 980–82.
[63] Ibid. p. 754.
[64] Ibid., pp. 755–60; Tonan ajiya chosakai, pp. 5/13–5/14.
[65] See Nobuo Tomita et al., "The Liberal Democratic Party: The Ruling Party of Japan," in Ronald J. Hrebenar, *The Japanese Party System: From One-Party Rule to Coalition Government* (Boulder, Colo.: Westview Press, 1986), pp. 248–69.

candidates. This boosts the amounts of energy and money invested in election campaigns both by individual LDP candidates and by the factions, and that in turn indirectly but substantially helps the LDP as a whole to keep winning against the opposition as consistently as it has been doing.

Among Japan's opposition parties, the two older ones, the JCP and, especially, the JSP, have experienced periodic bouts of factional conflicts, sometimes resulting in the expulsion or defection of dissidents and general weakening in each party's electoral performance.[66] The much younger CGP and DSP have fared considerably better in this respect, but to the extent they have been affected by factionalism, both have clearly suffered at the polls.[67]

The LDP's experience with beneficial effects of intraparty factionalism is thus unique even among Japanese parties. For other parties in Japan and other countries, factionalism almost invariably hurts, rather than benefits, them electorally and otherwise. In the case of India's venerable INC, factional conflict led to formal splits in 1969 and 1977, giving birth to splinter parties known, respectively, as the INC-Organization and the INC-Urs, subsequently renamed INC-S after the name of Urs's successor, Sharad Pawar.[68] It was not until 1986 that these two splinter parties were reunited with the INC-I and the latter's predominant position was stabilized.

The impacts of factionalism on the INC-I's main opposition are quite similar. The Janata party has been afflicted with destructive factional conflict ever since the coalition party was founded in 1977.[69] In 1980, a protracted dispute between those associated with the former Indian People's Union (Bharatiya Jana Sangh) and those associated with the former Indian People's party (Bharatiya Lok Dal) led to the fall of the Janata party government led by Morarji R. Desai. Shortly thereafter, the party lost one of its most influential leaders, and a former INC stalwart, Jagjivan Ram, in a continuing factional dispute. The tradition of factionalism has been inherited by the two parties that have split off the Janata party—the People's party (Lok Dal) and the Bharatiya Janata party.[70] The same tradition even pervades India's communist opposition, as the presence of multiple competing communist parties—the Communist Party of India, the All India Communist party, the Communist Party of India-Marxist, and the Communist Party of India-Marxist-Leninist—suggests.[71]

Pakistan's PML has a similar, and even worse, record of crippling factionalism that has over the years given rise to a host of splinter parties,

---

[66] See J. A. A. Stockwin, "The Japan Socialist Party: A Politics of Permanent Opposition," and Peter Berton, "The Japan Communist Party: The 'Lovable' Party," in Hrebenar, *The Japanese Party System,* pp. 83–115, 116–44.

[67] See Ronald J. Hrebenar, "The Komeito: Party of 'Buddhist Democracy,' " and "The Democratic Socialist Party: Enigma of the Center," in Hrebenar, *The Japanese Party System,* pp. 147–208.

[68] Fukui, vol. I, pp. 330–37; Banks, p. 264.

[69] Fukui, vol. I, pp. 340–42.

[70] Banks, p. 265; Fukui, vol. I, p. 302.

[71] Fukui, vol. I, pp. 308–15; Tonan ajiya chosakai, pp. 11/6–11/7.

each bearing a PML label with a suffix.[72] These include the PML-Convention and the PML-Council, both formed in 1962; the PML-Qayyum, which split off from the PML-Council in 1964; and the PML-Chatha, the PML-Qasim and the PML-Forward Bloc, all formed in 1978. A similar proclivity for fragmentation characterizes Pakistan's opposition, especially the coalition of the major opposition parties, the Movement for the Restoration of Democracy.[73] Almost as soon as it was formed in 1981, the 12 parties, and their subdivisions, making up the grand coalition began to fight each other. This made it virtually impossible to develop a coherent program of action against the government. The tradition continues to the present day in both the PML and the opposition coalition.

Sri Lanka's United National party has, since the early 1950s been spared open and damaging factional strife. Then, the party was nearly paralyzed by a severe factional struggle under the leadership of Dudley Senanayake and John Kotelawala.[74] In the UNP's traditional rival, the Sri Lanka Freedom party, there was a period in the early 1980s of intraparty conflict between those supporting the former party leader and prime minister, Sirimavo R. D. Bandaranaike (then deprived of her civil rights on charges of corruption), and those rallying behind the interim party leader, Maithripala Senanayake.[75] The conflict has apparently been overcome. The main threat to party unity, both in the ruling UNP and in the opposition, including the Communist Party of Sri Lanka, now comes from the escalating Sinhalese-Tamil racial tension.[76] The issue in fact threatens the physical unity of Sri Lanka itself.

It is too early to try to identify the patterns of intraparty conflicts, not to mention measure their impacts, in the Philippines' PDP-Laban, Bangladesh's National party, Vanuatu's Vanua'aku Pati, and their respective rivals. It is almost certain, however, that the long tradition of factionalism in the Philippines and Bangladesh will continue to shape party politics in both countries.[77]

Parties in similar positions in the seven two-party systems found in the area resemble one another as much as those in the one-party and hegemonic party systems and far more than those in the predominant party systems. Australia and New Zealand have provided not only a model party system but, to an important extent, also model party organization and behavior for the four island countries that have adopted a two-party system.

In the 1987 House of Representatives election in Australia, the Australian Labor party won 58 percent and the Liberal party 29 percent of the

[72] Fukui, vol. II, pp. 918–24.
[73] Banks, p. 446.
[74] Fukui, vol. II, pp. 1048–55.
[75] Ibid., p. 1043; Banks, pp. 552–53.
[76] Bruce Matthews, "Radical Conflict and the Rationalization of Violence in Sri Lanka," *Pacific Affairs* 59, no. 1 (Spring 1986), 28–44; Robert N. Kearney, "Territorial Elements of Tamil Separatism in Sri Lanka," *Pacific Affairs* 60, no. 4 (Winter 1987–88), pp. 561–77; Tonan ajiya chosakai, p. 10/1.
[77] Fukui, vol. I, pp. 40–41, vol. II, 950–52; Tonan ajiya chosakai, p. 14/3.

148 seats.[78] This may appear to give the ALP what amounts to a position of predominance. In the tradition of federal elections in Australia, however, this kind of spread is perfectly normal and does not mean by any means that the LP has been wiped out, nor, for that matter, the National Party of Australia, which won the remaining 13 percent of the seats.[79] Not only are the shares of the two opposition parties quite respectable, but, more importantly, those two parties have a long history of alliance against the ALP. In fact, the ALP's 1987 victory was won largely thanks to a split between the LP and the NPA, but after the election they have patched up the conflict and restored the traditional alliance.[80] Finally, the ALP's popularity has been on the wane since the election, as suggested by its defeat in an important state legislative election in New South Wales in 1988. There is thus every likelihood that the well-established two-party tradition will survive for many more years, if not indefinitely. Exactly the same statement applies to the Labour party's victory in the 1987 New Zealand House of Representatives election. Labour's share of 60 percent and the National party's 40 percent of the 97 seats represent a perfectly normal division in this two-party system.[81]

The high degree of stability and predictability of the two-party systems in Australia and New Zealand is a result of the ideological moderation and pragmatic bent in the two parties' (particularly the labor party's) approach to politics in both countries. Over the years, domestic economic and social issues, as distinguished from highly emotional or ideological issues, have dominated parliamentary debates and election campaigns in normal times in both countries, especially in the last two decades. In this and other respects, the two systems and the two pairs of parties are nearly interchangeable not only in appearance but also in behavior.

Western Samoa's currently ruling Human Rights Protection party and its only opposition party, the Samoan National Development party, also pragmatically interact with each other in a manner conducive to a two-party system.[82] Unlike their counterparts in either Australia or New Zealand, most (45 out of 47) of Western Samoa's Legislative Assembly members are elected by a group of family heads, known as the *matai*, rather than by the people. As the likelihood of universal adult suffrage in the near future increases, the future of this country's two-party system becomes more problematical, particularly considering the generally weak party identity among Legislative Assembly members.

Fiji's two-party system is even more problematical, as already suggested. Here the cause of the uncertainty is the latent, but increasingly manifest, racial tension between Indians, who are a bare majority among the total population but control much of the island's economy, and Fijians, who are a minority in their native country, although they still own the bulk of the

[78] Banks, p. 34.
[79] Fukui, vol. I, pp. 22–24.
[80] Banks, p. 32.
[81] Ibid., p. 422.
[82] Fukui, vol. II, p. 1197; Banks, p. 668.

land.[83] While the two major parties, the Alliance party and the National Federation party, are both nominally multiracial in their membership composition and officially advocate multiracialism, the former is in fact predominantly Fijian both in membership and policy, while the latter is predominantly Indian.[84] Their leadership seems increasingly vulnerable to pressures from racial extremists among their own ranks. The 1987 coup d'état, and subsequent developments, is a sign of the trend. Moreover, the major parties are flanked by small but vocal extremist groups on the fringe, such as the Fijian Nationalist party and the Taukei Liberation Front. How much longer this two-party system may survive is open to question.

Among the four moderate pluralism systems found in the area, South Korea and Thailand share a tradition of military coups d'état and rule by martial law. Both, however, now appear to have finally outgrown that tradition and are moving into a system of electoral politics based on more or less free, and relatively pragmatic, competition among multiple parties. Thailand is less ambiguous on this score, thanks to the relatively longer history of its major parties.

Thailand's strongest contemporary parties are the oldest ones. Of the 15 parties that participated and won seats in Thailand's 1986 House of Representatives election, the Democrat party (Prachatipat), which won 29 percent of the 347 seats, was founded in 1946 and is the country's oldest party.[85] Both the second- and third-ranking parties after that election, Thai Nation (Chat Thai) with 18 percent of the seats and Social Action (Kit Sangkom) with 15 percent, were founded in 1975.[86] The remaining 12 are all younger parties, most of them formed just before the 1986 election. While some of these may not last very long, the presence and success of the older ones gives the Thai system of party pluralism an air of stability and durability.

In the case of South Korea, a more real sense of uncertainty lingers owing to the youth of both the system itself and the parties that constitute it, especially on the opposition side. The ruling Democratic Justice party was founded as recently as 1981, but it is the oldest surviving party in the country where the three opposition parties, the Party for Peace and Democracy, the Reunification Democratic party and the National Democratic Republican party, were all formed as recently as 1987, to help their respective leaders fight the presidential election held in December of that year.[87]

In both countries, parties are built around prominent personalities rather than on the basis of policy or ideology. In Thailand, such personalities come either from aristocratic families—as in the case of the founder of the Democrat Party, Khuang Aphaiwong, and the founder of the Social Action party, Kukrit Pramoj—or from the ranks of military leaders, as in the case

---

[83] Banks, p. 190; Kyodo tsushinsha, p. 268.
[84] Fukui, vol. I, pp. 273–74.
[85] Banks, pp. 583–84.
[86] Fukui, vol. II, pp. 1071–73, 1075–76.
[87] Banks, pp. 326–27.

of Major-General Pramarn Adireksan and his associates who founded the Thai Nation party.[88] South Korea does not have a surviving aristocracy comparable to Thailand's, but personalities play just as pivotal a role in the formation and maintenance of a South Korean party as they do in a Thai party. The DJP was launched originally as President Chun Doo Hwan's support group and has been inherited by the general's successor, Roh Tae Woo.[89] Likewise, the opposition parties, the PPD, the RDP and the NDRP, were formed by and for Roh's three challengers in the 1987 presidential election, namely, Kim Dae Jung, Kim Young Sam and Kim Jong Pil. This integral association with particular personalities works against institutionalization of party rules and functions, adding to the sense of uncertainty and unpredictability.

In the two Pacific island countries that currently have a system of moderate party pluralism—Papua New Guinea and the Solomon Islands—personal and local connections play an even more central part in politics in general and in the formation and development of political parties in particular.[90] Policy and ideology have a marginal role. Papua New Guinea's People's Democratic Movement, which currently leads the anti-Pangu ruling coalition, is a group that split off Pangu Pati in 1985 under the direction of the present prime minister, Paias Wingti.[91] The second ranking partner in the ruling coalition, the National party, and the third ranking partner, the Melanesian Alliance, are based, respectively, in the Highlands and Bougainville, while Pangu Pati's strength lies mainly in Port Moresby.

The Solomon Islands' parties are formed more closely around particular personalities. The Solomon Islands United party currently holds a plurality of seats in the national parliament; it was founded in 1979, and is still led by a former prime minister, Peter Kenilorea. Its principal rival, the People's Alliance party is a product of a 1979 merger of the People's Progressive party and the Rural Alliance party, founded and led, respectively, by Solomon Mamaloni (another former prime minister) and David Kausimae.[92] The other opposition party, the Solomon Islands Liberal party, has been led by a fourth prominent political leader in the islands, Bartholomew Ulufa'alu.

CONCLUSION

The brief sketches of political parties and party systems in Asia and the Pacific islands show that they are just as diverse and complex as the peoples who inhabit the area, despite a number of commonalities found among some of them. While the effects of a country's party system and individual parties on its society and economy cannot be discussed in a short article, they are no doubt just as diverse and complex. A glance at relevant data

[88] Fukui, vol. II, pp. 1057–59.
[89] Banks, pp. 331–32; Fukui, vol. I, p. 665.
[90] Fukui, vol. II, pp. 941–42, 999–1000.
[91] Banks, p. 456.
[92] Ibid., p. 523.

would quickly convince one that there is no simple and consistent relationship between the type of party system and parties a country has on the one hand and the conditions and standards of living on the other. While some countries without a legal party and party system may be poorer than some with a legal party and party system, the oil-rich Sultanate of Brunei and the phosphate-rich Republic of Nauru, both with no legal parties, have a higher gross national product per person than, respectively, Australia and New Zealand with model, two-party systems.[93] What kind of particular natural resources a country is endowed with, rather than what kind of party system it has, often determines its standard of living as measured by GNP per person. Likewise, India and Bangladesh, both with a predominant party system, have as low a GNP per person as their tiny party-less neighbors, the Maldives and Bhutan. Taiwan with an anticommunist hegemonic party system has achieved incomparably faster economic growth and a higher GNP per person than the People's Republic of China with a communist hegemonic party system.

As is the case with any other political institution, the social and economic impacts of a party system or of an individual party are thus indirect, subtle and extremely hard to trace and measure. Yet, a party system clearly matters to many people in Asia and the Pacific islands, as it does to those in other parts of the world, presumably because it is the most economical and reliable (if not necessarily the best) mechanism through which diverse and contending interests within a society can be peacefully and efficiently negotiated and adjusted. A brief survey of the different forms in which such a mechanism appears in Asia and the Pacific islands does not tell one which is better or worse. Rather, it does lead one to believe that a country does not choose but accepts a particular party system imposed by its particular historical circumstances. In short, the foregoing discussion implicitly argues as much for attention to the specific characteristics of each country's party system and the specific circumstances that account for such characteristics as for attention to general patterns and trends.

FURTHER READING

Banks, Arthur, S., ed. *Political Handbook of the World, 1987: Governments and Intergovernmental Organizations as of March 15, 1987*. Binghamton, New York: State University of New York Publications, 1987.

Day, Alan J., and Degenhardt, Henry W., eds. *Political Parties of the World*. Detroit: Gale, 1980.

Fukui, Haruhiro, et al., eds. *Political Parties of Asia and the Pacific*. 2 vols. Westport, Connecticut: Greenwood Press, 1985.

Inter-Parliamentary Union. *Parliaments of the World: A Reference Compendium*. Berlin and New York: De Gruyter, 1976.

[93] World Bank, *World Development Report 1988* (New York: Oxford University Press, 1988), pp. 222–23, Table 1. Basic Indicators.

RELIGION AND POLITICS
IN ASIA

JUDITH NAGATA

THE fact that religion and politics have a number of characteristics in common may contribute to the frequency with which they seem to invade each other's domains, creating loyalties which are sometimes conflicting, sometimes complementary. Both are essentially concerned with issues of power and authority at all levels, from that of the individual and local community to a larger zone whose limits may correspond with a political state or to the maximal, an imagined community of the faith such as "Christendom" or Islam's *ummat*. In principle, the kinds of power appropriate to religion and politics derive from different sources, one more transcendental, even thaumaturgical, the other preoccupied with matters more secular or profane. In practice, however, they often become entangled as much of the history of Asia attests. Both may rely on similar strategies and institutions for their effects, although their appeal may be based on substantially different myths and ideologies.

This raises a second point of comparison. Both religion and politics create systems of meaning and generate their own types of discourse, emotions, rationalities and blueprints for existence. Above all, they provide sources of legitimacy for authority and social action, often of compelling urgency. Religious and political systems are rich in symbolism, through which their goals are mediated and justified. Finally, both also tend to assume moralistic tones that are judgmental, ethical and immune to further question.

Occasionally it happens that the boundaries of a nation coincide with, and are legitimated by, a single religious faith. But more commonly, the religious "community" is less physically compact and cuts a swath across several countries. This may be referred to as an "imagined community,"[1] in the sense of an ideological, moral universe transcending the barriers of mundane, nonsacred communities and interests. In matters of identity, citizenship in a state may compete with religious loyalties, and in the rela-

---

[1] Benedict Anderson, *Imagined Communities: Reflections on the Origin and Spread of Nationalism* (London: Verso, 1983).

tionship between these often lie some of the most contentious and divisive social problems of a nation.

THE MAJOR RELIGIONS OF ASIA

In the study of comparative religions there is a basic distinction between so-called "universalistic" and "particularistic" faiths. Universalistic religions are those ideally that recruit and evaluate their memberships exclusively on the basis of acceptance to their tenets and on meritorious practice of these doctrines. It should be a body of believers and practitioners of a shared moral tradition and behavior, irrespective of other identities or loyalties, whether political, ethnic or social. Orthodoxy thus is judged purely on performance, not on birth or other kinds of status. In theory such religions are culturally neutral in that the religious ethos is supposed to transcend lesser distinctions of local custom, ethnic preference and, of course, national obligations. In certain cases, too, the very processes of involvement in intense religious experiences and rituals generate emotions of an order different from those of secular society, setting up a kind of religious kinship independent of preexisting social ties.

Religious particularism by contrast is found where a faith is exclusively identified with, or appropriated by, a specific social, ethnic or political group, thus reinforcing the community's boundaries. Recruitment is restricted, usually by birth; legitimacy is symbolized by faith and cult. The faith here is as much an expression of a status and identity as a creed or set of beliefs alone, and this can produce a formidable combination of loyalty and interest. For obvious reasons, proselytization and conversion are not encouraged, although these aspects are customary in universalistic religions.

Of the four principal religions found in Asia, three—Buddhism, Christianity and Islam—fall into the universalistic category, whereas Hinduism represents a closer approximation of the particularistic variety. At the risk of overgeneralization, it could be argued that followers of Hinduism (which is itself something of a composite, obscured by a single label applied by outsiders) are more likely to be members by birth in an Indian community, in India or overseas. Full participation in Hinduism can only be achieved through membership and kinship in Indian life. Recognition of the intimate relationships among religion, caste, occupation, genealogy and other uniquely Indian social institutions underscores the obstacles facing any potential convert. Ideally, Hindu religion and society exist in a seamless whole from the individual to the state.

A possible parallel to Hinduism is Shintoism whose integral role in Japanese cultural history reinforces the unity and uniqueness of Japanese society at a level of intensity and meaning deeper than that of the Buddhist and other institutions later grafted upon it.

The apparent dichotomy between particularistic and universalistic religions, however, must not be overdrawn. It cannot be assumed a priori that in practice Islam, Christianity and Buddhism are much more detached from the social and political identities of their followers than is Hinduism from the Indian community in actual situations. In fact these three religions have become so thoroughly absorbed, in symbol and practice, into the local customs and political cultures of particular peoples and nations that it often makes little sense to attempt to abstract "religion" as an independent category of ideas, behavior and institutions.

In most Asian societies, especially in Southeast Asia, Islam, Theravada Buddhism and certain forms of Christianity have become substantially indigenized to the extent that religious and political systems have come to draw heavily upon each other's resources and are mutually supportive. The symbols of the one provide reference points for the other, and the religious ethos frequently sets the tone for society at large. Thus Theravada Buddhism supplies the ethical and institutional underpinning of Thai society as well as a thread of continuity capable of weathering the vicissitudes of monarchical, civilian and military government crises. Likewise, Burmese Buddhism exerts a continuous modifying effect on the socialist character of the country's official regime, and still governs much of the behavior at the village level. In a more disturbing manifestation of particularism, Buddhism has assumed a central symbolic role for the Sinhalese population of Sri Lanka in its ongoing struggle for national identity and dominance vis-à-vis "alien" Tamil immigrants.

Islam plays a comparable role in Malaysia and to some extent in Indonesia where it is identified with certain segments of the local population that now regard it as an inalienable part of their ethnic identity, a quality acquired by birth and blood. Thus Islam reinforces the cleavages among Malays, Chinese and Indians in Malaysia, and among certain core groups in Indonesia and some of the peripheral outer island populations.

In the Philippines it is Catholicism that has shaped much of the country's colonial and recent history and politics. In a very literal sense, the church has become so indigenized regarding local customs, that a uniquely native Aglipayan branch of the church emerged around 1900. In removing "Roman" from its brand of Catholicism, and by asserting local power and authority over that of the pope, the church has become more Asian than European. More recently, the proclivity of Catholicism to generate and promote new saints has found expression in cults of local Filipino political heroes. Among these are cults of José Rizal, a liberator of the Philippines from Spanish rule, and Benigno Aquino, slain opponent of the Marcos regime; shrines and chapels have been dedicated to both of these men.

In all of the above cases, a major world religion of apparent universalistic character has become particularized for the identity and needs of a specific nation or people. The end product bears a closer resemblance to Hinduism or Shintoism than might be anticipated. From another angle, Malaysian and Indonesian Islam have, for example, developed their own distinctive characters, recognizably different from the Islam of Pakistan, Afghanistan or Iran. And Buddhism too has its own national variants. The process of indigenization represents forms of practical religion, not necessarily fully in line with (and occasionally even counter to) the theology and practices of their respective faiths, to the point where they may be considered by some purists as certainly less than orthodox. In the religions with the strongest literate and legal traditions, particularly Islam and Christianity, such discrepancies have often been the sources of debate and discord. One prominent example of extreme political controversy arises from the different interpretations of practices of Islam in Malaysia and Indonesia. In Malaysia the division is between those who infuse their Islam with local custom (*adat*) and the Koranic Muslims (represented by the Kaum Muda or by *dakwah* factions, depending on the era). Indonesian Islam is split among orthodox *Santri* and their "Indonesianized" coreligionists, aristocratic *priyayi* and village *abangan*. In both societies, these religious divisions have provided a frame of reference for pressing social and political issues, including those pertaining to local authority and the qualities of leadership.

This lack of perfect congruence between theological orthodoxy and social practices underscores the need of the political observer to pay attention to "practical religion,"[2] and it is to this mainly that the present essay will be directed. The relationship between politics and religion deals less with text than context, although the textual references are always available as sources of political ammunition and legitimation. For this reason, no attempt to provide theological accounts of the four religions under consideration will be made, but instead there will be a focus on their local manifestations as the bases for comparison.

RELIGION AS A LEGITIMATION OF POWER AND AUTHORITY

As noted above, religious and political communities are founded on different bases and principles: one on shared belief and practice, the other on territorial grounds; and these do not necessarily coincide. At worst, the two sets of loyalties result in tension, competition and conflict. This antagonism appears to enhance the strength of European-style nationalisms at the expense of traditional religious allegiances with their sacred cultures and languages. Despite pressures for detachment of religious from political affairs in Europeanized national bureaucracies and technocratic regimes created by colonial powers, the evidence suggests that religion plays a continuing and lively role in many Asian countries. Historically, Asian political cultures, in the manner of medieval Europe, accommodated blends of sacred and secular powers; this tradition appears to have been reinvigorated under the current climate of religious resurgence in Asia. Indeed, for most Asian peoples, at most times, religion has been a serious factor in society at every level, endowing almost all action with meanings transcending the narrowly secular.[3] The arrival on the scene of national states after the European model may thus be seen as something of an anomaly in the local political order, one that probably contributed to the tension in many contemporary issues.

[2] Roy Ellen, "Practical Islam in Southeast Asia" in *Islam in Southeast Asia,* ed. M. Hooker (Leiden: Brill, 1983), 50–91.
[3] T. N. Madan, "Secularism in Its Place," *Journal of Asian Studies* 46, no. 4 (1987): 745–60.

What is most striking is the extent to which religion has been harnessed to political regimes and causes as a source of moral strength and support in all periods. Sometimes overlooked, however, is the fact that political leaders in their turn have also advanced the causes and acceptability of certain religions in their own domains by promoting and disseminating new faiths (or variants) for their subjects. Of course, it also frequently happens that political opposition by minorities or dissidents retaliates by recourse to the same weapon; religion is often used as a buttress for deviant movements, revivals and other popular causes. Each of the four major faiths in Asia has long played, and continues to play, a critical role in the legitimation of the political order from local community and village to the national level.

Hinduism and the political order
As a system of ideology, a moral charter and indeed a guide for a total way of life, Hinduism has the capacity to bind together all the elements of the Indian social order and to endow it with coherence and meaning. Hinduism justifies the pervasive pattern of caste and hierarchical authority, and was used to validate the status and trappings of traditional Indian rulers. Rajahs and zamindars were often scions of the martial Kshatriya caste; this status allowed them to perform the coercive and defensive functions of leadership. The priestly elements of the Brahmin caste performed the crucial rites of sacralization of kingship in what was essentially a relationship of complementarity. The central position of the monarch in the divine cosmological order survives today in a somewhat attenuated form in Nepal although it is extinct in India. The Indic idea of kingship was also carried to pre-Islamic Southeast Asia where it supported the monarchs of such early states as Srivijaya, Madjapahit and Bali in the Indonesian archipelago, and the rajahs of the original Malay states.

Although the modern independent nation of India is avowedly secular, and one where even Mahatma Gandhi's style of spiritual-political action may today have less appeal, the symbol and spirit of Hinduism is still potent enough to mobilize large sections of Indian society for certain political causes, whether in opposition to Muslim or Sikh groups or as a more general rallying call to criticize and embarrass the incumbent Congress party and government. This approach is a specialty of the Janata party which has been quite successful in recent years in reinjecting Hindu sentiments into political issues, and thus challenging political secularism. Manifestations of this new Hindu fundamentalism are reflected in urban devotional movements (*bhakti*) and in the increased incidence of widow immolation (*suttee*) now resurfacing. Various forms of religiously inspired caste improvement associations have also tried to tie Hindu religious philosophy to modernization by using inspirational activities for self-interested material and often undeniably political ends, including on occasion the fielding of sympathetic political candidates. The religious element in Indian politics, however, is strongly counterbalanced by a variety of secular institutions, notably branches of the powerful communist party in several states.

Recent political and communal crises have dramatically underscored the persistence of religion as a stimulus to political action and as a symbol of identity in that action. The salience of appeals to Islam or to Sikhism seem far to outweigh economic or other inequalities, or else they become symbolic of these perceived inequities. In the case of the territorial status of the Punjab, for instance, almost all the rhetoric and moral concern is religious on both sides.[4] From the days of the moguls, when Islam was the official faith of the rulers, to the present, Muslims have remained one of the principal groups of opposition to Hindu authority. This antagonism led to the genesis of Pakistan. Unlike most Sikhs and Hindus, Muslims are of course members of a wider, international religious community (*ummat*) which competes for their loyalties as citizens of India, Pakistan or Bangladesh.

Islam and the political order
Islam has never recognized any distinction between the sacred and the secular, between church and state. Rather it claims to encompass and provide a plan for all of social and political life under a chain of authority from God through the prophet Muhammad to any just leader who follows and promotes Islamic principles. By extension Muslims who find themselves citizens or residents of non-Muslim nations are enjoined to resist any national obligations that would contravene Islam, using force if necessary. Similarly good Muslims are encouraged to unseat unjust rulers or those who have forsaken Islamic principles. A recent case in point is the dramatic switch from a less to a more righteous source of authority in Iran. The shah and the Pahlavi dynasty, although officially Muslims, sought legitimacy through mythical Persian roots; the regime of ayatollah Ruhollah Khomeini, on the other hand, is squarely in the Islamic tradition of the sacred ruler who derives his authority from God alone.

In the rest of the Asian Islamic world, mostly in the Sunni tradition, political leaders often invoke religious support for their authority, and use Islamic symbols in the ceremonial trappings of office. The history of the original Islamic penetration of Southeast Asia[5] illustrates how regional rulers appropriated Islamic doctrines and interpretations to this end. In the process of conversion to Islam, one kind of moral authority was substituted for another: rajahs became sultans and a certain measure of "Arabization" or emulation of things Middle Eastern characterized cultural elites. From the 14th century on, the royal courts of the Malay peninsula and the Indonesian archipelago—in particular the early states of Aceh, Bantam, Mataram, Melaka and Johor—adopted the formal tenets and *Sharia* law of Islam for themselves as well as for their subjects who invariably emulated

[4] It is worth noting here that the Sikhs originally emerged as a sectarian offshoot of Hinduism, later to become a fullfledged "ethnic" group with political, territorial and secessionist aspirations, creating yet another particularistic religion.
[5] See, for example, Leonard Andaya's account of Malaysia in this Handbook; also M. Hooker, *Islam in Southeast Asia,* and M. C. Rickleifs, "Six Centuries of Islamisation in Java," in *Conversion to Islam,* ed. N. Levitzion (New York: Holmes & Meier, 1979), 100–28.

them by following them into the new faith.[6] Along with the doctrines and laws came the necessary interpreters and administrators, a new class of religious teachers with direct connections to the Holy Land. These court ulama not only provided religious services and translated texts but, like the Brahmins serving the rajahs in traditional India, they provided a validation of royal power. In some cases, the requisite credentials involved new genealogies that would link the Muslim rulers to a more Islamic past, so that the rulers of Aceh in Sumatra were found to have ties with Iskander (Alexander the Great) or a closer connection with the Middle East,[7] while the sultans of Brunei discovered ancient family origins in Muslim kingdoms in India and elsewhere.[8] Such claims were further elaborated in amendments to the original annals and genealogical court histories *(hikayat)* that endowed the royal heroes with impeccable religious credentials. Most of the mediation, instruction and administration of the faith was left in the hands of the ulama who introduced the *Sharia* courts and religious schools to local communities (kampongs). This educational network *(pondok* in Malaysia, *pesantren* in Indonesia) made Islam the way of life for most villagers.

In the fervor of nationalism, immediately preceding and following independence from colonial rule, other identities sometimes intruded upon the religious, creating conflicts. Today the Muslim leadership in the countries of Asia again draws selectively upon Islam for their credentials.

Indonesia: In the gestation period for independence in the Dutch East Indies (1920s and 1930s), leaders of several movements appealed to different interpretations of Islam for their causes. The Sarekat Islam, founded in 1912, promoted the interests of the commercial sector of the Muslim population[9] through a more liberal interpretation of the scriptures, permitting modifications to suit the needs of a modernizing society.[10] Sarekat Islam carried its reformist message successfully to the countryside and remote areas while simultaneously promoting the commercial interests of Arab and other merchants against the competition by the "infidel" Chinese. With the religious mission there was a strong anticolonial message that in the following decades grew more intense. With politicization the rhetoric be-

[6] *Sharia* law represents the "living" side of Islam, the code of principles and behaviors that guide Muslims in all facets of social life: rules of family, marriage and inheritance; personal comportment and hygiene; punishment of offenders, both sinners and criminals; and so forth. It is normally interpreted and administered in local areas (usually politically defined) by accepted Muslim scholars *(ulama)* in special *Sharia* courts.

[7] A. C. Milner, *Kerajaan: Malay Political Culture on the Eve of Colonial Rule* (Tucson: University of Arizona Press, 1982).

[8] D. E. Brown, "Hereditary Rank and Ethnic History: Analysis of Brunei Historiography," *Journal of Anthropological Research* 29, no. 2 (1973): 113–23.

[9] Clifford Geertz, *The Religion of Java* (Glencoe, Illinois: Free Press, 1960).

[10] The question of whether and how far the original scriptures of the Koran and the Hadith (acts and sayings of the Prophet) can be reinterpreted in different cultures and places continues a debate almost as old as the faith itself. Those scholars who advocate unchanging adherence to the letter of the originals *(ijma)* remain opposed to any trend supporting updating according to need *(ijitihad)*.

came more militant and socialistic, although not radical enough for some of its followers. Eventually this radical fringe joined others of like mind to form new associations. Insulinde, for example, attempted to make the Koran read like the Communist Manifesto.[11] Along with these groups there emerged a more orthodox organization of religious teachers (Nahdatul Ulama), as an antidote to the radical elements but equally committed to the independence cause. Another organization, Muhammadiyah, successfully reinforced its Islamic reformist program with a strong interisland infrastructure of religious schools. It is worth noting that this group's educational pragmatism and humanitarian institutions have been attributed to competition with Christian (colonial) counterparts as an affirmation of Muhammadiyah's proindependence orientation. Although not overtly political in its program or goals, Muhammadiyah's training produced many of independent Indonesia's political leaders, notably Agoes Salim and Hamka. Following the declaration of independence in 1945 many of these leaders applied their political talents to Masjumi, a coalition of followers—from Sarekat Islam, Nahdatul Ulama, Muhammadiyah and the student organization Himpunan Mahasiswa Islam—that was so influential in the new Indonesia. All of these political groups represented different expressions of the same faith, Islam, and claimed legitimacy for their different conceptions of Indonesian leadership, ranging from local religious teacher to prosperous merchant or radical socialist—all of which contributed to the making of the modern Indonesian political elite.

Compared with this varied cast of political characters, the remnants of the old sultanic tradition, the *priyayi,* attempted to maintain a thread of continuity with the past. Islam had initially accommodated the earlier Indic royal style and, as with some contemporary Malay sultans, had been made compatible with some rather clearly un-Islamic mythic and historic antecedents. Most of the real power of the sultans was annulled at independence, but some of the aura of their status persists to the present. The rituals used for the 1987 burial of Mangkunegaran VII of Solo suggest a revival of respect for royal authority, while reminders of a distant kinship tie between the Solo royal family and President Suharto's wife hint at a continuity of legitimacy for the head of state.

Since independence Indonesia has had leaders whose public office is officially detached from any religious base. Beginning with Sukarno's radical philosophy of "marhaenism" and his brand of socialism, this position has its most recent expression in Suharto's Pancasila.[12] Yet as in India's officially secular political culture, religion in Indonesia lies close to the surface, and still colors much political party activity and ceremonial etiquette. Even in the breach, Islam is respected and has not been eliminated as an underpinning of the Indonesian identity. And although emasculated by the political arrangements of the Golkar party-military alliance of the late 1980s,

---

[11] Robert van Niel, *The Emergence of the Modern Indonesian Elite* (Leiden: Foris Publications, 1984), 160.

[12] The five tenets of Pancasila doctrine include "belief in God," but otherwise stress civic rather than religious virtues.

other political parties fight on, among them a religious coalition one of whose components is the still influential Nahdatul Ulama. In their own curious way, too, even followers of the pre-Suharto Communist party managed to combine their political beliefs with a form of nonpracticing or "lapsed" Islam to create a uniquely Indonesian hybrid called *abangan*.[13] Although at times reduced to an almost inert element, Islam still figures in political imagery even at the most basic level.

The religious-political relationship can work either way: religion can be invoked as a buttress of political authority and political authority can in its turn allow the easy dissemination of a particular faith or sect. Both sides exist in contemporary Muslim Southeast Asia. As Ibn Khaldun observed long ago, to the extent that cultural trends often move in the direction of power and influence, it follows that rulers and other political role models should favor religious association or conversion. Religion can thus become a form of cultural hegemony whereby the centers of power manipulate their subjects while they themselves become defenders of the faith. Undoubtedly this kind of halo effect aided the initial acceptance of Islam in Southeast Asia, along with an ancient esteem for teachers and learning that cleared the way for the incoming ulama at the village level.

Malaysia: While the early history of Islam in the Malay peninsula paralleled that of Indonesia, there has been a substantial parting of the ways in more recent times. In what is now Malaysia, Islam has progressively become more integral to the political process, and although Malaysia is not an Islamic state along the lines of Iran, Islam is the official religion. This arrangement has set the tone of political activity since the mid-1960s in particular.

The composition of Malaysia's population is notable for the relative size and salience of its Chinese and Indian minorities who are largely non-Muslim, in contrast to the monolithically Muslim Malays. To a greater degree than in Indonesia, ethnic and religious identities have become strongly politicized, reinforcing other cleavages often to the detriment of national unity. Since the end of the 19th century, ethnicity has been associated in the Malay peninsula with occupational and economic status, leading to abrasive resentments by Malay rice producers, isolated in rural kampongs, toward the more urban, commercial (and wealthy) Chinese and Indian communities. With independence in 1957 and the removal of colonial controls, simmering ethnic antagonisms came to a near boil, culminating in communal riots in 1969. Part of the colonial legacy too was a constitution that enshrined the political and symbolic dominance of the Malays in what is called a parliamentary democracy. In legal terms, Islam (along with the Malay language and customs) is an integral component of Malay identity; being Malay is critical for access to certain political privileges and positions.[14] Basic social institutions in Malaysian society tend to be divided

---

[13] Cf. Geertz, *The Religion of Java.*

[14] Among these are an assortment of occupational preferences, including a quota of 75 percent of Division I civil service posts, many kinds of licenses, scholarships and training schemes, all set aside for Malays to enable them to "catch up" with

along communal lines, including most of the major political parties. Three principal parties represent the ethnic trinity: the United Malays National Organization (UMNO), the Malaysian Chinese Association and the Malaysian Indian Congress. The parties have cooperated since independence in a fragile coalition at the national level.

Following the logic of a constitution that defines its politically favored ethnic community in purely cultural and religious terms, some trends toward ethnic assimilation might reasonably be expected to emerge in the direction of Malay conformity. Such a process would obviously run counter to the rationale of the Malays' special position which thus has to be defended vigorously on all fronts, including the religious and political. This situation helps to clarify many of the ethnic events of recent Malaysian history. It explains, for example, why conversion to Islam by non-Malays, especially Chinese, is seen by Malays as politically threatening. By the terms of the constitution this religious change could occasion a reevaluation of the ethnic status of the convert, who could also presumably learn the Malay language and cultural behaviors as many do in immigrant societies. In practice, however, birth and ethnic background are invoked by Malays in such cases to create a more insurmountable barrier. Thus a number of recent Chinese Muslim converts have been mostly relegated to permanent marginal status as new associates in the faith. Not being considered as full members of either the Malay or Chinese communities, these converts often live in social and ritual limbo. They are encouraged by Malay religious authorities to retain their Chinese surnames in order to avoid ethnic ambiguity or attempts at "passing" for ethnic Malays. This requirement preempts the principal alleged goal of many converts, that of gaining access to Malay political and economic privileges. If this has been the strategy of such converts, success has been extremely limited despite a courageous defense in the early 1970s on their behalf, based on religious grounds, by Tunku Abdul Rahman, the tolerant first prime minister of postcolonial Malaysia. Eventually it was the particularistic interpretation of Islam which prevailed in the delicate ethnic politics of the country.

The Indian Muslims (by birth) have also remained distinct—from both their Malay coreligionists and their fellow Indian Malaysians. They have created separate Indian Muslim associations (including a political party) and some mosques with Indian cultural and linguistic orientations. Offspring of mixed Malay-Indian Muslim marriages are marked by peculiarly hybrid ethnic terms (e.g., *Kling*), again highlighting the extent to which religion serves ethnic-political interest.

Religion thus plays a central role in the validation of Malay ethnic and political status, one that has intensified under the Islamic resurgence (*dakwah*) of the 1980s. In Malaysia fundamentalist Islamic activity has been directed exclusively toward the Malay population and not Chinese or Indian Muslims, driving a deeper wedge among the communities. On the other

non-Malays under the New Economic Policy in force until at least 1990. The prerogative of providing the prime minister, deputy prime minister and most state chief ministers is also guaranteed to Malays.

hand, conversion of non-Malay indigenous tribal populations has been officially encouraged, as in the mass conversions in Sabah in the 1970s. This strategy of course helps to inflate the demographic proportions of indigenes (Malay and non-Malay) versus immigrants (Chinese and Indian) to a more psychologically acceptable majority. Here the ease of assimilation (if desired by the non-Malay indigene) contrasts glaringly with the difficulties faced by the Muslim Chinese in gaining an entrée into the Malay community.

While Islam is indisputably central to the legitimacy of the Malaysian state and its government, what is disputed in the Malay community is who is the most Islamic. UMNO, the dominant Malay party, was born before independence. It was created as a party of modern technocrats and had little in the way of a religious platform; its members then regarded cooperation with the other ethnic communities as ultimately in the best interest of the Malays. Over the past decade, under the pressure of Islamic revitalization, UMNO has been cornered into increasing protestations of its own Muslim character and moral base. It has been forced to generate a series of projects ranging from mosque building and establishing Islamic banks and an international Islamic University to programs of religious education, Koran reading competitions and enforcement of *Sharia* law—all to impress the party's Muslim credentials upon the Malay electorate. So far, however, UMNO has resisted the pressure to declare Malaysia an Islamic state, aware that as in the cases of the Libya and Iran, this could invite a political takeover by the ulama. Specifically this would mean political ascendancy for the opposition Malay Islamic party whose followers are mostly in rural areas where the traditional ulama are prominent local leaders in both secular and religious-moral community affairs. In the kampongs, political party contests are invariably over issues of religious ideology and moral righteousness as indicators of qualifications for leadership.

In fact, Islam still remains a controversial influence in the concept of the ideal and just ruler in Malay society. Modern Malaysia retains a rotating kingship drawn from the nine sultans whose authority within their respective states resides in their custodianship of Malay religion and customs. Their moral authority has been questioned in recent years by many non-royal aspirants to political power who depict the sultans as remnants of a feudal, patronage-based and amoral elite, identified historically with un-Islamic escapades that embody more closely an ancient ideal of the Malay hero.[15] Prime Minister D. S. Mahathir and UMNO have been involved in a number of acrimonious encounters with certain sultans, and this has been generalized as a problem of royal authority with moral overtones. Despite their historic role in the introduction of Islam into the peninsula, the sultans still bear part of the burden of the older, autocratic tradition that religious purists find inappropriate in a just Muslim ruler. But this image of the autocrat is not at odds with Malay views of a good ruler. In this

---

[15] Cf. Chandra Muzaffar, *Protector? An Analysis of the Concept and Practices of Loyalty in Leader-Led Relationships within Malay Society* (Pinang: Aliran, 1979); Shaharuddin bin Maaruf, *Concept of a Hero in Malay Society* (Singapore: Eastern Universities Press, 1984).

respect, the sultans have the advantage of a dual source of legitimacy: partially incompatible views of the ideal Muslim and the ideal Malay leader.

Several of the recent Muslim revival *(dakwah)* groups have also challenged the legitimacy of the present government system, in both its parliamentary and royal aspects. What all these criticisms have in common, however, is their invocation of Islam in some way to justify their goals and actions, but each group according to its own interpretations and needs.

Pakistan, Iran and Afghanistan: Pakistan, created by the partition of British India in 1947, is heir to a dichotomous political tradition already observed in Indonesia and Malaysia. One strand, represented by Mohammed Ali Jinnah and the Muslim League, espoused a secular form of government and maintained a modernist, Westernized, development-oriented outlook. As a country of Muslims, many of whom had fled India on religious grounds, there is a competing vision of leadership inherited from the tradition of the caliphates. The ideal caliph was an example of the just ruler who promotes and protects the cause of Islam in the exercise of his temporal powers. Although this tradition was current in the writings of Muhammad Iqbal, one of the foremost modern Muslim exegesists of South Asia, and a major inspiration for the founders of Pakistan, it is somewhat ironic that Jinnah originally had no intention of making the new country into an Islamic state in the strict sense. Yet in the events leading up to partition, Jinnah was swayed by the communal, political and religious passions of his followers. The character of Pakistan's rural and village leadership is very much determined by local ulama and *pirs,* respected religious authorities who oppose a secular central government.

At its founding the nation itself assumed responsibility for reestablishing and reinforcing Islam after generations of laxity under British colonial rule, and Pakistan is once again beginning to call upon Islamic authority to buttress its own credentials as its image blurs. Islam did provide an overriding sense of unity and legitimacy for the disparate tribal and ethnic populations of the various provinces of the new nation, including Sindhis, Baluchis, Pathans, Punjabis and, even more important, the immigrant *mujahirs* from India, and the physically separate Bengalis in what then became East Pakistan. Since 1947, however, Pakistan has lurched somewhat unevenly in the direction of greater "Islamization," from the third constitution of 1973 to the harnessing of Islam to the military regime of General Mohammed Zia ul-Haq. Islamic law has been gradually extended and more rigorously enforced throughout most of public and private social life, from the criminal justice system and financial institutions to personal morality, family patterns and codes of behavior for women. In some instances, these trends have strengthened the rural ulama and the more traditional Islam cultivated by them, although somewhat paradoxically, this development has been turned against the central state authority whose Islamic credentials are considered motivated by self-interest and opportunism. Increasingly, too, national leaders from Zulfikar Ali Bhutto to Zia have had to accommodate the demands of the Jamaat, a fundamentalist Islamic movement drawn from a variety of Muslim groups, in shaping the national image and policies. As a pressure group, the Jamaat is a continual religious thorn in the side of the incumbent regime and claims to be a moral standard-bearer. The need for moral reinforcement pushed Zia further in the direction of Islam, and culminated in a 1984 referendum that equated approval of Islam with a de facto acceptance of his regime. With the secession of East Pakistan (as Bangladesh) the remaining part of the country has looked increasingly toward the Middle East for cultural inspiration. For example, the Arabic language is now used frequently. In addition there are connections in political and economic policy. Pakistan is as much preoccupied with events in Afghanistan as in India; its religious scholars study in the Holy Land or Egypt rather than in Deoband, India; and its workers seek employment in the Gulf states rather than farther east. The loss of East Pakistan also illustrated the limits of the unifying power of the Islamic faith against the competing force of Bengali culture, language and ethnic identity.

In two other Asian nations Islam assumed a dramatic central role following periods of internal political conflict and social disorganization in which the faith received a battering at the hands of competing groups and interests. Despite the popular strength of Shiite Islam with its peculiarly local cults and rituals, the regime of Shah Mohammed Reza Pahlavi in Iran appealed heavily to the pre-Islamic Persian era for legitimacy and roots. Under Khomeini the country is one of the closest approximations of an Islamic state anywhere, and a model and reference point for fundamentalist movements throughout the Islamic world. In Afghanistan, tribal chiefs and khans had for centuries used their own brands of Islam and employed their own mullahs for specific political ends. Prior to the Soviet invasion in 1978, the Khalq party had officially disengaged the state from religion, although Islam continued to be respected and still set the moral tone of public life. Islam's most recent role in Afghanistan has been as a rallying call for resistance to the Marxist regime, although internal tribal differences add many complications. The Soviet period can be seen as yet another in a historical series of colonial occupations since British control in the 19th century. Whatever the nature of the official government based in Kabul, most of the real political life continues to thrive independently in the tribal areas where power is expressed in local idioms of religion and honor.

For all its international appeal as a faith that accepts in theory national boundaries, Islam in the real world is nonetheless solidly rooted in and identified with specific political communities, and even co-opted by them as a powerful bastion of their legitimacy.

Buddhism and the political order

While Buddhism is the dominant faith in many Asian nations, in both its Mahayana and Theravada forms, it has lost its strength as a legitimator of incumbent rulers and governments in most of these countries, with the major exception of Thailand. Once Buddhism was identified with royal power and the underpinning of kingship in Korea, Burma (now Myanmar), Cambodia, Laos and Ceylon, as well as the theocracy of Tibet, and in these countries it still has deep popular roots, independent of many political changes beyond the local level.

In Thailand, Buddhism remains strong as the country's "civic religion"[16] and as the ideological base for the monarchy, which is no longer actually a divine kingship. In the historical perspective of coups, crises and changes in regime through which Thailand has moved since the palace revolution of 1932,[17] Buddhism has undoubtedly provided a thread, sometimes a lifeline, of continuity and strength.

As far back as the mid-19th century the resources and prestige of the Buddhist clergy (sangha) in Thailand were utilized by the monarch for political goals, notably under King Mongkut in rural development programs among the peripheral populations in the hills to the northeast. Political expansion in this area went hand in hand with Buddhist evangelization among the largely animist tribes, as priests spread the prestige and strength of the monarchy. In the process, the sangha was organized into an administrative hierarchy amenable to political control in Bangkok. This relationship was later pressed into service in counterinsurgency activities against communists. There seems to be some justification for the conclusion that it is partly due to the pervasiveness of Theravada Buddhism in the political culture that Thai authorities are less repressive of minorities than are some of their Asian neighbors. Certainly the tolerance shown to surrendered communist guerrillas is in marked contrast to the policy of Malaysian authorities to the south. The Buddhist Thai also have a relatively favorable record regarding treatment of immigrants and members of other religions, such as Chinese and Malay Muslims in the southern part of the country; this contrasts strikingly again with the fate of such minorities in Malaysia and Indonesia, or of Muslims in the mostly Catholic Philippines.

The salience of Theravada Buddhism as a basis for state legitimacy has forcefully resurfaced in Sri Lanka. Despite the fact that the Sinhalese have, under successive Portuguese, Dutch and British colonial influences, diluted their religious unity as a people with substantial Protestant and Catholic admixtures, and even compromised the purity of some of their Buddhist practices, the anti-Tamil opposition in the late 1980s caused the Sinhalese to close ranks under the single banner of Buddhism. The Sinhalese situation is reminiscent in several respects of that of the Malays in Malaysia, where an indigenous majority attempts to assert its political, linguistic and cultural dominance over a large and highly competitive minority that has historically often eclipsed it in educational and occupational achievements. Further, the Tamils, like the Chinese throughout Southeast Asia, were encouraged to migrate by the colonial powers. Since the early 1970s, however, the Sinhalese have by skillful political manipulation and constitutional and other legal measures managed to attain political and military

---

[16] Charles F. Keyes, "Buddhism and National Integration in Thailand," *Journal of Asian Studies* 30, no. 3 (1971): 551–68.

[17] In 1932 a coup by a small corps of army officers and bureaucrats succeeded in replacing the autocratic kingship with a form of parliamentary democracy under a constitutional monarchy.

dominance. In addition they have had the support of the Buddhist *sangha*. Indeed, a rising and highly chauvinistic political party, the Janatha Vimukhti Peramuna, more extreme in its anti-Tamil sentiment than the government of J. R. Jayewardene, distills a powerful kind of Sinhalese nationalism in a very distinctive Buddhist format. A number of otherwise unrelated Buddhist revival movements also suggests Sinhalese regroupment under a Buddhist banner. This ethnic coalescence far outweighs any other residual religious links (for example Christian) that might once have joined individual Sinhalese and Tamils across ethnic lines. The pressure is strong for a monolithic reinstatement of Buddhism as the single spiritual and moral foundation of Sinhalese identity.

In Burma, long after the dissolution of the indigenous monarchy at the hands of the colonial British, Buddhism has been resurrected as a rallying call on several occasions, first in the independence movements throughout the early 20th century and then under U Nu as a basis for his educational and development programs. Subsequently Buddhism has also been invoked to muster various student protests, although the late 1980s were generally marked by significant tension between *sangha* and government.

Christianity and the political order
In Asia, the Philippines is the only country in which Christianity commands the allegiance of the majority of the population and for whom it sets the cultural and moral tone. In other countries, such as Vietnam and, lately, South Korea, Christianity has played a significant, but not dominant role in social and political life, more in opposition to rather than as legitimation of established authority. Various forms of Christianity are also embraced by certain minority populations in India, Burma and Indonesia.

The Spanish, in colonizing the Philippine islands, used Catholicism as an instrument of domestication through conversion. Conversion in this context was as much a social as a spiritual process, symbolizing acceptance of both new authorities—clerical and secular—as well as symbols of a Western religious and political culture. Evangelical politics managed to incorporate many indigenous spiritual and ethical ideas into the new order, although the use of the Spanish language and terminology in key religious and political spheres pointed out the center of power. For three centuries, from the 16th to the end of the 19th, the Spanish Philippines was effectively ruled by a variety of church orders, notably the Dominicans and Franciscans, whose regional control was accompanied by policies of cultural "Hispanicization," especially among the upper strata of the local population. Much of the cultural change was effected through church schools. But within the velvet glove of religious teaching lay an iron fist of coercion, often physical, by bought henchmen. By the mid-19th century, the legitimacy of the church and its teachings had been thoroughly assimilated by most of the local population at all levels of society, and provided in fact much of the infrastructure of the colony. But by the latter part of the 19th century the style and techniques with which the colony was administered faced growing challenges from a ground swell of indigenous leaders rising out the educated Filipino elite. Among these was José Rizal, novelist and Catholic—with an impeccable command of the Spanish language and understanding of Spanish culture. This first anticlerical independence movement in the Philippines was ended by the Spanish-American War (1898). Under United States colonial control the Catholic church enjoyed no special privileges, and during the new regime the church witnessed the birth of the indigenous Filipino Aglipayan Church. Remaining Catholic in its principal doctrines and rituals, it abandoned the "Roman" authority; likewise the leadership of the new Aglipayan Church was totally indigenized. A similar local church later emerged as an offshoot of some of the mainstream Protestant churches introduced by American missionaries. Today Iglesia Ni Kristo holds considerable wealth, has a following of two to three million, and allegedly has the power to control votes and political constituencies in a number of key areas.

Probably the most dramatic recent manifestation of the power of Christianity in Philippine politics was the temporary alliance in the mid-1980s of the Catholic church, under the guidance of Cardinal Jaime Sin, with the anti-Marcos faction led by Benigno Aquino. In the popular imagination, however, the fusion of the Catholic spirit with a social consciousness has led to the rise of indigenous cult movements, centered first on Rizal and more recently on Aquino. The dedication of churches and shrines to local heroes amounts almost to a beatification in the evolved folk Catholicism of the country.

In other areas of Filipino society religious and nonreligious values and terms have also fused. Thus in the ubiquitous patronage system that permeates Filipino life, from the highest chambers of state to local landholders and their tenants, the ethical imperative of reciprocity in honoring social obligations according to status penetrates both religious and social matters, and is particularly salient in political matters. In this, the government of Corazon Aquino differs little from that of Ferdinand Marcos or other preceding regimes.

Elsewhere in Asia where Christianity has gained any substantial foothold, it has mostly been at levels lower than the state, and its penetration has tended either to reinforce the legitimacy of, or else be legitimated by, the status of local leaders. A partial exception occurred briefly in South Vietnam under President Ngo Dinh Diem. Such is the case with Christianity in several Indonesian ethnic groups whose identity has become bound up with or even strengthened by their religion. Among these are the Toba Batak of Sumatra, and the Toraja, Minahasa and Ambonese of the eastern outer islands where entire peoples followed their leaders at once into one form of Christianity or another, without substantially modifying traditional social and local political relationships. Just as Islam in its initial penetration in Southeast Asia profited from the effects of status emulation, some early Christian missionaries achieved the same results. The most successful of these became folk churches with relatively early indigenization of the pastorate. Unlike in neighboring Malaysia, the Indonesian ministry of religious affairs has fully recognized Catholics and Protestants as official religions on a par with Islam. Indeed, several important political figures have been Christian, including Adam Malik, a past vice-president, and Benny Moerdani, former chief of the armed forces and present minister of defense.

Aside from the above illustrations, Christianity has had a limited impact upon Asian societies except as a minority or oppositional religion. In other cases where missionaries attempted, without success, to gain allegiance from the indigenous elites, such as the Buddhist royal families of Thailand, Cambodia and Burma, they failed to make a mark on the majority populations.

RELIGION AS A SYMBOL OF OPPOSITION

If religion has often been used to support the status quo, it has also been a favorite tool of opposition movements and interests throughout Asia. Paradoxically the same nominal faith is frequently invoked by two or more sides in a conflict, by opponents with distinct even irreconcilable political interests. Thus we find Muslim pitted against Muslim, Christian against Christian within the same country, engaged in ingenious exercises of theological casuistry and mutual excommunication. And with changing political conditions, regimes and ideals, today's duly recognized authority may be tomorrow's opposition, or the reverse. This shift can create negative consequences for the orthodoxy of a particular sect or cult. Finally, there are occasions when purely religious (sacred) power challenges its secular opponents with morality as the prime issue. Both Sunni and Shiite Islam and Catholic and Protestant Christianity have long traditions of internal theological conflicts that have motivated these religions to support a variety of political causes.

Islam

Pakistan: In Pakistan, the original tenuous unity of the new nation was soon broken by an assortment of regional ethnic and tribal divisions, each with its own dual spiritual and secular leaderships. This complex situation was compounded by the separate claims of immigrant Indian Muslims, the *muhajirs,* most of whom settled in Karachi as merchants, and a selection of sometimes dissident sectarian groups such as the Shiite, Sufi, Ahmadiyah and Qadiani sects. Many of the ethnic groups, in their political competition with one another, tried to make their points more cogent by claims of being more orthodox than their neighbors.[18] Further, from the 1960s to the 1980s, successive national regimes, including those of Bhutto and Zia, have had to come to terms with the Jamaat movement, a heterogeneous coalition of rural ulama, army officers, students and later a large cohort of fundamentalists of the ripening Muslim resurgence, all of whose principal common interest lay in their challenge to the authority of the incumbent national leadership. When there were open elections, the favors of the Ja-

[18] Richard Tapper, "Holier Than Thou: Islam in Three Tribal Societies," in *Islam in Tribal Societies: From the Atlas to the Indus,* ed. Akbar S. Ahmed and David M. Hart (London: Routledge and Kegan Paul, 1984), pp. 244–65.

maat have always been courted by the principal political candidates. Zia's successor, Benazir Bhutto, seems to be at the center of the more secularist forces. Many of Pakistan's Muslims persisted in judging Zia's escalated program of "Islamization" as a hypocritical manipulation of religious symbols to validate his personal authority, as so transparently displayed in the 1984 referendum. The ultimate irony is that all of the dissident ethnic and other political groups resort equally to theological rationales for their actions. All claim a common identity in Islam although each creates a unique exegesis, and the universality of the *ummat* comes to serve highly specific and even selfish group interests.

India: Meanwhile, since partition, the Muslims who remained in India have, as a religious and social community, been largely demoted from their past position as a highly educated occupational and even political elite to a rather formless, unmobilized and sometimes disadvantaged group with a relatively low political profile. The image of Hindu-Muslim hostility generally reflects the culmination of a host of local economic and social issues articulated in religious terms, and often publicly acted upon as such. Otherwise, Indian Muslims rarely identify with strategic social or legal matters affecting their community as a whole, nor have they formed a political party. Their main mode of opposition lies in their tendency to support opposition groups in different states, even including the Marxists. Today, India's Muslims are not clearly concentrated in any region and in general display a far lower level of militancy and political mobilization than do the Punjab-based Sikhs. Presumably, Khalistan today represents for the Sikhs what Pakistan did for the Muslims in the late 1940s: the culmination of a politicized religion and a process of ethnogenesis.

Malaysia: Although Islam is Malaysia's official religion, there exist several strands of political culture, each one claiming greater religious purity and orthodoxy than the others in a kind of perpetual "holier than thou" contest. The rather painless brand of Islam followed by the technocratic UMNO leadership is described above, as is the more traditional, ceremonial and theatrical style of the hereditary Malay sultans.

Since independence, however, UMNO has been continuously confronted by an opposition Malay party representing a more traditional, rural Malay constituency whose Islam includes some Sufi elements as well as a strong injection of pre-Islamic custom *(adat).* The typical kampong is a social and moral community with its own patterns of religious behavior, worship and leadership. The combination of the sacred and secular in daily life has been achieved by the ulama whose religious credentials, often derived from years of study in the Holy Land, have been transformed into local power and authority. Some of their Middle Eastern connections are reflected in the distinctive titles they adopt that endow them with unique personal, and potentially political, identities.

The political party most representative of this group is the rather chauvinistic Malay Pan-Islamic party (PAS) for whom the government's variety of Islam is illegitimate and tainted by accommodation to the interests of other ethnic and religious communities as well as to Western influences.

1071

UMNO followers for their part can retaliate by pointing to the syncretic character of rural Islam. Thus each questions the other's orthodoxy and fitness to rule, with the moral challenge masking the dispute over authority. This antagonism is often most intense in some Malay villages where both UMNO and PAS are represented, leading followers to refuse to pray in the same mosque or use the same wells together. Members of one party will even declare meat slaughtered and marriages solemnized by the other as invalid. Some even accuse their political opponents of being infidels *(kafir)* in an vilification process known as *kafir-mengafir* or mutual excommunication. Despite PAS' appeal in the heavily Malay states of the north, particularly Kelantan, Kedah and Trengganu, it has never scored significantly in national elections, although for several years the party controlled the state government of Kelantan. Were PAS to form a national government, there is speculation as to if and how its leaders would be able to implement a fully Islamic state, and to what extent they would abandon Western structures for finance, development and education. The Khomeini model would be less easily replicated in Malaysia, if only because of Malaysia's greater ethnic diversity. One of the tasks of a nationally victorious PAS would be to handle non-Malay, non-Muslim populations and interests. In the 1986 elections, PAS tried to diversify its platform to include all Malaysian Muslims, even fielding one or two Chinese Muslim candidates, but this rather feeble and cosmetic exercise did little for the party's electoral fortunes.

A highly publicized recent development in rural Malay religious politics has been the episodic eruption of local, idiosyncratic religious movements and events, often under a powerful ulama who declares opposition to all external secular authority. One of the most dramatic and bloody was the Memali incident in Kedah in 1986 by the aptly self-styled leader Ibrahim Libya who drew his moral strength from the wider *ummat* for his version of local Malay Islam.

A more widely recorded assertion of political power through religious means has been in the form of an Islamic revival *(dakwah)*. *Dakwah* ideas were originally imported into Malaysia in the early 1970s mostly by students who had studied overseas. Abroad they had been exposed not only to Western colleagues and ideas but also to other Muslims from countries such as Iran, Libya and Pakistan. These students were also the first major cohort of young Malays to benefit from the New Economic Policy of the early 1970s that sought to bring Malays the perceived wealth and privilege of non-Malays. In the 1960s, Malay campus activists had successfully fought for Malay as the national language. In the 1970s they sought gains in another cultural domain, that of religion. It so happened that this stage of Malay political development and self-awareness coincided with an unprecedented period of economic prosperity, fostering the sudden growth of a new Malay middle class of educated professionals and bureaucrats, male and female. Many of them came from rural backgrounds and had few role models to emulate. It also coincided with the Islamic revival in other parts of the Muslim world. These events created the Malay form of *dakwah*. For the first generation of revivalists, *dakwah* provided a clear sense of identity, a gauge for behavior and a guide for living in uncertain situations. Through shared experiences with peers confronting similar problems, various strategies evolved and crystallized in several religious movements; at all times the memberships were exceedingly fluid as the groups constantly revised their ideas and borrowed from one another.

The best known of these groups in the early 1970s was the Young Malays' Muslim League (ABIM), the creation of Anwar Ibrahim whose own politicization came during involvement in the Malay language movement as well as in the communal riots of 1969. ABIM was further inspired by then fashionable antiwestern sentiment and, more positively, by the Islamic resurgence in the Middle East, notably in Iran. Anwar's group also aligned itself in opposition to the perceived secularism of Malaysia's technocratic government during a period when Malay elites cooperated with non-Malays in ethically disturbing ways. Such criticisms led members of ABIM into social and political activism, demonstrating support of the poor as in the 1974 march to publicize the plight of starving Malay peasants in Baling. At the time Malay elites failed to comprehend why their youth, so expensively educated and pampered, could "bite the hand feeding them". In 1974, Tunku Abdul Rahman made an unsuccessful appeal on behalf of the government to urge Anwar to join UMNO, an action that one of his successors, D. S. Mahathir, was able to achieve only in 1982. By this move, Mahathir managed to inject into his avowedly secular government a new shot of Islamic legitimacy that had the threefold effect of emasculating ABIM, satisfying Anwar's personal political aspirations and providing UMNO with moral reinforcements.

The second major *dakwah* movement began about the same time as ABIM but has drawn more heavily from the rural Malay religious tradition. Its original leader, Ustaz Azahari, more closely resembles the typical kampong ulama and appeals to middle-class Malays with village roots. Darul Arqam operates a number of residential retreats and communes, with their own schools and clinics, that attempt to produce much of their own pure food for both consumption and sale. Darul Arqam aims at near self-sufficiency, but particularly tries to be independent of all Chinese products and commerce. In its physical and social encapsulation and its preoccupation with its own internal affairs and symbolic rejection of worldly concerns, Darul Arqam is nevertheless perceived as a threat by UMNO, partly as a countercultural group with a strong moral and ethnic platform, and partly due to its potent connections with potentially "subversive" countries such as Iran and Libya.

The third principal *dakwah* movement, Tabligh, began in India and was carried to Malaysia by missionaries who claim to be nonpolitical. Tabligh's international network links many of the more troubled and troubling Muslim minorities of the world, including those in the southern Philippines and southern Thailand, and occasionally becomes embroiled in those internal problems. Unlike ABIM and Darul Arqam, however, Tabligh is less exclusively directed toward Malays, and thus contributes less to the ethnic polarization that has accompanied the revitalization activities of the other two *dakwah* groups.

1073

The rise of the youth-oriented *dakwah* movement has been regarded as a challenge to the older generation as well as to established authority in general in Malaysia. In their zeal for religious orthodoxy and obedience to Islamic authorities outside of Malaysia, many young revivalists have come to view traditional rural Malay Islam as either lapsed or syncretic. Such arrogance is inevitably resented by parents and ulama alike, and has given rise to disturbing conflicts between them and young people returning to their home communities; these conflicts have led to their chastisement as "deviants" by authorities in the national government to the kampong level. The political establishment, in conjunction with the more compliant members of state religious councils, has devised as an antidote its own official *dakwah* program to counter the deviance. Much rhetoric continues among the various religious and political organizations, although most of the principal leaders now appear to have moved toward more central positions, with the government more sensitive in the 1980s to religious interests, and amid signs that the intensity of religious excitement has probably peaked. In the larger perspective of Malay history one can observe similar religious revivals that rose and waned, such as the Kaum Muda movement in the first part of the 20th century.[19]

Indonesia: In post-Sukarno Indonesia, and especially since the demise of the Masjumi coalition, the formal oppositional role of Islam has waned. Unlike in Malaysia, the religious resurgence has played a minor public role. The remnants of the four principal religious parties of the preindependence era have coalesced into the United Development party (PPP) that is riven by internal dissent and provides only a weak opposition to Golkar. In the 1987 elections, one of the PPP's components, Nahdatul Ulama, was persuaded to adopt the secularist Pancasila philosophy of the government, creating a crack in the political fabric that would permit the return of the Sukarno-era Democratic party. Even Muhammadiyah has become domesticated, devoting its activities almost exclusively to its educational and charitable institutions and showing no signs of political ambition. Today, Indonesia's Muslim intellectuals are largely alienated from the ulama who have become disenchanted with the new PPP arrangement. Even Abdurrahman Wahid, the head of Nahdatul Ulama, is not a religious leader. In contrast with Malaysia and elsewhere in the Muslim world, there are no youth organizations comparable to ABIM or Darul Arqam. This is sometimes referred to as Indonesia's "lost generation of Islam." Finally, Islam plays little more than an incidental role in ethnic conflicts in Indonesia where several religions cut across ethnic affiliations to a greater extent than in Malaysia.

Thailand and the Philippines: Thailand and the Philippines both possess small but active Muslim minorities whose ethnic and regional interests have become politicized in the name of religion. Among the many problems of the Philippines, that of Mindanao in the south has always been depicted as a religious conflict between Christianity and Islam, or an ethnic conflict between Christians and Moros. This picture conveniently ignores the blatant and unpopular land seizures as well as other discriminatory economic and political measures used by northern Christians to control the south. This has led the Moro National Liberation Front (MNLF) under Nur Misuari to seek support first from neighboring Sabah's sympathetic Muslim government under Tun Mustapha, and subsequently to look for assistance from fellow Muslims elsewhere, notably in Libya. The MNLF is also negotiating for full recognition by the Islamic Conference, an international group that transcends secular national boundaries. Mindanao is also part of the international Tabligh network with missionaries from Malaysia, in addition to the financial aid from the Middle East. Declaration of martial law by Marcos led to an intensification of the Christian-Muslim conflict and further alienated the Moros despite the less publicized fragmentation of leadership among them.

A somewhat similar situation can be found in southern Thailand where ethnic (Malay) and religious (Muslim) interests coincide in a condition of geographic and economic marginality. At least four active Muslim movements, some with connections to Malays across the border, engage in sporadic conflict generally less violent than in the southern Philippines. Some of the claims for greater linguistic, educational and religious rights have been partly acceded to by Thai authorities. Furthermore it is not entirely clear how seriously total political separation is being pursued by the groups. However the question of Malay irredentism is one of the border problems that will no doubt simmer for years to come.

Buddhism

In contrast to Islam, the other major Asian religions generally have lower political profiles concerning political opposition. Buddhists in India represent a dissident untouchable (Harijan) caste centered in Agra. In Indonesia and Malaysia, Buddhism has undergone a revitalization lately partly in response to Islamic domination moves. Malaysian Buddhism is largely associated with the ethnic Chinese whose perceived ethnic, political and commercial disadvantages at the hands of the Muslim Malays have, on occasion, been phrased in Buddhist symbols. An interesting change among Malaysian Chinese Buddhists has been a turning toward Theravada Buddhism among younger better educated Chinese and away from the traditional Mahayana form favored by the older generation. In this respect Buddhists bear some resemblance to their counterparts in the *dakwah* movement. Within the parameters of Theravada Buddhism, these young followers also cultivate an international network of fellow Buddhists that includes peripatetic monks in Thailand, Burma, Sri Lanka and even Australia. Again, these trends suggest a growing sense of a religious community that transcends political boundaries. Indonesian Buddhists likewise are identified principally with the Chinese minority, but the impressive attendance at the annual Wesak festival in Borobudur, Java, might even be drawing out a residual pre-Islamic religious substratum among the Javanese who are well known for religious eclecticism and mysticism under their Muslim surface. Recent violence in Borobudur has been attributed to a latent and pervasive hostility by more militant Muslims against this perceived recidivism in the local populations. Another strand of Buddhism that appears to be enjoying expansion in Asia and the West is the Tibetan variety. But this cannot be totally separated from the cause of the Tibetan people and their homeland, as represented by the exiled Dalai Lama.

Christianity

With the exception of the Philippines, Christianity has remained a minority faith in Asia. Quiescent and docile most of the time, it has nonetheless on occasion been invoked in local conflict. Some Christian converts, for example, in India, Burma and Indonesia took the colonial side in their country's independence movements. However, the fact that Asian Christians tended to be missionary educated and exposed to Western ideas primed them for political awareness and nontraditional ideologies. Peoples whose exposure has led them to activism include the Baptist Karen and Kachin minorities of Burma, and some of the tribes of the Indian state of Assam; all have used their religious identity in their struggle for greater autonomy. At times some of these movements took on a millenarian zeal, with visions of divine deliverance from oppression backed by a mixture of Christian and indigenous prophecies such as the episode of Ariya and the Golden Book in the Chin Hills of Burma.[20] The millennial flavor has, however, given way to more blatantly political forms in the Karen rebellion. In many parts of India, conversion to Christianity has often been equated with attempts to escape from less privileged Hindu castes. Missionaries have evidently been most successful among the lower and untouchable castes. Ironically these converts have merely been reincorporated into the caste system under the label of the "Christian caste," but with no fewer disabilities. The tenacity and pervasiveness of the caste system is powerfully illustrated by the case of Goa where the mass conversions of entire communities to Catholicism under the Portuguese resulted in a society of Brahmin, Kshatriya, Vaisya and Sudra Christians.

In the Philippines various Christian movements have played a part in political events of the late 1980s. A pervasive dissatisfaction with the Marcos regime found expression in the creation of Basic Christian Communities whose joining of Christian morality and radical social ideals resembles some of the liberation theology of Latin America. Another tendency is the support by some Philippine clerics for the New People's Army, lending it a greater legitimacy and credibility at the popular level. The intervention of Cardinal Sin, with the full weight of the mainstream Catholic church, in political events at the close of the Marcos era was of incalculable significance. Similarly the 1987 South Korean national elections turned the main Catholic cathedral in Seoul into a rallying point and a sanctuary. It appears that the country's Christians, estimated to be 40 percent of the population in 1988, are becoming more politically assertive.

Singapore provides yet another example of the increasing salience of Christianity in the political arena. In the perception of authorities the so-called "Singapore Sixteen" represent a growing and often troublesome

[20] Theodore Stern, "Ariya and the Golden Book: A Millenarian Buddhist Sect among the Karen," *Journal of Asian Studies* 27 (1968): 297–328.

movement of socially conscious young Christians concerned with local community issues. Whether or not they are connected to Marxist ideologies, as alleged by the state, this particular group does seem to be alienated from both formal political channels of expression as well as from their own official church leadership. In contemporary Singapore church organizations are among the few alternatives allowed for political expression beyond the official People's Action party.

As in Singapore, a growing cohort of young (and often Western-educated) Malaysians and even Indonesians find in Christianity an accessible mode of organization and a potential power base. Now that church pastorates are more or less indigenized, and free of European and American constraints, local Christians can turn their attention from doctrinal topics to pressing social and political concerns. A growing preference for independent, evangelical churches allows for greater lay and female participation as well as control over religious and community affairs, both of which appeal to minorities in authoritarian regimes.

In Malaysia, where Christians have always been forbidden to proselytize among Muslims and have been kept at arm's length in general, the Islamic resurgence has deepened the religious-ethnic cleavage further. Of late, there has been something of a backlash, a reassertion of religious rights by Christians and other non-Muslims. Some of these groups have undergone revivals of their own, all of which serve to reinforce ethnic differences. The recent formation in Malaysia of a Joint Consultative Council of Buddhists, Christians, Hindus and Sikhs was a direct attempt to defend such matters as religious education, burial rights and language of worship which are seen as being eroded. The 1980s also saw an escalation of accusations by Malays concerning prohibited Christian evangelism among Muslims, a further expression of deteriorating ethnic and religious relations. Another example of the religious paranoia that has invaded Malaysian politics erupted on the victory of the predominantly Christian party of Joseph Kitingan in Sabah in 1986, precipitating a strong Muslim backlash in the state and an abrasive reaction from the prime minister. The election victory also meant the loss of a friendly neighbor and sanctuary for the dissident Muslims of Mindanao across the sea.

Indonesian Christianity, by contrast, is recognized as two official religions (Protestant and Catholic) by the ministry of religious affairs. While there are strong correlations between ethnicity and religion, crossethnic evangelism and cooperation are more common than in Malaysia. Reports of church or mosque burnings and other violence are usually only of local significance and rarely assume national importance. Many more ethnic Chinese have converted to Christianity, particularly since 1965 following the fall of Sukarno when it became expedient for suspect Chinese to associate with either Christianity or Islam to avoid the taint of communism.

RELIGIOUS REVIVALS

The Islamic resurgence of the 1970s and 1980s has probably had the strongest political impact, both in individual countries and as an international movement. As noted above the Malaysian government has had to steer its policies cautiously in the face of the challenges to its authority arising out of the various *dakwah* movements, and through fear of more extensive subversion from contacts with revivalists from overseas. The government has also had to modify some of its approaches to economic and social development under the critical glare of the new Islamic fundamentalism, and continues to tread a precarious path between the technocratic and religious extremes. The revival has also provided a convenient forum for an assortment of otherwise unrelated causes arising out of regional, ethnic and generational problems. The more deliberately secularist public policies of Suharto's Indonesia have kept the Islamic resurgence at a subpolitical, more personal level. Nevertheless the government keeps an apprehensive eye on Islamic developments overseas. In Pakistan, on the other hand, Zia's use of "Islamization" to achieve his personal political ends partly coincided, partly conflicted with the goals of the Jama'at and the fundamentalist revival, illustrating again how theologies are quickly appropriated by political interests. The youthful character of many revivalists tends to reinforce a more radical image than may be warranted. In its international form, the image is at worst one of a terrorist conspiracy, indebted to extremist states such as Iran and Libya, and potentially destabilizing to Muslim and Western nations alike. At its broadest, Islam provides the most accessible and convenient tenets and symbols of opposition capable of uniting otherwise dissimilar Asian interests in their differences with the West. Yet this view is balanced to some degree by the fundamentalists' accompanying moralistic ethos that led many of these radical youth along paths more socially and politically conservative than those chosen by their elders, to the extent that even highly educated young professionals may decide to reject promising secular careers and material comforts voluntarily in order to retreat into a new submissiveness. While the international profile of the *ummat* has undoubtedly grown, at least symbolically, through recent events, this development must not be overestimated. Within individual nations it is evident that the resurgence is in fact multifaceted and fragmented along lines of preexisting local interest groups. To each village the international Islamic revival has different meanings and is deployed for different ends.

The intensity, impact and high international profile of the Islamic resurgence is nowhere approached by any of the other major religions of Asia. In several countries Christianity is unquestionably finding new strength and converts, particularly in the more independent churches, while even the older mainstream churches are moving in novel directions and seeking nontraditional functions. Where real political power is otherwise inaccessible, the substitute may be a resort to a thaumaturgical manipulation of power, as in Singapore, the Philippines and South Korea. Christianity also provides a voice for some of the disaffected ethnic Chinese of Southeast Asia. As in the case of Islam, revivalism is particularly evident among the young and relatively well educated. Not surprisingly too, where the Islamic revival has made "Arabization" culturally more fashionable, Asian Christians are more receptive to Western ideas and culture, notably in matters such as the status of women, trade unions and business associations. Where institutional and personal connections still link local Christians with their Western counterparts, there is a heightened sensitivity among some Asian political leaders of the potential subversive impact of these connections.

Buddhist revivals of great variety have occurred throughout history, and in the last decade of the 20th century several Buddhist nations are the scenes of a flurry of revivalist cults, most quite localized. Thailand is particularly rich in such movements (e.g., the Forest Monks and a growing number of urban cults) but few have made political marks except in diffuse ways. Possibly more remarkable is the recent cultivation of a more "rational" type of Theravada Buddhism by youth of Mahayana backgrounds, especially among Malaysian and Singaporean Chinese. Like many *dakwah* followers and some born-again Christians, these young Buddhists, usually well educated, middle class and fairly cosmopolitan, seek new symbols and meanings for elusive or eroding identities. This new cohort of Buddhists has a strongly practical, rational, even moderately materialist orientation; they are concerned with successful careers and prosperity and are very much of this world.

Hinduism, too, outside the Indian heartland, has undergone transformations; Malaysian Indians in particular have developed elaborate temples and festivals (as in Thaipusam) and devotional movements *(bhakti)* in all social strata. Many established middle-class Indian professionals in Malaysia have been attracted to the Sai Baba movement, suggesting a reevaluation of their identity and ethnic status in a country where they are a minority. In Java and Bali, remnants of the pre-Islamic Indic mystical cults have provided outlets for feelings of local powerlessness under the growing centralization and secularization of Suharto's regime.

What all these revivals have in common is their ability to create an imagined spiritual community that transcends the boundaries of secular states and provides identities that compete with the legal ties of citizenship. Such identities, especially when intertwined with ethnic and kinship loyalties, are powerful enough to stir feelings of apprehension and even paranoia on the part of some national governments, thus putting religious and secular powers in direct confrontation with each other. Finally, there is the question as to how independent these revivals are, and how much one revival is antidote to or fuel for another. To a degree, all revivals may be symptomatic of basic social, political and ethnic tensions within specific countries. But a religious movement often responds to developments in another faith, and may even imitate some of the patterns of the "competitor." Ultimately some of these responses become backlashes, leading to further politicization, or they may form unlikely and uneasy coalitions.

CONCLUSION

In Asia the political character of much religious activity is marked by its preoccupation with power and authority; political ideologies often draw freely on religious symbols, rituals and doctrines for their support. The relationship between politics and religion ranges from mutual legitimation to opposition or conflict. Most of the time, the two are in a situation of creative tension, with secular and spiritual authorities making mutual adjustments and changes. The modern political state in the European mold is not always in harmony with religious loyalties or identities, especially those that cut across natural boundaries or eclipse the importance of citizenship. Within a nation different constituencies may harness religious principles, even from the same religion, in their individual quests for power and influence; the result is either cooperation or dissonance. In this way, even the most universalistic faiths are particularized to narrow goals. This dichotomy goes beyond simplistically linking political powerlessness with embracing religion, a view favored by some interpreters of spiritual revivals. Rather it is an assertion that religion and politics are but two expressions of a pervasive and common set of needs having to do with control over the destinies of individuals, groups and their beliefs.

FURTHER READING

Esposito, John L., ed. *Islam in Asia: Rebellion, Politics and Society.* Oxford and New York: Oxford University Press, 1987.

Geertz, Clifford, ed. *Old Societies and New States: The Quest for Modernity in Asia and Africa.* New York: Free Press, 1963.

Hooker, M. B. ed. *Islam in Southeast Asia.* Leiden: Brill, 1983.

Keyes, Charles F. *Thailand: Buddhist Kingdom as Modern Nation-State.* Boulder, Colorado: Westview Press, 1987.

Mendelsohn, E. Michael. *Sangha and State in Burma: A Study of Monastic Sectarianism and Leadership.* Ithaca, New York: Cornell University Press, 1975.

Nagata, Judith. *Malaysian Mosaic: Perspectives from a Poly-Ethnic Society.* Vancouver: University of British Columbia Press, 1979.

———. *The Reflowering of Malaysian Islam: Modern Religious Radicals and Their Roots.* Vancouver: University of British Columbia Press, 1984.

Rizal y Alonso, José. *The Social Cancer: A Complete English Version of "Noli me tangere" from the Spanish of José Rizal.* Rev. ed. Manila: Philippine Education Company, 1974.

Rudolph, Lloyd I., and Rudolph, Susanne Hoeber. *The Modernity of Tradition: Political Development in India.* Chicago: University of Chicago Press, 1967.

Sukarno. *Nationalism, Islam and Marxism.* Ithaca, New York: Modern Indonesia Project, Cornell University Press, 1970.

Tambiah, S. J. *World Conqueror and World Renouncer: A Study of Buddhism and Polity in Thailand against a Historical Background.* Cambridge and New York: Cambridge University Press, 1976.

von der Mehden, Fred R. *Religion and Modernization in Southeast Asia.* Syracuse, New York: Syracuse University Press, 1986.

———. *Religion and Nationalism in Southeast Asia.* Madison: University of Wisconsin Press, 1963.

REGIONAL COOPERATION IN EAST ASIA

MARTIN E. WEINSTEIN

SINCE the 1970s, trade and investment in the Pacific Basin have surpassed that crossing the Atlantic. By the late 1980s it had become clear that the combined GNP of the Pacific Basin countries was larger and growing faster than any other region. Although it may be premature to assert that the center of gravity of world politics has shifted from the Atlantic to the Pacific, these economic facts and trends do indicate the prominence that East Asia has attained in world affairs and the major role that it will play in the future.

These economic achievements in Asia and the Pacific would not have been possible without a relatively orderly and stable international security environment. This is not to suggest that East Asia has been totally peaceful since the end of World War II. On the contrary, the large-scale hostilities in Korea in the early 1950s and the prolonged fighting in Vietnam from 1945 until 1975 were among the most serious conflicts in the postwar period. Nevertheless, the Korean War and the Vietnam War were both limited, local conflicts which did not disrupt the stability of the Asia-Pacific region as a whole. However, these two wars had enormous influence in shaping United States security policy in East Asia, that in turn has had the greatest impact on the power configuration and the security arrangements in the region.

THE U.S. PERSPECTIVE

Indeed, one way to view the international politics and security arrangements in East Asia over the past 40 years is to see them in the light of U.S. political and military commitments and deployments. From 1945 until the Korean War broke out in June 1950, it was unclear what role the United States was going to play. The naval and air forces which the United States had built to defeat Japan and the American occupation of Japan gave the United States an overwhelming, seemingly unchallengeable military predominance in the Western Pacific and along the coast of East

Asia, from the Bering Strait, across the Korean peninsula and Taiwan to the Strait of Malacca. In 1945 the United States expected to build an international order in Asia based on close, cooperative relations with its wartime Asian ally China and on continued U.S.-Soviet cooperation.

By 1946-1947 it began to appear that the civil war in China was making it unlikely that this plan would materialize, but there was no new American plan to replace it. By 1949, when the Soviets had clearly become the adversary in the cold war and the Chinese civil war ended in a communist victory, there was no longer any possibility that the postwar order in Asia could be built around U.S.-Soviet-Chinese cooperation. Japan, the recently defeated enemy, had become the central focus of U.S. Asian policy, and Japanese economic recovery was being encouraged. It was unclear, however, whether Japan would be enlisted as an American ally or encouraged to play a neutral role in the cold war.

President Harry Truman and Secretary of State Dean Acheson seemed to expect a period of calm following the communist takeover in China while the new government consolidated its position. Since Soviet and U.S. forces had largely withdrawn from North and South Korea in 1948–1949, the American government concluded that the Korean peninsula would serve as a buffer zone between the free world and the communist camp in Asia. It was this belief that led Acheson to declare in January 1950 that the United States' defense perimeter in Asia ran from the Aleutian Islands through Japan and Taiwan to the Philippines—making no mention at all of Korea. In Washington's view, it seemed that the central and crucial confrontation between the superpowers was in Central Europe, and that given the weakness of their forces in Asia, the Soviets would want to avoid any conflict in that region.

When North Korean forces invaded South Korea in June 1950, the expectation that the Korean peninsula would serve as a buffer in Asia also proved a vain hope. U.S. troops stationed in Japan were rushed to fight in Korea under the auspices of the United Nations, and Japan thus became the logistical base for UN operations in Korea. The Korean War dispelled American uncertainty about its policy in Asia. It elevated East Asia to a major theater in the cold war, transformed the 38th parallel in Korea into the principal military frontier in Asia, and clarified the position of Japan and South Korea as U.S. allies. When Chinese forces massively intervened in the war in the winter of 1950, China became identified in the American mind as the main enemy in Asia—an identity that was to remain unchanged for two decades.

The war raged up and down the Korean peninsula, from the Pusan perimeter in the south to the Yalu River in the north, and resulted in enormous casualties and destruction. For several months after scoring a dramatic victory against the North Koreans at Inchon in the fall of 1950, General Douglas MacArthur, the UN commander, pushed his forces rapidly up the peninsula almost to the Yalu River, the Chinese border. It was at this point that the Chinese entered the war, inflicted heavy losses on the UN forces, and advanced deep into South Korea before being pushed back to the 38th parallel. When hostilities were terminated by an armistice agreement in 1953, however, both sides were back at the place where the war began. Since the basic objective of the UN military action was to repulse North Korea's attack and to protect the security of South Korea, the action by the United Nations was successful.

From the conflict in Korea until the closing stages of the Vietnam War in the mid-1970s, security arrangements in East Asia remained essentially those defined by the Korean War. The Soviet-Chinese treaty of friendship, alliance and mutual assistance, the basis of cooperation during the Korean fighting, was concluded in February 1950. The U.S.-Japanese mutual security treaty and the ANZUS pact were signed in September 1951, and the U.S.-South Korean mutual security treaty in October 1953.

Although the split between China and the Soviet Union was apparent by the early 1960s, it did not alter U.S. security commitments or military deployments in the Asia-Pacific region. The United States continued to view both the Soviet Union and China as military adversaries and threats. During the years of large-scale American combat involvement in Vietnam (1965–1970), the United States operated on the assumption that both communist giants were assisting North Vietnam. From Washington's perspective, East Asia was divided into two camps, communist and free. The United States saw itself as leading the free world nations in Asia and the Pacific: these included Japan, South Korea, Taiwan, Australia, New Zealand and two members of the Southeast Asia Treaty Organization (SEATO)—the Philippines and Thailand—along with South Vietnam, Laos and Cambodia as protocol nations. SEATO provided the legal basis for U.S. military involvement in Vietnam.

The Vietnam War was essentially an armed struggle by the communist party in Vietnam to gain control of a unified country. The first phase of the conflict began immediately after World War II when Japanese forces left Vietnam and the French, who had ruled Vietnam as a colony since the mid-19th century, attempted to reestablish their colonial government. The French were defeated and withdrew in 1954, under the Geneva peace accords that led to the establishment of a communist government in Hanoi and a noncommunist government in Saigon, with the 17th parallel as the demarcation line between them.

The U.S. government decided that the prevention of a communist takeover of South Vietnam was a vital element in its global containment policy, and began to send economic and military aid to the Saigon regime. The communists in the north persisted in their goal of unification, employing a combination of subversion, terror and conventional military actions as well as supporting the guerrilla activities of the Viet Cong in the south. By 1964 it was clear to the United States that unless American forces intervened directly, North Vietnam would soon prevail. By 1967, although there were 525,000 American troops in Vietnam, with supporting naval and air forces, North Vietnam was still able to carry the war into the south, as it dramatically demonstrated in the Tet offensive of February 1967. Although the Tet offensive failed in its objective of capturing South Vietnamese provincial capitals, and cost North Vietnam heavy casualties, it was a major setback for the United States which had mistakenly convinced itself during the fall and winter of 1967 that it had broken Hanoi's offensive capability.

The war was bitterly controversial in the United States. In the spring of 1968, Lyndon Johnson, who had initiated direct American involvement, announced the decision to begin withdrawing U.S. forces while seeking a political solution. When the administration of Richard Nixon took office in early 1969, it continued this policy, leading to withdrawal of U.S. forces under the Paris peace accords of 1973 and the communist victory in Vietnam in 1975.

In Vietnam, the United States had undertaken to prevent a communist takeover of the south by employing a strategy of attrition. But in a war of attrition victory requires the willingness to take casualties and to endure. In Vietnam, the United States proved unwilling to pay the price in human lives and to endure. The domestic controversy over the Vietnam War led to a substantial modification of U.S. security policy in Asia that also had the effect of restructuring the international politics of the region. The Nixon administration was determined to disengage U.S. forces from Vietnam and in the process to shift the focus of American and world attention from a war that Washington had decided could not be won to a more productive and positive U.S. foreign policy. In the spring of 1969 China and the Soviet Union clashed over Damansky Island in the Ussuri River that marks the border between them. In the aftermath of this fighting the Soviet Union rapidly augmented its Far Eastern forces, increasing its army units from 18 to 42 divisions by the end of 1970. Soviet diplomats reportedly spoke to U.S. officials about a possible preemptive strike at Chinese nuclear facilities and missile bases on the grounds that the Chinese were too irresponsible to be trusted with a nuclear arsenal. At about the same time that the Soviet Union was seeking American understanding on its China policy, Beijing also began to court Washington, indicating that there would be mutual benefits to ending the acrimony in U.S.-Chinese relations that had persisted since the fighting in Korea.

To Nixon and his national security advisor Henry Kissinger the willingness of the Soviets and the Chinese to seek symbolic, diplomatic support from the United States in the midst of the increasingly bitter Soviet-Chinese struggle furnished a promising opening for a dramatic U.S. foreign policy initiative. First the Nixon administration exploited the Soviet willingness to improve relations by energetically negotiating the SALT I agreement and declaring that this nuclear arms agreement marked the end of the cold war and the beginning of a new era of détente in U.S.-Soviet relations and in world politics. In the latter stages of the SALT I negotiations, in June 1971, Kissinger made a secret trip to Beijing, following which he announced that Nixon would visit China in early 1972. The Nixon visit to China in February 1972 led to the signing of the Shanghai Communiqué that initiated trade and informal diplomatic relations between the United States and China. This opening to China was described as a rapprochement. Thus, while the United States was withdrawing troops from Vietnam and attempting to negotiate a satisfactory solution to the war, it was able to announce to the American public and to the world that it had initiated a generation of peace. Within a few years, however, it was apparent that détente and rapprochement had been oversold. The Paris peace accords did not provide the United States with a satisfactory political solution in Vietnam. The SALT I agreement did not stop the nuclear arms race or prevent regional adventures by the Soviets. However, rapprochement with China did produce limited but real benefits. The most substantial benefit of rapprochement was that it ended the U.S. policy of treating both the Soviet Union and China as enemies in Asia. This enabled the United States to reduce its armed forces in the Asia-Pacific region without undermining its security guarantees to Japan and to South Korea and the stability that has been the prerequisite for economic growth in the region.

THE SOVIET PERSPECTIVE

Although the Soviet perspective on security in East Asia has not been spelled out by public policy debates, Soviet actions and official statements do suggest a comprehensible pattern of behavior. It should be noted that at the end of World War II, the Soviet Union was much more preoccupied with Germany and Eastern Europe than was the United States, and had relatively few resources and little attention to spare for Asia. Indeed, American eagerness to involve the Soviet Union in the final battles against Japan was a major factor drawing the Soviets into Asia at the end of the war. At the Yalta Conference in February 1945 Franklin Roosevelt urged Joseph Stalin to bring Soviet forces into action against Japan immediately following the expected German surrender. Stalin demurred. The Soviet Union had previously concluded a neutrality pact with Japan, the Soviet Union was exhausted from its effort against Germany and, according to Stalin, the Soviet people would not understand or support a war in East Asia. Stalin was finally persuaded to pledge military action against Japan by American promises that such action would regain southern Sakhalin and the Kuril Islands for the Soviet Union—territories lost in the Russo-Japanese War of 1904–1905.

As it turned out, Soviet military intervention was not necessary to end the war against Japan or to reduce American casualties in the planned invasion. United States atomic bombs dropped on Hiroshima and Nagasaki in August 1945 abruptly ended the war. Truman had been informed of the successful atomic bomb test during his meeting with Stalin at the Potsdam Conference in July 1945 but did not consider releasing Stalin from his reluctant commitment to attack Japan. Consequently, Soviet troops invaded Manchuria and accepted the surrender of the Japanese forces there. The weapons captured from the Japanese were turned over to the Chinese communists operating in northern China and were used in the civil war against Chiang Kai-shek's nationalist armies.

Despite this Soviet help to Mao Zedong and Zhou Enlai, available evidence suggests that Stalin did not want or expect the Chinese communists to win control over a unified China. Stalin, considering a unified Communist China a potential threat to the Soviet Union, had already shown a deep distrust of Mao and Zhou. Until late in the civil war, he maintained rela-

1085

tively friendly, open ties with Chiang. Stalin preferred a divided China and probably would have been willing to cooperate with the United States in 1947–1949 in imposing such a division on the communists and nationalists as the basis for settling their civil war. In the event, in April 1949, Chiang abandoned the nationalist forces deployed on the Chang Jiang (Yangtze River) and in December fled to Taiwan with his personal military units; there he established the Kuomintang government in Taipei. The United States disengaged itself from the war in China. This led to the collapse of the nationalists there. The communists assumed control of a unified China (minus Taiwan) in October 1949. Within a few months of the communist victory, in February 1950, Moscow and Beijing concluded a treaty of alliance directed primarily against Japan and the revival of Japanese militarism.

The Soviet role in the Korean War still remains shrouded in secrecy, but most Soviet specialists agree that North Korea could not have attacked South Korea in June 1950 unless Stalin had directed or approved the action. North Korean forces were armed with Soviet weapons, advised by Soviet officers and dependent on Soviet ammunition and fuel. Stalin may have believed that a Korea unified by Kim Il-sung's communists would remain sufficiently weak and dependent on the Soviet Union and that a Soviet satellite in Korea would help to offset U.S. military superiority in East Asia, and would also help to keep the Chinese in line. He almost certainly did not anticipate a vigorous U.S. military response.

As noted above, the Korean War led to a large-scale U.S. military buildup in the Asia-Pacific region and to the conclusion of military alliances with Japan, South Korea, Taiwan, the SEATO nations, Australia and New Zealand—all directed against Soviet aggression and expansion. Indeed, American military superiority in East Asia vis-à-vis the Soviet Union was more pronounced after the Korean War than it had been before. China's massive intervention in the Korean War and its initial victories against U.S. forces reinforced Chinese national pride and made China less susceptible to Soviet influence. Moreover, since Stalin carefully refrained from deploying any Soviet forces in Korea, the war probably deepened Chinese resentment and suspicion of the Soviets who seemed quite willing to fight on in Korea to the last Chinese.

Stalin's death and the Korean armistice in 1953 do not appear to have marked the end of Soviet difficulties in northeastern Asia. The new Soviet leadership under Nikita Khrushchev seemed intent on correcting Stalin's errors. They were aware of the suspicion and resentment in Beijing, and attempted to put Soviet-Chinese relations on a more comfortable, friendly footing by providing economic and technical assistance to China in its efforts to industrialize and by treating China's leaders in a more fraternal manner. Khrushchev soon realized, however, that Mao considered himself the heir to Stalin as the ideological leader of world communism, and that it would be extremely difficult to achieve amicable relations. Moreover, the Soviets discovered that while they wanted to reduce tensions and the danger of war with the United States, Mao was willing to risk war with the United States in his efforts to gain control of Taiwan. It appears that Mao demanded that the Soviet Union provide China with the technology to build atomic bombs, and that Mao also expected full Soviet military support in his plans to invade the island. Mao wanted the Soviet Union to warn the United States that if it interfered militarily in defending Taiwan, the Soviets would also find it necessary to intervene on behalf of their Chinese ally. Mao clearly shook the Soviet leadership by his comments on atomic warfare: he reportedly said that while the United States and the Soviet Union would be wiped out in a nuclear war, even if 400 million Chinese were killed, 400 million Chinese would survive to carry on the revolution. Consequently, by the time that Mao ordered the bombardment of Quemoy and Matsu in 1958, Khrushchev had refused Chinese demands for nuclear technology, had cut off technical and economic assistance and had refused to back Mao on his Taiwan policy. The Soviet-Chinese conflict intensified, and Stalin's misgivings about the danger of a unified communist China seemed to be materializing.

During the same period of the mid- and late 1950s, the Soviet Union had an opportunity to improve its relations with Japan, and perhaps to loosen the U.S.-Japanese alliance. Since it had not signed the San Francisco peace treaty in 1951, the Soviet Union was technically still at war with Japan. When Prime Minister Ichiro Hatoyama formed his cabinet in December 1954, he was intent on ending this legal state of hostilities with the Soviet Union, on regaining for Japan the southernmost Kuril Islands that the Soviets had captured in 1945 and on reducing Japanese dependence on the United States. The four island groups off the northern tip of Hokkaido had never been Soviet territory and therefore did not come under the terms of the Yalta agreement.

The southernmost islands, Shikotan and the Habomais, are little more than rocks jutting out into the Pacific. The more northern islands, Kunashiri and Etorofu (Iturup), are large enough to serve potentially as military bases. It is likely that the Hatoyama government would have been willing to conclude a peace treaty with the Soviet Union and to have entered into normal diplomatic and trade relations if the Soviets had been ready to give Shikotan and the Habomais back to Japan. The Soviets, however, refused to budge on the territorial issue and insisted that a peace treaty with Japan would only be possible if Japan terminated its military alliance with the United States. Soviet intransigence only convinced the Japanese that the Soviet Union was as dangerous and threatening as the Americans claimed, and had the effect of bolstering the U.S.-Japanese relationship. Eighteen months of grueling negotiations produced only an agreement reestablishing diplomatic relations between Moscow and Tokyo.

When the 1960s began, therefore, East Asia probably did not present a comforting picture to Soviet leaders. Relations with China were bad and getting worse. The Soviet military position in Asia was decidedly inferior to that of the United States. The Soviet Far East continued to be economically undeveloped and strategically vulnerable. The U.S.-Japanese alliance was solid and Japan was doing very well economically. South Korea was beginning to emerge from the ruins of the war, while Kim in North Korea was proving a difficult protégé. The one consolation for Moscow was that the United States still seemed to believe that there was a powerful, unified Soviet-Chinese bloc, and seemed to be restrained by the phantom of communist power in East Asia.

From the Soviet perspective, the deepening U.S. involvement in Vietnam, that culminated in massive direct U.S. military intervention by 1965 and defeat in 1975, was a decided plus. Before the Vietnam War, U.S. military power in Asia seemed unchallengeable, and America's security guarantees to its allies were unshakeable. By the end of the Vietnam War, American power and influence, although still formidable, were clearly reduced. The Soviet Union was able to use North Vietnam's need of modern weapons and military assistance to establish an influential presence in Hanoi. Moreover, since North Vietnam had a long history of conflict with China, the Soviets gained a strategically placed communist ally in the Soviet-Chinese conflict. When the war ended, North Vietnam agreed to Soviet use of the large, modern naval base the United States had built at Cam Ranh Bay. This facility enabled the Soviet navy to operate in the southwestern Pacific and in the Indian Ocean, and lent credibility to Soviet claims to being a Pacific power.

While the United States was losing its war in Vietnam and then reducing its military presence in Asia between the early 1960s and 1975, the Soviet Union became a major naval and air power in the Pacific. Following the Soviet setback in the Cuban missile crisis of 1962, the Soviets appear to have decided on a large-scale, long-term naval and air buildup that would enable them to project power overseas and also to threaten interdiction of the sea lanes necessary to the United States and its allies. In 1965, before the United States began its escalation in Vietnam, it had 900,000 tons of naval shipping and 950 military aircraft in the Pacific compared to 700,000 tons of naval shipping and 1,430 aircraft for the Soviet Union. In 1965, Soviet naval forces were generally short range and technically inferior, and their aircraft were also short range and concentrated on the Chinese border. By 1975, U.S. naval tonnage in the Pacific had declined to 600,000 tons and aircraft to 500, while the Soviets had increased their naval tonnage to 1.2 million tons and aircraft to more than 2,000. The new Soviet ships and aircraft had far greater range and firepower. They were capable of challenging American power in the Western Pacific, and their presence began to create doubts about the reliability of American security guarantees in East Asia.

As noted above, before the Vietnam War ended, the rapprochements between China and the United States, and between China and Japan, had materialized. However, given China's economic and military weakness in the 1970s, the largely symbolic quality of the U.S.-Chinese rapprochement, and the doubts that then existed about the steadfastness of American commitments in Asia and the Pacific, such a rapprochement did not appear very threatening in Soviet eyes. The Soviet view of rapprochement was not well understood in Washington. In 1978 the Jimmy Carter administration attempted to strengthen its hand in the SALT II negotiations by establishing formal diplomatic relations with Beijing—playing what it considered to be its China card. This ploy had no observable effect on Soviet arms reduction policy. The Carter administration realized the extent of its misperception of Soviet policy and the China card in December 1979 when Soviet forces invaded Afghanistan.

In the 1980s the Soviet Union continued its steady naval and air buildup in Asia while its diplomatic stance became more flexible and imaginative with Mikhail Gorbachev's coming to power in 1985. Gorbachev moved gradually and carefully toward less hostile, tense relations with China. He even suggested the possibility of settling the dispute over the southern Kuril Islands with Japan, and has revived talk about Japanese participation in Siberian economic development. He has also moved to improve Soviet economic relations with South Korea, seeing in that country a promising source of the technology and industrial products necessary for the economic development of the Soviet Far East. In the INF treaty the Soviet Union agreed to remove its SS-20 missiles from Asia as well as Europe. At the same time, however, the Soviets continued to increase their naval and air forces and operations in the Western Pacific. Gorbachev has repeatedly asserted that the Soviet Union is a Pacific power and that it will play a major role in the future of the Asia-Pacific region. Despite an impressive Soviet military presence in the region, its economic and political influence will continue to be limited unless China and/or Japan decide to improve fundamentally their relations with the Soviet Union.

THE CHINESE PERSPECTIVE

The Chinese perspective on regional security has been essentially different from that of the two superpowers. Since taking power in 1949, China's communist leadership has consistently criticized superpower hegemony as a threat to world peace. Despite their ideology, Mao and Chou were almost as fearful of close ties to the Soviet Union as they were opposed to what they saw as excessive American power in Asia. Their mission was to create an independent China, relying on its own economic and military power and not dependent on any foreign nation.

In the broadest of terms, Mao offered three general maxims for Chinese security. First, identify the main foreign military and political threat to China, and do not allow China to be embroiled in conflicts of less than vital interest. Second, avoid international isolation and outright confrontation with one or both of the superpowers. And third, lean toward the less threatening and more helpful of the two superpowers but never in an irrevocable fashion. In practice, Mao did not always heed his own advice, and neither he nor his successors have always accurately understood or anticipated Soviet or U.S. policy. Nevertheless, Chinese security policy since 1949 can be viewed as an imperfect effort to follow these theoretical maxims.

When they succeeded in unifying China in late 1949, the communists found themselves with very little room to maneuver on foreign policy. They saw the United States as the main military threat to their survival, and saw no alternative to alliance with Stalin. The United States had supported Chiang and the nationalists throughout the civil war, and by 1949 it appeared to Mao that the United States was rearming Japan to help stop the spread of communism in Asia. Although the Chinese communists had suffered repeated betrayals and treachery at the hands of Stalin, the Soviet Union appeared to be the only country they could turn to for the military and economic help needed to consolidate their rule. It was in this spirit of necessity that they entered into alliance with the Soviets in February 1950.

The leadership in Beijing needed a period of peace to organize a government and to begin to deal with the country's terrible economic problems. They did not regard the outbreak of war in Korea in the summer of 1950 as being in China's interest and it was unlikely that they were consulted by the North Koreans. When they intervened in November 1950, they did so at the urging of the Soviets and in the belief that it was necessary at all costs to prevent American intrusions into China across the Yalu River. The Chinese army suffered heavy losses in Korea, and thus their recovery from the war with Japan as well as their own civil war was delayed despite Soviet military and economic aid. Nevertheless, the Chinese took great pride in having battled U.S. forces in Korea to a stalemate at the 38th parallel. They emerged from the war more confident of their own legitimacy and authority in China, and less psychologically dependent on the Soviets. Stalin's use of China as a military proxy in the Korean conflict deepened China's suspicion of the Soviet Union and strengthened its determination not to be further exploited by its erstwhile ally.

Stalin's death in 1953 hastened what was probably an inevitable split between Beijing and Moscow. With Stalin's passing from the scene, Mao viewed himself as the senior communist leader and refused to defer to Stalin's successors. He saw Khrushchev's efforts to put Soviet-Chinese relations on a basis of fraternal equality as evidence of Soviet weakness, and mistakenly insisted on demanding atomic weapons and Soviet military support in the planned invasion of Taiwan as conditions for Soviet-Chinese cooperation. In Mao's view, the Soviet leaders were not alone in seeking control of China. Khrushchev's interest in peaceful coexistence with the West also offered clearcut evidence of Soviet and American collusion in a plan to consign China to subordinate status in both global and Asian politics.

By the end of the 1950s, China was beginning to build its own nuclear capability and was bombarding the nationalist-held islands of Quemoy and Matsu in defiance of the U.S. Seventh Fleet at the same time Khrushchev was cutting off trade and technical assistance. The result of Mao's misjudgments was that China found itself at odds with both superpowers, too weak to complete its unification policy by invading Taiwan, and virtually cut off from the economic and technical assistance necessary to build its economy. There is evidence that China hoped that its informal contacts with American diplomats in Warsaw would help improve relations with the United States. However, China's denunciation of peaceful coexistence, its outspoken support of wars of national liberation against American imperialism and its cavalier attitude toward nuclear war ensured that no improvement of relations would occur.

Consequently, in the late 1950s and early 1960s, China found itself in an international position that was in some ways more dangerous than at the end of the Korean War. It was weak, isolated and on tense, almost hostile terms with both superpowers. Beijing's defiance was fueled by internal politics. Mao was not only defying Moscow in international affairs, he was also trying to purge the communist party of those opposed to the increasing radicalization that would subsequently lead to the xenophobia and chaos of the Cultural Revolution. In a marked departure from a decade of effort to forge expanded relations in the Third World, China increasingly withdrew from international involvement, leaving itself isolated and vulnerable in the midst of domestic turmoil and violence.

In the mid- and late 1960s, as the United States began to intervene directly in Vietnam, many predicted that the war in Southeast Asia would mute the Soviet-Chinese conflict and draw Beijing and Moscow closer together. However, Mao publicly rejected the calls of Khrushchev's successors for joint Soviet-Chinese action to oppose the United States in Vietnam, even though his intransigence spelled the demise of the Soviet-Chinese alliance. China sent the small assistance it could afford to Vietnam on its own, while it warily allowed limited shipments of Soviet military aid to pass through its territory. At the same time, China let the United States know that it wished to avoid a wider U.S.-Chinese conflict. In the eyes of Chinese leaders, America's Vietnam involvement was doomed to failure from the outset. It seemed to the Chinese that despite American declarations to the contrary, Southeast Asia was not strategically vital to the United States and that North Vietnam had the resources and strategy to make U.S. involvement excessively costly.

This evaluation was vindicated in the late 1960s and early 1970s. As a result, however, the Soviet Union steadily augmented its military power without provoking serious U.S. reactions. Even worse for Chinese interests, much of this growth in Soviet power occurred along China's northern frontier. Soviet alarm over the xenophobia of the Cultural Revolution—exacerbated by Mao's references to Chinese territory that had been seized by the czars and was still held by the Soviets—led Moscow to upgrade its defenses along the thinly manned border with China. Beijing's worst strategic nightmare was coming to pass. China, convulsed in internal disarray and without credible allies or powerful friends, faced acute political pressure on separate geographic fronts from both superpowers.

The Chinese themselves were largely responsible for these inauspicious developments. China's dual adversary foreign policy had led to severe isolation, internal dislocation, and a societal vulnerability tempting to external adversaries. China was far weaker than either the United States or the Soviet Union, yet Beijing's internal and external course alienated and affronted both superpowers and precluded effective collaboration with either. All three of Mao's cardinal rules of international strategy were being neglected.

The full implications of China's isolation and vulnerability began to be felt in the late 1960s. The Soviet invasion of Czechoslovakia in 1968 and a series of bloody clashes along the Ussuri River on the Soviet-Chinese border in 1969 made it abundantly clear that China faced a major Soviet military challenge to its north. Soviet-Chinese differences had now been transformed from a war of words and ideologies into a potential war with guns. China therefore had to put its domestic house in order as well as make a series of difficult but critical choices in its foreign policy strategy. Overtures from Beijing to the newly elected Nixon administration were answered. Both countries were prepared to enter into political dealings for mutual advantage, culminating in the Nixon visit to China in February 1972.

Thus, China's long-sought independence and leverage had finally been achieved, but only after a period of acute internal and external crises (with the help of the Vietnam War) had led the United States to welcome an opening to China. Within China, the political disgrace and death in 1971 of Defense Minister Lin Biao, who had been Mao's designated successor, marked a turning point in foreign policy. Lin was the apparent architect of China's dual adversary strategy toward both superpowers and, not accidentally, the major political beneficiary of China's convulsive course at home and abroad. Both Mao and Zhou had increasingly realized the acute danger inherent in China's continuing to pursue a policy of defiance and hostility toward both the Soviet Union and the United States.

Mao's and Zhou's overtures to the United States reflected classic balance of power calculations and bore little relation to the ideological pronouncements that Beijing had held dear for much of the 1960s. A posture of informal alignment with the United States would permit China to have vital breathing space at a time of acute vulnerability. It could thus seek to deter any further escalation of Soviet-Chinese hostilities to the north, as it progressively eased tensions with the United States to the east and the south. In fact if not in name, Beijing was willing to form a security alignment with Washington, even as the United States was still trying to salvage a political victory in Vietnam against China's erstwhile communist ally.

In grasping such opportunities the Nixon administration not only capitalized on the possibilities inherent in the Soviet-Chinese conflict since the late 1950s, it also accorded China an independent strategic value in the Asian and global balances of power. Although China from the first realized that the U.S. agenda in forging ties with Beijing differed from its own, this did not diminish the fact that the new U.S.-Chinese relationship also marked the realization of China's long-sought strategic objective. China could no longer seek to parlay its relationship with the United States into more effective opposition to the growth of Soviet power in Asia. What is more, the American connection also accorded Beijing unparalleled international stature and legitimacy in both the communist and capitalist worlds. It is little wonder, therefore, that Mao's creation of this revolutionary line in China's foreign policy remains among the few areas where his role in Chinese politics still remains sacrosanct.

The U.S.-Chinese rapprochement made Asian security arrangements more complex and yet more stable. The superpowers now had to weigh the implications of their actions toward China against the effect of these actions on their relations with each other. China itself was acting in a less militant fashion and at the same time both superpowers had greater reason to refrain from using their military power against China. However, the new security arrangements created problems as well as opportunities. In view of the ominous Soviet military position on its border, it was crucial to China that its improved ties with Washington should temper rather than provoke Moscow. On this score it became extremely important to China that U.S. policy toward the Soviet Union in Asia and around the world should be based on strength and firmness and yet avoid provocations, since excessive U.S.-Soviet antagonism was now more likely to embroil China than in its period of defiant isolation.

Consequently, the Chinese leadership needed to weigh carefully not only its own interests in U.S.-Chinese relations but also how it perceived American interests and strategies toward both China and the Soviet Union. In this regard, Beijing was persuaded that the United States at long last intended to disengage from Vietnam, and in other respects would curtail its military activity in the Western Pacific. In addition, to the extent that the United States pursued better relations with Beijing and Moscow, new pressures needed to be placed on Hanoi to negotiate with Washington. The Chinese also understood that the Nixon administration gained additional leverage in its dealings with the Soviet Union by enjoying access to China's leadership.

Thus, another risk for China was that the United States would simply use its ties with Beijing to improve dramatically its relations with the Soviet Union, leading to another Chinese security nightmare—U.S.-Soviet collusion at China's expense. In 1970–1972, when the United States concluded the SALT I agreement with the Soviet Union, and Nixon and Leonid Brezhnev met in Moscow to announce the end of the cold war and the opening of a new era of peace, Chinese anxieties about superpower hegemony were aroused. By the end of 1973, following the clash of U.S. and Soviet interests and policies in the Middle East at the time of the Yom Kippur War, Beijing's fears on this point receded. Following the fall of Saigon in 1975 and a string of successful Soviet interventions in Africa and Latin America that had gone unanswered by the United States, Beijing began to fret over a third problem in its new relationship with Washington. The United States, in the view of many Chinese observers, was becoming a defensive and perhaps a declining power. Some in Beijing questioned whether the United States was still enough of a superpower to be a credible partner for China. Nevertheless, despite these doubts and other potential difficulties, Deng Xiaoping, now at the top of the Chinese leadership, decided that on balance it was necessary to forge lasting and important ties with the West, particularly the United States, while avoiding intimacy and dependence.

It was clear to Deng and his colleagues that after the upheavals of Mao's Cultural Revolution and the reign of the Gang of Four, China's economic development was inadequate and potentially a source of political and military vulnerability. Japan's economic success and dynamism accentuated China's poverty and industrial weakness. The Soviet naval and air buildup, and particularly the technological improvements in new Soviet weapons, underlined China's technological backwardness. China needed new sources of technological and economic assistance, and the only possible providers were the West and Japan. Thus, the improvement of U.S.-Chinese relations in the late 1970s, and the consolidation of these good ties in the 1980s, was based to a large extent on the conjunction of China's internal and external needs for development, stability and security.

THE JAPANESE PERSPECTIVE

Japan entered the postwar period as a defeated nation, stripped of its empire, its industries and cities destroyed by American bombing, its merchant marine sunk by submarine warfare, and its people demoralized by hunger, defeat and bereavement culminating in the atomic destruction of Hiroshima and Nagasaki. The allied occupation of Japan, under the command of MacArthur, was predominantly American although it included small contingents of British and Australian forces. The purpose of the occupation was to demilitarize and democratize Japan and to ensure that Japan never again posed a military threat to its neighbors and the world.

The first major decision concerning Japan's postwar security in East Asia was taken in Washington a few weeks after Japan's surrender in September 1945, when Truman refused Stalin's request for a Soviet zone of military occupation in northern Hokkaido. Truman's decision saved Japan from becoming a divided country like Germany, and ensured that Japan would enter the postwar period with its home territories essentially intact. However, Soviet forces did capture four small Japanese island groups north of Hokkaido over which they had no previous claim. Soviet refusal to return these islands to Japan has continued to be a major sticking point in efforts to improve Soviet-Japanese relations.

The second major decision affecting Japanese security policy was taken in 1947 when the occupation sponsored a new constitution for Japan where in Article 9 Japan "forever renounce[d] war as a sovereign right of the nation," and undertook not to maintain "land, sea and air forces, as well as other war potential." Although Japan was to begin rebuilding its armed forces during the Korean War, on orders from the U.S. occupation forces, Article 9 has continued to embody and symbolize a pacificist approach to international politics in Japan, and has been a major obstacle to expanding the size, equipment and function of the country's Self-Defense Forces.

In 1947–1948, as U.S.-Soviet relations deteriorated and the communists gained the ascendancy in the Chinese civil war, MacArthur and others realized that a Japan without industry—which they had been planning—would be intolerably poor and politically unstable; thus they decided to promote the rebuilding of Japan's industrial economy. When the Korean War broke out in the summer of 1950, U.S. forces in Korea began to place orders in Japan for uniforms, military equipment and vehicle and ship repairs, all of which gave the shattered Japanese economy a big lift.

It was the Korean War that made Japan an ally of the United States. The San Francisco peace conference, which legally ended the war between Japan and the allies (with the exception of the Soviet Union), was concluded in September 1951 along with the first U.S.-Japanese security treaty.

In the security treaty negotiated by Prime Minister Shigeru Yoshida and Ambassador John Foster Dulles, Japan agreed to have U.S. military bases on its territory, while the U.S. agreed to use these bases for the defense of East Asia, including Japan. This treaty did not, however, provide for cooperation in defense matters between the United States and Japan, nor did it provide a clear U.S. guarantee of Japan's defense in the event it was attacked. In fact, apart from the military basing agreement, the treaty reads more like a joint communiqué than a legal document.

As early as 1947, Yoshida and several of his colleagues had come to the view that the United States and the Soviet Union would be rival superpowers, and that the best way for Japan to provide for its security when it regained its independence was to enter into an agreement with the United States. The terms of this agreement were put into a memorandum prepared by the foreign minister, Hitoshi Ashida, that was sent to Washington in that year. Japan was so devastated and demoralized by its recent defeat that the question of rearmament was not raised. The Ashida proposal was based on the premise that as long as the United States remained the major naval and air power in the Western Pacific, a U.S. guarantee of Japan's defense against attack would suffice to deter a Soviet threat or attack against Japan. In exchange for the American guarantee, Japan was prepared to agree to continued U.S. military bases as well as administrative control of the Ryukyu Islands. Moreover, since Japan was in extremely shaky economic and political condition during the early years of the occupation, it was also proposed that Japan would establish an internal security force and would take sole responsibility for protecting its newly democratized government. In 1947, Washington was still hoping to patch together relations with Moscow, and the Ashida proposal was put aside with neither response nor comment.

The basic ideas in this memorandum have shaped Japanese security policy to the present. Japan's leaders were quick to see the emergence of a bipolar international system. They were intent on finding a way to reestablish an independent, respected Japan, one that would be economically viable and reasonably safe from attack. They decided to cast their lot with the United States not only because they believed that U.S. military power could protect Japan, but also because they believed that membership in a United States-led coalition of democratic nations with market economies offered the best hope for Japan's economic recovery and future prosperity.

Following the communist victory in China in 1949 and the outbreak of the Korean War in 1950, the United States was determined to have Japan as an ally, but not on the terms proposed by Ashida in 1947. When he came to Japan to negotiate the security treaty in 1950–1951, Dulles insisted that Japan must rearm to protect itself against a Soviet-Chinese threat, and must join a northeastern Asian treaty organization similar to NATO, meaning a collective security agreement in which all the parties would guarantee one another's security. Yoshida argued that Japan was economically, morally and constitutionally unable to rearm, and that given its lack of armed forces and the lingering animosity of its neighbors, it could not enter a regional collective security agreement. However, the prime minister did believe that it was vital to Japan's security that South Korea be in friendly hands, and he was willing to give the United States whatever bases it needed in Japan to wage successfully the war in Korea. Yoshida wanted a treaty that would provide for consultations and cooperation between the United States and Japan on the use of American bases in Japan as well as military security and economic matters. Much to his suprise and chagrin Dulles discovered during negotiations in Tokyo in early 1951 that MacArthur agreed with Yoshida on rearmament. Japan would not commit itself to rebuilding its armed forces and it would not join a regional security organization; consequently, Dulles refused to agree to consultations and cooperation on security matters. Dulles insisted that the United States would use its bases in Japan in whatever way it decided was necessary to maintain peace and security in East Asia.

As a consequence of these bruising negotiations and the less than satisfactory 1951 security treaty, Yoshida decided that it would be necessary for Japan to undertake some kind of rearmament in order to maintain a workable alliance with the United States. In 1954 the Japan Defense Agency and the Self-Defense Forces were established. Their mission was to raise the threshold of a Soviet attack against Japan to a sufficiently high level that it would guarantee U.S. military response, and to provide visible evidence to the U.S. Congress that Japan was prepared to fight in its own defense and was willing to share the burden of its defense with the United States.

In 1955–1956 Prime Minister Hatoyama attempted to reduce Japan's military dependence on the United States by negotiating a peace treaty with the Soviets. As observed above, the Soviets rebuffed the Hatoyama initiative and refused to budge on the issue of the northern islands unless Japan terminated its security treaty with the United States. That step Hatoyama refused to consider. In 1958–1960 Prime Minister Nobusuke Kishi entered into negotiations with the United States to change the 1951 security treaty into a more mutual, cooperative arrangement, closer to what Yoshida had wanted but failed to achieve. By this time Dulles was prepared to admit that Japan's economic recovery was impressive and that the Self-Defense Forces helped to share the defense burden. Moreover, Washington had also come to see that the Japanese were loyal and cooperative allies and that a more equitable agreement was indeed appropriate. Thus Kishi was successful in negotiating the revised 1960 U.S.-Japanese security treaty that has continued in effect to the present. The 1960 treaty provides for consultations and cooperation in both security and economic issues, and clearly commits the United States to use its bases in Japan to defend Japan against attack. In a note appended to the treaty, the United States also agrees to gain Japan's prior approval for any substantial changes in the weapons and manner of deployment used by U.S. forces in Japan including the introduction of nuclear weapons into the country. By 1960 there was a keen appreciation in Washington that Japan had become the United States' most important ally in the Asia-Pacific region, and there was a willingness to treat Japan as a partner (although a junior partner) and not as a military dependent.

Ironically, however, despite his diplomatic success in achieving the security relationship with the United States that Yoshida had once sought, Kishi was forced to resign as a result of domestic political battles generated during the ratification of the 1960 treaty. Neither his colleagues in the ruling Liberal Democratic party (LDP) nor in the opposition parties wanted Kishi to get credit for his success. LDP leaders delayed and quibbled over the treaty while the socialist opposition organized rallies and demonstrations all over Japan, many of them aimed at Kishi more than at the treaty. Kishi had been a member of Japan's wartime cabinet and had been arrested but not tried as a war criminal. He was an easy target for the opposition. The LDP ultimately used its majority in the Diet to ratify the treaty, but only on the understanding that Kishi would step down as prime minister.

During the decade of the 1960s Japan's economic recovery continued beyond all expectations and was transformed into an economic miracle—a decade during which Japan's national and per capita production more than doubled. Japan spent less than one percent of its GNP on defense and enjoyed a high degree of security, largely because of the farsighted and intelligent security policy that its government had pursued since 1947. There is little doubt that Japan's very small military budget combined with strong international and domestic security continue to contribute greatly to its economic success. The 1960s saw the beginning of massive U.S. intervention in Vietnam, a move than eventually failed in its effort to maintain a noncommunist South Vietnam. Most of the Japanese public did not see Vietnam as vital to Japanese or U.S. security, and tended to regard the war as a case of a huge, rich and powerful United States trying to crush a poor Asian country. The Japanese government also had doubts about how critical Vietnam was in Asian security arrangements, but it cooperated to support the United States in order to sustain U.S.-Japanese security arrangements and economic ties. The greatest concern of officials in Tokyo was that the United States was squandering its military forces in an unneccesary war, and that if the United States should lose in Vietnam it might decide to reevaluate its entire strategy in Asia and decide to withdraw from South Korea and Japan.

In the 1970s it sometimes seemed to Tokyo that this nightmare might materialize. Although public opinion in Japan was enthusiastic about détente and rapprochement, the Japanese government tended to view these developments with skepticism. The Nixon Doctrine stated that the United States would limit its military help to allies to naval, air and nuclear forces. It clearly implied the withdrawal of U.S. ground forces from South Korea, something that Japanese officials anticipated would destabilize the peninsula and probably lead to another war. The secret Kissinger visit to China in 1971, the Shanghai Communiqué of 1972 and the subsequent U.S.-Chinese rapprochement all indicated that the United States might turn to China as an ally in place of Japan, or might try to organize a regional Asian balance of power while withdrawing its forces from the western Pacific. The collapse of Saigon in 1975 and the failure of the United States in Vietnam could not but raise questions about the reliability of the United States as an ally for Japan. And in the late 1970s the Carter administration seemed determined to withdraw U.S. ground forces from South Korea; it was only stopped by the combined opposition of virtually the entire foreign and defense policy community in Washington.

It is not suprising, therefore, that when Ronald Reagan took office in 1981 on a platform that rejected détente and rapprochement and pledged to rebuild American military power and relations with its allies, the Japanese government was relieved. Nevertheless, it was clear to Japanese leaders—including prime ministers Zenko Suzuki, Yasuhiro Nakasone and Noboru Takeshita—that the basis of Japan's security had shifted from a simple reliance on U.S. military power to a more complex arrangement. From the Japanese point of view, U.S. commitments and forces in Japan and South Korea remain essential and central to the security of the two countries, but not sufficient.

Following Nixon's visit to Beijing in 1972, Japan moved quickly to improve its own relations with China, and also quickly came to see China as a counterweight to Soviet power in Asia. By the 1980s, Japan became the largest aid donor and foreign creditor in China in an effort to contribute to China's economic development, independence and stability. Although Japanese public statements stress the economic and humanitarian purpose of this aid, it also has a strategic dimension. Japan is also the major foreign investor in South Korea, Taiwan, and in most of the member countries of the Association of Southeast Asian Nations, not only because it is good business, but also because it enhances Japan's international security and helps to compensate for the relatively weakened U.S. military position in Asia.

The Japanese government has also concluded that it is necessary to pay the growing yen costs of U.S. bases in Japan. By 1988, Japan was spending U.S.\$2.5 billion on this while the United States was spending about \$3 billion on its military forces in Japan. Moreover, the Self-Defense Forces, although representing about one percent of Japan's GNP, had assumed shared responsibility with the United States for the protection of the Western Pacific sea lanes, 1,000 miles out from Japan. In addition the forces were contributing more effectively to Japan's air and naval defense and were using their sophisticated air and naval equipment to control the strategic waters near Tsushima, Tsugaru and Soya. These are the straits through which the Soviet Pacific fleet must pass if it is to operate in the Pacific and Indian Oceans.

CONCLUSION

Looking back over more than four decades of international relations in East Asia, it appears that the security arrangements in this region have undergone several major changes. Between the end of World War II in 1945 and the outbreak of the Korean War in 1950 there were no well-defined security arrangements in Asia. The United States, which had a predominant military position in the region as a consequence of its victory over Japan, was pinning its hopes for regional security on cooperative relations with the Soviet Union and China. The Soviet Union, which was then extremely weak in East Asia, was working with both the communists and the nationalists in China, and seemed prepared to live with a weak, divided China. Japan was economically and politically prostrate as a result of its recent defeat, but Japan's leaders correctly anticipated that the United States and the Soviet Union would be rivals in Asia, and they began planning and working toward an alliance with the United States. China was torn by a brutal civil war that resulted in victory for the communists, who—contrary to both U.S. and Soviet plans—established themselves in Beijing as the government of a unified China (except for Taiwan) in October 1949.

The Soviet Union then moved swiftly to pull China into its orbit; it also seems to have initiated the North Korean attack on South Korea which led to the war. For a brief period in 1949–1950, it may have seemed to Stalin that American dominance in East Asia would evaporate in the confusion that followed the communist takeover in China and the initial communist military successes in Korea. Unexpectedly, however, the United States decided to fight in Korea and in order to win the United States built and deployed powerful land, sea and air forces across the Pacific and created a network of Asian alliances, centering on a close economic and military relationship with Japan. By the end of the 1950s it was clear that as a result of the Korean War, U.S. military power in the Asia-Pacific region had become virtually unchallengeable, Japan was recovering economically and remaining a close ally of the United States and China was determined to be independent of the Soviet Union. The Soviets seem to have realized that they were at a decisive disadvantage in Asia, but the United States still believed that it faced a monolithic Soviet-Chinese enemy.

The U.S. failure in Vietnam in the mid-1970s marked the end of a period of unchallengeable U.S. power in the region, but not the end of the security arrangements that it had fostered. The U.S.-Japanese alliance survived the Vietnam War, and in the mid-1970s a disillusioned United States found itself cooperating with China to oppose Soviet attempts at hegemony in Southeast Asia and East Asia. Although there was little possibility of such Soviet dominance, the Chinese decision to lean toward the United States ensured that the Soviets would remain relatively isolated and politically weak in Asia irrespective of military deployment on the Chinese border. Consequently, during the 1980s, East Asia flourished economically under a set of security arrangements that resembled the Pax Americana of the 1950s and 1960s—despite a reduced U.S. military presence in Asia and the Pacific, and despite an impressive Soviet naval and air buildup in the Western Pacific. Japan's economic success, political stability and policy of close cooperation with the United States—combined with China's decision to link its economic future to Japan and the West—seem to have compensated for the reduction of U.S. power and appears to hold the system together.

FURTHER READING

Acheson, Dean. *Present at the Creation: My Years in the State Department*. New York: Norton, 1969.
Borden, William S. *The Pacific Alliance: United States Foreign Economic Policy and*

Japanese Trade Recovery, 1947–1955. Madison: University of Wisconsin Press, 1984.

Boyd, R. G. *Communist China's Foreign Policy*. New York: Praeger, 1962.

Buhite, Russell D. *Soviet-America Relations in Asia, 1945–1954*. Norman: University of Oklahoma Press, 1981.

Dulles, Eleanor Lansing. *American Foreign Policy in the Making*. New York: Harper & Row, 1968.

Hellman, Donald C. *Japanese Foreign Policy and Domestic Politics: The Peace Agreement with the Soviet Union*. Berkeley: University of California Press, 1969.

Hinton, Harold C. *Peking-Washington: Chinese Foreign Policy and the United States*. Beverly Hills, California: Sage Publications, 1976.

Kennan, George F. *Memoirs: 1925–1963*. Boston: Little, Brown, 1972.

Pollack, Jonathan D. *Security, Strategy and the Logic of Chinese Foreign Policy*. Berkeley: Institute of East Asian Studies, University of California, 1981.

Ulam, Adam B. *The Rivals: America and Russia since World War II*. New York: Viking, 1971.

Weinstein, Martin E. *Japan's Postwar Defense Policy, 1947–1968*. New York: Columbia University Press, 1971.

———. *The United States and Japan: Decisions for the Next President*. Washington, D.C.: Significant Issues Series, Center for Strategic and International Studies, June 1988.

REGIONAL COOPERATION IN SOUTHEAST ASIA: ASEAN

R. A. LONGMIRE

AT first glance Southeast Asia would appear to be an unlikely candidate for any kind of regional arrangement. An area of great ethnic, religious and cultural diversity, its peoples have had no sense of regional identity such as has existed in Europe for centuries, however submerged by rival nationalisms. During the European colonial era Southeast Asia was considered a part of the Far East and was divided up by the imperial powers: Britain in Burma (now Myanmar), Malaya and Singapore; France in Indochina; the Netherlands in Indonesia; and the United States in the Philippines. Only Thailand remained independent, adroitly fulfilling the role of buffer state between the British and French possessions on its doorsteps. The phrase "Southeast Asia" did not exist as a geographical term until the formation during World War II of the South-East Asia Command in the fight against the Japanese.

Against this unpromising background, what was it that has given rise to a regional grouping in this part of the world? The first seeds were sown by the United States in the aftermath of the Geneva Conference of 1954 when Secretary of State John Foster Dulles urged the establishment of the Southeast Asia Treaty Organization (SEATO), whose aim was to block further communist advances after the Vietnamese victory over the French and the withdrawal of the latter from Indochina. Unfortunately SEATO clashed with the ideas of nonalignment then gaining strength in the Third World. Indonesia, host to the Bandung nonaligned conference in 1955, regarded SEATO with great suspicion and refused to join, thereby seriously weakening the whole project from the start. Only three Asian nations did become members—Pakistan, Thailand and the Philippines, all countries widely known at the time for their pro-American sympathies. Malaysia and Singapore subsequently stood aloof when they obtained independence from Britain a few years later. The upshot was that SEATO, however useful as a symbol of American and European attempts to contain communism and

1101

as a channel of Western technological and medical aid to the Asian member nations, remained flawed by its image as an instrument of U.S. policy.

By the early 1960s most of the noncommunist nations of the region were aware of the need for a regional organization that would, they hoped, be free of the influence of outside powers. In 1961 Malaya, Thailand and the Philippines formed the Association of Southeast Asia with the accent on economic, scientific and cultural, rather than political, collaboration. The association suffered, however, from too close an alignment with the United States and once again the largest country in the region, Indonesia, was absent. Two years later, on the initiative of the Philippines, another organization, Maphilindo, came into being. The members were the predominantly Malay countries of Malaya, the Philippines and Indonesia but it was quickly aborted by Sukarno's hostility toward, and military confrontation with, the newly expanded nation of Malaysia, formed in 1963 and consisting of Malaya, Singapore, Sarawak and Sabah (Singapore seceded in 1965).

Thus far the cause of regional cooperation in Southeast Asia had proved singularly unsuccessful. The picture changed, however, with the formation in 1967 of the Association of Southeast Asian Nations (ASEAN). It embraced all the noncommunist countries of the area with the exception of Brunei (which eventually joined in 1984 on attaining independence from Britain), and Burma which clung steadfastly to its nonaligned isolation. The reasons why ASEAN took root where other groupings had failed are not far to seek. By this time the United States was fully enmeshed in Vietnam and it was not at all clear what the outcome of the conflict would be. Prudence dictated that the countries of Southeast Asia draw together in the interests of regional solidarity and security. Another important consideration was that the political climate in Indonesia had drastically altered as a result of the failure of the procommunist coup of 1965. The subsequent fall of Sukarno, the ending of the confrontation with Malaysia and the pro-Western (and sharply anti-Chinese) mood of the Suharto regime all helped to secure Indonesia's active participation. Additional motivation must also have come from the example of the European Community which had already changed the framework of interstate relations in Europe, as well as from the experience of regional groupings elsewhere—the Organization of African Unity and the Latin American Free Trade Association.

INAUGURAL MEETING OF ASEAN

ASEAN was formally established by the foreign ministers of Indonesia, the Philippines, Singapore and Thailand and the deputy prime minister of Malaysia at a meeting in Bangkok in August 1967. They signed the Bangkok declaration which set forth the aims of the association and the machinery for bringing them to fruition. In the order in which they appear in the document these aims are: to accelerate economic growth, social progress and cultural development in the region; to promote regional peace and stability by a respect for justice and the rule of law in the relationships among member states; to collaborate actively in the economic, social, cultural, technical, scientific and administrative fields; to help one another with technical, educational and other kinds of training and research; to work for the greater utilization of agriculture and industry; to expand trade and improve transportation and communication facilities; to further Southeast Asian studies; and to maintain close cooperation with similar international and regional organizations elsewhere.

The highest policymaking body was to be an annual meeting of foreign ministers held in each member nation in rotation; special meetings were to be convened as required. In between these meetings decisions were to be made by a standing committee under the chairmanship of the foreign minister of the host country or his representative, the committee's members the ambassadors of the other member countries accredited to the host country. There was also provision for ad hoc committees and permanent committees of specialists and officials on specific subjects. In each country there was to be a national secretariat to deal with ASEAN affairs and to service the foreign ministers' meeting and the standing committee. Finally, ASEAN was to be open to participation by all nations in Southeast Asia which subscribed to its aims and principles—a formula which could be elastic or restrictive, according to its interpretation by the member nations.

This, then, was both an optimistic and a practical document meant to set the scene for regional collaboration in Southeast Asia. Its authors evidently looked for progress in economic, cultural and scientific matters rather than purely political collaboration, and they were careful not to diminish in any way the power of the national state. Indeed, they expressly referred to their determination to "preserve their national identities in accordance with the ideals and aspirations of their peoples." ASEAN was to be no more than the sum of its parts. With respect to military collaboration they trod with equal if not greater wariness. The phrase as such did not appear at all but the preamble made it clear that the member nations were "determined to ensure their stability and security from external interference in any form or manifestation." At the same time they also displayed some disquiet for fear that countries outside the association might see it as some kind of military threat. All foreign bases, they declared, were temporary, remained only with the "expressed concurrence" of the countries concerned and were not intended to be used directly or indirectly to subvert the national independence and freedom of countries in the area.

For most of the late 1960s until the late 1970s ASEAN adopted a low profile. True, the foreign ministers duly met every year and were productive of some local publicity. Eleven permanent committees were established to cover subjects such as agriculture, shipping, air transportation, commerce and industry, science and technology and tourism. Ad hoc committees dealt with the challenge of synthetic rubber to the natural variety, cooperation in the sugar industries, the ASEAN attitude toward the General Agreement on Tariffs and Trade and, subsequent to the signing in 1973 of the Paris peace accords ending the war in Vietnam, the problems connected with the reconstruction of the nations of Indochina. It has to be said that not much in the way of concrete results came out of all these deliberations and indeed ASEAN tended to be dismissed by many commentators as not much more than a forum for discussion. Part of the trouble seems to have been that although the various committees were active enough, they worked in isolation from the policymakers in their own governments. Ministers for economic affairs, for instance, were rarely consulted or knew what was being discussed in the way of measures for economic cooperation within ASEAN.

ZOPFAN

One important initiative that ASEAN did take in the early years—and that in the political field, contrasting the general flow of its interests which were then economic—was the attempt to ensure that Southeast Asia became a neutralized zone, free from interference by outside powers. This concept was the brainchild of the Malaysians who clearly felt somewhat exposed by the 1968 British withdrawal "East of Suez" and, like their fellow members of ASEAN, were increasingly worried by the prospect of an American debacle in Vietnam. Using the formula of a zone of peace, freedom and neutrality (ZOPFAN) they sought the endorsement not only of their neighbors Thailand and Indonesia but also of the Nonaligned Movement to which they were admitted in 1969.

The idea was formally presented at the fourth ASEAN ministerial meeting in March 1971; the following November the ASEAN foreign ministers convened in Kuala Lumpur in order to issue a declaration of their determination "to exert initially necessary efforts to secure the recognition of, and respect for" ZOPFAN. The somewhat lukewarm phraseology lends credence to the view that the other members of ASEAN had doubts about the feasibility of the Malaysian concept but subscribed to it in the interests of group solidarity. Nonetheless ZOPFAN now became part of ASEAN's official policy. In this context it is of some interest that the preamble to the declaration contains a passing reference to the principles of peaceful coexistence enunciated at the Bandung conference of 1955 and also to the significant trend toward establishing nuclear-free zones in, for example, Latin America and Africa.

U.N. REPORT ON ASEAN

The withdrawal of U.S. troops from Vietnam in 1973 and the fall of South Vietnam to the communists two years later deeply affected the member nations of ASEAN. As early as 1972 a report on ASEAN economic cooperation by a U.N. study team had called for greater efforts by member nations in this field. It pointed out that although their total foreign trade amounted to US $18 billion annually, only 15 percent of it was among themselves (and only 6 percent if Singapore's entrepôt trade was not included). Imports of manufactured goods amounted to $5 billion annually but only about 3 percent of this market was being met from within the region by import-substitution manufacturing of simpler goods. Close industrial integration was not recommended, however, nor was the region politically or economically ready to become a free trade area, a customs union or a common market. Instead it was suggested that the member governments negotiate measures of trade liberalization in selected commodities; that industrial complementary agreements be reached with the help of the business communities, and by means of tariff concessions by the governments where necessary; and that joint industrial projects be promoted. One result of this report was that the economic ministers of the member nations were increasingly brought into ASEAN planning and decisionmaking. As the discussion on the U.N. findings developed, Singapore emerged as the firmest supporter of an ASEAN free trade area with the Philippines and Thailand also in favor. Indonesia, however, was bitterly opposed to this notion, fearing that it would be subjected to the full blast of Singaporean competition in its home market.

The eighth ASEAN ministerial meeting, held in Kuala Lumpur in May 1975, two weeks after the fall of Saigon, requested the permanent committees give priority to projects that would contribute to the liberalization of trade and industrial complementation. A draft agreement on the establishment of an ASEAN secretariat was approved as was a draft treaty of amity and cooperation. The proposal by Adam Malik, the Indonesian foreign minister, that a meeting of ASEAN heads of government be held for the first time was a further reflection of the seriousness of the international situation. As Lee Kuan Yew put it during a visit to Singapore by Thai Prime Minister Kukrit Pramoj in 1975, "the countries of ASEAN are at a crossroads." Lee added that the region was facing "great changes after the momentous events in Indochina."

BALI SUMMIT

The heads of government met in Bali in February 1976. Three documents were signed: a declaration of ASEAN concord, a treaty of amity and cooperation in Southeast Asia and an agreement on the establishment of an ASEAN secretariat. The declaration of ASEAN concord, the most important and detailed of the three, began by setting out the "objectives and principles in the pursuit of political stability." These included the elimination of threats posed by subversion in each member nation; the improvement of living standards and the promotion of social justice by intensifying cooperation in economic and social development; the relief of member nations when afflicted by natural disorders and other major calamities; the broadening of the complementarity of their economies; and the peaceful settlement of intraregional differences. The document then went on to delineate a program of action for ASEAN cooperation under various headings—political, economic, social and cultural. The political section mentioned among other things the improvement of ASEAN machinery to strengthen political cooperation and the possibilities for developing judicial cooperation including an ASEAN extradition treaty. It spoke of "immediate consideration of initial steps toward recognition of and respect for ZOPFAN wherever possible," a formulation which reflected the wording of the ZOPFAN declaration of 1971 and which interestingly appears to be less firm than that used in the preamble on principles (referred to above) where it is stated that "Member states, individually and collectively, shall take active steps for the early establishment of ZOPFAN." Obviously this was a subject that called for some fancy footwork by the drafters of the document.

The economic sections covered cooperation on the supply of basic commodities, particularly food and energy. Member nations should also cooperate in the establishment of large-scale ASEAN industrial plants to meet regional requirements of essential commodities. On trade, the member states were to progress toward the establishment of preferential trading arrangements as a long-term objective through negotiations, "subject to the unanimous agreement of member states." They were also to improve access to markets outside ASEAN by striving for the elimination of all trade barriers in such markets. In addition there was to be cooperation in the field of technology and production methods to improve the quality of exports from ASEAN countries. There should be joint approaches in the United Nations and elsewhere to international commodity problems and the reform of the world trading and monetary systems, "with a view to contributing to the establishment of the New International Economic Order." The machinery for economic cooperation was placed on a more organized basis in the shape of regular meetings of ministers for economic affairs.

The declaration also included a section on social matters dealing briefly with cooperation concerning the expansion of productive employment with fair remuneration, the problems of population growth and the prevention and eradication of the abuse of narcotics and the illegal trafficking in drugs. This was followed by a cultural section that looked to the promotion of the study of ASEAN and the languages of the region in schools. ASEAN scholars, writers, artists and the media were to be encouraged to foster a sense of regional identification and fellowship. The section on security, as befitted an organization that took care not to stress this aspect of its activities, consisted of a single sentence that merely looked to a continuation of cooperation among its members on a non-ASEAN basis "in accordance with their mutual needs and interests."

The second major agreement signed at Bali, the treaty of amity and cooperation, was designed "to promote regional peace and stability through abiding respect for justice and the rule of law and enhancing regional resilience." It acknowledged its debt to the Charter of the United Nations, the Ten Principles of Peaceful Coexistence adopted at Bandung, the Bangkok declaration of 1967 and the Kuala Lumpur declaration of 1971. Inevitably, perhaps, much of the treaty is couched in vague generalities ("peace," "harmony," "stability") and goes over ground already covered by the declaration of ASEAN concord. But it does make clear (possibly with the Philippine claim to Sabah in mind) that each signatory nation "shall not in any manner or form participate in any activity which shall constitute a threat to the political and economic stability, sovereignty, or territorial integrity" of another signatory nation. Disputes should be prevented from arising but if they did arise there should be no threat or use of force and they should be settled by friendly negotiations. A high council, comprising a representative at ministerial level from each member nation, was to settle disputes through regional processes and, where direct negotiations failed to affect a solution, by offering its good offices or, with the agreement of the parties to the dispute, by constituting itself into a committee of mediation, inquiry or conciliation. The treaty was to be open for accession by other nations in Southeast Asia thus echoing the Bangkok declaration. Generally thought to be a gesture toward Burma and the countries of Indochina, the treaty must be seen as rather a forlorn hope, given the prevailing circumstances in those countries.

The agreement on the establishment of an ASEAN secretariat was necessitated, according to its preamble, by "the rapidly growing activities of ASEAN" since its inception. A permanent secretariat would, it was hoped, lead to "more efficient coordination of ASEAN organs and more effective implementation of ASEAN projects and activities." Jakarta was chosen as its site—an acknowledgement, no doubt, of Indonesia's position as by far the largest member nation. The host country was responsible for the capital outlay connected with the building, furnishing and major maintenance of the headquarters; recurrent expenditure (salaries, office requisites, annual maintenance and all other administrative expenses) was to be shared by all member nations. The secretary-general was to be appointed for two years by the ASEAN foreign ministers on a rotational basis in alphabetical order (Dharsono of Indonesia became the first incumbent). There were to be three bureaus—economic; science and technology; and social and cultural, in that order of rank—each headed by a director. There was also to be a foreign trade and economic relations officer, an administrative officer, a public information officer and an assistant to the secretary-general, all of at least first secretary rank, nominated by the member nations and appointed by the standing committee. Apart from the secretary-general, all these appointments were for a term of three years with the possibility of extension for another full term but no longer. This steady flow of changing personnel at the upper echelons meant that no one could make a career in ASEAN and that the association would remain in a subordinate position vis-à-vis the member countries.

In their final communiqué the heads of government noted with satisfaction what had been achieved at the meeting and expressed their belief that it was essential for the member states to move to "higher levels of cooperation." On ZOPFAN they managed to marry the two formulas used in the declaration of ASEAN concord which gave the impression that, on balance, they were in favor of its early establishment. The events in Vietnam were evidently still very much on their minds. They averred their readiness to develop "fruitful relations and mutually beneficial cooperation with other countries in the region" and expressed the hope that "other powers would pursue policies which would contribute to the achievement of peace, stability and progress in Southeast Asia." Their main emphasis, however, was on the economic development of ASEAN. They agreed that the economic ministers should meet in Kuala Lumpur the following month to consider ways of implementing the decisions of the Bali meeting. In particular they were to consider appropriate measures for the establishment of large-scale industrial projects for the production of urea, superphosphates, potash, petrochemicals, steel, soda ash, newsprint and rubber products. Regarding preferential trading arrangements they mentioned such methods as long-term quantity contracts, purchase finance support at preferential interest rates and the extension of tariff preferences. Priority should be given to the stabilization of export earnings of ASEAN commodities.

The documents signed at the Bali summit conference provided a framework for ASEAN policies that has continued to the present. The heads of government built upon and carried further the decisions of the inaugural meeting in Bangkok nine years previously, although in several important respects there was little change. The economic development of ASEAN, slow though it was, continued to receive more attention than its political, social and cultural concerns. The emphasis was still on the national state as the basis of the association and the subject of regional security, although very much in the minds of many, was given little public airing in ASEAN forums.

ECONOMIC AFTERMATH OF BALI

Immediately following the Bali meeting the economic ministers met as arranged in March 1976. Already each member nation had chosen its industrial project: Indonesia, urea; Malaysia, urea; the Philippines, superphosphates; Singapore, diesel engines; and Thailand, soda ash. The economic ministers agreed to establish a group of experts to examine the feasibility of these projects and to consider other possible projects, namely machine tools, fisheries, tin plating, tires and electronic components. But this initial enthusiasm was not maintained. The text of the basic agreement on ASEAN industrial projects was agreed by the economic ministers only in 1978. The first project to be approved was Indonesia's in 1977; the second was Malaysia's the following year, when the Thai rock salt soda ash plant was also accepted. The Philippines, having had a superphosphate fertilizer plant approved as the fourth ASEAN project in 1979, changed its mind when it looked as though prices would not be competitive on world markets and substituted for it an integrated pulp and paper project at the 1980 economic ministers' meeting. The Philippines had third thoughts the following year when it decided on a copper fabrication plant, which was approved by the economic ministers in 1982. Singapore had very soon decided against its diesel engine project because of the likelihood of sharp competition from similar plants in other member nations, notably Indonesia. It made no immediate attempt at substitution and it was not until 1984 that its token suggestion for a small hepatitis B vaccine plant was approved as the fifth ASEAN industrial project. The Thais, too, had problems with the soda ash project, which they mulled over for several years. It was scaled down in 1984 but the *Far Eastern Economic Review* stated in December 1987 that it had been officially dropped "for complex feasibility and environmental reasons." Thus only the Indonesian and Malaysian projects were actually completed and are in production by the end of the 1980s. The Philippine copper fabrication project was reported to be still in the planning stage as of 1986.

Another significant economic initiative set in motion at Bali was the preferential trading arrangement (PTA). After consideration in draft form by each of the economic ministers, an agreement was signed at a special meeting of foreign ministers in Manila in February 1977. By the following June the first tariff concessions were made, involving 71 products; later the same year the economic ministers agreed to establish a target of 50 products to be added for each round of negotiations on tariff preferences. In 1980 the economic ministers agreed that trade in products of less than $50,000 in value be subject to a 20 percent cut in existing tariffs across the board. Two years later these cuts were applied to items having an import value of up to $10 million. The system of ASEAN-wide negotiations on exchanging tariff preference items on products was replaced by bilateral negotiations between member nations. A maximum tariff reduction of 50 percent was established for nonfood items already under the PTA and for products approved in the future. The result of these measures has been that the list now covers thousands of items (more than 12,000 by 1983). Although this looks impressive it covers only two percent of intra-ASEAN trade and in any case the latter amounts to no more than about one seventh of total ASEAN trade. The member governments have tended to exclude a broad range of items on the plea of sensitivity, while items put forward for inclusion have, generally speaking, been those which would not affect customs revenue unduly.

As noted above, industrial complementation had been mentioned in the U.N. report of 1972. It was also taken up by one of several special committees established by the economic ministers in 1977, namely that dealing with industry, minerals and energy. The committee identified possible projects in a whole series of sectors, including motor vehicles, agricultural machines, telecommunications equipment, newsprint, fertilizers, steel and rubber. The idea was that business and government in the member nations would cooperate in the establishment of industries in which each country would play a complementary part in production and subassembly. The finished product would enjoy intra-ASEAN tariff protection. The involvement of the private sector took some time to organize, however. Even after the formation of the ASEAN Chambers of Commerce in 1972 it was three years before a working group in complementation was established. This latter eventually concentrated on a proposal for an integrated automobile industry, which was finally given the approval of the economic ministers in 1980. Negotiations followed with Japan, the country which exported most cars to the region, but the decision by Malaysia to produce its own automobile dealt a serious blow to the whole scheme.

The economic ministers were also keen to promote joint ventures between domestic and foreign investors. The ASEAN industrial joint venture (AIJV) scheme, approved in 1983, provides for the submission of a list of products by the private sector through the ASEAN Chambers of Commerce to the committee on industry, minerals and energy for approval by the economic minister. Two or more ASEAN countries may participate in any AIJV project which can be located in any of the participating countries. AIJV products are granted a 50 percent minimum tariff preference by participating countries for a period of three years, after which this preference is extended to all plants in the ASEAN region producing the product whether they are AIJV or not. The first two projects, with majority shares owned by Malaysians were begun in 1984 and produce constant velocity joints and rack and pinion steerings. Thailand also started two AIJV projects: one, a $7 million plant producing pottery glazes, represents cooperation between Thai, Malaysian and Japanese interests; the other, a motorcycle electrical parts project, has majority Thai and minority Malaysian interests. In 1985 three new AIJV projects were approved by the economic ministers: paper (Malaysia and Brunei), potash feldspar quartz (Thailand and Indonesia) and slaughtered meat (Thailand and the Philippines). The next year the economic ministers agreed to increase the margin of preference for AIJV projects from 50 percent to 75 percent to encourage foreign investment.

Other ASEAN economic initiatives after Bali included a swap arrangement or standby credit facility established in 1977 by the ASEAN central banks and monetary authorities to help members bridge temporary international liquidity problems. The arrangement was backed by the sum of $100 million ($20 million from each of the five members) and credit was to be made available for a period of up to six months. A member nation could borrow up to double the amount of its contribution. Another precautionary measure was a sharing scheme for rice and oil (or oil products) to meet emergencies and shortages.

POLITICAL DEVELOPMENTS

So far the thoughts of ASEAN leaders had been mainly directed toward economic matters even though the actual results were modest. The single political initiative, ZOPFAN, often seemed more of a chimera than a solid policy. The early 1970s also saw the establishment of a series of "dialogues" with friendly powers. That with the European Community (EC) was started in 1972; with Australia in 1974; New Zealand in 1975; and Canada, Japan and the United States each in 1977. Each ASEAN member was responsible for a particular part of the dialogue coverage: Indonesia with Japan and the EC; Malaysia with Australia and South Asian countries; Philippines with the United States and Canada; Singapore with New Zealand; and Thailand with the U.N. Development Program, UNCTAD and ESCAP. Basically forums for discussion of matters of mutual interest, these dialogues also covered various aspects of development cooperation and technical aid, research projects and the expansion of trade, including the organization of, for example, trade fairs. While the actual achievements of these dialogues might be somewhat less than the printed word would suggest, they represented a useful stage in the molding of an ASEAN attitude toward the outside world.

The tenth anniversary of the founding of ASEAN was celebrated in style with the holding of a second heads of government meeting, this time in Kuala Lumpur in August 1977. Since it was only eighteen months since the previous summit its deliberations covered much the same ground and the final communiqué was a far less important document than those issued at Bali. The ASEAN heads seized the opportunity to express their concern over the "protectionist tendencies" of the developed countries and, in a reference to the growing problem of Vietnamese refugees ("boat people"), called on the U.N. High Commissioner for Refugees and other similar agencies to help with the speedy resettlement of these unfortunate people in third countries. On intra-ASEAN affairs the heads of government praised the initial efforts of member nations at regional cooperation in communications and transportation (for example, the development of the ASEAN submarine cable and regional satellite systems) and cooperation in railways, shipping and aviation; they also drew attention to the ASEAN declaration of principles on the combatting of drug abuse.

One initiative was an invitation to the heads of government of Japan, Australia and New Zealand to meet the ASEAN leaders for the first time, after the main summit meeting. Prime Minister Malcolm Fraser of Australia, Prime Minister Takeo Fukuda of Japan and Prime Minister Robert Muldoon of New Zealand all attended. This was mainly an exercise in public relations in the interest of boosting the association's international image. However, Fraser announced that existing Australian bilateral aid to ASEAN member countries would be increased from A$90 million to A$250 million; and Fukuda promised Japanese assistance to the ASEAN industrial projects program to the requested amount of $1 billion, subject to confirmation by feasibility tests.

The most unexpected political aspect of the Kuala Lumpur summit conference was President Ferdinand Marcos' offer that the Philippines would drop its claim to Sabah. This problem had bedeviled relations with Malaysia since the latter's formation in 1963. The then Philippine government, claiming to be the heir of the sultan of the Sulu Islands, part of whose territory Sabah had once been, averred that the province should revert to the Philippines. The dispute continued quietly over the years but was certainly never allowed to disrupt ASEAN solidarity. It did, however, cause some coolness between the two countries. Marcos' gesture was therefore received with great satisfaction, not only in Kuala Lumpur but also in the other ASEAN capitals. As time went on, however, Malaysia's satisfaction was tempered with frustration in that the Philippine government made no effort to amend documents wherein Sabah was listed as part of Philippine territory. The Malaysians were not reassured by soothing statements from Manila, including one in 1984 by Foreign Minister Arturo Tolentino that the claim had been dropped. In 1987 the government of Corazon Aquino introduced a bill that for the first time defined Philippine boundaries without Sabah but it met with strong opposition in congress. To help toward an affirmative vote Malaysia made a tentative offer to establish joint border patrols (as requested by Manila) in the drive against piracy, smuggling and gun running but to no avail. Malaysia and the Philippines also have competing claims for the Spratly Islands in the South China Sea and each country reportedly maintains a small naval presence there.

Undoubtedly the greatest political test which ASEAN has had to undergo arose from events in Indochina. The victory of the communists in Vietnam caused the members of ASEAN to draw closer together. At first Hanoi was deeply suspicious of the association, dubbing it a tool of the Americans, and refused to have anything to do with it, although it established or normalized relations with the member nations individually. For their part the ASEAN countries were ready to deal with Vietnam, Cambodia and Laos "on a constructive and productive basis," in the words of Lee Kuan Yew. Vietnam began to have second thoughts about ASEAN in 1978 as a result of deteriorating relations with Cambodia and China. During a visit to To- kyo in July of that year Deputy Foreign Minister Phan Hien said that his country was ready to have dealings with ASEAN at any time and even called for a new regional economic organization to include ASEAN, Indo- china and even Burma. Two months later Prime Minister Pham Van Dong toured the ASEAN countries on a fence-mending operation. He assured them that Vietnam would not interfere in their internal affairs (interpreted as no longer supporting communist insurgencies), urged the conclusion of treaties of friendship with member nations and spoke of the need for a zone of peace, independence, freedom, neutrality, stability and prosperity in the region. The inclusion of the reference to "independence" in this gloss on the ZOPFAN concept was seen as inferring that so long as U.S. bases continued to exist the region was not truly free.

This attempt at rapprochement was soon nullified by the Vietnamese invasion of Cambodia in December 1978, the overthrow of the Khmer Rouge regime and the installation of the Heng Samrin puppet government in January 1979. The ASEAN countries roundly condemned the Vietnam- ese actions and found themselves on the same side of the imbroglio as China, a staunch supporter of the Khmer Rouge, and against the Soviet Union which had signed a treaty of friendship and cooperation with Viet- nam the previous November. Unlike the Chinese who undertook a limited punitive "expedition" against the Vietnamese early in 1978, ASEAN con- fined its activities to the United Nations where with U.S. help it sponsored two Security Council resolutions calling for the withdrawal of foreign troops from Cambodia; both resolutions were vetoed by the Soviet Union. There- after the battleground shifted to the General Assembly which, at ASEAN insistence, voted against recognition of the Heng Samrin regime as the representative of Cambodia and passed a resolution calling for the total and unconditional withdrawal of Vietnamese forces from Cambodia as a precon- dition for negotiations.

It was also as the result of ASEAN efforts that a U.N. conference on Cambodia was held in New York in 1981. ASEAN tried to follow a con- ciliatory line of inviting representatives from the four Cambodian factions but China would not agree to a member of the Heng Samrin government attending. The final declaration represented something of a compromise between ASEAN's "conciliation" and China's "intransigence." It called for a ceasefire by all parties, the withdrawal of all foreign troops from Cam- bodia under U.N supervision and the holding of free elections also under U.N. auspices. Subsequently China joined ASEAN in urging the three factions opposed to Heng Samrin to form a coalition, which they eventually did in 1982. Throughout the 1980s ASEAN tried through patient diplo- macy to bring the coalition group and the Phnom Penh authorities to the negotiating table. This policy was maintained despite differences of opinion in the ASEAN ranks: on one side Indonesia and Malaysia have kept open their lines to Hanoi in the conviction that Vietnam could provide a shield for Southeast Asia against China; and on the other side Thailand cultivates China as an insurance policy against Vietnamese military power. The whole situation significantly altered following the Chinese-Soviet rapprochement in 1989 and the announcement by Vietnam that, if a political settlement could be reached, it would withdraw all its troops from Cambodia by 1990. It can be reasonably argued that ASEAN has helped to bring about these events by its steadfast refusal over the years to accept the Vietnamese occupation of Cambodia or to allow the rest of the world to forget it.

The twentieth anniversary of ASEAN was celebrated by the convening of a heads of government meeting in Manila in December 1987. Postponed from the previous July because of the volatile internal situation in the Philippines, it was apparently held on the insistence of Suharto who wished to demonstrate ASEAN's support for the Aquino government. It was notable for being the first visit to Manila of a Malaysian prime minister (a reflection of the Sabah issue) and for the fact that the only foreign visitor to meet the ASEAN leaders afterward was Japanese Prime Minister Noboru Takeshita (a reflection of that country's importance to Southeast Asia). The Japanese guest brought promises of $2 billion worth of aid, although, as with Fukuda's gesture in 1977, it is difficult to know how and to what extent such large sums are to be disbursed. For the rest, there were no major political initiatives. No further progress was made with ZOPFAN, the leaders still hoping for its "early realization." Efforts toward the early establishment of a nuclear-free zone were also mentioned but Aquino's hopes for ASEAN endorsement of the importance of the U.S. bases in the Philippines—or maybe even an assumption of an ASEAN collective responsibility for them—received no encouragement. The Sabah dispute—that "fishbone in the throat," to use the words of Malaysia Prime Minister D. S. Mahathir—was left in abeyance. On the economic front there were no major steps forward. Instead the declaration confined itself to pious hopes for the future: to expand the PTA to cover half of intra-ASEAN trade within the next few years; to freeze and gradually reduce nontariff barriers to intra-ASEAN trade; to harmonize guarantees for intra-ASEAN investment; and to arrange for non-ASEAN partners in AIJV schemes to be allowed to hold 60 percent of the equity.

ACHIEVEMENTS AND PROSPECTS

What then has been achieved by ASEAN during the first twenty or so years of its existence? Looking back on the record, it has clearly been less of a success in the economic, than in the political field. Most of the ASEAN economic agreements have been statements of principle or of intent rather than decisions producing tangible attainments. Nothing seems to be completed. Only two of the ASEAN industrial projects were actively in production by 1990 and the range of PTAs looks more impressive on paper than in actuality. The individual economies of the member nations remains largely untrammeled by ASEAN regulations. Since the aim has so far been economic cooperation rather than economic integration, talk of a free trade zone, a customs union or even a common market for ASEAN still seems unrealistic. The member nations remain stubbornly competitive in the production of commodities and the development of their manufacturing industries.

In the political arena the balance sheet looks much brighter. The member countries have certainly learned to "think ASEAN" and to present a united front in international affairs. This is not to say that they see eye to eye on every issue. As indicated above, the Philippines and Malaysia have continuing problems over Sabah and the Spratly Islands. Malaysia and Indonesia view China (and Vietnam) rather differently than does Thailand. And in November 1986 Singapore gave great offense to its Islamic neighbors by receiving the Israeli president on a state visit (the Aquino government cancelled a similar visit to Manila in the light of Malaysian and Indonesian reactions). The point to make here, however, is that none of these disagreements has been allowed to go beyond a certain point or to dent ASEAN unanimity in the eyes of the rest of the world. This solidarity was evident during Indonesia's takeover of East Timor in 1975 and at various times has sustained Thailand in its role as front-line nation against the Vietnamese and the Philippine government in its struggle against communist insurgency. It received its most striking expression over the Cambodian situation which has tested ASEAN patience for over ten years. The habit of forming a political consensus has taken root among the member nations (however wayward and individualistic they remain, economically speaking) and, what is equally important, the rest of the world has got used to ASEAN as an entity. The Soviet Union and Vietnam, once so scathing about the association, have come round to recognizing it as a valid interlocutor on the international stage and even to court its good opinion. Japan and the United States, its two biggest markets, continue to cultivate it for political, strategic and economic reasons. Japan, also its main aid donor, sends its prime minister to ASEAN summit meetings and the United States has even expressed the idea of an ASEAN-U.S. free trade zone.

ASEAN's greatest achievement, however, is that it is difficult to conceive of a situation where the member nations, whatever their disagreements, would resort to the use of arms against one another. In this it parallels Europe where it is now unthinkable that war would ever break out within the EC itself, however complicated some of its internal problems are. Perhaps therefore it is not too fanciful to suggest that ASEAN, despite its present economic divergencies, may even pursue the goal of becoming an economic community by 2000 as Aquino and Suharto have suggested. But given ASEAN's slow rate of change this seems problematical. More distantly the association may one day become part of a wider Pacific Basin community. Meanwhile ASEAN will probably continue cautiously to develop its internal cohesion, to eschew the role of military organization and to seek stability for its region by obtaining general recognition as a neutral and nonnuclear group. Its attainments so far justify a certain optimism.

FURTHER READING

Broinowski, Alison, ed. *Understanding ASEAN*. London: Macmillan, 1982.

Harris, Stuart, and Bridges, Brian. *European Interests in ASEAN*. Chatham House Paper No. 19. London: Routledge & Kegan Paul for the Royal Institute of International Affairs, 1983.

Jorgensen-Dahl, Arnfinn. *Regional Organisation and Order in Southeast Asia*. London: Macmillan, 1982.

Leifer, Michael. *ASEAN and the Security of South-East Asia*. London: Routledge, 1988.

Palmer, Ronald D., and Reckford, Thomas J. *Building ASEAN: 20 Years of Southeast Asian Cooperation*. New York: Praeger, 1987.

Simon, Sheldon W. *The ASEAN States and Regional Security*. Stanford, California: Hoover Institution Press, 1982.

Skully, Michael T. *ASEAN Financial Cooperation: Developments in Banking, Finance and Insurance*. London: Macmillan, 1985.

Tilman, Robert O. *Southeast Asia and the Enemy Beyond: ASEAN Perceptions of External Threats*. Boulder, Colorado: Westview Press, 1987.

Wawn, Brian. *The Economies of the ASEAN Countries: Indonesia, Malaysia, Philippines, Singapore, and Thailand*. London: Macmillan, 1982.

REGIONAL COOPERATION IN SOUTH ASIA: SAARC

SUMIT GANGULY

ORIGINS

THE notion of regional cooperation in South Asia is an odd one. After all, this is one region of the world that has witnessed not only its fair share of intrastate discord but four wars of some consequence (the three Indo-Pakistani conflicts of 1947–48, 1965 and 1971 and the Sino-Indian border war of 1962). The states in the region have had varying degrees of difficulty in achieving national integration. From the time of their independence in 1947, India and Pakistan have both sought to integrate the state of Kashmir. Also India had to use force in 1947 to integrate Hyderabad and Junagadh, two recalcitrant princely states. Later, when negotiations failed, India again resorted to force to evict the last outpost of Portuguese colonialism in Goa in 1961. More recently, India has been faced with a series of autonomist movements in its northeast where rebel Naga and Mizo forces have challenged the extension of state authority. These conflicts appear to be subsiding. However, another, and indeed worse problem, that of the Punjab, threatens Indian unity. Pakistan's fortunes in the area of national integration have not been as successful. A combination of economic, cultural, primarily linguistic, grievances led to a secessionist movement in East Pakistan, culminating in the genesis of Bangladesh in 1971. In the post-1971 era Pakistan has continued to witness the periodic rise of autonomist sentiment in its western province of Sind. Bangladesh too has not escaped ethnic and regional discord. Today tribals in the Chakma Hill tracts resist the imposition of central authority. However, the most compelling ethnic conflict raging in South Asia, with the possible exception of the Punjab, is in Sri Lanka. Here the Tamil minority seek to redress what they perceive to be Sinhalese attempts to deny them equal socioeconomic and political status.

Many of these internal conflicts are not self-contained but percolate through porous borders. In 1971 India actively aided the East Pakistani *mukti bahini* (freedom force) and there was considerable support for Bengali nationalism in the adjoining state of West Bengal. Today there are widespread allegations of Pakistani support for Sikh terrorists in the Punjab. Until the signing of the Indo-Sri Lankan accord, there was also evidence of tacit Indian support for the Tamil guerrillas in Sri Lanka. Conflict and discord rather than cooperation and harmony have characterized the relations of the South Asian states in the postindependence era.

It is hardly surprising that this region should be characterized by such fissiparous tendencies.[1] It is often said that the region is a patchwork of religious persuasions, linguistic differences and consequent cultural heterogeneity. Such cultural diversity can lead to violent conflict. One has to only to look to the European experience to find compelling historical antecedents.

Despite the prevalence of internal discord and external conflict for nearly three decades, efforts have been under way to obtain a degree of cooperation and harmony in the region. The immediate origins of the South Asian Association for Regional Cooperation (SAARC) must be traced to the initiatives launched between 1977 and 1981 by the assassinated Bangladeshi leader, General Ziaur Rahman. However, the idea of and efforts toward regional cooperation in South Asia long precede General Ziaur's legacy.

The discussions about regional cooperation in Asia in general, and South Asia in particular, were debated at the Asian Relations Conference held in New Delhi in late March and early April 1947. Organized under the auspices of the semiautonomous Indian Council for World Affairs, the conference drew delegates from some 25 Asian nations. This conference had an obviously anticolonial tone and the delegates, many of whom were nascent heads of state, proudly proclaimed the arrival of free Asia on the world scene. While proclaiming their newly acquired status as independent states they also expressed misgivings about the possibilities of being dominated by the larger Asian powers. In turn, the two largest Asian nations in attendance, India and China, discovered that, despite professions of amity, there were important and concrete differences that divided them. Specifically, the Indians and the Chinese clashed on two issues. First, on a general level, they were in contention about their respective desires to assume the leadership role in Asia. Second, and more particularly, the Chinese objected to a map that showed Tibet to be a separate state.[2] Both issues were to take on much greater significance in the years that followed and ultimately culminate in the Sino-Indian border war of 1962.

The conference ended without any concrete proposals for action. If anything, the smaller nations were interested in limiting the freer movements of populations in Asia. At best, all the states in attendance celebrated independent Asia's resurgence. No specific proposals for increased cooperation emerged, let alone concrete efforts toward regional integration. The results should not have come as a surprise. Most of the delegations were led by individuals who had recently brought their nations to independence.

[1] Selig Harrison, *India: The Most Dangerous Decades* (Princeton, N.J.: Princeton University Press, 1960).
[2] Sisir Gupta, *India and Regional Integration in Asia* (Bombay: Asia Publishing House, 1964), p. 36.

At this time they were hardly likely to concede any hint of their hard-won sovereignty to a supranational organization. In the words of Sisir Gupta, an Indian scholar-diplomat, "Viewed from the angle of regional integration, the conference was evidently more important for exposing the problems involved in any such attempt than in achieving concrete results."[3]

The conference was scheduled to meet again in China in 1949. Owing to the civil war and the Chinese revolution, it failed to transpire. It maintained a notional existence until 1957 when it was quietly disbanded. The idea of regional cooperation, however, was not extinguished and continued to persist, as was evident in the Baguio Conference of May 1950 held in the Philippines. The conference was attended by India, Pakistan, Australia, Indonesia, Thailand and Ceylon (later Sri Lanka). By this time, the winds of the cold war were being felt in Asia and there was a greater sense of discord among the Asian nations. The Philippines and Australia were distinctly pro-American and anticommunist, whereas the other states were neutral to varying degrees. In substantive terms this conference could only encourage greater cultural cooperation.[4]

The idea of regional cooperation underwent a shift at this point. Instead of emphasizing the evanescent possibilities of regional integration, the focus turned to the possibilities of shielding Asia from cold war tensions. India's prime minister, Jawaharlal Nehru, played a major role in stressing the need to keep Asia free from superpower competition. His principal fear was that economic development in Asia, for which there was a great need, would suffer a major setback if Asia was drawn into the vortex of superpower competition. This fear in turn stemmed from the belief that involvement with the superpowers and their conflicts would lead to the militarization of Asian societies. Peace in Nehru's view was "an emergent necessity."[5] Nehru's ideas, though unacceptable to both superpowers, found favor with some Asian leaders. In keeping with the sentiments espoused by Nehru, the prime minister of Ceylon convened a conference in Colombo in April 1954, attended by Burma, India, Pakistan and Indonesia. The conference agenda included such diverse issues as the threat of the hydrogen bomb to international security and the problem of international communism. Again national perspectives and interests quickly overshadowed the larger goal of seeking peace and amity in Asia. To the Ceylonese and the Pakistanis the spread of international communism was the principal concern. Also Pakistan sought to bring up its bilateral problem with India over the unresolved question of Kashmir. The bilateral differences and the divergent views about the cold war limited the cooperative dimensions of this conference. Over the next several years these differences, particularly those of a bilateral nature, grew. The participants of this conference, with the exception of Paki-

[3] Ibid., p. 37.
[4] Ibid., p. 47.
[5] D. R. Sardesai, *Indian Foreign Policy in Cambodia, Laos and Vietnam* (Berkeley: University of California Press, 1968), p. 68.

istan, met again in 1956. Again there was desultory talk about increasing cooperation but it amounted to little.[6]

In the interim, in 1955, President Sukarno of Indonesia had convened the Bandung Conference. The conference addressed a large and diverse set of goals, most of them relating to building a sense of solidarity between newly independent African and Asian nations. From the standpoint of regional integration the delegates enumerated a long agenda of cooperative ventures. They included suggestions for mutual technical assistance, the establishment of regional banks, the creation of regional training institutes and the possibilities of collective bargaining in specific issue areas.[7] However, no machinery or institutional means for achieving such ends were actively considered.

In large part this may have simply stemmed from the twin political and economic difficulties of supporting such organizations. The political problems would have been caused by a diversity of specific interests; the economic problems would have arisen from the paucity of funds that were available to these nations. Despite the inability of the Bandung Conference to make much headway in the area of regional integration it nevertheless provided the basis of what came to be known as the Non-Aligned Movement (NAM).

The only other effort at regional integration in Asia, of any note, was attempted under the aegis of the British Commonwealth. At a Commonwealth foreign ministers meeting in Colombo in 1950, discussions were held about possible means of enhancing economic development in Asia. To this end, the foreign ministers made bilateral arrangements to provide technical training and direct technical and economic assistance. While this program met with varying degrees of success, it remained largely a set of bilateral arrangements and has not fundamentally contributed to regional integration.

REKINDLING AN IDEA

After the mid-1960s it was difficult to conceive of the possibilities of regional integration in South Asia. Discord, both internal and external, characterized the region. Not until the early 1970s did the region experience any degree of political stability. Despite this political stability, the region remained one of the poorest in the world. The initiative for regional cooperation came from Bangladesh, the poorest nation in the region. Three distinct reasons can be suggested for the timing of this initiative. First, General Ziaur Rahman had come to power in a military coup in 1975, overthrowing the civilian regime of Sheikh Mujibur Rahman, founder of Bangladesh. India, the dominant regional power, had seen the overthrow of Sheikh Mujibur Rahman as a major foreign policy setback. India had supported him prior to the creation of Bangladesh, and saw his regime as

[6]Gupta, p. 53.
[7]Ibid., p. 65.

sympathetic to its interests. The new military regime could not be counted on to pursue policies congruent with Indian concerns. Thus, it was perhaps with a view to allaying Indian misgivings that General Ziaur decided to explore the possibilities of a regional organization devoted to regional co-operation. Second, Bangladesh would be more likely to get a better hearing on certain outstanding problems that it faced with India if these problems could be raised in a multilateral forum. Third, the moment was propitious for discussing the idea of regional cooperation because of the regime in India. The Janata party was in office there and was pursuing a more conciliatory foreign policy toward India's neighbors than had been the case during Indira Gandhi's regime. Specifically, as far as Bangladesh was concerned, it was during this time that an important accord on sharing the Ganga River waters was signed between India and Bangladesh. Despite domestic opposition in India, the Indian government made significant concessions to the Bangladeshi demands for a greater share of the river's waters.[8]

Despite the Indian government's willingness to make significant concessions on the Ganga River waters, suspicions about General Ziaur's regime remained. Thus when General Ziaur first suggested a cooperative venture he was met with a less than enthusiastic response from India. The smaller countries of the region—Nepal, Bhutan and Sri Lanka—were more forthcoming. (Initially, the Maldives was not approached.) Both Pakistan and India viewed this proposal with a mixture of caution and suspicion. India feared that this proposed forum or organization would be used by its smaller neighbors to gang up against India and air their grievances. Pakistan, in turn, feared that India might dominate the organization and turn the smaller states against Pakistan. Despite this initial suspicion and caution both nations, after careful scrutiny of the proposal, gave their consent.

The fact that the two larger powers in the region should have viewed Ziaur's proposals with circumspection is indicative of the difficulties of promoting regional cooperation. What distinguishes South Asia from other areas is that, as a region, there is a lack of economic complementariness and a perceived security threat. Nevertheless, the Bangladesh foreign ministry's memorandum, which formally proposed the creation of the South Asian Regional Cooperation (SARC) organization, pointed out that:

> while other regions had evolved institutional arrangements for consultations on matters of mutual interest and cooperation in the economic, social and cultural fields on a regional basis, and had consequently benefited immensely from such cooperation, the only region which did not have any such arrangements for regional cooperation was the South Asian region which comprised one-fifth of the world's population.[9]

[8] Nandita Bhatnagar, "Development of Water Resources in South Asia," in Bhabani Sen Gupta, ed., *Regional Cooperation and Development in South Asia,* vol. 2 (New Delhi: South Asia Publishers, 1986), pp. 233–34.

[9] Government of the People's Republic of Bangladesh, Ministry of Foreign Affairs, *A Paper on the Proposal for Regional Cooperation in South Asia,* Dhaka, November 1980, p. 2.

The memorandum also contended that if South Asia achieved a degree of regional cohesion it could hope to have a more effective voice at the United Nations and in other multilateral forums. Finally, it alluded to the common values enshrined in the cultural, ethnic and historical traditions of the region and sought to use them as a basis for regional cooperation. Interestingly enough, it did not seek to smooth over existing differences. It merely suggested that through regional cooperation it might be possible to ameliorate the differences that had characterized the relations of the states within the region. The memorandum was also careful in spelling out that:

> Regional Cooperation in South Asia as elsewhere in the world should in no way intrude on the existing bilateral and multilateral relations of the countries in the region: nor does the proposal envisage either the substitution or the disruption of existing cooperation between or amongst the countries of the region in other forums.[10]

In substantive terms, the memorandum delineated the possible areas of cooperation. These areas had been previously identified when General Ziaur's personal emissary visited various South Asian capitals (as well as in notes exchanged subsequent to his visits). They were as follows: telecommunications, meteorology, transport, shipping, tourism, the agricultural/rural sector, joint ventures, the promotion of markets for selected commodities, scientific and technological cooperation, educational cooperation and cultural cooperation. From this list it is apparent that the proponents of this organization had started with a strong functionalist bias. Clearly the hope was that by focusing on relatively noncontroversial and apolitical areas, the greatest degree of cooperation could be achieved. The hope and expectation was that success in these areas would promote a degree of amity and trust, and thereby have positive spillover effects into other more contentious areas.[11]

GETTING STARTED

Despite its laudable goals, the organization had a timorous beginning. Initially it was decided that the first meeting of the organization would take place at the bureaucratic level. It is interesting to note that the principal opponents to a political-level meeting were India and Pakistan.[12] This meeting of the foreign secretaries of the seven South Asian states was held in Colombo April 21–24, 1981. From the outset it was obvious that the bilateral differences, which had long characterized the region, would continue to have an impact on the workings of this nascent organization. Both India and Pakistan expressed reservations about institutionalizing the SARC organization. Instead they suggested that certain basic principles of how the

[10] Ibid., pp. 2–3.
[11] The theoretical literature on regional integration and functionalism is vast. A good critique and application of this body of literature can be found in Chimelu Chime, *Integration and Politics Among African States* (Uppsala: Scandinavian Institute of African Studies, 1977).
[12] Imtiaz H. Bokhari, "South Asian Regional Cooperation: Progress Problems, Potential and Prospects," *Asian Survey* 25, no. 4 (April 1985), 374.

proposed organization would function be decided before any institutional arrangements were put in place.

Accordingly the joint communique released at the conclusion of this meeting spelled out the rules of discourse within the organization. Among other matters, it stated that all decisions would be taken on the basis of unanimity, that "bilateral and contentious" issues would not be discussed under the aegis of SARC and that regional cooperation was not intended or expected to be a substitute for bilateral and multilateral cooperation. [13] Using the paper prepared by Bangladesh, the delegates agreed to set up five study groups and coordinators to explore the issue areas proposed in the paper: agriculture (Bangladesh), rural development (Sri Lanka), telecommunications (Pakistan), meteorology (India) and health and population activities (Nepal). The purpose of the study groups was to examine the scope and potential for cooperation in the respective issue areas and to make recommendations at the next meeting of the foreign secretaries. Simultaneously a Committee of the Whole was appointed, with Sri Lanka as the coordinator, to explore other possible areas of cooperation. The Committee of the Whole, though composed of senior officials from all seven countries, was seen as a consultative and not a deliberative body. Accordingly, its report stated that final decisions on all issues would be made by the foreign secretaries. Also in keeping with the overall spirit of the SARC organization the rule of unanimity would also apply to the deliberations of this committee.

The next meeting of the foreign secretaries was held in Kathmandu November 1–4, 1981. At this meeting the foreign secretaries affirmed the importance of continuing the SARC venture stating that regional cooperation was "beneficial, desirable and necessary." [14] The mere fact that this meeting was held as planned indicated that despite bilateral differences between the key nations in the region a certain commitment to the SARC process had developed. At this time Indo-Pakistani relations had sunk to a new low over their different responses to the Soviet invasion of Afghanistan and the renewed U.S.-Pakistani strategic nexus.

At this meeting it was decided to convert the existing study groups into working groups. It was also agreed that the chairs of the study groups would be on a rotating basis with the periodicity being initially determined by each group. The initial coordinators of the various study groups were made the chairs of the working groups. The purpose of these working groups would be to draw up programs for cooperative action.

The commitment to the SARC process was also evident in that the foreign secretaries had the mandate from their respective national governments to expand the scope of the organization's activities. At the Kathmandu meeting they decided to expand the ambit of SARC. To the existing agenda

[13] Joint Communique Issued at the Conclusion of the First Meeting of the Foreign Secretaries, Colombo, April 21–23, 1981, p. 2.
[14] Joint Communique Issued at the Conclusion of the Second Meeting of the Foreign Secretaries, Kathmandu, November 2–4, 1981, p. 2.

they added the following: transport (Maldives), postal services (Bhutan) and scientific and technological cooperation (Pakistan). At this meeting, the foreign secretaries also agreed to hold their next meeting within the next six to eight months; and it was decided that a foreign ministers meeting would be held in 1982.

The foreign secretaries met again in Islamabad August 7–9, 1982. In his keynote address, the Pakistani foreign minister, Sahibzada Yakub Khan, spoke of the "equal stake of all the countries of the region in the preservation of peace and security." There is little question that this allusion to shared concerns about regional peace and security was a veiled reference to the fundamentally different positions that India and its neighbors had taken on the Soviet invasion and occupation of Afghanistan. Though the Indian position had evolved since 1980, it was a far cry from that held by its neighbors, particularly Pakistan. With the exception of Bhutan, which had also abstained from directly criticizing the Soviets, India's neighbors had all expressed their displeasure about the Soviet presence in Afghanistan to varying degrees.

Despite the obvious difference of perspectives on a crucial issue of regional security, the meeting marked the continuing evolution of the SARC process. At this meeting the foreign secretaries endorsed the reports of the study groups on transport, postal services and scientific and technological cooperation. They also decided to convert these study groups into working groups with the existing coordinators being made the chairs of their respective groups. The areas of cooperation were also expanded with the creation of two new study groups. One would deal with sports, arts and culture and the other with planning and development. At a procedural level, the conferees decided that the chairs of the working groups would be for a period of two years and would rotate in alphabetical order. In addition to these developments the Committee of the Whole was now charged with moving toward an Integrated Program of Action (IPA) in the areas that had been identified for cooperation. Specifically, it was asked to formulate the means, both organizational and financial, to implement the projected goals.[15]

In preparation for the ministerial meeting in New Delhi, two meetings were held. The first was a meeting of the Committee of the Whole at Colombo January 10–13, 1983. The second was a foreign secretaries' meeting held in Dhaka March 28–30, 1983. At the first meeting the committee sought to set up the mechanisms for cooperative ventures. It especially dealt with the financial obligations of members to defray the costs of the various proposed activities. Specifically, it recommended that national governments regularly allocate certain sums of money in their national budgets to the particular ministries responsible for cooperative ventures, that they make provisions for ad hoc allocations and that they provide scholarships, concessionary airfares and accomodations to individuals involved in SARC-

---

[15] Joint Communique Issued at the Conclusion of the Third Meeeting of the Foreign Secretaries, Islamabad, August 7–9, 1982.

related activities.[16] The Dhaka meeting expanded on the work of the Committee of the Whole; it sought to start the implementation of the IPA. Also it welcomed the offers of assistance to SARC that had come from the International Telecommunications Union and the European Economic Community (EC).

The first meeting of the SARC foreign ministers was not held at a propitious time. Ethnic violence against the Sri Lankan Tamils had inflamed sentiments in India, particularly in the state of Tamil Nadu, the home of some 50 million Indian Tamils. Apparently there were some doubts whether or not the Sri Lankan foreign minister would attend this meeting but eventually he did. In this meeting, and at two subsequent ones held at Male in July 1984 and Thimphu in May 1985, the groundwork was laid for the institutionalization of the organization.

In institutional terms, SARC became a three-tiered organization. At the bottom were the foreign secretaries, at the next level the foreign ministers and at the apex the prime ministers of the seven states. The top-level meetings are considered as the SARC (SAARC after 1985) summits. The first SARC summit was held in Dhaka in December 1985. At this meeting several important steps were taken to make this essentially consultative body into a formal organization, embodying a set of explicit goals, rules and procedures. As the bulk of preparatory work had been done earlier in the secretarial- and ministerial-level meetings, the summit basically ratified and gave formal assent to an agreed-upon agenda. Immediately, the members changed the name of the organization from SARC to SAARC (from South Asian Regional Cooperation to South Asian Association for Regional Cooperation). This meeting also produced a SAARC charter, which spelled out the rights and duties of the members. To a very large extent, the SAARC charter embodies the same principles that were contained in the original Bangladeshi proposal for the creation of a regional organization.

With a view to institutionalize the organization the members also decided to create a SAARC secretariat. Bangladesh and Nepal actively vied and lobbied for the right to house the secretariat and eventually it was agreed to locate it in Kathmandu. It was also at this meeting that national leaders, during the course of private and informal sessions, decided that the SAARC summits should be held once a year and that their respective foreign ministers should confer at least twice a year, more often if the need arose. The foreign secretaries were scheduled to meet three times a year.[17] These significant procedural developments suggested that the organization had successfully weathered the vagaries of regional and international politics ranging from the overthrow of General Ziaur Rahman (the proponent of the organization) to the Soviet intervention in Afghanistan to the assassination of Indira Gandhi.

On a substantive note, the meeting added two new possible areas of

---

[16] Report of the Meeeting of the Committee of the Whole, Colombo, January 10–13, 1983.

[17] Bhabani Sen Gupta, "Is India Serious about SAARC?" *Center,* December 15–January 15, 1987.

cooperation to the organization's agenda: control of the international narcotics trade and control of international terrorism. It is widely believed that the addition of these two areas was at the suggestion of the United States which was increasingly preoccupied with these issues in its own foreign policy. While the question of controlling the narcotics traffic was unexceptional and relatively noncontroversial, the same could not be said of the matter of terrorism. Observers of the SAARC process have questioned whether or not this issue indeed can be deemed to be noncontentious.[18]

The second SAARC summit held in Bangalore in November 1986 sought to expand the achievements of the Dhaka meeting. Despite incipient Indo-Pakistani tensions over border demarcations at Siachen Glacier in Kashmir and Indian accusations about Pakistan's alleged support to Sikh terrorists in the Punjab, the meeting was largely free of acrimonious exchanges. Neither did the continuing Sinhalese-Tamil ethnic violence in Sri Lanka color the proceedings in a demonstrable fashion. At the conclusion of the summit the Pakistani foreign secretary, Abdus Sattar, commented that, "Within the short time since its inception, SAARC has made impressive progress." His Indian counterpart, A. P. Venkateshwaran, concurred.[19]

Though free of angry rhetoric, the meeting made painfully slow progress on substantive issues. Despite the formal commitment to prevent politicization of the issues under discussion, the obvious difficulties with such a principle were evident. The national leaders and their aides failed to come up with an acceptable definition of terrorism, though this was hardly surprising. As alluded to earlier, with India accusing Pakistan of actively aiding and abetting the Sikh terrorists and Sri Lanka contending that it was justified in using force against the Tamil militants a quick accord on this issue was virtually impossible.

The other substantive issue on which the conferees made little headway was that of regional economic and industrial cooperation. India had made a cogent appeal on this matter but ultimately it proved to be a nonstarter owing to Pakistani intransigence. In Pakistan's view greater economic cooperation within SAARC would eventually call for the opening up of its markets to Indian manufactured goods. This, the Pakistanis feared, would simply mean the end of many of their domestic industries given India's more sophisticated and diversified industrial base.

Despite the lack of progress on issues on the formal agenda, the meeting (and the SAARC process in general) was beneficial to its members, and served as an important venue for informal contacts between the leaders of the various nations. It was these contacts that made possible small, positive shifts on many bilateral fronts. It was reported, for example, that Pakistan's prime minister, Muhammad Khan Junejo and Prime Minister Rajiv Gandhi of India privately dealt with the prickly question of terrorism and the normalization of Indo-Pakistani relations. In a multilateral context, the

[18] L. K. Sharma, "SAARC Is Increasingly Getting Politicized," *Times of India,* November 9, 1987.
[19] Dilip Bobb, "SAARC: Painful Progress," *India Today,* December 15, 1986, pp. 126–27.

nations present agreed to develop a joint strategy on global economic issues.[20]

The role of regional politics was underscored in the SAARC foreign ministers' meeting, which preceded the Kathmandu summit. Shortly before this meeting Indian air force planes had been used to drop relief supplies to Sri Lankan Tamils trapped on the Jaffna Peninsula. The decision to airdrop supplies (which involved at least a nominal violation of Sri Lankan airspace) had come in the wake of Sri Lanka's refusal to allow an Indian naval convoy to provide humanitarian assistance to the beleaguered population. Without entering into a discussion of the merits (or the lack thereof) of the Indian decision to airdrop relief supplies, it was clear that the mission had deeply offended Sri Lankan sensibilities.

On June 18, 1987, at the open session of the foreign ministers' meeting, the Sri Lankan foreign minister, A. C. Shahul Hameed, made a compelling plea to modify the SAARC charter. He contended that even though initially the members had decided to exclude all bilateral issues from this forum, recent developments necessitated a reconsideration of that principle.

> When conflicts confront us do we turn a blind eye? It could be argued that if we do not discuss issues and problems among us, then how do we strengthen our forum—surely we are not driving them to other forums. . . . SAARC must not end up as a deaf, dumb and blind organization. If we brush issues under the carpet because they are unpalatable, we will be taking the first step in crippling SAARC.[21]

The sentiments of the Sri Lankan foreign minister were echoed by his Pakistani colleague Sahibzada Yakub Khan. It was hardly surprising that the Pakistani delegate should have picked up on the Sri Lankan grievance. India's active interest and involvement in the Sri Lankan ethnic turmoil no doubt stirred not-so-dormant Pakistani memories of the Indian intervention in East Pakistan in 1971. The Indian foreign minister, Narayan Dutt Tiwari, strongly rebuffed the Sri Lankan and Pakistani suggestions for amending the charter. Eventually, it was the Bangladeshi foreign minister, Humayun Rashid Choudhury, who sought and succeeded in defusing this incipient crisis. While conceding that events in the region do influence stands taken in SAARC, it was vital to the continuing success of the organization that members adhered to the spirit and letter of the charter, avoiding "contentious and bilateral issues."[22] Despite Choudhury's sage counsel, recent developments suggest that his pleas, though of some effect in their immediate term, will carry little weight in the future.

The third meeting of the SAARC summit was held in Kathmandu in November 1987. The Kathmandu summit, while it had its detractors, did produce some concrete results. There were two significant achievements at this meeting. The first was the creation of a 200,000-ton buffer stock of food grains (the South Asian Food Security Reserve) to be used in the event

[20] Ibid., p. 127.
[21] Sumit Chakravarty, "SAARC Survives Subversion," *Mainstream* 25, no. 41, p. 4.
[22] Ibid., p. 5.

of national emergencies. The other was a regional convention on the suppression of terrorism. Both these subjects merit discussion.

The buffer stocks will exist independent of national reserves and will be supplied to fellow members on bilateral terms as the need arises. In emergencies, countries may themselves draw upon these stocks for domestic consumption. However, they are expected to inform all other members.[23] Most observers have noted that this agreement is a small but positive step, yet it has its detractors. They contend that the stock is painfully small, that there are no mechanisms for ascertaining that countries have indeed set aside the requisite amount and that the authority administering the buffer will have no means to assess the real needs of the country seeking resources.[24]

The other agreement, that dealing with the extradition of terrorists, appears to be a significant achievement. However, it is not without problems. In essence the members agreed to extradite those engaged in criminal acts of terror. The agreement will require the amending of the pertinent legislation in each nation and bilateral treaties between governments. Given the existence of a number of extant ethnic conflicts that transcend national borders in South Asia, this agreement—while agreed on at a general level—may be harder to implement on a national and bilateral basis. According to A. S. Abraham,

> The procedural nitty-gritty apart, what is the value of such a convention when there is no agreement on what constitutes terrorism and who a terrorist is? The Sikh terrorists who find such easy refuge in Pakistan, not to mention succour, are hardly seen in that light by Islamabad. In Sri Lanka, the Tamil militants have been regarded from the beginning as terrorists, an appellation never used of them, officially or otherwise in India.[25]

There is probably more than a modicum of truth to the line of criticism expressed above. Clearly, the definition of what constitutes terrorism is not free of political considerations. It would indeed put vast powers in the hands of a state if all the conferees had agreed with President Jayewardene who stated at this conclave that "any violence against the State is terrorism."[26]

Without entirely dismissing the significance of these two steps it is nevertheless possible to concede that they are fraught with difficulties. Unfortunately for the continuing success of SAARC, these are not the only difficulties that have surfaced. In certain areas the conferees could not even resolve their differences and produce an appearance of amity and concord. India had supported Afghanistan's inclusion in SAARC. This proposal was met with staunch Pakistani opposition, while being attacked with varying degrees of vigor by the other states. The ostensible reason for the Pakistani

[23] Salamat Ali, "Hands Across the Region," *Far Eastern Economic Review,* November 19, 1987, p. 39.
[24] A. S. Abraham, "Talk-Fest in Kathmandu," *Times of India,* November 14, 1987.
[25] Ibid.
[26] S. D. Muni, "SAARC Summit Perspectives," *Mainstream,* November 7, 1987, p. 6.

opposition to Afghanistan's membership was provided by Pakistan's minister of state for foreign affairs, Zain Noorani. According to him, while there was no inherent objection to Afghanistan's membership in the organization, at the present time it was not possible to consider it as the country was under Soviet occupation. Eventually, a face-saving gesture was made by a SAARC spokesman, a Nepalese diplomat. He stated that the issue could not be dealt with as no formal application for membership was pending before the body.[27]

There were other contentious issues that surfaced at this summit. Most of them were reflections of bilateral concerns. One such issue was Pakistan's proposal for a nuclear-free South Asia. This was a reprise of an old Pakistani stand largely designed to embarrass India. Though well aware that China looms large in India's strategic calculus, where nuclear weapons are concerned, Pakistan persists in this strategy knowing that it will place India on the defensive. Much to India's dismay, the King of Bhutan, Jigme Singye Wangchuk, picked up this issue in his speech. He pointedly remarked that SAARC members could not pontificate on this issue unless they themselves were willing to forswear the nuclear option. India, expectedly on the defensive, scored a debating point by stating that nuclear disarmament was a global and not a regional problem.[28]

Other bilateral problems also cropped up at the meeting. Bangladesh sought to bring up the issue of Himalayan water development. India sensed that this was an unveiled attempt to raise the issue of water sharing in the Ganges Delta. The Indian response was that as this issue did not concern all the SAARC member states it did not fall within the scope of the conference. Eventually, the members agreed to set up a committee to study a closely related issue, the causes and consequences of natural disasters in South Asia.

The fourth SAARC summit was held in Islamabad December 28, 1987–January 31, 1988. At the level of global issues, the summit called for stemming both the vertical and horizontal proliferation of nuclear weapons. It also decided to support the Group of 77's call for a special U.N. General Assembly session in 1990 to discuss strategies for reviving growth in the developing world. On a regional level, the leaders of the SAARC nations agreed to move toward enabling legislation to implement the antiterrorism accord that they had ratified earlier. (The accord came into effect on August 22, 1988.) Beyond these tangible measures, the members reiterated their mutual commitment to improving the quality of life in their respective nations by eradicating poverty, hunger, disease, illiteracy and unemployment.

Though not under the aegis of SAARC, India and Pakistan took several measures to improve bilateral relations. Most importantly, they signed an accord (which had been verbally agreed upon in 1986) not to attack each other's nuclear facilities. Also, the two countries agreed to expand cultural

[27] Salamat Ali, "Smoothed Over Summit," *Far Eastern Economic Review,* November 19, 1987, p. 40.
[28] Ibid., p. 41.

exchanges and avoid double taxation. Continued improvement in Indo-Pakistani bilateral relations may well have a positive impact on the SAARC process.

SAARC ACHIEVEMENTS

Beyond setting up the food buffer stock and reaching the accord on the extradition of terrorists, we must question whether SAARC has achieved anything else. In a region that has known more than its fair share of internal discord and external conflict, the creation and sustenance of this organization is an achievement in itself, and it offers hope for the future. It provides a forum to search for solutions to a range of problems that are endemic to the area. These range from the larger issues of environmental degradation to smaller ones such as telephone links within the region. Though accords on these issues may not be promptly forthcoming, SAARC is an invaluable forum to at least raise them and explore means by which solutions may be found. As a former Nepalese prime minister, Surya Bahadur Thapa, stated at the end of the Kathmandu SAARC summit,

> Granted that SAARC is far from tapping its full potential. But what is the alternative? It is in everyone's interest, especially of India's neighbors, that all the seven keep talking, because the alternative is even worse." [29]

There are also other low-level achievements with which SAARC can be credited. For the first time in the history of these nations, joint telephone and direct transportation links are being established. This may not appear to be an achievement worthy of heralding, yet it needs to be borne in mind that until recently it was easier to place a call from New Delhi (or any other SAARC capital) to the United States than to any of the other SAARC nations. Air links were of a similar character. Now in addition to improving these physical links a number of procedural changes will enhance regional people-to-people contacts. SAARC tourists traveling within the region will have to pay only half the normal airfare if they travel to more than two SAARC nations. Arrangements for group tours within the region are also under way, and yet another familiar difficulty of most tourists in the SAARC region—the paucity of foreign exchange—appears to be on its way out. It has been agreed that up to $400 worth of foreign exchange will be made available to each traveler. Visa procedures, which have also greatly inhibited travel within the region, are also being reviewed. [30]

Even these minor achievements have been criticized by the region's intellectuals. One long-time observer of the SAARC process complains that while these changes may be laudable enough they only affect a tiny fraction of the populations of the SAARC states. As he has stated: "After all what percentage of South Asian masses have an easy and assured access to air-travel, television, telephones, tourism and higher education? Very small indeed." [31]

[29] Ibid., p. 39.
[30] Ibid.
[31] Muni, p. 5.

Though it may sound like needless carping there is probably a large element of truth his criticism. Yet it is probably unrealistic to expect the national leaders of these states to act otherwise. Despite a professed commitment to eradicate poverty and reduce inequalities vast segments of the populations of these nations remain at the edge of subsistence. In India, the largest country in the region, close to 40 percent of the population lives below the officially defined poverty line. The situation is probably the worst in Bangladesh where close to 80 percent of the population lives below the official poverty line.[32] Clearly, national political elites in South Asia have not devoted the bulk of their efforts to improving the lot of these people in their endeavors at SAARC.

CONCLUSION

What lies in store for the future of SAARC? Unlike the other two successful examples of regional cooperation ASEAN (Association of Southeast Asian Nations) and the EC, SAARC lacks the common perceived threats of both. In the case of ASEAN there has long been a shared sense of threat from the Soviet Union and the People's Republic of China (PRC). The threat from the PRC looms especially large in Malaysia and Indonesia—both countries with large ethnic Chinese populations. Western Europe not only faces a common sense of peril from the Soviet presence in Eastern Europe but also is driven by the exigencies of postwar economic reconstruction. Additionally unlike the states of South Asia, which are in the very process of state building, the state in Western Europe (with the possible exception of West Germany) has reached its apogee. In South Asia the process of state construction is still largely in its infancy.

In the case of South Asia, as we discussed at the outset, the writ of many of these states is in question. In Clifford Geertz's terms these nations are "old societies and new states." The state structure of most of these nations is fragile, weak and under stress. Under these conditions, when the state is desperately seeking the loyalties of all segments of its population, it is difficult for it to be open to the possibilities of transnational cooperation. After all, such cooperation makes a state more porous and multinational ventures erode its exclusive authority. It is precisely this fear of the loss of national control of a range of activities that animates South Asian elites. In turn, this fear is simply compounded by the history of regional conflicts. Yet many of the problems that confront South Asia call for such multinational cooperation. Whether it is the prevention of soil erosion in the Himalayan *terai* region, the ability to track monsoonal cyclones, the prevention of regional crop diseases or even the international marketing of primary commodities like tea—multinational cooperation is indeed the crying need of the times.

For the very reasons spelled out above it is unlikely that any dramatic

[32] Pramit Chaudhuri, "India: Economy," and K. A. S. Murshid, "Bangladesh: Economy," in *The World of Learning: The Far East and Australasia* (London: Europa Publications, 1987), pp. 382–83, 217–18.

cooperative ventures will be launched in the foreseeable future. The seven nations will continue to meet, they will also continue to bicker and it is hoped they will find some small common ground on which to achieve cooperation.

FURTHER READING

Chopra, Pran Nath, ed. *The Future of South Asia.* Delhi and London: Macmillan, 1986.

Gupta, Sisir. *India and Regional Integration in Asia.* Bombay and London: Asia Publishing House, 1964.

Mishra, Pramod Kumar. *The Dhaka Summit and SAARC: A Broad Overview.* Calcutta: K. P. Bagchi, 1986.

———. *South Asia in International Politics.* Delhi: UDH Publishers; 1984.

Muni, S. D., and Muni, Anuradha. *Regional Cooperation in South Asia.* New Delhi: National Publishing House, 1984.

Sen Gupta, Bhabani, ed. *Regional Cooperation and Development in South Asia.* 2 vols. New Delhi: South Asian Publishers, 1986.

THE EVOLUTION OF ANZUS

F. A. MEDIANSKY

INTRODUCTION

In mid-1986 the U.S. Secretary of State George Shultz emerged from a closed meeting with New Zealand's Prime Minister David Lange to declare that the two countries were parting company as allies although they were parting as friends. By unilaterally cutting New Zealand off from the Australia–New Zealand–United States (ANZUS) security triangle, Shultz formally suspended perhaps the most cost-effective and, until the early 1980s, the most easily managed and cohesive American alliance framework in the Pacific. The outward reason for the breakup was the U.S. unwillingness to accept the New Zealand's desire to remain in ANZUS on strictly nonnuclear terms. Below the surface, more complex divergences had emerged between the strategic priorities of the Reagan administration and those of its South Pacific allies, which had elected more nationalistically inclined Labour governments in the early 1980s. While the differences between Australia and the United States are less fundamental and are kept in check by overriding interests, the alliance between them is now more complex and less easily managed than it was in the past.

ANZUS is a loosely structured alliance whose coherence traditionally has depended on extra-security factors. A shared language and parallel experiences in national development have contributed to compatible values and similar political institutions. Consequently the alliance relationship has been strongly supported, though not always well understood, by popular opinion in all three countries.

Economic linkages have also helped the cohesion of the Australia–New Zealand–United States relationship. Britain's entry into the European Community in 1973 compelled Australia and New Zealand to develop economic links with their Pacific neighbors. At the same time the United States has become increasingly attracted to the dynamic economies of the Pacific basin. By the mid-1980s two-way trade between the United States and Australia was around U.S. $8 billion while trade with New Zealand was about $1.5 billion. The level of U.S. and Australian investment in each other's economies has also reached substantial proportions. American investment in Australia had exceeded $9 billion by 1986, while Australian investment surpassed $7 billion and is growing rapidly. On current projections, Australia will have invested more than $30 billion by 1990, making it a major foreign investor in the U.S. economy. Australia and New Zealand have made enormous progress in integrating their economies since they embarked on a program for a closer economic relationship—the CER—in 1980. The CER is the most comprehensive bilateral trade agreement for both countries. Under this agreement the final steps were taken to eliminate tariffs on all merchandise trade in 1988. New Zealand exports to Australia have risen substantially under CER, and New Zealand now represents Australia's third largest export market and its largest market for manufactured goods. Two-way investment has also expanded significantly.

A complex of factors led Australia and New Zealand to establish a close security relationship with the United States in the aftermath of World War II. Both states have a long tradition of security dependence, dating back to the earliest days of European settlement. As members of the British empire, both countries looked to Britain to protect their external interests; this course engendered close political, economic and military cooperation with the mother country. Within this context Australia and New Zealand have traditionally defined their security interests in collective terms, the strategy behind the long-standing practice of contributing to the distant military campaigns of the great-power ally.

The collective security assumptions that made Australia and New Zealand depend on British protection failed alarmingly during World War II. The collapse of British power in Southeast Asia left the two dominions, for a brief time, alone against the southward drive of imperial Japan. As it turned out, the entry of the United States into the Pacific war saved the day, and Australia and New Zealand emerged on the winning side as minor American allies.

From the standpoint of the two dominions, the continuation of the war-time alliance with the United States made good sense. The British navy's ability to protect Australia and New Zealand was set to decline in the postwar years. At the same time, the decolonization of Southeast Asia marked the beginning of a new and more uncertain regional order. Against these considerations, the deeply ingrained habit of security dependence prompted the two states to look to the United States, which had emerged from the war as the preeminent power in the Pacific. Yet the postwar policies of the United States foreshadowed a complicated security partnership. American security interests in the more distant sectors of the Western Pacific were not clearly defined, and the two dominions differed with the United States over Japan's postwar role. U.S. occupation policy increasingly leaned toward a soft peace treaty while Australia, especially, was determined to ensure that Japan should never again be allowed to challenge the regional balance in the Pacific. Although divergent views about Japan's future role persisted through the early postwar decades, security concerns closer to home became increasingly more pressing. These concerns centered on the emergence of communist regimes on the Asian mainland whose influence was readily, though often simplistically, linked to the various communist-led insurgencies that were challenging the newly independent governments as well as the remnants of colonial power in Southeast Asia.

The Truman administration had little enthusiasm for a formal alliance with Australia and New Zealand during the early postwar years. Some American policymakers were uncertain about the advantages of allying the United States with two former British dependencies that supported continued British presence in the region. Not unreasonably, American strategists were concerned lest an alliance with the only two predominantly white countries in the Southwest Pacific might prove contrary to U.S. interests at the time when nationalist and anticolonial sentiments were running high in Southeast Asia. Such reservations were pushed into the background by the victory of the communist forces in China and the outbreak of the Korean War—events that quickly brought the divisions of the cold war into the Asia-Pacific region. The United States responded to these developments by forming a string of alliances along the western rim of the Pacific as part of its strategy for the containment of communism on the Asian mainland.

THE ANZUS TREATY PROVISIONS

Australia, New Zealand and the United States signed the ANZUS security treaty in San Francisco in 1951. Broadly worded, the treaty represents little more than a set of principles to facilitate security cooperation in whatever form seems most attractive to the three allies at any given time. The text states that an armed attack in the Pacific area on any of the partners would endanger the security of the others, and consequently each undertakes to "act to meet the common danger in accordance with its constitutional processes." The treaty calls on the partners, separately and jointly, to "maintain and develop their individual and collective capacity to resist armed attack." Provision is also made for regular consultations at the ministerial level, or whenever any member considers that its "territorial integrity, political independence or security . . . is threatened in the Pacific."

The broadly expressed provisions of ANZUS led to extensive unresolved debate in Australia and New Zealand about the degree of protection the treaty provides. The treaty's security provisions are essentially consultative and do not clearly delineate the circumstances under which the partners are obliged to provide substantive assistance to one another. Nor does the treaty indicate the nature or timing of such assistance. The text is sufficiently general to enable the three allies to respond to any contingency in the Pacific according to individual perceptions of what constitutes a threat and to assess the best way to provide support. Thus even during the cold war years, when Australia and New Zealand depended on U.S. security assistance far more than they do now, it was generally recognized that the commitment of troops by one partner did not automatically ensure the military support of the others. Thus, for example, Australia and New Zealand did not feel obliged to provide security assistance to the United States during the Chinese offshore island crisis. Likewise, the U.S. response to

1134

Australia's call to help resist Indonesia's claims to Western New Guinea fell short of Australian expectations.

As it emerged from the negotiating table in San Francisco, the ANZUS Treaty disappointed Australia and New Zealand in several respects. The loosely worded security guarantee was disconcerting to the two allies, which felt increasingly isolated and vulnerable as cold war divisions split the Asia-Pacific region. The United States also disappointed its new allies by its unwillingness to include Britain in the treaty framework and so extend its protection to the British possessions in Southeast Asia. The security of these territories was accepted as Australia's and New Zealand's obligation not only because proximity made them strategically important but also because both countries wanted to maintain a British military presence in Southeast Asia. They continued to see their strategic interests as being closely linked with their membership of the British Commonwealth.

From the American perspective, ANZUS was an element in the network of Pacific alliances. It formalized the U.S. security relationship with Australia and New Zealand in much the same terms as the relationship with other Pacific nations, such as the Philippines and Japan. These American bilateral treaties—later extended to South Korea and Taiwan—formed the Pacific security system, whose central purpose was to stem what was then seen as the relentlessly expanionist aims of monolithic communism.

THE COSTS AND BENEFITS OF ANZUS

For about the first 25 years of its existence, ANZUS proved to be an outstandingly easily managed and low-cost security arrangement. A complex of factors contributed to the agreeable nature of the alliance. First, the strategic objectives of the three countries have remained largely compatible over the postwar years—though priorities have diverged on many instances. Second, a strong tradition of security dependence accustomed Australia and New Zealand to look to a great power for protection and strategic leadership. Third, the location of Australia and New Zealand in an isolated and tranquil environment without recognizable external threats has meant that the security guarantees of the alliance rarely come close to being put to the ultimate test.

For Australia and New Zealand the undemanding character of the alliance has been attractive. The United States has placed few and relatively low cost expectations on its ANZUS partners, because of U.S. preeminence throughout the Pacific as well as the isolated location and the limited military capabilities of its South Pacific allies. Furthermore, as ANZUS lacks the kind of integrative mechanisms that constitute military interdependence, Australia and New Zealand were left free to define their defense forces without much regard for alliance-generated requirements.

In a security relationship between a global power and two regional states, considerable divergence about which elements of the alliance are most valued is not surprising. For its part, the United States has tended to value allied contributions that directly affect its strategic capabilities. By hosting a number of what are commonly described as joint defense communications facilities (discussed later), Australia contributes directly to the American global posture; for that reason the facilities are, for the United States, the single most important element of the ANZUS relationship.

Australia and to a lesser extent New Zealand have provided considerable support for the U.S. military interests in the Indian Ocean, Southeast Asia, and the southwestern Pacific. Although its western coastline is distantly located from the northwest Indian Ocean, which is the focus of U.S. interest, Australia nevertheless provides a useful contribution to the American regional presence. Both Australia and New Zealand have responded to the U.S. request to contribute to the Sinai multilateral peacekeeping force. Australia also provides port access to U.S. naval craft in the Indian Ocean, which use the jointly operated naval communications station at Northwest Cape. The Guam-based B-52 aircraft have exercising and staging rights in northern Australia that facilitate their movement throughout the region. The United States has also sought to pre-position fuel in Western Australia for the use of its naval vessels in the Indian Ocean.

The long involvement of Australia and New Zealand in Southeast Asia has helped to further U.S. regional objectives in several ways. Both countries have tried to foster a Western-oriented strategic outlook on the part of the regional states. Their regional programs, including defense aid and membership of the Five Power Defense Agreement (designed to support Malaysia and Singapore), have contributed significantly to Western influence. The continuous regular deployment of Australian—and until recently New Zealand—units in Southeast Asia has been welcomed by the United States as a valued contribution by its ANZUS allies whose regional credentials are widely accepted. Similar objectives have motivated Australian diplomacy to encourage a positive attitude among the Association of Southeast Asian Nations (ASEAN) toward the U.S. military presence in the Philippines.

As the major powers in the Southwest Pacific, Australia and New Zealand have been instrumental in extending the ANZUS presence throughout the region. The two countries maintain an unsurpassed level of diplomatic representation, and their economic and military aid programs are the most extensive in the South Pacific. In all, their influence has ensured that the island states look almost exclusively to the West in the realization of their political, economic and military interests. For these reasons Australia and New Zealand can claim considerable credit for imposing a large measure of strategic denial against Soviet influence in the South Pacific. Largely in response to growing external competition in the late 1980s, Australia and New Zealand have announced long-term commitments to enhance their surveillance and military deployments in the Southwest Pacific. These undertakings, together with the ongoing programs, benefit U.S. interests, as the American regional military presence in the area is intermittent and its political and economic links are confined to the larger regional island states.

One of the paradoxes of ANZUS is that the treaty itself is only loosely linked to the most valued elements of the alliance. Indeed, some of these elements predate the treaty, while others are only bilateral. Thus the most valued aspects of the security relationship could have taken place even if the three states had not signed the ANZUS Treaty. The main elements of the alliance fall under three headings: intelligence sharing, hosting of the defense communications facilities and major defense cooperation programs.

Until the mid-1980s cooperation between the ANZUS partners in intelligence matters was very close, and this element of the relationship was often cited as an example of the intimate character of the alliance itself. Intelligence sharing among the three countries dates from allied wartime cooperation in the Pacific and thus clearly predates ANZUS. The treaty does not mention intelligence cooperation, though such cooperation is clearly within the spirit of the alliance and can be carried out under Article II. The arrangements covering intelligence sharing are mostly secret, and some of the more important agreements include Western countries that are not in ANZUS. The intimacy of the intelligence sharing arrangements have been reinforced by the practice of posting liaison officers in each ANZUS country and by seconding staff to important collection facilities. Such highly integrated arrangements among partners with vastly disparate intelligence collection and assessment capabilities inevitably have placed Australia and New Zealand in a highly dependent relationship with the United States. As modern intelligence collection tends to be regional or even global in scope, Australia and New Zealand, along with other Western allies, contribute to a common pool managed by the United States, which in turn distributes the fruits of the collective effort. For small allies such integrated and centrally managed arrangements have costs as well as benefits. One enormous benefit is the opportunity to tap into the global intelligence system of the United States. Yet by doing so Australia and New Zealand open their national security decisions to influence by externally managed intelligence inputs.

Two factors have weakened intelligence cooperation within the alliance. One, intelligence cooperation between the United States and New Zealand was suspended when security cooperation between them ended. Since then, intelligence exchanges have become fully bilateral, with Australia endeavoring to maintain separate links with the United States and New Zealand. The second factor stems from the current Australian defense policy commitment to greater military self-reliance, a course that in turn emphasizes the need for independent and regionally focused intelligence capabilities. As both Australia and New Zealand are now embarked on a policy of military self-reliance, the integrative force of intelligence cooperation will no longer be as strong as in the past—even if the current disagreement between the United States and New Zealand is resolved.

Australia hosts a large number of U.S. defense communications facilities that now operate under joint management. The most important of these are the naval communication station at Northwest Cape, the signals intelligence facility at Pine Gap and the satellite ground station at Nurrungar. The major functions of these facilities include military communications, signals intelligence, early warning of ballistic missile attack and arms control verification. While the present Hawke Labor government has issued several statements aimed at lifting the veil of secrecy from the facilities, the public record regarding the function and management of the installations is far from complete. According to Desmond Ball, the leading authority on the facilities, Australia hosts more U.S. installations concerned with "military communications navigation, satellite tracking and control of various forms of intelligence collection" than "any other country except the United Kingdom, Canada, West Germany and Japan."[1] The choice of Australia as a location for such sensitive installations is undoubtedly due to a mix of political and technical factors. Politically Australia is attractive because it has proved itself to be a stable and accommodating host. Technical factors include the requirements of siting. The facilities have been commonly associated with the ANZUS Treaty in ways that suggest an organic linkage. Yet the facilities were established by separate agreements that have standing outside the treaty, and over the years these agreements have been amended without recourse to the treaty text. The separate basis of existence of the facilities was acknowledged for the first time by Australian Foreign Minister Bill Hayden, who noted that "Northwest Cape, Pine Gap and Nurrungar are not linked to any specific ANZUS obligation and that they are in any case bilateral arrangements as New Zealand is not involved."[2]

Although no party in government has opposed the hosting of the joint facilities, their presence has generated an ongoing debate in Australia. Those arguing for the facilities have claimed that the installations enhance strategic stability by contributing to American deterrence as well as to arms control verification capabilities. Critics, on the other hand, claim that the facilities contribute to U.S. war-fighting capabilities, that they make Australia a nuclear target and that they detract from Australian sovereignty. The debate cannot be resolved with any degree of certainty because of the dearth of public information about the functional characteristics and operating arrangements of the facilities. Also, the functions of the facilities change with technological developments and with changes in U.S. strategic policy. Ball's analysis tends to agree with government claims that the Pine Gap facility contributes to arms control by providing "unique" inputs to U.S. verification capabilities.[3] Ball assesses the arguments for Nurrungar as being "much more closely balanced"—while the facility does provide early warning of missile attack and helps reduce the risks of accidental nuclear war, it "also makes an increasingly critical contribution to the U.S. strategic nuclear war-fighting posture."[4] On the question of sovereignty, the Australian defense white paper of 1987 unequivocally stated the government's position that "all . . . [the] functions and activities [of Northwest Cape, Pine Gap and Nurrungar] require, and have, the full knowledge and concurrence of the Australian government."[5] However, Ball casts doubt on

[1] Desmond Ball, *The ANZUS Connection: The Security Relationships Between Australia, New Zealand and the United States,* SDSC Reference Paper no. 105 (Canberra: Australian National University, 1983), 16.
[2] Bill Hayden, "The Ministerial Review of ANZUS," *Backgrounder,* issue no. 400 (Canberra: Department of Foreign Affairs), x.
[3] Desmond Ball, *A Base for Debate* (Sydney: Allen and Unwin, 1987), 87.
[4] Ibid., p. 88.
[5] *The Defence of Australia 1987* (Canberra: Department of Defence, 1987), 12.

such all-encompassing claims. According to Ball, "Australia does not have access to the message traffic which passes through . . . [Northwest Cape and] hence the station is quite simply incompatible with Australia's sovereignty."[6] With respect to Nurrungar, Ball argues that because of the lack of

> Australian access to the station and the information produced, [we] cannot be sure that the information is not employed by the United States in ways that are contrary to Australian government policy—whether it be to provide an important data base for the SDI program or to enable the United States to more accurately characterise and assess so-called "limited" nuclear exchanges.[7]

It is now widely accepted that the facilities are nuclear targets. Australian governments, however, have argued that the risks associated with hosting the facilities are offset by the contribution made to strategic deterrence and to arms control.

The ANZUS countries have developed a wide range of cooperative measures that are discussed here under three headings: technology transfers and the supply of defense equipment, military exercises, and the regular use of allied military facilities. Cooperation in these fields is not explicitly called for by the ANZUS Treaty text and most of the arrangements are not trilateral; many are bilateral agreements, while a few programs encompass extra-treaty states.

Since World War II Australia and to a lesser extent New Zealand have increasingly looked to the United States to provide technically advanced military equipment. The United States has negotiated separate memorandums of understanding on logistic supply with its ANZUS partners; however, the status of the agreement with New Zealand has become uncertain since the United States suspended its treaty relationship with that country. Most of the sophisticated equipment in the Australian military inventory is American, including the long-range F-111 and the F-18 fighter aircraft.

Official Australian statements frequently stress the importance attached to technology transfers from the United States. For example, access to technology is helping Australia develop its over-the-horizon radar which, "for the first time in our history, holds the prospect of broad area surveillance of our approaches."[8] Yet major collaborative equipment projects between Australia and the United States are still in their infancy. The first is project Nulka, in which the two countries are working on the joint development of an anti-ship missile defense system. On the other hand, collaborative procurement and production programs between Australia and New Zealand have made significant advances. The two states currently are working toward the acquisition of a common light patrol frigate that would involve joint production arrangements.

Both Australian and New Zealand forces attach importance to exercising with larger allied forces. Such exercises provide opportunities for operational training on a scale and intensity that is precluded by the size of their

[6] Ball, *A Base for Debate*, 86.
[7] Ibid., p. 89.
[8] *The Defence of Australia 1987*, 4.

respective forces. Since the breakdown of the United States–New Zealand alliance relationship, trilateral ANZUS exercises have been suspended. Australia (at some additional expense) now conducts separate exercises with New Zealand and the United States. Australia regularly participates with the United States in multilateral exercises such as RIMPAC.

While the transfer of defense technology and equipment and the program of regular military exercise have benefited Australia and New Zealand far more than the United States, the reverse applies in the case of port visits. As regionally oriented powers, Australia and New Zealand have little operational interest in access to the more distant military facilities of the United States. The requirements of the American global posture, on the other hand, emphasize strategic access throughout the Pacific and Indian Oceans. Consequently the United States places importance on the regular access its ships and aircraft have to Australian base facilities; New Zealand's refusal to provide such access led to the suspension of U.S. treaty links with that country.

While defense cooperation remains an important part of the alliance, its role in fostering the cohesion of ANZUS has declined. The breakdown in the United States–New Zealand security relationship has suspended defense cooperation between those two states. Also, the commitment of Australia and New Zealand to a strategy of self-reliance is bound to diminish the scope for cooperation with the United States because self-reliance, as understood by Australia and New Zealand, calls for the maximizing of indigenous production capabilities—partly to enhance independence and partly to ensure the acquisition of equipment suited to local requirements. Thus Australia has embarked on an impressive range of major defense production projects, including the construction of six new submarines and eight new light, long-range patrol frigates. At the same time, Australia recognises that self-reliance requires the acquisition of sophisticated defense equipment that is well beyond its indigenous capabilities and that the United States is likely to remain the major source for much of that equipment. Self-reliance also emphasizes early identification of emerging threats. Therefore, current defense strategy in Australia and New Zealand seeks to improve national intelligence capabilities; to that end both countries have embarked on major programs.

THE ANZUS TRIANGLE

Although the ANZUS acronym implies trilateral cooperation, the alliance has developed essentially as a set of bilateral linkages. In practice the alliance conforms to the prevailing character of the American alliance system in the Pacific, which is essentially a set of bilateral security links between the United States and its regional allies. If the ANZUS security linkages are seen in terms of bilateral segments within a triangle, it is useful to recognize that not all segments were equally developed. Thus the Australia–United States segment is far more important to both states than their respective links with New Zealand. As regards New Zealand, its linkage with Australia has been, and remains, more extensive than that with the United States.

It is difficult to exaggerate the importance that Australia has placed on its security relationship with the United States. Australia has a long history of viewing its security in terms of its relationship with a great-power protector. This security dependence in turn has established the deeply ingrained habit of thinking about defense in collective terms. The Australian understanding of collective security was based on a number of assumptions that made it an outstandingly accommodating ally. Australia assumed that because security interests within an alliance were indivisible, the overriding obligation of the lesser ally was to give priority to the needs of the alliance. Thus collective security was interpreted as dependence on and subordination to the strategic judgments of the great-power protector. This in turn freed Australia from making independent judgments about its defense interests or from planning for its own defense. Because the locations, mode and timing of military engagements was determined by the major ally, Australia was absolved from having to make strategic judgments altogether; the judgments left to Australia were essentially military or tactical. Most important, the Australian contribution to any allied military operation—even to its own defense—was not expected to decide the outcome of the conflict.

Developments in the late 1960s began to seriously undermine the collectivist assumptions upon which Australian security had rested. Britain's decision to withdraw its forces from east of Suez, the Nixon administration's Guam Doctrine and the subsequent dismantling of the U.S.-sponsored coalition in the Asia Pacific, which was primarily aimed at containing China, had profound implications for Australia's security calculations. Though ambiguously worded, the Guam Doctrine was widely interpreted as signaling a lessening of U.S. security commitments in the Asia Pacific region. As Australian Defense Minister Kim Beazley recently observed, the Guam Doctrine "dealt a fatal blow to the premise upon which Australian defence policy had traditionally been based."[9]

The far-reaching changes foreshadowed by the Guam Doctrine emerged quickly during the 1970s. These included U.S. military disengagement from mainland Southeast Asia; the rapid normalization of Sino–U.S. relations and the emergence of a unified Vietnam as a major regional power formally allied to the Soviet Union. Taken together these changes represented a major realignment within Australia's security environment. The Australian response was outlined in the 1976 defense white paper that stated that because the nature of U.S. security assistance in a range of contingencies was sufficiently uncertain, more self-reliance military capabilities should be developed. Such judgments represented a major departure from Australia's long-standing assumptions about collective security. Nevertheless, the 1976 defense white paper had little impact on the alliance relationship for two reasons: the United States accepted self-reliance as an accommodating

---

[9] *The Australian,* 29–30 March 1986.

response to the Guam Doctrine, and the policy rhetoric of the conservative Fraser government greatly stressed alliance cohesion.

The alliance relationship became more difficult to manage in the 1980s largely because the Reagan Administration's maritime strategy in the Pacific is not easily reconciled with the Hawke government's emphasis on localized self-reliance. Under the Hawke Labor government the strategy of self-reliance has been developed with considerable energy in two recent documents—the 1986 Dibb Report on force capabilities and the 1987 defense white paper. These two reports have attracted more critical attention in the United States than any other Australian defense documents in recent memory.

Both the Dibb Report and the 1987 white paper endorse the previous policy judgments that advocate enhanced military self-reliance in response to the greater uncertainties that surround U.S. regional commitments. What sets the present Australian government's defense policy apart from that of its predecessors is its more stridently nationalistic tone, which implies a lesser willingness to participate in allied operations—especially in distant or "forward" locations.

The attraction of ANZUS for Australia and New Zealand has been motivated by considerations that diverge from American interests in the alliance. Notwithstanding the ambiguities of the treaty language, it has been widely accepted that the alliance does provide a degree of U.S. protection. For example, an Australian parliamentary report on ANZUS stated:

> The rationale for Australia's continuing contribution to the Alliance has been, and continues to be, the expectation that in a situation of grave danger facing Australia the United States will meet its obligations under the ANZUS Treaty and provide military support to help us deal with the threat.[10]

This judgment was reinforced in the 1987 defense white paper, which notes that while "the threshold for direct United States combat aid to Australia could be quite high in some circumstances," the existence of the treaty would nevertheless have a deterrent effect on a potential aggressor.[11] At the same time, Australia's current defense policy is based on the judgment that American response to lower-level threats to Australia is sufficiently uncertain as to call for a high degree of Australian military self-reliance. The reassessment of the security guarantees in the alliance has not led Australian defense planners to downgrade the relationship with the United States. On the contrary, the policy of self-reliance is seen as continuing to render Australia dependent on the United States. This apparent paradox is explained in the Dibb Report in the following words:

> It may appear to be a contradiction, but if Australia is to become more self reliant in its defence capabilities it will continue . . . to require the tangible benefits of defence cooperation with the United States. To be able to defend credibly a continent the size of ours, and with our small armed forces, de-

[10] Joint Committee on Foreign Affairs and Defence, *The ANZUS Alliance* (Canberra: Australian Parliament, 1982), 5.
[11] *The Defence of Australia* 1987, 5.

mands access to intelligence, high technology sensor and military equipment. For much of this the United States is the best source by far and for some, indeed, it is the only source. [12]

Current Australian defense policy of course recognizes that membership in the Western alliance community does generate wider security obligations. Such obligations are met by hosting the U.S. defense facilities that contribute directly to Western deterrence, as well as by supporting American ships and aircraft that constitute the American regional presence. Current policy also leaves the door open to token contributions to more distant allied operations. However, as such contributions cannot influence force development, the Australian capacity to contribute to out-of-area operations is bound to diminish.

Notwithstanding its critical dependence on the United States, Australian policy characterizes the relationship as an essentially balanced one. Increasingly the alliance is presented as a reasonably symmetrical tradeoff in which the United States provides privileged access to intelligence, defense science and technology, equipment and logistic support, and in return Australia hosts important defense facilities and provides access to ports and airfields on a reasonably liberal basis.

The Australian concern with self-reliance is less than optimally suited to the alliance strategy of the Reagan Administration. The current U.S. emphasis on anti-Soviet alliance mobilization and security interdependence in the Pacific does not fit well with the Australian emphasis on greater operational independence in a regionally confined area. American concerns with Australia's more independent mood were no doubt further exacerbated by its recent experience with New Zealand, where a similar defense policy, coupled with a strong antinuclear feeling, led to the breakdown of bilateral security cooperation.

Australia's policy of self-reliance was the subject of extensive discussion during the 1986 and 1987 Australia–United States ministerial talks, which have displaced the trilateral ANZUS council meetings. The final communique of the June 1987 meeting in Canberra endorsed the current thrust of Australia's defense policy, stating that the United States "agreed that the Australian Government's emphasis on defence self-reliance and modernisation, incorporated into the alliance framework and based on broad concepts of strategic responsibility and regional commitment, constituted a strong foundation for the defence of Australia and for Australia's execution of alliance responsibilities." [13]

On the face of it, these words represent a carefully balanced accommodation wherein Washington endorses Australian defense policy as long as that strategy does not mean opting out of Australia's broader strategic responsibilities. What such responsibilities might encompass is left unstated. Nevertheless, the issue is of major importance because it sets the scope for

[12] Paul Dibb, *Review of Australia's Defence Capabilities* (Canberra: Department of Defence, 1986), vi.

[13] Department of Foreign Affairs, *Australia-United States Ministerial Talks* (Sydney, June 22, 1987) 1–2.

peacetime military cooperation between Australia and the United States. The question is, how can Australia, with its limited resources and a policy of focusing its force capabilities on its immediate environment, hope to contribute to such distant U.S. preoccupations as the Arab/Persian Gulf and the Korean peninsula? The administration's maritime strategy, with its emphasis on forward naval deployments kept at a high state of readiness and on horizontal escalation, looks to a level of allied interoperability in the Northwest Pacific and Indian Oceans which is not easily reconciled with the Australian policy of self-reliance. These divergent preoccupations are clearly reflected in U.S. and Australian characterizations of the alliance. Contrast, for example, the presentation of the alliance in the Dibb Report and the defense white paper, which sees the alliance primarily as a tradeoff that facilitates self-reliance, with Secretary Shultz's opening statement at the 1987 bilateral ministerial talks:

> ANZUS continues to be a key link in the global network of alliances . . . important as these alliances are in deterring aggression, their strength . . . derives from a common recognition that peace is indivisible and that collective efforts are necessary to ensure the common good.[14]

The divergence of views on military cooperation is further amplified by the differing appreciations of the Soviet Union in the southwestern Pacific and in Southeast Asia.

Although a reading of the last two communiques of the Australian–United States ministerial defense talks suggests a harmony of outlook on the southwestern Pacific and an endorsement of Australia's leading role in that region, several points of difference have emerged. In the first place, both the Dibb Report and the defense white paper brush aside the security implications of Soviet activities in the region. Yet these activities have aroused considerable concern on the part of the United States,[15] which has now heightened its interest in the region. Secondly, the Australian outlook diverges significantly on a number of regional issues, such as the French policies in New Caledonia and Australia's support for the South Pacific nuclear-free zone.

A similar pattern of divergent outlooks is apparent in the Southeast Asia region. In contrast to U.S. assessments, neither the Dibb Report nor the defense white paper accords much military significance to the Soviet presence in Vietnam. Differences with the U.S. were recently discussed by Defense Minister Beazley, who said, "The United States simply doesn't see it our way. They see it primarily in military terms. We see it as a serious political problem, as a serious political threat."[16] Other regional differences include divergent policies on the Cambodian settlement and the U.S. concern with the regional interest in a nuclear-free zone proposal, which

[14] Text of Secretary Schultz's opening statement, First Plenary Session, *Australia-United States Ministerial Talks* (Sydney, June 22, 1987) 1.
[15] See, for example, USIS interview with Admiral James Lyons, Commander in Chief, U.S. Pacific Fleet, on June 3, 1987.
[16] Peter Hastings, "Threats to the North—Military and Political," *Sydney Morning Herald,* 5 March 1987.

Washington sees as having been inspired by the South Pacific model, which in turn is very much an Australian-inspired model.[17]

Historic links and geographic proximity support the traditionally close relationship between Australia and New Zealand. The relationship was formalized in 1944 by the bilateral Canberra Pact, which outlined the common security interests of the two countries and their commitment to a collaborative relationship in the South Pacific. Although the Canberra Pact was largely superseded by ANZUS, the suspension of the United States–New Zealand segment has led Australia and New Zealand to revert to the 1944 segment as the basis for their ongoing security relationship. Close links are maintained by a regular program of consultations between the two defense ministers and their most senior military and civilian advisers, and by a wide range of bilateral exercises, exchange training programs, maritime surveillance, exchanges of technical and operational information, and cooperation in intelligence, defense science and technological matters. The two countries have also embarked on wide-ranging equipment production and procurement programs that will substantially further their commitment to maximize military interoperability.

Although Australia and New Zealand maintain an impressive range of bilateral security links, the wider framework for cooperation has diminished, in part because the common linkage to such organizations as the British Commonwealth no longer generates the same requirements for defense planning as in the past. Both states have abandoned collective security strategies that have led to collaborative forward deployments on the Malay peninsula and in Indochina. Instead, both countries now embrace similar strategies of self-reliance that nevertheless have led to divergent security outlooks. Although Australia is conscious of its extended Indian Ocean coastline and its proximity to Southeast Asia, New Zealand's isolated location in the Pacific has prompted more circumscribed defense concerns.

Undoubtedly the most serious strain on current defense cooperation stems from the breakdown of the United States–New Zealand security relationship. Australia has, from the outset, disassociated itself from New Zealand's policy on nuclear ship visits while maintaining trans-Tasman security links. Such a course is not without difficulties. For example, the U.S. decision to cut its flow of intelligence to New Zealand has severely limited cooperation in this field. Likewise, the suspension of ANZUS exercises by the United States obliges Australia to conduct separate and often parallel exercises with its ANZUS allies.

For a number of reasons the United States has tended to regard its security links with New Zealand as secondary to its broader-based links with Australia. Situated in a remote area, New Zealand is isolated from instability and great-power competition, and its image as a strategic backwater is reflected in infrequent deployment of U.S. military units in its vicinity and by few naval visits to its ports. With a population of little more than 3 million, it can only maintain modest military forces and does not host

[17] Nicholas Rothwell, "ASEAN Dramatises Pacific Rift," *The Australian,* 20–21 June 1987.

U.S. installations as strategically important as those in Australia. Consequently Washington has tended to regard New Zealand as little more than an adjunct to Australia in the ANZUS alliance. At the same time, New Zealand's record as a gallant but modest ally that is prepared to concentrate its efforts on the smaller island states of the South Pacific has been appreciated by its two larger allies.

The genesis of New Zealand's more stridently nationalistic and antinuclear attitudes is commonly linked to the radicalizing influence of the Vietnam War. Since then minor parties with a central commitment to nuclear disarmament have gained wider support; some of these parties have been openly opposed to ANZUS. These attitudes have gained currency within the leftwing elements of the New Zealand Labour party, which has passed motions calling for the withdrawal from ANZUS, the termination of military exercises with nuclear forces and the shutdown of the Antarctic support base in New Zealand that is used by the United States. While the Labour government has resisted most of these resolutions, party opinion has forced the present government to ban the visits of nuclear-powered ships as well as those with nuclear weapons from New Zealand ports. In the 1984 elections some two-thirds of the vote went to parties opposed to visits by nuclear-powered and nuclear-armed ships. At the same time, about 70% of public opinion favors continued membership in the ANZUS alliance.

The Labour government of Prime Minister Lange came to office with a commitment not to permit nuclear ships into New Zealand harbors. Aside from the nuclear ships issue, the government hoped to maintain the existing range of alliance links with its ANZUS partners. The Lange government has argued that as a small and isolated nation, living in a nuclear-free environment and committed to keeping the South Pacific nuclear-free, New Zealand finds that its security interests—and those of the West—are best served by keeping nuclear forces out of New Zealand. The government has also stressed that as its stance reflects its special strategic circumstances, its example should not be taken as a precedent by other Western allies.

The United States rejected New Zealand's position from the outset, arguing that given its long-standing policy to neither confirm nor deny speculation about the nature of weapons carried by its ships, the nuclear ban can only result in the blanket exclusion of all U.S. Navy vessels from New Zealand. Such an exclusion amounts to strategic denial, an action clearly incompatible with New Zealand's status as an ally. After allowing a decent interval for the Lange government to consider its position, the United States proposed, in early 1985, a visit by the conventionally powered destroyer, the *USS Buchanan*. The proposed visit was turned down because the New Zealand government could not conclusively determine that the ship was not nuclear-armed. The American response was not to tender any further ship visits and to break off security cooperation.

Negotiations aimed at resolving the issue proved unsuccessful. The United States became increasingly alienated by New Zealand's handling of the problem and especially by the steps taken to enshrine the antinuclear policy into legislation. Secretary of State Shultz met Prime Minister Lange in

Manila in 1986, and at the end of that meeting the United States unilaterally withdrew its treaty-based security guarantees from New Zealand.

The United States viewed the anti-nuclear ship policy from a wider perspective. Because its policy to neither confirm nor deny is a global one, it could not make an exception for New Zealand without risking repercussions with more important allies such as Japan and Australia, which also have vocal antinuclear constituencies. The United States was also concerned that the failure to stand firm with New Zealand would complicate arms control negotiations with the Soviet Union and that the success of New Zealand's policy could enhance the Soviet strategic objective of encouraging regional denial.

Australia supports the U.S. position on the nuclear ships ban. At the same time both Washington and Canberra decided not to discard the trilateral ANZUS Treaty; instead they reaffirmed, by exchange of letters in 1986, their desire to continue cooperation within the treaty on a bilateral basis. Under this formula the trilateral ANZUS framework remains but the New Zealand chair is left vacant. Several considerations prompted this course. In the first place both Australia and the United States wish to leave the door open for New Zealand to modify its stance and rejoin the alliance. Secondly, both realized that the negotiation of a new bilateral treaty would subject both administrations to the political uncertainties of their respective ratification processes.

CONCLUSION

The outstanding characteristic of the ANZUS alliance is its adaptability to changing circumstances. Negotiated at the outset of the cold war in the Asia Pacific region, the alliance proved cohesive especially while all three states subscribed to collective security strategy. Undoubtedly the underdeveloped nature of the formalized arrangement contributed to its adaptability. ANZUS lacks most of the characteristics that typically bind alliances. It is without routinized joint planning arrangements, it does not require joint military deployments and it has few clearly defined agreements for sharing burdens. Instead, alliance cohesion has been facilitated by a wide range of extra-security factors such as the affinity between the peoples of the treaty partners, economic links and compatible political values.

The flexibility of the alliance was demonstrated in the ability to cope with the breakdown of the United States–New Zealand security relationship in the mid-1980s. Having worked more as a set of bilateral linkages within a triangle, the breakdown of one segment has done little practical damage to the remaining linkages. To be sure, Australia's willingness to maintain its security links with the United States and New Zealand on a bilateral basis has minimized the damage to the interests of its two closest allies. In turn both the United States and New Zealand now attach greater importance to their links to Australia.

For both Australia and the United States the alliance serves to formalize the close bilateral relationship that has developed between them—though the most valued elements of the relationship could as well take place outside the ANZUS Treaty. The stability of the bilateral relationship rests on the recognition of security interdependence. Although Australia continues to regard the ambiguous security guarantees in ANZUS as important, it increasingly emphasizes its privileged access to American intelligence, scientific and technical information and logistic support—all of which facilitate its strategy of self-reliance. For the United States, the security guarantees it extends under the treaty have never proved onerous. What makes Australia an increasingly important ally is the support it provides to the conventional regional postures of the United States as well as its willingness to host the defense facilities that directly contribute to American strategic interests. The stability of the relationship rests substantially on the appreciation by both sides that the relationship serves respective core interests that cannot be changed unilaterally without endangering the entire relationship. The lack of a similarly balanced interdependence between the United States and New Zealand has contributed to the more asymmetrical nature of that relationship.

The underlying divergences within ANZUS were evident at the outset. These stem from the inevitable differences in the global concerns of the United States and the more regionally focused concerns of Australia and New Zealand. Different outlooks emerged after World War II over the peace with Japan, an issue that reflected the different preoccupations about the nature of security and order in the Pacific. Such differences were submerged while the three allies pursued a common strategy of containment, a strategy based on the fundamental assumption that the security interests of the ANZUS allies were indivisible. The Guam Doctrine made these assumptions much less tenable. The subsequent disaggregation of security preoccupations and the inevitable divergence of priorities emerged as U.S. strategies in the Asia Pacific region reflected its global perspective, while Australia and especially New Zealand have focused their security strategies on their immediate environment.

FURTHER READING

Albinski, Henry S. *ANZUS, The United States, and Pacific Security*. New York: University Presses of America for the Asia Society, 1987.

Ball, Desmond. *A Base For Debate*. Sydney and London: Allen & Unwin, 1987.

————, ed. *The ANZAC Connection*. Sydney and London: Allen & Unwin, 1985.

Dorrance, John C. "ANZUS: Misconceptions, Mythology and Reality." *Australian Quarterly* 57 (Spring 1985).

Mediansky, F. A. "Australia and the United States: Implications for New Zealand." In Ann Trotter, ed. *New Zealand, Canada and the United States*. Dunedin, New Zealand: University of Otago Press, 1987.

————. "The Defence of Australia and the American Alliance." *Australian Outlook* 41, no. 3 (1987).

————. "Nuclear Weapons and Security in the South Pacific: Problems for the ANZUS Alliance." *Washington Quarterly* (Winter 1986).

Thakur, Ramesh. *In Defense of New Zealand: Foreign Policy Choices in the Nuclear Age*. Boulder, Colorado, Westview Press, 1986.

THE POLITICAL FUTURE OF THE PACIFIC ISLAND STATES

WILLIAM NESTER

INTRODUCTION

ONE of the most dramatic developments of the postwar era has been the rise of the Pacific Basin to a central role in world politics and economy. No region on earth has experienced faster economic and trade growth: In 1986 the Pacific Basin countries enjoyed 60 percent of the world's GNP and 40 percent of its trade, exceeding that of the Atlantic Basin by one third.[1] Over U.S. $200 billion worth of goods flows within the Pacific Basin each year, a figure that is supposed to more than double by the year 2000. It is no wonder, then, that analysts are now calling the 21st century the Pacific century. But the Pacific Basin's economic dynamism is not equally distributed. The triangular relationship among the United States, Japan and East Asia is the dynamic core of economic actors in the Pacific Basin, with Australia, New Zealand, Canada and Mexico playing supporting roles, and the rest of Latin America with mere walk-on parts.

In comparison, the 20 Pacific island countries and territories scattered from the Mariana Islands to the north, Papua New Guinea to the west and French Polynesia to the east, are seen as remote, tranquil tropical play-grounds for wealthy jetsetters. These small, isolated islands depend largely on tourism, foreign aid and the export of a few primary products for their livelihood; altogether, they contribute less than one percent to the Pacific Basin's GNP.

Despite the microstate image, there is actually great population, economic and cultural diversity within the region. Most of the inhabitants live in Papua New Guinea (population 3.5 million), which also dwarfs the other Pacific island countries in land area and GNP. Fiji, the second most populous country, has a population of 592,000. Nauru, Niue and Tuvalu, on the other hand—each with a population of less than 8,000—are among the world's smallest countries. As measured by GDP, the region can be divided among "large economy" countries such as Nauru, Papua New Guinea,

---

[1] Direction of Trade Statistics, 1979–84; *International Monetary Fund Yearbook*.

Fiji and New Caledonia, with GNPs of around $500 million; "medium economy" countries such as French Polynesia and Western Samoa, which fall within the $40 million to $50 million GNP range; and "small economy" countries such as Niue and the Solomon Islands, with GNPs of around $1 million.[2] Culturally, the region is divided among Polynesians in the east, Melanesians in the west and Micronesians in the north.

Traditionally, the Pacific islands have been considered politically stable, democratic and pro-American. One by one, starting with Western Samoa in 1962, 14 Pacific island states achieved either full or partial independence. By the 1980s nine countries were fully independent: Western Samoa (1962), Nauru (1968), Tonga (1968), Fiji (1970), Papua New Guinea (1975), the Solomon Islands (1975), Kiribati (1978), Tuvalu (1978) and Vanuatu (1980). Five states chose independence in free association with a larger country responsible for its defense and foreign policy: The Cook Islands (1965) and Niue (1974) were associated with New Zealand, whereas the Federated States of Micronesia (1986), the Marshall Islands (1986) and Palau (1987) were associated with the United States. For all these countries, independence was achieved peacefully and relations remained close with former colonial or administrative powers. Residents of the Marianas voted to remain with the United States as the Commonwealth of the Northern Mariana Islands. Guam and American Samoa are U.S. territories. The territories of New Caledonia and French Polynesia, however, remained firmly under French rule.

Throughout the 1980s the Pacific islands experienced a series of challenges that changed their image as sleepy economic and political backwaters. The South Pacific Forum, a regional organization of the newly independent Pacific island states plus Australia and New Zealand, negotiated two very important treaties: the South Pacific Nuclear Free Zone (SPNFZ) Treaty in 1986, which was aimed largely at continued French nuclear tests on Mururoa Atoll; and the Fisheries Treaty with the United States in 1987, by the terms of which Washington agreed to recognize the Pacific islands' 200-mile/322-km. economic enterprise zones (EEZs) for jurisdiction over tuna fishing. In doing so the United States solved a long-standing conflict caused by American tuna boats poaching throughout the region. In addition, the forum unanimously declared its support for an independent New Caledonia in 1986.

The forum's newfound political activism was matched by that of several of its members. New Zealand declared itself a nuclear free zone in 1984, starting a heated conflict with the United States that led Washington to repudiate Wellington's membership in the ANZUS defense alliance two years later. Kiribati and Vanuatu made considerable waves when they signed fishing agreements with the Soviet Union in 1985 and 1986, respectively. Combined with the steady buildup of the Soviet Pacific fleet in the 1980s and Secretary-General Mikhail Gorbachev's 1986 Vladivostok speech, in which he declared that the Soviet Union would become an increasingly active Pacific power, these two fishing agreements were seen as the first

[2] *U.N. Statistical Yearbook, 1986.*

stage of a long-term Moscow strategy to gain influence in the Pacific. Vanuatu made headlines again in 1987 when it openly considered allowing Libya to establish an embassy in Port-Vila.

Several Pacific island countries have experienced political instability. Fiji's parliamentary system and the fragile relationship between the native Fijian and Indian communities were shattered by a military coup in May 1987 that followed an election victory in late April by the largely Indian-backed Fiji Labour party over the largely native Fijian Alliance party, which had governed Fiji since independence. After the coup the new government struggled to overcome severe economic disruptions and form a new political arrangement acceptable to both groups. In Vanuatu, growing estrangement between Prime Minister Walter Lini and Communication Minister Barak Sope, which had been building for over a year, broke into rioting in May 1988. At Lini's request, Australia and New Zealand rushed in riot equipment and police, and the disruption was quelled. But Vanuatu remained plagued by political uncertainty. Papua New Guinea was wracked by corruption and presided over by a seven-party coalition that frequently threatened to break up in open conflict.

These developments revealed a political future for the Pacific islands filled with both promises and perils. The first section of this essay will examine the South Pacific Forum's past successes and future challenges in fulfilling its goals for increased regional political and economic integration and development, as well as the implications of political instability in Fiji, Papua New Guinea, Vanuatu and elsewhere. The second section will analyze the constellation of large outside powers competing to achieve their respective goals in the region.

REGIONAL ISSUES, SUCCESSESS AND CHALLENGES

For over 40 years there have been attempts to achieve greater regional cooperation and integration in the Pacific. The South Pacific Commission was created by the region's colonial powers in 1947 to integrate and develop the region economically and culturally. The South Pacific Forum was created in 1971 to deal with many of the political issues avoided by the conservative commission. The commission has become increasingly moribund as the forum focuses on key regional political and economic initiatives. General policies are decided at annual forum meetings and then committees are formed to implement the specific proposals or programs. Since 1971 the forum has attempted to promote regional development and integration by initiating telecommunications, foreign investment, transportation, bulk processing, free trade and education. The forum's membership rose to 15 countries at the Apia (Western Samoa) meeting in May 1987 when it admitted two new countries, the Federated States of Micronesia and the Marshall Islands, to its ranks. The forum came of age in 1986 and 1987 when it successfully concluded SPNFZ, and the Fisheries Treaty with the United States; each had evolved as issues over the previous decade.

On December 11, 1986, SPNFZ came into force when Australia became the eighth nation to ratify the pact. Although SPNFZ evolved quickly from

Australia's introduction of the concept at the Canberra forum meeting in 1983, to the document's signing at Rarotonga in 1985 and its ratification a year and one-half later, it represented the culmination of government and popular antinuclear sentiments that had been developing in the Pacific region since the early 1970s. The forum has been officially opposed to nuclear testing and dumping in the Pacific ever since its first meeting in 1971. The South Pacific has been the only other region to declare itself a nuclear free zone since Latin America became the first with the Treaty of Tlatelolco in 1967.

Although SPNFZ is an important step in the South Pacific's development as a politically active and cohesive region, its significance as an arms control measure is primarily psychological. SPNFZ represents a compromise between countries such as New Zealand, Papua New Guinea, Vanuatu and the Solomon Islands that preferred a more ambitious arms control arrangement, and Fiji, Tonga, Western Samoa, Niue and the Cook Islands that were reluctant to sign any treaty for fear that it might affect regional security arrangements.[3] Only Vanuatu refused to sign the treaty, saying it did not go far enough to control the nuclear presence in the Pacific. While clearly declaring its opposition to the presence, testing or dumping of nuclear arms in the South Pacific, the treaty allows each country to determine its own policy regarding visits by nuclear-powered or nuclear-armed ships. Freedom of transit of such vessels is left untouched. The nuclear status quo remains largely unaltered. SPNFZ does impede further nuclearization of the South Pacific by requiring signers to renounce the right to acquire nuclear weapons or allow foreign countries to introduce nuclear weapons into their respective countries.

SPNFZ was primarily directed against continued French nuclear testing; both the United States and Britain officially stopped their nuclear test programs in the Pacific in 1963. All the French tests were conducted at or near Mururoa Atoll in French Polynesia. Between 1966, when the first explosion occurred, and 1975 the French detonated 40 nuclear devices in the atmosphere over Mururoa and one over the nearby Fangataufa Atoll. Thereafter, in response to a 1975 joint effort by Australia, New Zealand and Fiji to take France before the International Court of Justice, the French conducted all their tests underground. From 1975 through 1987 there were 57 underground explosions, 60 at Mururoa and two at Fangataufa.[4]

Despite the limited effect of SPNFZ on nuclear arms in the Pacific, in February 1987 the United States announced its refusal to sign, citing fears that SPNFZ would undermine deterrence, disrupt the balance of power and encourage more sensitive, strategic areas like Western Europe to create their own nuclear free zones. About the same time both Britain and France, citing similar concerns, also announced they would not sign SPNFZ. Scoring important public relations coups, the Soviet Union signed the treaty

[3] Greg Fry, "Towards a South Pacific Nuclear-Free-Zone," *Bulletin of the Atomic Scientists* (Spring 1986): 62.
[4] Greg Fry, *A Nuclear-Free Zone for the Southwest Pacific,* The Strategic and Defense Centre Working Paper no. 75 (Canberra), 17–19.

in December 1986 and China in February 1987. The United States' refusal to sign SPNFZ was a disappointment to the Pacific island countries and undercut, to a certain extent, the relief and goodwill created by the recent conclusion of the long-awaited Fisheries Treaty between the United States and the forum countries.

The fisheries issue originated in 1976 when the forum decided to coordinate its members' fisheries policies. It was not until 1979, however, that the Forum Fisheries Agency (FFA) was established to implement forum fishing policy. Between 1977 and 1984 all of the forum countries declared the right to regulate fishing and mining within 200-mile EEZs around their territories. It is estimated that the annual unprocessed tuna catch within the Pacific island countries' EEZs is about 650,000 tons, valued at $450 million, almost all of which is caught by foreign fishing fleets. One of the FFA's objectives was to obtain at least five percent of the annual catch in licensing fees from the foreign tunaboat fleets. Unfortunately, until recently it was beyond the abilities of the Pacific islands to patrol their vast EEZs, so they only received about two percent of the catch's value.[5]

In 1980 the U.S. tuna fleet began to move its operations from the strictly regulated west coast of Latin America into the South Pacific. The American tuna fishers, represented by the American Tunaboat Association (ATA), succeeded in getting Congress to pass the Magnusson Act in 1976. The act declared that migratory tuna were beyond the jurisdiction of the EEZs, and called for mandatory trade cutoffs with any country that interfered with the "right" of America's fishing fleet to catch tuna anywhere it pleased. By 1984, 65 American tunaboats were taking an annual $150 million of unprocessed tuna in the South Pacific without paying any fees.

The FFA opened negotiations with Washington in 1984 in an attempt to force the United States to recognize its right to regulate migratory tuna within the EEZs. The ATA exerted considerable pressure on Washington to resist FFA demands, which caused anti-American sentiment to rise throughout the region. These feelings were exacerbated when the United States imposed trade embargoes on both the Solomon Islands and Papua New Guinea after those two countries seized American tunaboats illegally fishing within their respective EEZs. Both countries had to sell back the boats to their owners for a nominal price to end the embargo.

Over the course of the negotiations between 1984 and 1987, when the treaty was signed, Washington policymakers gradually realized the damage a continued hard-line approach was causing American interests in the Pacific. Finally, in April 1987 the United States signed a treaty with the FFA, by the terms of which it agreed to provide the Pacific island countries with over $60 million during the next five years for the right of American tunaboats to operate there. Of this amount the industry would provide about $2 million and the U.S. government about $10 million a year for the next five years. The government funds included $1 million in economic development assistance and $9 million in cash, to be divided among the

[5] John Rob, "Fisheries Development in the South Pacific," in *The Emerging Marine Economy of the Pacific,* ed. Chennat Gopalkrishnan, 111–12.

islands. The industry would pay a minimum of $1.75 million a year in boat fees, and a flat $250,000 a year in technical assistance to fishery-related projects. These fees were based on a minimum rate of $50,000 per vessel. There were at the time 64 active purse seiners in the American fishing fleet, and it was expected that at least 40 of them would seek licenses. Beyond 40 vessels the price would go up to $60,000 a vessel. Fifteen percent of the total package would cover the administrative costs of the FFA in Honiara (Solomon Islands) as well as equal division among the signatories, producing about $100,000 a year for each of the governments. The remaining 85 percent would be distributed according to the location of the catch, which changes from year to year. Papua New Guinea and the Federated States of Micronesia were expected to receive about half of the 85 percent.[6]

This treaty provided an important economic boost to the region, particularly to small countries like Kiribati and Tuvalu whose fees amounted to as much as half their government revenues. The treaty resolved a worsening sore spot in United States-Pacific islands relations, and was an important symbol for regional cooperation. The United States was the last fishing country to sign a treaty with the FFA. In addition to the United States, five other distant-water fishing nations had access agreements with Pacific island states: Japan had agreements with 10 of these, Taiwan with seven, South Korea with three, and the Soviet Union and Mexico with one each.

Unfortunately, however, American boats continued to fish illegally in the EEZs while the treaty awaited ratification by Congress. In May 1987 the American boat *Tradition* was seized by Kiribati for illegally fishing in its waters, while about 10 other American boats got away. The *Tradition's* catch was confiscated, and the ship's owner and captain were each fined $A150,000. This time there was no official reaction from Washington.

The South Pacific Forum could be judged a success if one examined only its many economic development projects and its united stand on political issues such as the Fiji coup or independence for New Caledonia. But with its fishing treaty with the United States and its nuclear free zone treaty, the forum can be regarded as the world's most successful regional international organization after the European Community. Yet despite these efforts the forum may have reached its limits of cooperation or integration. The member-countries are too distant and small to form any viable economic integration, and too culturally diverse to form a larger political union. Ethnic groupings are conceivable but unlikely. The Melanesian Spearhead Group—which included Papua New Guinea, Vanuatu and the Solomon Islands—talked about some sort of subregional union, but most observers considered it a pipe dream.

Despite the unlikelihood of any greater degree of integration, the forum faced major challenges in the future from both regional and outside powers. Among the independent Pacific island nations themselves, Papua New Guinea, Fiji and Vanuatu either attempted to challenge the regional status quo or had the potential to do so.

[6] *Pacific Islands Monthly* (April 1987): 28.

Papua New Guinea

With the largest population and land area of the Pacific island countries, Papua New Guinea can become a significant regional political and economic power in the 1990s. Papua New Guinea contains rich but largely unexploited mineral, forestry, human and energy resources. In the last few years Papua New Guinea has been following a growing independent foreign policy, vowing to create positive relations with all the powers, including the Soviet Union, China, Japan, the United States and neighboring Indonesia. Communications Minister Gabriel Ramoi said that foreign policy "must be conducted in such a way that it secures and protects PNG's national interest. While we have been debating this, Australia, for example, has been sending businessmen to the Soviet Union."[7]

Central to this policy was the need to shed Papua New Guinea's traditional dependence on Australia. A March 1987 statement of principles signed between the two countries was designed to reorient Australia-Papua New Guinea relations on a more equitable basis. This may in part have been a reaction to Australia's cutback in aid to Papua New Guinea in fiscal year 1987–88, after Prime Minister Robert Hawke had agreed two years earlier to a five-year aid package during Papua New Guinea's ten-year independence celebration in 1985. The official policy was to reduce Australian aid from 19 percent of GNP to about five percent, and make up the difference with mutually advantageous trade.[8]

Papua New Guinea also intended to lessen its traditional dependence on Australia to ensure its military security. In early 1988 it invited an American special forces team to help train its military in jungle tactics. With its own 13,000-member military force, an additional 4,600 paramilitary troops and a 300-member navy using five patrol boats, Papua New Guinea posed no regional military threat and seemed unlikely ever to become one since it will always be dwarfed by its huge neighbors, Indonesia and Australia. The Papua New Guinea military was primarily designed to provide internal security and to contain border problems with Indonesia.

Papua New Guinea's border problems with Indonesia were indeed a troublesome security issue. Indonesian troops violated the border a number of times in pursuit of Free Papua Movement (OPM) guerrillas. Port Moresby was flooded with several waves of refugees, particularly following an abortive 1984 OPM uprising in the provincial capital of Jayapura. Jakarta continued to be irritated by Port Moresby's apparent toleration of the OPM and open sympathy for their "Melanesian brothers" and the OPM cause. The friendship, cooperation and mutual respect treaty signed between the two countries in March 1987 helped alleviate some distrust, in that both nations pledged never to use force against each other. Indonesia subsequently curbed its policy of hot pursuit of guerrillas into Papua New Guinea. The issue rested with the U.N. High Commissioner for Refugees. In addition, Indonesia provided Papua New Guinea with industrial and agricultural technology, and aided several rural development projects.

[7] Ibid., February 1988, p. 22.
[8] Ibid., January 1988, p. 36.

Nevertheless, tensions flared again when the OPM launched a violent raid in March 1988 on an Indonesian transmigration settlement at Arso, near Jayapura, which in turn triggered an Indonesian counterraid across the border on an OPM camp. Although the government of Papua New Guinea formally protested the Indonesian incursion, it also moved about 1,000 border-camp refugees to a new settlement deeper within its territory.[9]

Papua New Guinea was interested in maintaining good relations with Indonesia for more reasons than military security and economic assistance. Geographically straddling the frontier between the South Pacific and Southeast Asia, Papua New Guinea intended to become as active in the latter as it has been in the former. The council of the Association of Southeast Asian Nations (ASEAN) considered a Papua New Guinea request to sign the ASEAN treaty of amity and cooperation, although Papua New Guinea was said to be hesitating on whether or not to become a full ASEAN member. Meanwhile, Papua New Guinea continued to maintain a high profile in both the South Pacific Forum and the Melanesian Spearhead Group. It helped initiate the August 1986 forum call for New Caledonian independence and was the first government to grant full recognition to the new Fijian republic.

Papua New Guinea was expected to succeed in achieving its ambition to break its dependence on Australia and create a broad web of relations with the superpowers and Southeast Asia, alongside its continuing ties with the Pacific islands. But it faced a number of domestic economic and political challenges that impeded early maximization of its goal. Over 87 percent of the population lived a subsistence existence in the countryside, and the rapidly swelling cities became centers of crime, poverty, unemployment and corruption.

Papua New Guinea shared with other developing countries throughout the world the same conflicts created by rising expectations, and was ill-equipped politically to handle them. The political system focused on patronage; nepotism, graft and vote buying were widespread. There were open auctions for support, in which one's political loyalty went to the highest bidder, until the next came along.[10] In 1986 Ted Diro, who had held several government portfolios, including defense and foreign affairs, resigned after a commission of inquiry charged him on three counts of perjury concerning timber sale payoffs. But because of the delicate balance of power among political blocs in parliament, Diro and his People's Action party were readmitted into the government's seven-party coalition later that year.

There seemed a growing chance that either a suspension of the constitution or a coup could take place if Papua New Guinea experienced further economic and political instability. In December 1987 a censorship law was enacted that enabled the government to determine the content of all publications and broadcasting, and required foreign control in any mass media to be reduced to 50 percent immediately and nationalized within 10 years.

[9] *Far Eastern Economic Review* (May 26, 1988)
[10] *Pacific Islands Monthly* (January 1988): 32–36.

Two daily newspapers, the *Papua New Guinea Post-Courier* and *Niugini Nius,* both foreign owned, were affected by the new legislation.

Fiji

The military had never played a significant role in any Pacific island nation until the May 1987 coup in Fiji. In fact, Fiji was lauded as a model democracy with a multiracial society and a developing economy. Its 1970 constitution was one of the world's most complex, in that it attempted to maintain a fair representation among ethnic Fijians, Indians and minority groups. Although recent population figures showed Indians comprising 48.7 percent of the population, slightly larger than the native Fijians at 46.1 percent, the Fijian Alliance party led by Ratu Sir Kamisese Mara had continually won elections since independence in 1970.[11] In the April 1987 election, however, the Indian National Federation party and the mixed-race Fiji Labour party joined to win 28 seats, whereas the Alliance party won 24 seats. Dr. Timoci Bavadra, an ethnic Fijian, then formed a coalition government that included both parties and ethnic representatives.

On May 14, Lt. Col. Sitiveni Rabuka and 14 men shocked the world by storming parliament and seizing the new cabinet. Rabuka justified the coup by claiming that the Bavadra government would eventually take away the land rights of ethnic Fijians. The coup was supported by the Taukei movement of ethnic Fijians who favored stripping the Indians of their political rights and returning Fiji to rule by the Great Council of Chiefs, which under the 1970 constitution had an only symbolic role. Following the coup, Fiji's 3,100-member armed forces were beefed up with reserves to around 8,000. Rabuka ruled through a council of Fijian leaders until, tired of the political impasse over constitutional reforms, he staged a second coup on September 26. On October 6 he declared himself head of the new republic of Fiji and the 1970 constitution void.

Both coups were greeted with condemnation by the Western powers. The forum countries also denounced the coups, although the Melanesian Spearhead Group expressed reservations about interference in Fiji's internal affairs and offered to send a mediatory delegation to Suva if requested. The Commonwealth of Nations, meeting in Vancouver in mid-October, voted to expel Fiji, but in private British diplomats were more conciliatory as they negotiated for a return to democracy.

On December 5, 1987, Rabuka announced his abdication and turned power over to former Governor-General Ratu Sir Penaia Ganilau, who became the first president of the republic of Fiji. Ganilau accepted the position after being assured that the new constitution would guarantee the rights of all Fijian citizens. Mara accepted the prime ministership with the assurance he would be free to select his own cabinet and to set a schedule for returning the country to parliamentary democracy. Ganilau promised that Fiji would reestablish links with Britain and the Commonwealth.[12] There was a good chance that the new government would create a consti-

[11] Ibid., p. 22
[12] Ibid., p. 10.

tution to restore both democracy and the delicate balance between the Fijian and Indian communities.

Although the political damage was reparable, the coup inflicted lasting damage on Fiji's economy. Afraid of the violence, tourists kept away. Hotel occupancy averaged only about 10 percent in June 1987, compared to its normal level of 70 percent. Indian sugarcane farmers, who made up more than 70 percent of the growers, refused to harvest the crop, jeopardizing Fiji's most important export and the economy's backbone. Sugarcane accounted for 15 percent of the GNP, 60 percent of total export earnings and 25 percent of the labor force. The harvest delay was estimated to have cost Fiji anywhere between $30 million to $50 million out of a total crop value of around $200 million. [13]

The government countered the recession by devaluing the Fijian dollar 17.5 percent, and enacted strict financial controls to impede a massive flight of capital and to stimulate exports. In addition, the government announced a 20 percent cutback in government services and a 25 percent pay cut. Despite these actions, Fiji's foreign reserves fell from $F170 million on the day of the coup to $F113 million six weeks later. [14] The government deficit was over $100 million for 1987, almost $25 million higher than the projected deficit of $F77 million. After the second coup the Fijian dollar was devalued a further 15.25 percent and foreign reserves fell to a little over $F100 million.

Fiji's economic future looked bleak, with tourism the only sector of the economy that might recover in the short term. Stimulated by cheap round-trip fares from Australia and New Zealand, as well as the devalued Fijian dollar, as early as July 1987 hotel occupancy was up to 35 percent and by late spring 1988 hovered around 60 percent, slightly less than the normal May average. [15] But all other economic sectors were mired in a deep recession. After the May coup, both foreign and domestic investment came to a standstill and there seemed little prospect of significant future investments as long as Fiji's political situation remained unstable. While foreign investors could benefit from the devalued Fijian dollar, they feared further disruptions and an inability to repatriate any profits. On paper, inflation rose less than expected, only six percent for 1987 compared to earlier fears that inflation would reach 20 percent. But the devaluations of the Fijian dollar were offset by a lack of buying power. Because inflation for essential goods did rise to over 20 percent, while the prices of luxury goods dropped considerably, the overall inflation rate did not seem significant. The recession caused a huge shortfall in taxes and contributed to a record budget deficit. The Finance Ministry attempted to raise revenues through a variety of excise, export and import taxes, but its immediate effect was to boost inflation.

Perhaps the worst long-term economic effect was the steady migration of the most capable and wealthiest Indians, leaving a severe shortage of

[13] Ibid., August 1987, pp. 21–24.
[14] Ibid., p. 22.
[15] Ibid., March 1988, p. 7.

doctors, accountants, engineers, pharmacists, lawyers and other professionals. The Indians felt they had no future in Fiji, and after the coup they were exposed to open discrimination and, at times, violence.[16] This brain drain caused considerable harm to Fiji's future economic development.

Fiji used the coup to try to break its traditional political dependence on Britain, and its economic dependence on Australia and New Zealand. "Foreign Policy Initiatives for the Republic of Fiji," issued in October 1987, stated, among other things, that Fiji would establish and promote new patterns of trade, develop new campaigns to bring tourists to the country, and attempt to attract foreign investment and technical assistance from sources other than Australia and New Zealand. The report was promptly followed by trade missions to the forum and ASEAN countries; and Suva declared its intention to create closer ties with China, Taiwan and South Korea.[17]

The United States, Australia and New Zealand all condemned the coups and urged a prompt restoration of democracy to Fiji. Yet they tried to keep enough pressure on Suva to restore democracy without pushing the country to pursue a completely independent line. The fear was that Fiji could turn to the Soviet Union or Libya if pushed too hard. While there was little possibility of Fiji's leaders ever going that far, the French offered Suva $A12 million in aid in an attempt to replace Australia as Fiji's largest aid donor. Paris, of course, used the economic assistance to influence Fiji to diminish its criticism of continued French control over New Caledonia and nuclear tests on Mururoa.[18] Australia sought to offset the French play for influence by changing the basis of its diplomatic relations with other countries from one of recognizing governments to one of recognizing nations. By making this change Australia would be able to resume the aid and defense agreements with Fiji that were suspended following the coups.[19]

Kiribati

Kiribati and Vanuatu sharply disturbed the region's political tranquility by their respective agreements with Moscow allowing Soviet fishing boats access to their EEZs. Kiribati's action occurred after the ATA refused to renew its 1982–84 fishing agreement with Kiribati, the Federated States of Micronesia and Palau, largely because the ATA objected to paying for a license when there was little chance of getting caught for poaching. The loss of the ATA licensing fees forced Kiribati to seek other parties interested in purchasing fishing rights, and so it responded favorably to Moscow's request for access. The Soviet Union had unsuccessfully approached other countries in the Pacific—including Fiji, Papua New Guinea, the Solomon Islands, Tuvalu and Western Samoa—to establish fisheries.

Negotiations for a tuna fishing agreement between Kiribati and the Soviet Union started in Australia in February 1985, continued in May in

[16] *Independent* (March 14, 1988).
[17] *Pacific Islands Monthly* (December 1987): 16.
[18] Ibid., February 1988, p. 11.
[19] Ibid., p. 11.

Singapore and concluded in Manila in August. Kiribati's deal with the Soviet Union was similar to other distant-water fishing agreements in force in the Pacific island region. The Soviet Union paid $1.5 million in access rights. At the agreement's expiration in October 1986, the Soviets did not renew because Kiribati refused to lower the fee for the following year. The commercial value of the fish caught by the Soviets was about $600 a ton but the Soviets paid almost $800 a ton (or $2.4 million) for it. Kiribati rejected a Soviet renewal offer of $1 million, less than half of what it had paid the previous year.[20]

The negotiations and eventual agreement between Kiribati and the Soviet Union stimulated both domestic and international opposition. Washington gravely warned Kiribati that such an agreement would lead to greater Soviet intelligence gathering activities in the region and could lead to eventual port access arrangements for the Soviet fleet. The U.S. State Department hastily tried to put together an aid package to offset the Soviet offer. The U.S. Agency for International Development offered to assist Kiribati's domestic tuna industry, but was later reluctant to offer cash because of its restricted foreign aid budget and fear that it would encourage other countries to enter into negotiations with the Soviet Union as a means of gaining access to American aid coffers.[21] Other international response to the agreement was mixed. Although Papua New Guinea and Vanuatu openly supported Kiribati, most other Pacific island countries expressed concern. Australia and New Zealand strongly opposed the agreement and offered their own aid programs. China also protested the agreement and offered Kiribati aid valued at $350,000, as well as interest-free loans for development purposes.[22] For political and strategic reasons the United States, Australia, New Zealand and China wanted to minimalize Soviet presence in the Pacific islands.

There was significant domestic opposition to the government's fishery deal with the Soviet Union as well. A vote of no confidence during the August 1985 parliament session was defeated by a narrow margin. In an unusual move, the Protestant and Catholic churches, prior to the signing of the agreement, petitioned Kiribati's president to delay ratification until Kiribatians had considered the full implications of the agreement. Opponents of the agreement cited Soviet aggression in Afghanistan and Poland and the possibility of the country's EEZs being dominated by foreign fishing vessels. The president of Kiribati, in the face of internal and foreign criticism over the agreement, claimed that it had been concluded: (1) out of economic necessity; (2) as a reaction to persistent illegal fishing by American purse seiners in Kiribati's EEZ; and (3) as a direct result of the collapse of the ATA agreement.[23] In its national interest Kiribati sold fishing rights

---

[20] Ibid., February 1987, p. 25.
[21] David Doulman, *Some Aspects and Issues Concerning the Kiribati/Soviet Union Fishing Paper,* East West Center Paper (Honolulu, August 1986), 14.
[22] Ibid.,
[23] Ibid., p. 11.

to the highest bidder; the highest bidder was the Soviet Union, even though the ATA had been given the first option.

Vanuatu

Vanuatu signed a similar fishing deal with the Soviet Union in January 1987—worth $1.5 million—but this time the criticism was muted and less widespread. An editorial in the *Pacific Islands Monthly* called Vanuatu's fishing agreement with the Soviet Union inevitable, and added that in "the absence of better offers for access to the nation's very valuable resource, it makes common commercial sense to conclude a deal with the highest—or only—bidder." The editorial pointed out that independent states should be free to deal with any country they wish: New Zealand and other industrialized countries have fishing agreements with the Soviet Union, why not Vanuatu?[24]

Vanuatu's attempts to create close ties with Libya, on the other hand, provoked a storm of international criticism. Vanuatu was the only forum country that was a member of the nonaligned bloc. In March 1987 Prime Minister Lini's plans to send 30 or 40 Vanuaaku Pati officials, journalists and bodyguards to Libya for training became public, unleashing protests from other Pacific island nations and the United States that such actions would militarize the region.

Australia went so far as to send back a party of eight Vanuatuans who were traveling to Libya via Sydney. After the party returned to Port-Vila, Lini felt compelled to declare that Vanuatu would never become a Communist or a terrorist state. He said Vanuatu's relations were in line with his government's policies of nonalignment, and accused the Western media of waging a deliberate propaganda campaign against Muammar al-Qadhafi and countries with which Libya had relations. Barak Sope, the left-wing secretary-general of the Vanuaaku Pati, added:

> This group is going mainly to look at their political system, and later they [the Libyans] will come and see how the Vanuaaku Party works. . . . In a short time Libya will establish a People's Bureau in Port-Vila. . . . We have similar ideals, of helping countries who fight for their independence. . . . We also think we can have economic gain from having diplomatic ties with Libya . . . as a small but rich country they provide aid to many African countries—why not to Vanuatu? . . . If Australia can have diplomatic relations with Libya and Russia, why not us?"[25]

In April 1987 two Libyan diplomats arrived in Port-Vila, uninvited and unannounced, with the intention of setting up a People's Bureau. Lini, angered that proper protocol had not been followed, and under diplomatic pressure from Australia and the United States, did not receive the representatives, and later said he was indefinitely postponing plans to let Libya open an embassy. New Zealand, meanwhile, with annual exports to Libya

[24] *Pacific Islands Monthly* (February 1987): 5.
[25] Ibid., February 1987, p. 19.

of $30 million, declined to join its allies in denouncing the Libyan presence.[26]

Sensational as a Libyan presence in the Pacific might seem, Lini had practical reasons for nurturing ties with Qadhafi. Vanuatu's economic problems were severe: In 1986 it suffered a $60 million deficit; and a hurricane caused $200 million worth of damage. Australia's annual $6 million aid package simply was not enough to overcome the country's chronic problems. So when Qadhafi approached Lini at the September 1986 nonaligned movement meeting in Zimbabwe with an offer of $40 million in aid and subsidized oil shipments, cheaper than any Vanuatu then received, Lini indicated he was interested.

Even were diplomatic ties established, they would probably not have seriously affected Vanuatu's solidly capitalist economic development strategy. Vanuatu's seemingly radical foreign policy contrasted sharply with domestic economic plans to break away from its dependence on foreign aid by advertising itself as a tax haven offering tough banking secrecy laws similar to those of Bermuda or the Bahamas, a tourist center, and a flag of convenience haven where over 70 ships were registered.[27]

It was conceivable, however, that recent political instability could lead to a new regime that would attempt to align Vanuatu economically as well as politically with Socialist countries. Lini suffered a stroke in February 1987 and Sope took advantage of the situation by consolidating power. Sope repeatedly called for closer ties with Libya and other nonaligned countries. He also advocated a federation of Melanesian states that would include not only the Solomons Islands, Papua New Guinea and Fiji but also, more problematically, an independent New Caledonia under Kanak rule and an Irian Jaya free from Indonesian control.[28]

Sope was said to have been behind a May 1988 march by over 2,000 people (some armed with iron bars and clubs) through Port-Vila after he lost control of the Vila Urban Land Corporation—a semiofficial agency and an important source of patronage for him. The government abolished the corporation on grounds of mismanagement, and transferred its control to the state. Although the government compensated the landowners, Sope encouraged the tribes to believe that the government was taking their traditional lands. One person was killed and nine injured during clashes with the police when some protestors began looting local businesses. Prime Minister Lini called for help from Australia and New Zealand, which quickly airlifted police, riot-control gear and medical supplies to Port-Vila.[29] Although Sope's most recent power play was defeated, his growing popularity, combined with Lini's frailty, meant continued political instability and uncertainty for Vanuatu.

[26] Los Angeles Times, 17 July 1987, p. 12.
[27] Economist, May 28, 1988.
[28] Time, May 30, 1988.
[29] Independent, May 18, 1987.

OUTSIDE POWERS IN THE PACIFIC

Outside powers have been crowding into the Pacific ever since Captain James Cook's voyages in the mid-18th century. By the late 19th century the region had been completely carved up by the imperial powers. Political change came slowly to the Pacific region. Although some colonies changed hands after each world war, the major decolonization efforts occurring elsewhere in the world did not reach the Pacific until the early 1960s. By 1987, however, 15 Pacific island countries had achieved independence. French Polynesia and New Caledonia were the largest remaining foreign dependencies.

Until the 1980s, because of Britain's withdrawal west of Suez and the United States' preoccupations elsewhere, Australia and New Zealand generally dominated trade, economic assistance, defense and cultural relations with the Pacific island states. The United States, warmly welcomed during World War II for liberating the region from Japanese imperialism, withdrew its presence after 1945 to its trusteeship over Micronesia north of the equator. In 1954 Washington signed the ANZUS pact with Canberra and Wellington, but its major concern was Southeast Asia; Australia and New Zealand would be responsible for Pacific military, economic and political security. France was and remained the unwanted outsider. Its continued nuclear testing at Mururoa Atoll and colonial rule over French Polynesia and New Caledonia made it the pariah of the Pacific.

In the later 1980s however, the old relations among the United States, Australia and New Zealand became strained over several issues, while new outsiders—the Soviet Union, Japan, Indonesia and Libya—attempted to work their way into the region. By playing one outside power off against another, the Pacific island countries benefited from increased great-power competition. For example, the sudden emergence of perceived Soviet and Libyan "threats" to the Pacific islands generated keen interest by Washington in this long-neglected region: The United States signed the generous Fisheries Treaty with the forum and, along with Australia and New Zealand, stepped up its aid, trade and diplomatic presence. But some outsiders also benefited from great-power rivalry and domestic problems; Japan, France and Indonesia took advantage of the political and economic problems in the Pacific to increase their own influence in the region. This heightened competition among the outside powers raised important questions that affected the political future of the region. Was there a Soviet and/or Libyan threat, and if so what was it? What were American interests in the Pacific, and what policy changes, if any, would occur? Would France continue to hold nuclear tests and territory in the region? What objectives did older powers such as Australia and New Zealand and newcomers such as Japan and Indonesia have in the Pacific? Underlying all these questions, what would their impact be on the political future of the region?

Soviet Union

Imperial Russia never showed much interest in the remote South Pacific. Although Russian explorers reached the Pacific coast as early as the 17th century, Moscow did not begin to build up its Far Eastern military forces until the late 19th century. It was only in the 1960s that the Soviets began to build a Pacific-based blue-water navy. By 1986 the Soviet Pacific fleet was the largest of the country's four fleets, and consisted of 85 surface combat vessels—including two aircraft carriers—589 auxiliary ships, 32 ballistic missile submarines and 90 attack submarines (almost all nuclear powered). These were supported by an air force of over 300 bombers and 1,200 fighters. Most of the fleet was based at Vladivostok, but since its 1978 treaty with Vietnam, the Soviet Union had maintained a portion of the fleet at Cam Ranh Bay, including 20 to 25 surface combatants, three to five submarines, a squadron of MiG-23 fighter-interceptors and antisubmarine aircraft, as well as about 7,000 personnel.[30]

What threat, if any, did the Soviet Pacific fleet pose to the West or the Pacific islands? As with all navies, the Soviet fleet has both political and strategic objectives. In peacetime the Soviet fleet's mission is to show the flag and impress all observers with Moscow's power and prestige. Strategically, both the Soviet Pacific fleet and air force have four primary missions: to protect sea approaches to the Soviet Union, to intimidate opponents in a crisis; to contain China; and, in wartime, to tie down U.S. naval forces and attack sea lanes. How effective is the Soviet fleet in achieving these missions? Showing the flag can have political costs as well as benefits. As the Americans found out in New Zealand and elsewhere, the presence of foreign ships, particularly if they are suspected of carrying nuclear arms, can create a popular backlash in the host country. No Soviet naval ships have appeared in the South Pacific since the 19th century, and the appearance of one now would incur for the Soviets tremendous political damage. Militarily, the Soviet Pacific fleet was vastly inferior to the U.S. Pacific fleet, which in wartime would be augmented by Japanese, Australian and other allied forces. American submarines and aircraft could quickly sink most Soviet ships at sea in both the Indian and Pacific Oceans, while American bombers based in the Philippines could destroy the Soviet forces at Cam Ranh Bay. Soviet ships based at Vladivostok could easily be contained, and probably eliminated in the Sea of Japan. The Soviet submarine fleet ran quieter thanks to Toshiba's sale of technology, but the United States continued to have the edge in submarine warfare. Despite the size of the Soviet submarine fleet, it suffered from poor maintenance and morale, and only a fraction of the fleet could operate at sea at one time. Thus, even the Soviet submarine fleet could quickly be eliminated in the event of hostilities.

But if the Soviet military posed no real political or military threat, what about the Soviet attempts to increase their diplomatic and economic presence? In his major policy speech at Vladivostok in 1986, Gorbachev declared that the Soviet Union was a Pacific power and would seek to establish a presence throughout the region. In August 1987 Australian Foreign Minister William Hayden claimed he had no doubt that the Soviet Union "aspired to drive out the U.S. presence and influence in the region . . .

---

[30] *Pacific Islands Monthly* (April 1987): 26.

in order to reap the security, political, and economic benefits of its own proximity and military predominance."[31]

Just as the Soviet military presence posed a relatively limited threat to the West, despite the seemingly alarming increase in its size and presence over the past decade, Soviet political initiatives suffered similar obstacles. The Soviet Union was limited in both its means and ability to influence Pacific politics to its advantage. For the most part, Soviet attempts to influence the region consisted of propaganda warning of the dangers of continued alignment with the United States, combined with attempts to make fishing, aviation or trade deals with the various Pacific island countries. The Soviets no doubt hoped the agreements would be followed by increased influence over the recipient country. But this strategy stood little chance of success. The Pacific island nations were generally deeply religious and strongly anticommunist, and they depended on the West for practically all their trade, investments and aid. Thus, the Soviets were caught in a dilemma: Any increased presence, however seemingly innocent, automatically heightened suspicions that they posed some sort of threat to the region. Mass media such as the major Australian and New Zealand newspapers and magazines, the *Fiji Times,* and the *Pacific Islands Monthly,* among others, loved to spotlight the latest Soviet moves in the region.

The fishing agreements with Kiribati and Vanuatu showed Moscow's mixed, but largely unambitious goals in the Pacific, and its limited abilities to achieve even those goals. Soviet fishing boats had actually been in the Pacific since the 1970s. The Soviets approached most of the island countries for access after those nations began declaring 200-mile EEZs, but the Soviets only succeeded in completing two deals. The fact that they allowed their fishing agreement with Kiribati to expire when they failed to catch their limit shows they were primarily interested in fishing. The treaty with Vanuatu, however, seems to have been for espionage rather than commercial purposes: it is well known that Vanuatu's waters have no significant fish stocks, but they do provide a strategic listening position to monitor U.S. ship movements in the North Pacific.[32] Still, neither agreement posed a threat to Kiribati, Vanuatu, the Pacific region as a whole or American security interests. Both deals prevented the Soviets from establishing any on-shore facilities or an actual presence. The Soviets had fishing agreements with over 100 countries, and generally followed strictly the terms of the agreements. The presence of Soviet fishing boats caused no noticeable adverse political side effects in any of those countries.

The Soviet Union was, however, slowly dispelling the negative image that continued to haunt any of its diplomatic initiatives in the region. Pacific islanders realize that the regional hysteria that greeted the fishing agreements might have been overdone: the treaties did not turn the Pacific Ocean into the Red Sea. Moscow's decision to sign SPNFZ further softened its negative image, particularly when contrasted with Washington's contin-

[31] Ibid., January 1988, p. 38.
[32] Per interview with Professor Kilafati Etuate, University of the South Pacific, Suva, June 6, 1987.

uing refusal to do so, despite the fact that the treaty was carefully constructed so that it would not affect American ship movements in the region. But the Soviet Union never gained a significant presence—no region of the world is of less importance to the Kremlin's geopolitical strategy—and, despite frictions, the Western powers remained popular.

Libya

If the Soviet Union posed no threat to the Pacific island nations, what about its sometime ally, Libya? Qadhafi had made a number of largely unsuccessful attempts to increase his influence in the region. He had offered money to help Australia's aborigines and New Zealand's Maori to set up independent homelands within their respective countries. He had also supplied military training and funds to the Kanak independence movement against France in New Caledonia and the OPM against Indonesia in Irian Jaya. Qadhafi had also entertained delegations from Vanuatu, Fiji, Tonga and the Solomon Islands, and had financed a new, union-based party in the latter. Although he was rebuffed in his attempt to set up a People's Bureau in Port-Vila in 1987, Vanuatu remained a prime target for the Libyan leader because of its role as an international tax haven and banking center—ideal for laundering money for terrorist groups.[33]

It may seem strange that Qadhafi was interested in such a remote region filled with microstates. But because they are microstates, they would seem to be easier to influence than larger countries. By interfering in the region, Libya could make trouble for its two key enemies: France, which frustrated Libyan ambitions in Chad; and the United States, which bombed Libya and has skirmished twice with Libyan jet fighters. In doing so, Qadhafi could deflect attention from domestic economic problems and enhance his popularity as a "world leader." But despite all these efforts, Libya did not succeed in gaining any significant foothold in the region, and like the Soviets, was unlikely to become a prominent player in future regional affairs.

United States

Since neither the Soviet Union nor Libya posed any threat to the region, would the South Pacific remain an "American sea?" In the eyes of Washington policymakers, the Pacific Basin was fast becoming as important as the Atlantic Basin, mostly because of its increasingly dynamic role in the world economy and its geostrategic role as a huge moat providing a defense for America's west coast. But the Pacific was also vital as the main route to the rich oil fields of the Arab/Persian Gulf. Since the early 1950s, five of Washington's 18 mutual-security agreements have been with Pacific Basin countries: Japan, Thailand, and Philippines, Australia and New Zealand.

To back these interests and security pacts, the United States maintained about 77,000 ground troops and 168,000 navy forces in American territory

[33] *Los Angeles Times,* 17 July 1987, p. 12.

within the Pacific Basin, and 109,000 ground troops and 20,000 navy forces in other Pacific countries. The largest American troop concentrations in foreign countries were Japan (48,000), South Korea (43,000), the Philippines (16,000) and Australia (700). American naval forces include the Third Fleet, the Seventh Fleet and the Pacific Submarine Force. The Seventh Fleet, based at Yokosuka, Japan, included eight submarines, two carriers, 20 surface combatants, and nine amphibious and six support ships. It was the largest of the U.S. fleets and included almost 40,000 personnel—almost half of the entire overseas U.S. Navy. The Third Fleet, based in Hawaii, with support bases on the west coast and Alaska, generally included 28 submarines, four aircraft carriers, 72 principal surface combatants, and 26 amphibious and 32 support ships. Finally, the Pacific Submarine Force included up to 42 attack submarines—39 of which were nuclear powered—and eight strategic missile submarines. The Pacific Air Force, based in Hawaii, had about 300 fighter, ground attack and reconnaissance aircraft. The United States had access to 55 shore installations in the Pacific.

Virtually all of these forces were based in the North Pacific; strategically, the South Pacific was of secondary importance. The sea lanes from the west coast of the United States to Southeast Asia and the Middle East beyond run directly through the North Pacific. Although the South Pacific would seem to provide a vast hiding place for American nuclear submarines, none spent any time there because their missiles could not reach the Soviet Union from south of the equator.

The ANZUS security treaty, signed in 1952 by the United States, Australia and New Zealand, was originally designed in the postwar era to contain the Soviet Union. The ANZUS pact provided the United States with access to ports and airfields in Australia and New Zealand that served as stepping stones to the American military presence in the Indian Ocean and Arab/Persian Gulf. Of its two regional allies, Australia was of far more strategic significance to the United States than New Zealand. The communications and intelligence-gathering facilities in Australia at Pine Gap, Nurrungar and the Northwest Cape were vital links in America's nuclear strategy. New Zealand's contribution, on the other hand, was more psychological than strategic. New Zealand's remote location made it arguably the least important of all of America's allies. Thus, Wellington's 1984 declaration that New Zealand would be a nuclear free zone had no really significant effect on the nuclear balance of power.

Despite almost 40 years of benign neglect, capped with depredations by its tuna fleet in the 1980s, the United States remained relatively popular throughout the Pacific islands. Memories of America's wartime role might be fading, but the newer generation, though more critical than older islanders of Washington's policies, was captivated by America's material affluence and mass culture, as were many young people elsewhere. The 1986 Fisheries Treaty alleviated many of the hard feelings previously caused by rapacious American tunaboats; the $60 million worth of aid and fishing fees spread out over five years would be a significant and much-needed

1167

economic boost for the region. From the beginning of its program of economic assistance to the Pacific island nations in 1978 through the Fisheries Treaty, Washington contributed $65 million.

U.S. popularity was also strengthened in 1986 when Washington decided to end the trusteeship it had held over Micronesia since 1945, and to implement the Compact of Free Association with the Marshall Islands, the Federated States of Micronesia and Palau. Under the compact, the United States controlled defense and had a veto power in foreign affairs in case of conflict. In August 1987 Palau voted to suspend its constitutional nuclear ban that had prevented the Compact of Free Association from passing.

France

Pacific enthusiasm over the fishery and compact agreements was only temporarily overshadowed by Washington's refusal to sign SPNFZ, and its hard line against Wellington's antinuclear policy. The labor governments of Australia and New Zealand were much more disappointed than the generally conservative Pacific islanders. For its continued nuclear testing program at Mururoa and colonial hold over New Caledonia and Polynesia, France, not the United States, remained the real villain of the South Pacific.[34]

France's regional military was relatively small: It was composed of a naval force of three frigates, three minor surface combatants, some amphibious support ships and five reconnaissance aircraft. About 4,000 navy personnel were supported by about 8,000 troops in New Caledonia, and 5,400 in French Polynesia. It was the more than 60 nuclear tests conducted at Mururoa and two at Fangataufa since 1975, rather than France's small conventional military presence, that continually stoked Pacific antinuclear and anti-French sentiments. Australia initiated SPNFZ largely because of the Labor government's opposition to French testing. The *Rainbow Warrior* incident of 1985, in which France blew up a Greenpeace ship that was going to monitor French nuclear testing, further inflamed anti-French sentiment in the region. In response, Paris repeatedly stated that its nuclear tests were conducted on French territory, posed no threat to nearby countries and would continue indefinitely.

In 1986, the same year SPNFZ was signed, the South Pacific Forum unanimously called for independence for New Caledonia. The forum agreed to ask the United Nations to add New Caledonia to the list of territories that were not yet self-governing. The forum sponsored a General Assembly resolution reinstating New Caledonia on the decolonization committee and affirming the territory's right to self-determination and independence. The French played tough in trying to gain support against the resolution, including threatening Antigua with deferral of a French loan, telling Zimbabwe that a Peugeot plant was at risk, and informing Nigeria that Paris would not cooperate with debt rescheduling.[35] The French went on to crit-

---

[34] *Pacific Islands Monthly* (January 1988): 38–40.
[35] Ibid., February 1987, p. 13.

icize Australia and New Zealand for their policies against aborigines and Maori. The General Assembly resolution passed by an 89 to 24 vote.

Paris considered New Caledonia to be an integral part of France. It argued that although officially Melanesians represented 43 percent of the population, Europeans 38 percent and Polynesians 12 percent, in reality a century of intermarriage had resulted in a multiracial society. Thus, according to Paris, to reduce the political situation to Kanak versus non-Kanak was absurd. New Caledonia was democratically run, divided into four administrative regions—north, central, south and the Loyalty Islands—which governed themselves through regional councils elected by direct universal suffrage with proportional representation. The Assemblée Territoriale consisted of the regional representatives and was responsible for the administration of socioeconomic policies. The French language was considered essential to unite a territory with 28 Melanesian dialects. The governor, appointed by France, actually ruled New Caledonia.[36]

Throughout the 1980s the Kanak Socialist National Liberation Front (FLNKS) incessantly campaigned for New Caledonian independence. In the March 1983 elections FLNKS-supported candidates won 18 of the 32 communes outside of Nouméa, while the pro-French party took all 45 seats in Nouméa. In the September 1985 election FLNKS candidates won three of four regions; only the Nouméa region was controlled by the pro-French party. But FLNKS support peaked in the mid-1980s.

FLNKS repeatedly called for a referendum on independence by indigenous Kanaks and those with one Kanak parent. In the spring of 1987 the government of Jacques Chirac took up the FLNKS challenge and decided to allow a referendum in which all French citizens with over three years of residence in New Caledonia would be allowed to vote. With the political deck obviously stacked against it, FLNKS responded by demanding a boycott of the referendum. It thus became an important test of actual FLNKS support: If more than 50 percent boycotted the referendum it would be seen as a victory for FLNKS, less than 50 percent a victory for Paris.

Chirac's government did all that it could to ensure a pro-French victory. In August 1987, six weeks before the September 13 referendum, Overseas Territories Minister Bernard Pons announced in Nouméa that Paris would supplement its 1988 aid package of $A70.3 million with an additional $A32 million. Meanwhile, New Caledonia was treated to a massive construction and beautification campaign. The government position was constantly promoted in the controlled or influenced mass media. Only the FLNKS-run Radio Djiido and underground newspapers presented the pro-independence viewpoint. A planned FLNKS-led march was banned. Pons backed these efforts by dispatching an additional 1,300 troops to New Caledonia, bringing the total to well over 8,000—to control a population of only 145,000 people. In September FLNKS led several demonstrations, in defiance of a ban on public political rallies, but only attracted a few hundred participants.[37]

[36] Ibid., September 1987, p. 21.
[37] Ibid.

Although there was no doubt that the referendum would reaffirm New Caledonia's ties with France, few expected how large the pro-French vote would be: 98.3 percent of the 59.1 percent of the total enrolled electorate who voted. Only one-quarter of the Kanak population seemed not to have voted. Thus, it was clear that FLNKS support had waned considerably since 1984 and 1985, when a series of violent mass proindependence demonstrations shook New Caledonia. The majority vote for continued ties with France was a severe blow to FLNKS and its international supporters in the forum and United Nations. If, for example, the forum continued its unanimous call for New Caledonian independence, it faced the dilemma of being accused of disregarding the majority's will. The vote reinforced Paris' political desire to stay in the South Pacific.

FLNKS remained torn by political, religious, ethnic and ideological factions, and appeared unable to present any constructive programs that had popular appeal. The more moderate proindependence Kanak Socialist Liberation party attracted followers from FLNKS' ranks, while FLNKS itself was polarized by moderate and hard-line factions. In late April 1988 a radical FLNKS faction took 23 hostages and demanded independence for New Caledonia. On May 5 a French rescue team succeeded in freeing the hostages, at the cost of 17 lives, all but two of them Kanaks. It seemed clear that Paris was prepared to do anything to co-opt Kanak moderates while acting tough against FLNKS terrorism. New Caledonia would undoubtedly remain French for a long time.

French Polynesia's independence movement attracted only about 15 percent of the population, but in the long term proved more successful than that of New Caledonia. The 185,000 Polynesians made up 68.5 percent of the population, compared to 14.4 percent mixed race and 11.6 percent European. A political generation gap emerged between the conservative older population that generally accepted French rule and policies and an increasingly radical younger group restless for economic benefits and political change. Whereas previously the word was taboo, independence was now regarded as the panacea for Tahiti's problems. The Polynesian Liberation Front, which wanted both independence and an end to nuclear testing, now had the support of at least 15 percent of the population.[38]

Tahiti had the same socioeconomic problems faced by most other Pacific island countries: rising unemployment with a rapidly growing population; spiraling economic and political expectations that the government was increasingly unable to fulfill; and continued dependence on France for capital and aid. Tahiti's economy rested on both tourism and nuclear testing, hardly the basis for stability and prosperity. Over one-third of the population depended either directly or indirectly on the French military presence for a livelihood. About 150,000 tourists spent over $A240 million in French Polynesia each year. Little of the money from the enclave industries of defense and tourism trickled down to the people. Paris pumped in $A1.2 billion a year to prop up the economy. The bankruptcy rate continued to

[38] Ibid, December 1987, p. 11.

climb: It averaged 30 a month in 1987 compared to only 30 or 40 a year before 1984.[39]

Rioting by unemployed workers and malcontents in October 1987 caused an estimated $A70 million in damage and destroyed a number of businesses in Papeete. Continued economic problems and the October rioting led progressive Alexandre Leontieff to replace the conservative Gaston Flosse as president of the Territorial Assembly in December 1987. Leontieff favored a development strategy that lessened Tahiti's economic and political dependence on Paris. His patchwork party coalition, however, included the Ia Mana party led by Jacqui Drollet, which advocated eventual independence for Tahiti and removal of the French nuclear test center. The victory of François Mitterrand and the Socialist party in the May and June 1988 elections resulted in policies and appointments that reflected the progressive views of the Leontieff government. Radical leaders in the government, such as Jean Juventin, the speaker of the Assembly, and Emile Vernaudon, another prominent assemblyman, began to tilt Tahiti's politics to the left. The success of Leontieff's policies succeeded in transforming Polynesia from economic dependency to self-sufficiency; the independence movement was diluted. His failure would have meant that Polynesia became polarized between pro- and antiindependence forces. Although demographics and continued economic stagnation fueled the independence movement, France would not give up Polynesia without a real struggle.

Australia

Australia and New Zealand continued their role as the region's most important political supporters, economic partners and aid donors. With over 70,000 ground troops and 15,000 naval forces deployed almost evenly between the Pacific and Indian Oceans, Australia was the region's largest power. The fleet included six submarines, three destroyers and nine frigates; the air force had 22,000 service people and 225 combat aircraft. Australia had been the economic superpower of the South Pacific as well. In 1985–86 Australia's exports to South Pacific Forum members, including New Zealand and Papua New Guinea, amounted to $A321 million, while imports were only $A127 million. In 1985 both Australia and New Zealand responded to continuing Pacific island complaints about Australia's trade deficits by liberalizing import regulations to accord duty-free and unrestricted access to almost all island exports. The decision revitalized the existing South Pacific Regional Trade and Economic Cooperation Agreement (SPARTECA), in effect since 1981. The agreement was a preferential nonreciprocal arrangement among Australia, New Zealand, and the other forum countries to achieve duty-free and unrestricted access to the markets of Australia and New Zealand. SPARTECA provided island exporters with help to promote trade and cooperation in projects. In 1982, 97 percent of the goods exported by Pacific island countries was handled under the agreement.[40]

[39] Ibid.
[40] Ibid., July 1987, p. 34.

Canberra was also the Pacific's largest aid donor. Australian aid to the Pacific islands increased from $13 million in 1977 to $86 million in 1986–87. But this aid was severely cut back to $A50 million for the following fiscal year. Australia provided separate assistance to Papua New Guinea, totaling $A300 million.[41] Australia's reduction of aid to needy countries—most obviously Papua New Guinea and Fiji—cost Canberra prestige and economic opportunities, and opened the way for other countries, particularly France and Japan.

Australia generally supported forum views on political issues. Canberra initiated SPNFZ, supported the Fisheries Treaty with Washington, came out strongly against the Fiji coup, favored independence for New Caledonia and opposed any Libyan presence in the Pacific. At the same time it remained firmly committed to the ANZUS pact. A 1987 white paper on defense identified the South Pacific and Southeast Asia as strategically equal in importance to Australia, and declared that Canberra would actively continue to promote and defend its interests in those regions. The report was followed by a July 1987 visit of Defense Minister Kim Beazley to Papua New Guinea, the Solomon Islands, Vanuatu, Tuvalu and Kiribati. Beazley reiterated Australia's commitments to the region. Defense cooperation topics included Australia's contribution of patrol boats, engineering projects and communications assistance.

Because of its size, resources, strategic position and historic relationship, Papua New Guinea continued to receive the lion's share of new Australian agreements. Australia beefed up Papua New Guinea's navy with four new patrol boats in October 1987, and changed its military mission in Papua New Guinea from that of adviser to an exchange relationship similar to that with its industrial allies. An Australia-Papua New Guinea defense pact was signed in late 1987 formalizing the new equitable relationship.

New Zealand

New Zealand remained Australia's junior partner in supporting the Pacific island countries, while taking an independent line when its own interests were directly affected. Geographically and culturally New Zealand is much closer than Australia to the South Pacific. New Zealand is home to the largest concentration of Polynesians; over 12 percent of the population is Maori. After Australia, New Zealand has been the largest market for Pacific products; 81 percent of Wellington's financial aid went to the region. New Zealand had total armed forces of 12,600 regulars and 9,000 reservists. There was an army of 5,800 troops; a navy of 2,600 personnel, with four frigates and four large patrol boats; and an air force with 4,200 servicepeople and 43 combat aircraft. Wellington employed its fleet to aid several of the island countries in patroling their EEZs.

In July 1984 David Lange's Labour party came to power and immediately fulfilled its campaign pledge to prohibit any nuclear-armed or nuclear-powered ships from visiting New Zealand. Executive policy became law in June 1987 when parliament passed legislation declaring all of New

[41] Ibid., June 1987, p. 33.

Zealand a nuclear free zone. The resolution was supported by over 70 percent of the population. Negotiations for some sort of compromise continued between the United States and New Zealand throughout the first half of 1986. The failure of both sides to resolve their differences at a June 1986 meeting between Lange and U.S. Secretary of State George Shultz led to the announcement that the United States would withdraw its security umbrella from New Zealand. "We part as friends," Shultz said, "but we part company so far as the alliance is concerned." This was followed by a formal announcement in August 1986 that the United States was suspending its defense commitment to New Zealand.[42] Parliament's passage of legislation making New Zealand a nuclear free zone occurred June 1987. In an October 1987 visit to Hawaii, Lange attempted to soften New Zealand's antinuclear stand when he said that under certain conditions U.S. ships would be permitted to enter New Zealand waters, since the antinuclear legislation gave the prime minister great latitude in determining whether or not a ship was carrying nuclear weapons.[43]

Japan

Japan was the new power in the Pacific that eventually proved to be the most dominant. Tokyo embarked on a trade, aid and diplomatic campaign in the region designed to take over economically while dispelling wartime memories of the Japanese occupation and atrocities. Just as it had in East Asia and elsewhere, Japan eventually overcame its economic rivals in the Pacific, while covering up regional resentments and mistrust of Japanese expressions of cultural superiority and economic exploitation.[44]

Japanese officials visiting the region kept up a constant refrain that Tokyo's interests were purely altruistic and designed to promote the prosperity of both Japan and the Pacific. In a January 1987 speech before the forum, Foreign Affairs Minister Tadashi Kuranari promised an aid package of $2 million for development projects, targeted particularly toward telecommunications and transportation, and $1 million for technology research and for visits by young Pacific islanders to Japan. This offer capped an aid program to the Pacific that increased over 10 times in five years, although it began with a very low base. Most of the aid was tied to the purchase of Japanese goods and services. In response to complaints by islanders about Japan's trade surplus and closed domestic markets, Kuranari said he hoped Pacific island businesses "would make every effort to sell goods to Japan, which the government in Tokyo was prepared to encourage."[45] Similar promises to other regions suffering persistent trade deficits with Japan, however, failed to be honored; the Pacific's trade deficit with Japan was likely to be huge and permanent.

Most Pacific islanders saw Japanese aid and trade as a Trojan horse de-

---

[42] Richard Fisher, "Responding to New Zealand's Challenge to Western Security in the South Pacific," *Asian Studies Center Backgrounder* (Summer 1987): 3.

[43] *Pacific Islands Monthly* (November 1987): 17.

[44] Ibid., February 1988, p. 32.

[45] Ibid., p. 26.

signed to put the region into Tokyo's commercial empire. Tony Siaguru, the leader of Papua New Guinea's League for National Advancement, described the altruistic tone of Japanese officials as an attempt to deflect attention from the "aggressively self-seeking approach of Japanese industrial and commercial interests." He recalled the attempts of a giant Japanese conglomerate to buy Papua New Guinea from Australia in the 1960s, while another Japanese group sought to lease it for 50 years in order to "develop" it.[46]

Tokyo proved to be even more intransigent on the fisheries issue than Washington; it threatened the forum with aid and trade sanctions if it insisted on raising the license fees to a commercially viable level. The Japanese Fishing Association rejected all suggestions of compromise; meanwhile, it took $50 million worth of tuna annually from Papua New Guinea alone. The Japanese stand on fishing rights compared unfavorably with that of the United States, which resolved its long-standing tuna issue by promising to supplement commercial fees with an official aid component. Japan refused, insisting on keeping the two separate.[47]

Siaguru also complained bitterly of the "outrages committed by Japanese timber firms: of areas logged, then abruptly left without the furniture factories, wharves, mills and the reafforestation that had been an integral part of the agreement. . . . Instead of the development they had been promised they have been left with denuded lands, eroded soils and ruined reefs." As a result, Pacific islanders viewed the Japanese with a mixture of cynicism and fear. Siaguru went on to say that Japanese officials claimed to have no control over commercial interests, but he countered this by noting that if that was really true then they should "recognize the insincerity of the altruism they preach. . . . Surely the logic cannot be that there are two types of Japanese—the good guys who pat island nations on the head and the bad guys who stab them in the back."[48]

Part of Tokyo's strategy was to use Australian expertise for its own penetration of the region. Kuranari led a delegation to Canberra in January 1987, ostensibly with the objective of coordinating the two countries' efforts to offset increased Soviet presence in the Pacific, but in reality to gain Australian assistance in administering aid projects in the region. Tokyo wanted the two countries to form "a North-South axis in the Asia-Pacific area based on shared values of democracy and free trade." The two-day conference in Canberra suffered a severe strain when Japan failed to live up to its declared commitment to free trade and to make the economic concessions that Australia had wanted. Australian leaders pointed out to Kuranari that unless Japan opened its markets to the free flow of Australian goods—particularly iron ore, coal and beef—Australia would not help Japan with its aid projects in the Pacific region.[49]

Despite Tokyo's heavy-handed approach it eventually succeeded in be-

[46] Ibid., p. 32.
[47] Ibid., May 1987, p. 16; Ibid., February 1988, p. 32.
[48] Ibid., p. 32.
[49] Ibid., p. 43.

coming the economic hegemon in the Pacific. Japan's government and its businesses long ago perfected a partnership that was designed to make other countries and regions dependent on Japanese trade, investments and aid. None of Japan's economic rivals was able to overcome Tokyo's long-term economic offensive.

Indonesia

Indonesia might not be able to compete with Japan's economic steamroller, but it attempted steadily to increase its political and military influence in the Pacific. Although most of its 280,000 troops were used for internal security, its army was over four times larger than that of Australia. About 20,000 troops were deployed in East Timor. The navy, with forces totaling 26,000, was organized into two fleets equipped with six guided missile frigates and six conventional frigates. The air force, with forces of 27,000, was equipped with 84 combat aircraft.[50]

Overtures by Indonesia to Fiji and Papua New Guinea were seen in Canberra as blatant attempts to gain influence in the region at Australia's expense. Indonesia moved swiftly to establish links with the new Fijian republic. A high-level trade mission flew to Suva after the second coup, offering incentives to increase trade and economic cooperation between the two countries, including a possible collaboration between Indonesia's Garuda Airlines and Fiji's Air Pacific. In addition, there was an offer of 25,000 tons of rice and special trade finances; most disturbing for Australia, there was a promise to supply the republic with an unspecified number of ships and planes.[51] A $200,000 "donation" by the Indonesian commander in chief to Ted Diro, Papua New Guinea's foreign minister, sparked a major scandal and fueled fears in Canberra and elsewhere that Indonesia was attempting to buy or muscle its way into the Pacific region.

With its population of one hundred fifty million, vast resources of energy and raw material, and a growing industrial base, Indonesia saw itself as a global giant in the 21st century. It hoped to become the center of a single Indian Ocean-Pacific Ocean "hemisphere" stretching from Madagascar to Easter Island—the geographical limits that Malayo-Polynesian peoples reached in their ancient oceanic wanderings. Jakarta's military-sponsored Center for Strategic and International Studies targeted the South Pacific as the primary short-term goal for Indonesian economic and political expansion, hoping to assume the leadership position in the Pacific that it had in Southeast Asia. Although Indonesia's economic presence slowly broadened, Jakarta was unable to realize its ambitions for political and military hegemony in the Pacific. The forum countries were as wary of Indonesia's strategic ambitions as they were of Japan's economic ambitions. With its economic dependence on other nations, Indonesia could never have afforded an outright annexation of Papua New Guinea, nor would forum nations have stood for any Indonesian political power plays.[52]

[50] Ibid., January 1988, p. 41.
[51] Ibid., December 1987, p. 5.
[52] Ibid., March 1988, pp. 26–28.

CONCLUSION

The Pacific region clearly faced a number of internal and external political and economic challenges. The South Pacific Forum had been quite successful in overcoming a number of obstacles to negotiate SPNFZ and the Fisheries Treaty with the United States, as well as a host of regional economic and social programs. In the short term it seemed probable that the forum would negotiate a fishing treaty with Japan similar to that with the United States. Despite the tough, seemingly intransigent position Tokyo had taken, Japan was too concerned with its international image and stake in the region to jeopardize these over a few treaty concessions. The forum countries also forged close economic and political ties in subregional units such as the Melanesian Spearhead Group.

Unfortunately, the Fiji coup established a precedent for the military in other Pacific island countries restless as a result of political corruption or economic stagnation. Papua New Guinea and Vanuatu experienced increased political instability and violence, and were prime candidates for possible coups. Paris seemed temporarily to have contained self-determination pressures in New Caledonia, but French Polynesia's independence movement continued to grow. Economic expansion and a more equitable distribution of income, however, kept both territories firmly tied to France.

Most Pacific island countries, however, remained politically stable even though all experienced severe economic development problems. Migration continued to act as a safety valve, but it was usually the best and brightest who left their native islands. Because of their small land areas, populations and resource bases, most Pacific island countries remain aid recipients. Only Papua New Guinea and Fiji had enough human and natural resources to stand on their own economic feet; continued political instability in both countries, however, undermined development.

Such development problems made the region dependent on—rather than interdependent with—the outside world. The increased competition among outside powers enabled the Pacific island countries to play one against the other. The Soviets continued to fish, but neither Moscow nor Tripoli gained any significant political, economic or strategic assets in the Pacific. The forum countries, including Vanuatu (despite its rhetoric), were basically conservative and anticommunist. They had the potential to gain from new regional powers such as Japan and Indonesia who competed with old-timers such as the United States, Australia, New Zealand and France. Japan displaced Australia as the region's economic hegemon. Whether this was to the Pacific's long-term advantage or not, familiar complaints of insensitivity, unfairness and exploitation were expected to haunt the Japanese. Overall, though, the Pacific island countries have generally met successfully most of the challenges that faced them.

FURTHER READING

Ally, Roderic. "A Nuclear Free Pacific." In Hearn, T. Y., ed. *Arms and Disarmament in New Zealand*. Dunedin, New Zealand: University of Otago Press, 1983.

Benjamin, Roger, and Kudrele, Robert T., eds. *The Industrial Future of the Pacific Basin.* Boulder, Colorado: Westview Press, 1984.

Bergin, Anthony. "Fisheries of the South Pacific." *Asia Pacific Community* 22 (Fall 1983): 20–32.

Chesneaux, Jean. "France in the Pacific: Global Approach or Respect for Regional Agendas." *Bulletin of Concerned Asian Scholars,* special issue, 1987.

Doulman, David J. *Fishing for Tuna: The Operation of Distant Water Fleets in the Pacific Islands Region.* Honolulu, Hawaii: East-West Center, 1986.

Fry, Greg. "The Pacific Challenge: A Transnational Future." *Asia Pacific Community* 21 (Summer 1983): 36–44.

———. "Toward a South Pacific Nuclear-Free-Zone." *Bulletin of the Atomic Scientists* 41, no. 6 (June/July 1985): 16–20.

Gopalkrishnan, Chennet, ed. *The Emerging Marine Economy of the South Pacific.* Ann Arbor: Michigan Science Books, 1984.

Kiste, Robert C. and Herr, R. A. "The Potential for Soviet Penetration of the South Pacific Islands: An Assessment." *Bulletin of Concerned Asian Scholars,* special issue, 1987.

Thakur, Ramesh. "A Nuclear-Weapon-Free South Pacific: A New Zealand Perspective." *Pacific Affairs* 58 (Summer 1985): 216–38.

Woodard, Garry. "The Pacific Community: Start, Stop, Start?" *Asian Pacific Community* 25 (Summer 1984): 116–24.

THE SOVIET UNION
AND ASIA

GERALD SEGAL

IT is not surprising that Soviet policy in Asia since 1945 has been deeply confused. The reasons for this lie in the nature of the Soviet Union and the region. When regarding the vast stretch from Afghanistan to Japan, the Soviet Union perceives the huge variations in types of states and cultures. It would be unfair to expect a coherent foreign policy toward such diverse states, and the Soviet Union has at least had the courage to admit as much.

The confusion in Soviet policy is also the result of the peculiarities of Russian history and the changing, modern Soviet Union. Looming over both Europe and Asia, the Soviet Union is the only Eurasian power. Although it is by far the largest Asian state in geographic terms (one-third of Asia is Soviet territory), the majority of its people are not Asian (about 10 percent are of Asian nationality); and an even larger portion of Soviet GDP is generated in its European regions. Thus, the Soviet Union has consistently remained far more interested in European and superpower politics than in the complex events in Asia.

While the Soviet population in Asia is enough to make it among the largest Asian states, Soviet Asians have been largely cut off from fellow Asians by virtue of Soviet policy. While almost all previous European colonialism in Asia has been reversed, with the granting of independence to Asian states, the USSR has retained its gains and incorporated them into the Soviet Union. Such a historical tradition has always given Soviet appeals for decolonization elsewhere in Asia a discordant sound.

Asia has also given the Soviet Union some of its most significant "gains" in the postwar strategic balance, as well as its major losses. The presence of seven other Marxist-ruled regimes (as many as in Eastern Europe) is accentuated by the fact that these states combined cover far more territory and contain a far larger population than do Soviet allies in Europe. Yet the largest of these states, China, has behaved erratically, and the Sino-Soviet division was the single greatest strategic setback to postwar Soviet foreign policy.

Yet with all this confusion in Soviet foreign policy in the region, there have been some more relatively stable patterns. Most important, the hier-

1178

archy of national interests in Asia has remained remarkably unchanged for more than 40 years. In the first tier are the three great powers with a major role in Asia, the Soviet Union, China and the United States. In the second tier are the very different potential powers of Japan and India. In the third tier are a number of developing states—such as Indochina, Korea, Pakistan or Afghanistan—whose political unrest has forced them to be of more immediate concern to Moscow. Finally, there is everything else, including the Association of Southeast Asian Nations (ASEAN) and the states of the South Pacific.

Another complicating factor for Soviet foreign policy in Asia has been its own changing leadership and domestic priorities. While few fundamental changes took place in the transitions from Stalin to Khrushchev to Brezhnev to Andropov/Chernenko, there may now be signs that Mikhail Gorbachev is more serious about modernizing Soviet policy. The extent of Gorbachev's task, and the options available, are best understood by an assessment of the legacy of his predecessors' attempts to confront the predicaments of Soviet power.

THE IMPORTANCE OF SOVIET ASIA

The size and strategic location of Soviet Asia is an important basis for Moscow's claim to be a genuine superpower and to take an active part in Asian politics. Unlike the United States, the Soviet Union is a power in Asia and the Pacific as well as Europe by right of geography and not by invitation of allies.

The Asian Soviet Union is also a vast storehouse of minerals and thus holds the basis of Soviet economic independence, as well as the promise of future development. The exploitation of these resources and the ability to develop a successful economy in Asia also becomes a vital test of the Soviet system and the appeal of its ideology.

It has been a cause of major concern, therefore, to the Gorbachev administration that the Soviet Union has been unable to meet the test. In his July 1986 speech at Vladivostok, Gorbachev made it clear that the Soviet Union had failed to develop its Asian territories and new strategies were now required. The U.S. $359 billion project announced in 1987 was the most recent and most ambitious in a long line of such plans to make the area more self-sufficient and productive. It called for greater investment in regional infrastructure and cooperation with foreign neighbors in joint ventures and far-reaching investments.

Like the rest of the country, Soviet Asia is involved in the new reform programs proposed by Gorbachev. The success of the reforms will be no less vital to Soviet Asia than to the country as a whole. To a large extent, the importance of such political and economic questions will determine the fate of all the major foreign dimensions to Soviet policy. But it is also clear that reforms in foreign policy can help create an environment more conducive to domestic reform. Soviet policy in Asia is a complex mix of domestic and foreign factors.

THE IMPORTANCE OF SINO-SOVIET RELATIONS

When Soviet leaders think of neighbors in Asia, they think first of China—the only other serious rival on the continent. The importance of China has deep historical roots, for Russia reached the Pacific across the north of China before it penetrated into the old central Asian khanates. The Chinese Empire, even more than the British, was the main rival to Russian power until the collapse of the Qing dynasty in the early 20th century.

Although the Soviet Union was unable to hold onto all of the territory it had grabbed from China before 1945, the Russian Empire had made important gains when the age of colonialism was ended. Yet all the territory that the Soviet Union retained was populated by ethnic minorities rather than Han Chinese and so did not touch "core" China. Of course, the loss of land still rankled with China, but it was not a primary issue in Sino-Soviet relationships at the end of World War II.

China was then absorbed in its civil war, and the Soviet Union took the opportunity to grab Manchuria from an all-but-collapsed Japanese Empire and relocate the industrial plant in the region for the regeneration of the European Soviet Union. With the triumph of communism in China, the Soviet Union was eventually to return all the territory and extraterritorial rights it had taken in Manchuria, but the Soviet presence as a major military power in the northern Pacific and in northeast Asia was established. Manchuria, that old cockpit of Asia, also became the focus of Soviet cooperation with the new comrades in China.

Mao Zedong's Communists came to power under their own steam, but their route maps owed a great deal to Soviet ideological leadership. Stalin was the undisputed leader of international communism at the time, and China was prepared to play younger brother to the more experienced revolutionary sibling in Moscow. A friendship pact in 1950 did not give China everything it wanted, but for a Soviet economy staggering after the war, the aid was generous. By and large, the Soviet Union was satisfied that China was not an unreasonable ally, and certainly its friendship was the most important gain for postwar Soviet foreign policy.

The Korean War (1950–53) was the first foreign-policy test for the alliance, and the Soviet Union could be pleased that the direct involvement of Chinese troops meant that the Soviet Union itself did not have to get dragged in. Of course, the Soviet Union provided massive military aid to its allies, including advisers and air cover for China, but Moscow could concentrate on the European cold war and the building of alliances in Eastern Europe.

The death of Stalin in 1953 helped bring an end to the Korean War, but it also destabilized the Sino-Soviet relationship. China was less willing to acknowledge the leadership of Khrushchev, as Mao was now seen as the most important Communist leader. But at least until the late 1950s the Soviet Union went out of its way to accept that China was more important than the East Europeans and had to be accorded more exalted status as number-one ally.

Relations went from strength to strength in the mid-1950s, as the Soviet

Union provided increased military aid and a model for development that reached every level of Chinese society, from education and the arts to the armed forces. This honeymoon can be seen to have ended in 1956 with Khrushchev's de-Stalinization, a major change in ideology undertaken without consultation with China. In the ensuing instability in the Communist world, China too reassessed its adherence to a Soviet model and began experimenting with a Sinicized Marxism.

Thus, the key challenge to Soviet power in East Asia came from changes in ideology and the new experiments in domestic Chinese policies. The 1958 Great Leap Forward was undertaken in the teeth of Soviet opposition, but Soviet aid continued and the two Communist giants still coordinated foreign policy on most international issues. Chinese attempts to regain off-shore islands from U.S.-supported Taiwan drew Soviet backing but also Soviet displeasure at the unnecessary aggravation of international tension: For a Soviet Union preoccupied with events in Europe, distractions in the Pacific were not appreciated.

It was Khrushchev's exploration of détente with the United States and the playing down of revolutionary struggle that first made the Sino-Soviet split apparent. By 1960 it was also clear that the Chinese domestic scene had abandoned Soviet models, even though its own revolutionary model had ended in the disaster of 20 million to 30 million deaths due to famine. As China drifted to radical solutions, the Soviet Union was guided to more realistic accommodation with the capitalist world.

One of the earliest and most revealing manifestations of these divergences in ideology and practice was the Sino-Indian war of 1962. The punishment of India for border encroachments was a sign of increased Chinese dominance in Asia and the world of developing states, but it put the Soviet Union into a bind. The war took place just as the Soviet Union needed full support from its allies in the Cuban Missile Crisis. Moscow verbally supported China in the border war, but when the Cuban crisis had been defused the Soviet Union adopted a more even-handed position on the Himalayan war, which was interpreted as support of India. The strategy was to entice India into closer relations with the Communist world and away from its roots in the Western and British-oriented world.

The 1962 war and the open Sino-Soviet split in 1963, therefore, were salient points along the turning circle of Soviet policy in Asia. The move toward moderation meant the loss of China, though it was made in the hope of finding new friends in the nonaligned world and obtaining benefits from less tension with the capitalist world. It was a choice that Moscow would rather not have made, but the radicalization of Chinese politics made the hard choice inevitable.

The loss of China as an ally was devastating to Soviet foreign policy. Communist parties around the world were ripped apart, and although the Soviet Union invariably picked up the largest pieces, it also never recovered from the blow struck against the ideological claims for the inevitable forward march of world revolution. What is more, China as an adversary began to remember old territorial disputes and raised the specter of border conflict.

From the Soviet defense planners' point of view, with a relatively stabilized European balance, nothing could be more worrying than a hostile China with close to a billion people threatening to flood the vast open spaces of the vulnerable Soviet Far East. Thus, in the mid-1960s the Soviet Union began deploying more troops along the Sino-Soviet frontier and Mongolia. China responded with its own far larger deployment. Military matters were brought to the fore with the escalating war in Vietnam, where, although both Communist powers denied it, they competed with each other in aiding the Communist North Vietnamese. It was, in fact, the Vietnam conflict that finally brought the break in Sino-Soviet party-to-party relations in March 1966—that ultimate sign of a serious split in inter-Communist relations.

The clearly vulnerable Soviet position in East Asia was most apparent when China inflicted a minor but very visible defeat on Soviet border troops along a disputed portion of the Ussuri River in March 1969. The Soviet Union responded with a massive counterstrike and in the ensuing months tried to scare the Chinese into sitting down to negotiate a more stable arrangement along the frontier. Although at first the Chinese refused to be pushed around, by August the Soviet Union let it be known it was considering a surgical strike against China's nascent nuclear weapons program. China soon capitulated and agreed to talks.

This Asian version of the Cuban Missile Crisis was won by the Soviet Union, but only at the cost of increased military expenditure. Some 80 percent of the growth in Soviet defense spending in the decade from 1969 was for the anti-China theater. By 1979 roughly one-third of all Soviet military forces could be said to have an anti-China task. The damage to Soviet foreign policy wrought by the 1963 split was fully visible on the battleground. The risks of a two-front war, which Stalin had struggled so hard to avoid in World War II, now loomed over Brezhnev and his Kremlin colleagues.

After Mao's death in 1976, China began to abandon its radical domestic politics, but its foreign policy swerved further into yet another type of extremism. Relations with the capitalist world were improved to an extent never contemplated by the Soviet Union: Western arms sales to China, strategic cooperation and China as NATO's 16th member all seemed possible. The coalition of Japan, the United States and China that seemed to form by 1979 marked the low point for Soviet policy in Asia.

The recovery from these depths was only partially an achievement of Soviet policy, and mostly the result of changes in Chinese domestic and foreign policies. China announced officially in 1982 that it had decided to reassess its international position in order to create the best environment for the pursuit of its four modernization programs. The key link in the new strategy was the view that the Soviet Union, bogged down as it was in Afghanistan, with aging leaders and a declining economy, was less threatening than first thought.

This reassessment allowed China to pick up the overtures made by the dying Brezhnev in 1982. The Soviet leadership was impressed with the return to sensible domestic socialism in China and was prepared to recognize China once again as a socialist state. From 1982 on Sino-Soviet détente has been healing every part of the original split.

This transformation of the Soviet position in Asia was nearly as striking as the split in 1963. By 1986 China had once again become the Soviet Union's main trading partner in East Asia. Soviet advisers were returning to China, and aging plants were being refurbished with Soviet assistance. Soviet and Chinese experts began close examination of each other's reforms, and diplomatic discussions were regularly undertaken at increasingly higher levels, culminating in May 1989 with President Gorbachev's visit to China.

Even in military terms, the border became quiet and both sides began withdrawing considerable numbers of troops. China's reduction of its armed forces by one million was matched by the thinning out of Soviet divisions and some withdrawals from Mongolia. When border incidents did threaten to flare up, both sides met at a local level to keep the peace. In more general foreign-policy matters—for example, in much of the developing world or on some arms-control issues—China increasingly took an independent position, which meant sharper differences of opinion with the United States and greater tacit cooperation with the Soviet Union.

To be sure, acute disputes remained, and China continued to claim there were three obstacles to the normalization of relations. The first two, the Soviet invasion of Afghanistan and the presence of Soviet troops along the Sino-Soviet frontier, were by 1987 consigned to the margins of the dispute. The main obstacle remained Soviet support for the Vietnamese occupation of Cambodia, but even here there was considerable progress.

As the Soviet Union approached the 40th anniversary of relations with Communist China, it seemed that the "midlife crisis" had been overcome, even though it happened at an unnaturally early age. The Gorbachev leadership undertook repeated initiatives to improve relations with China, and the success of the venture was apparent. The Soviet position in East Asia was stronger than at any time since 1963, because it felt less threatened by a two-front war. China had become an important trading partner and possibly even a friend in beating back American and Japanese dominance of the Pacific.

Of course, just as the Sino-Soviet split led to gains for the Soviet Union elsewhere in Asia (in India, for example, and Vietnam), the Sino-Soviet détente also caused problems for the Soviet Union in the region. But the balance sheet must be seen as overwhelmingly positive, and quite the best thing to have happened to the Soviet position in the world in general and Asia in particular since the original triumph of communism in China in 1949.

THE IMPORTANCE OF SOVIET-AMERICAN RELATIONS

The Asian Soviet Union stretches across to the continent's easternmost tip, nearly touching the United States across the International Date Line. But the meeting of the two giants of the northern Pacific is incidental, as their real relationship has focused on conflicts in Europe and global superpower rivalry. Their confrontation in Asia has always been indirect, subordinate to more important dimensions in Europe and on the global level.

Yet events in Asia have had an important impact on superpower relations, even if both superpowers often felt it was a distracting sideshow. In the arcane game of superpower gains and losses, it seems that the two superpowers have come out about even. But more important, both have learned a number of vital lessons.

The first and most painful lesson for the Soviet Union came in 1950 with the outbreak of the Korean War. The use of force by a Communist state to change the postwar boundaries shocked many Western Europeans into meeting American demands for greater defense spending. The war galvanized the European alliance at an time when some had begun to feel that the Soviet Union and communism might not be a serious threat. Of course, the war also helped build alliances in the Communist world, but by and large the Soviet Union saw conflict in Asia as a distraction for itself and its friends from the more important battle in Europe.

A second lesson, also derived from sporadic crises in Korea after 1953, was that the superpowers had to get a grip on their allies or risk further tension. North Korea was particularly adept at tweaking America's nose, then sitting back and waiting for an American reaction, and drawing Soviet and Chinese support. Moscow soon found that, especially in an era of détente with the United States, such antics were not in the best Soviet interest.

The resulting belief in the efficacy of superpower crisis management was more strongly held in the United States than in the Soviet Union. But both superpowers appreciated the need to control conflict, especially of a nuclear kind, when the issue arose during Sino-American crises in the Taiwan straits. The Soviet Union raised its nuclear umbrella over its allies as promised but with increasing reluctance, as Sino-Soviet relations deteriorated.

A third lesson for the Soviet Union was the importance of backing the winning party in a local conflict. In the initial Indo-Pakistan wars, the Soviet Union was certainly not supportive of Pakistan, an American ally, but it only gradually became a supporter of India as Sino-Soviet relations deteriorated and the ban on closer relations with Delhi was lifted. By the time of the 1971 war in Bangladesh, the Soviet Union had signed a friendship treaty with India and was able to deter United States intervention in support of failing Pakistan. The Soviet Union found, as had the United States in the Arab-Israeli wars, that it was far easier to deter an opposing superpower than to try to coerce it to undo an unwanted act.

To some extent, the Soviet Union played the same game in the Vietnam wars. As the United States found it could not win the limited war in the 1960s, it tried escalating the conflict by bombing more important targets in North Vietnam. The Americans took the risks while the Soviet Union merely had to deter anything that threatened to destabilize the Communist regime.

When the United States wanted the Soviet Union to force North Vietnam to moderate its negotiating demands in the early 1970s, the Soviet

Union refused to be taken in. Although the Americans made a great deal of the supposed Soviet cooperation in pressing Hanoi to negotiate in exchange for a superpower arms-control deal in 1972, the Soviet Union had merely considered the superpower deal on its merits and let Vietnam get on with its war. The eventual defeat of the U.S.-supported regime in South Vietnam in 1975 only confirmed the Soviet belief that it is far easier to manage superpower relations in the developing world when you are backing the winning team.

Similarly, when the United States expressed its displeasure over the Vietnamese occupation of Cambodia in early 1979 and the Soviet invasion of Afghanistan, at the opposite end of Asia, in the last days of that year, the Soviet Union realized that there was little risk of the two conflicts getting out of control. Certainly in the case of Cambodia, the United States was unlikely to exert itself in behalf of the genocidal Pol Pot regime, which had in turn defeated the American ally Lon Nol in 1975.

The Afghan case was more complicated. To some extent, like the Korean War 30 years earlier, the Soviet action had unfortunate consequences in the more important European and superpower theaters. The death of the SALT II agreement was deplored by the Soviet Union when the invasion of Afghanistan raised the level of anti-Soviet propaganda in the United States. But a persuasive case can be made that superpower relations were already failing because of events in Africa and the growing Sino-American relationship. The death of superpower détente was only partly due to Soviet actions in Afghanistan and its support for Vietnam in Cambodia.

Since the low point in 1979, superpower relations stumbled through the Reagan presidency toward a late-blooming détente in the new era of Gorbachev's daily détente initiatives. Yet in Asia there has been a strange calm in superpower relations. The retreat of the United States from continental engagements has no doubt helped reduce tension; and the near absence of open warfare—except guerrilla wars in Afghanistan, Sri Lanka and Cambodia—has meant that the superpowers can more easily ignore their differences in Asia.

This maturation of the superpower relationship is in part due to the mutual learning of the lessons noted above. It is also due to the shift of the rivalry into the more theoretical games of naval peacetime balances in the Indian and Pacific oceans. Ever since the increase of Soviet military deployments in the Pacific to meet the perceived Chinese threat, there has been new concern in Japan and the United States that the Soviet Pacific fleet poses a major threat to the sealanes. Few analysts suggest that Western forces could not prevail in wartime against the Soviet fleet, but the arguments over the "threat" helped make possible a huge increase in the U.S. navy.

A similar story of exaggerated perceptions of threat and a basically stable superpower deterrence is also apparent in the Indian Ocean. Calls for the region to be declared a zone of peace have never gone beyond rhetoric, and in any case the new technologies of war have made deployment in the Indian Ocean less important than in the 1970s.

Perhaps a further sign of maturing superpower relations is the increasing discussion of arms control in Asia. For much of the 1960s and 1970s, there was sporadic musing about how nice it would be to control local wars and weapons and to extend the benefits of superpower detente and arms control to Asia. Such ethnocentric ideas were regularly rejected until the late 1980s, when the superpowers became more serious about their proposals.

The 1987 superpower deal on land-based intermediate-range weapons for the first time meant the elimination of at least a part of the superpowers' Asian arsenals. The benefits to Asians, and most especially the Japanese and Chinese, are immediately apparent. What is more, the Soviet Union under Gorbachev became more reasonable in the type of proposals for further confidence-building measures. His speech in Vladivistok in 1986, as well as further statements in 1987, suggested that the Soviet Union was willing to accept a Helsinki-like agreement on international security that included the United States. This was not likely to mean the elimination of many weapons, but it was symptomatic of the extent to which the superpowers had returned to the path of détente in Asia. Europe had long seen such a mix of competition and coexistence in superpower relations, but it was relatively rare in Asia to see quite as much cooperation and quite so little conflict.

THE IMPORTANCE OF JAPAN

Japan holds a special place in Soviet perspectives on Asia. Russia was the first non-Asian victim of Japanese imperialism in 1905 and a regular rival for the bones of the Chinese empire. Japan was the Soviet victim in 1945, allowing the Kremlin to claim the spoils of victory in the Pacific war. It therefore provided the excuse for the Soviet role in Korea and in the vital northeast Asian nexus. Japan was also the joint enemy of Communist Asia and was explicitly cited in the 1950 Sino-Soviet friendship treaty as the cutting edge of imperialism. As a close ally of the United States, Japan was also the focus of worries about revitalized militarism, and these were exacerbated by the American success in shutting out the Soviet Union from the postwar management of Japan (which had not happened in Germany).

It was not until the normalization of Soviet-Japanese relations in the mid-1950s that this negative image of Japan began to soften. The incentives for Moscow were both economic and political. Politically, the idea, as in Western Europe, was to see if there were any room in which to drive a wedge between the United States and its allies. In economic terms, Japan, like Western Europe, was a possible trading partner and eventually a provider of competing high technology.

The main Soviet problem with Japan has always been the lack of means to attract Japan out of its close alliance with the United States. Unlike a divided Germany, which the Soviet Union has held hostage against the good behavior of West Germany and its NATO allies, there was no similar card to play with Japan or any other American ally, for that matter.

Apart from a few northern islands, all the Soviet Union could offer was the prospect of a more independent foreign policy to those few Japanese who wanted to reduce the risks of nuclear devastation and to find a more independent international position. The Soviet Union could also offer itself as a market for Japanese goods; but given half a chance, the Japanese would overburden the Soviet economy, as they did to China in the early 1980s.

The only offer the Japanese eventually took up was the prospect of finding alternative sources of energy and minerals in the Soviet Far East at a time of rising oil prices and possible restrictions on strategic minerals. The boom in Soviet-Japanese relations was short lived, however, and the friendship stumbled into decline in the late 1970s, more for economic than for political reasons. The problem was the difficulty in extracting resources at competitive prices, and in an atmosphere of deteriorating East-West relations there was little incentive to swim against the tide of U.S. policy.

The most salient excuse offered for the new freeze in Soviet-Japanese relations was the northern territories issue: three islands and one group of tiny islands north of Hokkaido that the Soviet Union had obtained at the end of World War II. Although some compromise over the smaller Habomais and Shikotan islands was possible, the Soviet Union has steadfastly refused to place any concessions onto the bargaining table. Japanese skeptical of Soviet policy continue to stress the issue as the main block to Soviet-Japanese détente, although it was most useful as a means of raising Japanese consciousness about the otherwise minimized "Soviet threat."

The block began to show signs of shifting in the mid-1980s with the new Gorbachev initiatives in the Pacific. The concessions to China in 1986 over the definition of their river border was not matched by an offer to Japan on the islands, but it did suggest that cosmetic but well-packaged offers might get the Soviets off their Japanese hook. There was much evidence that even a minor territorial concession would split the Japanese northern territory lobby and help feed Japan's broader desire for a more independent foreign policy.

More intriguing still to the Japanese was Gorbachev's recognition that Japan has arrived as a world economic power and had transformed the international relations of the Pacific. Gorbachev now welcomed the economic development in many ideologically hostile states of the region and took a more positive approach to Pacific cooperation. The attempt to join organizations for Pacific economic cooperation might be greatly assisted by lifting the Japanese veto, but that would require some sort of Soviet initiative that at least flattered Japan and would perhaps even appear to meet real Japanese demands.

Once again it was the economic motive that drove Soviet-Japanese relations. Japan, like many other observers of the Gorbachev reforms, was impressed by the seriousness of intent and was keen to exploit the possibilities for trade. A return to a 1970s-like arrangement was possible, although energy prices were now much reduced. What is more, the nature of the Japanese economy changed rapidly in the late 1980s, and the types of goods the Soviet Union could export or import were not the same as a decade earlier. But Gorbachev's talk of Japanese involvement in Soviet equivalents of joint ventures on the Chinese model suggested that there were fresh ideas in Moscow on how to play a realistic part in the Pacific. As the Japanese economy develops, the Soviet Union will not only lose its lead as Asia's largest economy, but it will also slip to number three in the world. Soviet-Japanese relations may remain frozen for a while, but the Japanese challenge, especially in economic terms, to the Soviet Union has certainly forced itself onto Moscow's agenda.

THE IMPORTANCE OF INDIA

The jewel in the crown of Soviet relations with the developing world has been India. But it was a jewel that took a long time to acquire and one that often cut the Soviet Union when it tried to handle it too roughly. For a long time the extent of Soviet-Indian relations was a function of Soviet relations with China, but eventually it came to stand, albeit uncertainly, on its own.

The delay in cultivating Indian contacts was due to Stalin's suspicions of any so-called nonaligned states in a world of cold war. By the mid-1950s, however, Khrushchev had taken a special interest in India, and his 1955 tour went a long way toward building the basis for closer relations. So long as China and India remained on good terms, as they were in the mid-1950s, the Soviet Union paid little price for cultivating this friendship. But growing Sino-Indian territorial disputes and rivalry for the leadership of the developing world in the later 1950s made China wary of Soviet-Indian relations.

By the time of the Sino-Indian border clashes in 1959, close Soviet relations with India was seen by China as a sell-out of the revolutionary cause. The Soviet Union did not understand any ideological need to restrain relations with Delhi, but in the attempt to hold Sino-Soviet relations together, it became inclined to support the Chinese radicals' view. But, as already explained, 1962 was the watershed for Soviet-Indian relations, as Moscow decided to pursue its Indian friendship despite the damage to relations with China.

India proved an attractive trading substitute for China in the mid-1960s, and it quickly emerged as Moscow's main trading partner in the developing world. Soviet arbitration in the 1965 Indo-Pakistan war was appreciated by India, even though it was not particularly successful. It was certainly preferable to the leading role that the United States played in supporting India against China in 1962.

Although Pakistan sought to stay on decent terms, it was India under Indira Gandhi that was most serious about developing ties with the Soviet Union. Her inclination toward the Soviet side in the cold war, an inclination that was seen by the West as excessive, was best seen in the 1971 friendship treaty. The treaty was part of Brezhnev's scheme to build an anti-China collective security arrangement. India saw through the plan, but it also saw the advantage in cooperating with the Soviet Union in order to deal with Pakistan free from outside pressure.

India's calculations were finely executed, and the creation of Bangladesh in the 1971 war was achieved in part because the Soviet Union was holding the United States at bay. India and the Soviet Union were so successful that Pakistan was driven into even further cooperation with the United

States and helped arrange for the Nixon visit to China. The spiral of escalation in competing alliances led to increased polarization in South Asia but no more wars, as Pakistan had been so seriously scarred by its defeat that it could not seriously challenge India on the battlefield.

Soviet-Indian trade reached new peaks in this period, and complex co-production deals were made for military equipment. India became by far the Soviet Union's main trading partner in the developing world, and a symbol of the benefits that friendship and mutual respect with Moscow made possible. But the process was not without its strains, and certainly the Soviet Union was on its best behavior. India had to "teach" the Soviet Union how to treat another large and proud people with respect, a trick the Chinese were only beginning to master by the late 1950s. But India was always obliged to hold the Soviet Union at arms' length and avoid leaning so far to the Soviet side as to be horizontal.

It came as somewhat of a shock to India when the Soviet Union began exercising its option to seek other friends in Asia less to India's liking. The main change, of course, was the return of China as a trading partner. Indian anxieties about Chinese intentions were in no way reduced by a decrease in the size of Beijing's armed forces. India's convincing defeat in 1962 remained a sore spot, and many officials were spoiling for a return match, especially after the disastrous showing of the Chinese armed forces in their war with Vietnam in 1979.

The Soviet Union was not interested in seeing the two Asian powers go to war, if only because Moscow was coming to believe it could maintain its good relations with India while improving ties to China. This tricky task was largely successful, although Soviet-Indian trade had begun to stagnate just as Sino-Soviet trade took off. Yet Gorbachev took care to keep a balance among his friends in Asia. The overtures to China in 1986 were matched by a trip to India and a return trip by Rajiv Gandhi to Moscow, an apparent indication that all was still normal in Soviet-Indian relations. The smiles of cordiality were sometimes strained as Rajiv Gandhi suggested he was more interested in balancing relations with the superpowers than his mother had seen fit. The complex link of India, China and the superpowers was every bit as intricate as it was in 1971. But in the 1980s it was in the cause of détente rather than confrontation.

In the 1980s Soviet-Indian relations suffered from success in that they appeared more normal and even "boring" than the new détente between the Communist giants. But India had achieved a great deal in establishing such normal relations with the Soviet Union, and the benefits are arguably also enjoyed by China. The new Sino-Soviet détente was on a far more equal basis than the earlier honeymoon, and the Soviet Union had apparently learned from two decades of Indian teachers some lessons about how to treat proud Asian giants.

THE IMPORTANCE OF EAST ASIAN COMMUNIST STATES

One of the more striking trends in postwar Asia has been the establishment of Marxist regimes of one variety or another. Apart from Mongolia and the

Soviet Union, which were Communist before 1945, similarly oriented regimes were then established in North Korea, China, North Vietnam (later a united Vietnam), Cambodia, Laos and finally Afghanistan. This has been not quite a fulfillment of the domino theory that so motivated American action in the Vietnam war in the 1960s, but there were clearly gains for socialism that were not replicated anywhere else, except for sporadic cases in the developing world.

In all but the Afghan case, a friendly regime was created where one had not existed before. But in the case of China the friend turned enemy, and in Korea the friend became somewhat distant in an effort to lean to the Chinese side of the Sino-Soviet split. Nevertheless, the Soviet Union could be pleased that the tide of history was moving its way, even if it could not control all the ebbs and flows.

The main problem for the Soviet Union was that almost without exception these new friends were among the poorest states in Asia, and all brought as many problems as advantages for Soviet foreign policy. All the newcomers to Marxism were involved in conflict of one sort or another and requested Soviet assistance. All were economic drains down which a great deal of precious Soviet resources were poured. Few provided vital rewards except for their friendship (the exception being bases in Vietnam).

By far the most important and difficult of these allies was Vietnam. As the third-largest Communist state (in population terms, and only since 1975), and the only one to have defeated the United States in combat, Vietnam had truly earned a special place in Soviet schemes for Asia. Soviet support for Communist North Vietnam in its attempt to take over the whole country was complicated not only by superpower relations but also by Sino-Soviet relations. In the 1950s, and especially at the 1954 Indochina settlement in Geneva, the Soviet Union, like China, conspired to support Vietnam while preventing it from achieving its full objective. Hanoi soon recognized its Communist patrons as equivocal allies.

During the anti-American phase of the war in Vietnam, in the decade from 1964, Hanoi received most of its military support from the Soviet Union. Moscow tried to limit the damage to superpower relations while drawing China into a "united action" in support of Vietnam. The Communist rift slowed up the Vietnamese war effort, but it also allowed Hanoi to play off one ally against the other. The Soviet Union, with its superior ability to deliver aid, was eventually to win the battle against China for Vietnamese favor.

While the Soviet Union did not send combat troops to help fight the war (as China sent anti-aircraft units), advisers were killed by American bombing raids and Soviet ships were hit when Vietnamese ports were attacked. It is probably fair to say that North Vietnam could not have won the war without Soviet support; and certainly it would have been a much more protracted conflict without Soviet arms and financial support.

At the end of the war, in 1975, China and Vietnam were well on their way to a serious split, and the Soviet Union remained Hanoi's main supporter. As conflict with China developed, Soviet aid remained just as essential as it was in the 1960s. From the Soviet point of view, the gains it made in terms of Vietnamese friendship had to be balanced against continuing antagonism with the far more important China. In fact, this dilemma for Soviet policy remained and indeed was accentuated in subsequent years.

With the Vietnamese occupation of Cambodia in 1978–79 and the Chinese attack on Vietnam in early 1979, Vietnam became even more dependent on Soviet aid. Vietnam joined the Council for Mutual Economic Assistance (COMECON)—and became the only Asian member apart from Mongolia—and signed a friendship pact with the Soviet Union. In 1978 the Soviet Union wrote off $1.5 billion in debts, and gross disbursement of COMECON aid in 1985 was also $1.5 billion. In the 1980s the Soviet Union sent millions of dollars of aid every day and received in return basing rights in Cam Ranh Bay. But Moscow also received a bad press in the region for its support of Vietnamese aggression and suffered for having a close ally that was shunned in most of the Pacific and Asia.

The extent of the damage to Soviet policy was only recognized when Soviet leaders began improving the image of the USSR in the Pacific in the 1980s. Andropov and, in a more sustained fashion, Gorbachev decided to press Vietnam for some concessions in its regional policy. In late 1986 the Vietnamese Communist party was shoved into reforms as suggested by Moscow. The Soviets waved both carrot and stick and found it relatively easy to make headway, as the Vietnamese economy was obviously in such sad shape. The Soviet Union was still unable to force Vietnam out of Cambodia, but in July 1987 Gorbachev made it clear that Vietnam would be kept to its pledge to evacuate by 1990. Certainly the pace of reform at home in Vietnam was set at a cracking pace, and it suggested that reform in foreign policy was not far behind.

Vietnam remained the Soviet Union's closest major friend in Asia, although it was less close than Mongolia and less important than India. But by virtue of its crucial role in local conflicts, Vietnam continued to take up far more Soviet attention when it might have been relegated to a more peripheral role. For the first time since the mid-1960s, the Soviet Union tried to throw some of its weight around in order to ensure that the Vietnamese tail did not constantly wag the Soviet dog.

The two other states of Indochina, Laos and Cambodia, were far less important to the Soviet Union, and their fate was very much tied up with that of Vietnam. Soviet influence in both these states was controlled by either China or Vietnam at various times until 1975. With the triumph of communism in both states in 1975, the Soviet Union tried to extend its own direct links to the regimes. Laos was very firmly under Vietnamese control, although it, too, depended heavily on Soviet aid. As one of the poorest states in the world, it was not a Soviet priority and hardly a fine example of the benefits of socialism.

Cambodia was and remained a far more difficult problem. Its ruling Communist party under Pol Pot in the last half of the 1970s was more in the Chinese sphere of influence than in that of Vietnam or the Soviet Union, and with the growing Sino-Soviet split, Cambodia became even less of a Soviet friend. The brief war between Vietnam and Cambodia resulted in the imposition of the Vietnamese-supported regime of Heng Samrin. When the Soviet Union tried to establish its own links to the regime, Vietnam had the Soviet "friends" purged. Moscow was still expected to pump aid into Cambodia ($110 million of COMECON aid in 1985) and to underwrite the Vietnamese action, but it was left with little control in the area. Communism had tipped the Indochinese dominoes, but it was far from Soviet-style or Soviet-controlled communism.

The two other East Asian Communist states are, yet again, different types of regimes for the Soviet Union to handle. North Korea was established before China became Communist, and has been almost as much bother without the compensating benefits of being an important power. It seems clear that Stalin had primed the North Korean gun in 1950, and Kim Il-sung then set it off to begin the Korean War at a time of his own choosing. Kim then managed to balance Soviet and Chinese interests—which at the time were mostly in common—to see if the war could be won, even following the Chinese intervention.

The failure to achieve a victory set the pattern of complex inter-Communist and international relations in this vital region of the Pacific. The Soviet Union could not afford not to pay great attention to the area because of its own vital interests, as well as because of the participation of Japan, the United States and China. Kim managed to delay a ceasefire in the conflict, but he was not able to prevent the Soviet Union pulling the plug on the war in 1953.

Kim managed thereafter to drag the Soviet Union into crises in the area that involved all the major powers. The Soviet Union had long had an interest in the control of Asian conflicts, if only to allow the concentration on more important issues in Europe. But Kim extracted arms and aid that made North Korea a threat to South Korea and a reasonably successful Communist economy. It was the most successful economy in the Communist developing world, although with one of the more reprehensible governments. It was difficult for the Soviet Union to hold it up as an example for others, but was at least less of an economic drain than Vietnam.

During the period of Sino-Soviet rivalry, North Korea was able to manipulate its patrons into providing support short of a new war against South Korea. But with the Sino-American détente, both China and the USSR tacitly came to agree that the reunification of Korea had to be peaceful and that Korean policy should not get in the way of improving relations with other states in the Pacific. While China built a billion-dollar unofficial trade with South Korea, the Soviet Union discussed Korean issues with the United States in order to keep the region calm. Under Gorbachev there were signs that the Soviet Union also wanted to explore improving relations with South Korea, although also on an unofficial level.

The Sino-Soviet détente of the early 1980s had already begun to push North Korea into a corner as its ability to play off its patrons was circumscribed. The Soviet Union and China both urged economic reform on Kim as the once fast-growing economy began to grind to a halt. The aging Korean leadership was even less flexible than that in Vietnam, and much seemed to depend on the successor to Kim Il-sung. Korea was no longer the major problem for Soviet foreign policy that it was in the 1950s, but there was no guarantee that it would not suddenly explode again.

Mongolia, the first of the Communist East Asian states, remained unusual for a number of other reasons. As a COMECON member, it was at one time closely integrated into the Soviet economy but was curiously cut off from the rest of the region. It was useful to the Soviet Union as a supplier of raw materials and a strategic buffer, of sorts, against China. In the 1960s it was a convenient base for Soviet divisions deployed against China, and a useful ally in the Communist world when taking on the China challenge.

But in the new Soviet atmosphere of reform in the 1980s, Mongolia became more of a problem. Its need for reform at home was pushed hard but was met with obvious delay from Ulaanbaatar. When the Soviet Union first stressed improved relations with China, the Mongolians managed to sabotage the policy. A change in the Mongolian leadership was engineered, and thereafter Mongolia was more helpful in supporting the new Soviet line.

The result of this shift was the marginalization of Mongolia. At a time when Soviet relations with China and the Pacific states were developing, Mongolia had little to offer and was to be kept quiet while the Soviet Union withdrew troops from the country and reoriented its trade patterns. Without reform in Mongolia, the area threatened to become a major loser in the new Soviet foreign policy in Asia.

THE PROBLEMS OF AFGHANISTAN

Afghanistan was nothing but a problem for the Soviet Union. Until the 1970s it was a quiet Soviet neighbor (one of only four land neighbors in Asia) that knew it had to keep on the good side of the superpower to the north. Its monarchy was also friendly with China and to some extent with the West, but it was little cared about by all.

The 1973 coup that removed the monarchy moved Afghanistan somewhat closer to the Soviet orbit, but it was apparently not a state of affairs that the Soviet Union particularly sought. The next coup in 1978 brought an even more radical regime to one of the world's poorest states and forced the area into the attention of Soviet foreign-policy planners.

This new addition to the Marxist world would have been welcomed by the Soviet Union if it somehow brought prosperity, power or influence. Regrettably, from the Soviet point of view, it merely brought problems of instability and debt. The main instability was due to the imposition of an increasingly atheistic government on a population that believed in fundamental Islam. It was also a regime deeply divided by factional politics and gradually losing control of a country that never enjoyed a strong central rule.

The dilemma for the Soviet Union was whether to intervene in Afghanistan and reorder the country's politics or to let it drift into its own solution. The problem with the latter option was that revolutionary trends should not be allowed to be undone, and in any case Afghanistan bordered on the Soviet Union and could not be allowed to fall into hostile hands. Hence, when the ever-twisting factional politics in Afghanistan threatened to take it closer to a newly Islamicized Iran and out of the Soviet orbit, the Soviet Union decided to intervene in December 1979.

Yet the invasion by over 100,000 Soviet troops was hardly an ideal solution. It was the first major use of Soviet troops in combat in Asia (apart from border clashes with China), and it did serious damage to Moscow's reputation in the Islamic world. It was the first Soviet attempt to directly control a developing state, and it brought out all the problems encountered by the American intervention in Vietnam: guerilla war in mountainous terrain with a predominantly poor peasant population favors low-tech solutions. The Soviet Union soon found that it could control the cities and the main highways, but its troops were never safe from surprise attack. The country could not be sealed off from its hostile neighbors, who were supported by an almost equally hostile Islamic and Western world eager to undermine the Soviet Union.

As a result, the Soviet Union found itself for the first time the only great power to be involved in regular combat. This, and the other dubiously exclusive predicaments, were apparent to many Soviet leaders right from the start of the operation. The possible gains from this sorry situation remained limited. At best, the Soviet Union would get a quiet, pro-Soviet neighbor—which was where it started before the 1970s. Some felt the Soviet Union was actually working up to incorporating Afghanistan into the Soviet Union, as Russia had done with other central Asian khanates in previous centuries. Nearly a decade into the Soviet occupation, there were merely signs of creating an ideologically sound state on East European lines, not an integral part of the Soviet Union.

The damage to the Soviet position in the world was clear by the time Brezhnev died in 1983. Thereafter, there were regular signs that the Soviet Union wanted to get out of its predicament in Afghanistan. Mikhail Gorbachev was more serious than any of the Brezhnev successors in pursuing this goal, and he finally secured a phased withdrawal of Soviet troops, ending in 1989. The key problem was the nature of the regime in Afghanistan after the Soviet withdrawal. The Soviet Union wanted a friendly regime, while the very divided rebel groups wanted an Islamic state that would, perhaps, be as independent of the Soviet Union as Iran or even as hostile as Pakistan. The rebels were unable to agree among themselves on this issue, but the Soviet Union was unwilling to discuss anything but a friendly regime. The obvious compromise, a return to a monarchical government, was suggested by Gorbachev, but turning back the clock is a notoriously difficult and often fruitless process.

The Soviet Union remained stuck and bleeding in Afghanistan for a decade. It was the one part of Asia that went most disastrously wrong for Soviet foreign policy, especially since relations with China had improved. Afghanistan was, of course, not of vital strategic importance, compared to other theaters, but it was still on the Soviet frontier in an area of rising Islamic unrest. The risk of contagion to Soviet central Asia was ever present and a reason for the often super-cautious Soviet response to possible solutions.

No one had a vested interest in helping the Soviet Union out of its Afghan impasse, while many were happy to see it stuck. Short of a military victory, only major concessions freed the Soviet Union from its problem, and even then it was unlikely to look back on events as worthwhile. The Afghan quagmire was one of the great disasters of Soviet foreign policy in Asia.

THE IMPORTANCE OF SMALL NON-COMMUNIST STATES

The remainder of the Asian states are as diverse as those already considered, and most have been seen by the Soviet Union as special cases. Most were regarded as friendly to the United States and/or China and therefore difficult to woo. Some, such as Pakistan, the Philippines or South Korea, had mutual security treaties with the United States. Only one, Burma (now Myanmar), was never the focus of some sort of Soviet concern.

Pakistan was perhaps the most important of these states, bordering on Afghanistan and just kept off the Soviet frontier by the artificially drawn Wakhan Corridor. As a U.S. military ally, it was seen in an unfavorable light; and as an enemy of India and Afghanistan, it was seen as an enemy of a friend.

Yet for these very reasons, the Soviet Union recognized that it must get along with Pakistan, and at times it even tried to entice it away from the United States and China. In 1965 Soviet mediation at Tashkent was intended to do just that, but this effort was unsuccessful. As Pakistan drifted into civil war and then dismemberment by Soviet-supported India in 1971, the Soviet Union's hope for a better relationship with Pakistan faded. The Islamization of Pakistani politics and the Afghan war ensured that the gulf remained wide. Thus, Pakistan, though important for Soviet policy, remained a state with some of the most hostile feelings toward Moscow. This was not a successful area, needless to say, for Soviet foreign policy.

Perhaps the next most important state for the Soviet Union was Indonesia, the maverick in ASEAN that tried to mediate in the Indochina impasse. It is also a mainly Islamic state, and one therefore that is opposed to the Soviet state and its actions in Afghanistan. But unlike Pakistan, it is as far from Afghanistan as Korea and is really much more interested in Indochinese events.

Indonesia, of course, had its own brush with communism in 1965, when a failed coup led to the suppression of the Communist party. But China was seen as the main culprit, and the Soviet reputation was relatively free from taint because of the Sino-Soviet split. Yet the suspicion of communism remained, and the Soviet Union was merely seen as a useful counterweight to American and above all Chinese power. Indonesia, like India in South Asia, had regional aspirations that required playing off one superpower against the other.

The Soviet Union knows these games are played, and it has largely been unwilling to be manipulated. It treated ASEAN as a sideshow and an unpromising one at that. The change came with the Gorbachev administration and the attempt to break the Indochina deadlock. Indonesia, as the main moderate in ASEAN on an Indochina settlement, took on a special and more positive role in the Soviet perspective. Yet it remained distant from direct Soviet interests, and Moscow recognized its limits of influence in this distant theater.

No other state in the region showed much prospect for Soviet influence, but each represented different dimensions of the Soviet dilemma in Asia. Thailand and the Philippines were poor states, concerned with the growth of Soviet military power. Both relied on the United States for protection and were concerned about Sino-Soviet détente. Thailand was at the front line of the Cambodian conflict, and the Philippines had the largest American bases outside of the United States.

Taiwan, South Korea and the smaller newly industrialized countries (NICs) of Hong Kong and Singapore have long been off-limits to Soviet foreign policy. They are all closely aligned with the Western security system, whether formally or tacitly. Above all, they are upsetting examples of the success of the capitalist world and the need for change in the Soviet Union and its approach to Asia. This has encouraged the Soviet Union to minimize South Asia and try to understand the East Asian success stories more carefully. It has helped the Soviet Union push its allies into reform in order to meet the challenge of the NICs and Japan. Their steady integration into a type of Pacific economic community has upset the Soviet Union and led it to explore the idea of Pacific cooperation in a more positive fashion. Above all, the NICs represent the challenge as Gorbachev sees it in East Asia. To the extent that the challenge is being properly met, relations with these states are likely to improve.

NEW DIRECTIONS?

Before the death of Brezhnev it would have been hard to write positively about Soviet thinking regarding Asia. But it is increasingly clear that new ideas have reached Soviet foreign as well as domestic policy, and they have been applied in Asia before anywhere else in the developing world. In such an atmosphere, trend spotting is more dangerous than usual.

The main Soviet gains in Asia since 1945 have, in order, been the following: (1) friendship with India and (2) new Communist regimes in China, Korea and Indochina. The main losses have been (1) China as an adversary and (2) the war in Afghanistan. Yet such a summary skims over the major changes in the strategic balance in the interim. China might once have been counted as an ally and therefore a major gain, or as an enemy and thus a major loss; it is now classed as a problem, albeit a far less serious one than it used to be. It is therefore more useful to highlight the main agenda for the Soviet Union in Asia, again in order of priority.

(1) Relations with China need to be improved further. There is still much room for improvement, and the effect of healthier contacts will be felt in almost every sphere of Soviet-Asian relations.

(2) Communist Asia, apart from China, needs to be revitalized. The

1196

reforms already made need to be followed up with additional energy, or else Soviet friends will slip further behind their Asian neighbors and be less useful as supporters of the Soviet Union in economic, political or even military terms. Vietnamese withdrawal from Cambodia should be seen as part of this agenda.

(3) Very much related is the Soviet need to build bridges to non-Communist Asia, especially Japan and the NICs. The economic benefits are obvious, as any observer of Soviet relations with Western Europe will note. Relations with the United States in Asia are no longer particularly important, except as part of the most vital global question of keeping the superpower relationship stable.

(4) The withdrawal from Afghanistan in 1989 must be followed by attempts to improve the Soviet image in the Islamic world and in Asia as a whole. South Asia remains less important for Soviet interests than either East Asia or the Arab/Persian Gulf, but the effects of the Afghan war are wounds that must be healed if the Soviet Union is to project a more peaceful international image and if its economy is to prosper.

Even if only some of these most important challenges are met by the Soviet Union, it will improve its position in Asia. Despite regular statements about the need to see the region in terms of collective security, the Soviet Union has learned that the area is far more diverse than any other part of the globe. This is of course a problem for Moscow, but it is also encouraging in the sense that the Soviet Union can become more easily integrated into the region. In order to become a more genuine Asian power, as opposed to a power in Asia, it will need to show that it has a more constructive role to play.

FURTHER READING

Bok, Georges Tan Eng. *The USSR in East Asia.* Paris: Atlantic Institute, 1986.

Buszyinski, Leszek. *The Soviet Union and Southeast Asia.* London: Croom Helm, 1986).

Segal, Gerald. *Sino-Soviet Relations After Mao.* Adelphi Paper no. 202. London: International Institute for Strategic Studies, 1985.

————, ed. *The Soviet Union in East Asia.* London: Heinemann; Boulder, Colorado: Westview Press, 1983.

Swearingen, Rodger, ed. *Siberia and the Soviet Far East.* Stanford, California: Hoover Institution Press, 1987.

Whiting, Allen. *Siberian Development and East Asia.* Stanford, California: Stanford University Press, 1981.

Zagoria, Donald, ed. *Soviet Policy in East Asia.* New Haven, Connecticut: Yale University Press, 1982.

THE UNITED STATES AND ASIA

GRAHAM HUTCHINGS

THE importance of Asia to the United States, both historically and at the present time, is easily demonstrated. It was in Asia that the United States seized its first and only major colony. An Asian country was the first to threaten U.S. security interests in modern times. Conflict in Asia in the 1950s marked a turning point in American foreign policy by tipping the scales in favor of the global containment of communism. And, 15 years later, another Asian war proved to be the longest the United States has ever fought, the least successful, and the most divisive at home. In the late 1980s, three of the regional conflicts in which the Soviet Union and the United States confronted each other, although indirectly, were to be found in Asia. Afghanistan, Cambodia, and Korea are either occupied by foreign powers or divided arbitrarily as a consequence of superpower rivalry.

These are remarkable developments in view of the fact that the United States had no developed policy toward Asia before the late 1890s and maintained an isolationist foreign policy for decades afterward. American interests and commitments in the region nonetheless quickly eclipsed those of the traditional European imperial powers who became involved in Asia in the first half of the 19th century. The growth and development of these interests, which have been concerned mainly with East and Southeast Asia, and in particular with China, Japan, the Philippines, Vietnam, and Korea, form the subject of this essay. Its aim is to give an account of two centuries of involvement in Asia by the United States, what such involvement has meant for the Asian countries concerned, and its bearing on the general pattern of international relations in the region.

RIGHTS WITHOUT RESPONSIBILITIES: EARLY U.S. POLICY TOWARD CHINA

Although it inaugurated direct trade with both China and the Philippines in the late 18th century, the United States remained a decidedly secondary imperial power in the region for most of the next one hundred years. The early decades of the 19th century were years of domestic rather than foreign expansion. This is not to say that overseas and overland adventures were

1198

unrelated. Access to Asia via the Pacific rather than the Atlantic acted as a stimulus to the development of the American interior. The acquisition of the Oregon country in the late 1830s and California a decade later brought Asia closer to the United States, and thus gave rise to the idea of continental *and* maritime empire. Asia suddenly became the United States' neighbor, separated only by a large placid intervening ocean that seemed very inviting to American steamships.

However, while pioneers explored continental frontiers, successive U.S. governments were content to follow in the path of the established European powers in China, attempting to share whatever commercial advantages they might win from the declining Qing dynasty. This decline was of the utmost consequence for the balance of power in East Asia. It formed the backdrop to a century of imperial rivalry and domestic upheaval in the region, in which the United States played a major part. On the whole, early U.S. policy toward China was successful. The United States won a substantial share of the illegal market for opium in China following the arrival of the first American-owned cargo in Guangzhou (Canton) in 1805. And in 1844, Caleb Cushing, leader of the first U.S. diplomatic mission to China, signed a treaty which secured all the rights Britain had to fight for but none of the historical opprobrium.

This set a pattern for much of the remainder of the century. Britain, and to some extent France, did the groundwork. These powers were "responsible" for China. The United States followed at some distance and maintained altogether smaller military resources and personnel in the country. This made it easier for the United States to express abstract principles as far as policy toward China was concerned. It could emphasize moral and sympathetic rather than material interests in China. Indeed, American material interests in China were negligible for most of the 19th century. Bilateral trade increased by only US$10 million during the period 1875–1895 to reach $25 million. This is not to say economic factors were unimportant. The United States wanted at least a reasonable share of what its rivals got, and more if possible. There was also the promise of China, the lure of a vast market. From the first half of the 19th century, China was regarded as the world's last great untapped market for manufactured products.

The real basis of U.S. interests in China, however, was less concrete. It had to do with the extent that the United States felt it could change China into a more unified, modernized, independent nation. American missionaries, who soon outnumbered their rivals from other countries, felt they had a vital part to play in this process. Their presence in the late 1800s was not regarded as accidental. China was widely believed to be at a crucial point in its history; it was set for change and the United States was glad to be there to help. However different this approach was from that of the other European powers, it presented no challenge to the framework of the Western presence in China. Many U.S. diplomats in China complained about British methods in the country, but all of them accepted the fruits of wars and treaties won by others. And at least one of them was quite candid about it. George F. Seward, ambassador to Beijing from 1876–1880, confessed: "I should think less of Western civilization and of Western manhood if it were not pushing and aggressive in China."

The U.S. encounter with Japan began on an altogether different basis from that with China. Whereas merchants and missionaries led the way in China, Japan was opened to American commerce by an official mission. It included notable scientists and involved one quarter of the entire U.S. navy. The 1853 visit of Comm. Matthew Perry's fleet to Tokyo Bay proved that the United States, too, could resort to gunboat diplomacy. In 1854, Perry forced the Tokugawa rulers to sign the Treaty of Kanagawa, marking the formal conclusion of two centuries of Japanese isolation from the outside world. From the point of view of the powers, the treaty was markedly inferior to the Treaty of Nanjing which opened China. But in an exact reversal of the situation there, Britain, Russia, and eventually the Netherlands, were quick to follow the U.S. lead and secure equal benefits.

Advantages in Japan similar to those won in China through wars and occupation came in 1858. Again it was the United States that set the pace. In 1856 Townsend Harris began to impress Japan with the need to sign a full commercial treaty. He told the authorities that if they refused the moderate conditions offered by the United States, the British were bound to appear and impose harsh terms. American policy, on the other hand, was unique because it was based on a special friendship with Japan. After protracted negotiations Harris concluded a commercial treaty in 1858 which opened Japan fully to trade. He subsequently became the first U.S. ambassador to Japan and opened a legation in Tokyo.

In keeping with the way in which Japan was "opened," it was American rather than European influence that was felt most in the post-treaty period. Unlike China, moreover, Japan had an inquisitive, almost acquisitive, attitude toward the latest foreign ideas and techniques. This was generally admired by the growing number of Americans in Japan. They found the increasing influence of American educational methods particularly encouraging. It seemed to imply an inevitable development in the direction of democratic liberalism. The deeper perception that Japan was mainly interested in such ways of the West as might contribute to strengthening the state was less apparent.

In China the Western presence added a new complexity to a gradual process of imperial decline; the American-led intrusion in Japan, on the other hand, sparked a profound political change. This had been long in the making. Lethargy and indecision had gripped the bureaucracy of the Tokugawa shogunate several decades before the arrival of Perry. Economic changes had weakened its authority and financial base. The Western presence compounded the domestic crisis but also hastened its resolution. In 1868 the shogunate was overthrown and the emperor, little more than figurehead in the Tokugawa era, was restored to power. During the next 25 years, an energetic elite carried out a program of modernization that, by the close of the century, made Japan a force to be reckoned with in East Asian politics.

In terms of international politics, the Meiji restoration was perfectly timed. The West had proved powerful enough to act as a catalyst for political change but not powerful enough, nor indeed interested in, further Asian territorial acquistions while Japan was in turmoil. In the case of the United States, interest in Asia waned as the civil war raged at home. In Europe, too, there was concern with the consequences for the European balance of power with the rise of Germany. When the "new imperialism" emerged during the late 1880s and 1890s, Japan had become too formidable a power to humble with a show of strength in Tokyo Bay. Indeed, Japan was prepared to do some humbling itself. The relative lack of American interest, though not of influence, in Japan during the late Tokugawa and early Meiji periods, contributed to good relations between the two countries. It was an era of amiability between Washington and Tokyo. Toward the end of the century, bilateral trade came to surpass that between the United States and China. Two Americans, Henry Williard Denison and Durham W. Stevens, were key advisors to the Japanese foreign ministry in the 1880s. They helped Tokyo win a treaty revision in 1894. Extraterritoriality was abolished in 1899, and tariff autonomy secured in 1911. From certain perspectives, therefore, Japan seemed to be a "model student"; no other Asian nation could match its rapid and dramatic development into modern statehood.

U.S. MILITARY POWER IN ASIA: THE PHILIPPINES

Until the 1890s the United States might have been regarded as an "interested observer" in Asia. It had great aspirations in China, but more real influence in Japan. There was no significant contact with other countries in the region. As the century came to a close, however, the domestic frontier disappeared and exponents of America's "manifest destiny" looked farther afield. This attitude was reinforced by Capt. Alfred Mahan's *The Influence of Sea Power upon History* (1890), which argued that the state, through its navy, had a responsibility to promote overseas commerce as an outlet for overproductivity at home. A section of American public opinion thus clamored for overseas expansion at a time when the pace of imperialism was also quickening on the part of the European powers. Social Darwinism, very much in vogue during the 1880s and 1890s, held out bleak prospects for nations unable to keep up.

U.S. attention focused on Cuba, long ruled corruptly and inefficiently by Spain. Sympathy for Cuban independence, American investment in sugar, tobacco, and the iron industry, and "popular clamor," all combined in 1898 to produce what President Theodore Roosevelt later admitted was not much of a war, but one that was quickly won. The logic of war with Spain demanded the elimination of the Spanish fleet. This might have been an inconsequential matter for students of U.S. involvement in Asia were it not for the fact that the fleet was then in Manila Bay in the Philippines, another ineptly ruled Spanish colony. A small section of American opinion had long regarded the Philippines with interest, but for most they were little heard and known. This situation soon changed. By 1900, two thirds of the U.S. army was fighting there, but fighting Filipinos, not the Spanish.

While Adm. George Dewey destroyed Spanish power at sea in April 1898, Filipinos overthrew it on land. This presented the United States with a dilemma. In the current climate it was hardly to be expected that so vulnerable a country could remain independent. And although the islands themselves were thought to be of little value, they seemed to be a gateway to Asia's glittering wealth; viewed in this light, they were too valuable for the United States to pass over. There was also the duty of civilizing peoples less fortunate than Americans. But the United States was not so different an imperialist power from Britain or France that it consulted the views of those it chose to civilize. Filipinos found U.S. rule no less disagreeable than Spanish; for the next three years they waged a bitter guerrilla war against their new masters.

In quite a remarkable way, the American experience in the Philippines immediately after the defeat of Spain foreshadowed much of what later followed from the U.S. struggle in Vietnam. Domestic opinion was bitterly divided between imperialists and those who held that to govern people without their consent violated a cardinal principle of American democracy. If liberty was stamped out abroad, opponents argued, it would surely suffer at home. The administration's censorship of news from the new colony to conceal from a domestic audience the real nature of the rebellion against U.S. rule tended to bear this out. Such arguments were of no avail. The United States had acquired a firm stake in Asia and was not about to relinquish it. The insurrection was put down. After the controversy surrounding its acquisition, the Philippines never again became an important issue in American domestic politics. Moreover, there were no further uprisings against U.S. rule. Meanwhile, the war with Spain led the United States to annex Hawaii and acquire a harbor in Samoa, bringing crucial staging posts in the Pacific under American control.

U.S. MORAL POWER IN ASIA: THE OPEN DOOR POLICY

Four years before the United States gained its first major colony, Japan dealt China a crushing blow in a short war over supremacy in Korea. Japan's success showed how well it had adopted Western techniques in the development of industry, weaponry, and military affairs and, conversely, how China had failed in this regard. Most Americans (and many Europeans) interested in Asian matters welcomed Japan's victory; Asia's "top student" had thrashed sluggard China. But it soon became clear that this new revelation of China's weakness had implications for the balance of power in East Asia. The treaty system, which had evolved earlier in the century as a result of the long decline of Chinese power, depended on at least the fiction of a strong central government in Beijing. It was now clear that a new order was needed. The powers attempted to establish one by entering into regional arrangements with China, usually and more colorfully referred to as the "scramble for concessions" or "spheres of influence."

Although the United States was rapidly becoming a power to be reckoned with in Asian affairs during this period, it was in no position to join this scramble, even if it wanted to. American material interests in China were modest at the end of the 19th century, however evaluated, and the same is true of Asia generally. In 1900 there was still five times as much European capital in the United States than American capital overseas. Most U.S. exports were still agricultural products, and most went to Europe rather than to Asia. However, this did not mean that the United States was going to be squeezed out of any future arrangements in China. Indeed, the United States sought a larger, although different, sphere of influence in Chinese affairs than that of the established powers as imperial rivalry intensified at the close of the 19th century. In 1897 and 1900, the United States issued diplomatic notes to all the powers involved in China setting out what came to be known as the Open Door policy. The first note called mainly for the preservation of equal foreign economic opportunity in China, irrespective of spheres of influence. But the second referred to the need to maintain China's "territorial and administrative integrity." It seemed, therefore, at least in American eyes, that the United States was a protector of China against the ravages of the imperial powers. The second note, issued at the height of the Boxer crisis, also provided a rationale for U.S. participation in the allied occupation of Beijing following the lifting of the siege of the diplomatic quarter. U.S. intervention could be seen as a form of backing for the shaken, disintegrating Qing government against both its internal and external foes.

Although it was accepted only grudgingly by some of the European powers, the Open Door principle became a key theme of U.S. policy toward China for at least the next half century. Moreover, it has exercized a curious and tenacious hold on the American mind as the foundation of a special relationship with China. The Open Door policy, so its proponents maintained, prevented the dismemberment of China when it was most vulnerable. This altruistic view of U.S. China policy has not survived the examination of modern historians unscathed. Given the relative weakness of U.S. power in Asia when the Open Door notes were issued, they ought to be regarded as "foot in the door" notes according to some authorities. In this view, the Open Door principle was a form of cost-effective imperialism conducted on the basis of relative military weakness. Secretary of State John Hay's notes were an attempt to keep markets open for American evangelization and trade in the face of superior European competition.

Certainly, both at the time they were issued and subsequently, the notion that the Open Door notes formed the basis of a special relationship between the United States and China was more apparent to Americans than to Chinese. Moreover, American citizens at home had anything but a special relationship with the ordinary Chinese they encountered. Chinese immigrants in the United States, who numbered at least 100,000 by the time the first Open Door note was issued, faced tougher laws than any other ethnic group. Acts of 1882, 1888, and 1892 suspended immigration of

Chinese laborers and prevented the naturalization of those already in the United States. Such harsh domestic treatment led, in 1905, to one of the earliest stirrings of Chinese nationalism when merchants and workers in Shanghai and Guangzhou organized a comprehensive boycott of American goods. But it will not do to be too cynical about the Open Door policy. It was a legitimate expression of American "sympathetic" interests in China, and reflected a desire to see an end to conventional colonialism and an independent, friendly China. The European powers sometimes shared these sentiments, but they did not always choose to make them a categorical and public principle of foreign policy.

THE BEGINNING OF THE END OF EUROPEAN ASCENDANCY IN EAST ASIA

On the surface, the scramble for concessions and the allied occupation of Beijing following the Boxer uprising represented the zenith of European influence in China. In fact, this power was more tenuous than it seemed. There was a change of axis in international relations in East Asia in the early years of the 20th century. The European powers, including Russia, had stretched their economic, technological, and military resources to the limit and, generally speaking, were in no position to take over any more territory. British naval and maritime supremacy, long the principal factor of East Asian politics, had begun a gradual decline and would soon concentrate in European waters where Germany was vigorously developing its sea power. Britain's power in China and East Asia was not by any means spent—it was to some extent preserved through an alliance with Japan—but it began to lose its vigor in the early 20th century. By way of contrast, the United States, apparently only able to issue notes at the close of the 19th century, increasingly made its power felt in the region. In this context, American participation in the eight-power occupation of Beijing marked a stage in the rise to global power of the United States.

Yet even more striking during this period was the rise of Japan. In 1902, Tokyo signed a treaty with London, the first to be concluded between a Western and non-Western power on a basis of equality. It insulated Britain from the threat posed by the rise of other naval powers in the region, but was much more important to Japan. The treaty acknowledged Japanese interests in Korea and promised British neutrality in the event of war with Russia. It was therefore an essential prelude to the Russo-Japanese War of 1904–1905 which almost overnight secured world power status and full equality for Japan. Tokyo became an imperialist power with colonies (in all but name) in Korea and Taiwan, and valuable "rights" in southern Manchuria. The days when Japan could be denied the spoils of war, as happened in 1898 when Russia, France, and Germany insisted Tokyo give up what it had exacted from China in the Treaty of Shimonoseki, had gone.

This first defeat of a Western by an Eastern power was formalized in the Treaty of Portsmouth, which the belligerents signed in 1905. They were brought together by the good offices of President Theodore Roosevelt. Roosevelt's efforts won him a Nobel peace prize, but more important, they marked the first interaction of American, European, and Asian politics.

That a dispute between Russia and Japan over Korea and parts of China was resolved in the United States foreshadowed the global politics of the later 20th century. The Treaty of Portsmouth also marked the earliest stirrings of unease between Tokyo and Washington. On a practical level, a section of Japanese opinion was irritated by the American failure to extract a financial indemnity from the Russians at Portsmouth. Such indemnities had long been a feature of previous wars in the region, and the Japanese saw no grounds for exception in this case. In the United States, on the other hand, there were the first signs of concern that the Japanese *samurai* tradition, strengthened by growing economic power, might present a challenge to American interests.

On a more theoretical plane, two embryonic, competing nationalisms began to develop in Washington and Tokyo in the early 20th century. One involved a pan-Asian revival of Asian values; the other, a westward course of empire based on liberal democratic politics and free market economics. There were many years to go before the exponents of these views came to blows. When they did, it was only partly over such grandiose visions. But such opposing views helped reinforce the main theme of U.S. involvement in East Asia during the next 40 years: growing closeness to China; growing coolness toward Japan.

COOPERATION AND COMPETITION IN CHINA

What has been described as American "sympathetic" interests in China grew appreciably in the early 20th century. They were symbolized by the American missionary effort and, what often stemmed from the same thing, programs of educational aid designed to help China help itself. Such programs were partly financed by the remission of the U.S. share of the Boxer uprising indemnity in 1904 and 1924.

There were 150 American missionaries in China in 1872. By 1898, this figure had increased to 967. Just over 20 years later Americans accounted for one half of the estimated 6,600 Protestant missionaries in China. They were the largest group of Americans Chinese came into contact with prior to World War II. The same period also saw the climax of the American educational effort. Cornell University aided Nanjing University; Princeton and Harvard supported Yanjing. From 1913 money from the Rockefeller Foundation helped create Asia's finest teaching hospital, Beijing University Medical College. By the early 1930s, around $37 million had been invested in the college. Selskar M. Gunn, a Rockefeller Foundation vice president during the 1930s, gave expression to the belief which underlay both these secular and spiritual endeavors when he said: "China has become plastic after many centuries of isolation and rigid conventionalism." Again, the image of China in American eyes was conducive to America's transforming role: Washington would ensure China's territorial integrity while American philanthropy would mold this "plastic" nation into a modern, friendly state.

Meanwhile, however, the diplomacy of imperialism in East Asia had been unsettled by World War I. To be sure, the war's consequences in Asia were not as severe as in Europe, but among its results was the further decline of Russian influence as czarist rule gave way to Alexander Kerensky's government, the Bolshevik seizure of power, and two years of fierce civil war. British power was also attenuated by the exhausting struggle on the European continent. For Japan, however, the European powers absorption with the defeat of imperial Germany created new opportunities for expansion. With allied approval, Tokyo seized the German concessions in Shandong, and followed this with the Twenty-One Demands which showed Western diplomats the full extent of Japanese ambitions in China. Japan's determination to retain what it had gained from Germany in China sparked a new kind of nationalism which rocked the Beijing government and proved a major irritant in East Asian politics. In particular, it marked an important stage in the worsening of relations between Tokyo and Washington.

American distaste for the imperialist disputes of Europe militated against U.S. involvement in World War I. As was to happen in World War II, however, self-complacent isolationism gave way to intervention. Washington began to feel that only when military autocracy threatened Europe was democracy at home in danger. American power eventually tipped the scales in favor of the allies. But prior to this, President Woodrow Wilson had enunciated in January 1918 his Fourteen Points, which he envisaged would eradicate the basis for future war. Whatever their implications for Europe, the fact that Shandong was not restored to Chinese rule at the Versailles Conference (1919) showed that Wilson's principles had only limited applications when it came to non-European peoples.

U.S. acquiescence in Japan's hold over Shandong weighed heavily on the conscience of those who saw the United States as China's special friend. But it was not until the Washington Conference in 1921 that Japan, reluctantly, gave up its hold on the peninsula. The Washington Conference, organized on the initiative of Secretary of State Charles Evans Hughes, was an attempt to revise the diplomacy of imperialism and create a new international order in East Asia based on cooperation. It involved the abrogation of the Anglo-Japanese alliance and, insofar as it called for a ratio of naval vessels at 5:5:3 on the part of the United States, Britain, and Japan, it can be seen as another stage in the substitution of American for British power in Asia. The Open Door policy was reaffirmed at Washington, and the powers looked toward the creation of a united, independent China. They did not, however, feel it was yet time to abolish extraterritoriality or grant China tariff autonomy. The Washington settlement has been regarded as an Asian equivalent of the Versailles settlement in Europe. Both called for collective security and internationalism in trade; both were undermined about the same time by the aggression of powerful, militarized states.

Immediately after the Washington Conference, however, Soviet influence, especially in China, seemed the greatest challenge to the new Asian order. As opposed to the revision of imperialist diplomacy offered by the Western powers at Washington, Soviet leaders practiced revolutionary diplomacy, encouraging nationalist and revolutionary forces in China to unite the country and expel foreign influence. China's national revolutionaries soon found they had less in common than either they or the Soviet Union thought, and the experiment quickly degenerated into protracted civil war.

But the different paths to modernization and independence held out to China by Washington and Moscow in the mid-1920s foreshadowed the greater, more protracted struggle between West and East, capitalism and communism, that dominated Asia and Europe after World War II.

While from the U.S. point of view the Soviet Union remained an important factor in East Asian politics during the 1930s, the real concern was nevertheless with the restless militarism of Japan. The basis of the Washington settlement was gradually eroded by economic slump and, what was often a consequence, the collapse of parliamentary government and the growth of military power. The fact that both censure and persuasion failed to dislodge the Japanese army from Manchuria following its invasion in 1931, suggested that the era of cooperation was coming to an end. This is not to say that the United States was ready to intervene in Asian affairs any more than it was in Europe where the policy of isolation was regarded as especially virtuous. Indeed, a process of *withdrawal* from Asia began in 1934 when the Tydings-McDuffie Act changed the Philippines from a colony into a self-governing commonwealth and promised full independence by 1945. With this act, the United States became the only big power to cede independence voluntarily to an Asian country and set a timetable for its attainment.

But against this apparent willingness to at least reduce American commitment to Asia must be set the growth of popular sympathy toward China. This was especially marked when Japan extended its occupation of Manchuria into an attack on China proper in the summer of 1937. Pro-Chinese and anti-Japanese feeling crystallized further at the close of the year when Japanese aircraft sank the United States gunship *Panay* while it was sailing down the Yangtze River with Chinese refugees on board. Opinion polls in the United States showed a much greater willingness to fight for China against Japan than for the European democracies against fascism.

Until 1938, however, it seemed unlikely that such fighting would take place. U.S. policymakers were not thinking in terms of military commitment to Asia any more than they were to Europe, even though there was greater public support for the former. Indeed, in spite of such bodies as the United States Committee for Non-Participation in Japanese Aggression—an organization with a curiously neutral, isolationist name—vital raw materials continued to reach Japan from the United States until mid-1940. Nonetheless, a new U.S. policy toward Asia was in the making during 1939–1940. Washington began to move from a passive to an active role, although exactly when it happened remains disputed by historians. An important sign of this change came at the close of 1938 when the United States extended a $25 million loan to China—the first material pressure the United States applied to constrain Japan. Six months later, the bulk of the U.S. fleet was assigned, fatefully as it turned out, to Pacific waters.

Alongside these practical steps were key speeches by President Franklin Roosevelt that helped erode powerful isolationist sentiments at home. The

United States could not be a "lone island in a world dominated by force," the president told his audience at the University of Virginia in the summer of 1940. And in a "fireside chat" in December of the same year, the United States was pictured as the "arsenal of democracy" aiding the democracies in their struggle with the Axis powers. These speeches demonstrate America's decision to support the beleaguered democracies, in particular Britain. Their relevance to U.S. involvement in Asia stems from the fact that Washington had begun to couple developments in Asia with world politics (i.e., European politics) in a new global concern with security.

With the outbreak of war in Europe, Britain and France were absorbed increasingly in European affairs. Even the Royal Navy's resources were unable to guard all of Britain's overseas possessions. From the U.S. point of view, there were worrying revelations of British weakness: notably, the closure, in June 1940 and at Japan's request, of the Burma Road, a vital lifeline to unoccupied China. The European war also made European colonies in Asia vulnerable to Japan. There was a growing feeling that the United States would have to move to counter Japanese aggression. But any U.S. action would not be for the sake of Asia itself. For all the genuine sympathy and self-delusion about China, the United States and Japan did not fall out over Tokyo's violations of the Open Door policy. Rather, Japan's regional attempts at hegemony were seen as of a piece with those of Germany and Italy in Europe. German Nazis and Japanese militarists were part of the same conspiracy—they were in formal, though inconsequential, alliance from September 1940—and had to be stopped.

U.S. moves against Japan are best understood therefore in the context of a determination to beat Adolf Hitler and his allies. Indeed, had the Axis powers not threatened European democracy and Japan launched a first strike against the United States at Pearl Harbor in December 1941, Tokyo's ambitions in Asia may well have faced little physical resistance from the United States. In the event, they ushered in an era of fundamental U.S. involvement in Asia and the Pacific which resulted in the destruction of Japanese military power.

THE ERA OF FUNDAMENTAL COMMITMENT: THE STRUGGLE AGAINST JAPAN

Japan's alliance with the Axis powers and the logic of its conquests in Asia made war with the United States and the established imperial powers inevitable. Tokyo's demand for raw materials to sustain its ambitions on the Asian continent meant that it would have to seize European colonies in Southeast Asia and deal with United States naval power in the Pacific. The attack on Pearl Harbor temporarily secured Japan a free hand. But though devastating, it was not a knockout blow. Coupled with Germany's declaration of war against the United States amid Japanese euphoria of the attack, it made only one thing certain: the inevitability of Japan's defeat.

Yet by the spring of 1942, Japan appeared invincible. U.S. air power in the Pacific, based in the Philippines, was crushed in a lightning raid shortly after Pearl Harbor. The next day, the British battleships *Repulse* and *Prince of Wales* were sunk off the coast of Malaya. The European empires collapsed in the face of stunning offensives. Japan soon threatened India in the north and Australia in the south. China was cut off from the outside world. After bitter fighting, American and Filipino forces under General Douglas MacArthur were driven out of the Philippines. Japan achieved overnight a degree of control over Southeast and East Asia which had proved quite beyond any of the traditional imperial powers during the previous century.

The sudden collapse of European power in Asia at one level brought an uncharacteristic simplification to international politics in East Asia. From the start of 1942, only two powers counted: Japan and the United States. This was not easily accepted in Britain, by now the only power with significant interests in Asia which had not succumbed to the Japanese military. British officials resented reports from their embassy in Chongqing, suggesting that ordinary Chinese now regarded the United States as China's only friend. Indeed, Anglo-American coolness was an important subtheme of the war in the East. American sensitivity to the idea but not necessarily to the practice of imperialism, led to suspicion about the real purpose of the South East Asian Command (SEAC) set up by the British in Calcutta in August 1943. Many Americans, including noted anglophobe General Joseph Stilwell who was deputy supreme commander, felt SEAC was an acronym for "Save England's Asian Colonies." Stilwell's mistrust was shared by MacArthur.

But while Winston Churchill's government made no secret of the fact that it was not in business to preside over the dissolution of the British Empire, either in Asia or elsewhere, in the immediate term there were far more pressing concerns in Europe and North Africa. And to be sure, the defeat of Nazism was also a priority of the United States. This was not altered by Pearl Harbor. During the early stages of U.S. military involvement in the war, first place in the allocation of resources went to the deployment of strategic air power for strikes against German industry. Only when plans for a second front in Europe were shelved did the U.S. command authorize offensives in the Pacific theater of war. These offensives, notably the naval battles of the Coral Sea and Midway, began to turn the tide against Japan and paved the way for a two-pronged "island-hopping" attack on the home islands. The first was a thrust across the Central Pacific through the Marshalls, the Carolines, and the Marianas to Iwo Jima. The second, north from New Caledonia in the South Pacific, returned MacArthur to the Philippines in June 1944. MacArthur insisted on the early liberation of the Philippines—which had admittedly been promised independence—with the kind of dogged determination Americans found unacceptable in British officials who demanded that former colonies be returned to British sovereignty following their liberation from Japanese rule.

CHINA IN U.S. STRATEGY

The allied strategy of Europe first, the Pacific second, and, as it seemed, China last, irritated Chiang Kai-shek, the beleaguered Chinese leader. In fact, the policy stemmed from an accurate perception of China's military role. To be sure, China had been invaded as early as 1937 and had consequently suffered more than most from Japan's aggression. But it was also clear to many observers, Stilwell possibly excluded, that the most the Chinese Nationalist armies could do was tie down large numbers of Japanese troops. Chiang's best forces were blockading the Communists or watching the semiindependent forces of regional leaders on whom the generalissimo was now forced to rely. To expect this situation to change was to show a lack of perception, a naiveté even, concerning the nature of the Nationalist regime. Stilwell thought more could be expected of the Communist forces in north central China. But they, too, were mindful of domestic politics, and any attempt to establish even a loose American command over them was bound to fall foul of Chiang. These military realities eventually meant that China was bypassed in the advance on Japan, leaving the Nationalists, with U.S. support, to compete with the Communists in the struggle to fill the vacuum created by the defeat of Japan.

This somewhat phlegmatic view of Chinese military capabilities had long been understood by the British to mean that China was relatively unimportant in the task of defeating Japan. China's collapse was obviously to be avoided. But the idea that the China of Chiang Kai-shek should be considered as one of the "powers" was absurd from London's point of view. Quite a different view occupied the minds of policymakers and public alike in the United States. The myth of a free China had been building gradually in the United States during the late 1930s. It reached new heights with the triumphal wartime American tours of Madame Chiang Kai-shek, once a *Time* magazine "Wife of the Year." From Washington's point of view, it was quite appropriate to recognize China as one of the great powers, as happened at the Moscow meeting of foreign ministers in October 1943. The formal renunciation, at the Cairo meeting the following month, of the privileges deriving from the unequal treaties, was a natural corollary.

There were many facets to the United States' China illusion. That Chinese farmers were land-loving democrats in the American mold, that the Communists were at heart agrarian democrats, and that, above all, China could be turned into a major, friendly power in the region given adequate American assistance, were chief among them. The last of these in the end proved the most calamitous. China's "great power" status was something of an American fiction. To realize it the United States was obliged to intervene in Chinese domestic politics. When this failed and China was considered "lost," there were serious consequences in terms of both U.S. domestic politics and foreign policy.

PLANNING FOR POSTWAR ASIA

Although the U.S. Air Force started regular bombing of the Japanese home islands beginning in late 1944, there were no illusions in Washington about the difficulty of forcing a quick unconditional surrender by Japan. Roosevelt therefore had hinted during 1944 that the Soviet Union should enter the war against Japan once Germany had been beaten in the west. Soviet participation, along with many other proposals which had a lasting impact on East Asia, was discussed at the Yalta Conference by Roosevelt,

Stalin, and Churchill in February 1945. Regarding East Asia in particular the Yalta Conference provided the formal framework of a bipolar world which seemed inevitable once Japanese power had finally been crushed. In short, the protagonists at Yalta envisaged that the United States would be dominant in the Pacific and in Japan, while Soviet influence would prevail in northeastern Asia. A unified and independent China would be a gray area where Soviet and American influence would meet. Hopefully, the two powers would cooperate rather than collide in China. To this end, Stalin was persuaded to sign a treaty with Chiang Kai-shek acknowledging the legitimacy of the Nationalist government. Little was said at Yalta about Korea, except that some sort of trusteeship was envisaged. It was also assumed, though not stated, that France and Britain would relinquish their Asian colonies following the defeat of Japan.

Washington's immediate task, however, was to secure the unconditional surrender of Japan called for at the Potsdam Conference in the summer of 1945. From the spring of that year, Japanese cities had been subject to unprecedented bombing. In one particular raid, Tokyo was all but destroyed by incendiary bombs. But it was not until the first atomic bomb flattened Hiroshima on August 6 and the Soviet Red Army attacked Japan's Kwangtung forces two days later, that the peace party in Tokyo began to get the upper hand. Once satisfied that the allies were unlikely to insist on the abolition of imperial institutions, and mindful of the threat of a Soviet invasion, Emperor Hirohito conceded to his subjects that "the war situation has developed not necessarily to Japan's advantage." Japan would have to "endure the unendurable."

U.S. ASCENDANCY IN ASIA

In terms of intact economic power, the United States was the only real victor when Germany and Japan surrendered in 1945. A principal cause of the defeat of the Axis powers had been the swift gearing of the American economy to war production, and the scientific and technological developments that flowed from this change. It was thus no surprise that, following the defeat of Japan, the U.S. presence in Asia was very different from the situation five years earlier, America was inevitably drawn into the vacuum created by the collapse of Japan.

In the first place, the United States "occupied" Japan, introducing a novel form of Western presence in Asia. Although nominally an allied operation, U.S. authority in Japan was unaffected by its partners. This was either because of relative disinterest, as in the case of Britain, or because Washington expressly ruled it out, as in the case of the Soviet Union. A different form of U.S. occupation appeared in Korea south of the 38th parallel, where American troops confronted those of the Soviet Union north of the line. In China, meanwhile, substantial American efforts were directed toward creating the united China envisaged at Yalta. In the Philippines, which had been devastated by the war, independence from American rule was followed by the signing of an agreement in 1947 providing for U.S. military bases on the islands.

Yet in spite of these new interests in the region, U.S. demobilization proceeded at a rapid pace. By early 1947, the army had been reduced from eight million to one million; the navy from three million to one and one-half million; and the air force from more than 200 to fewer than 50 combat groups. Comforted by its monopoly of the atomic bomb, Washington at first felt able to execute its new responsibilities without vast conventional forces.

THE "LOSS" OF CHINA

However, the bomb soon proved all but useless in the achievement of regional objectives in U.S. foreign policy in Asia or elsewhere. Certainly it was far too unwieldy a weapon to play the delicate role required in China. Here, U.S. policy was designed to produce a coalition government. This involved a long mediation effort by George Marshall, one of the architects of victory in World War II. It failed primarily because the two protagonists in the civil conflict had no intention of sharing power. Divisions between the Communists and Nationalists, imperfectly understood by many Americans, were too deep and bitter to be easily resolved by powersharing arrangements. But it also failed because Marshall's well-intentioned efforts were prejudiced by U.S. re-equipping of Chiang's armies. In terms of American domestic politics, this made the defeat of U.S. policy in China even more difficult to accept. The fact was, however, in the context of overall U.S. foreign policy, China was not considered important enough to warrant direct intervention. At the same time, very largely because of sympathetic interests, it was considered too important to abandon. U.S. policy therefore faced a no-win situation.

By August 1948 both President Harry Truman and Marshall had long abandoned mediation and expressed publicly their opposition to Communist participation in any future Chinese government. Mao Zedong, meanwhile, identified the Communist cause with that of proletarian internationalism led by Moscow. As the People's Liberation Army overwhelmed Chiang's demoralized forces, American hopes sank along with the aid squandered by the Nationalists.

Taken in isolation, the collapse of Chiang's control might not have been so important in American eyes. But it acquired a new seriousness against the backdrop of events in Europe. While Mao's armies were winning the Chinese civil war, Eastern Europe had fallen under Soviet control. Greece, it seemed, was heading for the same fate. And on the eve of Mao's victory, the Soviet Union broke the American monopoly of the atomic bomb. These setbacks for U.S. foreign policy, coupled with vocal Republicans sore at being out of presidential power for so long, made for a new climate of suspicion at home. Overseas, they made for a foreign policy which regarded communism as monolithic and the idea that a country could be both communist *and* independent—especially one like China with supposedly powerful affinities with the United States—a contradiction in terms.

In this context China was indeed "lost." Conservatives wanted an explanation and found it in a conspiracy of communist-leaning State Department officials. Subsequently, the foreign policy establishment, along with many other areas of American life, fell prey to the hysteria of Joseph McCarthy. As the example of Greece showed so clearly, the United States had moved decisively into the vacuum created by the decline of Britain. In 1947, Truman pledged U.S. support to free peoples everywhere who were under pressure from armed minorities or outside pressures. This meant containment of the Soviet Union, whose leader, Stalin, was increasingly spoken of as another Hitler. This time, however, there would be no concessions.

CONTAINMENT AND ROLLBACK

Yet it was not until June 1950, when North Korean forces suddenly invaded South Korea, that the struggle against communism was understood to be truly global. To be sure, the previous April had seen the publication of a National Security Council paper which spoke of the need for an immediate and large-scale buildup of U.S. power as a deterrent to the Soviet Union. But a few months earlier, Secretary of State Dean Acheson had excluded Taiwan together with all of continental Asia from the U.S. defense perimeter. The North Korean attack ended these ambiguities in U.S. Asian policy. It showed that although Europe might be the cockpit of the Cold War, the real fighting was going to be in Asia.

For Koreans the war of 1950–1953 was just the latest in a series of calamities. Their country had been bitterly fought over in the mid-1890s and again 10 years later. From 1910 until 1945 it was ruled harshly by Japan. When the Japanese withdrew, the peninsula was divided arbitrarily at a point for which there was no geographical, historical, or cultural basis. With the North Korean attack, the country became a theater of struggle between the superpowers that left between three and four million dead.

The speed of the North Korean advance in the summer of 1950 nearly administered a knockout blow to the defending forces. But U.S.-led troops, nominally under United Nations command, quickly recovered lost ground in bitter fighting. By late October, General MacArthur had taken Pyongyang and approached the Yalu River. Containment seemed about to give way to rollback. Such fancies were soon dispelled by the sudden intervention of Chinese "volunteers." Only five years after its wartime alliance, the United States was at war with China in a conflict that shaped the attitudes of the two countries toward each other for the next two decades. It was indeed an ironic fulfillment of U.S. policy of creating a strong, united China.

By mid-1951, U.S. forces again established a defensive line along the 38th parallel. But the fighting dragged on for two more years until President Dwight Eisenhower threatened to use the bomb against the North. This threat, combined with war weariness on the Chinese side and pressure from the Soviet Union, resulted in an armistice in July 1953.

LEANING AGAINST CHINA: ENTANGLING ALLIANCES

The war in Korea naturally hardened the United States' already inflexible policy toward China. Washington was now determined to isolate Beijing, which was henceforth perceived, somewhat simplistically, as an agent of the Soviet Union and thus America's chief Asian adversary. Soon after the North Korean invasion, Truman ordered the United States Seventh Fleet into the Taiwan Strait both to restrain Chiang Kai-shek and to forestall an expected attack from the mainland. For the next 20 years it was the principal task of U.S. foreign policy in Asia to refuse to recognize Beijing, exclude the People's Republic of China from the United Nations, support Chiang Kai-shek, and encircle the mainland with military bases and formal alliances.

The first of these alliances was a mutual defense treaty in August 1951 between the United States and the Philippines. Washington's need for secure military bases in the islands meant helping the Filipinos put down the Huk insurgency, most of whose members were drawn from the wartime Anti-Japanese People's Liberation Army. This was largely achieved by 1954, thanks to American backing for the anticorruption drive and rural development program of Ramon Magsaysay, the Philippine president. Instability and insurgency, however, remained prominent features of Filipino political life long after the Huk rebellion was crushed.

A few days after the treaty with the Philippines was signed, Washington concluded the tripartite ANZUS pact with Australia and New Zealand. This alliance with two Commonwealth countries was another striking example of the substitution of U.S. influence for that of Britain in East Asia and the Pacific. It provided for collaboration between the three parties in the event of "an armed attack in the Pacific area."

The policy of containment also quickened the development of amicable relations between the United States and Japan. This process was underway before a shot was fired in Korea and was one of the most remarkable developments of the postwar world. During the occupation, U.S. authority was imposed easily over a Japanese government largely intact and still functioning. By the time the United States withdrew in March 1952, Japan had a new, supposedly nonnationalistic education system and a democratic constitution. In legal terms at least, the emperor was just a figurehead. The constitution renounced war and stipulated that Japan would not maintain armed forces other than those for self-defense. In September 1951, the former belligerents signed a mutual security pact. Tokyo requested the retention of U.S. forces in Japan as a defense against attack from overseas, and Washington expressed the hope that Japan would "increasingly assume responsibility for its own defense."

South Korea quickly became another of the key links in the chain around China. In 1953, Washington and Seoul concluded a mutual defense treaty thus cementing a relationship which, by the eve of Sino-American rapprochement in 1970, had secured South Korea an estimated $3 billion of military aid and $5 billion in ordinary economic assistance.

A further, and from China's point of view, even tighter link was forged when Washington's support for the Nationalist government on Taiwan was formalized with the signing of another mutual defense treaty in 1954.

SUPPORTING THE VIETNAMESE "DOMINO"

The United States was not content simply to build a *cordon sanitaire* around Chinese communism. It was also necessary to shore up countries prey to internal turmoil and thus vulnerable to communist takeover. In Southeast Asia this was designed to prevent the collapse of the "dominoes"—the noncommunist countries in the region. Adherence to the domino theory meant U.S. involvement in what were essentially revolutionary civil wars associated with the struggle for national independence. But this was not how Washington viewed them. Rather they were aspects of the global struggle between democracy and monolithic communism. And wherever communism was considered to have advanced, U.S. security interests were deemed to have suffered. American involvement, therefore, was not undertaken for the sake of the country itself, but in order to guarantee broader geopolitical and strategic interests. There was a feeling that if one failed to fight communism in Southeast Asia, one might soon have to do so in California.

In this context, the United States could not ignore the weakening of French authority and resolve in Vietnam. Indeed, the country came to be seen as a vital testing ground of American commitment. It became a laboratory for turning economic and military power into political influence. Since the stakes were thought to be so high, it was quite acceptable to prop up unrepresentative social and political elites, irrespective of the fact that they were often symbols of a discredited traditional pattern of authority.

There are many ironies associated with America's longest Asian war. Outside of the Philippines, the United States had little significant contact with Southeast Asia until World War II. Even then, American involvement was confined and temporary. In 1943, Roosevelt said that Indochina should be placed under a trusteeship after the war. He charged that the French had had the region for one hundred years but the people were worse off than they were at the beginning. By 1950, however, Washington's view of French policy had not changed. The development of the Cold War in Europe, the rise of Mao in China, and communist uprisings in Burma, Malaya, the Philippines, and Indonesia all lent a new interpretation to the startling successes of Ho Chi Minh against the French. One month before the outbreak of hostilities in Korea, the United States extended military and economic aid to the French. Four years later, the United States was financing about 80 percent of the cost of the war, clearly with little effect. As the French collapse loomed at Dien Bien Phu, Secretary of State John Foster Dulles implied that U.S. air power, and perhaps even low-yield nuclear weapons, might be used to secure a reprieve.

As it turned out, a reprieve was won at the Geneva Conference in 1954 which provided for French withdrawal and the partition of Vietnam at the 17th parallel. The Cold War thus produced two Vietnams, just as it had two Germanys, two Koreas, and two Chinas. The United States responded with the Southeast Asia Treaty Organization (SEATO)—an Asian equivalent to the North Atlantic Treaty Organization (NATO) to restrain China—

and increased support for Ngo Dinh Diem in the southern half of Vietnam. But Diem's family rule, which involved vigorous drives against armed religious sects and the Chinese community, alienated important sections of the population and led to the growth of terrorism and communist rural insurgency. This in turn required greater backing from the United States as American politicians, aware of the domestic consequences of the "loss" of China, determined not to "lose" Vietnam.

By the time Diem was assasinated in November 1963, there were 15,000 American personnel in South Vietnam. Two years later 125,000 men were on active service; by the close of 1966 this figure had risen to more than 400,000. Meanwhile, systematic bombing of North Vietnam on an unprecedented scale had begun in an attempt to neutralize opposition to the Saigon government. Moreover, neighboring Laos and Cambodia were quickly dragged into what was becoming a war for all Indochina. Geography probably made it impossible for these two countries to avoid direct involvement in the Vietnam War. But in the struggle against monolithic communism the United States viewed the idea of neutrality—especially when espoused by small nations—with extreme prejudice.

Washington had undermined the only genuine opportunity to create a neutral and unified Laos in 1957. And when U.S. ground troops were committed in Vietnam, communist-held areas of Laos were bombed heavily. Indeed, the scale of American intervention in Indochina was brought into sharp relief by the bombing campaign in this tiny, landlocked country. More than 2 million tons of bombs were dropped on Laos. This was more than the total tonnage dropped by American aircraft throughout World War II. The United States also used guerrilla bands formed from ethnic minorities in Laos to support the royal Laotian army in its fight against the Pathet Lao.

Cambodia, which under Prince Norodom Sihanouk combined a measure of neutrality with the presence of "sanctuaries" used by Vietnamese communist forces, was also bombed heavily, and secretly, from 1969. The following year, Sihanouk was overthrown by Lon Nol, who had a more combative attitude toward both the Vietnamese communists and the Cambodian Khmer Rouge whom the Americans urged him to fight. This escalation of the conflict eventually left Cambodia devastated and paved the way for the rise to power of the Khmer Rouge.

However, by 1968, although massive intervention had prevented the collapse of South Vietnam and even enabled it to survive the communist Tet offensive, it could not continue indefinitely, American involvement in Vietnam was becoming increasingly unpopular at home. Whereas the "loss" of China led to an acrimonious examination of U.S. foreign policy, the scale and consequences of intervention in Vietnam raised questions about the very nature of a society that could produce such a conflict. No American war since the Civil War a century earlier had proved so divisive at home. One of the reasons for this unpopularity was television. Indeed, some analysts have argued that the graphic images of the conflict in Vietnam portrayed by television—the first war to be covered systematically by the medium—eventually secured the Vietcong victories they could not have won on the battlefield alone. This view, sometimes held by those who believed that the United States should have done more rather than less on the battlefield, gained popularity when Vietnam, along with Cambodia and Laos, fell under Soviet influence.

Domestic political pressure undoubtedly played a part in the attempts of President Richard Nixon and Henry Kissinger to secure withdrawal from Vietnam. They did this by starting peace talks while building up the South Vietnamese forces. As this process got underway, and ironically at the same time as the war was spread into Cambodia, Nixon hinted at a new United States policy toward Asia. Known as the Guam Doctrine, it reaffirmed American intentions to keep treaty commitments, maintain the nuclear umbrella, and offer aid against communist insurrection. However, Nixon insisted that there would have to be an indigenous solution to insurgency, and that U.S. ground troops would not be committed.

THE GREAT POWER TRIANGLE IN ASIA

Although public opinion created pressure for withdrawal from Vietnam, this withdrawal and the Guam Doctrine with which it was associated, was based on a much more fundamental change in U.S. foreign policy behind which there were no domestic pressures. This was rapprochement with the People's Republic of China. The realignment of American policy, symbolized by Nixon's 1972 visit to Beijing, marked another major change in the axis of international politics in Asia. From at least the late 1950s it had become clear to observers that communism was far from monolithic. The unsettling effects in China of Nikita Khrushchev's 1956 denunciation of Stalin, and Soviet uneasiness over China's claim to have set up a communist society as a result of the 1958 Great Leap Forward, were not the world's best kept secrets. That all might not be well between China and the Soviet Union was also apparent from Moscow's failure to back Beijing's attempts to take Quemoy from the Nationalists in 1958, and its guarded support for India during the 1962 border war with China. Yet Washington policymakers were slow to pick up these signals. It was not until the war of words between Moscow and Beijing was stepped up in the mid-1960s that the old policy of isolating China, based ultimately on the belief that Beijing was a puppet of Moscow, was shown to be at best anachronistic and at worst seriously misguided. A warmer relationship between Washington and Beijing could have evolved during this period, had it not been for the Vietnam War and China's absorption in the domestic upheavels of the Cultural Revolution.

As the Vietnam War dragged on, however, and China and the Soviet Union were brought to the brink of nuclear war over their own border dispute, there was a genuine community of interests between Washington and Beijing. Both sought a reduction of tensions in the region. Washington was concerned to win President Nguyen Van Thieu of South Vietnam a "decent interval" between U.S. withdrawal and the inevitable communist takeover, and reduce its military commitment generally in Asia. Beijing sought backing against Soviet ambitions in East Asia and the withdrawal of American support for Taiwan pending eventual reunification.

Some of these goals were realized. Although the United States continued to bomb North Vietnam after the signing of the Shanghai Communiqué of 1972, and remained involved in the anticommunist struggle in Laos and Cambodia, Nixon formally ended U.S. participation in the Vietnam War in January 1973. Three years later U.S. influence in Southeast Asia was sharply curtailed by the voluntary withdrawal of military facilities in Thailand and a series of communist victories in Indochina.

For its part, China secured U.S. recognition that there was but one China with Taiwan as a part, and a promise to reduce U.S. military installations on the island. Thus the way was paved for the termination of the mutual defense treaty with Taiwan, and the formal switch of U.S. diplomatic relations from Taipei to Beijing which took place in January 1979. This did not signal the end of American commitment to Taiwan. But the Shanghai Communiqué effectively de-internationalized the Taiwan issue. Consequently, it became more of a purely Chinese problem than at any time since the arrival of Chiang Kai-shek's defeated troops in 1949. This was a heavy blow for Taiwan's rulers, long used to unconditional, though not uncritical, American support. But, buoyed by the island's economic strength, they began a cautious program of political reform in 1986 which, subject to reactions from China, held out the prospect of Taiwan's international rehabilitation.

RENEWED COLD WAR?

In spite of the mutual benefits accruing from the resumption of relations between Washington and Beijing—and here one must not overlook the feeling in certain American circles that the United States had once again linked hands with its "natural" ally in the region—the implicitly anti-Soviet tone of the rapprochement hardly checked Moscow's authority in Asia. By the end of 1975, communist victories in Vietnam, Cambodia, and Laos pointed to a worrying expansion of Soviet influence for both Washington and Beijing. The domino theory quickly acquired new adherents when, immediately after signing a treaty of friendship and cooperation with the Soviet Union in November 1978, Vietnam invaded Cambodia and replaced the Khmer Rouge government with one of its own choosing. Any benefits this might have brought the people of Cambodia by at least toppling the genocidal rule of Pol Pot were inconsiderable factors in regional power politics. China sought to "teach Vietnam a lesson" by launching a limited border war in February 1979. But as it happened, this proved more of an education for Beijing than Hanoi. China, in common with the United States and other governments supposedly more attached to human rights, kept Pol Pot and the Khmer Rouge in business as the most formidable military faction in the Cambodian resistance to Vietnamese rule. Tragically, the continued strength of the Khmer Rouge, only partially camouflaged by the low profile of Pol Pot and the high visibility of Prince Sihanouk, official leader of the resistance coalition, remained a major obstacle to the resolution of the Cambodian problem in the 1980s.

These developments in Southeast Asia occurred against the backdrop of the new approach to U.S. foreign policy by President Jimmy Carter. In general terms, the Carter administration sought to substitute the notion of world order and American moral leadership for the old doctrine of containing the Soviet Union. For conservative critics, bolstered by the spectacular failure to free kidnapped American embassy staff in Tehran, this was far too self-effacing an approach. The Vietnam experience could hardly be forgotten, but too much emphasis on the supposed limits of U.S. power was regarded as unhealthy. This case was strengthened by the failure of Moscow to play by the new rules espoused by Carter. Indeed, the projection of Soviet power into Southeast Asia during the 1970s was complemented at the end of the decade by Moscow's intervention in Afghanistan. This was regarded as a very serious matter in both Washington and Beijing. Analysts tended to overwork the analogy with Vietnam in the early stages of the Soviet intervention, but there were some unmistakable similarities: a poor country, fought over not for itself but for wider geopolitical interests; technologically-superior occupying forces tied down by guerilla units financed by external powers; and an enormous, debilitating commitment for the invading power.

It was therefore in the shadow of a series of perceived failures in foreign policy that President Ronald Reagan took office in 1981. The new administration regarded the 1970s as the decade of neglect, and was committed to the resurgence of U.S. military power and traditional world leadership. High on the agenda in Asia was a determination to support the guerilla resistance against the Soviet-backed government in Kabul. By 1987, this operation had become the Central Intelligence Agency's biggest covert commitment. It also meant that South Asia acquired a higher profile in U.S. foreign policy.

Traditionally a British sphere of influence, South Asia had always been second to East and Southeast Asia in American priorities. However, Washington had hardly ignored the region. Attention focused on Pakistan, which was seen as a vital, vulnerable link between the Middle East and Southeast Asia. If the Soviet Union advanced in this region, perhaps in search of oil or "warm water," both NATO and SEATO would be outflanked. In the Baghdad Pact of February 1955, therefore, Pakistan was enrolled in the Middle East Treaty Organization (METO). This alliance brought together Britain, Turkey, Iran, Iraq, and Pakistan. Theoretically, it created a northern tier of defense against communism along 3,000 miles of the Soviet Union's southern border.

Although it supported the pact, the United States itself was not a signatory. Washington felt that full participation would complicate the already difficult objective of reconciling support for Israel with the desire to win the Arab world to the cause of the West. However, Egypt's growing coolness toward the West, the Suez affair, and the 1958 revolution in Iraq, led to a firm U.S. commitment to the "reliable" METO members. In August 1959, the alliance (minus Iraq) was renamed the Central Treaty Organization (CENTO). This strengthened Pakistan, South Asia's weakest state, and gave it confidence with respect to India, its giant neighbor. Washington had reason to be concerned with India. Bound to the Soviet Union by a treaty of peace and friendship, India was the only Asian country outside of the Soviet bloc where Moscow wielded considerable influence. Under the auspices of CENTO and the bilateral agreements associated with it, Pakistan received substantial U.S. economic and military aid. As with the United States' underdeveloped anticommunist allies elsewhere in the world, this strengthened the control of the military over society. It thus helped undermine poorly-rooted democratic institutions in Pakistan, led to excessive spending on defense, and ultimately created a regional imbalance.

However, the Soviet invasion of Afghanistan gave a new lease of life to the strategic relationship between Washington and Islamabad. In 1980 ties were strengthened and military sales increased. American enthusiasm for arming Pakistan was tempered by fears that Islamabad was developing its own nuclear capability. But the Soviet presence in Afghanistan and continued influence in India counted for more in American eyes.

THE AGENDA OF CHANGE

Whatever the merits of the resurgence of conservatism in U.S. foreign policy, there is no doubting the Soviet buildup in Asia and the Pacific during the late 1970s and early 1980s. It led to demands, particularly from the Philippines and other member countries of the Association of Southeast Asian Nations (ASEAN), that the United States reaffirm its commitment to the maintenance of a military presence in the region. At the same time, however, political, economic, and social changes in all the countries then host to U.S. military facilities, and many of those that were not, suggested the need for a new kind of relationship with Washington. Tentative signs of these new relationships were apparent at the close of the 1980s.

Japan

This was particularly the case with Japan, the United States' closest Asian ally. By the early 1980s there was an incongruity at the heart of this relationship which could no longer be ignored. It was that the world's biggest debtor nation was responsible for much of the defense of the world's biggest creditor nation. Japan's status as an economic superpower was underlined every time the United States posted its trade figures. In spite of apparently genuine attempts to look favorably on American imports, Japan continued to run an enormous surplus in trade with the United States.

Japan has enjoyed low-cost high security by the simple expedient of allowing the presence of U.S. military installations in exchange for the protection of the nuclear umbrella. These installations, which in 1988 numbered more than 100 and ranged from radio stations to a port capable of accommodating a battle carrier group, have proved of inestimable value to Washington. They have given the United States the option of exerting a throttling effect on the key sea lanes used by the Soviet Pacific fleet based at Vladivostok. Nevertheless, Washington has pressed Tokyo to adopt a higher defense posture and assume a more active role in Pacific security. There has been some willingness on the part of the Japanese government to respond to these suggestions. But Japan's neighbors, particularly China, remain sensitive to any signs of renewed militarism. These fears are not groundless. If Tokyo were to spend only three percent of its GNP on defense, it has been estimated that it could create a military force capable of facing the Soviet Union on its own.

However, U.S. attempts to beef up Japan's military role have not lacked ambiguity. The United States protested strongly when Japan indicated that it would develop its own jet fighters to replace aging American planes. American defense planners seem keen for Tokyo to develop a strong defense, but not, apparently, an autonomous one. Many Japanese politicians, on the other hand, are keen to retain the nuclear umbrella, but dislike continued reliance on U.S. military hardware. New directions in the relationship between the United States and Japan have therefore been signposted, but exactly where they might lead, other than toward a generally enlarged security role for Japan, remains unclear.

China

U.S. relations with China have experienced perceptible, but less marked changes in the decade following the establishment of diplomatic relations in 1979. The idea that Washington and Beijing might embark on some kind of firm, anti-Soviet strategic alliance did not survive long, even though limited military cooperation has taken place based on a genuine community of interests in the region. The Beijing-Washington axis has remained generally stable while subject to turbulence caused by the Taiwan issue, recurrent threats of American protectionism in trade, U.S. embargoes on the export of high technology, and occasional objections to China's record on human rights.

A new factor in the late 1980s, however, has been a thaw, slow at first, in relations between China and the Soviet Union. Under the reformist leadership of Mikhail Gorbachev, Moscow has adopted a conciliatory approach in its border dispute with Beijing and has attempted to relate its own efforts at economic reform to those pursued by Deng Xiaoping and his colleagues. President Gorbachev's visit to Beijing in the spring of 1989 began the slow process of normalization. But it is far from clear that the complete healing of the 30-year rift between the two giants of world socialism can be resisted for very long by Beijing's aging leaders. Rapprochement with the Soviet Union, very much on the agenda for the late 1980s or early 1990s, will enable China to pursue a more equidistant relationship between Washington and Moscow, something it has long had in mind.

South Korea

U.S. relations with South Korea, apparently long frozen in a mold by the military threat from the North, are also in flux. With the possible exception of Cuba in 1963, no other part of the world has seemed so likely to spark a conflagration between the superpowers during the last 35 years as the Korean peninsula. Indeed, since the formal end of hostilities, the United

States has yet to strike up any coherent dialogue with the government of North Korea.

The scars from the Korean War have not healed as quickly as those from the war in Vietnam. To be sure, the resumption of diplomatic relations between Vietnam and the United States still seems some way off. But senior U.S. officials visited Hanoi in 1987 to discuss the fate of U.S. servicemen missing in action and to clear the ground for talks on aid for Vietnam's battered economy. No such developments have occurred respecting North Korea. The stalemate in Korea has been due mainly to the enigma of Kim Il-sung. The activities of the "Great Leader" have concerned Chinese and Soviet backers as much as they have defense planners in Seoul and Washington.

The consequences of this for South Korea have been considerable. Perhaps most striking has been the infringement of South Korean sovereignty arising from U.S. command over South Korean troops, control over nuclear weapons on South Korean soil, and American domination of the regular talks at Panmunjon on the border between North and South. This has given rise to occasional anti-American demonstrations. Much more noticeable, however, has been the unprecedented political development in South Korea during the late 1980s, associated with generally free and fair presidential elections. The growth of popular opinion in South Korea has all but undermined the once unanswerable claim of right-wing dictators as the only force capable of resisting communism, and thus the only worthy recipients of U.S. aid. President Roh Tae Woo is as anticommunist as his less agreeable predecessors. He differs from those before him in his determination to bring South Korea into a new, less dependent relationship with the United States.

The Philippines

Analogous processes of change are at work in the Philippines more than 40 years after independence from U.S. rule. The political awakening of the islands associated with the overthrow of Ferdinand Marcos in 1986 occasioned some deft footwork from Washington in switching allegiance to Corazon Aquino. It soon became apparent that Aquino represented a new kind of Filipino leader, ready, at last, to throw off the psychology of colonialism which had survived formal independence and which had been encouraged by her unsavory predecessors.

In the first years of her presidency Aquino seemed to perceive the future of her country more in terms of the ASEAN regional grouping than as a strategic outpost of the Western world. This did not mean that she was opposed to the U.S. presence in the country. Aquino shared with the leaders of other ASEAN nations the view that as long as the Soviet Union maintained substantial bases at Danang and Cam Ranh Bay in Vietnam, there was a need for the American naval base at Subic Bay and Clark Air Force Base. The bases protect Japan's commercial lifelines and facilitate the projection of U.S. naval power into the Indian Ocean where, at Diego Garcia, the United States maintains major air and naval support facilities courtesy of Britain. Nonetheless, the future of the Filipino bases came under intensive discussion in 1988, pending renewal of a 25-year military base agreement in 1991. Manila, unsuccessful in persuading other ASEAN countries to share the burden of U.S. military facilities, has sought increased compensation for their presence. Several analysts warned that this might prove counterproductive. In view of Washington's shrinking foreign aid budget, they argued that excessive demands might agitate isolationist sentiment and prompt a U.S. military retreat from the region, possibly as far back as the Mariana Islands.

This may also be the outcome of the demand from some ASEAN nations that the Southeast Asia be designated a nuclear-free zone or a zone of peace, freedom, and neutrality. If so, it would be something of a repeat of the situation in 1985 when New Zealand refused to allow visits of U.S. nuclear-powered or nuclear-armed vessels. Washington regarded this as hostile to the ANZUS pact and suspended, although on a temporary basis, cooperation with Wellington.

Asia and the World

The foregoing account of two centuries of U.S. involvement in Asia has attempted to show that there is no "state of rest." U.S. relations with Asia have been subject to increasingly rapid change; there is every indication that even more dramatic transformations lie ahead. Indeed, complex regional developments have occurred against a background of fundamental changes in the wider pattern of international relations. At the close of the 1980s, the Washington and Moscow summits of 1987 and 1988 were frequently interpreted as the swan songs of a bipolar world. No longer, analysts maintained, would the Soviet and U.S. superpowers be able to impose their joint dominion over the affairs of the world. The financial costs of superpower hegemony have had adverse effects on the American and Soviet economies. When, at the end of World War II, the United States produced about half of the world's manufacturing output, it made sense for Roosevelt to remark that "there is not a single problem, military or political, in which the United States is not interested." Nearly half a century later, not every problem in the world can be regarded as a problem for U.S. foreign policy. The Soviet Union, too, has discovered that its security interests are served better by a program of economic modernization and limited nuclear disarmament than by a continually escalating military budget and costly imbroglios such as that resulting from the invasion of Afghanistan.

That a new international order is emerging is incontestable; its exact shape remains shadowy and uncertain. The most likely scenario for the 21st century appears to be one reminiscent of the 19th: four or five great powers in flexible but uneasy balance. Unlike the 19th century, however, not all of these powers will be based in Europe or North America.

Asia and the Pacific, long recognized as a future economic epicenter of the world, seem set to become a crucial focus of world power in the 21st century. China's Deng Xiaoping has suggested that Japan, rather than the Soviet Union or the United States, is likely to be the main focus of China's foreign policy in the next century. There is a rather agreeable symmetry to the idea that East Asia might again be dominated by regional rather than international powers. Naturally it begs many questions. Not least among them is how a Japan with the military might to match its economic muscle would get on with an equally formidable China. But it would be something of a throwback to the traditional East Asian world order. According to this interpretation, the Western presence in Asia, which began when this order started to crumble in the late 18th and early 19th centuries, and which the United States once represented at its peak, will seem something of a brief interlude between more "normal" patterns of relations in the region.

FURTHER READING

Blaufarb, Douglas S. *The Counterinsurgency Era: US Doctrine and Performance, 1950 to the Present.* New York: Free Press, 1977.

Chay, John, ed., *The Problems and Perspectives of American-East Asian Relations.* Boulder, Colorado: Westview Press, 1977.

Cohen, Warren I., ed. *New Frontiers in American-East Asian Relations: Essays Presented to Dorothy Borg.* New York: Columbia University Press, 1983.

Hess, Gary R. *The United States' Emergence as a Southeast Asian Power, 1940–1950.* New York: Columbia University Press, 1987.

Iriye, Akira. *The Cold War in Asia: A Historical Introduction.* Englewood Cliffs, New Jersey: Prentice-Hall, 1974.

Kahin, George McT. *Intervention: How America Became Involved in Vietnam.* New York: Knopf, 1986.

Karnow, Stanley. *In Our Image: America's Empire in the Philippines.* New York: Random House, 1989.

Kolko, Gabriel. *Vietnam: Anatomy of a War, 1940–1975.* London: Allen & Unwin, 1985.

Leifer, Michael. ed. *The Balance of Power in East Asia.* London: Macmillan, 1986.

May, Ernest R., and Thomson, James C. eds. *American-East Asian Relations: A Survey.* Cambridge, Massachusetts: Harvard University Press, 1972.

Thomson, James C., Stanley, Peter W., and Perry, John Curtis. *Sentimental Imperialists: The American Experience in East Asia.* New York: Harper & Row, 1981.

THE EUROPEAN COMMUNITY AND ASIA

ERHARD LOUVEN

SINCE January 1967 when three independent communities—European Economic Community, European Atomic Energy Community and European Coal and Steel Community—merged to form the European Community (EC), there has been a remarkable expansion of community activities into new fields. But through the accession of Spain and Portugal to the community in 1986, a common policy of the member nations toward the outside world has become more complicated. The community is the world's biggest trading region: if trade among the member nations themselves is excluded, the community accounts for about 23 percent of world trade. It is the most important trading partner for many Third World countries, among them many Asian nations.

The EC, with its 12 member nations each having an individualized trade structure, is in Asia confronted with highly different countries, from centralistic socialist China, to developing countries like Bangladesh, to newly industrializing countries like South Korea, to a laissez-faire entrepôt like Hong Kong. Nonpreferential trading agreements were signed with Bangladesh, India, Pakistan and Sri Lanka between 1973 and 1976. Under the 1986 program of aid to nonassociated developing countries (other than the 66 African, Pacific and Caribbean countries associated with the EC under the Lome Conventions) the EC allocated 210 million ECU (European currency units) for the whole of Asia, principally for agricultural projects. It is understandable that the EC as a powerful association has concentrated its interests on the larger and most important countries and regional associations in Asia.

JAPAN

The only Asian nation that by now has reached a status that can be compared with a modern Western industrialized country is Japan. This country, whose historical and geographical heritage strongly formed it as a monolith, represents a permanent challenge to the EC. Because of its enormous successes in international markets and a high surplus in the trade balance with the EC, it is no wonder that the relations between the EC and Japan

1225

Table 1
JAPAN'S TRADE WITH THE EC
(billion U.S.$)

	Export	Import	Balance
1973	4.400	3.177	1.223
1974	5.968	3.982	1.986
1975	5.675	3.371	2.304
1976	7.234	3.623	3.611
1977	8.736	4.195	4.541
1978	11.105	6.072	5.033
1979	12.685	7.581	5.105
1980	16.650	7.842	8.808
1981	18.894	8.552	10.342
1982	17.064	7.560	9.504
1983	18.523	8.120	10.402
1984	19.405	9.334	10.071
1985	20.016	8.893	11.123
1986	30.675	13.989	16.686

Source: Ministry of Foreign Affairs (Tokyo, 1988).

are characterized as asymmetrical. The image the Europeans have of Japan is determined by suspicion-minded attitudes. On the one hand, idylls evocative of cherry blossoms and quiet temples prevail; on the other hand, the idea of Japan as a dangerous offshoot of the West now trying to supersede Europe is common. There exists an asymmetrical state of knowledge: the Japanese systematically began to study Western ideas, manners and technologies in the last century, whereas a similar approach by the Europeans only gained momentum when it was obvious that Japan had become an economic superpower which threatened established positions in the world market. Europe has politically, economically and culturally influenced the history of Japan to a significant extent. Individual European countries were of utmost importance to Japan.

A scathing reference to a country of "workaholics" and unacceptable Japanese living conditions ("What Westerners would regard as little more than rabbit hutches") contained in a confidential internal document which leaked to the press in 1979, expressed something of the bitterness felt in Europe.[1] The problem of trade surpluses, however, is structural, and Japan is likely to be more sensitive to criticism from the United States and mainly indifferent to complaints from the EC.

Japan as a supplier to the EC ranks fourth and as an outlet for the EC it holds thirteenth place. The bilateral trade primarily comprises manufactured goods, although the EC exports considerable quantities of meat and

[1] Endymion Wilkinson, *Misunderstandings: Europe versus Japan* (Tokyo, 1981), 221–22.

alcoholic beverages to Japan. The exports of the community primarily comprise organic chemical products and pharmaceutical goods, textiles, mineral products, metals, machines, vehicles and garments. Japan mainly exports office machines, acoustical and telecommunication instruments, electrical machines, vehicles, photographic equipment, chemical products, rubber products, iron and steel and precision instruments.

In the 1960s the balance of trade of the EC to Japan was positive, but in the 1970s the balance became negative to an ever increasing extent. From the mid-1980s Japan could realize trade surpluses to the amount of more than U.S. $10 billion. The exchange of services rapidly increased. A major part of EC's surplus is due to its traditionally strong position in the service sector such as banking and insurance. While the surplus in these invisible transactions with Japan increases, the Japanese service sector is developing rapidly. This could lead to a decreasing Japanese deficit with the invisibles due to improved operations of Japanese banking and insurance groups.

It is, then, no wonder that different bodies in the EC demand more balanced trade relations. Japan, so it is argued, is not integrated in the world market to a sufficient extent. This is evident since there exists in Japan a tremendous surplus of domestic savings, which is illustrated by rather low consumption for private households and low expenditures for housing and the social infrastructure. In spite of considerable surpluses, high economic growth, low rates of unemployment and inflation and a dynamic industrial and technological basis, Japan does not play an important role in the international economic and monetary framework.

The EC demands that Japan build up the yen—as well as the ECU—as an international reserve currency. A multilateral trade system should be established through a better linking of the individual economies. The relationship of Japanese investments in Europe to European investments in Japan is 10 to 1. The Europeans claim that some 80 percent of all Japanese investments go into the trade and service sectors. As a result more investments in the manufacturing sector are demanded. The reasons for relatively low European investments in Japan are the host of barriers established by the Japanese. In Japan licenses are given preference and direct investments in the manufacturing sector are discouraged and extremely difficult.

After the Japanese had only reacted verbally and evasively toward the many instances of moral persuasion on the side of the Europeans, in July 1986 the council of EC foreign ministers authorized the EC to take concrete actions against Japan. According to the General Agreement on Tariffs and Trade proceedings were taken against Japan. These measures pertain to Japanese imports of wines and liquors on which high protective duties are imposed. The means by which the Japanese successfully restrict imports of European wines and liquors can be taken as an example of procedures regarding other commodities. Japanese customs authorities distinguish between three quality degrees: "special," "first class" and "second class." The tax for "special" beverages is twice that for "first class" and seven times that of "second class." Scottish and Irish whisky automatically fall under the category "special" and are therefore subject to the highest tariff. There

Table 2
DIRECT INVESTMENTS OF JAPAN AND THE EC,
1950–85 (million U.S.$)

	Japan's direct investments in the EC	EC countries' direct investments in Japan
Denmark	16	n.a.
West Germany	1,342	238
Greece	95	n.a.
France	818	133
Ireland	262	n.a.
Italy	180	n.a.
Netherlands	1,687	164
Belgium	744	7
Luxemburg	1,216	n.a.
Britain	3,141	359
TOTAL	9,501	n.a.

Source: Calculated from data by Tsutomu Hata, *Japan-EC Relations: A Japanese Perspective* (Tokyo: Ministry of Foreign Affairs, 1986).

exist similar quality degrees and tariffs for brandy and cognac. In all cases the protection is strengthened through high customs duties, which are far higher than the EC customs duties.

In July 1985 the Japanese announced a three-year action program which provided for a series of measures to open up their markets. However, Japanese authorities claimed that they were unable to guarantee positive results of these measures. In October and December 1985 measures were announced in Tokyo aimed at boosting domestic demand. But the effects of these measures only touched the foreign trade imbalance marginally. The Japanese government estimated the additional imports at about $2 billion whereas according to private Japanese research institutes these would only amount to less than $1 billion.

In September 1986 the third comprehensive report by the EC on trade and economic relations between the EC and Japan suggested a coherent customs strategy toward Japan.[2] Additionally antidumping measures were proposed.

The Japanese skillfully use the differences in foreign trade policy among the member nations of the EC so that a global foreign trade agreement has not been accomplished up to now. With the exception of Ireland, all EC members have healthy bilateral foreign trade agreements with Japan. The failure to bring about a global foreign trade agreement has had serious

[2] European Parliament, *The Moorhouse Report,* Document no. A2-86/87 (July 10, 1986).

consequences for a precise delimitation of competences within the community. The EC considers necessary an offensive strategy in trade policy toward Japan. But this could only be successful if the members of the EC offer, as a compensation, a liberalization of a number of import restrictions on Japanese goods. On account of strong national attitudes in most of the countries there is no readiness to support such a policy.

The Japanese have developed a near perfect system to guard both society and economy against foreign intruders. In addition their complex distribution system presents barriers to the opening up of the Japanese market to foreign producers. Of primary importance in this area are the large numbers of small intermediaries, the unusually long and expensive distribution channels that work through several wholesale levels and the intricate web of personal relationships between suppliers and customers. Domestic and foreign producers must deal with these circumstances to the same extent. But recently the situation has improved for foreign producers, as the previously dominant role of wholesale trade in the importing of consumer goods has become rather shaky.

The Japanese claim that their enterprises operating in Europe find that similar cultural barriers exist. But Japanese companies have accepted them as part of the given, something one had to live with. When faced with such difficulties, Japanese managers did not bring their complaints to their own government for solution but preferred to emphasize market research and development and other self-help approaches. Supported by an adaptable, export-oriented approach, about 33,000 Japanese businessmen are stationed in Europe, while the number of European businessmen in Japan only amounts to about 2,000. This low number clearly demonstrates that the enthusiasm of EC enterprises to penetrate the Japanese market is much less than that with which they call on their governments or the EC to exert pressure on Japan at the official level.[3] The comparison is even more striking when one compares the number of the two groups of businessmen who are able to speak the local language. Another key factor to the success of Japanese enterprises is the enhancement of their local presence, especially the founding of subsidiaries, thereby establishing local sales networks. It was noteworthy that increased exports of German automobiles coincided with the establishment of a local sales company in Japan.

Because of these and other difficulties that Europeans encounter in the Japanese market, since 1979 the EC has maintained an export promotion program (EXPROM) to impart a better knowledge of the market and living conditions to European businessmen. The principal item of this program is an executive training program, in the framework of which young European businessmen spend 18 months in Japan. The first part of this program consists of a 12-month crash language course in Japanese coupled with seminars and visits. In six months of the second part the businessmen work in Japanese enterprises so that they can become acquainted with the various aspects of Japanese business life. Through EXPROM there are also

[3] Tsutomu Hata, *Japan-EC Relations: A Japanese Perspective* (Tokyo: Ministry of Foreign Affairs, 1986), 5–6.

visits of European businessmen to Japan, marketing studies (such as in foodstuffs, machine building and wine and liquors) and various practical studies. Since 1979 the EC has spent some 20 million ECU on such programs.

Cooperation with Japan in science and technology is difficult because public research in Japan is distributed among numerous competitive ministries, such as the Bureau for Science and Technology, the Ministry of Education, the Ministry of International Trade and Industry, the Ministry of Agriculture, and others. In January 1983 the EC came to terms with Japan about the promotion of cooperation in science and technology. Later issues of antiradiation precautions and science policy were discussed. In 1985 negotiations took place aimed at a closer cooperation in the field of nuclear fusion, resulting in the mutual exchange of six scientists. Other fields, such as fine ceramics and biotechnology, might be subjects of cooperation, but industrial and economic interests are relatively strong in these areas so that a common handling would probably be excluded. In general the expenditures for research and development by the Japanese government in priority areas correspond to those by the EC.

With regard to macroeconomic problems and coordinating foreign and security policy issues the process of rapprochement could be intensified. Partially concerted actions in the field of international politics were made in the Afghanistan crisis, the hostage affair in Iran, the proclamation of the state of emergency in Poland, and the downing of the South Korean aircraft. The initiative primarily started in Japan, but, especially in the Iran crisis, was extended beyond a policy of declarations and consultations to real bilateral crisis management. Britain, West Germany and France had already in 1982 begun talks with Japan on a bilateral basis. When U.S. President Ronald Reagan asked the Japanese to join the economic embargo against Libya, Tokyo showed reserve and waited for the reaction of the Europeans before formulating its own answer.

In March 1983 the foreign ministers of the EC agreed to hold semiannual political consultations between the chairman of the council of EC foreign ministers and the Japanese foreign minister on issues of political cooperation regarding the community. In May this formal inclusion of Japan into European political cooperation led to a meeting with Japanese Foreign Minister Shintaro Abe.

Both sides had explicitly committed themselves in the Ushiba-Haferkamp communiqué of March 1978 to expand their cooperation in the field of macroeconomics.[4] At the economic summit conference held in Versailles in 1982 a common front was built up against the U.S. policy of high interest rates. The same thing happened at the summit conference in Williamsburg in 1983, when the U.S. government imposed stringent import restrictions on finished steel against European and Japanese competitors. The move by the Reagan administration in September 1985 against the EC and Japan to put an end to alleged unfair trade practices formed a new coalition between both parties.

[4] *Official Journal of the European Community,* Document no. L123 (May 11, 1978).

Japan's endeavors to define more clearly its political and military role led at the economic summit in Williamsburg to a common declaration on disarmament and arms control as well as to the so-called "double decision" by NATO. It was the first time that Japan in an official document declared itself a quasi-honorary member of that alliance. Prime Minister Yasuhiro Nakasone offered this move as a signal for cooperation in arms policy with the West.

Since the beginning of the 1980s the European-Japanese dialogue has entered a new phase. This dialogue is strongly embedded in the alliance of the three big industrial regions: North America, Western Europe and Japan. Though this trilateral relationship is still anchored on the United States, the intensified communication between the Western Europeans and the Japanese has led to a calmer attitude toward divergences in the realm of trade policy. The susceptibility to friction within the European-Japanese dialogue has been reduced to the same extent as the contacts in the field of foreign and security policy have increased. A new kind of European-Japanese self-confidence is about to emerge.

CHINA

After the establishment of the European Economic Community in 1958 most of its members were unwilling to interact with China. Any attempt by China to adopt a favorable attitude toward the Community would have been tantamount to defiance of the Soviet Union. After the split with the Soviet Union, the Chinese communist party in 1964 expressed interest in the establishment of some kind of cooperation with Western Europe and various other countries. Mao Zedong's intermediate zone theory, which had originally been advanced in 1946, was revitalized. An authoritative statement, which appeared in the Chinese press perceived Western Europe as having developed sufficient common interests and purpose to be characterized as the second intermediate zone trying to free itself from U.S. control. Even more significant was the emphasis laid on the possible benefits of links with all countries other than the United States.

In 1963 and 1964 there were several contacts between Western European industrialists and Chinese administrators to discuss establishing trade missions and extending trade. But because of pressures from the United States the member nations of the EC were cautious about establishing relations with China. The contacts came to an end when the turmoil of the Cultural Revolution began in 1966. A systematic strategy of harassment of foreign diplomats was begun by the Chinese. Western European diplomats became the primary target. The most serious act was the burning of the chancellery building of the British legation in Beijing.

In the late 1960s, when the heat of the Cultural Revolution was spent, the moderate wing of the party succeeded in separating foreign affairs from internal affairs. Thus it was possible for China to formulate a more open attitude toward the outside world, while power struggles concerned with internal problems continued. After China's admission to the United Nations in October 1971 it adopted a new position on the EC, which was singled out as the most positive and important element in Western Europe. In the newly revised Maoist theory of the three worlds in 1974, members of the second and third worlds were eligible to become alliance partners with China. The superpowers belonged to the first world. They were, in the Chinese view, characterized by enormous potential and the determination to use this potential to the disadvantage of other nations. The second world consisted of the intermediate powers such as Japan and the industrialized nations of Western Europe.

The EC was perceived as one of the two intermediate zones with which close relations were ideologically permissible. In the opinion of the Chinese leadership Western Europe was especially threatened because it could be the main scene of action in the hegemonistic conflict of the superpowers and thus the primary goal of Soviet expansion. This was based on Western Europe's strong economic position—in the eyes of Chinese leaders. If the Soviet Union wanted to dominate the world, it first had to dominate Western Europe. Capital, industry, agriculture, science and technology were, according to the Chinese view, relatively concentrated in Western Europe. The country that controlled Europe could make use of its human, material, and financial resources to wage a world war.

In May 1973 Prime Minister Zhou Enlai announced China's wish to establish diplomatic relations with the community. Soon afterwards talks began to explore the possibilities of formal implementation of relations. This was a reasonable move by the Chinese because, since the beginning of 1973, the EC had taken over the responsibility to formulate and implement the principles and general direction of the trade policy of the members of the community. Nevertheless, the individual member countries kept the right to conclude bilateral agreements with China. The community reacted positively because major obstacles had been removed (for example, the attitude of the United States had become accepting of the EC's policy) and the vast Chinese market was a strong attraction.

One obstacle for closer relations between the two parties was the Taiwan issue. In 1970 the EC had concluded a textile agreement with Taiwan which expired in October 1973. China wanted to be sure that the EC had no intention of preserving any ties with Taiwan. When it had become clear in bilateral talks that the community considered the Beijing government the only government of China, the Chinese formally invited in May 1975 Christopher Soames, vice-president of the EC commission in charge of foreign affairs, to visit China. Despite informal assurances previously given by members of the EC delegation, the Chinese insisted that Soames formally and publicly declare that Taiwan was geographically an integral part of China. The EC delegation was reluctant to do so because it had no legal mandate to make any declaration that involved territories. The stalemate was overcome with a statement by Soames to the effect that the community did not have any official relations with Taiwan and that the community recognized the government of the People's Republic as the sole legal government of China.

In September 1975 the Chinese ambassador to the community, Li Lianbi, presented his credentials in Brussels. With the exception of Ireland, all other member countries of the EC had already established diplomatic relations with China. In January 1976 negotiations began between officials of the EC and the Chinese mission to conclude a trade agreement. After interruptions in the negotiations due to the deaths of Zhou and Mao, the trade agreement between the EC and China was eventually signed in February 1978.[5] The concluding of this agreement was an important event because it made way for an intensive dialogue between two strong forces outside the superpower structure. The EC was successful in obtaining the inclusion of two clauses that could be applied if heavy trade imbalances occurred. The matter had to be examined by a joint committee so that measures could be recommended in order to improve the situation. There was a restrictive regulation dealing with prices of Chinese imports: goods and services were to be delivered and implemented at market rates.

Political differences emerged regarding the Sino-Vietnam war in 1979. All nine foreign ministers of the community called in the Chinese ambassadors and asked China to end the incursions into Vietnam. When China began a campaign to push EC members to adopt an anti-Soviet position, the Western Europeans took the view that it was not reasonable to encourage the Chinese to increase the high level of Sino-Soviet tension. The British, West Germans and French made a concerted attempt to assure the Soviets that they were not accomplices of the Chinese in an attempt at encirclement. In 1978 Chinese military delegates presented impressive shopping lists for the most modern weapons to the Western Europeans. But the Europeans were reluctant and refused to conclude any major weapons deal. Eventually the Chinese lost interest because they lacked the foreign exchange and the prices of sophisticated weapon systems were high.

In January 1980 the textile agreement between the community and China went into effect. This agreement defined a framework applicable for five years for imports into the community of Chinese textiles and garments of cotton, wool and artificial fibers.[6] Although it guaranteed significantly increased access for Chinese products to the community market, the agreement took full account of the considerable difficulties faced by the clothing and textile industries of the member nations. The Chinese negotiators had accepted a safeguard clause for products not subject to the quota. This would allow the community to keep textile and clothing exports from China at a level not exceeding the highest thresholds guaranteed to the community's suppliers by the multifiber agreement.

The EC had calculated that China badly needed an agreement, partly to neutralize the adverse political and economic effects of abortive Sino-U.S. textile negotiations, and partly to maintain the momentum of Sino-EC rapprochement. With China's entry into the highly saturated international market, the EC feared that considerable damage might be caused to the community's relations with Third World countries if it were to lose out to China. Therefore, it was clear that it was politically and economically impossible for the EC to accept the quota of 60,000 tons of textiles the Chinese

[5] Europe Information, External Relations, 42/81. pp. 81ff.
[6] General Agreement on Tariffs and Trade, Document no. COMTEX/SB/601.

Table 3
TRADE OF CHINA WITH THE EC
(billion U.S.$)

	Export	Import	Balance
1980	2.363	2.814	−0.451
1981	2.502	2.714	−0.212
1982	2.168	2.178	−0.010
1983	2.508	3.390	−0.882
1984	2.232	3.323	−1.091
1985	2.283	6.151	−3.868
1986	3.993	7.661	−3.668

Source: Central Statistical Bureau of China (Beijing, 1987).

had wanted. The final agreement limited the Chinese exports to 40,000 tons per year. China also guaranteed to supply minimum quantities of textile raw materials, such as silk, cashmere and angora, at appropriate prices for the European processing industry.

In October 1984 a trade and economic cooperation agreement between the EC and China was concluded. It replaced the trade agreement of 1978. Total trade in both directions had doubled between 1975 and 1979. It then stagnated until 1982. From 1985 there was a sharp rise in Chinese imports from the community, which led to a deficit in the Chinese balance of trade. This is why the Chinese again and again demanded of the Western Europeans that they increase their imports from China.

In order to attain its ambitious foreign trade goals, China had to allow, or even to develop, new forms of economic cooperation at home. All cooperation forms are now in use in China, among them joint equity ventures, compensation trade, processing of raw or semifinished materials, barter, and contractual joint ventures (specially created by the Chinese). The Chinese prefer joint equity ventures as a means to transform quickly and upgrade technology and business procedures.

In December 1987 a symposium on investment was held in Beijing, jointly organized by the commission of the EC and the Chinese Ministry of Foreign Economic Relations and Trade with the aim of deepening and intensifying mutually beneficial cooperation between the two parties. This symposium was the first opportunity for the 300 participants to express their views on this subject in China within the framework of the EC. In several round table talks the Europeans could explain their manifold difficulties concerning joint ventures, such as the initial negotiation process, manpower and foreign exchange problems. The Chinese participants, mostly from high administrative ranks, promised to study the issues and to try to solve the problems.

The Chinese leadership has abandoned its policy of playing one European country against another and has made it clear that it would be more disposed to conclude contracts with Western European countries than with Japanese or U.S. enterprises. In a way the EC is politically in a more advantageous position than either Japan or the United States, as it has constituted itself into an autonomous force within the international system. It has thus contributed—together with China—to getting rid of the bipolar system dominated by the superpowers.

INDIA

The relations of the EC with the second largest country in Asia, India, are much older than those with China. For 25 years the relations have comprised a variety of aspects and are continuously developing. Thus the framework of cooperation does not only include trade and regional policies but has widened to the world economy and international politics.

In 1962 India established diplomatic relations with the then community of six Western European countries. At that time India aimed foremost at preserving access to the British market even after Britain's entry into the community. It is remarkable that the failure of the entry negotiations with Britain in 1961–1963 did not mean the end of India's relations with the EC. On the contrary, in 1964 the community exempted one of India's main export commodities, unpacked tea, as well as certain spices and hides from customs duties. This was followed by bilateral agreements first on jute and then on coconut fibers. Upon India's application the community opened up duty-free quotas for handmade silk and cotton fabrics as well as arts and crafts products. After the introduction of the general system of preferences by the EC in 1971 India became one of the main beneficiaries of this system. Before that India had played a major role in negotiations that led to the UNCTAD decision on general preferences.

Until 1972, when Denmark, Britain and Ireland entered the community, trade negotiations between the EC and India had reached a stage where both in the EC and in Britain the attitude was generally accepted that the existing network of bilateral and other agreements were sufficient to guarantee India an easy access to the British market. Thus, the EC confined itself—together with Britain—to a common declaration of intent. In this declaration the intention of the community was expressed to extend and to strengthen trade relations with India and other developing Asian countries and to examine trade-related issues in order to seek common paths. The cooperation agreement concluded in 1973 between India and the EC was the first of a whole generation of new agreements the community concluded with other countries.[7] This agreement strengthened common trade activities to a considerable extent. One example for this was the establishment in 1980, with financial assistance by the community, of an Indian trade center in Brussels.

On the occasion of the visit of Indian Prime Minister Morarji Desai to the EC commission in June 1978, talks were held aimed at giving the

[7] European Parliament, Document no. L82/84.

cooperation a broader basis. Further talks and negotiations ended in the signing of a nonpreferential five-year agreement on economic and trade cooperation in June 1981.[8] This agreement provided for new joint endeavors in the fields of trade, industry, science, energy and development. The agreement of 1981, which replaced that of 1973, was a model for a new generation of cooperation agreements.

The agreement was supervised and implemented by a joint EC-Indian committee newly created for that purpose. The committee had to promote the development of relations in all of the above mentioned fields and to supervise the fulfillment of the agreements additionally concluded between India and the community. The first meeting of the mixed committee took place in 1982 in New Delhi. At the second meeting in 1983 in Brussels this body concluded an extensive program for the promotion of trade with India. A third meeting took place in 1984 in New Delhi on the ministry level. With regard to India's permanent trade deficit vis-à-vis the community the committee decided to continue technical testing of individual products in order to allow a better penetration of community markets. Additionally a program for industrial cooperation was concluded that provided for the further promotion of the Indian investment center in Frankfurt as well as seminars on investments in industry and on technology transfer.

An essential purpose of the agreement on economic and trade cooperation was to stimulate the interest of Western European economic circles in forms of cooperation offered by Indian enterprises, such as joint ventures and license agreements. In January 1982 the EC for the first time organized in Bombay, New Delhi, Calcutta, and Madras seminars on problems and development prospects of Indian-EC relations. At that time the council of EC chambers of commerce in India was founded.

The agreement on trade with textile products, negotiated within the framework of the multifiber agreement, was initialed in September 1982.[9] It came into force in January 1983 and ceased at the end of 1986. It contained a program of voluntary self-restraint for certain categories of commodities. India was, as a compensation, permitted a guaranteed access to community markets and an improvement on conditions of access.

In November 1982 the community participated for the first time in the International Trade Fair in New Delhi. The stands of the then ten member nations of the EC were integrated into a single European pavilion. Also in November the community initiated the first stage of an important program for the promotion of economic cooperation aimed at informing businesses about the improved investment conditions in India. In Düsseldorf, Paris and Stratford-upon-Avon the community organized seminars where industrialists could obtain information on potential cooperation in India's industrial sector.

More than half of all imports from India to the community are finished products such as clothing, carpets, cotton and jute fabrics, cut diamonds and leather. The remaining are agricultural products (tea, oil cake, raw

[8] European Parliament, Document no. 328/81.
[9] Europe Information, External Relations, 85–86, pp. 3ff.

Table 4
INDIA'S TRADE WITH THE EC (billion ECU)

	Export	Import	Balance
1973	0.644	0.688	−0.024
1976	1.428	1.140	0.288
1979	1.839	2.009	−0.170
1981	1.880	3.363	−1.483
1983	2.196	3.823	−1.627
1984	2.905	4.630	−1.725
1985	2.672	5.560	−2.880
1986	2.621	6.314	−3.693

Source: Eurostat (Brussels).

tobacco, etc.) and mineral oil products. The community exports to India mainly machines, transportation vehicles, equipment, and finished products as well as chemical products, food, oils, etc. Some of these exports are within the framework of the food aid program of the EC; others are normal exports in the form of commercial trade deals.

With the expansion of trade volume, the foreign trade deficit of India vis-à-vis the EC increased. This deficit conforms with the overall trade deficit of the country since the introduction of a liberal import policy. With regard to this situation India repeatedly voiced grave concern. In addition it expressed a desire for easier access to community markets and demanded increased support for sales promotion.

India receives the most funds from the EC program for trade promotion. Since 1980 about six million ECU have been spent for projects of trade promotion, among them the Indian trade center in Brussels. This center endeavors to promote Indian exports to the EC. It is managed by Indian consultants. Its activities are directed toward machine-building, electronics, leather and leather articles, products from jute and coconut fibers, textiles and agricultural products. The program of the center also includes visits from trade delegations, marketing studies, organization of seminars as well as the participation of India in fairs and exhibitions in Europe.

Since 1984 the EC has endeavored to combine financial help and technical help. In 1984 such an integrated project was launched dealing with technical and trade aspects of Indian mica in building materials. There exist two more integrated projects: technical help in the treatment of seafood, and technical help in the packaging of agricultural products.

Among the nonassociated countries of Asia, India is placed first with regard to development aid from the community. Financial and technical assistance (in 1985 about 60 million ECU) is paid in the form of nonrepayable grants and primarily covers projects of rural development, particularly those that are carried through by nongovernment organizations. A major part of this assistance is made in deliveries of artificial fertilizer. The proceeds of the sale of these deliveries are invested by the Indian government in rural development projects.

Food aid is given within the framework of Operation Flood (for example, 20,000 tons of milk powder and 1,000 tons of butter oil in 1985). By means of Operation Flood the community has rendered help first via the World Food Program and afterwards directly. From 1970 until 1985 this help amounted to about 628 million ECU. For India Operation Flood has been successful in many ways: the incomes of the peasants have grown, living conditions in rural areas have improved, and the food situation in urban areas as well as the quality of the products are guaranteed.

First contacts of the European parliament with the Indian parliament date back to 1962 when a delegation from the European parliament visited India. Since then numerous meetings at the level of both parliament and government have taken place. At the beginning of 1984 the European parliament issued a report on urbanization problems in the Third World. This report dealt with the sensitive situation of Indian cities. The findings of the report have become the basis for development projects in this field.

India is a member of the South Asian Association for Regional Cooperation and hopes increasingly to participate in international bodies. The EC approves of this group and promotes it by means of financial aid for regional projects in energy and transportation.

ASEAN

The development of relations between the EC and the Association of Southeast Asian Nations (ASEAN), to which Indonesia, Malaysia, Thailand, the Philippines, Singapore and Brunei belong, can be divided into three phases. The first phase dates from the establishment of ASEAN in 1967 until 1972. In this period interactions between both groups practically did not take place. The first years of ASEAN were characterized by internal conflicts so that there was no room for orientation toward the outside world. The relations of the EC toward ASEAN were confined to the level of relations between individual nations.

The second phase began with the establishing of direct contacts between the two groups in 1972. This change of relations coincided with a reorientation of ASEAN aimed at becoming more independent both of Japan and the United States. Because of Britain's entry into the EC relations with the former British colonies of Malaysia and Singapore had to be readjusted, since these countries were afraid of losing Commonwealth preferences. In the declaration on Britain's entry agreement the EC determined to solve all relevant problems in an appropriate way as well as to extend and strengthen the trade relations of such countries. The second phase was, particularly in the beginning, characterized by talks with the special coordinating committee of the ASEAN nations and in a common study group consisting of representatives of the EC and the ASEAN governments. In 1975 the EC decided to extend the principle of cumulative origin of goods to imports from regional associations, among them ASEAN. This was a demonstrative step to promote the development of regional integration among developing

Table 5
ASEAN's TRADE WITH THE EC (billion ECU)

	Export	Import	Balance
1974	2.319	2.727	−0.408
1977	4.130	3.845	0.285
1980	6.857	5.369	1.488
1981	6.646	7.152	−0.506
1982	7.102	8.470	−1.368
1983	7.920	9.269	−1.349
1984	9.662	9.886	−0.224
1985	9.032	8.513	0.519
1986	10.463	9.279	1.184

Source: Eurostat (Brussels).

countries. The relations were politically upgraded to the level of ministers when in 1978 a meeting of the foreign ministers of both organizations took place. The EC then recorded ASEAN as a regional organization that played a prominent role in maintaining stability in Southeast Asia. This meeting was the breakthrough for the development of a framework and general directions for the future cooperation of both organizations. Both sides agreed to create a more formal basis for their relations.

The third phase in the relations began with the conclusion of a cooperation agreement in 1980 at the second meeting of the foreign ministers.[10] The main goals of the agreement, through which the interactions between EC and ASEAN were institutionalized, are economic cooperation and cooperation in the field of development policy. Since the signing of the agreement ASEAN has been able to realize export successes in certain fields such as machines and vehicles, but altogether has had to put up with a trade deficit for much of the time.

The ASEAN countries receive a significant portion of the EC's aid to developing countries. In the program for financial and technical aid to non-associated countries an ever increasing share has gone to the ASEAN countries since 1976. Such funds have been used in organizing ASEAN export trade missions, supporting participation in European trade fairs and exhibitions, providing experts in various fields, and carrying out feasibility studies on overseas markets for ASEAN products.

The ASEAN countries are all included in the community's scheme of tariff preferences by means of which the community grants special treatment in the form of a reduction or total exemption of tariffs on imports of many processed agricultural products and finished or semifinished products. This does not, however, mean that products from the ASEAN countries can flow freely into EC markets. The scope of the preferential treatment is

[10] *EC Bulletin* (December 1979), pp. 9ff.

limited by a ceiling system that restricts the volume of preferential imports in order to adapt them to those quantities that the market can absorb.

In comparison with their competitors from Japan and the United States, European suppliers seem to have followed a suboptimal strategy regarding the ASEAN countries. This is marked by too few representatives and sales branches in the region, an insufficient adaptation of products and prices to the requirements of the target markets, and the preference of license agreements to the disadvantage of direct investments. The last aspect is of utmost importance concerning the relatively poor success of European suppliers. Foreign direct investments promote the exchange of commodities between country of origin and recipient country by an induced demand for capital goods and intermediary goods.

The investment strategies of Western European businesses in the ASEAN countries have a low priority. While the direct investments of West German and British enterprises in 1981 to 1983 amounted to under $1 billion to slightly more than $2 billion in the region, Japanese and American enterprises invested $8 to $11 billion. The investments of the other EC countries were negligible. In addition the investors from the community concentrated on the raw material and service sectors and, within the industrial sector, on the chemical industry. Advantages which could have been realized in such labor-intensive products as textiles and clothing, electrical products, plastic goods and toys were not made by the Western Europeans, but definitely by Japanese and to a lesser extent by American enterprises.

The reasons for the low propensity of European enterprises to invest in the ASEAN countries can primarily be found in the considerable economic advantages they can realize in the EC itself, such as in Ireland and the Mediterranean countries, and in Eastern Europe.

More than progress in economic relations was reached in the political interactions between the two regional organizations. The EC-ASEAN relationship can be regarded as a model for relations between regional associations that contributes to international stability and the balance of interests between industrial and developing countries. A growing international interdependence has led to the greater influence of both associations in the international field. The interaction between them was influenced both by factors inside the associations and by factors in the international arena such as the polarization of the superpowers in Southeast Asia. An important aspect of the relationship has been the unequivocal condemnation of any endeavors to establish spheres of influence by the superpowers and the emphasizing of relations on the basis of the equality of the partners.

Both associations are characterized by the absence of hegemonial pretensions. Through cooperation an increasing emancipation from the superpowers is possible. Formalized interaction schemes contribute to diversifying political and economic relations, particularly of ASEAN. This is seen as the central role of the EC in the partnership. The homogeneous voting pattern in essential issues of international politics has made it clear that both communities can play an important role. In the United Nations the communities form a block of 18 nations, representing a total population of more than 580 million.

Since the conclusion of the cooperation agreement an institutional organization has taken shape. The political level is constituted by the EC-ASEAN foreign ministers meetings, the dialogue between the associations after the yearly ASEAN ministerial meeting, the meeting between the European Parliament and the ASEAN interparliamentary organization and the joint consultative committee. The economic level is handled by the EC-ASEAN economic council and the several conferences, seminars and other programs jointly organized by the EC and ASEAN.

The meetings of foreign ministers is the central body of interaction between the communities. This meeting was not only the first of its kind on a ministerial level between two regional groups, but it symbolizes the principles of regular consultations on the highest level between regional economic associations. The first meeting of foreign ministers took place before the conclusion of the EC-ASEAN cooperation agreement. This illustrates the foremost importance of the EC-ASEAN meetings of foreign ministers.

The proposal for a dialogue after the yearly ASEAN foreign ministers meeting came from ASEAN. This dialogue is integrated into the framework of ASEAN talks with the most important industrial countries and ASEAN trade partners such as the United States, Canada, Japan, Australia, New Zealand, and the EC; its main subjects are economic issues. In this dialogue the EC is only one partner among six. At the talks about Pacific cooperation in 1984 the European delegation was excluded—an indication among others of a recent reorientation of ASEAN toward the Pacific regions. From this region ASEAN seems to expect a stronger impetus than from Europe.

The third institution within the framework of relations can be seen in the meetings between the delegation of the European Parliament and the ASEAN interparliamentary organization, which has taken place every 18 months since 1979. These meetings are not stipulated in the cooperation agreement but have become a forum of exchange of political views below the level of government. The European Parliament plays an important role in formulating common programs in education, culture, science, research and technology. It is the opinion of the two parliamentary groups that their contacts should be made a component of the cooperation agreement. The delegation of the European Parliament holds the view that ASEAN's organization is important as there are many reasons to believe that this body will gradually change into the parliament of ASEAN.

The parliamentary delegations regard the joint consultative committee as a body that does the main work in implementing the agreement. Therefore, they demand that parliamentary members take part in the meetings. The committee has a key position on the economic level insofar as it concludes concrete measures to implement the agreement. As representatives from executive organs of both the EC and ASEAN work in it and form the general regulations and conditions for economic relations, the committee belongs to the political level.

Since the concluding of the cooperative agreement the political relations between the two associations have been institutionalized and extended to a wide area. On account of their common voting procedures the relationship has become a model for political interaction between regional groups. Economically the ASEAN countries seem to look increasingly eastward. The examples given by Japan and South Korea are quite attractive, whereas the problems and issues of economic integration with the EC are basically regarded as insurmountable.

AUSTRALIA, NEW ZEALAND AND THE PACIFIC

Australia's relations with the EC were troubled as early as the mid-1960s when the consequences of the EC's common agricultural policy led to increasing difficulties for Australia's agricultural exports. The EC had become more than self-sufficient in a number of important agricultural products. This caused pressure in world markets and contributed, in Australia's judgment, to a considerable decline in the prices of sugar, cereals, meat and dairy products. When Britain became a member of the EC, the loss of preference in and access to the British market particularly for foodstuffs was considered a significant threat to Australia's trading interests.

The traditional agricultural exports to Britain by Australia and New Zealand clash with community preferences, although the community has made some concessions on meat and butter. Regular consultations are held with Australia at ministerial levels. In 1986 Australia received assurances that the EC would not extend its export subsidies to markets in Asia. Talks were to be held on improving access to the EC markets for Australian beef. Also in 1986 an agreement was reached on maintaining the community's imports of butter from New Zealand, despite the surplus of dairy products within the community.

Eight Pacific nations (Fiji, Kiribati, Papua New Guinea, Solomon Islands, Tonga, Tuvalu, Vanuatu and Western Samoa) adhere to the Third Lome Convention, which went into effect in March 1985. Under the three Lome Conventions the EC provides funds for aid and investment and takes measures to safeguard mineral exports of the Pacific nations. During 1986 discussions conducted with the South Pacific Bureau for Economic Cooperation, the representative agency designated by the nations of the region, concluded that the priorities of the EC in the Pacific were regional cooperation, development of natural resources, transportation and communications.

FURTHER READING

Akrasanee, N., and Rieger, H. C., eds. *ASEAN–EEC Economic Relations.* Singapore: Institute of Southeast Asian Studies, 1982.

Burnett, Alan. *Australia and the European Communities in the 1980s.* Canberra: Department of International Relations, Australian National University, 1983.

Hanabusa, Masamichi. *Trade Problems between Japan and Western Europe.* London: Royal Institute of International Affairs, 1979.

Kapur, Harish. *China and the European Economic Community: The New Connection.* Dordrecht, Holland, and Boston: M. Nijhoff, 1986.

Maull, Hanns W. *Europe and Japan: A Relationship in Search of Roles.* Tokyo: University of Tokyo Press, 1984.

Nordin Sopiee, Chew Lay See, Lim Siang Jin, eds. *ASEAN at the Crossroads: Obstacles, Options and Opportunities in Economic Co-operation.* Kuala Lumpur: Oxford University Press, 1987.

Rothacher, Albrecht. *Economic Diplomacy between the European Community and Japan, 1959–1981.* Aldershot, Hampshire: Gower, 1983.

Stevens, Christopher, ed. *The EEC and the Third World: A Survey.* London: Overseas Development Institute, 1988.

Tsoulakis, Louis, and White, Maureen, eds. *Japan and Western Europe: Conflict and Cooperation.* London: Francis Pinter, 1982.

Wilkinson, Endymion. *Japan versus Europe: A History of Misunderstanding.* Harmondsworth, Middlesex: Penguin, 1985.

Yahuda, Michael. *Towards the End of Isolationism: China's Foreign Policy after Mao.* London: Macmillan, 1983.

THE ARMS RACE IN ASIA

JONATHAN D. POLLACK

WITH Europe, Asia ranks as the most heavily armed continent.[1] At all points of the compass, the nations in the various Asian regions continue to develop or acquire new weapons, even as many among them perceive improved prospects for peace and economic development. Three of the world's avowed nuclear powers (the United States, the Soviet Union and China) deploy nuclear weapons on the Asian land mass or in the Pacific; a fourth (France) tests its weapons in the Pacific; India has tested a nuclear device, although it has not deployed operational weapons; and Pakistan has continued development of a covert nuclear capability. Of the world's seven largest standing armies, five (China, India, Vietnam, Iraq and North Korea) are exclusively Asian, and a sixth (the Soviet Union) deploys approximately a half million soldiers east of the Ural Mountains.

Asia has also been the venue of repeated military conflicts, including the United States' prolonged involvements in Korea and Vietnam, its two principal combat experiences since World War II. Twice since the 1960s, major communist powers have engaged one another militarily: The Soviet Union and China in 1969 and Vietnam and China in 1979. Throughout the 1980s the Soviet Union sought to subdue rebel forces in Afghanistan and prop up its client regime there; Vietnam tried to do the same in Cambodia. India and Pakistan have fought three border wars, though none since 1971. Iran and Iraq engaged in an inconclusive but exceedingly bloody armed struggle for a full 10 years ending in an uneasy truce in 1988. Internal insurrections still fester in the Philippines, Sri Lanka and elsewhere, and a highly armed confrontation remains undiminished between the two Koreas. Finally, the United States and Soviet Union continue to maintain highly capable naval and air forces directed against each other in the waters and air space of the Northern Pacific Ocean.

Yet the widely prevalent term "arms race" seems misleading. Although Asia has repeatedly witnessed military conflicts over the past 40 years, the inhibitions on a direct clash between the superpowers are only marginally less potent in Asia than in Europe. Viewed as a whole, Asia at present seems inclined more toward peace and stability than at any point since

[1] The opinions in this essay are those of the author, and do not reflect the views of the RAND Corporation or its governmental sponsors.

1244

World War II—but it is a heavily armed peace. Much of the arms acquisition under way reflects a determination by various regional countries to defend and assert their own interests; these efforts generally suggest an evolutionary, deliberate approach to enhancing national power rather than any feverish planning for war. Although concerns about the possible proliferation of nuclear weapons persist, the candidate nuclear weapons nations (India and Pakistan) continue to refrain from outright demonstrations of such capabilities, undoubtedly reflecting an appreciation of the risks and uncertainties that an overt program would entail.

At the same time, the superpowers seem disinclined to augment their Asia-oriented deployments much beyond present levels. In considering their military requirements in Asia, both superpowers have confronted two principal limiting factors. First, for historical and political reasons, Washington and Moscow deemed Europe rather than Asia more important to their long-range global interests. Second, for geographic and logistic reasons, open-ended military deployments in Asia entailed major demands on U.S. and Soviet defense resources, since both had to deploy forces over vast distances and without a well-developed local infrastructure to support these deployments. Although decades of effort and changes in technology have modified these constraints, Asia continues to lack the centrality of Europe in the thinking and military planning of the global powers.

Indeed, both superpowers appear to be redefining the scope and character of their regional military commitments, but for different reasons. The United States, the principal beneficiary of the extraordinary economic dynamism evident along the Pacific Rim, no longer deems it necessary to uphold the security of its regional allies on an all-inclusive basis. As Washington's regional security partners have grown in strength and self-confidence, they have assumed more responsibility for their own defense, shifting the United States away from a front-line role. This trend is most visible in South Korea where Seoul's leaders actively seek a redefinition of the U.S.-Korean security relationship along more equitable lines, but it also extends to Japan, Australia, and other countries of the region. Such trends seem likely to diminish the direct American contribution to regional security.

The Soviet Union confronts more vexing choices. Having at great cost and effort built up a major Asia-Pacific military presence since the late 1960s, Moscow has begun to reassess the value of some of these deployments, especially those opposite China. With its presence in the area disproportionately military, the Soviet Union is remarkably isolated from the highly dynamic economies of Asia and the Pacific. As a consequence of Mikhail Gorbachev's efforts to build a political bridgehead in the region (especially with the Chinese), the Soviet Union over time seems likely to reduce the scale of its military activities east of the Urals. But Soviet actions appear equally induced by the budgetary and manpower demands of sustaining such a large regional military presence that yield small discernible gain to Soviet political interests.

Regardless of the specific policy calculations of Washington or Moscow, the ability of either superpower to dominate the Asian political and security landscape in the future seems likely to diminish. The security dynamics of the Asia-Pacific region, therefore, require understanding in a more differentiated context.

MILITARY POWER AND THE PROSPECTS FOR REGIONAL SECURITY

The vastness and diversity of the Asian continent makes generalizations about war and peace difficult. Unlike Europe, Asia lacks a clear-cut political or geographic demarcation that unambiguously defines the concept of regional security. The absence of multilateral security arrangements akin to the North Atlantic Treaty Organization (NATO) and the Warsaw Pact has made the Western Pacific appear a more diffuse and less vital region for both Washington and Moscow. In addition, the ambiguities and discontinuities in the strategic roles of Japan and especially China have further complicated the military requirements of the superpowers. Concepts and strategies derived from the European theater of the Cold War have long dominated U.S. and Soviet defense planning, but the threats and opportunities in the Asia-Pacific region have frequently been very different.

Even if Asia has been deemed less important than Europe to both global powers, it does not make the region unimportant to either. Neither nation is able to exclude the other's presence, and neither is willing to leave the other's power unchecked. But the major factors originally spurring U.S. and Soviet military deployments in the region were local wars (in Korea, in Vietnam, and along the Soviet-Chinese border) rather than the prospect of a direct clash between Moscow and Washington. The drawdown of U.S. ground and air forces in the aftermath of the Korean War and the Vietnam War reflected an expectation that the United States would not directly engage in large-scale regional hostilities. Similarly, pressures on the Soviet Union to reduce its Asian forces indicate diminished concerns about the likelihood of armed conflict with China rather than a reduced challenge from U.S. air and naval power.

Indeed, with several notable exceptions, most countries in Asia judge particular neighbors more pressing security concerns than either superpower. Asia is less an integrated whole than separate clusters of nations that compete within specific geographic domains, with Soviet and U.S. military involvement constituting an additional factor in several strategically significant locations. At the same time, three Asian actors (China, Japan and India) have political ambitions that transcend the region. The logic of a multipolar world is most keenly manifested in Asia, and especially among these three nations. But the military reach of all three remains circumscribed by political, economic and technological constraints that impose limits on the extent of their national capabilities and presumed spheres of influence. The military balance in Asia, therefore, derives largely from various regional or local power configurations rather than predominance exercised by any one single country.

Thus, the propensity of Asian nations to arm and of the superpowers to maintain significant regional military presences suggest a range of motivations and purposes. The deployments of the Soviet Union and the United States reflect the global character of their rivalry, with neither prepared to leave the other's power unchallenged within the world's most dynamic economic region. Both also commit forces as insurance or outright protection for regional allies who otherwise fear domination by more powerful neighbors. In addition, Moscow and Washington view their access to locations and military facilities as contributing to a larger, interlocking structure of deployments stretching from the Northern Pacific to the Indian Ocean to the Persian Gulf. For emergent powers such as China and India, the enhancement of national defense strength is deemed an absolute prerequisite of independent power status, without which their asserted claims to major power roles would lack credibility. Japan, although exceedingly wary of moving toward a military posture independent of the United States, is also committed (in the context of the U.S.-Japanese mutual security treaty and related security understandings) to achieve an enhanced self-defense capability in nearby waters, air space and strategic passageways.

In northeastern and southeastern Asia the consequences persist of past local conflicts that prompted interventions by various great powers. The Korean peninsula, the most heavily armed area in Asia, vividly reflects 40 years of antagonism between North Korea and South Korea, with most of Pyongyang's armies deployed in or near the so-called demilitarized zone. Seoul's imposing ground and air units stand guard to the south, assisted by the only remaining U.S. forces deployed on the Asian mainland. In Southeast Asia most countries maintain far more modest levels of manpower and arms, but all recognize the absence of an outright guarantor of their security. Within this region, only Vietnam possesses forces in very large numbers. Hanoi's total divisional strength numbers 65, two and a half times its strength at the end of the Vietnam War in 1975. But the demands imposed by the military rivalry with China and the continuing effort to dominate Indochina have led Hanoi to maintain more than a million men in uniform.

Thus, the arms competition in Asia reflects the conflict-ridden history of the past four decades. It also suggests the determination of various regional nations to deter the exercise of coercive power against them, as well as the belief that the use of force cannot be precluded in the future. Perhaps most important, few nations see credible alternatives to maintaining a certain level of armament, especially as countries throughout Asia emerge as industrial and technological powers in their own right. The prospect for long-term regional stability, therefore, seems likely to depend on three distinct but interrelated issues. First, will the Soviet Union and the United States move toward a compatible concept of their respective political and military roles in Asia and the Pacific? Second, will the shifting relationships among the prospective major powers in Asia lead to increased rivalry and military competition, or to a framework for relations where various national ambitions mesh rather than clash? Third, will those Asian countries whose recent history has been dominated by war and revolution find a means to achieve less antagonistic relations with their neighbors?

Quite apart from the continued growth of regional military strength, major armed conflict in Asia seems less likely at present than at any point since the end of World War II. The internal instability prevalent in numerous countries during the 1950s, 1960s and 1970s has diminished, with most nations seeking to turn attention toward their domestic programs. The prospect of future external interventions comparable to the Indochina or Afghanistan conflicts seems increasingly remote. At the same time, three decades of Soviet-Chinese hostility are drawing to a close, with both countries prepared to test the possibility of accommodation and diminished military tensions.

However, the economic and political changes among numerous Asian countries, most particularly those of the Pacific Rim, constitute the largest factor altering the region. Since the early 1960s, Japan has moved to the front ranks of the world's industrial and technological powers, and it is beginning to assume an international role commensurate with such power. Fueled by export-led growth, the newly industrializing economies of South Korea, Taiwan, Hong Kong and Singapore have become a potent force in global trade; comparable breakthroughs have also begun to occur in Thailand and certain coastal regions of China. These changes indicate a larger, long-term shift in the international balance of power: East Asia looms much larger in the global economic and technological equation than it did only as recently as the late 1970s. These changes confront both superpowers with major policy challenges, beginning with the continued relevance of their regional military deployments. To consider the inhibitions and opportunities facing Washington and Moscow, the character of U.S. and Soviet regional security strategies require more extended discussion.

THE REGIONAL SECURITY ROLE OF THE UNITED STATES

There are two principal dimensions to U.S. conventional defense planning in Asia. The first concerns the global military rivalry with the Soviet Union as it is manifested in locations deemed vital to American security interests in Asia. (The U.S.-Soviet nuclear weapons competition in the Pacific, although bearing on the conventional forces that the superpowers deploy in the region, is a distinctive issue in its own right, and is discussed separately below.) The second concerns the capacity of regional or local powers aligned with the United States to withstand threats to their territorial integrity and political viability. Given the implications of a direct U.S.-Soviet military conflict or of the use of U.S. forces against an ally of the Soviet Union, the first dimension has received disproportionate attention. Viewed in the context of America's past involvements in Asian conflicts, the latter dimension looms much larger. Moreover, the capacity of Soviet forces to pose a direct threat to U.S. forward deployed power has been a predominant concern only since the mid-1970s, as Moscow's naval and air deployments have grown in size and sophistication.

In contrast to the first two decades of the postwar era, the U.S. regional presence is no longer dominated by security obligations that (at least in theory) sought to emulate the NATO alliance structure. The essence of these security arrangements (for example, the now defunct Southeast Asia Treaty Organization) was a unilateral U.S. commitment to uphold the security of highly vulnerable societies with virtually no will or capacity to defend themselves. This concept proved increasingly questionable in light of the U.S. intervention in Vietnam where a disproportionate American effort ultimately led to a policy failure.

Simultaneous with the rapprochment with China and the effort to disentangle from Vietnam, the Richard Nixon administration began to redefine U.S. obligations to regional security. The Nixon Doctrine entailed a general commitment to assist nations under threat, but with responsibility for national defense resting principally with the specific country rather than with U.S. forces. As these countries grew in economic strength and political resiliency, the direct U.S. security contribution was expected to diminish. Although the United States remained politically committed through various bilateral security agreements, these pacts assumed that the nations of the region would contribute most of the forces required for their own defense.

The intervening two decades since the Nixon Doctrine have brought these assumptions much closer to fruition. The United States maintains formal alliances with Japan, South Korea, the Philippines and Australia, and also continues to uphold more general commitments to the security and territorial integrity of other Asian and Pacific nations. Beyond these statutory and declaratory obligations, however, U.S. forces deployed in the region are specifically committed only for the most threatening of contingencies—that is, the threat of Soviet long-range aviation to U.S. naval and air power in the western Pacific, Soviet threats to air and sea lanes in northeastern and southeastern Asia, threats to freedom of navigation in the Persian Gulf, and the threat of North Korean offensive capabilities directed against South Korea. In South Asia and Southeast Asia the United States has facilitated the efforts of local powers to build up their own defense capabilities, with especially active security assistance programs in Pakistan and in Thailand. But there is an explicit recognition that the United States cannot assume a direct role in upholding the national security of various nations over such a vast geographic expanse.

The risks to American interests are deemed greatest in northeastern Asia. U.S. forces remain concentrated in Japan, South Korea and the Philippines although the importance attributed to these three countries varies substantially. Japan remains the conceptual and locational cornerstone of U.S. regional military policy. Were the United States unable to operate in Japanese waters and from bases in Japan, execution of U.S. roles and missions in East Asia would be next to impossible. At the same time, the emergence of Japan as a global industrial, technological and economic power has led Washington to urge Tokyo to contribute more on behalf of the common security interests of the two countries.

Despite a underspread public perception that Japan receives a "free ride" in its defense relationship with the United States, its contribution is far from negligible. In budgetary terms Japanese defense expenditures (when calculated according to NATO criteria) already surpass U.S. $40 billion, an amount that exceeds the military budget of Great Britain or West Germany. Tokyo contributes $2.5 billion to defraying the costs of the approximately 50,000 American military personnel stationed in Japan—some 40 percent of the total expenses. Although these statistics in part reflect the upward valuation of the yen relative to the dollar since the mid-1980s, the trends are clearly in the direction of an enhanced Japanese contribution. Tokyo also committed itself to increased purchases of U.S. defense equipment and weapons systems during its 1986–1990 defense plan, as well as to sharing Japanese technological know-how in selected areas of defense research and development.

The more important trend, however, is Japan's willingness to broaden the scope of its defense cooperation with the United States. In the spring of 1981 Prime Minister Zenko Suzuki committed Japan to assume responsibility for defense of its territory, air space, and sea lanes to a distance of 1,000 miles. Japan's increased purchase of P-3C Orion patrol craft and of modern fighters (including the F-15) reflect the commitment to enhance the nation's air and sea lane defense capabilities. But implementation of this goal remains a long-term policy objective because Japan lacks the requisite forces to fulfill these obligations and because Japan studiously avoids the acquisition of power projection capabilities. In addition, there has been a steady expansion of intelligence sharing, joint exercises, and other forms of institutional collaboration. Brushing aside Soviet criticisms and warnings, Tokyo has also assented to the deployment of two squadrons of U.S. air force F-16Cs at Misawa in northern Honshu, thereby signalling an increased Japanese readiness to facilitate possible U.S. wartime roles and missions.

Despite these developments Japanese officials demonstrate continued reluctance to be drawn unambiguously into U.S. military operations against the Soviet Union. In a wartime environment, the soviet Pacific fleet would confront the problem of egress through the Soya, Tsugaru and Tsushima straits, the three major choke points lying between the Sea of Japan and the Pacific Ocean; at the same time, Soviet aircraft would need to breach Japanese air space en route to their targets. In 1983 Prime Minister Yasuhiro Nakasone decided that Japan should prepare for interdiction operations against Soviet naval and air forces. Tokyo agreed to set up a defensive screen against hostile aircraft and to bottle up the Soviet fleet in coastal waters by increasing its mine-laying capabilities. But debate persists about Japan's obligation to fulfill these responsibilities whether in response to an immediate threat to its own security, or in the face of a more generalized Soviet threat to regional security. To some observers, this debate is unnecessary in that Japan is augmenting its early warning, air defense and anti-submarine warfare capabilities that would be needed in either scenario. But the absence of Japan's explicit identification with U.S. wartime strategy suggests continuing political inhibitions concerning the scope of U.S.-Japanese defense cooperation.

On the Korean peninsula the presence of U.S. ground and air forces and the assurance of automatic U.S. involvement has been central to maintaining an uneasy peace ever since the armistice of 1953. The principal objective of American policy in South Korea remains the deterrence of North Korean attack and (in the event of deterrence failure) timely assistance for South Korean ground forces that would assume principal responsibility for repelling any North Korean advance. U.S. deployments in South Korea comprise close to half the U.S. combat aircraft inventory in the Pacific, much of it upgraded in recent years. Operation Team Spirit, the annual U.S.-South Korean exercises conducted since 1976, involve close to 200,000 troops from all three services; much to Pyongyang's frustration, the exercises demonstrate an impressive U.S. capability to reinforce its military presence in a potential crisis.

But the logic of the Nixon Doctrine vividly applies on the Korean peninsula: U.S. support is deemed essential to maintaining peace, but the local power assumes principal responsibility for its own defense. In money, matériel and manpower, South Korea makes a substantial contribution even though U.S. officials call for further burden sharing efforts. Indeed, as South Korea's strength and self-confidence have grown, so have calls to redefine the terms of the U.S.-South Korean security relationship. Responding to growing public pressure and nationalist sensitivities, South Korean officials have increasingly urged changes that would upgrade Seoul's status and responsibilities in the alliance. For example, the two governments are considering revisions in the Combined Forces Command structure. These changes would give senior South Korean military officers a more equitable and active voice in the command arrangements, which are presently reserved for U.S. generals. Over the longer run, a gradual withdrawal of the residual U.S. ground force presence seems a likely prospect. But any such decisions will be taken in the context of improved opportunities for meaningful tension reduction on the peninsula.

In both the Japanese and South Korean cases, therefore, the United States' regional allies are assumed to have come of age. At the same time, however, it is not expected that either can stand alone. Indeed, concerning the Japanese, there are compelling reasons for avoiding such a state of affairs, or even the perception that the United States plans to move in this direction. Thus, regional stability continues to depend on a predictable U.S. presence, with key allies prepared to assume an important but delimited range of defense responsibilities on a step-by-step basis.

From Washington's perspective, therefore, a credible U.S. presence remains based on a mutual compact: the United States sustains its security role provided that U.S. forces are able to operate freely within the region. But this expectation has begun to encounter criticism or outright opposition among a number of countries. The most salient issue at present concerns the continued ability of American forces to operate from bases and facilities in the Philippines. Since the end of World War II, U.S. naval and air power has enjoyed access to Clark Air Force Base, Subic Bay and other locations. These arrangements have enabled U.S. and allied forces to train, as well as furnishing excellent facilities for ship repair and matériel replenishment. In the absence of this access, the forward deployment of U.S. power in the Western Pacific and Indian Ocean could prove far more difficult. There is clearly no adequate alternative for facilities developed over such a prolonged period of time. However, the crucial issues concern location and infrastructure, not replacement costs. Although many in Manila support a continuation of the base agreements after their 1991 expiration date, public opinion within the Philippines remains deeply divided. Under such uncertain circumstances, the value of the facilities could diminish considerably, leading the United States to reassess its long-term options for maintaining the regional presence deemed crucial to the credibility of American power in the Pacific.

Thus, the history of the past 20 years bespeaks the maturation of a framework for regional politics, commerce and security: the sustaining of a maritime balance that permits the unimpeded movement of goods, raw materials and energy resources; the deterrence of major military conflict that would jeopardize political stability and internal economic growth; the denial of opportunities for any country to intimidate or coerce its neighbors; and the maintenance of the territorial integrity of individual nations—are all central to this process. U.S. regional security policy, therefore, has become more adaptive and collaborative and less unilateral, in particular by working with allies and other friendly countries in sharing complementary security objectives and needs and by moving toward understandings with nonaligned nations whose political and military goals are generally deemed compatible with the interests and objectives of the United States.

The largest challenge for U.S. regional security policy, therefore, is to mesh the separate requirements entailed in two very different military domains. On the one hand, the United States seeks to fulfill regional expectations of a continued American political and military presence. This has involved an open-ended U.S. commitment to maintain forces in the area and to assist the defense needs of various Asian countries. On the other hand, U.S. military planners retain a predominant concern for denying potential Soviet objectives in wartime in the context of the global military competition with the Soviet Union. Regional support for the first goal has not implied automatic assent to the second policy objective. Many countries desirous of a continued American presence express unease that they could be drawn into a conflict neither of their own choosing nor related to their own security. Given the unavoidable necessity of the forward deployment of U.S. naval and air power, especially from bases and facilities in the western Pacific, the role of these forces in any potential conflict with the Soviet Union looms as a pivotal issue in U.S. regional defense planning. To address these considerations more directly, attention needs to turn to the U.S.-Soviet military rivalry in the Asia-Pacific region.

U.S.-SOVIET MILITARY COMPETITION

For the Soviet Union and the United States the military forces both deploy in Asia and the Pacific constitute the ultimate expression of the value each attaches to the region. Even though the Asian dimension of the global U.S.-Soviet rivalry has aroused concern in some countries about the risks of confrontation, the possibility of a direct military clash between the superpowers remains highly remote. Given the size and diversity of the Soviet and U.S. force postures, however, the purposes and implications of these military deployments necessitate further discussion and assessment.

In contrast to the 1950s and 1960s, when U.S. naval and air power were virtually unchallenged in the Pacific, the U.S.-Soviet balance is much more complicated today. The first change occurred along the Soviet-Chinese border. Beginning in the mid- to late 1960s, Moscow began to augment its defenses opposite China, which until that date were thinly manned and minimally equipped. By the end of the 1970s, Soviet ground forces in Asia comprised approximately 50 divisions and nearly 500,000 men, one quarter of Soviet ground force strength, with modest augmentations continuing to occur in the early to mid-1980s. The period of sustained increases in Soviet ground force strength coincided with the withdrawal of U.S. forces from Vietnam, and with the steady diminution of the residual U.S. presence on Taiwan that had been directed against China. Although these trends were independent of each other, they fostered an impression of Soviet advance and American retrenchment. But these patterns extended to the growth of Soviet air, naval and nuclear systems as well. In the aftermath of the Soviet-Chinese border clashes of 1969 and uncompromising Chinese hostility toward the Soviet Union, Moscow began to prepare for possible conflict with China in a full range of potential contingencies.

Even more telling, Soviet forces in Asia were increased and modernized without drawing upon military units deployed along other fronts. In the late 1970s East Asia was formally designated a separate theater of military action. The Soviet Union did not make a choice among its various potential military fronts; it augmented its power on all of them simultaneously. In addition, military units in Asia for the first time received front-line combat equipment almost simultaneously with new equipment introduced in the European theater. At the same time, the logistic network and infrastructure for Soviet Asian forces were significantly improved, although the ground units were still maintained at a much lower level of readiness than those along the European front.

Over time, the logic of Moscow's regional buildup extended to other potential conflicts and adversaries. As the United States and Japan strengthened their ties with China in the late 1970s, the leadership in Moscow voiced mounting concern about the possibility of a U.S.-Japanese-Chinese quasialliance arrayed against the Soviet Union. In retrospect, the Soviet Union's anxieties were very likely exaggerated for political effect since they helped justify steady increases in the full array of Soviet power deployed in the region. Soviet naval capabilities had already begun a major enhancement during the mid-1970s as the Soviet Union replaced large numbers of obsolescent vessels in what had previously been an antiquated coastal defense force. By the end of the decade, Moscow had created a more comprehensive capability directed simultaneously against the air and naval challenge of U.S. forces deployed in Japan and the Western Pacific as well as the ground based Chinese challenge. Notwithstanding more recent changes in Moscow's political strategy in the region, these deployments remained largely intact at the end of the 1980s.

The cumulative results of these military deployments have proven very impressive, both quantitatively and qualitatively. As a consequence of this prolonged buildup, Soviet forces amply exceed the capabilities required for

China-related contingencies. This conclusion is even more germane in light of an improving relationship with Beijing, with Moscow no longer professing much concern about the possibility of a coordinated U.S.-Japanese-Chinese military strategy directed against the Soviet Union.

The most dramatic changes, however, pertain to the U.S.-Soviet military rivalry in the region. At present, approximately one third of Moscow's air and naval units are located east of the Urals and in nearby Pacific waters. For the first time, these forces (especially medium- and long-range aircraft and attack submarines) pose a credible threat to U.S. military assets in the area. Approximately 45 TU-22M Backfire bombers are stationed west of Lake Baikal, along with an additional 40 assigned to Soviet naval aviation; there are also in excess of 200 SU-24 fighter-bombers. More than one third of Soviet land-based and sea-based missiles targeted against the United States are deployed in Asia as well. However, 171 SS-20 multiple warhead missiles as well as shorter-range nuclear systems are now being dismantled as part of the 1987 U.S.-Soviet INF treaty.

Thus, the trends in ground deployments have been matched or exceeded by the enhancement of air and naval power. Of the nearly 2,000 Soviet tactical aircraft presently assigned to East Asia, more than 90 percent are modern fighters and fighter-bombers, including the MiG-23, MiG-27, MiG-31, SU-17, SU-24 and SU-27. These aircraft are stationed not only on Soviet territory but on islands just north of (and claimed by) Japan and in Vietnam. Medium-range bombers and long-range reconnaissance aircraft have also been transferred to airfields at Cam Ranh Bay. Yet the growth and increased visibility of Soviet naval power deployed in the region (including more than 120 attack submarines and approximately 90 major surface combatants) best testify to Moscow's determination to contest U.S. strength in the western Pacific.

Its naval and air presence in Vietnam typifies the changes in the Soviet Union's regional military deployments. In the immediate aftermath of Chinese-Vietnamese military hostilities in early 1979, Soviet vessels first began to drop anchor at Cam Ranh Bay, one of Asia's best natural harbors and one of the most important U.S. facilities during the Vietnam War. In the subsequent decade Moscow has undertaken a slow but steady augmentation of its military presence there, with its forces in place constituting the largest deployment of Soviet power outside the territory of the Soviet Union or its Eastern European allies. Although Soviet spokesmen repeatedly insist that the country's military presence is only temporary and intended largely for logistic support, minor ship repairs and the like, the scale and scope of Soviet activities appear of greater consequence, especially in light of Vietnam's long-standing aversion to an open-ended foreign military role on Vietnamese territory.

While not a full-fledged locale for Soviet power projection, Cam Ranh Bay has become a very useful asset for Soviet military planners. The Soviet naval and air presence underscores Moscow's determination to enhance its political presence in the region; it inhibits potential Chinese military actions against Vietnam; it is a vital location for Soviet intelligence gathering against U.S. and Chinese military forces; it places Soviet forces near Southeast Asia's sea lines of communication; and it serves as an important staging point for Soviet naval and air operations into the western Pacific and the Indian Ocean. Perhaps most important, an undiminished Soviet presence at Cam Ranh Bay would prove of incalculably greater value militarily and politically should the United States ultimately terminate its base arrangements in the Philippines.

Thus, regardless of the original factors that spurred the Soviet Union to upgrade its regional forces, this buildup has come to serve a broad range of political and military objectives. First, Moscow has increased its ability to neutralize U.S. capabilities to project power in the western Pacific, especially the threat of carrier-based air power to Soviet bases and related military targets. Second, the surface navy and the submarine fleet help protect Soviet strategic missile submarines deployed in the Sea of Okhotsk. (Many observers believe this mission is now the primary objective of Soviet regional deployments.) Third, these forces aid in defending Soviet territorial waters, air space and conventional military assets against intrusion and encroachment. Fourth, Soviet operations now include military targets in China, Japan and other nations without recourse to central strategic systems. Fifth, the Soviet Union has acquired a capability to impede U.S. interdiction operations directed against Soviet forces in wartime. Sixth, Moscow has enhanced its capacity to deter major Chinese military actions to either the north or south, thereby encouraging Beijing's neutrality in the event of U.S.-Soviet hostilities. Finally, the Soviets hope to impinge upon Japanese freedom of action in wartime, thereby limiting Japanese support of U.S. military interests and encouraging Tokyo's neutrality in the event of U.S.-Soviet hostilities.

Despite Moscow's incentives to avoid major hostilities with the United States in the region, there is an interaction between Soviet wartime and peacetime calculations. A major Soviet presence in East Asia underscores Moscow's claim to great power status within the region; it reduces the exposure of vast expanses of Soviet Asia to encroachment or intrusion; and it demonstrates Soviet determination to reduce its long-standing vulnerability to the forward deployment of U.S. military power.

However, the size and diversity of Soviet forces also reflect the extraordinary strategic dilemmas confronted by Moscow in East Asia and the western Pacific. Lacking buffer states along its eastern borders, facing a still partly contested boundary with China, frustrated by the constraints on Soviet freedom of action imposed by the forward deployment of U.S. naval and air power, concerned about the long-term implications of the growth of Chinese power and aware of the potential consequences of a political and military alignment among the United States, Japan and China, the Soviet Union has assembled a massive force posture in Asia that affords it far more military options, but does not provide a meaningful solution to its strategic problems. Indeed, the sheer scale of the Soviet buildup over the past 20 years has been the principal factor contributing to regional support for the U.S. political and military presence, especially the deepening of U.S.-Japanese military cooperation. In the murky realm of debate between capabilities and intentions, the size and scope of the Soviet buildup continue to outweigh Soviet insistence that its military forces pose no threat to the countries of Asia and the Pacific.

To a much greater extent than his predecessors, Gorbachev has demonstrated increased awareness of the intractability of the Soviet Union's Asian security problems. Moscow has emerged as a multifront great power, but its military capabilities have not conferred any particular political advantage among the countries of the region; nor does the Soviet Union seem appreciably more secure than in the late 1970s. The cumulative economic costs of enhancing the Soviet regional military presence have also been substantial; in the context of heightened concern with laggard rates of economic growth, sustaining this acquisition and deployment process is perceived as increasingly burdensome. Since the mid-1980s, the rate at which the Soviet Union has introduced advanced weapons systems into the region has slowed, and Soviet naval activities in the Pacific have also diminished. There have also been some reductions in Soviet forces deployed in Mongolia since 1986, and Soviet military exercises near the Soviet-Chinese border have been scaled back. At the end of the 1980s, for the first time in 20 years, the logic of continuing to augment Soviet military power in the region was openly questioned at senior leadership levels, although it seems extremely unlikely that the Soviet Union will accede to earlier Chinese demands that Soviet forces return to the level maintained prior to the late 1960s buildup.

In the longer run, therefore, Soviet defense needs in East Asia will very likely be dominated by the challenge of U.S. military power. Unlike the 1970s when the United States responded fitfully and inconsistently to the increases in Soviet capabilities in the Pacific, the subsequent decade witnessed sharp alteration in this pattern. The naval component, long the most powerful element in the U.S. Asian-Pacific force posture, has been substantially upgraded, including the recommissioning of several U.S. battleships and the addition of more modern frigates and destroyers. The Seventh Fleet, operating from bases in Japan, the Philippines and Guam, has augmented its carrier-based air power, reconnaissance and antisubmarine warfare assets. With the deployment of 48 F-16s at Misawa, the inventory of the Pacific Air Force has increased to approximately 300 aircraft. Tomahawk cruise missiles have been added to U.S. surface ships and attack submarines, enabling regional commanders to broaden significantly their options against Soviet targets. Similarly, B-52G aircraft based on Guam are now equipped with highly accurate short-range attack missiles that will further supplement other forms of offensive power already deployed in the Pacific.

Although U.S. naval and air forces remain significantly smaller in absolute numbers than their Soviet counterparts, by most military criteria they are far more capable and diversified. In the context of any potential hostilities, U.S. forces (especially the tactical fighter wings deployed in Japan and South Korea) enjoy considerable geographic advantage too. Thus, even as Soviet forces (especially the naval Backfires and the Su-24s) pose an increased threat to U.S. capabilities to project power in Asia (especially the carrier battle groups), the United States has responded by an appreciable augmentation of its own offensive striking power. As the growth of Soviet capabilities in northeastern Asia testifies to the enhanced strategic importance of the region to Soviet planners, so too have U.S. incentives to neutralize or preempt such capabilities in the event of a major U.S.-Soviet confrontation. Hence the dilemma for both superpowers: U.S. forces deployed in locations proximate to Soviet territory pose a threat that the Soviet Union must counter, with the United States in turn not wanting to permit such forces sanctuary.

These shifting circumstances have contributed to a significant redefinition of the role of U.S. regional forces in a potential U.S.-Soviet war and in ways that the Soviet Union finds difficult to counter militarily. As explained by American defense planners, the principal role of U.S. forces in a global conflict would be to deny the Soviet Union any prospective opportunity to "swing" its Asian-based forces to other fronts or to initiate offensive hostilities in the Pacific. Although the plausibility of either scenario is questioned by many military observers, U.S. strategy assumes the early use of naval and air power against Soviet targets in a U.S.-Soviet crisis, thereby preempting any potential actions that Soviet forces might otherwise initiate. Such a "horizontal escalation" scenario posits that the United States should not allow Soviet forces sanctuary. Considered in this context, therefore, northeastern Asia has become far more important to U.S. global strategic calculations than in the past.

Soviet policymakers appear increasingly mindful of the challenge posed by these changes in U.S. defense strategy, and are actively seeking to deflect it by political means. In a major speech at Vladivostok in July 1986 Gorbachev presented proposals for nuclear-free zones in East Asia, restrictions on antisubmarine warfare activity and negotiated reductions in conventional military forces, especially opposite China. In another speech at Krasnoyarsk in September 1988, he proposed a cap on the deployment of nuclear and naval systems, restrictions on the levels and activities of air and naval forces in northeastern Asia as part of a system of confidence building measures and (in the event of a U.S. withdrawal from bases in the Philippines) a withdrawal of Soviet forces from Cam Ranh Bay. Former Chief of the General Staff Sergei Akhromeyev offered parallel proposals in September 1988 to reduce the scale of naval activity in areas proximate to U.S. and Soviet territory, including the outright prohibition of antisubmarine warfare activities directed against missile-carrying submarines.

Although Gorbachev's proposals contained a number of self-serving aspects (in particular, the grossly asymmetrical "trade" of Cam Ranh Bay for U.S. bases in the Philippines), they reflected a growing Soviet concern about the ability of U.S. forward-based power to place vital Soviet military assets at risk, especially Asian-based strategic nuclear weapons. Such issues seem likely to be uppermost in Soviet concerns when and if Moscow and Washington should agree to discuss their respective military deployments in the northwestern Pacific.

In broader terms, moreover, Soviet arms control initiatives directed toward Asia and the Pacific reflect the political aspects of Moscow's regional position and the corresponding need to place recent declarations in the best possible light. At one level these appeals are part of a larger effort to support Soviet claims of reasonable sufficiency and the supposedly defensive orientation of its military forces. However, the Soviet Union remains vexed by its inability to garner much support within Asia for its regional arms control prospects. Many of Moscow's overtures are based largely on appeals either to antinuclear sentiment, especially in the southwestern Pacific and Southeast Asia, or to a more generalized fear among smaller nations of great power domination. Moreover, the seemingly inexorable growth of Soviet regional forces since the late 1960s has abated only recently. Most countries in the region therefore seem disinclined to move very far in Moscow's direction and appear likely to await actual measures in the military arena that would attest more conclusively to changes in Soviet policy.

At the same time, however, geography imparts a certain political advantage to Moscow. The United States has no alternative to its maritime orientation in the Pacific, whereas the predominantly land-based character of Soviet power affords it alternative military options. In addition, the United States has long been more politically and economically active in the region and is therefore more vulnerable when the Soviet Union resorts to issues that have nationalistic appeal. At bottom, the intent of Soviet proposals seems clear: Moscow hopes over time to restrict the ability of U.S. forces to operate in the western Pacific and the Indian Ocean, which as a practical consequence would limit the American presence throughout the region. For this reason alone most Soviet initiatives find very few takers.

Indeed, despite Moscow's appeals to regional antinuclear sentiment, Soviet defense planners undoubtedly recognize that the role of nuclear weapons in Asia and the Pacific is very different from that in Western Europe. Although the concept of extended deterrence has assumed importance in East Asia (especially in Japan), the regional powers have never called for American nuclear deployments equivalent in size or scope to those deployed in the NATO countries. Thus, when SS-20 mobile missiles were introduced in Soviet Asia during the late 1970s and early 1980s, it provoked genuine concern among those countries principally affected by these deployments, especially Japan and China. But no serious calls were heard within the region for the United States to deploy the Asian equivalent of Euromissiles. Rather, the U.S. regional nuclear presence has remained more ambiguous, concentrating largely on offshore, submarine-based deployments rather than any on-the-ground presence of cruise missiles or intermediate-range missiles. Even in South Korea, where it is widely assumed if never officially confirmed that the United States maintains selected tactical nuclear weapon capabilities, the long-term trend in U.S. policy has been to reduce any reliance on such weapons, especially as South Korea has grown more confident about its own self-defense capabilities.

Thus, the predominant role of nuclear weapons in the region has remained associated with nuclear deterrence at a strategic rather than a theater level. In this context, both superpowers retain significant portions of their sea-based strategic nuclear forces either in the Pacific Ocean or the Indian Ocean, or in both. In addition, both retain elements of their nuclear capable bomber forces in the region, and the Soviet Union continues to deploy some of its land-based ICBM force east of the Urals. Despite recent steps toward a strategic nuclear arms control agreement, both Moscow and Washington appear determined to uphold the credibility and integrity of their Asian-based strategic nuclear deployment. This has led the United States to stand by its commitment to "neither confirm nor deny" the presence of nuclear weapons on any of its Pacific-based naval forces, lest American nuclear deterrence requirements be undermined or otherwise eroded. In a different context, Soviet concern about the risks posed to its sea-based nuclear forces by American forward deployed air and naval power partly explains Moscow's calls for restrictions on U.S. military activities in locations proximate to Soviet territory.

In both word and deed, therefore, both superpowers recognize that East Asia remains integral to their thinking about war and peace. Regardless of factors that seem likely to inhibit future growth in the conventional power that the United States and Soviet Union deploy within the area, neither country sees an easy alternative to their prevailing strategic rivalry. This conclusion seems even more relevant in light of Asia's growing industrial and technological importance, and in view of the determination of the region's emergent major powers to develop military power commensurate with their long-term national goals. Attention, therefore, needs to be turned to the prospective contributions of China and India to the regional power equation.

CHINA AND INDIA: THE EMERGENT MAJOR POWERS

Among the region's major powers China and India aspire to autonomous security and foreign policy roles. Although both maintain or seek closer relations with the superpowers, neither desires a highly encumbering relationship, especially in the national security realm. In this respect Chinese and Indian aspirations remain distinct from Japan's since Tokyo shows little inclination to move toward an independent strategic position. For Beijing and New Delhi, therefore, enhancement of their autonomous defense capabilities remains a *sine qua non* in their pursuits of great power status. Even as both maintain attention to the prodigious tasks of societal and economic development, the enhancement of their military strength remains a central national goal.

In the case of China, there have been significant changes n the 1980s in Beijing's thinking about national security. As concerns about military hostilities with the Soviet Union have diminished, the Chinese have reoriented their defense planning toward the long-term requirements of a credible, more professionalized military force. This shift has entailed significant departures from the past emphasis on deterrence at the two poles of "people's war" and nuclear weapons, and toward a broader array of defense needs. On the one hand, Beijing seems certain to maintain attention to narrowing the imbalance of forces between itself and the Soviet Union and to upholding the credibility of China's independent nuclear deterrent. On the other hand, however, the military leadership appears convinced of the need to upgrade appreciably its air and naval forces, which continue to derive largely from Soviet technology initially supplied to China in the late 1950s and early 1960s. These efforts have included measures to accelerate the flow of advanced technology from the West, including purchases of military equipment or components in areas where China is especially deficient.

Thus, China appears intent on gradually developing a modest power projection capability. An enhanced capacity to deploy forces in various potential "local war" scenarios (for example, in defending claims to contested islands in the South China Sea, or in the event of renewed border tensions with India) has created concern among China's neighbors about its power ambitions. Not unexpectedly, Beijing insists that such military strength is intended only to uphold Chinese sovereignty and territorial claims. Viewed in a larger perspective, it reflects the leadership's conviction that Chinese power will never be credible in the absence of a more technologically sophisticated, professionalized defense force encompassing the full array of military needs. Given China's present level of technical and industrial capabilities—not to mention Beijing's compelling need for regional stability to advance its broader goals in national development—concerns about a more powerful, highly assertive China generally remain long term rather than immediate. A crucial political task for China, therefore, is the augmentation of its national power without alarming its neighbors, at the same time that it hopes to sustain a strategic position independent of both superpowers but antagonistic with neither.

India seems equally committed to its national power goals. Having long been the beneficiary of extraordinarily generous military assistance from the Soviet Union—including licensing arrangements for coproduction of advanced combat aircraft and leasing of a nuclear-powered submarine—New Delhi seems intent on achieving a more balanced relationship between Moscow and Washington. A significant improvement in U.S.-Indian relations in recent years—including major changes in American technology transfer policy—seems likely to afford India much more diversified political and strategic options in the future.

As New Delhi has reassessed its security goals, there has been a pronounced shift away from its past preoccupation with Pakistan, and even to a certain extent away from its competition with China. Having built up its ground and air forces to a position of unquestioned predominance on the subcontinent, the leadership has turned its attention to a broader Indian Ocean role. This role includes the capacity to deploy air mobile forces to quell insurrections in neighboring locales (e.g., Sri Lanka and the Maldives), and the development of a far more powerful navy, thereby underscoring India's determination and conviction to become the dominant power in the region.

In the background, however, the option of an avowed nuclear weapons capability also looms. India's 1974 nuclear detonation signalled New Delhi's determination to be accorded great power status. Although the leadership has avoided any decision to pursue an outright weapons capability, the country has made enormous strides in the intervening period to acquire the wherewithal for a full-scale program. This has included a major growth in India's supply of fissile material and significant advances in potential delivery systems, including missiles.

However, the development of this nuclear potential has not been free of negative consequences. In the aftermath of the 1974 test Pakistan began a highly determined effort to acquire a covert nuclear capability. These efforts entailed a wide array of illicit activities designed to provide Islamabad with the requisite materials for a rudimentary weapons program, all in defiance of U.S. nonproliferation policy. Most estimates credit Pakistan with having achieved such a capability, a point that the late President Zia virtually admitted.

The fact that neither New Delhi nor Islamabad has chosen to exercise opening its nuclear option attests to a mutual recognition of the potential risks to both countries. In the long term, however, it remains to be seen whether either or both will continue to maintain this restraint. The existence of "near nuclear" capabilities has conferred certain political advantages to both nations; given the increased possibility of an improvement of Indian-Pakistan relations in a period of diminished regional tensions and with a new government in Islamabad, the threshold may yet not be breached. However, in the absence of explicit understandings and agreements between both countries, the prospect of an overt nuclear competition in South Asia remains a distinct possibility, bringing with it highly unsettled long-range consequences. Although the paradoxical logic of nuclear deterrence might apply with equal force to newcomers in the weapons arena, the prospect of such an outcome leaves many observers discomfited. It remains to be seen, therefore, whether and how India can achieve its power ambitions without resorting to such a consequential step given the attendant uncertainties that would follow in its wake.

CONCLUSION

For better or worse, military power occupies a central position in the international politics of Asia and the Pacific. The existence of such military competition (especially the U.S.-Soviet rivalry) seems an inescapable dimension of the Asian landscape, and this seems unlikely to change in the near future. Indeed, the pursuit of far-reaching national objectives on the part of numerous countries in the region is inseparable from the development of such capabilities. As a component of national power, however, the military instrument is too blunt to stand alone. Viewed in this light, the prospects for long-term regional stability are dependent on a broader array of political, economic and technological achievements.

The difficulties in Soviet Asian policy goals is evident in this context. The deployment of large military forces in the region attests to Moscow's claims to global political equivalence with the United States; by virtue of such power, it cannot be ignored. But the singular concentration on the military dimension of Soviet national power—though now leavened by a more active and constructive political and diplomatic posture—leaves Moscow with a narrow range of options. Having staked its claim to military preponderance in relation to its neighbors, Moscow faces a daunting task in altering the geopolitical circumstances it helped create. The test will be to devise a political concept for its regional security role acceptable to its neighbors and the United States. But this concept cannot exclude U.S. power from the region and cannot insist upon compliance by its neighbors as the price of good relations with the Soviet Union.

For the United States, the problems are somewhat different. It faces the difficult tasks of alliance management, a problem compounded by potentially very contentious trade and technology issues, especially with Japan. But it, too, sees no easy alternative to the continued maintenance of military power in the region. Given the expense and complexity inherent in deploying sophisticated capabilities over such long distances, the burden sharing argument will remain acute, especially with Japan and South Korea. Yet unrelenting pressure on a nation such as Japan to do more could have adverse political consequences, a point clearly understood by policymakers in both Washington and Tokyo.

In a larger sense both Moscow and Washington will adapt to the power of Asia's indigenous actors. However, given the impossibility of predicting the precise configurations of national power, the superpowers will undoubtedly seek to maintain substantial military strength in Asia and the Pacific. Put simply, the region looms too large in global trends for either country to abdicate its claim to regional presence and position, if not predominance. For this reason alone, the regional arms competition will remain a crucial if admittedly imperfect means for maintaining peace and stability.

FURTHER READING

Asian Security, 1988–89. London: Brassey's Defence Publishers for the Research Institute for Peace and Security, Tokyo, 1988.

East Asia, The West, and International Security: Prospects for Peace. Adelphi Papers 216–218. London: International Institute for Strategic Studies, 1987.

Kihl, Young Whan, and Grinter, Lawrence, eds. *Security, Strategy, and Policy Responses in the Pacific Rim.* Boulder, Colorado: Lynne Rienner, 1989.

Nuclear Weapons and South Asian Security. Washington, D.C.: Carnegie Endowment for International Peace, 1988.

Solomon, Richard H., and Kosaka, Masataka, eds. *The Soviet Far East Military Buildup: Nuclear Dilemmas and Asian Security.* Dover, Massachusetts: Auburn House, 1986.

Spector, Leonard S. *The Undeclared Bomb.* Cambridge, Massachusetts: Ballinger Publishing Company for the Carnegie Endowment for International Peace, 1988.

Stuart, Douglas T., ed. *Security Within the Pacific Rim.* Aldershot, Hampshire and Brookfield, Vermont: Gower, 1987.

ISLAM IN ASIA AND THE SOVIET UNION

GEORGE JOFFE

INTRODUCTION

WITHIN the world of Islam the Muslim populations of Asia and the USSR represent its most significant demographic component. Out of an estimated worldwide population of 860.39 million Muslims in 1987—17.2 percent of the total world population and distributed among 172 different countries—the Muslims of Asia totaled 571.15 million, with those of the USSR providing a further 31.67 million—70 percent of the world total.[1] Although these figures, which are based on U.N. definitions of East Asia and South Asia, include Muslims in the Asiatic Middle East (who number about 145 million), Asia and the USSR still account for 53 percent of the world total of Muslims when Middle Eastern Muslims are excluded.

Although only four countries have no Muslim population at all, only seven Asian countries have a Muslim majority in their populations. Of these, two (Brunei and the Maldive islands) are very small states indeed, and in one (Malaysia) the Muslim population is merely a bare majority—a situation that has caused constant political problems. In fact, the only true Muslim states in Asia are clustered around the Indian subcontinent (Afghanistan, Pakistan and Bangladesh) or form one of the great Asian island states (Indonesia). Three of them (Bangladesh, Indonesia and Pakistan) are, nonetheless, the largest Islamic states in the world and they thus give to Asian Islam a vital role within the Muslim world overall.

The population figures for the USSR present an anomaly, however. Although the figures given above—taken from U.N. sources originally—indicate a total Muslim population of 31.67 million in 1987, most observers concur in suggesting that the true figure for the Soviet Muslim population should be at least 45 million.[2] According to the 1979 census the figure was even then 45.54 million, with a projection of between 64 million and

---

[1] *Britannica Book of the Year, 1988,* p. 303.
[2] M. Feshbach, "Trends in the Soviet Muslim Population: Demographic Aspects," in *The USSR and the Muslim World,* ed. Y. Ro'i (London: George Allen and Unwin, 1984), 94; S. Akiner, *Islamic Peoples of the Soviet Union* (London: Kegan Paul International, 1986), 40.

MUSLIMS IN ASIA AND THE USSR, 1987

Country	Muslims (millions)	Total population (millions)	Percent
Afghanistan	10.50 (Sunni) 3.55 (Shiite)	14.19	98.9
Bangladesh	91.25	105.31	86.6
Bhutan	0.07	1.34	5.2
Brunei	0.15	0.24	62.5
Burma	1.50	39.22	3.8
Cambodia	0.15	7.69	2.4
China (including Hong Kong and Macao)	25.70	1.078.25	2.4
India	88.88	783.04	11.4
Indonesia	150.03	172.25	87.1
Japan	—	220.27	—
North Korea	—	21.38	—
South Korea	—	42.07	—
Laos	0.31	3.75	1.0
Malaysia	8.75	16.54	52.9
Maldives	0.20	0.20	100.0
Mongolia	—	1.98	—
Nepal	0.45	17.56	2.7
Pakistan	102.79	106.19	96.7
Philippines	2.47	57.36	4.3
Singapore	0.43	2.64	16.3
Sri Lanka	1.24	16.54	7.6
Thailand	2.04	53.73	3.8
Taiwan	—	19.63	—
USSR	31.67	282.80	11.2
Vietnam	0.63	62.46	1.0

Source: *Britannica Book of the Year, 1988,* pp. 762–63.

75 million for the year 2000, depending whether the growth rate is 2.6 percent or 2 percent per year. It is a prospect that already frightens Soviet planners, since the average Soviet annual growth rate is expected to be only 0.7 percent; the result will be that the proportion of Muslims in the Soviet population will then have reached 21 percent.

The reason for the anomaly between national and U.N. figures is more difficult to determine. It is clear that the national census figures reflect ethnicity rather than religious practice and thus include many people who are no longer practicing Muslims. According to one recent analysis of religious attitudes in the Muslim republics of the USSR, 56.5 percent of the populations regarded themselves as, in some sense, believers; and up to

85.1 percent still paid at least lip service to Islamic practice[3]—about 38 million people. Furthermore, the census figures do not always differentiate between Muslim majority populations and non-Muslim minority populations, so that the Muslim total can easily be overstated. The U.N. figures, however, attempt to define actual adherents, and this difference of definition may well explain the significant demographic anomalies described above.

ISLAM IN ASIA BEFORE COLONIALISM

The advent of Islam into Asia easily dates from the initial Arab defeat of the Sassanid Empire in Persia. At the same time, it took place against the background of the internal struggles between the successors to the Prophet Muhammad and in the context of the civil wars that marked the first century of Islam as an international religious force. In AD 634, just 2 years after the death of the Prophet, the Arab armies destroyed the military might of Sassanid Persia (already enfeebled by a prolonged struggle with Byzantium between 602 and 628) at the Battle of Qadisiya in southern Iraq. The victory opened up the whole of the Iranian plateau to Arab conquest, although effective occupation of eastern Persia-Khurasan was to be delayed for a further 50 years by the Riddah war (632–34) and the first and second Fitnah wars (656–61 and 683–92): internal struggles over control of the caliphate that eventually ended in the creation of the Umayyad dynasty.

The crucial event was the penetration of the Arab armies across the Oxus River into Transoxania and Bukhara, Herat and Kabul. The first moves in this direction came at the end of the 670s under the first Umayyad caliph, Muawiya. However, despite further advances under his son, Yazid, the real occupation came at the start of the eighth century with the occupation of Bukhara and Samarkand, and an Arab thrust from present-day Afghanistan into Sind. Under the caliphs Abd el-Malek and Walid, the attempts of the Transoxanian city-states to use Chinese support to counter Muslim advance was finally overcome, and Islam had found a permanent place in Asia with its eastern limits drawn around Bukhara and Samarkand in central Asia, and along the Indus River further south.

However, although Islam had found a permanent place in Asia, Asian society still had many convulsions to go through before it took on forms similar to those that exist today. Not only were Iran and Afghanistan the cradles of the first great schism in Islam—the development of Shia and Kharajism as a result of the struggle between the Umayyads and the descendents of the Prophet's cousin, Ali—but it was in Asia that Islam had to come to terms with the fact that survival depended on its ability to transcend its Arab origins. The initial Arab occupation of Sassanid Persia had forced Arab leaders both to confront the consequences of assimilating an alien and sophisticated culture, and to establish some way of controlling

[3] A. Bennigsen, "Unrest in the World of Soviet Islam," *Third World Quarterly* 10, no. 2 (April 1988): 772.

vast alien territories and populations with a numerically limited and scattered Islamic Arab elite.

The Umayyad solution was to create an Arab ruling caste, an Arab kingdom[4]—located in special garrison encampments, the *amsar,* or on estates held under the *qatai* system in which title depended on cultivation and taxation—to which access was only possible by ethnic link. The masses of the conquered populations were persuaded to adopt Islam by the tax advantages it offered (Muslims were exempt from certain taxes), but as *mawali* they were still excluded from full membership in the Arab Muslim community. Those who did not convert to Islam became *dhimmis,* protected populations who enjoyed a normatively inferior status within the Islamic world. The *mawalis,* however, as Muslims, were aware of their right to egalitarian treatment under Islam and resented their economic disadvantage when compared with the status of the Arab ruling caste.

The *mawali* communities turned to Shia and Kharajism as means to express their resentment. Under Omar II (r. 717–20), the Arab-dominated Umayyad caliphate recognized the lack of viability in the system it had created by allowing the *mawalis* effective equality with Arabs in Khorasan. The damage had been done, however, for Shia had found a permanent home in Iran and parts of Afghanistan. The *mawalis* in Khorasan, dissatisfied with the Umayyad concessions, supported an extremist Shia movement, the Hishamiya, which eventually destroyed the Umayyad caliphate, replacing it with the Abbasid caliphate by the middle of the eighth century.

The crucial factor for the spread of Islam in Asia in the creation of the Abbasid caliphate was that the domination of the Islamic world by an Arab elite was broken. Although it would be quite wrong to suggest that the underlying reason for the Hishamiya rebellion was a racial conflict—it had far more to do with economic resentment among the *mawalis* and some Arab groups who felt themselves to be the victims of discrimination—it is certainly the case that an important by-product was, in the east at least, that the Arab domination of the political system was removed. A further by-product was the growth of local non-Arab centers of power as Abbasid power declined and the new capital at Baghdad (the Umayyad capital had been in Damascus) lost control of the periphery.

One reason for the increased autonomy shown by the eastern elements of the Abbasid caliphate, particularly around Khurasan, was that the province acted as the main core of Abbasid military power—thus displacing the Arabs from what had been a key role in their control of Islamic affairs. However, equally as important was the massive growth in trade, in which the Islamic world acted as a focus for the surrounding regions and where the east of that world was the most important component. Iran and Afghanistan provided the silver, iron and copper on which the Abbasid Empire depended. The east was also the focus of international trade, controlling the silk road from China; silks, spices, aromatics, wood and tin from

[4]The phrase was coined by Bernard Lewis; see his *The Arabs in History* (London: Hutchinson, 1970), 64.

southeast Asia by sea; and skins, furs and amber from Scandinavia. It was in the Euphrates-Tigris region—the Jazirah—that the Abbasid Empire developed a comprehensive banking system that further stimulated trade.

The actual breakup of the Abbasid Empire came about after the caliphate of Harun ar-Rashid in 813, in what are known as the fourth Fitnah wars. By 820, Tahir, a Persian general from Khurasan had set up an autonomous dynasty there, and thus ushered in the epoch of local dynastic struggles and the loss of the universal Islamic political vision. It was an event that, paradoxically, provided the eastern Islamic world with the catalyst it needed to stimulate further expansion. By breaking away from the straitjacket of Arab domination, the development of an indigenous political system in Khurasan within the Islamic world provided the dynamism to expand the frontiers of that world.

The expansion northward

The expansion of Islam into what is now the USSR began shortly after the death of the Prophet, with Arab armies conquering the predominantly Christian areas of Azerbaijan in 639 and occupying Dagestan in 643. The advance was stopped at the town of Derbent in 686, as the Arabs found themselves confronted by the nomadic Khazars to the north and by the Christian powers of Armenia and Georgia to the west.

Under Arab occupation the population of Azerbaijan rapidly accepted Islam, although conversion in the mountains of Dagestan was far slower, being completed only in the 12th century. Further east—to the east of the Caspian Sea in Central Asia, where the populations professed a variety of faiths (Zoroastrianism, Buddhism, Manichaenism and Christianity)—the Arab armies occupied Bukhara in 676 and reached as far as the Syr Darya River, beyond the Oxus, by 716.[5] The area soon accepted Islam in place of its earlier multiple religious confessions.

The next stage of Islamization began in the 10th century and was pacific in nature, expanding along the trade routes—north along the fur road and the Volga River, and east along the silk road. The resistance of the Khazars to the north was sidestepped as merchants converted the Volga Bulgars to Islam in 920,[6] in the lands now occupied by the Tatar population of the USSR. In the 10th century Islam also penetrated through trade into the Urals, around the modern Bashkir Republic. Further south, Islam spread along the silk road, north of the Syr Darya River, into Kirghizstan and eventually reached Xinjiang in China. Full Islamization of these new areas, however, was only achieved in the early 19th century.

The spread of Islam was then interrupted by a cataclysmic event—the 13th-century Mongol invasion of Central Asia. At a stroke, the rulers of the region ceased to be Muslim, becoming instead, Buddhists and Nestorian Christians. The Islamic response was to transform itself into a popular

[5] A. Bennigsen and C. Lemercier-Quelquejay, *Les Musulmans oubliés: L'Islam en Union Sovietique* (Paris: Maspéro, 1981), 11.
[6] M. G. S. Hodgson, *The Classical Age of Islam,* vol. 1 of *The Venture of Islam* (Chicago: University of Chicago Press, 1974), 311.

religion by means of Sufism. Sufi mysticism had long played a role in popular Islam, with Mery and Bukhara as traditional centers for the Sufi orders. Now these orders, particularly the Naqshbandi and the Qadiriya, acted as the guarantors of Islamic tradition among the mass of people living under Mongol rule.

Within a century, however, rulers of the Golden Horde and the khanate of Chagatay had become Muslim, thus restoring Islamic uniformity. Islam then expanded further into the Crimea, the southern Russian steppes and western Siberia. At the same time, the Islamization of the Caucasus began, aided in the 15th century by the growth of Ottoman influence along the northern Black Sea coast. By then, although Islam had not reached its maximum extent in the north, it had reached its apogee and would soon have to confront the aggressive expansion of Muscovy.

The expansion eastward

The expansion of Islam into the Indian subcontinent also began under the Arab kingdom at the start of the eighth century. In 712 an Arab army occupied Sind and then, during the century, pushed up into the northern Punjab. Attempts to move into Kashmir were, however, repulsed. It was really only with the development of local and autonomous political entities in Afghanistan that a determined effort was made to overcome the buffer principalities, such as Hindu Shahiya, that now prevented any Islamic expansion eastward.

The development of the ethnically Turkic Ghaznavid state in Afghanistan in 977 marked the beginning of the real Islamic conquest of the Indian subcontinent. The Ghaznavis were descendants of a Turkic slave military caste that took over power in west Khurasan and Afghanistan, with their capital at Ghazna; they were the first of the great Turkic Islamic dynasties in the region. They were soon to be followed by the Seljuk Turks, pastoral nomads in the Oxus basin who forced the Ghaznavids out of Khurasan and then expanded westward in the 11th century. The Ghaznavids annexed Transindus and parts of Hindu Shahiya, while raiding annually between 1000 and 1026 into the Punjab and down to the coast at Somnath. Any plans for occupation, however, were hindered by the Rajput clans, and a permanent Islamic base was not to be achieved for at least a century.

Eventually the Ghaznavids, because of the loss of Khorasan, were forced to move into the Punjab plains to exploit the Hindu plainsmen for taxes to support their Muslim armies.[7] A new capital was set up at Lahore at the end of the 11th century, but the Ghaznavid state was soon taken over by Iranians from the Ghur region. Moving into the Punjab via the Gomal Pass from Afghanistan, rather than via the more usual Khyber Pass, the Ghuri carried their jihad into the Punjab, conquering Sind in 1182, Lahore in 1185 and Delhi in 1192.

The occupation of Delhi marked the beginning of a permanent Islamic presence in India. The Delhi sultanate was a ruling elite formed from Turks

[7] Hodgson; *The Expansion of Islam in the Middle Periods,* vol. 2 of *The Venture of Islam* (Chicago: University of Chicago Press, 1974), 41–42.

settled in Afghanistan and the indigenous Irano-Afghani nobility, supported by a mercenary army of Turks, Persians and Afghans.[8] It was to last until the 16th century, extending its control and influence over Gujarat, the northern Deccan, Jaunpur, Malwa and, intermittently, Bengal. Although the sultanate depended on its links westward to Afghanistan, it constantly had to face threats from the Rajput clans, the rump Ghaznavid state in Afghanistan and the breakaway of independent Turkish sultanates from its sovereign territory.

At the end of the 13th century the Delhi sultanate found itself cut off from Afghanistan as a result of the Mongol invasions of the Punjab between 1270 and 1306, and by Tamerlane in 1398. Thereafter there were a series of dynasty changes, ending with an Afghan takeover in 1451 by the Lodis—a situation that profoundly enfeebled the sultanate. The constant breakaways also damaged it—with Bengal becoming independent in the 13th century, Gujarat and Malwa breaking away, and the Deccan breaking up into five small states under the Bahmanis (an Afghani group) between 1311 and 1538.

The sociopolitical structures of the Delhi sultanate did little to strengthen central power, for it was based on a variant of the *qatai* system. *Iqta* grants (grants of estates on feudal terms) to *muqti* (local governors) diffused central power. The tax system worsened this by isolating the Muslim elite. In addition to the Muslim taxes of *ushur* (a tax of between 20 and 50 percent on agricultural produce), *zakat* (a tithe of 10 percent) and booty (20 percent of all booty taken), the state depended on the *jiziyah* tax, a poll tax paid by non-Muslims. The tax system was sufficiently important to persuade the Delhi sultans to discourage conversions, which otherwise reduced its tax base.

Indeed, the inherent weaknesses of the Delhi sultanate were such that it eventually succumbed to renewed attacks from Afghanistan where Babur Timuri, a Mongol descendant and founder of the Timurid Mogul dynasty, had taken power in Kabul and Kandahar in 1517. After an unsuccessful invasion in 1523–24, Babur tried again in 1525–26 and destroyed the armies of Sultan Ibrahim of Delhi at the battle of Panipat. In the following year Babur also destroyed Rajput power at the battle of Kanwaha. By 1530 he had constructed a new Muslim empire stretching from the Indus to Bengal; this, although subjected to dynastic dispute under his son, Humayun, between 1540 and 1545, was to form the core of the Mogul Empire for the next 200 years.

The final construction of the Mogul Empire was carried out by Humayun's son, Akbar, who conquered Jaipur in 1568, Gujarat in 1572, Bengal in 1576, Kashmir in 1586, Orissa in 1592 and Sind in 1595. The Hindu Deccan kingdoms were taken over in 1605. Mogul control of the dynasty's homeland in Kandahar, however, became increasingly tenuous and eventually ceased completely in 1649.

The Mogul Empire represented a period of great stability in northern and central India, and its success was based on the subtle way in which its

[8] R. Thapar, *A History of India* (Harmondsworth, Middlesex: Penguin, 1966), 1:237.

rulers exploited their joint Muslim-Hindu heritage. In fact, the empire was based on Afghan soldiers and Rajput Hindu administrators.[9] There was a formal equality between Muslims and Hindus, and the *jiziyah* for non-Muslims was abandoned. Hindus participated in the emperor's privy council, provided provincial governors and even acted as military commanders (around 30 percent of the officer corps was Hindu), thus forming an administrative aristocracy—the *mansabdars*. They were prevented from forming a hereditary caste by being dependent on a state salary or by being rotated around the empire; and by being subject to heavy death duties, so that inherited wealth could not acquire a political significance.

The essential catalyst for the system was the personality of the emperor. He held the balance of power, defined the vital atmosphere of mutual tolerance and sustained the normative culture of his empire. Under Akbar this was Persian, although he himself was of Turkic origin. Indeed, he even tried to enshrine the role of the emperor in a kind of personality cult dedicated to the divinity of the monarchy. The cult never extended beyond his own circle, but the fact that he created it indicates the primordial role accorded to the institution of the emperor.

The 17th century was the Mogul golden age. Nonetheless, even then the empire faced serious problems and threats. The Sikhs in the Punjab began to create their own distinctive religion and revolted against the Moguls in mid-century. The Sikh revolt was only crushed finally in 1716. By that time, however, the decline of the Mogul Empire, which began in 1712, was already evident. The Hindu populations on the fringes of the empire exacted a revenge through the Marathas, whose marauding bands eventually sacked Delhi, the Mogul capital, in 1738—while invasions started from Persia in the same year and from Afghanistan 10 years later. At the same time, the British presence in India was beginning to make itself felt. Finally, in 1757, Afghan invaders brought the Mogul Empire to an end.

Islam in Malaysia and Indonesia.
Unlike the situation in Central Asia or the Indian subcontinent, Islam in Indochina and the great Pacific archipelagos spread largely as a result of trade contacts with India and the Arabian Peninsula. Islam was able to establish itself in the region because of its cultural sophistication, which appealed to the great urban-based kingdoms. However, its popular appeal arose—particularly in Malaysia—because of its diffusion through Sufi *tariqas* and because it was able to incorporate local popular religious tradition.

The spread of Islam throughout this area owed much to the cultural dominance of its precursor, the Hindu and Buddhist Indic culture that had been brought there by Indian trading communities. In fact, it was partly because Islam was introduced by the same communities that it progressed so effectively inside Malaysia, Java and Sumatra.[10] Indeed, as Clifford Geertz

[9] P. Spear, *A History of India* (Harmondsworth, Middlesex: Penguin, 1970), 2:52.
[10] Hodgson, *The Expansion of Islam,* p. 543; see also C. Geertz, *Islam Observed: Religious Development in Morocco and Indonesia* (Chicago: University of Chicago Press, 1968), 11.

suggests, "in Indonesia Islam did not construct a civilization, it appropriated one."[11] Islamization of the coastal regions began in the 14th century. Islam had become a major force in Malaysia by 1500 and in Java a century later.

The crucial event was the breakup of the Buddhist mercantile state of Sri Vijaya, which had controlled trade through the straits of Malacca at the end of the 12th century. It was replaced by independent city-states vying for control of the vital waterway that connected the Indian and Chinese commercial worlds. In the latter part of the 13th century two cities on the Sumatran side of the straits adopted Islam, to be followed by Melaka, the dominant city on the straits.

From these footholds on the coast, Islam was spread more widely by itinerant Sufi preachers attached to the dominant trading communities. They provided Islam with an immediate popular appeal and, conversely, marked Islam in the region with a strong mystical tradition that combined with the Indic cultural legacies to produce the typical eclectic and malleable character of Indonesian and Malaysian Islam. This was particularly significant in the case of Malaya and Sumatra, where the spread of Islam was helped by a certain linguistic homogeneity through the generalized use of Malay. The result was that inland sultanates developed, in which popular sentiment was attracted to Islam by its ability to integrate folk tradition and myth—thus preserving the continuity of a certain level of popular culture.

Further north, in Indochina, things were very different, although along the coast Muslim communities based on trade also grew up. Inland, Islam made very little headway, even though the king of Cambodia did, on one occasion, convert to Islam. The main reason for this was that these kingdoms did not depend on coastal trade. Instead, they were based on agrarian activities in which regional trade played little part. As a result, the normal methods of Islamic diffusion could hardly apply.

In Java the process of Islamization was also different and depended on the introduction of European influence into the Indonesian archipelago. As a result first of Portuguese settlement on the coast and then, 50 years later (in 1596), of Dutch settlement in search of spices, the trading patterns of the coastal areas changed. The Muslim coastal trading principalities along the north Javanese coast—Bantam, Tjirebon, Demak, Djapara, Tuban, Grisik and Surabaja—had already converted to Islam but had been welded into the Muslim sultanate of Mataram, a single state based on an agrarian economy, in which trading had become a peripheral economic activity by 1582. The arrival of the Dutch along the coast intensified this tendency toward an internalized agrarian economic base. Thus, Islam in Java acquired its introspective character as a result of growing Dutch pressure on its periphery. By the middle of the 18th century the sultanate had become a satrapy of the Dutch East India Company.[12]

[11] Geertz, *Islam Observed,* p. 11.
[12] L. H. Palmier, *Social Status and Power in Java* (London: Athlone Press, 1969); 4.

THE COLONIAL CHALLENGE

Islam in Asia had a quite different colonial experience from Islam in other parts of the Islamic world. Outside Asia, colonialism developed really as a result of European expansionism in the 19th century, in the wake of the Napoleonic Wars and as a result of the development of capitalism in Europe. In the Mediterranean, it is true, the maritime confrontation between Christianity and Islam—the "forgotten frontier" [13]—continually threatened the integrity of the Muslim world. It was, however, never breached, except for transient Spanish and Portuguese settlement on the North African coast. In Asia, the integrity of the Islamic world was breached long before—first by the Muscovites in Russia and Central Asia, then by the Dutch in the East Indies and finally by Britain in India.

The Russian threat

The crucial factor that distinguishes the Russian reaction against Islam from that elsewhere—except for that of the Balkans—is that much of the future Russian population had spent three centuries under Muslim control before the reaction developed and thus had an intimate knowledge of their enemy. Contrary to popular belief, however, the rule of the Golden Horde and of the Tatar khanates was not oppressive or brutal. In fact, there was a considerable degree of interdependence, as the Mongols and Tatars relied on indirect rule through the indigenous political structures of their Russian vassals, while at the same time continuing to practice religious tolerance. The reconquest was to result from the personal vision of the ruler of Muscovy in the 16th century, Ivan the Terrible. His vision was the result of the Byzantine inheritance of his state, in which religion and nationality were fused, and of his personal determination to expand the realms that he controlled.

Furthermore, the state of Muscovy was, in a sense, a recognized element within the 16th-century Central Asian world. Ivan was described by his Muslim neighbors as the "White Khan." Indeed, surrounding Muslim states did not see Muscovy as a threat because it was Christian, but assumed instead that it was merely expansionist like any other state. This was strengthened by the fact that Ivan was completely tolerant of Islam within his dominions, although missionary activity was encouraged. The result was that there was no generalized resistance to Russian occupation, once it had begun, simply because there was no general awareness of its implications.

In 1552 the khanate of Kazan was annexed and Muscovy occupied all the land up to the Volga River. In 1556 it was the turn of the khanate of Astrakhan, the Volga Valley and the northern approaches of the Caspian Sea. Then, in 1584, the khanate of Sibir, in western Siberia, was taken

[13] The phrase comes from Alexander Hess's *The Forgotten Frontier* (Chicago: University of Chicago Press, 1978).

over. Only the Crimean khanate, of all the former Tatar khanates, held out—as a result of aid it received from the Ottoman Empire. The northern Caucasus eventually became a Muslim stronghold against further Russian expansion.

The Russian conquest had serious repercussions. First, the Muslim world lost control of the valuable fur trade, which now became a Muscovite monopoly. Second, the Sunni Muslim world was split in two, with the Ottoman Empire losing contact with its Uzbeki origins, while the silk road was closed and Islam in Central Asia declined into isolation and stagnation. This particular consequence of the Muscovite success was furthered immeasurably by the alliance forged between Muscovy and the Shiite Safavid dynasty in Iran, which itself was engaged in a lengthy struggle with the Ottomans. Within the conquered territories things changed as well, particularly after the death of Ivan in 1584. His successors were not prepared to offer the same political toleration of Islam within a normatively Christian state as he had been. Soon, Muslims were forced into an inferior status within the Russian state, while intense missionary activity was launched to convert them and mosques were destroyed. The Muslim nobility suffered economic destruction. Inevitably there were uprisings, which, in turn, were met with ever heavier repression.

For the next two centuries, however, the Russian expansion against the Muslim world stopped. This was, first, a consequence of the collapse of the Muscovite state during the "Time of Troubles" and, second, a result of the Romanovs (who had succeeded to the Muscovite state) desiring to extend their lands to the west rather than to the south or the east. Peter the Great began the drive against Islam again. He met with failure in 1711, however, when he tried to force his way through to the Black Sea, although he did establish a temporary foothold in a parallel drive toward Iran. It was left to Catherine II to recover the initiative.

Within a few years the relentless Russian threat pushed southward from Siberia into Kazakhstan. The Russian armies built fortresses at Omsk (1716), Semipalatinsk (1718) and Ust-Kamenogorsk (1719). Then, in 1783—41 years after the Kazakhs had been forced to accept Russian suzerainty—the khanate of Crimea was destroyed, 12 years after seeking Russian protection. Thereafter the conquest of the northern Caucasus began. Despite ferocious resistance from Naqshbandi-led mountain peoples, the region was eventually subdued in 1856. In Central Asia, in 1865, Bukhara and Samarkand were forced to submit 10 years after the new campaign into the region began. In 1873 Khiva was occupied, and in 1880 the khanate of Kokand. Turkoman territory was finally occupied in 1864, and in 1900 the Pamirs were annexed to Romanov Russia.

The newly conquered territories were at first relatively well treated under Catherine II. She, like Ivan the Terrible, realized that the stability of her state rested on toleration of religious differences among its various ethnic groups. She allowed the free practice of Islam and reversed the assimilationist policies of her predecessors. In 1783 she also established a Central Muslim Spiritual Board in Orenburg and encouraged the Tatar populations to find a future inside the structure of Romanov Russia.[14] Her policies were rewarded by an economic and cultural renaissance of the Tatars during the 19th century. These policies were, however, replaced by the renewed assimilationist ones of her successors that, while abandoning the attempt to Russianize the Tatars, aimed at their conversion to Orthodox Christianity, in the hope of integrating them into the state. A similar policy was followed among the Kazakhs after 1820; at the same time, however, Russian Slav peasants were encouraged to settle the steppes, thus forcing the indigenous population into an ever more difficult situation. There was, further, a lack of coordination over the policies to be followed. In Central Asia, for example, the policy was one of rejecting assimilation; in Turkestan it was one of keeping the local population isolated from the rest of the Russian Empire. The result was that the incoming Soviet administration had to find a coherent alternative.

Developments in India

The collapse of the Mogul Empire in 1757, as the Marathas and Afghan invaders joined swords, also marked the beginning of the growth of British power in India. The remnants of the Mogul Empire dissolved into its component elements—either preserving an independent existence under their former viceroys (the *subadars,* now renamed *nawwabs*) or falling prey to the Marathas, the Sikhs or others, while the East India Company began to expand its interests in Bengal. The company had long been established in Madras, where it had successfully vied with French traders for influence. In 1717 it had received permission from the Moguls to set up in Bengal, and there in the 1750s, as Mogul influence waned, a dispute broke out with the local *nawwab*. Eventually, after the Battle of Plassey in 1757, the company was able to impose its military power, and a new political dispensation was achieved whereby the *nawwab* maintained administrative and legal power—but under the company's military aegis and in return for access to the state's revenues and free access to European merchants.

The East India Company's sway over India was gradually extended by warfare and alliance, as the various principalities either sought protection or succumbed to the company's armies. By 1818 the company effectively controlled all of the Indian subcontinent except for the Punjab, Sind and Kashmir, and was already contemplating the need to extend its control to Afghanistan and Burma. Afghanistan was to become a particular concern because of the growing threat to their new dominion from Persia and Russia perceived by the British rulers of India. Both Persia and Russia had already begun to cast eyes on Afghanistan and the waters of the Indian Ocean. As a result, the conquest of Burma was to be delayed until 1886, while attention was diverted to the Punjab and the situation further west. Sind was annexed in 1843 and the Punjab in 1849, after two fierce but brief wars against the Sikhs.

At this juncture the East India Company was forced to confront its own

[14] A. Bennigsen and M. Broxup, *The Islamic Threat to the Soviet State* (London: Croom Helm, 1983), 23.

inadequacies as the political authority in India. The Sepoy Mutiny in 1857–58 was a measure of how far the new British authorities had distanced themselves from the Moguls, their political predecessors in India. Mogul power was based on the principle that indigenous institutions were to be incorporated into the state, not destroyed by it. Although the initial British administrators of India—Robert Clive, Warren Hastings and Richard Wellesley—had begun with similar ideas, these had changed after 1818 when Bentinck had begun to alter Indian society radically and introduce European culture and technology. There had been massive economic change as well, which had resulted in considerable hardship and disorientation. Traditional structures and practices had been disrupted. The mutiny, when it came, was as much an expression of popular unrest as a deliberate plan to destroy the British presence in India, in which Muslim revivalism played a significant role in the great Muslim areas.

The primary result of the mutiny was to accelerate the integration of India into the British imperial system, with the East India Company being discarded as an obsolete relic of a past era. But there were other changes too, not least a desire to slow down the pace of change and to reassert such traditional symbols of authority as religion. Traditional political structures were also revived, so that India entered the modern era half-transformed by the reforms carried out by Lord Bentinck and Lord Dalhousie in the first three decades of the 19th century, and with its traditional political and religious divides half-preserved by the viceregal policies followed by the new British administration of the raj—now controlled by the government in London.

One important consequence was that, as new modes of political opposition began to appear on the Indian scene, the old distinctions between Muslim and Hindu also reappeared. In part this was because Muslims formed only one-quarter of the total Indian population. Furthermore, the British occupation had severely disadvantaged them: As the old Mogul administration was replaced, the role for Muslims in it declined, with Hindus, who were more ready to adapt to English rule, taking over. Finally, the Muslim community was considered by the bulk of British administrators as being responsible for the Sepoy Mutiny. The community's growing isolation from the mainstream of Indian life also seemed, to many Muslims, to threaten Islam with assimilation into the new secular culture introduced from the West in the face of the threat of competition from Hindu doctrines.[15]

The response was introspective, as Indian Muslims sought to use Islam to renew the intellectual and political integrity of their community. The reaction against Hinduism went back to the 18th century and was led by Sufism, which attempted to use Islamic mysticism to counter the mysticism of Hinduism. One branch of the Sufi movement sought an activism typical of the Wahhabi movement in Saudi Arabia, which aimed at returning Islam to its original purity; the other branch was more peaceful and resulted in the heterodox Ahmadiya order at the end of the 19th century. The Western threat was confronted by Sayyid Ahmad Khan in Delhi in the

---

[15] Spear, *History of India,* vol. 2; p. 224.

second half of the 19th century. He sought to reconcile Islam and Western secularism so that Muslims could exploit the new opportunities offered by the British raj in order to reaffirm their Muslim identity.

As part of this process, the sayyid founded the college in Aligarh in 1875 as a focus for modernist Muslim education. He also argued strongly for a separate Muslim political identity within India, pointing out that in any democratic system the demographic preponderance of Hindus would condemn Muslims to an inferior status. In this sense he was, perhaps, the first proponent of an independent Muslim state in the Indian subcontinent. This aspect of his ideas became particularly important at the end of the 19th century, as the indigenous population of India sought to organize a political movement to articulate political aspirations in the face of British rule.

The Indian Congress movement was founded in 1885 and had become an important factor in Indian politics by 1900. Muslims sought to create a counterorganization to Congress, which they saw as being Hindu-dominated; in 1906 they founded the Muslim League. The British authorities bowed to this separatist sentiment in their proposals for membership in the Indian councils—the legislative councils in which Indians were to participate as part of a process of gradual devolution—in 1909. These councils were to be provided with special representation for Muslims on a communal basis; the balance of the membership was to be elective, with the franchise being based on property qualifications. This was held by Muslim leaders to be unfair because Muslims generally suffered from a far greater degree of poverty than Hindus, and would thus suffer unequal and discriminatory representation.

This issue reemerged in the wake of World War I as Indian nationalists called for some political initiative to acknowledge the sacrifices made by Indian troops during the hostilities. This was particularly significant for Muslims who had seen their loyalties strained by Turkey's participation in the war on the side of Germany; this seemed to offer an Islamic justification to Germany's claims, which Indian Muslims had loyally resisted. Calls for internal self-government began to be voiced, and in 1916 Congress leaders concluded the vital Lucknow pact with Muslim leaders, whereby, in any future self-government system, Muslims would have separate electoral constituencies.

The Lucknow Pact was to guarantee cooperation between Muslim and Hindu nationalists, and after the massacre of Amritsar in 1919 the new Congress leader, Mahatma Ghandi, found himself enjoying widespread Muslim support when he called for a policy of noncooperation with the raj authorities in the wake of an ambivalent British response to the massacre. Muslim sentiment had turned progressively anti-European as a result of the proposed dismemberment of Turkey in the Treaty of Sèvres; and the non-cooperation issue became a convenient platform from which to voice their anger. It was articulated through the Khilifat movement, organized by Muhammad and Shaukat Ali; this movement sought to bypass the Muslim League (which many poorer Muslims felt had become too pro-British) and aimed at a far more specifically Muslim revivalism through adherence to pan-Islam and the concept of the Ottoman sultan as caliph of the Islamic world.

The collaboration with Congress soon collapsed, however, when the mainline Congress supporters rejected the idea of separate electorates in a constitutional proposal—the Motilal-Nehru proposal—put forward in 1928. This turned several Muslim leaders, such as Mohammed Ali Jinnah, against further collaboration with Congress. However, the Muslim community lacked close contacts with the British authorities in the wake of the destruction of the Ottoman sultanate by Mustafa Kemal Atatürk in 1924. Most Indian Muslims had supported this institution, and they felt it had been seriously weakened by British actions. It was, in short, leaderless and the Muslim League was virtually moribund. At this juncture the idea of an independent Muslim state was revived by the poet and philosopher Muhammad Iqbal in 1930. At the same time, a name—Pakistan—was coined for this new entity by Muslim Indians studying at Cambridge University.

Within five years the opportunity for a revival of Muslim identity developed, as Britain proposed further administrative devolution through the 1935 Government of India Act. The extent of the reforms proposed in the act made it clear that full-blown political autonomy could not be far distant, and Jinnah seized the opportunity to revive the Muslim League as the future vehicle of Muslim aspirations. He offered Congress a last chance for collaboration on India's future in the 1937 elections. The offer was refused, and thereafter he argued that Indian Muslims formed a separate nation. By March 1940 he was prepared to articulate Indian Muslims' claim for their own state—Pakistan—once independence had been won.

Colonialism in Malaysia and the Indonesian archipelago

The colonial experience in Malaysia and Indonesia was dominated by the issue of trade. Indeed, except for control of the central Javanese sultanate of Mataram, Dutch interests in the Indonesian archipelago remained limited to the coast until the 19th century; and until it collapsed in bankruptcy in 1799, the Dutch presence was controlled by the Dutch East India Company, which had originally been created to exploit the spice trade. In 1755 the sultanate was brought under direct Dutch control and was divided into two estates: Surakarta and Jogjakarta. In this new colony the Dutch merely held the reins of ultimate control, for day-to-day administration was carried out by an indigenous administrative class drawn from the former aristocracy, while the Indic-Muslim symbols of authority of the Mataram sultanate were retained as legitimizers for the new colonial dispensation. The system was retained even after the Dutch crown took over responsibility for the Company's possessions after 1799.

Within this Dutch-controlled colonial entity, however, change did occur. Partly because the Dutch had seized control of long-distance trade, the original Javanese traders had created a domestic trading network that also served as the vehicle of Islamization and of a purification of Islam's more arcane Indic and Javanese accretions. This development paved the way for the reassertion of Islamic orthodoxy and the destruction of the influence of the Sufi orders in the later 19th and 20th centuries. It also meant that the bazaar traders—now acting as an Islamic countertradition[16]—were to become the precursors of the radical reformists of the later colonial period and the early years of independence.

During the Napoleonic Wars Britain began to express a strategic interest in the region and in 1811 took over control of Java from the Dutch. At the same time, British interest in the Strait of Malacca and the Malay Peninsula began to increase because of growing trading interests in the Far East, particularly for the East India Company in Bengal. In the aftermath of the Napoleonic Wars, in 1816, Java was handed back to Dutch control, while Britain, by retaining Singapore, began to create the Straits Settlements. Later, toward the end of the 19th century, Britain began to control the Malay Peninsula through a process of indirect rule in which the original Muslim sultanates were provided with British political advisers. The Dutch were, in short, to be excluded from Malaysia, particularly from the future port of Singapore, and would have to content themselves with the Indonesian archipelago.

In Indonesia, particularly in Java—which was to act as the focus of the Dutch colonial empire in Indonesia—Dutch interests changed from trade to agrarian exploitation in 1830. A system of forced cultivation, the "Culture System," was introduced for the production of coffee, sugar and rubber. The system, under state control, was aimed at satisfying growing European demand as the industrial revolution began to make its effects felt. Forty years later the inherent inefficiencies of the system resulted in its being abandoned for private capitalism. In social terms this direct interferences with the economic order found its echo in social disruption as the symbols of indigenous authority lost their significance and the Javanese sought alternatives. These tended to derive from Islam and, in effect, enlarged the influence of the bazaar traders, for Indonesians under Dutch rule increasingly turned away from the mystical version of Islam, suffused with Sufism and pre-Islamic ritual and dogma, toward an austere reformist and anticolonial vision.

This change was stimulated by the vast improvement in communications, particularly after the 1850s. Indonesia ceased to be so remote; Makkah was accessible; and pilgrims began to flock there (2,000 in 1860; 10,000 in 1880; and 50,000 in 1926). Those who took advantage of this new ease of access to the Islamic heartland returned to Indonesia determined to further the Islamic revival through the institution of the modern Muslim school. They formed a new orthodox Islamic leadership, the ulama, or *kijaji*.

This development blended in with a far older tradition, the Santri movement—religious scholars who diffused Islamic orthodoxy through the country via the mosques associated with the bazaar economy. This tradition had long acted as a brake on the heterodoxy of the Javanese peasantry or the Indic traditions of the privileged classes. The same tendencies developed in Sumatra, where the movement also became anti-Malaysian. Strikingly, these indigenous anticolonial reformulations of Islamic doctrine anticipated the

[16] Geertz, *Islam Observed*, p. 42.

Islamic revival introduced elsewhere in the Islamic world by Jamal al-Din al-Afghani in the 1880s.

During the 19th century this renewed and purified Islamic movement became the vehicle of an increasing hostility toward the Dutch colonial presence, which had now centered on Java as the core of the Dutch East Indies empire. Between 1820 and 1880 there were four major and many minor Santri insurrections. In West Sumatra, between 1821 and 1828, a rebellion against the local potentate was only broken by a Dutch military invasion. Between 1826 and 1830 a Mahdi who had failed in a bid for the Javanese throne declared jihad against the Dutch authorities. On two occasions in northwestern Java, in the 1840s and the 1880s, local ulama incited massacres of the European population and Javanese administrators. From 1873 to 1903 the northern Sumatran population maintained a sporadic war against the Dutch authorities.

By the 20th century the Dutch had begun to undertake a series of reforms designed to correct the errors of the past. State control of the agrarian economy was introduced, and later an "ethical" social policy was instituted in an attempt to counter local grievances. Indonesian nationalists, however, were modernizing their approaches to the Dutch presence. In the 1920s the Islamic Union (the Saraket Islam), the first mass nationalist movement, was created by H. O. S. Tjokroaminoto. In 1929 Sukarno founded the Nationalist party of Indonesia and forced the Dutch to arrest him for political activities. By the end of the 1930s there was a full-scale and effective nationalist movement agitating for independence, and this received an enormous boost in 1942 with the Japanese invasion of Indonesia and humiliation of the Dutch administration there. By 1945, even though the Japanese attempt to crush European colonialism in Asia had collapsed, the damage done by World War II to European prestige made independence inevitable. Indeed, the nationalist movement had become so powerful that it was able to declare independence and resist Dutch attempts to reimpose control.

In Malaysia, which had been under British control, political direction was imposed by indirect rule in the Malay Peninsula and directly in the Straits Settlement of Singapore, while British economic interests developed the natural resources of Malaya—tin, rubber, hardwoods. There the political revival was not so intense. The British presence was less obtrusive than that of the Dutch in Indonesia, and nationalist agitation was confined to the cities. Furthermore, the Chinese-Malay split in the population diffused much of the potential Islamic feeling, while the effects of the war and the Japanese occupation resulted in an anticolonial Communist-led movement. In any case, before the war much of the tension was occasioned by economic hardship as a result of international market movement: the price of rubber, for example, falling from 12 shillings per pound at the end of the 19th century to as little as two pence per pound in 1932. The Communist-led insurrection was eventually crushed as a result of British army activity, in conjunction with locally recruited forces, during the Malay emergency after the war was over.

THE POSTCOLONIAL PERIOD

Islam in Asia and the USSR suffers from the melancholy distinction of being the only part of the Islamic world where full independence has not been achieved. In the USSR itself, despite the creation of autonomous republics after the revolution in 1917, the reality has been that Islam has faced constant attempts to destroy its influence and role in society. It was only in the 1980s that this policy was reversed. The same was true in those areas of the People's Republic of China where Islam still played a major role: 60 percent of the population of Xinjiang, for example, was Muslim.[17] At the same time Asia has also been one of the areas of major Islamic innovation, particularly over the issue of the relationship of Islam to the modern concept of the nation-state. The most important manifestations of this have been the creation of an Islamic state in Pakistan, the creation of a new state in Bangladesh, and the growth of Islamic sentiment in Malaysia and Indonesia in recent years. Asia is also the region in which Islam has demonstrated, once again, its vitality as an instrument of national liberation—in the lengthy struggle against Soviet occupation in Afghanistan.

Islam in the USSR

Islam under Soviet control has experienced a complex history of resistance and compromise, and is now poised for a renewed assertion of its separate identity as a result of the Gorbachev regime's policy of *perestroika*. Up to the October Revolution three strategies were applied to preserve the *dar al-Islam* within the Russian Empire: armed resistance, including jihads organized by the Sufi orders; the defense of Islam from competing ideologies; and cooperation with the dominant political order in order to preserve Islam for a future revival. Under Soviet rule the choices open to Muslims have been circumscribed, because the efficiency of the Red Army has made armed resistance a futile option. However, ideological confrontation and cooperation have remained valid strategies, and both have played a role in the renewed confidence now being demonstrated by Islam under Soviet rule.

Armed resistance began in the mid-16th century in Tatar areas and continued in succeeding centuries in the middle Volga region, the Urals and the Kazakh steppes. The leadership of this resistance came originally from the traditional secular ruling elite, itself grounded in feudal social structures and derived usually from Mongol stock—largely because the issue was seen as one of resistance to alien occupation. The Tatars rebelled in 1553–57, 1571–72, 1574, 1580, 1584 and 1608–10 at the same time that the Crimean khans moved against Muscovy. Later in the 17th century, Tatars and Bashkirs played an important role in the Razin revolt and then the emphasis switched to the Bashkirs, with uprisings in 1678, 1705–22, 1735, 1737, 1742 and 1755. Once again, Tatars and Bashkirs united to support the Pugachev rebellion at the end of the 18th century. Finally, resistance switched to the Kazakh steppes where the khans rebelled repeatedly until

[17] Bennigsen and Broxup, *The Islamic Threat to the Soviet State*, p. 118.

1839. The ultimate traditional type of rebellion among the Muslim nobility took place in Dagestan in 1877–78, but it was easily suppressed.

From the 18th century onward, however, the nature of the struggle changed, with the issue of the survival of an Islamic polity becoming dominant; as a result, resistance took on the cloak of jihad. The leadership became far more populist, with the Sufi orders dominating the struggle in the Caucasus and Central Asia: first the Naqshbandi *tariqa* and then, from the late 18th century onward, the Qadiriya *tariqa* as well. The first jihadist movement broke out in Chechnia in 1785, and although it was successfully crushed by 1790 new unrest was fomented from the Ottoman Empire. This resulted in the Murid movement, which caused sporadic violence between 1824 and 1859; its failure then forced the Sufi movement underground. In addition, the Qadiriya *tariqa* began to take over the leadership of militant Islam from the Naqshbandi order, a change that led to collaboration with the feudal nobility in the Dagestan-Chechnia rebellion in 1877–78.

The Naqshbandiya took a new lease on life, however, once Soviet power had appeared in Dagestan; and in 1920–21 a major Naqshbandi rebellion turned on the Red Army, after first opposing occupation by the White Russian Army. Although effectively suppressed in 1921, resistance smoldered on until 1925. It coincided with another major uprising in Central Asia, the Basmachi movement, a popular uprising in which the Sufi orders had considerable influence although, unlike the situation in the Caucasus, they did not control it. The movement, which had begun in 1918, lingered on until 1928 in the former emirate of Bukhara and persisted in southern Uzbekistan until the mid-1930s. It was in the northern Caucasus, however, that the last jihadist resistance persisted, with a rebellion in 1928 and others in 1934 and 1940–42. In these the Qadiriya played a major role, alongside former members of the National Communist movement—a movement that had attempted to reconcile Muslim nationalist aspirations with Bolshevik principles until dismantled by Stalin.

This violent resistance was only one part of the overall struggle to preserve a Muslim identity, however. Parallel with it ran attempts to conserve Islamic values, including adherence to the *dar al-Islam,* with the Ottoman caliph being treated as the supreme religious authority in the Crimea and the emir of Bukhara taking a similar role in Central Asia. Elsewhere this fiction was difficult to maintain, and instead Muslims either fell back on a passive religious conservatism—as occurred in the Tatar regions with the Qadimiya, or traditionalist, movement— or sought revival through adherence to the ideas that began to revive Islam elsewhere in the Muslim world toward the end of the 19th century in the Salafiya movement.

Within the Russian Empire, however, many of these ideas appeared from indigenous sources and, to some extent, predated similar developments elsewhere—such as the Salafiya movement spearheaded by Jamal al-Din al-Afghani in Iran and Turkey in the late 1860s and 1870s.[18] The main inspiration for this revivalism came from the Volga Tatars. It was started

---

[18] E. Mortimer, *Faith and Power: The Politics of Islam* (London: Faber & Faber, 1982), 109–17.

by Abu Nasr Kursavi in Bukhara in the mid-19th century and its most famous exponent was to be Ismail Bey Gaspraly, a leading voice within what became known as the Jadidiya (new, or modernist) movement toward the end of the century. The new movement led to a profound split within the Muslim community under Russian control, with the Qadimiya conservatives continuing loyal to the imperial regime, while the Jadidiya liberals were prepared to make common cause in opposing it. Hand in hand with the growth of Jadidist sentiment, the Muslim communities, particularly the Tatars, experienced a cultural revival that by 1905 left Russian Islam with 25,000 mosques and over 50,000 clerics, together with thousands of modernized schools, a sophisticated press and literature in the revived national languages.[19]

The October Revolution caused a radical realignment in the Russian Muslim world. The likely tensions within this world had been made clear during two Muslim congresses, held in May 1917 and July 1917, in the wake of the February revolution. The first congress had involved representatives from all the major Muslim communities. This congress had proposed that a federation of Muslim states under a common Muslim council should be created. The second congress, however, was attended only by Tatar groups and sought instead a single Tatar Muslim state. The result was that, once the October Revolution exploded, the Muslim world had no coherent political options to present to the Bolsheviks. In short, the pan-Islamic movement that had begun among the Volga Tatars in 1904 had collapsed, and the various local political movements that had started at the same time were individually and collectively threatened with absorption by the far better organized socialist movements that had grown up alongside them.[20]

At the same time, the Qadimiya conservatives and the Jadidiya liberals were soon absorbed by the October Revolution. Both were replaced by new movements, better adapted to the new revolutionary circumstances. One obvious response that was adopted in the face of efficient repression by the Red Army was a move underground. As Bolshevik control was instituted over the Muslim territories of the Soviet Union—often against considerable resistance—radical conservative elements sought to preserve their Muslim values within the Sufi *tariqas*, which themselves faced repression. The *tariqas* became unofficial institutions and, as a result, provided a limited arena in which Muslim values—since they fell outside official control—could be preserved. Four have come to dominate the scene: the Naqshbandiya, with traditions stretching back to the 14th century in Russia and Central Asia; the Qadiriya, which, although dating back to the 12th century, was only introduced into the Caucasus in the mid-19th century and is now split into three separate *tariqas*; and the Yasawiya and the Kubrawiya, both of which have very long pedigrees but are limited to a purely local audience in Ka-

[19] Bennigsen and Broxup, *The Islamic Threat to the Soviet State,* p. 71.
[20] Bennigsen and Lemercier-Quelquejay, *Les Musulmans oubliés: L'Islam en Union Sovietique,* pp. 30–47.

zakhstan and Turkmenistan. The Yasawiya also gave birth to a terrorist offshoot—the Chachtuu Eshander—in the wake of the Basmachi rebellion in the late 1920s. All these movements, defined by Soviet sources as "parallel Islam," are traditionalist and conservative, but will mark any more movement that may arise as a result of glasnost.

The other reaction has been one of cooperation between Muslims and the Soviet authorities. Its most famous exponent was the Muslim National Communist movement, which played a significant role in the new Soviet Muslim world between 1918 and 1928.[21] Its best-known representative was Sultan Galiev, a Tatar; but its membership was drawn from the Jadidiya movement and from the various political parties created in the latter part of the 19th century in many of the Muslim areas. Apart from Azerbaijan, where there had been members of the Bolshevik movement before the Revolution, all those involved came into the Communist party during the civil war up to 1920.

The National Communists were particularly concerned to create an ideology applicable in societies in which the conventional proletariat did not exist. They argued that colonial oppression created the equivalent of a proletariat and that struggles for national liberation were, in effect, socialist revolutions in societies in which, since class distinctions did not exist, there could not be a conventional class struggle. Furthermore, although conventional Marxism considered that the national question would be resolved by the revolution and the dictatorship of the proletariat, the National Communists did not agree. They argued that the experience of Russia itself proved this not to be the case and that national aggression was not, therefore, the consequence of capitalist imperialism and would be automatically removed by a socialist revolution. As far as Islam was concerned, they also rejected conventional Marxism, arguing that Islam could be reconciled with Marxist thought through *ijitihad* (independent reasoning derived from the basic elements of Islamic dogma—the Koran, the *Hadith,* the *Sharia* and the *Sunna*), an argument that referred back to Jadidist doctrine. Islam was, in short, to be secularized—with its reactionary elements eliminated, and moral, social and political influence retained.

The National Communists anticipated that their doctrines—which today bear an uncanny resemblance to the left-wing ideologies that have informed post-World War II national liberation movements in the Third World—would enable the spread of the socialist revolution into the colonial and underdeveloped world. They also believed that Europe would never be amenable to revolution and that the correct arena for this would be Asia, not least because success there would hinder any attempt by the non-Muslim Bolshevik movement in Moscow and Leningrad to reimpose the type of relationship that had existed under the czars. By 1923 the latter consideration had come to dominate the National Communist perspective, and Sul-

---

[21] For a full discussion of this movement, see A. Bennigsen and S. Enders Wimbush, *Muslim National Communism in the Soviet Union: A Revolutionary Strategy for the Colonial World* (Chicago: University of Chicago Press, 1979).

tan Galiev, for example, now considered the USSR to be dominated by a European protocolonial vision that would only work to the detriment of the oppressed.

Bolshevik reaction was not delayed. Orthodox Marxists rejected the National Communist theses, and from 1919 onward open confrontation became more and more frequent. The class struggle could not be delayed; and the concept of "proletarian nations"—Sultan Galiev's description of the oppressed colonial populations that sought national liberation—was rejected, while Bolshevik leaders reiterated that the West was the appropriate arena for revolution. By 1923 the confrontation became more violent, with the arrest of Sultan Galiev; after his release there was a period of uneasy truce. By 1928, however, Stalin had decided on a widespread purge of the National Communists and of the Muslim intelligensia. The National Communist movement was finally eliminated in 1930. The next 10 years saw the destruction of the Muslim intelligensia and the end of the cultural revival that had begun in the late 19th century among the Tatars.

A faint revival began in 1942 as Stalin acceded to requests to create a system similar to that provided for the USSR's Orthodox Christians. Persecution of Muslims and anti-Islamic propaganda ceased, and an Official Islamic Administration was created to look after Muslim interests. It consisted of four boards, three of which are Sunni and cover (1) Tashkent, Central Asia and Kazakhstan; (2) Ufa, European Russia and Siberia; (3) Malach-Qala, northern Caucasus and Dagestan. The fourth board is for Sunnis and Shiites, in Baku and Transcaucasia. These boards are staffed by persons close to the Jadidiya tradition, and they seek to achieve at least one of the National Communist traditions: the use of *ijitihad* in reconciling Islam and Marxism. In terms of resources, Islam now faces a parlous situation, with only about 400 to 500 mosques still permitted (one source claims as few as 365[22]), two *madrassahs* to educate new clergy, and one religious periodical. It remains to be seen if the Gorbachev reforms will make a significant difference.

Change will indeed occur. Ever since the Islamic revolution in Iran, the authorities in Moscow have been very anxious about reactions within the USSR itself. Perhaps the most serious arena for this would have been Azerbaydjan, since links with the other half of Azerbaydjan, under Iranian control, have continued to be strong. Even more important has been the catastrophe of the war in Afghanistan, which has had a wider effect as Muslims serve in the Soviet forces there. Surprisingly, however, the real danger seems to have been a return of nationalist aspirations, rather than of some fundamentalist version of Islam. Nonetheless, the danger still persists, as Islam could easily become the cloak for nationalist aspirations.[23] For the Soviet authorities, however, the crucial consideration will be to retain the terri-

[22] A. Bennigsen, "Unrest in the World of Soviet Islam," *Third World Quarterly* 10, no. 2 (April 1988): 775.

[23] The riots in Alma-Ata in December 1986, and later in Tadzhikistan, were apparently inspired by Islamic militants; see A. Bennigsen, "Unrest in the World of Soviet Islam," p. 771.

torial integrity of the USSR. For the sake of that, they will certainly be willing to make superficial concessions over Islamic practice.

Islam in Afghanistan

Modern Afghanistan is perhaps, after the Islamic revolution in Iran, the best-known example of the resurgence of Islamic sentiment in the world today. In large measure this awareness stems from the Afghan resistance to the Soviet occupation of their country since December 1979. However, Afghanistan's identity as an independent Islamic state reaches back to the mid-18th century. Afghanistan broke away from Iranian control in the wake of the death of Nadir Shah, who had first accepted non-Shiite participation within his official Shiite state. In Afghanistan, this had allowed the growth of a Sunni-dominated confederate political structure among the Abdali Pathans. Under the leadership of Ahmad Shah, the founder of the Afghan monarchy, or Durrani, the Pathans seized power in 1747 and created an independent state.[24]

From its base at Kandahar, the Durrani confederacy attempted to expand eastward into India but was prevented from doing so by the growth of Sikh power there. In the mid-19th century, however, it did incorporate Turkic groups north of the Hindu Kush. Expansion westward was prevented by Shiite Iran. From the early 19th century the Afghan monarchy had to struggle against encroachment from the British, based in their new possessions in India. The British role was stimulated, first, by a desire to expand westward, but later reflected anxieties over Russian ambitions toward Afghanistan. As the Russian armies pushed south through Central Asia, British officials feared that the Russian Empire would eventually attempt to extend its control down to the Pacific coast of Asia. The three wars between Britain and Afghanistan, in 1839–42, 1878–80 and 1919, reflected these twin objectives.

After the 1919 war Afghanistan found itself thrust into the political currents of the modern Islamic world. From a brief spate of pan-Islamic sentiment during World War I, Afghan leaders turned to deal with the difficult issue of modernization. In this context, the ruler Amanullah attempted first to create a modernized Islamic constitution and then to emulate the changes being wrought elsewhere—in Turkey by Kemal Atatürk and in Iran by Reza Shah Pahlavi. There was an inevitable fundamentalist reaction, and after a short civil war in 1929, Amanullah's successor, Nadir Shah, issued a constitution in 1931 that formalized the role of Islam and the ulama in Afghan political life.

Nonetheless, pressure began to develop during the 1940s for a more liberal, secularized system. First came demands for greater liberalization, then calls for political participation. The People's Democratic party of Afghanistan (PDPA), with its two factions, Parcham and Khalq, appeared,

---

[24] For details on Afghanistan, see D. Hiro, *Islamic Fundamentalism* (London: Paladin, 1988), 227–69, and E. Naby, "Islam within the Afghan Resistance," *Third World Quarterly* 10, no. 2 (April 1988): 787–805.

indicating the growth of Soviet influence. Tensions developed with neighboring states—particularly with Pakistan, then a completely new nation with which Afghanistan anticipated border problems and the growth of political tensions. The tensions were occasioned not least because of the growth of Islamic political sentiment within Afghanistan as a result of the growing secularization of Afghan society. Afghan Muslim leaders turned toward Pakistan for inspiration, seizing on the philosophy of Said Abu l-Ala Mawdudi and the support of the powerful Jamaati Islami movement in Pakistan. Other Afghan religious leaders—particularly those associated with Kabul University—looked toward the Egyptian thinker, Sayyid Qutb, the leader of the Ikhwan Muslimin movement.

In 1973 the monarchy was overthrown by Muhammad Daud Khan in a coup that, despite promises to preserve Afghanistan's Islamic system, soon bore all the marks of growing secularization and pro-Soviet socialism, given PDPA Parchami support for the Daud regime. In 1974 he crushed the fundamentalist movement, forcing its leaders into exile in Pakistan from where they tried to launch an unsuccessful rebellion in 1975. Afghanistan under Daud proved itself flexible in foreign policy—with improved relations both with Iran and Pakistan, together with an attempt to balance Western and Soviet interests in Afghanistan—but inflexibly opposed to Islamic pretensions to political power at home. Eventually the regime collapsed in 1978 as the result of a pro-PDPA military coup, because of fears that Daud was about to move against the Afghan political left.

The new regime accelerated the pace of reform and turned openly toward the PDPA for political support. This soon stimulated further conflict between the Khalqi leaders (President Nur Muhammad Taraki and Premier Hafizullah Amin) on the one hand and the more radical Parchami leaders (such as Babrak Karmal) on the other. At the same time the reforms began to stimulate growing Islamic resistance within the country at large, and Afghanistan also began to experience clandestine violence controlled by Afghan exiles in Pakistan, influenced increasingly by Mawdudi's doctrines. By 1978–79 rebellions in Nuristan and the Hazarajat region had brought local Islamic supporters into direct conflict with the authorities in Kabul, while an uprising in Herat, controlled from Pakistan, caused considerable anxiety in Moscow.

The USSR had, in fact, chosen to support the Parchamis and by 1979 had clearly decided that the Taraki-Amin government would have to go. Amin anticipated their plans by taking over power, while Soviet troops began to move into Afghanistan to support the Afghan army. In December 1979 the Brezhnev regime, in a move clearly designed to protect the secular government in Kabul from its own inability to control Afghanistan, occupied the country and removed the Amin regime, replacing it with a puppet Parchami government led by Babrak Karmal. Soon refugees were streaming out to Pakistan and Iran, and the support base for the Islamic resistance had been born. During the 1980s, despite the fact that it was never united, it was able, with Pakistani, Iranian and U.S. support, to force the USSR to accept that it could no longer control Afghanistan's future. Despite a change of government and a pro-Islamic initiative by the new Najibullah regime, it is likely that the departure of Soviet troops will cause an Islamic takeover in Afghanistan.

The problem was that the complexion of the new regime was very unclear, because of the plethora of Islamic resistance groups. Three main factions existed: pro-Iranian groups, pro-Pakistan groups and traditionalists. The traditionalists, who had powerful links in the countryside as well as with conservative urban groups were tied to the former royal regime and to the Qadiriya movement. They formed three separate parties enjoying support from Saudi Arabia, Egypt and the United States. Ranged against them were the pro-Shiite groups in the western Hazarajat, dominated by the Sazman-e Nasr and the Sejah-e Pasdaran, who sought to create an Iranian-style Islamic republic; and the Pakistan-based Sunni groups who wished to form a Pakistan-style Islamic state. There were three main parties: the Jamaati Islami, led by Borhanuddin Rabbani and based on Mawdudist principles; the two factions of the Hizb-e Islami, created by Gulbuddin Hekmatyar, a former student leader who was strongly influenced by the Ikhwan Muslimin movement and split between him and Maulavi Yunis Khalis after a dispute over tactics in 1979. It was very difficult to see which group could dominate in a post-Najibullah Afghan regime; nor could a coalition easily be created. Indeed, many observers wondered if Afghanistan would not, as a result of its competing Islamic influences, decay into its component parts and then fall prey to its neighbors.

Islam in Pakistan

With the end of World War II the new Labour government in London realized the time had come to hasten independence for Britain's Indian empire. It was also clear that the Congress movement had not gained the trust of India's Muslims and that Jinnah's claim that there were two nations on the Indian subcontinent was accurate. Congress, however, believed that Jinnah's support could be split and that an independent Pakistan was not a necessary concomitant of independence. Riots in 1946 finally convinced Congress that a two-state solution could not be avoided, and in 1947 Lord Mountbatten was sent out to negotiate the creation of independent India and Pakistan by August 1947. Punctually, independence was declared— accompanied by appalling massacres as population exchanges took place in the Punjab between Muslims and Sikhs. An estimated 500,000 were killed, as vast voluntary migrations took place: 5.5 million migrating each way in the Punjab; 500,000 Hindus moving out of Sind; and 1 million Hindus leaving East Pakistan (now Bangladesh) for Indian Bengal.

The new state faced many problems, not least over the question of Kashmir, which it claimed and for which it was to find itself in conflict with India. The real problems, however, were to be over the nature of the new state. Although some leaders sought a secular dispensation, most knew that the new nation would be explicitly Islamic. They were further persuaded by the emergence of Said Abu l-Ala Mawdudi as the philosopher for the new state. He had a fundamental vision of what it should be, based on the Koran and the *Sharia,* with *ijitihad* playing a very restricted role in modifying the rigors of the system.[25] The confrontation began over the issue of Kashmir; the modernist, Western-educated leaders of Pakistan, while calling on the local Kashmiri population to engage in jihad against Indian occupation, disclaimed all responsibility for the resulting disorder. Islamic leaders, such as Mawdudi, called the government's bluff by pointing out it was failing in its duty to support jihad and, if it were not, then the struggle in Kashmir could not be defined as one of jihad.

Although the government imprisoned Mawdudi for his comments, it had to bow to Islamic sentiment; in 1949 it produced a draft constitution that effectively provided the basis for an Islamic state. However, the institutions for such a state were to be delayed. Instead, a far more acute crisis developed over the status of a heterodox sect, the Ahmadiyas, who had been condemned by the ulama but were reluctantly protected by the government. The government also turned against the idea of implementing Islamic rule; but in 1958 it was overturned in a military coup lead by Muhammad Ayub Khan.

Ayub attempted to introduce a modernist Islamic state but eventually bowed to ulama opposition. In fact, he faced opposition from both the Mawdudi-aligned Jamaati Islami and a new party that had developed in West Pakistan under Zulfikar Ali Bhutto. This movement—the Pakistan People's party (PPP)—sought a socialist solution and, to protect itself from ulama attack, claimed that its socialism was Islamic in content and concept. The ulama nonetheless condemned the PPP as anti-Islamic.

Popular attitudes over the issue were put to the test in 1969, when Ayub stepped down and called elections to resolve the constitutional crisis. The PPP won impressively in West Pakistan against the fundamentalists, while in East Pakistan Sheikh Mujibur Rahman's national Awami party scored a landslide victory. The government, now headed by another military figure, Agha Muhammad Yahya Khan, stumbled into a civil war which it lost as India stepped in on the side of East Pakistan and assisted at the birth of a new Muslim nation, Bangladesh, in 1970. Bhutto took over in West Pakistan where he aligned PPP policy with Islamic rules as he lost support. Although Bhutto's PPP won a further election in 1977, it was accused of electoral fraud and the army stepped in once again.

The coup carried out by Mohammed Zia ul-Haq on July 5, 1977, was to mark the complete transformation of Pakistan into an Islamic state along the lines proposed by Mawdudi. The transformation was slow but permanent, with profound changes taking place in Pakistani institutions over a decade. Pakistan introduced an Islamic financial system, and the political system took on an ever more significant Islamic caste. Even though a limited democratic system was permitted for several years in the mid-1980s, the controlling hand continued to be that of Zia ul-Haq; and the state he created reflects the conservative and puritan perspective of its ideological progenitor, Said Abu l-Ala Mawdudi.

[25] E. Mortimer, Faith and Power: The Politics of Islam (London: Faber & Faber, 1981), 200–06.

Islam further to the east

Islam also underwent a revival in the Malay Peninsula and in the Indonesian archipelago during the 1970s. Most observers consider that these changes reflected the social and economic changes attendant upon development, although specific political circumstances also played a role: the Malay-Chinese ethnic confrontation in Malaysia; the aftermath of the Sukarno regime in Indonesia; and the corruption of the Marcos regime in the Philippines, where the Moro have been struggling against the central government ever since the 1960s.

In Malaysia the Islamic movement first came to prominence after 1973, in part as a result of the economic hardship caused by the oil price crisis in that year. Four parties came to the fore—the Parti Islam Semalaysia (PAS), the Malaysian Islamic Youth Movement (ABIM), the Tabligh movement, and the Darul Arqam. Only PAS and ABIM have played a role in political life, with the other two movements acting as cultural pressure groups. PAS has combined Malaysian nationalism with Islam, while ABIM has sought to base itself on Pakistani experience and on the *Ikhwan* movement in the Middle East. ABIM has supported PAS in elections and as a result, by 1978, Islamic deputies had become a significant power within political life. It was in 1982, however, that the power of PAS and ABIM was demonstrated by the policies introduced by the new administration of Mahathir bin Mohammad on behalf of the dominant United Malays National Organization. In short, the Mahathir administration outflanked PAS and ABIM in producing its own Islamic program, which prevented Islamic fundamentalism from taking control.[26]

In Indonesia the situation has been the reverse, with the Suharto government determined to prevent an Islamic resurgence. The result has been an attempt to control Islamic political sentiments within the state's official ideology. However, although the organized Muslim political movement might have been dismantled, there has been a Muslim revival since the 1970s.

FURTHER READING

Akiner, Shirin. *Islamic Peoples of the Soviet Union*. London: Kegan Paul International, 1986.

Dawisha, Adeed, ed. *Islam in Foreign Policy*. Cambridge and New York: Cambridge University Press for the Royal Institute of International Affairs, 1983.

Bennigsen Alexandre, and Broxup, Marie. *The Islamic Threat to the Soviet State*. London: Croom Helm, 1983.

———, and Lemercier-Quelquejay, Chantal. *Les Musulmans oubliés: L'Islam en Union Soviétique*. Paris: Maspéro, 1981.

———, and Wimbush, S. Enders. *Muslim National Communism in the Soviet Union: A Revolutionary Strategy for the Colonial World*. Chicago: University of Chicago Press, 1979.

[26] J. K. Sundaram and A. S. Cheek, "The Politics of Malay's Islamic Resurgence," *Third World Quarterly* 10, no. 2 (April 1988): 843–68.

Geertz, Clifford. *Islam Observed: Religious Development in Morocco and Indonesia.* New Haven, Connecticut: Yale University Press, 1968.

Hiro, Dilip. *Islamic Fundamentalism.* London: Paladin, 1988.

Hodgson, Marshall G. S. *The Venture of Islam: Conscience and History in a World Civilization.* 3 vols. Chicago: University of Chicago Press, 1974.

Ro'i, Yaacov, ed. *The USSR and the Muslim World: Issues in Domestic and Foreign Policy.* London and Boston: George Allen & Unwin, 1984.

Lewis, Bernard. *The Arabs in History.* London: Hutchinson, 1970.

Mortimer, Edward. *Faith and Power: The Politics of Islam.* London and Boston: Faber & Faber, 1982.

Spear, Percival. *A History of India.* Vol. 2. Harmondsworth, Middlesex: Penguin, 1973.

Thapar, Romila. *A History of India.* Vol 1. Harmondsworth, Middlesex: Penguin, 1966.

PART FOUR

ECONOMIC AFFAIRS

JAPAN AND THE WORLD ECONOMY

CHRISTOPHER HOWE

INTRODUCTION

THERE are now many striking indications of Japan's changing significance in the world economy and of the shift in relative economic power between itself and the United States.[1] One, is that whereas between 1960 and 1980 Japan's share of world economic output rose from 3% to 10%, that of the United States declined from 33% to 22%. A second indicator is the stock market capitalization of companies in the two economies. Japan now accounts for 44% of the *Financial Times* Actuaries World Index as compared with 31% for the United States. And finally, in international financial terms, while Japan is now the world's largest creditor, the United States is increasingly concerned with the problem of servicing net international indebtedness. These statistics all reflect the rise of a major new actor in the world economy and the relative decline of another. The main purpose of this article is to consider the Japanese origins of this shift and the readjustment it implies for Japan's economic partners, both worldwide and in Asia.

A broad picture of Japan's changing economic, demographic and land resource position is shown in Table 1. The data show that the shift in the global shares of GNP reflect Japan's comparatively high growth rate over the whole of the postwar period. This growth may be divided into three periods: High-Speed Growth (1955–74), Post–Oil-Shock Readjustment (1974–79) and Export-Led Growth (1979–86). What is remarkable is that in each of these phases, although the domestic rate of growth shifted, it remained above the U.S. and most other rates. Only the newly industrializing countries (NICs), whose structural circumstances were very different, outperformed Japan at certain periods. Thus while at first sight it is the

[1] Materials for this paper have been collected as part of a larger project on Japanese foreign trade. I am grateful to The School of Oriental and African Studies and the Nuffield Foundation for enabling me to make several visits to Japan during the 1980s. I am also very grateful to the Foundation for Advanced Information and Research, Japan, for support as a Visiting Scholar in October 1988, and to Tokyo University for academic hospitality as a Visiting Researcher. None of the above has any responsibility for errors or opinions in this article.

Table 1
JAPAN IN WORLD PERSPECTIVE

Population and land	Japan	United States	EC	USSR	China	World
Population (millions, 1984)	120	237	272	275	1,049	4,763
% of world total	2.5	5	5.7	5.8	22	100
Population density (overall per sq. km.)	318	25	164	12	108	36
Expectation of life (males)	74.54	71.6	71	65	66	

Gross National Product	Japan	United States	OECD	NICs	China	
Share of world total (%) 1960	3	33	26	3	5	
1980	10	22	31	4	6	

Growth Rates (% per year)	Japan	United States	West Germany	Britain	Italy	China
1950–70	9.17	3.85	7.26	2.29	5.96	6.17
1974–78	3.4	2.8	2.1	1.0	2.1	6.28
1979–83	4.1	1.3	1.2	0.8	1.6	7.36

Per capita income (U.S. $) at 1983 level and rate	Japan	United States	Britain	India	China
	9,717	14,093	8,140	242	235
At 1987 $:yen exchange rate	17,715	14,093	—	—	—

Shares of world output of major products (%)		Japan	USSR	United States	West Germany	China	South Korea	Index of World growth
Crude steel	1971	15.4	20	19.3	7	3.7	—	100
	1981	14.9	22.1	16.3	6.1	5.3	—	119
Ships	1971	48.2	—	—	6.6	—	—	100
	1981	51.9	—	—	3.9	—	7.2	69
TV	1971	27.3	13	19.5	5.7	—	0.5	100
	1981	17.6	9.9	22.3	5.6	6.5	9.3	184
Cars	1971	14.2	2	32.9	14.1	—	—	100
	1981	25.2	4.8	22.6	12.9	—	—	147

Sources: Bank of Japan (1984); State Statistical Bureau (1985); Keizai Koho Center (1986).

ultra fast growth of the first phase that is most striking—particularly in historical perspective—Japan's relative performance since 1974 is at least as remarkable and as much in need of explanation.

When the national income data are put on a per capita basis, we get an indication of the extent to which postwar progress has enabled Japan to catch up with the advanced economies. Although there is continuing controversy about the interpretation of such comparative measures of welfare, it is clear that Japan is becoming one of the world's richest countries. Per capita income in 1983 was ahead of Britain and about two-thirds of the U.S. level. Moreover, these calculations are based on the contemporary exchange rates. If 1987 dollar/yen rates are used, the Japanese per capita income rises to over U.S. $17,000. This is substantially above the U.S. level of income. Current rates have clearly taken the yen beyond purchasing power parity and more sophisticated comparisons suggest that real per capita income in Japan is approximately 70% of U.S. levels. However, this recent shift in Japan's nominal affluence has not gone unnoticed, and it is a real factor in trade frictions.

Two other features of Japan brought out by Table 1 are its demographic maturity and land shortage. Japan's expectation of life is now very high, remarkably so in view of Japan's population density and shortage of housing and infrastructure, which might have been thought to have kept expectancy down somewhat. Looking at the land data, Japan is one of the world's most densely populated countries, although parts of other countries match the highest Japanese densities. And in terms of agricultural land (data not shown), only China among major economies has a ratio of land to agricultural population as low as that in Japan. This land shortage (and associated agricultural and taxation policies) are reflected in land prices that have become a major domestic and international issue since the mid-1980s.

The emergence of Japan as one of the world's most advanced economies has given rise to a variety of scenarios of the future. The pessimists see many problems. They regard Japanese trade imbalances as a permanent destabilizing factor in the world economy. They see Japanese capital outflows in all their major forms (aid, direct investment and portfolio investment) as carrying with them a variety of adjustment difficulties and possibilities for confrontation. They also believe that Japan is not capable of matching economic and financial power with mature behavior in the political and strategic spheres. Against this one can suggest a more optimistic scenario. The trade balance should be containable in the medium term given the maintenance of a multilateral system. Capital outflows can be valued for their positive, productivity enhancing effects, whether they take the form of direct investment, aid or supplementation for U.S. or other savings shortfalls. And, finally, evidence can be cited to show that Japan has already assumed a more active and visible regional and international role, and that this is likely to continue.

HIGH-SPEED GROWTH

Japan's achievements in the phases of High-Speed Growth are displayed in Table 2. Three domestic results of High-Speed Growth are shown in lines

Table 2
THE MAIN PHASES OF JAPANESE POSTWAR
GROWTH, 1955–87

Growth per year	High-speed growth			Crisis	Adjustment and export-led growth		
	1955–59	1960–64	1965–69	1970–74	1975–79	1980–82	1982–86/7
GNP	8.7	9.7	12.2	5.1	4.9	3.7	3.8
Retail prices	1.5	6.1	5.4	11.5	6.8	1.3	1.7
Investment (rate)	11.4	14.8	18.1	18.2	—	—	—
Capital:output ratio	1.3	1.5	1.5	3.6	—	—	—
Unemployment (rate)	2.0	1.3	1.2	1.4	2.1	2.3	2.7
Private consumption	7.7	8.3	9.7	6.0			
Private sector investment: plant and machinery	22.6	8.7	22.8	0.9			
Government consumption	2.9	7.1	5.1	5.6			
Public capital formation	13.8	16.0	10.8	6.7			

Sources: Hisao Kanamori (1984); Yutaka Kosai (1985); Economic Planning Agency, *Keizai Hakusho* (1986); Ministry of Finance, *Monthly Finance Review* (Nov. 1987).

1297

1, 2 and 5. Total output between 1955 and 1969 not only grew very rapidly, but is seen to be accelerating and actually touched a peak of 13.7% in 1968. In long term perspective, this movement represented the highest phase of a series of accelerations originating before the First World War. Second, this growth was accompanied by low levels of unemployment. Even allowing that use of American or European conventions of measurement would raise the Japanese rates of unemployment by at least 30%, rates below 2% are low for a modern, market economy. Not surprisingly, rapid growth and low unemployment were accompanied by substantial inflation. In judging these one must bear in mind that Japanese price data are unusual in the divergence between the retail and wholesale indices, nonetheless, these retail price increases are very substantial bearing in mind that during the 1960s, inflation rates of 3% in Europe and the United States were regarded as representing a crisis. Finally, from line 6 it will be observed that the Japanese economic miracle was not the result of a cumulative and systematic expansion of heavy industry at the expense of the consumer. Although consumer spending grew less slowly than national income, it too grew at accelerating rates, achieving almost double digit growth in the late 1960s. Rising consumer welfare was reflected not only in national income data, but in high levels of availability of consumer goods and in a growth of the percentage of disposable income available for expenditure on nonessential goods and services.

The causes of High-Speed Growth were a mixture of technical, organizational, social and international factors. It is essential in a first approach to separate these out in analytically convenient ways. But the more the issues are studied, the more interrelated the various domestic factors appear to have been. In particular, technical innovation involved many mutually supportive linkages between attitudes, business organization and strategy and strictly technological factors.

In quantitative terms, the most striking explanatory statistics in Table 2 are the rising levels of investment and the low capital requirements for additional units of output (line 4). Moreover, to private sector investment we must add public investment (line 9), which was particularly important in the early years. Why was private sector investment so buoyant? In general terms, businessmen must have perceived that the environment provided opportunities for growth and profitability for successful firms. Official policy played an active role in this, not only by demand management, but by the effective insulation of the home from the world market by fiscal incentives and by the provision of the positive role in the economy played by government agencies—especially the Ministry of International Trade and Industry (MITI) and the Economic Planning Agency (EPA). The roles of the latter were complementary. MITI provided planning at the sectoral and micro levels—especially in metallurgy, chemicals, shipbuilding and industries dependent on imported technology. Compliance with this framework was secured by subsidies, financial policies, controls on transactions involving foreign exchange and the system of "administrative guidance." The EPA, in contrast, had no significant resources at its disposal, but produced a series of macro plans, of which the most famous was the Ikeda Income

Doubling Plan of 1961–1970. Of the five plans produced before 1970, all were overshot by a hyper-responsive private sector.

In addition to the favorable domestic environment, firms' behaviors were influenced by a variety of other postwar changes. The dissolution of the *Zaibatsu* and the consequent decoupling of economic and financial concentration were particularly important, even though some of these linkages were restored by the formation of *Keiretsu*. The immediate effect of the dissolution was to bring to power a new generation of business leaders and professional managers and to release competitive forces not known in the large scale sector in the prewar economy. Whether postwar firms have been maximizing growth and market share or profitability is an interesting issue for economists, but with hindsight it appears that the difference between these objectives resolves itself into questions of timescale. The headlong, competitive pursuit of growth was so powerful in the 1960s that it produced the unique Japanese phenomenon of "investment surges"—movements in which investment seemed to confirm the market share rather than profitability theory of firm motivation. The herd investment instinct and the long time horizon remain features of the Japanese firm commented on by Western analysts.

Another element that contributed to High-Speed Growth was technology. Japan had been isolated since before the Second World War and by the 1950s and 1960s had accumulated a backlog of investment opportunities. Firms were encouraged to embody these new techniques in their investment by the relative security of the domestic market and also by taxation provisions that violated Western ideas of fiscal neutrality but greatly enhanced the profitability of such investment. The impact of new technology was to transform basic industry by dramatic increases in the scale of production and corresponding cost reductions. The existence of scale economies was part of the rationale for investment bunching, and explains why MITI felt obliged to control rapidly changing sectors by limiting new entrants and to some extent by managing the market. The development of the heavy sector, especially metallurgy, chemicals and the heavy electrical industries, laid the foundations for the growth of downstream industries such as vehicles and the domestic electrical and electronic industries, which were to be so important in the growth of the trade sector.

The other important contribution to High-Speed Growth was from human resources. In demographic terms, the situation was initially influenced by the postwar surge in births—a surge that was short lived and went against the long-run trend of downward fertility. In the short run, food shortage and world economic uncertainty made this a matter for anxiety. But in the medium run it provided an important contribution to demand, and when the surge in numbers reached working age, it made a major contribution to the supply side of the economy. As Table 3 shows, the population of working age grew at 3.5% per annum during High-Speed Growth. Rising participation in education at first lessened the impact of this on actual workforce growth but, even so, workforce growth was 1.4%.

While educational participation lowered numbers of new workers, it improved quality. Japan has a long history of high standards of basic literacy.

Table 3
LABOR FORCE AND POPULATION, 1955–82
(thousands)

	Population age 15+		Work force		Number of employees	Work force population 15+
1955	100 ⎤		100 ⎤		100	71%
1960	157 ⎬ 3.5% per year		108 ⎬ 1.4% per year		133	69%
1972	179 ⎦		127 ⎦		195	64%
1982	201 1.2% per year		141 1.1% per year		230	63%

Source: Ministry of Labor, *Rodo Hakusho* (various years).

In the postwar years the expansion of education led to rapidly rising numbers in high school and tertiary institutions. These gave Japan one of the highest participation rates in tertiary education in the world and corresponding levels of labor quality.

The rapid growth and marked structural shifts of employment would, in most market economies, have been difficult to secure without destablization of the labor market and a tendency for money wages to outstrip productivity increases. This did not happen in Japan. For although money wages in the productive sectors advanced rapidly, the trend in real wages during High-Speed Growth remained well below the growth of labor productivity. The system thus provided for both workforce incentives and investment profitability. This satisfying outcome was a reflection of two factors: the relatively elastic supply of labor in the 1950s and 1960s, and collective bargaining arrangements in which much power was decentralized to the firm level, and in which centralized influences operated in a manner that allowed for ritualized confrontation in the annual *Shunto*—"Spring Offensive"—but which nonetheless remained basically cautious and responsive to economic objectives.

Various estimates of the sources of Japanese growth based on the original Dennison method have been made for Japan. A recent example that updates the Dennison analysis is shown in Table 4. The data for the 1960s may be taken as proxy for High-Speed Growth, and these show the relative contribution to growth of labor, capital and productivity increases. It will be seen that although capital and labor increases were large, they only accounted for a third of total growth, the balance being productivity increases associated with new technology, economies of scale and the reallocation of resources between low and high productivity sectors. Not shown here is the interesting result of Dennison's work that showed that, in comparative terms, Japan's superiority to other Organization for Economic Cooperation and Development (OECD) economies did not rest on any one source of growth, but reflected superior performance in all sources.

Table 4
SOURCES OF GROWTH

Contributions	1960–70	1970–80	1980–90 (est.)
Labor	1.31	0.73	0.80
(Education)	(0.19)	(0.22)	(0.13)
Capital	2.44	1.24	0.94
Land	0	0	0
Productivity	6.87	2.93	3.26
(Knowledge advance)	(6.02)	(2.43)	(2.94)
Real GNP	10.62	4.90	5.00

Source: Hisao Kanamori (1984).

THE OIL SHOCK AND THE END OF HIGH-SPEED GROWTH

Between 1970 and 1974 the Japanese economy suddenly experienced low growth of output and consumption, and a collapse of private investment. At the same time unemployment and inflation moved upwards. In the broad sweep of events this major shift of direction is often attributed to the Oil Shock of 1973–1974, and to the "Nixon Shock" of 1971. (During the latter the United States came off the dollar-gold standard and forced a general revaluation of all currencies against the dollar.) Important as both of these events were, other significant shifts in the forces underlying the upward trajectory of the postwar economy can be identified. In 1960, Japan was the fifth largest market economy in the world. By 1968 it was the second. This striking advance stimulated a major revaluation of a policy regime that concentrated almost exclusively on the maximization of conventionally measured GNP. For many in Japan, the results of this regime in terms of wider measures of welfare appeared no longer commensurate with the costs. The growing gap between welfare and growth is illustrated by estimates in Table 5, which show the relative movements of GNP and "Net National Welfare"—a measure that adds leisure and other nonmone-

Table 5
GROWTH AND WELFARE, 1955–75
(billion yen—1970 prices)

	1955	1970	1975	1955–75 (growth per year)	1970–75 (growth per year)
Gross national product	17,268	72,144	93,260	10%	5.3%
Net national welfare	18,036	47,548	73,231	6.7%	9.3%

Source: Hisao Kanamori (1978).

Table 6
PRICE MOVEMENTS, 1970–74

	Wholesale	Retail	Land	Money supply	Shunto wage increase
1970	−.8	6.0	15.7	15.9	18.5
1971	.8	4.6	13.2	24.3	16.9
1972	15.9	11.8	25.1	24.7	15.3
1973	31.3	24.3	23.0	16.8	20.1
1974	3.0	11.9	−4.3	11.5	32.9

Source: Yutaka Kosai (1985).

tized benefits to GNP, but subtracts values for pollution, urbanization and negative costs ignored by conventional accounting. The data demonstrate that while positive contributions to welfare were growing, so were negative ones. The result is that up to 1970, GNP measures were overstating welfare improvement by almost 50%. The general perception of the gap between growth and welfare was reinforced in the public mind by a series of specific pollution scandals and by first-hand experience of air pollution which, in Tokyo, reached its all-time measured peak in 1970.

Attitudes engendered by these factors were a product of generational shifts as well as the problems themselves. In the 1970s the emergence of a new class of students and workers and the passing of the first postwar generation of bureaucrats and business leaders produced new expectations, norms of behavior and a rethinking of some of the basic postulates of the High-Speed Growth. By the late 1960s, the labor market was also influenced by the growing inelasticity of the labor supply, while demographic movement foreshadowed economic and social change to come. The absolute increment to the labor force peaked in 1973, and, between 1970 and 1975, the net reproduction rate fell below one, reflecting the dominance of the long-term downward trend in fertility and indicating an eventual decline in population.

Finally, the other significant domestic factor in Japanese growth was the more than doubling of the capital requirement for growth. This reflected many factors, but the demand that investment take account of environmental considerations was a particularly important one. The high ratio implied that even if a high rate of investment had been sustained, its effect on economic growth would decline.

The destabilization of the economy that occurred in 1970–1974 is illustrated by data on prices, wages and the money supply (Table 6). These confirm that land prices and wages were growing very rapidly *before* the shocks, and that the money supply was being allowed to accommodate these. In 1972 and 1973 imported oil and commodity prices extended the destabilization first to wholesale, and then to retail prices. In 1974 these price increases reinforced the *Shunto* trend leading to a 32.9% wage increase in that year. The combination of these extraordinary movements in output, prices and wages, together with world economic uncertainties, produced a profound reaction in Japan, a reaction that put the economy on a new course from 1975 to 1986.

STABILITY AND EXPORT-LED GROWTH

Since 1974 the rate of economic growth in Japan has been consistently less than half the rate achieved during High-Speed Growth (Table 2) and the sources of growth have changed significantly. In the immediate aftermath of the oil shock, private and inventory investment fell sharply and demand was sustained by private consumption and exports. Between 1976 and 1978, both private and public investment picked up. Since 1978, the main features of internal demand have been the low, frequently negative contributions from housing and public investment and a low, erratic level of private investment in plant and equipment. In the case of public fixed capital formation, in six of the eight years 1979–1986, its contribution to demand was negative. For private housing, four of the eight years were negative; while increases in private consumption, though positive, were smaller than before 1973 (Table 7).

The implications of these figures for the structure of the economy and its external sector have been profound. During 1970–1975 the share of manufacturing in total output fell by 6%, while that of services rose by 5%. Since then the broad structure has stabilized, but inspection at a lower level of detail shows structural and corporate change occurring with speed. Many of these changes were the direct result of the oil price rise, which immediately shifted comparative advantage away from Japanese industries that used fuel intensively. These changes were often more acceptable because they echoed and reinforced the earlier shift of emphasis from raw material and pollution intensive industries, and, in many cases (for example, aluminum smelting), the required adjustments were facilitated by MITI under special legislation. Apart from structural readjustment, the other major contribution of MITI since 1973 has been its comprehensive program for energy. This program and market forces have substantially reduced Japan's energy requirements per unit of GNP and kept Japan at the forefront of energy related technologies.

We can see from price data that the violent instability of the 1970s has given way in the 1980s to stability and to a progressive reduction in inflation. Retail price increases fell from 7.8% in 1980 to zero in 1986, while wholesale prices also fell. These trends partly reflect the benefits of oil and raw material price reductions; they also reflect recent willingness of companies to accept lower profit margins in order to maintain market presence and share under conditions of severe yen appreciation.

The net effect of developments in the past 15 years has been to change significantly the relative contributions of internal and external sources of demand. A broad measure of the new significance of external markets to Japan is the fact that whereas in only 1 of the 8 years 1966–1973 did

Table 7
NATIONAL PRODUCT AND COMPONENTS,
1983–88 (%)
(calendar years, 1980 prices)

	1983	1984	1985	1986	1987	1988 (forecast)
Gross national product	3.2	5.1	4.9	2.4	4.3	(3.8)
Private final consumption	3.2	2.7	2.7	3.2	3.9	(3.8)
Government final consumption	2.9	2.8	1.7	6.5	-0.5	—
Gross fixed capital formation	-0.3	4.9	5.8	6.0	10.3	—
Private fixed capital formation	0.3	8.1	10.4	6.6	10.9	—
FCF in dwellings	-6.2	-2.0	2.5	8.4	20.6	(1.9)

Sources: Economic Planning Agency, *Nihon Keizai Shihyo* (1988), No. 2, p. 122; Ministry of Finance, *Zaisei Kinyu Tokei Geppo* (1988), No. 435, *orikomu*.

external demand make a positive net contribution to the growth rate, in only 2 of the 12 years between 1975 and 1985 did it fail to do so.

By 1986, the Japanese found this new pattern to be unsustainable. Externally, Japan's economic partners have had problems in accommodating bilateral and regional trade imbalances. In some cases the capital outflows from Japan have also been controversial. Even the United States, which required the outflow to cover part of its fiscal deficit, found that, ultimately, dependence on yen savings led to instabilities in bond and other financial markets. This was an experience analogous to the American discovery in the late 1960s that the global accumulation of dollar balances, while convenient in the short run (to finance the Vietnam War) could not be sustained indefinitely.

Internally, one effect of export-led growth was that the share of exports in output was growing and the dependence of some individual industries on foreign markets became very high indeed. (The exported shares of the output of the household electronics and office equipment industries have risen to over 50%, while the vehicle industry has been exporting approximately a quarter of its total output). This growth and concentration of trade dependency has meant that private sector investment in plant, machinery and inventories have become highly sensitive to the external sector—in which developments are often not determined by predictable factors, but by politics, the shocks of trade restriction, currency movements and factors beyond the reach of conventional forecasting.

The stock market problems of October 1987 revealed a number of other potential dangers, including the difficulties that world financial instability could create for Japanese exporters who, finding their core businesses seriously undermined by exchange rate movements and protectionism, have begun to speculate in financial markets. This speculation was not only undertaken with internal cash flow, but with funds raised in the market. In 1986, for example, Toyota derived one-third of its profits from financial operations, and in 1987 raised 200 billion yen to expand them. Good performance in financial investment can maintain company probitability, but clearly the consequences of a downturn in financial markets could be very serious for companies whose industrial activities are central to the performance of the Japanese economy.

JAPAN AND THE WORLD ECONOMY

Until relatively recently, the functions of the trade sector have been to facilitate the import of raw materials and foreign technology. The commodity structure of trade and its postwar evolution is shown in broad terms in Table 8. In the early 1950s raw materials accounted for 87.8% of imports, and as recently as 1980, the figure was 77.1%. Of the balance of manufactured goods, most were capital goods, frequently embodying new technology. Within the primary product group it will be seen that the relative importance of fuel increased sharply in the oil shocks. (As recently as 1980 fuel accounted for half of the total import bill.) From 1981 to 1986, however, there was a greater shift in the import structure than in

Table 8
STRUCTURE OF TRADE BY COMMODITIES
1951–86 (% share)

	Imports Primary	(Fuel)	(Food)	Manufactures	Exports Primary	Manufactures	(Textiles)	(Light industry)	(Heavy industry)
1951–55	87.8	11.3	26.9	12.2	3.6	96.4	38.6	17.4	40.0
1966–70	70.8	20.6	14.4	29.2	2.4	97.6	14.4	12.2	68.0
1980	77.1	49.8	10.4	22.8	2.2	97.8	4.8	12.2	84.0
1986	58.2	29.2	15.2	41.8	0.7	99.3	3.2	10.2	87.0

	Imports Chemicals	Iron, steel, metal products	Exports All types of machinery	Vehicles	Electrical	Ships	Scientific instruments
1976	5.6	19.6	58.9	13.2	6.5	10.5	2.8
1980	5.2	16.4	62.8	17.9	6.1	3.6	3.5
1986	4.5	8.7	74.1	20.4	6.9	2.3	4.1

Sources: Ministry of International Trade and Industry, *Tsusho Hakusho* (various years).

the previous 20 years. This was the result of primary and fuel product price declines, domestic demand transformations, and some trade liberalization—all of which enabled the share of manufactures in imports to double.

Although the main source of demand during High-Speed Growth was internal, and although the share of exports in Japan's domestic product was only about half the level found in Western Europe, export growth was critical in facilitating raw material imports, and in this sense constituted a ceiling on the growth rate. (The changing structure of exports is shown in Table 8.) During this era, the performance of the export sector far surpassed early postwar expectations—partly because few foresaw either the rate of growth of world trade or the efficiency with which Japan would respond to those opportunities.

This efficiency has had many dimensions. One has been the quality of the early policy decisions to encourage the continued restructuring of the economy in favor of industries in which the rate of technical progress was high, in which returns to scale were steep and for whose products world income elasticity of demand was high. These policy decisions, moreover, were not implemented in a way that seriously prejudiced the flexibility of the economic structure so that both inter- and intrasectoral structural change in response to market decisions continued rapidly. Further, Japan's price competitiveness benefited from the original decision to fix the rate for the yen at 360 per U.S. dollar, and from world acquiescence at the maintenance of this rate for more than two decades.

One net effect of these real and financial factors is shown in Table 9. Here we see that, as of 1965, vis-à-vis its European and U.S. competitors, Japan had a substantial advantage in its *general level* of industrial labor costs. In relation to the United States, costs were little more than half U.S. costs, and in the sectors and firms competing in export markets the advantage was probably larger. This advantage remained substantial in 1975 (after the breakdown of the fixed exchange rate system) and although yen appreciation has continued inexorably (at different rates against different currencies), other sources of improvement have kept Japan competitive against all countries until very recently, when the depreciation of the dollar against the yen finally passed the point where U.S. cost levels were below Japanese ones.

Important aspects of the favorable world environment began to change in the late 1960s and 1970s. Because Japanese exports were concentrated in specific products, the expansion of the scale of the export effort led to a series of trade frictions, first in textiles, televisions and steel, and later in automobiles and electronics. Moreover, Japan's membership in the international economic community and its formal organizations meant that the government came under irresistible pressure to remove quantitative and tariff barriers to trade. But the major factors in the transformation of Japanese trade and payments were the oil and commodity price shocks and the long run implications of this shift to floating exchange rates. The first oil shock raised the cost of fuel from one-fifth to one-half of the total import bill and, in value terms, the oil bill rose sevenfold between 1970 and 1975. In 1972, equally alarming, although now almost forgotten, world food

Table 9
RELATIVE LABOR COSTS IN JAPAN,
UNITED STATES, WEST GERMANY AND
GREAT BRITAIN, 1965–88

	Japan	United States				West Germany				Great Britain			
	A	A	B	C	D	A	B	C	D	A	B	C	D
1965	100	179				143				198			
1975	100	120	(+33	+15	+18)	138	(+ 3	−36	+39)	164	(+17	+39	−22)
1980	100	127	(− 6	+21	−27)	171	(−24	+12	−36)	262	(−60	+21	−81)
1984	100	151	(−19	+ 5	−24)	129	(+25	+20	+ 5)	183	(+30	+40	−10)
1988	100	78	(+48	+45	+ 3)	123	(+ 5	+14	− 9)	152	(+17	+22	− 5)

Note: Column A shows Japan's labor costs in manufacturing relative to those in the United States, West Germany and Great Britain for selected years (pre-Vietnam boom, post-oil shock, post-second oil shock, pre-U.S. dollar fall). This data is derived from more complete data in Donald J. Daly, *Japanese Manufacturing Competitiveness: Implications for International Trade*. Professor Daly's data is derived from U.S. Bureau of Labor data, which he has updated to spring 1988. I am very grateful to Professor Daly for permission to use these figures and for discussion of their significance.

Column B shows the shift in competitiveness since the previous quoted year; column C represents the shift attributable to exchange-rate movements; column D indicates the balance, attributable to changes in productivity and domestic labor cost.

I have taken the exchange-rate data from *Nihon Tokei Nenkan* and the current press.

output grew less rapidly than population, leading to a rapid rise in food prices. (Between 1970 and 1975, Japanese import prices of sugar, wheat, maize and cotton rose by 5.1-, 2.4-, 1.8- and 1.6-fold respectively.) These commodity price changes not only represented a serious burden on the balance of payments, they also revived prewar fears about the physical security of the Japanese economy. And while the Americans publicly undertook to guarantee food supplies, no one could do the same for oil because the whole non-OPEC world was equally threatened by the disintegration of the conventions governing the oil market and equally uncertain about the future.

The oil crisis presented Japan with three problems: how to restore short-run domestic stability; how to handle the "oil deficit" and how to find national and corporate strategies appropriate to a world economy depressed by the deflationary impact of the oil price rise and which no longer offered the certainties of fixed exchange rates. Of these, the latter were crucial, because it was the response to these that led to the pattern of export-led growth that now has to be reversed at considerable transitional cost. At the level of macro policy, the general direction of monetary and fiscal policy has been cautious, while at the company level, low domestic demand led to an intensification of activity in foreign markets. In the short run, companies reduced internal costs by pressure on subcontractors and the application of new managerial techniques. For the longer term, they began heavy investment in R-and-D to transform export competitiveness through innovation.

As we have seen, investment in borrowed technology had already led to the creation of a new range of process and product technologies, which reduced costs in established industries and resulted in the appearance of new products. (Over 40% of the components of the 1970 Index of Industrial Production were not in the 1950 Index.) What was new after 1974 was the heightened level of domestic research and the intensive effort, not only to produce new products but to sharpen competitiveness by accelerating model changes and supporting these with more sophisticated marketing. Although Japan's total research effort tends to look low in international perspective because of the absence of defense research and the small role of government in R-and-D, by 1978 Japan's spending on R-and-D (exclusive of defense) was well ahead of Britain and not far behind the U.S. Further, when we look at the data for the corporate sector we find that corporate spending as a proportion of gross revenues exceeded both American and British levels. These data support MITI surveys of business opinion, which show that Japanese business leaders regard innovation as the key to growth through both cost reduction and enhancement of product variety, both at home and overseas.

Central to this technological drive have been Japanese efforts in electronics. In this field, the Japanese initially felt disadvantaged vis-à-vis the United States precisely because of their lack of defense and government supported research. Consequently, in 1976, MITI mounted a major program that coordinated and supported the development of VLSI chips in the private sector, while at the same time effectively excluding American imports.

Table 10
TECHNOLOGY TRADE, JAPAN, UNITED STATES
AND GREAT BRITAIN (%)

	Japan	United States	Great Britain (to 1984)
Annual rate of growth of imports 1976–86	8.7	−11.6	3.6
Annual rate of growth of exports 1976–86	11.4	3.3	1.8
Ratio of exports to imports 1986	.28	40.27	1.09

Note: These flows represent payments for licenses, patents etc.
Source: Agency for Science and Technology, 1987 *Kagaku Gijitsu Hakusho* (Tokyo, 1988).

This program produced chips that set new standards of quality in the industry, and it came on stream at a low point in the American electronics cycle. The result was rapid penetration of American markets for certain products. Because of the MITI role in the program and because of the perceived unfair advantage that Japanese integrated electronics companies have in being able to cross-subsidize components and finished products, this led to serious trade frictions.

The vitality of Japan's technology trade can be seen in Table 10. Here we see that the rate of growth of technology exports is high and that the vitality of trade is reflected in buoyant technology imports. In looking at this data, it is important to realize that the current ratio of exports to imports (the "balance of technology trade") is a reflection of contracts entered into many years ago. Data on current contracts show Japan as a technology exporter. It should not be assumed from all this that Japan has any sort of overall superiority over U.S. technology. The evidence is quite the contrary, and at a detailed level of disaggregation of visible trade data we find that many U.S. imports are relatively standard components, that are then incorporated in high-value added, final products. Nonetheless, Japan's growing strength in technology trade and penetration of markets for high technology goods is important, not only for the future of these sectors themselves, but also for the future of more traditional industries that can be transformed by new techniques. It is this total effect that has given rise to some alarm and provides an edge to American technology protectionism.

In Table 11 one perspective is enlarged to include the overall Balance of Payments. At the top of the table, commodity trade balances are shown. It will be seen that a relatively comfortable balance was achieved in the early 1970s; that there was a dip in the oil crisis; but that thereafter the surplus increased almost exponentially until 1986. It is expected to have grown slightly in 1987 and to fall modestly thereafter.

The other important line is that for the long-term capital balance. From

Table 11
BALANCE OF PAYMENTS (billion U.S. $)

	1966–70	1971–75	1976–80	1981–83	1984	1985	1986	1987 (est.)	1988 (est.)	1989 (est.)
Trade balance	2.725	5.383	11.153	23.232	44.257	55.986	92.827	101.68	94.85	89.52
Nontrade balance	−1.310	−3.665	−8.015	−10.826	−7.747	−5.165	−4.932			
Current balance	1.240	1.382	2.326	10.881	33.003	49.169	85.845			
Long-term capital balance	−0.721	−3.894	−5.356	−13.072	−49.651	−64.542	−131.461			
Basic Balance	0.519	−2.512	−3.030	−2.191	−14.648	−15.373	−45.616			

Sources: Ministry of Finance *Monthly Finance Review* (November 1987); Ministry of International Trade and Industry, *Tsusho Hakusho* (1984).

this it will be seen that the trade balance and the capital outflow expanded proportionately up to 1985, but that in 1986 net capital outflow went sharply ahead of the trade balance.

The composition of the outflow is shown in Table 12. Direct investment is seen to expand very rapidly but to be small in relation to the outflow for bond purchases. The striking feature of the data on inflow is how small its value is. If we take data for 1985 and 1986, for every dollar invested in Japan, the Japanese invested 12 abroad. Another surprise is the minute share of foreign investment in Japan that takes the form of direct investment. This extreme asymmetry is highly important, but its existence tends to be overshadowed by the trade figures and associated issues.

Finally, one other line of the Balance of Payments of great interest is the net balance of nontrade items. These have always been negative and have tended to depress the current balance. In 1981–1983 the nontrade balance reduced the current balance by 47%. By 1986, however, the return on Japanese investments reduced this to a mere 2%. Given the relatively recent time profile of direct investment and the growth of Japanese activity in the financial services sector, decline in the trade balance could well be significantly offset by further improvements on the nontrade balance.

To appreciate the global significance of Japan's economy we need to examine the regional distribution of trade and investment flows. For current tensions, the trade balance is the more important (Table 13). The data for 1960 are of interest because at the time Japan's overall balance was negative but small. We see that in this situation Japan ran negative balances with the developed countries, the Middle East and the Communist Bloc. These were partly offset by trade with developing economies. By 1972 the overall balance was strong and 59% of this was accounted for by trade with the U.S. By 1986 the balance was enormous, but the U.S. *share* was only marginally larger. The share of other developed countries increased, while that of developing countries declined. The significance of the U.S. time series is that it illustrates that part of the problem of U.S.-Japanese relations is a question of scale rather than proportion. In 1972 the U.S. deficit with Japan was uncomfortable in some sectors, but by 1986, although the U.S. share of the deficit was only marginally larger as a proportion of the total deficit with Japan, in absolute financial terms it was 17 times larger.

JAPAN AND THE ASIAN ECONOMIES

Japan's Asian economic partners are a large and varied group of countries. The broadest group is somewhat misleadingly classified by the Japanese as *Tonan Ajia*. This includes Southeast Asia, Korea, Taiwan, Hong Kong and India. The People's Republic of China is classified separately as a bloc economy. Differences of scale, demographic and economic characteristics and political organization among these economies are so large that they have to be broken down into broad groups. The most convenient of these are: (1) the Newly Industrializing Countries (NICs)—Hong Kong, Korea, Taiwan and Singapore; (2) the ASEAN group—Brunei, Indonesia, Malaysia, Phil-

Table 12

LONG-TERM CAPITAL MOVEMENTS 1977–86

(billion U.S. $, calendar year)

	Outflows			Inflows		
	1977	1983	1986	1977	1983	1986
Total	5.247	32.459	132.095	2.063	14.759	0.634
O.w. direct investment	1.645	3.612	14.480	0.021	0.416	0.226
Bonds	0.735	12.505	93.024			
Securities and shares				1.577	20.274	−15.213

Source: Bank of Japan *Kokusai Shushi Tokei Geppo* (October 1987).

Table 13
GLOBAL TRADE BALANCES, 1960–86
(million U.S.$)

	1960	1971	1986
Balances with:			
Developed economies:	−660	+3,627	+68,916
United States	−452	+2,996	+51,402
Great Britain	+22	+478	+3,074
Developing economies:	+274	+1,275	+7,993
Middle East	−271	−2,317	−8,632
Communist bloc	−52	+216	+5,832
Total	−436	+5,120	+82,743

Sources: Bank of Japan, *Kokusai Shushi Tokei Geppo* (various years); *Tokei Nenkan* (Statistical Annual) (various years).

ippines and Thailand; and (3) India and China treated individually. (Singapore is a member of both ASEAN and the NICs.)

The main feature of the NICs as a group has been their persistently high growth rates and the even higher rates of growth of their external sectors. Between 1973 and 1983 their average growth rate was 8.3%. In the 1970s, their export growth rates were about three times the rate of domestic growth, and in the first part of the 1980s, all except Singapore, which had a structural crisis, maintained export elasticities of more than one. Because of their relatively small populations and, except in the South Korean case, their lack of primary and agricultural sectors, externally oriented industrialization is the only economic strategy available to these countries if they are to take advantage of economies of scale. The open international environment between the mid-1950s and the first oil crisis enabled them to grow rapidly. Their internal (especially wage) flexibility enabled them to adjust quickly to the post–oil-shock world, and, in the 1980s, they had the added benefit of improvements in the terms of trade and of market opportunities created by the American deficit. It is interesting to note that economic performance among this group has not been affected by domestic political crises.

The contrasting feature of the ASEAN economies is their dependence on agriculture and raw materials and their much larger populations (in total, four times the size of the NICs and less mature in demographic characteristics). In spite of these differences, the growth performance of the group has until recently been impressive. The average (weighted) growth rate 1973–1983 was 6.8%. Since then, however, Indonesia and Malaysia have been severely affected by declining oil and primary prices, and the Philippines by revolution.

How does Japan relate to this environment? First, it must be emphasized that relations between Japan and all Southeast Asian countries are greatly influenced by the past. Prewar and wartime experiences, economic, political and military, weigh heavily and add an overtone of politics and nationalism to relations that would otherwise be purely commercial. The main trade patterns can be seen in Table 14. These show the data for the whole of the *Tonan Ajia* group, for China and for representative NIC and ASEAN economies. We see that as a group, they account for a quarter of Japan's exports and that there has been no shift in this trend during the past decade. This aggregation, however, is misleading, because the figures are greatly influenced by the ability to pay of the ASEAN fuel and primary commodity exporters, whose purchasing power has been declining in the 1980s. In contrast, South Korea, Hong Kong and Taiwan have been absorbing a growth of Japanese imports of 12% to 13% per annum. These are therefore very rapidly growing markets, which because of the general soundness of their balance of payments, are likely to be important in the future. Insofar as these NIC imports consist of inputs of traded goods, the potential demand of these economies is not limited by their domestic markets, but only by their ability to expand their own exports. In contrast to Japanese exports, the trend of Asian imports to Japan is clearly upward. The share of the group rose from 22.8% in 1976 to 27.8% in 1987. Moreover, this rise has been achieved in spite of the fact that Indonesia (which accounts for one-third of the region's exports to Japan) has seen exports fall by one-half since 1980, mainly because of oil prices. This loss has been offset by a vigorous growth of exports from other sources, especially Korea and Taiwan, whose exports have been growing at an annual rate of 10.7% and 14.7% since 1976.

If we turn now to the balance between exports and imports, we see, in Table 15, trends in the net relationship between Japan and the region. In aggregate, in 1986 the region had a deficit of $12.3 billion, in spite of Indonesia's positive balance of $4.65 billion. This deficit is the source of serious regional friction, particularly between Japan and the formally organized and articulate ASEAN group. These anxieties, while understandable, can easily be exaggerated. It is not surprising that a group of developing countries have a deficit with a highly developed neighbor who is capable of providing aid and private capital flows. Moreover, the Asian share of the world deficit with Japan has declined substantially from 26.4% of the deficit in 1976 to 14.9% in 1986.

ASEAN concern about its trade with Japan is not simply a matter of the deficit, but of the overall structure. For the group as a whole, to take 1983 as a typical year, mineral and fuel exports to Japan accounted for 51% of total exports and other primary products for a further 28%. Manufactures only account for about one-fifth of exports. In contrast, over 80% of Japanese exports are heavy industrial goods. It is this "colonial" structure that the ASEAN group wishes to change. There are signs that change is occurring. Close analysis of movements in the Japanese import structure since yen appreciation began in September, 1985, show that the developing countries as a whole are rapidly expanding their share of the market for imported consumer goods in Japan. Yen appreciation has been particularly helpful to Asian economies strictly or loosely linked to the dollar, and micro surveys in Japan confirm that the prospects for further penetration

Table 14
JAPAN'S TRADE WITH ASIA 1976–86
(million U.S. $)

Imports from Asian Partners

| | SEA | PRC = | Total | of which: | | | |
				ROK	Tai	Indo	Phil
1976	13,410	1,370	14,780	1,920	1,190	4,090	790
1980	31,750	4,320	36,070	3,000	2,290	13,710	1,950
1986	29,490	5,650	35,140	5,290	4,690	7,310	126,410

Exports to Asian Partners

| | SEA | PRC = | Total | of which: | | | |
				ROK	Tai	Indo	Phil
1976	14,050	1,660	15,710	2,820	2,280	1,640	1,140
1980	30,910	5,080	35,990	5,370	5,150	3,460	1,680
1986	41,790	9,860	87,640	10,480	7,850	2,660	1,090

Note:

SEA = *Tōnan Ajia* (see text)
PRC = People's Republic of China
ROK = Republic of Korea (South)
Tai = Taiwan
Indo = Indonesia
Phil = Philippines
Source: Bank of Japan *Kokusai Shushi Tokei Geppo* (October 1987).

Table 15
ASIAN TRADE BALANCES WITH JAPAN
1976–86 (million U.S. $)

	SEA	PRC	ROK	Tai	Indo	Phil
1976	−640	−290	−900	−1,090	+2,540	−350
1980	+840	−760	−2,370	−2,860	+9,710	+270
1986	−12,300	−4,210	−5,190	−3,160	+4,650	+130

Note:

    SEA = South East Asia
    PRC = People's Republic of China
    ROK = Republic of Korea (South)
    Tai = Thailand
    Indo = Indonesia
    Phil = Philippines
Source: Bank of Japan *Kokusai Shushi Tokei Geppo* (October 1987).

are good. For some developing countries, the share of manufactures in their exports to Japan are 50% and above. Moreover, yen appreciation has also helped exports of agricultural goods, with spectacular increases in Philippine chickens for Japan's *yakitori* bars and in sales of Philippine bananas and Indonesian plywood. Nonetheless, dissatisfaction remains. The Japanese are unable to accept the full domestic readjustment that Asian economies require to take advantage of their price competitiveness in agricultural and some labor intensive sectors, and the Asians also fear that, because of their inferior political bargaining power, Japanese liberalization vis-à-vis the Americans will worsen their relative ease of access to the Japanese market.

The other source of discontent in Asian-Japanese relations is in the field of direct investment. In the early stages of growth, the main purpose of such investment was to secure stable supplies of raw materials for Japan. Investment thus reinforced the colonial structure of trade. Since 1985 the attraction of many Asian economies to Japanese direct investors has been cheap and relatively skillful labor and their ability to absorb a range of industries rendered uncompetitive in Japan by yen appreciation and land prices.

One result of Asian investment has been to stimulate exports to Japan. As Japanese multinationals elaborate their own international division of labor, controlling and predicting Japanese trade flows becomes more difficult as does judging the balance of advantage from the emerging pattern of trade and investment. In spite of Asian concerns about this pattern, the Japanese have their anxieties too. A 1987 edition of ESP *(Keizai, Shakai, Seisaku)*, published by the Economic Planning Agency, included a special symposium entitled "Will the NICs overtake Japan?" These anxieties are particularly focussed on South Korea which alone among the NICs has a substantial population base. Seen from the standpoint of the non-Asian

1317

economies it appears that, on balance, current patterns of increasing horizontal specialization in East Asia are mutually beneficial and serve to strengthen the competitiveness of the region as a whole against the developed economies.

JAPAN AND CHINA

Japan's economic links with China are more politically sensitive than those with any other country. The Japanese retain a sense of national and often personal responsibility for Japanese actions in China from the late nineteenth century to the end of the Sino-Japanese war, a fact of which the Chinese have always made the fullest use in diplomatic and other forms of exchange.

The Japanese and Chinese economies have strong complementarities. Japan is land scarce and requires raw materials, markets and investment outlets. China needs foreign exchange, inputs for industrialization, aid and technical assistance. Although Japan is much smaller than China in terms of population and land, its economy is much larger and at a far superior technical level. There is therefore a rough overall equality between the two that is not found in other bilateral Japanese links in East and Southeast Asia. The only exception to this might be the Soviet Union, and among the three countries there is an uneasy, triangular rivalry.

Japanese trade received its first boost in China as a result of the collapse of the Sino-Soviet accords. During the 1960s, two-way trade grew rapidly, in spite of the fact that no diplomatic relations existed, and, within China, anti-Japanese propaganda was officially promoted and very popular. Surmounting all difficulties, two-way trade rose to account for approximately one-fifth of all Chinese trade, although exports to China accounted for only 2% of total Japanese exports.

On July 15, 1971, Nixon delivered one of the most famous of his "shocks": news of Henry Kissinger's visit to China and the impending reopening of relations with China. Japan, to whom this was a change of stupendous political importance, was given only hours of notice that it was to be announced. No time was wasted, however, before Japan mended its own fences and the first of three "China booms" was under way. Hailing Mao's China as a "huge, dynamic, reborn nation," the Japanese immediately won orders for 12 petrochemical plants and began large scale exports of chemicals and steel. In 1974 they committed themselves to supplying a rolling mill for the modernization of the Wuhan iron and steel plant. In return, Japan bought textiles, raw materials, light industrial products and, most important of all, oil. Until the development of the Taching field, China had been dependent on oil imports from the Soviet Union. When Taching, and later Shengli, came on stream, the Chinese found themselves in a position to become exporters at almost exactly the same time as world markets were affected by the oil shock of 1974. For the Japanese, at their moment of crisis, the prospect of regional, non-OPEC supplies of oil made China an irresistible trading partner.

In 1978 the Japanese and Chinese signed a Long-Term Trade Agree-

Table 16

JAPAN'S EXPORTS, IMPORTS AND TRADE
BALANCE WITH THE PEOPLE'S REPUBLIC OF
CHINA, 1976–86 (million U.S. $)

	Exports	Imports	Balance
1976	1,663	1,371	+292
1980	5,078	4,323	+755
1983	4,912	5,087	−175
1984	7,217	5,958	+1,259
1985	12,477	6,483	+5,994
1986	9,856	5,652	+4,202

Source: Bank of Japan *Kokusai Shushi Tokei Geppo* (October 1987).

ment. Under this, two way trade of $20 billion was planned to take place over eight years. On Japan's side, the main exports were to be steel and capital goods, and the treaty was appropriately signed by Yoshihiro Inayama, the senior figure in the Japanese steel industry. On the Chinese side, the agreement was to be financed mainly by oil sales, which were expected to rise to from 7 to 15 million tons in 1982. The Chinese anticipated some need for deferred payments, but, broadly speaking, trade was conceived in balanced terms. The main group of contracts that were signed under the agreement were those for the integrated steelworks of Baoshan, on the outskirts of Shanghai, the Baoshan plant being an important part of the Chinese 10-year plan (1975–1985), to raise steel output to 60 million tons.

The agreement was only partially successful. Oil exports to Japan fell short of the plan by one-third. In February 1979, the Chinese suspended Baoshan and other contracts for four months, and, in 1981, as part of the "readjustment," they cancelled phase two of Baoshan—a phase never even recognized by the Japanese.

In 1982 and 1983, high-level visits were made to Tokyo by Zhao Ziyang and Hu Yaobang. During these visits the two sides agreed on the "four principles" to govern their relations. In direct reference to Baoshan, and other economic disputes, these included both "mutual benefit" and "mutual trust." In 1984, Prime Minister Nakasone visited Beijing. This high-level diplomatic activity did little to improve relations, and frictions continued. The Chinese criticized Nakasone for his higher defense spending and international profile. To which Nakasone replied: "Having watched your process of trial and error, I must say that, while you have anxieties about Japan, we have similar emotions about your country." In 1985, Chinese student protesters launched an anti-Japanese campaign reminiscent of the 1920s, and further disputes occurred in 1986 and 1987.

The growth of two-way trade in Japan is shown in Table 16. We see that trade has grown rapidly, with sharp fluctuations and a growing Chinese deficit. Rapid as growth has been, Japan's share seems to be permanently in the range of one-quarter of China's trade. The deficit that has opened reflects on the one side the failure of oil exports to perform well, and, on the other, the skill of Japanese companies in taking advantage of China's strong demand for both capital and consumer goods and the periodic collapse of planning control. The most striking example of the latter effect can be seen in the data for 1985.

Although by 1987 there had been a substantial improvement, the Chinese seemed to accept the structural character of the deficit, to some degree. However they look to the Japanese to compensate with capital flows. The Chinese, we might say, wish to be treated like the rest of the world. The Japanese have not fulfilled these expectations, in spite of some notable successful direct investments such as the Hitachi television plant in Fujian province. Between 1979 and 1984 the Japanese accounted for only 7% of the direct foreign investment in China. In 1986 and 1987, there was an investment "strike" by the Japanese in response to uncertainties and experience of operating problems on existing investments. In 1987, a senior Japanese adviser, Keiichi Konaga, visited China and expressed regret for this, but underlined that the reason for lack of investment was Chinese failure to create an attractive investment climate. There has been some upturn of interest since that visit, and in 1988 the two countries agreed upon a system of investment protection. Nonetheless, the current flow of investment in China is still less than 4% of Japanese total investment and what is now so interesting is that the Japanese position as direct investors in China is basically the same as that of other foreign investors. The fact that Japan can make and act on such objective, apolitical assessments in this matter is a break from the past and an indicator of a new phase in Sino-Japanese relations. From the viewpoint of the Japanese direct private investor, the whole of Asia is now a "level playing field."

CONCLUSIONS AND PROSPECTS

The prospects for a rapid return to global equilibrium in trade and finance are not good. On the Japanese side, the authorities are relying on the rising exchange rate (*endaka*), and on fiscal and other measures to influence directly the restructuring of the economy and a movement toward international equilibrium. Structural change, however, cannot be achieved overnight. Moreover, excessive reliance on the exchange rate in preference to other policy instruments could have the effect of making the yen adjustment overshoot by a wide margin.

This will mean that, in addition to problems arising from the length of the J-curve effects (the lagged response to price changes), businessmen's actions could lead to structural adjustments that are inconsistent with internal equilibrium in the longer term. As we have seen, the data in Table 9 suggest that, in terms of the dollar, yen appreciation has already gone substantially past the point at which the general level of costs is lower in the US than in Japan. Although European levels are still higher, what is striking about the British data is the extent to which the precipitous rate of decline in competitiveness has been halted. (Britain lines 1980–1988, column D). In the U.S. case, column D actually shows a small improvement in 1984–88, thus reinforcing the impact of yen appreciation on U.S. export potential to Japan.

Several other factors need to be borne in mind in considering the future of U.S.- and Euro-Japanese relations. One is the significance of nonprice factors in trade. To the extent that Japanese investment in R-and-D and in marketing sharpen Japanese competitiveness, the impact of domestic cost and exchange rate trends will be diminished. If the Japanese are the only producers of octolingual word processors the price will not be important; and if the relative deterioration of the British human capital stock continues, no rate for the pound against the yen will stimulate British exports from knowledge-intensive activities in either goods or services. Second is the significance for the future of the interaction between direct exports, the invisible balance and Japanese foreign investment. The visible balance in the short run and the invisible one in the longer term. In the European case the issue is further complicated by the planned creation of the common internal market in 1992. The precise nature of this and its trade creating and diverting effects is far from clear—partly because 1992 has become such a major factor in bilateral bargaining between Japan and the European Community (EC).

In the case of the US, improvement will require further action on both sides.

We have now seen a three-year period of dollar devaluation in relation to the yen and no major improvement in the U.S. external position, or its bilateral balance with Japan, has been achieved. This suggests that if U.S. output and absorption trends are not brought in line, under almost any exchange-rate conditions, there will be an American deficit in which Japan will have some share. A great deal of emphasis (and hope) has been placed by Japanese and foreign politicians on Japan's market opening measures as a means to reaching a better trade balance. As quantitative and tariff barriers have disappeared, there have been calls for further measures including positive discrimination by Japanese buyers. While there is some room for discrimination in public sector purchases, the problems in the private sector are complex. For the US and Europe the difficulty is that surveys of private sector purchasing trends show that in many sectors, potential export markets have already been lost to the export sectors of developing countries. For Europe and the US, it would appear that the most sensible strategy has to be to accept some level of trade imbalance and to optimize the use of the Japanese capital outflow.

The Japanese have made enormous investments in public relations and political lobbying in the Western economies, and while some in Europe and America are already critical of the Japanese, others are busy establishing incentives for even more direct investment or are benefitting in the services sector from Japanese trade and investment activities. Nonetheless, one cannot exclude the possibility that a sharp move toward protectionism might take place in the 1990s. The likelihood of this will be enhanced if real oil prices continue to fall and if the post-Reagan politics do not allow the US to come to grips with the fiscal deficit. In these circumstances,

Japan's response is likely to include intensified trade and investment efforts throughout the whole of Asia, and we could then see the emergence of new systems of regional trading blocs that would lead to substantial misallocation of world resources, and whose structure, once supported by domestic vested interests, might take many years to modify.

FURTHER READING

In English:

Chong, N. K. and Hirono, Ryokichi, eds. *ASEAN-Japan Industrial Cooperation: An Overview.* Singapore: Institute of Southeast Asian Studies, 1984.

JETRO China Newsletter, Tokyo.

Kanamori, Hisao. "Japanese Economic Growth and Economic Welfare." In Tsuru, Shigeto, ed. *Economic Growth and Resources.* Tokyo: University of Tokyo Press, 1978.

Keizai Koho Center. *Japan 1986: An International Comparison.* Tokyo: University of Tokyo Press, 1986.

Minami, Ryoshiu. *The Economic Development of Japan: A Quantitative Study.* Basingstoke, Hampshire: Macmillan, 1986.

Monthly Finance Review. Tokyo: Ministry of Finance.

Nakamura, Takafusa. *The Postwar Japanese Economy: Its Development and Structure.* Tokyo: University of Tokyo Press, 1981.

Ohkawa, Kazushi, and Shinohara, Miyohei, eds. *Patterns of Japanese Economic Development: A Quantitative Appraisal.* New Haven, Connecticut: Yale University Press, 1979.

Patrick, Hugh, and Rosovsky, Henry, eds. *Asia's New Giant: How the Japanese Economy Works.* Washington, D.C.: Brookings Institution, 1976.

Sekiguchi, Sueo. *ASEAN-Japan Relations: Investment.* Singapore: Institute of Southeast Asian Studies, 1983.

Shinohara, Miyohei. *Industrial Growth, Trade, and Dynamic Patterns in the Japanese Eoconomy,* Tokyo: University of Tokyo Press, 1982.

Yamanura, K. *The Political Economy of Japan: The Domestic Transformation.* Stanford, California: Stanford University Press, 1987.

In Japanese and Chinese:

Bank of Japan. *Kokusai shushi tokei geppo.* (International balance of payments monthly.) Tokyo.

Bank of Japan. *Nihon keizai o chushin to suru kokusai hikaku tokei,* (International comparative statistics with the Japanese economy as the focus.) Tokyo, 1984.

Chinese State Statistical Bureau. *Zhongguo tongji nianjian.* (Chinese statistical yearbook.) Peking, 1981—.

Economic Planning Agency. *2000 nen no Nihon.* (Japan in the year 2000.) 8 vols. Tokyo, 1983.

————. *Keizai hakusho.* (Economic white paper.) Tokyo.

————. *Seikai keizai kokka nihon e.* (Japan on the way to being a global economy.) Tokyo, 1986.

ESP. (Keizai, shakai, seisaku.) Tokyo, monthly.

Funahashi, Naomichi. *Tenkanki no chingin mondai.* (Wage problems in the period of transition.) Tokyo, 1971.

Kanamori, Hisao. *Nihon keizai dai tenkan no jidai.* (The era of great change in the Japanese economy.) Tokyo, 1984.

Keizai Semina. *Kaisetsu tsusho hakusho.* (An explanation of the trade white paper.) Tokyo, 1986.

Keizai Semina. (Economic seminar.) Tokyo, monthly.

Komiya, Ryutaro. *Gendai nihon keizai kenkyu.* (Research into problems of the modern Japanese economy.) Tokyo, 1975.

Kosai, Yutaka. *Kodo seicho no jidai.* (The era of high speed growth.) Tokyo, 1985.

Ministry of International Trade and Industry, *Tsusho hakusho,* Trade white paper), Tokyo.

————. *Waga kuni kigyo no kaigai jigyo katsudo.* (Our country's enterprises overseas undertakings.) Tokyo, 1984.

Ministry of Labor. *Rodo hakusho.* (Labor white paper.) Tokyo.

Statistics Bureau, Management and Coordination Agency. *Tokei nenkan.* (Statistics yearbook.) Tokyo.

Yamazawa, I. *Nihon no keizai to kokusai bungyo.* (Japanese economic development and the international division of labor.) Tokyo, 1983.

Zhungguo dui wai jingji maoyi nianjian. (Chinese foreign economic relations almanac.) Peking, 1984—.

Zhungguo jingji nianjian. (Chinese economic almanac.) Peking, 1982—.

THE ECONOMIES OF ASIA'S NEWLY INDUSTRIALIZING COUNTRIES

EDWARD K. Y. CHEN

INTRODUCTION

THE experience of economic growth in the Asia-Pacific region in the 1970s and 1980s has truly been most impressive by any standard. The Asia-Pacific region in this context means the Western Pacific Basin, which runs from South Korea in the north to Indonesia in the south. Specifically this region contains 10 countries (the Asia-10): Japan, China, Hong Kong, South Korea, Singapore, Taiwan, the Philippines, Malaysia, Thailand and Indonesia. These countries have by and large recently enjoyed much faster economic growth than countries in other parts of the world. In the 1950s and 1960s Japan surprised the world with its economic growth at a rate of 10 percent or more. In the 1960s and 1970s Asia's newly industrializing countries (NICs) known as the "Four Little Dragons" (Hong Kong, Singapore, Taiwan and South Korea) demonstrated that they were also capable of achieving similar or even greater success. Since opening up in 1977, China has also been growing at an average rate close to 10 percent. Four of the countries that comprise the Association of Southeast Asian Nations (ASEAN) (Thailand, the Philippines, Indonesia and Malaysia) are latecomers (although the Philippines in fact started industrialization earlier than any of the four Asian NICs), but their potential should not be underestimated. Thailand has undoubtedly turned its latent heat into strong energy. Thailand should very soon be Asia's fifth NIC, or little dragon number five.

Can the general experience of economic growth in these Asia-Pacific countries be used as a lesson for other developing countries? The answer depends on what level such a generalization is to be made. If one confines oneself to the observation of what has happened concomitantly with rapid growth in income, one can easily make the generalization that the rapid economic growth of an Asia-Pacific country is based on export-oriented industrialization, specifically the export of light, labor-intensive products.

Table 1

COMPARATIVE ECONOMIC PERFORMANCE
(Average Annual Growth Rates, 1960–85)

	GNP	Per capita income	Manufactured exports
4 ANICs	9.0	6.9	25.8
ASEAN-4	6.0	3.9	19.6
China	6.4	4.8	11.8
South Asia	4.1	1.5	11.0
Latin America	3.9	1.7	10.5
Africa	3.2	0.7	4.2
North America	3.6	2.1	14.9
European Community	3.6	2.3	12.3
Japan	6.9	4.7	16.0
Australia	3.9	2.0	11.5

Source: World Bank, *World Development Report,* various years.

Some simple comparative statistics shown in Table 1 are sufficient to support an assertion of export-led growth. Countries or groups of countries that have higher rates of growth in manufactured exports are also those that enjoy higher rates of GNP growth. Of course, this association of economic growth with manufactured export growth is no definite proof of export-led economic growth in the sense that the direction of causation runs from the growth of manufactured exports to the growth of income. But on the basis of some econometric and time series causality analyses, there is strong evidence that export is the engine rather than the handmaiden of economic growth.

Among the Asia-10, the most spectacular export-led growth based on labor-intensive manufactures is found in the Asian NICs (ANICs). It is the purpose of this paper to focus on the experience of the ANICs, and discuss the economic policy and other noneconomic, institutional aspects that have led to their economic miracles. Although the experience of the ANICs is the major concern, this chapter will also look at the implications of the ANIC model for other developing countries in the region. First, is the ANIC model in theory transferable to other developing countries? Second, if it is in theory transferable, then is it in practice possible, considering that the world market for manufactured exports is limited? Before these questions can be answered one must examine the Asian experience of export-led industrialization and the factors contributing to its success.

EXPORT-ORIENTED INDUSTRIALIZATION

Development strategies for industrialization can be broadly divided into import substitution and export orientation, strategies that are not mutually exclusive. Import substitution is a strategy in which products produced by newly developed industries are mainly for the domestic market, thus replacing the products that have to be imported. Export orientation is a strategy in which the newly developed industries target their sales for overseas markets. Increased foreign exchange earnings will then be able to support an even greater amount of imports. Import substitution can further be divided into a first stage of "easy" import substitution, during which nondurable consumer goods are produced, and a second stage of "difficult" import substitution for the production of durable consumer intermediate goods and capital goods. The first stage of import substitution (IS1) is easy because production is roughly in line with the prevailing comparative advantage. The second stage of import substitution (IS2) becomes difficult because of rapidly increasing costs brought about by limited economies of scale, dependence on foreign resources and expertise, and development of monopolistic controls. Import substitution is associated with a package of policies aiming at protecting infant industries and discriminating against exports. Such policies include overvalued exchange rates, multiple exchange-rate systems, import controls, high tariffs and quantitative restrictions on imports. These measures discriminate against exports because they force exporters to face import prices of inputs above the world level.

Export orientation can also be divided into a first stage of exporting manufactures that are more labor intensive (EO1) and a second stage of exporting products that are more capital and technology intensive (EO2). This second stage has a phase (EO2 complex) in which import substitution of capital and intermediate products (secondary import substitution) occurs at the same time as export orientation. Concomitantly, sectors providing financial, technical and other professional services may grow. The EO2 complex stage may take place after EO1 or some time after EO2 has begun.

Thus, for industrialization in developing countries, four possible stages of development exist: IS1, IS2, EO1, and EO2/EO2 complex. Generally, countries pass through the various stages in the order here listed. Latin American countries went from IS1 to IS2 for some time before switching to EO1, during which high growth rates were experienced. But it seems that they went from EO1 to EO2 so readily and extensively that they got themselves into trouble. The ANICs did not go through IS2. Hong Kong did not even pass through IS1, and in Singapore the IS1 stage was very short. Both South Korea and Taiwan moved into EO1 when the stage of easy import substitution was over. As early as the beginning of the 1970s both South Korea and Taiwan began to diversify into capital- and technology-intensive industries, and therefore in some ways went into the stage of EO2/EO2 complex. South Korea and Taiwan have been more cautious than Latin American countries. Thus, despite some setbacks in some of their heavier industries, particularly the energy-intensive ones, they have managed to succeed in establishing some capital- and technology-intensive industries and in upgrading many of their existing light industries. Hong Kong and Singapore began to move into EO2 after the late 1970s. Indeed, the common problems facing all ANICs at the end of the 1980s and into the 1990s are related to the economic transformation from EO1 to EO2, and it seems that this transformation is more intriguing than that from IS1 to EO1.

In the process of industrialization Hong Kong constitutes the only exception among developing countries in not having gone through an import substitution stage before export orientation. The beginning of industrialization in Hong Kong was the result of historical factors that included the Communist takeover in China and the Korean War. The change of regime in China gave rise to a reduction in entrepôt trade, and to massive flows of capital, labor and entrepreneurship from China into Hong Kong. The Korean War resulted in a U.N. embargo, which further reduced Hong Kong's volume of entrepôt trade. Thus, it was for survival that Hong Kong had to industrialize, taking advantage of the inflow of production factors for industry.

Under a typical colonial administration it was not expected that the government would play an important role in directing the transformation of the economy. Fortunately, because of laziness or laissez-faire attitudes of the government, no measures were taken to protect the newly established firms and industries, and hence no biases against exports were created. Under these circumstances, Hong Kong could fully exploit its comparative advantage from the beginning for export-oriented industrialization. Given the small size of the domestic market, lack of resources and the possibility of obtaining imported inputs at world prices, entrepreneurs certainly will go for export orientation to maximize their earnings.

Although Singapore is smaller than Hong Kong in size and population, it went through a brief period of import substitution. With the establishment of self-government in 1959 Singapore attempted to promote industrialization through active government programs. In the years 1960–63 protective tariff and quantitative import restrictions were introduced. An important reason for Singapore's pursuit of import substitution policies then was the hope of establishing a common market with Malaysia. For two years after Singapore's independence, in 1965–67, more import duties and restrictions were introduced. The common market never came into being. Singapore was then forced to adopt an export-oriented development strategy. In the Economic Expansion Incentives Act of 1967 the tax rate on profits was reduced from 40 percent to four percent. At the same time there were other tax concessions related to expenditures on research and development and capital equipment. Although tariffs on some imports remained, the incidence of import quotas was gradually reduced. .

In South Korea and Taiwan the switch from import substitution to export orientation necessitated a reform in exchange-rate policy in addition to import liberalization and export incentives. The policy changes in South Korea took place in 1960–61 with the commencement of the Park Chung Hee government. It was believed that (1) the easy stage of import substitution was completed and it was difficult to turn to a higher stage of import substitution, and (2) under these circumstances the balance-of-payments problem could only be solved by export promotion. It turns out that the belief was correct. To promote exports, first, the won was devalued in 1961 (from 62.5 won to 130 per U.S. dollar) and again in 1964 (from 130 won to 256 won per U.S. dollar); second, measures to liberalize import restrictions were taken, especially after the devaluation in 1964; and third, various export incentives were introduced. These included tariff and tax concessions granted to imports of raw materials by exporting firms, accelerated depreciation and various export credit subsidies. An interesting form of export incentive is the assignment of export targets to industrial associations, firms and regions. When export targets are not met, measures are taken to rectify the situation, ranging from threats of sanctions to provision of additional incentives and government actions to remove bottlenecks.

Rigorous import substitution policies were pursued by the Taiwan government in 1951–57. Strict import controls were imposed in 1951, accompanied by a multiple-exchange-rate system. Import substitution was generally a success during this period, leading to a doubling of manufacturing production.

By 1958, however, easy import substitution came to an end and the manufacturing sector was faced with many problems, including falling prices and runaway competition. A series of policies switching to export orientation was adopted in 1958–60. They were preceded by the 1955 regulations for the rebate of taxes on export products, which provided for the rebate of import duty, defense surtax and commodity tax for exporting products. Like any package of measures aiming at export promotion, these taken by the Taiwan government included reforms in exchange-rate systems, import liberalization and export incentives. First, the multiple-exchange-rate system gradually evolved into a single-rate system, and the exchange rate applicable to the bulk of imports and to exports by private enterprises was devalued from around NT$25 to NT$40 per U.S. dollar. Second, the government gradually liberalized and finally abolished the commodity import quota system. Import controls were also liberalized. In 1961 domestic manufacturers seeking protection had to show that they were capable of satisfying domestic demand and that their prices did not exceed the prices of comparable imports by more than 25 percent. In 1964 this was reduced to 15 percent, in 1968 to 10 percent and in 1973 to five percent. The reduction in tariffs was reflected by the decline of the ratio of net customs revenues to total imports, from 42 percent in 1955 to 28 percent in 1960; 22 percent in 1965; 18 percent in 1970; and 14 percent in 1976. Third, the provision of export incentives included the setting up of three export processing zones in Kaohsiung, Nantze and Taichung; cheap loans for exports; further tax concessions for some export products; and export insurance and promotion by government organizations.

The most important generalization arising from the experiences of the four ANICs is that only under export-oriented industrialization can sustained fast economic growth be achieved. Under import substitution any success is short-lived. An important question is why export orientation is a better policy. If one goes by the traditional static trade theory, the gain from international trade will only lead to a once and for all increase in income as a result of improvement in resources reallocation. On the contrary, the infant-industry argument hinges on the dynamic effects of a learning process that will lead to higher economic growth. Similarly, the superiority of export orientation has to be explained on the basis of dynamic effects. A. O. Krueger, in an article published in 1981, gives the following explanations.[1] First, export promotion is a better policy because it involves incentives rather than controls, and because measures can be applied more generally across the board. Whereas import substitution policies discriminate against exports and create market distortion, many export promotion policies give similar incentives to production for domestic and export markets. Also, whereas import controls are usually highly selective, export incentives usually do not differentiate much among individual export commodities. Second, it is easier to detect the effectiveness of export promotion policies because export performance can be easily observed. Thus, policy mistakes of export promotion can be more quickly corrected. Third, export promotion gives industries the opportunity to enlarge their markets and achieve greater economies of scale. Fourth, export-oriented development forces industries to compete in the international market and achieve greater efficiency.

These explanations are not the complete story. To explain the generation of sustained growth under export orientation, a virtuous-circle hypothesis is needed. It has been shown that the export sector usually has a high rate of profits and a high propensity to save. This can perhaps be explained by Krueger's analysis that exporting firms achieve greater economies of scale and efficiency. In the ANICs, the rapid growth of exports was accompanied by a high rate of capital formation. Foreign capital (aid, loan or investment) was crucial to the development of all four ANICs at certain stages. But the level of domestic saving always rapidly increases as exports grow. It seems that a two-way relationship exists between saving and investment on one hand and export growth on the other, giving rise to a virtuous circle of development.

The superiority of export orientation over import substitution can also be explained by a two-gap model. The model, at the risk of simplification, asserts that export growth will generate foreign-exchange earnings to overcome the foreign-resources constraint that for developing countries is more binding than the domestic-resources constraint. The model implies that export growth will enable a developing country to import capital and intermediate goods, and technology for growth in productivity, and therefore income. It has been shown that these hypothesized relationships did exist in the ANIC.[2] Thus, inasmuch as the availability of foreign resources is a binding constraint, export orientation is a better policy than import substitution. The gain from trade in this case is not only static but also dynamic, in the sense that export growth will initiate a dynamic process of capital accumulation and technological progress.

[1] A. O. Krueger, "Export-led Industrial Growth Reconsidered," in *Trade and Growth of the Advanced Developing Countries in the Pacific Basin,* ed. W. Hong and L. B. Krause (Seoul: Korea Development Institute, 1981), 3–27.
[2] Edward K. Y. Chen, "Export Expansion and Economic Growth in Some Asian Countries: A Simultaneous-equation Model," *Measurement, History, and Factors of Economic Growth,* ed. R. C. C. Matthews (London: Macmillan, 1980), 284–93.

Even if export orientation is a better policy, one might still ask whether the stage of import substitution is necessary as a precondition for export orientation. Economists increasingly believe that import substitution is not really necessary. This is an issue difficult to generalize. It depends on the initial conditions of the country and the types of industries developed. It is certainly difficult to conceive that manufactured products can be produced immediately at world competitive prices without some previous industrial base. Even if one can cite examples, such as garments and electronic products, that can penetrate world markets successfully without first being produced for the home market, these products could not have been manufactured at such competitive prices without an industrial base and infrastructure created by the manufacture of other products under import substitution. In Hong Kong and Singapore an infrastructure favorable to export-oriented industrialization was built during the entrepôt stage of economic development. Also, Hong Kong and Singapore are special cases because industrialization was to a large extent triggered by the inflow of entrepreneurs from Shanghai to Hong Kong and from developed countries to Singapore. A stage of import substitution for the breeding of indigenous entrepreneurship could therefore be avoided. Thus, Hong Kong did not undergo an import substitution stage, and Singapore could have done without one if it had so chosen.

EXPLANATIONS FOR THE ECONOMIC SUCCESS OF THE ANICs

Even if export orientation is in theory a better strategy, there is no assurance that a country adopting the strategy will experience fast economic growth. A complicated set of economic, political, and cultural factors seems to be important in assuring the success of export-oriented industrialization.

As expected, it did not take long for neoclassical economists to realize that the economic success of the ANICS demonstrated a great victory for neoclassical economics, which emphasizes automatic adjustments and free market forces. It is true that the adoption of an export-oriented industrialization strategy implies getting the prices right so that the products can be competitive in the world market. But it is not true that this can be achieved through automatic adjustments. The role of the government has been important in getting the prices right, in setting objectives and in implementing policies. For example, monopolies have to be destroyed, labor and capital market imperfections have to be removed, overvaluation of exchange rates has to be corrected, trade restrictions have to be reduced, and incentives for exporting have to be established. Thus, what is important is a kind of neoclassical interventionism rather than the invisible hand of the classical school. But the experience of the ANICs does lend strong support to the classical and neoclassical conviction that competition is better than protection, and therefore export-oriented industrialization is better than import substitution.

Yet it is certainly no easy task for a developing country to adopt export-oriented industrialization at an early stage of development. As indicated above, the role of the government is important. And above all, popular response to government policies is even more crucial. If successful economic development is as simple a matter as export orientation and getting the prices right, there would be very few low-income countries today. Besides economics, some investigators are beginning to believe that there must be some noneconomic elements bringing about the economic success of the ANICs. The cultural factor of course comes to mind. But the cultural commonality of the ANICs is Confucianism, which for decades has been accepted as an inhibiting rather than moving force for economic development. Thus, one must have courage and determination to challenge Max Weber if one attempts to associate the economic success of the ANICs with Confucianism. Futurologist Herman Kahn was the first, in 1979, to explain explicitly the economic success of East Asia on the basis of Confucian ethics.[3] This view was echoed by Roderick MacFarquahar in 1980[4] and elaborated on by Peter Berger[5] in 1983. Philosophers and historians have added further insights to the Confucianism explanation of economic success in East Asia. Following Berger, one gets around Weber's hypothesis by arguing that the old imperial, or state, Confucianism has evolved gradually, because of changing political, economic and social circumstances, into a new form called secular, or vulgar, Confucianism that is much more inducive to economic development and the rise of modern capitalism. In essence, the culturalist school emphasizes the following aspects of Confucianism: (1) work ethic and self-discipline; (2) hierarchy and obedience; (3) respect for scholarship; (4) familialism; (5) thriftiness; and (6) flexibility and adaptability.

As Figure 1 points out, the adaptability of entrepreneurs within a Confucian culture can be related to world attitudes and the dimension of rationalization of Confucianism. Confucianism is "world affirmation" in the evaluation of the world, uses adaptation to the world as the method for pursuit of the highest good and is cognitive regarding the dimension of rationalization. Christianity, on the other hand, is "world abnegation," stresses ethics and uses mastery of the world for pursuit of the highest good.

Recently, political scientists have participated in the analysis of the economic successes of the four ANICs. The beginning of this contribution can be traced to a 1984 paper by Chalmers Johnson.[6] Johnson attempted to establish a link between political institutions and economic development. Combining economics and politics is of course not new. But their applica-

---

[3] Herman Kahn, *World Economic Development: 1979 and Beyond* (Boulder, Colorado: Westview Press, 1979).
[4] Roderick MacFarquahar, "The Post-Confucian Challenge," *The Economist,* 9 February 1980, pp. 67–71.
[5] Peter Berger, "Secularity: East and West," in *Cultural Identity and Modernization in Asian Countries: Proceedings of Kokugakuin University Centennial Symposium* (Tokyo: Institute for Japanese Culture and Classics, 1983), 28–47.
[6] Chalmers Johnson, "Political Institutions and Economic Performance: The Government-Business Relationship in Japan, South Korea, and Taiwan," in *Asian Economic Development,* ed. R. A. Scalapino (Berkeley, California: Institute of East Asian Studies, 1985), 63–89.

Figure 1
CONTENTS OF RELIGIOUS WORLD VIEW

Methods for pursuit of highest good / Evaluation of the world	Active	Passive	Dimension of rationalization
World abnegation	Mastery of the world: e.g., Christianity	Flight from the world: e.g., Hinduism	Ethical
World affirmation	Adaptation to the world: e.g., Confucianism	Theoretical grasp of the world: e.g., Greek philosophy	Cognitive

tion to East Asia as well as Johnson's conclusion that an autocratic government is inducive to economic development are indeed interesting. It is argued that a development-oriented autocratic "hard" state is necessary for economic development because it provides a stable environment for investment and machinery for the effective implementation of policies.

In the ANICs, South Korea and Taiwan were until the late 1980s under autocratic military governments. In Hong Kong the rule of law and personal freedom exists but the government has been under a benevolent colonial autocracy. Before the decision was made to return the colony to Chinese sovereignty in 1997, the governing bodies (executive and legislative councils) consisted entirely of members appointed by the governor who in turn was appointed by the British government. In Singapore the government has been controlled by a single party since 1959. One thing all four ANICs have in common is that there exists a class of highly educated, well trained and efficient bureaucrats to handle effectively the implementation of policies.

Besides the systematic economic, cultural and political theorization of the economic success of the ANICs, there are also other less formal explanations that emphasize preconditions (such as the Japanese occupation of Taiwan and South Korea and the British colonial control of Hong Kong and Singapore), geographic location, country size, natural resources endowment and so forth. While these factors may be of some significance, their dominant role can largely be refuted on the basis of historical, empirical and theoretical analyses.

AN ECLECTIC MODEL

The explanations discussed above in terms of economics, culture and politics suffer from two weaknesses:

1332

1. Each theory is a partial explanation, in the sense that it does not give due consideration to other factors. Even if it does recognize the significance of other factors, no attempts have been made to show their interactions.
2. Each theory is supposed to be universally true, applicable to all types and stages of economic development. For example, if Confucianism is inducive to economic development, it does not matter whether it is import substitution or export-oriented industrialization.

There is a model that does not suffer from these two weaknesses. It is an integrated or eclectic model that shows the importance of economic and noneconomic factors and how these factors are interrelated. More important, it can be argued that the takeoff and the most rapid economic growth of the ANICs took place under EO1, that is, export-oriented industrialization on the basis of labor-intensive manufactured exports, and hence that any development model explaining the economic success of the ANICs should be confined to the stage of EO1. Any attempt to overgeneralize will invariably encounter serious difficulties.

The starting point for the eclectic model is that in the stage of EO1 the most important factors of production are entrepreneurship and labor. Capital is of course necessary for any production, but it is relatively less important because the scale of production is generally medium or small in EO1. The technology used is standardized and production is not land intensive because factories can be housed in multistory industrial buildings. The characteristics of EO1 can be summarized as: (1) exporting labor-intensive manufactured products, based on realizing the existing comparative advantage; (2) demand-determined export growth, in the sense that exports react passively to what the markets want; and (3) continuous export growth sustained by a process of rapid adaptations by entrepreneurs resulting in rapid product diversification. Essentially, the success of EO1 depends on the supply of flexible and adaptable entrepreneurs, the supply of skilled and docile workers, and an adequate supply of capital and standardized technology.

The structure of the model is illustrated in Figure 2, and can be explained in terms of how the interplay of economic and noneconomic factors facilitates the type of factor supplies that are essential for the success of EO1.

ENTREPRENEURSHIP

1. An autocratic government provides a stable political environment and a set of consistent economic policies for entrepreneurs to grow and to invest.
2. Neoclassical interventionism provides a framework of economic freedom and a private enterprise system.
3. Secular Confucianism gives rise to a class of entrepreneurs who are flexible and adaptable. The existence of family firms enables prompt

Figure 2
ANIC MODEL UNDER EO1

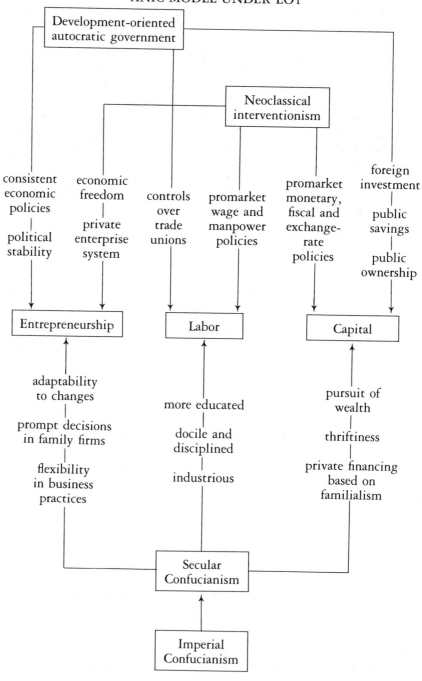

decisions to be made. Informal (very often verbal) contractual agreements facilitate flexibility and confidentiality in business transactions.

Labor

1. Only an autocratic government can effectively keep trade unions under control so that wage increases will not be out of line with increases in labor productivity.
2. Neoclassical interventionism provides a set of policies to ensure that the labor market is working under competitive conditions and that no unrealistic minimum wage laws are legislated.
3. Confucian values such as self-discipline, obedience, commitment to work and family, old age protection dependent on family ties, and so forth give rise to an industrious, docile and productive labor force. Moreover, the labor force in Confucian societies has been shown to have higher educational attainments than in other societies in the developing world. Higher educational standards generally result in greater productivity and adaptability.

Capital

1. An autocratic government is in a better position to mobilize public savings through schemes such as a central provident fund, and to take up public ownership in activities where large capital investment is required. An autocratic government is also in a better position to promote foreign investment by giving concessions to foreign investors in the absence of strong opposition parties.
2. Neoclassical interventionism provides a set of competitive market monetary, fiscal and exchange-rate policies, which are inducive to domestic saving and capital accumulation.
3. In a Confucian society thriftiness is a virtue. Moreover, in a society where an autocratic government prevails, the pursuit of political excellence is substituted for the pursuit of greater wealth and business excellence. Familialism also facilitates the private means of financing investment through the pooling of resources; such a means is adequate for the establishment of small and medium-sized firms.

In summary, the specific cultural and political institutions in conjunction with the appropriate economic policies that minimize factor price and exchange-rate distortions have produced in the ANICs an adequate supply of capital; plentiful, productive and docile labor; and an available class of adaptable and resourceful entrepreneurs. As a result, a most favorable environment has been created for the first stage of export-oriented industrialization, in which mainly labor-intensive products are made and production is largely determined by the extent and type of demand prevailing in overseas markets.

The question that remains to be answered is: Will the ANICs be able to

Table 2
EO1 VERSUS EO2/EO2 COMPLEX

EO1	*EO2/EO2 complex*
Export labor-intensive light manufactured products based on existing comparative advantage.	Export capital-, technology-, and knowledge-intensive light and heavy manufactured products based on the acquisition of dynamic comparative advantage.
Growth is largely demand determined.	Growth is substantially supply determined.
Growth is sustained by rapid *adaptations* (products and techniques).	Growth is sustained by rapid *transformations* (industry and technology).
Tourism and personal services are of some importance.	Importance of the service sector, especially financial services, increases.
Capital goods and intermediate products are mainly imported.	There is some degree of secondary import substitution.

achieve smaller or greater success in the next stage of development, in EO2/EO2 complex?

The differences between EO1 and EO2/EO2 complex, as given in Table 2, must first be examined. In this new stage of development a different type of neoclassical interventionism is necessary for the acquisition of an economy's dynamic comparative advantage. A class of entrepreneurs of a different caliber is necessary to face the problems imposed by a type of economic growth that is based on the supplier's ability to direct the market. And these entrepreneurs must not only be able to adapt but must also be able to create and transform. Technological creation and transformation, as well as highly trained and educated manpower are essential for the second stage of export-oriented industrialization. If all these conditions are needed, one can no longer have as much optimism as before about the economic future of the ANICs. For instance, Confucianism may be too soft a cultural system to effect transformation; the autocratic political institution may be too closed to formulate and implement policies for the emergence of a complex industrial structure.

But such a static analysis need not be accepted. The world is constantly changing, and the ANICs have been the most dynamic and resilient. Political institutions will change and cultural systems will undergo evolutionary processes when the economy moves toward a higher stage of development. The political democratization and economic liberalization movements in South Korea and Taiwan are part of this dynamic process. If Confucianism has already evolved from an imperial to a secular form, then there is every reason to believe that it will undergo further change to cope with the needs of a higher level of export-oriented growth. Thus, from a dynamic point of view there is ample reason to believe that the rapid economic growth of the ANICs will be sustained in the future.

THE "FLYING GEESE" PATTERN OF THE SUBREGIONAL DIVISION OF LABOR

The success of export-oriented industrialization depends crucially on the availability of world markets for manufactured products. Since the early stages of their industrialization the ANICs have accounted for a rapidly increasing share of the world trade in manufactures. A new wave of protectionism consisting mainly of nontariff barriers has been set forth in the developed countries that are the major markets for the manufactured exports of developing countries. The first question that comes to mind is: How were the ANICs able to maintain their rapid economic growth through the 1970s and 1980s? The second question is: Even if the ANICs themselves survive, can the ANIC model be transferred to other developing Asia-Pacific countries so that the entire region can engage in export-oriented industrialization and not be subject to a zero-sum game?

The experience of economic growth in the Asia-Pacific region seems to suggest that, as far as the competition for markets is concerned, it is possible for the entire region to engage in export-oriented industrialization and at the same time achieve rapid economic growth. The reason is a simple one. A high degree of sophisticated subregional division of labor has developed in the region in the course of economic growth. One can of course also ask if Confucianism and a development-oriented "hard" state are absolutely necessary for export-oriented industrialization to work. As is commonly known, it is difficult for political institutions and almost impossible for cultural systems to be transferred. One should perhaps take the view that countries without the cultural and political environment of the ANICs would find it much more difficult to succeed in EO1. But there are always alternative means to the same end. The presence of ANIC communities and foreign direct investment might be a close substitute for the inheritance of a Confucian culture; an efficient and effective democratic government might be a close substitute for a "hard" state. Moreover, most developing countries are today embarking on a EO-cum-IS strategy rather than a pure EO1 strategy.

Many economists believe there is a possible limitation to the spread of export-oriented industrialization from the ANICs to other developing countries because of the fallacy of composition. This means that while export-oriented industrialization may work well if pursued by a limited number of countries, it may break down if a large number of developing countries pursue it at the same time. There is certainly an element of truth to this argument, considering that the capacity of the Western markets to absorb manufactured imports has been decreasing and that protectionism has been rising. But it should be observed that all developing countries do not reach the same stage of economic development and produce the same type of industrial products. Even within the ANICs a high degree of industrial

Figure 3

THE FLYING GEESE HYPOTHESIS

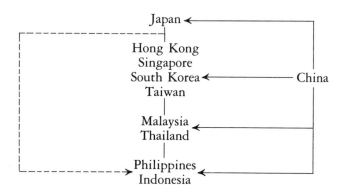

and product differentiation exists. The importance of markets in the developing countries should also be observed. With China adopting an open-door policy, the potential of the Chinese market, for example, should not be underestimated.

Thus, it is safe to conclude that even if most of the Asia-Pacific developing countries adopt the strategy of export-oriented industrialization, these countries will still be able to achieve rapid growth at the same time because of the possibility of complementarity in such industrial growth. Most important, such complementarity is not necessarily a result of deliberate regional economic cooperation but may simply be the result of the different stages of economic development existing in different countries and the changing comparative advantages in countries over time.

The idea of different stages of economic development in this region can best be illustrated by the so-called flying geese hypothesis. In terms of today's situation, one may envision the following pattern:

The leader of the flock of geese is undoubtedly Japan, followed by the ANICs. Of the ASEAN-4, Malaysia and Thailand not only have higher per capita income levels than the Philippines and Indonesia but also have much better economic and political infrastructure for industrialization. In the 1950s the Philippines had the highest degree of industrialization, but the country has been falling behind the others since then: This is shown by the dotted line in the diagram. China is not a goose but a huge bird flying alongside the geese. China has the potential of complementing and competing with the various groups of flying geese at different levels of industrial production. In some areas China is competing or can potentially compete with Japan and the ANICs. On the other hand, China is also producing labor-intensive products in competition with the ASEAN-4. This is shown by the solid lines in the diagram.

Industries can be classified as early (e.g., food, textiles and leather goods), middle (e.g., chemicals and petroleum refining) and late (e.g., clothing,

Table 3
STAGES OF INDUSTRIAL GROWTH IN
ASIA-PACIFIC COUNTRIES

Country	Stage 1986	2000
Indonesia	early to middle	middle to late
Philippines	middle	late
China	early, middle, and late	late to high-tech
Thailand	middle	late to high-tech
Malaysia	middle to late	late to high-tech
Hong Kong	late	late to high-tech
South Korea	late to high-tech	high-tech
Taiwan	late to high-tech	high-tech
Singapore	late to high-tech	high-tech
Japan	high-tech	high-tech

consumer durables, and capital and intermediate goods). To these can be added a fourth stage, high-tech industries (e.g., information technology, biotechnology and material science). A modified "flying geese" pattern is depicted in Table 3. China in the late 1980s was in the early, middle and late stages and will be in a late to high-tech stage in 2000. South Korea and Taiwan are now ahead of Hong Kong and Singapore in technological capability. It can be seen that developing countries in the Asia-Pacific region are engaged in different stages of industrial development. Even for countries in the same stage of development, specialization is normally possible for the achievement of complementarity.

A subregional division of labor is carried out in all the major industries in the Asia-Pacific region. A good example is in the manufacture of semiconductors, with its four distinct phases of production: design and mask making, wafer fabrication, assembly, final testing. What is significant is that each stage requires different levels of skill and different factor intensities. The design and mask-making stage requires a relatively high level of design and production engineering. The wafer fabrication stage is capital intensive, and requires a high standard of precision and product quality control. The assembly stage, which involves mostly bonding, is very labor intensive. The final testing stage requires skilled labor and considerable investment for the acquisition of equipment.

To take advantage of lower wage rates in developing countries (even after consideration of productivity), U.S semiconductor manufacturers moved the assembly stage of production to Asia at a very early time. Hong Kong was the first place where offshore semiconductor assembly was begun, when Fairchild established a plant there in 1962. Wafers were shipped to Hong Kong and the assembled products were sent back to the United States for final testing. In 1964 Fairchild and Motorola invested in South Korea. Many U.S. semiconductor manufacturers set up assembly plants in Taiwan in 1967–69. In 1968–69 National Semiconductor, Texas Instruments and Fairchild opened facilities in Singapore. In the early 1970s numerous facilities were built in the ASEAN-4 countries. By 1974 there were eight U.S.-owned offshore assembly plants in Hong Kong, nine in South Korea, three in Taiwan, nine in Singapore, 11 in Malaysia and six in the rest of Asia. Japanese and European semiconductor manufacturers did not exactly follow the strategy of U.S. firms. While Japanese companies did operate facilities in South Korea, Taiwan and Malaysia, and European firms in Malaysia and Singapore, the extent of offshore production of U.S. firms was considerably larger. At the same time Japanese semiconductor firms responded by automation in the assembling process, and improved technology and design.

In Asia, and especially in the ANICs, indigenous firms were established to assemble semiconductors and compete with foreign multinational firms. There were at first small backward and forward linkages. Since the early 1980s efforts have been made in the ANICs to integrate backward assembly with wafer fabrication through the establishment of indigenous or joint venture firms. In Hong Kong three fabrication plants were set up in 1981–82 and one in the late 1980s.

In South Korea the government took a keen interest in the development of an integrated semiconductor industry. In 1982 a semiconductor industry promotion plan was announced. A new 2,000-acre electronics industrial park was established in Gumi, southeast of Seoul. The government also created the Korean Institute of Electronics Technology. By 1985 there were four fabrication plants in the country, all major South Korean corporate enterprises having the capability and willingness to invest heavily in research and development on a long-term basis. These plants acquire the technology through licensing, subcontracting and joint-venture relationships.

Taiwan's fabrication industry stems from U.S. direct investment in offshore plants. Once started, the local fabrication industry in Taiwan has not been concentrated in a few major large corporations, as in South Korea, but has become widespread, consisting of many medium- and even small-sized firms. The Hsinchu industrial park was established in 1980 and from the very beginning attracted a few Taiwan-United States joint ventures engaged in the production of semiconductors. Above all, the government-supported Electronics and Research Service Organization fabricates wafers at Hsinchu.

Singapore had been an assembly and testing center for semiconductors for many years, relying mainly on investments by transnational corporations. The Singapore government was anxious to develop an integrated semiconductor industry but attempts were largely in vain. Finally, in the early 1980s, Italy's SGS-Ates agreed to set up a fabrication plant in Singapore and later a facility to design chips for the regional market.

In general, in the mid- to late 1980s, a pattern of subregional specialization in the semiconductor industry in the Asia-Pacific region emerged. The ANICs integrated the industry backward to wafer fabrication and design, and forward to final testing, and increasingly concentrated their efforts in this direction of development. This is, in fact, a matter of course in view of their changing comparative advantages. The assembly of semi-conductors has more and more been taken up by the ASEAN-4, especially the Philippines and Malaysia. Thus, in the development of the semiconductor industry in this region, the flying geese hypothesis works. Japan takes the lead in the development of the industry. The ANICs first engage in assembly and then pass this work on to the next tier of economies, the ASEAN-4. Today, foreign direct investment in electronics in the ASEAN-4 is not confined to the United States, Japan and Europe. The ANICs, especially Hong Kong, invest considerably in assembly facilities in the ASEAN-4. Meanwhile, the ANICs take after Japan in engaging in the design and fabrication of wafers, and Japan focuses on innovations in design and production technology.

ECONOMIC GROWTH AND INCOME DISTRIBUTION

While a high rate of economic growth is undoubtedly a primary objective of developing countries, researchers and policymakers are increasingly concerned with the question of equity, that is, the distribution of the fruits of economic growth. It is clearly not a satisfactory situation if the rich get richer and the poor get poorer in the course of rapid economic growth. In 1955 Simon Kuznets[7] hypothesized an inverted-U relationship between the levels of income and income inequality in the course of economic growth. Kuznets claimed that inequality increases with income growth at first but decreases with income growth later on. The implication is that growth and equity are not compatible in the early stage of economic development.

It is interesting to note the change in income inequality over time in the ANICs. Income inequality is usually measured by the Gini coefficient (G), a relative measurement taking into consideration the income shares of different income groups in the economy. G ranges from 0 to 1. When G=0, every household/individual (depending on which is the unit of measurement) has the same income as every other one. When G=1, a single household/individual earns all the income. Developed Western countries typically have G ranges between 0.3 and 0.4, and developing countries between 0.4 and 0.7. Table 4 gives time series data on G in the ANICs. In Taiwan, for example, income inequality has been falling consistently and continuously since the beginning of the country's industrialization. In the late 1980s income inequality in Taiwan was not only very low by the standard for developing countries, but in fact it was among the lowest for developed capitalist economies. There is therefore no evidence of Kuznets' inverted-U relationship.

The level of income inequality is also quite low in South Korea; and the change over time shows a significant trend of decreasing inequality at first, but somewhat increasing inequality since the early 1970s. Hong Kong and Singapore have higher Gini coefficients than South Korea and Taiwan. What is most interesting is that the change in income distribution in both Hong

[7] Simon Kuznets, "Economic Growth and Income Inequality," *American Economic Review* 45, no. 1 (March 1955): 1–28.

Table 4
CHANGES IN INCOME DISTRIBUTION

Hong Kong		South Korea		Singapore		Taiwan	
Year	Gini coefficient	Year	Gini coefficient	Year	Gini coefficient	Year	Gini coefficient
1966	0.487	1961	0.438	1966	0.498	1953	0.558
1971	0.439	1965	0.344	1972	0.443	1961	0.461
1976	0.435	1970	0.332	1973	0.457	1964	0.360
1981	0.481	1976	0.381	1974	0.434	1966	0.358
1986	0.482	1980	0.389	1975	0.448	1968	0.362
						1970	0.321
						1972	0.318
						1974	0.319
						1976	0.307
						1978	0.306
						1980	0.303

Sources: Hong Kong: L. C. Chau, "Rising Income and Rising Inequality in Hong Kong," Discussion Paper no. 17 (Department of Economics, University of Hong Kong, 1983). The 1986 figure is calculated by the present author. South Korea: Korea Development Institute, Seoul. Singapore: Bhanoji V. V. Rao and M. K. Ramakrishnan, *Income Inequality in Singapore*, (Singapore: Singapore University Press, 1980). Taiwan: Shirley W. Y. Kuo, *The Taiwan Economy in Transition* (Boulder, Colorado: Westview Press, 1983).

Kong and Singapore follows the same pattern as in South Korea: income inequality decreased at first but increased later on. This situation also contradicts Kuznets's generally accepted hypothesis. Since this is observed in all four of the ANICs, the evidence cannot be discarded as an exception to the rule.

This is not the place to discuss in detail the pattern of income distribution at a more disaggregate level and the factors underlying the changes in income distribution in the Asian NICs. Extensive individual country studies exist. Suffice it to say that probably not the *level* of development but the *type* of development is important in affecting income distribution. The export-oriented development strategy pursued by the ANICs has given rise to rapid increases in employment. This type of development strategy is therefore more in line with the factor endowment of the countries. At the same time, a type of economic development that devotes a good deal of attention and resources to agricultural development—such as that which took place in South Korea and Taiwan—would surely further improve the pattern of income distribution because of the narrowing of the rural-urban income gap.

An additional factor in Taiwan is the country's attempt to decentralize its industries at the early stage so that the rural population can participate in industrial activities without moving far. In doing so, Taiwan has largely avoided urban unemployment problems facing other developing countries, where industrialization is mostly confined to the capital cities.

Increasing inequality in Hong Kong and Singapore is probably related to their recent development as financial centers and movement toward EO2/ EO2 complex. This change in type of development has resulted in a lower rate of labor absorption and an increase in the importance of the financial sector, which typically has a higher income inequality. In South Korea increasing income inequality is probably related to the development of capital-intensive industries at a somewhat early stage of development in the early 1970s. It has been argued that mismanagement of credit rationing in favor of arbitrarily selected heavy industries is responsible, at least partly, for South Korea's worsening income distribution. Generally speaking as the ANICs move from EO1 to EO2/EO2 complex, a trend of increasing income inequality is likely. For how long and to what extent this will occur depends on the type of policies that individual countries pursue. The implication seems to be that income inequality in the course of economic development will vary with the four different types of development strategy (IS1, IS2, EO1 and EO2), but that it may be possible to make some generalization about these relationships.

CONCLUSION

This paper has described export-oriented industrialization in Asia with reference to the four Asian newly industrialized countries: Hong Kong, Singapore, Taiwan and South Korea. It has been argued that while export orientation is a better strategy than import substitution, the realization of rapid growth under export-oriented industrialization is not an easy matter. First of all, promarket economic policies aiming at eliminating market distortions must be implemented. But some noneconomic factors are probably equally important in ensuring the success of the first stage of export-oriented industrialization. Specific political institutions (a development-oriented hard state) and cultural values (Confucianism) appear to be relevant in this connection. An eclectic model has been developed to explain the success of the ANICs under EO1. Further, a high degree of sophisticated subregional division of labor in the flying geese pattern helps explain sustained growth in the ANICs and the spread of rapid economic growth to other developing countries in the Asia-Pacific region. Moreover, rapid economic growth in the ANICs has also been accompanied by decreasing inequality in income distribution, although more recently there has been the indication of a reversing trend, probably due to changing economic structures and new types of economic growth in these countries' economies.

FURTHER READING

Balassa, B. *The Newly Industrializing Countries in the World Economy*. New York: Pergamon, 1981.

Chen, Edward K. Y. *Hyper-Growth in Asian Economies*. London: Macmillan, 1979.

————. ed. "The Economic Setting." In Lethbridge, David, *Business Environment in Hong Kong*. Hong Kong and London: Oxford University Press, 1984.

————. "The Newly Industrializing Countries in Asia: Growth Experience and Prospects." in Scalapino, R. A., ed. *Asian Economic Development.* Berkeley, California: Institute of East Asian Studies, 1985.

Chen, P. S. J., ed. *Singapore Development Policies and Trends.* Singapore: Oxford University Press, 1983.

Corbe, V., et al., eds. *Export-oriented Development Strategies: The Success of the Five NICs.* Boulder, Colorado: Westview Press, 1985.

Galenson, W. *Foreign Trade and Investment: Economic Growth in the Newly Industrializing Asian Countries.* Madison: University of Wisconsin Press, 1985.

Hansan, P., and Rao, D. C. *Korea: Policy Issues for Long-Term Development.* Baltimore, Maryland: Johns Hopkins University Press, 1979.

Ho, Samuel P. S. *Economic Development of Taiwan, 1860–1970.* New Haven, Connecticut: Yale University Press, 1978.

Hofheinz, R., and Calder, K. E. *The East Asia Edge.* New York: Basic Books, 1982.

Kahn, Herman, *World Economic Development: 1979 and Beyond.* Boulder, Colorado: Westview Press, 1979.

Kuo, Shirley W. Y. *The Taiwan Economy in Transition.* Boulder, Colorado: Westview Press, 1983.

Lau, L. J., and Klein, L. R., eds. *Models of Development: A Comparative Study of Economic Growth in South Korea and Taiwan.* San Francisco: Institute for Contemporary Studies, 1986.

Tu, Wei. *Confucian Ethnics Today: The Singapore Challenge.* Singapore: Federal Publications, 1984.

Turner, L., and McMullen, N. *The Newly Industrializing Countries: Trade and Adjustment.* London: Allen & Unwin, 1982.

THE MARKET ECONOMIES OF SOUTHEAST ASIA

HANS CHRISTOPH RIEGER

INTRODUCTION

THE term "Southeast Asia" was apparently first used during World War II in connection with the establishment of the allied South East Asia Command in 1943. There does not seem to have been any indigenous historical concept for the region previously. By singling out the market economies of Southeast Asia we are thus, in fact, selecting from a rather arbitrary base. And since there is no hard and fast dividing line in practice between market economies on one hand and nonmarket economies on the other, some initial explanation of the terms used in the title of this article is needed.

Southeast Asia in this context refers to the six member countries of the Association of Southeast Asian Nations (ASEAN), that is, Indonesia, Malaysia, the Philippines, Singapore, Thailand, and Brunei; to Burma (now Myanmar) and to the Indochina states of Laos, Cambodia, and Vietnam. There are great economic differences among all of these countries in terms of both resource availability and economic organization. Nevertheless, three typical forms of economic organization are prevalent. Burma has decided on its own socialist mode of economic development. Although the country would probably not be capable of survival without its flourishing black market, the official economic policy, despite occasional statements of intent regarding economic reforms, is oriented toward centrally planned socialist forms of production. Very much the same holds true for Vietnam. The market system here is for the most part "black" too, although it is no less important in bolstering the crumbling economy. Although greater pragmatism may be expected in the future, Vietnam continues to have a socialist economy. As for Laos and Cambodia, both economies are dominated by Vietnamese occupation forces. The present form of economic organization is certainly nearer to the socialist pattern than to the market-oriented pattern, but it would perhaps be unfair to suggest that this is the direction these countries have chosen. Therefore it seems preferable to classify them as "dominated" economies. The remaining countries of Southeast Asia, to a greater or lesser degree, have chosen a market-oriented path to economic development. This should not be confused with a pure capitalist approach in which the government takes no active part in the economy beyond the enactment of laws regulating markets and enforcing contracts. On the contrary, even Singapore, the most market oriented of the group, is an example of an economy in which the government plays a very active part, sometimes to the exclusion of local would-be capitalists. The main distinguishing feature of the market economies of Southeast Asia is that they make use of market forces to generate economic activity and dynamic development in the direction preferred by their respective governments.

The purpose of this article is to take a closer look at the market economies of Southeast Asia, to describe the existing similarities, differences, and interlinkages among them, and to examine their attempts to cooperate in the process of economic development in the ASEAN organization. However, because Brunei joined the ASEAN group only in 1984, and because with its comparatively small population of some 232,000 its weight in the group is not greatly significant, the discussion will focus on the original member countries of ASEAN, that is, Indonesia, Malaysia, the Philippines, Singapore, and Thailand.

BASIC ECONOMIC STRUCTURE

The ASEAN countries of Southeast Asia emerged from very different historical experiences. Thailand always managed to avoid coming under colonial rule; Indonesia emerged from the Netherlands East Indies; Singapore, Malaysia, and Brunei were carved from the Straits Settlements and Federated Malay States; and the Philippines is a product of colonial rule by Spain and, later, the United States. It is not surprising that the different colonial powers imprinted their own stamp on the countries under their rule, and this contributed to the kinds of economies that emerged. Large plantations rather than subsistence farms in many parts of Sumatra and peninsular Malaysia, United States bases in the Philippines, and the harbor infrastructure in Singapore are all evidence of this. But the form of public administration, the way things are done, and the legal system for the dispensation of justice reveal perhaps more subtle differences that are no less important.

The main resources of any country are its land area and its population. Table 1 presents the vast differences existing in the ASEAN region.

At one end of the scale is Indonesia, the fifth largest country in the world with nearly two million square kilometers of land area and an average per capita income of US$ 490 per year. At the other end are Brunei and Singapore, the former with about 232,000 inhabitants with relatively high average incomes and the latter consisting of no more than a small island with a completely urbanized population of under three million having the highest income level in Asia (after Japan and excepting Brunei).

With the exception of Singapore, all the ASEAN countries are blessed with abundant renewable and nonrenewable natural resources. Indonesia, Malaysia, and Brunei are exporters of oil and natural gas; Indonesia is a member of the Organization of Petroleum Exporting Countries. Although

Table 1
BASIC COMPARISON OF ASEAN ECONOMIES

	Brunei	Indonesia	Malaysia	Philippines	Singapore	Thailand	ASEAN
Area (1,000 sq. km.)	6	1,919	330	300	1	514	3,069.4
Population (millions, mid-1986)	0.2	166.4	16.1	57.3	2.6	52.6	295.2
Average population density (persons/sq. km.)	34	87	49	191	4,333	102	96
GNP per capita (U.S. $)	15,400	490	1,830	560	7,410	810	724

Source: World Bank, *World Development Report 1988.*

the other ASEAN countries are importers of oil, the region as a whole is a net exporter. Indonesia, Malaysia, and Thailand are among the world's major tin producers, making the ASEAN region the world's largest exporter. There are substantial coal deposits in Sumatra. Bauxite, copper ore, chromite ore, barite ore, gypsum, and manganese are mined in several of the ASEAN countries. Regarding renewable resources, the region is rich in tropical hardwood, palm oil, and coconut products, and is the world's largest exporter of natural rubber. Until recently, Indonesia was the world's largest rice importer, but has now become self-sufficient regarding food grains.

The ASEAN group has been acclaimed as the fastest growing region in the world, although a slowdown in the mid-1980s temporarily dampened growth optimism. Table 2 provides an overview of the economic growth rates of the ASEAN countries.

With the exception of the Philippines, which was set back severely toward the end of the Ferdinand Marcos regime in the mid-1980s, all ASEAN countries have done remarkably well in terms of their per capita GNP growth since the mid-1960s. The particularly impressive achievement of Singapore is due to a large extent to the successful policy of controlling population growth. This is demonstrated in a comparison of population growth figures in Table 3.

Population growth has been curbed in Singapore to such an extent that in the absence of significant levels of immigration the present age structure of population will cause an absolute decline in the coming decades, a prospect that is causing the political leadership in that country considerable concern. In the Philippines the situation is more complex. On one hand, the failure to reduce drastically poverty levels continues to make large families attractive as an old age insurance. On the other hand, a century of Spanish rule brought Catholicism to the Philippines, so that socioreligious barriers to contraception exist. Nevertheless, World Bank projections for the turn of the century indicate that after the first decade of the 21st century population expansion will stabilize in the ASEAN region at a level somewhere over 600 million, or just about twice what it is today.

With the exception of Singapore and, to a large extent, Brunei, agriculture still plays an important role in the ASEAN region. In general, however, the contribution of agriculture to GDP is considerably smaller than the share of employment and has been shrinking rapidly in importance in comparison to the contribution of industry and services to GDP in some ASEAN countries—particularly Indonesia and Thailand (and probably Malaysia too, although there are no comparable figures available). In part this is the result of conscious industrialization efforts of the ASEAN countries in their drive toward economic development. Because industrially organized activity is able to generate higher levels of value added than is possible in traditional forms of agricultural production, and because more efficient agriculture requires larger land areas per agricultural worker, industrialization is regarded as the main instrument of economic develop-

Table 2
ASEAN ECONOMIC GROWTH RATES
(percent per year)

	Indonesia	Malaysia	Philippines	Singapore	Thailand	ASEAN*
GDP 1965–80	7.9	7.4	5.9	10.4	7.4	7.2
GDP 1980–86	3.4	4.8	−1.0	5.3	4.8	3.4
GNP per capita 1965–86	4.6	4.3	1.9	7.6	4.0	4.0

*GDP growth rates weighted by 1965 and 1986 GDP values, respectively. GNP per capita growth rates weighted by 1986 population.
Source: World Bank, *World Development Report 1988*. Values for Brunei not available.

Table 3
ASEAN POPULATION GROWTH RATES
(percent per year)

	Indonesia	Malaysia	Philippines	Singapore	Thailand	ASEAN*
1965–80	2.3	2.5	2.9	1.6	2.7	2.6
1980–86	2.2	2.7	2.5	1.1	2.0	2.2
Projection 1986–2000	1.8	1.9	2.3	0.8	1.6	1.9
Projected year of reaching net reproduction rate of 1	2005	2005	2015	2030	2000	2030
Hypothetical size of stationary population (millions)	335	33	137	3	99	607

*ASEAN population growth rates weighted by 1986 population.
Source: World Bank, *World Development Report 1988.* Values for Brunei not available.

ment. The structure of production in the ASEAN countries is depicted in Table 4.

The role of services appears to have decreased in some countries and risen in others. The main reason for this is that to some extent services are a residual category and may include many different items that vary from country to country. It is therefore useful to focus attention on the development of manufacturing, a subsector of the industry category. This is done because manufacturing is generally regarded as the most dynamic sector in economic development. Manufacturing has increased in importance in all ASEAN countries and now contributes close to one fifth of ASEAN GDP. It is interesting to note that Indonesia is the country with the fastest increase in manufacturing share of GDP, although, of course, it grew from a significantly lower base than in other ASEAN countries. The level at 14 percent is still significantly below the ASEAN average of 19 percent. Although manufacturing as a share of GDP appears high in the Philippines, nearly equaling that of industrialized Singapore, much of it is still concentrated in the agricultural sector and is a reflection of the large food crop plantations and canning industries characteristic of the Philippines. That is evident from a look at Table 5, in which the structure of manufacturing in the ASEAN countries is presented in greater detail.

Although the proportion of food- and agriculture-based manufacturing was even higher in Thailand than in the Philippines in 1970, the Philippines now has the largest proportion of manufacturing in the region, that is, over one third in 1985. At the other end of the development spectrum, Singapore and Malaysia have significant proportions of their manufacturing industries geared toward the production of machinery and transport equipment—close to 50 percent in the case of Singapore and nearly 25 percent in the case of Malyasia. The rapidity with which this area has expanded in the countries mentioned may be an indication of the importance of this sector as an engine of growth in the process of development.

Another indication of development and industrialization is energy consumption. Although all countries are attempting to curb energy input after the experience of the energy crisis in the early 1970s and 1980s, industrialization by its very nature makes use of nonhuman energy for the production of goods and services. The speed with which energy consumption rises is therefore a good indication of the rate of industrialization. Table 6 presents the appropriate figures for the ASEAN countries. The figures are revealing regarding the very large spread among ASEAN countries, with Singaporeans consuming, on average, ten times as much energy as Filipinos. Of course, it must not be forgotten that Singapore is highly urbanized and that a large proportion of energy consumption is used for air conditioning rather than for production, although air conditioning of offices and factories for highly skill-intensive activities can also be considered a production input. But the most interesting feature is that, while all other ASEAN countries have at least doubled and, in one case, quadrupled their energy input per person, the Philippines has remained stagnant at a comparatively low level. Once above the ASEAN average, the level is now well below it. This appears to be an indication of the slow spread of industrialization in the

Table 4
ASEAN STRUCTURE OF PRODUCTION
(percent of GDP)

	Indonesia	Malaysia	Philippines	Singapore	Thailand	ASEAN*
1965						
Agriculture	56	28	26	3	35	34
Industry	13	25	28	24	23	23
(Manufacturing)	8	9	20	15	14	14
Services, etc.	31	47	46	73	42	44
1986						
Agriculture	26	N.A.	26	1	17	21
Industry	32	N.A.	32	38	30	32
(Manufacturing)	14	N.A.	25	27	21	19
Services, etc.	42	N.A.	42	62	53	47

*ASEAN values weighted by respective GDP for respective years.
Source: World Bank, *World Development Report 1988.* Values for Brunei not available.

Table 5

ASEAN STRUCTURE OF MANUFACTURING

(percent of manufacturing value added)

	Indonesia	Malaysia	Philippines	Singapore	Thailand	ASEAN*
1970						
Food and agriculture	N.A.	26	39	12	43	35
Textiles and clothing	N.A.	3	8	5	13	8
Machinery and transport equipment	N.A.	8	8	28	9	10
Chemicals	N.A.	9	13	4	6	9
Other	N.A.	54	32	51	29	36
1985						
Food and agriculture	23	21	34	6	30	25
Textiles and clothing	11	6	10	4	17	11
Machinery and transport equipment	10	23	11	49	13	16
Chemicals	10	10	11	8	6	9
Other	47	40	34	33	34	39

*ASEAN values weighted by respective manufacturing value added for respective years.
Source: World Bank, *World Development Report 1988*. Values for Brunei not available.

Philippines in the 1970s and 1980s. Thailand, which is often compared to the Philippines because of many structural similarities, was once the ASEAN country with the lowest energy consumption per person. In the space of 20 years the figure has increased fourfold and Thailand is now well above the ASEAN average.

Table 6 also gives an idea of the degree to which ASEAN countries have to rely on imports to meet their energy requirements. Next to Singapore, which has no sources of energy of its own, it is the Philippines that has to devote an above average proportion of its imports to energy. One might well ask whether a high energy bill is the reason for low Philippine energy consumption. A comparison of ASEAN merchandise trade figures in Table 7 shows fairly clearly, however, that it is a comparatively low level of foreign merchandise trade that accounts, at least statistically, for the high percentage of energy imports in total Philippine imports.

While merchandise imports of all ASEAN countries grew between 1965 and 1980, there was a slowdown in the first half of the 1980s. This was most marked in the Philippines which saw a reduction of imports at an annual rate of six percent in spite of a continued moderate growth of exports. This is a reflection of the economic difficulties experienced in the Philippines in the wake of economic mismanagement during the Marcos era. Loss of confidence caused foreign direct investment to lag, and the remaining trickle of foreign capital was insufficient to offset the perennial negative trade balance. Consequently, austerity measures had to be adopted to reduce the level of imports.

All countries generally incur external public debts in the course of development. For well-known reasons connected with the United States budget deficit and the overvalued dollar as well as the recycling of so-called petrodollars in the late 1970s and early 1980s, one-time reasonable levels of lending have created heavy debt burdens. Indonesia and the Philippines have been the worst hit in the ASEAN region. In the case of Indonesia falling oil prices caused a loss of expected revenue from petroleum exports, income that had been earmarked for development projects. The rupiah needed to be devalued, thus immediately increasing dollar-denominated debts in rupiah terms. In the case of the Philippines, external public debt was accumulated over several years and the crisis of confidence attending the final years of the Marcos era led to an erosion of the peso. But Malaysia has also been hit by falling oil and other commodity prices, and its current debt service charges are second only to Indonesia in the region. Malaysia also has the highest ratio of debt service payments to GNP of the ASEAN group, but Indonesia and the Philippines, in that order, top the list regarding the ratio of debt service payments to exports of goods and services. Details are provided in Table 8.

The international community has assisted the ASEAN countries in their development efforts by providing both technical and financial assistance. The Philippines has been the main beneficiary in recent years, both in terms of absolute amounts as well as per capita receipts. Table 9 presents the relevant figures for the ASEAN countries in 1986.

The relatively high per capita amount for the Philippines is perhaps not

1354

Table 6
ASEAN ENERGY CONSUMPTION AND IMPORTS

	Indonesia	Malaysia	Philippines	Singapore	Thailand	ASEAN*
Energy consumption per capita (kg. of oil equivalent)						
1965	91	312	160	670	81	120
1986	213	762	180	1,851	325	271
Energy imports as a percentage of merchandise exports						
1965	3	11	12	17	11	11
1986	14	4	17	22	13	15

*ASEAN per capita energy consumption weighted by 1986 population, energy imports by merchandise exports. Values for Brunei not available.
Source: World Bank, *World Development Report 1988.*

Table 7
ASEAN MERCHANDISE TRADE

	Indonesia	Malaysia	Philippines	Singapore	Thailand	ASEAN*
Exports 1986 (U.S. $ million)	14,824	13,874	4,771	22,495	8,794	64,758
Imports 1986 (U.S. $ million)	13,371	10,829	5,394	25,511	9,178	64,283
Balance (U.S. $ million)	1,453	3,045	−623	−3,016	−384	475
Average annual growth rates						
Exports						
1965–80	9.6	4.4	4.7	4.7	8.5	6.0
1980–86	2.0	10.2	−1.7	6.1	9.2	6.0
Imports						
1965–80	14.2	2.9	2.9	7	4.1	7.0
1980–86	−1.0	5.2	−6.0	3.6	2.0	2.0

*ASEAN growth rates weighted by 1986 export and import values, respectively.
Source: World Bank, *World Development Report 1988*. Values for Brunei not available.

Table 8
ASEAN EXTERNAL PUBLIC DEBT AND
DEBT-SERVICE RATIOS 1986
(U.S. $ million)

	Indonesia	Malaysia	Philippines	Singapore	Thailand	ASEAN*
External public debt						
(U.S. $ million)	31,901	16,759	19,828	2,120	11,023	81,631
As percentage of GNP	44.4	65.7	66.2	11.8	27.4	44.3
Interest payments						
(U.S. $ million)	2,047	1,173	962	174	751	5,107
Debt service as percentage						
of GNP	6.2	8.7	5.3	2.3	4.8	5.8
Exports of goods and services	27.8	13.7	18.3	1.4	16.1	13.3

*ASEAN values weighted by 1986 GDP and export figures, respectively.
Source: World Bank, *World Development Report 1988*. Values for Brunei not available.

Table 9
ASEAN OFFICIAL DEVELOPMENT ASSISTANCE
(ODA) RECEIPTS 1986
(U.S. $ million)

	Indonesia	Malaysia	Philippines	Singapore	Thailand	ASEAN
ODA from all sources (U.S. $ million)	711	193	956	30	496	2,386
Per capita (U.S. $)	4.3	12.0	16.7	11.5	9.4	8.1
As percentage of GNP	.1	.8	3.2	.2	1.2	1.3

Source: World Bank, *World Development Report 1988*. Values for Brunei not available.

surprising. But that Singapore, unquestionably the most advanced of the ASEAN countries, should receive an above average amount per capita is remarkable. One of the reasons is probably the advantage of being small, since development assistance is frequently allotted by country rather than according to population or need. Part of the development assistance granted Singapore is, of course, also intended for the region as a whole (regional training centers, for instance) so that there is some statistical bias in the Singapore figure. In terms of development assistance receipts as a percentage of GDP, the figures look decidedly more reasonable, with the more advanced countries (Singapore and Malaysia) both well below the one percent level.

Developing countries are usually reluctant to release data regarding their distribution of income. It is therefore difficult to compare this component in the ASEAN countries. Table 10 presents the figures available along with the years to which the distribution figures apply. Comparable figures are unavailable for Singapore and Brunei. The ASEAN figure calculated in the last column of Table 10 is somewhat arbitrary, necessarily assuming that figures dispersed over a decade are comparable. As is well known, income distribution tends to become more skewed in the course of development. This is a normal trend closely linked to the nature of the development process itself.

A far more important question is whether the number of persons living in poverty can be reduced in the course of time. Although the poverty line is a rather arbitrary concept, the need to reduce the number of people living below that level is not. Studies suggest that in Indonesia the proportion of persons below the poverty line was reduced both in rural and urban households and both in and outside Java in the period studied from 1970 to 1976.[1] In peninsular Malaysia the picture is similar, with the percentage of both urban and rural households below the poverty line falling substantially in the period from 1970 to 1984.[2] In Singapore a 1988 publication indicates that in the decade 1972–1973 to 1982–1983 the incidence of poverty fell from 32 percent to 7.2 percent.[3] In the Philippines the trend is less clear, with a fall in the incidence of poverty from 1961 to 1965 and a subsequent rise in 1971.[4] A 1988 confidential World Bank study is said to come to the conclusion that with the present relatively high birthrate the situation is worsening in that there are more poor people in the Philippines today than at any time in recent history.[5] In Thailand there was a reduction in the number of households below the

[1] World Bank, *Employment and Income Distribution in Indonesia* (Washington, D.C., 1980), 77.
[2] *Fifth Malaysia Plan, 1986–1990* (Kuala Lumpur), 86.
[3] Lim Chong Yah and others, *Policy Option for the Singapore Economy* (Singapore: McGraw-Hill, 1988), 394.
[4] Edita A. Tan, "Income Distribution in the Philippines," in José Encarnación and others, *Philippine Problems in Perspective* (Manila: Institute of Economic Development and Research, 1978), 225.
[5] James Clad, "Poor Get Poorer," *Far Eastern Economic Review*, 18 August 1988, p. 34.

Table 10
ASEAN INCOME DISTRIBUTION

	Indonesia 1976	Malaysia 1973	Philippines 1985	Thailand 1975–76	ASEAN*
Lowest 20 percent	6.6	3.5	5.2	5.6	6.0
Second quintile	7.8	7.7	8.9	9.6	8.3
Third quintile	12.6	12.4	13.2	13.9	12.9
Fourth quintile	23.6	20.3	20.2	21.1	22.3
Highest 20 percent	49.4	56.1	52.5	49.8	50.4
Highest 10 percent	34.0	39.8	37.0	34.1	34.9

*ASEAN values weighted by 1986 population.
Source: World Bank, *World Development Report 1988*. Values for Brunei and Singapore not available.

poverty line in the period studied from 1962–1963 to 1975–1976 both in rural and urban areas.[6] Thus, with the exception of the Philippines, the evidence suggests that all ASEAN countries seem to have been successful in reducing poverty, even though there may have been a trade-off with an increase in the inequality of income. The ASEAN countries as a whole compare favorably with a number of countries in Asia (and indeed Southeast Asia) that had set out to attain social goals in a more direct way and, to date, have achieved neither the reduction of poverty nor the equitable distributions they had initially proclaimed.

ECONOMIC POLICY AND DEVELOPMENT STRATEGY

By definition the market economies of Southeast Asia are similar in terms of economic and development policy in the sense that their economic organization is market oriented. Nevertheless, there are significant differences in the degree to which they rely on market forces and in the way these are supplemented by government intervention and involvement in the economy. At one end of the scale there is Singapore which has eliminated nearly all customs tariffs and is open to direct foreign investments, and at the other there is Indonesia where monopolies owned or granted by government severely hamper the undistorted development of the economy. In between these two the other four ASEAN countries manifest varying degrees of economic liberalism and government control in the economy. In addition to these differences, there have also been quite important changes in economic development strategy within each country over time.

Independence from colonial rule had the effect of reinforcing the desire of ASEAN governments to create within their countries a national economy with a solid and integrated industrial base capable of producing the consumer goods required by the population and the intermediate and capital goods necessary for production and further development. This national economy required the initiative, active participation, and protection of the government because indigenous entrepreneurs were not available or financially too weak and because aggressive competition from the industrially advanced countries entailed the danger of reinstating foreign domination in the economic sphere just after it had been eliminated in the political. The development strategy associated with this policy of building a balanced national economy is that of import substitution. Instead of continuing to spend scarce foreign exchange needed for the import of industrial equipment and machinery on importing consumer goods from the world market, the domestic market would increasingly be supplied by domestic producers. To encourage local entrepreneurs to invest in the production of these goods, protection from competition by foreign firms would be provided through tariffs and other import restrictions

At the other extreme, a body of thought by intellectuals of the ASEAN countries sent abroad for academic training considered the narrowly nation-

[6] World Bank, *Income, Consumption and Poverty in Thailand, 1962/63 to 1975/76* (Washington, D.C., 1979), 52.

alistic economic structure as suboptimal in terms of growth potential within the world economy. According to this view, the newly industrializing countries, rather than replicating the structure of the fully industrialized countries of the West, with heavy industries providing the materials and machines for intermediate and consumer goods production, should concentrate on producing those goods in which they had a comparative advantage and exchange them for goods more cheaply produced elsewhere. This export-oriented strategy would require more liberal trade policies. A disadvantage of "plugging in" to the international system would be the dependence on foreign markets and sources of supply as well as susceptibility to the fluctuations of the world economy. But the strategy would ensure that economic growth would remain essentially free of distortions in the allocation of resources that are characteristic of industrial structures built behind high tariff walls.

The choice between these contending strategies was complicated by two factors. First, economists were far less agreed among themselves on the superiority of export orientation over import substitution than they are today; even the World Bank then advocated import substitution strategies in the initial phases of industrial development. Second, adopting the path of import substitution in most cases turns out to be a road of no return in the sense that protection generates the need for protection. Strong vested interests are created that governments subsequently find difficult to ignore even when they become convinced of the rationale for more liberal policies.

The ASEAN countries provide interesting case studies of the perennial conflict between narrow nationalistic economic policies supported by privileged interest groups and the need to avoid or remove the distortions and inequities that in the long run curtail economic growth. The following discussion is restricted mainly to the actual policies pursued as evidenced by legislation and other measures. A thorough analysis of the decision-making processes in the political economies of each ASEAN country, not possible within the framework of this article, has been undertaken recently elsewhere.[7]

GOVERNMENT INVOLVEMENTS IN ASEAN ECONOMIES

There are several ways in which a government can get involved in the economy and exert a strong influence on the direction of economic development. First, the government can—and must—spend on activities such as defense, education, health, housing, and those social and economic services not undertaken by the private sector. Second, the government can engage in commercial activities by owning or having equity shares in industrial enterprises. Third, the government can steer the economy in certain directions by means of economic policies. And fourth, the government can intervene in certain markets by fixing or otherwise manipulating prices.

Table 11 presents a breakdown of central government expenditures in

[7] Richard Robison, Kevin Hewison and Richard Higgott, eds., *Southeast Asia in the 1980s: The Politics of Economic Crisis* (Sydney: Allen and Unwin, 1987).

Table 11
ASEAN CENTRAL GOVERNMENT
EXPENDITURES FOR 1986
(percent of GNP)

	Indonesia	Malaysia	Philippines	Singapore	Thailand	ASEAN*
Defense	2.5	N.A.	1.3	6.0	4.4	3.1
Education	2.3	N.A.	2.2	5.7	4.2	3.1
Health	0.5	N.A.	0.6	1.7	1.2	0.8
Housing, social security and welfare	0.4	N.A.	0.2	1.5	1.0	0.6
Economic services	5.2	N.A.	4.8	4.7	4.9	5.0
Other	16.0	N.A.	1.7	6.9	5.9	9.9
TOTAL	26.9	N.A.	10.8	26.5	21.6	24.6*

*ASEAN values weighted by 1986 GDP. Last column total includes Malaysia.
Source: Calculated from World Bank, *World Development Report 1988*. Values for Brunei not available.

most ASEAN countries in 1986 according to major categories. Data for Malaysia, which has the highest level of government expenditure, are not available for individual categories. Government expenditure as a proportion of GNP was by far the lowest in the Philippines. In fact, it has been low by Asian standards all along. While this probably encouraged the growth of the private sector, infrastructure and social services remained underdeveloped. Many economic activities that in other countries are in the hands of the government, such as utilities and transportation, developed in the private sector. In the meantime the government has taken over most of the utilities sector, such as electricity and water, as well as some of the transportation sector.[8] Thailand's proportion of government expenditure in GNP is also below the ASEAN average. In fact, the government's stated policy is to give the private sector the primary role in the development of the economy. Education and defense, however, are important areas of government expenditure in Thailand. The defense proportion is only exceeded by Singapore, which spends as much as six percent of GNP on defense. Given the liberal image of Singapore's economic regime, it is interesting to observe the strong level of government involvement in the economy. Social services in Singapore such as health, housing, and education are at the highest relative levels in the ASEAN group, and this reflects the stage of development reached by the island nation. As more and more people come to expect and actually obtain public goods, the proportion of government expenditure in GNP tends to rise. At the other extreme, Indonesia is only able to spend a relatively small proportion of its GNP on social services; only the Philippines has still lower levels.

All ASEAN governments are involved to some extent in commercial activities in their economies. The rationale for this is generally that the private sector is incapable or unwilling to set up enterprises deemed by the government to be of strategic importance for the development of the economy. In some cases the government may also be tempted to exercise its licensing rights in order to reserve especially lucrative industries for itself. And frequently governments are not prepared to become dependent on the private sector in sensitive industries such as those related to defense.

Government involvement in the economy is high in this respect in Singapore. For example, in 1968 the government established the public International Trading Company (INTRACO) to help develop overseas markets for Singapore-made products and to find cheaper sources of raw materials for local industries through bulk buying. In 1969 a 100 percent government equity public limited company, Neptune Orient Lines, was established to expedite foreign trade and ensure low freight charges for Singapore-manufactured goods. Other initiatives have been the Development Bank Of Singapore, Keppel Shipyard, National Iron and Steel Mills, and the Post Offices Savings Bank. Furthermore, statutory boards play an important role in areas such as housing, industrial land development, ports, telecommunications, and urban development. The Singapore government be-

[8] Brian Wawn, *The Economies of the ASEAN Countries: Indonesia, Malaysia Philippines, Singapore and Thailand* (London: Macmillan, 1984), 76.

lieves that it can have an important catalytic role. In introducing its development plan for the 1980s, this role was made clear: "As we want to restructure and upgrade our economy quickly, the State must resume its role as an entrepreneur, not to supplant private enterprise but to encourage and assist entrepreneurs to venture their capital on new machinery with labour saving devices."[9] In Indonesia the dramatic rise in the price of oil (1973–1974 and early 1980s) furthered state-led economic nationalism. The oil bonanza meant a surge of funds for state revenues and therefore the state's capacity to invest. This led to the emergence of important public conglomerates in the oil sector (PERTAMINA), in petrochemicals, and in steel (Krakatau Steel) and other metal industries. The government controls major components of large-scale manufacturing such as aviation, cement, fertilizer, and so forth. In the Philippines government ownership and control of business increased during the Marcos era when the government had to bail out numerous uneconomical enterprises. Malaysia in the late 1970s provided over one third of domestic funds for private investment, partly in the form of equity and loans from organizations geared toward the furthering of the Malay population, such as Perbadanan Nasional Berhad (PERNAS), and partly through others such as the Urban Development Authority and the State Development Corporation. In this way the government owns important parts of manufacturing. It plays a leading role in oil and natural gas production through the National Petroleum Corporation (PETRONAS) as well as in banking and in the production, processing, and/or marketing of many agricultural goods (e.g., rice, rubber, palm oil, and tobacco). In 1981 the government set up the Heavy Industries Corporation of Malaysia to promote heavy industries, alone or in conjunction with the private sector. The much criticized production of the Malaysian car, the Proton Saga, is another example of the Malaysian government's involvement in the economy.

INDUSTRIALIZATION POLICIES

Economic policy in all ASEAN countries initially followed a pattern of import-substituting industrialization. To a greater or lesser extent, all of these countries have now switched or are in the process of giving greater emphasis to export-oriented industrialization. Nevertheless, important differences remain. As expected, Singapore, which has no hinterland of its own, relies on free trade for its very survival. There was only a brief import substitution phase in the early 1960s, and even in this period protective tariffs and quota restrictions were moderate. After the adoption of export-oriented industrialization, Singapore's manufacturing sector grew at an average rate of 12 percent yearly and its contribution to GDP increased from 12.8 percent in 1960 to 20.5 percent in 1970 and to 24.1 percent in 1980.[10] Unemployment was virtually eliminated. In 1979 Singapore's in-

[9] Quoted in ibid., p. 109.
[10] Romeo M. Bautista, "Recent Shifts in Industrialization Strategies and Trade Patterns of ASEAN Countries," *ASEAN Economic Bulletin* 1 (July 1984): 7.

dustrialization strategy was augmented by an effort to restructure the economy. By means of a high-wage policy and the introduction of various tax concessions and incentives, the government promoted a rapid shift in the direction of higher value-added protection. Because of the rapid success of export industrialization and mass employment creation, Singapore has frequently been held up as a shining example of an economic policy to be emulated by other developing countries. However, it should be borne in mind that Singapore represents a special case, particularly in terms of its size and the absence of an agricultural base.

In Malaysia, which initially had been intimately linked to Singapore, the first major industrialization measure enacted was aimed at promoting and accelerating the overall industrialization process, that is, to encourage the establishment and development of industrial and commercial enterprises by way of income tax relief. Efforts in this direction were erratic and haphazard, but a clearly discernible thrust toward import substitution industrialization emerged. The rationale for the strategy adopted was to encourage foreign manufacturers to set up production, assembly, and packaging plants in the country to supply goods that had previously been imported. To promote import-substituting industries, the government directly and indirectly subsidized the establishment of new factories and protected the domestic market.[11] But by the mid-1960s the inherent contradictions of the strategy were becoming clear. In 1968 an Investment Incentives Act was passed to encourage the expansion of manufactured exports, and this signalled the switch from import-substituting industrialization to export-oriented industrialization. This new emphasis was reinforced by the country's second economic plan (1971–1975), which introduced the so-called New Economic Policy. In early 1986 the Malaysian government presented an industrial master plan. While the export-led industrialization strategy remains, the 1986 plan envisages cutting down protection on import-substituting industries, many of which currently enjoy handsome profits behind high tariff walls.[12]

Among the ASEAN countries the Philippines has the longest history of active policies to encourage industrial development. In response to a severe balance of payments crisis in 1949, import-substituting industrialization was introduced. What was initially viewed as a curb on the consumption of nonessential imports soon became a protective device to encourage production of their substitutes.[13] The policy continued until the 1970s, although manufacturing growth was sluggish. Even in 1980 Philippine industries had an average rate of effective protection of more than 70 percent and had not declined from the levels of the mid-1960s. In 1970 a number of incentive measures were introduced to encourage exports of manufactures, but in the absence of corrections to the distortions caused by protec-

---

[11] Jomo Kwame Sundaram, "Economic Crisis and Policy Response in Malaysia," in Robison, *Southeast Asia in the 1980s,* p. 137.
[12] Ibid.
[13] Bautista, p. 9.

tionism, these were inherently contradictory.[14] In 1979 the government agreed to undertake a major tariff reform program that would substantially reduce the average level of protection. However, almost at the same time, the government declared its intention to develop 11 major industrial projects, largely in the field of heavy industry; this move had a strong import substitution flavor. The ventures included aluminum and copper smelters, an integrated steel mill, diesel engine manufacturing, and a petrochemical complex. Although these ambitious plans eventually had to be dropped because of financial constraints, their proclamation indicated a lack of clear purpose on the part of the government regarding its industrialization strategy.

Import-substituting industrialization in Thailand does not seem to have been the result of deliberate government policies but rather the outcome of pressure for protection exerted by prominent businessmen in Bangkok. When announcing increased tariffs in late 1960, the Thai finance minister stated that the decision had been taken following strong representations by local industrialists.[15] The decline of the import substitution strategy was the result of domestic and international developments. In Thailand excess capacity had become a major problem; growth in the manufacturing sector had dropped and there were corresponding falls in manufacturing investment. Simultaneously, growing trade deficits forced the government to turn to an export-oriented industrialization strategy. The formal endorsement of greater export orientation was contained in the country's third economic plan (1972–1976), even though it was conceded that import-substituting industrialization was not to be completely given up. In the fourth plan (1977–1981) export industries received special state promotional privileges.[16]

Indonesia is the ASEAN country in which there is as yet little hope for a more dynamic export-oriented industrialization strategy. The nationalistic policy of building up an integrated industrial base almost as a replica of the world economy behind high tariff walls was made possible and reinforced by apparently endlessly rising revenues from oil exports. It was only after oil prices collapsed in the early 1980s that serious rethinking began to take place. By this time, however, a politico-bureaucratic elite had become entrenched in the prevailing system, wielding power and earning attractive rents from the administration of licenses, the taxation of imports, and the control of state concessions for the private sector. Although the Indonesian leadership may intellectually recognize the need for reforms and a greater liberalization of imports, the pace at which it can afford to proceed is severely inhibited by the economic interests of the ruling elite. Nevertheless, recent moves have been in the direction of greater efficiency

[14]S. K. Jayasuriya, "The Politics of Economic Policy in the Philippines in the Marcos Era," in Robison, *Southeast Asia in the 1980s*, p. 99.
[15]Kevin Hewison, "National Interests and Economic Downturn: Thailand," in ibid., p. 55.
[16]Ibid., p. 56.

and transparency in the collection of customs duties as well as in the gradual removal of the system of privileged imports under which the right to import certain strategic inputs for production was granted to particularly favored individuals. There is still a long way to go, but a start in the right direction has obviously been made.

TRADE REGIMES

For a number of reasons, it is difficult to gain a comprehensive and comparative picture of the tariff structures of the ASEAN countries. A pioneering study undertaken by the Philippine Tariff Commission was updated in 1985.[17] A number of insights can be gained from this work. Table 12 presents the average levels of tariffs in ASEAN countries by major commodity groups.

Unfortunately, the calculation of tariff averages over a large number of individual tariff lines raises some methodological problems. First, duties are frequently collected on imported items for reasons other than that of protection. Thus all ASEAN countries, including Singapore, have extremely high duties on beverages and tobacco, with Malaysia at the head of the list. However, these are in the main fiscal duties rather than protective measures. As such they tend to distort the comparison of protective duties to some extent. Second, a country's tariff schedule may contain items that are relatively unimportant or not traded at all. For this reason it is preferable to weight individual items by the amount actually traded. But to the extent that the tariff has the effect of reducing or restricting trade volumes, this method underestimates tariff levels. In the extreme, a prohibitively high tariff would receive a weight of zero and not affect the average level at all. Table 12 contains simple overall averages of tariffs in commodity groups for each ASEAN country. The bottom line, however, provides an average for each country on the basis of individual tariff lines weighted by trade volume; this is a better indication of the degree of protection of the individual ASEAN countries. A comparison with the simple averages five years previously permits some insight into the direction of change. On the basis of simple and trade weighted tariffs, Indonesia is the most protective of the ASEAN countries and Singapore the least. Thailand, the Philippines, and Malaysia have roughly similar trade weighted averages of tariffs.

Although Indonesia has a high absolute level of protection, there has been a small decrease in the simple average level since 1978. Compared to 1978 there has been a large increase in the proportion of tariff lines with 1 to 10 percent duty rates that was compensated for by a decrease in the number of tariff lines in the 11 to 20 percent duty range. There was a significant increase in the beverages and tobacco commodity group from 46 to almost 62 percent. Significant reductions have occurred in the commodity group of chemicals and related products (from 26.8 to 10.6 percent),

[17] Philippine Tariff Commission, *Tariff Profiles in ASEAN—An Update* (Quezon City, 1985).

Table 12
AVERAGE LEVELS OF TARIFFS IN
ASEAN COUNTRIES
(percentages)

Commodity group	Indonesia	Malaysia	Philippines	Singapore	Thailand	ASEAN
Food and live animals chiefly for food	47.9	13.7	40.6	0.6	50.6	30.7
Beverages and tobacco	61.9	1,361.6	55.2	593.2	52.6	424.9
Crude minerals, except fuel	14.5	4.0	21.6	0.1	16.7	11.4
Mineral fuels, lubricants and related materials	8.5	4.9	17.0	0.8	15.5	9.4
Animal and vegetable oils, fats and waxes	28.8	1.0	28.1	0.0	23.6	16.3
Chemicals and related products	10.6	8.1	18.0	1.5	20.7	11.8
Manufactured goods classified chiefly by materials	42.2	16.7	33.2	0.1	32.4	24.9
Machinery and transport equipment	20.0	10.2	21.9	0.5	24.0	15.3
Miscellaneous manufactured goods	49.8	12.5	35.0	0.8	39.9	27.6
Commodities and transactions not listed elsewhere	28.5	7.2	36.7	0.0	22.1	18.9
Overall average 1983	32.6	25.0	29.2	6.4	30.7	24.8
Overall average 1978	33.0	15.3	44.2	5.6	29.4	25.5
Trade weighted average 1983	38.5	24.4	20.9	0.8	22.6	21.4

Source: Philippine Tariff Commission, *Tariff Profiles in ASEAN, An Update*, 1985. Values for Brunei not available.

but in the industrially important commodity group of manufactured goods classified chiefly by materials, the average tariff was raised from 38 to 42.2 percent.

There has also been a significant rise in the average Malaysian level of tariffs, but this reflects to a large extent the more than triple increase on products in the commodity group of beverages and tobacco—from 347 to over 1,300 percent. There has also been a substantial decrease in the proportion of duty-free tariff lines (from 48.3 percent to 38.3 percent of all tariff lines) and a corresponding increase in the proportion of lines imposing a 1 to 10 percent duty.

The Philippines implemented a tariff reform program in 1981 and this led to a general reduction of tariff rates almost across the board. It is only in the commodity group of mineral fuels, lubricants, and related materials that a slight increase in tariffs has occurred. Compared to 1978 when only 40 percent of the tariff lines had rates equal to or less than 20 percent, this proportion increased to close to 50 percent in 1984. There are now no longer any tariffs greater than 70 percent. As can be seen from Table 12, the trade weighted average of tariffs in the Philippines is lower than all other ASEAN countries with the exception of Singapore.

The simple average figures for Thailand reveal little change over the period 1978–1983. But in fact the proportion of tariff lines imposing rates between 21 and 30 percent decreased from nearly 44 percent to less than 23 percent. At the same time, however, the number of items with tariff rates between 51 and 70 percent increased from 129 to 651, that is from 8.9 percent of total tariff lines in 1978 to 29.2 percent in 1983. These structural changes compensated each other, so that the average tariff rates per commodity group remained essentially the same. Incidentally, Thailand was the only ASEAN country to reduce its tariffs on beverages and tobacco—from 363.4 percent in 1978 to 52.6 percent in 1983.

Singapore exhibited very little change in the structure of its tariff rates mainly because 90 percent of the 2,584 tariff lines are already free of duty. The only change was an increase in the commodity group of beverages and tobacco from 458 percent to 593.2 percent. If the high duties for this group of commodities were disregarded, the national average would be less than one percent.

It is clear from this comparison that all the ASEAN countries with the exception of Singapore still have ample room for reducing the protection of their domestic industries, thereby taking steps to eliminate gradually the distortions in their industrial structures associated with tariff protection.

ATTITUDES TOWARD FOREIGN CAPITAL

Investment by foreigners in the form of setting up plants in the domestic economy is nearly always a controversial matter. On the positive side, such investments bring in capital to augment the funds available from domestic savings. The balance of payments effect is positive because foreign currency is brought in. Technical and management know-how otherwise not available domestically is transferred so that industrialization can be promoted. On the negative side, reliance on foreign enterprises stifles the development of domestic entrepreneurs. Long-term balance of payments effects are negative because profits, royalties, and interest payments on capital in excess of initial investment amounts are eventually transferred to the foreign investor. Large-scale multinational corporations exert influences on economic and political decision making to the detriment of the domestic producers. Although the discussion of this issue by economists is far from over, the prevalent view seems to be that opening up the economy to foreign investments is one of the important ways of bringing about dynamic economic development.

All of the ASEAN countries have expressed keen desires to obtain foreign direct investments to enhance the development of their domestic economies. However, the conditions under which foreign capital is permitted to enter vary from country to country. The country in which it is welcomed most is Singapore, which has practically no legal restrictions on foreign equity participation. Investment in the manufacturing sector is particularly welcome, especially in the production of higher value-added products employing medium to higher range technology. There are minimum controls on the operations of enterprises, both local and foreign. Singapore, which was the first country in Southeast Asia to set up industrial parks now has over 20 of them providing infrastructure for new ventures. The economic policy of Singapore in this area has been informed by the recognition that a relatively unrestricted flow of investment provides better opportunities for directing it to desired directions.

The oppositive view seems to prevail in Indonesia where it was assumed that foreign investors should identify with Indonesian development aspirations rather than be guided by the ulterior motives of profit. It was argued that investment in capital, intermediate, and even high-technology goods could be generated only by deliberate state intervention and could not be produced by the free operation of an international marketplace which in reality would be dominated by transnational corporations.[18] Through the introduction of priority investment lists, the government reserved certain sectors, either partially or totally, for domestic investors. Foreign investors were increasingly restricted to those sectors that required special technologies and skills or large amounts of capital not available domestically, or they were located in sectors with export earning potential. Furthermore, the government has made it mandatory in practice for foreign investors operating in Indonesia to have local partners. All new foreign capital investment in Indonesia, other than investment totally for export production, must take the form of a joint venture in which the equity participation of ethnic Indonesian individuals or companies is to rise to 51 percent within ten years after the start of commercial production. The initial Indonesian participation is usually required to be at least 20 percent. Shares held by

[18] Richard Robison, "After the Gold Rush: The Politics of Economic Restructuring in Indonesia in the 1980s," in Robison, *Southeast Asia in the 1980s*, p. 30.

Indonesian investors of Chinese or other nonindigenous origin are not treated as forming part of the *pribumi* equity percentage.[19]

In Thailand the Alien Business Law of 1972 restricts the participation of non-Thai nationals in three defined categories. In the first category, comprising basic agricultural trades, real estate, and so forth, a minimum 51 percent Thai ownership is required, and the majority of managerial positions must be held by Thai nationals. In the second category, which includes the processing of several basic agricultural and mineral products and the manufacture of basic construction items, garments, and shoes (except for export), all new ventures must have majority Thai ownership unless they have obtained promoted status from the board of investments. In the third category, comprising most residual businesses, 100 percent foreign-owned ventures may be established after obtaining special permits. Some of the activities are not clearly defined, giving rise to unnecessary uncertainty. In recent years, the Thai government has acted to make Thailand more attractive to international investors.

The situation is similar in Malaysia where preference is accorded to manufacturing proposals organized on a joint venture basis between Malaysians and foreigners. The extent of foreign capital ownership permitted depends on the nature of the project, that is, dependence on the Malaysian market or depletion of Malaysian resources. The government encourages foreign investment particularly in the manufacturing sector where local investors may lack the technical know-how, management expertise, or export market outlets.[20] Malaysia has created more than 80 industrial parks to provide suitable sites for industry and a number of free trade zones to enable export-oriented industries to operate with minimum customs formalities attaching to the import of raw materials and the export of finished goods.

In the Philippines enterprises in pioneer areas may be fully owned by foreign investors at the outset, but at least 60 percent of voting stock must be transferred to Philippine nationals within 30 years from registration of the investment. In the case of nonpioneer enterprises, only 40 percent of voting stock may be held by foreign investors. Exceptions are made if the foreign enterprises export 100 percent of their production. The Philippines has adopted a policy of developing export processing zones in various parts of the country. There was reluctance to bring new capital into the Philippines in the mid-1980s, due in part to the fears of foreign investors of political instability in the final years of the Marcos regime.[21]

INDUSTRIAL RELATIONS

The way in which the management of industrial enterprises brings about the combination of capital and labor to produce goods is to a great extent constrained by legislation on industrial relations. Governments, through

[19] Philip B. Gurney, *Joint Venture Investment in ASEAN* (Singapore: Institute of Southeast Asian Studies, 1982), 7.
[20] Ibid., p. 28.
[21] Sundaram, p. 96.

appropriate laws and other measures, can have an important influence on the way in which enterprises are operated and on the extent to which they contribute to economic development. Whether trade unions are permitted and strikes are tolerated as legitimate means of collective bargaining are important aspects of economic development policy. In general, the ASEAN governments are of the view that mutual cooperation between management and labor in the determination of wage levels, supported by government mediation if necessary, is superior to strikes in bringing about agreements on wages and working conditions. Strikes not only disrupt production, but they are likely to send the wrong signals to potential foreign investors. In addition they manifest an open antagonism that is considered alien to cultural values. It is therefore not surprising to find that industrial relations among workers, managers, and owners in ASEAN countries are regulated within fairly narrow boundaries.[22]

In Indonesia the right to strike is fundamentally guaranteed by law, although there is a restriction concerning workers in "vital industries." However, strikes are not tolerated because industrial conflict is incompatible with the five tenets of the state's *Pancasila* philosophy: one supreme God, just and civilized humanity, the unity of Indonesia, democracy guided by representatives, and social justice for the people. Since 1974 the government has been actively promoting *Pancasila* labor relations. The essence of this policy as spelled out in various government publications is that workers and employers are partners in production and profit, and both have a responsibility to God, to the nation, to the community, to their fellow workers and their families, and to the establishment where they work.[23] The all-pervasive method of conflict resolution in Indonesia is compulsory arbitration under a 1957 act for the settlement of labor disputes.

In Malaysia trade unions have the right to strike provided that two thirds of the members entitled to vote are in favor. It is illegal for unorganized workers to strike, and since the organized sector is very small, most workers in fact cannnot exercise the right to strike. Moreover, the registrar of trade unions is vested with the power to deauthorize labor organizations. Consequently it is very difficult for workers to organize any protest. Collective bargaining generally takes place at the enterprise level in Malaysia. Trade unions in pioneer industries, that is, industries set up under privileged status by foreign investment, are barred from negotiating matters such as promotion, transfer, new hiring, assignment of duties to employees, dismissal, retrenchment, and reinstatement. The government's Look East policy has led to the promotion of supposedly Japanese work ethics and related campaigns (such as quality control circles) intended to boost labor productivity. The encouragement of in-house unions is another example.

In the Philippines unionization is fairly respectable by ASEAN standards. However, this has not always been so. After the declaration of mar-

---

[22] Basu Sharma, *Aspects of Industrial Relations in ASEAN* (Singapore: Institute of Southeast Asian Studies, 1985).
[23] Ibid., p. 44.

tial law by the Marcos regime, industrial labor relations were tightly controlled. Trade union activists were arrested, most strikes were made illegal, and an atmosphere of repression and intimidation prevailed. As worker resistance increased, more radical unions were organized as alternatives to the tame "official" unions. By the end of the 1970s, militant unionism had spread even to the export processing zones, forcing "official" union leaders to adopt a tough stance in wage negotiations in response to the threat posed by the rival, more radical leadership. The escalation of working-class activities in open defiance of the government was one factor that moved the regime to lift martial law and restore the right to strike (with limitations) in 1981.[24] Under the present law, a new trade union can be registered if it represents 30 percent or more of the qualified employees. Given the instability of the government of Corazon Aquino, and the present poor economic situation, political issues are likely to dominate union activity in the Philippines for some time to come.

The development of industrial relations in Singapore has been tightly controlled by the government in order not to inhibit the inflow of foreign capital. The militant and politically dominated trade unionism of the early postindependence period was restrained by the introduction of a series of labor laws restricting many of the activities of labor organizations. Most notably the Employment Act of 1968 withdrew many of the benefits and privileges gained by unions during the anticolonial political struggle; in the new law emphasis was placed on efficiency and productivity. Singapore's two largest unions, the Singapore Industrial Labour Organisation and the Pioneer Industries Employees Union, were dissolved to make way for nine smaller industry-based unions. The government also introduced house unions wherever possible, and tightened its direct representation in and control over the National Trades Union Congress.[25] The role of a trade union has been redefined from an organization whose main objective was to promote, organize, or finance strikes to an organization "that seeks, among other things, to promote good industrial relations and raise productivity for the benefit of employees, employers and the economy of the Nation."[26]

Initially in Thailand, too, the government deliberately encouraged weak and small labor associations formed either on an establishment or a provincial basis. But the Labor Relations Act of 1975 allowed greater freedom to organize and to bargain collectively. It provided protection for trade unions against tort and criminal actions and contained provisions for conciliation and arbitration in case of labor disputes. Two types of unions are now allowed: company unions and industrial unions. Unorganized workers have the same rights and privileges as unionized workers, so that there is no great incentive to join a union. This has weakened the power of trade unions to bargain effectively, and the degree of unionization relative to

---

[24] Jayasuriya, p. 103.
[25] Garry Rodan, "The Rise and Fall of Singapore's 'Second Industrial Revolution,' " in Robison, *Southeast Asia in the 1980s,* p. 160.
[26] Industrial Arbitration Court, quoted in Sharma, p. 65.

Table 13
INDUSTRIAL RELATIONS IN ASEAN COUNTRIES

	Indonesia	Thailand	Philippines	Malaysia	Singapore
Pattern of labor-government relations	Political	Conflictual	Conflictual	Conflictual	Accommodative
Nature of labor movement	Unified	Fragmented	Fragmented	Fragmented	Unified
Employer associations	Very weak	Very weak	Weak	Strong	Strong
Power of trade union registrar	Small	Small	Small	Considerable	Considerable
Statutory limits on bargainable issues	Procedural	Procedural	Procedural	Substantive	Substantive
Strikes	Not tolerated	Allowed	Allowed	Most allowed	Allowed

Source: Basu Sharma, *Aspects of Industrial Relations in ASEAN* (Singapore: Institute of Southeast Asian Studies, 1985), 79. Information for Brunei not available.

total employment is consequently very low. Because of this, collective bargaining is generally conducted at the enterprise level in Thailand.

Table 13 provides an overview of industrial relations in the ASEAN countries. The dominant mode of industrial relations in these nations in the late 1980s is tripartite, with government mediating between management and labor wherever possible or deemed necessary. Strikes are technically legal in all ASEAN countries, but are generally frowned upon. Expressions of open conflict are considered contrary to the Asian style of dealing with differences. In addition, work stoppages are considered against the national interest because of the need to attract foreign capital for industrialization programs.

ASEAN ECONOMIC COOPERATION

In 1967 the ASEAN countries signed a declaration agreeing to cooperate economically and politically. Although the first objective in the declaration is "to accelerate the economic growth, social progress and cultural development in the region," it is clear from the political background of ASEAN's formation that the peaceful resolution of existing conflicts and the creation of political stability were overriding concerns. There are three major programs of ASEAN economic cooperation: the ASEAN industrial projects; the ASEAN Industrial Complementation Scheme together with the ASEAN Industrial Joint Venture Scheme; and the preferential trading arrangements.

The ASEAN industrial projects were conceived as large-scale enterprises to produce commodities generally required in the ASEAN region. Each member country was to set up one such project with equity participation by the other ASEAN countries. The funding was to be from a $1 billion grant provided by Japan. To date, large fertilizer complexes have begun production in northern Sumatra (Indonesia) and in Sabah (Malaysia). However, the other industrial projects have been bogged down by a number of difficulties. Singapore, which initially proposed the production of diesel engines, withdrew temporarily from the scheme because Indonesia refused to renounce its production of diesel engines. Subsequently Singapore participated with only one percent equity in the other ASEAN industrial projects. Singapore has recently proposed a production unit for hepatitis vaccine that has been accepted by ASEAN. The equity participation of the other ASEAN countries in this case will be limited to one percent. Thailand originally proposed a soda ash plant but this was dropped because of lack of demand and because its viability had been questioned by the private sector. The Philippines, which initially also considered a fertilizer project, next decided upon a pulp-paper project, and is now actively contemplating a copper purification plant. The idea behind the ASEAN industrial projects is that the products would be free of tariffs within the ASEAN region. However, since these projects have to be government-run enterprises because of their size, they are looked upon with suspicion by some ASEAN partners. Singapore, for instance, feels that the industrial projects would misallocate resources that the private sector could utilize more economically and effectively.

The ASEAN Industrial Complementation Scheme is geared to the private sector. The idea behind the scheme is that private enterprises in the ASEAN countries should divide among themselves products in an industrial sector to avoid unnecessary duplication. An attempt was made to achieve this in the automotive industry, where individual items were distributed among entrepreneurs in various ASEAN countries. However, the scheme relies on the acceptance of the proposed complementation arrangements by ASEAN as well as on the support of individual ASEAN governments that must reduce tariffs on the items exchanged. Because ASEAN decisions and individual government actions take time, they are frequently out of date by the time production could start. In general the ASEAN Industrial Complementation Scheme has suffered from the sluggishness of the decision-making process needed for its implementation. Because of these difficulties, the ASEAN Industrial Joint Venture Scheme was inaugurated. It permits private entrepreneurs in two or more member countries to undertake joint ventures, the products of which would be accorded preferential tariffs within the ASEAN region for a period of five years. This program seems to have far more promise because the degree of consensus required is much lower than in the complementation scheme. A number of items are now being produced under this scheme, and the private sector is well aware of the possibilities inherent in it. It is expected that this scheme will become a major aspect of ASEAN economic cooperation.

ASEAN endeavors to increase intra-ASEAN trade have focused mainly on providing the members of the group preferential access to one another's markets. This has been done by reducing the tariffs on items produced by ASEAN member countries. An agreement on preferential trading arrangements was signed in 1977. The number of items offered and exchanged in negotiations is well over 8,000. Not satisfied with the progress of this item-by-item approach, ASEAN finance ministers in 1980 agreed on across-the-board tariff reductions for "lightly traded" items, that is, on commodities with annual import values of less than $50,000 (using 1978 trade statistics). In 1981 the cutoff ceiling was raised to $500,000, in 1982 to $1 million, in 1982 to $10 million, and since 1986 the ceiling has been removed completely.

The number of items exchanged, the progress made at meetings of the finance ministers, and the apparent lack of open conflict in the many discussions and negotiations preceding decisions have all been impressive. The overall progress achieved by ASEAN has silenced the cynics who expected economic cooperation to break down at the point where words had to be transformed into deeds. One cannot expect, however, the actual economic effects of these achievements in increasing intra-ASEAN trade to be very significant. In fact, the level of intra-ASEAN trade as a percentage of total ASEAN trade has remained low.[27] The main reasons for this are that the

[27] Hans Christoph Rieger, *ASEAN Co-operation and Intra-ASEAN Trade* (Singapore: Institute of Southeast Asian Studies, 1985), 5.

margins of preference for ASEAN goods are generally low (about 24 percent on average) and that the across-the-board tariff cuts have been restricted to "nonsensitive" items. Since each ASEAN country decides whether an item falling under a tariff cut is sensitive or not, the impact of the preferential measure is reduced by the extent to which member countries make use of this option. All countries except Singapore and Brunei have utilized this escape clause, with more than half of all eligible goods being excluded. Finance ministers preparing for the 1987 ASEAN summit proposed an increase in the margin of preference to 50 percent and a reduction of the exclusion lists to no more than 10 percent of the number of traded items in each country and to no more than 50 percent of intra-ASEAN trade value. The proposal was subsequently accepted by the heads of governments meeting in 1987.

As tariffs are successively reduced, nontariff trade barriers tend to have an increasing effect on limiting trade expansion. Another disadvantage of the incremental approach is that uncertainty regarding future progress inhibits long-range planning by the private sector—or even the public sector, for that matter. For this reason the effects of the liberalization measures occur much later than would be the case if these measures followed a plan. It is clear that the economic success of the ASEAN countries cannot be attributed in any substantial way to the existence of the association as an economic regional group, but rather to the economic policies of individual national governments. Nevertheless, ASEAN does have real potential once member governments realize that cooperation is not a zero-sum game in which one gains what another loses.

FURTHER READING

Dahm, Bernhard, and Draguhn, Werner, eds. *Politics, Society and Economy in the ASEAN States.* Wiesbaden, Germany: Harrassowitz, 1975.

Martin, Linda G., ed. *The ASEAN Success Story: Social, Economic and Political Dimensions.* Honolulu, Hawaii: East-West Center, 1987.

Robison, Richard, et al. *Southeast Asia in the 1980s: The Politics of Economic Crisis.* Sydney, London and Boston: Allen & Unwin, 1987.

Spinanger, Dean. *Industrialization Policies and Regional Economic Development in Malaysia.* Singapore, Oxford and New York: Oxford University Press, 1986.

Wawn, Brian. *The Economies of the ASEAN Countries: Indonesia, Malaysia, Philippines, Singapore, and Thailand.* London: Macmillan, 1984.

ASIAN SOCIALIST ECONOMIES: CHINA, VIETNAM AND NORTH KOREA

R. F. ASH AND CHRISTOPHER HOWE

PEOPLE'S REPUBLIC OF CHINA

Macroeconomic overview

THE economic situation facing China in 1949 reflected the disruption occasioned by civil and international wars during the preceding decades, but also a secular process of decline that had been going on since the middle of the 19th century. These facts shaped both the short- and long-term strategies of the new communist government. The immediate objectives were to reduce unemployment (especially in the cities), combat hyperinflation and reestablish a sound monetary system, reverse infrastructural collapse and restore levels of agricultural and industrial production to their peak levels of the mid-1930s. For its long-term objectives China shared the aspirations of other developing countries: to transform a poor, traditional and agriculturally-oriented economy into a modern, industrial system capable of operating an independent and advanced military sector. The means toward all of these ends were shaped by the ideological underpinnings of a government committed to communism and by the international environment in which it had to operate.

The extent to which the long-term objectives have been met is suggested by the fact that as of 1987, China possessed the seventh largest GNP in the world; was the fifth largest industrial producer (after the United States, Soviet Union, Japan and West Germany); and led the world as an agricultural producer. Tables 1–3 serve to indicate in more specific quantitative terms the degree of economic growth and structural change achieved since 1949.

The data suggest profound structural change underlying a growth performance, which, if not exceptional, bears favorable comparison with the postwar records of many developing countries. It is a performance that has been financed by an extraordinarily high rate of accumulation, as Table 4 shows.

1379

Table 1
THE GROWTH RECORD, 1949–86

| | Average annual rate of growth | |
	1952–86	1978–86
National income	6.6%	12.6%
Gross value output	8.7%	13.1%
Agricultural	4.8%	16.4%
Industrial	11.0%	11.7%
Light industry	9.9%	12.8%
Heavy industry	12.3%	10.7%

Source: State Statistical Bureau.

What the data in the Tables 1–4 do not show is the very erratic course which China's economy has followed since 1949. The major watershed undoubtedly occurred in 1978 at which time a distinct change in the pace and direction of development became observable. The change was a reflection of the impact of economic reforms that emerged in the wake of the Third Plenum of the Eleventh Chinese Communist party central committee in 1978 and that has reflected the primacy of Deng Xiaoping. The reforms embody an economic philosophy that has become increasingly distant from the ideological motivation and mass mobilization techniques associated with Mao Zedong's more radical approach to economic development.

Mao's ideas shaped economic thinking and policy in China from 1949 to his death in 1976. In the largely hostile international environment fac-

Table 2
STRUCTURAL CHANGE IN THE CHINESE ECONOMY, 1949–86

Percentage contributions of agriculture, light industry and heavy industry to combined gross value output of the agricultural and industrial sectors

	Agriculture	Light industry	Heavy industry
1949	70.0	28.1	7.9
1952	56.9	27.8	15.3
1957	43.3	31.2	25.5
1965	37.3	32.3	30.4
1978	27.8	31.1	41.1
1981	32.5	34.7	32.8
1986	35.0	30.5	34.5

Source: State Statistical Bureau.

Table 3
STRUCTURAL CHANGE IN THE
INDUSTRIAL SECTOR, 1949–86

*Percentage contributions of light and
heavy industry to industrial gross
value output*

	Light industry	Heavy industry
1949	73.6	26.4
1952	64.5	35.5
1957	55.0	45.0
1965	51.6	48.4
1978	43.1	56.9
1981	51.5	48.5
1986	46.9	53.1

Source: State Statistical Bureau.

ing China in the early 1950s, it was politic to adopt a highly centralized planning system and a strategy of development that derived overwhelmingly from the practice of the Soviet Union. This debt was most evident in the first five-year plan (FYP) (1953–1957) which also relied heavily on Soviet assistance to provide the financial, material and technological means for the projected economic expansion (especially in heavy industry). But the approach was unbalanced; in particular, the reliance on institutional change—the process of collectivization—to promote agricultural growth was not successful. In the face of agricultural bottlenecks that threatened to impede overall advance, Mao launched in 1958 a new strategy (the Great

Table 4
THE RATE OF
ACCUMULATION

*As percentage of
national income*

1953–57	24.2
1958–62	30.8
1963–65	22.7
1966–78	31.2
1979–85	31.2
1978	36.5
1981	28.3
1986	34.3

Source: State Statistical Bureau.

Leap Forward) that he considered better suited to China's resource endowment and level of development. It sought to use massive labor mobilization and ideological motivation to promote agricultural and light industrial growth, while simultaneously maintaining the momentum of heavy industrial expansion through the allocation of most state investment funds to that sector.

The initial positive impact of the new strategy was short-lived and soon gave way to severe economic depression—a collapse that owed the most to policy mismanagement, although it was also exacerbated by adverse natural conditions and the withdrawal in 1960 of Soviet assistance. Much of industry came to a halt, construction activity dried up and urban unemployment reached serious proportions. Most catastrophic of all, the mismanagement of agriculture caused a sharp decline in grain production that led to the deaths of some 15 to 20 million people between 1959 and 1961.

The events of the late 1950s and early 1960s forced upon Chinese planners a revision of economic priorities in favor of the agricultural sector. Indeed, the adoption of especially pragmatic policies during 1962–1965—policies that in the countryside anticipated post-1978 rural reforms—generated rapid recovery. But pending the reemergence of Mao, who was in temporary eclipse after the Great Leap Forward, to center stage, the long-term impact of these measures was vitiated. Instead, in 1966 the Cultural Revolution—essentially a radical campaign designed to stem what Mao regarded as the ideological backsliding of the preceding years and to prevent China from proceeding farther along the road to capitalism—was launched. This movement, with its attendant political factionalism, caused considerable disruption in the industrial and transportation sectors, especially during 1967–1969.

From the outbreak of the Cultural Revolution until Mao's death and the subsequent arrest of the radical Gang of Four, both the spread and direction of economic development were adversely affected by the ideological and political constraints imposed by the radical left. Nor was China's basic economic situation, despite fresh initiatives, altered during the brief leadership of Mao's successor, Hua Guofeng (1976–1978). Only at the Third Plenum in 1978 was it finally recognized, in the face of admitted economic disorder and imbalance, that future development would best be served by a period of retrenchment. Accordingly, 1979 heralded a revision of China's modernization program in favor of "readjustment, restructuring, reorganization and up-grading," designed to lay the foundation in the 1980s for more rapid growth in the final decade of the 20th century.

The sixth and seventh FYPs (1981–1985 and 1986–1990) have reflected the fundamental change in emphasis that is implicit in China's reform program. In place of the supposedly "blind expansion" of capital construction and excessive emphasis on heavy industrialization, leading to unbalanced development, greater priority has been attached to the growth of agriculture and light industry. This reordering of priorities has been underpinned by important institutional reforms—the almost universal establishment of contractual arrangements with individual households in agriculture, the encouragement of independent and private economic activities and delegation of decision making to the lowest level. Officially, planning remains the prime force behind economic change; in reality, there is an increasing awareness of the limitations inherent in centralized planning and a corresponding willingness to rely on prices and markets in order to determine production. There have been significant reform initiatives in banking and fiscal systems. In the area of China's foreign economic relations, there have also been dramatic changes, China's "open door" policy signifying not merely a major expansion in trade, but also—and more radically—active encouragement of various forms of foreign investment.

The impact of recent reforms on living standards has been notable, although sizable pockets of poverty continue to exist and differentials have widened. From 1952 until 1976, the per capita consumption of peasants grew on average by a mere 1.2 percent a year; for urban residents, the figure was about 2 percent a year. By contrast, from 1981 to 1985 average per capita income rose, in real terms, by 22.3 percent—and that of peasants by 90 percent. Increases in grain consumption and access to a more varied diet, a significant expansion in the demand for some consumer durables and very large rises in urban and rural savings deposits further attest to the effect of the new economic policies upon social and personal welfare.

Population

The size, structure and rate of increase of any country's population (but especially that of a developing country) has critical implications for virtually every area of economic activity. In the case of China, the most populous country in the world, two quantitative indicators may serve to indicate the burden implied by its demographic profile. First, in order to meet the basic consumption requirements of its population, China's agriculture has to feed about 22 percent of the global population with a mere five percent of the world's cultivated land. Second, notwithstanding the remarkable decline in the birthrate since the 1970s, even now something like 60 percent of increased aggregate consumption in any year is absorbed by population increase. The same factor exacerbates the shortage of farmland and housing, and further limits employment and educational opportunities.

Population density varies enormously within China, the most marked contrast being that between the eastern seaboard, and the west and northwest. The high mountains, plateaus and arid basins of Tibet, Xinjiang and Nei Mongol account for about half of China's total surface area, but contain little more than five percent of its population. By contrast, the availability of fertile land in the east is reflected in very high population densities, especially in the alluvial plains where intensive agriculture has traditionally been practiced. Table 5 presents official estimates of China's total population and associated vital growth rates for selected years since 1949.

Although China remains a predominantly rural society as a result of the economic development and structural changes that have occurred since 1949, considerable urbanization has taken place. For example, the proportion of urban population in the total increased from 10.6 percent in 1949 to 23.5

Table 5
CHINA'S TOTAL POPULATION AND VITAL GROWTH RATES

	Total population (thousands)	Birth rate	Death rate	Rate of natural increase
		All growth rates given per thousand		
1949	541,670	36.0	20.0	16.0
1952	574,820	37.0	17.0	20.0
1957	646,530	34.0	10.8	23.2
1965	725,380	37.9	9.5	28.4
1978	962,590	18.3	6.3	12.0
1981	1,000,720	20.9	6.4	14.5
1982	1,015,410	21.1	6.6	14.5
1983	1,024,950	18.6	7.1	11.5
1984	1,034,750	17.5	6.7	10.8
1985	1,045,320	17.8	6.6	11.2
1986	1,060,080	20.8	6.7	14.1
1987	1,080,000	21.04	6.65	14.39

Source: State Statistical Bureau.

percent in 1983. After 1983, the official definition of "urban" changed so that current statistics show urban population accounting for more than 35 percent of the total.

During the last 40 years official policy toward population growth has changed dramatically. During the 1950s Mao took the view that rapid population increase, far from posing a threat to economic development, was instead a means of effecting revolutionary transformation: "It is a very good thing that we have a large population; we are quite prepared to cope with a population that is several times larger than our present one." Those who argued to the contrary were castigated as reactionary neo-Malthusians. It is true that the first birth control campaign dates from as early as 1956 and was followed by others during the 1960s. The impact, however, was slight and the rate of natural increase continued to rise, reaching a peak of 28.5 per thousand in 1965. It was not until the 1970s and the end of the most disruptive phase of the Cultural Revolution that attempts to curb population growth began to take real effect. Control measures then generated quite a dramatic decline, the rate of natural increase falling from 25.83 per thousand in 1970 to 12.66 just six years later. This rate of decline was maintained and by the end of the 1970s the figure was marginally below 12 per thousand. This is a remarkable record by any standards, probably unmatched anywhere in modern times.

The urgency of the population issue is evident in the attention that it received from government leaders and planners throughout the 1980s. Attempts to reduce the rate of increase of China's population had initially been based on the propagation of effective contraception techniques. Subsequently, more emphasis was placed on the advocacy of late marriages. By 1980, notwithstanding the success of earlier policies, it had become apparent that an average of two children per family would lead to a total population in excess of 1,500 million by the middle of the 21st century. With these statistics in mind the leadership decided upon a policy of adopting "one child per family" to reach the goal of keeping total population at or below 1,200 million by the end of the 20th century—thereafter reducing it by some 500 million during the course of the next one hundred years.

The task implied by this target is an enormous one. It must be a matter of concern that recent years have seen a rise again in the rate of natural increase (see Table 5). This has led some officials to speak of a new demographic crisis facing China. It is clear that maintaining a rate of growth as low as 12 per thousand was always going to be extremely difficult, given the evolving age structure of the population and the increasing numbers of young people reaching marriageable and childbearing ages. But the renewed increase in births can also be attributed to some extent to the failure to implement the one child per family policy as strictly as is necessary.

Part of the difficulty arises simply from the unpopularity of the single-child policy, although the problem has been exacerbated in the countryside by the process of decollectivization accompanying the nearly universal establishment of household responsibility systems in agriculture. This change put a premium on family labor, especially sons. In the first half of the 1980s, implementation of the single-child policy was underlined by the imposition of punitive economic sanctions against those who failed to adhere to the new policy. However, since 1985 this has given way to a more relaxed attitude and an attempt to introduce more flexible rules that would be better suited to the varied demographic conditions in China. In practice, this has meant the continuation of a one-child rule in the cities, but a two-children rule elsewhere.

Such uncertainty suggests that the urgency of the population issue will persist into the foreseeable future. The Chinese government in fact faces a difficult dilemma. Continued relaxation of the official policy will result in China's population far exceeding the planned level of 1,200 million by the end of the 20th century—with all the attendant difficulties that this figure implies. But fulfillment of the target goals will require the reintroduction of stringent measures that could push planners in a direction contrary to the spirit of prevailing reforms.

Industry

Historical as well as economic factors dictated that the industrial sector inherited by the communist government in 1949 was small, geographically highly concentrated and, in terms of both organization and techniques, premodern. There existed a heavy industry base in the northeast (Manchuria) developed largely by Japanese expertise and investment during that country's occupation of the region (1931–1945). Elsewhere production was dominated by light industry.

Table 6
RATES OF INDUSTRIAL GROWTH

*Average annual rate of
growth of industrial
gross value output*

1952–78	11.4%	
1952–57		18.5%
1957–65		10.3%
1965–78		9.4%
1979–85	10.1%	

Sources: Data for years up to 1978 from C. Riskin, *China's Political Economy* (London: Oxford University Press, 1987), 264. Data for 1979–85 from State Statistical Bureau.

Many of these features changed in subsequent years under the impact of an economic strategy that attached high, and sometimes overwhelming, priority to industrialization, especially the expansion of heavy industry. By the end of the first FYP in 1957, industry had displaced agriculture as the largest economic sector. The importance of light industry also rapidly gave way to that of heavy industry. Such changes reflected Stalinist emphasis on heavy industrialization that was central to the first FYP's strategy—an approach that betokened increases in both the average size and technical sophistication of industrial activity. But attempts to achieve a more rational geographical distribution of industry—rational in the sense of propinquity to sources of raw materials—met with limited success. Even at the end of the 1980s perhaps three quarters of industrial output came from the northeast, the eastern seaboard provinces and the three great industrial centers of Beijing, Tianjin and, above all, Shanghai.

Tables 6 and 7 provide quantitative indicators of China's industrial performance since 1952, the point at which economic rehabilitation was complete and the economy poised for net growth.

The period of most rapid industrial growth was, not surprisingly, that of the first FYP, with an average annual growth rate in excess of 18 percent. Thereafter the rate of increase slowed to around 10 percent a year—by no means an unimpressive figure. Since 1952 the expansion of heavy industry has easily outstripped that of light industry, although with the revised economic priorities of the post-1978 period, that pattern has been reversed.

However, such aggregate measures of industrial growth give no indication of changes in efficiency. Attempts have been made to investigate this crucial aspect of Chinese industrial performance and they reveal that from

1386

Table 7
TOTAL OUTPUT OF SELECTED
INDUSTRIAL ITEMS

	1949	1952	1957	1965	1978	1987
Heavy industry						
Coal	32	66	131	232	618	920
Crude oil	0.12	0.44	1.46	11.31	104.05	134
Electricity (million KWh)	4.3	7.3	19.3	67.6	256.6	496
Steel	0.16	1.35	5.35	12.23	31.78	56.02
Rolled steel	0.13	1.06	4.15	8.81	22.08	43.91
Cement	0.66	2.86	6.86	16.34	65.24	180.0
Chemical fertilizer	—	0.04	0.15	1.73	8.69	17.03
Light industry						
Cotton yarn	0.33	0.66	0.84	1.30	2.38	4.32
Cloth (billion m.)	1,890	3,830	5,050	6,280	11,030	16,700
Sugar	0.20	0.45	0.86	1.46	2.27	5.11

Note: All figures in million metric tons except where noted otherwise.
Source: State Statistical Bureau.

1952 to 1978, labor productivity increased, on average, by 4 percent a year, while output per unit of capital fell by 1.1 percent a year. The implication is that industrial growth during this period derived mainly from physical increases in the factors of production. Indeed, even the rise in labor productivity was associated with an almost fourfold rise in the capital-labor ratio. Nor is there any evidence that this pattern has significantly altered since the late 1970s when reform and readjustment began. On the contrary, official reports have continued to speak of industry's poor economic results, as measured by material and energy consumption norms, profit rates, cost reduction, quality improvements and so forth.

There is also evidence that the higher priority given to light industry since 1978 has not been consistently maintained and at times growth in heavy industry has threatened once more to run ahead of that in light industry. Despite increases in the output of many consumer durables, such as washing machines, televisions and refrigerators, the expansion of light industry has not always kept up with the rise in purchasing power. For several years official sources have voiced concern about the allegedly excessive scale of capital construction activity, especially in initiating projects outside the state budget. This practice is wasteful of resources and may serve only to deprive key sectors of urgently needed funds and material.

The magnitude of the problem is suggested by a recent revelation that of 26 large and medium-sized projects launched in the first half of 1987, only one had been officially sanctioned by the state council.

Individual industries have also been beset by problems. Coal and steel are two notable examples. The production of coal, which even today remains by far the most important source of primary energy, reached a peak in 1960, but was in decline throughout the next decade and did not re-attain this level until 1972. The stagnation in steel production was even more dramatic, recovery from its 1960 peak not taking place until 1978. More than a decade of zero growth in these crucial industries has had serious repercussions throughout the rest of the economy. The reasons for such poor performances lie in low levels of productivity resulting from inadequate investment, exacerbated initially by the effects of the withdrawal of Soviet assistance.

For the present and the foreseeable future, the most serious constraint on industrial expansion will be posed by the energy sector. In contrast to the buoyant performance of the rest of the economy, the rate of increase in primary energy production during the first half of the 1980s actually fell below the previous long-run trend rate of growth. Most serious undoubtedly has been the disappointing performance of the previous spectacularly successful oil sector. For example, between 1978 and 1983, crude oil production experienced virtually no growth at all, and although recovery has subsequently taken place, the average annual rate of increase since 1983 has been a mere 5.84 percent, compared with 23.4 percent a year during 1953–1978. With coal and electricity production growing only modestly, a pessimistic view of future energy supplies seems unavoidable.

For most of the past 40 years, China's industrial organization has been shaped by the Soviet model, providing for vertical lines of control and with key enterprises under the sole authority of the central bureaucracy in Beijing. As a means of chaneling scarce resources into designated priority areas, this arrangement has had obvious advantages. But as a means of encouraging initiative and innovation (especially at the local level) as well as enhancing efficiency and achieving proper horizontal integration, it has been less effective. These are problems that current reform measures seek to overcome.

Earlier attempts to improve industrial organization and management focused on the search for the most appropriate degree of decentralization in decision making, the use of material incentives and the distribution of responsibility within industrial enterprises. In general, a more collectivist approach toward decision making was pursued during radical movements and reached its apogee during the late 1960s when revolutionary committees (made up of representatives of the People's Liberation Army, party cadres and peasants) temporarily took over the running of enterprises. It was at such times too that the use of material incentives was downgraded in favor of ideological motivation. By contrast, in the more relaxed economic atmosphere that followed this period, material incentives were revived and accompanied by a renewed emphasis on the need for specialist skills.

Since 1978 the main tasks of industrial reform have again been to reduce excessive centralized control over enterprises, to separate the functions of government from those of management in enterprises, to establish clear lines of responsibility and to break down barriers built up over previous years between departments and regions. A major reformist theme has been the need to make enterprises fully independent units, operating under the sole control of their directors and fully responsible for profits and losses. The pragmatism inherent in current reforms is also evident in the expansion of leasing and contractual arrangements with individuals, the introduction of share issues and even the experimentation with bankruptcy. So too is the expanded scope of market-oriented production that has accompanied the decline in mandatory planning. Nevertheless Chinese planners have yet to confront directly the need for comprehensive price reform—the essential adjunct of the kind of changes envisaged in the industrial sector.

Industrial reform has only moved to a central position in China's program of economic reform since 1984. It would be premature to attempt an assessment of the measures that have so far been introduced, although some of the difficulties that stand in the way of their successful implementation are already becoming apparent. Two such difficulties are evident: resistance from entrenched interests, either administrators in the old bureacratic hierarchy or workers whose previous job security (the "iron rice bowl") may be threatened by the more competitive climate in which enterprises must now operate; and the reluctance or inability to rationalize prices in such a way as to enable them to serve as arbiters of production and distribution and so enhance enterprise performance.

Agriculture

China's experience since 1949 demonstrates the fundamental position occupied by agriculture in a developing economy and the dangers of ignoring its basic developmental role. At the most general level, the agricultural sector has to meet the demands of food for a rising population; provide raw materials, such as cotton and tobacco, for light industry; and make available an export surplus that will help pay for imports. For much of the time since 1949, China's agriculture has been underfunded and this, combined with an organizational framework that too often offered little scope for individual peasant initiative, resulted in rates of growth which could not support industrial and broader economic expansion on the scale looked for. It is true that reforms implemented since 1979 have had a positive impact on many branches of agricultural activity, but it has yet to be shown that these gains can be maintained without the emergence of major new problems.

Tables 8 and 9 provide quantitative indicators of agricultural rates of growth and the total output of selected agricultural products since 1949.

During the 1950s, the official policy toward agriculture was dominated by the belief that growth could be secured on the basis of institutional change (collectivization), without the need to divert scarce state investment funds from the priority sector of heavy industry. The disappointing rates of growth actually achieved during the first FYP and the emergence of

Table 8
RATES OF AGRICULTURAL GROWTH

| | Average annual rate of growth | |
	1953–78	1979–85
Agricultural gross value output	3.2%	10.0%
Food grains	2.4%	3.2%
Cotton	2.0%	9.7%
Oil-bearing crops	0.8%	17.1%
Sugar crops	4.5%	14.2%
Pork, beef and mutton	3.6%	10.8%
Aquatic products	4.0%	5.9%

Source: State Statistical Bureau.

agricultural bottlenecks suggested that this strategy was misguided. But under pressure to maintain the momentum of industrial expansion, investment priorities were adhered to and the hoped for agricultural breakthrough was sought through further institutional change (the creation of communes) and mass mobilization of labor on an unprecedented scale. Only in the wake of a preciptious decline in food production and widespread famine was a revision of priorities eventually forced on planners who for the first time gave explicit recognition to the pivotal economic role of the agricultural sector.

Evidence of this shift is afforded in the fact that in 1962 the agricultural sector received 21.3 percent of total state investment, compared with a mere 8.6 percent in 1957. However, the allocation of state funds to agriculture almost immediately began to decline—to 14.6 percent in 1965 and less than 10 percent by the mid-1970s. Admittedly, the growth of grain production showed a more consistently upward trend after 1965, but this was only achieved at the expense of extending the grain area to the detriment of both industrial crops and livestock production. Little consideration was given to the financial costs of so one-sidedly emphasizing the grain

Table 9
TOTAL OUTPUT OF SELECTED AGRICULTURAL PRODUCTS

	1949	1952	1957	1965	1978	1987
Food grains	113.18	163.92	195.05	194.53	304.77	402.41
Cotton	0.44	1.30	1.64	2.10	2.17	4.19
Oil-bearing crops	2.56	4.19	4.20	3.63	5.22	15.25

Note: All figures in million metric tons.
Source: State Statistical Bureau.

Table 10
STRUCTURAL CHANGE IN
THE RURAL SECTOR

Percentage contribution of each sector to agricultural gross value output

	Crop husbandry	Forestry	Animal husbandry	Fishery	Sidelines Total	Brigade and team industry
1949	82.5	0.6	12.4	0.2	4.3	—
1952	83.1	0.7	11.5	0.3	4.4	—
1957	80.6	1.7	12.9	0.5	4.3	—
1965	75.8	2.0	14.0	1.7	6.5	—
1978	67.8	3.0	13.2	1.4	14.6	11.7
1986	45.4	3.4	13.9	1.9	35.4	29.8

Source: State Statistical Bureau.

sector. Faced by high procurement quotas and low procurement prices, peasant morale suffered accordingly.

This was the general background against which far reaching reforms were introduced in the agricultural sector starting in 1979. These have embraced both institutional and economic changes. On one hand agricultural operations have been effectively decollectivized and contractual arrangements have been introduced by means of various household responsibility systems that give much greater scope to individual peasant initiative. This has been accompanied by a move toward greater specialization and by a major extension of private activities. On the other hand, economic incentives have been improved through tax and price adjustments. Most far-reaching of all was the abandonment in 1985 of the 30-year-old state monopoly procurement scheme for agricultural and sideline products, and its replacement by contractual arrangements with individual households.

There is no doubt that in general the impact of such policies has been dramatic: there has been a marked acceleration, although at a declining rate, in the output of virtually all major farm products. This is all the more impressive in that it has been based on increases in unit area yields and indeed often accompanied by declining sown area. No less important are the structural changes that have also taken place under these reforms. Prior to 1978 agriculture was dominated by crop husbandry and any move in the direction of diversification was modest. During the 1980s, as Table 10 shows, the rural sector has become highly diversified.

The most striking change has been the expansion of rural industrial undertakings. This is a development that must be seen in the context of a high degree of agricultural underemployment. Official estimates have indicated that as many as 30 percent of China's agricultural labor force (about 100 million people) may be surplus to requirements. This massive surplus cannot simply be moved into the large cities; in any case labor absorption by the industrial sector is a gradual process. The key to resolving the problem is seen in increasing the occupational and geographical mobility of agricultural labor within the rural sector. In particular, in addition to readjustments in the production structure of agriculture (as shown in Table 10), township enterprises must rapidly be developed to accommodate more laborers—according to one estimate as many as 30 million during the seventh FYP (1986–1990).

Nobody would deny the marked effect which reform measures have had on output and productivity in the rural sector. Equally, there is no doubting the large improvements in peasant incomes and living standards. However, the cost of these improvements has become increasingly apparent and agriculture at the end of the 1980s faces a number of serious problems that must be resolved if the momentum of the decade is not to be lost and if rural restructuring is to continue. Land utilization is one such problem. Natural resource constraints have always inhibited China's agricultural development and one of the most serious of these has been the shortage of arable land. Between 1957 and 1977 the arable area fell by more than 2,900,000 hectares. The impact of post-1978 reforms was to intensify this decline; during the first half of the 1980s an average of about 490,000 hectares were lost each year. This accelerated decline was in large measure the result of rural industrial capital construction, house building by peasants, illegal land sales and transfers and simply the abandonment or neglect of farmland as peasants moved from farming to more profitable pursuits.

This last factor highlights what has become perhaps the most pressing—though hardly unfamiliar—problem facing agriculture: the availability of grain. The abandonment of the state monopoly procurement scheme in 1985 was announced in the wake of a series of bumper harvests that had generated supposedly unmanageable surpluses of grain. In retrospect such surpluses may have been more illusory than real, for the evidence of the years since 1985 is that peasants have become increasingly disclined to grow grain, preferring to move into the cultivation of higher income crops (e.g., tobacco) or, most preferable of all, to seek employment in the burgeoning rural industrial enterprises. Such a response is perfectly rational in a profit-maximizing sense, but it is also one that poses a real dilemma for China's leaders. With incomes continuing to rise, it is inevitable that the demand for a more varied diet (especially the consumption of meat and dairy products) will increase. The pressure of demand on grain for indirect use—especially to provide feed for animals—will correspondingly rise. In short, given the continuing central position of grain production, measures must be devised to guarantee current and future food supplies. If these are not forthcoming, the state may have to reintroduce more direct control methods in order to ensure that such priorities are upheld.

Finally, there is evidence to show that a consequence of agricultural decollectivization has been a drop in agricultural investment and a deterioration of the rural infrastructure. The decline in irrigated area is perhaps the most serious manifestation of this phenomenon. Official projections make it clear that the most important source of future investment in agriculture will be funds accumulated within the rural sector itself; by contrast, the state's role will remain very much a subordinate one. The high level of private rural savings deposits indicates that lack of funds for investment is not a problem. Rather, the issue is one of mobilization. Whether the problem can be resolved without the reimposition of a collectivized framework remains to be seen. It would however, be an irony if the emergence of such difficulties compelled a return to policies that in their advocacy of more centralized methods of control were the very antithesis of the reformist spirit of the 1980s.

Foreign trade and investment
The role of the trade system in China since 1949 has been to facilitate the export of primary products and labor-intensive manufactures, and to import capital goods and raw materials for industrial development. At the same time as importing capital goods, China has also needed to acquire the whole range of skills necessary for industrialization and modernization of the economy generally.

The Soviet Union played the key role in China's trade development during its first decade. For political, ideological and strategic reasons, the first FYP was based on a close relationship between the two countries. This was reflected in very high levels of Chinese trade dependence on the Soviet Union and Eastern Europe. It was also reflected in a comprehensive program of technical assistance, training and technology transfer. During the 1950s the Chinese gained great benefits from this relationship. Not only did the Soviets assist the Chinese in the renovation of their older industries, such as metallurgy, but they transferred plants and skills that enabled China to acquire completely new industries and the technologies necessary to maintain and manage them.

During the 1960s trade took a much lower profile in the Chinese economy. Problems in agriculture made export availability low, while such foreign exchange as was available had to be used for grain imports and the oil and raw materials necessary for minimal industrial performance. This change of emphasis was reflected in new ideological concepts of self-reliance and self-strengthening. In industrial terms this meant new emphasis on indigenous techniques and a minimization of the role of imported technologies.

During the 1970s there was much confusion in the management of the foreign trade sector and in associated policies. On one hand it was recognized that in certain sectors (e.g., fertilizer technology) major plant imports were essential and that, more generally, the problem of China's deteriorating technology position could not be handled without substantial expansion of foreign trade. Also, by the mid-1970s the availability of oil for export was beginning to transform China's capacity to import. During 1970–1976, however, the question of foreign trade became politically contentious. The ideology of self-reliance still had a strong grip and factions within the communist party (and within the ministry of foreign trade) would not support the perpetuation of commodity trade patterns of a "colonial" character—a pattern implied by the expansion of oil exports.

After Mao's death, first Hua, then Deng, advocated and implemented a

Table 11
IMPORTS, EXPORTS AND THE TRADE BALANCE
(billion U.S. $)

	Imports	Exports	Total	Balance
1978	10.9	9.8	20.7	−1.1
1981	22.0	22.0	44.0	0
1985	42.3	27.4	69.7	−14.9
1986	42.9	30.9	73.8	−12.0
1987	43.2	39.5	82.7	−3.7

Source: State Statistical Bureau.

new "open door" policy. Since 1978 the expansion of international economic relations has been a basic tenet of Chinese policy. Moreover, the "open door" is not defined in narrow economic terms. Trade, foreign investment, technology transfer and foreign cultural relations are all understood to be essential to the process of modernizing China.

The results of the "open door" policy in trade terms can be judged from the data in Table 11. Total trade expanded by more than fourfold with an annual growth rate of approximately 17 percent. The impact of this on the Chinese economy has been to raise the share of foreign trade in the economy from under 10 percent to nearly 20 percent (exports and imports as a share of national income). This shift obviously represents a major effort to catch up with the opportunities lost in the 1960s and early 1970s when the world economy was expanding trade and China's share was declining rapidly. Looking to the future, it is unlikely that a continuation of this process will be possible, although it may continue at a slower rate if China is successful in unlocking its potential for trade still further.

The other feature of Table 11 shows the tendency of the trade account to be in deficit. Deficits in trade are not new in China, but before 1978 they tended to be exceptional, unforeseen events, that were reversed as rapidly as possible. However, after 1980, only in 1982 did China achieve a significant trade surplus, and this was the result of a violent swing in policy to tighten control on imports as part of the readjustment. Of the seven other years, in two trade was virtually balanced and in five there was a substantial deficit. In 1985 and 1986 the deficits were very large, substantially larger than could be accommodated by prudent use of reserves. Thus after 30 years of very conservative management of the external sector, the policymakers now seem to accept that at this stage of China's development deficits can be permitted, although in external as in internal budgetary plans, the target in the current plan for 1990 is a balanced position.

Table 12 shows long-term trends in the structure of trade as well as the most recent developments. If 1952 is compared with 1965, a strong rise in the proportion of processed agricultural materials and a decline in pri-

Table 12
TRADE STRUCTURES
(percentage shares)

	Manufactures and minerals	Processed agriculture	Exports Agriculture	Capital goods	Consumer goods
1952	17.9	22.8	59.3	89.4	10.6
1959	23.7	38.7	37.6	95.7	4.3
1961	33.4	45.9	20.7	61.9	38.1
1965	30.9	36.0	33.1	66.5	33.5
1980	51.8	29.5	18.7	78.9	21.1

Exports	1985	1986	Imports	1985	1986
Primary	50.6	36.4	Primary	12.5	13.2
(Food)	(13.9)	(14.4)	(Food)	(3.7)	(3.8)
(Fuel/minerals)	(26.0)	(11.9)	Industrial	87.5	86.3
Industrial	49.4	63.6	(Machinery)	(39.1)	(38.4)
(Light/textile)	(16.4)	(19.0)	(Steel)	(16.9)	(15.7)
(Misc. clothing)	(12.8)	(16.0)			

Source: State Statistical Bureau.

mary, agricultural exports is evident. Moving to 1980, the jump in manufactures and minerals reflects the growth of oil exports and the high oil price in that year. On the import side nearly all imports before 1959 were industrially related but, thereafter, the import of grain and other agricultural raw materials is reflected in the changing balance in the import structure.

The data for 1985–1986 show that between those two years the share of primary products in exports fell sharply. This is partly the result of the growth of manufactured exports, but mainly it reflects the decline in the world oil price, thus illustrating the problems for China inherent in being a significant exporter of primary products whose prices are subject to major, short-term fluctuations. In quantity terms the fall in oil exports was less than 5 percent but in value terms, oil exports fell by half.

The other feature of China's trade in the 1980s has been the emergence of China as a major world exporter of textiles and related products. In 1986 and 1987 textiles and garment exports achieved growths of 60 percent and 20 percent, and although they have now encountered serious restrictions in the United States, Japan and Europe, China's success does reflect economic logic. With the long-run combination of China's low labor costs and Hong Kong's technical, marketing and financial skills, these sectors are likely to continue to make progress at the lower end of the market.

On the import side recent change has been much less dramatic. Since

Table 13
REGIONAL DISTRIBUTION OF TRADE
(percentage shares)

Exports by country/region		*Imports by country/region*	
United States	13	United States	10
Japan	20	Japan	32
Western Europe	9	Western Europe	16
West Germany	2	West Germany	6
Great Britain	1	Great Britain	1
Hong Kong	36	Hong Kong	23
Singapore	7	Singapore	1
Rest	12	Rest	11
Total	100	Total	100

Source: State Statistical Bureau.

the 1960s the share of industrially-related imports has shifted back toward the 1959 pattern. One surprising feature of the import structure, however, is the continuing importance of steel. This partly reflects errors in China's metallurgical policy going back many years, together with a demand for some higher quality steels in which Japan has a clear comparative advantage.

In Table 13 China's total trade is allocated by trading partners. The data show the situation in 1985. A very clear pattern emerges. First, in terms of both imports and exports there is a dominance of regional trade partners. Trade with Asia and the United States accounts for 76 percent of exports and 65 percent of imports. Even if the U.S. figures are subtracted, the shares are reduced but not substantially. This pattern has been determined by the following factors: the proximity of the Asian partners, the extraordinary role played in China's trade by Hong Kong and the competitive strength of Japan. The interdependence of the Chinese and Hong Kong economies increased quite dramatically in the 1980s. One indicator of this is a recent estimate that the total number of people in Guangdong province working in some way related to the Hong Kong economy, is about one million, of whom 300,000 are in the knitwear and textile trades. U.S.-Chinese trade ties are also very strong, although they are from time to time disrupted by political disagreements. In structural terms Chinese demand for American capital goods and technology remains strong.

The role of Europe in Chinese trade is relatively small, but not insignificant. West Germany and France in particular have worked assiduously to advance the scale of their two-way trade. A major obstacle to the expansion of Chinese-European trade, however, is the limited ability of Western Europe to absorb Chinese exports. Apart from the long-standing trade in certain primary products, overall trade is relatively small because European markets tend to be too sophisticated for Chinese manufactured products.

During the 1980s the Chinese have repeatedly tried to reform their foreign trade organization. From the early 1950s to the late 1970s the essentials of the trade system remained unchanged. The main feature of the system was the highly centralized ministry of foreign trade, working through a group of specialized trade corporations responsible for detailed management of exports and imports. The corporations worked by ordering commodities required for export from enterprises and internal trading organizations and by allocating imported goods in accordance with an import plan that took account of expressed needs of user enterprises and central judgments about China's import priorities. To understand the significance of this system it is essential to appreciate that the exchange rate in China does not perform the function of linking the domestic to the international price system. Thus exports often require subsidies to enable the producer enterprise to cover losses, and imports are often repriced upward to match domestic prices. Under this arrangement, "profits" on imports and "losses" on exports can be balanced centrally. However, as soon as the system is decentralized, domestic enterprises will find themselves faced with an international price system that induces excessive imports and often discourages exports, which are more profitable to sell domestically. Apart from this, the traditional centralized system also has the flaw that by centralizing information and power, producers of exports and users of imports do not have the ability or incentive to play an effective role in maximizing the gains from trade. No factory dependent on a ministry for information on its markets can be expected to sell effectively, and no purchaser of imported capital goods dependent on central judgments on its requirements is likely to use foreign exchange to the best advantage.

One important step in reform has been the creation of new institutions. In trade the key institution is now the ministry of foreign economic relations and trade; in the early stages of reform there was a significant decentralization of the power of the foreign trade corporations, local governments and even some individual enterprises. There was also an attempt to categorize exports into groups with retention of central control restricted to those with the highest priority. In 1984 a dual system of control was instituted allowing direct trade by "foreign trade enterprises" and trade by other enterprises through official intermediaries, often the old corporations. At the same time export subsidies were reduced. The net effect of these changes was to discourage some types of exports, but to encourage an inflow of imports on a very large scale. The impact of these changes shows up very clearly in the trade data for 1984–1985. The error of this reform, therefore, was that it decentralized important trade decisions without ensuring that appropriate microeconomic signals and incentives were in place. In 1986 a sharp recentralization was implemented that reimposed the old type of controls. The overall pattern of the trade system changes since 1979 was summed up by one Chinese writer as "chaos after deregulation, inertia after centralization."

The problem now facing the Chinese planners is a difficult one. This is because although in early 1988 the leadership made it clear that priority was to be given to trade reform, change in the trade system cannot effectively proceed without appropriate changes in the domestic system. Pricing in particular is central to both reforms. But there is at present no agreement on the exact goals for the general reform, either in terms of the ultimate nature of planning and the economy or in terms of the schedule to be followed to attain this goal.

At present the main agenda for trade reform is summed up in the "Draft Plan for the Reshaping of the Foreign Trade System in 1988" approved by the state council in November 1987. Under this plan three principles are to be introduced into trade planning. First, the foreign trade corporations are to become independent businesses responsible for profits and losses and, given appropriate freedom of action, expected to make profits. Second, instead of the old bureaucratic links between enterprise and corporations, future relations are to be contractual and freely entered into. Third, there is to be an attempt to end the division between enterprises and corporations, which presumably means that in the long run enterprises will tend to absorb the appropriate corporations with their internal structures (if they are large enough).

The net effect of this further reform is likely to be a strengthening of the role of the enterprise in the trade system. Enterprises designated as "trade enterprises" are to be allowed to sign foreign trade contracts directly, and the incentives for all enterprises are to be strengthened, partly by allowing even more foreign exchange retention, with the level of retention higher for higher value-added goods. These moves alleviate but do not seem to remove the old incentive difficulties. Enterprises under this system will be able to offset any losses on exports by their use of foreign exchange retention which can be used for imports. Thus the enterprise will become the focus for the balancing of losses and gains through inappropriate pricing and exchange rates rather than the corporation or ministry under the old system. However, in practice the new system is not likely to work so symmetrically, and the problems of small-scale exporters seem likely to remain. In the first stage of the new system, light industry, arts and crafts and the garment industries are to be the major centers of experimentation.

Thus how far the new initiative will go in solving the problems of the earlier reformed system remains to be seen. In the past two to three years, the further devaluation of the yuan (which is linked to the dollar) has negated some of the effects of earlier reforms because it has raised the yuan cost of exports and hence further undermined export profitability. Further, the precise responsibility of price determination is unspecified under the new system. And in the longer run the Chinese remain unclear as to exactly what the logical basis of their trade is. In the case of imports, technological catching up remains a powerful criterion, although the detailed interpretation of this will remain a problem as long as incentives to innovate domestically remain weak and as long as the central role in determining technological priorities has to be strong. Exports also remain a very difficult problem. Some Chinese economists have moved toward the idea of comparative advantage in traditional senses (Ricardo and Heckscher-Ohlin trade), others are hoping that China will be able to jump into product cycle trade and interact with foreign investment in the manner of the newly industrialized countries. Prime Minister Zhao Ziyang clearly embraced the general concept of export-led growth as the basis of current policy on reform in the trade sector.

The international links between market economies consist not only of trade but of investment relationships. Direct investment is particularly important for developing countries because it is one of the major vehicles for the transfer of technology. One can learn much directly from the import of machines, but often even more from a joint relationship in a direct investment.

In Mao's time the idea of direct foreign ownership or participation in the Chinese economy was unthinkable. Under Deng the concept has become an integral part of the "open door." The forms of direct participation and investment are numerous, ranging from joint activities to fully-owned foreign companies operating in China. One important form is compensation trade whereby a foreign firm invests in a plant in China and is repaid with the foreign exchange earnings of the plant. Deals of this kind have been commonplace in Eastern European economies for some years. In effect they offer economies on labor costs to the foreign partner and provide the Chinese with the benefits of superior marketing and technology. Also, from the point of view of the foreign participant, deals of this kind offer the prospect of access to markets in planned economies that are otherwise thought to be inaccessible. This has been an important motive in the Chinese case, and one that the Chinese have played upon with some skill.

Another important form of foreign participation in China is the equity joint venture. These are established in accordance with the joint venture law of 1979 and of its subsequent amendments. Equity joint ventures are run by boards made up of the Chinese and foreign partners, each of whom contributes to the joint capital. The foreign partner usually supplies equipment and foreign exchanges and the Chinese, land and other local resources.

The progress of direct investment in China may be judged from Tables 14 and 15. Table 14 reveals that the total flow of resources to China since 1979 has been relatively modest, with the inflow (commitments) peaking in 1985. Utilization of commitments seems persistently lower than would have been expected. To put the figures in some perspective, the total utilized flow of investment over the nine years is less than 8 percent of the capital outflow from Japan in the single year 1986. In Table 15 the breakdown of foreign investment by major categories confirms the equity joint venture as the most important form, closely followed by the contractual joint venture.

There is no doubt that if one subtracts from this inflow the inflow attributable to Hong Kong investors, the results of this new program to date have been extremely disappointing. In a long-term perspective, however, this is not altogether surprising. It was bound to be very difficult to introduce foreign capital into an economy that until the late 1970s had been embedded into a Maoist society with chaotic institutions, no effective systems of law and administration, and a resource allocation mechanism based mainly on physical planning. The adjustments required on both sides were

Table 14
FOREIGN CAPITAL IN
JOINT VENTURES
(billion U.S. $)

	Approved	Utilized
1979–87	25.64	10.37
1983	1.92	.91
1984	2.87	1.41
1985	6.33	1.96
1986	3.33	2.24
1987	3.68	1.90

Source: State Statistical Bureau.

substantial, and the Chinese have had to contend with the fact that, the Hong Kong investors apart, the options available to foreign investors in other countries have looked much more attractive.

The Chinese are still working to improve their absorptive capacity for foreign capital. They have formally made conditions more attractive, have endeavored to improve the relationship between foreign capital and the planning system and are now increasingly willing to allow foreign managements more or less complete independence. All this is vital because it was officially reported in December 1987 that one third of foreign investments were running at a loss and another third were hardly making any profit. Thus although there are strong underlying reasons for a successful partnership between China and foreign capital, to realize the potential gains the Chinese will certainly need to provide a far more effective framework than has been the case in the past.

SOCIALIST REPUBLIC OF VIETNAM

The victory of North Vietnam was the beginning of a disastrous phase in the development of the Vietnamese economy. Apart from the effects of the

Table 15
STRUCTURE OF FOREIGN INVESTMENT
BY CATEGORY, 1986
(percentage shares)

Equity joint venture	41.3
Contractual joint venture	40.8
Joint developmental projects	2.4
Wholly foreign owned	.6
Compensation trade	9.4
Total value	U.S. $3.33 billion

Table 16
ECONOMIC INDICATORS FOR VIETNAM

	National income	Food output (million metric tons)	Trade balance (billion U.S. $)
1975	100	11.6	n.a.
1976	115	13.5	−0.61
1980	113	14.4	−1.18
1984	144	17.9	−1.23
1986	n.a.	18.5	−1.77
1987	n.a.	17.4 est.	n.a.

Source: Data supplied by T. Kimura, Institute of Developing Economies, Tokyo.

war itself, the economy of the former South Vietnam was adversely affected by the communist takeover and the attempt to impose Soviet style economic planning and control. As early as 1975 basic food rations were reduced from 18 kgs to 13 kgs per month—a level below most measures of subsistence. As Table 16 indicates, between 1976 and 1980, however, national income is estimated to have declined in absolute terms. According to the best available estimates, national income fell by three percent while population continued to grow at about two percent a year.

In September 1979 a new effort was made to remove the worst effects of central planning. This probably reflected the influence of Tran Phuong, an economist who believes in incentives and who began to become influential at that time. In spite of these efforts, serious economic difficulties were reported to be persisting between 1979 and 1982. National income and output picked up somewhat in 1981, but consumption tensions were revealed by the fact that cloth rations were reduced from 7 m. to 3 m. per person and availability of sugar became a chronic problem.

During the mid-1980s agriculture did improve steadily. A more flexible system of planning was introduced that contained a mixture of tax, quota and above-quota purchases by the state. The incentives embodied in this quota system were an important factor in this improvement. In 1983 total food output is estimated to have been 17 million metric tons (mmt), of which 14.73 were rice. Government procurement in that year was estimated at 3.75 mmt—considered to be a satisfactory outcome. Nonetheless, a rice target of 18 mmt was set; it was based on calorie intake of 1800 per person, still not a high figure in terms of other Asian economies, but a great improvement since the mid-1970s. Anxiety continued at this time about the growth of population that, in spite of Malthusian food constraints, was estimated to be growing at 2.4 percent a year.

By 1986 the 18 mmt level for total food output had been reached, but in 1987 food output was estimated to have fallen by three percent, which may be an underestimate. The ambitious rice target has never been achieved.

The Vietnamese food problem is exacerbated by the fact that the Mekong Delta is the main rice area and there are great difficulties in getting the necessary regional transfers of output to the north. The situation in the nonagricultural economy in 1986 remained very poor. Output was low, inflation very high and an external debt of US $6 billion could not be serviced. Without Soviet and other aid complete collapse would have occurred.

In 1986 a new round of reforms began, a number of them modeled on China, which the Vietnamese are watching closely in spite of their hostile political relations. In the reform, central planning was relaxed, managerial autonomy increased and some private activities encouraged. Early signs suggest that the reforms are having a positive effect but real progress is bound to be a matter of years. Meanwhile inflation continues and unemployment is very high. In 1985 the black market value of the dong was 370 to the dollar; by 1987 the figure was 1300 to the dollar.

Vietnam continues to trade with Japan, Singapore, Thailand and Hong Kong, as well as with Eastern European countries. Japan is the main noncommunist partner, selling food processing and textile machinery, and buying seafood and coal. Some slight interest has been expressed by foreigners in direct investment, but by the end of the 1980s no serious commitments had been made.

In short, the Vietnamese per capita income remains very low—lower than China's, for example. Demographic growth continues and a high rate of inflation reflects the breakdown of the management of the economy. Some slow progress has been made since 1980 and may continue if reforms are consolidated. But continued population growth means ever greater pressure on the economy and further serious crises seem likely.

DEMOCRATIC PEOPLE'S REPUBLIC OF KOREA

North Korea's economic relationships with China and the Soviet Union have been shaping influences on the economic policies it has adopted during most of the period following the Korean War. In recent years its government has, however, been largely impervious to the kind of radical reformist pressures that have had such a dramatic impact on its neighbors' economies. Some signs of an "opening door" policy have been apparent in official calls for expanded economic cooperation (including the establishment of joint ventures) and assistance from the West and Japan. North Korea has also shown a genuine interest in maintaining an economy dialogue with South Korea. But there is no evidence that such initiatives are the prelude to more far-reaching reforms in domestic economic management. For the time being, the North Korean economy continues most closely to resemble the Maoist model that prevailed in China until the late 1970s; a model characterized by a strategy of economic development centered on the expansion of heavy industry, highly-centralized controls over production and distribution, advocacy of self-reliance (*juch'e* in Korean parlance) and ideological motivation.

Such factors offer clues to both the earlier economic successes of North

Korea and its more recent disappointing performance. Until the 1960s centralized controls, combined with a very high investment rate, enabled rapid economic growth to take place. Structural change was also profound: between 1946 and 1965 industry's share of national income rose from 16.8 percent to 63.5 percent, while that of agriculture fell from about two thirds to under 20 percent. But subsequently the constraints imposed by such a high degree of centralization and control have imposed a heavy cost in terms of inefficiency and the former growth rates have not been sustained. Thus, there is little doubt that the outcome of the latest development plan (1978–1984) has proved disappointing. North Korea's economic difficulties have also been exacerbated by its massive defense orientation. According to some sources, almost one quarter of the country's GNP is allocated to the military, and its armed forces total well over 800,000 men—equivalent to almost 10 percent of the total labor force.

The priority sectors identified in the most recent seven-year plan were agriculture, energy and raw materials, and transport and communications. No less important than the physical targets were the demands for qualitative improvements: for the modernization of production and management methods and the scientific application of up-to-date techniques. Such an emphasis might have betokened a reappraisal of North Korea's economic condition and capabilities. But in reality, the failure to devise specific measures to break existing bottlenecks and promote technical progress has led to results that were less than impressive. Neither the planned growth of net material product nor of industry seems to have been achieved. And production targets for a number of agricultural and industrial products remain unfulfilled.

North Korea's natural resource endowment suggests a comparative advantage in the production of industrial, rather than agricultural, products. Although the country contains 55 percent of the total surface area of the Korean peninsula, only about 20 percent of it is arable (about 2.1 million hectares). Further, prevailing climatic conditions make it impossible to remedy this arable deficiency through the extension of multiple cropping. The normal pattern is that a piece of land supports just one harvest a year.

Paralleling the experience of China, North Korea's agriculture was rapidly collectivized during the 1950s. The basic organizational framework established then has persisted to the present day and collective units now farm 90 percent of the cultivated area (the remainder are under the control of state farms). Within this framework a significant degree of modernization has been achieved, including electrification, the widespread use of tractors, intensive application of chemical fertilizers and the mechanization of certain critical farm operations (notably, rice planting).

The agricultural sector is overwhelmingly dominated by crop farming, and this, in turn, by grain production. By far the most important cereal is rice (accounting for 42 percent of total grain output), followed by corn (20 percent) and sweet potatoes (13 percent). Current levels of production seem sufficient to provide a satisfactory caloric intake for the subsisting population, although evidence suggests that the consumption of foods other than grain is very low. As of the mid-1980s the average production of grain

1403

(unprocessed) per person in the total population was around 650 kg; the corresponding figure per person in the agricultural labor force was in excess of 3,000 kg. Even allowing for an element of exaggeration in official statistics, such figures may indicate the impact of modernization, although it must also be borne in mind that unlike its Asian neighbors, North Korea enjoys a relatively low population density and consequently less pressure upon arable land.

In contrast to innately unfavorable agricultural conditions, North Korea possesses some 80 to 90 percent of major mineral deposits in the Korean peninsula, including rich deposits of coal, iron ore, lead, zinc, and others. The mineral resource base is probably potentially adequate to support an advanced and diversified industrial economy. This potential has, however, not yet been fully realized, in part because existing methods of resource utilization and management have proved insufficient to meet the demands placed upon them by North Korea's developmental goals.

The most critical resource constraint is that of energy. In the absence of native oil deposits, North Korea's petroleum needs must be imported (from China and the Soviet Union). A further corollary is that coal remains the source of about three quarters of North Korea's primary energy supplies— a much higher degree of dependence than that of most developed industrial economies. Against this background it is clear why the inability to raise productivity in the coal industry to levels commensurate with the targeted rates of industrial growth has been such a signal failure in recent years.

Given the very high accumulation rate sustained by the North Korean economy over several decades and the allocation of most available funds to heavy industry, levels of consumption have been severely squeezed. In the early 1980s there were signs that government leaders might be prepared to relax previous priorities and raise the share of light industrial investment in order to improve living standards. But the momentum has not been maintained and it is reasonable to view the entire period since the Korean War as one in which investment has overwhelmingly been directed toward the expansion of the heavy industrial base. The focus of this expansion has been the machine-building industry whose contribution to industry's gross value output is now more than one third.

If North Korea's industrial growth record in the 1980s has not been unimpressive, many planned targets have nevertheless remained unfulfilled. Technological deficiencies, exacerbated by increasingly outmoded methods of organization and management, have been the main contributory factors. A further constraint is that imposed by an inadequate infrastructure, in particular, transportation capacity falls far short of the needs of the further expansion of industry.

With such a heavy emphasis on self-reliance, it is not surprising that in both absolute and relative terms, North Korea's trade volume has remained small. For example, in the early 1980s the combined value of imports and exports was no more than $2.8 billion—a mere fraction of that of South Korea. The government of North Korea has used trade to fill the gaps which its domestic resources cannot meet—in other words, to provide for urgently needed development items. However, the decision, taken in the early 1970s, to accelerate the purchase of plant and equipment from the West and Japan generated a large trade deficit and attendant debt problems. Indeed, in 1976 North Korea was forced to default on its foreign debt—the first communist country ever to do so. Such difficulties have compelled the government to follow a more cautious approach toward foreign imports. At present, the chief trading partners of North Korea are the Soviet Union, China and Japan.

FURTHER READING

Joint Economic Committee, U.S. Congress. *China Under the Four Modernizations.* Washington, D.C.: Government Printing Office, 1982.

Joint Economic Committee, U.S. Congress. *The Chinese Economy in the Eighties.* Washington, D.C.: Government Printing Office, 1986.

Kraus, Willy. *Economic Development and Social Change in the People's Republic of China.* New York: Springer-Verlag, 1982.

Lardy, Nicholas R. *Agriculture in China's Modern Economic Development.* Cambridge and New York: Cambridge University Press, 1983.

Liu Suinian and Wu Qungan, eds. *China's Socialist Economy: An Outline History, 1949–1984.* Beijing: Beijing Review, 1986.

Rawski, Thomas G. *China's Transition to Industrialism: Producer Goods and Economic Development in the Twentieth Century.* Ann Arbor: University of Michigan Press, 1980.

Riskin, Carl. *China's Political Economy: The Quest for Development Since 1949.* Oxford and New York: Oxford University Press, 1987.

State Statistical Bureau. *Statistical Yearbook of China.* English ed. Annual.

Tidrick, Gene, and Chen Jiyuan, eds., *China's Industrial Reform.* New York: Oxford University Press for the World Bank, 1987.

Walker, Kenneth R. *Food Grain Procurement and Consumption in China.* Cambridge and New York: Cambridge University Press, 1984.

SOUTH ASIAN ECONOMIC DEVELOPMENT

TERENCE J. BYRES

THE ECONOMIES OF SOUTH ASIA

The seven countries of South Asia—India, Bangladesh, Pakistan, Nepal, Sri Lanka, Bhutan and the Maldives—all fall into the World Bank category of "low-income economies." This category encompasses the world's 42 poorest nations: that is, those with per capita annual incomes of U.S. $400 or less as of 1985. Indeed, three of the South Asian economies—Bangladesh, Bhutan and Nepal—are, by this measure, among the world's seven poorest countries. In each of the nations of South Asia awareness of the very low levels of per capita income, resulting from economic backwardness, has given rise to efforts to secure economic development and raise income. All have embraced a form of economic planning, at least on paper. The roots of that awareness are deepest in India and the attempts to plan economic development are the most sophisticated there. Nevertheless India's highly developed plan formulation has never been matched by a high degree of success in plan implementation. There are significant differences in South Asia concerning the methods needed to develop.

These countries also display a remarkable variety of population size, geographic area, economic and social characteristics, physical features and political systems. They also differ in the results they have achieved on the economic front. Their economic variety can be seen in Tables 1 and 2.

The broad indicators of Table 1 reveal that the countries of South Asia range as follows:

- In *population size,* in 1985, from India with a population of 765.1 million (second in the world to China) to Bhutan with 1.2 million and Maldives with 182,000
- In *area* (excluding Maldives), from India's vast, subcontinental 3.3 million sq. km. to Bhutan's landlocked mountain kingdom of 47,000 sq. km. and Sri Lanka's island of 66,000 sq. km.
- In *per capita* GNP, from Bangladesh with $155 and Bhutan and Nepal each with $160, to Pakistan and Sri Lanka each with $380

Table 1
THE ECONOMIES OF SOUTH ASIA:
SELECTED INDICATORS

Country	Population Millions 1985	Population Average annual growth rate % (1980–85)	Area (thousand sq. km.)	GNP per capita U.S. dollars (1985)	GNP per capita Average annual growth rate % (1965–85)	Life expectancy at birth (years, 1985)	Foreign trade ratio % (1981)	Development assistance as % GNP (1985)
(1)	(2)	(3)	(4)	(5)	(6)	(7)	(8)	(9)
India	765.1	2.2	3,288	270	1.7	56	8.5	0.7
Bangladesh	100.6	2.6	144	144	0.4	51	15.3	7.1
Pakistan	96.2	3.1	804	380	2.6	51	18.0	2.2
Nepal	16.5	2.4	141	160	0.1	47	13.9	10.1
Sri Lanka	15.8	1.4	66	380	2.9	70	38.5	8.2
Bhutan	1.2	2.2	47	160	n.a.	44	n.a.	12.9
Maldives	0.182	n.a.	n.a.	290	1.9	53	n.a.	n.a.

Notes: n.a. indicates that figures are not available. Column 8, the foreign trade ratio, is the average of exports and imports expressed as a proportion of GDP.

Sources: Columns 2, 4, 5, 6 and 7: World Bank, *World Development Report, 1987* (New York: Oxford University Press, 1987), Table 1, p. 202. Column 3: Ibid., Table 27, p. 254. Column 9: Ibid., Table 22, p. 244. Column 8: calculated from data in World Bank, *World Tables*, Vol. 1, 3rd ed. (Baltimore and London: The Johns Hopkins University Press, 1983), p. 505.

Table 2
THE ECONOMIES OF SOUTH ASIA: FURTHER INDICATORS

Indicator (1)	Pakistan (2)	Bangladesh (3)	Sri Lanka (4)	Nepal (5)	Bhutan (6)	India (7)
Average annual growth rate of production %						
a) Agriculture 1965–80	3.3	1.5	2.7	—	—	2.8
1980–85	2.1	2.8	4.0	—	—	2.7
b) Industry 1965–80	6.2	3.8	5.1	—	—	4.1
1980–85	8.8	4.7	4.2	—	—	5.4
Structure of production: distribution of GDP %						
1965 Agriculture	40	53	28	65	—	47
Industry	20	11	21	11	—	22
Services	40	36	51	23	—	31
1985 Agriculture	25	50	27	62	50	31
Industry	28	14	26	12	18	27
Services	47	36	46	26	32	41
Structure of labor force %						
1965 Agriculture	60	84	56	94	95	73

Industry	18	5	14	2	2	12
Services	22	11	30	4	4	15
1980 Agriculture	55	75	53	93	92	70
Industry	16	6	14	1	3	13
Services	30	19	33	7	5	17
Average annual growth rate of merchandise trade %						
Exports 1965–80	4.3	—	0.5	−2.3	—	3.7
1980–85	2.4	7.1	7.3	8.4	—	4.6
Imports 1965–80	0.5	—	−1.1	3.0	—	1.6
1980–85	3.9	3.1	1.5	7.8	—	2.2
Crude birth and death rates per 1,000 in 1985						
Birth rate	44	40	25	43	43	33
Death rate	15	15	6	18	21	12
Total long-term external debt service (public and private) in 1985 as % of						
GNP	3.2	1.3	4.1	0.5	—	1.4
Exports	30.0	16.7	14.7	4.0	—	12.7

Note: The relevant data are not available for Maldives.

Source: World Bank, *World Development Report, 1987* (New York: Oxford University Press, 1987), Tables 2, 3, 10, 18, 28, 32, pp. 204, 206, 220, 236, 256, 264.

- In *life expectancy at birth,* from Bhutan's 44 and Nepal's 47 to Sri Lanka's 70;
- In *average annual growth of per capita GNP* (excluding Bhutan), between 1965 and 1985, from Nepal's 0.1 percent and Bangladesh's 0.4 percent to Pakistan's 2.6 percent and Sri Lanka's 2.9 percent
- In *average annual growth of population* (excluding Maldives), between 1965 and 1980, from Bhutan's 1.5 percent and Sri Lanka's 1.8 percent to Bangladesh's 2.7 percent and Pakistan's rapid 3.1 percent
- In *foreign trade orientation* (excluding Maldives and Bhutan), from India's small foreign trade ratio (a feature of very large economies) of 8.5 percent to Sri Lanka's 38.5 percent

But such variation excludes neat generalizations. These countries vary in many other ways. India has a large and diversified industrial structure with an established heavy industry sector (steel, machine tools, chemicals, heavy engineering, and so forth) and a range of consumer goods industries. It is ranked as the tenth industrial power in the world, and in technology it is among the world's top six in its ability to manufacture complex equipment. No other South Asian economy can match this. Maldives, by contrast, has a precarious economic base, relying heavily on fishing, tourism and shipping services. Sri Lanka has a large plantation sector. Plantations exist elsewhere in South Asia but without the degree of dominance found in Sri Lanka. Bhutan has not shifted much from self-sufficiency and barter, while commercialization has penetrated large parts of the economies of the other six countries.

In December 1985 the seven countries of South Asia formed the South Asian Association for Regional Cooperation (SAARC) as a means of encouraging regional economic development. Economic cooperation had not been in evidence in the region previously. It remains to be seen whether SAARC is capable of becoming more than a token presence.

India's size and diversity dictate that it receive particular attention. Its population constituted 76.9 percent of the region's total in 1985 and its area 73 percent of the total area (excluding the Maldives). Indeed, within India the state of Uttar Pradesh has a population well in excess of that of the next largest country in the region, Bangladesh (123.1 million in 1986, compared with Bangladesh's 100.6 million in 1985). Of the other 21 Indian states (excluding the Union Territories), 13 have larger populations than Sri Lanka and Nepal, at least nine of them with double the population of these two countries.

India itself displays great variety. One of its distinguished historians has observed that the "endless variety is striking, often incongruous. Costume, speech, the physical appearance of the people, customs, standards of living, food, climate, geographical features all offer the greatest possible differences.[1] India includes differing patterns of economic development and contains areas of significant economic success as well as persistent stagnation.

[1] D. D. Kosambi, *The Culture and Civilization of Ancient India in Historical Outline* (New Delhi: Vikas Publishing House, 1970), 1.

Something of India's regional variety is shown in Table 3. Its features encompass the following examples of diversity:

- *Area.* From the massive states of Madhya Pradesh at the heart of the country and Rajasthan in the northwest with 443,000 and 342,000 sq. km., respectively, to narrow Sikkim (a Himalayan kingdom annexed in 1975 to become India's 22nd state, and Tripura with 7,100 and 10,500 sq. km., respectively
- *Population size.* Huge Uttar Pradesh (123.1 million in 1986) at one extreme and tiny Nagaland and Sikkim at the other (0.9 and 0.4 million, respectively)
- *Population growth.* Kerala growing relatively slowly at 19.2 percent over the decade 1971–81 and bigger states such as Assam, Rajasthan, Haryana, Gujarat, and Jammu and Kashmir growing quickly at more than 27 percent
- *Levels of per capita income.* Punjab, Maharashtra, Haryana and Gujarat in the vanguard with about Rs. 3,000 or more per capita in 1984–85, and Bihar and Orissa trailing far behind with about Rs. 1,500 or less
- *Degree and speed of agricultural development.* Punjab, Maharashtra, Haryana, Gujarat and Uttar Pradesh standing out with grain production growing (between 1970 and 1985) at about 3.5 percent a year or more; production in the first two expanding at almost six percent; very slow growth (under one percent a year), by contrast, in Bihar, West Bengal and Himachal Pradesh, and negative growth in Kerala
- *Extent and speed of industrialization.* Relatively high levels of industrialization in Gujarat, Haryana, Maharashtra, Tamil Nadu and West Bengal (all with daily factory employment of more than 15 people per 1,000 in 1983), and low levels in Assam, Bihar, Jammu and Kashmir, Orissa, Rajasthan, and Uttar Pradesh (all with under five per 1,000). Industrial growth between 1977 and 1983 relatively fast in Andhra Pradesh, Haryana, Jammu and Kashmir, Karnataka, Kerala, Punjab, and Tamil Nadu (all at more than six percent a year) and slow in Himachal Pradesh, Rajasthan and West Bengal (at under two percent)
- *Literacy rates.* From 70.4 percent in Kerala to under 30 percent in Andhra Pradesh, Assam, Himachal Pradesh, Madhya Pradesh, Rajasthan and Uttar Pradesh

Moreover, within the states of India there is other substantive variation. For example, eastern and western Uttar Pradesh stand in sharp distinction: the former is caught in semifeudal torpor while the latter is a significant and progressive area of India. In this essay concentration is focused first and largely on India and the features of its economic development since 1947. The other 6 economies of South Asia are then discussed more briefly.

THE INDIAN ECONOMY AT INDEPENDENCE; ECONOMIC STRATEGIES AND PERFORMANCE SINCE 1950

The Indian economy at independence

At independence in 1947 the Indian economy was characterized by an extremely low level of per capita income (Rs. 248 at 1948–49 prices or Rs.

Table 3
THE STATE AND TERRITORIES OF INDIA:
SELECTED INDICATORS

States/territories	Population		Area	Per capita	Irrigation
	Millions (estimate) 1986	Decennial growth % (1971–81)	(thousand sq. km.)	NDP (current prices) Rs. (1984–85)	ratio % (1981–82)
(1)	(2)	(3)	(4)	(5)	(6)
Andhra Pradesh	58.8	23.1	275.1	1,996	32.6
Assam	22.4	36.1	78.4	1,821	21.1
Bihar	77.7	24.1	173.9	1,385	38.2
Gujarat	37.7	27.7	196.0	2,997	22.3
Haryana	14.8	28.8	44.2	3,296	61.4
Himachal Pradesh	4.7	23.7	55.7	2,316	16.1
Jammu and Kashmir	6.7	29.7	222.2	2,075	42.9
Karnataka	41.4	26.8	191.8	2,047	11.1
Kerala	27.8	19.2	38.9	2,196	11.1
Madhya Pradesh	58.2	25.3	443.4	1,716	12.8
Maharashtra	69.7	24.5	307.7	3,232	10.5
Manipur	1.6	32.5	22.3	2,200	n.a.
Meghalaya	1.5	32.0	22.4	1,727	n.a.
Nagaland	0.9	50.1	16.6	n.a.	n.a.
Orissa	28.8	20.2	155.7	1,534	19.8
Punjab	18.5	23.9	50.4	3,835	81.0
Rajasthan	39.2	33.0	342.2	1,838	18.6
Sikkim	0.4	50.8	7.1	n.a.	n.a.
Tamil Nadu	52.6	17.5	130.1	2,070	47.2
Tripura	2.3	31.9	10.5	n.a.	n.a.
Uttar Pradesh	123.1	25.5	294.4	1,764	55.2
West Bengal	60.3	23.2	88.8	2,485	26.8
Union Territories	12.0	n.a.	119.5	n.a.	n.a.
INDIA	761.1	25.0	3,287.3	2,355	28.0

Notes: n.a. indicates that figures are not available. Union Territories include the following: Andaman and Nicobar; Arunchal Pradesh; Chandigarh; Dadra and Nagar Haveli; Delhi; Goa, Daman and Diu; Lakshadweep; Mizoram; Pondicherry. Column 6, the irrigation ratio, is the proportion of cropped area that is irrigated. Column 8 relates to Indian food grain production, the overwhelmingly dominant element in total agricultural production.
Sources: Columns 2 and 4, S. Muthiah, ed., *A Social and Economic Atlas of India* (Delhi: Oxford University Press, 1987), Tables 2 and 5, pp. 4 and 16. Columns

Annual sectoral growth %		Literacy rate %			Daily factory
Industry	Agriculture	Total	Male	Female	employment per
(1977–83)	(food grains)		(1981)		1,000 population
	(1970–85)				(1983)
(7)	(8)	(9)	(10)	(11)	(12)
6.7	3.24	29.94	39.26	20.39	10.1
5.8	1.90	n.a.	n.a.	n.a.	3.3
5.1	0.55	26.20	38.11	13.62	5.8
3.0	3.44	43.70	54.44	32.30	19.3
6.6	3.98	36.14	48.20	22.27	15.7
−1.9	0.68	42.48	53.19	31.46	n.a.
6.7	2.30	26.67	36.29	15.88	3.5
6.4	1.43	38.46	48.81	27.71	13.9
9.0	−0.39	70.42	75.26	65.73	11.0
3.4	1.63	27.87	39.49	15.53	8.3
2.9	5.97	47.18	58.79	34.79	18.2
n.a.	n.a.	41.35	53.29	29.06	n.a.
n.a.	n.a.	34.08	37.89	30.08	n.a.
n.a.	n.a.	42.57	50.06	33.89	n.a.
4.2	1.50	34.23	47.10	21.12	3.8
7.6	5.91	40.86	47.16	33.69	14.0
2.0	1.31	24.38	36.30	11.42	4.9
n.a.	n.a.	34.05	43.95	22.20	n.a.
9.5	−0.71	46.76	58.26	34.99	15.9
n.a.	n.a.	42.12	51.70	32.00	n.a.
5.7	3.93	27.16	38.76	14.04	4.5
0.1	0.46	40.94	50.67	30.25	15.8
n.a.	n.a.	n.a.	n.a.	n.a.	n.a.
3.0	2.66	36.23	46.89	24.82	10.4

3, 6, 7, 12, Tata Services Limited, *A Statistical Outline of India, 1986–87* (Bombay: Tata Press, 1986), Tables 3 and 25, pp. 7, 8, 34. Columns 5, 9, 10, 11, Government of India, Central Statistical Organisation, Department of Statistics, Ministry of Planning, *Statistical Pocket Book, India, 1986* (New Delhi, 1987), Tables 18 and 141, pp. 25 and 194. Column 8, S. Mahendradev, "Growth and Instability in Foodgrains Production: An Inter-State Analysis," Table 1, p. A–83, *Economic and Political Weekly* 22, no. 39 (September 26, 1987).

466 at 1970–71 prices) and showed few signs of dynamism. Income and assets were very unequally distributed and poverty was intense and widespread.

It was an economy dominated by agriculture: in 1951 83 percent of all Indians lived in rural areas; 69 percent of the male workforce was in the primary sector and 56 percent of net domestic product was generated there. Moreover, it was a backward agriculture that displayed very low yields (per acre and per head) and was virtually stagnant. Mechanization was almost totally absent; modern inputs had almost nowhere been applied; and, despite the much vaunted creation of irrigation facilities by the British, the irrigation ratio (the proportion of total cropped area irrigated) was only 17 percent.

In 1947 India had a tiny modern industrial sector. In 1951 only 13 percent of the male labor force was in the secondary sector, with 17 percent of net domestic product produced there. Modern industry was represented by a group of largely consumer goods industries (especially textiles). Although there was full knowledge of rich deposits of iron ore and coal, which could have been the basis of a heavy goods sector, Indian industry had virtually no capital goods component.

Indeed, the Indian economy at that time displayed a kind of stasis: the structure of the labor force (the proportions in agriculture and industry) had remained stubbornly constant since the beginning of the 20th century, although there had been some shift of the industrial labor force into modern industries. Capital accumulation was very limited, and net saving and investment rates were diminutive at around 6 percent. These showed no signs of increase. A considerable proportion of the existing surplus went into unproductive and speculative activity, with trading and money lending especially important.

At independence India, like other countries with very large populations, had a relatively small foreign trade ratio (the proportion of imports and exports to GDP) of less than 10 percent. In 1955 it was still only 7.8 percent. This did not signify the unimportance or irrelevance of foreign trade for the Indian economy. On the contrary, the capacity to import (for example, food in times of shortage, consumer goods not manufactured in India or capital goods for a variety of purposes) was of considerable importance. Those imports had to be paid for in foreign exchange that needed to be earned, largely through exports.

In 1950–1951 the structure of Indian imports was as follows: 26 percent were capital goods, the largest component of which was machinery (14.6 percent); 35 percent were raw materials and intermediate goods with cotton, raw jute and mineral oils of particular significance (respectively 16.2 percent, 8.8 percent and 4.4 percent); and 22 percent were consumer goods, dominated by foodgrains (13 percent). India, an overwhelmingly agrarian economy with sown acreage largely for good crops (76 percent in 1950), was at that time critically dependent upon imports of foodgrains.

Exports were dominated by tea, cotton goods and jute manufactures constituting 52 percent of the total (respectively 13.4 percent, 19.6 percent and 19 percent). Hides and skins, black pepper, tobacco and vegetable oils were also of some importance constituting 15.5 percent of the total. There was no evidence at that time of a dynamic export sector.

In 1950–1951 there was considerable private foreign investment in India, some 75 percent of which was British. Having previously built the railways and extended irrigation facilities, British capital was concentrated, in an obviously "colonial" way: in extractive industries (as opposed to manufacturing industries), in processing for export, in international trade, and in related ancillary industries. Statistically this meant that 25 percent was in tea and jute (together providing one third of Indian exports), 17 percent in trading, 8 percent in finance and management, 6 percent in utilities (mainly electricity), 6 percent in transportation (mainly shipping) and only 20 percent in manufacturing other than jute. Within the Indian business community there was some hostility toward foreign capital inasmuch as Indian capital had been discriminated against and dominated by British capital. But as independence approached, this hostility began to be modified somewhat, at least among India's stronger capitalists.

A public sector did exist, but it was small. It contained only five units in 1950–1951, and was the locus of some 23 percent of total gross capital formation (public and private) in India. That it represented such a high proportion of the total does not reflect any significance in its absolute size but, rather, the meager amount of capital formation generated by the private sector. Moreover, it was a public sector without strategic economic significance at that time: an amalgam of mainly nonmanufacturing enterprises that were the product of the pre-1947 colonial state concerned with irrigation, mail service and telegraphs, railways and ordnance factories.

The population grew between 1941 and 1951 at an annual compound rate of 1.25 percent: the outcome of a very high birthrate in 1950–1951 of 39.9 and a high deathrate of 27.4. Life expectancy at birth was 32.5 years for males and 31.7 years for females. The overall literacy rate was a very low 16.6 percent with 25 percent for males and 7.9 percent for females. For further statistics see Tables 4 and 5.

Economic planning in colonial India
Those who took formal political power in India in 1947—the Congress party under the leadership of Jawaharlal Nehru—were acutely aware of India's striking economic backwardness and of the crushing poverty that condemned the majority of the Indian people to the barest subsistence. Food scarcity was ever present and the specter of famine never far away: the great Bengal famine of 1943 had killed some three million people. Indian nationalists saw poverty and economic backwardness as the product of colonialism. There had been considerable discussion as to how these two might be eradicated but nearly all agreed that an essential prerequisite was the departure of the British and an independent India.

When the British went, poverty and economic backwardness did not go with them. Economic development was regarded as necessary if India were to cope with poverty. Development was perceived as crucial, moreover, if India were to survive as a political unit, defend itself adequately, and participate fully in world politics: in short, if India were to become a modern

Table 4

LONG-TERM GROWTH IN INDIA, 1950–51 TO 1985–86:
SELECTED INDICATORS

Indicator	1950–51	1960–61	1970–71	1980–81	1985–86	Growth rate 1950–51 to 1980–81	Growth rate 1950–51 to 1985–86
(1)	(2)	(3)	(4)	(5)	(6)	(7)	(8)
NNP at factor cost (1970–71 prices) Rs. crores	16,731	24,250	34,235	47,414	—	3.5	n.a.
Per capita NNP (1970–71 prices) Rs.	466.0	558.8	632.8	698.3	—	1.4	n.a.
Net domestic savings (% of NDP)	6.6	9.3	11.8	17.8	16.7	—	—
(revised series)				(13.5)	(13.3)	—	—
Net domestic investment (% of NDP)	6.4	12.7	12.9	19.6	18.6	—	—
(revised series)				(15.2)	(15.9)	—	—
Index of agricultural production (Base: triennium ending 1969–70)	58.5	86.7	111.5	135.3	161.7	2.8	3.0
Irrigation ratio (gross area irrigated % of total cropped area)	17.1	18.3	23.0	28.8	30.5	—	—
Index of industrial production (Base: 1980–81)	18.3	36.2	65.3	100.0	142.1	5.8	6.0
Imports (Rs. millions)	6,500	11,214	16,340	124,650	198,000	10.3	10.2
Exports (Rs. millions)	6,010	6,329	15,352	66,750	113,000	8.3	8.7
Availability per capita per day of food grains (grams)							
(a) cereals	324.9	399.7	417.6	416.2	434.2	0.8	0.8
(b) pulses	57.4	65.3	51.2	37.5	41.9	–1.0	–0.7
(c) total	382.3	468.7	468.8	453.7	476.1	0.6	0.6
Population (millions)	361.2	442.4	551.3	690.1	766.1	2.2	2.2
Birth rate (per 1,000)	39.9	41.7	36.9	33.9	32.5	—	—

Death rate (per 1,000)	27.4	22.8	14.9	12.5	11.2	—
Life expectancy at birth (in years)						
(a) Male	32.5	41.9	46.4	54.1	n.a.	—
(b) Female	31.7	40.6	44.7	54.8	n.a.	—
Literacy rate (percentage)						
(a) Overall	16.6	24.0	29.5	36.2	n.a.	—
(b) Male	25.0	34.4	39.5	46.9	n.a.	—
(c) Female	7.9	13.0	18.7	24.8	n.a.	—
Public Sector						
(a) Number of units	5	48	97	185	221	—
(b) Investment (Rs. crores)	29	953	4,682	21,102	42,811	—
(c) Number of employees (000s)	n.a.	185	660	1,839	2,107	—
(d) Gross capital formation % of total in India	23	44	39	44	51	—

Notes: n.a. indicates not available. Growth rates are compound growth rates calculated from the data in the table. The long-term growth rate figures are calculated for 1950–51 to 1985–86, rather than 1950–51 to 1986–87. This is partly because a full run of figures for 1986–87 is not available, and partly because 1986–87 was an unusually bad year in many cases and an obvious departure from the trend. The net domestic savings rate, net investment rate, imports and exports figures were unavailable for 1986–87. The agricultural production and net availability of food grains figures for 1986–87 were unusually low. The 1985–86 irrigation ratio and public-sector figures are actually for 1983–84. The 1985–86 figures are not available. The 1981 literacy figures exclude Assam. It is not possible to calculate a growth rate for net national product and per capita net national product for 1950–51 to 1985–86. A series using the same base year prices was not available for 1950–51 to 1985–86.

Source: With the exception of the literacy rate, irrigation ratio and public-sector figures, Government of India, Ministry of Finance (Economic Division), *Economic Survey, 1987–88* (New Delhi: Controller of Publications, 1988), Appendix, page S–1. For literacy rates, Tata Services Limited, *Statistical Outline of India, 1978* (Bombay, 1977), p. 29 and *Statistical Outline of India, 1986–87* (Bombay, 1986), p. 33. For irrigation ratio, 1950–51, Government of India, Ministry of Finance, Department of Economic Affairs, *India: Pocket Book of Economic Information* (New Delhi, 1964), Table 4.4, p. 36; and for 1960–61 and the other years, *Statistical Outline of India, 1986–87*, p. 58. For public sector, (a), (b) and (c), Tata, *Statistical Outline of India, 1982*, p. 82; *Statistical Outline of India, 1986–87*, p. 83. For (d), 1950–51, 1960–61 and 1970–71, Ram N. Lal, *Capital Formation and its Financing in India* (Bombay: Allied Publishers, 1977), Table 6.1, p. 107; and 1980–81 and 1985–86, *Statistical Outline of India, 1984*, p. 26, and *Statistical Outline of India, 1986–87*, p. 29.

Table 5
RURAL-URBAN DISTRIBUTION AND SECTORAL SHARE IN NET DOMESTIC PRODUCT AND MALE WORK FORCE IN INDIA, 1951 TO 1985

Category (1)	1951 (2)	1961 (3)	1971 (4)	1981 (5)	1985 (6)
Rural-urban distribution (percentage share)					
Rural population	82.7	82	80.1	76.7	n.a.
Urban population	17.3	18	19.9	23.3	n.a.
TOTAL	100.0	100.0	100.0	100.0	n.a.
Sectoral share in net domestic product (%)					
Primary	56.1	51.2	44.7	42.5	37.4
Secondary	17.3	20.1	22.9	21.1	23.0
Tertiary	26.6	28.7	32.5	36.4	39.6
TOTAL	100.0	100.0	100.0	100.0	100.0
Sectoral share in male work force (%)					
Primary	69.1	68.0	69.7	65.6	n.a.
Secondary	12.6	12.7	12.0	14.5	n.a.
Tertiary	18.3	19.3	18.3	19.9	n.a.
TOTAL	100.0	100.0	100.0	100.0	n.a.

Notes: n.a. indicates not available. Where the columns do not add up to 100, the difference is due to rounding. The figures for sectoral share in net domestic product are for 1950–51, 1960–61, 1970–71, 1980–81 and 1984–85. These relate to net domestic product at constant prices. For 1950–51, 1960–61 and 1970–71 they are at 1960–61 prices; and for 1980–81 and 1984–85 they are at 1970–71 prices. Figures for sectoral share in *male* work force are given because those for the full work force are not available. The primary sector relates largely to agriculture and includes forestry and fishing; the secondary sector covers mainly manufacturing industry, but includes mining and quarrying, construction and electricity, and gas and water supply; the tertiary sector covers services, including trade and commerce, banking and insurance, public administration, defense, hotels and restaurants, transport, etc.

Sources: Rural-urban distribution, for 1951 Tata Services Limited, *Statistical Outline of India, 1978* (Bombay, 1977), p. 29; for 1961, 1971 and 1981, Ibid., *Statistical Outline of India, 1986–87* (Bombay, 1986), p. 33. Sectoral share in net domestic product, for 1951, 1961 and 1971, V.K.R.V. Rao, *India's National Income, 1950–1980: An Analysis of Economic Growth and Change* (New Delhi: Sage Publications, 1983), p. 36; for 1981 and 1985, Tata Services Limited, *Statistical Outline of India, 1984* (Bombay, 1984), p. 18 and Ibid., *Statistical Outline of India, 1986–87,* p. 21. Sectoral share in male work force, for 1951 and 1961, Rao, *India's National Income,* p. 36; for 1971 and 1981, Sudha Deshpande and L. K. Deshpande, "Census of 1981 and the Structure of Employment," *Economic and Political Weekly* 20, no. 22 (June 1, 1985), p. 969.

power. Economic development would be capitalist. Despite much socialist rhetoric, there was never real doubt that economic development would be capitalist even if it were secured with considerable intervention by the state, by planning and by the creation of a large and economically strategic public sector.

There had been discussion of planned economic development before 1947, and there had even been a number of actual plans. In 1934 a plan prepared by M. Visvesvaraya (the dewan of the then princely state of Mysore) was published that placed great stress on the need for industrialization. In 1944 three private plans appeared: the Bombay plan, prepared by India's leading industrialists (a sign that capitalists were well aware of the need for industrial planning and state intervention); a people's plan, drawn up by M. N. Roy, one of India's earliest Marxist thinkers who had broken with the Indian communist party; and a Gandhian plan, produced by S. N. Agarwal (later known as Shriman Narayan). Also in 1944, somewhat belatedly, the imperial government formed a planning and development department (under Ardeshsir Dalal) and asked provincial governments to create planning organizations.

Following independence the government inaugurated a series of five-year plans (FYPs). Planning got under way with the start of the first FYP in 1951 (1951/52–55/56). With the seventh FYP (1985/86–1989/90) completed, the planning procedure begins its fifth decade. For a comprehensive look at selected indicators in India's five-year plans, see Table 6.

The performance of the Indian economy

In assessing the performance of the Indian economy since 1950 it is useful to observe three successive levels of aggregation. The first level is that of the individual five-year plans. The record of a FYP period points to weaknesses and strengths in the economy, problems of plan implementation and possible difficulties with respect to the chosen economic strategy. Formulation of a new FYP is an occasion for economic stocktaking and sometimes for new initiatives and changes in basic economic strategy.

The second level is that of longer subperiods. These become obvious as one examines the individual plan periods. During these subperiods persistent underlying trends and specific features of the economy may be detected giving an identity to the years in question. Between the subperiods changes in those trends and features may occur suggesting a new character.

Third, one may attempt an assessment of long-term growth and change over the whole period, from 1950 to 1987. Here attention is directed toward the overall rate of economic growth, the broad pattern of economic development that has emerged since 1950 and whether the economic transformation and structural change sought have been attained.

The First Three Plans

The first FYP (1951/52–1955/56) did not attempt to initiate any basic structural changes in the Indian economy. It was, for its time, a sophisticated document, underpinned by a Harrod-Domar model and written largely by the young and later eminent Indian economist, K. N. Raj. In essence

Table 6
INDIA'S FIVE-YEAR PLANS: SELECTED INDICATORS

Year and plan period	Net national product at factor cost (1970–71 prices)		Population (million)	Index of agricultural production (Base: 3 yr. ending 1969/70 = 100)	Index of industrial production (Base 1960 = 100)
	N.N.P. (Rs. crores)	Per capita N.N.P. (Rs.)			
(1)	(2)	(3)	(4)	(5)	(6)
1950–51 First Plan	16,731	466.0	361.2	58.5	52.0
1951–52	17,086	468.1	369.6	59.4	58.0
1952–53	17,699	475.8	376.0	62.9	60.0
1953–54	18,854	497.5	382.9	71.0	61.2
1954–55	19,328	500.7	390.2	72.2	65.4
1955–56	19,953	507.7	397.3	71.9	70.6
Growth rate	3.5	1.7	1.9	4.2	6.2
Second Plan					
1956–57	21,046	524.8	405.8	76.2	76.9
1957–58	20,587	503.3	414.3	70.8	80.0
1958–59	22,329	534.2	423.3	82.2	82.8
1959–60	22,676	532.3	432.7	80.1	89.8
1960–61	24,250	558.8	442.4	86.7	100.0
Growth rate	4.0	1.9	2.1	3.8	7.2
Third Plan					
1961–62	25,039	563.9	452.2	86.8	109.2
1962–63	25,414	559.8	462.0	85.3	119.8
1963–64	26,746	576.4	472.1	87.2	129.7
1964–65	28,808	607.8	482.5	96.9	140.8
1965–66	27,103	558.8	493.2	80.8	153.8
Growth rate	2.3	zero	2.1	−1.3	9.0
(to 1964–65)	(4.4)	(1.9)	(2.1)	(3.8)	(9.0)
Annual Plans					
1966–67	27,298	551.5	504.2	80.7	152.7
1967–68	29,715	587.3	515.4	98.9	151.4
1968–69	30,513	589.1	527.0	97.3	161.1
Growth rate					
(1964–65 as base)	1.7	1.0	2.3	0.1	4.6
Fourth Plan					
1969–70	32,408	612.6	538.9	103.8	172.4
1970–71	34,235	632.8	551.3	111.5	184.3
1971–72	34,713	626.6	563.9	111.2	186.1
1972–73	34,215	603.4	576.8	102.2	199.5
1973–74	36,033	621.3	590.0	112.4	200.4
Growth rate	3.4	1.1	2.3	2.9	4.5
					(Base 1970 = 100)
1973–74					114.3

Year and plan period	Net national product at factor cost (1970–71 prices)		Population (million)	Index of agricultural production (Base: 3 yr. ending 1969/ 70 = 100)	Index of industrial production (Base 1960 = 100)
	N.N.P. (Rs. crores)	Per capita N.N.P. (Rs.)			
(1)	(2)	(3)	(4)	(5)	(6)
Fifth Plan					
1974–75	36,590	617.0	603.5	108.6	119.7
1975–76	40,274	663.5	617.2	125.1	133.7
1976–77	40,429	652.1	631.3	116.3	147.7
1977–78	44,046	694.7	645.7	132.9	149.5
1978–79	46,533	717.0	660.3	138.0	150.2
Growth rate	5.2	2.9	2.3	4.2	5.6
1979–80	44,136	664.7	675.2	117.0	148.1
1980–81	47,414	698.3	690.1	135.3	154.1
Sixth Plan					
1980–81	110,484	1,627.2	690.1	135.3	100.0
1981–82	117,027	1,686.3	705.2	142.9	109.3
1982–83	119,619	1,687.2	720.4	137.5	112.8
1983–84	128,922	1,780.7	735.6	156.4	120.4
1984–85	132,367	1,791.2	750.9	154.6	130.7
Growth rate	4.6	2.4	2.1	5.7	7.0
Seventh Plan					
1985–86	138,611	1,835.9	766.1	161.7	142.1
1986–87	143,935	1,869.3	781.4	152.6	155.1

Notes: n.a. indicates not available. Growth rates are compound growth rates calculated from the yearly data given in the table. Attention is drawn to the following:
(a) For the third plan period growth rates are given both for the five years of the plan and up to the penultimate year, 1964–65, since the last year was an unusually bad one
(b) For the period of the annual plans (1966–67 to 1968–69, inclusive) growth rates are calculated with 1964–65 as base, rather than 1965–66, since use of the latter would exaggerate the performance
(c) In the sixth plan period growth rates for total net national product and per capita net national product, and for the index of industrial production are for four years, since the first year of the period had to be used as base year.
The population figures in column 4 relate to calendar years. The 1951 figure is given as that for 1950–51, and so on. Those for 1950–51 (i.e., 1951), 1960–61 (i.e., 1961), 1970–71 (i.e., 1971) and 1980–81 (i.e., 1981) are actual census totals. Those for other years are either projections made by the office of the Registrar General of India or estimates approved by the Indian Planning Commission. In columns 7–9, for the years 1980–81 to 1985–86, inclusive, the figures in brackets are those of a new series calculated by India's national accounts statisticians. They show lower rates of saving and capital formation than the series produced according to previous methods and given in the table; and they appear to be more accurate. The pre-1980/81 figures reproduced in the table have been calculated according to the previous method. In columns 13–15 the figures are for calendar years. The 1951 figure is given as 1950–51, etc.
Sources: Columns 2 and 3, Government of India, Ministry of Finance (Economic Division), *Economic Survey, 1987–88* (New Delhi: Controller of Publications, 1988), Appendix, Statis-

Rate of saving and capital formation (as % of NDP at current market prices)			Foreign trade (Rs. millions)			Availability per capita per day of food grains (grams)		
Net domestic saving	Net domestic capital formation	Net inflow of foreign capital	Imports	Exports	Balance	Cereals	Pulses	Total
(7)	(8)	(9)	(10)	(11)	(12)	(13)	(14)	(15)
6.61	6.38	−0.23	6,500	6,010	−490	324.9	57.4	382.3
6.09	7.97	1.88	9,709	7,289	−2,420	316.4	55.7	372.1
3.64	3.28	−0.36	6,713	5,273	−1,440	338.8	59.4	398.2
4.01	3.88	−0.13	5,758	5,262	−496	375.5	65.6	441.1
7.39	7.64	0.25	6,564	5,885	−679	361.4	67.2	428.6
8.83	9.36	0.53	7,064	6,039	−1,025	350.1	66.5	416.6
			1.7	zero		1.5	3.0	1.7
8.77	11.95	3.18	8,406	6,130	−2,276	363.1	68.2	431.3
6.38	10.50	4.12	10,849	5,845	−5,014	339.9	55.3	395.2
5.18	8.09	2.92	9,063	5,532	−3,531	384.2	74.4	458.6
5.01	6.77	1.75	9,608	6,299	−3,309	383.0	65.3	448.3
9.34	12.72	3.38	11,214	6,329	−4,975	399.7	69.0	468.7
			9.7	0.9		2.7	0.7	2.4
8.50	10.79	2.29	11,071	6,606	−4,465	398.9	62.0	460.9
9.61	12.35	2.74	11,356	6,853	−4,503	384.0	59.8	443.8
9.84	12.21	2.37	12,229	7,932	−4,297	401.0	51.0	452.0
9.29	12.04	2.75	13,490	8,163	−5,327	418.5	61.6	480.1
11.28	13.91	2.64	13,941	8,056	−5,885	359.9	48.2	408.1
			4.4	4.9		−1.9	−5.4	−2.5
			(4.7)	(6.6)		(0.9)	(−2.0)	(0.4)
11.96	15.50	3.55	20,784	10,949	−9,835	361.8	39.6	401.4
9.64	12.39	2.75	20,076	11,987	−8,089	404.1	56.1	460.2
9.61	10.94	1.33	18,616	13,579	−5,037	397.8	47.3	445.1
			11.3	19.1		−1.6	−7.1	−2.3
11.91	12.61	0.70	15,817	14,133	−1,684	403.1	51.9	455.0
11.84	12.88	1.04	16,340	15,352	−988	417.6	51.2	468.8
11.25	12.44	1.19	18,120	16,080	−2,040	419.1	47.0	466.1
12.50	13.17	0.67	17,333	19,708	2,375	380.5	41.1	421.6
12.40	13.12	0.72	29,553	25,230	−4,323	410.4	40.8	451.2
			9.6	13.2		0.6	−2.5	0.2

Rate of saving and capital formation (as % of NDP at current market prices)			Foreign trade (Rs. millions)			Availability per capita per day of food grains (grams)		
Net domestic saving	Net domestic capital formation	Net inflow of foreign capital	Imports	Exports	Balance	Cereals	Pulses	Total
(7)	(8)	(9)	(10)	(11)	(12)	(13)	(14)	(15)
13.43	14.42	0.99	45,180	33,288	−11,892	365.8	39.7	405.5
14.64	14.48	−0.16	56,250	40,430	−15,820	373.8	50.5	424.3
15.96	13.98	−1.98	56,740	51,460	−5,280	386.3	43.3	429.6
18.00	16.20	−1.80	60,250	54,040	−6,210	422.5	45.5	468.0
20.00	20.10	0.10	68,140	57,260	−10,880	431.8	44.7	476.5
			18.4	17.8		1.0	1.8	1.1
17.9	18.4	0.5	89,080	64,590	−24,490	379.5	30.9	410.4
17.6	19.3	1.7	124,650	66,750	−57,900	416.2	37.5	453.7
17.8 (13.5)	19.6 (15.2)	1.8 (1.7)	124,650	66,750	−57,900	416.2	37.5	453.7
17.2 (13.3)	19.1 (15.1)	1.9 (1.8)	136,080	78,060	−58,020	414.8	39.2	454.0
16.9 (11.1)	18.5 (12.7)	1.6 (1.6)	142,930	88,030	−54,890	396.9	39.5	436.4
16.4 (11.5)	17.8 (12.9)	1.4 (1.4)	157,630	98,720	−58,910	436.1	41.8	477.9
16.9 (10.9)	18.6 (12.5)	1.7 (1.6)	171,171	118,550	−53,160	415.6	38.1	453.7
			13.9	13.0		1.8	4.3	2.0
16.7 (13.3)	18.6 (15.9)	1.9 (2.6)	198,000	113,000	−85,000	434.2	41.9	476.1
n.a.	n.a.	n.a.	n.a.	n.a.	n.a.	429.3	36.2	465.5

tical Tables, Table 1.1, p. S–3. Column 4, *Economic Survey, 1987–88,* Table 1.16, p. S–23. All figures except for 1952 to 1960 inclusive. For 1952 to 1960, inclusive, V. G. Kulkarni, *Statistical Outline of Indian Economy* (Bombay: Vora & Co., 1968), Table II–8, p. 20. Column 5, Government of India, Directorate of Economics and Statistics, Department of Agriculture and Cooperation, Ministry of Agriculture, *Indian Agriculture In Brief* (New Delhi: Controller of Publications, 1987), Table 1.62, pp. 122–23. All figures except for 1985–86 and 1986–87. For 1985–86 and 1986–87, *Economic Survey, 1987–88,* Table 1.7, p. S–12. Column 6, 1950–51 to 1973–74, inclusive, John W. Mellor, *The New Economics of Growth. A Strategy for India and the Developing World* (Ithaca and London: Cornell University Press, 1976), Table 1–2, p. 8. Those for 1973–74 to 1980–81, inclusive, Tata Services Limited, *Statistical Outline of India, 1978* (Bombay, 1977), p. 61; *Statistical Outline of India, 1980* (Bombay, 1980), p. 63; *Statistical Outline of India, 1982* (Bombay, 1982); and *Statistical Outline of India, 1986–87* (Bombay, 1986), p. 72. Columns 7–9, 1950–51 to 1976–77, inclusive, S. L. Shetty, *Structural Retrogression in the Indian Economy since the Mid-Sixties* (Bombay: Economic and Political Weekly, 1978), Table 29, p. 35. 1977–78 to 1979–80, Tata Services Limited, *Statistical Outline of India, 1986–87,* p. 27. 1980–81 to 1985–86 from Government of India, Central Statistical Organisation, Department of Statistics, Ministry of Planning, *New Series On National Accounts Statistics With 1980–81 As Base Year* (New Delhi: Government of India Press, 1988), p. 37. Columns 10–14, 1950–51, Government of India, Planning Commission, *Fourth Five Year Plan. A Draft Outline* (New Delhi, 1966), Appendix 1, p. 419. 1951–52 to 1980–81, inclusive, V. N. Balasubramanyam, *The Economy of India* (London: Weidenfeld and Nicolson, 1984), pp. 187 and 194. 1981–82 to 1985–86, inclusive, Tata Service, *Statistical Outline of India, 1986–87.*

it was an attempt to consolidate by building upon the existing structure of the economy. Great emphasis was placed upon the need to raise the rate of saving. Foreign aid was sought and obtained to augment domestic savings, but did not loom large. Structural change and a concerted attempt at industrialization were put aside for future plans.

It was with the second FYP (1956/57–1960/61), associated with the name of P. C. Mahalanobis and the famous Mahalanobis model, that such an initiative came. That plan embodied a bold strategy of industrialization at whose core lay the creation of a capital goods sector. It also involved heavy recourse to foreign aid for the first time. The second plan has been criticized for its lack of attention to agriculture. This may, in part, have derived from the fortuitous success of agriculture during the first plan period (a success largely due to unusually good weather). The second plan marked the beginning of significant increases in the public sector as part of the program of industrialization.

The third FYP (1961/62–1965/66) continued the second plan's emphasis. It gave a new stress, however, to India's need for "self-reliance": that is, an ability to meet import requirements without resort to foreign aid. This was partly a response to the heavy recourse to foreign aid in the previous plan period as well as a growing perception of possibly undesirable implications of such a recourse. Yet, in the third plan resort to foreign aid continued to be substantial.

Performance during these three plan periods was varied, and there were moments of difficulty, especially the foreign exchange crisis during the second plan period. But, overall, the growth of real national income and per capita real national income in each of the three plan periods was relatively steady and showed progressive acceleration, at least up to the fourth year of the third plan. Growth of real net national product was 3.5 percent a year in the first plan, 4 percent in the second and 4.4 percent in the first four years of the third plan—averaging just under 4 percent a year. Per capita real income grew at 1.7 percent, 1.9 percent and 1.9 percent respectively, and averaged 1.8 percent a year.

Agricultural growth hovered at, or just under, 4 percent a year; and industrial growth accelerated from 6.2 percent to 7.2 percent to 9 percent in successive plan periods, averaging something over 7 percent a year. The rate of net domestic saving had risen from 6.6 percent in 1950–1951 to 11.3 percent in 1965–1966 and the rate of net domestic capital formation from 6.4 percent to 13.9 percent. Per capita availability of foodgrains per day (the outcome of domestic production and imports) grew from 382.3 grams in 1950–1951 to 448.3 in 1964–1965. This was hardly a dramatic rise over 14 years (a rate of growth per year of about 1.5 percent). But at least some perceptible growth had taken place.

The public sector grew, between 1950–1951 and 1960–1961, from 5 to 48 units, its investment from Rs. 29 crores to Rs. 953 crores and its share of total gross capital formation in India from 23 percent to 44 percent. The number of public sector employees stood at 185,000 in 1961. This number was tiny in relation to India's total working population, its share in total gross domestic product was only 11 percent, and its performance attracted considerable criticism. But that it occupied a key role in the Indian economy was beyond doubt. By 1965–1966 the number of public sector units had risen to 74, its investment to Rs. 2,415 crores, its share of total gross capital formation to 50 percent, and its employees to 471,000. In 1964–1965 its share of GDP had gone up to 12 percent.

Access to growing amounts of foreign exchange is critically important if an economic strategy of the kind attempted in India is to be successful. India did not prove capable of earning that foreign exchange through an adequate export performance. The value of imports was consistently and substantially in excess of exports, and up to 1964–1965 imports grew at an overall average rate of 5.4 percent and exports grew at only 2.5 percent. Exports were stagnant during the first and second plan periods, and started to grow only in the third plan years. Access to foreign exchange came, essentially, through foreign aid, mainly from the United States. Over the first plan period external resources (mainly aid) financed 9.6 percent of planned public outlay; during the second plan years this proportion rose dramatically to 22.5 percent; and in the third plan period to 28.2 percent. Here was reliance upon foreign aid with a vengeance. "Self-reliance," a proclaimed goal of the third plan, seemed ever further in the future.

Private foreign investment also grew over these years, but under government control and subject to a variety of limitations. Moreover, it changed its nature. By the mid-1960s, foreign capital was decreasingly British in origin and increasingly characterized by a multiplicity of national origins. It was now concentrated in a small number of industries: with plantations (mainly tea), manufacturing industries and petroleum together constituting some 81 percent of the total. Manufacturing industry's increased share, from 28 percent in 1947 to around 40 percent in the mid-1960s, is especially noteworthy. Within manufacturing, particular industries assumed special importance: the traditional textile industries (cotton and jute) lost capital whereas industries such as chemicals and drugs, cigarettes and tobacco, and electrical goods gained significantly. These favored industries were technologically complex, protected by patents and, very important from the viewpoint of the foreign investors (mainly multinationals), had large uncontrolled profit margins. The Indian government remained wary of foreign capital and attempted to control it. But Indian capital had lost its fear and sought lucrative collaboration with foreign investors.

By the mid-1960s, too, the structure of both imports and exports had changed. Capital goods were now 45 percent of imports, with machinery alone constituting 24 percent of total imports, a reflection of India's capital-intensive industrialization strategy. Raw materials and intermediate goods were down to 22 percent of the total, but oil and oil-related products had achieved considerable significance. Mineral oils were more than 10 percent of imports. Imports of fertilizers were growing rapidly in importance. By 1965–1966 they were 3.2 percent of total imports. Consumer goods, however, were roughly proportionate to their 1950–1951 figures, and were still dominated by foodgrains that in the last two years of the third plan were, respectively, 21 percent and 24 percent of total imports. India's heavy dependence on imports of foodgrains continued.

By 1965–1966 the three exports that had dominated in 1950–1951—tea, cotton goods and jute manufactures—had fallen from 52 percent of the total to close to 40 percent. India's "traditional" exports were giving way in importance to a variety of new ones. These latter exports included engineering products, iron and steel, chemical and allied products and iron ore. Changes were afoot, and these exports had some dynamism attached to them. But still, in the mid-1960s, they represented only 10 percent of total exports. Their dynamism was far from producing an Indian export performance that was, in overall terms, satisfactory.

Crisis and watershed in the mid-1960s

The end of the third plan in the mid-1960s is often seen as a watershed in India's post-1947 development. Certainly, immediately after it came a period of crisis in the economy. At this point several related features were in evidence. There was very poor agricultural performance, with agricultural growth more or less at a halt, and conditions approaching famine in some parts of India. Foodgrain imports were running at 34 percent and 26 percent, respectively, of total imports in 1966–1967 and 1968–1969. A sharp deceleration of industrial growth, to half the rate achieved during the first four years of the third plan, showed itself. There was a decline in the rates of saving and investment, and difficulties in obtaining aid (especially from the United States). Partly in response to these powerful strains, the rupee was devalued by 36.5 percent in June 1966. Population growth was obviously accelerating: the 1961 census revealed compound growth between 1951 and 1961 of 2.01 percent a year. Planning was suspended, and there were three years of a so-called "plan holiday" (1966/67, 1967/68 and 1968/69).

From the fourth to the seventh plan

By the mid-1960s a certain "plan weariness" had emerged. In the earlier years of planning the formulation of plans and the publication of plan documents had been the occasion of intense discussion and some intellectual excitement. By the end of the 1960s, however, this feeling had given way to disillusionment and even cynicism among Indian economists and, more generally, Indian intellectuals. The fourth FYP, originally scheduled for 1966/67–1971/72, eventually got under way in 1969/70. The alarming stagnation of Indian agriculture had given rise to a "green revolution" strategy that represented a determined attempt to secure agricultural growth through significant rises in agricultural yields, essentially in the dominating group of foodgrains. In the mid-1960s foodgrains still covered 75 percent of India's cultivated area. This strategy was at the center of the fourth plan. There was, nevertheless, a continued emphasis on industrialization. The relationship between the two rates of growth was recognized (the fact that a particular industrial growth rate required a particular minimum agricultural growth), and targets of industrial growth at between 8 percent and 10 percent a year and agricultural growth of 5 percent or more were set. The fourth plan also displayed a preoccupation with the need to slow down the rate of growth of population.

The fifth FYP (1974/75–1978/79) covered the period of a national emergency and was brought to a premature end one year early, in 1977–1978, when the Janata party came to power. It continued the "green revolution" strategy, and showed a new, official preoccupation with poverty; *garibi hatao* (abolish poverty) had been a call raised by Indira Gandhi in 1971. The sixth FYP (1980/81–1984/85) brought no significant changes in economic strategy. India's seventh FYP (1985/6–1989/90) was recently completed. The "green revolution" strategy in agriculture, the emphasis upon industrialization, and an awareness of poverty along with various poverty programs, have all been prominent features of the fifth, sixth and seventh FYPs.

In general, abstractions from this period show a gradual return to the performance achieved before the mid-1960s. In the fourth, fifth and sixth plans net national product grew at, respectively, 3.4 percent, 5.2 percent and 4.6 percent a year, an average rate of something more than 4 percent; and per capita national income was at, respectively, 1.1 percent, 2.9 percent and 2.4 percent, an overall rate of some 2.1 percent a year. Both overall rates are slightly better than in the period of the first three plans.

Agriculture appeared to be back, more or less, to the level achieved by the mid-1960s: growing at 2.9 percent, 4.2 percent and 5.7 percent, or overall at just over 4 percent a year. There is no evidence of its growing, on a long-term basis, at the targeted 5 percent a year or more set in the fourth plan. Industry grew at only 4.5 percent and 5.6 percent, respectively, in the fourth and fifth plan periods, and then at 7 percent in the sixth, and overall at 5.7 percent. This is a deceleration of growth, by comparison with the first period, and performance far below that of the 8 percent to 10 percent targeted in the fourth plan.

The net domestic savings rate and rate of capital formation have also moved upward: apparently, in 1978–1979, each reaching as high as 20 percent; and standing at 16.7 percent and 18.6 percent respectively in 1985–1986. But these very high rates have been questioned recently by India's official national income statisticians. Revised estimates suggest a considerable exaggeration, certainly for the years from 1980–1981 onward (and probably before then, too). These show the 1985–1986 figures to be only 13.3 percent and 15.9 percent respectively, and those for 1984–1985 only 10.9 percent and 12.5 percent.

The availability per capital per day of foodgrains grew at only 0.2 percent a year in the fourth plan period, 1.1 percent in the fifth and 2 percent in the sixth. Indeed, it had stood at 480 in 1964–1965, plummeted to 401.4 in the dark days of 1966–1967 and has yet to reach the 1964–1965 figure again. More than 20 years later, in 1985–1986, it stood at only 476.5, and fell again to 465.5 in 1986–1987.

The awareness of the need to moderate the rate of population growth has not been sufficient to bring about a change on this front. Population growth has shown no signs of abatement. The 1971 census revealed it to have grown at a compound rate per year of 2.2 percent between 1961 and 1971, while the 1981 census revealed a growth rate of almost 2.3 percent in the subsequent decade. The birthrate has, it is true, fallen from 41.7 in 1961 to 32.5 in 1981, but so too has the deathrate, from 22.8 to 11.2. India's total population, which was 361.2 million in 1951 and 690.1 million in 1981, is estimated at 766.1 million in 1986. If it continues to grow at 2 percent a year it will have reached 1,000 million by 2000.

Poverty remains deep and pervasive in the cities and in the countryside. Before the late 1960s the measurement of poverty in India was itself an activity limited in scope. Since then it has become a major preoccupation, and one that is contentious both in its techniques and in the results that it generates. It is often sophisticated in its procedures, but these are the subject of much controversy and attract considerable criticism from rival groups. Results are generated that vary considerably in the degree of poverty that they indicate in particular years and in the changes that they suggest between years (certainly in the degree of change but also in the direction of change).

The seventh plan document insisted that "removal of poverty remains a central concern of planning in India."[2] It noted that, according to National Sample Survey data, the proportion of people living below the poverty line (a line based on minimum caloric intake) in India was 48.3 percent in 1977–1978, with 51.2 percent below that line in rural areas and 38.2 percent in urban areas. The overall figure had fallen to 37.4 percent in 1983–1984, with a decline in the rural proportion to 40.4 percent and in the urban to 28.1 percent. With considerable equanimity the survey predicted that the overall proportion would fall to under 26 percent by 1989–1990.[3]

Many dispute these figures, arguing, for example, that the 1977–1978 overall figure was probably more than 50 percent, with the urban and rural figures higher than those indicated. Also, the National Sample Survey figures for 1983–1984 are not comparable with those for 1977–1978, and that the decline, if there has been one, has been far less than that suggested. There are those who maintain that the current figure overall is still close to 50 percent (with at least 50 percent below the poverty line in rural India), and that the possibility of reducing the overall poverty ratio to 25 percent by 1990 does not exist. Certainly, however, poverty in India remains massive, gross and disfiguring. Even in the sanguine figures of the seventh plan document, some 273 million people lived beneath a poverty line that, in its specification, does not err on the side of generosity.

The public sector has continued to grow. By 1985–1986 it contained 221 units, its investment was Rs. 42,811 crores, its employees numbered 2.1 million and its share of gross capital formation was 51 percent. At that time its share of GDP (at 1988 prices) had risen to 25 percent. Its performance continues to attract criticism. It is said to be inefficient and very costly and to contribute far less to total savings than it should. By comparison with its contribution of 25 percent to GDP and 51 percent to gross capital formation, its share of gross domestic savings is only 14 percent.

[2] Government of India, Planning Commission, *Seventh Five Year Plan, 1985–90, vol. 1* (New Delhi, 1985), viii.
[3] See Ibid., pp. viii and 4, for the prediction and the figures.

As elsewhere in the world, there is talk of privatization, but only a few token moves in that direction have been made.

The course of foreign trade became more favorable from the mid-1960s onward. The surplus of imports over exports continues year after year, but following on the improvement in the third plan years, the value of exports began to grow more quickly than imports: 19 percent a year compared with 11 percent over the three annual plan years, and 13 percent compared with 10 percent during the fourth plan period. During the fifth plan imports and exports both grew rapidly at more or less the same rate (just over 18 percent a year compared with just under 18 percent). In the sixth plan years imports grew at an annual compound rate of 14 percent and exports at 13 percent. Over the fourth, fifth and sixth plan years the annual growth of imports averaged 14 percent, and that of exports rather more at something under 15 percent. Export growth now matches that of imports.

Imports in the mid-1970s were dominated by four categories: mineral oils, lubricants and related products, metals, machinery and transportation equipment; foodgrains and fertilizers; and oil and capital equipment. Foodgrains varied in significance depending upon the nature of the harvest. They were as high as 26 percent of total imports in 1975–1976 and 18 percent in 1977, and then fell to 2 percent in 1977–1978. More recently foodgrains have shrunk to negligible proportions (under one percent of total imports), a result of apparent agricultural success. In 1985–1986 imports were dominated by oil and oil products (25 percent), fertilizers (7 percent), capital goods (22 percent), chemicals (6 percent) and iron and steel (7 percent).

By the mid-1970s manufactures were of considerable significance in the structure of exports, contributing 53 percent of the total in 1974–1975. The shift from traditional manufactures to nontraditional—for example, from jute and cotton textiles to chemicals and engineering goods—had been decisive. In addition exports such as cashews, tobacco, coffee, oil cakes and sugar were growing rapidly. But some economists expressed doubts concerning the likely future growth of these exports: the manufacturers because of their high costs and essentially uncompetitive nature, the others because their success at that time was based upon a series of unusual circumstances outside of India which were unlikely to continue. By 1985–1986 manufactures were close to 60 percent of total exports. But the doubts remain. Growing protectionism in industrialized countries and virtual stagnation in international trade flows placed great pressure upon Indian exports of manufactures in the late 1980s. India's export performance, although far better than in the first subperiod, remains problematic.

Foreign aid has declined in importance but is by no means eliminated. External resources as a proportion of planned public outlay fell to 12.9 percent in the fourth plan, 12.8 percent in the fifth and 7.7 percent in the sixth. Its targeted level during the period of the seventh plan was 10 percent. These proportions are far lower than those of the second and third plan years, although even in proportionate terms they are by no means negligible. In absolute terms they represent a large amount of foreign resources.

India has not yet become a self-reliant economy. This was underlined in November 1981 when India, under a barrage of criticism from its more radical economists, took a massive International Monetary Fund (IMF) loan (the largest loan ever negotiated by the government of India and the largest given by the IMF in its 36-year history), with stringent conditions attached to it. This was strong testimony to India's inadequate record of domestic resource mobilization and its inability to earn sufficient foreign exchange. Here was a loan of Rs. 6,000 crores, or US $5.8 billion. In one transaction India's total external indebtedness was raised by 40 percent. India's current overall external debt service ratios, of 1.4 percent of GNP and 12.7 percent of exports in 1985, are not crippling. Compared with Mexico, for example, where the figures are, respectively, 8.5 percent and 48.2 percent, or Brazil where they are 4.9 percent and 34.8 percent, India is, in this respect, relatively favorably placed. That portion reflects, perhaps, sound economic management. It may also reflect the greater difficulty India has had in the past in gaining access to the kind of bank sector lending that so-called middle-income economies have been able to obtain.

Private foreign investment continues to be made. The total stock of private foreign capital in India is less than in many far smaller countries (such as Malaysia), and significantly smaller than in countries such as Mexico and Brazil. Private foreign investment in India is not insignificant. It probably represents about 20 percent of the value of gross assets of India's joint stock companies in the private sector. It does not, however, occupy the dominating position or exert the distorting influence that it does in many other poor countries. Reliable information is difficult to obtain. It seems likely that the inflow has diminished appreciably since 1973 when the Foreign Exchange Regulations Act forcing foreign companies to limit their equity holdings in favor of local shareholders was passed. That trend, however, is changing as the government's attitude becomes more favorable.

Private foreign investment in India has come to be characterized by a large number of technical collaboration agreements between India and foreign firms for the import of technology and know-how. Reliable data on the precise content and provenance of these agreements are scarce, but the trends prior to the mid-1960s have continued. These collaboration agreements attracted criticism in earlier years for an excessive bias toward the production of commodities of "low social priority": a variety of consumer goods most likely to be bought by high-income groups (for example, cosmetics, toothpaste, soap, toys, footwear and soft drinks). That criticism, however, has become far less vocal. Technical collaboration is now significantly concentrated in certain technologically intensive fields of manufacturing such as electrical and nonelectrical machinery, machine tools and transportation equipment.

The government of Rajiv Gandhi has actively encouraged a large number of technical collaboration agreements with the aim of giving Indian industry ready access to the most modern technology. The number of foreign collaboration agreements approved rose from 183 in 1970 to 526 in 1980, 752 in 1984 and 1,024 in 1985. It seems likely that the flow of private foreign investment to India, largely through this source, has grown of late and will continue to increase.

Differences between the two subperiods
The second subperiod (1974/75 to the present) shows significant differences from the first (from 1950/51 to 1964/65): a declaration in industrial growth; a poorer performance with respect to per capita availability of foodgrains; an improved performance for exports; changes in the structure of both imports and exports, with a decline in foodgrains as a dominant element in imports; a decreased resort to foreign aid (although no transition to real self-reliance); an increasing incidence of technical collaboration agreements in the field of private foreign investment; and a more obvious preoccupation with the incidence and the eradication of poverty (although not necessarily marked by success).

There were further differences between the two subperiods. Firstly, in agriculture, the sources of growth changed significantly. In the first subperiod growth came from an extension of the cultivated area. That source of growth became increasingly difficult to tap by the mid-1960s. Thereafter the predominant source of growth became a steady increase in yields: the result of the "green revolution" strategy. Second, in industry there was a switch from growth predominantly in heavy industry, in the first subperiod, to growth in consumer goods (especially a group of largely luxury goods industries). In the first subperiod industrial growth was led by supply: the result of decisions and direction by the planners. Industrial growth, which diminished in the second subperiod, became increasingly led by demand: a response to upper-income groups and a reflection of India's very unequal distribution of income. Third, the extent that the rate of domestic savings has genuinely risen substantially reflects a significant increase in inventories in the second subperiod, at least through the end of the 1970s. A substantial rise in the level of stocks shows up as a rise in the savings rate. This does not, however, indicate any greater capacity or ability to secure a rise in real capital formation. On the contrary, it suggests that this is not taking place, that production potential already created is not being exploited. Such an enhanced capacity to accumulate would derive, rather, from greater success in domestic resource mobilization. That situation is not in evidence in India. The relatively low rates of savings in the 1980s, revealed by the adjusted estimates of the national income statisticians, suggest this strongly. The Indian tax effort and especially the taxation of agriculture have been conspicuously unsuccessful in both subperiods.

Growth, change and the pattern of economic development
Taking the entire postcolonial period, a compound growth rate of 3.5 percent a year for net national product and of 1.4 percent for real per capita national income mark a sharp break with the pre-1947 era. Broken down into agricultural growth at about 3 percent a year and industrial growth at

about 6 percent, these figures represent a departure from previous economic stagnation.

By comparison with the other countries of South Asia, India's overall performance has been reasonable but unspectacular. The only poor country of comparable size is China. India's average rate of growth of real per capita GNP at 1.7 percent a year from 1960 to 1985 is less than half of China's 4.8 percent. At these rates India's real per capita GNP doubles in 41 years while China's does so in 15 years.

A comparison with its 35 fellow low-income economies shows India to be well ahead of the average of 0.4 percent a year. In South Asia India has grown more rapidly than Bangladesh and Nepal (0.4 percent and 0.1 percent respectively), but more slowly than Pakistan and Sri Lanka (2.6 percent and 2.9 percent respectively).

Comparison with the 60 poor countries that fall into the World Bank's middle-income category (developing countries with a per capita real income in 1985 of $401 or more) is less flattering. On the average those countries grew at an annual average rate of 3 percent. Asian countries that achieved very high rates include Singapore (7.6 percent), South Korea (6.6 percent), Hong Kong (6.1 percent), Taiwan (figure not available), Malaysia (4.4 percent), Thailand (4 percent) and Indonesia (4.8 percent). India's economic performance is not on a par with these nations.

One must, of course, remember India's size and diversity. The performance of some states, which compare in size with the countries mentioned above, has certainly equaled that of the high performing middle-income developing economies. Precise comparison is not possible, but Punjab, Haryana and western Uttar Pradesh must be singled out as high performers, while Maharashtra and Gujarat have also performed well.

In agriculture the rise in the irrigation ratio from 17.1 percent in 1950–1951 to 31 percent in 1985–1986 has involved much effort. But the fact that some 70 percent of India's cropped area continues to be without assured water (through irrigation) means that a large proportion of India's agriculture is precariously based. Again, there are regional variations. The growth of Indian agriculture now derives from rising yields. That growth, however, although reasonable by historical standards, at about 3 percent a year, is far from the 5 percent that the Indian planners thought necessary in the mid-1960s. A rate of agricultural growth of 5 percent a year may still be deemed necessary if India is to raise significantly the per capita availability of foodgrains. India continues to be unable to do that by means of its export earnings. Whether, with such a rise, the poor would benefit significantly remains doubtful. The distributional mechanisms in a country in the early stages of capitalist development may not yield advantage to the poor so easily or so quickly. An agriculture growing at least at 5 percent a year is desirable for other reasons. It seems likely that only with such an agricultural growth will industry be able to grow more quickly—at a rate nearer the 10 percent a year that the planners thought possible before the advent of the crisis of the mid-1960s. It was then thought that these were balanced sectoral growth rates. It may now be the case that even with agriculture growing at 5 percent a year industrial growth of 10 percent would be difficult.

The raising of the net domestic savings rate from 6.6 percent in 1950–1951 to 13.3 percent in 1985–1986 is less of an achievement than many had recently thought. The much-cited 20 percent figure for 1978–1979 now seems to have been a considerable exaggeration and, to the extent that it was not, it reflected considerable accumulation of inventories. In fact it is at a rate consistently in excess of 20 percent, without such high inventory levels, that India should be aiming. That seems to be quite some distance away.

The rise in the rate of net domestic capital formation has been similarly exaggerated. The actual rise, from 6.4 percent to 15.9 percent, has been made possible by considerable inflows of foreign resources. These have not been sufficient to secure the desirable rate of something well in excess of 20 percent. India continues to depend on foreign resources. It will not, however, reach 20 percent until the domestic savings rate rises sufficiently. That, in its turn, will require considerably greater success concerning domestic resource mobilization than is currently the case.

India's rate of growth of population has, over the whole period, been 2.2 percent a year. This figure means a doubling of the population every 32 years. Using the years 1980–1985 India's 2.2 percent rate is lower than Bangladesh's 2.6 percent, Pakistan's 3.1 percent and the average of 2.7 percent of its fellow low-income countries. It is also lower than the 2.5 percent average of middle-income countries. But other poor countries are growing significantly less rapidly: China at 1.2 percent, Sri Lanka at 1.4 percent, South Korea at 1.5 percent, Singapore at 1.2 percent, and Hong Kong at 1.4 percent. India's planners underestimated the difficulties associated with keeping population growth down. A rate of 1.4 percent they would currently like to achieve, but it seems unlikely to be approached in the near future.

The rise in life expectancy at birth from 32.5 in 1951 to 54.1 in 1981 for males and from 31.7 to 54.8 for females represents some progress. So, too, does the increase in the literacy rate from 16.6 overall to 36.2 over the same period—for females from 7.9 to 24.8 and for males from 25 to 46.9. But there has not been a proportionate decline in the birthrate, nor has there been a sufficient assault upon poverty. In fact these changes have not really reached the large numbers of Indians who continue to exist in abysmal poverty.

Between 1951 and 1981 agricultural growth at just under 3 percent a year and industrial growth at just under 6 percent yielded a decline in the primary sector's share of net national product from 56 percent to 43 percent and a rise in the secondary sector's share from 17 percent to 21 percent—shares that by 1985 had changed to 37 percent and 23 percent respectively. Agriculture's share has declined substantially while that of industry has risen perceptibly, but not to the same degree. In fact, it is the tertiary sector—services—that has clearly taken agriculture's share, rising from 27 percent in 1951 to 36 percent in 1981 and 40 percent in 1985. The planners had intended agriculture's declining share, but it was industry, not services, that they had seen as the new dominating element. To that extent, industrialization has not achieved the intended structural change.

The structure of the labor force reveals a remarkable constancy in the postcolonial period. In 1951 69 percent of the male workforce was in the primary sector. This had not changed by 1961 or 1971. The 1981 census seems to show a slight decline to 67 percent, although this figure has been disputed by some authorities.[4] It is by no means certain that over three decades agriculture's share has changed at all. The shares of industry and services sector have remained equally constant. The structural stasis that was a feature of the half century from 1900 to 1950 has continued. India has failed, so far, to achieve the structural change that was the essential aim of planning and the strategy of industrialization. Agriculture's strong dominance as an employer of labor remains. Nearly 80 percent of Indians continue to live in rural areas.

PAKISTAN

Among the South Asian economies, in terms of per capita income, Pakistan ranks highest (with Sri Lanka), in 1985, with $380; its per capita growth rate, between 1965 and 1985, was 2.6 percent a year (close to Sri Lanka's 2.9 percent). This is respectable, but is less than the average performance of the middle-income poor countries and significantly less than the high performers in that group.

Pakistan's population, however, is growing at the very rapid rate of 3.1 percent a year, with a birthrate in 1985 of 44 and a deathrate of 15. This places it, demographically, among the most quickly growing poor countries. The difficulties associated with raising per capita income, increases on the pressure on the land and problems in employment are all intensified.

Like India, Pakistan has pursued a vigorous "green revolution" strategy essentially with respect to foodgrains. Between 1965 and 1980 agriculture grew at an average annual rate of 3.3 percent, but this fell between 1980 and 1985 to 2.1 percent. Pakistan's agricultural performance is roughly comparable to India's. Yields per hectare remain low (lower than in the bordering Indian regions). The government is attempting to deal with a shortage of irrigation that limits the spread of new technology. Fertilizers, seeds and pesticides have also been in short supply. Pakistan is the world's largest exporter of cotton.

Industry, by contrast, grew at 6.2 percent between 1965 and 1980, and accelerated to 8.8 percent a year between 1980 and 1985; in manufacturing industry the acceleration was from 5.3 percent to 10.1 percent a year. The industrial record is also comparable to India's up to 1980, but in the five years thereafter it was better. Industry remains structurally weak, however. There is little diversification; industrial activity is based mainly on the

---

[4]See, for example, J. N. Sinha, "1981 Census Economic Data," *Economic and Political Weekly* 17, no. 6 (February 6, 1982).

processing of agricultural products, especially cotton and food. Technology remains somewhat primitive.

These sectoral growth rates have not generated significant structural change. Here the experience is like India's. There has been some shift in the share of GDP away from agriculture, with a decline from 40 percent of GDP in 1965 to 25 percent in 1985. This was partly taken up by industry whose share rose from 20 percent to 28 percent, but also by services whose share increased from 40 percent to 47 percent. The structure of the labor force, however, has proved more resistant to change: agriculture's share falling from 60 percent in 1965 to 55 percent in 1980, industry's declining from 18 percent to 16 percent, and that of services rising from 22 percent to 30 percent. A precise comparison with India is not possible. But while Pakistan is experiencing a similar absence of significant sectoral structural change—the kind sought by strategies of industrialization—a smaller proportion of its labor force is employed in agriculture.

Pakistan's foreign trade ratio is quite high at 18 percent of GDP, although not the highest in South Asia. Between 1965 and 1980 its exports grew at an annual rate of 4.3 percent and its imports at only 0.5 percent. This favorable situation, however, was replaced in 1980–1985 by one in which import growth at 3.9 percent a year exceeded that of exports growing at 2.4 percent. Agriculture remains critically important, accounting indirectly for some 70 percent of total exports. Pakistan's major exports are cotton yarn, raw cotton, garments, cotton cloth and rice. With respect to imports there is a severe shortage of oil products and technical know-how.

Pakistan's level of development assistance, at 2.2 percent of GNP, is far higher than India's 0.7 percent. Its present overall debt service ratios, 3.2 percent of GNP and 30 percent of exports in 1985, are very high and significantly greater than India's 1.4 percent and 12.7 percent, respectively.

Pakistan has just ended its sixth FYP period (1983–1988). Its present stated economic priorities are to strengthen the economy's infrastructure, reduce rural-urban migration and improve the employment situation. A policy of Islamization requires banks to stop charging and paying interest on loans and deposits. Experience elsewhere suggests that ways around this are usually devised and, indeed, alternative forms of lending have evolved in Pakistan. Its savings and investment ratios, however, are among the lowest of developing countries in Asia, at 14 percent. These were targeted to rise to 16 percent by the end of 1988. Even at that level they would remain well below the desirable rate of 20 percent suggested for India.

BANGLADESH

The Bangladesh economy is beset by severe problems. The country is characterized by some of the world's worst poverty, by frequent natural disasters, and by the ever-present danger of large-scale starvation. The country was labeled in 1971, the year of its origin, by American officials as an "international basket case."

The per capita growth rate between 1965 and 1985 was negligible at

0.4 percent a year. Population growth is rapid at 2.6 percent a year currently, with the birthrate in 1985 at 40 and the deathrate at 15. Agriculture grew at only 1.5 percent a year between 1965 and 1980, about half of the rate of population increase. This speeded up between 1980 and 1985 to 2.8 percent, but was still only barely ahead of population. Industrial growth was modest at 3.8 percent from 1965 to 1980, and slightly better at 4.7 percent from 1980 to 1985. Development assistance, at 7.1 percent of GNP in 1985, is very large; Bangladesh is a major recipient of aid. Very preferential terms have yielded debt ratios that are not high by the standards of several other poor countries (1.7 percent of GNP and 16.7 percent of exports in 1985). Nevertheless, this adds to balance of payments pressures. Agriculture continues to generate 50 percent of GDP and industry only 14 percent. About 75 percent of the labor force is in agriculture with only 6 percent in industry and 19 percent in services.

The economy is based on a narrow range of agricultural commodities. The country possesses relatively few natural resources and has a savagely unreliable climate that often brings severe flooding. Bangladesh is currently completing its third FYP period (1985–1990). There is immense pressure on agricultural land, with most marginal land already cultivated. Yields are very low. Rice is the predominant food crop, although wheat production is now beginning. Self-sufficiency in foodgrain production is a constantly repeated goal; it remains but a distant possibility. Cash crop production is dominated by jute, of which Bangladesh is the world's largest supplier; and jute and jute products constitute more than 50 percent of exports. Attempts at cash crop diversification have mainly centered on the production of tea now representing 6 percent of exports. Fish resources are also of some importance with shrimp and prawns at around 8 percent of exports.

Industry is based mainly on the processing of agricultural products, especially jute and cotton. The production of cigarettes, paper, sugar, flour, edible oils, prepared fish and fertilizers is also of some importance. But in all industry remains of very minor significance. Bangladesh does possess substantial natural gas resources. Gas is used as a feedstock in the fertilizer industry as well as for power generation and general consumption.

Bangladesh's foreign trade ratio is relatively high at 15.3 percent. Currently the government is pursuing a strategy of export-led growth. Among other things this strategy entails the adoption of exchange rate policies that encourage nontraditional exports and that exempt from duties imports of goods that are used in the production of exports. Whether this can have any long-term success remains to be seen. Exports grew at 7.1 percent a year between 1980 and 1985, and imports at only 3.1 percent. But Bangladesh suffers from regular trade and current account deficits, and there is little likelihood that such a situation will continue.

For the foreseeable future Bangladesh's economic prospects are closely tied to the price of jute. But jute is subject to severe competition from synthetic substitutes. Unfortunately for Bangladesh the real price of jute fibers has declined over the last decade at an annual average rate of 8 percent. It is hoped in Bangladesh that more private foreign investment will be attracted and that more foreign markets will become available for the new nontraditional exports. Neither hope yet shows much sign of being realized.

SRI LANKA

The level of Sri Lanka's per capita income was, in 1985, $380, along with Pakistan's, the highest in South Asia. Between 1965 and 1985, its per capita growth rate of 2.9 percent a year was South Asia's most rapid. An important element in this is Sri Lanka's low rate of growth of population: at 1.4 percent a year between 1980 and 1985, the lowest in South Asia and among the lowest in the group of poor countries. Its agricultural and industrial growth have been reasonable, but not outstanding—on a par with India's general record but far less than that of several of India's states.

The structure, in sectoral terms, is similar to that of Pakistan: 55 percent of the labor force was in agriculture in 1985, 14 percent was in industry and 33 percent was in services. The GDP structure in 1985 was also similar to Pakistan's—27 percent, 26 percent and 46 percent respectively. There has been no significant shift toward industry in the last two decades, although there was some shift with respect to GDP, but none with respect to the labor force. Agriculture remains the backbone of the economy. The major industries are petroleum and chemical products, food processing, tobacco, beverages, textiles, leather and clothing.

Rice is the major foodgrain occupying 40 percent of the cultivated area. Self-sufficiency in rice production was attained in 1985, but that is by no means regularly the case. The three plantation crops—rubber, tea and coconuts—are the major cash crops and important earners of foreign exchange, providing more than half of export earnings and one third of government revenue. The transfer of the plantations to state ownership in the early 1970s, however, was followed by major difficulties. The plantations were run down; there was a failure to replant or to reinvest profits; and output had stagnated. Attempts have been made since the early 1980s to improve the situation but the gestation period for these crops is long. Meanwhile there has been some diversification into cocoa, spices and sugar.

Sri Lanka's birthrate of 25 in 1985 and deathrate of 6 are the lowest in South Asia. The country's life expectancy of 70 is by far the highest. Income is more equally distributed than elsewhere in South Asia. The record with respect to health care and general basic needs is good. But this needs to be put into perspective: all classes and ethnic groups do not participate equally. An official estimate indicates that at least 30 percent of the population live below the poverty line. Estate laborers, for example, continue to have chronic malnutrition, poor health services and low enrolment in schools.

Until the open outbreak in 1983 of ethnic disturbances that have continued to ravage the country, Sri Lanka's economic performance was looked at favorably by development economists. It combined concern for the poor with reasonable growth. The civil disturbances now threaten that record through direct disruption of production, a large increase in defense expenditure and a decline in tourist revenue. The rice-growing areas of the north and the east have been affected by the disturbances. In 1987 Sri Lanka had to import 80,000 tons of rice from China and Pakistan. In 1986 and 1987 tourist arrivals fell by an estimated 11 percent and 20 percent respectively. But even without the disturbances certain strains were already obvious.

Sri Lanka's very high foreign trade ratio of 39 percent makes it especially susceptible to possibly deteriorating terms of trade and fluctuating primary product prices. This is so in relation to its three major exports—tea, rubber and coconut products. The country benefited from high tea prices in the early 1980s but by 1985 these had started to decline. Recent world prices for tea and rubber have been low. Sri Lanka has also suffered from a reduction of workers' remittances from the Middle East.

Sri Lanka's dependence upon development assistance is very high (at 8.2 percent of GNP in 1985), and this has brought large external debt ratios (4.1 percent of GNP and 14.7 percent of exports in 1985). Negotiations with the IMF for structural adjustment funds have recently been completed. Encouragement of private foreign investment is a key element in government policy.

The government is committed to export-led growth, an open-market policy and a reduction of state intervention. There is some debate as to the impact of these policies upon economic performance. It is by no means clear that there are connections between them and any improvement in the economy.

NEPAL

Nepal has an overwhelmingly agricultural economy with 93 percent of its labor force employed in agriculture in 1980, and 62 percent of its GDP generated there in 1985. There is no sign of any structural change.

Population is growing quickly at 2.1 percent a year, and per capita income hardly at all (only 0.1 percent a year between 1965 and 1985). The foreign trade ratio is quite high at 14 percent. Recently economic growth has been accompanied by a deteriorating balance of payments. Development assistance is also very high, constituting 10 percent of GNP in 1985; because the terms are quite concessionary this has not produced a large debt service ratio (only 0.5 percent of GNP and 4 percent of exports in 1985). Foreign aid is expected to meet 60 percent of the expenditure under the seventh FYP (1985–1990). Life expectancy was 47 years in 1985. Only in Bhutan in South Asia is life expectancy less.

The economy depends on subsistence agriculture but the soil is poor and erosion is severe. The main crops are rice and other foodgrains, sugar cane, tobacco, potatoes and oil seeds. There is an absence of fertilizer, seed and irrigation. Storage facilities are poor and agricultural credit at reasonable rates of interest is limited. Roads are terrible and the infrastructure is rudimentary.

Tourism has become increasingly important as a source of foreign exchange and employment. Over 223,000 tourists visited Nepal in 1986, up

23 percent from the previous year. It is envisaged that this figure will rise to one million by 2000.

Nepal possesses few natural resources other than water power. But that water power has immense economic potential. It is thought to be capable of supplying the hydroelectric needs of the entire Indian subcontinent. A central part of the current development strategy is to increase export earnings through its exploitation. This, however, depends on India's cooperation since it is the only country in the region capable of absorbing the electricity generated. There is a proposed 3,600 megawatt project at Karnali that is still in the design stage. In the late 1980s India seemed to have withdrawn its support for the project.

India, indeed, exercises a powerful influence upon the Nepalese economy. In 1986 30 percent of Nepal's entire external trade was with India. Japan, however, is another major source of imports (23 percent), along with the United States (24 percent) and West Germany (15 percent). The main imports are manufactured goods, machinery and transportation equipment; the major exports are rice, jute, woolen carpets, hides and skins, handicrafts, food and livestock. The Nepalese rupee was previously linked directly to the Indian rupee. But in 1986 it was floated in accordance with the currencies that reflect the full composition of its foreign trade.

BHUTAN

Bhutan remains, to a large extent, a self-sufficient barter economy. About 92 percent of its labor force is in agriculture and 50 percent of its GDP is produced there. It has the lowest life expectancy in South Asia at 44 years. Among all of the world's poor countries only Guinea and Sierra Leone have lower life expectancies (each with 40). Bhutan's population is growing at 2.1 percent a year.

The sixth plan (1987/88–1991/92) is currently in operation. It stresses decentralization of development administration and encouragement of popular participation in decision making. The fifth plan had emphasized self-reliance on a district basis but was abandoned as a premature goal.

Bhutan's major crops are corn, rice, wheat, barley and potatoes. Industry (which generated 18 percent of GDP in 1985 and employed 3 percent of the labor force in 1980) concentrates, for the most part, on cement and wood production and on food processing. Several minerals are known to exist but quarrying is limited to limestone and dolomite. Bhutan possesses substantial hydroelectric potential, but nothing has been done to tap this. Tourism has superseded postage stamps as the main earner of foreign exchange. There is also some merchandise trade. The main exports are cement, minerals, timber and fruit. In 1985 India was the destination for 99 percent of Bhutan's exports, and the source of 90 percent of its imports.

MALDIVES

Maldives are a group of 1,200 coral islands of which 200 are inhabited. About 25 percent of the country's total population of 182,000 lives on

Male. The soil is poor and most food (including rice, wheat and sugar) has to be imported. Fishing, tourism and shipping services are the major earners of foreign exchange. The Maldives' main trading partners are Sri Lanka, Japan, Singapore, India and Thailand.

Fishing is the major element in the economy. Almost half of the labor force is employed in fishing which generates 25 percent of GNP. Output in this section more than doubled between 1982 and 1985, with the introduction of mechanized fishing boats. Fish processing facilities have been upgraded; processed fish constituted half of total fish exports in 1985 compared with one third in 1982.

Tourism accounts for 10 percent of GNP, and has expanded since the opening of Male's international airport in 1981 and the introduction of direct flights from Europe in 1984. Europe supplies 85 percent of the visitors to the Maldives. Arrivals have risen from 5,000 in 1973 to 42,000 in 1980 and 114,554 in 1985. The government's policy is to establish accommodations on previously uninhabited islands. There are now over 60 resorts providing more than 5,000 beds.

The shipping industry, which depends on third-country trade for 90 percent of its earnings, is facing a crisis. This is the result of the recession of the early 1980s, the war in the Persian Gulf, and an UNCTAD resolution limiting third-country carriers to 20 percent of international sea freight.

Although there is an awareness of the need to diversify the economy, there are limits to diversification. Agricultural development is constrained by a shortage of arable land, and the growth of industry by the small domestic market. Foreign debt remains low. The 1985–1987 three-year plan made improvements in the infrastructure a priority, particularly stressing sanitation and water supply.

FURTHER READING

Ahluwalia, Isher Judge. *Industrial Growth in India: Stagnation Since the Mid-Sixties.* Delhi and New York: Oxford University Press, 1985.

Balasubramanyam, V. N. *The Economy of India.* London: Weidenfeld & Nicolson, 1984.

Bhagwati, Jagdish N., and Srinivasan, T. N. *Foreign Trade Regimes and Economic Development: India.* New York: Columbia University Press, for the National Bureau of Economic Research, 1975.

Burki, Shahid Javed and Laporte, Robert, Jr., eds. *Pakistan's Development Priorities: Choices for the Future.* London and Karachi: Oxford University Press, 1984.

Byres, T. J. *The Green Revolution in India.* Milton Keynes, Buckinghamshire: The Open University Press, 1983.

Chakravarty, Sukhamoy. *Development Planning: The Indian Experience.* Oxford and New York: Oxford University Press, 1987.

Chaudhuri, Prasmit. *The Indian Economy: Poverty and Development.* London: Crosby Lockwood Staples, 1978.

Hartmann, Betsy and Boyce, James K. *A Quiet Violence: View from a Bangladesh Village.* London: Zed Press; San Francisco: Institute for Food and Development Policy, 1983.

Kidron, Michael. *Foreign Investments in India.* London and New York: Oxford University Press, 1965.

Ponnambalam, Satchi. *Dependent Capitalism in Crisis: The Sri Lankan Economy, 1948–1980.* London: Zed Press, 1981.

THE ECONOMIC FUTURE OF AUSTRALIA, NEW ZEALAND AND THE PACIFIC ISLAND STATES

CHRISTOPHER FINDLAY

INTRODUCTION

THE economic prospects of each member of the Oceanian group of countries in the Pacific Basin economy depends most importantly on its economic relations with the rest of the world. The relatively high degree of openness of the various national economies as well as the importance to them of resource transfers from the rest of the world, in the forms of investment, remittances or aid, are significant factors in this regard. Such a general outlook can be considered with reference to, first, the group's relationship to other countries, especially those with which the group as a whole has more intense economic relations—the countries of the Pacific Basin—and second, issues relevant to economic relations among the countries that comprise the group. The growing importance of the Pacific Basin region also raises a number of issues of global significance that necessarily reflect on the future of the countries of Oceania.

The Oceanian group of Pacific Basin countries accounts for a small share of the world output (1.6% of GNP in 1986) and world trade (1.6% of world exports in the same year); see Table 1. Although the group is as important in world output as the Association of Southeast Asian Nations (ASEAN) economies, its importance in world trade is about half that of ASEAN. Despite this comparison, the Oceanian group is relatively open: The ratios of exports of goods and services to GDP are 12% for Australia, 23% for New Zealand and up to 10% for the Pacific islands (compared to an average of 10% for the Pacific Basin and 14% for the world as a whole). While the Oceanian group has a degree of openness equal to or higher than other economies of a similar type, it is of relatively little significance in the world economy. This fact constitutes a formidable dilemma for the nations concerned. Their economic prospects are dependent on global economic activity, particularly the trade and industry policies of their larger trading partners; their economic size, however, gives them relatively little

Table 1
SHARES IN WORLD GNP AND EXPORTS,
RATIO OF EXPORTS TO GNP AND GNP PER
CAPITA, FOR SELECTED ECONOMIES, 1986

Economy	Shares in world GNP (%)	Exports (%)	Ratio of exports to GNP (%)	GNP per capita ($ U.S.)
Australia	1.4	1.2	12.3	11,118
New Zealand	0.2	0.3	23.4	7,739
Pacific Islands	0.03	0.08	36.0	831
Oceania	1.6	1.6	14.1	8,675
Japan	15.2	11.6	10.7	16,167
China	2.1	1.7	11.6	258
South Korea	0.7	1.9	36.5	2,287
Hong Kong	0.3	2.0	94.7	6,727
Singapore	0.1	1.2	125.1	6,959
Other ASEAN economies	1.3	2.2	24.5	578
East Asian	19.7	20.6	14.7	1,684
Canada	2.7	4.7	23.9	13,735
United States	32.6	11.7	5.0	17,489
North America	35.3	16.4	6.5	17,128
PACIFIC TOTAL	56.6	38.6	9.5	4,057
EC	26.6	39.8	20.9	10,692
Other centrally planned economies	0.7	1.2	22.8	1,979
Rest of World	16.0	20.3	17.7	969
WORLD	100.0	100.0	13.9	3,001

Source: International Economic Data Bank, Australian National University.

influence over either those policies or the political processes by which policies inimical to them might be amended or reformed. Their success in this arena of policy formation is fundamental to a positive economic outcome for the group as a whole. Of course, domestic policies are also important. However, pressures for domestic policy reform and policy responses to those pressures are also conditioned by events in the world economy.

As a consequence, it is necessary to examine in greater detail the mechanics of the connections between the countries of the region and the rest of the world. This discussion will focus on the other economies of East Asia; the similarity of economic interests between Oceania and East Asia will be noted. This is done despite the customary picture of Oceania as primarily a group of exporters of natural resource-based products, such as agricultural commodities, energy, minerals and base metals. In addition to their interests in resource-based products, agricultural commodities in par-

Table 2
COMMODITY COMPOSITION OF EXPORTS AND
REVEALED COMPARATIVE ADVANTAGE (RCA),
OCEANIA, 1986

	Pacific Islands	New Zealand	Australia	World
Agricultural Products				
%	54.9	72.7	41.1	14.9
RCA*	3.7	4.9	2.8	1.0
Metals				
%	9.9	4.8	7.0	2.6
RCA	3.7	1.8	2.7	1.0
Minerals				
%	32.0	1.6	34.9	14.5
RCA	2.2	0.1	2.4	1.0
Labor Intensive Products				
%	0.9	5.1	1.5	11.8
RCA	0.1	0.4	0.1	1.0
Other Manufactures				
%	1.2	15.0	13.6	54.5
RCA	0.02	0.3	0.3	1.0

*The ratio of the share of the commodity group in a country's exports compared to its share in world trade.
Source: International Economic Data Bank, Australian National University.

ticular, Oceania has many interests in common with exporters of manufactured products. This common interest may even offer a strategy for tackling the Oceanian group's dilemma concerning the importance of the world trade regime for its economic prospects compared to its lack of importance in world trade.

OCEANIAN TRADE

The exports of the Oceanian group are dominated by natural resource-based products, across the board in the case of Australia and the Pacific islands other than New Zealand, and agricultural products only in the case of New Zealand; see Table 2. Nearly three-quarters of the group's exports are accounted for by these commodities, a profile that is often typical of developing economies, especially in their early stages of growth. Some features of these stages of development are useful to note at this point. A very poor but growing economy will tend to export natural resource-based products in exchange for manufactures. It will export agricultural products (as in the case of the Pacific islands) or minerals according to its endowments. Over time it might switch to exporting manufactured goods, which are labor intensive. This is more likely when the country is relatively resource poor—

at least it will happen more quickly then. As the country develops its manufacturing base, it will tend to substitute capital-intensive for labor-intensive products. In the early stages, the manufacture of woolen or cotton clothing for instance, together with infrastructural needs, will create a demand for the import of raw materials. As the capital intensity of production rises, however, the demand for raw materials will tend to fall. In later stages growth is focused on human capital products, and agricultural imports might switch to food rather than items for further processing. Consider a group of economies such as those in East Asia, each with very different income levels: These countries illustrate different stages of this process.

The economies of Oceania display in the composition of their exports features typical of countries at the early stages of this development process. Yet some economies in the Oceanian group support high incomes: Australia and New Zealand are classified as "industrialized market economies." This is due to the large size and quality of the basic resource inputs into agriculture, minerals and energy, combined with a small population. In other words, Australia and New Zealand cannot be classified as natural-resource poor, and their competitiveness is retained in natural resource-based industries, extending perhaps to more highly processed forms such as the production of steel instead of ore and coal.

These features of the Oceania group's trade are also reflected in their indexes of "revealed comparative advantage." Such indices are calculated as the ratios of the share of a commodity group in a country's exports compared to its share in world trade. The Oceanian group has ratios greater than one for agriculture, and Australia has a high ratio for minerals and energy. The group also has high ratios for metals, although metals account for a very small proportion of world trade. (Metals are both resource intensive and relatively capital intensive—this might explain why the developing countries do not generally reveal a comparative advantage in metals whereas they do in agriculture, minerals and energy.) The group's share of manufactured goods in exports is very low compared to world averages. Clearly, these countries reveal a comparative advantage in natural resource-intensive products.

These similarities suggest that there will be limited opportunities for trade within the Oceanian group based on complementarity of economic structure—with perhaps the exception of minerals and energy. Despite this lack of complementarity, the trade among these countries is relatively intense. That is, the various economies account for a greater share of one another's trade than would be expected by their shares in world trade; see Table 3. For example, New Zealand has a share of Australia's exports that is nearly 12 times its share of world trade. Factors other than a complementary commodity structure account for this concentration of trade. One factor is that commodity classifications are rather too broad and that within them there is significant intraindustry trade; that is, items within a classification move in both directions. Another possibility is that trade is mutually biased due to policy factors (noted below) and other forces that reduce the barriers to trade. These forces include common colonial backgrounds,

Table 3
BILATERAL TRADE SHARES (%)

Origin	Pacific Islands	Shares in Exports Destination Australia	New Zealand	Pacific total
Pacific Islands	—	5.95	2.28	52.67
Austalia	2.78	—	3.47	58.92
New Zealand	3.45	15.57	—	64.73
Total Pacific	0.30	2.14	0.48	65.25

Destination	Pacific Islands	Shares in Imports Origin Australia	New Zealand	Pacific total
Pacific Islands	—	27.49	8.89	69.17
New Zealand	0.77	16.27	—	68.96
Australia	0.66	—	3.71	63.87
Total Pacific	0.11	2.06	0.52	64.11

Source: International Economic Data Bank, Australian National University.

which induce similar business practices and language, and the effects of shorter distances, which reduce costs of transportation and communication. Statistical analyses suggest that these biases overwhelm the lack of complementarity observed at the levels of commodity aggregation used here. These results apply to the Oceanian group as a whole.

This discussion refers solely to merchandise trade. There are other economic exchanges where complementarity will be higher. For example, intraregional tourist flows tend to be relatively intense. Also, Australia and New Zealand offer opportunities for the Pacific islands to export labor services.

The data on the commodity composition of trade suggests that the degree of complementarity will be much higher with other economies outside the Oceanian group. The importance of proximity as a source of trade bias further suggests that the trade of the Oceanian group will be concentrated in the Pacific Basin. In fact, in 1986 over 60 percent of the group's imports and exports came from or were destined for other economies in the Pacific Basin; see Table 3. This data refers to the recent direction of trade. With respect to the question of economic prospects for the region, consideration must be given to possibilities for future trade growth. The growth in demand for a country's exports will depend on the economic growth of its trading partners and on the degree to which those partners will open their economies to trade, or the degree to which they have already done so. On all counts, the countries of East Asia are likely to be the most important sources of trade growth for the Oceanian group. In East Asia the prospects for economic growth are strong and national economies are already very much open to the world economy, or, like China, they are going through a period of reform that will see them open up even more. As a result, an accelerated concentration of Oceanian trade with these East Asian countries is more than likely.

Such a process of growth and industrialization could also intensify the degree of complementarity between Oceania and East Asia, especially natural resource-poor northeastern Asia. Growth in that region will be associated with demands for raw materials for industry, especially fibers for processing (e.g., wool), minerals and energy. Opportunities will exist for Oceania to supply its traditional exports to new markets in that area. Furthermore, the industrialization of an economy tends to reduce the share of agriculture in production and therefore the degree of food self-sufficiency. Demand for food imports will grow over time as well. The commodity composition of imports in the more advanced and highly industrialized countries will shift from inputs to manufacturing. The degree of complementarity in those areas might consequently be expected to fall. On the other hand, because of the effects of growth on the composition of final consumption, new demands may be created. Already evident is massive growth in Japanese tourism in Oceania, a growth that could be mirrored in the future from South Korea and Taiwan. Other tradable services such as health and education may also come into demand. In other words, new forms of complementarity will tend to emerge. Interestingly, many forms may continue to have some link to resource intensity or at least to low population density, especially when this feature can be combined with the skills of high-income populations.

PROSPECTS

A powerful relationship binds the economic growth and outward orientation of the East Asia economies, especially those of northeastern Asia, with the economic prospects of Oceania. This is not to say that these economies are the only ones that matter. Clearly, traditional markets in other industrialized countries continue to be important. However, it is the rapidly growing and industrializing economies of East Asia that offer the greatest prospect for trade development. Factors that influence the growth of those economies will also influence growth in Oceania. As a result, Oceania and East Asia have a common interest in tackling the barriers to East Asian growth. One feature of the East Asian group is that the several countries are at varying stages of development. As a result, their export compositions are not only significantly different in profile but are changing as well because of rapid growth and industrialization. The implication is that newcomer suppliers from the region will tend to take over market share from traditional suppliers. This is already evident in the emergence of China in world textile and clothing markets.

This structural transition in production and trade has further implications for East Asian economies: They have a common interest in maintain-

1447

ing market access for their products. Their key markets are in North America and Europe, which account for about 60 percent of world imports. Japan is certainly an important destination for the East Asian group, but sustained growth will also require access to other industrialized markets. It seems unlikely that Japan alone as an export destination could sustain recent growth rates.

Immediate market access is not the only issue. A critical interest for East Asian economies is market access based on the principle of nondiscriminatory dealing. The changing export mixes of these countries mean that members of the group are continually moving into new product areas. Market access is required to make this transition possible. It will not be possible if newcomer suppliers are locked out of import markets by quotas to export that are given to older suppliers. This system creates short-run gains for preferred suppliers but can inhibit the change in the export mix of other countries at earlier stages of development. Thus, all these countries have a common long-run interest in nondiscriminatory market access. This interest spills over to Oceania as well because of its role as a material supplier to industrializing East Asia.

The Oceanian economies have a more obvious interest in the application of nondiscriminatory rules that also apply to import markets in East Asia. The United States has espoused bilateral (and therefore discriminatory) dealing in the Pacific region. This action is open to a number of interpretations. The United States could be aiming to stimulate the pace of commercial diplomacy in multilateral organizations. The General Agreement on Tariffs and Trade (GATT) could be the focal point of this strategy, with policies designed to isolate a number of markets in East Asia that could account for a significant part of Europe's exports in the 1990s. This is a legitimate tactic that could eventually promote trade, but it runs the risk of consolidating long-run trading arrangements that distort trade patterns, including those of the smaller countries in the Oceanian group overlooked in the negotiations. Second, U.S. initiatives could also reflect a growing interest in the Pacific economies. The challenge will be to sustain that interest without deferring to the United States by offering preferential access to markets in East Asia. The Oceanian group has a significant interest in these issues because it competes directly in some markets with the United States (e.g., coal, agriculture and beef in Japan, and some service markets). Thirdly, the United States may be attempting to manage the rate of penetration into its domestic markets. Such an arrangement would lock in the preferred suppliers and deny access to newcomers in the market (such as members of the rapidly growing East Asian group), and at the same time ensure for its own exporters some preferential access to East Asia, where there are trade issues associated with services and food. This interpretation lies farthest from the interests of Oceania.

Clearly, the Oceanian economies are critically interested in maintaining access for their agricultural exports, and for overcoming disruption in world markets for those products as a result of the actions of other countries. This is a familiar point and encapsulates Australian representations to European policymakers on the costs of the EC's Common Agricultural Policy, and the involvement of Australia, New Zealand, and Fiji in the Cairns Group of efficient agricultural exporters. In addition, however, the countries of Oceania have an interest in avoiding the use of discriminatory practices that inhibit trade between the East Asian economies and their industrialized country partners.

Thus, the Oceanian economies have a wide-ranging set of policy interests, and their prospects for growth depend on policy reforms not only in agriculture but also in the trade of manufactured goods. The fact that these economies have interests in common suggests that the Oceanian group may find it profitable to attempt to form coalitions in various international organizations, such as GATT, with their East Asian trading partners, who have much greater weight in the world economy. This common interest offers a strategy for tackling the dilemma that these small economies face in dealing with the rules of the international trading system. Pursuit of this strategy raises a number of questions about how it might be executed. Clearly, an option is to work through Pacific Basin institutions that handle economic issues in a way that involves the interests of many countries. An example is the Pacific Economic Cooperation Conference. Collecting agricultural exporters in the Cairns Group is another example of this sort of strategy. However, there are extra benefits if it is possible to put together a coalition of agricultural as well as manufacturing interests.

The Oceanian economies cannot involve themselves in these sorts of trade-policy initiatives without indicating a readiness to put their own houses in order. Obviously, reduced levels of protection afforded to the manufacturing sectors are necessary. Other actions that complement the efforts of commercial diplomacy are desirable. The Oceanian economies have already taken some initiatives with respect to regional trade agreements, in the form of Closer Economic Relations (CER) between Australia and New Zealand, the South Pacific Regional Trade and Economic Agreement (SPARTECA) among Australia, New Zealand, Fiji, the Solomon Islands, the Cook Islands, Kiribati, Nauru, Niue, Tonga, Tuvalu, Vanuatu and Western Samoa; and the Australia/Papua New Guinea Trade and Commercial Relationships Agreement (PATCRA).

The aim of SPARTECA is to facilitate the entry into Australian and New Zealand markets of as wide a range of products as possible from South Pacific Forum nations, either by removing duties or by providing extra margins of preference. The agreement is nonreciprocal. It has been interpreted as a device for diverting sources of imports to the South Pacific, thereby transferring tariff revenue to the Pacific island states, while attempting to limit the change in the level of protection afforded to industries in Australia and New Zealand. To some extent, therefore, it could integrate production in the Pacific islands with the import demands of the developed countries in the region. However, an assessment of the agreement is that it has had little impact on trade growth among Australia, New Zealand, and the Pacific islands. This is because market access has not been a problem for the types of items exported by these developing countries. SPARTECA might become more relevant if plans to build export processing zones for manufacturing textiles and clothing, especially in

Fiji, are fulfilled. In the past, the bigger problem has not been market access but rather the lack of marketing skills required to penetrate the markets of these two industrialized countries. An examination of alternatives to special trade deals, such as direct transfers to the Pacific island economies rather than via tariff revenue foregone, indicates that a greater boost to the economic prospects of the region is possible without distorting the location of production in the region.

CER came into effect in January 1983 and replaced an earlier agreement that had operated since 1956. The previous agreement had led to a reduction in tariff barriers among the countries. The new agreement was designed to stimulate this process by automatically including all goods in the agreement unless otherwise specifically negotiated. Also, the agreement was extended to include all quantitative import restrictions and export subsidies as well as tariffs. It has been argued that to maximize benefits the range of policies considered for "harmonization" will have to be extended even further.

There is the possibility of trade diversion as a result of this type of agreement in the Oceanian group. Trade diversion involves some costs, and the general interests of the region are to inhibit the growth of such policies in the world economy. However, a long-run benefit claimed for bilateral free trade is that it facilitates a more open policy to the rest of the world as well. In other words, the bilateralism that has been pursued in this case can be trade promotion in the long run. For example, free trade among these countries will tend to increase the rate of import penetration in various markets that could in turn hasten specialization in production and make each country more export orientated, and therefore more able to sustain an outward-looking set of economic policies. Assessments by CER suggest that this effect is greater in New Zealand than in Australia. One instance, in addition to the evidence of New Zealand's rapid growth in exports compared to Australia's, is the removal of severe quantitative barriers to imports into New Zealand as a result of CER. A further benefit claimed for structures such as CER is that they offer a basis for coordinated bargaining in other international organizations, which is important for these relatively small economies. These effects of integration of trade within the Oceanian group are therefore consistent with the swing to an East Asian orientation.

It is clear that despite the resource intensity of their production activities, the economic prospects of the Oceanian economies are not dismal; this is due to the demand for their exports created by the industrialization of East Asia. However, the economic prospects for Oceania, especially since its significance in the world economy is so small, depend critically on the application and maintenance of particular rules in the world trading system. Specifically, the Oceanian economies have a special interest in nondiscrimination, both in markets for exports of their East Asian trading partners and in the import markets of those East Asian economies as well. Those regional trading arrangements already developed by the group could actually promote further integration with East Asia.

The economic prospects for the region depend not only on the resolution of these issues, which are significant regionally and globally; domestic policy is also critical. However, the urgency with which domestic policy issues, namely policies that are inhibiting growth, are tackled is likely to depend on pressure from events in the world economy. For instance, the manufacturing sectors in both Australia and New Zealand have been highly protected. These economies cannot involve themselves in the formation of global policy initiatives without acting in a manner consistent with those initiatives themselves. Reduction in levels of protection is an obvious area, and in many cases such a reduction is possible. This can be traced to a number of factors. The industry in question might constitute an important input into the international competitiveness of another industry. In that case, exporter interests, most likely down the production line, will lobby for and support policy reform in the domestic political process. The development of a more outward-orientated industry as a result of such policy changes also carries some weight where a country is running large trade deficits and the improvement of export growth is a priority. A third factor supporting reform concerns the interests of a different group of exporters, the traditional export industries. They see their growth as contingent on sales to industrializing East Asia. As an exporter of manufactures often of high degrees of labor intensity, East Asia tends to be more highly protective of these sectors than nations within the Oceanian group. Their export prospects will be enhanced when their customers can gain access to more foreign markets, including those in Oceania. Thus, three forces for reform are important: the macroeconomic requirements; the interests of exporters in the manufacturing sectors whose competitiveness is held back by protection elsewhere in the sector; and the interests of traditional exporters.

Pressures for reform need not be restricted to the manufacturing sector. Similar arguments apply in the service sector of the economy. Australia and New Zealand have already acted to reduce the barriers to international trade in financial services. The regulation of the banking sector, especially in the presence of new technologies, inhibited the competitiveness of traditional banks in domestic and international markets. A more sophisticated finance market proved valuable in providing devices to transfer risks of dealing in a more open economy, in providing information on market opportunities in other countries, and in providing financial services in the foreign markets of the more internationally orientated Oceanian corporations. Similar pressures are emerging in other parts of the service sector, for example, in transportation and communications. In education, questions are being asked about how the services of education can be most efficiently exported to East Asia, and how domestic students in the system can be made more "Asia-literate."

SPECIAL PACIFIC ISLAND ISSUES

GNP per capita in the Pacific islands is of the order of U.S. $800. However, economic growth in the Pacific islands has been slow since the early 1970s. Slow growth over a long period is linked to special features of these economies, and clearly their growth prospects depend on the same set of factors. The key features of the Pacific island economies are their small size, their isolation, their concentration of production and trade in agricultural commodities, the significance of emigration and remittances, and the impact of foreign aid.

The population of the Pacific islands totals 5.1 million, compared to 3.1 million in New Zealand and 15.1 million in Australia. The land area of the islands is about 7 percent of that of Australia, but the sea area of the islands is huge—much more than the area of Canada and the United States put together, or about three times the area of Australia alone. The picture is therefore one of a small population spread over a vast area, with relatively low density on the land component. This combination has a number of implications. Small size means that these countries will have to focus on a few commodities for export in order to gain the benefits of access to world markets and the benefits of specialization. Size also means that the importance of the export sector in national output will tend to be high. The low population density and the command of a large area of sea resources suggest a specialization in primary commodities, as already observed in the aggregate data for the Oceanian group as a whole.

To some extent these expectations are borne out in the data. The major merchandise-export commodities are copper, gold, sugar, coconut, coffee, phosphate, timber, vegetable oils, and fish. Clearly, recent falls in commodity prices have had enormous effects on incomes and have necessitated major adjustments in these economies. These price falls have also reduced the apparent significance of exports in national output. Even so, the significance of exports is not uniformly high, being for example, for some countries in the range of 13 to 18 percent compared to around 40 percent for others. This is much lower than other island countries in Europe or the West Indies. It is important to identify reasons for the failures of the export sector to perform a leading role in growth over the long run.

The concentration in agricultural commodities has other implications. Because of the similarity among the island economies there is little intraregional trade. For the same reason, Australia and New Zealand are less significant as export destinations than they are as sources of imports. Colonial ties appear to be important in determining the major export destinations (e.g., the importance of Great Britain or France in some island exports). In some cases Japan is a major export destination but, in contrast to the picture for the Oceanian group as a whole, the East Asian economies are not major destinations for exports.

Examination of the unit export prices indicates that the quality of agricultural product exports is of lower quality than average in the world market. This will limit the access of the islands to new markets. Farther down the marketing chain, the prices received by farmers are also low. Prices received at the ports in the exporting countries are already low; they are often one-third below world prices. Farmers receive only a small proportion of this revenue because marketing boards take a significant proportion of the receipts. Thus agriculture, the likely area of greatest comparative advantage, is taxed by these policies. Land-tenure arrangements are also likely to impede productivity growth in agriculture, by reducing average lot sizes as population grows, sustaining subsistence agriculture, and inhibiting amalgamation and the adoption of new technologies.

However, it is not only supply-side factors that have reduced returns to exporting. The policies of other countries also have had enormous effects on the islands' exports. For example, Fiji has faced lower prices for sugar exports because of European Community policies. In addition, farm policies in Europe, Japan and the United States can be shown to increase the degree of instability in world market prices. Both directly and through substitution effects, these fluctuations feed into the export markets of the island economies.

A further barrier to export performance is the cost of overcoming geographic isolation. Given small volumes and the loss of sale economies in transportation, unit transportation costs tend to be high and to drive down the returns to exports as these small countries sell into a competitive world market. As a result, even if the countries are competitive producers of some items with free-on-board terms, they face offsetting disadvantages in terms of transportation costs. A combination of low density and long distances requires some careful transportation planning. At the same time, it might be expected that isolation would provide some natural protection for other import-competing industries; in that case, however, the disadvantage is the small size of the local market, and the problems of competing against much larger producers. Returns to exporting are lower than they might otherwise be because of these geographic features. This does not mean that a more inward-looking or self-reliant policy will promote growth; import substitution will direct resources into areas where the islands are even less competitive.

The high concentration of exports in agricultural products exposes these economies to a high degree of instability in returns to exports. Instability itself need not be an inhibitor of growth, but perhaps more important is the perception that instability is a problem that demands a policy response. These responses, however, can inhibit growth. Recommended strategies have involved the pursuit of diversification—in exports, the destinations of exports and in the structure of production—so that importable goods and services, which are difficult to purchase on world markets because of variation in export earnings, can be made available. However, such strategies can be highly distortionary (as noted above), and have a negative impact on growth rates.

To some extent, Papua New Guinea differs from the other island economies in that the country has the largest area and the lowest population density. Not surprisingly, it is also a large exporter of minerals, especially copper and gold. There is the prospect of another minerals boom with the discovery of new gold deposits. This will create a different sort of instability. Commentators have noted that if a boom does materialize, it will obviously be important to invest the funds in a way that will yield high returns and that will thereby sustain future growth when the boom disappears. Key issues include the value of investments in the social infrastruc-

1453

ture, including the education and justice systems, and the wage and exchange-rate policies in the country, as well as their impact on the competitiveness of the manufacturing and agricultural sectors.

One area of export in which it may be profitable for a number of the island economies to diversify is tourism, already a significant contributor to export credits in Fiji and the Cook Islands. Tourism is also another way of exporting more highly processed primary goods, such as local foods and handicrafts, which is a recommended form of diversification. However, the development of tourism also requires some careful strategic planning, especially in the construction of the infrastructure required, the training of staff and the building of complex transportation systems that permit tourists to visit a number of islands in one trip to the region. Tourism has another advantage in that it tends to be countercyclical compared to the prices of and demand for food exports, which are more influenced by cycles in the world economy.

This advantage is also true for aid flows and remittances. Both are high: Per capita aid flows to the island economies in 1985 equaled $148, compared to average GNP per capita of $1,220. These figures put the islanders among the highest aid recipients in the world. While in the short term aid has an important stabilizing influence, in the long term the significance of the flows is relatively unpredictable, politically motivated as they are. Given the small size of the recipient countries, aid flows have also had problematic effects on the exchange and structure of production similar to those of resource booms. Because the aid flows in the first instance to governments, the size of the public sector grows; wages rise, as a result of the demand for labor on public projects; and the rate of exchange remains high, biasing production against exports and in favor of imports. Overall, the private sector is constrained. Commentators also suggest that there have been problems in the procedure for the selection of projects and in the competition between donors for projects. These issues has become even more important as more aid becomes available, especially from Japan.

The combination of slow growth and a rapidly growing population has led many islanders to look outside their own countries for employment. Emigration has been described as essential for countries such as Tonga and Western Samoa. As a result of the export of labor services, the remittance line in the balance of payments is high, sometimes as important as the official aid flows (e.g., for Fiji, Tonga and Western Samoa). Overall, it would be expected that emigration would contribute to growth. Even though the labor supply contracts are in the home country and shortages of skills, which represent large budget outlays in the past, are unavoidable, the home country still receives the remittance, and later the benefits of savings and pensions when the retired workers return home. Population pressures at home are relieved as well. Yet a continuing contribution to growth from this source clearly depends on the future remittance pattern of the departing population.

In summary, the critical issues in the development of the Pacific island economies are: 1) the assessment of methods at the macroeconomic level to offset the effects of variable export earnings from the commodity groups in which they have the greatest competitiveness; 2) the reform of policies toward agricultural marketing and land tenure, which appear to be inhibiting incentives to invest in the rural sector; 3) the coordination of aid flows in ways that are even more countercyclical; 4) the selection of projects and the payments of aid funds in ways that do not exacerbate distortions in the structure of production and the biases against the private sector; 5) cooperative work on the development of transportation systems in the region for handling both tourists and freight; 6) the construction of the necessary infrastructure for the tourist industry; and (7) the impact of emigration, in terms of both the size of the flows and the patterns of remittance of those who leave home.

CONCLUSIONS

The countries of Oceania are rich in natural resources and generally have low populations relative to this resource base. Consequently, their exports are dominated by primary products such as agricultural goods, minerals, metals and energy. Their economies are also relatively open to world markets, with ratios of exports to output equal to or higher than average for similar economies. Thus, the economic prospects of these countries will depend very much on the prospects for their main export items. These commodities are also critical inputs into the process of industrialization. The East Asian economies are continuing to industrialize rapidly; this will reinforce the role of this region as a supplier to the Oceanian group of countries. This role is likely to be enhanced in the future, and the prospects for rapid growth in East Asia will spill over to Oceania.

This scenario is conditional on a couple of factors, both of which relate to government policies. One set of policies that is critical concerns the trade and industry policies of the industrialized market-economy trading partners of the East Asian exporters. Some of these policies deny access to these exporters, especially newcomer suppliers from the Pacific Basin region. This restricts growth not only in East Asia but also in countries that sell to it, such as those in Oceania. This means that the Oceanian economies have a strong interest in manufacturing-sector policies, in addition to their more obvious interest in agricultural issues. This mutual interest offers a way of dealing with the dilemma of being relatively small in the world but depending critically upon the world for growth. The second set of policies that is critical concerns the domestic trade and industry policies in Oceania. Reforms are important in the traditionally highly protected areas as well as the service sectors not presently exposed to trade because of regulatory barriers. Reform is likely to proceed rapidly where necessary in those policies because of the pressures created by the exporter groups, both in the manufacturing sector and in the traditional areas of export, who regard these reforms as methods of enhancing their international competitiveness.

In short, the prospects for growth in the Oceanian region are strong, despite recent slow growth and the peculiar composition of the region's production and exports. But growth is conditional on addressing some issues which have both regional and global significance. While this prognosis applies generally to the region there are some special issues for the Pacific island economies. These include concerns associated with the isolation and small size of these economies, the importance of aid to their growth, and the importance of population movements, both short-term visits by tourists and long-term emigration.

FURTHER READING

Anderson, Kym, and Garnaut, R. *Australian Protectionism: Extent, Causes and Effects.* Sydney: Allen & Unwin, 1987.
———. *Intensity of Trade between Pacific Basin Countries.* Canberra: Australian National University Press, 1983.
Drysdale, P. *International Economic Pluralism: Economic Policy in East Asia and the Pacific.* Sydney: Allen & Unwin, 1989.
——— and Patrick, Hugh T. *Evaluating a Proposed Asian-Pacific Regional Economic Organization.* Canberra: Australian National University Press, 1979.

BANKING AND FINANCE IN ASIA

ANTHONY ROWLEY

BANKING and investment structures are diverse in Asia, as is to be expected in a region that is itself rich in cultural, social and political institutions. If it is possible to generalize about these financial structures, the one thing that can be noted about their development is a steady shift from indirect to direct methods of financing—in other words, a shift from bank-dominated systems to ones where a variety of capital-market institutions coexist with powerful banks. Japan is the most obvious example of an Asian country whose financial structure has evolved to the point where the traditional role of banks as intermediaries has significantly diminished as users of capital have sought and obtained capital directly from both domestic and foreign investors. At the same time Japanese savers have come to expect considerably higher returns on their funds than those they enjoyed when banks were virtually all-powerful. It is to be expected that this pattern will also manifest itself in neighboring countries such as South Korea and Taiwan, widely regarded as the "new Japans" of East Asia. Hong Kong and Singapore are the only two Asian countries to have possessed a Western capital-market system for several decades because of their British colonial heritage. Here too there are peculiarities and distortions that differentiate these city-states from political units seen in the West. Elsewhere in Asia there exist a variety of different financial structures, most of which are bank-dominated. Pakistan is an exception to the rule in Asia in that it has evolved a relatively developed form of Islamic banking where the principles of debt and nondebt financing have become blurred within a system of profit sharing. How far these Islamic principles will penetrate into Southeast Asian finance, let alone into religious and social practices, is something hard to judge.

One remarkable feature of the Asian financial scene in the late 1980s was an ideological shift toward a belief in market mechanisms as an alternative to the allocation of funds through government budgets. To a certain extent this has been driven by the necessity for governments to reduce spending in line with reduced receipts, dictated in turn by deteriorating terms of trade and recessionary conditions. Privatization of loss-making public enterprises in order to reduce expenditures, and even to raise capital to pay off public debts, has been one result. This new respectability accorded capitalist ideas has not been solely a matter of expediency. The marketplace philosophy advocated by the administration of Ronald Reagan and the privatizing zeal of Margaret Thatcher's government have won adherents in many developing countries. There has been a new willingness in countries as diverse as Bangladesh, Papua New Guinea, Thailand and Taiwan to examine ways in which financial market mechanisms can assist national economic development. Nowhere has this transition been more unexpected than in China where parallel financial markets have sprung up alongside the official conduits of budgetary finance and where capital-market institutions of various kinds are now reappearing. It is premature to suggest that China is likely to evolve a liberal financial market system. The free-market segment of financing is still very small in relation to that controlled by the state. China is also undecided, even if it should permit some degree of independence for banking and investment institutions, whether it should opt for Japanese-style indirect financing or a more Western-oriented system of direct financing through capital markets.

FINANCIAL INSTITUTIONS IN JAPAN

Japan's ability to modify its own economic system so that direct and indirect forms of financing can coexist, as well as its ability to mix foreign financial institutions with peculiarly Japanese ones, is perhaps the most remarkable success story of all in Asia. It finds a parallel only in the way the Japanese have adapted their economy from one based on an exchange rate of 250 and more yen to the U.S. dollar (and on the stimulus of external demand) to one where the exchange rate hovers around 120 to one, and where domestic demand has been nurtured to take up the export slack.

Remarkable too has been the emergence of Japanese financial institutions on the international stage. At the beginning of the 1980s few outside of Japan could name a Japanese securities house other than perhaps Nomura; and few were familiar with Japanese banks others than the Bank of Tokyo. In less than a decade the names of securities firms such as Daiwa, Nikko and Yamaichi or banks such as Sumitomo, Dai Ichi Kangyo and Mitsubishi have become well known in the West. The nine largest financial institutions in the world, measured by stock market value, are Japanese and Nomura is the biggest among these. Nomura is also the biggest market-maker in the London-based Eurobond market, having dislodged Crédit Suisse First Boston from that position.

None of this success has been achieved with just posturing and fanfare or "positioning." The Japanese speak with almost clinical detachment when they declare their aim to become number one in most key areas of international banking and capital-market activity. It is as though they were simply working out a manifest destiny. As with their earlier penetration of United States and European markets for automobiles, electronics and other consumer goods, the Japanese have penetrated Western financial markets through careful preparation and painstaking strategy—plus a willingness and ability to accept very slender profit margins (sometimes in fact nonexistent) during the early stages. They carefully select an area of specialization and then put everything into conquering it before moving on to another.

One of the reasons why the transition from virtual obscurity to global preeminence has been so sudden is that the tidal wave of Japan's capital exports struck the world's financial markets with tremendous force. Between 1982 and 1986 Japan's gross external assets trebled to US$727 billion. The country's financial institutions are riding on the crest of this *tsunami* of money. Yet the Japanese yen is still far from playing a role commensurate with the global presence of Japanese financial institutions. The yen accounts for only seven percent of the reserve holdings of the world's central banks—perhaps only one tenth of the size of official holdings of U.S. dollars. And the yen's role as a transaction currency in international trade also remains tiny. This is partly because Japan chooses to denominate the bulk of its imports and exports in dollars but also because, until fairly recently at least, the world simply did not want yens. This situation is now changing with the decline of the U.S. dollar, and it seems inevitable that the yen will play a much greater role in the future as an international reserve and transaction currency.

As foreign borrowers become increasingly free to borrow yens from Japanese institutions, or to switch to yens through the huge swap markets, offshore holdings of yens will increase dramatically. The Japanese government is not altogether happy with this prospect. It is anxious to avoid the situation where a huge offshore yen overhang could become the tail that wags the dog of domestic monetary policy—but it is hard to see how this situation can be avoided.

Under Prime Minister Yasuhiro Nakasone, Japan abandoned some of its former defensive attitudes and resolved that, if it was going to achieve a bigger role on the world economic and monetary stage, it must be prepared to see the increasing internationalization of the yen. This is what is happening now, primarily through the issuance of yen instruments in the Euromarkets as well as through trade financing. With the growing internationalization of the yen will come the progressive decline of the enormous power exerted by the U.S. dollar, as well as the ability of the United States to continue funding its deficits by issuing debt-denominated instruments in its own currency and servicing them by the inflationary printing of money. Just what all this portends for the future stability of the international monetary system is difficult to predict although some believe that the system will be less stable without the presence of a single major numeraire of reserve value. Others believe that a multicurrency system based on the dollar, the yen and the European ECU will be inherently more stable.

Leaving such arguments aside it can be maintained with certainty that the international role of Japanese banks and securities houses will continue to expand in line with the growing internationalization of the yen. This will be apparent mainly in the Euromarkets although it is not inconceivable that Japan will open up its domestic financial markets in the next few years to the point where financial companies and institutions will be able to borrow freely or raise capital freely on the Tokyo market. Already Tokyo has launched its own offshore banking zone although it has remained fairly small in the first few years of its existence. It is no doubt intended as a controlled experiment until the Tokyo financial market proper is opened up to the outside world.

Certainly the sheer size of Japan's net overseas assets nowadays suggests that the further spread and eventual preeminence of Japanese financial institutions overseas is inevitable. In the same way that U.S. banks spread around the world in the late 1960s, at first supporting U.S. multinational corporations and then lending wherever there was a demand and to whomever seemed creditworthy, so Japanese banks seem destined to follow a similar route. The common factor is of course sheer wealth—first dollars and now yen—and the need to deploy them beyond the domestic economy. It is quite likely that the Japanese yen will become the principal currency in the so-called Asiadollar market—although some argue that this market is really an extension of the Eurodollar market—based in Singapore and Hong Kong, and begun by U.S. banks in the early 1970s.

At the end of 1986 Japan's net overseas assets totaled $180 billion (up from just $11 billion in 1981). Not since the oil crises of the 1970s has a shift in trade patterns had such a massive effect on the world's financial markets. The figure for Japan's net assets understates the size of international money flows. Between 1982 and 1986 the claims on Japan by the rest of the world somewhat more than doubled to $547 billion. Japan's gross assets meanwhile rose from $228 billion to $727 billion. Japan's markets were the major beneficiaries of the great surge in international liquidity during the 1980s. Japan's gross liabilities in the form of securities rose from $47 billion in 1982 to $146 billion in 1986 but this was far outweighed by Japan's own purchases of foreign securities. The amount of foreign securities held rose during the same period from $40 billion to $258 billion. Outflows of this magnitude are likely to continue as long as Japanese net savings continue to exceed investment requirements at home. Even with the sharp acceleration in domestic activity that began in 1987 it appears that outflows will continue at a very high levels into the early 1990s at least.

The bulk of Japanese financial investments have gone into U.S. markets, the short- and long-term bond markets primarily although also into equities. Elsewhere the Japanese have proved to be cautious investors, venturing only into the biggest and most liquid overseas markets, such as those for British gilts and Canadian or Australian bonds. They have ventured into equity markets to a limited extent. This too is changing slowly and Japanese institutions are maintaining an increasingly important presence in continental Europe fixed-interest and equity markets. Curiously the markets where the Japanese are most conspicuous by their absence are those virtually on their doorstep—namely in South Korea and Taiwan. However Japanese investors are becoming an important force in the Hong Kong stock market. Japanese institutions claim that the relative lack of liquidity in Asian stock markets (and the existence of anomalies in settlement systems) is a major factor keeping them out. In addition South Korea and certain Southeast Asian countries have deliberately discouraged Japanese portfolio investments for fear of being swamped by them and handing over some of their national assets to Japanese control.

The massive surplus of Japanese resources has coincided with the lifting of official ceilings on the proportion of assets that financial institutions can invest overseas. As a result all financial companies have rapidly increased their financial holdings although they are still well below the official ceilings in every case. Life insurance companies, with ¥8 trillion of foreign securities holdings as of mid-1987, are closest to the ceiling. They too will continue to increase the size of overseas holdings because of the need to find investment outlets for the fast-growing Japanese pension funds they control.

To put all this in perspective, Nomura estimates that Japan's net overseas assets will reach more than $550 billion by 1995. In other words Japan will become the world's paymaster in terms of overseas assets and, quite possibly, in terms of being home to the world's principal reserve currency before the end of the 20th century. This is especially likely if, as some observers suggest, Japan should become the center of a bloc in East Asia and Southeast Asia where the yen would be used as the chief settlement currency. Japanese banks and other financial institutions must inevitably develop harmoniously with this policy of national financial expansion.

FINANCIAL INSTITUTIONS IN CHINA

The overwhelming financial might that Japan has acquired since the mid-1980s suggests that it is in a singularly favorable position to influence and to participate in the development of financial structures in its neighbor China. So far this has not proved to be the case. North American and European banks, as well as those from Hong Kong, have penetrated China to a greater degree than have those from Japan. The Chinese, like the Koreans, appear to be wary of learning too readily from Japan, lest they fall under its influence. Strange as it may seem now, some Chinese see their country rivaling Japan some day as a financial power. Deng Xiaoping has declared that it is his ambition for China to become as important a trade center for the rest of Asia by the end of the 20th century as Japan is today. But there are enormous problems to overcome first.

Shanghai—China's traditional entrepôt and financial center—is presently caught between these fundamental contradictions. Many in Shanghai have the desire and ability to transform their city from a place where time almost stood still for 30 years to an important regional center of commerce again. Some of them would like to go further and see Shanghai rivaling not only Hong Kong and Singapore but even Tokyo one day.

From the day in 1979 when China announced its new "open door" policy toward the outside world and appeared ready to introduce elements of a market economy, it has been evident that the transition would be an extremely difficult one. Blending a centrally planned economy with market mechanisms is almost a contradiction in terms. Much the same difficulty applies to the idea that China's financing systems might be able to function independently of the nation's real economy. In a society that China's has been since the communist victory in 1949, financial markets have naturally been accorded very low priority. Not only were they long regarded as instruments of a defeated capitalist ideology but they were also considered functionally redundant in the sense that financial capital needed for productive enterprises could be provided directly by the state. The banking system, such as it was, existed only as a conduit to distribute funds decreed officially, to collect surpluses available in the personal sector for savings and to conduct external trade transactions.

The economic reforms since 1979 have led to changes in the system. In an effort to make industrial managers more performance conscious, government officials have attempted to make them aware of the cost of funds and of the need to generate a surplus on such funds. Finance is to be provided through the banking system rather than through the national treasury; enterprises are supposed to pay interest on loans received rather than simply reimburse the state through taxes. This system has been implemented to a degree, along with the reestablishment of more traditional roles for banks in China. They are no longer simply treasurers dispensing state allocations. Short-term money markets have also been introduced in certain centers, including rudimentary interbank and foreign exchange markets. At the same time long-term capital markets have reappeared in China with both stock and bonds being issued by enterprises and cooperatives. There is little secondary market trading as yet.

These reforms have occurred a little too quickly for China's own good in that they have already provoked something of a backlash and a slowing down of the pace of financial change. In the same way that China's "open door" policy led to a massive surge in consumer and capital goods imports during 1985 and to a subsequent official curb on imports during 1986, so both banking and capital-market reforms have provoked reactions at official levels. The effect of channeling funds to enterprises through the banking system led to its own form of distortion. Instead of bidding for funds on the basis of ability to pay, some enterprises were able to use their connections with high-level politicians and bureaucrats to obtain bank loans. In some cases such cadres appear to have directed banks to make loans in order to finance their own pet projects. The result again was a clampdown by high-level government officials. Much the same thing happened in the capital market where a flood of share issues by enterprises in the late 1980s led to fears in Beijing that the market experiment might be getting out of hand. From early 1987 an official moratorium was imposed on further issues of shares by state enterprises; only collectives and cooperatives (as distinct from state enterprises) were permitted to issue shares for the time being. Bond issues are, however, still freely permitted.

The upshot of all this is that China now appears to be trapped in a sort of holding pattern as far as its financial development is concerned. An optimistic view of this situation considers it simply a healthy pause in the pace of economic reform that gives China the opportunity to think more carefully about how far and how fast it wishes to go. A less optimistic view claims that state plan-oriented policymakers have gained the upper hand and that the great majority of funds for enterprises will continue to be allocated directly by the state. The latter view is supported by the fact that, according to sources in the People's Bank of China (the central bank), the basic characteristics of the Chinese financial system have not changed greatly despite the reforms. Over 90 percent of funds are still allocated directly by the state and only 10 percent through the independent operations of banks and capital markets. Statistics for this vary widely, however, and while it is difficult to gauge the exact size of the so-called parallel financial markets it does appear that they are growing.

They must grow if China is to overcome the shortage of funds that bedevil the attempts of many enterprises, including foreign joint ventures, to expand in China and to obtain sufficient working capital for their needs. This shortage is caused by budgetary restraint on the part of the central government which cannot yet be offset by the operations of the money and capital markets. Fiscal and monetary politics are still not coordinated. Along with the cautious reappearance of rudimentary share trading in Shanghai and many other centers there has been the reemergence of financial institutions such as insurance companies and pension funds that are an essential adjunct to any efficient capital market.

Perhaps the best way to judge China's progress in financial reform is to recall the Cultural Revolution in the late 1960s when just about anything that smacked of capitalism was abhorred and anyone suspected of having sympathy for its ideals was liable to be arbitrarily detained, tortured and even executed. Remnants of these attitudes persist to this day in China and thus it is obvious why reformers have to proceed with caution. Viewed in this light progress toward a less rigid form of communist-socialist ideology has been remarkable.

STOCK MARKETS ELSEWHERE IN ASIA

Looking beyond Japan and China to Asia as a whole, perhaps the best way to judge the progress made toward the development of modern financial institutions is to look at what has been achieved in the development of stock markets and the promotion of broad-based capital markets independent of banks. It is certain that the power of banks throughout the region is still formidable. This power has declined in Japan, relative to overall financing. But it is still firmly entrenched in South Korea. In Indonesia it is almost absolute. In Thailand, Malaysia, the Philippines and India banking systems are still very powerful.

To those accustomed to the liberal capital-market system of the United States and Britain, these Asian systems appear antiquated and overly rigid. To those accustomed to the more bank-dominated financing systems of continental Europe, the situation might appear different. Reforms that have taken place in Asia in the 1980s suggest that the region is evolving slowly but surely toward the U.S. and British model of financing rather than toward the continental system. (Even the financial structures of Europe are destined to become more open and liberalized under the plan for a single, unified market within the European Community beginning in 1992.)

Japan's stock market is Asia's biggest not only in absolute terms but in economy-relative terms too. Whereas the total capitalization of stocks on Wall Street is equivalent to roughly half of the value of the U.S. GDP, the value of Tokyo-listed stocks is about equal to Japan's total GDP—a remarkable fact in a country where the stock market was relatively under-developed until the beginning of the 1980s and where banks have traditionally been the dominant force in financing.

There is virtually no country of any significance in Asia (except those in Communist Indochina) that does not have a functioning stock market to-day. Even the Himalayan kingdom of Nepal has established one and Papua New Guinea, which came into contact with the modern world only 50 years ago, is thinking about one.

Hong Kong's is the biggest of the Asian stock markets after Japan's, yet as of mid-1986 its $35 billion capitalization was less than three percent of Tokyo's. The value put by the Japanese market on the shares of Dai Ichi Kangyo Bank alone in 1986 roughly equalled the combined capitalization of the Singapore and Kuala Lumpur stock markets. Although South Korea and Taiwan are often termed the "New Japans" of East Asia, their stock markets are tiny by comparison with that of Japan. For instance, the two markets put together amount to no more than a few percentage points of Japan's total capitalization. Much the same can be said for the stock markets of Hong Kong and Singapore. Yet by 1995 the combined exports of these four countries are likely to equal four fifths those of Japan. The stock markets of Hong Kong and Singapore are, however, large in relation to the size of the economies of these two city-states. (Hong Kong's population is around 5 million and Singapore's is roughly half that.) South Korea, with a market capitalization equal only to about 10 percent of the size of the economy, and Taiwan, where the ratio is around 20 percent, clearly have much more scope (and need) to increase the size of their stock markets if they wish to emulate Japan. The same goes for countries such as the Philippines, Thailand, India and Indonesia—the latter with the least developed of all Asian stock markets.

The obvious questions which arise are why the markets outside of Japan (leaving aside Hong Kong and Singapore) are so small and how it is that Asian countries have been able to finance the dramatic growth they have enjoyed in recent decades with apparently little help from their stock markets. The primary determining factor in almost all of the countries concerned is the dominance of banks, both government-owned and privately owned, and of debt financing. The power of Japan's banks was legendary until the mid-1980s when the huge export surpluses enjoyed by Japanese trading houses and manufacturing groups weaned the biggest corporations away from overdependence on overdraft financing. Some of them now have treasury departments that are richer than the commercial banks. Japan, however, is the exception rather than the rule in this respect. An Asian Development Bank study in 1986 of capital-market development in six Asian countries—Indonesia, South Korea, Pakistan, the Philippines, Sri Lanka and Thailand—showed that commercial banks controlled at least 40 percent of all financial institution assets in these countries. In Pakistan and Sir Lanka the figure was over 60 percent.

The domination of the banks has meant the subjugation of capital-market development in general and of stock market development in particular. Financial institutions such as pension funds, insurance companies and mutual funds, which in many Western countries absorb a large proportion of national savings and channel them into stock markets, either do not exist or are severely restricted in Asia. The massive preemption of national savings in Singapore and Malaysia by state-run provident schemes has cut deeply into the market of private provident funds and into the amount of disposable income available for securities investment. Generally in Asia neither insurance (especially life insurance) nor pensions is regarded as an essential form of financial provision, although this situation is changing slowly. Tax laws are still biased in favor of debt financing and against equity funding in most Asian countries.

On top of this there is an underlying distrust of stock markets among many bureaucrats. Stock markets are often seen as little better than casinos; consequently the government's role is confined to heavy-handed intervention aimed at controlling speculation. The irony is that the absence of capital-market institutions in itself increases the relative influence of individual investors and thus the volatility of stock markets. In both South Korea and Taiwan for instance governments have put much more effort into (often unsuccessful) attempts to control stock markets than into promoting capital-market institutions with long-term perspectives that could help to stabilize markets.

Fortunately this attitude is changing and the idea that capital markets do have a useful role to play is taking hold slowly across Asia. South Korea and Taiwan remain ambivalent in their attitudes toward market development. In both countries a strong suspicion of foreign influence continues to operate against the acceptance of foreign portfolio investment. In South Korea this translates into the acceptance of a huge—but now diminishing—burden of foreign debt rather than an acceptance of nondebt financing through foreign portfolio investment. In Taiwan it manifests itself in a fortresslike mentality toward national reserve building. There are, admittedly, national security considerations in Taiwan's case.

In the six members of the Association of Southeast Asian Nations rather different factors have impeded the growth of stock markets. Many of these countries have markets whose histories go back a long time. Indonesia for instance has had a stock market of sorts since 1912 and the Philippines since 1927, and Singapore knew share trading before the end of the 19th century. But these markets were legacies of the colonial systems under which all three (plus Malaysia) operated. The development of their economies in recent times has been financed largely outside of their stock markets. Although Singapore has a very substantial stock market in relation to the size of its economy, it has financed much of its infrastructure and industrial development through state savings systems while the local stock market has served largely as a theater of operations for Malaysian companies. In Malaysia itself a major program of industrialization on the east coast has been financed largely through borrowings from foreign banks thus adding to the country's rapidly growing debt burden. Similarly Thailand, whose stock market grew for a long time at a snail's pace, has a $1.2 billion eastern coastal development program to finance and appears to be doing so without the help it ought to expect from a fully developed stock market. The Philippines stock market, until 1973 one of the biggest in Asia, has declined sadly since then. In Indonesia the stock market is a virtual irrelevance in terms of total financing.

There is little doubt that a great deal more money is going to become available for investment in Asia's stock markets in the 1990s as East Asian export surpluses seek a home for investment and as portfolio managers in the West seek diversification of their assets. At present there are few if any stock markets in the developing world that can seriously challenge Asia's claims to provide economic growth along with relative political stability. The markets of Latin America—notably Brazil's—are, however, becoming better known and somewhat better trusted in the outside world and unless Asian governments make a determined effort to open their markets more to outside investment (through the removal of legal and tax barriers and other disincentives) they could find themselves bypassed by the huge pool of surplus liquidity which the world generated in the 1980s.

BANKS ELSEWHERE IN ASIA

To generalize about banking in Asia is to court the danger of oversimplification. The problems that Japanese banks face as they enter the mature stages of financial liberalization are quite different from those confronted by Chinese banks as they set out along an uncertain road toward modernization. And a fundamentally Islamic banking system in Pakistan has little in common with the rigorously government-controlled banking system in South Korea, other than perhaps inefficiency. Nevertheless in those Asian countries where banks do operate to a greater or lesser degree along modern, international lines the problems they confront at present are not very different from those facing banks in the Western world: continuing disintermediation, increasing competiton and declining margins. The extent to which the global stock market crash of October 1987 will alter this situation by discouraging the further securitization of debt and initiating a resurgence of the syndicated loans market remains to be seen.

Bank regulators meanwhile continue struggling to keep pace with the changes in the nature of banking and finance, hoping at least not to fall farther behind. Hong Kong has demonstrated perhaps the greatest awareness so far of the need for regular contacts among banking regulators in other countries. This is a welcome development given the ease with which crooked bankers and entrepreneurs have been able to exploit the lack of communication among different jurisdictions. This process still has a long way to go, however, in cementing better regulatory ties between Hong Kong and countries such as Malaysia, Thailand and Singapore where the overseas Chinese nexus is strong.

But in the more conceptual area of where banking is going in relation to capital-market development in general, regulators can only sit and watch what happens. International financial influences are so strong now in the more open of Asia's economies that any attempt to opt out of the global evolutionary process would be futile. Singapore and Hong Kong are forced to recognize this fact just as much as Tokyo, New York and London. Singapore and Hong Kong, being the principal offshore banking centers in Asia at present, are most embroiled in these changes. Singapore's $200 billion Asiadollar market moved significantly down the road toward debt securitization and away from loan syndication at the end of 1987. There has been something of a swing back toward loan syndication and away from securitization since then in global financial markets but this may only be a temporary reaction to the market crash of October 1987.

Banks have to win back business from the securities markets if they are to survive. Alternatively they have to assume a greater role themselves in securities underwriting and trading. They are presently prevented from doing so in Japan by Article 65 of the Securities Act which, like the Glass-Steagall Act in the United States, formally separates investment banking from commercial banking activities. The Glass-Steagall Act is likely to be repealed in the United States before long, however, and then it will be only a matter of time before Article 65 in Japan goes too.

In South Korea a turnaround to current account surplus for the country during 1986 following a decade or so of deficits left the financial system there awash with liquidity. This meant not only that the government was able to start repayment of its substantial debt but that, for the first time in country's history, savings exceeded investment. These changes have eliminated the two most important arguments used in the past to justify the tight control that the government exercises over banks. Because of previous reliance on foreign capital, it was argued that loans had to be made to those industries well positioned to earn foreign exchange, which in turn could be used to pay off the debt. In the past too it was argued that deposit interest rates had to be held at high levels in order to attract money into the banking system and away from the unofficial curb market and from property speculation.

The curb market has always been a major component of the South Korean financial scene. Arguably it is a product of rigid government control over banks and over the centralized allocation of loans. Those middle-sized and small enterprises that were not big enough to have bank loans directly had to turn somewhere for finance and it was to the curb. The system's brokers acted as go-betweens securing finance at very high rates for cash-hungry businesses and paying less high rates of interest to depositors, thereby making nice margins for themselves in the process. The curb market has in fact been such a lucrative source of profit for its organizers that many high-level politicians as well as business people have been drawn into it, thus ensuring protection from official interference. Successive scandals involving high-level figures in curb market failures eventually led to clamps on this informal sector. A similar situation exists in Thailand where the curb market consists of a network of "chit funds" subscribed to by housewives and others anxious to reap the maximum return on their savings. In Thailand's case this is not so much a reflection of the inadequacy of banking structures; it simply shows, once again, that senior political and military figures are willing to give protection to chit-fund operators. Government bureaucrats were for a long time powerless to move against such people even though recent curb market scandals in both South Korea and Thailand have led to pressure for reform.

Meanwhile the South Korean government has found it hard to cope with the sudden surplus of liquidity that the country is enjoying. Although the rationale for the government's presence in South Korean financial markets has been partly removed by the current account surpluses and the liquidity boom, it still appears that the institutional ties between the banks and the government will take more than a few years of current account surpluses to weaken. The country's four main commercial banks were state-owned until President Chun Doo Hwan came to power in 1980. These banks have since been partly hived off to private shareholders (in the name of deregulation) although their presidents continue to be selected by the ministry of finance, often from among its own ranks. Another factor that binds the South Korean banks closely to the government, apart from the fact that the government still sets interest rates and lending guidelines, is the large number of nonperforming loans that banks have on their books. These are a legacy of many years of lending decisions made on political and bureaucratic, rather than business, grounds.

In certain Asian countries the situation is even worse in this regard. In Malaysia for example commercial banks have for decades been compelled to lend to priority sectors such as agriculture and small holdings. Apart from the dubious commercial merit of such state-directed lending policies they can also be faulted on the grounds that they are linked to racial considerations. In an effort to encourage the native Malay (*bumiputra*) citizens (as distinct from either Indian or Chinese Malaysians) to become more involved in business and investment, the government compels banks to lend a certain proportion of their funds to this group. No matter how laudable this may be in terms of establishing social equity, in practice the result has led to undisciplined lending to *bumiputras* simply so that banks can fill their quotas. Many of the loans have never been paid back.

All of this illustrates a deficiency common to the financial systems of many Asian countries. Where governments have tried to nurture economic development (the case in most countries), they have assumed that financial capital is a commodity whose cost can be regulated through control of the interest rate structure and the banks. It has not occurred to them to encourage the development of a range of financial institutions competing for savings so that the cost of capital arbitrates priorities in the scale of national investment needs. This is understandable because politicians and bureaucrats find it easier to control a relatively small number of banks whereas a plethora of capital-market institutions—indicative of a balanced and dynamic financial system—are much harder to regulate.

Taiwan too is almost a textbook case of unbalanced financial development. Its huge export surpluses find relatively few attractive domestic channels of reinvestment so they tend to get channelled offshore where they add to the country's already huge surpluses. Despite its small size Taiwan presently has the second largest official reserves in the world. Taiwan has not gone in for the same sort of state-decreed investment in heavy industry as has South Korea but the lack of a balanced capital-market structure nevertheless tends to confine capital to a relatively small group of industries.

It cannot be denied of course that the newly industrialized nations of East Asia and various countries of Southeast Asia have achieved something of an economic growth miracle in recent decades—in spite of rather than because of their rigid banking and financial systems. A Confucian respect for authority (provided those in charge are able to deliver their part of the bargain by way of general prosperity), a willingness to accept pragmatic solutions to problems rather than to seek remedies in rigid ideologies, and educational systems that have produced intelligent government technocrats as well as skilled industrial workers have all been important factors. So too have been the comparative lack of labor disputes and the general desire to catch up and eventually overtake Western countries. A willingness to save and to accept comparatively small returns on savings through modest bank interest rates has also played a part.

These factors were very much part of the Japanese success story and thus the Japanese economy was able to succeed within the context of a somewhat outdated financial system. To their credit successive Japanese administrations—especially that of Yasuhiro Nakasone—permitted the financial system to evolve into one responsive to internal and external pressures for change and for deregulation. If other Asian countries would permit a similar evolution rather than trying to force their financial systems into rigid molds there is no reason why they too should not develop financial institutions and capital-market systems capable of carrying them into the mature phases of economic development: namely a shift toward more consumer and domestic demand-oriented growth as a counterbalance to overreliance on exports.

Elsewhere in Asia, and especially on the Indian subcontinent, banking reforms like most other things move slowly. Following Prime Minister Rajiv Gandhi's accession to power there were high hopes that India's financial sector, like its industrial and commercial systems, would be freed from the stranglehold of bureaucratic power and corruption. Such hopes have not yet been realized. Bankers also desired a dose of financial deregulation to bring India's inflated interest rates more into line with world norms. Such desires were fueled by reformist bureaucratic rhetoric. Recently, however, the Reserve Bank of India (the central bank) became alarmed at what it saw as the inflationary potential of lowering interest rates and allowing money supply to rise. Interest rate liberalization has been only halfhearted. The fact that most major banks in India remain under state control—bank employees frequently demonstrate in favor of nationalizing foreign banks in the country too—does not help efficiency. Developments such as computerization of bank services help only at the margin. The fundamental problem is that political and social objectives are all too often permitted to intrude upon what should be the basic function of banks: to collect and allocate savings according to where the funds can be used most efficiently, as determined by the price mechanism.

But if the Indian financial system is bound by ideology to a large extent, it is relatively liberal in operation compared to that of Pakistan. There Islamic banking is in formal operation. Banks in Pakistan are finding it difficult to maintain satisfactory rates of return on customers' deposits under the profit-and-loss sharing system of interest-free banking. The concept of interest (especially usury) is alien to Islamic law (Shariah), and therefore banks have to devise a mechanism of profit sharing in order to replace the principle of interest. The result is something between debt and equity financing, blurred at the edges and confusing one with the other.

In Bangladesh too pressure is mounting for the introduction of Islamic principles in banking. This has not been diminished by a recent ruling of an Egyptian court that interest is legal and does not amount to usury. Those banks in Bangladesh that already practice Islamic banking say that their thinking is guided more by the Shariah council (consisting of Islamic scholars) than by any temporal body. This is rather ironic because the first interest-free, Shariah-based bank was in fact established in Cairo in 1963. For ideological purity in banking principles, though, South Asian countries have tended to look to Iran rather than to Egypt in recent times.

In Iran itself there is fierce debate over the extent to which Islamic principles can be applied to the economy. If this situation should lead to a softening of Iran's own interpretation of Islamic financing, it would have the effect of permitting more liberal interpretations in countries such as Pakistan and Bangladesh. It is interesting to note that there are many eminent Pakistanis working in institutions such as the World Bank and the International Monetary Fund where they embrace Western concepts of financing that they would not apply in their own country.

At the opposite end of the spectrum to the state- and ideology-influenced banks of the Indian subcontinent are those in the British colony of Hong Kong. There the banking system continues to be dominated by the Hong Kong and Shanghai Banking Corporation and by the Chartered Banks, both British owned. Increasingly, however, their monopoly is being challenged within Hong Kong itself by the Bank of China and its 13 so-called sister banks in the colony. The size of their deposit base has grown enormously in recent years, assisted by sophisticated innovations such as electronic banking and computerization but also by the latent chauvinism of the Chinese and their preference to keep everything within one big Chinese family. Through Hong Kong, China is able to fund a not insignificant part of its capital needs by collecting deposits from Hong Kong savers and channeling them to China to finance productive enterprises. As the 1997 date for the restoration of Hong Kong to Chinese sovereignty draws near it can be expected that the colony will increasingly be called upon to assume the role of a financial center specifically for China rather than that of a freewheeling little financial entrepôt that seeks its profits where it can best find them.

There are questions too over how long Hong Kong can continue to serve as the premier loan syndication and offshore financial center for East Asia and Southeast Asia. This is not simply due to the increasing shadow which China casts over the colony but also because Tokyo is growing rapidly in importance as a regional and international financial center. It appears to be only a matter of time before Tokyo becomes Asia's premier loan financing center although Hong Kong is likely to maintain its supremacy as a portfolio fund management center, at least until such time as China deems otherwise. Hong Kong's liberal tax laws and generally free financing climate militate in favor of fund management remaining supreme there if it continues to be a free society. A wave of bank failures in Hong Kong in recent years has led to a tightening of financial regulations in the banking sector. The present British administration should be in position to hand over a smoothly functioning financial center to Beijing when the time comes.

One aspect of the banking failures has yet to be resolved, though, and it is one that has lessons for Asian financial centers other than Hong Kong. Many of the banks that failed have strong links with overseas Chinese bankers and entrepreneurs in countries such as Malaysia, Thailand and Singapore. Such is the extensive and intricate financial and business nexus of the overseas Chinese throughout Southeast Asia that it is impossible to separate transactions in one country (and within any one banking jurisdiction) from those in another. Money can and does flow swiftly and easily from one overseas Chinese group to another throughout the region. This constitutes a nightmare for banking regulators and monetary authorities trying to keep track of such funds. Money that may appear to have been lent to a safely diversified group of borrowers may in fact turn out to have been lent to a different but connected group. When there is a failure within such a group— or when there is outright fraud as sometimes happens—the regulators wake up to find that the lending institution is bankrupt and the directors have fled to a refuge where they remain beyond the law. There have been attempts by banking regulators to improve coordination in keeping track of such groups, but there is as yet a long way to go. Linked business groups— extended families of entrepreneurs might be a better term—among the Chinese is not purely an offshore phenomenon either. In Taiwan for instance the collapse of the Cathay Group in the mid-1980s embroiled many other business concerns in the country. Until some of these apparently sound firms collapsed the full nature of their links with defaulted core companies had not been appreciated. Accountancy rules are slowly being tightened, corporate disclosure improved and regulation stiffened in Taiwan.

Singapore has long applied draconian regulation to its banking and financial sector, to the point where some have suggested that it stifles all financial innovation. Nevertheless Singapore has managed to avoid significant banking or financial defaults. The so-called Pan-Electric affair in 1985, which brought about the downfall of this particular company and precipitated a dramatic crash on both the Singapore and Kuala Lumpur stock markets, was a major exception and one that resulted in further tightening of market regulation in Singapore. The question is whether Singapore can reasonably hope to pick up business that may avoid Hong Kong as 1997 draws near and the financial environment there becomes less free. At one time Singapore's chances looked good but the rise of Tokyo as a financial center will overshadow Singapore's prospects to some extent. On the other hand, there is always room for an enterprising financial entrepôt that thrives on the freedoms bigger centers linked to major economic hinterlands are

1471

not able to provide. If Singapore can cast off the more oppressive aspects of its government regulation, it could have a bright future as the new Hong Kong of Southeast Asia.

FURTHER READING

Asia Yearbook. Hong Kong: *Far Eastern Economic Review,* Annual.

Capital Market Development in Selected Developing Countries of the Asian Development Bank. Manila: Asian Development Bank, 1986.

Rowley, Anthony. *Asian Stockmarkets: The Inside Story.* Dow Jones-Irwin, 1987.

————. *Financial Centre Shanghai—Achievements, Problems and Prospects.* Shanghai: Freidrich Ebert Foundation, 1988.

Skully, Michael, ed. *Financial Institutions and Markets in the Far East.* Basingstoke, Hampshire: Macmillan, 1982.

The Japanese Financial System. Tokyo: Bank of Japan.

The World Economy and Financial Markets in 1995: Japan's Role and Challenges. Tokyo: Nomura Research Institute, 1986.

Van Agtmael, Antoine W. *Emerging Securities Market.* London: Euromoney Publications, 1984.

Viner, Aron. *Inside Japan's Financial Markets.* London: Economist Publications, 1988.

THE ASIAN
DEVELOPMENT BANK

ROBERT WIHTOL

Is it possible for a multilateral development bank, funded mainly by Japan and the Western industrial countries and lending to developing countries, to respond with flexibility to the diverse and changing needs for development finance in Asia? The Asian Development Bank (ADB) was set up in 1966 to fill a gap in the finance available for development projects in the region, mainly in the sectors of agriculture, infrastructure and industry. From relatively modest beginnings, its annual lending has expanded to over US $2.4 billion. In volume the ADB's present lending program is second only to that of the World Bank as a source of public development finance in Asia.

Over time the region's needs for finance have changed considerably. In the 1970s agriculture, rural development and energy were the bank's principal areas of lending. The agricultural sector and rural development continue to have high priority in most of the region's poor countries, but the steady growth in the region's middle-income and newly industrialized countries in the 1980s has led to a decline in demand for conventional project loans and the emergence of new financial needs. In recognition of these changes, at the urging of several of its donor countries the bank commissioned a team of international experts to prepare a study, completed in 1989, on the bank's role in the region in the 1990s.

As the gap between the region's rich and poor countries widens, and as the borrowing countries' needs become more diverse, two principal challenges will face the ADB. First, will the bank be able to mobilize the financial resources to meet the economic requirements for concessional finance in the poorest Asian countries? Only by continuing to provide substantial "soft" lending to the low-income countries can the bank hope to contribute to their agricultural development and social infrastructure, thus alleviating poverty and raising the living standards of the poor in the region. Second, will the bank be able to develop new forms of cooperation that correspond to the emerging financial needs of the middle-income and newly industrialized borrowing countries?

These questions and others of relevance to the ADB's future roles are examined in the light of the bank's past record and present situation. Following an outline of how the bank functions, its lending policies and operations are discussed at four levels: the policies and interests pursued by the individual member countries of the bank, the ADB's development policies, changing management policies under the ADB's four presidents and the bank's lending operations.

HOW THE BANK OPERATES

The ADB was established as the result of a series of preparatory meetings held between 1963 and 1966 under the auspices of the United Nations Economic Commission for Asia and the Far East.[1] On one hand, the bank was set up in response to the perceived need among the Asian countries for a source of development finance catering to the specific needs of the region. In the early 1960s there was considerable dissatisfaction among the Asian countries with World Bank lending, which in Asia was concentrated mainly in India and Pakistan and on infrastructure as opposed to agriculture or industry. On the other hand, the main incentive for the financial participation of the industrialized countries lay in the opportunity the bank offered as a means for promoting their development policies and economic and political interests. Japan played a central role in establishing the bank, due to the vital importance of the Asian developing countries both as a source of raw materials and food and as an outlet for expanding exports and foreign investment for the Japanese economy.

The ADB's principal mode of operation is the provision of capital assistance for development projects, in the form of loans on either ordinary or concessional terms. Loans from the bank's ordinary capital resources (OCR) have a two- to seven-year grace period and a maturity of 10 to 30 years, and carry interest rates varying from 6.875 percent in the late 1960s to 10.5 percent in 1983. In 1986 the bank introduced a standard variable interest rate which was initially set at 7.65 percent and revised in 1987 to 7.03 percent. Concessional loans from the bank's special fund resources have a 10-year grace period, a maturity of 40 years and carry interest only in the form of a 1 percent service charge. Ordinary loans are made for all sectors of bank activity, and have been made principally to the borrowers with a relatively high GNP per capita, particularly the Southeast and East Asian developing countries. Concessional loans have been granted mainly to the least developed members, particularly in South Asia, and are often more directly poverty oriented, focusing predominantly on agriculture and rural development. By the end of 1987 the bank had committed ordinary loans totaling $14,697.6 million and concessional loans worth $7,134.9 million.

In addition to its lending activities the bank provides technical assistance grants and has carried out various regional activities. Technical assistance is intended mainly to help the borrowing countries in project preparation and implementation, and has concentrated on the least developed member

[1] In 1974 the Economic Commission for Asia and the Far East was renamed the Economic and Social Commission for Asia and the Pacific.

countries. The bank's regional activities include undertaking or commissioning various regional surveys and studies, and organizing meetings, seminars and workshops. Technical assistance and regional activities provide the ADB with a means of influencing the formulation of development policies in its borrowing countries, and in the 1980s there has been a clear shift from the provision of policy guidance at the regional level to the enhancement of the bank's role in country-level policy formulation. Compared with the World Bank, which often makes loans conditional on policy changes, the initial thrust of ADB operations was at the project rather than the policy level. Recently the bank has increasingly attached policy conditions to its loans, and has to a limited extent started program lending. By 1987 the bank had provided $280.8 million in technical assistance grants, of which $235.9 million was for technical assistance to individual countries and $44.9 million for regional activities.

ADB operations are funded through these channels, which correspond to the bank's modes of operation. The bank's ordinary capital resources form the basis for ordinary lending operations, while the Asian Development Fund (ADF) provides concessional loans. Technical assistance grants are funded mainly through the bank's Technical Assistance Special Fund (TASF), and these are supplemented with grants from other sources, mainly donor countries' bilateral programs and the United Nations Development Program.

The bank's OCR consist of three main categories: subscribed capital stock, funds raised by the bank through borrowing and funds received by the bank as repayment and income from OCR loans. Based on its subscribed capital stock, the bank borrows on the international capital markets and lends to its developing members on terms which broadly reflect the bank's own borrowing costs and administrative expenses. Member countries' subscriptions to bank capital are divided into paid-in and callable shares, of which the paid-in portion has ranged from 50 percent of subscriptions to the original capital stock to 5 percent of subscriptions to the third general increase in 1983. The paid-in shares are paid partly in convertible currency and partly in the national currency of the member, while the callable shares in effect constitute a government guarantee from each member country. By 1987 bank members had subscribed to a total of $22,709.7 million of their entitlements, of which $2,752.4 million (12 percent) was paid in and $20,017.3 million (88 percent) was callable.

When the ADB was established, there was considerable disagreement among the member countries regarding the importance of special funds and the form such funds should take. Consequently, no general fund comparable to the World Bank's concessional window, the International Development Association, was established, and the ADB charter merely set out the general terms for eventual special funds. Once the bank was operational, in 1968 three special funds were set up, the Multi-Purpose Special Fund (MPSF), the Agricultural Special Fund (ASF) and the TASF. The MPSF provided loans on concessional terms for all sectors, while the ASF, which was funded mainly by Japan, provided concessional loans for agricultural projects. Initially donors contributed to the MPSF and ASF at their own initiative on a bilateral basis, and under terms that varied considerably. As the bank's concessional lending expanded the need to regularize the mobilization of additional resources for the special funds and achieve uniformity in the terms and administration of concessional lending led to the establishment in 1974 of the ADF, which gradually became the bank's only source of concessional loans.

ADF resources consist of contributions from donor countries, funds received as repayment and income from ADF loans, and a small allocation set aside from the bank's OCR. Because of the concessional terms of its loans, the ADF cannot sustain itself on repayments and income and is almost completely reliant on replenishments to maintain and expand its lending. Consequently, while ADF loans have accounted for only 32.7 percent of bank lending, as contributions to the fund are paid in full, by 1987 contributions to the ADF constituted 78 percent of funds actually paid in to the bank by its members. The replenishment negotiations for the ADF, which decide both the size of each replenishment and the formula for cost sharing among donors, are held at four-year intervals. The negotiations have proved sensitive to changes in donor policies and have become increasingly politicized, with some countries' contributions being used as a means of achieving leverage over bank policies, particularly in the case of the United States. Due to the ADF's direct dependence on contributions, delays in payments and in the replenishment negotiations have on several occasions restricted and even threatened to halt ADF lending.

THE MEMBER COUNTRIES

The ADB had 31 founding members, and by 1986 its membership had increased to 47, consisting of 29 Asian and Pacific developing countries and 18 industrial countries, three from the region (Japan, Australia and New Zealand), two from North America (the United States and Canada) and 13 from Western Europe (Austria, Belgium, Denmark, Finland, France, Great Britain, Italy, the Netherlands, Norway, Spain, Sweden, Switzerland and West Germany). The industrialized members constitute the main source of funds for bank operations, while the developing member countries (DMCs), with a few exceptions discussed below, are the bank's borrowers. Both the ADB's decision-making structure and the positions taken by its members on key institutional and policy issues highlight the fact that a fundamental conflict in the bank exists between the interests of the donors and the DMCs in exercising control over the bank's operations.

In examining the power structure of the ADB, a distinction should be made between formal voting power and actual influence on bank operations. Formal voting power is mainly proportional to financial contributions, and is based 80 percent on capital subscriptions and 20 percent on an equal distribution of votes. However, the formula does not reflect the real influence of the bank's dominant donors as it takes account of neither special fund contributions, which in fact constitute a much larger financial contribution from donors than capital subscriptions, nor the weight of the potential threat that a contribution will not be renewed unless a donor's policy requirements are met.

Table 1 compares member countries' voting power with their paid-in OCR subscriptions and contributions to the ADF. In the third column OCR and ADF contributions are summed up to show each country's total paid-in contribution. Two features stand out. First, while the donors wield about 55 percent of formal voting power they contribute about 91 percent of the bank's resources. In contrast the DMCs, with 45 percent of voting power, contribute only about 9 percent of the bank's resources. This very much enhances the influence of the donors. Second, while voting power is based on the formula for distributing member countries' capital subscriptions, contributions to the ADF are made on a different basis. For example, by 1987 Japan had contributed $5,318.4 million to the ADF, which far exceeded the U.S. contribution of $1,222.1 million, although their respective capital subscriptions entitled both countries to virtually identical voting shares of 12.4 and 12.3 percent respectively. Similarly West Germany and Canada both have smaller voting shares than Australia, although West Germany has contributed $708.4 million and Canada $575.4 million to the ADF, compared with Australia's total contribution of $265.0.

In recent years this has caused dissatisfaction among donors, some of which have called for special increases to allow a revised distribution of votes. Since the mid-1980s Japan has been pressing vigorously for a special capital increase to expand its voting share and formalize its dominance in the bank. The United States has opposed increasing Japan's voting share, and several borrowers have also expressed reluctance to increase Japan's formal influence in the bank. The issue has been further complicated by the fact that South Korea, Sweden, Taiwan and India are also asking for special capital increases.[2] The 1988 annual meeting postponed any decision on special capital increases and voting power by at least another year.

The bank's donors can be divided into three groups: Japan (12.4 percent of votes and 45.8 percent of contributions), the United States (12.3 percent of votes and 13 percent of contributions) and the other donors (30.3 percent of votes and 32.1 percent of contributions), although the countries in the last group can be subdivided based on policy differences. The objectives pursued by the donors in the ADB can also broadly be classified into three categories: political and strategic, economic and commercial, and developmental. Significant differences can be pointed out in the relative importance of these objectives to the different donors.

Owing to Japan's high level of economic reliance on the Asian region, its development policy is closely linked to the pursuit of Japanese economic and commercial interests. Japanese policy toward the ADB has remained relatively stable, which can be attributed to the fact that the Liberal Democratic party has continuously been in power in Japan and has followed a constant development cooperation policy, with emphasis on expanding ODA and the role of multilateral institutions. The two issues most actively pur-

[2] Philip Bowring, "Waiting for Wisdom," *Far Eastern Economic Review* (May 12, 1988): 62–64.

Table 1
BREAKDOWN OF MEMBER COUNTRIES'
CUMULATIVE PAID-IN FINANCIAL
CONTRIBUTIONS AND VOTING POWER IN
THE ADB
(as of end of 1987)

Member country	Paid-in ordinary capital contributions ($ million)	(percent)	Paid-in ADF contributions ($ million)	(percent)	Total paid-in contributions ($ million)	(percent)	Voting power (percent)
China	194.2	(7.1)	—	(—)	194.2	(1.6)	6.1
India	190.8	(6.9)	—	(—)	190.8	(1.5)	6.0
Indonesia	164.1	(6.0)	2.6	(*)	166.7	(1.3)	5.2
South Korea	151.8	(5.5)	4.2	(*)	155.9	(1.2)	4.9
Malaysia	82.1	(3.0)	—	(—)	82.1	(0.7)	2.8
Pakistan	65.6	(2.4)	—	(—)	65.6	(0.5)	2.5
Philippines	71.8	(2.6)	—	(—)	71.8	(0.6)	2.3
Thailand	41.0	(1.5)	—	(—)	41.0	(0.3)	1.6
Taiwan	32.8	(1.2)	1.7	(*)	34.5	(0.3)	1.4

Bangladesh	30.8	(1.1)	—	(—)	30.8	(0.2)	1.3
Other borrowers	99.2	(3.6)	1.1	(*)	100.3	(0.8)	10.6
Total borrowers	1,124.2	(40.9)	9.6	(0.1)	1,133.7	(9.0)	44.7
Japan	410.4	(14.9)	5,318.4	(54.5)	5,728.7	(45.8)	12.4
United States	407.8	(14.8)	1,222.1	(12.5)	1,629.9	(13.0)	12.3
Australia	174.4	(6.3)	265.0	(2.7)	439.4	(3.5)	5.5
Canada	157.6	(5.7)	575.4	(5.9)	733.0	(5.9)	5.0
West Germany	130.4	(4.7)	708.4	(7.3)	838.8	(6.7)	4.2
France	70.1	(2.5)	325.1	(3.3)	395.2	(3.2)	2.5
Great Britain	61.5	(2.2)	335.6	(3.4)	397.1	(3.2)	2.2
Italy	54.5	(2.0)	208.4	(2.1)	262.9	(2.1)	2.0
New Zealand	46.3	(1.7)	17.3	(0.2)	63.6	(0.5)	1.8
Netherlands	30.9	(1.1)	201.9	(2.1)	232.8	(1.9)	1.3
Other donors	84.5	(3.1)	570.5	(5.8)	655.0	(5.2)	5.8
Total donors	1,628.4	(59.0)	9,748.1	(99.8)	11,376.4	(90.9)	55.0
TOTAL	2,752.6	(100.0)	9,757.7	(100.0)	12,510.1	(100.0)	100.0

*Less than one-tenth of 1 percent.
Note: Figures may not tally owing to rounding.
Source: ADB, *Annual Report* (1987).

sued by Japan in the bank have been the mobilization of resources for bank operations, and the question of agricultural development and food production. Underpinning both issues is a concern for Japanese interests.

From the start of ADB operations, Japan assumed a leading role in mobilizing funds for the bank's concessional lending, and due to the continued low level of U.S. contributions this role has grown significantly over time. When the ADF was set up in 1974, Japan contributed one-third of its resources; by the mid-1980s this share had increased to 38 percent. Because of delays in the contributions of some other countries, by 1987 Japan's share of contributions actually paid into the ADF had risen to 54.5 percent. To a large extent Japan's central role in financing the ADB can be attributed to the close link between the bank and Japan's ministry of finance. The ministry was directly involved in establishing the ADB, and the link has been reinforced by the recruitment of ministry personnel to key positions in the bank, including three of the bank's four presidents.

In contrast to Japan's generous financial role, Japanese policies regarding the terms of lending, including procurement and consultant policy, have been more restrictive than those of many other donors, to safeguard the interests of Japanese companies in securing contracts for bank projects. The strong Japanese support in the bank for the agricultural sector is also a direct outgrowth of Japanese national interests. Japan is almost completely dependent on imports of livestock fodder and certain staple foods, and is therefore very sensitive to price increases caused by crop failures and foodgrain shortages. As Okita Saburo, who has served as Japanese foreign minister and its chairman of the team of international experts examining the bank's role in the 1990s, has observed, "If other Asian countries increase food production and reduce their grain imports, this will indirectly contribute to Japan's food security."[3] Consequently, in the ADB Japan has promoted an approach to agricultural development aimed at increasing food production, mainly in Southeast Asia, that is based on extensive investment in irrigation—as opposed to a poverty-oriented approach.[4]

U.S. participation in the bank is derived from the political and strategic importance of the Asian region to American interests. And while it also has clear economic objectives, the United States is not very dependent on trade with the ADB's borrowers. The relationship between successive administrations and Congress regarding multilateral assistance is particularly important in explaining U.S. policy. While administrations negotiate and agree on financial contributions covering periods of several years, the appropriation of individual instalments is subject to annual approval by Congress. This has given Congress, and particularly congressional opponents of multilateral aid, substantial leverage over the policies formulated by the administration. More important, the appropriation process has given the United States influence over the bank and enabled U.S. representatives to bring up policy issues in connection with funding negotiations, with the

[3] Okita Saburo, "The Proper Approach to Food Policy," *Japan Echo* 5 (1978): 56.
[4] Robert Wihtol, *The Asian Development Bank and Rural Development: Policy and Practice* (Basingstoke and London: Macmillan Press, 1988), 38–42.

implicit threat of endangering not only the U.S. contribution but the linked contributions of other donors. As Rowley puts it, "Washington's way of bringing the ADB to heel, as with the World Bank, is to drag its feet over contributions to their soft-loan windows, causing a delay in the linked contributions from the institutions' other member-countries, thereby gaining leverage to force its own policy prescriptions."[5]

Compared with Japan's stable, economically oriented policy, U.S. policy in the bank has been more openly political and subject to variation following changes in U.S. administrations. U.S. initiatives in the bank have concentrated on ensuring a high level of lending to countries of political and strategic importance to the United States, on promoting policies and projects developing market economies and on promoting the role of the private sector. The United States has also used the bank as an instrument of national policy in specific issues, for example legitimization of U.S.-supported regimes in former South Vietnam and Taiwan and opposition to Vietnam.

During the Johnson and Nixon administrations the United States strongly supported the bank, although owing to congressional opposition no commitments to the bank's special funds were fulfilled until 1974. This resulted in Japan taking the lead in financing the ADF. The Carter administration brought a change in American development priorities, with a stronger emphasis on poverty alleviation, low-income groups and the rural sector, as well as various directly political issues, particularly the question of human rights.

The advent of the Reagan administration in 1981 marked another shift in U.S. aid policy, with major cuts in public spending and multilateral aid and greater emphasis on bilateral, politically oriented assistance and the role of the private sector. This policy shift was evident in the ADB's 1983 general capital increase, which was 105 percent instead of the 125 percent originally planned, and the fourth ADF replenishment, which was reduced from $4.1 to $3.2 billion, with some other donors assuming a larger proportion than in previous replenishments. During its first term the Reagan administration mainly exercised financial leverage over bank policy. From 1985 until 1989, however, it openly used voting against loans on the bank's board as a policy instrument, to protect American private sector interests and to promote policy conditionality, including privatization in the borrowing countries.

The participation in the bank of the other donors—the Western European countries, Canada, Australia and New Zealand—is more clearly based on their support for multilateral assistance and the opportunity provided by the bank for them to further their own economic and commercial interests, and has been much less overtly political. The smaller donors have supported both the bank's capital increases and the replenishments of the ADF, and several have increased their share of the ADF as U.S. contributions have declined. The smaller donors have in general favored more lib-

[5] Anthony Rowley, "Ideology Before Need," *Far Eastern Economic Review* (February 14, 1985): 72.

eral lending terms than either Japan or the United States, particularly with regard to issues such as the untying of procurements and increasing lending for local cost financing, and they have pressed the bank to increase its lending to the poorest countries. In the 1970s the bank's smaller donors were to a significant extent behind the shift in the bank's agricultural lending toward rural development and poverty alleviation. In the 1980s, while the United States and several of the large European Community countries urged the bank to expand its role in determining the economic policies of its borrowers, many of the smaller donors adopted a more cautious stance.

Broadly the bank's DMCs consist of low-income countries eligible only for the ADF's concessional loans, middle-income countries eligible for either a "blend" of ADF loans and ordinary loans or for ordinary loans only, and nonborrowing DMCs. In the bank loan allocation is formally viewed as the process of a country "maturing" from ADF eligibility through "blend" status to hard loan status and, finally, "graduating" to become a nonborrower. This process is discussed in more detail below.

So far, three countries have shifted to nonborrower status: Taiwan has not borrowed since 1971, nor Hong Kong and Singapore since 1980. In addition, since the mid-1980s lending to other fast-growing and newly industrialized economies, particularly South Korea, Thailand and Malaysia, has declined. At the same time two nontraditional borrowers have emerged. When the bank was established, it was agreed that India would not be included among the borrowers mainly owing to the burden lending to India would have placed on the limited resources of the bank at that time. This policy was recently revised, and in 1986 the bank started lending to India. Following lengthy political negotiations, China joined the bank in 1986 under a formula which allows the simultaneous membership of both China and Taiwan, and started borrowing in 1987.

The policies pursued in the bank by the borrowers differ in many respects from those of the donors. Initially the borrowers were critical of donor efforts to tie procurements from bank-financed projects to their own goods and services. The borrowers have consistently advocated more flexible lending terms, including the full untying of procurements, various measures to increase the proportion of procurements from developing countries, greater use of national consultants, and increased financing of local costs. In the 1970s many of the borrowers called for increased lending directly toward poverty alleviation, and were critical of the bias inherent in many bank lending policies and practices in favor of capital-intensive technologies. In the 1980s the borrowers have been strongly opposed to efforts, particularly those of the United States, to increase the policy conditionality of lending.

The borrowers' own policies and development programs have both shaped and constrained bank lending. For example, the borrowers have pressed for many of the changes in ADB policies and practices which are essential in order to provide a framework for increasing the impact of bank projects on unemployment and poverty. At the same time, the policies pursued by the borrowers in the bank, the degree to which their national development programs have or have not effectively tackled unemployment and poverty,

1482

and the types of projects for which the borrowers are willing to borrow to a significant degree reflect national power structures and vested interests and have also constrained bank lending. At the policy level, the exclusion of land reform from bank programs is perhaps the best example of the influence exerted by the borrowers. At the project level, vested interests prevail not only on the selection of projects and project components for financing, but on the distribution of project benefits.

DEVELOPMENT POLICIES

The more than two decades since the ADB was established have witnessed significant changes in the international economic and political setting, in the international debate on development and the resulting policies and approaches underlying donors' aid programs, and in the national policies of many of the bank's borrowers. Against this background substantial changes have taken place in the ADB's development policies. This has been evident not only in the discussions and policy statements at the bank's annual meetings, but also in sectoral reports and documents of lending policy and, most important, in the bank's lending program.

During the late 1960s and early 1970s bank operations reflected the prevailing growth-oriented approach to economic development, on one hand, and a concern with establishing the bank and starting up a lending program, on the other. Policies of growth-directed ADB lending mainly to the "traditional" sectors of infrastructure and industry and, in the rural sector, to investment in increasing agricultural production through the introduction of the high-yielding foodgrain varieties of the "green revolution." This cautious policy was consistent with the concern of the bank's management to establish the bank's international credit rating. In 1967 the ADB made no loans and in 1968–1969 its lending program was modest. But in 1970 lending more than doubled to $245.6 million for 30 projects, marking the beginning of a substantial lending program.

Two developments in the early 1970s shaped bank policy and lending for most of the decade. The first was the oil crisis of 1973 that dramatically increased the import bill of many countries in the region and retarded growth in 1974–1975. The bank responded to the oil crisis in two ways. It rapidly increased its efforts to identify and develop indigenous energy resources in Asia, particularly coal, natural gas and hydropower. Lending for the energy sector doubled in 1975, and energy continued to account for over 25 percent of total lending until the mid-1980s. At the same time the bank stepped up its efforts to expand total lending. The ADF was set up in 1974 to coordinate donor contributions for soft lending, and the bank's ordinary capital was increased in 1977.[6]

The second development was the global food grain shortage of the early 1970s. In Asia rice production stagnated in 1971–1972 and declined in 1972–1973, and grain prices rose steeply. The food shortages heightened

[6] Dick Wilson, *A Bank for Half the World: The Story of the Asian Development Bank 1966–1986* (Manila: Asian Development Bank, 1987), 69–86.

international awareness that poverty and unemployment, particularly in rural areas, has increased in spite of growth-oriented development efforts. In the early 1970s it was also evident that while the "green revolution" had initially been successful in accelerating Asian rice production in the late 1960s, owing to unequal access to support services, the success had been confined mainly to relatively large holdings. This led the international donor community to undertake a major review of its rural sector policies, with a view to tackling more directly the problems of hunger, poverty and unemployment.

In the ADB this shift took the form of an increase in the allocation of funds for the rural sector and a revision of the bank's development policy. The ADB's initial rural sector policy was based on the *Asian Agricultural Survey*, undertaken by the bank in 1967–1968; it recommended a strategy of increasing agricultural production through large-scale investment in irrigation and agricultural inputs to supplement the introduction of new food grain varieties.[7] In the mid-1970s the bank undertook a second survey, *Rural Asia: Challenge and Opportunity*, that recommended a wider approach incorporating production growth, employment creation and income distribution.[8] In 1973–1975 ADB lending for agriculture increased substantially, and since then it has accounted for one-third of the bank's lending.

In the early 1980s, following the second oil crisis and global economic recession, there was a general tightening of donor countries' aid policies, including substantial cutbacks in contributions to international agencies and a growing emphasis on bilateral and commercially oriented assistance. This tendency was clearest in the changes introduced by the Reagan administration that included giving priority to bilateral, politically directed aid, increasing the policy conditionality of multilateral aid and stepping up pressure on multilateral agencies to adopt policies in line with the administration's political and economic priorities.

The World Bank has in many respects served as a model for the other multilateral banks, including the ADB. The retirement in 1981 of World Bank President Robert McNamara, who had adopted numerous policies in relative independence from congressional pressure, marked the beginning of a shift in the World Bank's policies. Under McNamara's successors, A. W. Clausen and, since 1986, Barber Conable, the World Bank has placed greater emphasis on the role of the private sector, policy conditionality and structural adjustment lending.

In the ADB a similarly accommodating line was adopted by Fujioka Masao, who assumed the bank's presidency in 1981. In addition to stressing the need to expand bank lending, Fujioka has placed considerable emphasis on strengthening the bank's ties with the private sector, including cofinancing with commercial banks and lending to support the private enterprises and privatization. While ADB loans are traditionally made either directly to governments or against a government guarantee, in 1986 the bank also initiated a modest amount of lending directly to the private

[7] ADB, *Asian Agricultural Survey* (Tokyo: University of Tokyo Press, 1968).
[8] ADB, *Rural Asia: Challenge and Opportunity* (New York: Praeger, 1977).

sector, without government guarantees. This trend was further enhanced in 1988 with the establishment by the bank of the Asian Development Equity Fund that is intended to promote private investment in the region. At the same time the bank's earlier emphasis on the rural sector and poverty alleviation has declined.

While the bank is in principle limited by its charter to lending for projects, it recently approved a ceiling of 15 percent of total lending for program loans and is also discussing adjustment lending. Both sector lending (for a sector rather than a specific project) and program lending have expanded significantly, and project loans are increasingly being tied to the adoption of policy changes by the borrowing countries. Several donors, particularly the United States, have put pressure on the bank to move into sectoral adjustment as well as structural adjustment lending. Other donors, mainly the smaller Western European donors, have advocated caution, pointing out that expanding the bank's policy role will require a significant expansion of its analytical capacity. The borrowers, again, have been opposed to expanding the bank's role in economic policy prescription.

Table 2 sets out the breakdown of ADB loan commitments by sector from 1968 to 1987, based on three-year moving averages. Several trends are apparent and reflect the changes in the bank's development policy. Lending for agriculture and energy increased in the early and mid-1970s and both sectors have since remained high, together accounting for over 54 percent of ADB loan commitments. Lending for social development (urban development, education, health and population) increased significantly in the late 1970s, while the share of water supply and sanitation has remained stable. At the same time lending for industry, development banks, and transportation and communication has declined. Interestingly, in a complete break with these trends, in 1987 lending for agriculture, energy and social development declined, while lending for the more conventional sectors of industry, development banks and transport and communications increased.[9] This can to a large extent be explained by the bank's recent emphasis on expanding its lending—industry and physical infrastructure projects are easier to prepare and implement than agriculture and social development projects. However, it is too early to tell whether this marks a long-term shift in the bank's lending priorities.

MANAGEMENT POLICIES

Changing development policies and priorities have led to a variety of pressures on the bank for project innovation. At the same time, however, the bank's organizational concern with effeciently mobilizing, committing and disbursing resources has given rise to institutional pressures and operational procedures which constrain rather than encourage project change. While changing development policies in the rural sector have called, for example,

[9] In real terms the shifts are marked. In Table 2 they are not as apparent, owing to the use of three-year moving averages that reduce annual fluctuations and highlight trends.

Table 2

DISTRIBUTION OF ADB ANNUAL LOAN
COMMITMENTS BY SECTOR, FROM 1968–1970
TO 1985–1987

(percent, based on three-year moving averages)

	Agriculture and agroindustry	Energy	Industry and nonfuel minerals	Development banks	Transportation and communications	Water supply and sanitation	Urban development, education, health and population	Multi-sector	Total lending
1968–70	19.5	12.0	15.0	23.4	24.1	5.3	0.7	—	100.0
1969–71	20.5	25.4	8.7	19.5	21.7	3.7	0.5	—	100.0
1970–72	15.7	33.1	5.0	14.0	21.5	9.9	0.8	—	100.0
1971–73	15.8	32.2	0.4	15.5	23.9	11.2	1.0	—	100.0
1972–74	18.8	26.7	4.0	15.1	21.3	13.3	0.8	—	100.0
1973–75	27.9	23.0	4.2	16.7	17.7	9.2	1.3	—	100.0

1974–76	29.3	21.3	5.5	17.4	16.6	9.1	0.8	—	100.0
1975–77	30.5	22.0	4.2	15.5	17.0	8.4	2.4	—	100.0
1976–78	27.4	21.5	7.2	14.4	16.0	9.0	4.5	—	100.0
1977–79	29.8	24.0	5.7	11.8	12.1	8.7	7.9	—	100.0
1978–80	30.9	24.9	3.9	11.0	12.4	8.0	8.8	0.1	100.0
1979–81	32.6	27.2	0.9	10.7	9.4	7.8	11.3	0.1	100.0
1980–82	34.0	27.7	0.7	10.0	11.5	6.0	10.0	0.1	100.0
1981–83	33.7	26.6	2.4	10.6	7.5	7.0	11.2	1.0	100.0
1982–84	34.2	29.0	1.9	7.0	12.1	6.0	8.4	1.4	100.0
1983–85	31.9	24.2	1.8	8.0	12.5	8.2	11.7	1.5	100.0
1984–86	34.8	24.8	0.4	6.2	14.2	5.9	11.3	2.4	100.0
1985–87	29.8	17.0	3.3	12.3	20.0	4.6	10.2	1.8	100.0
Total (1968–87)	30.6	23.8	3.2	11.4	15.2	6.7	8.2	0.9	100.0

Note: Figures may not tally owing to rounding.
Source: ADB, *Annual Report* (1984–87).

for smaller innovative, multicomponent projects, with specific target groups and incorporating experimental technologies, the continuously increasing resources at the ADB's disposal have led the bank's management to focus on the efficient—rather than the innovative—commitment of these resources. This has led to a tendency toward large-scale, uniform projects with a minimum of implementation difficulties that has worked counter to many of the operational changes called for in rural lending.

The organizational objectives pursued by the ADB's management have to a large extent been built around channeling resources to the borrowing countries. Broadly this can be broken down into three components: a concern with mobilizing resources, including funds for hard lending on international financial markets and funds for ADF lending directly from donors; a concern with committing resources, in the form of new loan approvals; and a concern with the rapid disbursement of resources. Together these comprise the fund-channeling cycle, although varying emphasis has been placed on different elements at different times.

In the initial years of the bank's existence, particularly during the presidency of Takeshi Watanabe from 1966 to 1972, there was a strong emphasis on establishing the ADB's reputation and credit rating on international financial markets, and the bank's reputation with its major donors as a suitable channel for ODA. This concern was reflected in Watanabe's acceptance speech when he was appointed president at the bank's inaugural meeting in 1966:

> It behooves us therefore, in our infancy, to step cautiously, exerting every effort toward establishing a high credit standing, and proving the worthiness of this institution. In this way, and only in this way, will the necessary additional resources, in all the various forms, be made available to the bank. It is my ardent desire that all developed countries, in every corner of the world, who are concerned with the welfare of Asia, will appreciate our efforts and continue to contribute generously to our common endeavor. [10]

The priority given by Watanabe to the different aspects of resource mobilization led him to adopt a cautious lending policy, focusing on traditional "bankable" sectors and projects. [11] Watanabe's concern with establishing the bank's financial reputation and credit rating, and its close link with the selection of infrastructure and industry projects and production-oriented agricultural projects, is also evident throughout his memoirs. [12]

By the first half of the 1970s regular increases in the bank's ordinary capital and a more or less regular flow of concessional funds from the donors had been established, as had the bank's credit rating. The latter was indicated by the fact that in the early 1970s the bank's bond issues were ac-

[10] The President's Acceptance Speech at the Inaugural Meeting of the Board of Governors, November 24–26, 1966, in ADB, *Paths to Progress, Selected Addresses by Takeshi Watanabe* (Manila, 1972), 5.
[11] Takeshi Watanabe, "The Asian Development Starts Functioning," *Contemporary Japan,* 28 (May 1967): 700.
[12] Takeshi Watanabe, *Towards a New Asia; Memoirs of the First President of the Asian Development Bank* (Singapore, 1977).

corded a triple A credit rating on international financial markets. Management's emphasis consequently shifted to ensuring that project departments were preparing a sufficient number of projects for approval each year, and that the disbursement of funds increased correspondingly. As a result the bank was able to expand loan commitments at an average annual rate of approximately 20 percent throughout the 1970s (see Table 3). Due to the rapid increase of loan approvals, however, management became increasingly concerned by the disbursement problem, that is ensuring that funds were being spent at the same pace as new loans were approved and more funds were requested and received from donors. President Inoue Shiro, who succeeded Watanabe, first drew attention to the low disbursement rate at the 1973 annual meeting, and subsequently initiated a number of measures to streamline loan administration. In his speech the following year, Inoue noted that the problem required changes in the bank's operational approach, including more emphasis on "quicker-yielding more directly productive projects." [13]

Following these measures the disbursement rate increased significantly in 1973–1975, but declined again in 1976, leading the next president, Yoshida Taroichi, to take further steps to speed up project implementation. These included allocating more staff time for loan administration, streamlining and simplifying procedures, conducting training courses for counterpart staff in borrowing countries, and introducing annual disbursement targets. Yoshida's address at the 1977 annual meeting indicated the significance of disbursements not only from the borrowers' viewpoint but from the point of view of mobilizing additional funds from the donors:

> I submit that [the low disbursement rate] is a matter which needs our serious consideration. Unless we can show to capital-exporting countries, and indeed also the tax-payers in developing countries, that projects once started will be expeditiously implemented, we will be inviting disillusionment. It would raise understandable doubts among the donors whether the demand for aid is commensurate with the capacity to utilise aid. Moreover, every investment that is delayed in implementation means a substantial economic loss to the developing country concerned; our developing member countries cannot afford such avoidable losses. [14]

At the beginning of the 1980s emphasis shifted from raising disbursements to stepping up loan commitments, mainly due to a significant drop in demand for ADB loans in the region, but also as one of a number of ambitious undertakings initiated by Fujioka who assumed the ADB presidency in 1981. Loan approvals had increased at a substantial rate in the 1970s, but following the global recession and cutbacks in government spending in many Asian countries, in 1982 ADB lending increased by only 3.2 percent over lending in 1981. [15] Fujioka expressed considerable concern

[13] Address by Inoue Shiro, in ADB, *Summary of Proceedings, Seventh Annual Meeting of the Board of Governors* (Kuala Lumpur, April 25–27, 1974), 21.
[14] Address by Yoshida Taroichi, in ADB, *Summary of Proceedings, Tenth Annual Meeting of the Board of Governors* (Manila, April 21–23, 1977), 39.
[15] ADB, *Annual Report* (1982) gives new approvals as $1,730.6 million; but annual

Table 3
ANNUAL LOAN APPROVALS, ANNUAL LOAN
DISBURSEMENTS AND AVERAGE SIZE
OF LOANS BY THE ADB, 1968–87

	Annual loan approvals ($ million)	Increase over previous year (percent)	Annual loan disbursements ($ million)	Increase over previous year (percent)	Disbursements as proportion of new approvals (percent)	Number of new loans	Average loan size ($ million)	Increase over previous year (percent)
1968	41.6	—	1.8	—	4	7	5.9	—
1969	98.1	136	7.5	317	8	19	5.2	−12
1970	245.6	150	17.1	128	7	30	8.2	58
1971	254.0	3	48.7	185	19	26	9.4	15
1972	316.1	24	61.1	25	19	32	9.9	5
1973	421.5	33	146.5	140	35	39	10.8	9

1974	547.7	30	187.5	28	34	39	14.0	30
1975	660.3	21	361.9	93	55	40	16.5	18
1976	775.9	18	326.6	−10	42	36	21.6	31
1977	886.5	14	356.2	30	40	45	19.7	−9
1978	1,158.7	31	462.2	30	40	52	22.3	13
1979	1,251.6	8	486.3	5	39	57	22.0	−1
1980	1,435.7	15	579.0	19	40	58	24.8	13
1981	1,677.6	17	667.1	15	40	54	31.1	25
1982*	1,730.6	3	795.1	19	46	56	30.9	−1
1983	1,893.2	9	936.9	18	49	53	35.7	16
1984	2,234.3	18	1,000.5	7	45	47	47.5	33
1985	1,908.1	−15	1,010.1	1	53	46	41.5	−13
1986	2,001.3	5	1,024.3	1	51	48	41.7	0
1987	2,438.5	22	1,231.4	20	50	48	50.8	22

* In the 1982 *Annual Report* loan approvals are given as $1,730.6 million, but in annual reports since 1984 the 1982 figure is given as $1,683.6 million, due to cancellations.

Source: ADB, *Annual Report* (1968–87).

over this in his 1983 address to the board of governors. He subsequently announced a target of annually increasing lending by 15 percent during the next five years, and introduced measures "to speed up project processing and other stages of the project cycle." [16] When in 1983, in spite of extensive pressure on bank staff by Fujioka, lending increased by only 9 percent, the target for 1984 was raised from 15 to 21 percent to make up for the shortfall of the previous year. [17] In 1984 lending increased by 18 percent, but in 1985 it declined by 15 percent and in 1986 it increased by only 5 percent.

According to bank staff annual lending targets have been translated by Fujioka into lending quotas for project divisions, against which professional performance is measured and on whose achievement career prospects hinge. In an interview in the *Far Eastern Economic Review* Fujioka denied imposing lending quotas and said that he has sought merely to "push staff hard and make them work more efficiently." [18] In addition to the annual expansion of lending, Fujioka has placed emphasis on the bank's "operational efficiency," defined as maintaining low staff and administrative costs in relation to the volume of lending and disbursements.

The emphasis on annual approval and disbursement targets and staff efficiency has led to considerable pressure on bank staff, particularly in project departments. The need to expand annual loan commitments has placed pressure on staff to prepare and process loans for approval before the end of the bank's fiscal year, in some cases with disregard for technical, institutional, economic or financial considerations, and has led to a phenomenon known as "bunching," the rushed submission of a large number of projects for board approval during the last months of the year. Recently there have been substantiated allegations that project departments and management have, in a number of instances, ignored or played down the importance of technical and economic considerations which might have slowed down project processing and even of the suppression and distortion of project data, in order to push projects through for board approval within the context of annual loan targets. [19]

Organizational concern with approvals and disbursement rates also has clear implications for decisions in the bank related to the sectoral distribution of loans. Loans for physical infrastructure, industry and energy are relatively straightforward to plan and implement, and in general have a higher disbursement rate and less implementation problems than loans for agriculture, rural development and social infrastructure. Consequently there

reports since 1984 give the figures as $1,683.6 due to cancellations. Thus, effective lending in 1982 increased by only 0.4 percent.

[16] ADB, *Address to the Board of Governors by Masao Fujioka,* Sixteenth Annual Meeting (Manila, May 4–6, 1983), 4–5.

[17] Rodney Tasker, "Lender of First Resort," *Far Eastern Economic Review* (May 17, 1983), 69.

[18] James Clad, "Unhappy Returns," *Far Eastern Economic Review* (November 27, 1986) 61.

[19] Ibid., and various other articles in *Far Eastern Economic Review* (November 27, 1986), 60–65.

THE ASIAN DEVELOPMENT BANK

has been a degree of conflict between management's concern with smooth implementation and high disbursements, on one hand, and the bank's developmental objectives and political pressure on the bank to undertake more innovative projects, on the other.

This observation is borne out by the composition of the 1987 lending program. Loan approvals showed a substantial increase in 1987. However, this was achieved by increasing average loan size and program and sector lending, by giving Indonesia marginal access to ADF loans, and by vastly expanding lending for transportation, communication, industry and mining projects. At the same time, lending for energy, argiculture and social infrastructure (health, education, population, urban development, water supply and sanitation) dropped sharply. Agriculture, which has received one third of ADB lending since the late 1970s, declined from $822.2 million in 1986 to $534 million or 21.9 percent of lending in 1987. Similarly social infrastructure, which has regularly accounted for over 17 percent of total lending since the late 1970s, dropped from $272.5 million in 1986 to $136.5 million or 5.6 percent in 1987. Projects in both sectors are of more direct benefit to low-income groups but are also more difficult to plan and implement.

The most important question is that of the relationship between quantitative lending targets and project quality. While the stress on annual lending targets has led to streamlined project planning and implementation, it has also forced staff to prepare projects within the confines of tight deadlines and management targets. It appears that the constraints have enhanced tendencies toward the preparation of large projects, easily manageable projects, projects with a high disbursement rate, projects with a relatively short cycle, "repeater" projects in which similar loans are given to a country at regular intervals, sector loans, and standardized projects in which a similar design is applied in different countries. There are arguments for and against each of the above tendencies, but often they conflict with developmental considerations and work against project innovation and change.

Management pressure for departments to meet annual targets has aroused strong objections not only among bank staff but also on the board of directors. Many donors have criticized annual lending targets for detracting from the quality of individual projects. The variance between management and donors on this issue is illustrated by the fact that in the early 1980s, while Fujioka was placing increasing emphasis on annual targets, at the insistence of numerous donors the bank introduced three-year planning figures in its annual reports in an effort to alleviate pressure on project departments to meet annual targets at the possible expense of project quality. Donor concern with deteriorating project quality culminated in 1986 in a delay in the approval of a $35 million edible oil project in Burma (now Myanmar) and the abstention of two executive directors on the approval of an $11 million aquaculture loan to Nepal, the latter a highly exceptional measure in the context of the board's consensus-oriented decision-making process. More recently other projects have been criticized by the board, and at the bank's 1987 annual meeting several donors, notably the United States,

Canada and Australia, voiced concern over the low quality of certain projects.[20]

The distribution of ADB lending by sector and by borrowing country are two of the principal indicators of how Bank money is spent. The former, set out in Table 2, is discussed above. The distribution of lending by borrowing country is set out in Table 4.

For purposes of lending the ADB divides the borrowing countries into three groups based on GNP per capita. The low-income (group A) countries are fully eligible for ADF loans, and include most Pacific island countries and countries with very low GNP per capita (Afghanistan, Bangladesh, Bhutan, Burma, Cambodia, Laos, the Maldives, Nepal, Pakistan, Sri Lanka and Vietnam). In addition some group A countries, mainly Pakistan, Burma and Sri Lanka, are eligible for a "blend" of ordinary and ADF Loans. Of the four middle-income (group B) countries, Papua New Guinea is eligible for ordinary and ADF loans while the Philippines, Thailand and Indonesia were marginally eligible for these loans until the early 1980s. Thailand last received an ADF loan in 1981, while the Philippines received a "blended" loan in 1986. In 1987, in recognition of their economic difficulties, Indonesia and the Philippines were again granted limited eligibility for ADF borrowing. The relatively high-income (group C) countries (Fiji, Hong Kong, Malaysia, Singapore, South Korea and Taiwan) are only eligible for normal loans, and three have already ceased to borrow.

Table 4 highlights several trends. Lending from the bank's ordinary capital has concentrated mainly on the high- and middle-income (groups C and B) countries, while lending from the ADF has concentrated on the low-income (group A) countries. Pakistan and Papua New Guinea have borrowed from both sources, while Indonesia, the Philippines and Thailand have supplemented substantial ordinary borrowing with some concessional loans. China and India have only borrowed from the bank's ordinary capital.

Total lending has concentrated on the relatively high-income borrowing countries. Per capita lending in 1967–1987 for group C is $47.5 and the corresponding figure for group B is $32.2, while per capita lending to group A countries is only $22.8. The concentration of lending in Indonesia, South Korea, the Philippines, Thailand and Malaysia is particularly marked. While these countries account for 46 percent of the borrowing countries' total population, they have received over 55 percent of all loans. The group A countries, with a per capita income in 1980 of less than $300, which account for 50 percent of the borrowing countries' total population (excluding India and China), including many of the most impoverished people in Asia, have received only 37 percent of all loans.

The unequal distribution of per capita lending is largely explained by the fact that ADF lending to the poorest countries has been limited by the

[20] Wihtol, *The Asian Development Bank,* pp. 104–107.

fund's resource constraints, while the relatively more abundant OCR loans have been earmarked mainly for countries with higher debt repayment capacity. It is important to note that ADF lending as a proportion of total ADB lending is significantly lower than the proportional lending of the concessional "windows" of the World Bank and the other multilateral banks. At the same time, the allocation of lending by country suggests that political factors have also played a role. Country allocation is most closely in line with Japan's bilateral priorities, particularly the high concentration of lending in South Korea and the members of the Association of Southeast Asian Nations. It is also closely in line with U.S. priorities, although U.S. bilateral aid has tended to concentrate more on low-income countries, particularly India and Bangladesh. On the other hand, many of the smaller donors give much lower priority to the middle-income countries and have urged the bank to increase its lending to the region's poorest countries.

Political factors have also determined various country-specific decisions. The facts that Vietnam has received no loans since 1974, that Cambodia has only received one loan in 1971 and that there is a relatively low level of lending to Laos are the result of U.S. opposition to lending to a socialist Indochina. The bank started a modest technical assistance program in Vietnam in the late 1970s, but this was discontinued following the Vietnamese intervention in Cambodia, and settling the Cambodian issue is a condition for resumed lending to Vietnam.[21] Following the Soviet invasion of Afghanistan in 1979, the bank halted both disbursements and new commitments to the Afghan government. It is also interesting to note that Taiwan has not borrowed since 1971, the year the people's republic took over the Chinese seat at the United Nations and the year before the Nixon administration normalized U.S. relations with China; on the other hand there was a long delay before the ADB in 1986 accepted the people's republic as a bank member, in part due to strong congressional opposition to such a move. The halt in ADB lending to Taiwan cannot be explained by GNP per capita alone, as both Hong Kong and Singapore continued to borrow once they reached the GNP level at which Taiwan stopped borrowing.

One of the main reasons for the donors' participation in the ADB—and one of the issues most actively pursued by these countries in the bank—is the opportunity the ADB offers for promoting their exports to Asia. Owing largely to the influence of Japan and the United States, the ADB's procurement policies and practices have strongly favored the donor countries. The bank has been slow to change these policies and only adopted a margin of preference for procurements from borrowing countries in 1986, over a decade later than most other international agencies. This is reflected in the breakdown of cumulative procurements for ADB project by supplier country. Of the seven leading suppliers, five are developed countries (Japan, the United States, West Germany, Great Britain and Italy) and two developing countries (South Korea and India). The lion's share of procurements of goods, related services and civil works for ADB projects are made from the donor countries. The DMCs' share has increased slightly from 10 percent in 1974

---

[21]Bowring, "Waiting for Wisdom."

Table 4
THE DISTRIBUTION OF ADB LENDING
BY BORROWING COUNTRY
(cumulative as of December 1987)

Borrowing country	OCR loans ($ million)	ADF loans ($ million)	Total loan approvals ($ million)	Share of total lending (percent)	Cumulative ADB lending per capita ($)
Group C					
South Korea	2,199.0	3.7	2,202.7	10.1	53.7
Malaysia	1,361.6	3.3	1,364.9	6.3	87.0
Singapore	178.1	3.0	181.1	0.8	70.7
Hong Kong	101.5	—	101.5	0.5	18.6
Taiwan	100.4	—	100.4	0.5	5.3
Fiji	60.5		60.5	0.3	86.4
Total Group C	4,001.1	10.0	4,011.1	18.4	47.5
Group B					
Indonesia	4,051.8	297.3	4,349.1	19.9	26.3
Philippines	2,342.0	129.3	2,471.3	11.3	45.2
Thailand	1,656.3	72.1	1,728.4	7.9	33.7

Papua New Guinea	142.3	140.3	282.6	1.3	83.9
Total Group B	8,192.4	639.0	8,831.4	40.5	32.2
Group A					
Pakistan	1,689.2	2,080.5	3,769.6	17.3	39.2
Bangladesh	11.4	2,181.3	2,192.7	10.0	22.2
Sri Lanka	14.1	660.6	674.8	3.1	42.6
Nepal	2.0	638.9	640.9	2.9	38.4
Burma	6.6	524.3	530.9	2.4	14.5
Laos	—	106.6	106.6	0.5	24.0
Afghanistan	—	95.1	95.1	0.4	5.2
Vietnam	3.9	40.7	44.6	0.2	0.8
Bhutan	—	28.0	28.0	0.1	21.9
Maldives	—	9.5	9.5	*	52.8
Cambodia	—	1.7	1.7	*	0.2
Total Group A	1,727.2	6,367.2	8,094.4	37.1	22.8
Pacific island countries	118.8	—	118.8	0.5	157.3
India	643.6	—	643.6	2.9	**
China	133.3	—	133.3	0.6	**
Total	14,697.6	7,134.9	21,832.5	100.0	30.5

Note: Figures may not tally owing to rounding.
* Less than one-tenth of 1 percent.
** India and China are not included in these calculations owing to their recent status as borrowers.
Source: ADB, *Annual Report* (1987) and *The World Bank Atlas* (1987).

to over 13 percent in 1986, but virtually no procurements have been made from the low-income countries. In addition to India and South Korea, six countries—Taiwan, Singapore, Thailand, the Philippines, Hong Kong and Malaysia—accounted for almost all procurements from the DMCs.[22]

The impact of ADB lending can be examined both in terms of whether projects have achieved their stated objectives and in terms of more broadly defined development objectives, such as increasing production, creating employment or contributing to a more equitable distribution of incomes. The bank itself assesses the impact of its projects as follows:

> . . . the most important post-evaluation finding is that over two-thirds of Bank-assisted projects have substantially achieved their physical, institutional and socio-economic objectives. Overall, projects have provided needed facilities and services that positively contributed to social development and economic growth; they have strengthened local organizations and firms that provide and maintain these facilities and services; and they have benefited millions of users.[23]

At the same time, in acknowledgment of the criticism leveled at selected projects, the 1986 annual report conceded that "there has been a tendency toward optimistic estimation of economic internal rates of return at appraisal."[24] There are also differences in project performance in different sectors. Rural development projects have encountered more difficulties than, for example, infrastructure and industry projects.

Viewed in terms of development objectives, bank projects have predominantly been concerned with promoting economic growth that in projects translates into increasing production or output in different sectors. On the other hand, ADB projects have paid little attention to less tangible objectives such as employment creation and income distribution. This can be attributed partly to the bank's project appraisal methodology that includes the calculation of economic and, where feasible, financial rates of return, but does not include social cost-benefit analysis. The bank's project identification criteria are also less innovative than those of many other international agencies.[25]

Given that bank projects are production oriented, they have tended to benefit those owning or controlling productive assets as well as socioeconomic groups that are fully integrated in the market economy. Marginal producers and low-income groups have benefited to a much lesser extent. In the agricultural sector, for example, projects have been designed mainly to step up agricultural production. Initially they benefited large producers, but gradually they also included relatively small-scale farmers. As projects

[22] This paragraph is based on figures from ADB, *Annual Report* (1986). In 1987, in an effort to make the borrowing countries' share of procurements appear larger, the ADB included locally awarded contracts under procurements from the borrowers, although these include substantial amounts actually spent on imports. For this reason, 1987 figures are not used.

[23] ADB, *Annual Report* (1986), 25.

[24] Ibid.

[25] Wihtol, *The Asian Development Bank,* pp. 89–93 and 168–69.

have not incorporated effective measures to promote land reform nor to create extensive off-farm employment, marginal and subsistence farmers and landless laborers have largely been beyond their reach.[26]

CONCLUSION

To play an effective role in development, a development bank should have a significant lending program and projects of high quality. However, recent years have witnessed a decline and stagnation in the lending program of the ADB, while at the same time serious questions have been raised about the substance—and the quality—of the bank's lending. The simultaneous dip in both performance indicators is a symptom of the severe identity crisis the bank is facing, and in 1986–1987 it led to repeated calls from donor countries for a thorough review of the bank's role and operations. It is also the main reason that the bank recently commissioned a high-level panel of international experts to undertake a study of its role in the 1990s.

Defining the bank's future role involves complex political, financial and technical issues, and solutions will have to be sought that meet the diverse needs of the bank's borrowers while continuing to attract financial support from donors who represent a wide political spectrum. Solutions will have to be based on precise quantitative and qualitative definitions of what is expected of ADB lending. In fact, such concepts may prove to be the only way of establishing performance objectives and priorities acceptable to the bank's 47 member countries.

The quantity problem is the combined result of the decline in demand for the bank's hard loans and the scarcity of resources for the Asian Development Fund's soft loans. While the ADB has had sufficient ordinary capital resources to expand lending, bank lending to traditionally large borrowers has declined. In the region's fast-growing and newly industrialised economies, particularly South Korea, Thailand and Malaysia, ADB loans face serious competition from commercial loans.

There is ample demand for the ADF's concessional loans among eligible borrowers that include the region's poorest countries. However, ADF lending has remained low owing mainly to the United States' refusal to participate fully in the replenishments proposed by the bank's management and other donors. This has reduced the size of ADF replenishments and led other donors to increase their contributions.

Throughout the 1970s lending in nominal terms expanded at an average annual rate of about 20 percent. The corresponding figure in the 1980s was about 8 percent. Following the virtually complete stagnation of new loan approvals in 1982, Fujioka applied considerable pressure on his staff to expand lending. As a result new approvals increased in 1983 and 1984, but dropped in 1985 and increased only slightly in 1986. Approvals increased again in 1987. In real terms, lending over the period 1981 to 1987 was almost stagnant.

The quality problem can be seen fundamentally as a question concerning

[26] Ibid., pp. 128–30.

for what purposes the bank should lend. The ADB was established to fill a gap in the capital requirements of the region. Its initial lending concentrated on infrastructure, industry and agriculture. In the 1970s agriculture, rural development and energy emerged as the leading sectors. While priority until 1988 continued to be on agriculture and energy, followed by physical and social infrastructure, during the 1980s ADB lending placed increasing emphasis on financial efficiency, supporting the private sector and attaching policy conditions to loans. This shift in part reflected the disenchantment of the international aid community with the often bloated and inefficient and sometimes corrupt public sector institutions that evolved in many developing countries abetted by the aid policies of the 1970s. It also reflected the changing political climate in many donor countries, particularly the policies of the Reagan administration.

The quality of individual projects has also been criticized. The bank's excessive concern with channeling funds to its borrowers, as reflected by the annual lending targets instituted by Fujioka, has led the bank to pay insufficient attention to technical and economic aspects of its projects. The ADB itself concedes that this has led to overly optimistic project planning, while bank staff and outside observers point to far more serious shortcomings. These include promoting loans where they are not needed or where key technical questions remain unresolved, and the distortion of project data to this end. It has also been pointed out that management's emphasis on moving increasing amounts of money has detracted attention from project formulation and restricted the bank to conventional sectors and projects. The latter observation is borne out by the composition of the 1987 lending program. In contrast, several other agencies, including the World Bank and many bilateral donors, have given more priority to innovation and change, particularly in their lending for the rural sector and social development, and to directing resources to benefit the poor.

In addition to lending targets, various broader attempts have been made to increase ADB lending. Lending terms have been made more flexible, to make ADB loans more competitive with commercial loans, and cofinancing with the private sector has expanded. In 1987, the Japanese government signed an agreement with the ADB providing for extensive cofinancing from the Export-Import Bank of Japan, in an explicit gesture of support for Fujioka's efforts to expand lending. The ADB has also significantly increased its use of rapidly disbursed forms of lending, particularly sector and program lending.

A number of fundamental questions about the bank's role must be addressed before any broad decisions can be taken on the extent to which lending should expand in the 1990s. First the borrowers' future capital requirements must be assessed. While demand for ordinary lending has recently been stagnant, the bank's scope for lending to its traditional borrowers in the longer term must be determined. So must the extent to which the bank plans to lend to its nontraditional borrowers (India and China). There are already indications that lending to India and China may not increase much more, owing to fears that concentrating excessively on these two borrowers could undermine the bank's multilateral nature and financial standing and might lead to a further politicization of the bank.[27] At the same time it is clear that the poorer borrowers will continue to require substantial capital, mainly on concessional terms.

Second, and closely connected to the above, lending practices should be examined. In attempting to expand lending and make its loans more competitive with commercial loans, the bank has significantly modified its lending practices. Consequently the distinction between ADB and commercial loans has become blurred. The bank needs a substantial loan portfolio in order to play an effective role in the region, but should expansion take place at the risk of obscuring the bank's developmental role? Should the bank simply seek to expand its lending by competing for fund projects for which commercial finance is available; or should it define its role more precisely and accept that the size of its loan portfolio may not expand annually? Reducing the emphasis on quantity would release much needed staff time for more thorough project identification, preparation and implementation.

At the bank's 1988 annual meeting, no decision was reached on the next general capital increase. Japan is the donor most strongly supporting the capital increase and an expansion of lending. However, its financial role in the bank, particularly the recent cofinancing arrangement with the Export-Import Bank of Japan, has been criticized by some borrowers as simply a means of increasing Japanese exports to the region. The United States, again, is opposed to a general capital increase, and has been reluctant to replenish the ADF and critical of project quality. Australia, Canada and West Germany have also questioned the need for a capital increase and criticized project quality, but have supported the ADF. Most other donors favor increasing both ordinary and soft lending.

Third, the bank should define its role with regard to adjustment lending. The expansion of program lending has significantly increased the ADB's role in policy advice and prescription. However, calls for the bank to undertake adjustment lending should be given careful consideration, particularly bearing in mind the bank's limited analytical capacity and the opposition of many borrowers. It is worth reiterating that while the ADB charter limits its role to lending for projects, it has already been interpreted broadly to allow the bank to give program loans.

Decisions must be taken on the sectoral and country focus of ADB lending, and on the bank's role in relation to other sources of finance. The bank's members need to decide whether to continue to expand project lending in areas where commercial finance is available, and whether to move into the policy domains of the World Bank and the International Monetary Fund. Steady growth by the region's middle-income and newly industrializing borrowers has led to a decline in demand for traditional project lending, and points to the need for the ADB to develop new modes of cooperation with these countries. In many of the region's poorest countries low economic growth has been accompanied by high population growth and rapidly increasing poverty and unemployment. A solid case could therefore also be made for narrowing the scope of lending, improving effectiveness

---

[27] Bowring, "Waiting for Wisdom."

of projects and concentrating on areas for which other funds are not available. These include social infrastructure, agriculture, rural development and poverty alleviation.

FURTHER READING

Asian Development Bank. *Bibliography on the Asian Development Bank.* Manila: 1987.
————. *Study of Operational Priorities and Plans of the Asian Development Bank for the 1980s.* Manila: June 1983.
Huang, Po-Wen. *The Asian Development Bank: Diplomacy and Development in Asia.* New York: Vantage Press, 1975.
Krishnamurti, R. *Asian Development Bank—The Seeding Days.* Manila: ADB Printing Section, 1977.
Watanabe, Takeshi. *Towards a New Asia: Memoirs of the First President of the Asian Development Bank.* Singapore: Dawn Publications, 1977.
White, John. *Regional Development Banks.* London: Overseas Development Institute, 1970.
Wihtol, Robert. *The Asian Development Bank and Rural Development: Policy and Practice.* Basingstoke, Hampshire: Macmillan, 1988.
Wilson, Dick. *A Bank for Half the World: The Story of the Asian Development Bank, 1966–1986.* Manila: Asian Development Bank, 1987.
Yasutomo, Dennis T. *Japan and the Asian Development Bank.* New York: Praeger, 1983.

BUDDHIST ECONOMICS

E. F. SCHUMACHER

"RIGHT Livelihood" is one of the requirements of the Buddha's Noble Eightfold Path. It is clear, therefore, that there must be such a thing as Buddhist economics.

Buddhist countries, at the same time, have often stated that they wish to remain faithful to their heritage. So Burma: "The New Burma sees no conflict between religious values and economic progress. Spiritual health and material well-being are not enemies: they are natural allies."[1] Or: "We can blend successfully the religious and spiritual values of our heritage with the benefits of modern technology."[2] Or: "We Burmans have a sacred duty to conform both our dreams and our acts to our faith. This we shall ever do."[3]

All the same, such countries invariably assume that they can model their economic development plans in accordance with modern economics, and they call upon modern economists from so-called advanced countries to advise them, to formulate the policies to be pursued and to construct the grand design for development, the Five-Year Plan or whatever it may be called. No one seems to think that a Buddhist way of life would call for Buddhist economics, just as the modern materialist way of life has brought forth modern economics.

Economists themselves, like most specialists, normally suffer from a kind of metaphysical blindness, assuming that theirs is a science of absolute and invariable truths, without any presuppositions. Some go as far as to claim that economic laws are as free from "metaphysics" or "values" as the law of gravitation. We need not, however, get involved in arguments of methodology. Instead, let us take some fundamentals and see what they look like when viewed by a modern economist and a Buddhist economist.

There is universal agreement that the fundamental source of wealth is human labor. Now, the modern economist has been brought up to consider "labor" or work as little more than a necessary evil. From the point of view of the employer, it is in any case simply an item of cost, to be reduced to a minimum if it cannot be eliminated altogether, say, by automation. From

[1] *Pyidawtha, The New Burma* (Government of the Union of Burma: *Economic and Social Board,* 1954) 10.
[2] Ibid., p. 8.
[3] Ibid., p. 128.

the point of view of the workman, it is a "disutility"; to work is to make a sacrifice of one's leisure and comfort, and wages are a kind of compensation for the sacrifice. Hence the ideal from the point of view of the employer is to have output without employees, and the ideal from the point of view of the employee is to have income without employment.

The consequences of these attitudes both in theory and in practice are, of course, extremely far-reaching. If the ideal with regard to work is to get rid of it, every method that "reduces the work load" is a good thing. The most potent method, short of automation, is the so-called division of labor and the classical example is the pin factory eulogized in Adam Smith's *Wealth of Nations*. Here it is not a matter of ordinary specialization, which mankind has practiced from time immemorial, but of dividing up every complete process of production into minute parts, so that the final product can be produced at great speed without anyone having had to contribute more than a totally insignificant and, in most cases, unskilled movement of his limbs.

WORK

The Buddhist point of view takes the function of work to be at least three-fold: to give a man a chance to utilize and develop his faculties; to enable him to overcome his ego-centeredness by joining with other people in a common task; and to bring forth the goods and services needed for a becoming existence. Again, the consequences that flow from this view are endless. To organize work in such a manner that it becomes meaningless, boring, stultifying or nerve-racking for the worker would be little short of criminal; it would indicate a greater concern with goods than with people, an evil lack of compassion and a soul-destroying degree of attachment to the most primitive side of this worldly existence. Equally, to strive for leisure as an alternative to work would be considered a complete misunderstanding of one of the basic truths of human existence, namely, that work and leisure are complementary parts of the same living process and cannot be separated without destroying the joy of work and the bliss of leisure.

From the Buddhist point of view, there are therefore two types of mechanization which must be clearly distinguished: one that enhances a man's skill and power and one that turns the work of man over to a mechanical slave, leaving man in a position of having to serve the slave. How to tell the one from the other? "The craftsman himself," says Ananda Coomaraswamy, a man equally competent to talk about the modern West as the ancient East, "the craftsman himself can always, if allowed to, draw the delicate distinction between the machine and the tool. The carpet loom is a tool, a contrivance for holding warp threads at a stretch for the pile to be woven round them by the craftsmen's fingers; but the power loom is a machine, and its significance as a destroyer of culture lies in the fact that it does the essentially human part of the work."[4] It is clear, therefore, that

[4] Ananda K. Coomaraswamy, *Art and Swadeshi* (Madras: Ganesh and Co., 1950), 30.

Buddhist economics must be very different from the economics of modern materialism, since the Buddhist sees the essence of civilization not in a multiplication of wants but in the purification of human character. Character, at the same time, is formed primarily by a man's work. And work, properly conducted in conditions of human dignity and freedom, blesses those who do it and equally their products. The Indian philosopher and economist J. C. Kumarappa sums the matter up as follows:

> If the nature of the work is properly appreciated and applied, it will stand in the same relation to the higher faculties as food is to the physical body. It nourishes and enlivens the higher man and urges him to produce the best he is capable of. It directs his freewill along the proper course and disciplines the animal in him into progressive channels. It furnishes an excellent background for man to display his scale of values and develop his personality.[5]

If a man has no chance of obtaining work he is in a desperate position, not simply because he lacks an income but because he lacks this nourishing and enlivening factor of disciplined work which nothing can replace. A modern economist may engage in highly sophisticated calculations on whether full employment "pays" or whether it might be more "economic" to run an economy at less than full employment so as to ensure a greater mobility of labor, a better stability of wages and so forth. His fundamental criterion of success is simply the total quantity of goods produced during a given period of time. "If the marginal urgency of goods is low," says Professor Galbraith in *The Affluent Society,* "then so is the urgency of employing the last man or the last million men in the labour force." And again: "If . . . we can afford some unemployment in the interest of stability—a proposition, incidentally, of impeccably conservative antecedents—then we can afford to give those who are unemployed the goods that enable them to sustain their accustomed standard of living."[6]

From a Buddhist point of view, this is standing the truth on its head by considering goods as more important than people and consumption as more important than creative activity. It means shifting the emphasis from the worker to the product of work, that is, from the human to the subhuman, a surrender to the forces of evil. The very start of Buddhist economic planning would be a planning for full employment, and the primary purpose of this would in fact be employment for everyone who needs an "outside" job: it would not be the maximization of employment or the maximization of production. Women, on the whole, do not need an "outside" job, and the large-scale employment of women in offices or factories would be considered a sign of serious economic failure. In particular, to let mothers of young children work in factories while the children run wild would be as uneconomic in the eyes of a Buddhist economist as the employment of a skilled worker as a soldier in the eyes of a modern economist. In either case, a "productive" person would be thought to be unproductively used from the Buddhist point of view.

[5] J. C. Kumarappa, *The Economy of Permanence,* (Rajghat, Kashi: Sarva-Seva-Sangh-Publication, 4th ed. 1958) 117.
[6] J. K. Galbraith, *The Affluent Society* (London: Penguin, 1962): 272–73.

While the materialist is mainly interested in goods, the Buddhist is mainly interested in liberation. But Buddhism is "the Middle Way" and therefore in no way antagonistic to physical well-being. It is not wealth that stands in the way of liberation but the attachment to wealth; not the enjoyment of pleasurable things but the craving for them. The keynote of Buddhist economics, therefore, is simplicity and nonviolence. From an economist's point of view, the marvel of the Buddhist way of life is the utter rationality of its pattern—amazingly small means leading to extraordinarily satisfactory results.

STANDARD OF LIVING

For the modern economist this is very difficult to understand. He is used to measuring the "standard of living" by the amount of annual consumption, assuming all the time that a man who consumes more is "better off" than a man who consumes less. A Buddhist economist would consider this approach excessively irrational: Since consumption is merely a means to human well-being, the aim should be to obtain the maximum of well-being with the minimum of consumption. Thus, if the purpose of clothing is a certain amount of temperature comfort and an attractive appearance, the task is to attain this purpose with the smallest possible effort, that is, with the smallest annual destruction of cloth and with the help of designs that involve the smallest possible input of toil. The less toil there is, the more time and strength is left for artistic creativity. It would be highly uneconomic, for instance, to go in for complicated tailoring, like the modern West, when a much more beautiful effect can be achieved by the skillful draping of uncut material. It would be the height of folly to make material so that it should wear out quickly and the height of barbarity to make anything ugly, shabby or mean. What has just been said about clothing applies equally to all other human requirements. The ownership and the consumption of goods is a means to an end, and Buddhist economics is the systematic study of how to attain given ends with the minimum means.

Modern economics, on the other hand, considers consumption to be "the sole end and purpose of all economic activity," taking the factors of production—land, labor and capital—as the means. The former, in short, tries to maximize human satisfactions by the optimal pattern of consumption, while the latter tries to maximize consumption by the optimal pattern of productive effort. It is easy to see that the effort needed to sustain a way of life which seeks to attain the optimal pattern of consumption is likely to be much smaller than the effort needed to sustain a drive for maximum consumption. We need not be surprised, therefore, that the pressure and strain of living is very much less in, say, Burma (now Myamnar) than it is in the United States, in spite of the fact that the amount of labor-saving machinery used in the former country is only a minute fraction of the amount used in the latter.

1506

PATTERN OF CONSUMPTION

Simplicity and nonviolence are obviously closely related. The optimal pattern of consumption, producing a high degree of human satisfaction by means of a relatively low rate of consumption, allows people to live without great pressure and strain and to fulfill the primary injunction of Buddhist teaching: "Cease to do evil; try to do good." As physical resources are everywhere limited, people satisfying their needs by means of a modest use of resources are obviously less likely to be at each other's throats than people depending upon a high rate of use. Equally, people who live in highly self-sufficient local communities are less likely to get involved in large-scale violence than people whose existence depends on worldwide systems of trade.

From the point of view of Buddhist economics, therefore, production from local resources for local needs is the most rational way of economic life, while dependence on imports from afar and the consequent need to produce for export to unknown and distant peoples is highly uneconomic and justifiable only in exceptional cases and on a small scale. Just as the modern economist would admit that a high rate of consumption of transport services between a man's home and his place of work signifies a misfortune and not a high standard of life, so the Buddhist economist would hold that to satisfy human wants from faraway sources rather than from sources nearby signifies failure rather than success. The former might take statistics showing an increase in the number of tons/miles per head of the population carried by a country's transport system as proof of economic progress, while to the latter—the Buddhist economist—the same statistics would indicate a highly undesirable deterioration in the *pattern* of consumption.

NATURAL RESOURCES

Another striking difference between modern economics and Buddhist economics arises over the use of natural resources. Bertrand de Juvenal, the eminent French political philosopher, has characterized "Western man" in words which may be taken as a fair description of the modern economist:

> He tends to count nothing as an expenditure, other than human effort; he does not seem to mind how much mineral matter he wastes and, far worse, how much living matter he destroys. He does not seem to realise at all that human life is a dependent part of an ecosystem of many different forms of life. As the world is ruled from towns where men are cut off from any form of life other than human, the feeling of belonging to an ecosystem is not revived. This results in a harsh and improvident treatment of things upon which we ultimately depend, such as water and trees.[7]

The teaching of the Buddha, on the other hand, enjoins a reverent and nonviolent attitude not only to all sentient beings but also, with great

[7] Richard B. Gregg, *A Philosophy of Indian Economic Development* (Ahmadabad: Navajivan Publishing House, 1958), 140–41.

emphasis, to trees. Every follower of the Buddha ought to plant a tree every few years and look after it until it is safely established, and the Buddhist economist can demonstrate without difficulty that the universal observance of this rule would result in a high rate of genuine economic development independent of any foreign aid. Much of the economic decay of Southeast Asia (as of many other parts of the world) is undoubtedly due to a heedless and shameful neglect of trees.

Modern economics does not distinguish between renewable and nonrenewable materials, as its very method is to equalize and quantify everything by means of a money price. Thus, taking various alternative fuels, like coal, oil, wood or water power, the only difference between them recognized by modern economics is relative cost per equivalent unit. The cheapest is automatically the one to be preferred, as to do otherwise would be irrational and "uneconomic." From a Buddhist point of view, of course, this will not do; the essential difference between nonrenewable fuels like coal and oil on the one hand and renewable fuels like wood and water power on the other cannot be simply overlooked. Nonrenewable goods must be used only if they are indispensable, and then only with the greatest care and the most meticulous concern for conservation. To use them heedlessly or extravagantly is an act of violence, and while complete nonviolence may not be attainable on this earth, there is none the less an ineluctable duty on man to aim at the ideal of nonviolence in all he does.

Just as a modern European economist would not consider it a great economic achievement if all European art treasures were sold to America at attractive prices, so the Buddhist economist would insist that a population basing its economic life on nonrenewable fuels is living parasitically, on capital instead of income. Such a way of life could have no permanence and could therefore be justified only as a purely temporary expedient. As the world's resources of nonrenewable fuels—coal, oil and natural gas—are exceedingly unevenly distributed over the globe and undoubtedly limited in quantity, it is clear that their exploitation at an ever increasing rate is an act of violence against nature which must almost inevitably lead to violence between men.

THE MIDDLE WAY

This fact alone might give food for thought even to those people in Buddhist countries who care nothing for the religious and spiritual values of their heritage and ardently desire to embrace the materialism of modern economics at the fastest possible speed. Before they dismiss Buddhist economics as nothing better than a nostalgic dream, they might wish to consider whether the path of economic development outlined by modern economics is likely to lead them to places where they really want to be. Toward the end of his courageous book *The Challenge of Man's Future,* Professor Harrison Brown of the California Institute of Technology gives the following appraisal:

> Thus we see that, just as industrial society is fundamentally unstable and subject to reversion to agrarian existence, so within it the conditions which

offer individual freedom are unstable in their ability to avoid the conditions which impose rigid organization and totalitarian control. Indeed, when we examine all of the foreseeable difficulties which threaten the survival of industrial civilization, it is difficult to see how the achievement of stability and the maintenance of individual liberty can be made compatible.[8]

Even if this were dismissed as a long-term view—and in the long term, as Keynes said, we are all dead—there is the immediate question of whether "modernization," as currently practiced without regard to religious and spiritual values, is actually producing agreeable results. As far as the masses are concerned, the results appear to be disastrous—a collapse of the rural economy, a rising tide of unemployment in town and country, and the growth of a city proletariat without nourishment for either body or soul.

It is in the light of both immediate experience and long-term prospects that the study of Buddhist economics could be recommended even to those who believe that economic growth is more important than any spiritual or religious values. For it is not a question of choosing between "modern growth" and "traditional stagnation." It is a question of finding the right path of development, the Middle Way between materialist heedlessness and traditionalist immobility, in short, of finding "Right Livelihood."

That this can be done is not in doubt. But it requires much more than blind imitation of the materialist way of life of the so-called advanced countries.[9] It requires, above all, the conscious and systematic development of a Middle Way in technology, of an "intermediate technology," as I have called it,[10] a technology more productive and powerful than the decayed technology of the ancient East, but at the same time nonviolent and immensely cheaper and simpler than the labor-saving technology of the modern West.

FURTHER READING

Bergmann, D., et al. *A Future for European Agriculture.* Paris: Atlantic Institute, 1970.

Brown, Harrison. *The Challenge of Man's Future.* New York: Viking, 1954.

Herbert, Lewis. *Our Synthetic Environment.* London: Cape, 1963.

Kumarappa, J. C. *Gandhian Economic Thought.* Bombay: Vora, 1951.

Pollution: Nuisance or Nemesis? London: HMSO, 1972.

Schumacher, E. F. *Small Is Beautiful: A Study of Economics as if People Mattered.* London: Blond & Briggs, 1973.

Wolstenholme, Gordon, ed. *Man and His Future.* London: J. & A. Churchill, 1963.

[8] Harrison Brown, *The Challenge of Man's Future* (New York: The Viking Press, 1954), 255.

[9] E. F. Schumacher, "Rural Industries," in *India at Midpassage* (London: Overseas Development Institute, 1964).

[10] E. F. Schumacher "Industrialisation through Intermediate Technology,"in *Minerals and Industries,* I, no. 4 (Calcutta, 1964); Vijay Chebbi and George McRobie, *Dynamics of District Development* (Hyderabad: SIET Institute, 1964).

PART FIVE

SOCIAL AFFAIRS

DEMOGRAPHIC TRENDS

GAVIN W. JONES

INTRODUCTION

ASIA and the Pacific hold a large and, until recently, growing share of the world's population. In 1980, this share was 56 percent, and it is expected to still be 56 percent in the year 2000, by which time the population of Asia and the Pacific is expected to have grown to 3.4 billion, equal to the total population of the world as recently as 1966. The reason why its share of the world's population has ceased to rise is that the growth rate has begun to fall, keeping pace with the decelerating growth rate in the world as a whole. The growth rate of Asia's population, equalling as it does that of the world as a whole, is well above that of Europe and North America, but well below that of Africa and the Middle East.

There is tremendous diversity in the population size and growth rates of the different countries that go to make up this massive region. The two largest countries in the world are in Asia: China and India, but so are some of the smallest, and in the Pacific, there are some very tiny nation states, including countries as small as Tuvalu (8,000 inhabitants) and Tokelau (2,000 inhabitants).

In terms of growth rates, there is also tremendous diversity. One of the most significant events of the 20th century—the beginnings of a downturn in fertility rates in the developing countries—began in the 1960s on this continent and appears to be gathering momentum. However, the decline is by no means universal and varies greatly in its speed and intensity. It both reflects and is itself reinforcing the increasing diversity of economic and social conditions in Asian countries. The diversity in fertility and mortality rates underlies the wide differences in rates of population growth, which are shown in Table 1. Over the period 1980–2000, the rate of population growth in Japan is expected to be only 0.5 percent, in China substantially higher at 1.4 percent and in India and Indonesia somewhat higher at 1.7 percent. All these rates of growth, however, are well below those for Asia as a whole during the late 1960s, when they peaked at 2.4 percent per year. Rates even higher than this still characterize countries such as Pakistan and Bangladesh.

If the countries of Asia and the Pacific are arrayed according to their passage through the demographic transition (the process whereby a country moves from a situation of high fertility and high and unstable mortality to

1513

Table 1
CRUDE BIRTH RATES IN MAJOR
WORLD REGIONS, 1980–85
(per thousand population)

Developed countries of Europe, North America	14.6
East Asia (China, Japan, etc.)	18.8
Latin America	31.6
Southeast Asia	31.6
South Asia, non-Muslim (India, etc.)	31.9
South Asia, Muslim	43.7
Arab countries	43.7
Africa	45.9

Source: United Nations, *World Population Prospects, Estimates and Projections as Assessed in 1984,* Table A-6.

one of low and stable fertility and mortality), almost every stage of the transition is represented. Countries such as Japan, Australia and New Zealand have completed the transition; countries such as China, the Republic of Korea and Thailand have largely completed it; countries such as Malaysia, Indonesia, Vietnam, India and the Philippines are well on the way; and countries such as Bangladesh, Pakistan and Afghanistan, though they have lowered their mortality rates substantially, have evidenced barely any fertility decline.

The population growth rate of 2.4 percent per year reached in Asia and the Pacific in the period 1960–1980 signified a basic and underlying instability in that it could not long be sustained. The acceleration in rates of population growth was due to success in lowering death rates to moderate levels. Such factors as improved sanitation and public health, vaccination campaigns and higher levels of nutrition contributed to these lower death rates. Birth rates in many countries, however, had not fallen very much, if at all. A continuation of the rate of 2.4 percent would, even in a time span as short as 100 years, have led to a population in Asia (over 20 billion as compared with the present 2.7 billion) that clearly could not be supported by available resources, not to mention problems of sheer physical crowding. Adjustments, then, had to take place and have been taking place. The nature of these adjustments will be a major emphasis of this article.

TRENDS IN MORTALITY

In the years following the end of World War II mortality rates fell sharply in many Asian countries. In 1950, it was the rule rather than the exception for one baby out of every five to die before reaching the age of one year. Over the following 25 years, expectations of life at birth in East Asia increased by 20 years and in South Asia by 11 years. Much of this improvement took place in the earlier part of the period. In Sri Lanka, almost 2 years were being added annually to the expectation of life over the period from 1946 to 1953, and in China, the population may have been gaining on the average 1.5 years of expectation of life for each calendar year during the 1960s and 1970s, though not without temporary fluctuations.

These declines in mortality—the source of the post-World War II "population explosion"—were far more rapid than the corresponding declines that had occurred much earlier in the developed countries, and they reflect death-control and disease-control technologies that are enormously more effective in low-income conditions than they were formerly. Health may not have improved to the extent commensurate with the mortality decline. But the extent to which mortality conditions are divorced from the underlying living conditions of the people should not be exaggerated. Mortality is much lower in the more prosperous Asian countries than in the poorer countries and, within any given country, much lower among the higher socioeconomic groups than among the poor.

For example, there is a 15-year difference in life expectancy in Java between the lowest and highest socioeconomic groups. Recent national survey data reveal a few instances (Bangladesh, Malaysia, Thailand) where child mortality among rural poor was more than 10 times higher than among the well-off metropolitan families. In the Philippines, it was 8 times higher. The gaps between sub-groups of the population showed no sign of narrowing during the period of rapid mortality decline.

There is no reason for complacency about the mortality situation in the Asia-Pacific region. Though in some countries—for example, Malaysia, the Republic of Korea, and China—the level of mortality is little higher than in Western industrialized countries; in others—such as Bangladesh, Cambodia, and Afghanistan—more than 1 baby in 10 still fails to reach the age of one year. In an intermediate group of countries, which includes India and Indonesia, the situation is improving but mortality rates are still a number of times higher than in the Western industrialized countries. Moreover, the incidence of many health conditions that are debilitating rather than directly life-threatening—such as intestinal parasites, blindness caused by vitamin A deficiency and skin diseases—is very high.

Public health experts have long stressed that a "primary health care" approach stressing preventive health care, use of paramedics and community participation, would do much more to lower mortality rates than the traditional curative, hospital-based approach. Though lip service is generally paid to the need for change, the strength of ingrained ideas and the conservatism of the medical establishment have prevented a really meaningful shift toward a primary health care approach in many countries. The low mortality rates in Sri Lanka, despite its low per capita income, serve as a reminder that efforts to meet basic nutritional and educational needs and to make health services widely available throughout the rural areas can succeed where expensive hospital-based services fail.

TRENDS IN FERTILITY

Fertility rates in the world as a whole have shown a downturn in recent years, but the downturn is not universal. As shown in Table 1, within Asia, countries can be divided into three distinct groups: (1) East Asian countries (dominated by China and Japan) where the crude birth rate has fallen to levels not far above those in the countries of Europe and North America; (2) Southeast Asia and the non-Muslim countries of South Asia (dominated by India), where birth rates have fallen to intermediate levels and are continuing to fall; (3) the Muslim countries of South Asia and the Arab countries of West Asia, where it is hard to detect more than a negligible decline in fertility. Trends in total fertility rates (which show the number of children an average woman would bear over her reproductive period if she were to bear children over that period at the age-specific rates prevailing in the year in question) in major Asian countries are shown in Figure 1.

Some of the fertility declines experienced in recent years in Asia have been extraordinarily rapid by historical standards. A steady contraction in the time taken for fertility rates to be halved once a fertility decline sets in has been observed in the world as a whole; it happens that many countries undergoing a fertility decline in recent years have been situated in Asia. Japan was the harbinger of precipitous fertility declines in Asia, although its hitherto unprecedented halving of fertility in a decade from the late 1940s is rather misleading as there was a baby boom in 1946 and 1947 following the end of World War II, and this gives an artificially high starting point from which to measure the decline. Japan's fertility had in fact already begun to decline in the 1930s.

Japan's postwar decline was followed after a brief interval by countries such as Taiwan, Hong Kong, Singapore and the Republic of Korea, in all of which fertility rates were halved in the short space of 10 or 15 years in the 1970s and early 1980s. But in many respects, the most remarkable of all have been the declines in recent years in the large countries of China, Thailand and Indonesia, not to mention a number of the large states of India. These are not city-states or small, manageable countries. They are relatively poor and far-flung territories posing formidable problems of transport and communications, provision of basic government services and, indeed, maintaining government control over heterogeneous and often troublesome populations.

Yet even in these large countries fertility decline is quite definitely in train (see Figure 1). The largest and sharpest declines have occurred in China. Shanghai, the pacesetter, matched the halving of fertility in a decade achieved by Singapore and Hong Kong. Beginning slightly later, China as a whole halved its fertility in nine years between 1968 and 1977, and by 1980 had virtually achieved replacement-level fertility. This would have to rank as one of the most dramatic events in world demographic history. Thailand has halved its fertility rate in 15 years to 1985 and is approaching replacement-level fertility. Indonesia and India achieved similar declines in fertility (about a 20 percent drop in fertility in a decade up to the late 1970s), though the fickle world press declared Indonesia's family planning program a success and India's a failure. It does appear, however, that since that time the pace of fertility decline in Indonesia has outstripped that in India.

Turning from these large countries to the small nations of the Pacific

Figure 1
TRENDS IN TOTAL FERTILITY RATES, 1965–85

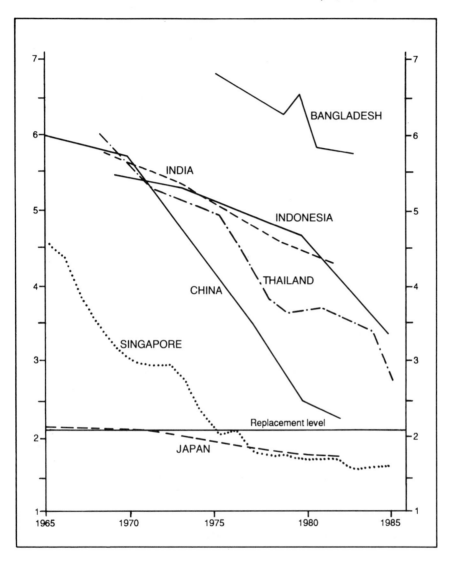

Ocean, one sees that fertility remains relatively high in most of these nations, with total fertility rates as high as six being quite common. However, there are exceptions, and total fertility rates appear to be as low as around three in Fiji, Guam, Tuvalu, the Cook Islands, Niue, New Caledonia and Nauru.

From the patterns of fertility observed in Asia and the Pacific, it is impossible to detect any unicausal explanations of fertility levels; instead, a mosaic of determinants has to be pieced together. The sharpest fertility declines in Southeast and East Asia tend to be in countries where rates of economic growth have been very rapid, but China has had very sharp declines with less rapid economic growth and some Muslim countries of the Middle East have had rapid economic growth without much fertility decline. Presence of a strong government program to reduce fertility rates has undoubtedly played an important role in countries such as China and Indonesia, but a long-standing family planning program in Pakistan appears to have had little impact. The Muslim religion is generally associated with persistence of high fertility, even in countries where economic growth has been rapid; but the largest Muslim country in the world, Indonesia, has seen impressive declines in fertility.

More nuanced explanations of the factors influencing fertility levels would have to allow for the variation in social development (e.g., expansion of female education) in countries experiencing rapid economic development; for the varieties of Islamic belief and differences in the role of women among countries falling under the rubric of "Muslim"; and for differences in transport, communications and public health infrastructure and patterns of income distribution, among different countries.

DETERMINANTS OF FERTILITY AND MORTALITY TRENDS

Demographic transition theory sees fertility transition as arising partly from the (lagged) downward adjustment of fertility following increases in numbers of surviving children, and also from the modernizing influences arising from urbanization, education and the growth of industrial society. Although many of the fertility transitions in Asia are not inconsistent with this general viewpoint, transitions in the larger and poorer countries do place considerable strain on the theory. Alternative, or at least supplementary, ways of explaining what has happened typically stress the communications revolution, the diffusion of innovative family planning behavior and the influence of government-sponsored family planning programs. The gist of the former argument is that aspirations and ideas can change sharply under the influence of altered means of communications, without necessarily waiting for the advent of urban-industrial society and the pressures on traditional life-styles and fertility regimes that this brings. The latter argument is that effectively organized government family planning programs can influence motivations to control family size and lower both the financial and psychological cost of controlling births.

A number of points regarding fertility transition may easily be overlooked. First, postponement of marriage has been an important means of reducing fertility, especially during the early stages of a fertility decline. Japan, China, Sri Lanka and the Malays in Malaysia are four examples where postponement of marriage has been very important. Second, abortion played a crucial role in fertility decline in Japan, where it was legalized in 1948 as a result of public pressure rather than as a government policy to reduce fertility. Abortion has also been very important in Singapore and China, in both of which it has been part of the government's anti-natalist

1518

armory. Third, family planning protagonists are naturally eager to claim a major share of the credit for fertility declines, and the role of well-run programs should not be underestimated. But it is well to keep in mind that the onset of major fertility declines in Asia preceded the main thrust of organized family planning programs.

Of the Asian countries where little progress has been made so far in lowering fertility rates, the Islamic countries of South Asia are the largest block. Even in the oil-rich Islamic countries, where incomes have risen dramatically, fertility remains high, perhaps partly because economic change has been so rapid that social change has been unable to keep up. A theory of "lagged response" enables us to be optimistic about eventual attainment of low fertility levels in these countries.

Not so, however, in Pakistan and Bangladesh, where—despite modest gains in female education, government support for family planning and some emphasis on improving women's social position—prospects for rapid economic development, with its attendant strains on the traditional social structure, are not good. Population growth could undoubtedly be slowed by dynamic family planning programs linked with a primary health care approach at the village level, and by basic changes in family and social structure. These are most unlikely without a "big push" in women's education, along with an increased freedom for women to plan and order their own lives. As long as the family structure remains patriarchal and women are dependent on men (first father, then husband and, after widowhood, sons) for their livelihood and place in society, the prospects for reducing birth rates are not good.

There is great ambivalence on the part of many political leaders in these countries about the need for such far-reaching changes, and traditional Islamic leaders are often strongly opposed to family planning. It has been argued that high fertility is no direct threat to the economic or political interests of kin and patronage groups at the village level, and that with a patriarchal family structure, society is transferring demographic costs forward in time, mortgaging its own future generations.

There are those who would argue that, in the poorer Asian countries, waiting for social and economic development to usher in lower birth rates will not be enough, especially because rapid rates of population growth will themselves hinder the process of economic development needed to bring population growth rates down. Many argue further that voluntary family planning will not be enough, and incentive and disincentive programs such as those of Singapore and China will be needed. Others go still further and argue that coercive measures will be needed. It should be noted, however, that few of the countries with apparently intractable population problems could be said to have vigorous family planning programs, or strong efforts to educate all women and provide them with meaningful roles aside from the bearing and rearing of children. In still fewer countries is the power of entrenched elites challenged or are attempts made to modify rural social structures in ways that will give poorer families a greater sense of control over their own destinies. Such programs should be pursued seriously before the need for more coercive measures is entertained.

GROWTH AND STRUCTURE OF THE POPULATION

The dimensions of the expected growth of population in the region over the period 1980–2000 is shown in Figure 2. The size of the populations involved can be read along the horizontal axis, the rate of increase along the vertical axis and the absolute growth from the area of the growth rectangle. Because of its enormous initial size, the absolute growth of China's population is expected to be very substantial, even though the rate of growth will be only modest. India's very large initial size, linked with a somewhat faster rate of growth, will result in even larger absolute growth. Substantial absolute growth will also occur in Pakistan and Bangladesh. Although they began the period with much smaller populations than Indonesia, they will experience greater absolute population growth because of their much faster rates of increase.

Another way of looking at population growth in the region is to graph the projected annual increments to the population of some of the larger countries in Asia (see Figure 3). China and India dominate by virtue of their enormous population size, not because of the fact that their population growth rates will be especially rapid by Asian standards. Because of its rapid fertility decline, the annual increment to China's population fell below that of India in the late 1970s. (Both countries are now adding slightly less than an Australia to their population each year.) In the same period, Bangladesh passed Indonesia's annual increment to population, and Thailand passed the annual increment of Japan. But the annual increments in Thailand are falling progressively further behind those in the Philippines, a country only slightly larger in population, because fertility decline in the Philippines has stalled.

The scale of projected population growth is not easy to comprehend. Bangladesh is currently adding 2.5 million people a year to a population living on a land area less than two thirds as large as Great Britain. By the turn of the century it is expected to be adding over 3 million a year. Growth of this order has alarming implications for poor, densely settled, rural populations. The continuing population growth in areas such as Java and Nepal is also cause for alarm. This alarm can perhaps be tempered by the knowledge that as early as the beginning of this century, observers were arguing that Java was overpopulated, yet its population has trebled since then and living conditions of the mass of the population, though not good, are certainly no worse, and probably better, than they were at that time. Nevertheless, the growth brings severe problems in its train: ecological problems (e.g., the cutting of forests and farming of oversteep slopes in Java and Nepal has led to severe erosion and has exacerbated problems of siltation and flooding in the lower reaches of the rivers); problems of expanding school and health systems to cater adequately for the whole population; problems of unemployment; and problems of urban growth (caused, contrary to popular belief, more by the natural increase of the urban population itself than by migration from the countryside).

As already shown in Table 1, the South Asian Muslim countries constitute a special group of countries that, like the Arab and African countries,

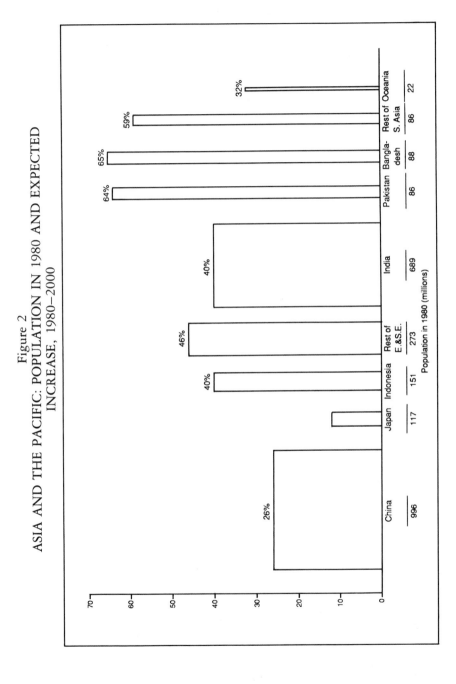

Figure 2

ASIA AND THE PACIFIC: POPULATION IN 1980 AND EXPECTED INCREASE, 1980–2000

Figure 3
PROJECTED AND ACTUAL AVERAGE ANNUAL INCREMENTS IN
POPULATION FOR SELECTED ASIAN COUNTRIES, 1960–2025.
U.N. MEDIUM VARIANT, AS ASSESSED IN 1984

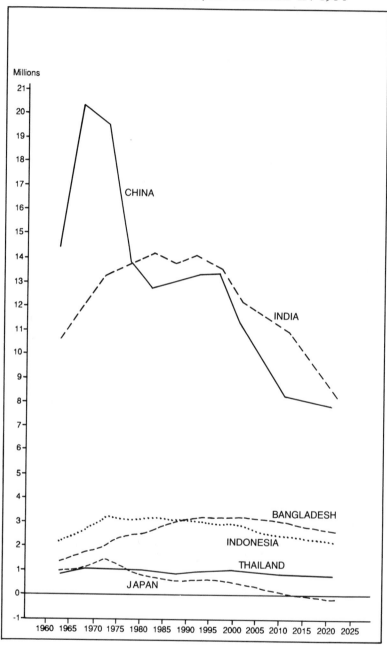

have very high fertility levels. At what point is population growth likely to stop in such countries? Answers to this question must remain speculative, because fertility remains high and it is hard to predict what forces will operate to bring it down and at what point they will become important. Nevertheless it is worth examining the expectations of U.N. demographers as reflected in recent population projections. The medium projection shows that, whereas the populations of East Asian countries are expected to grow by only 34 percent between 1985 and 2020, over the same period Pakistan's population is projected to grow by 97 percent and that of Bangladesh by 104 percent. Such a doubling would by no means represent the end of the matter; the projections indicate that after the year 2020, these populations would still be growing at rates exceeding 1.5 percent per year.

There is a built-in momentum to population growth that ensures that populations of Asian-Pacific countries (with a few exceptions, notably Japan) will continue to increase substantially for some time to come. This can be illustrated from the examples of Japan, Thailand and Pakistan. The population pyramids for these three countries reveal some sharp differences (see Figure 4). The population pyramid for Japan does not have growth momentum built into it, because the numbers of young people moving into the main reproductive age groups (with the exception of those aged 10–14 in 1985, whose births were an "echo" effect of the postwar baby boom) are not increasing from year to year. The population pyramid for Thailand still has growth momentum built into it because, although birth rates have been falling rapidly, this has had the short-term effect of increasing the proportion of the total population that is constituted by reproductive-age women. This makes for higher crude birth rates (and hence numbers of births) for any given fertility rates (i.e., number of births per average reproductive-age woman). However, eventually the growth momentum of Thailand's population will slacken as smaller birth cohorts move into the reproductive-age groups.

Pakistan represents a third situation in which population momentum remains high and there is no prospect of an early slackening in this momentum, because fertility is not declining appreciably and therefore each successive birth cohort exceeds the one born before it.

Population structure and growth have implications for economic welfare. These implications are many and complex but one aspect which is easily understood is the dependency rate. If we divide the population into potential workers (approximated by the age group 15–64 years) and dependents (those aged less than 15 and 65 and over) then the ratio of dependents to potential workers tells us something about the ease with which the potential workers can produce· for the needs of the total population, provided employment can be found for these potential workers. The dependency rate

$$\left(\frac{\text{population aged 0–15 and } +65}{\text{population aged 15–65}} \times 100 \right)$$ in Pakistan in 1985 was 87, in

Thailand 66 and in Japan 47. Thus Japan has a demographic advantage in providing high levels of average income for its population, in addition to its marked technological advantage. Thailand is entering a period where its dependency ratios will be declining for some decades because of its lowered

Figure 4

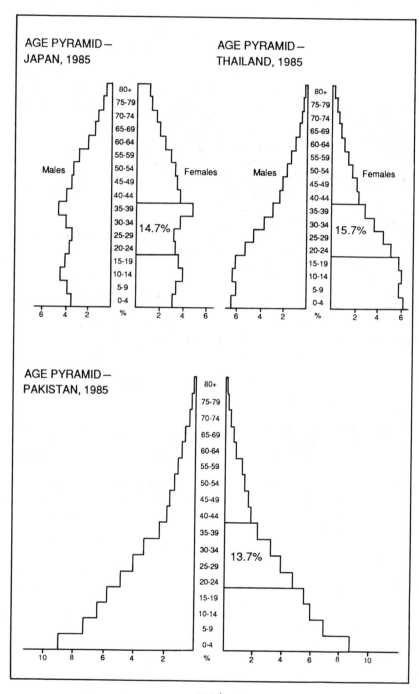

youth dependency ratio. Pakistan, by contrast, continues to suffer from high dependency ratios because of its failure to lower birth rates appreciably. Also, a smaller proportion of the potential work force is economically active in Pakistan, because of cultural barriers to women's participation in most economic activities.

As time goes on, of course, the advantage of a lowered youth dependency ratio will be partly offset by an increasing aged dependency ratio. This is happening at present in Japan, where the total dependency ratio is projected to fall from 48 in 1980 to 43 by 1990, but thereafter to rise steadily to 50 in the year 2000 and 62 in the year 2020. Thailand's population will age rapidly in the early decades of the 21st century. However, even by the year 2030 Thailand's dependency rate will remain below its 1980 level. Whatever the trend in total dependency rates, however, the shift away from high youth dependency and toward high aged dependency ratios will have many implications for consumption patterns, social security systems, structure of government expenditures and perhaps the degree to which rapid social change is tolerated in a society.

MIGRATION AND URBANIZATION

Traditional images of Asia are of peasants living their lives of toil in one village, never dreaming of shifting to another place and indeed rarely leaving the village even to shop or visit relatives. Evidence has been accumulating, however, that there is a great deal of mobility, and that this is by no means a new phenomenon, although improvements in systems of transport and communication have certainly fostered increased mobility in recent times.

The traditional image of immobility was partly due to the data used to analyze migration flows. Census data typically recorded permanent migration between major administrative districts in a country, thus missing much permanent movement that did not cross provincial or district boundaries, and also missing short-term and temporary mobility such as commuting from the fringes of large cities and beyond and moving for temporary employment during the agricultural slack season. But even using the low census-based estimates, in many Asian countries, more than one quarter of the population are lifetime migrants, or people living in a place other than their place of birth.

Though movement from closely settled agricultural areas to sparsely settled frontier areas has been an important component of population redistribution in some Asian countries—notably Thailand, Malaysia, Indonesia and Vietnam—in recent decades, in most of Asia there is little suitable land available, and this is increasingly the case as well in these Southeast Asian countries. Increasingly, then, the main focus of population redistribution is from rural to urban areas or between urban areas themselves.

Surveys reveal that economic motives are dominant in the decision to migrate. Since people tend to move from areas of lesser to those of greater economic opportunity, it is not surprising that poorer regions of a country usually experience net out-migration rates and wealthier regions (often metropolitan regions) net in-migration rates. The employment structure is changing gradually throughout Asia: the share of agriculture is declining and that of manufacturing and tertiary sector activities is increasing. Though an increasing share of such nonagricultural employment tends to be in rural areas, on the whole the movement out of agriculture is correlated with a movement to urban areas.

The evidence does not support another commonly held view: that most rural-urban migration stems from rural poverty and landlessness, and is therefore more due to rural "push" than urban "pull." While recognizing that the decision to migrate tends to result from a weighing of many different considerations, the "push" of poverty and destitution is less likely to be salient than the decision by a relatively well-off individual or family that they have something to gain by moving. The very poor are less likely to migrate, no doubt partly because they lack the resources to pay for transport and establishment in the city, partly because they tend to lack the contacts that are all-important in gaining urban employment, and partly because the destitute cannot afford to gamble with the risk of failure.

Asia remains one of the world's least urbanized areas. In 1985, only 28 percent of Asia's population lived in urban areas, compared with 41 percent in the world as a whole and 31 percent in the less developed regions as a whole. However, urbanization is proceeding steadily in Asia, and the urban population is projected by the United Nations to reach 35 percent in the year 2000 and 53 percent in 2025. This implies massive increases in the absolute numbers living in cities in Asia: from 791 million in 1985 to 2,397 million in the year 2025. Already, 10 of the world's 20 largest cities are in Asia, and the number is expected to increase to 12 by the year 2000 (see Table 2). Each of the 12 will have a population exceeding 10 million. Provision of infrastructure and basic services in cities of this size provides a difficult challenge to planners, particularly in poorer cities such as Calcutta, Dhaka, Manila and Jakarta.

EMPLOYMENT PROBLEMS

Throughout the Asia-Pacific region, the work force is continuing to increase rapidly. In the high fertility countries, this increase is matched by rapid growth in other sections of the population. But in those countries experiencing a sustained decline in fertility rates, the population structure is changing in a potentially favorable direction through a lowering of dependency ratios, as noted earlier. Though the number of aged dependents is continuing to grow rapidly, this is more than offset by the slower growth of the child population due to the recent declines in birth rates. However, the benefits of these declining dependency rates will only be realized if suitable employment is available for the rapidly growing work force. This is far from certain in many countries.

Employment issues have to be seen in the light of the educational and occupational structure of the work force. Education raises labor productivity, and in this light the notable gains in widening the educational system to cover an increasing proportion of the school-age population has been a

Table 2
WORLD'S 20 LARGEST CITIES, 1985,
AND PROJECTED TO 2000

1985	*Population (million)*	*2000*	*Population (million)*
*1 Tokyo/Yokohama	18.8	1 Mexico City	25.8
2 Mexico City	17.3	2 São Paulo	24.0
3 São Paulo	15.9	*3 Tokyo/Yokohama	20.2
4 New York	15.6	*4 Calcutta	16.5
*5 Shanghai	12.0	*5 Greater Bombay	16.0
*6 Calcutta	11.0	6 New York	15.8
7 Buenos Aires	10.9	*7 Shanghai	14.3
8 Rio de Janeiro	10.4	*8 Seoul	13.8
9 London	10.4	*9 Teheran	13.6
*10 Seoul	10.3	10 Rio de Janeiro	13.3
*11 Greater Bombay	10.1	*11 Delhi	13.2
12 Los Angeles	10.1	12 Buenos Aires	13.2
*13 Osaka/Kobe	9.5	*13 Jakarta	13.2
*14 Beijing	9.3	*14 Karachi	12.0
15 Moscow	9.0	*15 Dhaka	11.2
16 Paris	8.7	16 Cairo/Giza	11.1
*17 Jakarta	7.9	*17 Manila	11.1
*18 Tianjin	7.9	18 Los Angeles	11.0
19 Cairo/Giza	7.7	*19 Bangkok	10.7
*20 Teheran	7.5	20 London	10.5

*Asian cities.
Source: United Nations, *The Prospects of World Urbanization.*

very positive development. Issues arise, however, owing to the job expectations of the educated. When numbers of high school and college educated people were small, those who attained these levels of education could expect to find work in the professions, the public service or in clerical work of some kind. With the rapid expansion of the pool of well-educated, these expectations are no longer certain to be fulfilled.

POLICY ISSUES

A range of policy issues face Asian-Pacific countries with regard to the growth, structure and distribution of their populations. In the late 1960s and early 1970s, a number of Asian countries followed India, China (on and off) and Singapore in adopting policies to reduce the growth rate of their population. Many of these policies were designed to promote a decline in fertility. By the late 1970s, however, there remained a few countries (such as Burma and Afghanistan) that had not adopted a specific policy, and policy reversals occurred in Iran after the fall of the Shah and in Malaysia and the Philippines in the mid-1980s. In the latter two countries there is now an uneasy standoff between those favoring pronatalist and anti-natalist policies. In large countries including China, Vietnam, India, Indonesia, Pakistan, Bangladesh and Thailand, however, the strength of government resolve to actively promote fertility decline appears undiminished, though the programs adopted to this end vary greatly in their efficacy.

Programs to lower population growth rates have sometimes included efforts to increase the average age of marriage for females, and so delay the onset of childbearing. China is the most noteworthy example. But the main effort in most countries has been to lower fertility within marriage by means of promotion of the practice of contraception. Some of the best-designed and successful family planning programs have been those in China, Taiwan, the Republic of Korea, Singapore, Thailand and Indonesia. The Indian program has been more controversial, and its excesses helped bring down the Indira Gandhi government in 1977. However, in some states, the Indian program must be ranked among the region's best.

Reduction of population growth rates inevitably entails changing population structure. The proportion of children declines, and the proportion of the population in the working-age and the elderly-age groups increases. For a number of decades, the proportion of dependents to potential producers rises, as the growth of the working-age population is still driven by the higher fertility rates of previous decades. The realization of the potential advantages of lower dependency, however, is dependent on the capacity of the economy to grow fast enough to absorb the rapidly growing work force into productive employment. The problems of underutilization of labor are some of the most troublesome to economic planners throughout the region, but they will be ameliorated in a number of countries before the turn of the century by the decreasing rate of increase of the younger segment of the work force, as those born in the period of declining fertility begin to enter the work force.

Population aging is beginning to cause concern in a few Asian countries. In Japan, the proportion of the population aged 65 and above reached 10 percent in 1985, and is expected to double by 2010, by which time it will be among the highest in the world. China and Singapore face very sharp increases in the elderly proportion of their populations, though it will not reach 10 percent until after the year 2010. For other Asian countries, aging is definitely a problem for the 21st century rather than the present one.

Problems of urbanization and regional aspects of population distribution are causing concern throughout the region. Part of the problem is the natural increase of the urban population, but policy attention tends to be devoted more to the migration of people to the cities from the rural areas, leading to a gradual rise in the urban share of the population. Efforts to slow metropolitan growth have included attempts to hold people in the rural areas through agricultural and rural development programs, various decentralization and "growth pole" policies and even the barring of entry to metropolitan areas to people without jobs already arranged. But the impacts of broad economic and sectoral policies on migration flows has probably been greater, even though these policies usually do not have an explicit spatial objective. Thus "fine tuning" of urbanization trends and migration flows has proved to be impossible, and even to bring changes in the broad dimensions of these flows has large potential political costs.

There is increasing attention in planning circles to the qualitative dimensions of population, with the increasing recognition that human resource development plays a vital role in economic development. Thus investment in education and health is seen as contributing to economic growth, along with investment in physical capital. In all of the countries in the region where economic growth has been rapid, substantial progress has been made in expanding the educational system and in making health care more widely available throughout the community.

Finally, public policy must take into account the interrelatedness of population policy issues. Lowering of mortality, especially the increased survival of infants and children, undercuts the incentive to produce many children. In turn, elimination of childbearing at very young and very old ages and reduction of its frequency at other ages help reduce infant and maternal mortality rates. Lowered fertility and mortality assist in efforts to raise the quality of human resources through improved health and education. With better education, further mortality and fertility declines will come more readily. The effort must be made to allocate government investment in such a way as to maximize these and other synergistic effects.

FURTHER READING

Fuchs, Roland J., Jones, Gavin W. and Pernia, Ernesto N., eds. *Urbanization and Urban Policies in Pacific Asia.* Boulder, Colorado: Westview Press, 1987.

Hugo, Graeme J., Hull, Terence H., Hull, Valerie J., and Jones, Gavin W. *The Demographic Dimension in Indonesian Development.* Singapore, Oxford and New York: Oxford University Press, 1987.

Jones, Gavin W., ed. *Demographic Transition in Asia.* Singapore: Maruzen Asia, 1984.

Kane, P., and Lucas, D. "Population Problems in the South Pacific Islands: An Overview." *Journal of the Australian Population Association* 2(2), November 1985.

Kosinski, Leszek, and Elahi, K. Maudood, eds. *Population Redistribution and Development in South Asia.* Dordrecht, Holland, and Boston: D. Reidel, 1985.

Mitra, Asok. *India's Population: Aspects of Quality and Control.* New Delhi: Abhinav Publications, 1978.

Ross, John A., ed. *International Encyclopedia of Population.* New York: Free Press, 1982.

Urbanization in Asia and the Pacific. Bangkok: United Nations Economic and Social Commission for Asia and the Pacific, 1985.

ENERGY PROSPECTS
IN ASIA

SHARON L. HOFFMAN

INTRODUCTION

THE Asia-Pacific region has distinguished itself, particularly in the 1970s and 1980s, with both its economic and energy demand growth. This is especially notable as it is an extremely varied region. Not only does it include the industrialized nation of Japan and newly industrializing countries of South Korea, Taiwan, Hong Kong, and Singapore, but it also encompasses developing countries such as Indonesia, Malaysia, Thailand, Brunei, and the Philippines, all of which are dependent on exports of primary commodities.

Much of the high growth in economy and trade in the Asia-Pacific region has been attributed to efforts to stabilize energy supply and demand through energy development as well as through the introduction of alternative energy sources and energy conservation. In addition, the movement toward industrialization in many of the countries has also served to boost overall growth in GDP.

In the decade between 1973 and 1983, growth in energy demand in all of the Asia-Pacific countries was positive; the United States, on the other hand, exhibited a negative growth rate. Staggering annual growth rates of energy demand occurred in Taiwan (7.6 percent), Indonesia (7.5 percent), Singapore (11 percent), Malaysia (5.9 percent), and South Korea (6.8 percent). This coincided with equally high rates of growth in GDP for these countries of 7.4 percent, 6.6 percent, 7.8 percent, 7.0 percent and 7.5 percent respectively. In the same period, the United States experienced only a two percent growth in GDP.

There is always a positive correlation between GDP per capita and energy consumption per capita. As more of the countries in this region move toward industrialization and those currently undergoing this change progress, many adjustments will arise. Energy usage will be at the foundation of this progression. While all of the countries in the region share similar goals in terms of the desire to develop and industrialize, they do not, however, share equality in their individual capabilities to supply their growing economies with needed fuels. Some countries may manage their resources more adeptly. However, there are certain parameters of the regional and global energy situations that apply to all and will emerge as critical issues.

As for the individual energy situations of these countries, they are all as varied as the languages and cultures among them. Japan, a highly industrialized nation, is almost totally dependent on imported energy. Australia is well endowed with a variety of energy resources ranging from uranium to natural gas. New Zealand is oil poor yet has made commendable strides utilizing its domestic natural gas. The newly industrializing countries of the region, like Japan, are resource poor and thus import most of their energy. On the other hand, the region includes Indonesia, Malaysia, and Brunei, all of which are resource rich developing countries that need to vitalize their economies by promoting resource development dependent on energy exports as a leading earner of foreign currency.

China's situation in the region is unique in that it embodies enough energy resources to support its energy needs, but energy supply forms the most crucial factor in restricting the achievement of its economic development plan. To earn foreign currency for economic development, China must continue oil and coal exports while enduring internal shortages of energy supplies.

The Pacific islands as a group are also subject to special circumstances. For the most part (aside from Papua New Guinea), they have virtually no domestic oil or gas and must import all their needs, which is a very expensive task considering the remote location of these islands. While renewable energy is making inroads in many island nations, oil will remain the dominant fuel for the foreseeable future. Even when oil supplies are abundant, however, many Pacific islands still face further difficulties in terms of reliability of electricity supply. Current levels of dependability have served in many cases to hinder well-needed economic development.

The Asia-Pacific region indeed encompasses a great diversity of countries that differ not only in size and population, but in availability of resources and economic development. For the purpose of statistical analysis related to this discussion, the region will be further divided into subregions, namely Southeast Asia, South Asia, and Australasia. Southeast Asia comprises Brunei, Hong Kong, Indonesia, Malaysia, the Philippines, Singapore, South Korea, Taiwan, Thailand, Papua New Guinea, and the Southwestern Pacific islands. Japan, however, stands alone in terms of statistical reporting due to its large energy consumption. South Asia refers to Afghanistan, Bangladesh, Burma (now Myanmar), India, Nepal, Pakistan, and Sri Lanka. Finally, the term Australasia pertains to Australia and New Zealand.

ENERGY CONSUMPTION

The Asia-Pacific region follows to a degree the global trends in energy consumption. As with most regions, it has turned away from oil as much as possible in the past decade. Still, as with the rest of the world, oil is the dominant primary fuel. Table 1 indicates primary energy consumption

Table 1
PRIMARY ENERGY CONSUMPTION BY FUEL
(1986)

	Total world MMTOE*	%	Total Asia-Pacific MMTOE*	%	Asia-Pacific (excluding China) MMTOE*	%
Oil	2,881.0	38	508.5	33	409.3	47
Gas	1,507.1	20	102.2	7	90.1	10
Coal	2,309.1	30	792.9	51	261.7	30
Hydro	519.4	7	85.0	5	56.8	7
Nuclear	372.7	5	54.7	4	54.7	6
Total	7,589.3	100	1,543.3	100	872.6	100

*Million tons of oil equivalent.
Source: BP Statistical Review of World Energy, 1986.

by fuel for the world, the Asia-Pacific region, and the Asia-Pacific region excluding China.

One third of the region's energy comes from oil and over one half from coal. Coal's apparent dominance in the region, however, can be explained by China's enormous consumption of this fuel. If China is excluded, the region's energy profile changes dramatically; coal's use falls from over 50 percent to 30 percent, and oil usage is then 47 percent, far above the world average with China included. Once again, this type of analysis serves to demonstrate the wide disparities that exist in the Asia-Pacific region.

Table 1 appears to indicate that the Asia-Pacific region has far to go in ameliorating dependency on oil, but there are positive initiatives toward this end. As discussed at length in the section on natural gas, the region is abundantly endowed with this resource, yet it has not utilized it to the fullest. In fact, the Asia-Pacific region has the lowest natural gas consumption compared to any other region in the world—even lower than Latin America and Africa. But it is only a matter of time before this trend reverses itself.

Hydropower and nuclear power are not significant contributors to the overall energy supply of the region. In 1986, hydropower and nuclear power combined provided less than 10 percent of the total energy supply. This is not to say that their use is insignificant; for many countries they represent substantial energy sources.

MAJOR SOURCES OF ENERGY

Oil

The Asia-Pacific region is a major producer and consumer of oil. In terms of petroleum reserves, the region is not overly endowed, however. Table 2 provides estimates of the Asia-Pacific oil reserves in comparison to world

Table 2
PROVEN OIL RESERVES
(as of January 1, 1987)

Oil	Billion barrels	Share of total	R/P ratio
Total World	703.1	100.0	32.5
OPEC	477.7	68.0	68.7
Asia-Pacific	37.5	5.2	15.5
Brunei	1.4	0.2	25.6
Indonesia	8.3	1.2	16.7
Malaysia	2.8	0.4	15.0
India	4.2	0.6	18.0
Australia	1.7	0.2	6.8
China	18.4	2.6	18.5

Source: BP Statistical Review of World Energy, 1986.

reserves. Of the global proven oil reserves of 703 billion barrels, 5.2 percent of this is located in the region. More specifically, oil reserves in Indonesia and China account for nearly three-fourths of all proven reserves in the region. The reserve-to-production (R/P) ratio is 15.5 years in the region; this is approximately half of the world R/P ratio. Of world oil reserves, members of the Organization of Petroleum Exporting Countries (OPEC) hold 68 percent.

The Asia-Pacific region has four major oil producers: China, Indonesia, Malaysia, and Brunei. The only new producer on the horizon is Papua New Guinea, where recent discoveries by a consortium led by Chevron have raised prospects for a production level of around 100,000 barrels daily by the early 1990s. The major problem with the large producers of the region is that they are all large consumers themselves. Indeed, a large portion of

Table 3
ASIA-PACIFIC OIL BALANCE
(thousands of barrels daily)

	1982	1985–86	1990	1995	2000
Net oil exporters	1,608	1,874	1,914	1,423	377
Net oil importers	−5,817	−5,335	−6,080	−6,762	−7,400
Oil required from outside the region	4,209	3,461	4,166	5,339	7,023
Dependence on the Arab/Persian Gulf	70%	60%	65%	75%	85%–90%

Source: East-West Center, unpublished files.

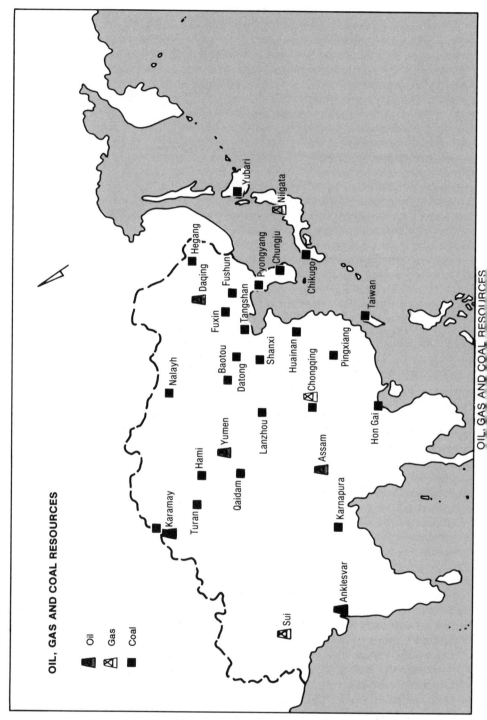

OIL, GAS AND COAL RESOURCES

OIL, GAS AND COAL RESOURCES

Oil
Gas
Coal

Yubari
Niigata
Hegang
Chungju
Pyongyang
Daqing
Fushun
Chikugo
Taiwan
Fuxin
Tangshan
Baotou
Shanxi
Huainan
Pingxiang
Nalayh
Datong
Chongqing
Yumen
Lanzhou
Hon Gai
Hami
Assam
Karamay
Qaidam
Turan
Karnapura
Anklesvar
Sui

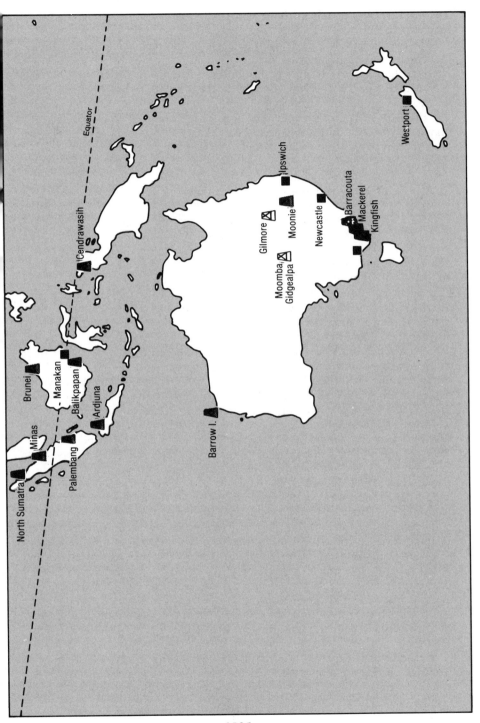

the growing production in the region goes to satisfying rising internal demand.

The overall supply and demand balance for the region is given in Table 3. These projections indicate that the net oil exporters of the region increased their exports from 1.6 million barrels daily (MMBD) in 1982 to 1.9 MMBD in 1985–1986. By 1990, these amounts will increase only slightly. A significant drop in production and exports is then forecasted. By the turn of the century, minor exports are expected from the current major producers: China, Indonesia, and Malaysia. The only sure exporters by the turn of the century are Brunei and very likely Papua New Guinea. Both countries could export oil well into the 21st century in that both have small internal demands.

As a result, net oil requirements from outside the region fell from 4.2 MMBD in 1982 to 3.5 MMBD in 1985–1986, before rising to 4.2 MMBD again in 1990. Thereafter, the need for outside oil jumps to 5.3 MMBD and 7.0 MMBD in 1995 and 2000 respectively. The change in the supply and demand balance illustrates why the Asia-Pacific region is referred to as the most import dependent region of the world. Dependence on Persian Gulf oil fell from 70 percent in 1982 to 60 percent in 1985–1986. This dependence is projected to rise rapidly to 65 percent in 1990, to 75 percent in 1995, and to 85–90 percent by the turn of the century. Clearly, the gulf is the major alternative source of supply for the region. While government policies could change the level of this dependence slightly, the geological fact remains that the Asia-Pacific region—much like the rest of the world—will become ever more dependent on the Arab/Persian Gulf. The overwhelming majority of the Asia-Pacific nations are oil importers, with Japan unequaled in the magnitude of its imports. Overall, as the projections attest, there is a declining oil production outlook for the region.

In specific terms, Chinese exports are expected to fall to approximately 600,000 barrels daily in 1990 and by 2000 are seen to decline to zero. This decline will be a direct result of increasing domestic consumption.

Indonesia is the region's only OPEC member. Its production has declined since 1984 due to OPEC controls on production and pricing. Domestically, Indonesia has managed to control oil consumption and it is expected that little growth in demand will occur. Despite effective measures controlling internal consumption, Indonesia is viewed as diminishing in importance in the oil market by the turn of the century.

Malaysia has enjoyed increased production in the past several years. In addition, the government is extremely interested in controlling domestic consumption. Despite such measures, exports are likely to be virtually nonexistent by the end of the century.

Brunei, on the other hand, foresees a stable production profile that, combined with small domestic consumption, will render it an oil exporter through 2000.

Myanmar once exported oil, yet is currently facing a crude oil shortage. To ward off oil imports, natural gas has been used in increasing quantities where possible. While never a significant exporter, Burma will probably join the majority of oil importers in the 1990s. This is due in part to governmental policies discouraging foreign investments.

Among the net oil importers, India shows the greatest potential for output growth. Production grew between 1982 and 1985 and India's future production is projected to rise as will domestic consumption. Thus, imports will begin to creep up as additional production will not be able to keep pace with demand.

While Australia's production has also increased in the past, petroleum geologists believe that the Gippsland Basin, the largest reservoir in Australia, will decline significantly by the end of the century. By that time, Australia's net oil imports will more than triple.

The Philippines and Thailand show only minor potential for increases in oil output. Philippine net oil imports have declined since 1982 and are expected to remain level over the next few years. Indeed, the Philippines' 1995 oil imports are expected to be lower than 1982 levels. Thailand's oil imports in 1986 were approximately 200,000 barrels daily, but are expected to increase due to growth in diesel demand.

Heretofore the discussion of oil in the Asia-Pacific region has been in broad terms regarding overall production, consumption, and trade, but there are also important trends that need to be examined within the general framework. One area in particular is the changing pattern of demand. An overview of petroleum product demand by light, middle, and heavy distillates is given in Table 4.

Since the late 1970s, the oil demand pattern in the region has undergone a shift away from fuel oil. In 1986, fuel oil demand of 4.5 MMBD comprised almost half of the total demand for petroleum products in the region. For the future, however, heavy fuel oil demand will rise from 4.5 MMBD to 4.6 MMBD in 1990 and 4.8 MMBD in 1995—an annual growth of 0.8 percent. Middle distillate growth of 4.5 percent annually will be the most pronounced, followed by light distillates at 3.2 percent.

The implications of this changing product demand are of great importance to Asia-Pacific countries and particularly to the refiners there. As the region demands more middle distillates, refinery upgrading plans must be directed toward middle distillate maximizing facilities, although light distillate production may still be profitable.

Coal
The coal industry in the Asia-Pacific region and in the world has grown significantly in the 1980s. The oil shocks of the 1970s produced large shifts in demand for coal not only through improved economics brought about by skyrocketing oil prices, but also through policy efforts initiated by governments of oil importing countries to move fuel consumption away from oil. The market responded rapidly as many consumers switched from oil and many newly planned facilities were designed with coal as the principal fuel.

To illustrate best the change in demand from the late 1970s to mid-1980s, Table 5 depicts coal imports for major consumers. The increasing

Table 4
PETROLEUM PRODUCT DEMAND
(thousand of Barrels Daily)

	1986	1990	1995
ASEAN*			
Light	196.9	254.7	295.8
Middle	598.3	796.9	961.4
Heavy	347.8	327.9	319.9
Total	1,143.0	1,379.5	1,577.1
AUSTRALASIA			
Light	317.4	320.6	320.7
Middle	228.6	246.3	281.2
Heavy	67.5	68.8	64.6
Total	613.5	635.7	666.5
EAST ASIA			
Light	1,624.1	1,945.5	2,214.7
Middle	1,842.9	2,425.9	2,738.4
Heavy	2,091.5	2,227.0	2,466.7
Total	5,558.5	6,598.4	7,419.8
ASIA-PACIFIC			
Light	2,138.4	2,520.8	2,831.2
Middle	2,669.8	3,469.1	3,981.0
Heavy	4,492.8	4,613.7	4,846.2
Total	9,301.0	10,603.6	11,658.4

*ASEAN (Association of Southeast Asian Nations): Indonesia, the Philippines, Thailand, Malaysia, and Singapore.
Note: Data for South Asia are not included.
Source: East-West Center, unpublished files.

role of the Asia-Pacific region can be seen especially in the case of Japan, the largest single coal importing country of the world. In Japan alone, imports rose from 52 million tonnes in 1978 to 91 million tonnes in 1986. For South Korea, Hong Kong, and Taiwan coal imports grew dramatically during the same period.

To support this massive increase in coal demand, many new mines in the world have been commissioned or brought on line. In the late 1970s, coal suppliers and energy analysts alike believed the trend in high oil prices would continue indefinitely. There seemed to be no impediments to the expansion of the coal industry.

What was not foreseen, however, was that global economic growth would not progress at steadily increasing rates. In addition, the coal industry had to contend with its own operational dynamics, specifically the time lag between the decision-making process and the actual development of mines and the beginning of production. The length of this time lag varies with

Table 5
MAJOR COAL IMPORTERS
1978–86
(million metric tons)

	1978	1979	1980	1981	1982	1983	1984	1985	1986
North America	16	19	17	16	18	17	20	17	15
Latin America	5	6	6	5	6	8	10	12	14
Total	21	25	23	21	24	25	30	29	29
Western Europe	83	94	108	112	110	100	117	127	121
Eastern Europe	38	40	34	29	30	35	39	41	38
Total	121	134	142	141	140	135	156	168	159
Japan	52	59	69	78	78	75	88	93	91
South Korea	3	7	8	12	11	11	13	19	21
Taiwan	1	3	5	5	6	6	8	10	11
Total	56	69	82	95	95	92	109	122	123
Other countries	4	3	11	19	9	15	15	26	30
Total world	202	231	258	276	268	267	310	345	341

Sources: Joint Coal Board, *Black Coal in Australia, 1984–85,* 1985. Joint Coal Board, *Black Coal in Australia, 1985–86,* 1986. Australian Coal Report, *Coal Marketing Manual 1987,* 1987.

the size, location, and geology of the deposit. In addition, environmental and political concerns had to be addressed and logistics were needed for the mining, washing, and transporting of the coal. Thus, it can take from five to ten years to bring a coal mine on line. During such a length of time, many events may occur which can alter significantly the economic viability of a project. For instance, the An Tai Bao mine in China was undergoing a feasibility study when oil prices were relatively stable. The mine actually opened in 1987, a time when the oil market had softened and coal prices had declined significantly. With the collapse in oil prices, there was both a reduction in coal demand growth and a decrease in price. Naturally the mine was hurt by these occurrences. As a result of such world events, many other coal-related projects, such as planned conversions from oil-fired boilers, never materialized.

Aside from the overall slowing down of the international coal market, which affected the Asia-Pacific region as well as the rest of the world, there were also a number of more subtle shifts, all of which have had an impact on regional dynamics. All of the changes have emerged in the decade between 1977 and 1986.

Certainly one of the changes witnessed in the region has been the dominance of Australia as the top coal exporting country. In 1977, the United States controlled almost one fourth of the export market. By 1986, however, Australia had usurped that position. While the United States targeted the European market for coal, Australia focused on the Asia-Pacific region. From 1977 to 1986, Australia's exports increased from 36 million tonnes to 92 million tonnes as compared to the United States which exported 49 million tonnes in 1977 and 78 million tonnes in 1986.

The second major change in the international coal market has been the shift away from Europe as an export market. The decline in European capacity has meant that imports from non-European sources have grown at a rate faster than overall coal demand in Europe.

A third trend, one which affects the Asia-Pacific region in particular, has been the emergence of export capacity of Canada and South Africa. Because Canadian producers are primarily located in western Canada, their exports are naturally targeted for the Pacific. While South Africa does not enjoy the same geographic proximity, it has nonetheless focused on the Atlantic and the Asia-Pacific regions as export markets. This is made possible because South Africa is well known for its low-cost mining facilities. Although this has been the case in the past, future political developments might dramatically alter the cost structure of South African coal.

The fourth structural change in the international coal market has been the emergence of what could be termed the newly emerging coal exporting countries. At present, the nation best fitting this description is China. In the past, coal exports have represented only one to two percent of China's total annual production. Of this exported coal, only 20 to 30 percent has been of coking coal quality due mostly to the fact that there is strong internal demand for this type of coal. Thus, emerging exports from China will be primarily steaming coal. Much of the coal presently exported is extracted from mines located west of Beijing near Datong in Shanxi province. The coal is transported by rail to Qinhuangdao where it is loaded on to vessels for export. The Asia-Pacific region seems to be the most likely target for sales of Chinese coal.

While China is seen as an upcoming force in the Asia-Pacific regional coal market, Indonesia could very well be another emerging exporter. At present, Indonesia is encouraging foreign investment in its coal mines, particularly in Kalimantan on the island of Borneo. Most of the coal in these deposits is steam quality; however, some areas hold coking coal. Inadequate infrastructure could prove limiting. In fact, when the mining companies first arrived in Kalimantan, there were no roads, railroads, ports, sanitation facilities, communication systems, or electrical power. These problems have not been completely solved and remain as major obstacles. In addition, the climate is not conducive to mine development in that high rainfall makes ground control and vehicular movement problematic. Kalimantan as a mining site also suffers from the fact that it is remotely located, meaning that technical maintenance and expertise must be brought in from the outside, thus driving up costs further. Naturally, if these obstacles could be overcome and the mines developed, exports would surely be targeted for the Asia-Pacific region, although exports to Europe are a small possibility.

With this variety of regional dynamics, the coal market may ultimately be controlled by the price structure in the oil market. Given the assumption that oil prices rise at controlled rates until 2000, the scenario for Asian countries would be as follows. In the region, Japan would remain the dominant importer of coal, with South Korea following. Taiwan would support the steaming coal market because the power sector there will need increasing amounts of steaming coal. Hong Kong's consumption is entirely import based and is comprised totally of steam coal, much of which goes to produce electricity. This utility sector would expand greatly. Of the ASEAN countries, only Singapore is without domestic energy reserves. Coal or lignite deposits are found in Thailand, the Philippines, Malaysia, and Indonesia, and have all been under development or consideration. Despite domestic reserves, all of these countries will need coal imports. Indonesia may be the exception in that it has first right of refusal to purchase its own exportable coal. China, with a centrally planned economy, could exercise enormous control over its coal production and export. However, much will depend on China's immediate need for foreign exchange, the level of internal demand, and the ability of the infrastructure to support exports. As with Indonesia, the future exports of Chinese coal could fluctuate greatly.

In conclusion, the Asia-Pacific region will be greatly involved with coal in the years to come. Australia, the world's largest producer, will strive to maintain that position, while new producers such as China and Indonesia will test the international waters. Meanwhile, the region will be a repository for large quantities of exports from outside the region, namely from Canada and possibly South Africa and the United States. Driving this demand will be industrialized Japan along with the newly industrializing nations of Taiwan and South Korea. The Pacific islands have never been reliant on coal and are not likely to begin to be so.

The international coal industry, however, is a mature industry; the focus will not be shortage of supply for the region or for the world. If China and Indonesia emerge as exporters and South Africa increases its exports to the region there may well be a surplus. While current weak oil prices have depressed the market somewhat, an increase in oil prices could certainly bring coal back to the fore. In that case, the Asia-Pacific region will be waiting.

Natural gas

Because diversification away from oil has been a primary concern for energy planners, natural gas has become a welcome contributor to the overall energy balance of the Asia-Pacific region. In fact, in the 1990s, the natural gas industry in the region will double in terms of volumes traded. Two major factors contributing to this expansion are the economics of shipping liquefied natural gas (LNG) and the energy policies of the various governments supporting the increased utilization of natural gas.

Table 6 illustrates the proven reserves of natural gas in the region. Over 3,600 trillion cubic feet of gas reserves exist in the world. Of the world total, approximately 6.4 percent, or 228 trillion cubic feet, lie in the region. Malaysia and Indonesia, with reserves of 49.4 trillion cubic feet each, have by far the largest gas reserves in the region. Next is China with 30 trillion cubic feet of reserves. India, Australia, Pakistan, and to a lesser

Table 6
NATURAL GAS RESERVES IN THE ASIA-PACIFIC REGION

	Trillion cubic feet	Share of total
Total World	3,615.2	100.0
OPEC	1,193.2	33.0
Asia-Pacific	228.7	6.4
Japan	1.1	—
Brunei	7.1	0.2
Indonesia	49.4	1.4
Malaysia	49.4	1.4
India	17.6	0.5
Australia	18.7	0.5
China	30.0	0.8
New Zealand	5.7	0.2
Bangladesh	12.7	0.4
Pakistan	18.7	0.5
Other Southeast Asia	18.3	0.5

Source: BP Statistical Review of World Energy, 1986.

extent Bangladesh each hold about one third the volume of gas reserves of Malaysia or Indonesia.

In the past several years, many of the regional nations have added steadily to their assessed proven reserves. This was mostly due to intensive exploration programs spearheaded by the need to move away from oil. While Malaysia, Indonesia, Australia, China, Pakistan, India, and Bangladesh all added to their reserves, Thailand witnessed a significant drop in reserves as the Erawan gas field was re-evaluated. Nevertheless, the Asia-Pacific region is relatively rich in natural gas reserves.

In the early 1980s, there were varying levels of commercial production of natural gas in the region. Indonesia and China were the largest producers followed by Australia, Pakistan, and Brunei. Lower levels of production were also found in Malaysia, New Zealand, India, and Afghanistan. Today, Indonesia remains a giant natural gas producer, with Australia moving close behind as the Northwest Shelf LNG project materializes.

Not all countries export the gas they produce: this has been the case for China, Pakistan, New Zealand, India, Bangladesh, Thailand, Taiwan and Myanmar. In fact, natural gas trade in the region exists only among a handful of nations. Dominant in this equation is Japan, which buys from the United States, Brunei, Indonesia, Malaysia, and soon Australia. In fact, Japan's natural gas imports have comprised up to 60 percent of global LNG trade, thus distinguishing the Asia-Pacific region in the international trade arena.

Because the geography of Asia is not conducive to the pipelining of natural gas, the trade of LNG, marked by lower shipping costs, has flourished. LNG projects, however, are not inexpensive. A high level of capitalization is involved; an LNG export chain typically requires a 20-year payback period. Thus, many investors are reluctant to outlay such funds and find it difficult as well to negotiate 20-year trade agreements in light of fluctuating political and economic climates.

The nations of the Asia-Pacific region, in terms of natural gas utilization, can be classified into those that are self-sufficient, those that trade, and those that are prospectively in the market. As noted earlier, self-sufficient nations include New Zealand, China, India, and Bangladesh. Japan's increasing needs to fuel its power sector have encouraged this regional industry and have established Japan as the center of world LNG trade.

For New Zealand, natural gas has been a welcome alternative to imported oil. This relatively small island nation produces only about one tenth of the oil it uses; however, transportation accounts for over 80 percent of its liquid fuel use. This could translate into real political and economic vulnerability. New Zealanders, however, have been well aware of this state of affairs and with the 1969 discovery of the Maui gas field off the west coast, have set forth on a plan of self-sufficiency. The government has planned a variety of end uses for the Maui gas: a synthetic gasoline plant, a liquefied propane gas facility, a compressed natural gas plant, a methanol plant for export production, and a pipeline system for eventual distribution to residential and industrial users. While the Maui plant has turned out to be quite costly, especially in light of recent weakness in oil prices, there will nevertheless come a day when New Zealanders will be very pleased with the current economics. For now, national pride and increased self-sufficiency will have to suffice.

China's approach to its utilization of natural gas has not been as directly focused as that of New Zealand. In fact, natural gas discovery was typically a by-product of oil exploration. The widest use of natural gas occurs in Sichuan province where regional reserves are sizable. Also, the northern and northwestern parts of China produce small quantities. There are hopes to find additional reserves in the South China Sea. With present levels of production there are no exports; all natural gas is consumed internally.

While Pakistan does not export any of its natural gas, it does utilize its Mari gas field for electric power production. Specifically, the US $362 million Guddu combined cycle project will use 300 megawatts of gas turbines. This project has been funded in part by the Asian Development Bank and the International Finance Corporation.

India's natural gas history has, like China's, followed somewhat along the lines of its oil exploration. The Bombay High oil fields have a great deal of associated gas which in the past was flared as there were no facilities to utilize it. However, a major development at Bombay High is the transport by pipeline of gas to the Hazira fertilizer complex.

Initiatives for greater gas utilization have also been strong in Bangladesh. As a result of policy measures to ensure greater utilization, natural gas usage has increased 20 percent in the commercial sector since 1979. The major impediment to further usage is the remote location of the field.

Burma would also like to increase its use of natural gas. Myanma, the national oil company, embarked on an oil and gas exploration program in 1982 with Japanese assistance. The result was the discovery of a gas field in the Gulf of Martaban. In addition, in 1984, an onshore gas strike was made near Rangoon. While the Martaban gas reserves could serve as exports, the Rangoon gas field will most likely provide fuel for power generation for the Rangoon area.

While the aforementioned countries are either producing gas for domestic use or are in the process of planning for production, there are a handful of Asian nations with very significant LNG export projects. Brunei actually started the industry in the region when the government formed a joint venture in 1970 with Shell and Mitsubishi. This venture, known as Brunei Coldgas, has signed an export contract with Tokyo Electric, Tokyo Gas, and Osaka Gas.

Since 1970, Indonesia has assumed dominance in the Asian LNG export industry. Production began at the Badak LNG plant in 1977. The Arun trains came on line in 1978. Today, Indonesia's LNG export capacity totals more than 19 billion cubic meters annually. Its sole market is Japan.

The wave of LNG developments in the region increased Japan's appetite both for volumes of gas and diversity of suppliers. Thus, in 1983, shipments from Malaysia's Bintulu LNG plant began heading for Japan. The Bintulu complex, built at a cost of $1.6 billion, is hoped to reap some $30 billion in income over the next 20-year period. Although Malaysia has looked upon gas as a major export earner, it also views this resource as an important domestic fuel. It is hoped that by 2000 natural gas will assert itself as the major fuel for thermal power production.

Several trade agreements are still under consideration. These include possible exports from Indonesia to South Korea and exports from Thailand to Japan and South Korea, to name a few. Table 7 provides likely scenarios of natural gas trade in the Asia-Pacific region up to 2000.

Even though Australian exports to Japan are termed prospective in Table 7, it is considered extremely unlikely that they will not come to pass. The gas will emanate from the Northwest Shelf, a discovery made in 1971–1972 at a time when oil prices made an LNG project attractive, especially to energy poor Japan. In the next ten years oil prices rose, and in such an economic climate a two-phase program was devised to pipe natural gas to domestic customers in Western Australia and then supply Japan with LNG. In 1981, eight Japanese utilities signified their intention to purchase LNG from the Northwest Shelf, and despite current low oil prices, top Australian energy officials have been assured that the Japanese will follow through on their intention to import LNG until about 1989. There are seven partners in this venture—BHP, BP, Chevron, Shell, Woodside, and Japan's Mitsui and Mitsubishi corporations. A project of such magnitude entails the investment of huge sums of money, so it would be difficult for Japan to turn away from it once it had begun. Although it can be expected that Japan will import the LNG, the price it pays will be of critical importance to Australia. Despite the financial uncertainties, the Australian phase of the

Table 7
NATURAL GAS TRADE IN THE
ASIA-PACIFIC REGION

Exporter	Importer	Volume (bcml/year) 1990	1995	2000
Operating LNG				
United States (Alaska)	Japan	—[a]	—[a]	—[a]
Brunei	Japan	6.9	—[a]	—[a]
Abu Dhabi	Japan	3.0	3.0	—[a]
Indonesia-Badak I	Japan	4.1	4.1	—[a]
Indonesia-Arun I	Japan	6.1	6.1	—[a]
Malaysia	Japan	8.1	8.1	8.1
Indonesia-Badak II	Japan	4.3	4.3	4.3
Indonesia-Arun II	Japan	4.5	4.5	4.5
Pipeline				
Afghanistan	Soviet Union	2.4	—	—
Subtotal		39.4	30.1	16.9
Prospective LNG				
Indonesia-Arun III	South Korea	2.7	2.7	2.7
Indonesia IV	Taiwan	—	0.8	0.8
Malaysia	South Korea	2.0	2.0	2.0
Australia	Japan	8.1	8.1	8.1
Soviet Union (Sakhalin)	Japan	—	4.1	4.1
Qatar	Japan, South Korea, Taiwan	—	8.1	8.1
Thailand	Japan	4.1	4.1	4.1
Canada	Japan	3.9	3.9	3.9
Pipeline				
Malaysia	Singapore	1.6	1.6	1.6
China	Hong Kong	[b]	[b]	[b]
Subtotal		22.4	35.4	35.4

[a] Assumes contracts are not renewed.
[b] Information unavailable.
Source: Fereidun Fesharaki and Wendy Schultz, "Natural Gas Supply and Demand Planning in the Asia-Pacific Region," *Annual Review of Energy* (1985).

massive construction program was completed in 1984, and gas now flows to metropolitan Perth.

Given the abundance of LNG projects proliferating throughout the region, the outlook is probably most favorable for Japan which has collected a handful of eager producers. In fact, in the 1990s and beyond, volumes of traded gas will double as will the number of exporters. This buildup in the market has several ramifications. By 1995, the region will face downward price pressure from at least two areas. Older projects will be paid off yet will still have productive facilities. Thus, they will be able to undersell new competition. Both Indonesia and Malaysia have enough natural gas resources to expand existing production at a lesser cost than a brand-new producer would face. As Japan is clearly in a monopsonistic position, the pricing schedules for natural gas may not be favorable to the producers. In addition, if continued weakness in the oil market persists, natural gas pricing may come under even more pressure. Suffice it to say, the Asia-Pacific region will not be suffering a shortage of natural gas in the years to come. If anything, it will be awash in it.

Nuclear power

The nuclear power industry, while at a relative standstill globally, has managed to thrive somewhat in the Asia-Pacific region. On a global basis, this lack of growth can be attributed to a variety of factors. For one, when adjusted for inflation, oil prices are less in the late 1980s than a decade ago. Also, despite the view which prevailed a decade ago that natural gas would run out, there has been instead an enormous availability of gas. For countries such as the United States, there has been an oversupply of electric power plants and refineries. The developed world is not stampeding toward the use of nuclear power as it had in the past. The reasons for this are manifold.

In general, over a 30-year lifetime, a nuclear power plant may be slightly cheaper than coal. However, nuclear power has a financial disadvantage in that the government or utility (and their financing parties) must spend more money per year for a nuclear plant than for a coal plant. For nuclear plants, construction time is somewhere around ten years, after which another 12 years must pass until the annual expenses are less than those for a comparable coal plant. If all goes according to plan, there are savings after 22 years. To many governments, this span of time is just too long. Another factor contributing to the global slowdown is precisely that the industry is a global one. If an accident happens anywhere, the entire world knows about it. Thus, the entire nuclear industry is vulnerable at the weakest point in the system.

It has actually been in the developing countries and specifically in the Asia-Pacific region that the most intensive nuclear programs have been developed. This is not surprising because economic development occurs when the economy grows faster than the population. Under these circumstances, energy use typically grows at an even faster pace. Electricity grows even more rapidly than total energy consumption. Thus, as witnessed in South Korea and Taiwan, electric power can grow at such staggering rates as 15 to 20 percent annually.

Regionally, the three major countries employing the most significant amounts of nuclear power are Japan, South Korea, and Taiwan. Japan has one of the oldest and largest nuclear power programs in the world. It has been operational since 1966, when the British natural uranium gas-cooled reactor came on line. At the end of 1985, Japan had 33 reactors with plans for eight additional ones to be completed by 1990. In terms of installed capacity, Japan comes fifth in the world hierarchy. This buildup in nuclear capacity has been steady. Between 1975 and 1983, more than one GW was added each year at an absorption rate of about one MW per $27 million (¥8 billion). Under the assumption that nuclear power cost about $500/kw in the earlier pre-1975 period and was $1000/kw in the post-1975 period, less than one percent of the annual increase in GNP and four percent during the post-oil-shock period was devoted to nuclear power plants.

While Japan's buildup of nuclear energy has been steady, the programs in Taiwan and South Korea, which started a dozen years later, are now the most aggressive nuclear power programs in the world. In Taiwan and South Korea, the annual rates of addition during the first six years (1978–1983) were 540 MW and 310 MW respectively. These represented absorption rates of one MW for approximately $2.6 million (0.1 billion NT$) and $3.7 million (1.8 billion won) respectively. Thus, Taiwan spent about 40 percent of each year's additional GNP in nuclear power and South Korea 25 percent. This represents a huge commitment on both parts. Interestingly enough, South Korea had even larger plans in the early 1980s. However, by 1983, the government announced an indefinite delay for a number of planned reactors. A major factor cited was the difficulty in raising the necessary capital with almost $40 billion in foreign debt. As of 1986, South Korea had four operating units which supplied some 26 percent of its electrical needs.

Taiwan also experienced a surge in electrical demand in the 1970s as it industrialized. Taipower had hoped to expand nuclear capacity to accommodate this demand. While ambitious plans were made, they were scaled down in the early 1980s, because to reach former targets set for 2000, Taiwan would have to build about one reactor each year. Plans for 1983 indicated that target capacity by 1990 would approximate 5430 MW and 10,100 MW by 2000. However, additional setbacks were incurred so that operable nuclear capacity will most likely remain fixed at 5100 MWe (gross) and 4900 MWe (net) at least into the late 1990s. This results from a lower growth rate for electricity demand and an increased reliance on coal.

Although these three northeastern Asian countries have similar economic development patterns, there are differences in the manner in which they have approached the development of their nuclear industries. For one, South Korea and Taiwan have been building up their industries much faster than Japan with a related increase in financial commitment. Thus, both of these countries are far more vulnerable financially regarding their nuclear power programs.

In addition to differences in financial commitment to nuclear programs, there are differences within the entire region in overall development. Taiwan's procedure has been to import the most advanced and largest reactors possible in order to support its general industrial development. On the other hand, India has been designing its own industry and wants to import as little as possible. With its refusal to sign the nonproliferation treaty,

India stands outside most of the world market for nuclear technology. Yet India has distinguished itself by being the first developing country to build a nuclear power plant. China has a diversified development scheme. It has an indigenous industry, but has recently ordered two French reactors. As with Taiwan, South Korea, and Japan, China will expect a good deal of technology transfer so that it can become increasingly more independent.

Aside from South Korea, Taiwan, Japan, China, and India, nuclear programs in the region are also found to one extent or another in the Philippines and Pakistan. The Philippines' nuclear program was launched after the first oil shock; the first unit was completed in 1985. In the current economic and political environment, however, the government has decided to abandon the program. Considerable interest has been expressed in Pakistan regarding its nuclear industry. In part, this concern has been related to a perceived nuclear threat from India. In addition, much controversy in the past has surrounded the proposition that Pakistan might produce nuclear weapons. Despite all political and economic discussions, Pakistan at present has just one 125 MWe reactor, located in Karachi. Plans for a larger buildup are unclear at present.

Lastly, the Pacific islands merit discussion regarding nuclear power despite the fact that no reactors exist there. Nuclear questions have plagued the Pacific not only because of the history of nuclear testing by the United States and France, but also because of storage issues. Palau, formerly part of the American trust territory but now in free association with the United States, has a clear antinuclear policy forbidding entry of nuclear-armed ships. The United States government has continually tried to sway Palau, but with little success. Just as unpopular have been the past proposals to use Palmyra Island as a storage site for spent fuel and to dump low-level radioactive waste at sea.

The future of nuclear power in the Asia-Pacific region lies with a handful of nations. Japan has a well-developed nuclear industry. It is also in a technical leadership position. But it is highly likely that Japan will compete increasingly in the international market. South Korea and Taiwan both have large nuclear commitments; however, growth has not been what was originally expected for each nation. China is combining domestic expertise with imported technology and may develop a sizable capability by 2000. China is seen as a potential market for nuclear imports. In addition, there is scope for nuclear waste disposal in the deserts of China.

As for regional trade, the United States will most likely relinquish its dominance to Japan as a technology exporter. Many Asia-Pacific nations upon observing the success in Japan, Taiwan, and South Korea may select nuclear energy especially in light of increased technology and safety coupled with rising environmental concerns about coal use. Nevertheless, it may be an onerous task for developing countries to institute the necessary management, financial, and regulatory environments needed to utilize and reap the benefits that nuclear power offers.

RENEWABLE ENERGY

Although on an overall basis, renewable energy is a small contributor to total energy supply, it is still extremely important to the Asia-Pacific countries that have substantial rural populations. Biomass, wind, solar, water, and geothermal power are all employed to one degree or another in the region. The success of the individual projects, however, depends largely on the skilled manpower pool of trained scientists, technicians, and mechanics available in each country as well as the commitment of each government toward promoting alternative fuels. Often these are difficult demands especially for developing countries. In particular, those renewable forms such as solar, wind, and geothermal energy that require high levels of technical expertise for maintenance and operation can prove problematic.

Regarding biomass energy, the Asia-Pacific region, along with the rest of the world, has experienced severe deforestation. This is a serious global problem. Large segments of the rural population in Asia depend on timber for fuel, and thus it is not surprising to find in Table 8 that substantial deforestation has occurred particularly in Australia, Burma, Malaysia, the Philippines, Sri Lanka, Thailand, Vietnam, Western Samoa, and Tonga. To ameliorate the problem in Asia, the United Nations Food and Agriculture Organization, among other groups, has involved itself in the establishment of programs to improve timber supply through tree farms, through enhanced cooking stove technology, and through agroforestry. Tree farms have become especially important in the Pacific islands in that wood is needed for traditional underground ovens. The United States Department of Energy has been active in the promulgation of tree farms in the former Pacific trust territory.

As for other renewable energy forms, hydropower has been harnessed successfully in several countries such as Western Samoa, Australia (Tasmania), and the Philippines. Solar power has found a particular niche in remote sites of the Pacific islands where central power grids do not extend. In addition, passive solar energy is being used increasingly for hot water. Active solar energy systems have not been as successful in the Pacific islands due to the need for technical support.

Although oil, coal, and natural gas dominate the energy statistics of the Asia-Pacific region, renewable energy will remain a vital source, especially for the more undeveloped areas. Indeed, there is a quiet revolution going on. For example, the Philippines derives almost half of its total energy supply from nonconventional sources. But as Table 8 indicates, deforestation is at a crisis level in the Philippines. While renewable energy usage does not stand out in the overall statistics, its benefits are felt by millions in the region.

CRITICAL ISSUES IN THE REGION

Oil vulnerability and dependence on the Arab/Persian Gulf
As the foregoing discussion of the oil situation illustrates, the nations of the Asia-Pacific region are heavily dependent on oil imports from the out-

Table 8
CHANGE IN FOREST AND WOODLAND
IN THE ASIA-PACIFIC REGION

Country	Land area $(10^5$ ha.$)$	Percent of forest and woodland 1964–66	1981–83	Change[a] in distribution (% between 1964–66 to 1981–83)
ASIA				
Afghanistan	648	3	3	
Bangladesh	134	17	16	
Brunei	5	93	79	−14
Burma	658	49	49	
China	9,326	12	14	
Hong Kong	1	10	12	
India	2,973	20	23	
Indonesia	1,812	68	67	
Malaysia	329	79	67	−12
Nepal	137	33	33	
North Korea	120	74	74	
Pakistan	779	3	4	
Philippines	298	57	41	−16
Singapore	1	7	5	
South Korea	98	68	67	
Sri Lanka	65	49	37	−12
Thailand	512	51	31	−20
Vietnam	325	43	38	−5
PACIFIC				
American Samoa	—	70	70	
Australia	7,618	18	14	−4
Canton Island	—	0	0	
Christmas Island	—	0	0	
Cocos Island	—	0	0	
Cook Islands	—	0	0	
Fiji	18	65	65	
Former U.S. Pacific Trust Territory[b]	2	22	22	
French Polynesia	4	31	31	
Guam	1	18	18	
Kiribati	1	3	3	
Nauru	—	0	0	
New Caledonia	19	51	51	
New Zealand	269	27	37	
Niue	—	19	21	
Norfolk Island	—	0	0	
Papua New Guinea	452	72	71	

Country	*Land area (10⁵ ha.)*	*Percent of forest and woodland 1964–66*	*1981–83*	*Change[a] in distribution (% between 1964–66 to 1981–83)*
PACIFIC				
Samoa	3	52	47	−5
Solomon Islands	28	93	93	
Tokelau	—	0	0	
Tonga	1	16	12	−4
Tuvalu	—	0	0	
Vanuatu	15	1	1	
Wallis Island	—	0	0	

[a]Only negative change of three percent or more indicated.
[b]The former U.S. Pacific Trust Territory includes the Commonwealth of the Northern Mariana Islands, the Marshall Islands, the Federated States of Micronesia, and Palau.

side world. In 1985, there was a need for an additional 3.4 million barrels daily of oil. This figure will expand to over 5 million barrels daily by 1995.

A critical political question concerns the origin of these imports. In the past, the Arab/Persian Gulf exporters have been the main source of supply for the Asia-Pacific region. In 1982, 70 percent of net imports originated from the gulf. This dependency fell to 60 percent in 1985. By 1990, however, it is expected to grow to 65 percent and by 1995, this dependency is expected to be as much as 75 percent, as oil consumption in the region surpasses that of Europe.

The impact of government policy on energy use

A key factor in the Asia-Pacific region affecting energy issues is government policy. Most countries in the region are highly interventionist in the energy sector. A combination of oil vulnerability and dependence on imported energy, together with government bureaucracy, has resulted in an elaborate regulatory system which is in force in many countries.

Strong government policies have been extremely effective in conserving energy and moving away from oil as much as possible. No country has been as successful as Japan, where the Ministry of International Trade and Industry (MITI) has created one of the most resilient energy systems in the world. In short, Japanese energy policy is described by MITI as a "flexible switching system." Essentially, this approach allows for flexibility in switching from one energy source to another in such a manner that a loss of one fuel supply can be tolerated without disruption to the economy. The core of the Japanese policy is the power sector where deliberate policies have been undertaken to (1) make the price of fuel oil uneconomical compared to other fuels; (2) use the regulatory system to encourage a massive buildup in nuclear power generation; (3) disallow new construction of oil-fired power plants and encourage lower utilization rates; (4) embark on a major buildup of natural gas-based facilities and begin many long-term contracts; and (5) use more coal for power generation but maintain use of excess capacity in coal-fired power plants.

Currently, Japan's base-load electricity supply comes from nuclear power. Oil-, gas-, and coal-fired facilities are run at less than 40 percent capacity. If one of the fuels, say oil, is cut off, the Japanese power sector can continue to function uninterrupted. The same is true for any potential cutoff of coal or natural gas. In the 1990s, natural gas will join nuclear power as a base load, while oil and coal will be relegated to peak-load fuels. The same kind of flexibility in fuel switching has not and cannot realistically be achieved in the industrial, transportation, and commercial sectors. Nonetheless, prudent government policy has resulted in an important shield for the Japanese economy. This defensive system has not been inexpensive. The Japanese consumer has paid for it through high electricity costs. But these costs must be compared with the small Japanese military budget to defend the oil lanes of the Arab/Persian Gulf. Indeed, Japan may have chosen the path to real energy security through an integrated and comprehensive domestic policy.

Can any other nation copy Japan's policy? South Korea and Taiwan have tried, but they are less than half way there. Massive investments and strong goal-oriented discipline in energy policy still remain a very Japanese feature. Nevertheless, the nations of the region can learn much from Japan's experience.

Given the strong regulatory nature of the governments in the region, energy price controls have become the most important tools of government policy. By controlling pricing through differential taxation, the governments have influenced the growth of oil demand and the ratio of consumption of different fuels. In many cases, arbitrary prices have resulted in economically unjustifiable ratios of petroleum product demand, with little resemblance to the international market. As oil markets begin to integrate, the results of mistaken policies are becoming too costly. In many countries, for instance, government policies to reduce gasoline demand have resulted in a much higher growth in diesel demand, requiring hundreds of millions of dollars of refining investments to match the now distorted demand pattern.

Deregulation

The distortions introduced in the energy system, through different types of controls, are resulting in a determination to lessen government controls and allow a certain level of market influence. The first major effort to deregulate occurred in Australia.

The Australian oil industry, which has only existed since the early 1960s, has been regulated since 1965, when all indigenous crude oil was marketed under the crude allocation scheme. This was fundamentally a voluntary arrangement between producers and refiner-marketers administered by the national government. Under this allocation scheme, producers were guaranteed a market for their products by the provision of a mechanism for equitably allocating indigenous crude oil to refining companies. As of 1988, the oil market was deregulated, whereby refiners are no longer obligated to accept certain quantities of Australian crude and domestic producers are free to seek markets internationally. Naturally, there are adjustments to be made under such a radical policy shift. Because Australia is facing a clear need to seek additional oil supplies by the end of the century, deregulation in 1988 aided in the country's transition to a lesser level of oil self-suffiency. A similar effort was the deregulation of the New Zealand oil industry also effective in 1988.

Finally, and most dramatically, the Japanese government decided to deregulate its oil industry in a five-year period beginning in 1988. Since Japan accounts for nearly one half of the oil consumption in the region, any policy change in Japan will have a major impact on the overall oil trade flow in the Asia-Pacific region. Currently, the proposed liberalization plan for the refining sector in Japan calls for a dismantling of most MITI controls over the industry by 1990. Although most of the MITI guidance system will be phased out, the continuing policy of allowing only refiners to import products will offer some financial protection domestically. However, the degree to which imported products can replace domestic production will be of critical importance not only to Japan but to the Asia-Pacific region and the world. Whether or not Japanese product exports can compete in the international marketplace is a crucial question. Japanese refiners are currently examining the possibilities of exporting gasoline and processing crude oil for China and Malaysia. This transition period for Japan will not be without cost. In the long term, as found in the United States and Australia, it is hoped that deregulation will provide a more streamlined and efficient refining industry that can flourish and adapt to the changing market in the future.

In summary, some of the governments of the region are slowly beginning to allow market forces to enter their energy systems, although many are still far from totally free markets. As long as most of the nations of the Asia-Pacific region remain so dependent on the outside world to supply their energy needs, governments will keep a firm grip on the energy business in their countries.

FURTHER READING

Brandt, Robin and Wilson, Thomas R. *Capacity, Complexity, and Flexibility: The Evolution of Global Refining, 1970 to 1986.* Honolulu, Hawaii: East-West Center, 1987.
Dorian, James P. and Fridley, David G., eds. *China's Energy and Mineral Industries.* Boulder, Colorado: Westview Press, 1988.
Fesharaki, Fereidun, Brown, Harrison, Siddayao, Corazon M., Siddiqi, Toufiq, Smith, Kirk R., and Woodard, Kim. *Critical Energy Issues in Asia and the Pacific: The Next Twenty Years.* Boulder, Colorado: Westview Press, 1982.

Fesharaki, Fereidun. *Refining and Petrochemicals in the Asia-Pacific Oil Market.* Honolulu, Hawaii: East-West Center, 1986.

Gary, James H., and Handwerk, Glenn E. *Petroleum Refining: Technology and Economics.* 2nd ed. New York: Marcel Dekker, 1984.

Hoffman, Sharon, and Fesharaki, Fereidun. "Deregulating Australia's Oil: The Implications for Global and Regional Markets." *The Economist Intelligence Unit,* special report no. 1120. London, 1987.

Isaak, David T., and Hoffman, Sharon. "World Production of Synthetic Fuels: A Realistic Assessment." *The Economist Intelligence Unit,* special report no. 143. London, 1983.

Smith, Kirk R., and Fesharaki, Fereidun. *OPEC and Asia: The Changing Structure of the Oil Market.* New York: Pergamon Press, 1986.

ASIAN AND PACIFIC ECOLOGY

PHILIP STOTT

The benefits that Man confers upon natural vegetation are very meagre but as an agent for destruction he is unparalleled.
—The forester N. L. Bor, writing about the
Aka Hills of Assam in 1938.

THE CAUSES OF CHANGE: CLIMATE AND THE RISE OF HUMAN SOCIETIES

CLIMATE, the form of the land, soil and the impact of human societies are the four main factors that determine the ecological character of any portion of the earth's surface. It is these, functioning together, that will account for the types of vegetation found, which in turn will provide habitats for wildlife and will largely control the sensitive links between the processes of the atmosphere, such as rainfall, and the elements of the land, namely rock, soil, hills, valleys and rivers. In any region, the resultant mosaic of ecological systems is very complex; in Asia and the Pacific this is particularly so. In Yunnan Province of Southwest China, for example, the ecosystems encountered range from lush, tropical, semievergreen rain forest, through a spectrum of subtropical monsoon forests, savannas (tropical grasslands), mountain conifer forests and alpine meadows, to lowland zones of intensive cultivation, with emerald green rice fields and terraces (Figure 1).[1] In fact, Yunnan, together with the mountains of northern Burma (now Myanmar) and the eastern Himalaya, is a meeting ground for much of the flora of Asia, a zone in which tropical and northern temperate species mingle in great diversity.

If one of the key ecological determinants changes, so too, in time, will the pattern of vegetation and the processes of nature it partly controls. At the height of the last Ice Age, some 20,000 years ago, northwest Siberia lay under a continental ice sheet, while across the remainder of Siberia, from the Yenisei Valley in the west to the Kamchatka Peninsula in the far east, winters were even longer and colder than they are today, and fierce winds blew over frozen steppes where only hardy grasses and dwarf shrubs

---

[1] For a recent account of the vegetation of Yunnan, see *Journal of Biogeography* 13 no. 5 (September 1986): 367–486.

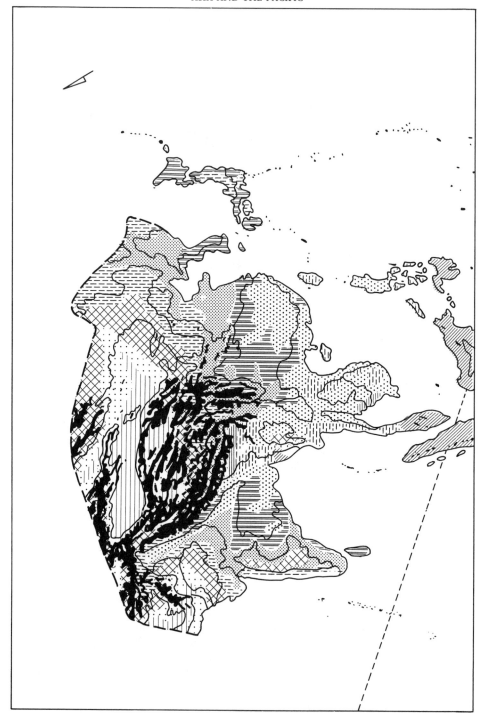

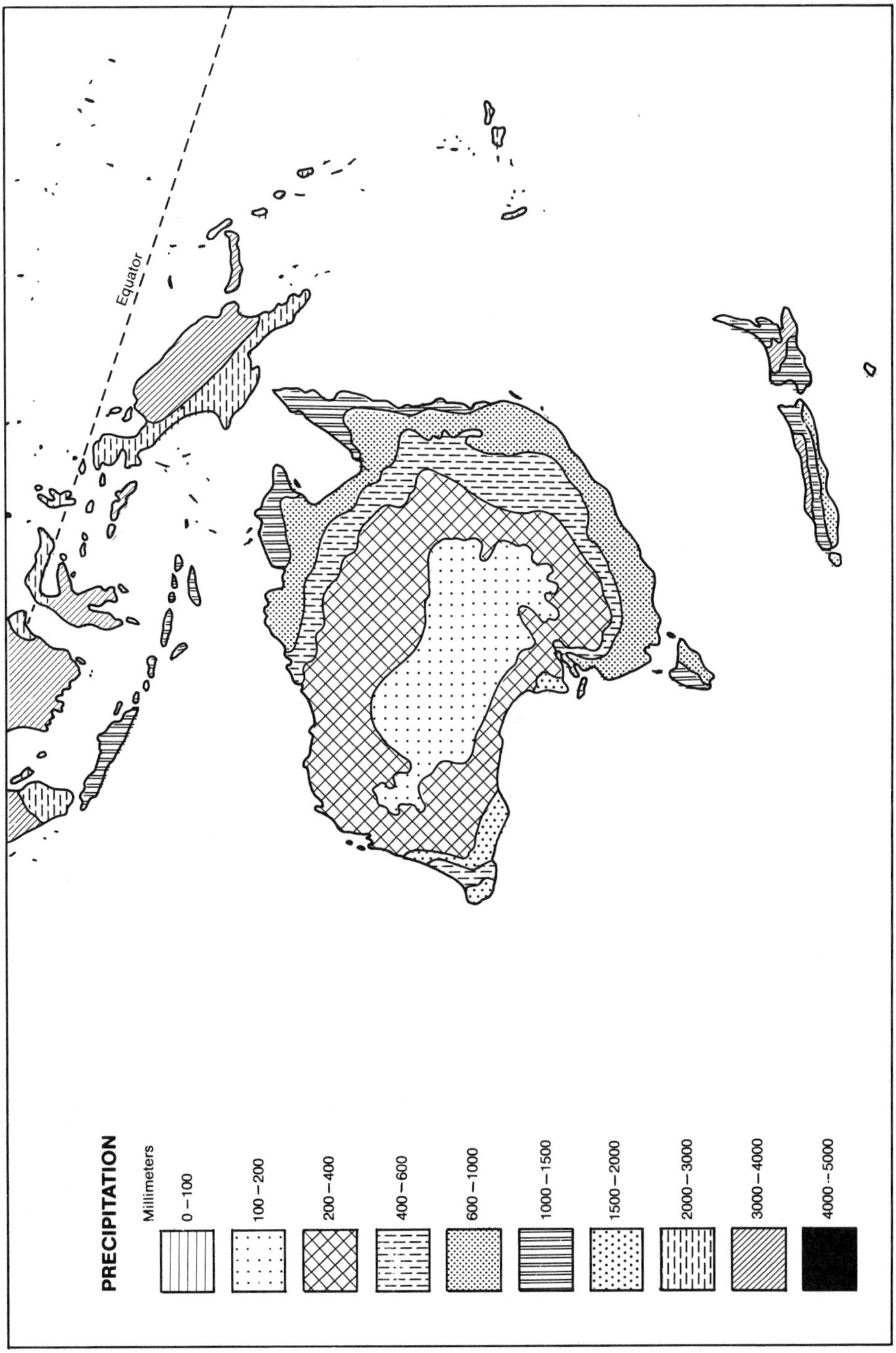

PRECIPITATION

PRECIPITATION

Millimeters

0 – 100

100 – 200

200 – 400

400 – 600

600 – 1000

1000 – 1500

1500 – 2000

2000 – 3000

3000 – 4000

4000 – 5000

Equator

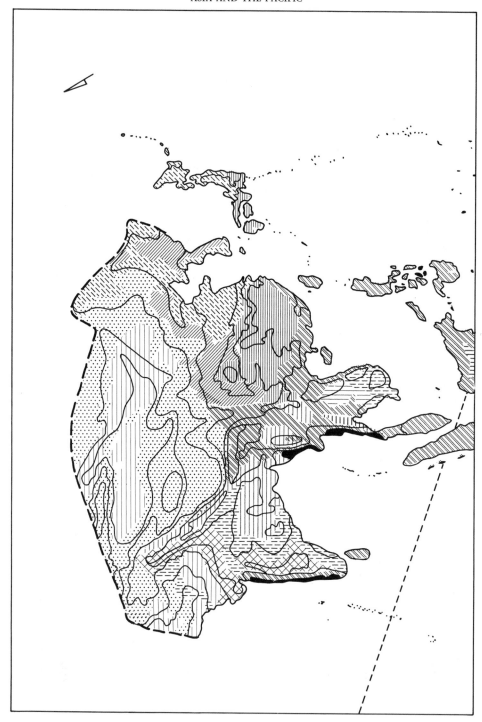

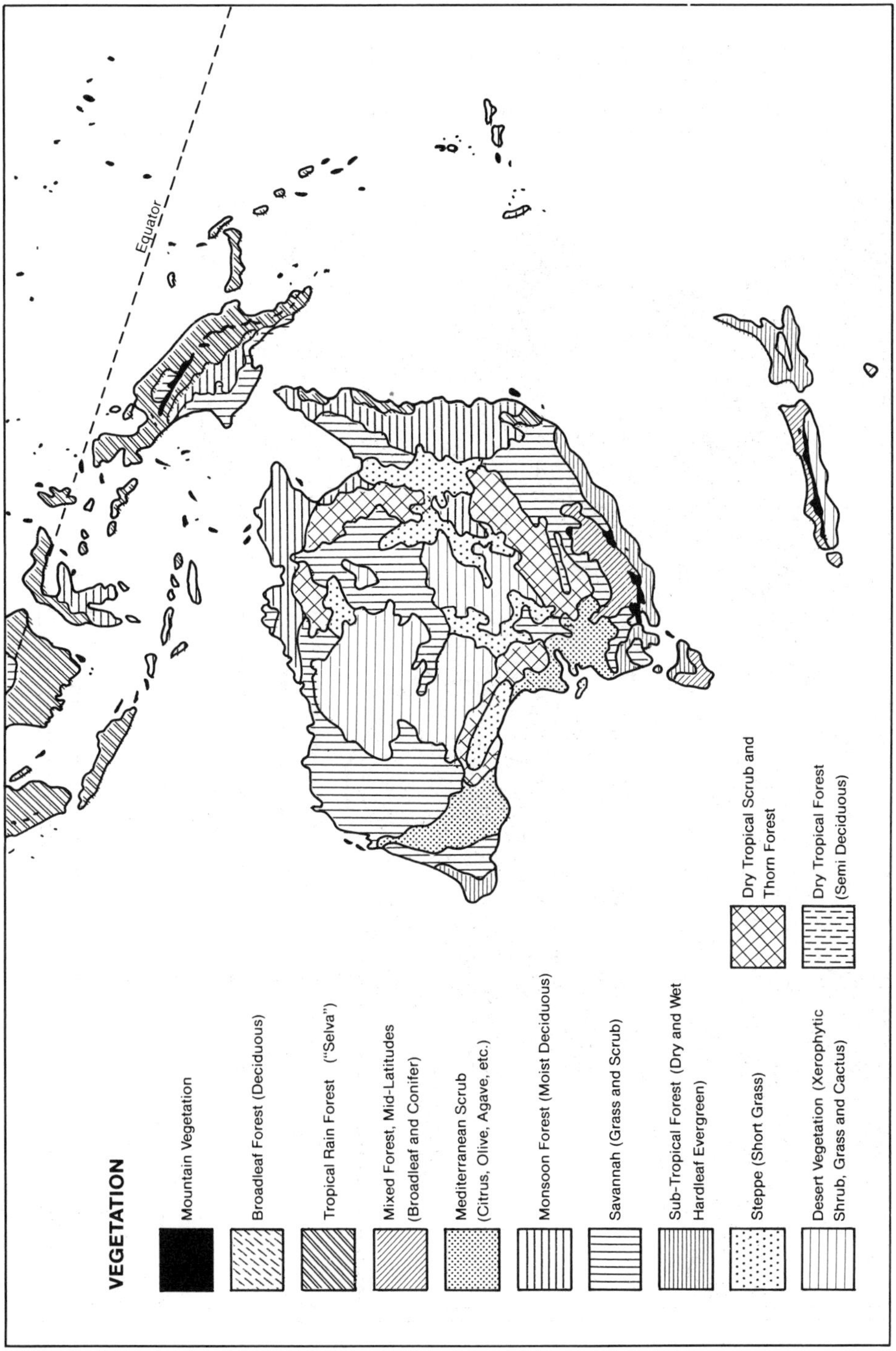

VEGETATION

VEGETATION

Mountain Vegetation

Broadleaf Forest (Deciduous)

Tropical Rain Forest ("Selva")

Mixed Forest, Mid-Latitudes (Broadleaf and Conifer)

Mediterranean Scrub (Citrus, Olive, Agave, etc.)

Monsoon Forest (Moist Deciduous)

Savannah (Grass and Scrub)

Sub-Tropical Forest (Dry and Wet Hardleaf Evergreen)

Steppe (Short Grass)

Desert Vegetation (Xerophytic Shrub, Grass and Cactus)

Dry Tropical Scrub and Thorn Forest

Dry Tropical Forest (Semi Deciduous)

Equator

Figure 1
THE JIGSAW OF VEGETATION: FOREST TYPES IN THE
SOUTHWEST OF YUNNAN PROVINCE, CHINA. © *JOURNAL OF
BIOGEOGRAPHY* 13, NO. 5 (SEPTEMBER 1986): 401.

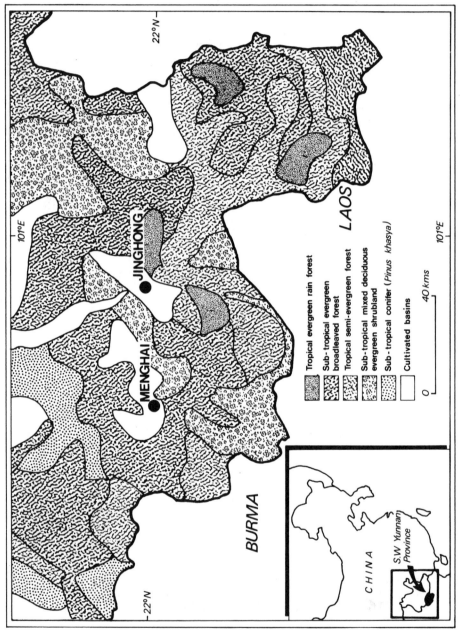

could survive. In this bleak land, Cro-Magnon peoples hunted large animals like the woolly mammoth *(Mammuthus primigenius)* and the steppe bison *(Bison priscus),* two of the nine mammals that later became extinct in Eurasia with the retreat of the ice about 10,000 to 12,000 years ago. When the climate warmed, the open vegetation, so suitable for big grazing herds, gave way to a new environment of birch and conifer forests. Overhunting may have further contributed to their ultimate demise. But the effects of the Ice Age had not been confined to the north of Asia. They had, in fact, penetrated deep into tropical Asia and the Pacific, lowering sea levels in the South China Sea; reducing temperatures in the mountains of Malaysia, Indonesia and Papua New Guinea by as much as 16°F/9°C; depressing tree limits; and possibly causing the cessation of the mighty southwest monsoon that brings vital rain to the Indian subcontinent, Southeast Asia, China and Japan.[2] Climatic change is thus one of the most potent factors in the ever-changing ecology of Asia and the Pacific.

Yet, during the last 10,000 years or so, beginning with the spread of Neolithic cultures and the development of agriculture—including the planting of roots like taro and yams in the Pacific and the cultivation of grains such as rice in tropical Asia, China and Japan, and millets in North China and India—it is the impact of human populations that has become the dominant theme in the altering ecology of the region. At first, while population densities remained low and technology simple, and while nomadic cultivators, using only a digging stick or hoe, harvested plots opened in the forest, this impact was limited. However, with the perfection of intensive cultivation systems such as lowland irrigated wet rice, population densities increased. Today, on an island like Java in Indonesia, for example, there is a mean population density of 690 inhabitants per square kilometer, with a population still increasing by 2 percent a year and a projected population density for the year 2031 of some 1,300 per square kilometer of habitable land—a figure that assumes that current birth control measures will actually prove effective.[3] Above all, it was the advent of intensive grain cultivation that facilitated the development of the first great city-states and civilizations in the region. These were often founded in conjunction with some of the world's great religions, Hinduism, Buddhism and Islam, and they brought both the benefits and the curses of urbanization to Asia and the Pacific. The present capital city of Thailand, Bangkok, or Krung Thep (City of Angels), may have many golden temples, *chedi* and palaces that reflect its Theravadan Buddhist heritage, but it also experiences severe flooding, subsidence, and one of the worst traffic and pollution problems known. Its inhabitants weave their way through crowded streets, often kneedeep in water, with handkerchiefs over their mouths for some protec-

[2] For climatic change in the tropics, see J. R. Flenley, *The Equatorial Rain Forest: A Geological History* (London: Butterworth, 1979), also *Progress in Physical Geography* 3 (1979): 488–509. For the early impact of human populations, see J. R. Flenley in *Journal of Biogeography* 15 no. 1 (1988): 185–97.

[3] For the population patterns of Java, see W. Donner, *Land Use and Environment in Indonesia* (London: C. Hurst, 1987), 32–52.

tion against the fumes and smells. A journey to work in this city of over 5 million people (one-tenth of the total population of the country) may take up to two or three hours.

With urbanization there has been growth of industry and the development of energy resources. In Asia and the Pacific these processes have been largely unregulated by government and law, and consequently have often led to ecological disasters and human devastation such as the explosion of a chemical factory in the Indian city of Bhopal and, in Japan, the infamous "Yokkaichi Disease" caused by photochemical smog and "Minamata Disease" brought about by mercury poisoning. The management of land, water and air has thus become a leading concern throughout Asia and the Pacific. Yet, even in the thronging cities of Japan, "natural monuments" survive in religious sectors—with shrine woods and parks covered with remnants of the old broad leaved evergreen forests, as at the Meiji-shrine and Rikugien-park.[4] Such wooded shrines, however, stand in stark contrast to Pacific islands made sterile by nuclear testing or, as on Nauru, by the relentless export of a valuable resource like phosphate. The following essay attempts to assess the balance between wisdom and folly in attempts to control the changing ecology of Asia and the Pacific.

THE RETREAT OF THE FOREST RESOURCE

During the last hundred years or so, the most obvious sign of human domination in Asia and the Pacific has undoubtedly been the clearance, destruction and exploitation of the forest resources. These range from the tropical rain forests of parts of India, Sri Lanka, Southeast Asia, Papua New Guinea, Queensland and Pacific islands like Fiji (Figure 2) through rich monsoon forests with teak *(Tectona grandis),* to the pines *(Pinus roxburghii)* and oaks (e.g., *Quercus incana*) of the high Himalaya. Until quite recently, tropical rain forests covered some 618 million acres/250 million ha. in Asia,[5] although in certain areas, such as lowland India, it would appear that a largely man-made landscape has been the pattern for hundreds of years, with forest remnants confined as "islands" to mountain fastnesses like the Western Ghats. The real process of destruction, however, began with the colonial exploitation of forest products: cloves, nutmeg, catechu *(Acacia catechu)* and tropical hardwoods. After World War II this process was accelerated by the drive of the newly independent nations to develop and modernize and by the insatiable demands of countries like Japan for timber.

The forests of the region are, however, one of the most diverse biological resources on earth. A Malaysian rain forest, for example, may house more

---

[4] For shrine woods, see the interesting paper by S. Iizumi in W. Holzner, M. J. A. Werger and I. Ikusima, eds., *Man's Impact on Vegetation* (The Hague: Junk, 1983), 335–40.

[5] For statistics of total tropical forest area, see A. Grainger in S. L. Sutton, T. C. Whitmore and A. C. Chadwick, eds., *Tropical Rain Forest: Ecology and Management* (Oxford: Blackwell Scientific, 1983), 387–95.

Figure 2
THE DISTRIBUTION OF TROPICAL RAIN FOREST.

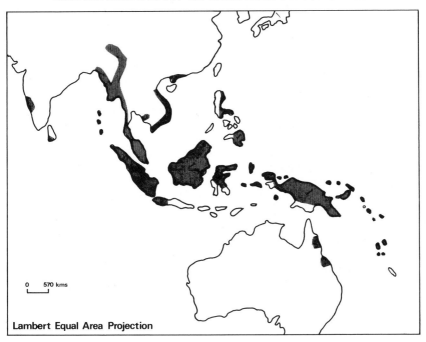

0   570 kms

Lambert Equal Area Projection

than 200 different woody species of plant in a single hectare,[6] while the monsoon forests of India, Burma, Thailand and Laos not only provide teak and many other valuable timbers, but are also rich in bamboos and a range of useful species. Moreover, fauna abounds. There is the hard-working Asian elephant *(Elephas maximus)*, so well portrayed by "Elephant Bill" (Lt. Col. J. H. Williams).[7] Wild elephants are rare today, with domesticated beasts mainly performing their tasks for admiring tourists. Several races of tiger, such as the Indian, or Bengal, tiger *(Panthera tigris tigris)*, the Amur, or Siberian, tiger *(P. t. altaica)* and the Chinese tiger *(P. t. amoyensis)*, prowl through forests of the region. Unfortunately, some types are probably now extinct, like the specialized island race of Bali *(P. t. bali)*. The endemic orangutan *(Pongo pygmaeus)* of northern Sumatra and Borneo is the largest of all arboreal apes and a near relative of human beings. Teak trees, however, now persist largely in plantations, and orangutans must be bred for survival even in their own forest domain at the Sepilok Rehabilitation Centre in Sabah. What humans first thoughtlessly destroy, they must then try to rehabilitate.

With the retreat of the forest, there is an inevitable reduction in the

[6] See T. C. Whitmore, *Tropical Rain Forests of the Far East,* 2nd ed. (Oxford: Clarendon Press, 1982).
[7] J. H. Williams, *Elephant Bill* (London, 1950).

vital genetic resources, the gene pool, which could well be exploited far more rationally in the future for foods, medicines and biochemicals. But for this to be possible, wild populations must be saved before it is too late. Most of the delicious indigenous fruits of the region are derived from forest species, the natural varieties of which are necessary for maintaining and improving commercial quality. Moreover, many species, including bananas (*Musa*) in Papua New Guinea, *Garcinia* in Malaysia, breadfruits (*Artocarpus*) in the Pacific and durians (*Durio*), remain to be properly developed. The medical potential of the forests is even greater, a fact well illustrated by the widespread traditional use of herbal medicines throughout the area.[8] *Rauwolfia serpentina*, for example, is already known as a treatment for hypertension.

The forests are, further, a biochemical storehouse for edible protein, lignin, cellulose and a range of pesticides, such as rotenone from *Derris* and *Millettia* and the newly extracted compound from the leaves of the Indian neem tree, recently developed at Imperial College of the University of London. Little is yet known about this hidden treasure trove, however, and a cure for cancer, for example, could be lost before it is found. The forests of Asia and the Pacific are thus a world resource; but it will be a nonrenewable resource if the habitats are destroyed.

In the animal kingdom, two particularly sad examples of extinction or near-extinction through human folly are Schomburgk's deer (*Cervus schomburgki*) and the kouprey (*Bos sauveli*). The former was a fine swamp deer known above all for its splendid, many-branched antlers. Until the 1850s it was common in the lowlands of the central plain of Thailand, but with the expansion of rice cultivation to meet increasing world demand following the signing of the Bowring Treaty in 1855, its natural habitat came under threat. During the monsoon floods, the reduced populations would become confined to small islands where parties of hunters, often riding on water buffalo or approaching in boats, would shoot, club and spear the trapped animals, whose complex antlers prevented their fleeing into the forest or scrub. It appears that the last specimen, a semiwild buck, was killed accidentally in 1938, although rumours persist of elusive sightings near the Cambodian border, which is also the territory of the kouprey. The kouprey was the last large mammal discovered by Western science; sadly, it is already on the list of the top 10 likely to become extinct. This large species of cattle has become the unwitting victim of the terrible conflict over Cambodia—many animals having been blown up by mines laid in the forest, or taken as food by villagers and the warring armies. There are probably less than 10 surviving specimens, although there are recent reports of a herd having been seen. Neither the case of the kouprey nor of Schomburgk's deer reflects well on human management of the natural heritage of Asia and the Pacific, although the king of Thailand has set aside a reserved area of forest to house the kouprey if some specimens stray across the border and can be saved. Of course, a disproportionate amount of effort

---

[8] See, for example, the excellent study by V. Brun and T. Schumacher, *Traditional Herbal Medicine in Northern Thailand* (Berkeley: University of California Press, 1987).

Figure 3
THE OFFICIAL AND UNOFFICIAL VIEW OF FOREST LOSS IN THAILAND.

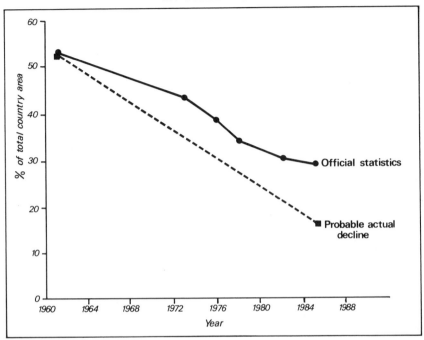

has gone into the conservation of one or two selected species, above all the giant panda, a Chinese endemic on the verge of extinction and symbol of the World-Wide Fund for Nature. Its cuddly, anthropomorphic image is easy to sell, and a specimen brings great financial rewards to any zoo owning one; but in many ways, this is a distraction from the real need: the maintenance of the rich forest habitats of Asia and the Pacific.

Rates and reasons for the retreat of the forest
It is extremely difficult to estimate with any accuracy the remaining area of undisturbed forest in the region, and even more problematic to assess the present rate of forest retreat. The reluctance of governments to release such statistics, the lack of any easily and widely applied international classification of forest types, and the near impossibility of actually collecting reliable data for many countries of Asia and the Pacific all help to compound the problem. Official figures often clearly differ from the observed reality on the ground—as is well exemplified in Figure 3, which contrasts the formal and the informal graphs[9] for forest decline in Thailand. What

[9] The informal graph is based on personal observations and discussions with the staff of the Faculty of Forestry at Kasetsart University in Bangkok; the official

is confidently termed "forest" is only that in a strict legal sense, and there is hardly a tree in sight. Much "forestland" is covered in secondary scrub, grassland and weeds of cultivation; it is of no productive use, either for agriculture or for forestry.

Yet, some countries retain a surprisingly high degree of forest cover. In Japan, no less than 62,417,460 acres/25,260,000 ha. (about 68 percent of the country) still carries woods and forests, giving a figure of 0.5 acres/0.2 ha. of forest per inhabitant.[10] The survival of so much forest in such a densely populated and industrialized country reflects above all the limitations placed on development by the steep and rugged mountain slopes that dominate much of the land. Nevertheless, most of this forest cover is far from natural, and some 88 percent of the plantation timber in Japan is less than 35 years old. There is a proliferation of small forest holdings, usually combining farming with forestry, which create a landscape patchwork of tiny plots and forest strips: 1.4 million owners manage woodlands of less than 2.4 acres/1 ha. Moreover, despite this home resource, the contribution of imports to total timber consumption in Japan rose from 12.1 percent in 1960 to over 50 percent in 1985, and Japan is now the biggest net importer of timber (in terms of volume) in the world. Other significant importers are South Korea and Taiwan.

As Figure 4 shows, estimates for the annual loss of forest in the countries of Asia and the Pacific range from less than 1 percent a year to nearly 4 percent, the latter figure being reached in such crucial countries as Nepal, where forests play so important a role in the management of watersheds.[11] At these rates, by the year 2010 it is likely that little undisturbed forest will persist in some countries, including Sri Lanka and Thailand, outside firmly protected national parks and wildlife sanctuaries. According to an estimate published in 1983, Asia and the Pacific as a whole had only 164 years to complete deforestation.[12] Moreover, the very sanctuaries themselves are often under threat when military and development needs press close on their borders, and when the growth of roads and the opening up of new land removes their buffer zones, so necessary to protect the core of any reserve. Unfortunately, the extension of agriculture remains a dominant process throughout the region. Pioneer frontiers exist in nearly all the remaining forest fringes and they are little subject to law and civil order.

The spread of agriculture is thus one of the main causes of forest destruction, particularly where marginal areas are being opened up by shifting cultivators, squatter farmers and settlers, However, while much of this largely pioneer settlement is uncontrolled, many such programs are actually

graph is based on *Thailand: Natural Resources Profile* (Bangkok: Thailand Development Research Institute, 1987) and government statistics.

[10] For statistics of Japanese forestry, see *Nihon Tokei Nenkan* (Japan Statistical Yearbook) and Rinno-cho, *Ringyo Hakusho* (Forestry White Paper), 1986. Trans. courtesy of J. Sargent.

[11] See J. C. Allen and D. F. Barnes, "The Causes of Deforestation in Developing Countries," *Annals of the Association of American Geographers* 75, no. 2 (1985): 163–84, for a good comparative account of deforestation statistics.

[12] Grainger, as footnote 5 above.

Figure 4
ESTIMATES OF RATES OF FOREST LOSS FOR COUNTRIES OF
ASIA AND THE PACIFIC.

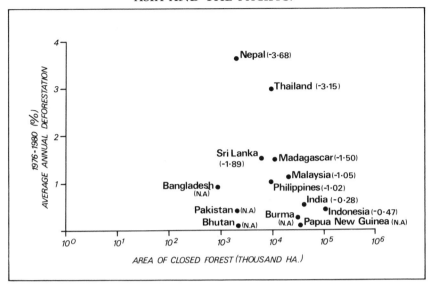

government directed, such as the transmigration *(transmigrasi)* policy in Indonesia. Here it is hoped to alleviate the population pressure on Java by moving people to new locations on the largely unpeopled outer islands of the country.[13] This often results in the opening up of forest areas in ecologically sensitive habitats, which are then badly farmed and managed. The policy has a long ancestry, going back to the Dutch and their resettlement schemes called *kolonisatie* or sometimes *transmigrasie*. The success of the Dutch schemes was limited, however, to the movement of only 200,000 people in 35 years. Today, the Indonesian government is seriously reassessing the effectiveness of the program. The net outflow from Java in the period between 1975 and 1980 was around 120,000 people a year. But the pressure to open up new areas is enormous throughout Asia and the Pacific. In China, for example, the estimates for the number of people per arable hectare have risen from 5.5 in 1952 to 9.8 in 1981, and will be around 12 by the year 2000. Such rural populations also have an insatiable need for firewood and charcoal—again imposing significant pressures on the forest resource.

In addition to these agricultural pressures, logging and the commercial extraction of timber remain a significant cause of forest loss. It is believed that between 1950 and the early 1970s the world consumption of tropical hardwoods quadrupled; and it is in Asia where the logging has been the heaviest. Both controlled and uncontrolled timber extraction involves the

[13] For transmigration policy, see Donner, chap. 11, as footnote 3 above.

construction of roads, which then, in turn, open up formerly protected areas to further damage. Moreover, a 10 percent extraction of timber will usually leave over 50 percent of a forest area damaged. Technology has also changed rapidly, with better log-hauling vehicles making the elephant redundant and one-man chain saws speeding up the felling. In 1983 the countries of ASEAN produced 1.5 billion cu. ft/42.5 million cu.m. of logs, 45 percent of the total production from the tropics. ASEAN has a total of 3,551 sawmills, with capacities of more than 17,657 cu. ft/500 cu.m. a year.[14]

Mining, the development of hydroelectric power, the spread of irrigation dams and other forms of exploitation—such as drilling for oil in Indonesia and the dredging of tin in Malaysia and southern Thailand—have also taken their toll of the forest resource, usually without the establishment of alternative or replacement forest systems. War has also played a part. In the late 1960s the military forces of the United States sprayed 18 million gallons/70 million litres of herbicides (mainly 2,4,5-T) on the forests of Vietnam, completely sterilizing the coastal mangroves, which are still barren today, despite replanting programs. Uncertainties about international boundaries have also allowed timber poaching along borders, as between Thailand and Laos. Corruption is rife in the forestry organizations of the region, and while many governments pay lip service to conservation needs, particularly in the international arena, they do little on the ground to stem the inexorable assault on the forest.

The shifting cultivators or swidden farmers of the marginal mountain regions of Asia and the Pacific are also much blamed for forest destruction along watersheds. It is certainly true that some groups, like the opium-growing Hmong (Miao) of the "Golden Triangle" in northern Thailand, Burma, Laos and southern China, are aggressive users of the forest resource. These peoples cut down the forest, then exhaust the soil through overcultivation, before moving on to repeat the destructive process in new areas. Many other peoples, however, are highly conservative in ecological terms; examples are the Ifugao in central Luzon in the Philippines and the Lawa in northern Thailand, who have traditional systems with a carefully worked out forest fallow in tune with the soil fertility of the region. In these instances, the blame should often lie, not directly with the hill peoples themselves, but with the dominant lowlanders and their governments, who so often force the highlanders onto smaller and smaller areas, thus causing them to abandon or to shorten their forest fallows and to alter their ancestral pattern of cautious land management. In fact, much modern agricultural development is far more destructive of the environment than the conservative practices of these shifting cultivators.

Finally, forest is often lost through fire and flood, disease, wind damage, volcanic action and climate change; it is quite difficult to distinguish the impact of humans from the impact of these natural causes. All forest systems have a natural cycle of a gap stage leading to a building stage and

[14] See F. Tesoro, "Tropical Timbers for Construction in the ASEAN Countries," *Unasylva* 39 (1987): 20–26.

then to mature forest. In many ways, shifting cultivators are simply mimicking the gap phase of forest regrowth. Many of the tree species that characterize the gap stage may have important commercial potential because they tend to be fast-growing pioneers.

Ecological consequences

The ecological consequences of this destructive impact on the forest resources of the region are, like the consequences for the maintenance of the gene pool already described, very serious—particularly on major watersheds such as the Himalaya. Forests are not only important in themselves as a timber and genetic resource, but they play a key role in controlling soil erosion, in regulating the flow of water into river systems and in affecting the local microclimate. Some 3.4 percent of the national territory of China is now estimated to be experiencing problems of desertification, nearly 40 percent of which is thought to be caused by forest destruction and overgrazing. In Australia this process began very early, with the arrival of aboriginal peoples from Asia around 40,000 years ago. Not only did these immigrants introduce such animals as the dingo, which threatened the native marsupial fauna—like the Tasmanian wolf (the largest marsupial predator)—but they also employed fire for hunting. Uncontrolled burns may well have spread the dry eucalypt forests at the expense of the rain forests, although care was exercised not to destroy vital food sites and known water holes. However, with European settlement after 1788, the whole process became markedly exacerbated by the clearance of coastal forests, overgrazing and the spread of farming.

Today, the ecological consequences of forest destruction are perhaps most vividly portrayed in the Himalaya, where the natural vegetation ranges from the tropical rain forests of Assam to deserts and high alpine steppe.[15] These form one of the world's greatest watersheds and they exemplify to the full the basic ecological principle that the ecological systems of one region cannot be altered without causing problems in another through a chain reaction. There is indeed a karma of ecological wrongdoing. The Himalaya are the catchment areas for the river systems on which the agriculture and the life of the people on the northern plains of India depend. It is the forest cover, above all, that filters and controls the snowmelt and precipitation that feeds these rivers, and thus ultimately the irrigation and flood-control systems on their lower reaches. If the forest cover is breached, the control system of the forest-soil relationship is destroyed, leading to soil erosion and gullying in the mountains, and then, way down on the plains, to alternate flood and drought. This truth was long ago recognized by local societies; the Sherpas of Khumbu, for example, organized forest guards, or *shingo naua*. Nevertheless, the pressures over the last hundred years or so have been enormous, including overgrazing by cattle, sheep and goats, particularly on the lower slopes of the the Western Himalaya, and the building of seasonal settlements for cultivation during the summer

[15] See U. Schweinfurth, "Man's Impact on Vegetation and Landscape in the Himalayas," in Holzner, et al., pp.297–309, as footnote 4 above.

months. There was also the development of British hill stations, like Simla and Darjeeling; the spread of roads and railways, especially after the Indian Mutiny of 1857; the overexploitation of timber; the uncontrolled use of fire; and, most recently of all, trekking and tourism. It is no wonder that thousands of people now die in India and Bangladesh because of floods in the lowlands beneath the denuded hills.

And yet, good land management is perfectly possible on even this, the steepest and highest of the world's mountain fastnesses. Human society can protect the fragile soil and its forest mantle by the correct use of fire in promoting stands of sal *(Shorea robusta)*—a tree of great economic value for its timber and resin—by terracing, by planting pines and bamboos, by controlling grazing, by conserving remaining stands of oaks and pines, and by managing shifting cultivation in the drier areas. But all this is difficult in an underdeveloped environment, where human activity so quickly destroys and great resources are needed to heal the wounds. Above everything else, there has to be a political and a social will to develop safely.

Soil erosion, in particular, is a major problem throughout Asia and the Pacific.[16] The annual loss of soil from the catchment of the Yellow River and its main tributaries in China has been estimated as over 17,000 metric tons per square kilometer, and for much of its course the Yellow River is little more than a mud slurry. The Red River catchment in Vietnam loses some 1,092 metric tons per square kilometer and the Brahmaputra in Bangladesh around 1,090 metric tons. In Java, the coastline is growing seaward by some 33 to 164 ft/10 to 50 m. every year as a result of the material being washed down from the mountain interior. The delta of the Punagara River in west Java has expanded by rates ranging from 0.11 to 0.34 sq. miles/0.28 to 0.89 sq. km. a year. In China 16 percent of the soil is thought to be seriously affected by erosion. The loss of this soil resource is unfortunate in itself, but the problem is more complex involving the downstream destruction of fisheries and rice fields by silt, the siltation of dams and canals, and the washing out of material to sea, where it does yet further damage to ocean fisheries and coral reefs.

Bare hills are of little value to human populations or animals. Sadly, one can travel many miles through the countries of Asia and the Pacific surrounded by a derelict land that has been raped and that has no long-term productive use. It would not be so galling if forest clearance was followed by a careful replacement program involving plantations, the development of agroforestry, the modernization of the shifting-cultivation principle, or the spread of forest villages. But more often than not the view is of a valley full of illegally cut logs ready for transport, lying under a haze from the uncontrolled forest and field fires blazing on the valley sides, and of hilltops bereft of any trees and reclaimed solely by coarse grasses and weeds. This is not a rational way to use the natural richness of a region for the ultimate

---

[16] See S. Nortcliff and A. C. D. C. P. Dias, "The Change in Soil Physical Conditions from Forest Clearance in the Humid Tropics," *Journal of Biogeography* 15, no. 1 (1988): 61–66.

benefit of its people. Short-term gain is the enemy of sound ecological development.

In addition to the slow but inexorable assault on forest, soil and genetic resources, the Asian/Pacific region has suffered and continues to experience major, sudden, natural and human-induced disasters that can have profound ecological consequences. In 1923 the entire city of Yokohama and over half of Tokyo were destroyed by earthquake and fire, which together claimed some 143,000 lives. (The even more gruesome parallel would be the dropping of the atomic bomb, first over Hiroshima on August 6, 1945, and then, three days later, at Nagasaki.) Flash floods in Bangladesh, volcanic eruptions in Indonesia, the Philippines and the Pacific islands, tidal waves in Japan, and the recent forest fires at Heilongjiang in China and on Borneo are similar in their awesome magnitude. Apportioning blame between nature and human action is difficult, for both the initial and the potential consequences of natural events are frequently reinforced by human action or inaction. The 1982–83 fire in the tropical forests of Borneo is a classic case in point. The initial cause of the fire was probably an unusual drought in East Kalimantan (eastern Borneo) in Indonesia, brought about by a climatic phenomenon known as the El Niño Southern Oscillation. Once started, the fire was spread by bad farming methods, shifting cultivation and lack of fire-control measures and education.[17] The result was a conflagration that raged from June 1982 to May 1983 and seriously affected some 7 million acres/3 million ha. of lowland tropical rain forest, swamp forest and peat forest. One of the local fires traveled 12 miles/20 km. in two months; another licked along at 547 yards/500 m. per day. The short-term and long-term ecological implications of this enormous fire have yet to be assessed, although recolonization and regrowth are likely to be very slow indeed if the experience of Krakatau (Krakatoa) is repeated.

The island group of Krakatau, lying west of Java, has become a field laboratory for studying the recovery of vegetation after complete obliteration.[18] In 1883 the whole island group was laid bare by a volcanic eruption that sent a cloud of dust around the world, intensifying sunsets even as far away as London. When Rakata, the main surviving island fragment, was visited a few months after the eruption, the only sign of life was a single spider; no plants appeared to have survived the holocaust. By 1886, however, there were 24 species of higher plants; by 1897 there were 50; by 1906, 99; and by 1936, 180. If all the island fragments were included, this last figure would have increased to 217. By 1979, nearly 100 years

[17] See L. Berenstain in *Biotropica* 18, no. 3 (1986): 257–62, also *Asiaweek* 10 (1984): 32–55.
[18] See J. R. Flenley and K. Richards, eds., *The Krakatoa Centenary Expedition: Final Report,* Department of Geography, University of Hull Miscellaneous Series no. 25 (Hull, 1982).

after the event, there were some 200 species on Rakata and around 370 in the islands as a whole. The rate of arrival of new species to the islands has been calculated at about 2.5 species a year, although this has been offset by an extinction rate of around 1.5 species annually. The net gain each year is thus rather paltry. It will take a long time indeed before the island once again becomes a lush tropical realm. Such unexpected and unpredictable events can thus alter the ecology of an area for many hundreds of years, and cause the complete disruption of plant and animal populations and of human cultures.

Diseases are also part of the changing ecology of Asia and the Pacific. Although great strides have undoubtedly been made in virtually eradicating some killer diseases, such as smallpox, certain modern developments have not always aided progress in this field. For example, agricultural improvement in India, using large pesticide applications, has actually caused a resurgence of malaria, which in the late 1960s was thought to be well under control. The indiscriminate employment of chemicals has enabled malarial mosquitoes to evolve a natural resistance to pesticides. In fact, since 1969, the number of cases of malaria in India has actually increased in direct relation to the use of DDT.[19] Dams and irrigation schemes have also provided new breeding grounds and have encouraged the spread of diseases and parasites involving aquatic snail vectors. In contrast, other diseases are so naturally prevalent that total control would be the only way of improving the situation. This is probably true for hookworm infestation in India, where there is a mean density of around 50 worms per person. Moreover, new diseases have been spread to the region, including AIDS, and the sexual license of some societies in the area could lead to an epidemic of this and other sexually transmitted diseases that, themselves, are constantly evolving new and more virulent strains. Diseases also seriously affect crop production, such as grassy stunt virus in cultivated Asian rice (*Oryza sativa*). Control is often effected by employing the gene pool of more resistant varieties and species, in this instance a wild species (*O. nivara*) from India. Here is another stark reminder of the foolishness of continuing to deplete available genetic resources.

Perhaps most alarmingly, the more advanced industrial societies of the region have created their very own gamut of diseases. Probably the classic example of such a disease is the terrible Minamata disease, brought about by mercury poisoning.[20] Minamata is a small city on the western coast of Kyushu in Japan. The disease was officially discovered there in May 1956, although there had been a long history of pollution and its side effects in Minamata Bay. Previously, the condition had been attributed to either a bacterial or viral infection, but in 1958–59 a British neurologist definitely established it as organic mercury intoxication brought about by eating contaminated fish. In October 1959, 2,000 fisherman in the city rioted and

[19] See G. Chapin and R. Wasserstrom in *Nature* 293 (1981): 181–85.
[20] For a moving account of the environmental problems in Japan, see N. Huddle and M. Reich, *Island of Dreams: Environmental Crisis in Japan* (New York and Tokyo: Autumn Press, 1975).

attacked the industrial corporation responsible. Yet it took until 1968 for the central government to recognize the disease and its cause formally. By January 1975, 793 Minamata victims had been certified, with a further 2,700 uncertified. Medical authorities, however, believe that many more had been affected in some way, probably numbering well over 10,000. Vast sums in compensation were paid by the corporation involved. This was an industrial disease of a rapidly industrializing society. The modern dream had become a nightmare for the people of Minamata. The physical and psychological agonies of its victims were excruciating and irreversible, and were often passed on to unborn children through the placenta, so that when they were born they could not speak, crawl or walk. Unfortunately, this story could be paralleled throughout Asia and the Pacific, for rapid industrial development too easily overlooks the ecological and human costs of progress. As elsewhere in the world, air pollution is another growing curse, often exacerbated in the countryside by the use of fires to burn fields and forest. The glorious sunsets over Burma and Thailand are not always what they seem; and Yokkaichi asthma has become a symbol, again from Japan, of the dangers of uncontrolled sulfur dioxide emission. On the positive side, however, better programs of hygiene and sanitation have much improved health and living generally. In South Korea, for example, the incidence of hookworm has fallen from 39 percent to 7 percent since 1949.

COASTS, SEAS, AND ISLANDS

As at Minamata, two sectors that need particularly careful monitoring are the coasts and the seas of Asia and the Pacific. The fringe of mangrove swamp that once characterized most sheltered bays and lowland coasts has been much destroyed and breached, with unfortunate consequences. Mangrove, with its stilt and breathing roots, acts as a protection against coastal erosion, and controls the movement of silt and waste products out to sea— thus safeguarding ocean fisheries and coral reefs. Moreover, it is an important habitat in itself for the spawning of many marine species, for the production of shellfish and for the manufacture of charcoal. A number of life-forms, such as the proboscis monkey in Borneo, confine their homes to this highly specialized habitat. In the Sundarbans of Bangladesh, Bengal tigers roam the mangroves feeding on swamp deer and unsuspecting fishermen. With increased soil erosion, it is ever more important that as much of the mangrove barrier be kept intact as possible. Mangrove swamps are thus a multipurpose resource needing sound management. As a source of firewood and charcoal they are often unsurpassed in countries where these elements provide over 50 percent of the energy requirements of the people.

Another particularly noteworthy habitat is the Great Barrier Reef, a complex of some 2,500 coral reefs exposed at low tide and covering about 96,525 sq. miles/250,000 sq. km. off the coast of Queensland. These spectacular reefs have developed over the last 20,000 years on much older foundations. North of the town of Cairns, they constitute a splendid wall of coral, with narrow openings into the sea, stretching for some 497 miles/ 800 km.; to the south, the reef is less continuous. Unfortunately, this famous habitat is threatened by a wide range of ecological pressures, including tropical cyclones, the attacks of the crown of thorns starfish, silt from the disturbed mangrove coasts and pollution. Luckily, much of the reef is protected by the Great Barrier Reef National Park, although the presence of oil reserves could prove the ultimate threat.

Sea pollution is, in general, a major problem, particularly along congested shipping lanes and especially on the routes that link industrial Japan with the oil-rich Middle East. It has been estimated that somewhere in the vicinity of 37,000 supertankers and other forms of shipping pass through the Malacca Straits every year, and there are the inevitable spillages, particularly of oil, such as that from the Japanese registered *Showa Maru* in 1975. Similar problems attend the widespread development of offshore oil and natural gas in the region. It is not surprising therefore that certain types of marine fauna appear to be threatened by pollution, and deformed fish have been noted along a number of coasts, possible omens of yet other Minamatas. In addition, many valuable species, such as turtles and ornamental tropical fish, which have a strong market in the developed world, are being hunted to extinction. Singapore often acts as an international trading center for such species. The protection of wildlife is difficult enough on the land; it is even more problematic at sea, where international laws and agreements are virtually impossible to enforce, as with the Japanese response to bans on whaling.

In the Pacific, in particular, there is an emerging marine economy that will require monitoring.[21] Reef and inshore fisheries have long been a mainstay of Pacific island peoples, including the traditional harvesting of bêche-demer, pearls and pearl shells from some atolls. The proper development of these resources could bring considerable wealth to the Pacific without over-exploitation and pollution. At present, however, progress is limited by political difficulties, the lack of local expertise and the absence of sufficient scientific research. One possibility is atoll aquaculture, not only of fish but also of marine plants such as seaweeds. The red algal genus *Gracilaria* is, at the moment, only harvested on a small scale for human consumption in Guam and Saipan, but it could form the basis for the development of an agar industry in Micronesia. Other new possibilities include the mining of manganese nodules, which occur in the deep waters of the Pacific. These nodules contain important reserves of copper, cobalt, nickel and manganese. Offshore gold is also found in alluvial deposits near the Solomon Islands and Guadalcanal. On land, the environmental impact of mineral exploitation has been devastating in the Pacific, with the mining of copper in Papua New Guinea, nickel in New Caledonia and, above all, phosphate in Nauru. The environmental problems associated with ocean-bed exploitation are as yet largely unknown. Even these require shore-based facilities, which could have deleterious effects. Finally, tourism brings in much foreign currency, but many governments remain skeptical about its real value, both economically and environmentally.

[21] See C. Gopalakrishnan, ed., *The Emerging Marine Economy of the Pacific* (Boston and London: Butterworth, 1984).

Island realms are in general susceptible to new introductions—not just of people but also of the plants and the animals they bring with them. Nowhere is this illustrated better than in Australia, where, for example, the chance introduction of the North American succulent genus *Opuntia* has helped to destroy many grazing areas, and where the arrival of the European rabbit proved devastating. New Zealand is another prime case, one disastrous introduction being the opossum *(Trichosurus vulpecula)* from neighboring Australia in 1858. This species was introduced to start a fur industry; but escaped animals have devastated both natural forests and plantations, severely defoliating stands of trees. Often, the best solution to some of these ecological scourges is the introduction of a controlling factor from the home environment. In the examples given above, the cinnabar moth was brought to Australia to control the prickly pear *(Opuntia),* and the virus disease myxomatosis to keep down rabbit populations. The introduction of domestic grazing animals, such as goats, cattle and sheep, has been especially damaging on some smaller islands—not least on the famous Galápagos Islands where Charles Darwin marshaled so much of the evidence for his theories of evolution. Here goats, feral cats and dogs have brought severe pressures to bear on the unique fauna of these isolated islands.

A PAST AND THE FUTURE

When population levels were still low, the peoples of Asia and the Pacific developed a number of indigenous land-use systems that were remarkable for their ecological diversity and soundness. Conservative systems of shifting cultivation, for example, while certainly destroying the prime forest cover, still managed to maintain the forest-soil relationship and to control soil fertility and soil erosion, even on very steep slopes in marginal mountain areas. Likewise, through the careful management of water, stubble, nursery bed and dry season, traditional systems of growing lowland wet rice were able to produce a crop year in and year out, and to support great civilizations. At Angkor in the 13th century, farmers were able to cultivate three rice crops a year. Moreover, these systems tended to be polycultures, with human beings entering the foodchain at many points. From the rice field, a village might take fish and shellfish, water vegetables and frogs, as well as rice. The aim was to produce a livelihood every year, whatever the monsoon; the change to having to produce a surplus for profit has been a significant one psychologically. These were truly sustainable systems.

From the 19th century onward, however, the story has been different, with population increasing rapidly and the development of modern agricultural systems—usually monocultures—industrial processing and the growth of great cities. In all this, much of the traditional ecological sense appears to have been forgotten or simply regarded as "primitive." It has been replaced by an urgent demand to open new land and to produce more and more as quickly as possible. The time is now surely ripe in the region to relearn ecological commonsense, and to seek systems that are not only highly productive and able to fulfill the imperatives of a modern world but which are equally sustainable through many generations, as were the older systems. The "mining" of timber must be replaced by more careful silvicultural techniques; by agroforestry, linking agriculture, forestry and, sometimes, fisheries as well; by social forestry; by the reservation of fully protected forest along sensitive watersheds; and by genetic conservation. The uncontrolled assault on the environment can no longer be allowed to continue; Asia and the Pacific is a rich area, but the natural resource is nearly exhausted and needs to be replenished by controlled development.

For this to happen, however, there must be the growth of indigenous philosophies of conservation and land management, which are developed on the old understanding of the relationship between humans and the land and which can be retaught through education. Such is now happening among the so-called forest monks of Buddhism, for the Buddha received enlightenment through the quiet, forest places of the world. But again, this will not be achieved without the development of mature governments that can plan for the long term and do not respond only to short-term demands. N. L. Bor's "agent of destruction" must turn into an "agent of reconstruction." In the words of His Holiness Tenzin Gyatso, 14th Dalai Lama of Tibet, "the world grows smaller and smaller, more and more inter-dependent . . . today more than ever before life must be characterized by a sense of Universal Responsibility, not only nation to nation and human to human, but also human to other forms of life."[22] In Asia and the Pacific the signs are less than fair, and there will be many more Minamatas before ecological sense prevails. Moreover, the recent recognition of the "greenhouse effect," of the hole in the ozone layer, and of global warming has shown just how interdependent we all are.

FURTHER READING

Deshmukh, Ian. *Ecology and Tropical Biology.* Palo Alto, California and Oxford: Blackwell Scientific Publications, 1986.

McAndrews, C., and Sien, Chia Lin, eds. *Developing Economies and the Environment.* Singapore: McGraw Hill International, 1979.

Myers, Norman. *The Primary Source: Tropical Forests and Our Future.* New York: Norton, 1984.

———. *The Sinking Ark.* Oxford: Pergamon Press, 1979.

Ranganathan, S. *Agro-Forestry: Employment for Millions.* Bombay: Tata Press, 1979.

Stott, P., ed. *Nature and Man in South East Asia.* London: School of Oriental and African Studies, 1978.

[22] See *Tree of Life: Buddhism and Protection of Nature* (London: Earl & Associates, 1987).

SOCIAL CHANGE AND THE ASIAN PEASANT

J. MOHAN RAO

INTRODUCTION

THE majority of Asians still live in villages, as they have for millennia past. But their lives are being rapidly transformed, especially when they leave their villages for towns. This transformation is far from complete in the populous nations of South and Southeast Asia. Scholarly research and debates have helped identify the causes and consequences of this process. In this chapter, the focus will be limited to the effects on peasants in Asian societies of economic and social change brought about by urbanization and agricultural transformations. Economic change is altering the work, livelihood and social relations of Asian peasants; these changes relate to the larger societies and polities of which Asian peasants are a part.

The term *peasant* in normal parlance applies indiscriminately to all agricultural producers. Specialists reserve the term to agricultural producers who own sufficient means of production to employ themselves but not enough to employ others. A variable but generally large fraction of agricultural families in Asia do not qualify as peasants in this narrower sense. They depend partly or wholly on others for their livelihood. When such producers work with leased-in land and borrowed capital, they must surrender part of what they produce to their landlords and creditors. Alternatively they may work for the well-to-do as wage laborers and produce a profit for their employers. Even peasants defined in the narrower sense frequently depend on merchants and moneylenders to arrange their sales and purchases.

All these groups may be included under the term *peasant*. What they share is their economic dependence and vulnerability. Excluded is a none-too-small proportion, in Asia, of rural families who are economically independent and are able to command the labor and surplus product of the others. Both peasants and nonpeasants thus defined are scarcely homogeneous groups; middle peasants and the landless differ in economic position, as do big landlords and rich peasants. Such class fragmentation differentiates peasants in terms of their economic possibilities and can significantly affect political consciousness and action. But we believe that our definition

1577

captures the most important form of class distinction relevant here. Other distinctions will be made where appropriate.

Asian peasants have been exposed to major waves of change over the past three centuries: Western colonialism, commercialization of production and the growth of markets, unprecedented population growth, anti-colonial and national struggles and technological changes. As a result, property relations, production organization and traditional village institutions have come under enormous pressure. Although economic and social differentiation in the traditional village remained stable and within well-defined bounds, this is no longer the case. Commercialization has presented opportunities to some rural social groups while posing challenges to others. As a result, the relations among these groups have also tended to change. For example, arm's-length employment of casual and migrant labor has grown at the expense of patron-client employment relations between the village well-to-do and laborers, which extended over lifetimes or even generations. Similarly, the decline in land/person ratios has induced changes in agricultural technology and state interventions. Thus villagers now depend far more on irrigation and developmental bureaucracies produced by these interventions. Many observers see a growing threat to the economic viability of peasants; peasants have had to adapt to these changes in ways that may also eventually undermine the very basis of their social existence.

Drawing lessons from the European experience of a century or two ago, social scientists from Marx onward supposed that capitalist development and modern economic growth would eliminate the peasantry as a social class. Market competition would force these changes as self-employed peasants and rural artisans became incapable of maintaining their livelihoods based on traditional techniques and small-scale production organization. The economic differentiation of the peasantry would develop proletarians and rich peasant-capitalists, quite apart from the growth of capitalism on large estates. Landless proletarians would also be increasingly absorbed by the urban industrialization that accompanied modern economic growth. These insights from past experience remain the fundamental starting points in the study of contemporary agrarian change. But this picture needs to be modified in the Asian context.

Economic growth in the Asian economies has been very uneven across countries, regions, the rural/urban divide and classes. Four decades of such growth have failed to raise significantly the living standards of the vast masses of rural Asians. The persistence of rural unemployment and under-employment is symptomatic of the failure of growth to "trickle down." Government policies, not rural structures and institutions alone, must be blamed, though policies and structures are interdependent. Growth tends to accentuate existing inequalities of access to resources, new opportunities and political power. In addition, the backwash effects of growth show up as absolute impoverishment of particular regions, sectors and groups. However, growth eventually does help reduce poverty, as the experience of the middle-income developing countries has demonstrated. But the pace at which this occurs is painfully slow and the human costs needlessly high. Studies of Bangladesh, India, Pakistan, Nepal, the Philippines, Sri Lanka, Indonesia and Thailand demonstrate growing inequalities within and between rural and urban areas. However, the increase is by no means inevitable, as the cases of Korea, Taiwan and China appear to demonstrate.

In Asian agriculture, both land and labor productivity have grown steadily during the past two or three decades, with land productivity growing significantly faster; agricultural production has grown in ways that economize on the limited supply of land relative to labor. The expansion of cultivated area has contributed at most 30 percent of output growth. At the same time, the rural sector has lagged significantly behind the urban. Thus, while nonagricultural labor productivity was 3.85 times agricultural productivity in 1964–66, this multiple had risen to 4.41 in 1982–84. This signifies, at least potentially, a long-term pressure on rural populations to migrate to urban areas. The reasons for this trend are threefold: (1) the political economy has not permitted a more rapid rate, or appropriate forms, of agricultural growth; (2) late-arriving developing countries have seen nonagricultural output growth of a type that has not generated much employment growth; and (3) agriculture continues to be the source of last-resort employment. Population growth is not the cause of rural poverty and underemployment; rather, these are consequences of the nature of the capitalist growth process itself.

In capitalist market economies, this point is best illustrated in relation to hunger. The growth of food output does not automatically satisfy the food needs of the hungry and the poor. A rise in their food purchasing power is required. Falling wages, declining employment opportunities, loss of assets or falling prices of cash crops produced by the poor signify a decline in the ability of the poor to purchase food. Such changes may occur even when food supply is rising. In fact, despite recent respectable rates of per capita food output growth, hunger and chronic malnutrition remain among Asia's most pressing problems. According to some estimates, about 1 billion people in the world live in absolute poverty, and more than 90 percent of these live in rural areas dependent on agriculture or nonfarm work partly linked to agriculture. Three-quarters of the world's poor live in Asia, they are distributed as follows: South Asia, 40 percent; China, 20 percent; and Southeast Asia, 15 percent. In India, food and calories supplied per capita have remained essentially stagnant over three decades despite the much-heralded Green Revolution. Southeast Asian countries have fared significantly better than South Asia in per capita food consumption, yet the decline in poverty has been small.

Most of Asia's poor are peasants and landless laborers, and most Asian peasants and landless workers are also poor. A large proportion of them live in rain-fed or semiarid regions where the growth of agricultural output and rural employment opportunities has failed to keep pace even with population growth. Even where rural output has grown at respectable rates, the benefits have been unequally distributed between the haves and the have-nots. In the Indian case, for example, the proportion of the population that is poor has not significantly declined despite steady if modest improvement in per capita living standards for over three decades. Part of the explanation is the failure of growth itself: in the 1960s, for example, agricultural growth exceeded 5 percent in about a third of the country's 281 districts, but output fell in a fifth of the districts and rose at less than 1 percent a year in another fifth. But this is certainly not the whole explanation. An ILO review of research on poverty and living standards in 10 Asian countries (including several Indian states) found no significant improvement in the incidence of poverty in most of them between the early 1960s and the mid or late 1970s. Even where the proportion of poor people has fallen (as in Thailand and the Punjab), its level remains high, and the reduction has been small. Growing landlessness, reduction in employment opportunities and the growth of casual (as distinct from durable) market employment are the most cited reasons for the persistence or growth of inequality and poverty.

The next section highlights the basic social framework within which Asian peasants eke out a living. Peasants live and work in villages, and village institutions have a life of their own that cannot be reduced to any simple, all-encompassing principle of morality, rationality or exploitation. Although economic change certainly accentuates conflict between peasants and nonpeasants within the village context, conflicts do not vanish when more impersonal market transactions replace the village in mediating the process of exchange. The transformation of village social relations, coupled with the growth of market relations, has raised peasant insecurity, reduced their economic viability and threatened their ability to cope with rapid change. In another section, the nature and consequences of the agricultural transformation in rural Asia is characterized in terms of class differentiation of the peasantry and the creation of an agricultural proletariat. This process of differentiation has been uneven over time and across regions; it has not, in general, led to a radically polarized class structure. The role of rural nonagricultural sectors, the impact of Green Revolution technologies and the consequences of mechanization and government growth initiatives in changing peasant livelihoods and social relations are also considered. Another section argues that the continuing incapacity of late-developing Asian economies to provide employment and decent living standards for their rural and urban masses is a direct consequence of their economic and political structures. The roots of the problem are not demographic or technological, nor should they be traced to insufficient investable resources or to politically based exploitation of the countryside by the town. The experiences of east Asia and presently developing Asian countries are contrasted. The final section summarizes conclusions.

AGRARIAN STRUCTURE AND THE PEASANTRY

In describing the salient features of the social and economic structure of the Asian rural economy and analyzing their consequences for the peasantry, three features merit special attention: the localization of economic transactions and the role of village social organization, the inequalities of land and wealth and the interaction between structure and rural factor markets in determining economic outcomes.

In the traditional rural economies of Asia, the village defined the matrix of relations within which economic and social transactions were conducted. Asian villages have been viewed not merely as geographical entities but also as political, economic and even moral units. Accordingly, unwritten rules of social conduct governed village-level economic transactions involving peasants, landlords, moneylenders and laborers. Of course, Asian villages were not autarchic and self-contained units; the village economy was tied to the outside world through networks of trade, local and supra-local politics, state taxation and other means. Nevertheless, the bulk of transactions involving access to the basic means of production—land, labor and finance—were localized within villages.

Two rather extreme models of such village economies have been defended by students of agrarian Asia. At one end, some authors have denied that the village economy can be understood in rational, individualistic terms. Village-level constraints on individual action and the villagers' commitment to shared moral values shape economic transactions. According to Scott, who studied the sources of peasant rebellion in Southeast Asia earlier in this century, the double threat of unpredictable nature and arbitrary and inflexible claims by outside political authority compelled peasants to concern themselves almost exclusively with assuring a socially acceptable subsistence level. Hence they developed norms of reciprocity and the right to subsistence. The moral economy of the peasant that these norms define is vastly different from a market economy governed by capitalist institutions and the profit motive. Scott argues that peasant uprisings are last-resort attempts to recover moral rights destroyed by capitalist development.

At the other extreme, some have suggested that self-interest and economic rationality govern the village economy. Asian peasants act individually on the basis of rational calculations of the practical consequences of their actions. Moreover, cooperative or collective action is seen as exclusively determined by the aggregation of individual economic interests. For example, where profitable opportunities for trade or improved productivity (say, through collective irrigation) exist, markets or marketlike institutions come into being to exploit such opportunities. Such arrangements may fail, however, without contradicting the hypothesis of peasant rationality. Thus the lack of development of insurance and welfare schemes in Vietnamese villages has been attributed to the problems of determining whether the poor were merely unfortunate or lazy and dishonest. Similarly, the rural rich acted as a cohesive group who exploited the others by virtue of their privileged access to political authority, a phenomenon consistent with rational action but not with moral economy. The growth of inequality, poverty and risks in 20th century southeast Asia, it has been argued, was due not to the growth of commercialization and markets but to the functioning of an unequal political system in colonial regimes.

The contemporary Asian village economy probably lies between these two extreme models. Even in contemporary Asia, the village remains a major arena within which economic transactions take place, though not quite to the same degree as in earlier times. Recent village surveys in West Bengal (India), for example, show that intra-village exchanges of labor, land and credit are the norm. Wages display a remarkable degree of dispersion across even contiguous villages, suggesting that markets remain fragmented. Although workers sometimes cross village lines, both employers and peasants prefer to confine their exchanges to their own villages. Economic transactions within this context are not characterized by anonymity, free mobility of economic agents and market competition; rather, personalized relationships, relative isolation and localized monopolies are the rule.

At the same time, economic change has loosened such traditional economic and social ties. As an increasing proportion of peasants find themselves bereft of land and other means of production, they must enter the market to search for employment outside their villages. Some eventually must sell their agricultural assets and move to urban areas in search of jobs. Technological changes also make the flexibility of casual employment relations more profitable for employers. Market growth and the increasing importance of production for exchange exposes rural producers to the compulsions of the marketplace. Hence, transactions based on caste, kin or village affiliations yield increasingly to those based on economic calculation.

These pressures for change affect peasants and nonpeasants in asymmetric ways. In most parts of Asia, the rural economy is characterized by substantial degrees of land inequality. A standard measure of land inequality (called the Gini coefficient) is as low as .3–.4 for Asian countries with reformed agrarian land-holding structures (Taiwan, China and Korea) whereas it is .5–.7 in other Asian countries. The inequality of rural incomes is strongly associated with the inequality of landownership, because landownership yields a substantial share of total incomes in a labor-abundant economy and because other forms of wealth ownership are also strongly correlated with the ownership of land: those who command much land also have the wherewithal to act as rural financiers, merchants and owners of rural small industries. Economic and social power reflected in land control impose narrow limits within which communal restrictions or values can play a role. The rich and powerful enjoy exclusive rights of disposal over their means of production and employment. Peasants who lose income, employment and assets are frequently left to their own devices.

In such a context, the claim for a moral economy seems extravagant. At the same time, however, the interplay of self-interest and political (power) imperatives must be recognized. Intra-village conflicts over access to land and employment or over the terms of such exchange are scarcely resolved by uncoordinated or purely selfish individual actions. For example, the conflicts between the landed and the land-poor may be resolved through compromise in which village institutions and rules play an important role. Some scholars also suggest the existence of significant differences across countries or regions in this respect. Hayami and Kikuchi argue that the relative ease with which land-augmenting and labor-using technologies are promoted in some parts of Southeast Asia compared to India is due to the strength of the village community in Southeast Asia—characterized by patron-client relationships, a traditional moral principle of mutual help and income-sharing—whereas caste and class divisions in India are major hindrances.

According to an interesting study of two Indonesian villages, adoption of new technologies is not explained only in terms of their private profitability. The new HYV technology under government sponsorship made rapid headway in Karang Sari, a favorably located village with highly polarized land distribution. The *bawon* system of harvest-sharing was displayed by market-based labor contracts for harvest work using the labor-saving sickle. In contrast, neither the new seeds nor the sickle found fertile soil in Suren, a village characterized by little differentiation and strong norms of reciprocity and sharing. Thus, the response to new technologies is influenced not only by landownership structure but also by the tenacity of noncapitalist institutions. Dramatic political realignments may be linked with technical change in an unequal agrarian context. Radical political changes since 1965 have assured the quiescence of the have-nots and transformed the relation between the agrarian classes in rural Java.

Although economic change certainly accentuates conflict between peasants and nonpeasants within the village, conflicts do not vanish when more impersonal market transactions replace the village in mediating the process of exchange. Recent research on rural factor markets in Asia demonstrates that economic outcomes—how resources are employed, who gains access to them, who gets what share of the product—are best seen as determined by the *interaction* between agrarian structure and market processes.

This is nowhere better illustrated than in the determination of employment and incomes. The different structural positions of peasants and nonpeasants fundamentally affects their behavior and responses. Few peasants remain outside the pale of the market economy. The view that Asian peasants are self-sufficient and independent of market conditions is no longer tenable, if it ever was. Peasants seek to make the most of their land and other assets in a market in which employment opportunities are limited and uncertain. Their main concern is to assure themselves a satisfactory level of income. The landless have no alternative but to seek whatever employment they can find in the market. Land-owning peasants seek, in addition, to ensure the viability of their own farms. To this end, they work their own lands as intensively as possible and, when this will not permit enough work, deploy their surplus labor in the market. Their limited holdings of land relative to their available supply of family labor ensures that, in a context of widespread unemployment, peasant farms are cultivated with a high degree of labor intensity. In contrast, because they must pay the prevailing wage, nonpeasant employers cannot hire labor beyond the point where it ceases to be profitable. The prevailing wage is not determined by market conditions (which, given unemployment, would imply a constant pressure to lower the wage) but by the relative power of employers and peasant laborers. To this must be added the problems of supervising and controlling the labor of hired workers. Hence, a gap, often substantial, exists in the perceived costs of labor between peasant and nonpeasant farms. These considerations also explain the willingness of the rural rich to mechanize agricultural operations and thus limit labor employment.

The belief that rural factor markets function efficiently and independently of agrarian structure is empirically false. Numerous studies have shown that small farms employ their land more intensively than large, labor-hiring farms. Although small farms have much stronger incentives to use labor effectively, they are at the same time restricted in their access to land and credit. Hence, the extent of unemployment of labor or underemployment of labor and other resources is intimately tied to the inequality of assets. Other consequences include wide variations in the efficiency of resources employed and reduced incomes for the poor.

Rural land and credit markets are also characterized by marked inflexibilities. In South Asia, for example, although there is a significant amount of land-leasing in the form of fixed rent or sharecropping tenancies, their effect on peasant access to the means of employment remains circumscribed; similarly, access to credit is closely linked to ownership/control of land. Hence, there is a connectedness between the ownership distribution of assets (land, total wealth) and their distribution in operational use. Rural moneylending takes the special form of seasonal credit—a substantial source of profit to the specialist moneylenders and a significant source of additional income to the landowners. Such credit had historically been a normal form of extracting surplus for those who had the holding power that comes from wealth. But with technical change, it also becomes a crucial lever for securing cheap labor and engrossing land at very favorable terms. Defaults further concentrate landownership, and the continuation of such credit is both a cause and a symptom of persistent poverty.

To sum up, the market and institutional setting within which Asian peasants eke out a living is neither benign nor equal. Economic and institutional changes have rapidly transformed peasant livelihoods. Many have lost their assets and must increasingly depend on others for a livelihood, through casual wage employment. Although the village continues to localize economic exchanges, peasants have to produce for distant markets and for employers largely motivated by profit. As a result, the social character of the village has also been transformed as it yields to the wider market. In the presence of large inequalities, market exchanges accentuate those inequalities by increasing unemployment and reducing efficiency. The most important consequence for the peasantry is rising economic insecurity, frequently accompanied by declining income that further reduces peasants' ability to cope with change.

AGRICULTURAL TRANSFORMATION: A VANISHING PEASANTRY?

Over the course of this century, agrarian structures have changed in rather complex ways under the pressures of a growing population, long periods of stagnation or slow growth, reforms in landownership and other state interventions. But the principal impetus for change comes from the process of accumulation and capitalist development to which Asian economies have been subject. Broadly speaking, this change can be characterized in terms of a class differentiation of the peasantry and the creation of an agricultural proletariat. Many peasants have become increasingly pauperized, have lost their assets and have joined the rural and urban proletariat. The proportion of purely landless laborers has certainly risen in both South and Southeast Asian countries. This category has grown mainly at the expense of the near-landless and the "middle" peasant group—those with the capacity to employ themselves. But this process of differentiation has been uneven over time and across regions. In some parts of South Asia, for example, middle and large farms have prospered, while in other regions, characterized by stagnation, relative positions and traditional structures have remained largely intact.

Two aspects of structural change require special emphasis. First, depeasantization takes place slowly and discontinuously; the continued survival of Asian peasants requires explanation. Second, the initiative in the agricultural transformation has not come exclusively or even mainly from the privileged class of large landowners; in many regions of Asia, middle and rich peasants have been more dynamic in taking advantage of growth opportunities and new technologies.

The internal logic of the peasant enterprise that is externally involved in the capitalist marketplace is the most plausible explanation for peasant survival. Social differentiation in the Marxist or Leninist sense pervades Asian peasantries. Peasant differentiation is not a purely cyclical phenomenon associated with random changes in family size or other such conditions facing individual peasants. Yet the persistence of family-labor enterprises even when they are involved in market exchanges contradicts the classic Leninist stance that class polarization is the normal form of agricultural development. This can only be understood as the outcome of adaptive peasant responses to capitalist expansion: peasants try to maintain their small landholdings as a fallback position, a base that gives them some security in an uncertain world. This gives rise to an involutionary pattern in which large farms and rich peasants grow by accumulating capital that adds little to the growth of employment while small peasant farms proliferate without access to credit or modern technology and heavily dependent on temporary wage employment. This pattern of growth does not lead to the "classical" outcome: there is pauperization but no wholesale depeasantization or polarization of the class structure. Fundamentally, it is explained both by the *resistance* of the peasantry to their proletarianization and by the *inability* of capitalist development to absorb the labor of the peasantry.

The persistence of the very small holdings in peasant agriculture is also a function of the polarization process itself. Although accumulation does lead to net land transfers from the poor to the rich (the polarization process), this process creates conditions by which even the smallest holdings may manage to survive. Thus, peasants losing their land resort to wage employment in both agricultural and nonagricultural activities. But they attempt, with the aid of such income-earning activities, to resist selling off their remaining holdings of land, as has been documented clearly with Bangladeshi evidence.

The second main feature of Asian agrarian change noted earlier is that the accumulation process is not always spearheaded by the top layers of the agrarian hierarchy. Growth and accumulation in Asian agriculture has had to proceed without an elastic land frontier, given already high person-land ratios. Land-augmenting investments are therefore the *leading* input for such growth. These include investments in irrigation, land improvement, agricultural research and extension, transport and electrification. Much of this takes place under state direction and financing. Even where the extension of arable land is physically feasible, it is frequently organized by public authorities. Private firms or farms have neither financial nor technical capability to make large investments in land-augmenting facilities. Thus the state has provided the resources and the organization for research, technical change, irrigation and other infrastructure and also provided credit, fertilizer and other subsidies. Hence, who will benefit from government initiatives in agricultural growth depends both on the prevailing agrarian structure of a region and on the pattern of spread of government development programs across regions.

Where peasants have access to such inputs, they have been as eager to adopt the new technologies as large farms are. In such cases, even small holders have adopted these inputs eventually. In fact, with their closer involvement in the management of their farms, the middle and rich peasantry have led the growth process in regions favored by government programs. Small size as such does not impose compelling disadvantages. But even where access is not biased in favor of large farms, as in parts of Malaysia and Indonesia, the absolute benefits tend, of course, to be much larger for them. Where they cannot or will not invest their surpluses elsewhere in the economy, large farms often buy up their smaller neighbors, thus contributing to the polarization process.

The advantage of large farms is not so much technological as institutional. This derives from their privileged access to nonlabor private and public inputs. Within traditional agriculture, large farms have not been notable for their direct interest in the production process or for productivity-raising investments. Under the impetus of the new HYV technology and related government initiatives, the large farmers' opportunities for manipulating local bureaucracies and markets have grown, further contributing to inequality. A good example is public irrigation. In many parts of Asia, government bureaucracies control canal irrigation. Problems of irrigation management and underuse are rampant—for example, in the wet and dry rice zones of Sri Lanka. But these problems may be induced by collusive actions of large landowners and local officials seeking to benefit themselves at the expense of small farmers and laborers. When excluded from access to the water, the small farmers are obliged to offer their surplus labor to the local landowners at lower wages.

Evidence from India and elsewhere support these observations. Agricultural development in India has persistently been extremely uneven. The pace of agricultural growth is broadly correlated with certain aspects of agrarian structure: notably, the regions of rapid growth are in the erstwhile *raiyatwari* (roughly, peasant-dominated) areas, especially northwestern India, while backward agricultural regions predominate among the erstwhile *zamindari* (roughly, landlord-dominated) areas, especially eastern India. Hence, Green Revolution technologies have widened interregional inequalities largely conditioned by the availability of complementary public inputs, though the areas of the Green Revolution were not exclusively the regions with the highest land inequality.

As noted earlier, lack of access to land and other means of production leads to considerable underemployment and unemployment. A fundamental problem of Asian growth has been the continuing inability of both urban and rural sectors to absorb unemployed and underemployed labor. Unequal land distribution and associated problems remain major obstacles to raising employment within agriculture and in rural industries. Given these structures, the employment elasticity of agricultural output under Asian conditions is rarely estimated to exceed 0.5. Thus, with the labor force growing at about 2 to 2.5 percent per annum, agricultural growth must be about 4 percent per annum to absorb the additions to the labor force—a rate of growth that few countries can sustain over long periods.

Japan absorbed increasing amounts of labor with continuous growth of its land and labor productivity in the early phases of its modern economic growth (1860–1917); other Asian countries hope to replicate that experience. Japan's increase in agricultural employment was accomplished by labor intensification of techniques, increased cropping intensity, and the production of labor-using infrastructure works. Taiwan after World War II and in post-revolution China had similar experiences. Yields and labor intensity in South Asia are considerably lower than those attained in Japan and China and at middling levels in Southeast Asia. In 1956, the average man-days per year per hectare in Japanese agriculture was nearly three times that in India, for example. Unfortunately, the general trend in both these late-developing regions is contrary to the east Asian experience. In contrast, labor input rose from 500 man-days per hectare in the 1950s to nearly 1,500 in the 1970s in the lower Yangtse valley.

Reasons for the difference include the failure of land reforms, early exposure to the use of labor-saving machinery on large farms and a reliance on trickle-down from urban-based industrial development, with attendant tradeoffs between growth and equity.

The social benefits of the Green Revolution technologies have been strongly conditioned by the policy and structural environment. In some countries, policymakers tended to favor large farmers because (1) they would adopt the new technologies faster and more completely, (2) their additions to output would directly add to the marketed surplus more than small farmers' gains and (3) they would save and invest at faster rates. During the initial phases of the Green Revolution, landlessness and land concentration increased because these assumptions proved right and because government policies for small farmers were unfavorable. In general, the new technologies have not raised rural wage rates significantly even when they have added to wage employment. In many cases, labor-saving mechanization motivated by the threat of rising wage rates has also aided this phenomenon. Government policies to add to stocks or to exports have also prevented prices from falling significantly, thus protecting the income gains of adopters at the expense of the well-being of poor consumers, including the rural poor.

Agricultural mechanization has historically increased land yields only in exceptional circumstances, as when its advent accompanies the use of other yield-raising inputs, such as fertilizers or new seeds. Its main effect is to substitute for human or animal labor. Mechanization is only partly determined by a country's changing accumulations of land and labor and nonagricultural demands for labor. It is also conditioned by the market prices of labor and capital, farm size and problems in using labor and organizing the production process. These latter elements are significantly related to the inequality of wealth and to agrarian structure. Where these inequalities are large, the private impetus to mechanize is strong if agricultural output growth occurs. State policy can strengthen or weaken the impetus. Thus, private profitability should not be confused with social profitability. Private profitability assumes ownership structures and control over the production process and state policy.

In densely populated rural Asia, mechanization probably will not be socially profitable in the foreseeable future. The demand for labor in recent decades has failed to keep pace with population growth. The abundance of labor is not likely to diminish, even with rapid labor-using growth of nonagriculture. But while governments may not resist the demand for mechanization where its private profitability is high, some policy actions raise private profitability without justification. Such policies contribute little to output growth while reducing employment.

The distinction between socially profitable biochemical innovations and socially unprofitable mechanical innovations has proved untenable in practice. Governments have been unable or unwilling to limit technical innovations to the former. The process by which biochemical innovations are introduced favors large farms because of their differential access to inputs and credit, thereby setting up strong pressures toward mechanization. This complementarity arises from problems in satisfying the increased demand for labor input, particularly at certain critical points in the production cycle, and in managing the labor process in these circumstances. Nevertheless, technological solutions may exacerbate conflict between workers and their employers. Such conflict is not easily resolved and will critically affect further developments.

Asian peasants are not limited, of course, only to agricultural activities. Peasant families and landless laborers also rely on incomes earned from rural nonfarm production and from remittances of migrants to the urban sector. Nonfarm activities include various cottage industries, agro-based processing activities and services (trade, transport and finance). Across Asian countries the importance of nonfarm employment varies widely; it accounts for between a fifth (India) and a half (Malaysia) of rural employment. But the predominance of part-time and female employment in such activities suggests that these are subsidiary sources of both employment and incomes. Not all of this production is organized on a family- or self-employment basis; wage employment is particularly prominent in nontraditional activities and in areas with a high incidence of landlessness. Many rural enterprises depend on merchants for their access to credit, inputs and markets. Labor productivity and capital intensity are low, and this is reflected in the low rate of labor earnings, which is frequently below the agricultural wage rate. In this respect, nonfarm activities serve as the rural employment source of last resort, much as the informal sector does in urban areas.

On the whole, modern economic growth tends to erode the relative economic importance of traditional nonfarm activities and, especially, their contribution to employment. One reason is the growth of competition for consumer incomes from urban-produced commodities. Another derives from the expectation that rural industries will adapt to such pressures by becoming more capital-intensive and less self-employment-oriented. Thus the nonfarm activities on which the rural poor partly depend will either decline or be transformed in ways that dilute their labor-absorbing nature.

But this conclusion applies only to the very long run: in the transition to a modern, largely urban economy, the rural, nonfarm sector may well play an important role as a contributor to rural incomes and employment. Whether this will be the case depends on what happens to the incomes of the rural poor, who provide a major part of the potential demand base for the nonfarm sector. The east Asian experience shows that the wider distribution of income gains in agriculture and the structural conditions favoring productive labor absorption increased the demand base for the nonfarm sector in the transition period. The growth of rural nonfarm employment was stimulated by and complementary to the specific institutional basis (aided by government policies in regard to infrastructure provision and land reforms) on which successful agricultural growth occurred.

In contrast, developing Asia has relied on trickle-down from urban-based industrial development with attendant tradeoffs between growth and equity. The failure to achieve growth with equity *within* agriculture has prevented the nonfarm sector from contributing further to growth or equity. The lack of vigor of the nonfarm sector—with continuing underemployment, low productivity and low earnings—largely reflects the similar problems plaguing agriculture generally and the peasant economy in particular. Much like the involuntary proliferation of tiny land-holdings, the persistence of these activities expresses the desperate struggle of the poor to survive and adapt to economic change rather than a healthy growth process in which they are full participants.

PEASANTS AND POLITICS

Though poorly endowed with land, even the poorer Asian countries have demonstrated an ability to take advantage of land-augmenting technological possibilities. Yet the gap between potential and performance remains distressingly large. Although the 1970s saw South Asia approaching self-sufficiency—domestic supply adequate to meet domestic market demand—in food production, the stagnation or slow growth of food consumption, despite high levels of undernutrition and poverty, reflects inadequate growth in both demand and supply. The middle-income Southeast Asian economies have achieved faster rates of growth of both output and consumption but, as noted earlier, the incidence of poverty has declined only slowly. In Asia, not only is rapid agricultural growth compatible with greater equality in agrarian structure, but also inegalitarian growth tends to be slow. The experience of post-reform Taiwan, South Korea, Japan and China bears testimony to this proposition.

The continuing incapacity of late-developing Asian economies to provide employment and decent living standards for their rural and urban masses is a direct consequence of their economic and political structures. Thus the fate of Asian peasantries is closely tied to the distribution of political power and the nature of state policies. The roots of the problem are not demographic or technological, nor are they to be traced to an insufficiency of investable resources or to a politically based exploitation of the countryside by the town. The view that rapid population growth is the villain, given limited supplies of land and limited technological possibilities, is patently false. The east Asian economies demonstrate what is possible even with much higher labor/land ratios than exist in most other Asian economies. And the potential of available technologies has scarcely been exhausted. The diagnoses based on "urban bias" and on insufficient resources are also flawed.

Asian agrarian societies remain heavily class-stratified. The economic plight of the poor is matched by their political oppression. Often this oppression is localized and isolated. The rural poor are subject to routine intimidation, discrimination and manipulation, and they are frequently threatened by violence or actually harmed. The rural powerful use the laws, village councils, local elections, police power and connections with state officials to gain and strengthen their advantages, often at the expense of the powerless poor. Resistance to the structures of power is rarely open or organized; such actions put peasants at considerable risk of outright repression by the powers of the state or the local elites. Most peasants act individually to cope with their economic and social condition. Their resistance often takes the form of individual acts of insubordination or noncompliance, in James Scott's formulation, "footdragging, dissimulation, false-compliance, pilfering, feigned ignorance, slander, arson, sabotage, and so forth."

The effects of such everyday forms of peasant resistance should not be underestimated. In the aggregate, they may significantly cost the rich in their efforts to extract a surplus. They can also cumulatively change the economic conditions of peasants and nonpeasants: the extent of mechanization, the reliance on wage labor rather than tenancy, the pace of productivity improvements, and so forth. There can be no assurance that they will benefit the peasantry in the long run. Only organized and visible forms of resistance by the poor, when they are successful, can provide such assurance. These are necessary to improve peasants' sense of security and well-being through local actions—the development of unions and cooperatives of the poor, access to local public goods, curbs on police powers—and to give the powerless a political voice in shaping national policies. Without a significant measure of such pressure from below, governments are unlikely to adopt programs that directly or indirectly fulfill the needs of the small farmers and the landless. As has been shown, government actions significantly influence, for better or for worse, the pace and pattern of agricultural development in Asian economies.

History shows that peasant rebellions and subsequent major political or economic reforms occur only after peasant poverty is stretched to broad limits. Nevertheless, the contradictions of unequal change have tended to raise peasant awareness of their plight and elicited political response. Asian governments have taken some actions to stabilize their political economies. The abolition of large estates—such as the zamindaris in India and the haciendas in Central Luzon—has been relatively easy because of their association with colonial regimes and the powerful demands for land reforms. In contrast, existing forms of inequality have been far more difficult to reform because larger landowners are more numerous and ally with rich and even middle peasants in successfully resisting reform efforts. The resistance of these intermediate classes and their political and bureaucratic control explain the continuing failure to introduce radical changes in structures. Governments have tried at best to shore up the positions of the middle peasantry who might also serve as a bulwark against organized resistance. They have attempted nominal reforms by imposing easily evaded land ceilings and have introduced protective legislation for tenants. In the main, these reforms have benefited middle and richer peasants while allowing governments to ignore almost completely the plight of a far larger segment of the rural poor—the landless and the nearly landless.

Incomplete land reform laws and regulations or the provision of subsidized inputs and credit have largely failed to benefit the poor and economically dependent majority. Commonly, the privileged classes in rural areas are in the best position to take advantage of these measures. Halfhearted attempts to regulate land rents, impose land ceilings or even redistribute land have tended to produce the opposite of the intended effects: eviction of tenants, increased proletarianization, and so forth. Indeed, the threat of land reforms may prevent a more effective use of labor, reduce the demand for labor and hence, increase inequality.

The agrarian structure, as defined by access to land, credit, employment and public inputs, adversely affects income distribution, poverty, labor absorption in both farm and nonfarm activities and technical change. Structural reforms may strengthen the individual peasant producer or create communal forms of production. South Korea, Taiwan and Japan fit the former type, while many socialist models of agricultural transformation have relied on the latter. But two lessons of history are well established. First, the *initial* step in the reform process must be the creation or rejuvenation of a peasant economy (direct transition to communal forms has proved practically impossible). Although the loss of output due to disruption tends not to be large, the marketed surplus tends to fall. Second, the natural tendency for such a peasant economy is to differentiate toward capitalist forms of production; if this is to be avoided, either communal forms must be established to limit the significance of private investment and private control, or accumulation must be controlled and overseen by the state to preserve the peasantry. Some observers believe that the proven benefits of a small-holder agriculture may be secured only if large landowners can profitably rent to tenants operating uniformly small units. Asian experience does not support this position. Neither does it warrant any faith in gradualist or piecemeal changes. Thorough land reforms require major political changes. But this presupposes that the beneficiaries are politically organized—exceedingly difficult in practice.

The preceding discussion pinpoints inequalities of economic and political power *within* agriculture as the main political constraint on agricultural change that can benefit the rural poor. Clearly, given the emphasis on the state's role in the agricultural transformation, this discussion also implies that the rural elites in Asia command significant power over the state. A rather different view is that the *economy-wide* pattern of growth has been both inequitable and inefficient and that this reflects the politically determined neglect of agriculture. The state, being dominated by the urban classes, acts to protect their interests. These actions consist of a wide array of "urban-biased" policies, including underinvestment in agriculture; underprovision of health, education and other services in rural areas; and industrial protection and cheap food policies that raise the prices received and lower the prices paid by rural producers. Such a strategy sacrifices major growth and employment opportunities in the rural and agricultural sectors.

This view should be rejected on several grounds. First, the rural elites are scarcely impotent, as the urban-bias thesis assumes. Nor are they merely junior partners of a political coalition dominated by urban interests. Second, rural and urban "classes" are not homogeneous interest groups; rather, exploitative class relations and fundamental conflicts of interest exist within each of these economic sectors. Third, it is not urban bias or rural bias that underlies the problems of slow growth and inequity, but class bias favoring the interests of rural and urban elites at the expense of peasants and workers.

In particular, governments have neglected certain types of agricultural growth. On the supply side, the increasing marginalization and poverty of Asian peasants results from the neglect of agrarian reforms, the privileged access of elites to public inputs and government reinforcement of the market/structural bias favoring the rich in the design and administration of growth programs. On the demand side, the low purchasing power of the majority poor constitutes a barrier to modernization. Because existing structures and policies do not permit the growth of the purchasing power of the poor, output growth in agriculture threatens to reduce land rents and agricultural profits by reducing agricultural prices. Growth may then be accompanied by an accumulation of stocks or subsidized exports; alternatively, growth policies will be reined in to keep pace with demand growth. Thus the neglect of agriculture is not a consequence of urban bias but of the imperative to protect the interests of rentiers.

The urban-bias hypothesis does not account for the fact that governments find ways to protect the interests of both urban and rural elites simultaneously. Governments use food subsidies and distribution to control wages of urban formal sector workers; thus, such subsidies benefit formal sector employers by keeping their money costs down and profits up. They do little to raise the food purchasing power of rural and urban informal sector workers or of poor peasants and the landless. At the same time, government subsidies and expenditures in the agricultural sector benefit larger landowners and rich peasants disproportionately. Such policies suggest that an alliance of urban and rural elites control Asian governments.

Nor can the inadequacy of investable surpluses in Asian economies account for the political economy of agricultural policies. Resources in agriculture and industry are heavily underused. Existing arrangements in agriculture lead to substantial misallocation of land, credit and irrigation, and to massive underemployment of labor. In the industrial sectors, capacity is similarly underused. Governments have also failed to tap the fiscal potential of untaxed rentier incomes. The activation of these surpluses has not been possible within the existing structures.

The east Asian experience may be contrasted with the experience of late-developing Asian countries. Before or along with industrialization, the east Asian economies experienced sustained increases in agricultural productivity, which created major sources of savings and demands for nonagricultural growth. Developing Asian countries have failed to register a similar record of agricultural success, especially when measured in terms of labor productivity. In addition, egalitarian land reform in east Asia was crucial in three respects: (1) it facilitated the absorption of new technologies and labor in agriculture; (2) it eased the problem of extracting a surplus from agriculture, via the terms of trade or directly; (3) it led to an egalitarian income base that stimulated both urban and rural industry. Lacking such an egalitarian distributive base, developing Asian economies find that neither agricultural growth nor industrial growth, rural or urban, significantly dents the problems of labor absorption or poverty. Finally, the early and rapid development of rural infrastructure in the form of transport, electricity and education contributed significantly to both rural growth and labor absorption. Not only is such infrastructure rare in developing Asia, but its benefits are also very unevenly distributed—recalling again the role of prevailing rural structures. Hence the further growth of infrastructure reproduces inequality, unemployment and rural poverty.

In effect, the east Asian path exploited both the supply and especially the demand complementarity between agricultural and nonagricultural growth. Rising rural incomes and employment fueled continued investment growth. Radical redistribution of rural assets, coupled with the judicious use of fiscal instruments to raise savings, considerably blunted the tradeoff between growth and employment. As a result, agricultural and rural industrial growth proceeded complementarily, and this helped achieve rapid growth with equity. No technical or financial constraints in the late-developing Asian countries preclude the adoption of similar structural and economic policies. Instead, the constraint is fundamentally political.

CONCLUSION

Asian peasants have been exposed to major waves of change over the past three centuries: Western colonialism, commercialization of production and the growth of markets, unprecedented population growth, anti-colonial and national struggles, and technological changes. National development strategies and state interventions have greatly accelerated change during the past four decades. As a result, peasants have had to cope with changes in property relations, production organization, and traditional village institutions.

1593

Economic and institutional changes have transformed the ways in which peasants make a living. Many have been rendered assetless, and hence must depend more on others for their livelihood, increasing casual wage employment. Although the village continues to localize economic exchanges, peasants often have to produce for distant markets and for employers largely motivated by profit. As a result, the social character of the village has also been altered as it yields to the wider market. Market exchanges accentuate existing inequalities by increasing unemployment and reducing the efficiency of resource use. The most important consequence for the peasantry is greater economic insecurity.

Peasant pauperization has not meant wholesale depeasantization or a radical polarization of the class structure. Although the landless proletariat has grown at the expense of the middle and poor peasants, an involutionary pattern whereby small-holders try to cling to their patches of land is a characteristic of Asia's ongoing agricultural transformation. Moreover, this process of differentiation has been uneven over time and across regions. In some parts of South Asia, for example, middle and large farms have prospered, while in other regions, characterized by stagnation, relative positions have not altered much and traditional structures have remained largely intact. At the same time, some middle and rich peasants, not the large landowners alone, have been at the forefront of technical and economic change in the Asian countryside.

Four decades of trickle-down growth have failed to raise significantly the living standards of the vast masses of rural Asia. Despite respectable rates of per capita food output growth in the recent past, hunger and chronic malnutrition remain among Asia's most pressing problems. Growing landlessness, reduction in employment opportunities and the growth of casual (as distinct from durable) market employment help explain the persistence or growth of inequality and poverty in developing Asia.

The roots of the problem are not demographic or technological; nor are they traced to insufficient investable resources or a politically based exploitation of the countryside by the town. The view that rapid population growth is the villain, given limited supplies of land and limited technological possibilities, is patently false. The east Asian economies demonstrate what is possible even with much higher labor/land ratios than exist in most other Asian economies. And the potential of available technologies has scarcely been exhausted. The diagnoses based on urban bias and on insufficient resources are also flawed. The continuing incapacity of late-developing Asian economies to provide employment and decent living standards for their rural and urban masses is a direct consequence of their economic and political structures. Clearly, the fate of Asian peasants is closely tied to the distribution of political power and the nature of state policies. The present conditions of Asia's poor are not inevitable. But it is doubtful that change for the better will come within existing structures.

FURTHER READING

Bhaduri, Amit. *The Economic Structure of Agricultural Backwardness*. London: Academic Press, 1983.

Byres, Terry J. "The New Technology, Class Formation and Class Action in the Indian Countryside." *Journal of Peasant Studies* 8 (1981), 405–54.

Cederroth, Sven, and Gerdin, Ingela. "Cultivating Poverty: The Case of the Green Revolution in Lombok." In Norlund, Irene, Cederroth, Sven, and Gerdin, Ingela, eds. *Rice Societies: Asian Problems and Prospects.* London: Curzon Press; Riverdale, Maryland: Riverdale Company, 1986.

Ghose, Ajit Kumar. "Agrarian Reform in Developing Countries: Issues of Theory and Problems of Practice." In Ghose, A. K., ed. *Agrarian Reform in Contemporary Developing Countries.* London: Croom Helm; New York: St. Martin's Press, 1983.

Griffin, Keith B. *World Hunger and the World Economy, And Other Essays in Development Economics.* New York: Holmes & Meier, 1987.

Hayami, Yujiro, and Kikuchi, Masao. *Asian Village Economy at the Crossroads: An Economic Approach to Institutional Change,* Tokyo: University of Tokyo Press; Baltimore: Johns Hopkins University Press, 1982.

Khan, Azizur Rahman, and Lee, Eddy, eds. *Poverty in Rural Asia.* Bangkok: International Labour Organisation, Asia Employment Programme (ARTEP), 1984.

Popkin, Samuel L. *The Rational Peasant: The Political Economy of Rural Society in Vietnam,* Berkeley: University of California Press, 1979.

Rao, J. Mohan. "Agriculture in Recent Development Theory." *Journal of Peasant Studies* 15 (1988), 238–57.

———. "Fragmented Rural Labour Markets." *Journal of Peasant Studies* 13 (1986), 5–35.

Scott, James C. *The Moral Economy of the Peasant: Rebellion and Subsistence in Southeast Asia.* New Haven, Connecticut: Yale University Press, 1976.

———. "Everyday Forms of Peasant Resistance." *Journal of Development Economics* 22 (1986), 41–86.

EDUCATION

CHRISTINE INGLIS

SINCE the end of World War II the Asia-Pacific region has experienced a major expansion in education. The trend, evident in such measures as the percentage of the population attending school, the level of schooling attended and expenditures on education, is illustrated in Table 1. Given the size of the region's population and the low levels of educational provisions in the 1950s, the expansion is a major achievement and reflects the extensive resources that went into producing it. Against this background this essay considers the major issues that currently dominate educational debate and policy in the Asia-Pacific region. The issues of access, equity, diversity, values, employment and quality require examination in the context of more general social and economic changes that exert a powerful influence on the formulation of and response to these issues.

The expansion of education is not unique to the Asia-Pacific region. The differences between Europe and North America, where extensive educational provision for formal schooling began much earlier, and other regions are narrowing as educational expansion is actively pursued worldwide. What is perhaps remarkable is that the system of formal schooling has developed in a period of less than 150 years. The rapid development of and the uniformities in the forms of educational expansion suggest considerable similarities in the social and economic processes producing them, including a shared belief in the efficacy of education to realize important socioeconomic goals. This belief is shared by educators, social reformers and, significantly to the extent to which the educational expansion has been the result of direct governmental intervention and activity, politicians.

The widespread belief in the efficacy of education was at its height during the 1950s and 1960s when optimism characterized attempts to improve society. The belief in the ability of society to progress was encapsulated in the use of the term "development" to signify the changes that were to be implemented. Education and educational development were seen as integral to the attainment of economic growth and development with education providing necessary skills as well as the values, motivations and other attributes essential to Western countries. Coexisting with these beliefs were others that regarded education as the means to develop social integration and unity among diverse populations that had become part of the same nation through immigration or the arbitrary imposition of borders under

1596

Table 1
THE EXPANSION OF EDUCATION, 1960–85

Regions	Enrollments[3]			Expenditures	
	First level	Second level	Third level	Percent of GNP	U.S. $ per inhabitant
Asia[1]					
1960	68.2	20.2	3.0		
1970	77.7	28.1	6.0	3.0	7
1980	86.0	34.5	8.1	4.6	38
1985	89.9	40.1	9.1	4.6	42
Oceania					
1960	101.6	53.1	9.9		
1970	103.5	68.1	13.9	4.7	103
1980	99.4	70.3	20.6	6.3	453
1985	97.2	74.5	22.9	6.3	436
Developed countries[2]					
1960	108.1	57.5	13.3		
1970	107.4	73.9	23.2	5.7	140
1980	108.6	78.5	29.9	6.1	471
1985	108.5	82.8	32.0	6.2	515
The world[1]					
1960	77.2	28.4	6.2		
1970	83.9	38.5	11.2	5.2	44
1980	92.6	43.8	14.1	5.6	143
1985	95.2	48.9	15.1	5.8	147

[1] Excludes China and North Korea.
[2] Includes all European countries, the Soviet Union, the United States, Canada, Japan, Israel, Australia, New Zealand, and South Africa.
[3] Based on gross enrollment ratios that are derived by dividing total enrollment by population of relevant age group. Ratios may be greater than 100 because of late entry, repetition and other factors.
Source: *UNESCO Statistical Yearbook* (1985).

colonial administrations. There was also the belief that education could further equity and justice for socially disadvantaged groups that would be able to advance socially and economically on the basis of their access to education.

Since that time there have been many changes in the understanding and assessment of efforts to produce social, economic and educational change. The resources that were put into educational expansion have indeed had an effect so that large sections of the world's population can now attend at least primary schools. This achievement has been accompanied, however, by a realization that many of the anticipated consequences of educational expansion have been overly ambitious or that the expansion has had unfortunate and unanticipated side effects. A similar awareness of the shortcomings of development planning in general has emerged. These reassessments, based on the actual outcomes of educational and economic programs, have included critiques of the theoretical frameworks and assumptions that guided so many of these early projects. The reliance on reproducing Western patterns to achieve economic growth and the ignoring of external factors that were limiting change have been identified as major shortcomings of the modernization theory that guided these projects.

In education critical assessments have led to a questioning of the extent to which education can actually change society, rather than merely reproduce existing social and cultural patterns. In such circumstances the ability of schooling to benefit the individual and society at large has been the subject of much scrutiny. During the 1970s such a concern produced a sense of pessimism and the word "crisis" was frequently used in writings about education. Since then, a more pragmatic and less idealistic approach has been evident but traces of the former pessimism still characterize many discussions of the subject.

Apart from critiques of earlier educational policies the identification of educational issues is affected by additional factors. Prominent among them is the changing world economic situation. The oil crisis of the early 1970s marked a watershed in the period of affluence and growth for many national economies. The subsequent constraints on spending by governments and by international agencies have had direct and severe repercussions on education. In addition the world recession of the 1970s resulted in high levels of unemployment especially among young people. Also important have been the diverse social and cultural changes that developed with the spread of technology and communication. These include changes in the status of women and, contrary to many expectations, continuing racial and ethnic divisions. The spread of industrialization, urbanization and popular cultural forms as well as changes in agricultural methods have all contributed to a situation in the late 1980s that is very different from that of 40 years ago. It is against the background of such changes that this essay examines some of the educational issues prominent in the Asia-Pacific region. Considerable social, economic and political diversity characterizes the countries of the region and this affects their educational responses to the changes. After identifying some key areas of diversity, attention is given to the educational issues and the types of educational priorities and policies associated with them in particular countries.

ASIA-PACIFIC SOCIETIES AND THEIR EDUCATIONAL SYSTEMS

The countries of the Asia-Pacific region differ dramatically in both the size and density of their populations, the basic parameters for educational provisions. These populations are not stable: more developed countries such as Singapore, Japan and Australia have experienced a marked decline in the size and proportion of the school-age population; in others such as Bangladesh and the Philippines the school-age population continues to increase both absolutely and relatively.

Granted a particular population profile, an important factor in the ability of countries to provide for the education of their population, especially in formal schooling, is their level of economic resources. Countries classified as "developing" may be recipients of special educational loans and aid both from other countries as well as from regional and international agencies such as the World Bank, UNESCO, or the Asian Development Bank. While some small Pacific island nations and others such as Bangladesh lack economic resources and are among the poorest nations in the world, the region also includes wealthy nations such as Japan, Australia and New Zealand (though the two latter economies rely more for their wealth on primary industry than on manufacturing, which has been so important in Japan's economic success). Between these two extremes are the newly industrialized countries (NICs) of Hong Kong, South Korea, Singapore and Taiwan that since the early 1960s have made major advances in achieving economic growth through industrialization. India is one of many other countries whose level of industrialization is increasing while agricultural methods and systems are also undergoing changes. Simple distinctions among developed, underdeveloped and developing countries are thus no longer adequate as a way of categorizing the countries of the region.

These economic changes together with new means of communication and technology have meant that many people are experiencing new patterns of life and being introduced to new cultural forms. At the same time the region is also characterized by diverse cultural traditions. These cultures range from the European Christian traditions dominant in Australia, New Zealand and the Philippines to Islam, Hinduism and Buddhism which have been major influences throughout the region. Cultural diversity is also a characteristic of many of these societies that contain within their political borders long-established ethnic and linguistic minorities or, like Australia and New Zealand, have undertaken extensive programs to increase their populations by immigration.

With only a few exceptions all the countries in the region are now independent nations. The majority have achieved independence since the 1960s but this has not always assured unity; many have experienced significant political unrest and disruption. A wide variety of political regimes exists ranging from parliamentary democracies to communist governments. Yet, while the governments may operate with rather different political ideologies and varied administrative processes, their educational systems display considerable similarity in the extent to which education is under the control of the state. Indeed it has been argued that a critical factor in the expansion of education that has resulted in the phenomenon of "mass schooling" has been the adoption of the European model of a national society in which "an expanded state educational system is essential to individual and national progress."[1] The similarity extends further for, even in countries such as China and India that have established traditions of schol-

---

[1] F. Ramirez and J. Boli, "The Political Contribution of Mass Schooling," *Sociology of Education* 60, no. 1 (1987): 2–17.

arship and education, the form of education that has been used as the basis for expansion is the formal model of the school developed in the West. This transfer was facilitated by the former colonial status of many Asia-Pacific countries whose educational systems developed under the influence of their former metropolitan powers. Even countries such as Thailand, Japan and China, which retained their political independence, were also exposed to, and sometimes actively sought, Western forms of education in the period before World War II.

Within given political and administrative forms the actual organization and procedures for financing, staffing and controlling education vary among countries. Not all education is necessarily financed or directly controlled by the national government; private schooling, often sponsored by religious groups, is strongly established in countries such as the Philippines and Australia. Yet, even in these countries, the general operation of private schools, and even much of their funding, may be controlled by the national government. An emerging trend recognizes the potential of education to constitute a service industry; in countries such as Singapore and Australia private educational institutions have been less subject to governmental control than has hitherto been evident in either country. In both Europe and North America similar moves emphasizing privatization and less government education spending have been seen as part of a trend away from the traditional European model to a corporate model in which the state's concerns shift from welfare to economic viability, restructuring education in response to changing economic circumstances.

ISSUES IN EDUCATION

Access
The diversified levels of enrollment in the Asia-Pacific region illustrated in Table 2 provide a starting point for considering what was initially the major concern in the establishment of national systems of education in the region. This primary concern was access. At the most immediate, quantitative level this involved making schools and staff available to large uneducated populations of children and adults. The physical and financial resources needed to provide buildings, train and pay staff and provide teaching materials were immense even for primary level education. Yet, an enormous amount has been achieved: primary education is now close to universal in the industrialized countries of Japan, Australia and New Zealand as well as in many other countries including Indonesia, the Philippines and Vietnam. But among poor countries such as Bangladesh with low enrollment levels, the ability to maintain even these levels has been jeopardized by continuing high rates of population growth that outstrip existing resources at the primary level. The aim of the 1960 Karachi Plan was to ensure that by 1980 primary education would be available to all—but this goal has had to be modified.

The importance attached to access to primary education derives from the coincidence of beliefs about the national and individual desirability of literacy and numeracy. The economic advantages believed to come from skills

Table 2
ENROLLMENTS IN THE ASIA-PACIFIC REGION
BY LEVEL OF EDUCATION, 1984[1]

Country	First level	Second level	Third level
Asia			
Bangladesh	62	19	4.9
Bhutan	25	4	—
Burma[2]	102	24	—
China	118	37	1.4
Hong Kong	105	69	12.8
India[2]	90	34	—
Indonesia	118	39	6.5
Japan	100	95	29.6
Laos[2]	91	19	1.4
Malaysia	97	53	6.1
Mongolia	105	88	—
Nepal	77	23	3.2[4]
Philippines[3]	106	65	38.0
Singapore	115	71	7.8[4]
South Korea	99	91	26.1
Sri Lanka[2]	103	65	4.6
Thailand[3]	97	30	19.6
Vietnam[3]	100	43	2.2[4]
Oceania			
Australia	107	94	27.1
Fiji	110	78	2.7[4]
New Zealand	106	85	35.1
Papua New Guinea	59[4]	12[4]	2.1

[1] Based on gross enrollment ratios.
[2] 1983 figures.
[3] 1985 figures.
[4] 1980 figures.
Source: *UNESCO Statistical Yearbook* (1985, 1986, 1987).

learned in primary education coalesces with a belief in the right of the individual to literacy as a means of ensuring personal liberation and development. Governments seeking to develop national integration also saw mass primary education as an obvious way to instill loyalty to the nation's values and identity and to encourage and develop the use of a common national language.

One response to the difficulties of achieving literacy and extending educational access in the absence of sufficient teachers or physical resources has been to explore ways of using the technology of television and radio. However, the costs involved in this technology and its unreliability where technical resources and skills are limited have led to a realization of the restricted ability of technology to provide a solution. Another approach has been the use of nonformal education. The rationale of nonformal education is to extend educational efforts outside the formal school setting and to contact adults and young people that the traditional schools have not reached. Literacy programs have been one important focus of nonformal education and have often supplemented others including health, social and agricultural education. All these programs are devised to have very immediate and practical returns for the participants and to avoid the irrelevance often seen as characterizing formal schooling. But unlike conventional educational enrollment, the effects of nonformal schooling are less easy to quantify. Indeed, the experience of UNESCO, which has had a special commitment to introducing literacy, reveals that definitions of literacy have changed over time as have the operations of programs developed to achieve it.[2] However, it is clear that neither technology nor nonformal schooling have seriously challenged more traditional formal schooling models.

As countries achieve success in establishing universal primary education, there is also a growth in the secondary and tertiary levels. As Table 2 shows the growth of the latter levels increases faster than the primary level might appear to warrant. This pattern highlights a tension that exists between individual countries and aid-giving agencies that, consistent with the sentiments embodied in the Karachi Plan, often emphasize primary education and literacy programs. This emphasis on primary education is not, however, always so enthusiastically shared by individual governments receiving aid; national leaderships often wish to put more resources into the secondary and tertiary levels of education. Their rationale lies in the belief that, especially at the postsecondary level, this is the area of educational investment that is most likely to produce immediate returns in economic growth and development. Support for this rationale can be found in the lending policies of the World Bank; it differs from UNESCO in its emphasis on funding educational projects that will contribute to human resource development. Governments are also subjected to pressures exerted by public demands from parents who wish their children to have access to what they perceive as important opportunities for economic mobility and success. Pressures from students and parents for access to higher levels of education are related to the phenomenon of "credential inflation" in which the extension of education is associated with progressively higher levels of qualifications required for the same job. Only a small amount of this inflation can be attributed to occupational needs created by advances in technology or expertise. Much of the inflation educators now realize is a result of competitive social pressures among the increasing numbers of educated young people seeking to improve or retain their social and economic position. Such pressures are reinforced by employers who have the opportunity to select from competing candidates. This inflation of qualifications occurs

[2] P. W. Jones, *International Policies for Third World Education* (London: Routledge, 1988).

especially in situations of high unemployment that have become common in the urban areas of developing countries but also in developed countries such as Australia and New Zealand. A popular strategy of parents and children is to continue their education during periods of high youth unemployment. This may also be influenced by government policies that seek to avoid the phenomenon of unemployed youth through encouraging continuation at school by a combination of positive and negative financial inducements. Such policies see unemployment as a result of inappropriate skills, or a lack of appropriate manpower planning that would be rectified by appropriate education. An alternative view that unemployment is a result of major structural changes in the economy has very different implications for schooling. Instead of a restricted and science- or technology-oriented curriculum to solve the lack of necessary skills, the educational prescriptions are commonly for greater diversity and flexibility in areas of study as a means of facilitating productive responses to the changed environment. This whole question of the relationship between school and work is a vital contemporary issue.

Access to education takes on a specific character in a country such as Japan with high participation rates and extensive individual competition for particular educational institutions. Such access is perceived as especially critical by parents and students where the educational system is very competitive and there is a clear set of prestigious institutions that act as gateways to social mobility in the absence of alternative paths. The pressures on students to succeed are considerable and are widely recognized as a source of major social problems, among them high levels of youth suicide. A similar widespread popular concern about the excessive pressure that students experience in the educational system also exists in countries such as Singapore, Taiwan and Hong Kong where there is considerable competition for the limited number of places in prestigious institutions.

The demand for longer education, particularly at the postsecondary level, is producing strains on the resources allocated to education even in the more affluent countries. Especially in some of the smaller and/or poorer countries the option of establishing a diverse system of postsecondary education is not feasible and may never be. One response is to participate in a joint regional institution such as the University of the South Pacific that has campuses in a number of Pacific island nations and that caters to students from the Pacific. A more usual solution followed by government or parents of students is for the students unable to be educated at home to be sent overseas for their training. This is especially likely to occur at the postsecondary and tertiary levels. Students may also study abroad earlier as a way of ensuring access to these institutions. A long tradition existed in Asia for students to go to major Islamic and other religious centers of learning; more recently students from the colonies went to the metropolitan powers for their further education. These patterns were facilitated by similarities in language and educational systems. With the expansion of educational opportunities many more countries now offer educational facilities.

Precise figures for the number of students studying overseas are difficult to obtain. In Hong Kong the proportion of students studying overseas is

Table 3
THIRD LEVEL FOREIGN STUDENTS
IN ASIA-PACIFIC COUNTRIES, 1984

Host country	Student numbers
Bangladesh	318
China	2,593
Hong Kong	208
India [1]	14,710
Indonesia	258
Japan	10,697
Philippines	4,640
Singapore [2]	3,992
South Korea	978
America Samoa	251
Australia	12,028
Fiji	16
New Zealand	2,408
Papua New Guinea	334

[1] 1980 figures.
[2] 1983 figures.
Source: *UNESCO Statistical Yearbook* (1987).

especially high with some 35,000 attending foreign universities and only 13,000 studying in the colony's two universities.[3] While the limited university facilities in Hong Kong contribute to this high rate, also important is the approaching change in the political status of the colony that will in 1997 become part of China. For many families an overseas education, especially in the United States and Canada, which have respectively 12,000 and 10,000 Hong Kong students in their universities, can be part of a strategy to increase migration opportunities. How many of these students will return to Hong Kong on the completion of their courses is unknown but the large number studying overseas helps account for the otherwise low level of tertiary educational enrollment in Hong Kong compared with the other NICs whose students can obtain access to tertiary education at home.

While the majority of overseas students still study outside the Asia-Pacific region in Europe and North America, increasing numbers are studying in the region. This can be seen in Table 3 which shows the numbers of foreign students (the majority of them from the region) actually studying within the region at the postsecondary level. While considerable prestige still attaches to study in Europe or North America, the introduction of expensive student fees and related costs has been a factor encouraging students to study in their own region where charges may be lower. Also,

[3] G. Postiglione, "Brief Report on the Sociology of Education in Hong Kong," *ISA Research Committee Sociology of Education Newsletter,* no. 10 (1987), 16.

certain regional governments provide scholarships for foreign students as part of their bilateral aid and diplomatic efforts in the region and this has been an important contribution to interregional student movement. The British-based educational systems in Australia and New Zealand are becoming increasingly important destinations and the majority of the overseas students in these two countries are from the Asia-Pacific region. In Australia most of the students are from Malaysia whereas Pacific island students are an important component in New Zealand. China has become an important destination for Hong Kong students since the end of the Cultural Revolution; recent figures show about 3,000 enrolled in two universities designed especially to cater to overseas students.[4] For many years Taiwanese universities also provided higher education opportunities for Hong Kong students, especially those educated in Chinese rather than in English. Among the large number of foreign students in India many are of Indian origin but come from outside the subcontinent. The increasing international influence of Japan is a factor in its ability to attract considerable numbers of overseas students even though they face the challenge of acquiring knowledge of the Japanese language.

The increase in students seeking to study overseas has raised significant educational issues. In the students' home countries there is official concern about the possibly destabilizing effects of studying overseas in often very different cultures and societies; also, in some cases, there is concern about the development of political opposition groups. Another issue in the potential host countries relates to the possibility of marketing educational services. The implications of treating education as a commodity, at least for overseas students, has important potential effects on the allocation of educational access to the local population, especially where there is an unmet demand for postsecondary education, and the lack of a tradition of private tertiary level institutions such as exist in Japan and the Philippines. The development of education as a service industry also has important implications for viewing education as a part of diplomatic relations.

Competing views related to the emphasis on education as a service industry are evident in Australia, which in recent years has had two major governmental inquiries touching on the position of overseas students and the implications of considering education as trade or aid. Furthermore, both private and public postsecondary and tertiary institutions are looking at ways of selling educational services for overseas students. This trend toward marketing has coincided with a move to reintroduce tuition for tertiary education. It was abolished in the 1970s as an equity measure for the local population, countering a belief that sees schooling as a resource to be paid for by the individual rather than a right. This approach is in conflict with the government's aim of encouraging the development of a skilled work force as a major contribution to economic development. The public debate has taken a different direction in Japan where there is an ambitious program to attract overseas students as a way of internationalizing society. In Singapore the emphasis on developing new service industries

4 Ibid.

is important to moves to privatize some schools and to attract tertiary level students. Experience in recent years has also shown that the skills these students acquire may be retained and used in Singapore which has always been a major importer of skilled professional labor from the region and the world.

When the movement of students overseas was couched in terms of aid the relevance of the curriculum for the work they would be doing on their return was a major concern, as was the expectation that they should be required to return upon completion of their courses rather than to stay overseas. With the development of the view of education as another service industry, the relevance of curriculum is measured in terms of individual market forces rather than by governmentally assessed needs. Planning then responds to these forces.

Equity
The ability of governments to provide universal primary education is closely related to their economic resources but the strength of the commitment to this level of education has ensured that few now question its desirability. At the higher levels of education the issue of how much of the country's resources should be committed to education, even in the wealthier countries, is far from settled and the decisions made by governments and private individuals concerning funds are the results of competition between educational and noneducational uses. In the absence of sufficient places for all those eligible for particular levels of education the issue of equity as well as the identification of those who fail to gain access and why become major social concerns. By the 1960s it was already evident that in the Asia-Pacific region; despite the rapid progress that had been made in extending educational access, not all groups were achieving equal participation rates nor similar levels of educational attainment. Initially, the cause was seen as the uneven geographical distribution of educational facilities—those in urban areas or more economically developed regions having readier access to the available places. But the issue of equity is more complex than simply providing sufficient places. The lesson learned by educators and policymakers in industrialized countries in the immediate postwar period was that a general increase in access to schooling was insufficient to produce equity in educational attainment or social outcomes among diverse social groups.

This awareness has now spread among countries in the Asia-Pacific region as they have extended their provisions for education. Groups such as women, individuals from rural areas, linguistic and ethnic minorities and the poor often display lower levels of educational participation and attainment, even though in theory the newly expanded educational systems are open to all. However, the issues that are identified as critical to determining lack of educational equity vary with the complexity and levels of development of the different national educational systems. While geographical factors affecting physical access are significant, the importance of economic, and especially, cultural factors limiting participation and achievement are only gradually being appreciated by educators and policymakers in the region. This is not surprising in situations where large sections of the population live well below the poverty level. Indeed poverty remains a critical factor limiting educational participation in many countries where families lack the money necessary for even small educational costs and are additionally unable to forgo the loss of income incurred as a result of a child attending school instead of contributing to family earnings through some form of work. But even in situations where economic need is not so urgent, the economic status of the family is typically found to be related to the level of educational participation and attainment—with children from wealthier families more likely to attain higher levels of education. Research in Australia and New Zealand, as in other industrialized countries, has demonstrated that this variation is not related solely to actual material resources but is also linked to disparate attitudes about the importance of education and the possession of a variety of cultural attributes that lead to success in schooling. These attributes include knowledge, language and behavioral forms that are valued in the school setting by teachers and are necessary for the actual curriculum and methods of assessment used.

Women are the social group most widely seen as being disadvantaged as a result of cultural beliefs that prevent or limit their participation in education. As Table 4 illustrates, between 1970 and 1985 there was an improvement in the participation of women in education in the Asia-Pacific region though rarely did they constitute 50 percent of the enrollment at the primary level. In the countries of South Asia, with the exception of Sri Lanka, the participation rate of women at the primary level is still very low. The relevance of Islam or Hinduism as an explanation should not be overstressed because low participation is also evident in countries with large rural populations such as China and Indonesia and several Pacific island nations. Furthermore, even though Islam is important in Indonesia, it is also important in Malaysia where participation rates for women are higher.

A variety of cultural factors apart from those linked to particular religious traditions can affect the participation of women and these are often related to the broader socioeconomic and political status of women as well as linked to beliefs about the type of economic role that is suitable for them. In the more industrialized countries, such as Australia, New Zealand, Singapore and Hong Kong, white-collar occupations are more attractive to women as a means of social mobility than skilled trades that often have lower educational requirements for entry. The effect of such occupational preferences is one factor accounting for women constituting 50 percent of the secondary level enrollments whereas they constitute less than half at the primary level. The equal participation of women in secondary schooling in many countries of the Pacific as well as the Philippines, Sri Lanka and Mongolia, which are less developed economically, is linked to the higher socioeconomic status of women in conjunction with the patterns of educational development that have characterized these countries. As the figures in Table 4 illustrate, the closer a country approximates universal schooling at a particular level, the greater the likelihood that women will participate equally. The third level of education, which in UNESCO statistics includes a variety of postsecondary and university education, is the level where universal participation is furthest from realization. It also tends

Table 4
CHANGES IN WOMEN'S PARTICIPATION
IN EDUCATION, 1970–85

| Country | Percentage of Women Students | | | | | |
| | 1970 | | | 1985 | | |
	First level	Second level	Third level	First level	Second level	Third level
Asia						
Bangladesh	32		10	40	28	18
Bhutan	5	3		34	17	5[1]
Brunei	48	45		48[2]	51[2]	62[2]
Burma	47	39				
China				45	40	30
Hong Kong	47	42		48[2]	50	35[2]
India	37	28		40[2]		
Indonesia	46	34		48[2]	42[2]	32[2]
Japan	49	49	28	49	49	34[2]
Laos	37	27	19	43[2]	40[2]	
Macao	47	45				
Malaysia	47	41		49	49	44
Maldives						
Mongolia				49[2]	51[2]	
Nepal	15			29[2]	23[2]	
Philippines			56	49	50	54
Singapore	47	48	30	47[2]	50	42[1]
South Korea	48	38	24	49	47	30
Sri Lanka	47		43	48	52	38
Thailand	47	42	42			
Vietnam				48	47	
Oceania						
American Samoa				47	47	
Australia	49		33	49	50	48
Cook Islands	51	48				
Fiji	48	42	28	49	50	38
French Polynesia	49	56		48[2]	54[2]	
Guam			48	48[1]	48[1]	
Kiribati		39		49	50	
Nauru				47	50	
New Caledonia	49	46		48	52	38[2]
New Zealand	48		39	49	50	44
Niue	49	44		44[2]	48[2]	
Papua New Guinea	37	27				23
Solomon Islands	36	26		42[1]	34[2]	47[2]
Tokelau		54		48[1]	50[1]	
Tonga	48	48		48	51	56

Table 4 (*continued*)

Country	Percentage of Women Students					
	1970			1985		
	First level	*Second level*	*Third level*	*First level*	*Second level*	*Third level*
Oceania						
Tuvalu				43^2		
Vanuatu	44	42			38^1	
Western Samoa	49	52	1	48^1	50^1	

[1] 1983 figures.
[2] 1984 figures.
Source: *UNESCO Statistical Yearbook* (1971, 1985, 1987).

to be the level where women are least represented. The most notable exceptions to this generalization are Brunei, the Philippines and Tonga where more women than men are enrolled. Significantly, the Philippines has one of the highest levels of tertiary enrollment in the region.

That the economically most developed and wealthiest countries in the region are not those with the highest levels of female participation in educators illustrates how diverse factors affecting women's roles in society influence their enrollment in higher education—a participation that is critical for access to high economic and social status and power. This is most strikingly illustrated in the case of Japan. The very different status of women in Japanese society compared with other industrialized societies such as Australia and New Zealand, let alone many other less wealthy and developed societies, is indicated by the fact that one third of Japanese students enrolled in tertiary education are women.

The cultural beliefs and attitudes that play such an important role in limiting women's educational participation and attainment are also evident in the areas of education they pursue. Statistics of the areas of specialization by those who graduate from the third level of education show that for selected Asian countries women are more likely to be concentrated in fields such as education and the humanities rather than in engineering—a pattern of enrollment that fits common stereotypes about particular female skills and abilities. In fields such as science women also tend to be underrepresented even though these areas are seen as critical to national economic development. Although such beliefs exist in the larger community attention is increasingly being directed to the actual role of primary and second schools—through curriculum, teachers and fellow students—in restricting the access of young women to scientific and technical subjects while encouraging them to follow the arts and humanities. In simple terms this involves them in being offered only a restricted set of subject choices in secondary schools where specialization frequently commences. However, even where these choices are widened, the preferences still continue. This means that educators must concern themselves with overcoming biased attitudes that exist in society as well as the often subtle way these attitudes are reflected in the process of schooling through the interaction of teachers and pupils in the classroom and the depiction of stereotypes in teaching materials and textbooks.

The educational disadvantages of women are now widely documented. But they are not the only group representing different economic levels and regions that experiences educational inequality. Although not usually highlighted in international compilations of educational statistics, inequalities in educational participation and attainment are also common among the ethnic and linguistic minorities that exist in most countries in the Asia-Pacific region. Especially where minorities are concentrated in particular areas these lower levels of participation have been attributed to lack of educational facilities such as schools. But, as in the case of women, this is only a partial explanation; it fails to explain the continuing differentials that continue even after the extension of educational opportunities. Explanations that focus on the cultural characteristics of the particular ethnic group have been especially common just as they have also been in the case of women and of those from lower socioeconomic backgrounds. These range from the frequently heard reference to a lack of interest or valuing of education to the view that the students may lack the cultural attributes or "capital" that are necessary for educational success. In the case of ethnic and racial minorities the language of schooling, which often differs from their own, is an obvious potential hindrance to educational success. The curriculum may emphasize material that is unfamiliar to students from different cultural backgrounds while the methods of teaching and learning, which are embedded in the process of schooling, may also be unlike those with which certain groups of students are familiar.

As in the case of women and other groups characterized by lower levels of educational attainment and participation, the explanations given for this phenomenon contain within themselves the prescriptions to be followed in ameliorating the situation. Although the immediate issue involves provision of physically accessible and affordable schooling, once these economic resources have been allocated, educators differ on what other provisions should be made to facilitate entry and attainment by the disadvantaged groups. Where the cultural characteristics of the group are perceived as a major factor hindering attainment, a common prescription is that programs should be developed that overcome the deficits in the cultural attributes of the group. These programs include second or foreign language instruction to assist in acquiring the language used in the school and curriculums to compensate for limited opportunities in science or mathmatics. More radical are the programs that see the cultural attributes not as deficits but as differences that can be overcome by changing the educational system to accommodate them rather than changing the individual students. Changes here can include alteration of the curriculum content, the language of instruction and the patterns of assessment. The use of positive discrimination to give access to higher levels of education typically involves a modification of assessment criteria to make access easier for member of a particular group seen as experiencing educational disadvantage. In practice a variety of methods may be used to achieve this effect. In Malaysia the requirement that students competing for tertiary places be tested in the national language (Bahasa Malaysia) was later supplemented by the use of quotas that allocated the majority of tertiary places to Malay or other *bumiputra* students rather than to non-*bumiputra* Malaysian students of Chinese, Indian or Eurasian background.

The relative power of particular disadvantaged groups is an important factor affecting both the identification of their disadvantage as an educational issue and, also, of the policy and practices that are proposed for responding to it. The limited provisions in the region for students with specific physical or psychological disabilities reflect the extent of their limited educational and political influence. Compensatory programs directed to ameliorating the cultural deficits of disadvantaged groups have been far more favored as ways of overcoming educational disadvantage than have programs that seek to alter the educational system and curriculum; the latter potentially conflicts with the interests of influential groups in the educational system as well as in society at large. The case of Malaysia is instructive in that the willingness and capacity of authorities to alter the educational system to overcome the educational disadvantage of the Malay population is a reflection of the political power of the Malay population that has grown since independence. Members of the group who were educationally disadvantaged were also in this situation members of the group with political control. While this change in internal political influence has occurred in other countries, the more typical situation has been that educationally disadvantaged groups continue to lack political clout.

Also affecting the type of program advocated are the goals of the particular disadvantaged group. Much of the concern in the area of women's education is thus directed to gaining access and success for women in the same educational arenas as men rather than in a reappraisal or establishment of alternative curriculum and educational arenas such as may be advocated by members of particular ethnic groups who seek separate curriculum or separate educational facilities. The potential of such proposals for introducing further divisions in societies where national unity is limited links concerns with equity directly to the issue of diversity and how to respond to it.

Diversity
The challenge of ethnic and religious diversity for education has taken different forms in the countries of the Asia-Pacific region. Provisions range from none at all to situations where completely separate school systems are maintained, either privately or with government funding. In between there is a variety of provisions that include teaching in a language other than the dominant or national language, courses that bring into the curriculum content from the diverse cultures and courses directed to the whole school population to make it more aware and accepting of the ethnic diversity. This variety of provisions depends on the existing patterns of ethnic and minority relations as well as the historical development of these relations.

Three different patterns can be distinguished. The most common occurs where disparate ethnic and religious groups were brought together under colonial administrations as in Indonesia, Malaysia, India, Fiji and Papua New Guinea. Associated with this diversity, varied forms of educational provisions had been set up by the colonial administration as well as by members of the various ethnic groups and other private bodies including outside religious groups. An immediate task confronting postindependence governments was to establish their legitimacy. This frequently involved the establishment of a distinct national identity and a unified nation out of a number of contending ethnic and minority groups. The second pattern is best exemplified by countries such as Japan, China and Thailand where there have been long-established bureaucracies and a sense of national identity. Although there are diverse ethnic groups, their political and social influence is limited and often is not associated with the existence of separate schooling provisions. The third pattern is that found in Australia and New Zealand, both of which were colonies that became major 19th-century destinations for white settlers from many parts of the world, especially Europe. More recently nonwhite immigrants from Asia and the Pacific have been welcomed. Although the indigenous populations differed in their ability to influence the initial patterns of ethnic relations that emerged, in neither case did the British settler population and its government perceive the need to establish its legitimacy or unity as a major political challenge. Even the post-World War II influx of diverse ethnic groups did not result in a major challenge to the existing political arrangements although these groups have become influential in seeking more recognition of the cultural diversity that now exists in both countries.

In the first group of countries education was regarded as an important means of achieving the government's political goal of handling often extremely volatile ethnic relations and creating authority. The establishment of a national language that would both unite the people and symbolize the departure of a foreign government was an important aim in many of these countries. In addition many nations also sought to develop a national ideology as a focus of loyalty among the population; schools were seen as a major agency for disseminating this ideology. Inevitably the selection of a national language belonging to a particular group led to concern among other groups that felt they would be disadvantaged by the choice. Language of schooling became an important symbolic focus for members of minority groups who felt their position in society jeopardized by the change in political control. From a governmental perspective the existence of private schooling, especially when associated with particular ethnic or religious minorities, was seen as a factor contributing to the maintenance of separatism, something to be avoided when associated with groups such as the overseas Chinese or Indians who played a minor role in the economy of many of the countries of Southeast Asia and the Pacific.

While new national governments had little difficulty in introducing various national symbols and ideologies (such as Indonesia's Pancasila) into the school curriculum, the success of attempts to introduce a national language or to eliminate alternative schooling was more problematic. Indonesia, the

Philippines and Malaysia all made concerted efforts to develop a system of national schools in which the national language would be used; all three countries have, in the course of doing this, witnessed the substantial demise of education in other languages, including Chinese and English. In Malaysia, however, the position is not necessarily settled as far as many sections of the population are concerned: Chinese schools and the possibility of establishing Chinese tertiary institutions continue to fuel significant political debates concerning those Malaysians of Chinese origin.

As the Malaysian situation illustrates the educational provisions for linguistic diversity arouse strong sentiments and the accommodations made may not be stable. In India the efforts by the government to establish Hindi as the national language and to replace English in schooling met strong opposition in southern India where there was a strongly developed English language educational system. Singapore, by contrast, began independence with a schooling system based on four languages, English, Chinese, Malay and Tamil; the last three are the mother tongues of the major groups in the population, but English is now the national language of education and the other three languages are taught only as subjects. The success of the Singapore government in using English to replace vernacular education has involved the demise of the once strong Chinese language schools and tertiary institutions, a situation that would have been unimaginable in the 1950s when bloody riots occurred concerning policy on Chinese education. An important factor in the dominance of English has been the government policy linking economic and social mobility with knowledge of English, and this in a population three quarters of whom are of Chinese background. The emphasis on English in Singaporean education has also been tied to a policy that seeks to reassure its Malay neighbor that it would not constitute a Chinese outpost in Southeast Asia. At the same time it serves the internal argument that no one of the major ethnic groups constituting Singapore's population is favored. The choice of English is also seen as a key part of the economic strategy that has been designed to establish Singapore as a major international manufacturing and service center with a skilled English-speaking workforce. By choosing English, Singapore has avoided the difficulties confronting other countries that have sought to introduce their national language as the language of instruction at the tertiary level and discovered the difficulties involved in ensuring adequate supplies of books and other resources.

In China the move to establish a national language based on the language spoken in the Beijing area was well advanced during the first half of the 20th century; the existence of a written form of Chinese common to the various regional languages further simplified the problem. The policy on language and education for the non-Han minorities, many of whom occupy autonomous regions, has changed as the emphasis on assimilating these minorities into Chinese society has varied. During the Cultural Revolution the emphasis was on complete assimilation but since then greater acceptance and support has been shown toward the existence of minority languages and cultures in general and in the educational system.

The dominance of a cultural assimilation approach to various minority groups has a long history in Japan too where the existence of ethnic diversity even tends to be denied and is seen as not an issue at all. Thailand, which remained independent of colonial rule during the 19th century, has also favored an assimilation policy stance. This policy has been most actively pursued during strongly nationalist periods when governments have sought to reduce the economic influence of the Chinese minority, many of whom have, over the years, been assimilated into Thai society. The exception to this policy is the case of the Muslim Malay population of southern Thailand that constitutes what is seen by the government as a potentially disruptive ethnic group. But the national leadership has been forced to make some accommodation to their claims for greater acceptance of their culture and language in the schools.

The issue of diversity in Australian and New Zealand education lies between the two other patterns. Both countries have a dominant British population and institutions although large-scale immigration from other countries has now introduced extensive cultural diversity. None of the ethnic minorities is seen as a major threat to the existing society. But they have been influential in the abandonment by both countries of what had been predominantly assimilation policies in favor of multiculturalism, which involves the acceptance of diversity in major social institutions. Debates continue over the emphases on cultural maintenance and equity and, also, over the resources allocated to these programs. In the case of the Australian aboriginal population the official policy is self-determination rather than multiculturalism, but many of the actual provisions are similar to those found in the multicultural programs although with a greater emphasis on social rather than language maintenance programs. The issue in this instance is the extent to which programs developed under self-determination should allow or facilitate eventual access to Australian society in general. Positions on this topic vary widely among the aboriginal population because it is involved in diverse situations ranging from those living in large modern urban areas to those living in the remote countryside in traditional conditions.

An important influence in the Asia-Pacific region is the dynamic nature of relations in each country resulting from the changing political, economic and social situations of ethnic groups. In turn this relates to the nature and extent of these groups' integration. Especially in situations where ethnic and racial issues have become major focuses of political conflict, education may become a critical political issue and rallying point for debate. That this is so reflects both the instrumental importance attached by all groups to educational attainment as well as the affective attachment to ethnic culture and the role education is perceived to play in its transmission.

Values and Moral Education
An important dimension of the emotive aspects of provisions for ethnic diversity concerns the cultural links through language and through historical awareness. These links relate directly to perceived core values of the community. The same concerns about the preservation of key values develop in society at large when values are seen to be threatened by social

change. Massive political, economic and social changes have been experienced by many countries of the Asia-Pacific region, especially when they have come into contact with the scientific and technical knowledge and structures of the Western world. Traditional values and morals are often regarded as confronting major assaults from the individualistic and alienating Western values. In countries such as Malaysia with a substantial Islamic population a special edge has been given to these concerns by their coincidence with the growth of Islamic fundamentalism. This has involved the establishment of the International Islamic University with its moral education curriculum. In many Pacific island countries with small populations and limited economic resources the issue is especially acute because of the need to rely more heavily on non-Pacific countries for education. This factor, combined with the development of tourism as a major economic resource, is felt to render traditional cultural values especially vulnerable.

Despite internal conflict between diverse ethnic and religious groups there is often much common ground in their shared non-Western attitudes as well as their agreement about their desire to combat rootlessness and antisocial behavior among the young. Concern with values transmission is especially evident in the diverse range of courses and emphases on moral education ranging from religion to ethics to civics courses being developed in the region. Indeed the emphases on moral and religious education in primary schools in the region is greater than in other regions of the world.[5] Australia and New Zealand with their European traditions are the exception. Yet there, too, there is a general concern about what is perceived to be a breakdown in the social fabric as evidenced by changes in the family structure and the increasing prominence of drugs and antisocial behavior among young people. So far this concern has not been translated into proposals for specific curriculum changes but there has been a variety of initiatives directed to development of pastoral care and counseling programs in the schools.

The concern with values and moral education is not only confined to retaining traditional values for their conservative link with a particular way of life. It is often closely connected to a belief that such traditional values can make an important contribution to economic development. In this regard the example of Japan's successful economic growth has been highly significant. The apparent retention of major elements of Japanese culture and the transmission of these through various forms of moral education are often regarded by countries inside and outside the region as a key factor in Japan's economic success. The key elements discerned in the success are the way the Japanese downplay individualism and operate with a high regard for authority and for the good of the group as a whole—elements clearly significant in the existence of an industrious and cooperative work force. The use of moral education for economic purposes is also evident in Singapore where a major feature of the government's economic strategy has

[5] J. L. G. Garido, *Primary Education on the Threshold of the 21st Century, International Yearbook of Education*, vol. 38 (Paris: UNESCO, 1986), 158.

been the development of a skilled, English-educated work force to assist Singapore in becoming a regional and world manufacturing and service center. As English language education has become universal there, the government has placed increasing emphasis on developing and extending the moral education component of the curriculum to protect traditional Eastern values held to be essential for continuing economic development. Indirectly, these include stressing family ties that lessen the need for the government to divert funds to welfare provisions and, directly, through the maintenance of a stable and cooperative labor force.

Employment and Economic Development

The links between education, work and the economy have long been a major focus of educators. This issue has been considered from the perspective of its relationship to access to education. Here the focus is with qualitative aspects concerning curriculum and its implementation. The central issues are those related to acquisition of skills and their relevance for both the individual and society. These concerns are not confined to the region's less developed countries as they attempt to determine the types of curriculums appropriate to their current economic conditions. It is also a major common concern shared by countries with apparently high levels of affluence such as Australia and New Zealand as they develop an awareness of their excessive reliance on primary production. The two groups of countries differ in their specific focuses of the education-economy nexus and the levels and types of integration favored for education and work.

The initial emphasis on primary education drew much of its impetus from a belief in the value of literacy and numeracy to equip individuals for the new jobs associated with modernization. It soon became evident that such jobs were limited in rural areas and where there was limited manufacturing—a situation typical of much of the region in the immediate postwar period. Simultaneously, the attractions of white-collar employment drew many to education and, even though not ensuring access to such jobs, their expectations were such that they did not want to undertake manual occupations. The concerns about appropriate forms of education to avoid such situations were already evident in British India in the 19th century and were continued in British Malaya in the debate about whether education should be in English or the vernacular. These earlier debates have continued and now revolve around the appropriate forms of education for rural populations, whether in traditional schools or in more informal or nonformal situations. The vocational and economic aspects of the skills to be acquired emphasize agriculture and health in conjunction with literacy for the community as a whole. The Chinese experiment to reform its educational system during the Cultural Revolution by integrating work and school was a notable attempt that ultimately failed; it was partly designed to address the issue of the overly academic nature of schooling in urban as well as rural areas.

In urban areas the relevance of an academic nonscientific curriculum beyond the primary level tended not to be questioned in the period just after World War II when few of the economies of the Asia-Pacific region had changed from the agricultural and commercial bases developed under colonial control. The job opportunities that existed in many of these countries for those with Western-style academic educations were limited then because major administrative positions and professional jobs were reserved for expatriates trained abroad. Clerical and teaching jobs were the major career openings available to the elite few with modern, rather than traditional, often religious, education.

As the colonies attained independence and, with other independent countries in the region, sought to expand their economic bases, the need for more and diverse job skills became evident. Partly these were skills related to taking control of the bureaucracy and engaging in politics but they were also related to the need for those with technical and scientific skills to develop new industries. One common response was to introduce a vocational strand into the schooling curriculum but, insofar as it existed parallel to the academic strand, it tended very often to be geared to lower-level technical skills and, moreover, it was given lower status by parents and students. As a result many of these offerings were abandoned or ignored by students and their families. Also, as the expansion of secondary and tertiary education continued, the possibilities of obtaining higher levels of technical and scientific training in postsecondary and university situations developed and it was these levels of higher and more diverse scientific knowledge that better fitted governmental strategies. For parents and students such education was also much more attractive.

Accompanying the widespread emphasis on scientific education has been an emphasis on the need for generally higher levels of educational attainment. This has been the case as countries such as Singapore and Australia seek to maintain or extend their relatively high levels of economic growth through economic strategies that involve moving into the tertiary service sector and high-technology manufacturing. The failure of the Chinese educational reforms of the Cultural Revolution reflects the reassertion by parents, students and government of alternative priorities for linking education and work to the economy.

The reorientation of economic strategies has been associated with moves to expand and/or reorganize university level education to ensure that it reflects more closely government priorities. These trends are not confined to countries where there has always been this emphasis but is also evident in Australia and New Zealand that have had considerable autonomy in government-supported tertiary institutions. The organizational structures of the governance of higher education institutions are being reorganized to extend government control designed also to influence curriculum. The preferred curriculum for developing a more educated work force generally is seen as involving a large component of mathematics and science with related areas of computer and electronic technology. Business management and accounting are also emphasized. The humanities and social sciences are viewed as a much lower priority. These developments at the tertiary level mark a reemergence of the earlier emphases in education on manpower planning and human capital and resource development. Linked to them is a major emphasis on efficiency and the search for its appropriate indicators and measurement. These trends in education are not confined to the Asia-Pacific region but resemble trends in Europe and North America where technocratic emphases now strongly characterize developments in education. This technocratic orientation is contested by those who assert the value of more humanistically oriented education. These educators assert not only the value of such education but question whether technocratic education is capable of the creative solutions and developments necessary to move national economies away from dependence on foreign innovations and scientific developments.

Another perspective from which one may consider the relationship between education and the economy is that of nonemployment. Prior to the oil crisis and subsequent world recession nonemployment was conceived in more developed countries to be a trend associated with the increased leisure occurring in conjunction with economic growth. Today the focus has shifted to nonemployment resulting from enforced long-term unemployment. As described above, educational policies have tended to concentrate on the issue as one linked to inadequate and inappropriate education rather than as a result of structural flaws in the economy. As a result school curriculum is becoming more prescriptive emphasizing what is seen as basic areas of skill and traditional methods of teaching. At the same time parents and students select courses they perceive will yield good employment prospects.

Quality of Education

With increasing success in the task of actually delivering universal primary education, attention has turned to the quality of the education that is delivered. At the physical level of resources this is associated with better buildings, smaller class sizes and more teaching resources and materials. Teachers are clearly important as the deliverers of education and concern to improve their quality is a widely recognized issue. Measures of quality are difficult to specify but there is general agreement that by increasing their preparation and training teachers are able to offer quality education. Where resources have allowed there has been an increase in the amount of preservice and in-service training for teachers. But the length of time available for training is only one factor affecting the quality of teacher preparation. Much can depend on what happens within that period of training. Educators are concerned with the emphasis placed on the components of teaching skills in contrast to the acquisition of "academic" knowledge of the material to be taught. There is also the issue of practical classroom training versus theoretical process of teaching.

An additional way of assessing the quality of the teaching force is the ability of the educational system to both recruit and retain people noted as effective teachers. An independent measure of effective teaching is extremely difficult to identify except in crude quantitative measures such as student success in examinations, levels of academic attainment and dropout rates. Instead the tendency is to rely on comparisons of teacher mobility and estimate the attractiveness of teaching against the educational qualifications of those in other occupations. Comparisons are made of salaries, social status, career prospects and various conditions of service. As these conditions depend directly on availability of economic resources for education and the allocation of resources among different educational areas the debate involves the overall budget priorities for education and thus directly places educational debate in the main political arena.

The costs of education in a period of economic constraint have ensured that discussions about improving educational quality in the 1990s are grounded very much in analyses of the efficiency and effectiveness of particular options and uses of resources. As an example, high student drop-out rates and repetition are widely seen as examples of inefficiency in educational systems; they involve waste of resources but equally they highlight issues concerning the relevance and quality of the education available. The quality of education depends both on the physical resources and staff as well as on the curriculum (including content, methods of teaching and assessment). Decisions as to what constitutes relevance are highly subjective and there is considerable dispute among politicians, educators, parents and students about the content of the curriculum and about methods of teaching and assessment. Education in the Asia-Pacific region has been characterized by traditional methods involving extensive reliance on rote learning. Even in countries where there has been greater use of more activity-based and discovery models of learning, these have also been under attack by politicians and parents who want to reemphasize more conservative teaching methods and more "basic" curriculum content.

FUTURE DIRECTIONS IN EDUCATIONAL ISSUES

The highly diverse and subjective nature of much of the debate about educational quality, especially once it moves beyond the physical provision of staff and resources, indicates the frequent lack of agreement and yardsticks for judgment among educators about what constitutes key issues and what are appropriate policies to pursue in handling them. The changing emphases in the identification of educational issues reflect not merely specific concrete differences in educational needs and the circumstances underlying them but the ability of different groups to bring to public attention specific issues. The actual identification of issues and the mobilization of support for specific policies to handle them are ultimately dependent on the influence and power of interest groups.

The issues described above reflect the tendency of educators and policymakers to focus on broad national concerns rather than on the concerns that characterize individuals involved in education as either students or teachers. Where the two levels of concern coincide the strategies and programs implemented may still only partially address the concerns of the latter group. These often relate to personal educational outcomes in the case of students and parents; for teachers they are the specifics of actual classroom educational experiences. For planners and politicians the focus tends to be on the practical and easily quantifiable aspects of education in conjunction with more overt subjects in the curriculum. This concern with the subject areas of the curriculum is shared by parents whose focus is very much on the outcomes they perceive resulting from their children's education and their assessment about how effectively their children are being taught. More detailed concerns and debates about the actual content and methods of teaching and assessment are very much the prerogative of educators. With the high priority placed on efficient implementation in the Asia-Pacific region, there is limited scope for critical evaluation by those involved in implementing educational programs. The reemergence in the 1980s of the emphasis on the economic implications of education for all of the countries in the region—not only those seeking to industrialize as a first stage of development—the issue of how education and the economy are, or should be, related has assumed a new significance. Although receiving less attention than the education-economy issue the nexus between education and political structures assumes increased importance as new developments in the economy call into question the state's existing policies and its claims to legitimacy.

At various times in the Asia-Pacific region educational issues have become the focus for heated and often violent political confrontation; students in countries as separate as Burma (now Myanmar), South Korea and China have become extensively involved in broad political movements as their immediate educational concerns have been extended into wider social, economic and political issues. Important as such events have been politically, their ultimate effect on the definition of key educational issues in the individual countries may well be more limited, despite evidence that even the quantitative aspects of educational provision are accorded different priorities dependent on the historical characteristics of the country's development.

Even if specific policies and programs adopted vary, nevertheless issues identified at any one period show considerable similarities considering the wide diversity in society and educational provisions in the Asia-Pacific region. As countries in the region have begun to meet the quantitative demands for schooling, less quantitative and more qualitative concerns involving curriculum and equity have become more significant. But the similarities do not fully reflect absolute necessities. Available physical resources provide the parameters within which decision making proceeds. The social and political structures within which this knowledge is formed and disseminated are varied but clearly highly effective. An important role is played by international agencies involved in funding educational changes because they have considerable autonomy in defining educational issues and appropriate solutions. Through discussions with these agencies and other policymaking bodies educators and government leaders concerned with education's relationship to other areas of society can influence the formation of officially recognized issues and, sometimes, even the development of responses to them.

As the Asia-Pacific region moves into the last decade of the 20th century, educational issues will change as will policy responses to proposed solutions. Thus, questions of access will continue but will focus on higher levels of education. As expansion is extended and quantitative demands met, attention will increasingly focus on issues directly involving curriculum and the quality of education. In the foreseeable future the importance of the link between education and the economy will be a continuing influence in the formulation of key educational issues in the region. Alternative issues relating to equity and social justice will not be entirely absent but it seems highly likely that any educational responses to them will be developed within the framework of broader concerns for national economic growth and restructuring. Indeed the reemergence of concerns about the relationship between education and work and economic development was a major trend in the late 1980s.

Whether nations in the region will continue to play such direct roles in educational provisions as they have up until now is unclear. Certainly indications from the more industrially developed and educationally developed countries in the world suggest a more limited role in funding at the same time there is near universal primary and secondary participation. Withdrawal from funding provisions may not, however, be linked to major reductions in state control. That is, the contemporary focus is not a result of a complete disillusionment about education and its ability to change as governments may wish. Rather it may be seen as a result of redirecting and restructuring of governmental activity similar to that which has been occurring in Europe and North America. The features of this reorganization include vocationalization, privatization and a growing link between the corporate sector and schooling institutions, more centralized directions and limitations on schooling expenditures.[6] Some of these trends have been evident for many years in various Asia-Pacific countries but resulting from somewhat different patterns of sociopolitical development. Whether there will be further convergence, at least in broad structural terms, remains an open question. Certainly the diverse levels of economic and social development and the variant relationship of the national economies with core economies and societies is an important factor. For example the economies of the NICs after a period of more limited growth in the mid-1980s now show considerable growth; if anything, countries outside the region may look to the major East and Southeast Asian economies and societies—including their educational systems—for guidance. Ultimately, however, the educational programs implemented will be affected significantly by the institutional and social structures that have developed in each country.

FURTHER READING

Altbach, P. G., Saldhana, D. and Weiler, J. *Education in South Asia: A Select Bibliography*. New York and London: Garland, 1987.
Coombs, Philip H. *The World Crisis in Education: The View from the Eighties*. New York: Oxford University Press, 1985.
Cowen, R., and McLean, M. *International Handbook of Educational Systems*. Vol 3, *Asia, Australasia and Latin America*. New York: Wiley, 1984.
Garrido, J. L. G. *International Yearbook of Education*. Vol. 38, *Primary Education on the Threshold of the 21st Century*. Paris: UNESCO, 1986.
Inglis, C. and Nash, R. *Education in Southeast Asia: A Select Bibliography of English*

[6] R. Sharp, ed., *Capitalist Crisis and Schooling* (Melbourne: Macmillan, 1986), 265.

Language Materials on Education in Indonesia, Malaysia, the Philippines, Singapore, and Thailand, 1945–1983. Aldershot, Hampshire: Gower, 1985.

Jones, Phillip W. *International Policies for Third World Education: UNESCO, Literacy and Development.* London and New York: Routledge, 1988.

Malkova, Z. A., and Vulfson, B. L. *International Yearbook of Education.* Vol. 39, *Secondary Education in the World Today.* Paris: UNESCO, 1989.

Parker, F. and Parker, B. J. *Education in the People's Republic of China, Past and Present: An Annotated Bibliography.* New York and London: Garland, 1986.

Sharp, R., ed. *Capitalist Crisis and Schooling: Comparative Studies in the Politics of Education.* Melbourne and London: Macmillan, 1986.

Singh, Raja Roy. *Education in Asia and the Pacific: Retrospect and Prospect.* Bangkok: UNESCO, 1986.

Thomas, R. M., and Postlethwaite, N. *Schooling in East Asia: Forces of Change.* London and New York: Oxford University Press, 1983.

HEALTH AND MEDICAL CARE

THOMAS W. MARETZKI

INTRODUCTION: A PERSPECTIVE ON HEALTH AND HEALTH CARE [1]

In the words of a long-time observer of international health:

> Since the end of World War II, great strides have been made in meeting health needs, particularly in Third World countries. . . . The death rate has fallen significantly, longevity has markedly increased, environmental sanitation has improved, maternal and child health facilities have multiplied, immunization programs increasingly protect children against common childhood diseases, and the incidence of many other diseases, such as malaria, has been notably lowered. [2]

This encouraging global assessment, however, is tempered by the ensuing observation that, "enormous health problems still confront most of the world, and it is highly unlikely that 'Health for All by the Year 2000' will be achieved." Our Western perspective, notably the North American outlook, imbues the realities of health conditions, and Western assistance to ameliorate them, with an excess of optimism. Even though some of its premises are misleading, the continued Western faith in the improvement of conditions serves as an effective stimulus to sustain needed national and international efforts to improve health care.

For Western people, the concepts of health, illness and medicine are linked by related connotations. Health, narrowly defined as soundness of body and mind, is highly valued and must be maintained or regained when lost. Illness, though always present, is mitigated by assurances that modern medicine can cure many conditions or reduce the threats of others. Medi-

[1] The author wishes to express his appreciation to his many colleagues, too numerous to name individually, who provided helpful information and suggestions for this chapter. To Carol Arnold, librarian at the University of Hawaii, School of Public Health, I owe thanks for her indefatigable and effective responses to my incessant quests for source materials. David Leake's assistance with a review was invaluable. Only the author, however, is responsible for the content of this chapter.
[2] G. Foster, "Bureaucratic Aspects of International Health Agencies," *Social Science & Medicine* 29, no. 9 (1987): 1039–48.

cine, a product of scientific knowledge and technological inventions, progressively gains in its capacity to contain and control ill health.

Idealized notions in the West that favorable conditions in health and illness are products of scientific knowledge, professional skills and material control are reiterated by the medical professions, by the media and by educational and political institutions. Until doubts about the undisputed value of medicalization[3] were voiced recently in the West, these connotations also guided Western thinking about health and illness in non-Western countries. The faith in modern medicine spread along an expansionary path traveled by Western medicine and gained acceptance in Asia. In this overview of health care in Asia and the Pacific some expansive medical idealizations are questioned. Cosmopolitan medicine (biomedicine) is one significant, often vital, contributor to attaining and maintaining an improved state of health; it is not the exclusive key to solutions.

The geographic region under discussion presents extreme variations in human and environmental conditions and human responses associated with health care. Relevant to these differences is the fact that health and illness are not absolute entities. High morbidity and mortality are associated with communicative diseases, malnutrition and unsanitary living conditions. These and other health risks to mothers, infants and young children remain the most immediate and overwhelming realities for populations in the developing countries. Although threatening endemic diseases and many other diseases are well defined by biomedicine, states of health and illness are best understood in a broader sense. Illnesses can be vague and relative, tied to individual functioning in various contexts. They are manifested in behaviors, feelings and reactions that are culturally shaped, socially defined, psychologically experienced and expressed.

This ethnomedical approach entails complexities because it implies that not all parameters of health and illness can be translated into objective, comparable and measurable phenomena. The epidemiological task of abstracting and comparing conditions of diseases, defining them and measuring their prevalence (occurrence in the population) and incidence (new cases arising during a given period) becomes more difficult, if not arbitrary, at the fuzzy edges of health and illness in different parts of the world. The World Health Organization (WHO), monitored by a broadly representative council with members from multiple national and cultural backgrounds, recognizing these broad implications, modified its original definition (viewing health as the absence of disease) by stating that: "Health is a state of complete physical, mental and social well-being and not the absence of disease or infirmity." Included in this definition are multitudes of existing subjective experiences and conditions. The move away from a primary emphasis on disease and curative orientation to the prevention of ill health, the removal of health risks and promotion of health through improved living conditions, has been the greatest overall shift to affect the health policies and programs of less developed Asian and Pacific countries in re-

[3] Medicalization refers to the conversion of diverse life problems to biomedical categories, with diagnostic and therapeutic consequences.

cent years. This approach also recognizes that health and illness parameters are shifting in response to other changes in societies, generally social, economic and political. Because of these changes, relatively slow in some countries yet extremely rapid in others, any health appraisal for a particular area is subject to change.

The universal transfer of biomedicine and the internationalization of health care involve shared factors for changes that, however, are everywhere shaped by distinct cultural traditions and institutions. References to cultural ideas and practices related to health maintenance and curing acknowledge that there are local indigenous traditions that may or may not overlap medical theory and practice approaches introduced from the outside. In relatively young nations, and in established countries, which have preserved their cultural traditions but lately accepted ideas from the West (Japan, Korea, China), the divergences resulting involve internal conflicts. National governments, which assume the task of developing health policies and coordinating their implementations, tend to be aware of these cultural tensions in health. They tolerate or negotiate maintenance of those traditional health beliefs and practices that do not jeopardize the achievement of basic and worldwide recognized health care goals and standards. Traditional medical practices are valued as a balance for too much or too rapid modernization. They may help to confirm and promote nationalism and even underscore politically fostered anti-Western sentiments. Traditional medicine, however, persists regardless of national sentiments.

The relative and optimal role of indigenous medical practices in total health care remains an unresolved puzzle in most countries. The International Classification of Disease (ICD), generated by the WHO, guides official policies in all nations. The recognition of local cultural styles for health care is independently and usually tacitly woven into the national pattern of each country. Policy changes are ongoing. In Japan, they are tied to the dominant control of health care by the biomedical professions and insurance carriers.[4] But overall, health care in this region can not be discussed without reference to the forces of cultural traditions and to the multitude of values, beliefs and practices.

Three major medical traditions, each culturally unique, retain a strong influence in Asian countries.[5] The legacy of Greek and Arab (Unani) medicine, which provides the historical basis for European medicine, has also been incorporated in various versions where Islamic religion prevails and exerts a cultural influence on populations in South and Southeast Asia. The Indian, or Aryuvedic, great medical tradition covers the South Asian subcontinent and Sri Lanka, with influences reaching other parts of Southeast Asia. A contemporary synthesis of Chinese traditional medicine plays a significant role in the health-care system of the People's Republic of China (PRC) and affects medicine in Taiwan, Hong Kong and other overseas areas

[4] M. Lock, "The Organization and Practice of East Asian Medicine in Japan, Continuity and Change," *Social Science & Medicine* 14B (1980): 245–53.
[5] C. Leslie, ed., *Asian Medical Systems* (Berkeley: University of California Press, 1976).

with Chinese populations; with modifications, it is also found as an alternative to biomedicine in Korea and Japan. These medical traditions have their own written texts and professional organizations with formal and systematic training of specialists.

Nowhere, perhaps, does contact between spreading biomedicine and continued non-Western medical traditions cause more political, as well as medical, reverberations than in the PRC. In policies related to the acceptance of the Western science model, cultural conservatism, Marxism and modernism meet head-on, and the internal struggles about the relative importance of each have not abated. Marxism rejects bourgeois metaphysical and social values of Western medicine on ideological grounds. Also, fundamentally different principles of knowledge applied in traditional medicine as compared with biomedicine create contrasting practical approaches to preventive and curative health care. A synthesis, now attempted, continues to seek appropriate adjustments in each. In other countries where major medical traditions prevail (India) or provide for cultural medical alternatives (Japan), the internal adaptations to contrasts are less dramatic, less internally inconsistent and less often subject to periodic politically or professionally inspired reinterpretations.

There are multitudes of minor or folk medical traditions in Asia and the Pacific, some covering broad areas, others being localized. They have produced a plethora of causal explanations and therapeutic practices that play a major role, though mostly unofficial, in the overall health care of most countries. Population movements over many centuries have spread ideas and practices from folk traditions resulting in a bewildering pluralism, a coexistence of many beliefs and practices. Biomedicine, more recently grafted with various degrees of penetration and effectiveness on all of these traditions, has nowhere fully replaced folk healing. A Western search for simplification of technological emphasis in biomedicine even resulted in a reverse diffusion of some traditional Asian ideas and practices. Acupuncture, perhaps the most prominent example, has been adapted in the West according to Western meanings. It is being scientifically legitimated in China.

These cultural factors are difficult to convey as realities to Westerners for whom "medical" means biological, science-based biomedicine with its association of systematic research, professional organizations and amply equipped clinical facilities. Equated with cultural superiority in the Western mind, biomedical science now becomes in its spread to Asia and the Pacific one index of modernization.

Another cultural set of factors relevant to health maintenance and health care in all countries is related to language. Regional languages and dialects abound, in some countries—Papua New Guinea and Indonesia, for example—amounting to several hundred discrete tongues. National languages have been chosen or developed in the newly established nations. For many nationals they are second languages, for some (who have not had formal schooling) they are unfamiliar. English provides much of the specialist vocabulary for many health settings. Because of the regional language variations, communications with outside health-care workers and professionals often have to be conducted in a third language for all parties involved. This may be the national language, or English or another lingua franca such as pidgin or creole. In India, where Hindi has been declared the official national language, English continues to serve unofficially as the dominant language of bureaucracy and of health care above local community levels.

Other dimensions in the variations of health care relate to levels of development and to political ideologies. Asian and Pacific countries in two of the WHO regions (South and Southeast Asia with regional offices in New Delhi; East Asia and Pacific with regional offices in Manila) cover the full range from highly affluent countries to the poorest nations in the world. Economic and political systems, which influence the nature of health-care policies and delivery, vary from communist to socialist to capitalist and entrepreneurial ideologies. These differences are particularly reflected in manpower, facilities and patient management. Moreover, change does not affect all areas at the same rate of speed and intensity. Within countries, change is concentrated in the growing urban areas, not in remote rural parts of a country. Health care reflects these conditions, with urban centers generally providing the most up-to-date biomedical health care.

PROBLEMS TO SOLVE

Health problems can be narrowly defined as diseases that fit the Western-derived taxonomy found in the ICD or much more broadly include social problems. The latter approach is more realistic. Health conditions of this heterogeneous region may be portrayed against the dimensions of economic development as well as different political ideologies. Those in the industrialized countries (e.g., Japan, Australia, Singapore) can then only be very generally compared with those in countries like Bangladesh, Burma or some of the small Pacific Island nations. That economic factors by themselves, however, need not determine the overall level of health conditions is illustrated by the example of the PRC where remarkable changes have been accomplished in a few decades by unique government policies of central directives and reliance on local implementation. The examples of the PRC at one level, and Japan at another, also exemplify that, for this area, there is not one continuum along which health problems may change, but several. It would therefore be an error to view the health conditions and health-care institutions of the modernized countries in the West as the models providing logical milestones and guidelines for parallel improvements.

A starting point for national health-care strategies in all countries (often laid down as part of a national development plan frequently updated every five years) is found in the need for effective health measures such as vaccinations, family planning, maternal and child health care, other innovative health care measures and related economic improvements. Urbanization and modernization require additional health strategies. Internal migrations of overflow populations, government planned, as in Indonesia, or unplanned, demand health-care intervention to facilitate adaptation to unfamiliar environments.

The endemic health problems of many countries in early stages of transition in Asia and the Pacific, like the health problems of most of the developing world, are associated with communicable diseases caused by infectious agents. Neither statistics nor long, fact-finding reports can truly render the realities of living with health risks that to large segments of the populations appear as the "normal" state of their existence. Perhaps only a qualified observer can convey the magnitude of problems and the chances of controlling them. Unmatched in their mixture of expertise and irreverence are some of the tales in Robert Desowitz's *New Guinea Tapeworms and Jewish Grandmothers*. Desowitz, a WHO consultant at the time, paid a visit to the Burmese minister of health:

> The minister estimated that in rural areas 75 percent of those seeking medical attention did so because of malaria. With each passing year more and more cases are resistant to treatment with the relatively inexpensive antimalarial drug chloroquine, and the newer, more effective drugs are beyond the pocketbook of both government and people. The minister was obviously preoccupied with malaria, but almost as an afterthought, he turned the conversation to the other problems that related to my consultantship in mosquito-transmitted infections. Dengue hemorrhagic fever from time to time sweeps through Rangoon, killing hundreds of children. Filariasis is always present in the large cities but may also be endemic elsewhere. No one is sure. Were there, I asked, problems with other, non-vector-borne infectious disease? Well, of course everyone had intestinal parasites, but they were too common to do anything about—a natural phenomenon. Water-borne bacterial intestinal infections are also taken for granted, although frequent outbreaks of cholera did give a dimension of urgency to that problem.[6]

No one area of knowledge provides a coherent perspective on the complexity of the existing health situation. The transfers of laboratory-produced knowledge and similar technological transplantations in isolation are doomed to failure as has, by now, been widely recognized. A greater promise for an understanding that may help to explain, if not solve, unwanted conditions lies in combining the products of pure science with an ecologically and behaviorally appropriate realism. Ecological, in that modifications of the natural environment may keep the instigators of diseases—parasites and their intermediate transmitters (vectors)—at bay in relation to potential human hosts. Behavioral, in that culturally founded customs—from nutritional habits to sanitary practices—affect the human role in the intricate cycles of offensive microorganisms and contact with the animals involved in transmission. Beyond these levels of influencing situations affecting health, and far beyond the effects of any preventive and interventive strategies of the many teams of health experts converging on the problems, are the behaviors of powerful technocrats and developers. Their projects, often government-initiated or supported, can change or destroy (under the assumption of improving) entire well-established and balanced ecosystems.

Medical technology to eradicate most of the diseases that are associated

---

[6] Robert Desowitz, *New Guinea Tapeworms and Jewish Grandmothers: Tales of Parasites and People* (New York: W. W. Norton, 1981), 13–14.

with parasite-induced and other infections is available today. The eradication of smallpox throughout the world in the mid-1970s is one example of what is possible. What stands in the way are the behavioral problems associated with successful introductions of health measures. The introduction of seemingly simple protective measures, such as the use of insect-repellant–impregnated mosquito bed-netting, may meet with failure when they are not used by those at risk or when mosquitoes are permitted access to dwellings earlier in the evening, prior to bed-net use. Examples of minor, but significant behavioral neglect abound in all disease prevention. Inappropriate behaviors occur among persons threatened or affected by diseases as community members or patients; they also occur among health-care providers, health officials, politicians and innumerable other categories of people contributing to economic and technological changes. Human engineering applied to medical problems so far has worked in some selected situations and in some demonstration projects; but more frequently problem behaviors still defy the untiring efforts of experts, including those who apply psychological and social welfare knowledge.

Where control of infectious and contagious diseases shows some degree of success in reductions of morbidity or mortality, other health problems either continue or new ones emerge in relation to modifications in environment, economic or general social circumstances. In some cases the peaks of epidemiological problem distributions may simply shift from those diseases now responding to health measures, which once were so dominant that they eclipsed other serious ones, to problems not yet responding and now gaining in urgency. Examples could be influenza, hepatitis, enteritic diseases or hemorrhagic fever. Among the emerging health problems are those associated with smoking, alcohol, environmental pollution and, in urban areas especially, occupational hazards, stress, cardiovascular problems and other so-called diseases of civilization. Few countries have sufficiently developed reporting systems to provide reliable detailed epidemiological statistics; but trends are apparent from national health statistics and clinical studies.

Reliable studies of associations between health status and such factors as modernization or urbanization in Asian or Pacific countries are rare. Given problems of methodology and interpretation, clear or simple relationships can not be identified although trends may be suggested. Furthermore, the small number of cases raises problems about generalizations. A modest study of a small sample of Cook Islanders suggests links between change toward modernization and negative health status.[7] More detailed evidence is available for Samoans from the American-affiliated part of the islands migrating to urban centers in Samoa and on to the United States.[8] Hypertension is reported to account for one-quarter to one-half of all deaths in the PRC each year and has been found to be increasing over the past 20 years. Blood

[7] T. D. Graves and N. B. Graves, "Stress and Health: Modernization in a Traditional Polynesian Society," *Medical Anthropology* 3, no. 1 (1979): 23–59.
[8] P. T. Baker, J. M. Hanna and T. S. Baker, eds., *The Changing Samoans. Behavior and Health in Transition* (New York: Oxford University Press, 1986).

pressure surveys show that city populations are at higher risk than those in rural areas.[9]

Many unresolved problems and questions suggesting the interaction between medical and cultural factors relate to what are narrowly conceived of as mental illnesses, but broadly translate into Western concepts as psychosocial problems. Aside from the medical complications associated with some tropical diseases that cause organic dysfunctions affecting the brain, other severe psychotic disorders are comparable to those of Western countries. Generally, mental illnesses are regarded as less significant public health and medical problems in the developing countries because they rank epidemiologically below other serious diseases and because of the stigma associated with them. Also, contrasting with symptomatologies of many population groups in the West, mental health problems may be present with somatic rather than psychological symptoms in the countries of Asia and the Pacific.

Mental illness categories were originally developed in the West by following the hierarchical and causal classification rationale used for other disease taxonomies regardless of whether organic causality had been ascertained; changes from a causal to a phenomenological mental illness classification are of recent date. Many conditions are categorized by behavioral manifestations, which are often the only basis for diagnostic assessment. Behavior, however, has its basis in cultural learning. It ranges over a spectrum of expressions that in local settings assume different meanings, so that a particular behavior may be accepted as normal even though in Western eyes it seems bizarre. Cultural evaluation of the significance of behaviors and their anchoring in generalized standards guiding health care is an ongoing challenge to psychiatrists who approach these problems biomedically, though increasingly they try to consider the significance of cultural factors. A number of cultural reactions—grief is one example, spirit possession another—and personal problems continue to be resolved in the local folk or traditional healing sector and by religious rituals. The widespread notions of what is translated as witchcraft (as in the Balinese *bebainan*) point to interpersonal or intrapersonal problems.[10] Whether these phenomena are best left to traditional therapies or need professional mental health attention is a much debated issue.

Many conditions arising in rapid changes from traditional to modern life-styles produce unfamiliar pressures on individuals assuming the status of new medical syndrome. In Japan, certain dysphoric behaviors, or conditions of suffering, appear now as medical categories such as, "moving-day depression," "child-rearing neurosis" and the "refusal-to-go-to-school"

---

[9]L. S. Liu and X. X. Jing, "Epidemiology and Community Control of Hypertension in China," *Public Health Review* 13 (1985): 293–308.

[10]L. K. Suryani, "Culture and Mental Disorder: The Case of *Bebainan* in Bali," *Culture, Medicine and Psychiatry* 8, no. 1 (1984): 95–113. See also M. Carstairs and R. L. Kapur, *The Great Universe of Kota: Stress, Change and Mental Disorder in an Indian Village* (Berkeley: University of California Press, 1976).

syndrome.[11] Such diagnoses reflect a medicalization of common, but disturbing experiences. Increasing attention and health resources are expended to deal with them. Once given a diagnostic status, these conditions are referred to specialists, mostly psychiatrists or psychotherapists, who provide professional treatment which—in the case of Japan—may be adapted to culturally appropriate therapies.[12] Self-help or informal support may be another way of responding, assisted by a growing "how to" literature. This situation, familiar in the West, is now replicated in Japan. Specialists are abundant and new medical market niches are being developed—an index of total modernization, but not necessarily Westernization.

In other countries, even though there are problems associated with stress, public health concern is minimal. Few diagnostic facilities exist for psychological stress conditions. They remain undetected, unresolved or transferred to alternative life domains. In the PRC, an ancient tradition of breathing control, associated with the Chinese concept of *Qi,* has recently been revived and gained acceptance as group therapy *(Qigong)* in some urban public settings.[13] Tolerated, but not endorsed by government and professional hierarchies, this folk practice seems to reflect an accumulation of what in the West might be conceived of as psychosomatic problems related to stress. These examples suggest that the reciprocal relationships of broad mental health problems to folk responses and emerging specialized services is difficult to disentangle for health-status assessments. A growing recognition of conditions, heretofore either not occurring or disregarded, and newly developing symptomatologies present epidemiological challenges.

Most serious, though also most difficult to document until long after their occurrence, are conditions of human suffering engendered by political circumstances. The Cultural Revolution in the PRC is one example of the impact of political excesses on the health of individuals.[14] The occupation of countries with the ensuing displacement of central religious values, as in Tibet, the uprisings and wars in other parts of the region, most recently in India, Sri Lanka and Afghanistan, and the continued violations of human rights in other countries must have an impact, yet to be ascertained, on mental health.

Between the extremes of health problems mentioned, we find a broad range of unsatisfactory health conditions whose amelioration will require large amounts of human energy and resources. Hunger, malnutrition and poor sanitary conditions are widespread; population pressures add to the

---

[11] M. Lock, "Faltering Discipline and the Ailing Family in Japan," *American Ethnologist* (forthcoming). See also M. Lock, "Protests of a Good Wife and Wise Mother: The Medicalization of Distress in Japan," in *Health, Illness and Medical Care in Japan,* E. Norbeck and M. Lock, eds. (Honolulu: University of Hawaii Press, 1987).

[12] D. Reynolds, *The Quiet Therapies* (Honolulu: University of Hawaii Press, 1980).

[13] Thomes Ots, *Medizin und Heilung in China: Annaeherung an die Traditionelle Chinesische Medizin* (Berlin: Deitrich Reimer Verlag, 1987).

[14] A. Kleinman, *The Origins of Social Distress and Disease* (New Haven, Connecticut: Yale University Press, 1986).

extreme disadvantaged conditions of families, particularly in South Asia and parts of Southeast Asia. Nutritional imbalances result in widespread problems such as anemias due to iron deficiency, blindness in children due to lack of vitamin A and iodine deficiencies causing endemic goiter or hyperthyroidism. These are among a long list of conditions putting infants and children at the highest risk. Cholera outbreaks are recurrent events in some areas. Severe diarrheas require regular intake of fluids (oral rehydration) to restore electrolytes, an imperative treatment that may conflict with customary responses. Statistics on infant mortality and overall limited life expectancies in populations reflect the extent of these problems in many countries. It is recognized that, in addition to the control of endemic diseases, improvement of child and maternal health and the provision of effective family planning demand the highest priority in less-developed countries. Furthermore, as has been suggested, it is recognized that improvements of overall health conditions cannot be considered separately from overall improvement of social and economic conditions. Crucial, too, for health education is an increase in literacy.

PRIMARY HEALTH CARE

Primary Health Care (PHC) is a recently introduced concept describing a worldwide approach to preventive and curative health services. Though touted as an innovative health-care approach for underdeveloped countries, PHC appears to return to the promising Community Development approaches of two decades ago.[15] PHC is essential health care made universally accessible to individuals and families in the community by means acceptable to them through their full participation and at a cost that the community and the country can afford. The concept was adopted as a novel approach to health care in a WHO-sponsored conference at Alma Ata, USSR, in 1978. Representatives from 134 nations and 67 organizations of the United Nations system met to plan strategies under the slogan "Health for All by the Year 2000" by which all citizens in the world would be able to lead socially and economically productive lives. This worldwide meeting acknowledged that health was directly related to the overall social and economic conditions of communities and that health promotion implied sweeping efforts towards development.

Significant for these goals is the concentration of health care at the community level and the collaborative involvement of residents as contrasted with predominant reliance on a centralized health-care organization and approach. Implied also is a denial that equating reliance on improved technology with quality of health care would lead to the desired improved conditions. Instead, technology needs to be adapted and made appropriate to different conditions. To translate the ideal goals and conceptions for health care into policies and services has become the planning challenge for most of the countries in Asia and the Pacific. In these countries, the changes

[15] G. M. Foster, "Community Development and Primary Health Care: Their Conceptual Similarities," *Medical Anthropology* 6, no. 3 (1982): 183–195.

have to be introduced gradually. For example, in Indonesia, a country of widely dispersed islands, each successive Five-Year Plan incorporates measures and budgets to widen the net of PHC services and facilities. Political decision making directly affects the distribution of health-care resources and efforts towards relative integration of the process. Internal political conflicts impinge on the realization of PHC in many countries in which the political leadership is unstable or where governments are overturned by political and revolutionary events. Even in relatively stable countries, PHC is not established without considerable difficulties involving trial and error.

The differences in political and economic foundations for government activities provide one overall factor in approaches and their responses to PHC introduction. Free-enterprise capitalism, socialism or an economy under guided democracy—each offers different conditions for realization of PHC. Nongovernmental organizations such as churches or international voluntary organizations, which in many countries also participate in these efforts, are allowed to function under opportunities or restraints that are not directly tied to government programs.

Complexities of political economy in each situation apply at a very general level. PHC will succeed only to the extent that it is adapted to the level of local customs and styles of communication. That means a true, culturally relevant understanding of populations and problems. Recognition of pertinent folk health concepts and localized support and communications systems is essential. The assumption that these are recognized by health officials has frequently proven erroneous.

Few persons, either within a country or from the outside, appear capable of abstracting the truly complex issues relating health to cultural conceptualizations. The following excerpt from the writings of an experienced and perceptive medical anthropologist gives an example of these complexities.

> Speaking of health is actually misleading. Just as a doctrine of multiple causality of illness exists in most cultures, so too multiple notions of health coexist. Most cultures entertain at least four overlapping concepts of health: health as the absence of socially disvalued symptoms, health as balance, positive health, and health as control.
>
> In order to understand health as the absence of symptoms one need first understand what are deemed normal body-mind signs within a culture. For example, the normal body signs—food transmit time, hunger, thirst, the color of urine, consistency of feces—of a poor South Indian farmer who consumes rice as a staple "superfood" are considerably different from those of a North Indian wheat eater or a cosmopolitan city dweller living off an eclectic diet. Yellow urine or hard feces may be commonplace, or at least not a health concern, to the latter, but are deemed a sign of illness to the former.[16]

This phenomenological understanding of health is important, Nichter writes, because of the lay person's perceived state of normality that serves

[16] M. Nichter, "Toward a 'People Near' Promotive Health within Primary Health Care," *First International Symposium on Public Health in Asia and the Pacific Basin, March 7–11, 1983* (Honolulu: School of Public Health, University of Hawaii): 10–11.

as a backdrop against which new foods, medicines and life-style advice are measured.

Health as balance refers to notions of humoral balance such as hot/cold, dry/wet, yin/yang, the balancing of tastes and what is consumed or not consumed with what else. Control refers to the folk knowledge that helps to build vitality by consumption of particular foods, tonics and medicines, while maintaining what are deemed routine bodily processes, purity as a state of control, resistance to and the ritual closing of space (the body, house, village) to malevolent influences. Such are examples at the level of culture that must be taken seriously. Much of the reasoning about health in the developing world is analogical. A preponderance of health communication relies on logical argumentation based on cause-and-effect relationships. Curative health services, which bring tangible results after a short time, are generally accepted more readily than promotive health services without immediate visible results. Appropriate styles of communication, adapted to different cultures, need to be developed and applied, but often are not. PHC—conceived and planned throughout in the lofty, though well-meaning, environment of a worldwide meeting—requires a realistic translation into individual field situations that may differ significantly even within one country. A few PHC-demonstration projects illustrate what can be achieved through an intensive, culture-sensitive approach. In the northwestern part of Thailand, the Lampang Health Development Project, sponsored by the Thai government, for several years (until 1981) developed the infrastructure and innovative community services by means of which health care was linked to other rural and provincial health facilities. Evaluation concluded that new community services were utilized as planned in contrast to control areas where there was an increasing reliance on centralized clinic and hospital care. The problem of financial resources, especially of local financial participation, was not fully solved by this project.[17] In Banjanegara, central Java (Indonesia), an integrated project innovatively combined separate services of unrelated agencies for health care, family planning and other community development. Education and services in all these areas are offered as orchestrated efforts.[18]

But the actual spread and successes of PHC in most if not all countries is slow and laborious. It remains a continued concern of planners, educators and health-service professionals who attempt to find ways for a realistic intersectoral collaboration between themselves and the various levels of less-specialized health workers to the participants in each community without whose full engagement the PHC programs can not succeed. The oral and written accounts of informed observers and participants in some aspects of PHC development in different countries are fascinating, but at times also discouraging in their realistic assessments of obstacles. Yet, it is widely

[17] Ministry of Public Health, Thailand, *Summary of Final Report on the Lampang Health Development Project* (Bangkok, 1981).
[18] A. Suwondo, "The Study of Selected Factors Influencing the Development of Primary Health Care in Rural Indonesia: The Banjanegara Experience" (Doctoral dissertation, School of Public Health, University of Hawaii, 1987).

acknowledged that there are no alternatives if sufficent and effective health care is to extend to all segments of all populations.

Even before PHC became an official policy of the WHO and its participant member countries, the PRC had developed an effective, integrated rural health community self-help model that attracted worldwide attention. In this nation with the largest population in the world, it was impossible to provide for all the services of specialized health professionals. Rural, secondary hospitals provided both primary health-care services and extension services for communities including the teaching of lay personnel. Impressive to the outside world was the development of lay helpers, the barefoot doctors, who became the providers of immediate curative care for problems that could be referred to higher institutional levels if they persisted, but who also symbolized and advocated the importance of prevention and intelligent self-care. In 1979, a visiting team from the United States, consisting of well-trained professional observers, visited China for a comprehensive overview of this country's health system and its amazing achievements. Fully aware of the communications and conceptual gaps existing, the report presents a remarkable summary of the situation at that time.[19] The relationship of community health-care experiences in the PRC to the general goals of the PRC is reflected in illustrations of strategies for health-care management in this agrarian country that faces conditions characteristic of many others in Asia. Uncharacteristic are the energetic efforts at problem resolution by utilizing existing or available knowledge and human resources. Their development is encouraged and guided with an emphasis on national autonomy. The report acknowledges "impressive achievements" of a system that depends on community initiation, community participation and community resource contributions in the prevention of diseases and maintenance of basic health. As an illustration of one set of problems recognized by this report, which may also indicate challenges for all PHC efforts, one reads:

> Yet, China's victory is far from total. China shares many of the difficult communicable disease problems faced by the United States, particularly hepatitis and influenza. Labor hygiene is still in its infancy. Furthermore, China needs to do much more in standardizing its records and statistics, a deficiency we found vexing on more than one occasion.[20]

MANPOWER, KNOWLEDGE AND KNOWLEDGE PRODUCTION

The term manpower, in spite of its unfortunate sexist connotation, summarizes the topic of health workers as a resource from the least trained to

[19] Committee on Scholarly Communications with the People's Republic of China, *Rural Health in the People's Republic of China* (U.S. Department of Health and Human Services, Public Health Services, National Institutes of Health, Publication No. 81–2124).

[20] *Ibid.*, p. 163. See also David Mechanic and A. Kleinman, "Ambulatory Medical Care in the People's Republic of China: An Exploratory Study," *American Journal of Public Health* 70, no. 1 (1980).

the most educated and professionalized and refers, of course, to both sexes. Most of the less-developed countries, including former colonial areas, did not begin to systematically deal with health-care manpower needs until two or three decades ago. Since then, training and upgrading manpower resources at all needed levels have had a high priority in all countries and have met with varying success. The development of health workers appropriate to specific situations of growth and development depends on a suitable and durable administrative and practice infrastructure that assures continuity. The responsibility for the education or training of health workers is mostly divided between ministries of health and ministries of education. Administrative planning and interdigitation requires frequent and effective communications between these and other agencies.

In all countries, training of health-care staff has a high priority, but there are differences in the educational facilities and types of programs available. The greatest need is for training of lower-level health-care staff, nurses, allied health-care professionals and—increasingly in recent years—community workers. Where colonial governments left a legacy of minimal or no training of health-care manpower, a totally new health educational system had to be put into place. Medical schools, schools of public health and training centers for nurses, laboratory technicians, nutrition specialists and other health-care workers have now been widely established in the larger nations, but few countries seem to have reached an optimal level of training facilities. Gradually, other therapists such as clinical psychologists and social workers are trained to staff mostly government and a few private agencies.

The training of health-care manpower is facilitated in member countries by advisory and material support from the WHO, including short-term training in India, Australia and European countries where English can serve as a common means of communication. A few countries—such as India, Thailand and the Philippines—produce an excess of physicians. They also train too many nurses with advanced degrees relative to available employment at their levels of skill. These surplus health experts who seek employment abroad—in America, Europe and elsewhere, including more recently in some Middle Eastern countries—are examples of brain drain. More common are inequities in physician availability as reflected in the following figures: in 1980, per 100,000 population, Bangladesh had approximately 8 physicians, the PRC 45, while the US had 200.

In recent years, a major change in dealing with manpower needs took place in many of the less developed countries. Where a professional and technological level, too high for practicality in many countries, was previously proposed by international agencies, the approach developed in the PRC became a widely recognized and sometimes overidealized model. The emphasis in building health manpower shifted from primary reliance on professionals to the role of paraprofessionals at the base of the health-care pyramid. The innovation of the barefoot doctor in the PRC during the 1960s followed a demand that greater attention be given to improving health care in the rural areas. Although reliance on minimally trained community workers turned out to be only a transitional phase in the highly practical approach to health care in the PRC, the shift of low-level health-care workers was introduced in other countries of Asia and the Pacific, though with varying results. A few medical schools—Udayana University in Bali is one example—have broken away from the narrow training models for physicians. They incorporate the learning of attitudes and skills for PHC during extended community placements.

With encouragement from the WHO, the role of traditional healers also began to be recognized in different countries. While in India, China, Korea and Japan a pluralistic medical system was left intact or accepted within set rules of training and practice, in other countries traditional healers continued their informal roles, but few among them gained formal acceptance or recognition from health officials. One exception were traditional birth attendants, individuals (female and/or male) who assisted with birth. They were contacted as valuable intermediaries between women giving birth and the professional midwives who would monitor pregnancies and birth. The attendants were offered minimal training in modern concepts of care during pregnancy, sanitation and attention to normal and unusual birth processes. Such measures reflect a transitional manpower solution.

The backbone of health manpower in preindustrialized countries today and in the forseeable future are nurses. Other key roles are provided by allied health professionals, the village health workers and other primary health-care volunteers. Physicians, important as they are in total health care, are not the frontline workers in preventively oriented health programs, but are rather the second- or even third-line of support. Many administrative coordinators of health-care policies and programs are physicians. Physicians may also be well connected to political leaders and structures.

While most countries have detailed long-range manpower plans to build staffing from the bottom up, many struggle with the coordination and sufficiency of their health manpower planning and training. A major challenge for these countries is effective distribution of limited resources in light of competing demands for health-care services. Though preventive public health measures and PHC are the basis for health care, medical curing plays a significant role in the actual manpower deployment of physicians. This emphasis grows with urbanization and modernization, with national health resources being drained from rural areas. Shortage of government funds for physician salaries is a chronic problem. Private practice of physicians in countries that allow entrepreneurial activities satisfies two realities: a growth in demands for clinical services and a need for personal income.

In developing countries, such as in Indonesia, government employment of physicians during part of the working day is mandatory during most of their lifelong careers. Physicians tend to cluster in urban areas for obvious reasons. But government efforts for a more equitable geographic distribution has met with some success. In Indonesia, as in most Asian developing countries, physicians upon completion of their training are obligated to serve an initial period in rural areas. During this time they assist with the staffing of PHC clinics and district government hospitals. The majority of hospitals in Asian countries is government owned. Eventual posting in more desirable provincial centers or the capital is customary. Physicians are permitted to supplement their modest government income through practice in private clinics or hospitals during afternoons and evenings. Physicians employed as faculty in university medical schools do not earn higher salaries than other government colleagues, but their high status assures them of a steady flow of private practice patients and medical consultancies.

FOREIGN AID FOR HEALTH-CARE WORKERS AND FACILITIES

Most countries in Asia and the Pacific look to international organizations for help and technical input, and to public and private agencies in major Western countries for foreign aid. In addition to providing some funding for health-care development, the WHO plays a central role in developing policies and supporting individual member countries in applying them. In recent years, the WHO staffing has shifted from a European specialist-dominated organization to one in which nationals from Asian and Southeast Asian countries have occupied leading positions, especially in the regional offices. This change may have aided in representing at central administrative levels a more balanced cultural and regional political emphasis.

Motivations and practices that guide the thrust of foreign aid organizations from Western countries are not easily characterized. Enthusiasm, commitment and willingness to contribute to innovative programs are among the positive qualities of many individual foreign workers in developing countries. Appropriately trained, they contribute needed skills and display necessary patience. Problems more likely arise at institutional levels. For example, the United States stands out for its politically dominated changing emphases in foreign policy. These inconsistencies can have negative repercussions. With each administration in Washington appear novel and often reversed policies tied to the monetary foreign aid that is intended to support particular health-related programs. These vacillations and changes create serious problems in the field. Although technical know-how has been an effective component of health-care export from the United States, it sometimes appears in dosages disproportionate to actual needs. At the same time, with experienced and persistent leadership, US government-generated assistance can have positive impact and continuity. An example is the MEDEX organization, which receives funding from USAID for its realistic, collaborative assistance with manpower development.

The impact of the United States on the health care and manpower development in the former Trust Territory of Micronesia (now a series of semi-independent Pacific island nations) and American Samoa (a dependency) illustrates a well-meaning, but overall misguided, American policy on health care abroad. It also illustrates some of the more general problems faced by small island nations in a modernizing world. In Micronesia, and also in American Samoa, the United States prevailed in bureaucratizing health care.[21] The Western-style allopathic health services, introduced by

[21] A. B. Robillar, "Foreign Medical Aid in Postmodern Capitalism: Some Ex-

the US Navy following World War II, began a trend that the succeeding US government continued. A bureaucratized, and initially centralized public-health administration was established in a climate of monetization detrimental to greater self-reliance on localized health care. The key to American influence was the transfer of ideas developed in the political and economic context of the States. Foremost among these was reliance on a salaried health-care staff, the introduction of technology and the spending of large, even totally disproportionate, amounts of funds for hospital facilities and technical equipment. (Even today, in Micronesia 50% of health budgets are spent on off-island referrals for a few tertiary-care patients and a few in-country dialysis patients.)

In the absence of indigenous physicians, American and other nationals spend brief periods in medical service in the islands, often too short to become adequately sensitized to the cultural needs of the local populations. An elite corps of male Micronesian high school graduates who received special paraprofessional training as medical officers—first in Fiji, more recently in Ponape—provides the basic medical services throughout all districts. These officers became the highest compensated indigenous public employees in the islands, receiving more than 10 times the average per capita income in addition to free housing and food allowances. Among their many problems are providing adequate coverage for the dispersed outer islands. Micronesian nurses are trained at the level of licensed practical nurse. Many of them are male. A few college-trained nurses, together with allied health professionals, some laboratory and x-ray technicians and physical therapists represent a replica of the US health care system, though at lower skill levels. Only now as Micronesians enter American colleges and US dominance has ended, can further changes be expected. How health officials will resolve the discrepancy between increased skills and demands for higher levels of technology on the one hand, and inadequate capital recources on the other, is one of many challenges these Pacific islands must face.

In the southern Pacific, less bureaucratized, less overfinanced health-care systems have developed with support from New Zealand and Australia. Political and economic upheavels threaten continuity in some of these programs; new countries like Papua New Guinea have tried to shed the colonially imposed health-care model. Australian health care of aborigines has been characterized as tied to culturally uninformed, blind policies in spite of substantial funding and staffing support. The direct participation in their health-care programs, suggested for aborigines by well-informed critics of government policies, has been met largely with doubts and resistance. Demands for taking responsibility for their own health care will increase as the rapidly reproducing aborigines gain the political influence they seek.[22]

amples from Micronesia," in *Foreign Medical Aid,* H. K. Heggenhougen, ed. (Dordrecht: D. Reidel, 1988).

[22] P. Schoeffel, "Dilemmas of Modernization in Primary Health Care in Western Samoa," *Social Science and Medicine,* 19, no. 3 (1984): 209–16. See also J. Reid,

THE GROWTH OF SPECIALIZED MEDICAL FACILITIES

The Western emphasis on medical technology and highest level professional staffing has met with different rates of adoption and with various practical solutions in each country. In addition to the United States, Australia and Japan are outstanding examples for their development of high-level technological and specialized medicine with clinics, hospitals and laboratories, which serve large segments of the populations. Economic, professional and political interests combine in the planning for such facilities. Different philosophies about equitable access are involved. Few countries can hope to achieve a relatively open access to tertiary facilities attempted in highly industrialized nations. When expensive equipment, such as kidney dialysis machines or sophisticated imaging devices, are imported by small Pacific islands or other poor nations, the question is: who will receive the benefits? The relevance of social worth of candidates for limited therapies, a topic of much ethical discussion in the West, is even more acute in these countries. Here the contrasts may be particularly sharp between capitalist and socialist political philosophies. Private health insurance or other government health-cost coverage programs known in the West are not available in many Asian and Pacific countries. Governments support basic health care. Private hospital care is limited to those who can afford to pay for their services. In the developing countries, the most modern equipment for public use is frequently found in hospitals affiliated with medical schools, most of which are government owned. Socially prominent and affluent individuals in developing countries who utilize the private clinics in the capital can also fly to Hong Kong or Singapore where totally modernized medical facilities are available. Most other residents in these countries have very limited access to specialized biomedicine.

KNOWLEDGE PRODUCTION: RESEARCH

The need for epidemiological data and other specific information on local health conditions, as well as appropriate educational materials, is linked to manpower training. A truly national research and knowledge distribution effort can only be developed with the establishment of universities, training centers and research institutes, staffed by qualified citizens. In most of the larger developing nations a critical phase was passed in the 1970s when key teaching and research positions could be assumed by those who had returned to their country from graduate training abroad. But there is a continued role for expatriate consultants, researchers and some specialty teachers. Individual countries maintain collaborative research and training programs with institutions in India, Japan, Australia, European countries and North America. There, some schools of public health, medical schools, institutes for medical research and institutes for demographic studies provide training and research collaboration. The human potential for learning

ed., *Body, Land and Spirit: Health and Healing in Aboriginal Society* (St. Lucia: University of Queensland Press, 1982).

appropriate research methods and for carrying out research and creating the needed knowledge bases is abundantly present in all countries. The greatest challenge is to provide career opportunities for returning individuals at commensurate salary levels to allow a full commitment to research and training. Personal opportunities begin with training of teachers and researchers, but so do personal and family sacrifices. Many graduates going abroad on modest fellowships, whether male or female, have to separate from families for an extended period to live in distant and unfamiliar places, often leaving spouses and children in the care of relatives. Another problem abroad is insufficient adaptation of training to the needs of Asians or Pacific islanders who will face different conditions for research than those who train them.

To the extent that specific cultural knowledge is relevant for individual countries in shaping health policies, training and services, Indian and Sri Lanka may be examples for research and knowledge development appropriate to the realities of their pluralistic system of traditional medicine with ancient texts and widely applied therapies. Established universities and research institutes for Aryuvedic medicine investigate conditions of health, including the nature and use of herbal medicines according to their concepts. In the PRC, research is carried out on ancient texts, the nature and use of traditional pharmaceuticals, and of therapies developed in traditional medicine. In Japan, where traditional Chinese medicine (known as *kampo*) is offered for diagnostic and treatment purposes, research is concentrated in specialized schools for East Asian medical training.[23] Commercial production of traditional pharmaceutical substances in several Asian countries also involves research. Research on sociocultural conditions related to health is carried out in a number of Asian and Pacific countries. Concepts and methods are borrowed from the Western social sciences, but sometimes applied with modified methodologies adapted to each situation. Ongoing field research projects of individual Western social scientists in Asian and Pacific countries may offer some stimulus for, and even collaboration with, local social science research. The WHO advises and supports several of these activities.

THE ROLE OF PHARMACEUTICALS AND SOME IMPLICATIONS

Pharmaceuticals are a necessity for some basic health care in the practice of clinical biomedicine. If left uncontrolled, they are also a severe threat to health. The WHO provides technical assistance for developing countries with policies for the management and control of pharmaceutical substances. A list of 27 essential drugs was published as a guideline (in 1985) by the WHO.[24] Essential drugs are those that satisfy health-care needs of the ma-

---

[23] M. Lock, *East Asian Medicine in Urban Japan* (Berkeley: University of California Press, 1980). See also P. Unschuld, *The History of Ideas in Chinese Medicine* (Berkeley: University of California Press, 1986) and Leslie, *Asian Medical Systems.*
[24] World Health Organization, *The Use of Essential Drugs,* Technical Report Series No. 722, (Geneva, 1985). See also other reports in this series.

jority of the population. They should be available in adequate amounts and in the appropriate dosage form. It is recognized that the choice of drugs depends on many factors, such as the diseases that need prevention and the nature of treatment facilities. In spite of these sensible and cautionary guidelines, effective control and appropriate distribution of pharmaceutical substances is fraught with problems in most countries. Only in a few, Singapore and Malaysia are examples, has enforcement of control been initiated with some success.

There are no clear solutions to the arguments about the extent to which pharmaceutical products are an aid or a danger to the promotion of health in non-Western countries. Any arguments, in fact, are weak defenses against actual onslaughts of the pharmaceutical companies, which have introduced their products through massive distributions and powerful advertising campaigns in all Asian and Pacific countries. The resulting acceptance and use of pharmaceuticals by a growing mass of consumers virtually overwhelms concerns about their potentially ravishing effects, which are only occasionally expressed. Moreover, the flooding of these products has powerful political connotations because the pharmaceutical industries are tied to large and important business interests in all countries. How did this overwhelming power, the almost unquestioned acceptance of pharmaceuticals and patent medicines become established? Until more substantive research findings are available, one can mostly speculate on the basis of a few studies about the myth of progress, the hopes for better cures, the skills of advertising campaigns and the translation of actual experiential knowledge into mass behavior. Widespread recognition of the positive effects of antibiotics raised expectations of people everywhere, whereas the increasing resistance of targeted bacterial organisms, which eventually reduced the efficacy of these drugs, did not register widely. Pharmaceutical products—pills—assumed a symbolic power that went far beyond scientifically established and responsibly claimed effectiveness. PHC workers, much as their colleagues in urban clinics and hospitals, recognize that any medication issued following a consultation has such powerful positive meaning to seekers of cures that it can not easily be refused. Prescriptions of vitamins and vitamin injections are commonplace as incentives to increase utilization of PHC health-care facilities.

In many cultures of the region, knowledge of natural substances, herbs and other sources for medicinal application long predates contacts with the West. A systematic knowledge of pharmacology (the effects of medical substances on the organism), related to the traditional correspondence theories, is known from early Chinese texts. Aryuvedic medicine had long gained an understanding of pharmacology based on flora and fauna. The use of herbs and other natural substances in many other cultures was an integral part of indigenous health care, an empirically based, balanced application of material medical remedies. These situations of an earlier period, though never static, have been totally altered by the introduction of synthetic pharmaceuticals.[25]

[25] P. U. Unschuld, *Medicine in China: A History of Pharmaceutics* (Berkeley: University of California Press, 1986).

The change to pharmaceutical industrialization in most of the countries of Asia and the Pacific is linked to a "commodification of health." This concept implies "the tendency to treat health as a state which one can obtain through the consumption of commodities, namely medicine."[26] In its simplest, crudest form applied to cultural ideas, translated into behaviors, "commodification" means that health is a commodity that can be obtained. Health no longer is centered in the person and in an individual's social context. Although data from observations in India can only serve as one example of the impact of health commodification, they are not atypical for many other countries. In these exacerbating situations, multinational pharmaceutical firms operating through affiliates and subsidiaries are shown to be overpromoting medications by exaggerated claims for extra indications while downplaying or outright omitting hazards. In India, when joined by Aryuvedically inspired patent medicines designed with cultural rationales and slogans, the compounded impact on a population in pursuit of health is frightening in terms of dangerous effects as well as economic sacrifices. With no objective evaluations in sight, perhaps not even possible, these ramifications appear to exceed any efficacious benefits of pharmaceuticals though this point will be vigorously debated and any negative implications denied by powerful commercial and industrial interests. (In some countries, physicians sell the pharmaceutical substances they prescribe to their patients.) Certainly, it can be demonstrated that in many countries there is a lack of quality control, laxity in prescription practices and a predominance of self-medication, given abundant free access to diverse pharmaceuticals and tonics. There is also a lack of detailed, understandable information about drug use. For example, a careful survey of drug prescription and self-medication for 600 Indian patients revealed widely varying, questionable prescription practices by physicians as well as the fact that 64% of the patients bought medicines over the counter without prescriptions, with variations between 30 and 90% from pharmacy to pharmacy.[27]

Considering the massive benefits achieved worldwide through vaccinations, their abusive applications, too, are easily disregarded. Though it is documented only sporadically, there are parallel examples of health commercialization in the unfettered use of injections. "Injection doctors" have been described for one area in Thailand as untrained agents (veritable quacks) who dispense injections for financial gain, testifying to the widespread dangers from uncontrolled technological fixes that in sound professional hands serve to preserve or restore health.[28] General and widespread misconceptions about vaccinations involve parallel risks and dangers. They illustrate the relationship between beneficial and destructive forces in modern medicine.

[26] M. Nichter, "Pharmaceuticals, Health Commodification, and Social Relations: Ramifications for Primary Health Care" (Unpublished manuscript, 1987).
[27] T. Greenhalgh, "Drug Prescription and Self-Medication in India: An Explorative Survey," *Social Science and Medicine* 25, no. 3 (1987): 307–18.
[28] S. van der Geest, "The Illegal Distribution of Western Medicine in Developing Countries: Pharmacists, Drug Peddlers, Injection Doctors and Others," *Medical Anthropology* 6, no. 4 (1982): 192–219.

While epidemiological surveys can demonstrate the impact of successful programs, it is more difficult to demonstrate the negative impact of false expectations, inappropriate beliefs and misleading use of metaphors related to vaccinations because illustrations must be drawn from careful and in-depth studies of populations rather than from survey research data. In the light of future hopes for new vaccine applications, this statement, introducing a discussion of vaccines in South Asia by an experienced, careful observer of that health scene, stands as a warning:

> . . . limited information is being presented to the community, misconceptions about the power of vaccinations abound, and false expectations and fears influence perceptions of vaccination efficacy and appropriateness. Compliance from one vaccination to the next is gained more by appeal, endorsement, and power relationships than adherence on understanding, felt need or perceptions of efficacy.[29]

Stressed in this presentation are the ramifications and inappropriateness of the military metaphor (e.g., fighting diseases, giving a shot to protect, and so forth) as a model for vaccination administration.

THE BOTTOM LINE FOR HEALTH CARE: CONCLUSIONS

Is there a bottom line, an overall measure for the level and impact of contemporary health care among Asian and Pacific populations? The opening quotation in this chapter offered the broad observation that increased life expectancy and reduction of specific risks to health is an undeniable outcome of concerted efforts toward better health. Essential knowledge gains in acceptance and leads to behaviors that will have positive health effects. As an example, in seven out of nine Asian countries surveyed, women knew of at least one modern family planning method and one-half of the women in several countries used family planning methods.[30] More contact with the outside world and targeted health education have an impact. Diseases are brought under control by vaccines. Although there are never enough, never sufficiently effective health-care services, they have increased in number and variety. Infants and children have a better chance of survival. They, and adults, are now better protected against some ravaging diseases, although exposure to continued precarious living conditions and new health risks continues. More people have more choices in their search for help. Their life span increases. This, in turn, will bring forth a new set of challenges for health care and welfare concerns. Whether it can be concluded on the basis of statistics alone that all individuals are better off living longer is questionable.

Thus, a bottom line to such global and largely philosophical observations cannot overlook the potential for individuals to experience changes in their lives in ways that have a positive impact on their health. It is a familiar problem of defining a partially filled glass as half empty or half full. One

[29] M. Nichter, "Vaccinations in South Asia: False Expectations and Command Metaphors" (Unpublished manuscript, 1987).

[30] *Population Reports,* Population Information Program, The Johns Hopkins University, XIII, 4 (Special Topics Series, M. No. 8, 1985).

side of the argument points to the large numbers of individuals in Asian and Pacific countries whose health, given the state of existing knowledge, is inadequate and needs to be improved through preventive and interventive actions. For many individuals, the positive impact of developmental changes, of more concerted community activities, of more education and of protection from exploitation are still distant possibilities. Clearly, not all changes result in an overall improvement of health conditions and health care. Given ongoing changes, there is no agreement on how to identify those countries that have the best potential for providing needed healthcare support in the process of modernization.

If we let countries speak for themselves through reports to the WHO about their health status, we obtain some measures based on surveys and assessments. In the Western Pacific region 10 out of 19 countries (N = 26) claim that at least 80% of their populations have adequate sanitary facilities at or near their homes; in 23 countries at least 80% of the population has access to health care, including availability of at least 20 essential drugs; in 11 out of 24 countries at least 90% of infants receive care from trained personnel.[31] But we also learn that the quality of care is still a problem. A corresponding profile of conditions is available for the Southeast Asian region.[32] Here we may also read that neither number of basic health units nor hospitals gives any measure of the quality of care.

There is no clear pattern, though there are obvious relationships between economic and health measures. The push toward modernization seems to work to a greater advantage for some populations or segments of populations. It may put other segments at a greater disadvantage in terms of health status and health care. The PRC experiment in modernization is still too new to detect clear trends in health care, though remarkable improvements were noted by the visiting teams of professionals. The comparative quality-of-life assessments as products of systematic research that would be needed for a bottom-line answer comparing different health conditions simply do not exist. Conclusions drawn from health and social welfare statistics depend on different viewpoints.

Access to modern knowledge and technology, whether health promoting or health inhibiting, combined with an existing variety of services, need to be given as choices to everyone. Access also implies restraint and control. These humanitarian goals depend on availability and allocation of resources. The choices in resource developments and applications, in control measures, in the relative role of traditional and modern concepts and practices—all these lie with each country. Intersectoral action within countries is essential. The need for international collaboration remains.

FURTHER READING

Committee on Scholarly Communications with the Peoples' Republic of China. *Rural Health in the People's Republic of China.* National Institutes of Health Pub-

[31] World Health Organization, *Evaluation of the Strategy for Health for All by the Year 2000: Seventh Report on the World Health Situation,* vol. 7: *Western Pacific Region* (Geneva; 1987).
[32] Ibid., vol. 4: *Southeast Asia Region* (Geneva; 1986).

lication no. 81–2124. Washington, D.C.: U.S. Department of Health and Human Services, 1980.

Evaluation of the Strategy for Health for All by the Year 2000. Seventh Report on the World Health Situation. Volume 1. Geneva: World Health Organization, 1987.

Henderson, Gail E., and Cohen, Myron S. *The Chinese Hospital: A Socialist Work Unit.* New Haven, Connecticut: Yale University Press, 1984.

Kleinman, Arthur. *Social Origins of Distress and Disease: Depression, Neurasthenia, and Pain in Modern China.* New Haven, Connecticut: Yale University Press, 1986.

————, et al., eds. *Culture and Healing in Asian Societies: Anthropological, Psychiatric, and Public Health Studies.* Boston: G. K. Hall, 1978.

Leslie, Charles, ed. *Asian Medical Systems: A Comparative Study.* Berkeley: University of California Press, 1976.

Lock, Margaret M. *East Asian Medicine in Urban Japan: Varieties of Medical Experience.* Berkeley: University of California Press, 1980.

Marsella, Anthony J., and White, G. M., eds. *Cultural Conceptions of Mental Health and Therapy.* Dordrecht, Holland: D. Reidel, 1982.

Ohnuki-Tierney, Emiko. *Illness and Culture in Contemporary Japan: An Anthropological View.* Cambridge and New York: Cambridge University Press, 1984.

Parsons, Claire D. F., ed. *Health Practices in the South Pacific.* Laie, Hawaii: Institute for Polynesian Studies, 1985.

Sidel, Ruth, and Sidel, Victor W. *The Health of China.* Boston: Beacon Press, 1982.

Unschuld, Paul U. *Medicine in China. A History of Ideas.* Berkeley: University of California Press, 1985.

————. *Medicine in China. A History of Pharmaceutics.* Berkeley: University of California Press, 1986.

ASIAN NEWSPAPERS AND JOURNALISM

JOHN A. LENT

HISTORICAL OVERVIEW

The first printing presses, newsletters and newspapers of Asia originated, as in other parts of the world, in the official surroundings of royal courts, colonial governments and foreign missionary societies.

Scholar-officials of China gathered news for the royal court; in South Asia Muslim rulers for centuries incorporated a newsgathering system of writers in various provinces, who kept the court informed. In Korea, Burma (now Myanmar), India and Pakistan most of the early newsletters were under royal patronage.

Handwritten and block-printed newssheets appeared before the advent of printing from movable type. In Japan, block printing dominated from at least A.D. 764 until the late 16th century. It was considered the domain of Buddhist authorities, who printed religious books. This type of printing was also used to bring out *kawaraban shimbun,* popular in Japan in the 17th and 18th centuries. Used to provide information to the public, not the royal courts, the *kawaraban* gave prosaic reports of social events and disasters (e.g., double suicides).

Ironically, European colonialists and missionaries introduced printing from movable type to Asia, though China had developed the process about A.D. 900 and Korea in the 14th century. Catholic missionaries published in Macao, Japan, the Philippines, China and India in the 16th century; later, their Protestant counterparts from Europe and the United States introduced the first presses and/or periodicals in Burma, Thailand, Malaya, Singapore, Indonesia and parts of China.

In India, Portuguese Jesuits brought a printing press to Goa as early as 1556; a Spanish lay brother of the Jesuit order set up a press in Malabar 20 years later; and Father John de Faria developed a press in the extreme south in 1587. Other Portuguese Jesuits launched printing in Japan and Macao. Diogo de Mesquita acquired a printing press while on a visit to Europe, and started a Japanese-language printing house in Nagasaki in 1586. About the same time Japanese soldiers returning from an invasion of Korea brought back a press with types. Roman Catholic printers operated in Macao from the 16th century. The first Macanese newspaper, *A*

Abelha da China, perhaps the first Western-language paper on the China coast, was published by the superior of the Dominicans in the early 19th century.

Another country where Catholic missionaries introduced printing was the Philippines. In 1593 the Dominican-established press in Manila published *Doctrina Christiana,* which was also the first work to come off other missionary presses in Asia. By 1611 the Franciscans and Augustinians had shipped presses to the Philippines.

With varying degrees of success Catholic missionaries continued printing operations into the 20th century. In Japan they met with resistance; printing from movable type lasted only from 1586 to about 1650, when the missionaries were expelled and the Japanese reverted to block printing. On the other hand, they prospered in the Philippines, bringing out about 550 book titles from 1593 to the 19th century.

With respect to the second wave of missionary-printers, representing Protestant denominations, Dutch Reformed Church personnel unsuccessfully attempted an Indonesian printing operation in 1624. Efforts to establish a printing firm were renewed in 1659, and shortly thereafter a *tijdboek* appeared that seemed to simulate a newsletter. By the 1690s the Seminary Press was developed in Batavia, but it was only in 1743 that this became functional. In the early 19th century Baptist missionary William Carey and Sir Thomas Stamford Raffles, in separate actions, further developed Indonesian printing.

It is virtually impossible to give an account of early 19th-century missionary printing in China without mentioning activities in Hong Kong, Macao and Melaka. The difficulty occurs because of the mobility of some of those presses and their printers among whom the dominating figures, the missionaries Robert Morrison, William Milne, Walter H. Medhurst, Charles F. A. Gutzlaff and James Legge, had something to do with most of the early 19th-century, church-related printing and periodicals started in China and Southeast Asia.

Modern printing came to China with the arrival of an East India Company press, with printer, in 1814. Dictionaries, vocabularies and, after 1831, the *Canton Miscellany* were issued. A second press arrived in 1825, responsible for the printing of the *Canton Register,* China's first modern newspaper. Of missionary-operated periodicals, the most prestigious and longest-lived was *The Chinese Repository.* Edited by an American missionary, Elijah Coleman Bridgman, the *Repository* promised an unbiased treatment of events, although, occasionally, it propagandized about the degraded nature of China and thus its need for Christianity. One of the most notable missionary editors in China was Young I. Allen, the American who, in 47 years in the later 19th century, founded and/or edited a number of periodicals, including the *North China Daily News and Herald* and *Chiao-hui hsin-pao.*

From 1815 to 1846 the Straits Settlements of Melaka, Penang and Singapore, as well as Indonesia, were used by the London Missionary Society as locations for the printing of literature meant for China. Periodicals from these presses (Anglo-Chinese Press of Malacca, Penang Press, Mission Press of Singapore) were among the earliest in East and Southeast Asia: the *Chinese Monthly Magazine,* the *Malacca Observer and Chinese Chronicle,* and the *Singapore Chronicle,* the last that settlement's earliest newspaper.

American missionaries brought the first presses to Burma and Thailand in the 19th century, although the latter had some printing in 1622, as a result of the efforts of the French Catholic Mission. In 1816 the American Baptist Mission in Burma received a new press and font of "Burman types," with which the Rev. George H. Hough printed a few religious tracts. More prolific, however, was Cephas Bennet, who started a press at Moulmein, from which emanated the *Religious Herald.*

Nineteenth-century printing in Thailand was associated with the medical missionary Dan Beach Bradley. Besides maintaining a medical practice, treating over 70 patients daily, Bradley founded a book bindery, type foundry and the country's first newspaper, the *Bangkok Recorder*—the latter in 1844.

In South Asia Protestant missionaries from England, Denmark, Holland and the United States succeeded the Portuguese Jesuits as early printers. A press started in India, which influenced other press development in South and Southeast Asia, was the Baptist Mission Press; it was inaugurated at Mudnabatty, in 1798 and moved to Serampore two years later. Missionary William Carey was the developer of the Serampore press, and by 1818 he and his group published a Bengali monthly and a weekly, the first periodicals published in an Indian language. Presbyterian missionaries did the first printing in the Punjab (now Pakistan). A press was established at Ludhiana in 1835, on which, the following year, appeared a Persian-language newspaper, *Lodiana Akhbar.*

The same Dutch governor who encouraged printing in Indonesia, Gustaaf Willem Baron van Imhoff, begged the Dutch East India Company to provide a press for the Dutch missionaries in Sri Lanka; it arrived in 1736. When the British occupied Sri Lanka 60 years later the London Missionary Society and other groups set up more presses. By the mid-19th century many of these presses, and the missionaries, produced most of Sri Lanka's literary periodicals.

While European and American religious orders initiated some of the first printing presses of Asia, they usually did not start the continent's pioneering newspapers. Civil servants, and sometimes private printers, accomplished that. For example, the first newspaper of the Philippines, *Del Superior Gobierno,* was issued in 1811 by the governor-general to satisfy Spanish colonialists' desire for information about Europe.

The early newspapers in what is now Pakistan were meant to maintain liaison among British colonialists; but the first one, *Kurrachee Advertiser,* in 1845, was sponsored by Sir Charles Napier to counter propaganda directed at him by British newspapers on the subcontinent.

It should not be surprising that Malaysia's first newspaper, the *Government Gazette* of Penang, was in English, although only 100 European merchants, planters and government personnel lived there. Like most colonial periodicals everywhere, the *Gazette* served as a house organ for the foreigners, advertising their wares, printing government notices and keeping them informed about England. Although printed at the Mission Press, the *Sin-*

gapore Chronicle was completely controlled by local authorities as an "exclusively commercial" newspaper.

In Sri Lanka, no record of a newspaper exists before the arrival of the British. Within three months after the island became a crown colony, the *Government Gazette* was founded, followed by the *Colombo Journal* in 1832. The latter had the encouragement of the governor. On the other hand, there was no official patronage behind the publication of India's first newspaper, *The Bengal Gazette or Calcutta General Advertiser,* which came out in 1780. James Augustus Hicky established the *Gazette* as a scandal sheet to strike out at members of the East India Company, the governor-general, and his staff.

The pioneer newspaper in Indonesia was *Bataviasche Nouvelles en Politique Raisonnementen,* published in 1744 under the sponsorship of Governor-General van Imhoff. It was short-lived because Dutch authorities in Holland would not sanction the paper. Over a century later, in 1861, another Dutch-language paper from Batavia (*Javasche Courant*) was the inspiration for Japan's first newspaper, *Batavia Shimbun.* Earlier, the Yosho Shirabe Jo (Institute for the Study of Foreign Books) hired copyists to record news translated from foreign newspapers; this news was printed in *Batavia Shimbun.*

Throughout the 19th century newspapers in non-Western languages appeared in Asia. Some of these later played an active role in nationalism and independence movements. In Hong Kong, newspapers published by Wang Tao were meant exclusively for non-Western audiences; his most important publication was *Tsun Wan Yat.* The Philippines had its first Tagalog paper in 1862, although it actually was bilingual. The honor of being the first daily in Tagalog alone belongs to *Diariong Tagalog,* published in the 1880s.

The first non-Dutch newspaper of Indonesia, *Bramatani,* appeared in 1855. It used Javanese, the language popular in the Indonesian press until the end of the 19th century, when newspapers began carrying Malay supplements. In Thailand Dr. Bradley brought out a Thai-language newspaper, as did King Mongkut—both about mid-19th century; while in Pakistan, *Koh-i-Noor* used Urdu as early as 1850.

Revolutionary, nationalist or independence movements took up much of the time and energy of Asians at the beginning of the 20th century and in succeeding decades. This was especially true in China, the Philippines, Burma, Indonesia, Korea, Singapore and Malaysia. In Sri Lanka, India, Pakistan and Vietnam, the revolutionary fervor was more acute between the world wars.

The press played an active role in many of these campaigns. During the last days of the Manchu dynasty, Chinese scholar-reformers such as Kang Yu-Wei and Liang Chi-Chao published newspapers in Shanghai and Beijing advocating political change. China's political problems were also important in Singapore and Malaysia, where a revolutionary press was on the scene by at least 1904, when Teo Eng Hock and Tan Chor Lam brought out *Thoe Lam Jit Poh.* Teo and Tan believed revolution was the only way to change China. In Malaya *Al Imam*'s appearance in 1906 changed the role of newspapers, pushing for religious and social reforms. In the 1920s and 1930s the Malay-language newspapers gradually moved out of Singapore, communicating a sense of the Malay consciousness on the peninsula.

Philippine journalists' roles in that nation's revolution are legendary. Many of the national heroes were journalists who helped lead the country from under Spanish rule in the 1890s. Jose Rizal, Marcelo del Pilar and Graciano Lopez-Jaena, who wrote for *La Solidaridad,* were chief among them. After the United States occupied the islands, other journalists and their periodicals campaigned against this intrusion.

In Korea So Jae-pil started the *Independent (Tongnip Sinmun)* in the 1890s as a nationalistic voice. As Korea's first newspaper, the *Independent* advocated an end to foreign dependence, protection of national sovereignty, elimination of class distinctions and expansion of civil rights. Another long-time advocate of Korean culture and independence was *Dong-a Ilbo,* which angered the occupying Japanese forces by reporting on proindependence rallies throughout Korea.

D. R. Wijewardene and his *Ceylon Daily News* were credited with sparking Sri Lanka's nationalist movement in the 1920s and 1930s. The *Daily News* promoted the aims of the Ceylon National Association and Ceylon Reform League, nationalistic groups founded by Wijewardene. Elsewhere in the subcontinent, nationalists such as Mohandas K. Gandhi, B. G. Horniman and Annie Besant used journalism to advocate a break with Great Britain. Muslim newspapers of the region have been credited with aiding the formation of a separate Muslim nation of Pakistan. During the early 20th century *Zamindar* performed this task and was accordingly punished, being required to deposit large sums of money with the government regularly as security.

Also in the late 19th and early 20th centuries, many Asian newspapers took on commercial aspects that aided big business, a characteristic of a large segment of the contemporary press. Nowhere was commercialism more pronounced than in Japan where by the 1890s there was a heightened capitalist aspect of the newspaper industry. Between 1895 and 1905 Japanese newspapers improved their facilities, bolstered sales and advertising, strengthened their organizations, sped up news reporting and developed a direct delivery system. As newspapers grew they became more dependent upon their investors and advertisers; in many cases business, circulation and advertising managers had more clout than editorial personnel.

Simultaneously, the Chinese-language press of China and Southeast Asia became profit-motivated, as did increasing numbers of Philippine, Indian and Sri Lankan newspapers. The result, in a few countries—especially Japan, the Philippines, India, Hong Kong and Sri Lanka—was a trend toward concentration of ownership. In the Philippines, Alejandro Roces, Sr., started the TVT media group of three dailies in the 1920s; it competed with the three dailies of the DHM group until World War II.

In the 1930s and 1940s the press, as did other institutions in nations occupied by Japan, suffered from Japanese military expansionism. Newspapers were closed and editors were interned or expelled. The Japanese usually kept in place a few newspapers in various languages, which were overseen by censors and were expected to propagate Japanese causes.

By 1941 most Chinese newspapers—of Hong Kong and Shanghai, for example—had already been closed by the Japanese, while some became mobile units, either following or receding from the front line. In Korea, occupied by the Japanese since 1910, an all-out effort was made in the 1930s to destroy the language, alphabet and press agencies of the country. By 1941 most newspapers were ordered to suspend, leaving Korea without an independent, Korean-language paper.

The Japanese were no less systematic at home. By 1937 most Japanese newspapers were forced or threatened into silence. As the war intensified Japanese authorities reduced the number of pages in dailies, and later, the number of newspapers: from 1,200 in 1937 to 52 in 1942. Various laws were enacted to restrict the press, and Domei News Agency acted as a contral mechanism.

After World War II there was a burgeoning of newspapers throughout Asia, as well as new press organizations and personnel. In Japan the press was completely changed—purged of militaristic and Communist elements, and guided by policies of the occupying supreme commander for Allied powers. At times, the post-war years were strenuous for the press. In Hong Kong newspapers were used in China's civil war, some taking sides with Mao, others with Chiang; in numerous other cases the press reacted to the difficult stages of the independence of their respective countries.

Sometimes newly independent states practiced authoritarianism nearly as severe as that of the colonialists and Japanese military. For example, Korean newspapers were restrained by the Rhee government until the April 1960 uprising, which left journalists in a privileged position. However, once the military took over in 1961, and especially after Park Chung Hee became president two years later, the press suffered harsh treatment. After 1949, when the Chinese Nationalist government evacuated to Taiwan, a new press era was started, and stifling legislation was enacted, modified only in 1987.

Laotian, Cambodian and Vietnamese newspapers experienced terrible government relationships because of colonialism, the Japanese occupation and continual civil strife, all of which did away with the principles of freedom of expression. Until 1988 Burma was a closed society, with a very subjugated press, which had been nationalized 20 years earlier.

CONTEMPORARY PERSPECTIVE

One of the big changes in Asian journalism in the 1980s was the transformation of the Chinese press from planned and controlled ideological and developmental aims to a marketing orientation that included sensational tabloids, use of advertising and increasing dependence upon outside forces.

Quantitatively, in less than a decade up to 1985, the number of dailies in China tripled to 661, with a combined circulation of 116.9 million. Altogether, there were 1,632 newspapers by the mid-1980s. Of greater importance, changes in policy and guidelines were made after 1980. Before that the press, organized around Marxist-Leninist-Maoist ideology, was a tool of the class struggle; in the 1980s it was designed to build spiritual and materialistic values in line with the state's modernization program.

Party dailies are still the main force of China, but other types of newspapers are available. Among these are organizational, professional, and university papers, as well as special-interest ones devoted to economics, science, business, advertising and law. Evening newspapers, many of which are tabloids, have prospered, carrying gossip and news of movies, fashion, dating, sex and crime. Sensationalism also plays a role in other newspapers.

Despite liberalization, press policies are formed by party executives, as they always were. In 1985 Party General Secretary Hu Yaobang said the press must retain its propaganda objective and provide veracity (by using 80 percent of the space for good news and 20 percent for criticism of seamy aspects of society). At the same time, newspapers should be timely instructive and interesting. Although tabloids offered an alternative to staid party and state newspapers of the Cultural Revolution, some basic premises on what makes news remained. For example, news values in China are based on how an event embodies the party line and whether it promotes modernizations; the role the event plays in the political and social progress of China; how it expresses public opinion and its effects upon social order, family life and morality; and how it helps people gain new culture.

Economics of the press
Another change in a large portion of Asia's daily press is its tendency toward big business orientation. In Japan, where *Asahi Shimbun* and *Yomiuri Shimbun* each top 12 million to 13 million in circulation, and a few other dailies also circulate in the millions, concentration of ownership has been prevalent for years.

This concentration and other big business practices have increasingly affected the press of other countries. Combines of government and of local business, and regional and multinational conglomerates have bought up parts of the press in Hong Kong, Taiwan, South Korea, Indonesia, the Philippines, Malaysia, Singapore and India.

In the mid-1980s the Australian media tycoon Rupert Murdoch bought Hong Kong's highly profitable *South China Morning Post* to add to his 80-plus publications and television operations scattered around the world. Previously the *Post* was owned by Hong Kong conglomerates, such as a bank, a diversified trading company and an airline, as well as Dow Jones, which had 22 percent of the shares. The *South China Morning Post* has a stable of properties, including the daily *Post, Sunday Post Herald,* 51 percent of the *Far Eastern Economic Review,* a third interest in a regional Sunday supplement *(Asia Magazine), Television and Entertainment Times, Asian Golf Digest* and *Welcome.* The group has links with the *Straits Times,* a Singapore conglomerate, and with the *Asian Wall Street Journal.*

Another large Hong Kong newspaper group is Sing Tao, founded by Aw Boon Haw. Among Sing Tao properties are *Sing Tao Jih Pao, Sing Tao Man Po,* Pacific Communications, Ltd., *Jetwind, Hong Kong Star,* a travel agency, *Hong Kong Standard,* editions of *Sing Tao* in eight major cities of the world, and a daily in Fiji.

In Taiwan, *United Daily News,* with a circulation of over 600,000, publishes four other newspapers and owns China Economic News Service and Lieking Publishing, one of the largest newspaper enterprises in Taiwan. Similarly South Korean media have become big business, with groups, cross-media ownership and conglomerate connections prominent. *Joong-Ang Ilbo,* with a circulation of over 600,000, owns a weekly, two student journals, one general audience monthly, a woman's magazine, an AM/FM radio station and a television channel. *Joong-Ang Ilbo* is part of Sansung Group, one of the largest corporations in South Korea. Other Korean newspapers are heavily involved in commercial dealings. *Hankook Ilbo* publishes *Daily Sports,* and runs a travel agency and a construction company; *Chosun Ilbo* owns a Seoul hotel; and the government-controlled *Seoul Shimbun* owns the daily *Sports Seoul.* Korea's six national dailies also own about 70 percent of all magazines in the country.

By the late 1970s commercial media conglomerates, such as *Sinar Harapan* and *Kompas,* began to dominate parts of Indonesia's press; later, in 1988, when commercial television was introduced to the country, Bimantara, the fastest growing Indonesian conglomerate, was responsible. Bimantara is involved with holding and investment companies, communications, electronics, transport and related services, insurance, leasing, petroleum, plastics, agriculture, forestry and manufacturing. Indonesian newspapers have been characterized as belonging to the "world of big business," most small regional newspapers being regarded as "small fry, which will eventually be gobbled up by the big fish of Jakarta and the other metropolitan countries." These large conglomerates had the "right connections" with military and civilian administrators.[1]

Philippine newspapers, for generations, have been tied to oligarchies. Before martial law in 1972, families involved in landownership, sugar, pharmaceuticals, utilities or beer, among other businesses, maintained print/broadcasting combines as political and business weapons. President Marcos closed the old media empires and developed new ones that for the last 13 years of his reign were headed by his cronies, who were also involved with shipping, telecommunications, electronics, the coconut industry and many other concerns.

After the revolution in February 1986, another set of newspapers appeared, a number of which were tied to big business. In fact, some of the entrepreneurial families of old returned to newspaper publishing. The Constitutional Commission of 1986–87 made efforts to limit ownership, and in 1988 a bill was filed in the Senate banning monopolization of broadcast media and calling for Philippine media ownership.

Diversification of press ownership suffered severely in Malaysia and Singapore during the 1980s, as both states further tightened ownership, management and control of mass media. Long-established, family-operated newspapers were replaced with new dailies in Singapore, and corporate control of newspaper groups was put in the hands of those close to government in both countries.

The three largest newspaper groups of Malaysia—New Straits Times, Star Publications and Utusan Melayu—have numerous other holdings and

---

[1] Andrew Goenawan, "The Indonesian Press, Indonesian Journalism and Guided Democracy," in *The Indonesian Press. Its Past, Its People, Its Problems,* Paul Tickell et al., eds. (Clayton, Australia: Monash University, 1987).

are closely tied to two political components of the ruling Barisan Nasional (United Malays National Organization and Malaysian Chinese Association). New Straits Times, owners of 70 percent of Sistem Televisyen Malaysia (the only commercial television channel), five dailies, many magazines, book publishing firms, a food products company and a major hotel chain, is a subsidiary of Fleet Holdings (a United Malays National Organization firm) and its investment arm, Fleet Group. Both had been chaired by Finance Minister Daim Zainuddin. Fleet, formed to wrest control of print media from the Chinese and foreigners, is made up of over 150 companies in areas such as investment, hotels, realty, telecommunications, trading, land development, motion pictures, shipping, recreational services, drilling, travel, car rental, construction, electronics, restaurants, credit companies, newsprint, insurance, banking, leasing, and computers—among others. In late 1987 Fleet and New Straits Times were accused of corruption, having contravened part of the Malaysian Companies Act.

Star Publications, publishers of the *Star, Tong Bao* and some magazines, was purchased in 1977 by Hauren Holdings, an investment subsidiary of the Malaysian Chinese Association.

A restructure of Singapore's press in 1982–83 was sweeping, encompassing the folding of three dailies and the establishment of a new company of three newspapers. After much manipulation, and the merging of Straits Times, Times Publications, and Singapore News and Publications, a new company, Singapore Press Holdings (SPH), was formed. It dominated the entire press scene, becoming the premier, publicly quoted, industrial company, with capitalization of about three-quarters of a billion dollars. SPH has ownership connections with large foreign companies, including Dow Jones of the United States, and Matra, the largest armaments company of France. The firm owns 10 percent of Dow's *Asian Wall Street Journal;* Dow, in turn, has shares in Straits Times and Times Business Publications, both part of SPH. Besides dominating the newspaper and publishing industries of Singapore, SPH has owned parts of newspapers in Thailand, Brunei, Malaysia and Hong Kong; large publishing companies in France, England, New Zealand and Australia; and newspaper dealerships in Tahiti and New Caledonia.

South Asia has had press and big business affiliations over the years. Indian groups of newspapers are owned by large conglomerates such as Tata and Birla; until government interference in the 1970s, 95 percent of Sri Lanka's press was controlled by three large concerns.

Japanese newspapers definitely are big business oriented, and for years, have been characterized by concentration and monopolization. The top five dailies—the national *Asahi, Mainichi, Yomiuri* and *Nihon Keizai Shimbun,* and the quasi-national *Chunichi*—account for about 60 percent of the total national circulation, have printing plants in numerous places and publish hundreds of regional editions daily. They have many media holdings in addition to their dailies and are involved in other businesses. *Asahi,* for example, publishes an English-language daily, three weeklies, three monthlies and 10 yearbooks, and maintains interests in 60 other enterprises, including radio-television stations, travel agencies and real estate firms.

Japanese press concentration has had the effect of denying outsiders entry into the newspaper business, at the same time piling up holdings by a few individuals or corporations. Newspapers often limit shareholding to members of their own organizations. In 1976, 17 dailies had 100 percent internal ownership; 24 others had 50 percent; and 28 had less than 50 percent. Since 1987 a few foreign concerns have collaborated with Japanese dailies; Dow Jones of the United States started printing and publishing the *Asian Wall Street Journal* in Japan in conjunction with *Nihon Keizai Shimbun;* and the *International Herald Tribune* of Paris commenced an edition there with the help of Mainichi Newspapers.

As Asian big business is concentrated in the major urban area or capital city of a country, so are daily newspapers. It is not rare to find outlying cities of a half-million or more people without dailies, while the major city is media-rich. After 1986 Manila published about 24 dailies regularly, while few existed in provincial cities—where 86 percent of the papers were weeklies, most with circulations between 1,000 and 2,000. Other cities are saturated with newspapers, making Asia unique in the world in the number of cities with 10 or more dailies.

For example, Hong Kong, with anywhere from 80 to 130 newspapers at any given time, has the highest density of newspapers per population in the world. Its bewildering array of newspapers includes horse and dog racing tip sheets, sex-oriented advertising sheets, daily editions of movie magazines, dailies used as weapons by their conglomerate owners, as well as others representing nearly every political hue.

At the beginning of the 1980s Taipei accounted for 16 of Taiwan's 31 dailies and about 80 percent of the aggregate circulation of all newspapers in the country. The 24 dailies of Malaysia are concentrated in Kuala Lumpur, with Penang as a secondary publishing city; and Jakarta and Bangkok each has between 15 and 20 dailies. Singapore has seven dailies. Similarly high concentrations exist in the major cities of India, Pakistan, South Korea, Japan and Sri Lanka. In Tokyo 24 dailies exist, 10 of which have multicity editions. At least another 100 newspapers are published in Japan, and altogether, they circulate 70.3 million copies daily, probably more than the total for all other daily newspapers of Asia.

Concentration of dailies in a few cities results in cutthroat competition, often detrimental to economic and professional growth. In many Asian countries dailies continue to edge, or keep even with, broadcasting in the rivalry for advertising. However, the large number of dailies means that each has a smaller slice of the aggregate revenue, and electronic media have rather quickly advanced in domination of national advertising budgets.

With diminishing proportions of advertising revenues, Asian newspapers have resorted to a number of strategies, not all of which are good for the profession. Some have woven themselves into the cozy cocoons of conglomerates, while others, especially in the Philippines and Hong Kong, have become more sensational, depending upon sleaze, gossip and innuendo to capture readership.

Hong Kong in the mid-1970s provides a case study of the consequences that occur when an abundance of dailies coincides with increased costs and lowered advertising moneys. In 1972–74 about 75 dailies closed, although some were replaced shortly after by new titles. Those that survived reduced the number of pages (e.g., the *Standard*), sought additional capital investment (e.g., the *South China Morning Post*), increased the price of newspapers (in 1981, 60 papers again raised the price, this time by 60 percent), or replaced senior staff with lower-paid young reporters. Low wages of editorial staff sometimes led to unprofessional behavior such as "palm greasing." (Similar complaints of reporters committing extortion, bribery and other ethical breaches are heard regularly throughout Asia. In the Philippines it has become known as "envelopmental journalism," with reference to reporters and editors who accept envelopes that contain bribes.)

Larger newspapers in many countries ride out the occasional periods of recession by transforming themselves into integrated information industries. Japanese newspapers and news agencies provide services that make information available to the public through personal computer networks, videotext, teletext and other new technology. News services, and some newspapers, elsewhere in Asia have undertaken similar ventures.

In the 1980s Bernama, Malaysia's news agency, set up many revenue-seeking branches that dispensed information. Among these were a public relations wire service, channeling news releases directly to media; a library and information service; an economic information service; a foreign news service; an Association of Southeast Asian Nations (ASEAN) file; a Japan service; and a package service of information of special interest. Bernama's Newscan, tailored for public places, hotels and offices, translates news and information over the television screen, including local and international news, tourist information and flight schedules. In 1987 Bernama set up Livecom, a database to provide packaged business information. It consists of Liveshares, providing information on the Kuala Lumpur stock exchange; Livebases, giving historical information on every public listed company; and Livecharts, charting data on listed companies. Additionally, Malaysia's New Straits Times Group of newspapers has a teletext service linked to the private television channel.

The Press Trust of India (PTI), a news service, linked with Reuter in 1987 to gain access to the Reuter Monitor. The latter service links 10,000 banks and other institutions in a worldwide network of data banks. PTI's Stockscan connects India's five major stock exchanges, displaying shares prices at each as they are traded; its Comscan provides tabulated information on the Indian and world markets; and its Newsscan relays the latest PTI news to hotels and airport lounges.

The press of Asia definitely has been smitten by the lures of new information technology. Japan has led in this area, having successfully computerized newsrooms in the early 1960s, and having earlier launched newspaper facsimile networks between Tokyo and Hokkaido. In the 1980s Singapore set as one of its national goals becoming the information technology center of Asia. Other countries followed the 1980s rush to new information technology. Remote places such as Bhutan used desktop publishing to bring out the national newspaper; the New China News Agency upgraded links between its Beijing headquarters and Hong Kong office via voice digitizers,

Singapore updated its newspaper offices with video display terminals; Japanese publishers replaced printed magazines with videocassette versions.

Such rapid technological advances have had undesired consequences. For one thing, much dialogue previously expended on the development of journalism, reportorial techniques or ethics, and freedom of expression, has shifted to discussion about information hardware—the best piece of equipment and its costs and capabilities. In some instances, heavy investment in new information technology has created a further drain on the economic base of newspapers and news services, often resulting in negative impacts upon news gathering. As an example, Malaysia's Bernama, which moved quickly and fully into new technology, faced financial difficulties by 1987 when it fell far behind in payments to foreign news services whose copy it distributes in Malaysia. Within a few months Bernama tried to recoup losses by radically pruning its network of overseas reporters.

Even with these shortcomings, economic gains in the production of Asian newspapers still outweigh those of consumption. Production capabilities have been enhanced by large city newspapers adopting modern printing equipment and tying in with new information societies, and by newsprint being somewhat more available as governments have helped in its manufacture. Thus, at least for a few capital city dailies in certain countries, press revenues have increased. The same cannot be said about progress made in the consumption of newspapers. Although overall, newspaper circulation shot up tremendously in most countries, so did population and newspaper prices, so that in most countries newspapers are still out of the reach of the masses.

Press-government relationships
During long stretches of colonial rule Asian newspapers seldom were their own masters, nor are the majority in the 1980s. The enormous increase in press ownership by businesses and local governments, prevailing "guided press" principles, newly enacted or amended press legislation, and instances of suspensions, arrests and other harassment, have lessened the chances of newspapers performing investigative functions.

The high costs of establishing and maintaining newspapers require that ownership be limited to those who have economic (and political) power. The close alliances between press barons and business, industrial, political and military powers mean a uniformity of ideas, continual press support of these power brokers and the status quo, as well as benefits such as lucrative government advertising, newsprint and foreign exchange allocations, access to officials and in some cases, enactment of legislation favorable to big business journalism.

Besides the big business connections already alluded to, government or ruling political party ownership and control prevail among much of the Asian press. Newspapers in the socialist states, such as China, North Korea, Mongolia, Afghanistan, Vietnam, Laos, Cambodia, and Burma are, or have been, state or party owned.

To lesser degrees, but threatening nevertheless, newspapers of other countries are owned or closely tied to government. Throughout South Asia, print media have had political party or government ownership over the years. The National Press Trust of Pakistan has owned from four to eight metropolitan dailies with many editions, and in Sri Lanka the Bandaranaike government of the 1970s passed a law providing the government 75 percent of the Lake House Group of newspapers. Also, a group of financiers, headed by the prime minister's son and including her nephew, bought controlling interest in a second group, Times of Ceylon. When a new government came into power in 1977, Lake House was placed under government control. The Gorkhapatra Sansthan, a government-owned corporation, owns newspapers in Nepal, but in 1983 the Bangladeshi authorities sold their seven periodicals—four dailies and three magazines—because some of them lost money.

The Taiwanese government purchased the outspoken *Taiwan Daily News* in 1978, thus significantly softening its tone; and Singaporean and Malaysian laws enacted in the 1970s gave authorities the power to own newspapers in those countries.

Government ownership of the press is a more subtle, and less noisy, form of control than closing newspapers or arresting journalists. So are misuse of development communication and the "guidance" offered the press by officials. Throughout Asia the press has been repeatedly instructed on the proper role it must play, especially that of being supportive of government goals. Asian authorities regularly stress that their societies are newly emergent, needing time to develop, during which period stability and unity must be sought, criticism minimized and public faith in government policies encouraged. This is especially evident in Southeast Asian countries. The press and other media are implored to cooperate by stressing positive, development-inspired news, by ignoring negative or oppositionist characteristics, and by supporting governmental ideologies and plans. In many cases the guided press idea is misused to perpetuate power concentrations, to initiate programs solely beneficial to domestic and foreign elites, or to develop and sustain cults of personality.

Some countries have national ideologies that officials rely upon to guide the press. Indonesia's *Pancasila* makes editors think twice before writing about issues such as the role of Islam, communism, upper-level corruption, the Chinese minority or political detainees. Editors realize they should never "MISS," meaning:

Menghasut—provoke agitation;
Insinuasi—report any insinuation;
SARA—spread racial or religious hatred;
Sensasi—report any sensation.

Guiding press control in Malaysia is the *Rukunegara,* which promotes belief in God, loyalty to king and country and upholding the constitution, the rules of law, good behavior and morality. In Nepal the *Panchayat* policy has a controlling impact upon the press; the policy promotes democratization and indigenization, among other concepts.

Additionally, different interpretations and styles of news have deleterious effects upon the free and responsible press in Asia. Objective reporting, an elusive goal anywhere, is even more problematic in many parts of Asia where journalists' relationships with government officials are cozier, the government participates more actively in press operations, and the repercussions for not favoring the authorities are more severe. Newspapers stay in line by practicing self censorship, while governments tend to keep journalists off stride—ignoring some sensational or negative news and clamping down on the reporting of others. The resultant self-restraint on the part of journalists is considered the worst type of censorship because of its subtlety and insidiousness.

Even in Japan, where laws restricting the press have been eliminated, self-regulatory customs of publishers and journalists, as well as consensus reporting, have been hindrances. "Institutional inhibitions" abound that do not permit criticism of the royal family or exposure of intimate relationships between right-wing gangsters and politicians.

Other subtle controls permeate government-press relationships. In most Asian countries government press offices have been expanded, enabling them to crank out even more handouts, to monitor the press and to guide editors in supporting the government.

Development communication, an expansion of development journalism conceived in the 1960s by Asian journalists, has also been used by authorities in pushing their ideologies and campaigns. Originally, development journalism was a means of covering a nation's development story in a simple style that had relevance, meaning and worth for the average citizen. By the 1970s it was bastardized to mean commitment to government, or "government-say-so-journalism."

Although on the wane, comparatively, overt press controls persist, often complementing more covert forms. New press laws or radical changes in old ones were ratified in the 1970s and 1980s and used for backup. Among these were regulations that licensed print media, prevalent in Taiwan, South Korea, Malaysia, Singapore, Indonesia, Bangladesh, Pakistan and the Philippines during the Marcos years; regulations that gave authorities the right to censor or close newspapers indiscriminately, at least in Thailand, Nepal, South and North Korea, Pakistan, Taiwan, Sri Lanka and Bangladesh; regulations that denied access to information by declaring it officially secret, as in Nepal, Malaysia and Pakistan; and regulations that allowed manipulation of libel and sedition to favor administrations, as in Singapore and Pakistan. In 1988 the Indian government was forced to withdraw a defamation bill meant to stop press disclosures of rampant corruption in government.

Arrests, suspensions and other harassment still exist in most parts of Asia. Individual journalists are arrested for what they write; in countries such as Malaysia and Singapore they are detained a minimum of 60 days, without being charged or arrested. Some journalists in those countries have served very long jail terms, and have been released when they confessed, on television, to subversion or similar charges. In the Philippines, during the last days of Marcos, many journalists were killed or simply "disappeared."

At various times in the past generation whole parts of newspaper operations were shut down in gigantic swoops: in Indonesia in 1965, when all Chinese dailies were closed; in Singapore in 1971; Philippines, 1972; Thailand, 1976; Malaysia, 1987; and China and South Korea in the 1980s.

Press freedom is an up and down affair in most parts of Asia, dependent upon each change of government and fluctuating internal situations. For example, newspapers in South Korea, Taiwan, China and the Philippines experienced better times at the close of the 1980s than they had in decades, while the press of India, normally least affected by government interventions, fought desperate battles.

After the ascendancy of a new president of South Korea in 1988, press controls were lifted, allowing the establishment of new publications. One that epitomized the liberalization was *Hangyoreh Shinun* (One Nation), which amassed its start-up capital of 3.7 million through a nation-wide canvas that brought in contributions from 20,000 people. Korea's Bureau of Information Policy, the censoring body, was abolished. After Taiwan's press laws were loosened in 1987–88 the first opposition newspaper in the nearly 40-year history of the nation was tolerated. China, in 1988, discussed a new press law that called for private ownership of newspapers, reporting of open meetings, right-of-reply to false news accounts and the creation of a press council, one-third of whose members would be journalists.

Cultural aspects of the press
Because of migration patterns, colonial experiences and the way cultures were split to form political units, most Asian countries are blends of various ethnic and linguistic groupings. In recent years—postindependence periods for a number of countries—there have been efforts to carve a national identity and unity out of these mixtures, at the same time abandoning (or at least minimizing) the influences of outside cultural factors. The press and other mass media have played various roles in these campaigns.

First, the press has been utilized to promote ideologies and campaigns built around national identity and consciousness. In many parts of Asia ministers and other officials go to the lectern regularly to implore the press to take up national campaigns, oftentimes, to preserve the local culture or to use and promote a national language. The press has done its part by carrying speeches or articles on the issues, by spearheading the campaigns, and by organizing national and regional press groups to discuss and recommend policies.

In Southeast Asia a Consultation on Press Systems in ASEAN was organized in 1988 to work on a press philosophy based on an understanding of "man in his cultural concept, rooted in his understanding of community, authority, and religion or spiritual belief." The delegates recommended that press and governments "always recognize the cultural context within which ASEAN societies develop, with a view of utilizing the cultures both as background for understanding, and as base for change." ASEAN presses were urged to support nation-building activities and be partners in national development, help mold a national identity, promote social harmony, and exercise "self-restraint and good sense" in reporting on issues bearing on racial, ethnic and religious matters.

1661

Many government officials and journalistic groups maintain that the pluralistic societies that make up Asia require a high degree of sensitivity among journalists. In some cases legislation has been passed to insure that the press does not promote ill will and hostility between the races and classes; in other instances the authorities remind journalists to be cautious in reporting sensitive issues, and journalists set their standards accordingly. For example, Southeast Asian editors and reporters devised the Davao Code in the early 1970s as a guide to reporting on sensitive ethnic issues.

Second, the press in many Asian countries uses or otherwise copes with, a multiplicity of languages. Obviously, a one-language press cannot reach the entire population of India, which has hundreds of languages, or the entire populations of the Philippines, Malaysia, Singapore, China, Pakistan, Sri Lanka and Hong Kong, all of which are multilingual. Traditionally some countries substituted English or Chinese for a national language, and the press was produced in those languages, but since independence that situation has changed.

Usually for political and nationalist reasons (the striving for national unity and identity), the press has been instructed or guided toward favoring one language over others. Indonesian prevails in that country's press, although tens of millions of readers know Javanese and Sundanese; and Malaysia's dominant language of the press is becoming Bahasa Malaysia, even though almost one-half of the population has Chinese or Tamil as original languages. English, Chinese and Tamil dailies survive in Malaysia, but their structures and functions have been drastically altered by the national language policy. In Singapore the press uses English, Chinese, Bahasa Malaysia and Tamil in a rather confusing language melange; Bahasa Malaysia is the national language even though it is ceremonial and English is the major language of the press, law, education and international trade, but over three-fourths of the people are Chinese, many of whom prefer one of the Chinese dialects. In 1979 Prime Minister Lee Kuan Yew decided the multidialect Chinese should use Mandarin to encourage linguistic unity.

The press of Thailand uses the Thai, Chinese and English languages, and on a few occasions favoritism in issuing printing permits was shown to Thai-language publishers. Philippine dailies usually are in English, with a few tabloids in Pilipino. More dailies were expected to publish in Pilipino after it was redeclared the national language in 1988. Indian has attempted to deal with language diversity by having a national daily in each of 14 major languages, although most large-circulation papers are still in English; while Pakistani newspapers use Urdu and English in the major cities and other languages to suit regional needs.

At times when authorities launch unified language campaigns, the press is used for promotional and instructional purposes. In the 1979 "Speak Mandarin" movement of Singapore, newspapers carried articles, speeches and editorials supporting the one Chinese-language policy. Similarly, in Malaysia in the 1970s and 1980s, newspapers wrote favorably about the use of Bahasa Malaysia and helped the public learn the language with daily lessons. Malaysia's "Love Our Language" movement resurfaced in 1987–88, at which time the newspapers gave it large amounts of space.

Third, Asian newspapers have attempted to control outside influences on their communication channels and to create a press climate that better reflects their cultures. In the 1970s and 1980s policies were set in motion to bar foreign ownership of the press, to replace foreign-made features with indigenous content and to establish binational or regional news and feature exchanges. Most Asian governments have relatively new legislation that requires local ownership of the press, but some of these laws have holes through which multinational conglomerates and others infiltrate. Important changes have been made in use of indigenous content, and Asian newspapers generally use more local comic strips (about one-half of the total in Philippine dailies), political cartoons, columns and other features than just a few years ago. Much of the boilerplate copy that used to be brought unchanged from England and the United States, and dumped into some Asian dailies, has all but disappeared.

National, binational and regional organizations such as the Confederation of ASEAN Journalists, Japan's Nihon Shimbun Kyokai or the Press Institute of India, among others, have included indigenization and professionalization of the press in their agendas. More ad hoc in nature were the Press Bulletin Service, launched in 1980 by Indonesia, Malaysia and the Philippines to promote news exchange; the earlier mentioned Consultation on Press Systems in ASEAN; or the 1979 arrangement worked out by the national news agencies of Malaysia, Thailand, the Philippines and Indonesia to increase cooperation in editorial staff exchanges, research and assistance to overseas staff members.

Certainly, Asian newspapers do not contain the high levels of foreign content that plague television. Nevertheless, outside influences linger, especially with English-language dailies, but also with the press in other languages. Some of the contents and the general looks of certain Asian newspapers retain the flavor of metropolitan country counterparts, and publishers and editors often have mind-sets akin to those of Western journalists when it comes to news judgment and selection. Also, many of the products the newspapers advertise create artificial needs for products of multinational corporations, and push Western notions of cleanliness, comfort, morality or beauty.

Fourth, the Asian press has made concerted attempts to control news and information, maintain fair flows of news in and out of their countries, and obliterate heavy dependence on foreign news services. The problem of news flow is not new to Asia. In the 1960s and even earlier editors met to consider the establishment of an Asian news agency. Their complaint was that the international agencies, especially the big four (Associated Press, United Press International, Reuters and Agence France Press), filtered Asian news through the biases of their home offices and their correspondents. Later, Asian journalists claimed that dependence on international news services made them "passive recipients" of world and their own national news.

In fact, Asia played a very pivotal role in the news flow controversy that raged during the 1970s. In 1975 a regional documentation and training center for media, based in Singapore, sponsored a conference on information imbalance in Asia; and one year later the Non-Aligned Countries

Movement set up a news pool of its members after a New Delhi meeting, where Indian Prime Minister Indira Gandhi said it was time for Africans to report upon Africa, Indians upon India.

Research studies in the late 1970s and early 1980s lent support to the proposal for a regional and/or continental news service. Two American scholars, Wilbur Schramm and Erwin Atwood, found that 90 percent of all identifiable sources for news stories in 18 Asian dailies emanated from the four large international agencies. A later study of the press of South Asia (including Burma, India, Nepal, Sri Lanka, Pakistan and Bangladesh) showed that the international news services were responsible for 50 percent to 90 percent of all foreign news published. Further, the study found that 20 percent of the international news related to South Asia, and that India used the fewest stories from the four international agencies.

Among actions taken in the 1980s to indigenize the news flow of Asia were the creation of national news agencies, so that they now exist in nearly every country; establishment of Asian wire services; lowering of telecommunications and other tariffs on the transmitting of news; upgrading of technology for news agencies; opening of more Asian branches of the international news agencies and hiring of Asians to work for them; and the setting up of regional press services.

Bernama of Malaysia, Antara of Indonesia, the Press Trust of India, Yonhap of Korea and Kyodo of Japan were among national news agencies that entered the computer age in the 1980s, while others, especially Xinhua News Agency of China, carried out large-scale modernization plans. After some pressure, during the discussions on the New World Information Order, the four major international agencies developed new regional offices in Asia and hired additional Asians as staff members.

Three regional news exchanges aimed at improving the flow of news and information came into existence in the 1980s: Asiavision, designed for broadcast exchanges; ASEAN News Exchange (ANEX); and Asian News Network (ANN). ANEX grew out of links between the Indonesian and Malaysian agencies in the early 1970s; because of some commonalities in culture and language, these two countries believed they should exchange news and information. The Philippine News Agency joined in 1978, and two years later the tri-lateral agreement became ANEX. Thailand News Agency completed the membership in 1981.

ANEX, a computerized, two-way transmission system, was to provide a balanced flow within ASEAN. However, by the mid-1980s the agency already faced severe criticism for its lack of speed in transmission and its journalistic quality. Made up of national news services, ANEX is seen by some as a propagandist for the ASEAN governments. Surveys have shown that Indonesian and Malaysian dailies did not publish many ANEX stories, and that dispatches of ANEX members Thailand News Agency and Philippine News Agency are not considered very credible. In 1985, eight Malaysian dailies still rated Reuters as their chief source, followed by Associated Press and then Bernama.

ANN is a news exchange sponsored by the Organization of Asia-Pacific News Agencies. It was started in 1981 and became fully operational the following year as a supplement and complement to other news sources. Like ANEX it is made up of national news services (24 in 20 countries), and similarly it receives criticism for being slow and progovernment in treatment. ANN's distribution system is cumbersome and complex, and as a result the agency is not able to compete with the large international services. On the positive side, ANN has prompted national news agencies to raise their performance levels.

CONCLUSION

Asian presses evolved from common backgrounds, having been started 200 years ago or less, by colonial officials and missionaries. Published in colonial languages, the early newspapers were designed to keep colonialists in touch with their metropolitan countries.

During the past generation much of the colonial mentality under which Asian newspapers operated has been changed as Asians replaced transferred European editors, as contents of dailies were indigenized and as foreign ownership was barred. Some aspects of the press that have had strong colonial influence still need to be revised.

Besides the colonial tradition, other commonalities of Asian journalism can be detected, including tendencies toward big business, with groups, cross-media and conglomerate ownership; toward integrated information industries, with newspapers and news agencies heavily involved in telematics; toward closely guided presses doing the bidding of governments under various guises; and toward newspaper saturation in a major city or two of most countries.

FURTHER READING

The Japanese Press. Tokyo: Nihon Shimbun Kyokai, annual.

Kuo, Eddie C. Y., and Chen, Peter S. J. *Communication Policy and Planning in Singapore*. London: Kegan Paul International, 1983.

Kurian, George Thomas, ed. *World Press Encyclopedia*. 2 vols. New York: Facts on File, 1982.

Lent, John A. *The Asian Newspapers' Reluctant Revolution*. Ames: Iowa State University Press, 1971.

———, ed. *Newspapers in Asia: Contemporary Trends and Problems*. Hong Kong: Heinemann Asia, 1982.

———. *Philippine Mass Communications: Before 1811, After 1966*. Manila: Philippine Press Institute, 1971.

Schramm, Wilbur, and Atwood, Erwin. *Circulation of News in the Third World: A Study of Asia*. Hong Kong: Chinese University of Hong Kong, 1981.

Tickell, Paul, ed. *The Indonesian Press. Its Past, Its People, Its Problems*. Clayton, Australia: Monash University Press, 1987.

REPORTING ASIA

JOHN A. LENT AND CHIEN-CHUNG TSAO

INTRODUCTION

To many Westerners, Asia elicits images of mystery, remoteness and ancient rituals. Since that first Western foreign correspondent Marco Polo reported upon Asia, Europeans, and later Americans, have had distorted perceptions of the continent and its people. With the assistance of modern technology, such as satellites, telephones, television and computers, many people have a slightly better understanding of Asia, but the misrepresentation and misperception generally remain unchanged.

Correspondingly, the misunderstanding of the West by Asians has resulted in serious ruptures in relationships. During the last half of the 20th century the West has played an important, if not critical, role in the development of many Asian countries. The resultant relationships can be characterized as controversial, cooperative or competitive. An understanding of these relationships is vital when looking at how and why Western media report Asia.

Any intercultural communication involves controversies, and the political dialogues between Asia and the West are not exceptions. Some critics believe that the way political dialogues are covered affects the way they turn out. For example, the 1940s China policy was believed to have resulted because the United States decided to withdraw support from the Nationalist government. A further reason some give for this change of policy is the way news reporting on China shifted, e.g., the Communists treated as "revolutionaries" instead of as "rebels." The Vietnam War brought another controversy; news reporting changed, affecting Americans' perceptions of the war, and perhaps the way the U.S. government reacted. Until the very late 1960s U.S. reporting of the Vietnam War was generally supportive of the U.S. military and government. But the Tet offensive and reporting of U.S. atrocities by the alternative media heightened opposition to the way the Pentagon carried on the war.

Many other examples could be provided, but one of the most significant pertains to the Philippines. For years the Western media sidestepped many of the corrupt and brutal actions of the Marcos regime, although some courageous Filipino media, and Filipino-American newsletters, brought them up regularly. When the Western press finally reported some of these abuses in late 1985 and early 1986, the international image of Ferdinand and Imelda Marcos and their cronies began to crumble.

Another type of relationship between Asia and the West has been cooperation. In the postindustrial era some Western nations realized that they could not dominate the world by ignoring the needs of less developed countries, while Asian nations realized that interdependence between East and West was one of the important factors in maintaining political stability and economic prosperity.

For instance, China reopened its doors to the West in the 1970s adding some capitalist qualities to the prevalent communism. Under this policy China invited Western capital and technology to help its modernization plans, simultaneously sending thousands of students to Europe and North American for study. Japan is another country that opened and then closed its door to the West, benefiting from the cooperative periods in between. During the Meiji Restoration after the mid-19th century, Japan cooperated with the West, gaining cultural, political and technological expertise. The country was sealed again during the Showa era but reopened in 1945, after which Japan grew in political and economic strength in its most cooperative period with the West.

Some other countries in Asia followed Japan's lead by maintaining close relationships with the West. Taiwan had very cordial relationships with the United States and Western Europe until China received recognition in the 1970s. But although the political status of the Nationalist government of Taiwan has been ignored by the West since the 1970s, the economic and cultural relationships were closely maintained. Similarly, South Korea, after the war on its soil in the early 1950s, miraculously prospered politically and economically, with close contact with the West. Singapore, Malaysia, the Philippines and Hong Kong, among many other countries, cooperated with the West, both to their benefit and to that of Western countries.

While the West was providing Asian nations with capital and technology, it may not have foreseen the fierce competition that would result later. Western nations lost some of their competitive edge, while some countries of Asia became economic powerhouses. In order to balance trade deficits, Western nations, particularly the United States, pressured Asian countries to buy more products from them. Trade protectionism became a key issue in the West's dealing with Asia, thus considerably complicating the relationships between the regions. To Asian nations, partly because of political motives, the West represented a major marketplace for their products, but the West's trade protectionism forced these Asian nations to open their markets to other areas, such as Eastern Europe, the Soviet Union and China. The result was that the ideological differences between Asia and Communist nations was blurred.

WESTERN MEDIA NEWS VALUES

Reporting in Asia became very important in the context of the debate between the Third World and the West regarding the New World Information and Communication Order. Western news media, particularly the four major international news agencies, have been heavily criticized for distorting Third World events on behalf of Western interests or to promote cultural and media imperialism.

Asian nations, and the Third World generally, are concerned about how Western media report their news events. As most Asian nations rely upon the West for economic and military aid, they are critical of the constant misrepresentation or distortion of their news, believing such coverage jeopardizes the confidence of Western nations in them. Further, Asian countries are sensitive about Western reporting, with governments and media organizations claiming that Asian journalism operates on different value systems. They point to the need for Asian journalists to be guided by government objectives and to use development journalism, the latter concept developed in Asia. They usually do not see that the function of journalism is to expose or investigate, but rather regard its function as one of cooperating with the authorities. Thus, when Western news agencies, operating on the idea that they should be adversaries of government, report negative happenings in Asia, the value systems collide.

A discussion of factors affecting international news reporting in the U.S. and European press can be approached from the perspectives of news values, national interests/government attitudes, cultural and geographic proximity, organizational constraints, national characteristics, political economy, or crisis orientation.

News value pertains to aspects of events that make them newsworthy. American and European researchers on journalism and the media have come up with a rather long list of these characteristics. Galtung and Holmboe, writing in 1965, believed news is based on factors such as frequency, threshold, unexpectedness, uniqueness, meaningfulness, personalization, elitism and negativism.[1] Ostgaard, in another 1965 study, echoed these factors, but further hypothesized that media exaggerate the importance of activities of Western leaders; portray the world as having more controversies and turmoils than actually exist; emphasize the use of forceful, rather than peaceful, means to solve conflicts; and simplify the world structure by suggesting dualities that divide it. Concerning the latter point, the world is divided economically and politically, as developed and underdeveloped; and is categorized into first and second worlds, rich and poor, or Communist and capitalist. Overall, Ostgaard believed sensationalism and simplification are the important factors deciding what news is selected.[2] Sociologist Herbert Gans takes a different path to discuss news values.[3] Gans' perspective is not based on an emphasis of neutral or impartial values of news, but on the enduring value the news implies. Enduring values, according to Gans, can be found in "many different types of news stories over a long period of time; often they affect what events become news and even help define the news." Moreover, these news values are not explicit and must be read between the lines by readers.

[1] J. Galtung and R. M. Holmboe, "The Structure of Foreign News," *Journal of Peace Research* 2 (1965): 64–91.
[2] E. Ostgaard, "Factors Influencing the Flow of News," *Journal of Peace Research* 2 (1965): 39–55.
[3] Herbert Gans, *Deciding What's News* (New York: Pantheon, 1979).

A number of enduring values may affect news selection processes, including ethnocentrism, altruism, democracy, responsible capitalism, individualism, and national leadership. Ethnocentrism is the value most explicit in international news, as media tend to evaluate foreign events from a national viewpoint.

National interest and government attitude are important factors in news selection. As indicated earlier, national interest means that journalists view foreign events from their own country's point of view; government attitude refers to actions taken by domestic or foreign governments that affect foreign correspondents' coverage.

Classifying the international news most often seen on television into seven different subjects, Gans said the top two subjects were American activities in a foreign country and foreign activities that affect Americans and U.S. policy. Chang et al., in their empirical study of U.S. coverage of international news, found that news stories relevant to the United States were important in determining international news coverage, especially in the print media—the *New York Times* chief among them.[4] Analyzing U.S. broadcasting network coverage of China and Taiwan, another researcher also showed that news was used when it had a connection to the United States.[5]

These foreign events are presented by the media through biases of the elite. In 1981 Paletz and Entman ennumerated three mechanisms by which this occurs: source, vantage point and language. Reporting that elite critics of administration policies (in the United States) are seldom sought, they added: "the only spokespersons for critical viewpoints are either representatives of unfriendly governments addressing their own people, or emotional Americans appearing in a setting which labels them as extremists."[6]

Further, people interviewed in foreign countries are usually officials from the home country, working in embassies or intelligence posts. Representatives of these agencies are not objective sources, yet diplomats and foreign correspondents often exchange information. Many diplomats have been known to use the media to change a nation's image or open a political dialogue with another country.

Reporters' vantage point also determines the questions that will be asked and the problems posed. In the United States the questions often revolve around the implications for U.S. interests as defined by the president and other top officials. The vantage point is compromised in cases where foreign correspondents are also on intelligence agency payrolls. In 1973 a Washington daily disclosed that the U.S. Central Intelligence Agency (CIA) had at least 40 U.S. journalists overseas on its payroll. Sometime later Carl

---

[4]T.-K. Chang, P. J. Shoemaker and N. Brendlinger, "Determinants of International News Coverage in the U.S. Media," *Communication Research* (August 1987): 396–414.

[5]Chien-Chung Tsao, "News Coverage of a Divided Country: A Content Analysis of the Commercial U.S. Television Network News Coverage of Taiwan and Communist China Before and After U.S. Rapprochement with Communist China" (M.A. thesis, Western Illinois University, 1983).

[6]D. L. Paletz and R. M. Entman, *Media, Power, Politics* (New York: The Free Press, 1981).

Bernstein of Watergate fame said that over 400 journalists had secretly carried out CIA work.

Also, reporters are prone to use in their coverage words provided by these biased sources, words that very considerably slant the news—e.g., the United States has "allies" whose freedom it "defends," and the Soviet Union has "satellites" that it "controls."

Cultural and geographical proximity also help determine how countries are covered in the United States and Europe. While Galtung and Holmboe speculated that Western editors select news stories that conform or are related to their own cultures, Ostgaard believed that this cultural conformity of editors is a worldwide phenomenon. He added that "cultural proximity" appears to be a major asset for a news story, and that the news media in any country will tend "to present the picture of the outside world as seen through the ethnocentric eyes of the receivers of the news." Lent broadened the perspective, claiming that a nation's "cultural heritage" also explains why many newly independent nations continually report on their former colonialists.[7]

Larson said a country closest to the United States in "perceptual distance" receives the most coverage in U.S. media,[8] while Peterson, surveying London *Times* journalists, found that 83 percent of the editors ranked Western news events as more "meaningful" than those in Third World nations. Based on the latter finding, Peterson concluded that cultural conformity shapes the decisions on news selections.[9] On the other hand, Chang et al. found that geographic distance is not an important factor in influencing international news in the *New York Times,* but is an important element on U.S. network news, more likely to be constrained by technical problems and limited budgets than the print medium.

Financial and structural characteristics of mass media have been known to shape international news coverage and usage. High communication expenses are given as a major reason why news events in remote nations are not covered, although this is difficult to fathom, what with the mind-boggling profits of mass media in the United States and Europe. For example, the huge Gannett newspaper group of about 100 U.S. dailies, including *USA Today,* chooses not to maintain a foreign staff. Others have provided rationales for the limitations of international news coverage. As Ostgaard pointed out, larger bureaus, normally in major cities (often in Europe), provide more news volume from which editors in home offices can select. But even if the large bureaus have more correspondents and larger budgets with which to file more news reports, a limit exists on the number of reports a correspondent can file in a day, no matter how many newsworthy events occur.

Riffe found that, because of a cutback in the number of U.S. foreign

[7] John A. Lent, "Foreign News in American Media," *Journal of Communication* 27, no. 1 (1977): 46–51.

[8] J. F. Larson, "International Affairs Coverage on U.S. Network Television," *Journal of Communication* (Spring 1979): 136–147.

[9] S. Peterson, "Foreign News Gatekeepers and Criteria of Newsworthiness," *Journalism Quarterly* (Summer 1979): 116–25.

correspondents in the 1970s, and foreign governments' censorship, news "borrowed" from foreign news media increased in the United States. The decreasing number of foreign correspondents and the placement of those who survive, cannot be explained simplistically. As indicated above, some large U.S. and European media, which definitely can afford to keep correspondents abroad, choose not to. The placement of correspondents is oftentimes curious; among U.S. media, over half of the correspondents have been concentrated in Europe (usually London or Paris), with other large groups in Tokyo and Hong Kong. After China opened its door to the West, foreign correspondents were stationed in Shanghai and Beijing, yet there were many other areas in Asia with no foreign correspondents. When correspondents concentrate in a few major cities, they practice a type of "firehouse reporting," racing here and there to cover the latest crisis.[10]

Certain characteristics of countries play significant roles in whether they are covered in the Western media. For instance, Ahern[11] and Larson found that the increase of a nation's GNP, economic productivity and political dialogue with the United States affect that nation's coverage in the U.S. press. Additionally, the use of public relations techniques by Third World governments has proved useful in getting them more coverage in the Western mass media. According to Albritton and Manheim, after several Third World countries hired U.S. public relations consultants, their news image in the *New York Times* "improved by a reduction in volume [of negative coverage], an increase in the percent of positive coverage, or its portrayal as a more cooperative nation." Other countries' international images also improved when they engaged U.S. public relations firms; among these countries were Indonesia, South Korea and the Philippines.[12]

In other efforts to obtain favorable coverage in the Western press, governments have used threats, intimidation or the staging of extravagant happenings. For example, Singapore has a law that can limit a foreign periodical's circulation in that country, if that newspaper or magazine carries information inimicable to Singapore's interests. In other cases, Asian governments, as well as those elsewhere, have censored foreign dispatches, detained or expelled correspondents, cancelled visas, denied access or threatened reporters' lives.

The theoretical basis of the political-economic perspective is that information, including news stories, has been treated as a commodity by Western news media. Since the major information markets are located in the United States and Europe, Western news agencies have to fulfill the commercial needs of these Western customers at the expense of social needs of Third World users.

The European, Canadian, Australian and United States mass media are

---

[10] D. Riffe, "International News Borrowing: A Trend Analysis," *Journalism Quarterly* (Spring 1984): 142–49.

[11] T. J. Ahern, Jr., "Determinants of Foreign Coverage in U.S. Newspapers," in *Foreign News and the New World Information Order,* ed. R. L. Stevenson and D. L. Shaw, (Ames, Iowa: The Iowa State University Press, 1984), 217–37.

[12] R. B. Albritton and J. B. Manheim, "Public Relations Effects for the Third World: Images in the News," *Journal of Communication* (Winter 1985): 43–59.

highly concentrated, with a few dozen entities dominating the flow of news and determining newsworthiness. They are large business enterprises, dependent upon advertising and closely linked to other large firms. Important members of the corporate community, these gigantic media reflect the interests of that community, often misrepresenting and distorting domestic and world news.

Finally, Western media have been accused of concentrating upon crisis news—the so-called coups and earthquakes syndrome. Various studies have shown that conflict, upheaval and other crises are the major fare of the large international wire services and of individual correspondents when covering the Third World. Complaints emanate from the Third World nations, which, having guided their own mass media toward reporting positive governmental goals, do not appreciate Western media harping upon their bad news. News reporting so conditioned by the sudden event or the upheaval has a difficult time dealing with the incremental, developmental, casual and evolutionary events that have a great deal to do with the usual course of life.

A Filipino information official said it well in the 1970s: "It is as if Western reporters feel their job in a developing society is to identify that society's weakest points and biggest problems and then make them worse by exaggeration and unremitting publicity."

A CHRONOLOGY OF REPORTING ASIA

In the recent debate on the New World Information and Communication Order, Third World countries criticized the foreign news coverage of powerful Western media for their imbalances in quantity and distortions in quality. Delegates from Asian countries, in particular, complained that their nations have always been the blank spot in international news. Some researchers have shown that this neglect of Asian affairs in Western media goes back several centuries.

Hester et al., in a study of three U.S. colonial newspapers for 1764–75, found that over 80 percent of the foreign news concentrated on Western Europe, and 2 percent or less on Asia. This finding is not surprising, yet it has several important implications. The obvious one is that the imbalanced news pattern found in the U.S. press today has a historical basis. It is understandable that international news in the U.S. colonial press was "Eurocentered." The newspapers were concerned about the British attitude toward the brewing American Revolution; in fact, three-fourths of all foreign news dealt with England. Further, the U.S. colonies were isolated geographically, and news from other regions was hard to obtain.[13]

Historical studies of Western Europe's press indicated a preference for coverage of European events. Wilkie, who compared news treatments in British, French and German newspapers with those of the United States

[13] A. Hester, S. P. Humes and C. Bickers, (1978): "Foreign News in Colonial North American Newspapers, 1764–1775," *Journalism Quarterly* no. 57 (1980): 18–22.

between the 17th and 20th centuries, reported that international news in all newspapers was centered on European events. Only later were other regions of the world reported, although Asia was ignored, for the most part, throughout the entire period. The newspaper that was the sole exception was England's *Daily Telegraph,* where the amount of Asian news increased dramatically, from 2 percent to 9 percent of the total foreign news.[14]

Western Europeans and Americans probably missed out on much information about Asia toward the end of the 19th and beginning of the 20th centuries, because turmoil plagued large parts of the continent. In China, a secret society, the Righteous Harmony Fists, was developed, later to become a force of social unrest against foreigners. While the Righteous Harmony Fists busied itself fighting with the Chinese authorities and an international force, Japan defeated Russia in 1904 to become a strong Asian power, and the United States was establishing a colonial outpost in Asia as it fought Filipino guerrillas for dominance. European correspondents were sent to Asia to cover these events. According to Philip Knightley, however, their assignments failed because of cultural barriers and government censorship, perhaps accounting for the reason why Asian news increased only moderately in some Western newspapers during that time.[15]

There was a major difference between the Western European and U.S. press regarding international news coverage during the three centuries Wilkie studied. As international news flow increased enormously in the Western European newspapers, foreign news in U.S. dailies was de-emphasized. Moreover, in some years, foreign dispatches far outweighed domestic news in newspapers such as the *Hamburgischer Correspondent, London Gazette* and *London Daily Telegraph.*

There are several explanations for the sharp contrast between international news coverage in Western European and American newspapers. First, government censorship in Europe severely suppressed domestic news, thus directing these newspapers' attention to foreign news. Second, European readers, particularly city dwellers, were interested in foreign news, and only later did they develop regional tastes because of political and economic factors. Third, U.S. isolationism was in full force at the end of the 19th century, with Americans primarily interested in opening up their own continent. Fourth, social problems during and after the American Civil War reinforced readers' preferences for domestic news. Of them all, U.S. isolationism, which flourished until World War I, might be the dominant reason why foreign news was ignored.

Additionally, the British influence on the U.S. press affected its international news coverage. For instance, after Reuters, a member of the European News Agency Cartel, obtained an exclusive right in the mid-19th century to gather and distribute news in both the United States and part of Asia, Americans had to view world events from a British perspective.

[14] J. Wilkie, "The Changing World of Media Reality," *Gazette* 34 no. 3 (1984): 175–90.
[15] Philip Knightley, *The First Casualty* (New York: Harcourt, Brace Jovanovich, 1975).

Further, Asian news flow to the West was monopolized by Reuters. During World War II the Associated Press terminated its relationship with the European News Agency Cartel, and became an active agency in its own right.

Of course, the big Asian story in the early 1940s was the Pacific War and Japan. Studying coverage of four East Asian nations in the largest newsmagazines in the United States (*Time, Newsweek* and *U.S. News & World Report*), Tsao, writing in 1982, found that in 1945 over one-half of the East Asian news concerned Japan. However, by 1949 China was the main story, each newsmagazine devoting at least 60 percent of its East Asian space to that country. Most of the China stories covered political issues and the Communist movement of Mao.[16] The American public's interest in China sparked an increase in stories about the revolution. In an analysis of four U.S. major city dailies, Hartgen showed that they devoted considerable space to the Chinese Communist movements in 1945–46, but that they concentrated on the visible and easily comprehensible events rather than giving a more in-depth analysis of social, political or economic problems. Correspondents' language deficiencies and cultural barriers blocked them from the wider perspectives.[17]

After the Communists took over in 1949 China was no longer a free zone for foreign correspondents, especially those from Great Britain, France and the United States. Most U.S. news bureaus were forced to move their Chinese operations from Shanghai or Nanjing to Tokyo or Hong Kong; and at best these latter bureaus could only gather Chinese news from secondary sources such as local newspapers, Western diplomats and tourists.

Almost simultaneously with the closing of China, Korea became a crisis news spot as war broke out in 1950. Imbalanced treatment of Asia was again the situation. A study completed by the International Press Institute showed that in 1952–53 the one British and three U.S. news services concentrated on the United Nations, NATO, the Korean War, Western Europe and Japan for most foreign news. The same study pointed out that many small U.S. dailies devoted nearly all their foreign news space to the war, which the U.S. press generally treated not as foreign news but rather as a story about the U.S. interests abroad.[18]

The way the Korean War was covered drew considerable criticism. Knightley went so far as to place some of the blame for the devastation of Korea on the correspondents, claiming they "got on side" with the U.S. military and never questioned what the war was about, how it was being conducted and the dominance of the United States in what was called a U.N. War. Knightley credited one or two British correspondents with

[16] Chien-Chung Tsao, "A Content Analysis of the News of East Asia—China, Japan, Korea and Taiwan—in Three American News Magazines (1945 and 1949)" (1982, unpublished paper).

[17] S. Hartgen, "How Four U.S. Papers Covered the Communist Chinese Revolt," *Journalism Quarterly* (Spring, 1979): 175–78.

[18] International Press Institute, *The Flow of the News: A Study by the International Press Institute* (Zurich, 1953).

assessing the justification of the intervention and providing a less emotional view.

U.S. press coverage of other parts of Asia came in for study and criticism in the early 1950s. For example, India, in the midst of nation-building despite numerous ethnic and religious divisions, received poor U.S. coverage; in fact, U.S. dailies were accused of giving a more inaccurate and distorted picture of the subcontinent than of any other part of the world. An Indian correspondent was quoted as saying that the U.S. press oversimplified Indian issues, played up those primarily with an American tie-in, ignored Indian domestic events, and stereotyped Indian culture from "mysterious" and outdated perspectives.

While India received negative portrayals on the news pages of many U.S. dailies, different treatment was given the country on at least one daily's editorial page. A study of the editorial treatment of India in the *New York Times*, from 1950 to 1962, found that a balanced picture was generally given, although India's relations with other Asian, as well as Communist, countries was given less favorable comment than its interests with the U.S.[19]

Elsewhere on the subcontinent, Pakistan was covered by U.S. media primarily in stories about its relations with India and the United States. Studying the three largest U.S. newsmagazines between 1962 and 1965, S. A. Mujahid wrote that they downplayed Pakistan's domestic issues, with *U.S. News & World Report* completely ignoring them. Only *Time* carried a few stories on Pakistan's internal affairs in its overall more extensive coverage. On the favorable side, all three newsmagazines kept a balanced editorial position on Pakistan, particularly on Indo-Pakistani relations.[20]

But the U.S. press was not alone in ethnocentric coverage of the subcontinent. News media in West Germany reported on India mostly when events were related to the European Community; and again, India's domestic problems or its connections with other parts of the world were not major concerns. A criticism of West German dailies' coverage was that it was too fragmentary to provide readers with even a basic understanding of the country. On the contrary, Indian news in the leading British dailies, such as the *Observer* and *Sunday Times* of London, was covered rather extensively, mainly because of the long historical ties between India and Britain.

In the mid-1960s three regions of Asia, designated as trouble centers, brought out several hundred Western correspondents. In Vietnam the war escalated; in Indonesia racial violence was on the rise; and in India and Pakistan the boundary issue kept relations tense. A long-time analyst of foreign correspondence, John Hohenberg believed that the American public was never more thoroughly informed regarding Asian affairs than in the mid-1960s, when all major news agencies and leading U.S. and European dailies assigned their foreign correspondents to these hot spots.[21]

[19] M. D. Lynch, and A. Effendi, "Editorial Treatment of India in the *New York Times*," *Journalism Quarterly* (Summer, 1964): 430–32.
[20] S. A. Mujahid, "Coverage of Pakistan in Three U.S. Newsmagazines," *Journalism Quarterly* no. 47 (1970): 126–30, 165.
[21] John Hohenberg, *Between Two Worlds* (New York: Frederick A. Praeger, 1967);

But overall, Hohenberg maintained, the U.S. public was still the most poorly informed in terms of Asian events because the majority of Asian countries were not covered. He states that when some regions, particularly China, were reported upon by Western media, the results were misrepresentation and distortion. Part of the problem was that access to information on China remained limited. Thus, foreign correspondents had to rely on secondary sources to draw conclusions about news events in China. As a French correspondent in Hong Kong said, he and his colleagues could report news about China only as they guessed and interpreted information gathered from secondary sources—travelers, refugees, "wall posters" and official news in the Chinese press.

Further, Western institutions were short of experts on Chinese affairs who could present useful and accurate information. Rosenblum pointed out that Western media were not willing to have their correspondents taught to speak foreign languages, which would have facilitated news gathering. Instead, reporters were shuffled from place to place so often that they did not become familiar with the language or culture of any one country.[22]

The access problem with respect to China continued into the 1970s. For example, in the middle of that decade, Western media relied on dispatches of 46 non-Chinese correspondents based in Beijing. Actually, most reports reaching Europe and North America were filed by 17 correspondents: four from England; three each from France and West Germany; two each from Italy, Canada and Scandinavia; and one from Australia. Most of these reporters were stifled by a lack of access to news.

If Asian news was previously concentrated in East and South Asia, it shifted in the mid-1960s to Southeast Asia, which remained the focus for a decade, with the U.S. involvement in the Vietnam War. A 1966 study by J. A. Hart, reporting on U.S. foreign coverage in 1964–65, showed that 24 percent of the foreign news slots of the *New York Times* and *Washington Post* was devoted to the "Far East" and Southeast Asia. In three U.S. dailies the Vietnam War already ranked as the number one foreign story, although this was not the case with the *New York Times,* which was still Eurocentered. According to Hart's study, the British dailies the *London Times, Guardian, Daily Express* and *Daily Telegraph* also paid more attention to news of Western Europe than Asia, although the latter ranked second.[23]

A few reasons come to mind for the lack of enthusiasm of the British press in covering Southeast Asia. First, none of the English dailies sent permanent correspondents to Vietnam, although the *Times* and *Sunday Times* assigned their Asian correspondents to look in on the country infrequently, and other reporters paid more attention to the war when it intensified. Second, as in the case of the Korean War, those British correspondents

"The Flow of News Between Asia and the West," *Nieman Reports* 3 (1967): 10–15.

[22] M. Rosenblum, *Coups and Earthquakes* (New York: Harper and Row, 1979).

[23] J. A. Hart, "Foreign News in U.S. and English Daily Newspapers: A Comparison," *Journalism Quarterly* (Autumn 1966): 443–48.

who did cover Vietnam were less emotional than their U.S. colleagues and covered the scene more objectively. Of course, such reportage could have been to their disadvantage; not taking sides with the U.S. military, and not being permanently posted to Vietnam, they may have had more difficulty moving about the country without U.S. military assistance.

British magazines took the same attitude regarding news coverage of Vietnam. None of them sent permanent correspondents, preferring freelance journalists and photographers instead.

Unlike the independent stance of the British press, the stance of three Swedish dailies, from 1963 to 1968, reflected a definite U.S. bias. Editorial themes and points of view in the Swedish dailies were remarkably similar to those in the U.S. press, probably because of the U.S. dominance of the international news flow and because of Sweden's strong ties to the West.[24]

Reporting the Vietnam War was a miserable and challenging experience for correspondents, especially those from the United States. For years reporters were undermined by the U.S. government and their own home-based editors, who often believed the official White House or Pentagon line rather than the actual dispatches from their correspondents in the field.

Further, military censorship, U.S. government pressure and the chaotic nature of the war prevented American correspondents from providing a true picture. Most importantly, as Knightley contended, U.S. correspondents were too patriotic to report the war objectively and, as in Korea, they dwelt on the effectiveness, rather than on the nature and significance, of the U.S. military intervention, or on the history or culture of the region.

A significant difference in how Vietnam was reported had to do with television. Much controversy revolved around this intrusive medium and its ability to bring into people's living rooms the brutality, desperation and frustration of war. Although it may have been a contributor to Americans' turnabout in views of the war, it was not the only, or the most important, factor.

Entman and Paletz, in a 1982 study, categorized U.S. television network coverage into phases of optimism, surprise and opposition with respect to the Tet offensive, Nixonization and sadness without lessons learned.[25] During the first phase (1963–67), the war was portrayed as an effort to stop a Communist invasion. Print and television journalists relied heavily upon official sources to interpret daily events and to forecast the future of the war. The tone of government officials and newspeople was optimistic, as they expected North Vietnam to pull back under strong pressure from U.S. forces. Television news legitimized myths that the South Vietnam and U.S. armies were invulnerable, and that North Vietnam would be quickly defeated. Although the networks sent crews to the front as early as

[24] E. Queckfeldt, " 'Vietnam': Three Swedish Newspapers' Views of the Vietnam Issue 1963–1968," *Nordicom Review* no. 1, (1982): 32–33.
[25] R. M. Entman, and P. L. Paletz, "The War in Southeast Asia: Tunnel Vision on Television," in *Television Coverage of International Affairs,* ed. W. C. Adams (Norwood, N.J.: Ablex, 1982), 181–201.

1963, they failed signally in presenting a true picture to audiences in the U.S.[26] In language and length of news treatments the networks supported the U.S. government position. Terms such as "enemy" and "Communist" were used in over one-third of all references to the people the U.S. were fighting. Most items read on television were extremely brief and superficial; less than 5 percent of the stories had more than 150 words, thus diluting complex issues into quickly presented and stereotyped formats.[27]

The second phase, according to Entman and Paletz, began at the early 1968 launching of the Tet offensive. For the first time U.S. audiences saw the vulnerability of South Vietnam and the uncontrollable nature of the war itself. This picture of the war was certainly different from those previously presented by the U.S. government; in an unprecedented manner television news interpreted an American war somewhat independently of government and military.

During the third phase of Nixonization (late 1969) the networks tired of covering the war, resulting in a drastic drop in the volume of Vietnam news. Several reasons can account for this decline, according to Entman and Paletz—among which are that the combat zone was moved from ground to air, cutting the possibilities for "interesting" visuals; journalists tired of doing repetitive stories and the Nixon administration included intimidation of journalists as part of its war policy. Other types of stories pushed the actual fighting off the screens—stories concerning U.S. atrocities, the Pentagon Papers, the antiwar movement in the United States and the contamination of the Vietnamese environment.

The fourth phase of television coverage occurred after the signing of the cease-fire treaty and the withdrawal of U.S. forces from Vietnam. U.S. network news now centered on the return of American POWs and the demise of South Vietnam.

After 1975 Vietnam—in fact, all of Indochina—seemed to disappear from U.S. newspaper pages and television screens. There was some thought in the late 1970s that it was difficult to market any Asian story in the U.S. media because of the humiliation of the Vietnam experience.

For whatever reasons, the massacres of millions of people in Cambodia and East Timor in the 1970s did not receive much U.S. coverage. The carnage in Cambodia between 1975 and 1978, which left 1 million to 3 million people dead was certainly downplayed; the three U.S. networks in three and one-third years devoted only 29 stories to this, for a total of about 58 minutes. (This averaged less than 30 seconds per month per network.) Genocide was addressed in only a little over eight minutes total airtime. Adams and Joblove commented that the networks dismissed the Cambodian story because they did not have good pictures, as the Khmer Rouge did not invite reporters inside their borders. Other reasons were that

[26] E. J. Epstein, *News from Nowhere: Television and the News* (New York: Longman, 1973).
[27] G. Bailey, "Television War: Trends in Network Coverage of Vietnam, 1965–70," *Journal of Broadcasting* (Spring, 1976): 147–158.

the networks followed the silence from both the White House and the prestige press, such as the *New York Times* and *Washington Post*.[28]

In 1976–77, when Indonesians massacred 50,000 to 100,000 citizens of East Timor, the U.S. press shunned the story for the sake of a client and ally, Indonesia. For example, the *New York Times* gave East Timor one-half of a column in 1976; the following year, five lines.

CONTEMPORARY SCENE

Studies of Western media bear out suspicions that their reporting of Asia has shrunk, that whole regions and many topics go virtually unnoticed and that coverage usually depends on a home-country angle.

For example, a comparative study of the three U.S. television networks revealed that in 1969, when they devoted 52 percent of their international news stories and 65 percent of their news times to the U.S. intervention in Asia, only 8 percent each of the news and time had to do with Asian events that did not have a U.S. angle. On the other hand, two to three times more stories were used about Western Europe, the Middle East or Eastern Europe.[29]

Within the period 1972–76 the three networks only covered Indochina (26 percent of their total foreign news) and China, India, Japan and Hong Kong (totaling 6 percent of total foreign news) to an appreciable degree. Exclusive of war news, Asian topics that made network news during this time were foreign relations, military and defense, economics and business, and natural disasters. Subjects such as labor, agriculture, fisheries, science and health, religion, education, the arts, and culture were downplayed or ignored.[30] Another study of the *New York Times, Washington Post,* ABC News and *Newsweek* in 1977 also reported very limited coverage on a few topics with tie-ins to the United States[31] Asian news continued to dwindle on U.S. television, so that between 1977 and 1981 only 10 percent of all foreign news dealt with the continent.[32]

Although much of the research on media reporting has concentrated on the U.S. television networks, content analyses have been done of Dutch, Japanese and British television, and of British radio. Some of the findings are familiar by now.

[28] W. C. Adams, and M. Joblove, "The Unnewsworthy Holocaust: TV News and Terror in Cambodia," in *Television Coverage of International Affairs,* ed. W. C. Adams (Norwood, N.J.: Ablex, 1982), 217–26.

[29] Adnan Almaney, "International Affairs on Network TV News in 1969," *Journal of Broadcasting* (Fall, 1970): 499–509.

[30] A. Hester, "Five Years of Foreign News on U.S. Television Evening Newscasts," *Gazette* 24, no. 1 (1978): 86–95.

[31] John A. Lent, and S. Rao, "A Content Analysis of National Media Coverage of Asian News and Information" *Gazette* 25, no. 1 (1979): 17–22.

[32] J. B. Weaver, C. J. Potter and M. E. Evans, "Patterns in Foreign News Coverage on U.S. Network TV: A 10-Year Analysis," *Journalism Quarterly* (Summer, 1984): 356–63.

For example, an analysis of Dutch television newscasts and current affairs programs in 1975–76 showed that only 13 of 221 news items dealt with Asia, while 102 covered Western Europe, supporting the thesis about the Eurocentric bias of Western media. Studying two each of Japanese and British television networks in 1980–81, another analyst showed that U.S. news dominated; and he justified this finding by the important international political roles the United States plays. It was found that on the Japanese networks the following Asian countries were mentioned: South Korea (38 times), China (26), Cambodia and Vietnam (seven each), Thailand (four), and North Korea and Bangladesh (two each). On the two British networks the mentions of Asian countries were of Japan (13) and Afghanistan (eight). Summarizing, the Japanese networks used 86 items about seven countries, while the British BBC and ITN used only 21 mentions of two countries.[33]

Home-country involvement was an indicator of foreign news reporting on Britain's "The World at One" radio show between 1975 and 1979, but less so with coverage of Asia and the Middle East than with other areas. For example, Britain was involved in nearly 74 percent of the stories on "White Africa," 57 percent of those on Latin America, 56 percent of reports on Western Europe, 53 percent of stories on "Black Africa" and 39 percent of reporting about Australasia. On the other hand, of the total of 195 stories on Asian countries (Vietnam, Cambodia, Pakistan, China, India and others), only 24.6 percent included a British connection. Not confirmed in M. Harrison's study of British radio coverage was the proposition that former colonies receive more attention. On British radio, India and Pakistan were featured when news merited it; there were no mentions of the former Asian colonies of Bangladesh or Sri Lanka. Asia ranked third among nine regions of the world in percentage of stories considered negative (disasters, crime, political violence or nonviolent political conflict). Forty percent of all radio news items dealing with Asia were in this category.[34]

A comprehensive study of foreign news in the media of 29 countries, conducted in 1979 by the International Association for Mass Communication Research, showed that U.S. media gave considerably more attention to Asia than did Western European media. After Western Europe and the Middle East—16 percent each of all foreign news—Asia was the third most important region in U.S. media, with 14 percent. But Asia was ranked after North America, the Middle East and Eastern Europe as a location of international news in dailies in Western Europe: Germany, Finland, Greece, Iceland, the Netherlands and Turkey.[35]

[33] K. Kitatani, "Assessment of the New World Information Order: A Content Analysis of International Affairs Coverage by the British and Japanese TV Networks" (Pullman, Washington, 1982, unpublished paper).
[34] M. Harrison, "A Window on the World?: Foreign Coverage by a British Radio Current Affairs Program," *Critical Studies in Mass Communication* (December, 1986): 409–28.
[35] A. Sreberny-Mohammadi et al., *Foreign News in the Media: International Reporting in 29 Countries* (Paris: UNESCO, 1985).

Two Western dailies considered "windows on the world," the *New York Times* and *Manchester Guardian,* present considerably different views of international events, including those of Asia. A 1979 comparison of these dailies showed that of the top 18 countries/organizations reported upon in the two papers combined, China ranked third, Vietnam sixth and Japan 18th. The *Times* had more stories than the *Guardian* on Asian dyads that figured in the cold war; China and Taiwan, North and South Korea, and India and Pakistan. On the other hand, the *Guardian,* which normally focuses more on smaller countries and former British colonies, still devoted more attention than the *Times* to Afghanistan, Cambodia, Indonesia, Thailand, Philippines, Singapore and Japan.[36]

Primarily to determine whether the total foreign news devoted to specific countries was positively correlated with level of trade, population and GNP, Robinson and Sparkes in 1976 studied 39 dailies from the United States and Canada. Their major finding was that for Canada the percentage of foreign news was moderately correlated with the level of trade; for the United States no such correlations existed. Except for Southeast Asia, which made up 11.35 percent of all foreign news in Canadian papers and 16.98 percent in those of the United States, the rest of Asia was not covered very frequently (5.93 percent of all foreign news in the Canadian press and 6.08 percent in the United States press). Specific countries treated in both were Japan, India, Pakistan and China.[37]

CASE STUDIES OF CHINA AND JAPAN

Perhaps the reporting of Asia by Western news media can be better understood by focusing on two of the continent's giants, China and Japan.

As indicated above, reporting about China was seriously hampered at various times, as for example from 1949 to the 1970s. In 1971 the United States ping-pong team, accompanied by some newspeople, slightly opened the door to China. The following year, when U.S. President Richard Nixon visited China, the U.S. press had a better opportunity to see the country, as planes full of U.S. television equipment and personnel were flown to Beijing. Also in that year Nixon and Chinese Premier Zhou Enlai signed an agreement giving U.S. newspeople the option to remain in China on short-term visas.

When President Jimmy Carter initiated full diplomatic relations with China in the late 1970s this expanded the possibilities of journalistic exchange between the two countries. It also meant a cooling of relations with the "other China," Taiwan, which had always been a blind spot to many Western media and was likely to become more so now. Tsao, in 1983, comparing U.S. network coverage of China and Taiwan, reported that while

[36] G. W. Hopple, "International News Coverage in Two Elite Newspapers," *Journal of Communication* (Winter, 1982): 61–74.
[37] G. J. Robinson, and V. M. Sparkes, "International News in the Canadian and American Press: A Comparative News Flow Study," *Gazette* 22, no. 4 (1976): 203–18.

in 1971 there were 629 news stories devoted to China and 146 to Taiwan, in 1980 the figures were 231 and 44, respectively. In both years network coverage of the two countries was heavily centered on U.S. involvement.

Most studies have shown that despite better relations between China and the United States, American media did not single out China for exceptional coverage, certainly not to the extent that China's CCTV reported on the United States. In 1985 an official at the national network said that CCTV devoted at least 25 percent of its foreign newscasts to the United States; most of the coverage was favorable, as China sought to open up more contacts with the capitalist West.

It is quite possible that China did not get more coverage because of the difficulties in covering the country. First of all, according to Chu, in 1984, the number of resident Western correspondents was not large compared to the immensity and diversity of China. In 1983, 19 U.S. news organizations sent 22 reporters to Beijing; the same number of resident correspondents represented Western Europe (England, France, West Germany, Italy and Spain).[38]

The correspondents regularly ran into problems such as the language barrier, isolation and government censorship. Because not many of the Western reporters spoke Chinese they relied upon translators, who, although competent and efficient, represented the Chinese Government. Foreign correspondents remained relatively isolated, being housed in a restricted area of Beijing. As a result, they were not always free to interact, socially, which hindered their newsgathering.

Further, the Chinese government took a sensitive attitude toward national security, and any information not already published in the national press was considered confidential. Individuals were still wary of making personal contact with foreign reporters. Because of these handicaps some correspondents, such as Takashi Oka of the *Christian Science Monitor,* tried other tactics; he reported the long-term social and economic problems instead of political issues, thus avoiding difficulties with the authorities, while providing U.S. readers more in-depth analyses.

Western correspondents arrived in Japan on the heels of its emergence from isolation in the 1860s and 1870s. By 1873 a telegraph system was in place in Japan, and shortly thereafter Britain's Reuters News Agency established an office in Yokohama and divisions in Nagasaki and Tokyo. Reuters' first permanent correspondent in Tokyo was hired in 1907. Although a few stringers and agents worked for the Western press in Tokyo by 1898, most foreign correspondents did not arrive until after 1900. By 1904 Reuters, the Associated Press, the *Times* of London, London *Daily Mail,* London *Standard, New York Herald, New York Sun* and Laffan News Bureau had assigned resident reporters or stringers to cover Japan.

As Japan's prestige on the international stage rose after defeating China and Russia, its government became image-conscious. In 1909 the Japanese government supported the formation of the International Press Association (IPA), which was to improve the level of correspondence from Japan to

[38] J. Chu, "The Gathering of News About China," *Gazette* 33, (1984): 87–106.

other countries and to prevent misrepresentation. Foreign correspondents were required to belong to IPA if they hoped to gather news from government offices and file reports abroad. Thus, the organization actually represented government control and censorship.

Today, even though an official censoring body similar to IPA does not exist, a number of no-less disturbing, subtle means of controlling foreign correspondents prevail. For instance, domestic reporters in Japan can agree to stop the leaking of news to foreign correspondents. Also, special press clubs, which cover different government branches, have a monopoly on who is invited to gather news at press conferences. If a foreign correspondent does not have a good relationship with these clubs, his or her Japan career ends immediately. It is reported that a Taiwanese correspondent was ousted from one such club in the mid-1970s to make room for correspondents from China when Japan normalized relations with the Chinese.

Whether it was for these reasons, Japan did not fare very well in post-World War II treatment in the U.S. press. U.S. correspondents did not, according to R. Armstrong's study of the press and Japan, give an

introspective look at what the Occupation [by MacArthur's SCAP] meant for Japan and what it showed Americans about themselves. The coverage of Japanese political movements and their intellectual background was superficial and keyed to demonstrations, cabinet changes and other events which could have had little meaning for their readers in the absence of fuller background and analysis.[39]

Armstrong contended that the coverage remained poor throughout the 1950s and 1960s, with editors' pens running "the well-worn ruts established in cold war exigencies." During Nixon's early years in the U.S. presidency, "crass business matters" dominated U.S. coverage of Japan; the stories remained of low quality.

The Lockheed scandal, of course, revived extensive interest in Japan, but Armstrong thought it also had a negative impact, because after Lockheed the U.S. press, for lack of visible political issues between the two countries, concentrated on "pop sociology." From 1977 to 1979 U.S. newspeople, already critical of Japanese economic strategy, were given support by the Carter administration, the result being bitterness in the tone of the reporting. Reviewing the situation, Armstrong pointed out that a number of U.S. daily newspapers maintained bureaus and regular stringer relationships in Japan.

U.S. press coverage of Japan has been criticized over the years as being exotic, quaint, inadequate and superficial. Hohenberg reported in 1967 that stories from Japan dealt with sukiyaki, geisha, cherry blossoms, Mount Fuji and paper lanterns, but seldom about the substance of daily life. Lee, in 1979, analyzing four major U.S. dailies between 1905 and 1972, found that the preponderant amount of Japanese news was conditioned by crises; war was the most frequently reported topic, and 50 percent of the stories

[39] R. Armstrong, "The American Press and Japan," *Keio Communication Review*, 1, (1980): 73–86.

were negative toward Japan, 36 percent were neutral and only 14 percent were positive.[40]

Nihon Shimbun Kyokai, in a survey of a week's run of newspapers of the world in 1979, found that the *New York Times* used 23 Japanese-oriented stories. Leading dailies of five other Asian countries used more stories than the *Times,* as did England's *Financial Times* (24). Only *Pravda* (eight), the *Frankfurter Allgemeine Zeitung* (11) and *Le Monde* (nine) had fewer stories. By comparison, Japan's *Asahi Shimbun* during that week had 112 stories mentioning the United States.[41] Another report claimed similar imbalances in television reporting. Japan's NHK aired, over a four-month period in 1980–81, 13 times more stories about the United States than CBS "Evening News" gave on Japan.[42]

Studying a period of economic conflict between Japan and the United States in 1978, Lee reported that three major U.S. dailies gave the plurality of their news to economics, followed by disasters. Other important spheres, such as foreign relations, politics and defense, were under-reported.[43] Lent and Tsao, analyzing the three-month trade war in 1987 between Japan and the United States, showed that eight major, regionally selected U.S. dailies carried a total of 790 stories on the subject. Over 52 percent of the trade-related stories appeared in the *New York Times, Wall Street Journal* and *Washington Post.*[44]

In an attempt to remedy Japan's being poorly represented in the foreign media, newspapers and news agencies have expanded overseas services. In 1982 *Asahi Shimbun* contracted with the New York Times Service to distribute in the United States and other countries a feature service on economics, technology and science, gleaned from that daily's pages. Also, Kyodo News Service and Jiji Press expanded outgoing information by providing, through their English-language services, materials that foreign correspondents in Japan could use and which would be directly distributed abroad. Nihon Shimbun Kyokai and other agencies have bilateral agreements with a number of countries, including the United States, on the exchange of journalists.

[40] S.-C. Lee, "The Japanese Image Projected in Four U.S. Dailies Over a Sixty-Seven Year Period (1905–1972)" (Ph.D. diss. University of Minnesota, 1979).

[41] Nihon Shimbun Kyokai, "Coverage of Foreign News by the Japanese Media—A Survey" (Tokyo, 1981).

[42] K. Kitatani, "A Content Analysis of Television News Flow Between Japan and the United States: Another One-Way Street?" *Keio Communication Review* no. 6, (1985): 55–68.

[43] S.-C. Lee, "The American Image of Relations with Japan Projected in Three U.S. Dailies," *Gazette* 25, no. 1 (1979): 31–45.

[44] John A. Lent, and Chien-Chung Tsao, "Coverage of Japan-United States Trade Dispute in Eight U.S. Metropolitan Dailies, March–May 1987" (Washington, D.C.: Center for Foreign Journalists, 1987).

CONCLUSION

To make conclusions about the West's reporting of Asia, using the enormous amount of information produced by researchers, is nearly impossible. Some of the research is almost unintelligible, as the researchers try to impress readers with their methodology, rather than to express their findings; some of it is tied to a "them-us" mentality, reminiscent of the first cold war period; and none of it can be generalized to apply to all the mass media. The latter factor is understandable in that resources have not been available to conduct such multidimensional and longitudinal research.

However, from some of the research cited above, from correspondents' observations and hunches, it can be gathered that there are many shortcomings in the way Western mass media report upon Asia. Foremost, probably, among these is the close alliance of foreign news with the home country's diplomatic, trade and military arrangements with countries being reported upon. Regularly in the research examples are given of events of global consequences that were downplayed, or even ignored, because the government (or/and "prestige" press) of the correspondent's home country remained mum. Even more often, Asian countries have entered the West's news flow primarily because stories about them had close connections to the United States or Western Europe.

Much of the reportage about Asia has been tied to crises. War usually generates a great deal of coverage, especially if it is a war "sanctioned," or participated in, by Western nations. Truthful, interpretative and investigative reporting usually does not coincide with war, as correspondents (sometimes out of necessity) ally themselves with the military, and present biased, patriotic reports that downplay conflicts and stereotype the opposition.

When coverage of war-torn areas, such as Korea in the 1950s and Vietnam in the 1960s, dominated Western European and U.S. media, most of the normal activity of the rest of Asia went unnoticed. In turn, the Koreas and Vietnams also receded into journalistic oblivion once conflicts upon their soil halted.

Foreign reporting, like most journalistic activity, thrives on conflict; if actual war is not available to feed the wire machines and video cameras, the next best thing is verbal confrontation. Much Asian reporting, especially in the U.S. press, has dealt with words tossed back and forth between cold war dyads—the two Koreas, the two Chinas, the two Vietnams the Aquino government and the New Peoples Army, and others. The result is that much coverage of Asia takes on negative characteristics.

Finally, it is not an easy task to report on Asia for reasons that have to do with home-country media owners' ignorance and greed, and with host-country governments' insecurity and paranoia. Foreign correspondents are rather scarce in most of Asia; therefore, they must perform extra duties, covering regions rather than countries or parts of countries. Such firehouse reporting does not allow them to become sufficiently familiar with any one culture or language.

In the case of U.S. media, owners and managers of newspapers and broadcasting stations regularly point to the great expense of maintaining correspondents as reasons for not doing more with foreign news. This is a lame justification when one takes into account the multimillion- and billion-dollar transactions taking place among media conglomerates, and the obscenely huge salaries paid executives, television anchor people and some favored reporters.

Correspondents have also faced problems of access to information because of censorship and other restraint policies of some Asian governments—for example, China, Singapore, Malaysia and Indochina.

TELECOMMUNICATIONS

DON M. FLOURNOY

INTRODUCTION

PHILOSOPHERS may argue whether people direct technology or technology directs people. In the developing world there is little doubt that technology is leading the way. Japan, Korea, Taiwan and Australia, the most technologically advanced countries in the Asia-Pacific region, all run very fast to keep up with the pace of invention. In terms of technological accomplishment, the lesser-developed Solomon Islands, Vietnam, Myanmar and Bangladesh must run fast just to keep within sight of their neighbors.

All the countries of the region go to great lengths to accommodate to the new developments and seemingly will, to the limits of their resources, do whatever is necessary to meet the demands of the technologies. Visible evidence of this accommodation can be seen in the hearty welcome being given to the new technologies of telecommunications. The bases of electronic communications today are microelectronics, artificial intelligence, digital systems and photonics. These scientific breakthroughs have made it possible for individuals as well as nations to produce and distribute their own voice, video and data communications using computer, satellite and fiber optic systems. The Asia-Pacific region has embraced these possibilities enthusiastically.

What is being adopted is more than just local improvements to postal, telephone and telegraph services. It is more than the installation of stronger transmitters for improved radio and television reception and the reduction of tariffs on the import of TV sets. A structural transformation is being accepted, which gives citizens of the region access to information, education and entertainment that will alter their way of life. The telecommunications involved are the VSATs (very small aperture satellite terminals), ISDN (integrated systems digital networks) and computer communications that standardize and give businesses increased speed, capacity and control over the management of information vital to their competitive positions as world players. They are the direct broadcast satellites (DBS) that give governments new ways to reach the public with development communications, long-distance teaching, distribution of news and sports and the sale of commercial goods. They are the personal computers, printers and modems, the video cameras, recorders and playback machines that give members of the public freedom to communicate with whomever they want, whenever they want.

To accomplish these various objectives using telecommunications, a great many changes must be made, both locally and regionally. The long-term effect of these changes is not yet known. It is understood, however, that the changes will be significant and permanent.

Within the Asia-Pacific region are nations with the wealth of Brunei, the populations of China and India, and the well-developed resources of Korea and Japan. There are the tiny attols of the Pacific and the large land masses of Papua New Guinea and Australia. There is the ethnic diversity of Indonesia and Singapore, and the inaccessibility of Tibet and Nepal. To treat these nations as if they were all the same would be an injustice, for they are diverse geographic, political, economic and social entities. Their systems of telecommunications reflect, and should continue to enhance, their uniqueness. What these nations do have in common is the desire to be in better control, to have more of a say in the direction the technology is to go, and to assume greater responsibility for its development.

TELECOMMUNICATION TECHNOLOGIES

A visitor to the region readily notes the evidence of change. The obvious symbols are the satellite-directed earth stations that can be seen on the way into town from the airport; the speed and clarity of international direct-dial telephone calls; the number of local and international program choices found on the television set; the availability of personal computers with modems in most offices; the presence of good quality videocassette recorders (VCRs), video production equipment and shelves full of recent movies in many homes.

These changes are occurring in more than just selected cities. Great strides have been made in the region to ensure that telephones, radio communications and even television programs are available to the most remote villages. Coverage, however, is still far from complete. In India in 1986 there were only 0.5 telephones per 100 residents, compared to 65 in Japan and 75 in the United States.[1] But the development of supporting infrastructure, giving the public increased access to channels of communication, is a near-universal priority, and progress has been extensive.

Radio is a medium well-suited to respond to the local needs of multilingual societies. It is a readily available technology that does not require literacy. With the advent of transistor sets that operate on batteries, radio communications have become almost universal in Asia. In fact, Asia has the largest proportion of radio receivers found in any of the Third World regions.[2]

[1] Arvind Singhal, Everett M. Rogers and S. Adnan Rahman, "High Technology Microelectronics Development in India" (Paper prepared for the International Communications Association national conference, New Orleans, May 1988), p. 7.
[2] W. J. Howell, Jr., *World Broadcasting in the Age of the Satellite* (Norwood, New Jersey: Ablex Publishing Corp. 1986), 166.

Television, however, is still a luxury in many countries. Television came to Fiji only in 1982 and in some of the islands of Oceania television is still unavailable.[3] Nevertheless, because of satellite distribution, it will be only a short time before the signals will be available everywhere. Having the means to broadcast nationwide is a strong incentive to governments to see that receivers are obtainable, and the availability of programming is an incentive to individuals to invest in TV sets. It is estimated that factories in China are now turning out 12 million television sets a year, mostly for domestic use.[4]

Today, there are few nations that do not use satellites in some form. Use in China, Japan, Indonesia and Australia is already widespread. INTELSAT, the international satellite consortium to which most of the region's countries belong, provides the means for nationwide distribution of telephone, data and video signals and is the link that almost all now use to be in communication with the rest of the world.

INTELSAT manages 16 ocean-bridging satellites worldwide, using a system of cross-subsidy charges that encourages the participation of both low-use and high-use nations. Domestic satellites operate with the region; one example is the Indonesian Palapa system whose excess capacity is leased out to Singapore, Malaysia, Thailand, Brunei and the Philippines. At the moment, only one of the satellites positioned over Asia (Japan's BS-2a) is broadcasting directly to homes, although backyard satellite dishes are beginning to dot the countryside. More TVROs will appear as programming in greater variety is transmitted on the open airwaves.

Fiber optic lines are also being put into place in Asia. These high-capacity channels, using light pulses rather than analog electrical waves, are replacing copper telephone and telex cables. They also reduce the need for microwave towers and will eventually compete with satellites for voice, video and data traffic. As of 1988, a new Hawaii 4/Transpac three-fiber cable system connected the Philippines, Guam, Japan and Hawaii to North America, with a Pacific channel capable of 40,000 simultaneous telephone conversations.[5]

Plans are under way to link Australia and New Zealand to the North American continent with the largest submarine cable network ever built—about 15,150 miles/24,376 km. of fiber optic cable. The Australia-New Zealand link will provide 57,000 voice circuits, compared to the 480 channels the TASMAN I cable currently provides. The Australia-New Zealand-Canada cable (ANZCAN) provides about 500 channels. The link to North America is expected to be completed in the 1990s.[6]

The presence of these cables, representing investments of literally billions of dollars, is in addition to the continuing investments being made

[3] Ibid., p. 173.
[4] "As the World Turns," *Channels (Field Guide 1987)*: 22.
[5] "Companies Sign Contracts to Lay Pacific Fiber Cable," *Communications News* (April 1986): 14.
[6] Benjamin Fukumoto, "Pacific Underseas Cables Play Vital Role in Communications Network," *Signal* (February 1984): 81.

in international satellites. The all-out effort now being made by large transnational corporations to build integrated business networks in Asia and the Pacific indicates the strategic importance of the region in their long-range plans.

So far, it has not been the long-distance carriers that have most affected the general public; rather, it has been the little VCR. The VCR is the one technology the public has some control over, a development that has caused great concern among regulators. The emergence of home video—that is, the availability of reasonably priced home production, recording and dubbing equipment—and a thriving market in (mostly pirated) entertainment-oriented videotapes has filled a void where entertainment channels are limited. Even in places like Hong Kong and Singapore, where multiple channels of programming are available, the VCR has enhanced and made viewing more flexible.

VCRs are popular because they are economical to purchase, easy to operate, give good quality sound and picture, and permit viewing at times and places that are convenient to the viewer. With home viewing, censorship is more difficult. Favorite videos may be played over and over, loaned to friends or, as is often the case, dubbed for resale. All over Asia, video shops have sprung up in large and small communities to supply the entertainment needs of the home viewer.

Home video, however, also has had an effect on the workplace. Where home video has emerged, corporate video has followed. Office staffs are not comfortable with VCRs. Schools and hospitals, government and military organizations, and private corporations have found that they can conduct employee orientation and training, distribute corporate news programs, release products to the market and provide direct instruction by this means. Corporate headquarters, even those from outside the region, can send videotapes and know that employees can watch them either at home or at the office.

In corporate communications, as well as broadcasting, the emergence of small-format video production equipment has made television seem less of a luxury for people in the less-affluent countries. Half-inch and quarter-inch cameras and recorders are available at reasonable cost, and the quality is acceptable for most nonbroadcast applications. The newer MII and BETACAM half-inch equipment, although more expensive than the consumer grade, is of broadcast quality and sufficient for international exchange of programs. These technologies were used extensively during the 1988 Olympics in Seoul, Korea.

The new cameras, switchers, recorders and tape editors are easier to use, require less training and less engineering, and are quite portable. These qualities make production of news, information, educational and entertainment programming much easier.

Cable is still underdeveloped in the Asia-Pacific region. Wiring of communities for cable distribution of satellite-delivered programming will, in fact, not happen in most of the Asia-Pacific countries. This is due in part to the cost of laying and maintaining cable, and in part to the scarcity of programming to go onto the cable. Mainly, however, it is due to the impending deployment of a more suitable alternative: direct-to-home satellite broadcasting.

Australia has no cable. Even in Japan, only 11 percent of the homes (about 3.3 million households) are estimated to be connected to cable, and these are of limited channel capacity used principally for retransmission of regular TV programs into areas with poor reception.[7] Hong Kong and Singapore have more developed cable systems designed to provide for their "information society" needs, linking videotex and facsimile terminals as well as providing for the distribution of video for entertainment and other purposes.

In Asia's postcolonial period, newspapers, radio and television have been among the most readily available tools of nation building. The mass media, in this regard, are thought to play a role different from their role in the West. The media are not used principally for public diversion and entertainment, but for the public good. With their diverse ethnic, religious and language groups, India, Sri Lanka, Malaysia, Indonesia and others in the region have needed ways to establish a core of political and cultural unity among their diverse constituents. Telecommunication technologies have been looked to as instruments for creating these new national identities and ensuring national integration. Entertainment is only a secondary consideration.

Even today, enhancements to broadcast technologies in the region are perceived to be an investment in the means for explaining national policies to the public, and for eliciting public support for those policies. Advancement of the goals of national development, national responsibility and discipline are primary mass media agendas in these countries. Inevitably, the particular political system and its communication system are closely linked. If they are not government-owned, the telecommunication technologies are carefully regulated by the government to ensure compliance with the national agenda.

In his opening remarks to the ministers of information of nonaligned countries meeting in Jakarta in 1984, President Suharto summarized Indonesia's mass media goals as intended "to inflame the spirit of dedication and struggle of the nation, consolidate the national unity and cohesion, enhance the sense of national responsibility and discipline, popularize the national culture and identity, and stimulate the participation of the community in development."[8] Suharto was only stating what was understood and approved by most members of the nonaligned group. That is, the mass media, newspapers as well as the telecommunications media, are there to promote the cause of national unity, to improve and assist the functioning

[7] "Japan," *Electronic Media* (January 10, 1985): 12.
[8] Quoted in Don M. Flournoy, "Satellites in the National Interest," *Satellite Communications* (February 1986): 34.

of the society and to facilitate national development. Any other purposes must take a back seat to these immediate goals.

Development programs at the community level have been a dominant initiative of the Suharto government. His "New Order" leadership, from 1965 until the present, has been oriented toward encouraging active participation of all the people in various development schemes. Thus, it is not surprising that the single national TV channel, distributed since 1976 by its own Palapa satellite system, is used to reach Indonesia's 163 million people, to explain to them the objectives of their government's programs, to enlist their support, and to encourage their constructive involvement in community and national affairs.

Indira Gandhi, at the time of the Jakarta conference was chairperson of the nonaligned movement. The reasons why "nonaligned countries have pioneered and effectively promoted the cause of a New International Information and Communication Order," she explained, is that "nonaligned countries are conscious of the special contributions the media can make to development and social change."[9] The promotion of a new information order, in which countries such as India have greater control over the communications that cross their borders, as well as increased opportunities to present themselves to the rest of the world, further explains the need for haste felt throughout the region to invest in the latest telecommunication technologies.

The first great stimulus to broadcasting in Malaysia was the outbreak of militant Communist activity in 1948, which forced rapid expansion of radio programming built around national security and national development issues. Such broadcasts were deemed pivotal during the period of independence from Great Britain (1957), the formation of the Malaysian state (1963) and the period of confrontation with Indonesia (1963–65).[10] Radio Malaysia was also extended—in 1952 and 1954—to the eastern states of Sarawak and Sabah, located on the northern coast of the island of Borneo. Because these non-Malay-speaking peoples are separated from the Malay Peninsula by the South China Sea, radio communication was seen as an important force for cohesion. Television broadcasting is now also used to help reassure eastern Malaysians that they are full members of the Malaysian nation.

In Asia, the mission undertaken by the national media goes well beyond the purposes of public diversion and entertainment. This is not to say that India, Indonesia, Malaysia, China and others do not import soap operas and serials, crime and adventure programs, game shows and cartoons, or that they do not now produce these shows on their own. Station programmers, however, understand that the first priority of the airwaves is to serve a larger purpose. The public airwaves are used to encourage family planning, promote health, increase agricultural productivity, stimulate reforestation, provide for education and prepare the way for modernization. At

---

[9] "COMINAC: Conference of the Ministers of Information of Non-Aligned Countries," Department of Information of the Republic of Indonesia, 1984, p. 31.
[10] John Lent, *Broadcasting in Asia and the Pacific* (Philadelphia: Temple University Press, 1978), 143.

the same time, television viewers are likely to be admonished by their leaders to become involved in the affairs of the community, rather than sit at home watching TV.

EDUCATIONAL APPLICATIONS

It is understood that to have a literate and informed public is the highest government priority. Among the people too there is often an unmet hunger for knowledge, for self-development and for international interchange. It has been interesting, for example, to observe that after years of isolation under the Cultural Revolution, the Chinese people have shown exceptional curiosity about the outside world and have made a strong commitment to catching up with that world. China's leaders have made a conscious effort to disseminate information, learning and even entertainment from one side of the country to the other. They have begun to position their country so that China can now more fully participate and compete as a global partner.

In 1987 the China Great Wall Industry Corp., a government organization offering satellite launch services, announced in the wake of the U.S. National Aeronautics and Space Administration (NASA) space shuttle and the European Ariane launch failures that they were prepared to "beat anyone's price."[11] Negotiations were underway with companies representing 19 different nations to place commercial satellites in orbit for them. The People's Insurance Company of China announced it was prepared to guarantee the service for an appropriate price.

China has been launching its own satellites for more than 10 years. Television coverage, using satellite and terrestrial transmissions, is now estimated to reach 60 percent of the population, or about 600 million people.[12] Although the official estimate of people with a college education is only six in 1,000 persons, student enrollments in China's Television University, full and part-time, was estimated at 673,600 in 1985.[13]

Nevertheless, it must be recognized, that for geographic, economic and political reasons, access to instruction, information and entertainment is in no way equally available throughout the Asia-Pacific region. Not all countries have equal capability. Television broadcast coverage is extensive in very few countries, with many having access to only a single channel. Almost all have limited broadcasting hours. Within the borders of a single nation, not all the population have the same levels of education or even speak the same language. Few countries have the facilities or the trained staff needed to respond to public expectations or wishes. These are serious limitations to the national development goals of education.

[11] "Launch News," *Via Satellite* (June 1987): 10.
[12] Lynne Reaves, "China: 200 Million Tune in to TV Renaissance," *Electronic Media* (April 4, 1985): 16.
[13] Deng-Jong, "Educational Use of Chinese TV Broadcasting" (Paper, School of Telecommunication, Ohio University, Athens, Ohio, 1986). See also Ma Chaozeng, "Television and Its Social Effects in China" (Paper presented to the 1986 International Television Studies Conference, London, 1986).

India, with its vast population, its limitations on facilities and its short-age of teachers, has sought to deemphasize degrees and degree programs, giving increased attention to nonformal education strategies. Emphasis is given to programs of vocational and continuing education that help to train adults without taking them out of their vocations. Satellite technologies are used for long-distance teaching, and broadcast directly to small dish receivers located at school sites. The intention, not yet substantially real-ized, is to connect villages electronically in ways that allow people to teach each other.

In the mid-1960s India initiated the now-famous SITE experiment, us-ing an ATS-6 satellite loaned by NASA to provide agricultural information to farmers. Some 2,330 villages viewed television in community-viewing situations, where the government found that literates and illiterates could learn equally well by way of TV.[14] Although this experiment lasted only a year, it has served as a model for numerous imitators. According to Yash Pal, science adviser to Indira Gandhi and later to Rajiv Gandhi, the tech-nology is not difficult; the hard part is the management of the system and the economic investment required to make reception equipment available in a nation of 700 million people.[15]

Taiwan has taken a different approach. It has announced its goal of put-ting a college degree within reach of Taiwanese citizens wherever they are on the island. Its University of the Air is a second-chance educational pro-gram for the two-thirds of high school graduates who never go on to col-lege. Patterned after Japanese and British open universities, the UHF-TV service is provided on one of three commercial channels. Chinese language, literature and history are stressed. Emphasis is on education through enter-tainment.[16]

Japan's University of the Air was begun in 1985 to provide alternatives in a society where education is valued, but admissions to institutions of higher education are limited. Japan is looking to satellite distribution to make this predominantly Tokyo-based program available nationwide in the future. Television classes have been designed so that credits are transferable to universities. Recently retired professors from prestigious Japanese uni-versities, where the mandatory retirement age is 60, are widely used. This increases credibility and ensures an experienced faculty.[17]

Due to mountainous conditions, a portion of Thailand's population has been difficult to reach with terrestrial telecommunications networks. Thai-land has sought to extend its broadcast coverage using the Indonesian Pa-lapa satellite to interconnect TV stations whose signals now reach 85 per-cent of the country. News, entertainment and educational programming is

[14] James Traub, "Beaming the World of Andhra Pradesh," *Channels* (May/June 1984): 42.

[15] Yash Pal, "Communication Technology for the People," *Communicator; Quarterly Journal of the Indian Institute of Mass Communication* (August 1986): 22–23.

[16] Robert King, "Taiwan Introduces TV University," *Chronicle of Higher Education* (January 25, 1984): 27–28.

[17] Peter Osterlund, "Japan's University of the Air Beams Learning to the Masses," *Christian Science Monitor*, 3 May 1985, pp. 23–24.

broadcast for eight hours a day, Monday through Friday, and 18½ hours a day on weekends. A new educational channel with no advertisements has been initiated.[18] Thailand's Open University broadcasts for four hours each weekday, with nonformal education transmissions carried for two hours on Saturday.

Asia has "staggering" educational problems, according to Vijay Menon of the Asian Mass Communications Research Center in Singapore. "Despite a doubling of enrollment between 1960 and 1982, nearly 400 million in the age group 5–24 in Asia remained outside the educational system."[19] Educational development, both formal and nonformal, ranks high on the national agendas of all the countries in the region. In reality, the impact of the media on formal education is still modest due to the cost and to deficiencies in equipment, lack of skilled workers and a shortage of educational programming.

LOCAL PROGRAMMING

National development priorities are apparent in the television schedules of these countries. Some nations place restrictions on the type and number of imported programming that may appear on the national broadcasting services, as well as when the programs may be shown. This means that indigenous programs will be clustered in prime early evening viewing hours. Content quotas are designed to stimulate local production, and to avoid the presumed negative consequences of foreign programs dominating local airwaves.

The purchase of foreign programs creates a number of problems. It exacerbates an often difficult balance-of-payments/foreign-exchange problem for the national government. It sets the stage for foreign imports to have undue influence over the tastes, and even the values, of viewers. In countries where there are insufficient local alternatives, it makes viewers discontent with the fare that can be offered locally.

To deal with these problems, Australia, for example, sets minimum percentages of programming that must originate within the country. The "points system" administered by the Australian Broadcasting Tribunal is a regulatory effort to protect local programming industries and to ensure the availability of home-produced material.[20]

China, like many of the countries in this region, is interested in foreign programs, but has been very selective about what it imports. Chinese program buyers like sports and noncontroversial programming dubbed in Chinese, such as Jacques Cousteau's "Sea Odyssey" and the BBC's "Anna Karenina." They do not like material with explicit sexual content and they try to avoid programs that display wealthy life-styles.

[18] Lynne Reaves, "Asia Offers Diverse Look at Television," *Electronic Media* (December 16, 1985): 54.
[19] "Broadcasting Development and Distance Education," *ABU Newsletter* 6, no. 3 (1987): 5.
[20] Jeff Pryor, "Kids' Hour Gets Kangaroo Punch from Australia," *Electronic Media* (January 24, 1985): 22.

In 1984 CBS sold a varied program package to the People's Republic of China on a barter basis. No cash changed hands. The package, which included 64 hours of programming over a 12-month basis consisting of basketball, movies of the week and selections from "60 Minutes," gave CBS the right to sell five minutes per hour of advertising. Since more than half of the world's population lives in Asia, and the world's largest single TV audience lives on the Chinese mainland, sponsors such as IBM, Kodak, Boeing, Weyerhauser, Stauffer Chemical and N. V. Philips were willing to underwrite the programs.[21]

To purchase a television set in China costs the equivalent of six month's wages, but owning a set ranks high among the priority items on the average citizen's wish list of refrigerator, sewing machine, bicycle, wristwatch and TV set. In China, families combine their savings and jointly purchase TV receivers. This is why an estimated 400 million Chinese viewed the 1984 Summer Olympics even though, officially, there were only six million TV sets in the country at the time.[22]

China's neighbor Nepal has a modest state-owned television service with some commercial programs. Its programs generally focus on agriculture, health, education and a little entertainment. The entertainment is used to encourage the people to watch the educational parts. Television sets must be provided for isolated villages and schools. In Nepal there is great fear of spoiling the youth with imported materials.

In general, locally produced programs are well received by the public and, even when scheduled against shows such as "Dynasty" or "Star Trek" still attract large viewing audiences. But locally produced programs are relatively more expensive than the imported fare and production efforts seldom match the demand.[23] It is cheaper to import "Sesame Street" and "Little House on the Prairie" from the United States, "Jewel in the Crown" from Great Britain and soap serials from Latin America than to write and produce anything close to comparable programs.

A syndication (rerun) market is needed to cover production costs of original programs that are not directly subsidized by the government or some other sponsor. In the United States, when the NBC commercial network orders a program or a series to be produced, NBC pays only about half of its actual cost. The remaining costs are absorbed by the production house, which retains the rights to the show and hopes to recover the other 50 percent (and considerably more) from domestic and international syndication.

There is an active international program exchange market. Producers are selling their shows because they want to recoup their initial investments.

[21] Dennis Chase, "China Central TV Returns to Shop at CBS," *Electronic Media* (December 9, 1985): 4. See also Eric Traub, "Overseas Barter, American Style," *Programmer* (April 1986): 40–41.

[22] Angela Newsome and Linh Ong, "TV Hooks World's Largest Audience," *TV World* (December 1984): 49–50.

[23] Kunda Dixit, "What TV Can Do for Katmandu," *Channels* (July/August 1986): 9–10. See also Arthur Unger, "TV Coming to the Fairy-Tale Kingdom of Nepal," *Christian Science Monitor*, 5 April 1985, pp. 23–24.

Fortunately for them, there is an exploding market for video material. This is due both to the longer hours of broadcasting now in effect around the world and the additional channels coming on line. Executives are looking for good programs that will fit the requirements of their particular broadcasting schedules.

In Singapore, where there are four official languages, there is an acknowledged responsibility for informing each segment of the population in its own language. Some 60 percent of television programming is imported. Chinese films are acquired from Hong Kong and from Taiwan for the majority population; Malay films are brought in from Indonesia and Malaysia for the Malay-speaking viewers; Tamil and Hindi films are imported from India for those of Indian origin. For the others, English films are shown, which come principally from the United States and Great Britain, and are subtitled.[24] Because of the population mix, importing programming is a necessity for Singapore. It is not reasonable to assume that this small island nation would be able to originate such a quantity and diversity of TV programs.

Within the region, however, there are extremes. New Zealand, with its two national channels, imports 75 percent of all programming shown; Japan, with a similarly homogeneous culture and a single language, used almost no programming from abroad as reported in 1986.[25] Import quotas are being looked at in Asia just at the time when the public is asking for greater variety in programming. The public wants some choice, which means more than one selection. This puts increased demands on local origination and, when this falls short, it forces broadcasters to look elsewhere for usable material.

REGIONAL PROGRAMMING

Asian and Pacific programmers do, at times, cooperate to develop original programming. But it is not easy to produce pan-Asia and pan-Pacific programming, and the difficulty is not just the cost. There are also problems of ethnic and language diversity and political difficulties associated with coproduction. The reasons that these countries have been going slowly in the implementation of DBS, for example, is not just that the system is expensive; they recognize that if they open the skies to satellite-distributed programming they will have a hard time finding a common denominator and may get a lot of programs—and advertising—that they would rather not broadcast.

One area of cooperative programming that has been immensely successful has been sports. The Asian Games of 1983 are reported to be one of the factors that speeded India's TV expansion and its move to color TV.[26] As

[24] Ministry of Culture, *Singapore 1985* (Singapore: Singapore National Printers, Ltd., 1985), 179–180.
[25] Howell, *World Broadcasting,* p. 79. See also Harvey D. Shapiro, "Japan's Closed Television World," *Channels* (October 1987): 12.
[26] Binod Agrawal, "Planning Strategies for Democratizing Communication in India," (Ahmadabad: Indian Space Research Organization, 1986) 3.

the location of these games moves from country to country, each broadcast organization tries to improve its technological capabilities so as to bring to viewers back home the best possible coverage. Sports in Asia are considered to be an important nation-building activity. Sports competitions are seen as a rallying point for national pride and international exchange. There is competition among the countries to host such events. Australia and New Zealand took great pride in 1987 in being hosts for the World Rugby Cup and in being able to offer video distribution to Western Europe, Africa and North America. Some 3,600 athletes from eight nations were in Jakarta for the SEA Games in the summer of 1987.

Another example of regional cooperation and cross-border communication, and one that can be pointed to as radically changing Asia's traditional dependence on foreign programming, is Asiavision. In April 1984 India, Pakistan, Bangladesh, Sri Lanka, Brunei, Malaysia and Indonesia began exchanging television news stories once each week via the Pacific Ocean and Indian Ocean INTELSAT networks. These are countries with diverse, and sometimes conflicting, cultural and political backgrounds and very different technical systems for broadcasting. Among them, all three television standards—625 PAL, 625 SECAM and 525 NTSC—are represented.[27]

In spite of these inhibitors, by following the principle of "free to offer, free to receive or to refuse," news editors took the initiative to share with others stories they had collected for their own use. Shared items were, for the most part, those produced within a country and thought to be of interest to others in the network. Those countries are now exchanging news on a daily basis—and sometimes twice daily. At about the same time the People's Republic of China, North Korea, Japan, Hong Kong, Australia, and New Zealand formed a similar network. They, too, are now trading news on a regular basis.

Asiavision is modeled on the successful Eurovision and similar satellite networks in the more developed world. The network's momentum is largely due to sponsorship by the United National Educational, Scientific and Cultural Organization (UNESCO), to the organizing work of the broadcasting unions, to the availability of INTELSAT channels, and to the financial, logistic and moral support given by the individual countries involved.[28]

Such exchanges, made possible as a result of satellite technologies, are now testing traditional assumptions about periphery-to-center relationships. The capability for collecting and sharing their own news gives these countries a way to break out of the usual "dominance-dependence" relationships characteristic of news flow, and makes possible what has been so difficult to manage until now—horizontal exchanges between neighboring or near-neighboring states.

Several countries in Asia, in cooperation with each other, now control the instruments of information production and distribution that formerly

[27] Don M. Flournoy, "Asian Countries Form Local News Exchanges," *Electronic Media* (October 7, 1985): 15, 20.
[28] Yrjo Lansipuro, "Asiavision News Exchange," *Media Asia* 14, no. 1 (1987): 46–52.

were controlled by others. The implication is that more news about Asia will be appearing on Asian television sets. Also, because of the capabilities for reverse feeds into the international distribution channels, regional news that has been collected by Asians will be made available to editors of TV news programs in other parts of the world.

The CNN World Report, which was inagurated in 1987, receives and redistributes news from Asia and the rest of the world unedited and uncensored. The result is a greater democratization of the media. Few of the countries of Asia will wish to give up their affiliations with the international news agencies, but with Asiavision and the CNN World Report in place they will have greater program choice and the opportunity for balanced coverage.

CROSS-BORDER COMMUNICATIONS

Fear of outside cultural domination and influence is still a big issue in Asia. "Cultural imperialism" is much discussed since few countries that do not import programs offer a significant schedule of programming, especially a choice among programs in the same time slot. New Zealand, for example, faces a triad of influences—American, British and Australian—whose combined programs take up 75 percent of the schedule on New Zealand airwaves.

When, in 1985, New Zealand celebrated its 25th anniversary of television reception, some newspapers satirically characterized the event as a celebration of "25 years of foreign programming in NZ."[29] And Ian Cross, former chairman of BCNZ, was quoted as saying New Zealand should "beware of satellites bearing gifts. . . . New Zealand must not regress by the twenty-first century to what it was in the nineteenth century by becoming a colony, not of the Old Empire, but of satellite communications."[30] Interestingly, New Zealand is among those nations listed with the British and the Australians whose influence over the communications of Papua New Guinea, Fiji, Kiribati, Tuvalu, the Cook and other Pacific islands has led to concerns of "cultural colonization."[31]

Television sets manufactured in Taiwan for domestic use have only three usable VHF channels. This is to ensure that the people of Taiwan cannot pick up television programming originating from the mainland. Whereas the Republic of China and the People's Republic of China seem to be

[29] Geoffrey Lealand, "Foreign Television Programmes on New Zealand Television: Windows on the World or Wicked Imperialism?" (Paper presented to the 1986 International Television Studies Conference, University of London, July 1986), p. 17.

[30] Ibid., p. 18.

[31] Jim Richstad, "International Broadcasting in the Pacific Islands" (Paper presented to the Association for Education in Journalism and Mass Communication 1986 Conference, University of Oklahoma, Norman, Okla., August 1986). See also Geoffrey L. Martin, "TV Battle Brews in South Pacific," *Electronic Media* (September 8, 1986): 18.

edging toward reconciliation, the Taiwanese government still feels it must protect its people from influence by the Communist regime.

South Korea seeks to protect itself from programming originating in the North and in Japan. Korea, once under Japanese rule, is still sufficiently concerned about Japanese "cultural aggression" that the government prohibits the showing of Japanese films and monitors the importation of Japanese publications for "adverse cultural effects."[32]

In July 1987, NHK-Japan started 24-hour programming one of its two DBS channels, the BS-2a, making it the first TV station in the world to launch a full-scale DBS service. BS-2a channels operate at 100 watts of power, sufficient to deliver a clear video signal to small (3 ft/1 m. or smaller) parabolic antennas located on the rooftops of Japanese households.[33]

As of 1987 DBS channel 1 provided 11 hours of news per day (importing news from ABC and CNN in the United States, and BBC in Britain) with NHK anchor persons introducing the correspondents. There also are classic movies, relays of theatrical performances (musicals, Kabuki and operas), concerts with digital sound and sports events. "Dynasty," the popular American soap opera, also is featured as an exclusive release to Japan on this channel. Channel 2, the other DBS channel, rebroadcasts both general and educational programs selected from Japanese terrestrial services, for viewers in remote areas and on islands where conventional signals are weak. At the end of May 1987 about 140,000 households in Japan were equipped to receive the DBS broadcasts. One million households were expected to have such capability by 1990.

In January 1984 Japan launched its first DBS satellite, whose signals can easily be picked up in Korea. The South Korean government promptly banned the selling of reception equipment and declared that it would jam the signal if necessary.[34]

The advent of satellites with more powerful and steerable antennas makes it much easier to transmit signals into the airspace of neighboring nations. If those signals are uninvited, affected nations have reason to be concerned. In 1981 Indonesia eliminated all commercial advertisements from the national service; it will not welcome a commercial-based enterprise using direct broadcast satellites to transmit programming into its territory. Since the Indonesian leadership worries about the adverse cultural effects of promoting consumerism beyond what the economy of the country can hope to satisfy, neither the programming nor the advertisements of spillover broadcasters, nor those aimed specifically at potential Indonesian audiences will be welcome.

Spillover does inevitably occur. Malaysia's new third channel, TV3, a commercial broadcast channel, has as its largest audience the people of Singapore. From transmitters in Johor, the southernmost Malaysian state, Singapore is easily within the path of its signal. TV3 has a potential viewing audience of over 2 million people among the citizens of its neighbor,

[32] "Seoul, Korea, Bans Japanese TV," *Video Age* (April 1984): 12.
[33] "NHK Launches 24-Hour DBS Satellite," *ABU Newsletter* 6, no. 4 (1987): 4.
[34] "Seoul, Korea, Bans Japanese TV," p. 12.

and it fully intends to compete with the Singapore Broadcasting Corp. (SBC) for that country's U.S. $40 million advertising market.[35] Much of the programming on TV3 is in English, consisting of programs purchased abroad that are designed to be competitive in a market where entertainment has a high priority and the public has some choice in what they view. The government-controlled SBC has been aggressively importing more U.S. made-for-TV movies to counter those acquired by the Malaysian channel, such as "Dynasty" and "Hill Street Blues."

RTM and SBC signals are also broadcast into Indonesian airspace, and are received in Sumatra to the west across the narrow Strait of Malacca, and in Riau, Batam and other islands to the south. Philippine signals also can be picked up in Indonesian territories to the northeast, as can those of Papua New Guinea to the east and Australia to the south.

Advertisements are a problem for Indonesia, but of even greater significance is the fact that the programs Indonesians view from outside make them discontent with what is offered on TVRI. TVRI's limited entertainment fare, aimed largely at its majority rural population, cannot compete with the quiz shows, serials, movies and sports that dominate the airwaves of its neighbors.[36] In addition, production qualities, although professional, do not compare favorably with the fast-paced timing and special effects of commercial competitors.

The biggest long-range threat, as far as Indonesia is concerned, is from the satellite. By 1987, enterprising Indonesians of Chinese extraction in central Java had purchased their own receiving dish, aimed it at Chinese satellites, and were rebroadcasting China Central Television (CCTV) signals to local subscribers by way of a low-power five-watt transmitter.[37] Satellite reception equipment is now being sold in home-assembly kits, and components are readily available. Since Singapore, Malaysia and Thailand use the Indonesian Palapa satellite to distribute their own television programs, there is little hope that TVRI viewers will resist the temptation to draw down those programs as well. In fact, the Indonesian government has been buying dishes for those villages that receive the weakest terrestrial broadcast signals, and has supported the right of private individuals to purchase parabolic antennas to receive TVRI satellite signals. There is no way of knowing whether the public is viewing TVRI or the programming of other countries carried on the Palapa satellite.

COMMERCIALIZATION

There are few nations of Asia and the Pacific that do not now permit commercial advertisements in some form. From a political and social point of view, most would prefer that program sponsorship come entirely from the government. However, since government funds are not forthcoming—at least to the extent needed to provide the type of programs and the quantity

[35] Reaves, "Asia Offers Diverse Look at Television," p. 54.
[36] "Videos Go to the Village," *CAJ Quarterly Newsletter* (October 1984): 6.
[37] Personal interview with TVRI Director K. S. Ishadi

demanded by the viewing public—and since additional taxes on receivers and increased license fees do not seem a likely source of new revenue, advertising sponsorship of programming is almost inevitable.

In 1984, when Indira Gandhi made a big push at the time of the Indian elections to increase reception of TV signals from 23 to about 70 percent of the population, she relied on "sponsored" programs and commercial advertisements to carry the weight of these developments. Doordarshan, India's television broadcaster, began to make money by charging for airtime. This was met with public approval at a time when there was a growing consumerism in India, when the middle class aspired to emulate Japan and the Western countries. Rajiv Gandhi's government has also responded to these middle-class interests by helping to make consumer products more readily available.[38]

The problem with commercial sponsorship in a poor country is that consumerism is promoted beyond the people's capabilities to purchase. Thus, the poor are left with unmet expectations, class tensions develop and the government in power becomes the object of public discontent.

SBC's third channel, a cultural channel, is supported both by advertising and by the mandatory license fee. Channel 12 has been having trouble attracting viewers due to its limited audience appeal. With an insecure funding base, its future is therefore uncertain. The problem with commercial support is that it exists only to the extent that the programs deliver an audience to the advertiser.

In the Philippines, where broadcasting has been a commercial enterprise from the start, the government gives a high priority to providing service to rural areas. Since advertisers prefer to stick to programs that attract the largest possible audiences, however, rural broadcasting is not a priority for the commercial sponsors. In a struggling economy the advertising industry also is strapped. The economic support of the media is weak, resulting in low-cost productions and programming for the largest available audiences.[39]

Although Niugini Television Network (NTN), Papua New Guinea, only came on air in 1987, a second commercial station, Media New Guinea (MNG), is expected to be on the air in 1988. NTN broadcasts only in the area of Port Moresby, but plans to expand to the highlands are in place.[40] There were estimated to be only 20,000 television sets in the country as of 1987, most of which were used for showing home videos for entertainment. Half of the NTN organization is owned by the Australian company PBL Pacific Television, which intends to cover the entire country by satellite.[41]

[38] James Traub, "New Delhi Gold Rush," *Channels* (July/August 1986): 34–35.
[39] Ibarra M. Gonzalez, "Democratization of the Philippine Media 1986" (Paper presented to the 1986 conference of the International Association for Mass Communication Research, New Delhi, Summer 1986).
[40] "Niugini TV Begins Broadcasts," *ABU Newsletter* 6, no. 2 (1987): 18.
[41] "Second Commercial TV Station for Papua New Guinea," *ABU Newsletter* 6, no. 4 (1987): 10.

A related development, reflecting changes occurring in other parts of the world, is a not-so-tentative move in the direction of privatization. Privatization is a way of transferring to the private sector, or allowing private enterprises to manage, those activities normally assigned to government agencies. From the legislator's point of view, shifting responsibility to (properly regulated) for-profit organizations is not simply a way to transfer costs from government; it is a way to reduce the bureaucracy, to spread the risk of failure and to increase the efficiency with which services are delivered. In Asia and the Pacific there are numerous examples to point to, including instances of turning postal services over to franchised operators and contracting out telecommunications services. There are also instances of competition being permitted or even encouraged, with those services provided by government monopoly.

In a move toward privatization, New Zealand will have a third television channel to compete with the two state-run channels. New Zealand's PTT, which incorporates the New Zealand Post Office, the Post Office Bank and the Telecom Corporation, was restructured in 1987 and the remaining PTT segments were released to be run as businesses rather than as government agencies.[42] TV3, due [which went] on the air in 1989, is a privately owned network consisting of four already existing regional companies. The new service will be supported by advertisers.[43]

The government of Macao has announced its intention to sell its Chinese-language radio and television service to the private sector, while keeping its Portuguese-language service. Teledifusao de Macau (TDM), which consolidated radio and television broadcasting under a single government organization in 1983, currently transmits five hours of programs daily in Cantonese and Portuguese.[44]

The Nippon Telegraph and Telephone Public Corporation (NTT) of Japan was legally restructured and (subjected to competitive telecommunications) in 1986. Earlier, NTT had been permitted to operate as a monopoly; guaranteed adequate profits and freedom from competition in exchange for implementation of universal telephone service. NTT will now have competitors, including competition from cable television and data transmissions companies that will build new telecommunications networks capable of carrying services other than TV programs. Market requirements and forces are expected to define the new service arrangements to be offered.[45]

Deregulation and competition with government monopolies come with demand for increased information services, which, in Asia and the Pacific, arises with the advent of satellite, fiber optic and digital communications.

---

[42] "New Zealand Announces the Restructuring of its PTT at Annual Pacific Telecommunications Council Meeting," *Communication News* (March 1987): 24.
[43] "Tele-Vid Three Awarded NZ Third Channel," *ABU Newsletter* 6, no. 4 (1987): 6.
[44] "Macau: Towards Semi-Privatization," *ABU Newsletter* 6, no. 2, (1987): 17.
[45] Megumi Komiya and Jean-Luc Renaud, "Privatizing Japanese Telecommunications," *Intermedia* (March 1986): 14–17.

These technologies are, in fact, the basis of the demand. Before the technology existed, the demand was not there because this kind of technology was considered merely science fiction.

Integrated services digital networks, now being installed on a global scale, are science fiction come true. ISDN offers the capability for moving vast quantities of voice, video and data reliably and quickly, which means that the information resources of the world may ultimately be made instantly available to the most remote corner of the planet. Asian countries wishing to participate in the emerging "world information society" have no choice but to adopt the world telecommunication standards, since all parts of the network must be compatible.

The intent of deregulation and competition is to stimulate the development of local telecommunication services and equipment, to increase the number of user options and to encourage participation of new players in the market.[46] Among the less-affluent countries the worry is that such new product developments will make physical plants and operating equipment obsolete. They fear that they will be left behind with outmoded telecommunications facilities, and without the resources to compete. However, the investment capital required to replace still serviceable but noncompetitive telecommunications technologies is sorely needed elsewhere. These countries face the prospect that they will forever be user and consumer nations rather than being the producers and developers.

This is why the issue of new television standards—that is, adoption of high-definition television—has sent such tremors throughout the Third World. The International Radio Consultative Committee, a deliberative committee of the International Telecommunications Union (ITU), is considering the issue of a world standard for television transmission.[47] Such a standard would give manufacturers the basis for building, and broadcasters the basis for using, television technologies that would produce a substantially better picture. Specifically, the television screen would be wider and the number of scan lines in the TV set would be increased from 525–625 lines (based on the 40-year-old American/European standard) to the new 1,000-plus line standard of the Japanese.[48]

Unfortunately, if a 1,125, or similar, line standard is adopted, it will mean the virtual abandonment of the existing system—a system that was only recently put into place, at great cost, in many Third World countries. The prospect that still-functional cameras, control rooms, transmitters, home antennas and receivers will automatically be rendered obsolete and incompatible is devastating for the electronics consumer nations.

These nations must not only raise the funds for the new equipment, but they will have little or no involvement in its manufacture. Certainly, in

---

[46] Ron Grawert and Brian Hughes, "Private Networks: A Changing International Perspective," *Telecommunications* (November 1987): 31–34.

[47] "High-Definition TV: Politics Muddies the Clear Picture," *Channels (Field Guide 1987)*, p. 54.

[48] John Parry, "U.S.-Japanese HDTV Pushed as Global Standard," *Electronic Media* (October 21, 1985): 36.

the beginning, those who will benefit are Sony of Japan, Philips of the Netherlands, RCA of the United States and others well positioned to compete in such ventures. The development will be a net drain on the resources of countries such as Bangladesh, Macao, Burma (now Myanmar) and Fiji, who must once again follow the lead of the more developed countries. While pressures are mounting for engineers to come up with an enhanced TV system that can be put into place without throwing out the existing one, there are also pressures to set the new standard quickly. To fail to adopt a universal standard that benefits the largest number of people is to face the prospect that Japan and others will proceed with, and in effect force, a de facto standard that may have less than universal support.

JOINT VENTURES

In order to take more competitive positions, the lesser-developed countries have little choice other than to make deals with those that have the technologies they need. While there are a few countries manufacturing and exporting telecommunications equipment in competition with European and North American businesses, and doing so successfully in a global market, most Asia-Pacific business ventures have their basis in cooperative arrangements with other more developed nations.

In South Korea the penetration rate for television broadcasting is 97.5 percent, with some 7.7 million television sets in place. Through joint ventures, technical cooperation, transfer of technology and strong government backing for private arrangements with foreign companies, the country has now gained reasonable self-sufficiency in telecommunications. Cooperative arrangements, such as the Gold Star Tele-Electric agreement with Siemens of Germany that began in 1970, have given the nation its great leap forward. There are currently more than a dozen joint-venture firms in operation in South Korea engaged in the production of telecommunications equipment.[49]

Global corporations, which appear in Asia as they do in other parts of the world, include large telecommunications companies, with offices in multiple locations, carrying out international business. In order for these businesses to function effectively, they require politically stable governments, trainable workers, supportive infrastructure and the ability to integrate their communication systems. The host countries, for their part, work very hard to be accommodating because of the presumed benefits that follow.

In China, technology transfer has been a key expectation as it enters into manufacturing and other arrangements with external organizations. Spar Aerospace Ltd. of Canada has provided China with both hardware and installation for voice, video and data networks. An agreement for transfer of technology, provided that the Chinese be taught not only how to use the equipment but how to make it, was a requirement for doing business in China. Philips, the Netherlands' giant electronics firm, and manufacturer

---

[49] "Korea Takes Sight at the 21st Century," *Business Korea* (November 1984): 66.

and developer of audio compact disc technologies, has developed a similar such joint venture with Beijing.[50]

India has had a series of successful joint ventures in space with the United States, the USSR, West Germany and others. NASA provided the satellite used for India's SITE experiments, and Ford Aerospace was responsible for INSAT 1. The USSR assisted with the 1975 Aryabhata astronomical satellite, and the Bhaskara I (1979) and II (1981) satellites used for remote sensing. India's goal, however, has been and continues to be autonomy and self-sufficiency in space operations.[51]

NEC Corporation of Japan and RCA Astro-Electronics have jointly worked on a high-powered DBS satellite (BS-3) since 1981. Japan now has some 30 satellites in orbit; 16 of them have been put into space using its own facilities. It is already building and operating launch vehicles using American, European and Soviet expendable boosters. In 1992 Japan expects to lift a two-ton geostationary satellite into orbit using all-Japanese technology. In this country, where private companies now work with the government in space development, plans are already being made for the 21st century, when it expects to have developed its own reusable reentry vehicle for space exploration.[52]

Japan is engaged in cooperative research on the Spacelab, including the development of experiment modules that it hopes to man for the United States/international space station. Already Japan has launched several space science missions, including two Halley's comet probes. Plans have been drawn up for advanced astronomical and solar observation spacecraft, using Japanese technology, with an eye to unmanned missions to the moon and eventually to Venus.[53] Thus, Japan has moved beyond the point where it is dependent on joint-venture relationships with more developed nations to realize its technological objectives. Rather, the reverse is true; others, even those with the most advanced economies, look to Japan for high-technology licenses and cooperative projects. Even with its ancient enemy, China, the Japanese have found a ready partner for trade and cooperative ventures.[54]

INFRASTRUCTURE

A sophisticated electronic infrastructure must be in place in order to sustain an information-intensive society. The 1988 Olympics illustrates this very well. Management of the Summer Games by South Korea required the use of some of the most advanced telecommunication technologies in the world today—including telephones, telegraph, radio, television, microwave and

[50] Vladimir Liska, "East Meets West," *Satellite World* (December 1985): 24–25.
[51] Theo Pirard, "India Rich in Telecommunications," *Satellite Communications* (May 1986): 29, 32.
[52] Takashi Oka, "Japan Pushes to Catch up with U.S. and Europe in Space," *Christian Science Monitor,* 9 March 1987, pp. 15–16.
[53] Craig Covault, "Japan: Emerging Space Power," *Commercial Space* (Summer 1986): 16–22.
[54] Clifford Jones, "China: A New Competitive Opportunity," *Broadcasting* (March 3, 1986): 12.

satellite—and all those technologies had to work well. To produce, record and relay the games from Seoul, there had to be a well-trained staff and a thoroughly disciplined organization.

As host, the Korean Broadcast System (KBS) was entrusted with the production of signals, sound and pictures for radio and television, and transmission of commentary in the multiple languages of the participating teams, using multiple transmissions circuits. KBS was aware of the organizational problems that had faced the 1986 World Cup Soccer championships in Mexico. In that event, which proved to be an embarrassment for the host country, approximately 25 countries got the wrong commentary or none at all; certain video feeds featured the wrong games; and thunderstorms interrupted some of the broadcasts.

Few countries would dare to embark upon such an undertaking as the Olympics broadcasts. Yet, it was a point of pride for South Korea. Others, at a similar stage of development, will wish to emulate Korea's accomplishment. CCTV has a new 22-story TV center, which opened in 1987 in Beijing; the Pakistan Television Corporation (PTV) has a new TV complex in Islamabad. It is only logical to assume that a greater number of international quality productions will originate from such centers.

Portability of equipment and interchangeability of signals are necessary criteria for such participation. Hong Kong, whose English and Chinese stations each air up to 10 hours of sports a week, send TV crews to other nations in order to meet this demand. For example, a crew was sent to Mexico for the 1986 Soccer finals, and to the 1986 Asian Games in Seoul, where the Hong Kong stations entered into coproduction agreements with CCTV and shared production facilities provided by KBS. In Hong Kong the Asian Games attracted 2 million viewers.[55]

Reasonably priced small-format cameras and recorders have made television production possible for even the smallest stations. Australia's first aboriginal-owned commercial TV station, headquartered in Alice Springs, involves 40 remote communities in its video productions. Using an outside broadcast van and portable equipment, programs are being produced of sufficient quality to be distributed locally and shared with the Australian Broadcasting Corporation. Because of the new broadcast technologies, grassroots participation in broadcasting is now a practical possibility.[56]

TRAINING

Changing technologies require new skills. Singapore has a new $5.8 million training school with seven studios for radio and television production, broadcast journalism, dance and speech.[57] Instructors are drawn from Hong Kong, Japan and Great Britain. Even small Nepal has established a media training center with help from UNESCO, Japan, France and Norway.

One of the organizations that has worked hardest at helping the Asia-

[55]"How HK Stations Serve Up Sports," *ABU Newsletter* 6, no. 2 (1987): 8–9.
[56]"Aboriginals' CAAMA Comes on the Air," *ABU Newsletter* 6, no. 4 (1987): 14.
[57]"Singapore: New Chairman, Facilities, Ad Rates," *Video Age* (April 1984).

Pacific countries develop skills in telecommunications has been the Asia-Pacific Broadcasting Union (ABU). The ABU is the youngest of the international broadcasting groups, in the pattern of the European Broadcasting Union and Intervision, the Eastern bloc countries' TV network. ABU is a private association with a mandate to assist in developing cooperative programs in the region, to encourage the use of broadcasting for national development, and to foster international understanding and good will through broadcasting activities. It also joins such organizations as UNESCO and the ITU in seeing to it that regional broadcast staffs have the requisite training so that these goals may be fulfilled.

The most important force for training in the Asia-Pacific region is its Asian Institute of Broadcast Development (AIBD). Headquartered in Malaysia, AIBD is a regional broadcasting training center aimed at upgrading broadcasting personnel and systems. Founded in 1977, it has provided training for more than 9,000 participants from 38 countries within the region. Its purpose is to assist member-countries to improve their professional capabilities through training and research in broadcast management, programming and production, engineering and operations, news and current affairs, and research and program evaluation. A conscious effort is made to orient the work of broadcast organizations toward educational and development goals, and to create collaborative networks among participating nations.

An example of this kind of training, consistent with the national development emphasis of AIBD, are the "Pop Com Radio" (population and development communications) regional courses executed with UNESCO support. The purpose is to increase the involvement and use of the electronic media, especially radio, in the management of population problems. One of these courses was held in March–April 1987 in Sri Lanka; it was attended by representatives from Brunei, China, India, Iran, Malaysia, Pakistan, Papua New Guinea and Thailand. Five of these courses have thus far been carried out in the region.[58]

Another example of training is the AIBD management course for heads of stations in the Pacific region aimed at upgrading radio standards. Thirteen professional managers from nine countries were given a two-week workshop on personnel, regulations and technologies, hosted by Fiji Broadcasting. Participants also came from Ponape, FSM, Nauru, Kiribati, Samoa, Tonga, Solomon Islands, Papua New Guinea and Niue.[59]

In 1986, a three-week course aimed at upgrading the skills of TV engineers was given in Kuala Lumpur at an AIBD training center. The purpose was to familiarize staff with signal/transmitter measurement techniques. Sixteen participants were drawn from 11 countries—Bangladesh, China, India, Korea, Malaysia, Pakistan, the Philippines, Singapore, Sri Lanka, Thailand and Vietnam.[60]

---

[58] "Pop Com Radio: Sri Lanka," *Asia Calling: AIBD Bulletin,* August 1987): 4–5.
[59] "Management Course for Heads of Stations," *Asia Calling: AIBD Bulletin* (August 1987): 8.
[60] "Upgrading TV Measurement Skills," *Asia Calling: AIBD Bulletin* (August 1987): 9.

FURTHER READING

Katz, Elihu, and Wedell, George. *Broadcasting in the Third World.* Cambridge, Massachusetts: Harvard University Press, 1977.

Head, Sydney W. *World Broadcasting Systems.* Belmont, California: Wadsworth, 1985.

Howell, W. J. *World Broadcasting in the Age of the Satellite.* Norwood, New Jersey: Ablex, 1986.

Ishadi, K. S. *Touches of the Third Wave: The Information Society, Its Significance in Developing Countries,* Jogjakarta: Griya Cipta, 1986.

Lent, John A., ed. *Broadcasting in Asia and the Pacific.* Philadelphia: Temple University Press, 1978.

Martin, L. John, and Chaudhary, Anju Grover, eds. *Comparative Mass Media Systems.* New York: Longman, 1983.

McCavitt, William E. *Broadcasting Around the World.* Blue Ridge Summit, Pennsylvania: Tab Books, 1981.

Moses, Charles, ed. *Diverse Unity: The Asia-Pacific Broadcasting Union, 1957–1977.* Tokyo: Nippon Hoso Kyokai, 1980.

Shepherd, Frank, ed. *Technical Development of Broadcasting in Asia-Pacific, 1964–1984.* Kuala Lumpur: Asia-Pacific Broadcasting Union, 1984.

THEATER AND FILM

JAMES R. BRANDON

FROM prehistoric times, the performing arts have played a vital role in Asian civilizations. In Western and non-Western languages alike the word *play* (Malay *main,* Japanese *asobi,* Korean *nori,* Chinese *xi*) has the double meaning of an activity that provides refreshing release and an art form that symbolically and publicly re-creates the spiritual and social world. Theater has transmitted values and ideologies, religious tenets, codes of social behavior and prevailing aesthetics. Before mass literacy and film, radio and television, theater was the most powerful mass medium available. Being educated or cultured has traditionally meant having knowledge of music, dance and theater, often as a performer. Theater, therefore, has never been merely a frill, but is a functional part of the social system, and theater practitioners have filled a practical role as much as priests, princes, farmers or merchants.

Close ties between traditional performance and society underlie the continuing popularity and vitality of theater in the post-industrial age. By conservative estimate, 15,000–25,000 professional and amateur theater troupes function today in Japan, the People's Republic of China (PRC), Taiwan, North and South Korea, Hong Kong, India, Sri Lanka, Bangladesh, Pakistan, Burma (now Myanmar), Thailand, Cambodia, Laos, Vietnam, Malaysia, Singapore, the Philippines and Indonesia. (East Java province in Indonesia alone registered 3,586 theater troupes in 1964.) Theater in Australia and New Zealand is patterned after British theater. Theater is not developed in the Pacific Islands area, where song, chant and dance are important. Film is a major cultural and artistic force in every country: in 1985 Asian and Pacific filmmakers produced 2,015 feature films. Major film industries have grown where there is both a financial base and a sufficient population in the language of production, notably India, Japan, the PRC, Taiwan, the Philippines, Pakistan and Hong Kong.

The aim of this article is to provide a framework for understanding which types of traditional theater have survived and why they remain popular, the place of modern theatrical forms, and the role of film. The current status of theater and film will also be sketched country by country.

BASES OF SOCIAL AND ECONOMIC SUPPORT

A theatrical troupe requires some contractual understanding with the community it serves. Folk troupes from within a community perform for that community on special occasions, often for no payment other than prestige: *chhau* masked dances in Seraikella, Purulia and Baripada villages in northeast India; ritual *barong* trance performances in Kuta, Bali; *hat cheo* comic improvisations in a north Korean village; lunar festival masked performances of demon-quelling *sato kagura* in northern Japan—these are some of thousands of current folk performances. Religious festivals and the continuation of traditional village life are usual preconditions for such performances. The amateur performance by students and an urban elite suggests itself as a modern parallel. Amateur recitals of *no* and comic *kyogen* plays, for example, outnumber professional performances by five to one, and professionals now depend on income from teaching to live. In Indonesia, perhaps one in 15 shadow puppeteers *(dalang)* is professional, the rest are amateur. The great majority of all theater in the PRC—traditional opera, revised opera and spoken drama—is performed by amateur club or factory troupes. High artistic standards can be maintained under folk-amateur conditions.

Private support is a second type of social contract. Commercial theaters, in which a producer provides a performance (usually daily) at a certain hour in exchange for a ticket purchase, are found in most urban areas. Lavish *kabuki* extravaganzas in Tokyo, Osaka and Kyoto; popular modern plays in urban proscenium theaters in New Delhi, Bombay, Jakarta, Kuala Lumpur, Sydney, Wellington, Seoul, Taipei and Manila; and commercial troupes doing *tamasha* and *jatra* in north India, *wayang orang* in Java, *pya zat* in Burma (now Myanmar), *mohlam luong* in Laos, *lakon bassac* in Cambodia, *cai luong* in Vietnam and *lakon jatri* and *likay* in Thailand are all supported by commercial systems. The contract between spectator and theater troupe is fleeting and monetary. Such commercial enterprises are more affected by economics than by political changes or government policies. In Korea, Japan, Hong Kong, Taiwan and Thailand, with flourishing economies, many new private theater buildings are being built. Professional theater is also arranged by private sponsors who pay performance costs for a personal benefit: a shadow play *(wayang kulit)* in Java or Malaysia for a wedding ceremony, a popular opera *(mohlam luong)* in Laos or Thailand as a religious offering.

The third major social basis for theater support is institutional. Asian rulers patronized theater that glorified them or propagated their values. Korean kings of successive dynasties, Silla (668–935), Koryo (935–1392) and Li (1392–1910), supported masked plays *(sandae)* at court. No was the official art *(shiki gaku)* at Japan's samurai court for four centuries before the Meiji restoration. The refined court dance dramas of southeast Asia were all products of lavish princely support over generations: Lao and Burmese court drama, Cambodian Royal Ballet *(lokhon kbach boran)*, Thai classical dance drama *(lakon* and *khon)* and Javanese dance dramas *(wayang wong)*.

1711

Today these genres have found (or are struggling to find) alternative means of social and economic support as monarchical patrons have disappeared.

Institutional support today comes from government ministries of culture, arts and education. Until recently in communist China, Korea, Vietnam, Cambodia and Laos, troupe members were salaried government employees and productions received full subsidy. Beginning in 1987, and in line with general liberalization and decentralization of the nation's economy, troupes in the PRC must earn much of their income through ticket sales. Government support in Australia, India, Indonesia, Hong Kong, Taiwan, the Philippines and Japan tends to take the form of subsidizing the infrastructure of theater—building new theaters, offering monetary prizes to theater artists, giving some production funds, awarding "living national treasure" status and setting up theater schools. Thus, in India the national government has built large "Tagore" theaters in each state capital city, Hong Kong has constructed the futuristic and splendidly equipped Academy of Performing Arts, the Philippine Cultural Center was built in Manila during the Marcos era, the Sydney Opera House is internationally famous, national theaters have been constructed in Seoul and Pyongyang, a modern National Theater and Concert Hall complex was inaugurated in Taiwan in 1986, the Japanese government has built three national theaters (for *kabuki, no,* and *bunraku*) and the Taman Ismail Marzuki complex of five theaters was constructed by the Jakarta city government. In Australia the National Theatre Trust supports a permanent national theater troupe, Hong Kong directly subsidizes a Chinese opera and a modern drama troupe, and the Japanese education ministry pays whatever is necessary to keep the country's single *bunraku* troupe operating.

In the 1980s the lines between these kinds of economic support are blurring: communist societies are relying more on market economics to provide income for theater, while capitalist countries—especially those with booming economies—are increasing the levels of institutional support to previously private theater groups. Tourism plays an increasingly important role. Australia draws an international clientele to the Sydney and Perth festivals. Hordes of tourists jet into Bali, Kerala and Kathmandu and pay high prices to see folk and ritual performances. In New Guinea the traditional mud dance, a folk event, has been transformed almost completely into a tourist attraction based on a cash exchange with outsiders. Tourism throughout the Pacific islands is profoundly altering local music and dance, with simpler, contemporary forms being favored over traditional genres that tourists are not expected to appreciate.

ARTISTIC CHARACTERISTICS

Unlike theater in the West, where each new generation "cannibalizes" the performing styles of the past in a continuing quest for the new, Asian culture characteristically has continued traditional forms of theater into the present. Further, traditional theaters are distinctive to a region or language area. No Indian would mistake the hip-swinging dance of *kuchipudi* in Andhra Pradesh state for the delicate group dances of *ras lila* in Uttar Pradesh state, though they portray similar subject matter. A genre is defined by its "codes" of performance: the music, dance, gesture, song, speech, costuming and makeup patterns used by the performers. Codes are learned at a young age, become ingrained habits and are passed on to the next generation, often to a son or daughter, thus preserving the genre's form and dramatic content. Artistic tradition is respected, and change comes gradually. In recent years deliberate attempts to break the barriers between genres have been part of the avant-garde movement. Theater performers may also work in film and television.

Traditional forms of theater perpetuate fundamental legends, myths, religious stories and literary works. The exploits of god-heroes Rama, Arjuna and Krishna are dramatized in classical Sanskrit drama and folk plays in India, in Thai and Cambodian masked dance plays, and in Malaysian shadow plays. In Java the heroes of the dozen cycles of shadow puppet dramas trace their genealogy back 60 generations to Adam and Allah. The chief figure in the auspicious *no* play *Takasago* is the spirit of a Pine Tree revered in Shintoism. The hero of a Thai dance drama is looked on as Buddha in a former life. Filipino folk performances depict the crucifixion of Christ. Secular *kabuki* in Japan and opera forms in China stage plays drawn from national history known to every audience member.

Traditional theater resists Western analysis that, by reducing an object to its constituent parts, opens the way for the dissolution of the object of study. Fusion of text with performance, music with dance and sound with movement produce highly flexible performance patterns that tend to persevere. The young performer in Japan or Indonesia is taught the total scene, the entire dance, not "steps" or "parts," thus tending to preserve the integrity of the form.

Direct and indirect connections to religion and ritual practices also perpetuate the performing arts. Ritual dances of offering are performed today before spirit altars at the most modern international hotels in Bangkok. The origin of Indian dance is credited to Siva. The first dance (*kagura*) occurred in Japan when a goddess performed suggestively to draw laughter from her fellow deities. Current shamanic performances in Korea (*kut*), Samoa (*fofo*) and Sri Lanka (*kolam*) are healing rituals. Spirits possess performers and guide their actions in *barong* in Bali, *prahlada nataka* in Orissa state in India and *menora* in Malaysia. Throughout Asia and the Pacific, performances are given to placate the gods or to assure a fruitful harvest or a prosperous new year.

DIFFUSION AND BORROWING

Much theater is a product of a historic and continuing interplay between internal (centripetal) and external (centrifugal) forces. Common elements are often traceable to borrowings, in time intermingled with local styles. Theater performers traveled the Silk Road, bringing Indian Buddhist and Brahmanic performance into Nepal, Tibet and China. In the early centuries of the Christian era, Indian dance style and the *Ramayana* and *Mahabharata* epics were transmitted to Burma, Thailand, Cambodia, Malaysia and Indonesia in southeast Asia, where they became major sources of dramatic inspiration. In the seventh and eighth centuries, Chinese performance was carried to Korea, and Korean performance to Japan. In this century, Chinese and Korean students studying in Tokyo brought Western theater back to their homelands—*Uncle Tom's Cabin* (1907), for example—thus completing the circle. Cambodians in the 15th century taught Thais their dance style when the kingdom of Angkor fell, and in 1767 Burmese learned Thai court dance from captured Thai performers. Javanese shadow theater spread to Bali, the Malay Peninsula and Cambodia. Chinese, Vietnamese, Thai and local styles intermingle to form Cambodia's popular urban-creole *lakon bassac*.

Western theater reached Asia and the Pacific via two separate streams: popular and elite. Commercial producers adapted Western popular entertainments aimed at a working-class audience—vaudeville, musical revues and melodrama—to local materials. The British musical hall and melodrama traditions continue in India today in trashy popular plays of Calcutta's Biswaroopa, Rung Mahal and Star commercial theaters and in the lavish popular melodramas of the huge National and Ennessen troupes in Madras. British and American popular artists who toured Australia and New Zealand were soon imitated. *Zarzuela* operetta, brought from Spain to the Philippines in 1878 and performed in Tagalog as early as 1899, was Manila's most popular commercial theater until replaced by vaudeville *(vodavil)* introduced by American performers and producers in 1916. Popular *kich* melodramas evolved in southern Vietnam during the 1920s as an amalgam of French boulevard theater and local song traditions. A craze for Western-style operetta and musical revues hit Japan between 1910 and 1930, a tradition that continues today in the highly successful Takarazuka Girls Opera (the subject of the film *Sayonara*) and the International Girls Revue (Kokusai Kagekidan).

Local elites striving to emulate the high theatrical culture of Europe and the United States introduced serious Western drama. Opera, ballet and Shakespearean translations were part of the borrowing, but the major influence was the psychological realism of Chekhov, Ibsen and Stanislavski (in Australia and New Zealand, Shaw, Pinero and Robertson as well). Original plays were written in the European style. The first serious modern Indian drama, *The Disguise (Chhadmabes)* was staged in Calcutta in 1795. In 1872 the National Theatre of Calcutta toured cities in the north with a production of *Mirror of Indigo (Nildarpan)*, banned for its harshly realistic depiction of British labor brutality. As early as 1890 students at the Teacher's College in Bandung, Indonesia, organized amateur performances of plays *(komedie)* they had written concerning divorce rights in a Muslim society and faults of colonial rule—themes from daily life. Osanai Kaoru studied realistic theater in Europe in 1899 and again in 1902 and returned to Tokyo to form the Free Theatre (Jiyu Gekijo), named for Antoine's Théâtre Libre, where he directed *John Gabriel Borkman* (1909) and *Lower Depths* (1910). Filipino playwrights wrote in the modern dramatic form to rouse audiences against American military rule in 1902–06. By the 1920s and 1930s, hundreds of student dramatic societies and semiprofessional troupes existed in India, Burma, Indonesia, the Philippines, China, Korea, Japan, Australia and New Zealand. Audiences were too small to support professional troupes.

Independence from European and American colonial rule after World War II brought confidence in local culture and released a pent-up desire to create a significant modern theater. Young theater directors, actors and playwrights received theater training in Western Europe, the Soviet Union and the United States, and new groups formed. Audiences increased, but by the 1960s dissatisfaction with "imported" or "foreign" realistic drama emerged, even in Australia and New Zealand. In India, Indonesia, Thailand, Korea, Malaysia and the Philippines, traditional theater was reexamined in a search for indigenous roots. Through the 1970s and 1980s daring directors such as Suzuki Tadashi and Terayama Shuji in Japan, Kim Jeong-ok and An Min-su in Korea, Rendra in Indonesia and Utpal Dutt and Ebrahim Alkazi in India created new performing styles based on a melding of Western and local theatrical traditions.

In retrospect, Western spoken drama has not been assimilated, except in Australia and New Zealand. Mass audiences, even in communist countries that support realism, find "sitting and talking" plays lifeless compared to the theatricality of traditional performance. The international influence of happenings, environmental theater and mixed-media performance art has impinged as well. In particular, authors and performers in India, Bangladesh, Pakistan, Malaysia, Burma and the Philippines have turned away from English-language drama in favor of vernacular language that relates to local ideologies and melds with traditional theater.

Today in every country various forms of theater simultaneously coexist, each patronized by different segments of the total population. The practical effect is that popularity in one genre does not carry over to others, especially in multilanguage countries. Government efforts to promote a "national" genre of theater in Indonesia, India, the PRC, Taiwan, Malaysia and the Philippines have met with little success.

FILM

Film has been a part of Asian life for nearly a century—almost as long as in the West. In 1896—two years after they were first seen in New York—flickering celluloid images from the Edison Kinetoscope were displayed in Tokyo, and short dramatic films made in France by the Cinematographe Lumiere were shown outdoors in parks in Shanghai and commercial theatres in Bombay. By the turn of the century, stage plays were filmed in Japan, and by 1920 local organizations making feature films were well established in China, India and Japan. Today these three countries, along with the Philippines and Taiwan, make up five of the seven major film producers in the world: in 1985 some 912 feature-length films were made in India, 319 in Japan, 152 in the Philippines, 150 in Taiwan and 127 in the PRC (400 were made in the United States and 160 in the Soviet Union).

The development of home video and VCR technology is profoundly affecting Asian and Pacific film production and viewing habits. In countries where home viewing on VCRs is extensive—Japan, Taiwan, the Philippines, Malaysia, Hong Kong, Thailand, Singapore, Australia and New Zealand—cinema attendance has declined precipitously. In Japan, where half of all households own a VCR, film production dropped by two-thirds between 1965 and 1985. In India, however, film production increased two and a half times between 1970 and 1985.

Few early locally made films were intended to have cultural significance. In the 1920s *kabuki* stars Onoe Kikugoro V and Ichikawa Danjuro IX were documented performing the *kabuki* plays *The Maple Viewing* and *The Maid of Dojo Temple,* and the great Beijing opera actor Mei Lan-fang played scenes from the operas *The Peony Pavilion* and *Heavenly Maiden Strews Blossoms* in the Shanghai studios of the New Asia Film Company. But traditional theater did not translate well to film; exaggerated makeup and costumes, stylized acting, painted stage settings and female impersonation appeared false on film. The chief aim of the new industry was the mass production of cheap films, showing local life in simple, realistic fashion, designed to appeal, as in the West, to a mass audience. In every country the serious art film is still the exception.

Intraregional exports of film are strong in three areas: Chinese-language films to Chinese overseas communities, Indian-language films to Indian overseas communities and Indonesian films to Malaysia and Singapore. Some Japanese action and monster films are also exported. But generally films do not export well, and most are seen only by local audiences. Governments restrict imports into Pakistan, Bangladesh, Indonesia, the PRC, Korea and Taiwan to protect local film producers and as part of broader programs of political and moral censorship. Distinctive artistic and aesthetic principles operate in the different Asian and Pacific cinemas (*rasa* in Indian film and Zen principles of restraint and quietude in Japan). A very Japanese film like Akira Kurosawa's *Rashomon,* Satyajit Ray's uniquely Indian *Pather Panchali,* or *The Great Wall* from China, suggest that a play or film that is true to its cultural heritage can elicit a universal response in foreign spectators. Yet the truly international film in Asia and the Pacific is imported from Hollywood. International film and theater festivals have assumed major importance and are well established, often on a yearly or biannual basis, in Perth and Adelaide, Osaka, Hong Kong, Singapore, Seoul, New Delhi and Manila.

SOUTH ASIA

Vital theatrical traditions in South Asia exist within folk and religious contexts related to Hinduism, Buddhism or Islam. Regional forms of dance and sung theater are widespread; each language area usually has its own distinct forms. Modern drama is restricted to the larger cities. Film is an important indigenous medium that reaches mass audiences in cities and villages.

India
India, the largest country in South Asia and the source of much of the region's culture and art, supports an exceptionally rich and varied theatrical

life. The ancient techniques for staging the great Sanskrit dramas written by Bhasa *(Vision of Vasavaddata,* third century), Kalidasa *(Shakuntala,* fourth century), Shudraka *(The Little Clay Cart),* Harsha *(Ratnavali,* seventh century) and Bhavabhuti *(The Later Deeds of Rama,* eighth century) are lost today. Some Sanskrit plays are performed by traditional *kudiyattam* artists in Kerala state in the south and as *ankiya nat* in Assam state in the northeast. Their performance follows the cardinal principle laid out in the third-century treatise on Sanskrit theatre, *The Art of Theatre (Natyasastra),* that the actor must express emotion *(bhava)* through varied means—song, dance, speech, gesture, costume and makeup—to elicit a response of aesthetic joyfulness *(rasa)* from the knowledgeable spectator.

Regional language theater forms are numerous and varied. Southern India is known for sophisticated dance dramas that alternate sections of pure dance *(nritta),* executed for their beauty, with storytelling mimetic dance *(nritya).* Each word of a song is expressed through an elaborate system of hand gestures *(hasta* or *mudra).* In Kerala state perhaps a dozen members of the Chakyar caste of Hindu priests perform excerpts from Sanskrit plays as *kudiyattam.* A clown *(vidushaka)* translates dialogue into local Malayalam language to improve comprehension. Small troupes of six to eight actors and musicians give all-night performances when commissioned for a festival or by a private sponsor. The Kerala Academy of Arts (Kerala Kalamandalam), supported by the state government, offers systematic instruction. *Kathakali,* created from *kudiyattam* by the Raja of Kottarakkara in the 17th century as a more accessible form of theater, is performed in Kerala by several hundred dancers and musicians, notably at the Kerala Academy of Arts and in the Trivandrum area. *Kathakali* is seen at festivals and holidays and on religious occasions, its popularity deriving from a vigorous dance style, use of vernacular Malayalam throughout, and plays of epic grandeur taken from the *Ramayana, Mahabharata* and *Puranas.* The voluminous costumes, halolike headdresses, and vividly colored makeup are easily recognizable adaptations from *kudiyattam.* Actors do not speak but mime lyrics that are sung by two side-singers. In Kerala, *krishnattam,* performed by a single Hindu temple troupe in the town of Guruvayur, and *cavittunatakam,* performed by numerous small Latin Catholic groups, are variations of *kathakali* adapted to plays about Krishna and Christianity.

Other dance dramas in the south that dramatize *Ramayana* and *Mahabharata* stories include *yakashagana* of Mysore (Kannada) state, performed by scores of professional and semiprofessional troupes at harvest time, and *therukuttu* street plays of Tamilnadu state. Stamps, leaps, and twirls in masculine style *(tandava)* abound in these vigorous performances. In contrast, the folk dance drama *kuchipudi,* performed by Brahmin males of the village of Kuchipudi in Andhra Pradesh state, and the recent *kuruvanji* dance plays choreographed by the late Rukmini Devi at her Kalakshetra Academy near Madras, emphasize sensuous female dance *(lasya)* appropriate to repertoires devoted to episodes in the life of Lord Krishna, eighth incarnation of the god Vishnu. Their common theme is human and devotional love of Krishna. Shadow plays are performed in the south in Kerala, by small opaque figures *(tholapavu koothu)* and in Andhra Pradesh and Mysore by large, colorful, translucent puppets *(tholu bommalattam)*. Family troupes travel to festivals or are hired for private celebrations.

Ram lila, celebrating the life of Rama, the seventh incarnation of Vishnu, and *ras lila,* depicting Krishna's flirtations with Radha and her milkmaiden friends, are devotional folk dramas of north India. The *ram lila* takes place in various locations of a host city over a period of up to 30 days. Rama and Sita, played by a preadolescent boy and girl, are vessels of the gods, and hence their acting is little significant. *Ras lila* performances provide numerous opportunities for worshipper-spectators to join the hymn singing and dancing with devotional fervor.

In north India numerous folk opera troupes, featuring virtuoso singers, travel from town to town on a commercial basis. *Tamasha* in Maharashtra state is performed today by several hundred well-organized professional companies. *Tamasha* stars are female singers whose double-entendre jokes and suggestive dances are for a predominantly male audience. The word *tamasha,* from Persian, means "fun." *Tamasha* singers borrow sentimental film songs to be up-to-date, and film composers adapt *tamasha* songs when they want to be risque. Dozens of large *nautanki* troupes in Uttar Pradesh, Rajasthan and Punjab states (and in neighboring Pakistan as well) sing operas extolling heroes of the Moghul period. Traveling *bhavai* troupes perform for large audiences in towns in Gujerat state, north of Bombay. Plays show ordinary people in daily situations. *Jatra* is the major theater form of the 80 million Bengalis who live in Calcutta and surrounding Bengal, Assam, Bihar and Orissa states. The repertoires of the scores of traveling professional companies encompass history, legend, religious epics, bourgeois domestic life and political agit-prop. *Jatra* singing, which takes place on a central stage surrounded by an adoring audience, is exceptionally powerful.

India's first important modern plays were written by Nobel laureate Rabindranath Tagore (1861–1941), who fused European technique with Indian folk materials in the *Red Oleanders* and *Sacrifice,* which he directed at his school at Santiniketan with amateur casts. Active amateur and academy-related drama troupes in India today include New Delhi, Hindi language (National School of Drama); Calcutta, Bengali language (Bahurupee, Nandikar); and Bombay, Gujerati language (Indian National Theatre, Prasthan) and Marathi language (Rangayan, Theatre Unit, Avishkar). Commerical troupes are concentrated in Bombay, including Parsi language troupes, and Calcutta.

One of India's most influential directors in the post–World War II period is Ebrahim Alkazi, a student of British theater, who headed the National School of Drama and pioneered in training actors in both Western realism and Indian forms. Utpal Dutt, in Calcutta, has guided his communist-affiliated People's Little Theatre to immense poular success, staging radical political plays within a traditional *jatra* format. Actor-director Sombhu Mitra and his actress wife Tripti Mitra stage Indian and Western classics in the Bengali language. Since the 1960s playwrights and directors Mohan Rakesh, Badal Sarkar, Shanta Gandhi, and Girish Karnad have incorporated elements of regional theater *(tamasha, yakashagana, bhavai)* into their works. K. N. Panikkar has trained his Sopanam acting company in *kudiyattam* and Keralan martial arts to perform folk plays (*Karimkutty, 1983*). Regional dance styles are used to revitalize Sanskrit classics by directors Ratan Thiyam, *manipur* dance in Bhasa's *Broken Thighs (Urbhanga)*; Shyamananda Jalan, *odissi* dance in Kalidasa's *Shakuntala;* and Girijia Devi, *kuchipudi* dance in *Shakuntala.*

Until the 1970s most of India's film industry was concentrated in Bombay, where Hindi language films were turned out. This monopoly was challenged by regional production centers, and by 1985, of the 912 feature films made in 23 languages, 70 percent were produced in the south in regional languages—Telugu, Tamil, Malayalam and Kannada. The majority of films are formula comedies or mythological musicals that star film idols and are turned out on shooting schedules as short as two weeks. As escapist entertainment they are economically profitable despite the cost of dubbing into other regional languages and a 177 percent entertainment tax on tickets imposed in 1986. The first nonmusical film was not made until 1954: K. A. Abbas's *The Lost Child*. Until recently only a handful of serious films depicting social problems have reached domestic audiences: K. A. Abbas's *Untouchable Girl* (1936), Bimal Roy's *Two Acres of Land* (1953) and V. Shantaram's *The Unexpected* (1937) about young girls forced into marriage, and Nimai Ghosh's *The Uprooted* (1950), concerning refugees of the partition of India and Pakistan in 1949.

A "new Indian cinema" concerned with honest portrayal of modern life began with Satyajit Ray's *Pather Panchali* (1956) and *Aparajito* (1957), which artfully blended realism with lyricism. When European film festival prizes honored Ray's unique film vision, serious film in India achieved new status. The Film Institute of India was established at Pune in 1961, and one function of the national Film Finance Corporation, set up in 1960, was to underwrite significant films, such as Satyajit Ray's *Charulata* (1964), Mrinal Sen's highly regarded *Bhuvan Shome* (1968), and M. S. Sathyu's *Garm Hawa* (1973). Regional government subsidies supported Girish Karnad's *Kaadu* (1973) and other productions. In 1981 the National Film Development Corporation (subsuming the Film Finance Corporation) began to schedule film festivals, encourage art film distribution, and help finance international coproductions, David Lean's *Gandhi* being the first.

Sri Lanka

Sophisticated and vigorous Kandyan dance was patronized by the royal court at Kandy between the 16th and 19th centuries and today is a treasured Sinhalese national art form. Sri Lanka is close to south India, and Kandyan dance has affinities with *kathakali*. Dramatic depictions of animals and scenes from the *Ramayana* of Rama crossing from India to Lanka are enacted in the repertoire. Pre-Buddhist beliefs underlie several exorcistic dances that retain their ritual efficaciousness in present-day performances: in *sanni yakku*, a series of humorous masked impersonations expel demons of disease, the *kohomba kankariya* appeases the god Kohomba to ensure prosperity *bali* propitiates celestial deities; and in rituals to the Demon of Blood (Riri Yakka) masked dancers leap and twirl while carrying blazing torches. In southern

Sri Lanka the ritual *kolam* performance is more popular than ever. Masked dancers portray a procession of human and demonic figures throughout the night, leading to the climax when the guiding shaman *(kattadiya)* calls on the Buddha to subdue and banish the manifested demons that cause a host's sickness or poor fortune. The scholar-author Ediriwira Sarachchandra helped revitalize the form in the 1960s, writing and staging new plays in *kolam* style, such as *Maname.*

Although modern theater is not developed (Henry Jayasena and A. J. Gunawardana are two playwright-directors), a modest film industry has produced local films since World War II—40 Sinhalese-language films in 1980 being the largest output in any year. Lester James Peries's *Line of Destiny* (1956), *Between Two Worlds* (1966), and the Buddhist morality tale *Yellow Robe* (1967) have gained both foreign awards and local audiences. Peries was the first director in Sri Lanka to shoot on location rather than in studios, as was usual in India. The unsettled economic and political situation in Sri Lanka is not encouraging to filmmaking.

Pakistan and Bangladesh

Pakistan and Bangladesh both have large Moslem populations, but their performing arts differ. In Bangladesh, professional *jatra* companies (some from India) travel from city to city and perform traditional operas about Moslem kings and Persian legends, as well as contemporary social and political plays. Modern theater is descended from the Bengali dramatic tradition of Calcutta. In Pakistan, virile *kathak* dancing, originally of the Pathan tribe, is one of many types of regional male dance. Popular commercial theater in the Urdu language began with the opera *Indra's Celestial Court (Indrasabha)*, written by the poet Agha Hasan Amanat in 1855. It was staged using northern *kathak* dance. Because Islam discourages the representation of human form, these types of theater originated in Persia to the west or Hindu India to the south.

Before partition of India and Pakistan, Lahore was the largest producer of Urdu language films and the third largest film center on the subcontinent. Today some 100 feature films are released yearly in Pakistan, with production evenly split between Karachi in the south and Lahore in the north. The film industry in Bangladesh has always been under the shadow of Calcutta and its huge film output; nonetheless, it maintains vital creativity that is part of its strong historic and cultural ties with Indian Bengal. Both the Pakistan and Bangladesh film industries have been hard hit by stringent censorship and by illegal showings of Indian videotapes at prices that undercut film showings.

SOUTHEAST ASIA

Traditional dance drama, opera, masked play and shadow theater genres, some a thousand years old, are widely performed in Southeast Asia. Sophisticated performing groups cluster in former and present court cities— Jogjakarta and Surakarta in Java; Ubud, Pliatan and Gianyar in Bali, Phnom Penh, Luang Prabang, Rangoon and Mandalay. Traditional commercial troupes settle in the new metropolises of Jakarta, Bangkok and Ho Chi Minh City and tour to the hinterlands as well. India's epic literature, the *Ramayana* and *Mahabharata,* and dance style have influenced Indonesian and Malaysian traditional theater, with an added Hinayana Buddhism overlay in Thailand, Cambodia, Laos and Burma. Vietnamese traditional theater is historically linked to Chinese opera. Modern drama groups, especially important in the Philippines, are active in each country but audience support is lacking. Vernacular language films are produced in each of the eight countries of Southeast Asia.

Indonesia

Hundreds of professional puppeteers and accompanying *gamelan* musical ensembles on the densely populated islands of Java and Bali perform ancient shadow plays *(wayang kulit)* depicting the heroes Arjuna, Krishna, and Rama. Sponsors commission and pay for an all-night performance containing elements of ritual and magic for a village festival, a circumcision, a wedding or a birth. In the 1980s there have been attempts to revive the magnificent court dance plays *(wayang wong)* of Jogjakarta, which borrowed wholesale the puppet theater's mythological heroes, their clown-seer, sidekick servants, the elegant iconography and patterns of movement, music and styles of elocution. Politically impotent sultans of Jogjakarta and Surakarta had sponsored lavish performances between 1921 and 1939. In Bali, performances of traditional dance and dance drama are intrinsic parts of religious festivals *(odalan)*: sacred ritual dances *(rejang, pendet, baris, sanghyang* and *gabor)* are offered in a temple's sacred inner courtyard; great dance dramas that conclude the sacred ceremonies are performed in the middle courtyard (Panji stories danced as *gambuh,* masked *topeng,* and classical *wayang wong* based on the *Ramayana)*; and secular, commercial entertainment such as *arja* operetta is set up outside the temple grounds. Special *Ramayana* ballets are staged for tourists in the summer months at the temple complex of Prambanan in Central Java and at Pandaan in East Java, while on Bali hour-long *Ramayana* ballets, *ketjak* money dances, and secular *barong* dance plays are staged daily for tourists. Traditional music, dance and drama are encouraged at government National Music and Dance Academies (ASTI) in Bandung, Yogyakarta, Surakarta and Den Pasar (Bali).

Today, four traditional theater genres are sung, sometimes danced and acted in bravura style in commercial theaters to audiences of merchants and workers: an estimated 30 troupes perform adaptations of court *wayang wong* (usually called *wayang orang)* in Central Java, 120 perform historical melodramas *(ketoprak)* in Central Java, 30 perform improvised urban comedies *(ludruk)* in East Java and 20 perform a mixed repertoire of classic *wayang* stories and melodramas *(sandiwara)* in West Java.

Censorship laws in effect since colonial times have periodically restricted theater to acceptable content. Rustam Effendi's *Bebasari* (1926), a verse play that opened Indonesia's era of modern drama, was banned by Dutch authorities for its allegorical criticism of their rule. Although plays by Mohammed Yamin, Sanusi Pane and other writers of the New Literati group in the 1930s were intended to lead Indonesia into the modern world, few people saw them staged. In the relatively free era since independence, the first modern theater school in Southeast Asia, the Indonesian National Theater Academy (ATNI), was founded (1955) to introduce Stanislavskian acting, Chekhov, Gogol, and Sartre. In the early 1960s, under President Sukarno's Guided Democracy, the doctrine of socialist realism was required of all modern plays; a complete about-face occurred with Sukarno's overthrow, and the previously numerous and influential communist and leftist theater groups were banned. The Jogjakarta poet-playwright-director Rendra has been alternately praised and condemned for productions of his Bengkel Teater Jogjakarta. His first major production was *Bip-Bop* (1968), a collectively developed nonlinear collage of movement and sound. Turning to traditional sources, he mediated *Oedipus Rex* and *Waiting for Godot* (both 1969) via Balinese *topeng* masks and Javanese *wayang* clowns. His more politically explicit productions *The Struggle of the Naga Tribe* (1974) and *District Secretary* (1977), were not tolerated by the Suharto government: he was placed under house arrest for six months and his work was banned for seven years. *Moths* (1970) is playwright Arifin Noer's imaginative investigation of the contemporary underdog, melding folk legends, children's games and village songs and dances into a truly modern Indonesian creation. Rendra, Noer's Theater Kecil, N. Riantiarno's Theater Koma, and Balinese actor-director Putu Wijaya's Teater Mandiri are able to attract popular audiences to avant-garde works.

Centered in Jakarta, Indonesia's film industry released 63 feature films in 1985; it is a major exporter to Malay-speaking audiences in Malaysia and Singapore. Local and foreign films (201 imported in 1985) play in 426 cinema houses. Usmar Ismail was the first important stage director to move to films in the 1950s; Arifin Noer continued this trend with *A Patient in A Mental Hospital* (1980). In 1983, Teguh Karya, director of *November 1928* (1979), commemorating the beginning of the Indonesian independence movement, was given a retrospective showing of his films at the Hong Kong International Film Festival, the first Indonesian director to be recognized at a foreign festival.

Thailand

Female *lakon* and male masked *khon*, two major forms of classical Thai dance drama developed at courts of princes and kings, are now taught at the Department of Fine Arts' Academy of Music and Dance in Bangkok and given spectacular productions three or four times a year, for two to four weeks, at the Silpakorn (National) Theatre in Bangkok. Excerpts from the *lakon* repertoire of romantic Panji stories (originally from Java) are also staged at hotel and dinner shows. The archaic shadow play *(nang yai)*, ritually performed at court funerals in the past, is performed by a single troupe in central Thailand. Performers are supported by a Buddhist temple, and the large puppets (4 × 5 feet), on which are incised entire scenes from the *Ramayana,* are stored there as well. The troupe consists of two narrators, four to six musicians, and eight to ten puppeteers, who hold the puppet scenes high overhead while dancing before and behind a lighted screen. Professional *lakon jatri* troupes (20 estimated) enact the Buddhist

1722

Jataka story about the half-bird, half-human princess Manora as dance drama at fairs in southern Thailand. An estimated 100 professional troupes perform *likay* throughout the country, usually traveling from town to town or from fair to fair. *Likay* is a commercial opera form, developed during the 20th century, that melds singing and dance to classical *pin peat* music. Actors playing historical figures improvise entire plays. In northeast Thailand, *likay* plays are performed to the music of the Lao reed organ by professional *mohlam luong* troupes (40 estimated).

Thailand has the second largest film industry in Southeast Asia, producing an average of 80 feature films a year. Of the 281 foreign films imported in 1986, some 150 were Chinese-language films from the PRC, Taiwan and Hong Kong. Writers, actors and directors easily move between film, televison, and modern drama (perhaps this is why modern theater has little identity). There is a strong star system, and top actors average 40 films a year, year in year out. Most films are formula action melodramas or domestic comedies. Admission prices are low at 900 theaters, and censorship is flexible. Despite the industry's insularity, such films as Euthana Mukdasnit's *Butterfly and Flower* (1985) are reaching international festivals.

Malaysia

Malaysia's provinces are the home of traditional theater. *Wayang kulit* is performed by 200–300 puppeteers and *gamelan* ensembles in Kelantan and Kedah states in the northeast. Although this shadow play is derived from the Javanese form, its language is Kelantanese dialect Malay mixed with Kawi (old Javanese) and, in religious invocations, Arabic. Although the majority of Malays are strict Moslems, *Ramayana* stories are the most popular part of the repertoire. Plays may last three or four hours, or all night. Puppet figures of Rama, Sita and Ravana range from close copies of Javanese pupppets *(wayang jawa)* to wholly indigenous designs *(wayang siam)*. It is a close cousin to the shadow theater *(nang talung)* of Thailand to the north. *Ma'yong,* a female dance drama from the courts of the rajahs of Kelantan and Trengganu, nearly died out after World War II. Elderly performers trained a new generation of actor-dancers, and now performances are occasionally arranged in Kelantan and Kuala Lumpur. In Kelantan and surrounding provinces animistic belief underlies shamanic healing performances of *main puteri.* To cure an illness the female medium *(bomoh)* enters trance or becomes possessed while singing and dancing. *Menora,* the shamanistic dance drama twin of Thai *lakon jatri,* is preferred entertainment for ritual occasions in Perlis and Kedah. It is Buddhist in subject matter, and its usual audience and performers are ethnic Thais living in Malaysia.

Theater in urban Kuala Lumpur and Penang is either commercial Chinese opera, staged in the open for religious-communal celebrations and free to the public, or amateur modern drama. Historical plays *(purbawara)* written in the 1950s celebrated Malaysian national heroes. Usman Awang's often revived *Death of a Warrior* (1964) presented the 15th-century traitor Hang Jebat in the modern guise of a rebel against tyranny. In reaction to these poetic plays, which showed the influence of the recently defunct *bangasawan* melodrama, Mustapha Kamil Yassin, a teacher and author, championed Western realism *(drama moden)* in social comedies like *Brick House* (1963), in which conflicts of city-country, Malay-Chinese, old-young were optimistically addressed. The ethnic riots of May 1969 challenged the facile assumptions of realistic *drama moden,* leading to a new contemporary theater *(teater kontemporari)* of the 1970s and 1980s that is experimental in technique while attempting to skirt official censorship and powerful Malay-Moslem taboos against extreme modernism. Syed Alwi's *Tok Perak* (1975) used mixed media and elements of folk theater to convey the message that society must be supported; Noordin Hassan in *Don't Kill the Butterflies* (1983), produced at the Drama Centre in Kuala Lumpur, tested the possibilities of an Islamic mode of theater; the charismatic author and director Dinsman created partially absurdist figures through sensational theatrical images in *Not Suicide* (1974) and *Ana* (1976). It is too early to tell whether the first English plays to be written and staged in a decade, K. S. Maniam's *The Cord* (1984) and Kee Thuan Chye's politically stringent *Here and Now* (1985), presage greater pluralism in Malaysian theater.

Malaysian filmgoing habits are in flux: the 716 cinemas that were operating 10 years ago have dwindled to 126. Film production is small (12 films a year) in comparison to a flood of imports (350 in 1986). Othman Hafsham, Azmil Mustapha, Kamal Ariffin, and Rahim Razali are young directors showing a willingness to try new concepts appropriate to Malaysian multicultural audiences.

Philippines
Indigenous theater in the Philippines was largely erased by 300 years of Spanish and American colonization. Some tribal traditions of epic recitations—the *Hudhod* and *Alim* of the Ifugao of Central Luzon, the *Ibalon* of the Bicolanos, and others—remain viable examples of performance prior to European contact. The epics have been passed on orally by tribal elders and priests from generation to generation. Two Christian folk genres, introduced by Spanish priests, are performed on religious festival days in many parts of the country, attesting to the power of the Catholic faith. *Comedia* is a scripted folk play, written in octosyllabic verse, eight lines to a stanza, that is performed by young adults of a village or church parish during the fiesta honoring a saint's day. The first *comedia* was given in mixed Latin and Spanish in 1598. Vernacular *comedia* that are seen today are set in medieval Europe and show the victory of a Spanish Christian prince over a Moslem (moor) prince (hence also called, disparagingly, *moro-moro). Cenaculo,* a dramatic pageant of the passion and death of Christ, introduced from Mexico and Spain in the 18th century, is presented through Holy Week in scores of villages today. The climactic events of Good Friday—self-flagellation by penitents and nailing Christ on the cross—may be literally recreated as acts of personal contrition by parishioners. Another Lenten folk performance, *moriones* on Marinduque Island, depicts the conversion and beheading of Christ's Roman centurion guard Longinus.

Occasional revivals of the once commercially popular *zarzuela* operetta are performed in Manila and other regions. Modern drama began when

1724

plays about independence were written in Tagalog by an educated elite (*ilustrados*) to protest American annexation. Juan Abad's *Golden Chain (Tanikalang Ginto)* (1902) is typical of their idealistic symbolism: the hero, Filipino Revolution, rescues the damsel, Light of the Philippines, from the villain, Greedy America. As a result of the "second American occupation" (English-language education), the best playwrights from the 1920s through the 1950s wrote in English, including post–World War II authors of psychological realism Wilfrido Guerreo, Alberto Florentino, and Severino Montano. A major change began in 1966 with Rolando Tinio's staging of bold Tagalog translations of plays by Tennessee Williams and Garcia Lorca. The following year the Philippine Educational Theatre Association (PETA), led by Cecile Guidote Alvarez, inaugurated its policy of staging "national theater" for mass audiences. Martial law proclaimed by President Marcos in 1972 failed to suppress a growing popular theater presented in vernacular languages. In the face of censorship and social tumult, PETA mounted new productions: *Monster* (1971), directed by Isagani Cruz, stunned with its amalgam of *zarzuela, vodavil,* epic, absurdist and Broadway devices; *Sinaculo* (1977) showed a radicalized Christ taking up arms. *Nuclear II* (1985) protested construction of a nuclear power station. A rock opera *Hero (Bayani)* (1984) featuring composer-singer Jim Paredes linked the contemporary situation with Jose Rizal, the Philippine national hero. The troupe Peryante performed in the streets wherever an audience existed. *Dula-dula* staged by the University of Philippines Repertory Company, led by Benh Cervantes, went back to the folk verse form of that name. An involved audience has been created for modern theater out of political crisis, the ferment of which continues into the "people power" government of Corazon Aquino.

The Philippine film industry is the largest in Southeast Asia (152 features in 1986), and it has entrenched patterns of turning out escapist entertainment. Although some 900 cinemas are operating, 320 films were imported in 1986, and attendance has dropped by 30 percent over three years. Studios play no role in production, but directors have to work within strict censorship regulations. Within an otherwise lackluster industry, two directors have made quality films that also appeal to the mass audience: Lino Brocka, *Insiang* (1978), *Jaguar* (1980) and *Clutching a Knife* (1983), and Ishmael Bernal, *Speck in the Water* (1976). *Insiang* and *Jaguar* were the first Philippine films to be shown at Cannes.

Cambodia and Laos

Cambodia and Laos share similar circumstances regarding theater today. They are small nations whose cultural traditions have been tragically fragmented by recent wars. In each country a classical female dance drama (*lokhon*) had been supported at the royal court, and a form of popular traditional theater (*lokhon bassac* in Cambodian and *mohlam luong* in Laos) had been widely performed by commerical troupes. Cambodian kings, ruling much of what is now Vietnam, Thailand and Cambodia during the Angkor period (802–1432), also supported male masked dance plays (*lokhon khol*) and plays of large shadow puppets (*nang sbek*) that parallel similar forms in neighboring Thailand. Female palace dancers, likened to the heavenly dancing

1725

nymphs *(apsaras)* carved on the bas reliefs at Angkor Wat, mystically engendered prosperity of the king's realm through their sacred dances. This function was lost in 1970 when the monarchy was abolished and all performance ceased during the bloodbaths of Khmer Rouge rule. The situation is only gradually clarifying, but it appears that inside Cambodia and Laos, as well as in refugee camps in Western countries, the classical dance drama is being restored as a secular art and a symbol of national identity. Both the Cambodian and Laotian governments are providing some degree of support to the classical dancers and musicians who remain. The status of popular troupes is not known.

Vietnam

Theater in Vietnam suffered greatly from the nation's long civil war, but unlike neighboring Cambodia and Laos, no theater forms were in danger of extinction. Government data for 1980 listed 62 professional theater companies in Vietnam. The three traditional opera troupes (called *hat boi* in the south and *hat tuong* in the north) are far fewer than existed a decade earlier, confirming a long-term decline in popularity of this old-fashioned genre. Although Vietnamese opera is strongly indebted to China—in 1285, Chinese opera actors, captured in battle, taught their art to their Vietnamese captors—over seven centuries *hat boi* has evolved as distinctly Vietnamese. Today its old Sino-Vietnamese language, fixed character types and sterotypical musical and movement patterns related to Chinese opera are difficult to adapt to the tastes of modern audiences. Twenty-three professional operetta *(cai luong)* troupes indicate that this southern form has not lost its appeal under a new communist government. *Cai luong* has been Vietnam's most popular theater since it was created in 1918 by adapting the haunting southern melody *vong co* (sung many times in each performance) to melodramatic plays about history and contemporary life. Modern spoken drama *(kich)*, based on the model of socialist realism, was performed by 23 troupes, many more than in the past. The government supported 16 *hat cheo* troupes in the north, but observers have noted that interest in this folk form is declining. In addition, 12,526 amateur theater groups were listed, supported by cooperatives, companies, schools and clubs. It is difficult to know how much genuine theater activity the figure represents.

Major theater buildings that were bombed during the war have been renovated. Newly written plays in *cai luong* and *kich* stress patriotism, the struggle to achieve economic reconstruction, resistance against Chinese aggression and other topical themes. Although government officials exercise direct control of the theater, including choice of play content, traditional plays continue to be staged in *hat boi* and *cai luong*. Sizable resources have been committed to support theater during a time of economic hardship, but enthusiasm and creativity are minimal, and, according to a 1980 government report, the "quality of artistic and cultural performances was not high."

The Ministry of Culture and Information and the private sector Hanoi Feature Film Studio produce about 35 black and white feature films a year. Most are set during the war and embody strong political and revolutionary content. Recent films that have achieved notice outside Vietnam are Dang What Minh's *October Won't Return* (1986), and *Karma* (1986), directed for the Ministry of Culture by Swiss citizen Ho Quong Minh.

Burma

Burmese classic dance drama is performed on special occasions by the national troupe of the State School of Music and Drama at Jubilee Hall or other locations in Yangon (Rangoon). This delicate, occasionally humorous, masked version of the *Ramayana* epic originated equally in Burmese dance and Thai *khon*. Many popular troupes perform extravaganzas of singing, dancing and clowning in huge temporary theaters. An all-night performance consists of a modernized romantic play *(pya zat)* in which a prince overcomes magic wizards to win a bride and a traditional dance drama *(zat pwe)* accompanied by a classical court musical ensemble of bronze xylophones and tuned drums. In recent years a dozen of these private troupes, lead by idolized star performers, have toured the country performing for a week or two at a time at major Buddhist temple festivals. How many popular troupes are performing today is not known.

New *zat* based on traditional materials were written in the years immediately before British annexation of Burma into the Empire in 1866: in three plays U Kyin U depicted the value of Buddhist renunciation in the midst of worldly strife and in *The Water Seller* U Pon Nya used free verse and a natural view of character. Writing modernized plays for professional *pya zat* troupes that were formed after the country fell, U Pok Ni created the popular *Konmara* and U Ku composed *The Orangoutan Brother and Sister* (1875). British touring companies introduced examples of spoken drama early in this century, leading to the writing, in English, of several short plays that followed Western realistic convention; of these, U Nu's *The People Win Through* (1950) is best known.

The government's overall policy of isolating Myanmar from outside influences has provided the small film industry with considerable security. The 45 feature films made in 1986 (down from a high of 70 in 1980) compare with only 20 foreign imports. Audience attendence is high, the average Burmese going to one of the 400 state-owned cinemas once a week. Although few Burmese films are sent to international competitions, the country has capable directors, notably U Myint Soe and U Thu Kha.

EAST ASIA

China, Korea and Japan share similar animistic, Confucian and Buddhist backgrounds that provided impetus to the development of court and folk theater. Direct exchanges of performing arts have continued over many centuries. When urban centers burgeoned in size and wealth, they provided the milieu in which *kabuki* and puppet theater in Japan and traditional opera in China developed. Western drama has made profound converts in East Asia, and film is a giant industry in China and Japan.

China

How much religious theater remains in the People's Republic of China (PRC) is unknown, but ritual performances are being acknowledged for the first time in nearly 40 years. By far the commonest type of theater in China is traditional opera *(xiqu)*, in which stories of the Monkey King, war tales from the *Three Kingdoms* and stories of faithful love are sung by actors and actresses. Regional operas in more than 300 languages follow similar acting conventions and role types (female, male, clown and painted face) but differ in musical and singing styles. Two "national" styles are southern operas *(kunqu)*, created by scholars in the 17th century who fit gentle southern music, featuring the flute, to expansive plays of up to 50 scenes, and Beijing opera *(jingju)*, developed by professional actors and musicians from rhythmic musical styles at the end of the 18th century. Today scenes are often excerpted for performance.

The number of troupes and the size of audiences in the PRC depends greatly on the level of government subsidy. In 1981, when financial support was strong, official records listed more than 2,000 traditional opera companies. For instance, Beijing had 16 companies and Shanghai 26 companies (8 Beijing opera, 2 *kunqu* opera and 32 regional-style opera), while 130 traditional troupes were registered in Sichuan province. Amateur companies made up the vast majority, while a small number of professional troupes—the Beijing Opera Theater of Beijing, the Shanghai Beijing Opera Theater, the Shanghai Kunqu Opera Theater, the Shanghai Yueju Opera Theater, and large regional companies—received virtually total support. Beginning in 1987 troupes have been expected to pay their way at least partly through box office income. Already some troupes have disbanded and the number of troupes will probably decline further under a free market policy.

For 40 years artists and policymakers have attempted to suit the content and artistic features of traditional opera to contemporary life. During the Cultural Revolution (1966–76) traditional plays with their aristocratic characters were banned and replaced by new "model revolutionary Beijing operas" that portrayed workers, peasants and soldiers as heroes (e.g., *Red Lantern, Taking Tiger Mountain by Strategy, Shachiapang, On the Docks*). The fall of the "Gang of Four" (1967) brought restoration of most of the traditional repertoire, but the problem of attracting audiences remains. To draw young audiences, newly written operas continue to be composed and staged (they comprise a quarter of the repertoire of the Experimental Sichuan Opera Company). In 1986 opera troupes from three provinces gathered in Shanghai to perform innovative adaptations of Shakespeare (the Shanghai Kunqu Opera Theater toured its *Macbeth* to Europe in 1987).

Western-style spoken drama *(huaju)* receives strong government encouragement: 175 spoken dramas were staged in 1981. Modern drama had a hard beginning in China: the first amateur spoken drama production was staged by students in Shanghai in 1907. Not until the 1920s were women allowed to appear on stage, or, for that matter, to enter a public theater as spectators. In the 1930s, Cao Yu seriously examined China's social problems in such plays as *Thunderstorm* and *Peking Man*. In the "One Hundred

1728

Flowers" period (1957–58) of the PRC, Lao She wrote a realistic montage of life during the war, the highly acclaimed *Teahouse*, which has toured Europe and the United States. Leftist criticism of Wu Han's *The Dismissal of Hai Rui* (1960) signaled the beginning of the Cultural Revolution. In the 1980s playwrights are looking both outward and inward in their attempts to address concerns of contemporary Chinese society. Sha Yexin's *If I Were Real*, an adaptation of Gogol's *Inspector General*, produced in 1979 during the government's "Open Door" policy, boldly satirized the mendacity and prejudices of communist cadres. Although criticized for "negativism," Sha's play was tolerated. Gao Xingjian directly challenged the ideology of realism in *Bus Stop* (1983), an absurdist drama that echos *Waiting for Godot*, and the Artaudian *Wild Man*, which incorporates primitive dance and ancient shamanic ritual into a modern tale of forest ecology. *Wild Man* was written during the "Campaign Against Spiritual Pollution" (1983–84) and could not be staged until 1985. Gao's most recent play, *The Other Side of the River*, was taken out of rehearsal because of its uncompromising non-realism when the "Campaign Against Bourgeois Liberalization" began in 1987. Paradoxically, the theatricalism that is praised in traditional opera is not yet accepted in spoken drama. Major professional companies are the Beijing People's Art Theater, the Shanghai People's Art Theater, the Central Experimental Spoken Drama Troupe and the China Youth Art Theater. Training is provided at the Central Drama Institute in Beijing, the Shanghai Drama Institute, the Zhejiang School of the Arts in Hangzhou and other regional institutes. In the 1980s contacts with the world theater community were reopened and Western plays are again being staged (beginning with *The Glass Menagerie* in 1981, *The Tempest* in 1982, *Death of a Salesman* in 1983 and Pinter's *The Dumb Waiter* in 1985).

Film production in China virtually ceased during the Cultural Revolution, and almost the only films produced were documentaries of the eight model revolutionary works (among them the ballet *The White Haired Girl*, 1972). In 1985 official figures show that the state-run film industry employed 500,000 workers in several organizations encompassing production, distribution and managing 8,000 movie theaters with 20 billion annual attendance. State studios in 16 regions plus 40 nongovernment studios served 400 directors (hence creating intense competition for access to facilities). The China Film Bureau was responsible for financing, censorship, international exchanges, production (127 feature films in 1986), exports (400 films), imports (50 films) and supervision of the Beijing Film Institute's four-year training program. Working within this immense bureaucracy, writers, directors and performers have had to balance innovation and creativity with governmental expectations for socially useful films.

There have been five "generations" of film directors in China. The first generation in the 1920s made opera documentaries and silent films. The second, working in Shanghai in the 1930s, is known for patriotic and socially conscious films *(Wild Torrent, Outcry of Women, Twin Sisters,* and Yuan Muzhi's *Street Angel).* Under wartime conditions of great hardship, the third generation created resistance films in the 1940s, influenced by study in Russia *(Light Spreads Everywhere* and *Daughters of China).* The work of the fourth generation, following establishment of the PRC in 1949, was useful and politically safe (*Girl Basketball Player No. 5, Serfs, By the March 8 Canal,* Ling Zifeng's *Rickshaw Boy*). Xie Jin's *Two Stage Sisters* (1964) was made during the Cultural Revolution but not released until 1978. Directors and writers of the fifth generation, members of the first graduating class of the Beijing Film Institute in 1982, have achieved international notice with such films as Chen Kaige's *Yellow Earth* (1984), Huang Jianxin's *The Black Cannon Incident* (1986), and Yan Xueshu's *Wild Mountains* (1986).

Mao Zedong's charge at the Yan'an Forum on Literature and Art (1942) that theater should be both revolutionary and artistic has proven difficult to put into practice. The debate between conservatism and reform, official ideology and artistic vision, social good and personal fulfillment continues after 45 years.

Taiwan, Hong Kong, and Singapore
Until recently 30 to 40 professional Taiwanese-language opera troupes (*ko tsu hsi* or *gezixi*) toured urban theaters and professional puppet theaters (*pu tai hi*) set up in city streets in Taipei; they are now seen mostly at festivals in the countryside. Related to mainland Chinese theater, these unique Taiwanese (Formosan) forms have received little official assistance from the nationalist government, a sore point with native Taiwanese. Beijing and regional styles of mainland opera are also performed, matching the language of the emigré Chinese audience: southern opera styles in Hong Kong and Singapore for southern audiences and Beijing opera in Taiwan for Mandarin speakers who left China when the PRC was established. Mainland performers, now old, are being replaced by graduates of three Beijing opera schools in Taiwan and one Cantonese opera school in Hong Kong.

Modern drama in English is performed in Hong Kong and Singapore. In Singapore Lim Chor Pee and Goh Poh Seng wrote in English through the 1960s, while Stella Kon's *Emily of Emerald Hill* (1985) brought national attention to English theater. In one-person shows in "Singlish" (Singapore English), iconoclastic playwright-director-actor Kuo Pao Kun, who was imprisoned 1976–80 as a "leftist," satirized Singapore's bureaucracy in *The Coffin Is Too Big for the Hole* (1985) and *No Parking on Odd Days* (1986). The Singapore Amateur Players laid the groundwork for realistic drama in the Mandarin language in the early 1950s. Kuo directed epic productions in Mandarin before his detention, teaching workers and farmers at the Practice Performing Arts School.

Hong Kong, which once produced 260 films in the Cantonese language each year, is still an important center of Cantonese filmmaking (100 films in 1986). During the 1960s, Shaw Brothers made kung fu action films in Mandarin that dominated the market, but today their studios are closed, and Mandarin films are rarely made. Recent work by director Allen Fong (*Father and Son* and *American Heart*) stands out among noncommercial films. The Taiwanese film industry sprang full blown when Shanghai film workers emigrated in 1949. Some 150 feature films were produced in 1985 (281 foreign films were imported). Films of the 1970s, celebrating urban hedonism, especially of the young, gave way to new wave directors seeking, as in Hong Kong, more personal, honest expression in the 1980s. Portmanteau films sponsored by the government's Central Motion Picture Corporation, *In Our Time* and *The Sandwich Man*, helped establish directors Edward Yang, Chang Yi, Wan Jen, Tseng Chuang-hsiang, and Hou Hsiao-hsien.

Japan

In a high-technology nation, village-based folk theater is still performed in several thousand localities: Shinto-based masked exorcistic dances and sketches (*sato kagura*), calendrical ritual enactments (*namahage* at lunar New Year), village *no* (Kurokawa village), regional puppet plays (Sado and Awaji islands), and farmers' *kabuki*. Tourists increasingly attend, often overwhelming local facilities.

Classical forms have found niches of support in contemporary society that assure their continuation. *Bugaku* court dance groups are supported at the Imperial Palace in Tokyo and at Shinto shrines in Nara, Kyoto and Osaka. In addition to ceremonial performances, *bugaku* is performed for the public at the National Theatre in Tokyo once or twice a year. The refined, Zen-influenced *no* dance drama and companion comic form *kyogen* are flourishing financially. The five schools of *no* (Kanze, Komparu, Kongo, Hosho and Kita) maintain their own theaters in Tokyo and other major cities where public performances are staged by both professional masters and amateur students. The *no* audience is small, but wealthy and educated.

Kabuki is a major form of commercial theater, produced monthly at two or three theaters (Kabukiza, National Theatre, Shimbashi Embujo in Tokyo; New Kabukiza and Nakaza in Osaka; Minamiza in Kyoto; Misonoza in Nagoya). A five-hour program includes several plays, and some theaters schedule programs twice a day, hence an aficionado can see a hundred *kabuki* plays in a year. New plays and staging techniques, such as the actor Ichikawa Ennosuke III's radically conceived *Takeru of Yamato* (1986), bring welcome excitement and young audiences to *kabuki*. One *bunraku* puppet troupe performs for two-week runs four times yearly at the Osaka National Bunraku Theatre and the Tokyo National Theatre. Large commercial theaters, such as the Imperial, Meiji, Nisei, Parco and Sunshine City (all in Tokyo), produce monthly bills of popular plays and musicals. Comic storytellers (*rakugo*), epic reciters (*kodan*), vaudeville duos (*manzai*), jugglers and other traditional artists perform at a dozen variety theaters (*yose*). American musicals (*Fiddler on the Roof, Oklahoma, A Chorus Line, Pajama Game,* etc.), are exceptionally popular with mass audiences. *Cats,* produced by the Shiki Theatre Company, ran to sold-out houses for a year and a half in a theater especially constructed for the play.

In smaller theaters, serious modern drama troupes (Art Theatre Company, Literary Theatre Troupe, Actors' Theatre, People's Theatre Company) stage translations of Western dramatic literature and works of established Japanese playwrights: the realist Kunio Kishida (*Mr. Sawa and His Two Daughters,* 1935), the folk plays of Junji Kinoshita (*Twilight Crane,* 1949), psychological studies by Yukio Mishima (*Five Modern Noh Plays,* 1956; *Madame de Sade,* trans. 1967), Chikao Tanaka's socially conscious dramas

(*The Head of Mary*, 1959, about the atom bombing of Hiroshima), and riotous spoofs of traditional theater by Hisashi Inoue (*Makeup*, 1983). The orthodoxy of this Western-derived literary theater *(shingeki)* has been aggressively challenged by innovative younger writers, directors and actors of a variety of persuasions since the 1960s. Avant-garde playwright-directors Tadashi Suzuki, Kobo Abe, Shuji Terayama and Shogo Ota formed acting companies and developed special training systems to create new performance styles. The feminist two-woman troupe, Two Rabbits, improvises plays under simple conditions. Fragmented, oppressed urban life inspires the grotesqueries of playwrights Makota Sato (*Elephant*, 1962) and Juro Kara (*The Beggar of Love*, 1970). Improvisation, rock musicals, radical deconstruction of traditional plays, media happenings, "dark soul" dance *(buto)* and political theater are part of the contemporary theater scene.

Theater in Japan is exceptionally open and free-wheeling, and government involvement is minimal. Characteristic of Japanese society, theater artists work in groups (which may be short-lived). As a result of Japan's economic prosperity, many imaginative new theater structures now serve the varied requirements of different theater performances. Over any two-week period, Japanese journals list 150–200 theater events in Tokyo and more in other cities. Ticket prices are high: $70 for *kabuki*, $100 for an important *no* program, $20 for an average modern play.

Modern and commercial theater in Japan is highly centralized. The *buto* troupe Byakkosha is in Kyoto, *bunraku* is in Osaka, but the vast bulk of theater is created in Tokyo and tours from there to cities throughout the country. In the past decade most municipalities have constructed cultural centers that include modern theaters.

The Japan Foundation subsidizes foreign tours of *kabuki, bunraku, no, kyogen,* the Takarazuka Girls' Opera, *buto,* and avant-garde theater. A recent phenomenon is designing fusions of Japanese and Western theater specifically for foreign tours (*Queen Medea*, Rome and Athens, 1983; *Macbeth*, London, 1987).

Japanese film came to world attention when Akira Kurosawa's *Rashomon* was awarded the Venice Film Festival Grand Prix in 1951. But film was a serious art long before that. Minou Murata's *Souls on the Road* (1921) innovatively cast actresses, rather than the usual *kabuki*-style female impersonator, and worked in a restrained, realistic mode unusual for silent films. Paradoxically, the time when the government was preparing for war in the 1930s was a golden age of humanistic films: Yasujiro Ozu's *Where Now Are the Dreams of Youth* (1932), Kenji Mizoguchi's *Osaka Elegy* (1936), Yasujiro Shimazu's *Our Neighbor Miss Yae* (1934).

Six major studios controlled the film industry in the 1950s: Shochiku (which controlled *kabuki* and *bunraku* as well), Toho, Shin Toho, Nikkatsu, Daiei and Toei. Each made two or three features a week (a total of 893 in 1965). Yet in the midst of this outpouring, great films were produced that include Ozu's *Tokyo Story* (1953), Kurosawa's *Seven Samurai* (1954) and *Throne of Blood* (1957), Mikio Naruse's *Mother* (1952) and Kon Ichikawa's *Harp of Burma* (1956). Kurosawa continued with *Kagemusha*, which won the Cannes Grand Prix in 1980, and *Ran* in 1985. After the 1960s cinema reflected an increasing sense of fragmentation of society: surrealism in Teshigahara Hiroshi's treatment of *Woman in the Dunes* (1964) from Kobo Abe's novel; the sexual revolution within multidimensional time in Yoshishige Yoshida's *Eros Plus Massacre* (1970); a documentary style in Shohei Imamura's *History of Postwar Japan as Told by a Bar Hostess* (1970); sadomasochism in Nagisa Oshima's *The Realm of the Senses* (1976); and gentle satire of Juzo Itami's *The Funeral* (1986).

Japan's film industry has great strengths: it is technically sophisticated and has large financial resources. Despite commercial imperatives, film artists are free to pursue serious moral and artistic inquiry into the nature of people and society, and the stature of their achievement appears only faintly in other regional Asian and Pacific cinema. Still, the future cannot be confidently predicted. The most innovative directors are not supported by the studio system, and cinema attendance continues to fall.

Korea

Significant national efforts are being made to improve the status of theater in Korea and to increase audiences in a culture where theatergoing is not a strong habit and where the oppressive legacy of colonial rule and wartime destruction is only now being overcome. In South Korea, training and performances sections of the National Theatre were established in 1950 for elegant court dance (dating from the period of the Three Kingdoms, 57 B.C.–A.D. 668), classical masked dance plays *(sandae)* from the Koryo period (935–1392), traditional opera *(chang guk)*, and folk *pansori*, a solo dance narrative accompanied by drum, originally from Cholla and Namwon in the southwest. Private organizations, such as the Institute for Korean Masked Dance, receive financial support from the Cultural Assets Maintenance Bureau. Local communities maintain traditional folk groups that perform masked dance plays in Yangju near Seoul, Pongsan in the north, and Kyongsang in the south. In loosely linked scenes venial monks and corrupt feudal officials are ridiculed. The rapidly moving scenes offer scope for farcical dancing and erotic singing.

Approximately 40 active troupes, led by the National Theater troupe, make modern drama *(singkuk)* the most lively branch of theater in South Korea today. Modern drama began in Korea 80 years ago when Korean students in Tokyo found that *A Doll's House* and *Uncle Tom's Cabin* addressed problems that existed in their society; returning home, they began staging Korean translations of Western plays in 1908. Actors and scholars, led by Yoo Chi-jin and Seo Hang-seog, formed the Society for Research in Dramatic Arts, which actively supported Western drama from 1931 until it was suppressed by the Japanese military in 1939. About 100 amateur troupes formed during this period. Modern drama's social and political link has continued through Japanese propaganda troupes in the 1940s to the choice of Western plays staged today: Pinter's *The Caretaker* (1973), Buchner's *Woyzeck* (1975), Fugard's *Blood Knot* (1980) and Lorca's *Blood Wedding* (1988). The bureaucratic censorship of successive military governments hampers playwriting. Nonetheless, authors and directors resourcefully find ways to engage the minds of an avid theatergoing public, increasingly re-

1733

turning to traditional culture. O Tae-suk's *Order* (1974), directed by Yoo Duk-hyung, introduced avant-garde theatricalism (the play was later done at La Mama in New York City). *Invocation of the Spirit* (1980), conceived and directed by An Min-su at the Drama Center, demonstrated how protest against oppression could be effectively conveyed by choral repetition of a single word (*aigo*, alas). Chae Yun-il's *0.917* (1983) was a grotesque exploration of how children view adults in contemporary Korean society; it ran for 200 performances, the longest run in modern Korean theater. The conflict between traditional values and today's materialism was the theme of Hwang Suk-yong's *The Dream of a Strong Man* (1984), produced by Theatre Friends. *Beggar's Song* (1983), a one-person play written and performed by Chun Pal-man, using traditional song styles, has been revived several times to increasing success. Two large, professional troupes doing pageant plays (*madang guk*) have adapted the songs and dances of villagers (*namsadang*). Folk Troupe's *All Kinds of Birds Are Flying In* (1983) and annual spectacles of the Culture Broadcasting Company Folk Troupe attract audiences of 5,000 to 10,000. Echo Theatre, Freedom Troupe and Reform Troupe are veteran companies today. Theater training is offered by the Drama Center (established in 1962) and the Seoul College of the Arts, both private theater academies, and in university theater departments—unusual in Asia. Sejong Cultural Center, Munye Theatre, Silhom Theatre, Elcanto Living Theatre, Cecil Theatre, Korean Culture and Arts Foundation and the National Theatre are major theater buildings. Government funds support playwriting contests, annual theater competitions and international theater festivals.

Theater in North Korea follows president Kim Il-sung's *juche* philosophy that art should represent socialist construction, should be nationalist, and should provide enjoyment. As in China at the time of the Cultural Revolution, only ideologically correct works may be shown, and these must be understandable to the masses (building on the 1930s popular tradition of sentimental *sinpa* plays). The repertoire consists of a small number of "model" works that are repeatedly staged. Their grandiose style may be called romantic realism. Only a few themes are appropriate: the struggle against Japanese imperialism, the liberation war against the south and the United States, and the joy of life in Korea today. New theatrical genres have been created to carry out these aims: contemporary "revolutionary opera," such as *Sea of Blood*, which features a massed chorus (*pangchang*); "music and dance drama," such as *Song of Paradise*, containing traditional dances like the drum dance that are woven into a sung story; and "music and dance epic" composed of a sequence of linked scenes enacted through singing and dance and accompanied by Korean traditional instruments (*Song of Glory*). All three forms are produced on a monumental scale: *Song of Glory*, a paean of praise to Kim, has a cast of 5,000. Children's theater is important in education: there are special children's theaters, and children often perform (they take all roles in the dance drama *Brother and Sister in Mount Kumgang*). Major theaters in Pyongyang are Pyongyang Grand Theatre, House of Culture and Mansudae Theatre.

Korean language film began in 1919. The admired director Ra Un-gyu made the realistic *Arirang* (1926) and a critique of colonialism, *The Owner-*

less Ferryboat (1932), during Japanese rule. Film facilities destroyed during the Korean conflict were rebuilt by 1960, in Seoul in the south and in Pyongyang in the north. In South Korea in 1985, some 60 private companies produced 80 feature films (down from 200 in 1960). Most are bland historical dramas and domestic melodramas. Im Kwon-taek's *Mandala* (1981), about a worldly and a pious monk, has received wide international recognition. Kim Su-yong's *Mountain Fire* (1973) is the best of this director's 100 films. I Tu-yong's *First Son* (1984) is a sensitive exploration of family relationships amid crumbling traditional values. In North Korea today, films are made that will inculcate current government themes. During the Korean conflict, support of the war was the theme of documentaries *(Righteous War, Announcing to the World)* and feature films *(Partisans,* 1951; *Again to the Front,* 1952; *Scout,* 1953). Recent themes are the anti-Japanese struggle *(An Jung-gun Shoots Ito Hirobumi, Story of a Detachment Commander),* the desire for national reunion *(Thaw, Flesh and Blood),* and praise for Kim's new society *(Road to Happiness, Love the Future).* As in the Cultural Revolution, a model theater piece, *Sea of Blood,* has been filmed. Films are made for local audiences, and only a few are shown abroad at film festivals in communist countries.

THE PACIFIC

In the 1980s theater and film in Australia and New Zealand remain closely related to those arts in Britain, the United States and Europe, rather than to neighboring Asian countries.

Australia

Western-style theater in Australia is 150 years old. Australia's early professional theater looked to London, and later Broadway, for standards, plays and players. Later a local drama, written and performed largely by amateurs, sought to define the Australian character and national experience.   ·

The pattern of importing professional companies to perform melodramas, Shakespearean works, opera, operettas, musical comedies, burlesques and pantomimes began in the 1830s. The entrepreneur George Seith Coppin drew huge popular audiences by importing celebrities from Britain and the United States in the 1850s, a practice that the J. C. Williamson organization (established in 1882), has continued to the present in its chain of theaters. In the period 1883–1914, visiting and Australian professional troupes toured circuits of theaters in 20 to 30 cities (theaters in Melbourne and Sydney could seat 15,000 to 20,000 spectators). Playwright-actor-managers such as George Darrell (*The Sunny South,* 1884) and Alfred Dampier (*Robbery Under Arms,* 1890) toured plays about the Australian outback as far as South Africa, England and the United States. The most widely performed of all bush plays was the comedy-melodrama *On Our Selection* (1912), its rough-but-honest Rudd family becoming popular icons of a nostalgic, vanished past.

Amateur productions of Australian plays between 1904 and the 1950s provided some encouragement to local playwrights. Government support of theater began in 1955 with the establishment of the Australian Elizabethan Theatre Trust. It produced the highly successful *Summer of the Seventeenth Doll* (1955) by the then-unknown Ray Lawler and other plays of working-class realism, *The Shifting Heart* (1957) by Richard Beynon and *The One Day of the Year* by Alan Seymour (1960). Today such subsidized professional theaters, as the Sydney Theatre Company at the Sydney Opera House and the Melbourne Theatre Company, provide a mixed repertoire of West End, classics and contemporary Australian plays. Alternative theater groups of the 1970s, at La Mama and Pram Factory in Melbourne and Jane Street Theatre and Nimrod Street Theatre in Sydney, grew in part out of theater experiments in universities in the 1960s, which produced theatrically charged celebrations of Australian character such as the National Institute of Dramatic Art's *The Legend of King O'Malley* (1970). David Williamson's *The Removalists* (1971), a study of erupting violence in suburbia, Jack Hibberd's *White with Wire Wheels* (1967), about three young executives' mindless conformity to a macho image and Alexander Buzo's *Norm and Ahmed* (1968), contrasting Asian and local mentalities, attempted to define Australian national character. Active playwrights include Louis Nowra (*Visions*, 1978), Patrick White (*Signal Driver*, 1982), Stephen Sewell (*The Blind Giant Is Dancing*, 1983), and aboriginal author Jack Davis (*The Dreamers*, 1981; *No Sugar*, 1985).

Film in Australia, like theater, began as a "colonial" stepchild. *On Our Selection* spawned four successful films in the 1920s and 1930s, but not until the 1960s did Australian filmmakers assert an independent attitude and style. Government subsidies in the 1970s encouraged Ken Hannam's *Sunday Too Far Away,* Peter Weir's successful *Picnic at Hanging Rock,* and Fred Schepisi's *The Chant of Jimmie Blacksmith.* The 1987 film *Crocodile Dundee,* starring Paul Hogan, once again uses the bluff outback hero as a popular image of Australia.

New Zealand

New Zealand theater and film have developed along paths similar to those followed in Australia. The arts are expected to measure up to international standards and at the same time express New Zealand's special cultural identity, aims that are often in conflict. New Zealand's first theater, the Royal Victoria, opened in Wellington in 1843, three years after the landing of British colonists. Five years later James Marriott's *Marcilina,* locally written, was produced there. George Leitch's *The Land of the Moa* (1895) was notable as a play that treated the Maori wars but did not cast the Maori as stage villains. New Zealand locales remained the exception in professional theater: frontier and gold rush audiences preferred the diversions of musical and melodrama companies from England or Australia or an imported serious play, such as *A Doll's House* starring the British actress Janet Achurch in 1890. Commercial theater dwindled in the 1930s, replaced as a popular art by film and by amateur societies committed to staging literary plays of social seriousness: Wellington Repertory, established in 1926; the leftist Unity, 1944; Community Arts Service, 1947; New Zealand Players, 1952.

The British Drama League, established in 1932, encouraged playwriting through regular competitions. In the 1940s and 1950s Ngaio Marsh at Canterbury University and other university theater groups trained young writers and directors who became important in government-subsidized and alternative theatres of the 1960s and 1970s. Bruce Mason's honest depiction of Maori life *Awatea* (1968) incorporated dancing and Maori ceremonial language. First staged at the Downstage in Wellington with the assistance of the Maori Theatre Trust, it has reached new audiences in many revivals. The line between professional and amateur theater has blurred, and the best theater is intended to be both meaningful and popular. Recent work of note, often supported by Arts Council grants, is diverse: Roger Hall's popular satire of bureaucracy, *Glide Time* (1976); Joseph Musaphia's black contemporary comedy *Mothers and Fathers* (1975) at the Fortune Theatre, Dunedin; *O! Temperance!* (1972) a collective musical developed by students at the Training School of the professional Court Theatre, Christchurch; *Song of A Kiwi* (1975), by the Amanus group, inspired their visit to Jerzy Grotowski's theater workshop in Poland.

The first New Zealander to direct a feature film was John O'Shea (*Broken Barrier*, 1952). Films about the New Zealand experience in the 1970s include Michael Firth's *Off the Edge* and Geoff Murphy's *Wild Man*. Murphy's *Utu*, a ferocious horror comedy about the pillage of a Maori village by colonial soldiers, and Roger Donaldson's *Sleeping Dogs* have received some international recognition. Recent films have also been made of popular stage plays: Tony William's *Solo*, Roger Hall's *Middle-Age Spread*, and James Baxter's *Jack Winter's Dream*.

FURTHER READING

Arnott, Peter D. *The Theatres of Japan*. London: Macmillan; New York: St. Martin's Press, 1969.

Bandem, I Madé, and deBoer, Fredrik Eugene. *Kaja and Kelod: Balinese Dance in Transition*. Kuala Lumpur and New York: Oxford University Press, 1981.

James R. Brandon, ed. *On Thrones of Gold: Three Javanese Shadow Plays*. Cambridge, Massachusetts: Harvard University Press, 1970.

————. *Theatre in Southeast Asia*. Cambridge, Massachusetts: Harvard University Press, 1967.

Ernst, Earle. *The Kabuki*. Honolulu: University of Hawaii Press, 1974.

Gargi, Balwant. *Folk Theatre in India*. Seattle: University of Washington Press, 1966.

Keith, A. *The Sanskrit Drama*. London and New York: Oxford University Press, 1970.

The Korean Theatre Past and Present. Seoul: Korean Centre of the International Theatre Institute, 1981.

Komparu, Kunio. *The Noh Theater: Principles and Perspectives*. New York and Tokyo: Weatherhill/Tankosha, 1983.

Mackerras, Colin, ed. *Chinese Theater: From its Origins to the Present Day*. Honolulu: University of Hawaii Press, 1983.

McNaughton, Howard. *New Zealand Drama*. Boston: Twayne Publishers, 1981.

Sarachchandra, E. R. *The Folk Drama of Ceylon.* Colombo: Ceylonese Department of Cultural Affairs, 1966.

Scott, A. C. *The Classical Theatre of China.* London: Allen & Unwin, 1967.

West, John. *Theatre in Australia.* Sydney: Cassell Australia, 1978.

Zoete, Beryl de, and Spies, Walter. *Dance and Drama in Bali.* London: Faber & Faber, 1952.

TOURISM AND
BUSINESS TRAVEL

LINDA K. RICHTER

INTRODUCTION

No other regions of the world offer more dazzling combinations of cultural and ethnic diversity, scenic splendor, remnants of ancient civilizations and fabled excesses in temples and palaces than the nations of Asia and the Pacific.

Nor are any regions in a better position to capitalize on their attractions for the development of tourism than these countries. If the 21st century is truly to be the century of the Pacific—and few challenge that—then these nations, which include both the oldest and the youngest civilizations, are at the very beginning of a massive commercial boom of which tourism will be one of the most important components.

Tourism is usually considered a cultural phenomenon by the general public, an activity more than an industry. Historians of Asia celebrate the great journeys of Marco Polo or Fu Hsien, or even the revelations of Rudyard Kipling or Somerset Maugham; the travel journals and novels of Robert Louis Stevenson or Herman Melville shape our images of the Pacific. When scholars have thought about *tourism* in Asia it has often been in the context of these great journeys or the summer exodus of colonialists to the hill stations of South and Southeast Asia; Darjeeling, Simla, Baguio and Kandy have colored our notions of touring in Asia.

But travel and tourism in Asia and the Pacific, no less than elsewhere, have also had their economic and political aspects. After World War II, the emergence of dozens of newly independent nations meant altered economic and political situations, followed soon after by the technology and economics of jumbo jets that made international travel available to a mass market.

Tourism is today a U.S. $2 trillion business—the largest industry in the world; as of 1987 more than two times as much money is being spent on world tourism as on armaments.[1] Nor is spending on world tourism likely to decline. All social indicators suggest that discretionary spending and

[1] Somerset Waters, *Travel Industry World Yearbook, 1987* (New York: Child and Waters, 1988), 11.

leisure time are both certain to increase, even as the value people place on travel has accelerated. Moreover, even in an age of computers, conference calls and satellite teleconferences, there has been more rather than less business travel; so the very forces that encourage the growth and development of Asian and Pacific countries are contributing to the belated but dramatic upsurge in tourism there. While tourist arrivals in the region represent only a small fraction of the world's travel flows, both the absolute numbers of tourists globally and the region's share are increasing rapidly (see Tables 1 and 2).

Tourism statistics must be considered carefully, however. Countries like India and China report international tourists primarily, relatively ignoring enormous numbers of domestic travelers, or only haphazardly measuring intraregional travel, as Pakistan and Nepal do. Tourism statistics also show almost no relationship between attractions and the level of tourists' interest. The tiny city-state of Singapore and the British colony of Hong Kong get more international tourists than any other nations in Asia and the Pacific—more than 3.4 million each. What they offer the visitor is a prime location; good value in accommodations, shopping and food; and, of greatest importance, security. As Fiji, Sri Lanka, Cambodia and the Philippines have learned all too well, the finest scenery, richest history, loveliest beaches and most elegant accommodations matter little if tourists feel insecure. The tourist can always go somewhere else.[2]

The importance of tourism to a country's economic and social development is also only loosely correlated with the absolute numbers of tourists. Both tiny Nepal, with 233,000 tourists, and giant India, with 1,000,000 tourists, have relatively low levels of international tourism, but tourism is still the leading source of foreign exchange in each of these countries.[3] India in particular benefits from one of the world's longest average length of tourist stay: 27 days. Thus, tourism's impact needs to be measured not only in absolute numbers but in terms of revenue and costs, and in comparison with other economic sectors. When such comparisons are made, it is clear that tourism is of vital concern to Asia and the Pacific. In Nepal, Maldives, Thailand and Burma (now Myanmar), tourism is also the leading source of foreign exchange. In Fiji it is the second-largest source; in Singapore, Hong Kong and the Philippines it ranks third;[4] and in Malaysia it is fourth.[5]

These numbers tell only part of the story. With the volatility and decline of major agricultural exports, most of these nations have needed sectors that can earn foreign exchange, absorb large numbers of relatively unskilled laborers and capitalize on the less industrialized parts of countries, and that are compatible with environmental and cultural preserva-

[2] Linda K. Richter and William Waugh, "Terrorism and Tourism as Logical Companions," *Tourism Management* (December 1986): 230–38.
[3] Waters, *Travel Industry World Yearbook, 1987,* 104; Raj Chengappa, "Busting Records," *India Today* (January 31, 1987): 63.
[4] "By the Million," *Asiaweek,* 20 September 1987, 65.
[5] "PATA [Pacific Area Travel Association] Fever," *Asiaweek,* 4 May 1986, 67.

Table 1
INTERNATIONAL TOURIST ARRIVALS, 1981–86

Region	1981	1982	1983	1984	1985	1986
World						
Total	288,848	286,958	293,944	315,359	332,991	340,000
% world total	100	100	100	100	100	100
% change	1.4	−0.7	2.4	7.3	5.6	2.1
Index	100	99	102	109	115	118
(1981 = 100)						
Africa						
Total	8,046	7,646	7,854	8,618	9,070	8,800
% world total	2.8	2.7	2.7	2.7	2.7	2.6
% change	13.8	−5.0	2.7	9.7	5.2	−3.0
Index	100	95	98	107	113	109
(1981 = 100)						
Americas						
Total	53,464	50,896	51,276	52,055	52,794	55,650
% world total	18.5	17.7	17.4	16.5	15.9	16.3
% change	−0.5	−4.8	0.8	1.5	1.4	5.4
Index	100	95	96	97	98	104
(1981 = 100)						
East Asia and the Pacific						
Total	23,446	24,521	26,839	31,302	36,985	39,500
% world total	8.1	8.5	9.1	9.9	11.1	11.6
% change	17.4	5.0	9.5	16.6	18.2	6.8
Index	100	105	114	134	158	168
(1981 = 100)						
Europe						
Total	195,289	194,490	199,433	214,405	224,488	227,500
% world total	67.6	67.8	67.8	68.0	67.4	66.9
% change	−0.4	−0.4	2.5	7.5	4.7	1.3
Index	100	100	102	110	115	116
(1981 = 100)						
Middle East						
Total	6,160	6,983	6,053	6,513	7,115	6,000
% world total	2.1	2.4	2.1	2.1	2.1	1.8
% change	5.8	13.4	−13.4	7.6	9.2	−15.7
Index	100	113	98	106	116	97
(1981 = 100)						
South Asia						
Total	2,443	2,427	2,489	2,466	2,539	2,550
% world total	0.9	0.9	0.9	0.8	0.8	0.8
% change	7.2	0.7	2.6	−0.9	3.0	0.4
Index	100	99	102	101	104	104
(1981 = 100)						

Notes: 1981–85: Revised figures; 1986: Preliminary estimates.
Source: World Tourism Organization, as quoted in Somerset Waters, *Travel Industry World Yearbook, 1987* (New York: Child and Waters, 1988), p. 6.

Table 2
VISITOR ARRIVALS TO EACH PACIFIC ASIA
TRAVEL ASSOCIATION (PATA) REGION,
1975–85

PATA Region	1975		1985		Annual growth rate 1975–85 (%)
	Visitor arrivals	Percent of total	Visitor arrivals	Percent of total	
East Asia	4,009,258	29.2	9,387,298	34.7	8.9
South Asia	896,855	6.5	1,827,734	6.8	7.4
Southeast Asia	4,400,911	32.1	8,074,164	29.8	6.3
South and Central Pacific	682,629	5.0	1,069,999	4.0	4.6
Australia/New Zealand	893,634	6.5	1,818,558	6.7	7.4
Hawaii	2,830,000	20.7	4,884,000	18.0	5.6
Total	13,713,287*	100.0	27,061,753*	100.0	7.0

*Excluding Canada.
Source: Pacific Asia Travel Association, in Somerset Waters, *Travel Industry World Yearbook, 1987* (New York: Child and Waters, 1988), 100.

tion. Development of tourism has been encouraged in nearly every nation for its potential in these respects.

Thus, in the 1980s, nearly all Asian and Pacific nations have established cabinet-level ministries or departments concerned with tourism. In the process, these nations have learned much about the pitfalls of tourism. Because most of these nations have emphasized luxury in their development plans, rather than campgrounds or hostels, or more modest hotels, vast sums of foreign exchange have been committed to the development of deluxe infrastructure. Foreign-exchange leakage, as a result, has been very high except in countries like India, which made a conscious and sustained commitment to import substitution.

The quality of employment generated has been an issue as well. It has been discovered that the vast bulk of this work is low-paying and unskilled. Labor unrest, as in Tahiti, New Zealand and the Philippines, has been associated with specific problems related to tourism. There have also been complaints about tourism development spawning dramatic increases in prostitution, including that of children in Sri Lanka, Thailand, the Philippines and Korea.[6]

Some developing nations in the area have found in tourism many neocolonial features. Ownership and management of much of the tourist sector may be in foreign hands. The former colonial power may continue to generate the largest share of tourists, as in the case of India or the Philippines; and the largely white tourist-generating countries are also disproportionately conspicuous in this non-white part of the world. Even Australians and New Zealanders are sometimes perceived as intruders because of their racial and cultural distinctiveness and their relative affluence. This is heightened because the non-white peoples of both countries are also less likely to travel than those of Caucasian background. Further, the relative spending power of the tourist vis-à-vis the average citizen may exacerbate consumer demands or increase feelings of citizen alienation.

Tourism has offered both positive and negative examples of intraregional impact as well. In South Asia there have been a few tentative efforts at regional and bilateral cooperation, but Pakistan has tended to link its fortunes with the Muslim states of the Middle East since its 1971 civil war, while Sri Lanka's ethnic struggle has precluded much regional planning with other South Asian nations.

In East Asia no tourism has been permitted between North and South Korea, but the 1988 Olympics in Seoul have stimulated some discussion in that direction. However it is finally resolved, the most noteworthy result is the growing willingness of both Koreas to work together on an issue; that represents a peaceful milestone in their post-division contacts. Between the People's Republic of China and Taiwan, there has also been a thawing of rhetoric and the initiation of some one-way travel to the mainland.[7]

[6] Peter Holden, Jurgen Horlemann, and Georg Friedrich Pfafflin, eds., *Tourism, Prostitution, Development* (Bangkok: Ecumenical Coalition on Third World Tourism, 1985).

[7] Carl Goldstein, "Hands Across the Strait," *Far Eastern Economic Review* (August 6, 1987): 18.

The ASEAN nations of Malaysia, Singapore, Thailand, Indonesia, the Philippines, Hong Kong and Brunei have established a tourism committee to thrash out regional tourism problems and facilitate travel and tourism in the region. Such efforts include moves to permit the use of any of the regional currencies in member nations, establish an ASEAN passport, and initiate better but less competitive airline routings among member nations. Most of these initiatives have not been implemented, however, despite the significant levels of regional travel. In fact, Malaysia, Thailand and the Philippines have charged large exit fees to their own citizens who wish to travel abroad. Singapore and Hong Kong, with much smaller populations but critically dependent on tourism, have been vocal in opposing the "protectionist policies" of the other ASEAN nations.

Japan, on the other hand, enjoys such an embarrassingly large balance of trade vis-à-vis Asia and the Pacific, as well as the United States, that it has actually been encouraging its citizens to travel abroad. This is a policy in sharp contrast to the barriers it erected to foreign travel during the two decades after World War II, when it badly needed to conserve foreign exchange and encourage savings.

The Pacific Area Travel Association has also been extremely active in encouraging tourism, and in overcoming obstacles to joint promotion and facilitation of travel and to developing incentives for cultural and historical preservation.

Competition, not cooperation, has been the norm, however. In the process, the tourist and business traveler has literally seen skylines changed, beaches shifted, mountains leveled and villages moved in an effort to attract more tourism. Sometimes, in the process, the very romance and exotic nature of a destination has been lost.

SINGAPORE

In Singapore, for example, the building boom of the 1970s and early 1980s all but eliminated the traditional neighborhoods, the architectural remnants of colonial rule, the flavor of the old city and the promise of bargains to be found in the clutter of tiny shops. Instead, a clean, tidy, almost sterile Singapore, replete with malls and high-rise hotels, awaits the visitor. In fact, the greatest complaint visitors have is that there are few tourist attractions. For business travelers, Singapore is relentlessly efficient and comfortable; for tourists, aware of its colorful history, there is disappointment. Recently, Singapore was working to complete a $200 million beach resort on Sentosa Island, and trying to salvage what remains of the old Arab and Indian sections of town.[8] It also began, hurriedly, to compile an inventory of historical buildings that had escaped the wreckers, in an effort to develop and retain tourist attractions.

Singapore is also making a great effort to capture a larger share of the lucrative tourism market from outside the region. Tourism is already the

[8]Somerset Waters, *Travel Industry World Yearbook, 1986* (New York: Child and Waters, 1987), 104.

third-largest revenue source for the ministate, which has invested heavily in related infrastructure. So fine are the facilities that Singapore was voted the best convention center in Asia. The very success of tourism in the past has created a heavy dependence on it for the future. However, Singapore is not inviting everyone. It retains its reputation for courting only conventional tourists. Hippies, drifters and other low-budget travelers are not welcome.

THE PHILIPPINES

Politics, both domestic and international, have also played a major role in dictating the pace and timing of tourism in Asia and the Pacific. Former President Marcos of the Philippines was especially adroit in using tourists and tourism promotion to garner praise and support following his declaration of martial law in 1972. Within months, a cabinet-level Department of Tourism was subsidizing visits to the Philippines, launching a massive hotel building spree, and countering claims of social unrest with a travel slogan billing the Philippines as the place "Where Asia Wears a Smile."[9]

Marcos realized that tourists are impressed by what authoritarian regimes can deliver: an aura of law and order in specific zones frequented by travelers; beautification; and modern infrastructure. Tourists are generally ill-prepared to evaluate press censorship, human rights abuses, economic conditions in the countryside, or the strength of democratic institutions.

In eight years of unbridled tourism spending, the Philippines under Marcos achieved a 500 percent increase in tourist arrivals, and won the praise of tourism organizations worldwide. But the costs were enormous. Most of the luxury hotels went bankrupt and were reclaimed by the government. Corruption associated with their development made the entire tourism sector a target for opposition violence, which led to a rapid decline in tourism in the 1980s. Protests against tourist-related prostitution, foreign-exchange leakage and guerrilla activities led to the further decline of tourism.[10]

Since President Aquino came to power, tourism has made a modest recovery. The president has wisely argued that the health of the tourism sector should be linked to alleviating the needs of the Filipino people. She has sought to privatize tourism by selling off the bankrupt but extravagant infrastructure built during the Marcos era.[11] The government has also moved against organized sex tours and pedophiles, and has reoriented the government's once quite exploitative promotion toward less sensational advertising.

The Aquino administration is not above using tourism for scoring polit-

[9] Linda K. Richter, "The Political Uses of Tourism: A Philippine Case Study," *Journal of Developing Areas* (January 1980): 237–57.
[10] Linda K. Richter, *Land Reform and Tourism Development: Policymaking in the Philippines* (Cambridge, Mass.: Schenkman, 1982).
[11] Susan Blanco, "Aquino's Privatisation Plans," *Asia Travel Trade* 23 (December 1987): 18. See also Jose Galang, "Come Back, Come Back," *Far Eastern Economic Review* (November 19, 1987): 110.

ical points, however. Malacanang Palace—the governor's residence during the Spanish and American colonial regimes, and the lavish home of Philippine presidents—has become a premier tourist attraction. Opened for the first time to the public by President Aquino, it has become a museum of the excesses and idiosyncrasies of the Marcos era. Along with the special tours of the sites of the four-day "People Power" Revolution in 1986, the palace has become both a major tourism money-maker and a source of political support for the Aquino government.[12]

The future of Philippine tourism should be bright indeed. A high percentage of the country's population speak English; travel expenses are, for Asia, very modest; and business travelers to Manila and Cebu will find the finest in hotels and convention facilities. The spectacular rice terraces of Benaue and Bontoc, the many tribal groups, the colorful *vinta* boats of Zamboanga, and the Muslim culture of much of the south are just a few of the many attractions awaiting visitors to the country.

SOUTH KOREA

South Korea's development of its attractiveness as a tourist destination has also been strongly influenced by a desire to improve the country's political image. Hosting the 1988 Summer Olympics was designed to do just that. It provided a national goal—a focus for major infrastructure development including hotels, stadia, roads, subways and even foreign-language training. Over $3 billion was spent on the Olympics.[13] Ironically, this also raised the stakes for opposition groups, whose importance grows as the need for political tranquillity increases.

South Korea already enjoys over two times the number of annual visitors the Philippines receives (1.66 million to less than 800,000), but that is still far below what the country expects to receive, given its many scenic and cultural attractions.[14] Tourism, which also received a boost from the country's hosting of the 1986 Asian Games, is also benefiting from lower oil prices and an exchange rate that makes South Korea a bargain for its major market, Japan.[15]

Still, there was concern that simultaneously building nine five-star hotels in Seoul alone would create in South Korea the kind of massive hotel glut that plagued the Philippines. Optimists, who prevailed, argued that tourism's growth of over 10 percent a year meant that supply and demand would be relatively equal by the next decade—a scenario depending on political serenity and continued economic success.[16]

The travel of Korean citizens continues to be sharply controlled accord-

[12] Linda K. Richter, "Bureaucracy in the Post-Marcos Philippines," *Journal of Southeast Asian Studies* (forthcoming).
[13] Waters, *Travel Industry World Yearbook, 1987*, 109.
[14] "Revealing an Asian Secret," *Asiaweek*, 20 April 1986, 60.
[15] Jung-nam Chi, "Agents Lose Out on Tourism Boom," *South* no. 84 (October 1987): 63.
[16] *Ibid.*

ing to the government's foreign-exchange concerns. Before 1981 only a privileged few were allowed to go abroad. After that, passport privileges were relaxed, and because of the pent-up demand the government soon felt a drain on its foreign-currency reserves. In 1983, restrictions were reimposed and only those under the age of 45 were allowed to travel abroad. That action forced many new Korean travel agencies out of business. In 1988 the government promised to extend the age limit to 50 and to abolish the requirement of large deposits for going abroad;[17] but as long as the freedom to travel depends on state whim, Korean entrepreneurs will be reluctant to plan and citizens afraid to hope.

NORTH KOREA

North Korea has pursued isolation, instead of soliciting tourists or business travelers, since the peninsula was divided in 1948. However, since 1986 there have been indications that the Pyongyang government of Kim Il-sung is gradually opening up. In 1987 the nation hosted not only traditional socialist conferences but one on denuclearization of the Pacific, a World Health Organization Conference and meetings of other foreign groups.[18]

The most tangible evidence of a sustained retreat from isolation, however, is the current hotel building boom, which includes a luxury hotel built by the French. Further, its own preparations for the 1988 Olympics included a 30-story youth hostel, a 650-room hotel and 10 enormous stadia that were built on an 847-acre/350 ha. site on the outskirts of Pyongyang. A huge new airport and several bridges were also prepared.[19]

JAPAN

Japan receives relatively modest numbers of international tourists (2.06 million in 1986) because of the high cost of traveling there and the strength of the yen against other currencies.[20] Even Japanese tourists find travel outside Japan much cheaper than vacationing at home; indeed, over $5 billion was spent in 1985 on travel overseas. There is also a particular glamor to overseas honeymoons, which has created a boom for such destinations as Guam and Hawaii. The high rate of savings has also kept Japanese tourism well below what it could be.

The Japanese government is thus faced with the enviable task of encouraging its citizens to spend more, work less, and travel and relax in greater numbers. It has even created a Leisure Development Center to generate ideas for encouraging Japanese to take vacations. Currently, the average Japanese worker takes little more than half the available vacation time. Companies are also being encouraged to give longer vacations and two-day weekends. However, with Japanese children in school five and one-half days

[17] Ibid.
[18] "Isolation Gives Way to Olympian Vistas," South no. 86 (December 1987): 35.
[19] Ibid.
[20] Waters, Travel Industry World Yearbook, 1987, 108.

a week, 10 months a year, tourism cannot change dramatically without the social structure being altered as well.[21]

TAIWAN

Tourism in Taiwan is not primarily an economic phenomenon, for the country has very strong foreign-exchange reserves. Though it earns nearly $1.5 billion dollars a year from international tourism, the government has needed to spend little on promotion. Shopping facilities, the famed Taroko Gorge and the beauty of Sun Moon Lake wooed over 1.3 million visitors to Taiwan in 1985; add to that the attractions of National Museum, which ranks as one of the world's finest with its priceless and enormous collection of Chinese art. Government support of tourism may be growing, however, as Taiwan relaxes visa requirements for overseas Chinese and begins to allow Taiwanese citizens to visit the People's Republic of China. The Taiwan World Trade Center, complete with convention facilities, exhibit halls and massive hotel, will soon be competing with other fine hotels for a share of the tourism pie. With occupancy rates dropping in many of the hotels, the government may need to offset the hotel glut with more promotional activity.[22]

Since there is little unemployment, however, tourism is not crucial as a source of income. Tourism attractions and resorts are being developed, nevertheless, to ease the claustrophobia of Taiwan's own crowded population. This is especially true of young males, who cannot leave Taiwan at all before completing their military service.

PEOPLE'S REPUBLIC OF CHINA

The contrast between the relatively leisurely pace at which tourism has proceeded in Taiwan and its frenetic course in the People's Republic of China during the early 1980s could not be more marked. For three decades following the Communist takeover of the Chinese mainland, tourism was minuscule, confined almost exclusively to those with the proper political credentials. Those favored few were treated to tours of communes and factories, and highly structured and preselected interviews with acceptable Chinese counterparts.

During the Cultural Revolution, not only were Western influences restricted, but some of the greatest architectural treasures were vandalized and destroyed by the xenophobic and antielitist Red Guards. Even during this internal struggle, however, diplomatic relations with most nations were thawing and becoming normalized. Thus, with the death of Mao Zedong in 1978 the stage was set for a new era in Chinese relations with the rest of the globe.

From having only a few empathetic visitors to coping with millions of curious and often critical capitalist tourists has required a major change in

[21] *Ibid.* See also "Venture Capital," *The Economist* (August 8, 1987): 58–59.
[22] Waters, *Travel Industry World Yearbook, 1986,* 107.

the tourist-receiving structure and in the development of needed infrastructure.[23] The tourism ministry, which first sought to centralize tourism decisions, is now decentralizing the processing of tourists, albeit according to a central reservation and planning process. Visas have become much easier to obtain on short notice, and the number of cities tourists can visit has been greatly expanded. Factory and commune tours are no longer de rigueur, but special-interest academic and professional tours remain common. While guided tours remain the norm for non-Chinese international tourists, solo or family travel is no longer rare.

Tourists continue to favor Beijing, with its nearby Great Wall and Ming tombs; Soochow and Wuxi, famed for their gardens and embroidery; beautiful Hangchow and Guilin; Xian, with its archaeological excavations of an ancient full-size terra-cotta army; and of course the commercial and cultural centers of Shanghai and Guangchou.

The only major setback to the expansion of tourist destinations has been with respect to Tibet. During the early 1980s, foreign travelers, averaging about 1,500 a year, were allowed in Tibet. This skyrocketed to 15,000 in 1985 and 30,000 in 1986, and in the same year a Holiday Inn opened in Lhasa.[24] However, 1987 and 1988 saw the reemergence of opposition by Tibetan nationalists; by early 1988, foreign journalists had been expelled and only a few guided tours were still visiting Tibet.

Elsewhere in China classic Marxist economics has yielded to more pragmatic development, which includes a number of joint ventures in hotel construction. Individual vendors have also been active in the selling of souvenirs and food to tourists. Right now, the new hotels alleviate the crucial need for international-standard accommodations, but there is concern among some development analysts lest China forgo too much foreign exchange by building luxury hotels, and end up neglecting the less fickle and far more massive domestic and overseas Chinese market.

VIETNAM

Vietnam's tourism program has barely begun, with an estimated 30,000 tourists in 1987, of whom 10,000 were overseas Vietnamese.[25] Despite the long war, remnants of the French colonial period remain in the wide boulevards of Ho Chi Minh City (formerly Saigon) and in the faded beach resorts. These, in addition to interest in Buddhist culture, the war and the colonial past form the underpinnings for the new tourism development.

Currently, economic conditions allow for little domestic tourism, but overseas Vietnamese are the nucleus of the small but growing international

[23] Linda K. Richter, "The Political Implications of Chinese Tourism Policy," *Annals of Tourism Research* 10 (1983): 395–413. See also Alan A. Lew, "The History, Policies, and Social Impact of International Tourism in the People's Republic of China," *Asian Profile* 15, no. 2 (April 1987): 117–26.

[24] Wu Naitao, "Tibet Opens to the Outside World," *Beijing Review* no. 42 (October 19, 1987): 16.

[25] "Vietnam," in *Asia 1988 Yearbook* (Hong Kong: Far Eastern Economic Review), 256.

tourism. The government is now encouraging the 1 million Vietnamese living abroad to visit, and to send goods and money to their relatives in Vietnam; in 1986, overseas Vietnamese responded with $300 million.[26] The Hanoi government, like the Chinese, appears to be moving toward joint ventures and a foreign investment code that will attract overseas businesses. If this continues, tourism is almost certain to be one of the participating sectors.

"Alternative tourism," or socially conscious tours by Western church groups, not-for-profit organizations and students, are also the base of today's tourism clientele, and they too encourage aid and assistance to the battered economy.[27]

BURMA

Burma, with its fabled "road to Mandalay," its temple city of Pagan, and the faded glory of Rangoon with its massive Schwe Dagon Temple, attracted fewer than 50,000 travelers in 1988, because of the inertia of the government.[28] It is not that the government is profoundly xenophobic; it simply fails to recognize the fact that its policies are miserably failing. In 1987 the silver jubilee of retired Gen. Ne Win's so-called socialist revolution was scarcely celebrated, and was certainly no occasion for tourist promotion.[29]

Tourism development, which might have brought in badly needed jobs and foreign exchange, was stymied by a combination of political unrest among non-Burman ethnic groups in the northern half of the country, by a shortage of accommodations and transport, and by a government policy that still allows visitors only seven days in Burma at a ridiculously punitive exchange rate.[30]

Burma's not-so-splendid isolation may be ending, however, as the government reluctantly concedes it has little to show for its rigid policies. In 1987 the government moved toward a policy of decontrol of agriculture; and it has hinted that other major, even constitutional, changes may be in the offing. If tourism is among the sectors targeted for stimulation, visitors will find in Burma a rare opportunity to explore a rich and varied culture that has—except for a thriving black market—been relatively sheltered from the "Coca-colonization" of Asia.

THAILAND

Neighboring Thailand has not been shy about encouraging tourism. Thai tourism was initially oriented to its culture: the Buddhist temples; the

[26] Ibid.

[27] Arthur Frommer, The New World of Travel, 1988 (New York: Prentice-Hall, 1988), 19.

[28] "Burma," in Asia 1988 Yearbook (Hong Kong: Far Eastern Economic Review), 110.

[29] Linda K. Richter, "Myanmar," in Americana Annual Yearbook 1988 (Canada, Grolier Incorporated), 157.

[30] "Burma," in Fodor's Southeast Asia, 1985 (New York: Fodor's Travel Guides, 1986), 250.

ruins of earlier capital cities, as at Ayudhya; the boat tours along Bangkok's busy canals. However, during the Vietnam War, Thailand became a rest and recreation center for war-weary American servicemen; culture receded as an attraction, and the Thai government's reluctance to acknowledge and monitor its seamier attractions has led to the country's unhappy reputation as the "brothel of Asia." Despite the fact that it has been officially illegal in Thailand since the 1930s, prostitution, centered particularly in Bangkok, the resort cities of Pattaya and Phuket, and the lovely hill city of Chiang Mai, involved a significant number of the tourists visiting in Thailand in 1988.[31]

Over 80 percent of these tourists are males, most from elsewhere in Southeast Asia, but also from Germany, Japan, Australia and the United States. Many are business travelers. Because tourism has surpassed rice as the leading source of foreign exchange, the government has been reluctant to crack down on live sex shows and prostitution. This may be costly and difficult, but in the age of AIDS it is necessary to try. Today, many sex tours avoid Thailand because of fears of disease, while many more conventional tourists bypass the country because they erroneously feel there is no escape from sex tourism.

Its historically laissez-faire attitude notwithstanding, Thailand has been moving toward greater government involvement in tourism since about 1985. The country has tripled its special tourism police to curb crime, and has imposed one of the world's highest hotel taxes on the industry. It is trying hard to keep and enlarge the annual billion-plus dollars in tourism revenue, while encouraging an image of Thailand more likely to enhance its ability to preserve its genuinely rich natural beauty and cultural treasures.

This is not a puritanical reaction, but a capitalist reckoning that Thailand's tourism future had to have healthier roots. It was also a course reputedly desired by the popular and proud monarchy. To that end, government financing of the Tourism Authority of Thailand sharply increased; in 1987, over $1 million was allocated for special promotion of festivals, fairs and other special events designed to encourage tourism built around the celebration of the king's 60th birthday.

MALAYSIA

Malaysia wants to have it both ways. This Muslim country enjoys one of the highest volumes of international tourists (3.2 million in 1988)—many of them business travelers from every country in Asia and the Pacific.[32] Yet it has slapped a high travel tax on its own nationals going abroad—a policy that has been strongly resented in Thailand, where Malaysians constitute one-quarter of all visitors, and in Singapore, which also receives a major portion of its travelers from Malaysia. These two countries alone constitute

[31] "Thailand," in *Asia 1988 Yearbook* (Hong Kong: Far Eastern Economic Review), 251.
[32] "Malaysia," in *Asia 1988 Yearbook* (Hong Kong: Far Eastern Economic Review), 183.

70 percent of Malaysia's visitors. It is a policy that invites retaliation, which Malaysia cannot afford. Malaysia, like so many nations that have become suddenly enthralled with tourism, has an enormous glut of hotel rooms.[33] Kuala Lumpur and Penang have become major convention destinations. Still, the country does not have the promotion budget or the attractions to woo Western markets.

INDONESIA

As the fifth-largest country in the world, with enormous natural resources including oil, Indonesia for a long time was relatively indifferent to tourism. Getting a visa was difficult, and obtaining reliable and current information was often impossible for some kinds of travel and excursions. This began to change significantly in 1983 when the government created a cabinet-level Ministry of Tourism, abolished visas for over 20 countries, devalued the rupiah and opened up the country to foreign airlines.[34] Even before that the World Bank had been instrumental in financing lavish tourist infrastructure development on the Hindu island of Bali, which attracts 60 percent of Indonesia's over 700,000 annual visitors.

Indonesia now draws tourists most heavily from Australia; but its expansion of flights to the United States is likely to reap rewards when Americans discover that Indonesia offers opportunities to sample a panoply of Islamic and Hindu cultures plus those of a wide variety of ethnic and tribal groups. Beyond that, the nation has beautiful mountains and beaches to tempt the most jaded traveler. Indonesia should also be a magnet for archaeology buffs, thanks to its excavations of impressive temple and palace complexes throughout the country. The ninth-century temple of Borobudur, discovered in 1815, is today, thanks to the international restoration efforts of UNESCO and many individual nations, a major world landmark, rivaling Angkor Wat in Cambodia and Pagan in Myanmar.[35]

Business travelers to Indonesia will find excellent accommodations, and banking and satellite facilities in key cities, but should expect negotiations and discussions to require a conservative approach and much patience.[36]

SOUTH ASIA

South Asia (India, Pakistan, Bangladesh, Nepal, Afghanistan, Bhutan, Sri Lanka and Maldives), despite its size and abundant tourist attractions, has never developed a firm foothold on international tourism. Distance from the major tourist-generating markets of Japan, North America and Europe

[33] Waters, *Travel Industry World Yearbook, 1987*, 105.
[34] Ginny Bruce, Mary Covernton, and Alan Samalgalski, *Indonesia: A Travel Survival Kit* (Berkeley, California: Lonely Planet, 1986), 55; Waters, *Travel Industry World Yearbook, 1987*, 106.
[35] *Fodor's Southeast Asia, 1985*, 354.
[36] Elizabeth Devine and Nancy L. Braganti, *The Traveler's Guide to Asian Customs and Manners* (New York: St. Martin's Press, 1986), 108–109.

has been a major factor. The media have to share some of the blame also; press coverage has been erratic and rare except when natural disaster or political unrest occurs. Thus, relatively few travelers from outside the region are aware that India, the world's largest democracy, is also the tenth-largest industrial power in the world, with the second-largest railway system. Nor do they realize that South Asia's tourist attractions range from the storied Himalayan hill stations of Kashmir, Swat and Darjeeling to tropical beach resorts in the Indian states of Goa, Kerala and Madras.

The region has, however, been a haven for the curious traveler for over two millennia. To this day, despite the general poverty and almost non-existent discretionary incomes of the majority of the people, domestic tourism flourishes. Even if only five percent of the region's over 1 billion people can afford to vacation frequently, that translates to 50 million domestic tourists. Many others avail themselves of inexpensive modes of travel for religious pilgrimages, a tradition for centuries. The major religions of Hinduism, Buddhism and Sikhism all had their origin in India; thus, a major part of tourism for the faithful and the curious alike consists of visiting the elaborate shrines, temples, holy centers, architectural wonders and relics of over 6,000 years of religious practices. The Buddhist center of Sarnath, the holy Hindu city of Varanasi, the Sikh Golden Temple at Amritsar, or the exquisite Muslim mosques in Delhi and Lahore testify to the faith of South Asia's devout.

Nor does the region lack secular attractions. The erotic sculpture of Khajuraho, the sublime beauty of the Taj Mahal, the palaces of the numerous maharajas who once ruled in South Asia, the excavated civilizations of Harappa, Moenjodaro and Taxila only suggest the wealth of cultural attractions the region offers. Bird and animal life—including white tigers and rhinoceroses—is still abundant in the region's many game parks, bird sanctuaries and wildlife preserves. Some, like Tiger Tops in Nepal, have acquired international reputations; other, like Jim Corbett National Park in India, are relatively unknown despite their excellence.

While South Asian governments have occasionally attempted to promote the region as a destination, international politics has often stood in the way. For years the hostility between India and Pakistan made collaborative planning impossible, and there was continued friction over which should control the once princely state and major tourist site of Kashmir. Secular India controls most of this largely Muslim state, while Pakistan retains only a portion of Kashmiri territory. As Indian and Pakistani relations improved in the late 1970s, revolution in Iran and the Soviet invasion of Afghanistan effectively stopped all overland journeys from Europe, though India and Pakistan continue to ease travel across their mutual borders.

Nepal and Bhutan have had their tourist travel strongly influenced by India because all access to Bhutan, and almost all to Nepal, is via India. Sri Lanka has been more independent, since, unlike the others, it has permitted charters—which has allowed the nation to market tourism separately from other South Asian nations. Tiny Maldives was until the mid-1980s dependent on India and Sri Lanka for air access, but now has flights direct to the capital city, Male. Bangladesh has air ties with several nations.

India

International tourism to India seems likely to do extremely well in the near future. In 1987, foreign visitors to India increased an incredible 29 percent (to 1,080,000).[37] Domestic and regional tourism are increasing, too, as the country continues to build on a decade of strong economic achievements. Business and convention tourism is also thriving, following the enormous and costly hotel building spree for the ninth Asian Games in 1982.[38]

The central government can claim some of the credit for the upturn in Indian tourism. Under Prime Minister Rajiv Gandhi, himself once a commercial pilot, tourism development has received serious attention. Now recognized as a major source of foreign exchange, tourism was seen as a significant possible side effect of the two-year Festival of India that traveled abroad in 1987. In the United States alone it visited 90 cities in 37 states, and seemed to have stimulated much interest in travel to India.[39] Such films as *Gandhi* and *A Passage to India,* and the television series "The Jewel in the Crown" also appear to have quickened interest in travel to India.

The state governments have also initiated innovative tourist programs, and have encouraged development that is geared not only to luxury-seeking tourists but also to those of more modest means. Goa is an apparent exception; many there feel displaced by lavish hotels that have been built with cavalier disregard for those who have lived and worked on the land and who previously had access to the coast.[40]

Computerization of India's domestic airlines has also facilitated international travel beyond the gateway cities of Delhi, Bombay, Calcutta and Madras.

India has been fortunate in inheriting from the British a well-developed rail system and an infrastructure of hill resorts. It also amassed a superb collection of palaces from the two-fifths of the country that had been princely states until independence. Many of these palaces have been converted to magnificent hotels or museums. It is on this base that the central government, the states and an active private sector have acted to stimulate and modernize tourism in India.[41]

Pakistan

Tourism in Pakistan theoretically had some of the same foundations as that in India; but because of domestic political instability, coups, civil war and

[37] R. K. Raju, "The Year of a Million Tourists," *Indian and Foreign Review* 24 (February 28, 1987): 4–5, 27.

[38] Sharat G. Lin and Nageshwar Patnaik, "Migrant Labor at Asiad '82 Construction Sites in New Delhi," *Bulletin of Concerned Asian Scholars* 14, no. 3 (July–September 1982): 23–31.

[39] Waters, *Travel Industry World Yearbook, 1987,* 103.

[40] "The TATA Land Grab at Candolim," *Contours* 1, no. 3 (1983): 6–7; "Update on Goa," *Contours* 1, no. 7 (1984): 14–15.

[41] Linda K. Richter and William L. Richter, "Policy Choices in South Asian Tourism Development," *Annals of Tourism Research* 12, no. 2 (1985): 201–17.

the current struggle to cope with 3 million Afghan refugees, tourism development has never been seen as more than peripheral to Pakistani interests.

Since 1977, when the fundamentalist government of Gen. Zia ul-Haq seized power, tourist facilities have had to adapt to strict Islamic customs, including the prohibition of alcohol, of dancing and of eating in public during Ramadan. Pakistani women are increasingly veiled, and Western women touring the country should expect to be extremely circumspect if they are to avoid unwelcome attention.[42]

On the other hand, Pakistan's Himalaya attract many trekking and holiday groups, while its ancient cities, shrines and mosques deservedly impress both domestic and foreign visitors. The latter totaled only about 110,000 in 1987, but they brought in nearly $200 million in foreign exchange.[43]

Bangladesh
Once described by Henry Kissinger as "a basket case among nations," Bangladesh, while enormously fertile and lush, is an extremely poor country due to its serious overpopulation. It is also tragically and routinely vulnerable to natural catastrophes (like typhoons) and to political instability: coups and assassinations of its top leadership.

Though Bangladesh has tourist attractions and such scenic attractions as the Chittagong Hills, tourism development appears designed less to attract roaming travelers than to cater to the rest and recreation needs of the large expatriate community of international and not-for-profit agencies trying to aid the country. Even so, approximately 129,070 tourists visited Bangladesh in 1987.[44] Very low earnings in foreign exchange (about one-ninth that of similar numbers of visitors to Pakistan) suggest that most were traveling on the Bangladesh currency, the taka—which probably means they were there in an official capacity.

While the capital, Dacca, and several other cities have international-standard hotels, the conservative culture, pervasive poverty and political instability discourage tourism development. A Bangladesh travel poster reads "Visit Bangladesh Before the Tourists Come"; there appears to be still time.

Nepal
Tourism has been absolutely critical to the economy of this largely mountainous and landlocked kingdom, with high unemployment and very little arable land. Nepal was closed to tourism until the 1950s, and even into the 1970s there were less than 200 miles of paved road in the whole country. Today, tourism is the major source of foreign exchange. While Kath-

[42] Linda K. Richter, "The Potential and Pitfalls of Tourism Planning in Third World Countries: The Case of Pakistan," *Tourism Recreation Research* (March 1984); Devine and Braganti, *The Traveler's Guide*, pp. 177–87.
[43] Waters, *Travel Industry World Yearbook, 1987*, p. 104.
[44] "Bangladesh," in *Asia 1988 Yearbook* (Hong Kong: Far Eastern Economic Review), 98.

mandu continues to receive the bulk of the nation's 223,000 visitors, trekking in the Himalaya has become a growth industry and a vital source of employment for the Sherpa guides and porters in the high country.

Major ecological and social problems have resulted from these seemingly innocuous trekking tours, however. Deforestation, littering, begging and dependence on tourists for medical supplies have been just a few of the problems compounded by large numbers of tourists traveling through ecologically fragile terrain and encountering a tradition-bound society.[45]

Bhutan

Bhutan has vowed to avoid dependence on tourism and the social and ecological problems it associates with Nepal's tourist development. On the other hand, it does not want to forgo foreign contacts, if only to establish its precarious independence from India. It has seen the principality of Sikkim absorbed by India and hopes to avoid a similar fate. What Bhutan has done is to limit the number of tourists at any one time in the country to 200 and to charge hotel rates of nearly $200 a night so as to maximize revenues from the approximately 2,500 tourists it accepts annually. In 1987 the National Assembly voted to accept the recommendation of the Special Commission for Cultural Affairs that would prohibit tourists from going to temples, monasteries or religious and meditational centers, or even from climbing sacred mountains. Also, because tourism demand exceeds access, and in order to save foreign exchange, tourist offices abroad are being closed. Bhutan badly needs foreign currency, but it wants even more to protect a way of life Bhutanese feel tourism might threaten.[46]

Sri Lanka

Sri Lanka has all the ingredients experts say is essential for tourism development: "sun, sand, sea and sex." And for a while it seemed that Sri Lankan tourism could not miss. Sri Lanka attracted over 300,000 visitors in 1982 with its beautiful beaches, mountains and monuments of Buddhist culture. Even then some said that Sri Lanka was building too many hotels, that tourism was growing too fast to be absorbed, and that the hedonistic beach resorts were luring youngsters away from schools and families into begging and prostitution.

By 1983, when the civil strife between the dominant Sinhalese and the minority Tamils broke out, concern was less about morals and more about holding the country together. By 1988 "the beautiful country," associated with serendipity and delight, was left with scores of almost empty tourist resorts and hotels, reminders of a time when Sri Lanka tried to develop tourism with luxury hotels and charter flights—both so vulnerable to fickle tastes and political unrest.

[45] Linda K. Richter, *The Development and Administration of Tourism Development in South Asia,* East-West Center Working Paper Series (Honolulu: University of Hawaii, 1986).
[46] "Bhutan," in *Asia 1988 Yearbook* (Hong Kong: Far Eastern Economic Review), 102.

Maldives

Maldives illustrates that if "no man is an island," no island nation—no matter how small—is really removed from the political environment of its region and the world. With a tiny population, scattered over 800 miles of atolls, the Republic of Maldives has attempted the almost impossible. Poor soil, a remote and fragmented location, and a conservative Muslim population do not augur well for agriculture, heavy industry, high tech or trade. Instead, Maldives is capitalizing on what it has in abundance: coastline, unspoiled tranquillity, a snorkeling and diving paradise; tourism is being developed. Since the islands are small, the pattern has been to develop a single resort per island, staff it with a totally male crew and make each resort a self-contained unit. The underlying logic was that Maldive culture, which prohibits pork, alcohol and dancing, could be kept intact, away from the mores of strangers; and that Maldivian women need never see tourists nor they the women.

This seemed to work, but problems are emerging. The Muslim male employees miss their families and the families worry about them, isolated in their resorts with hedonistic transients. The problems of coping with litter and sewage, and supplying fresh water to tourists are threatening to close some resorts. The foreign currency brought in by tourism is also leaking out to serve tourism development, since almost nothing for the resorts is available in Maldives themselves. Sri Lanka's tourism decline has had a pronounced effect on Maldives, which previously received many tourists who also had Sri Lanka on their itineraries.

Maldives is far from giving up on tourism, however, and visitors wax rhapsodic about the colorful fish and nearby reefs; but the islands are now attempting to diversify, both so that some tourist needs like food and furnishings, can be produced locally, and so that they will become less dependent on the tourism sector.

PACIFIC

Many of the island nations of the Pacific have tourism histories not unlike that of Maldives: They have tried to develop tourism to offset dependence on volatile agricultural commodities such as sugar. Others saw tourism as a way to absorb their unemployed or as a way of turning liabilities—remoteness, unassimilated minorities and underdevelopment—into economic assets.

Some of the island nations have succeeded; many have not. The desire to develop the limited coastal land for tourist purposes may conflict with its traditional use for fishing or with ritual uses. Land ownership becomes another controversial issue; traditional leaders may manage communal lands, but if they sell or lose control of the land, serious problems can arise for the developers and the former owners. Foreign-exchange leakage to develop and serve tourism is extremely high. Airlines can demand such great concessions for developing air links that little is retained by the countries involved. Ultimately, the smaller nations remain hostage to the whims and routes of the major carriers. Even cruise ships no longer have set destinations but travel to where they can get the best bargains in port attractions for their passengers.

The dress of leisured guests, and their behavior, is often offensive to some island peoples. The islanders resent living in a goldfish bowl, or being forced to trade or work on Sundays or other religious holidays in order to accommodate air and cruise schedules.[47] Yet the uncooperative also know what it is like to become a non-destination; to be suddenly dropped from the itineraries of air and boat cruises, to have a tourist industry but few tourists.

Despite many of the difficulties Pacific societies have in developing tourism, most of these countries see its potential as exceeding either the problems associated with it or alternative development options. Indeed, the South Pacific has known more dramatic increases in tourism than almost anywhere else on the globe.

The numbers, but not the percentages, of tourists are likely to increase sharply in the years ahead as population growth continues to accelerate. In the year 2000, six of every 10 people in the world will be living in and around the Pacific Rim.[48]

Hawaii

Capturing by far the greatest number of tourists in the Pacific is the state of Hawaii. Hawaii in 1987 welcomed over 5 million tourists, or nearly five times its number of citizens. Hawaii draws most heavily from the U.S. mainland, but has become almost a second home to the Japanese. A weak dollar relative to the Japanese yen has led to a commanding ownership position for the Japanese in Hawaii; nearly every major hotel in Waikiki is Japanese-owned, with restaurants and ground transportation also largely in Japanese hands.

For several years Hawaii has had a lively debate over its growing dependence on tourism. Yet tourism to Hawaii has led to a revival of Hawaiian identity in music, dance, language and culture; ethnic Hawaiians have had more results in getting the state government to protect their sacred *heiaus,* support the language and recognize the importance of preserving not only a facade of Hawaiiana but the genuine culture itself.

Although the massive increase in tourism has been relatively confined to about 10 percent of the islands' area, many protest that inflation, crowding, crime and increased ecological damage are the result of this acceleration.[49] Some communities on the islands of Kauai and Molokai have actually forced developers to retreat in the face of their opposition. However, other equally opposed communities have been forced to capitulate because alternative sources of employment were not available.

Increasingly, there is a need for better data on the *net* costs and benefits

[47] Cynthia Biddlecomb, *Pacific Tourism: Contrasts in Value and Expectations* (San Francisco, Calif.: Pacific Council of Churches, 1981).
[48] Waters, *Travel Industry World Yearbook, 1987,* 98.
[49] See Noel J. Kent, *Hawaii, Islands Under the Influence* (New York: Monthly Review Press, 1983).

of tourism. As Hawaii has had to develop more and more roads, bridges, water and electricity supplies, police units, trash and sewage disposal systems, and health facilities for the tourist industry, taxpayers are recognizing that tourism implies more than simply the presence of money-spending machines. There is also more awareness of foreign-exchange leakage through imports, and ultimately through the export of profits when Hawaii's tourism infrastructure is owned by outsiders.[50]

Australia and New Zealand

A major tourist boom has engulfed Australia and New Zealand—two nations whose own nationals have formed the bulk of their tourism customers. The wanderlust of these nationals has also been important to the development of Pacific tourism in general, especially in the Cook Islands, Fiji and Tahiti.

In the mid-1980s major tourism increases occurred—whether because of terrorism and high prices in Europe or because of political stability and shrewd promotion at home is not entirely certain. In any event, there has been a rage for things Australian. Also contributing was the enormous success of the film *Crocodile Dundee*. Its star, Paul Hogan, became an immediate hit in a series of Australia tourist promotions.

Events also conspired to focus the media's attention down under. The America's Cup races in early 1987 off Perth, in Western Australia, received more than cursory attention because it was the first time the race had been held outside U.S. waters. Journalists and tourists, based in Perth and touring Australia, found an immense continent of exotic wildlife, elegant and dynamic cities like Sydney and Melbourne, and unforgettable sights such as the Great Barrier Reef or Ayers Rock and the eerie loveliness of Kakadu National Park.

Their reports made it even more likely that the 1988 Bicentennial of the first European settlement in Australia would be a huge success. Less thrilled were the aboriginal populations, whose life-style, crafts and sacred sites intrigued visitors, but who received little of the revenues from tourism and found nothing to celebrate in the white conquest of Australia.

In addition to aggressive national promotion, the state governments of Australia have also been active in the stimulation of tourism. The national government is currently thinking of deregulation of the airlines because the national carrier, Qantas, can currently carry only those holding international tickets. This protects Australia's domestic airlines, but leads to inefficiencies in routings and loads that have become major problems for Qantas and the Australian touring public.[51]

New Zealand[52] has experienced a welcome increase in tourism from abroad at a time when the country's important agricultural base has been eroding.

[50]Governor's Conference on Tourism, December 10–12, 1984.
[51]Comments on Australia are based on personal interviews with state and federal tourism offices, February–March, 1987, throughout Eastern Australia.
[52]Comments on New Zealand are based on a series of personal interviews conducted from March 19, 1987, to April 8, 1987, throughout New Zealand.

The New Zealand dollar's devaluation has kept more nationals at home, however, where they have found it difficult to compete with the Japanese, Europeans and Americans for tourist facilities that have sharply increased in price. Most of the new accommodations being planned are not the bed and breakfast type or the simple housing favored by the domestic population, but rather the five-star luxury hotels business and group tours support.

Bus tours to such picturesque destinations as Milford Sound, Mount Cook or the Franz Joseph Glacier already cause major traffic and parking jams because the two-lane roads were designed for far less traffic. While many if not most New Zealanders welcome the influx of tourists as a needed economic and social stimulus, it has caused others to urge caution and sensitivity in New Zealand's tourism development. One such group, Justice in Tourism, based in Wellington, has assumed the two-fold task of educating New Zealanders about the impact of tourism on fragile South Pacific islands and about the impact of tourism at home on New Zealand culture and values.[53]

For example, Maori traditions must be respected and protected from trivialization designed to entertain tourists. The life-style of New Zealanders, which includes generally quiet weekends with family and friends, is difficult to reconcile with the tourist industry, which operates seven days a week. Labor unions have sought to insure that work on Saturday or Sunday be considered overtime; tourism establishments insist that ordinary shifts must include weekends.

Tourism brings badly needed jobs and entertainment to a quiet and beautiful country that admits it needs more of both; but New Zealand also wants to insure that the place they affectionately call "God's Own" remains a very special place at the end of the earth.

Fiji and Tahiti

The major beneficiaries of the spillover from traffic now heading down under to Australia and New Zealand have been Fiji and Tahiti. Fiji, independent from Britain since 1970, has seen impressive tourism growth since 1985—reaching over 260,000 in 1986.[54] In 1987 two military coups devastated the idyllic image that Fiji had struggled to develop. Tourist numbers plummeted and several airlines that came into Nadi's international airport threatened to discontinue stopovers. The most crushing long-term effect is expected from the cancellation of $500 million worth of new resort construction following the initial coup.

The political problem is based on the multiethnic character of Fiji. Though one would never know it by reading the tourist brochures featuring smiling, handsome Fijians, Fiji has acquired an Indian majority over the years. Until 1987 political power rested predominantly with ethnic Fijians, though economic power has shifted to the Indians and outside tourist interests.

[53] Justice in Tourism organization meeting, April 3, 1987, in Wellington, New Zealand.
[54] "Fiji," in *Asia 1988 Yearbook* (Hong Kong: Far Eastern Economic Review), 127.

The spring 1987 election put that pattern in doubt and a military coup followed. For the rest of the year, power shifted uneasily in response to negotiations and outside pressures—not the least of which was a precipitous decline in tourism, Fiji's second most important industry.

Tahiti, on the other hand, has seen its decades-long tourist doldrums shaken off by the new interest in the Pacific, and recognition that it is an ideal place for a stopover for tourists heading down under. Unlike many other destinations that are loosening entry barriers, however, Tahiti is following the French lead: attempting to curtail terrorism by requiring visas of most foreign nationals. It is not the visa that is the biggest barrier for tourists, however; it is the tremendous cost of food, accommodations, taxis and tours. Though a few small hotels have been built in the capital city, Papeete, and on some of the other islands by the French chains of Sofitel and Ibis, even they are only relative bargains.

Of course, most items must be imported; but even with that caveat, Tahiti remains extremely expensive. Only the large ferries to nearby Moorea and Bora Bora represent tourist values. Many of the large cruise lines are bypassing Tahiti because of the complaints of passengers about the cost of shore visits or longer stays on the island. There is virtually no business travel to Tahiti, though it has become a rest and recreation locale for the French Foreign Legion, charged with monitoring nuclear testing in the region.[55]

CONCLUSION

While this brief survey of Asian and Pacific tourism can only touch on the dramatic and powerful changes tourism has brought to these countries, it is also important to acknowledge the tremendous changes in sensitivity that have occurred in the host-guest relationship.

Few countries, industry developers, travel writers, or tourists themselves remain naive about the impact tourism can have, and many are attempting to make that impact a more benign and just one for both visitor and visited. Increasingly, countries are including advice to travelers about their customs and values, and what constitutes appropriate dress and behavior. Thoughtful tours and corporations should be applauded for insisting that those served by and connected with them behave with taste and decorum. Nor are Western visitors the only ones being encouraged to do so. Japanese businessmen, for example, are learning that New Zealanders do *not* consider the hotel lobby an extension of one's room, where pajamas are permitted, anymore than Sikhs will allow hatless and shoe-wearing tourists in their temples.

In fact, business travelers would do well to heed a whole range of dos and don'ts relating to gift-giving, punctuality, entertaining and other varieties of commercial etiquette. For example, the informal gesture of back-slapping, certain ways of eating, or touching someone with one's left hand could lose a person esteem in large parts of Asia where familiarity, espe-

[55] Comments on Tahiti are based on personal travel in April, 1987.

cially touching, is considered gauche, or where using one's left hand (which is considered unclean) is perceived as crude. (It is a difficult region for the left-handed.) Similarly, visitors should not assume that Asian men holding hands is any sign of their sexual preference, or that friendly Western gestures are interpreted the same way in the East.

Today, there are excellent guidebooks and sources of travel information designed for almost any clientele. The travel sections of libraries and bookstores have tripled in just the last 10 years; travel magazines and newsletters are proliferating.

While there is no longer any acceptable excuse (if there ever was) for being ignorant or culturally boorish, many well-intentioned travelers do not consider how their life-styles, traveling expectations and degree of sensitivity to people may still prove troublesome, given the tremendous numbers of travelers visiting the most popular destinations.

Several organizations have been active in preparing films, magazines, workshops and reports designed for work with nations in supporting a tourism industry beneficial to visitors and host populations alike. These groups include the Coalition for Third World Tourism, based in Bangkok; the Center for Responsible Tourism, in California; Tourism Ecumenical Network, in Europe; Equitable Tourism Options, in India; Justice in Tourism, located in New Zealand; and the Centre for the Advancement of Responsible Travel, in Great Britain.

FURTHER READING

Business Travel Guide. Uniglobe Series. Toronto: Summerhill Press, 1987.

De Kadt, Emanuel, ed. *Tourism, Passport to Development: Perspectives on the Social and Cultural Effects of Tourism in Developing Countries.* London and New York: Oxford University Press, 1979.

Edwards, Anthony, and Cleverdon, Robert. *International Tourism to 1990.* New York: Ballinger, 1982.

Fodor's Travel Guides. New York: McKay. Available for most countries in Asia and the Pacific.

Lea, John. *Tourism and Development in the Third World.* London: Chapman & Hall, 1988.

Lonely Planet series. Oakland, California. Available for most countries in Asia and the Pacific.

USEFUL ADDRESSES

Center for Responsible Tourism, 2 Kensington Road, San Anselmo, California 91201.

Centre for the Advancement of Responsible Travel, 70 Dry Hill Park Road, Tonbridge, Kent, TN10 BBX, England.

Coalition for Third World Tourism, P.O. Box 9–25 Bangkhen, Bangkok 10900, Thailand.

Equitable Tourism Options, 96 Main Road, India Nagar, Stage 1, Bangalore 560 038, India.

RELIGION IN ASIAN LIFE AND SOCIETY

BRUCE MATTHEWS

RELIGIOUS experience and its interpretation are integral to the human community. Although in Asia the power of religion may be diminishing in the face of modernization and Marxism, its relevance to society and the individual remains substantial, and often massive. Because religion is so closely tied to cultural norms of understanding life and the world, it cannot be successfully isolated and examined, especially in Asia, apart from the living tradition in which it is rooted. No religion is just a stone falling from heaven, somehow apart from the processes of change and social, artistic and intellectual metamorphosis. To be understood, the religions of Asia must be seen as living organisms exposed to the strains of adolescence, maturity and old age. They are not fixed devices that have somehow resisted the toil and nemesis of history. Nor are they hermetically sealed from the influence of other religions, or from the characteristics of the modern age such as science and its deepest consequences—technology, secularization and philosophical materialism. To reach out to Asia's religions is to come into contact with life itself—vibrant, fecund, complex, sometimes full of pain, sometimes incoherent and contradictory, not always beautiful or elegant, but nonetheless expressive of the ways human experience and destiny are grasped by this great part of humankind.

This chapter encompasses three perspectives. First, some observations on the nature of religion in general are drawn. A distinction is made between the Great Tradition of the primary civilizations such as India and China, and the Little Tradition of folk or village-level religion. This leads, secondly, to a review of certain characteristics of the Little Tradition. Third, the major religions associated with Asia's Great Tradition—Buddhism, Hinduism, Confucianism, Taoism, Shinto, Islam and Christianity—are examined, largely from a phenomenological perspective.[1]

Some observations on what religion means are necessary. Many interest-

---

[1] Descriptive phenomenologists investigate religious data or "phenomena," but resist making judgments about the level of sophistication or value of religion. At the same time, phenomenology tries to penetrate the experiential heart of a religion by being responsive to its claims and by seeking out recurrent themes shared by various religions.

ing attempts to provide such a definition aim by intellectual abstraction and generalization to summarize simply something as complex as religion. Two important but very different examples from the early 20th century show the range of opinion encountered.

On the one hand, in a classical study, sociologist Emile Durkheim distinguished between "the sacred" (which includes those "personal beings" called gods or spirits, as well as an undetermined number of "sacred objects," such as rites or customs), and everything else ("the profane"). He argued that the sacred originates as a symbolic projection of the clan or tribal group, and that, according to its cultural and psychological needs, a society continuously fabricates the sacred by venerating certain objects, ideas, or even people. This constitutes religion. On the other hand, concurrently, theologian and phenomenologist Rudolf Otto maintained that religion cannot be reduced to the mere expression of certain tribal or sociocultural needs. Religion as experience and embodiment is rather a response of awe and fascination to a power ("the holy") that stands beyond the human realm and transcends the human condition and human creative artifice. Each human being has a special spiritual capacity to experience the holy, yet it is never the unique property of one person, one culture or one religion.[2]

In many ways, Durkheim and Otto set the stage for the modern analysis of religion, in Asia as elsewhere. Both help to interpret what religious life means. Durkheim is correct in maintaining that religious behavior and thought must not be interpreted apart from everyday conduct. Others have expanded upon this horizontal or worldly feature of religion by showing how conceptions of the divine can be related to the social and economic conditions under which people live,[3] or even to the climate of their region.[4] But living religion is surely more than this. It has a vertical dimension that looks beyond the quotidian world. A religious account attaches its expression to a further reality, to the ontological ultimacy of this reality as the world's source or ground, Brahman, Tao or nirvana. This feature, too, must be considered to appreciate Asian religions. Primary religious experience is something that is known or felt as a whole and cannot be reached by ratiocination alone. Representation of this experience, whether academic or popular, is always secondary. Reports, whether iconic, artistic or theological, are at best thin, and should be understood as indications of a felt and known reality that is beyond full characterization. Asiatic religion is mostly lived and not just thought about. Thus the life of religion, as cultural formation (ritual, artistic artifact, institution) and as experience

[2] See Emile Durkheim, *The Elementary Forms of Religious Life* (New York: Collier, 1961) and Rudolf Otto, *The Idea of the Holy* (New York: Oxford University Press, 1958).

[3] Max Weber, *The Sociology of Religion* (Boston: Beacon Press, 1963).

[4] See Klaus Klostermaier, *Hindu and Christian in Vrindaban* (London: SCM, 1969), 40: "The theologian at 70°F in a good position presumes god to be happy and contented, well-fed and rested, without needs of any kind. The theologian at 120°F tries to imagine a god who is thirsty and hungry, who suffers and is sad, who sheds perspiration and knows despair."

(individual or collective), points to the linked pair of the human and the divine, the immanent and the transcendent.

Whatever its source and foundation, two observations about religion can be made. First, all religions, whether from the Great or Little Tradition, provide a worldview (*Weltanschauung*), or way to understand the universe— time and space, the natural order, life and death, the paradox of the human condition. A worldview provides self-definition for the individual and collective definition for the community. It gives enduring answers to pain, suffering, injustice and distress at both individual and communal levels. Ninian Smart observes that the worldview is often shown in beliefs and symbols that form a deep part of the structure of human consciousness and society.[5] A worldview may be expressed in myth, custom or ritual. World-views are so rich in indicating a culture or society's spiritual needs that they stand at the center of the modern study of religion. A central objective of this chapter is to articulate the major worldviews that undergird Asia's complex religious heritage.

Secondly, religion should not be spoken about and studied as just an "ism" (Buddhism, Confucianism, etc.). Every religion is concrete, made up of people and embodied ideas. Religions have a temporal, conditioned character and therefore undergo change, sometimes quietly, often dramatically. W. C. Smith has noted that no two centuries have been religious in the same way, neither have two communities or even two persons. "So much is this so," he writes, "that I have found myself pushed to dropping the word 'religion' as a concrete noun altogether, since I find nothing on earth, or in Heaven, that will consistently answer to those names" (i.e., "isms").[6] Indeed, in a celebrated theory, Smith proposes that the word *religion* be replaced altogether by two more descriptive terms—*cumulative tradition* and *faith*. The former is "the entire mass of overt objective data of the past religious life of the community in question . . . temples, scriptures, theological systems . . . anything that can be transmitted from one person, one generation to another, and that the historian can observe."[7] Faith, on the other hand, is the individual, personal indwelling of religious experience, the dynamic interior life, and, like love, it is essentially indescribable.

Although for many people a religion may appear essentially theological, monolithic, unchanging and knowable, a seamless entity come into the present, it is not. Convictions about the nature of reality and ethical values are shared for generations, to be sure. But intellectual, political and economic circumstances often stretch a religion's rationale and strain its worldview. Despite their venerable histories, Asian religions are not in a time warp. They are fully exposed to pressures requiring basic adaptation and redirection. This can be seen, for example, by the development in Japan of

---

[5] See Ninian Smart, *World Views: Cross-Cultural Exploration of Human Beliefs* (New York: Scribners, 1983), 2.

[6] W. C. Smith, *Toward a World Theology* (Philadelphia: Westminster, 1981), 4.

[7] W. C. Smith, *The Meaning and End of Religion,* (Toronto: Mentor, 1963), 141.

new religious sects *(shinko shukyo)*, like the Buddhist Soka Gakkai ("Value Creation Society"), the Shinto Tenrikyo ("Religion of Heavenly Wisdom") or by the slight, if uneven, loosening of caste restrictions in Hinduism, a process set in operation by Mohandas Gandhi some 50 years ago. Sometimes the change may appear to retreat to an abandoned norm or an archaic custom (like the wearing of the *hijab*—the Islamic female headdress revealing only the face, in contemporary Malaysia).[8] Whether or not such changes seem progressive to the outsider, they express the living response of a collective tradition and the assent of its adherents who wish to keep that faith efficacious and enduring. The religions of contemporary Asia in their current "human" context need to be seen in this light. A historical perspective is needed, especially to situate the great paradigmatic teachers and the doctrines that flowed from their initial vision; they are best appreciated when they are viewed not merely as begetters of systems of thought and doctrinaire "isms" but as *fons et origo* of living, developing traditions. The faithful strive to continue to keep in good repair the bridge over the turbulent waters of the sacred and the profane.

ASPECTS OF THE LITTLE TRADITION

In a leading study, Robert Redfield writes,

> In a civilization there is a great tradition of the reflective few and there is the little tradition of the largely unreflective many. This great tradition is cultivated in schools and temples; the little tradition works itself out and keeps itself going in the lives of the unlettered in their village communities. The tradition of the philosopher, theologian and literary man is a tradition consciously cultivated and handed down; that of the little people is for the most part taken for granted and not submitted to much scrutiny or considered refinement and improvement.[9]

There are other doublets that state the dichotomy expressed here (such as "high" and "low" cultures, "learned" and "popular" traditions, "hierarchic" and "village" religion), but the point is always the same: religion in Asia has two polarities, the doctrinal, canonical, classical religions of the sages and the literati, and the pursuit of religion at the level of the villager, peasant or aborigine. In between lies a vast range of religious interpretation and practice. Another distinction can be made between a Little Tradition associated with an untouched "primitive," "aboriginal" or "pagan" reli-

---

[8] Clifford Geertz notes that "stepping backward in order better to leap" is an established principle of cultural change. "Our own Reformation was made that way. But in the Islamic case the stepping backward seems often to be taken for the leap itself." In other words, there is no leap forward. "Islam, in this way, becomes a justification for modernity, without itself actually becoming modern." *Islam Observed* (Chicago: University of Chicago Press, 1968), 70.

[9] Robert Redfield, *Peasant Society and Culture* (Chicago: University of Chicago Press, 1956), 70.

gion,[10] and a Little Tradition that reflects elements of this "aboriginal" religion that have been absorbed by the Great Tradition. "Aboriginal" religion can still be found in Asia among some tribal people.[11] The Little Tradition is also encountered in the survivals of certain aboriginal indigenous religious ideas in the Great Tradition, as expressed through myths, customs and rituals. Despite the acceptance by a devotee of a "canonical" religion like Hinduism or Buddhism, the retention of some archaic beliefs affects that individual's worldview.[12] The religions of the Great Tradition have adapted to this reality, as Ananda Coomaraswamy can claim about India when he observes:

> Nor could the "higher religions," when from systems of pure thought and of monastic discipline they developed into popular faiths, have succeeded in securing the adhesion of the mass of people had they not both tolerated and reflected popular beliefs. Iconolatry, ritual, devotion, profound preoccupations of the popular non-Aryan consciousness, made of Buddhism, Jainism and Hinduism what they are, and that is something other than they were in their initial inception.[13]

Some of the more important aspects of the Little Tradition are animism, spirit cults, magic and folklore. They reflect beliefs and superstitions about an immense unseen spirit world that directly affects the individual and the community's sense of security. Briefly put, animism attributes a living soul to inanimate or insentient objects such as rocks, ravines, rivers, trees and rice and grains, or to the powers of nature ("kratophanies"), such as thunder and lightning. Spirits are an extension of the animistic understanding of the world and can include the spiritual essences or souls of the dead, malevolent forces, devils, goblins, fairies and angels. Magic or magical animism is a technique for coping with malignant powers and disorder in nature, but especially in the human sphere. Folklore represents an accumulation of custom, myth, ritual and folk medicine, among other things.

[10] "Pagan" is not used in a pejorative sense, but in its etymological sense from the Latin *paganus* ("peasant"), and thus "religion of the people of the land." See John Langerway, *Taoist Ritual in Chinese Society and History* (New York: Macmillan, 1987), v.

[11] For example, among some of the Orang Asli ("original people") of mainland Southeast Asia, or the Dyaks of Kalimantan (Borneo). See C. F. Keyes, *The Golden Peninsula* (New York: Macmillan, 1977), 13–14, on a whole range of aboriginal societies, and their religious beliefs, especially the Semang, the Chin and the Karens.

[12] In this regard, R. F. Gombrich and others aver that the affective aspect (the "religion of the heart," implied by actual behavior) is often different from the cognitive aspect (what people say about their beliefs and practices). See *Precept and Practice* (Clarendon: Oxford University Press, 1971), 220. Ursula Sharma notes, "This is an important point, since it has always been a besetting sin of Western scholars . . . to impute to Buddhism and Hinduism a stronger and more rigid sense of orthodoxy than actually exists." W. Foy, ed., *Man's Religious Quest* (London: Atheneum, 1978), 43.

[13] Ananda Coomaraswamy, *Origin of the Buddha Image* (Delhi: Manoharlal, 1972), 14.

Much of the population of contemporary Asia is still apprehensive about spirits, thought to lurk in any number of locations. For example, in rural areas of the Philippines, a Little Tradition persists (even after centuries of dominant Roman Catholicism) that focuses on such spirits as the *manku-kulam* (a witch who causes sickness and death), the *aswang* (spirits who wander at night, settling on the rafters over someone's bed), and the *tianac* (spirits who, though they live in the woods and chirp like birds, delight in obstructing birth and in murdering the newborn). Apotropaic acts or rituals to dispel or placate evil spirits include sealing the house and slashing about its perimeter with sticks to frighten them away. Charms and amulets *(anting-anting)* protect against witchcraft.[14]

Buddhist cultures offer some of the most striking examples of a Little Tradition's interest in spirits, something that coexists with the Great Tradition in a complicated but often close everyday arrangement. Burma has its celebrated 37 *nats* (initially regarded as impersonal animistic spirits, but later identified with notable persons or culture heroes), Sri Lanka its *pretas* or *yakhas,* and Thailand its *phii,* all representative of a whole cosmogonic level of spirit-world activity understood as involved in the course of events. For example, in a brilliant work, S. J. Tambiah shows how in Thailand the *phii* are associated with the consciousness *(winjan)* of a deceased person. He notes that the *phii* as a general category are highly differentiated, and their attributes extend from benevolent and disciplinary guardianship to extreme capricious malevolence.[15] Consistent with Buddhist doctrine, ultimately the *phii* are said to be reborn in another life, but in the interim they must be avoided or propitiated, depending on circumstances. To help in this task, devotees, through rites of exorcism conducted by the village diviner, can turn to benevolent angels *(thewada),* who help combat the mischief of the *phii.*

Likewise, in Sri Lanka several strata of pre-Buddhist beliefs from a Little Tradition can be easily identified. They include animistic worship of spirits, practice of astrology, and rites of pacification and protection. C. G. Seligmann argues that the aboriginal religion of Sri Lanka was based on ancestor worship, and that the spirits *(yakhas)* were thought to be "relatives as deities" (this still survives today among some Sinhalese, in the Bandara cult).[16] Disliking ancestor worship or its analogues, Buddhism has transformed this so that now the *yakhas* are more generally identified as goblins or demons. Canonical Buddhism has never recognized these spirits as real, but in popular Buddhism they continue to serve as agents of sickness or disaster. The same can be said for the "presiding deities" of the planets *(rukusu)* or the "evil eye" *(vas),* the object of important masked plays and curative ritual.[17] In this way, a person visited by misfortune could claim

---

[14] See A. S. Lardizabel, *Readings on Philippine Culture and Social Life* (Manila: Rex, 1970), 105.

[15] S. J. Tambiah, *Buddhism and the Spirit Cults in North-East Thailand* (London: Cambridge University Press, 1970), 59.

[16] C. G. Seligmann, *The Veddas* (London: Cambridge University Press, 1911), 203.

[17] See E. R. Sarachchandra, *The Folk Drama of Ceylon* (Colombo: Government Press, 1966).

that an external evil force was responsible, rather than one's karma or the nemesis of previous deeds. Oddly, even some Buddhist monks will participate in rituals of magical animism (such as chanting sacred passages to keep the spirits at bay) and engage in astrology and the casting of horoscopes. (Astrology is taken very seriously in Buddhist South and Southeast Asia. For example, parliamentary sessions in Sri Lanka are convened only at the astrologically propitious moment.)

Most remarkably, in contemporary Thailand, the following practices are not untypical. Protective formulas are sometimes placed within an effigy of the Buddha, endowing the image with magical, defensive potency. Amulets blessed by certain charismatic Thai Buddhist monks are thought to have similar powers. Some monks are active in such festivals as the annual propitiation of the traditional rain god in the renowned Bun Bang Fui or skyrocket festival.[18] Commenting on this, Michael Ames concludes that Buddhism serves not only the literati or the sophisticated; it also embraces the magical-animist practices and spirit cults of the village folk. In ordinary life Buddhism and magical animism are often fused. The Buddha's superiority over magic and the spirit cults is recognized, but because magical animism claims only to deal with the "misfortunes of daily life" and not with the Buddhist concern with "personal destiny" or salvation, the two can quite happily coexist.[19]

Chinese folk religion also affirms a range of animistic phenomena, much of which has become institutionalized by being attached to the Great Tradition, which includes Confucianism, Taoism and Buddhism. This is, for instance, exhibited in the concept of two souls for each deceased individual, and in rituals to keep these souls appeased and contented. Briefly put, a distinction is made between the *yin* or *kuei* (ghost) soul thought to follow the corpse to the grave, and the *yang* or *shen* (spiritual) soul assumed to reside both in heaven *(ti)* and in a spirit tablet. This is based on the age-old Chinese custom of the veneration of ancestors ("worship" of ancestors is too strong and misleading) and the doctrine of filial piety *(hsiao)*. At the heart of this belief is the domestic cult of ancestor veneration (which refers to the personal relationship an individual might have with immediate forebears) and the lineage cult (representing an individual's entire patrilineal ancestry, shared with others in a much larger kin group). Spirit tablets for the *yang* soul of adults are usually placed first on a domestic shrine hallowed by the presence of the household deity (the kitchen god Tsao shun). After

[18] See W. J. Klausner, "Popular Buddhism in Northeast Thailand," in F. S. C. Northrop and H. H. Livingston, eds., *Cross-Cultural Understanding* (New York: Harper and Row, 1964), who notes: "The world of spirits and magic is never far away . . . in some cases, certain charmed miniature Buddha images are kept as talismans to keep one from harm that might arise in the form of accidents, theft, bullet wounds, and the like."

[19] Michael Ames, "Magical-Animism and Buddhism: A Structural Analysis of the Sinhalese Religious System," *Journal of Asian Studies* 23 (1964), 41. Ames argues that because magical animism is "profane" and "non-meritorious," it is not part of the sacred and highly systematized Great and Little Traditions of Buddhism. "It caters to both types of Buddhists," and can therefore be seen as a "third kind of 'tradition.' "

several generations the tablet may be ritually disposed of or, for a wealthy clan, moved to an ancestral hall. On the other hand, the *yin* soul accompanies the body in burial, permanently in the earth as a mystified set of bones (although it is also thought to be able to hover above the grave). For this reason, much care is given to the correct siting *(feng-shui)* of the grave in relation to the direction of the wind, water runoff, magnetic forces and other meteorological phenomena. Carelessness in this could irritate or antagonize the spirit, with ill consequences for the living.[20]

Chinese folk religion also provides interesting examples of village and regional guardian spirits. This includes the earth god *t'u ti,* who is sometimes described as a multiple deity because of his appearance as a village or district guardian spirit. *T'u ti* is known more formally as *sheh shen* (community god), represented by such regional deities as, for example, Ma-tzu of Fukien province (also venerated in Taiwan by people of Fukienese origin). Community concerns can be brought to him, and his image is also commonly found in pious households under the domestic altar, as close to the earth as possible to protect the house and its inhabitants.[21] The *dinh* (spirit shrine) cult of traditional Vietnam has a similar aim. Charles Keyes points out that such a village guardian spirit could be a heavenly divinity who had become the village patron or a deified spirit of a deceased man venerated for his virtue or power. Traditionally the emperor "appointed" the spirit to the village, so the *dinh* was also a symbolic bond between village and emperor.[22]

The Little Tradition has so far been described largely in terms of animism and spirit cult. The power of myth also is important in explaining the spirit world. Myth functions as a source of basic, ultimate verities— how the universe came into being and where it is heading, how a particular society came to exist and why the human condition is so miserable.[23] Although admittedly an ill-defined category, myths are essentially ways of expressing the inexpressible shared by both the Little and the Great Traditions—perhaps the single most important source for establishing the worldview of any religion, aboriginal or canonical, in any culture. This was recognized by Bronislaw Malinowski in his classic study of society in the Trobriand Islands of Pacific Melanesia. He identified key concepts in the language of myth that guided and sustained this aboriginal culture, such as the mystic, impersonal power of *mana,* a potency that is the property of

[20] See Maurice Freedman, "Ritual Aspects of Chinese Kinship," in W. E. Lessa and E. Z. Vogt, eds., *Reader in Comparative Religion, An Anthropological Approach* (New York: Harper and Row, 1979), 400.

[21] L. G. Thompson, *Chinese Religion: An Introduction* (Belmont: Dickenson Press, 1969), p. 57. Local deities or spirits who failed to demonstrate sufficient protective power could be unceremoniously replaced by new deities. Although some of these notions undoubtedly survive in the People's Republic of China, more obvious examples are to be found in Taiwan and among the "overseas Chinese" communities in Southeast Asia and the Pacific Rim.

[22] Keyes, *The Golden Peninsula,* 190.

[23] See Paul Ricoeur, "Myth and History," in M. Eliade, ed., *The Encyclopedia of Religion,* vol. 10 (New York: Macmillan, 1987), 223.

all things, and *tabu,* which refers to objects and acts that are ritually forbidden, such as touching a newborn child or the tribal chief. Expanding on this, Malinowski writes:

> Myth fulfills in primitive culture an indispensable function: it expresses, enhances and codifies belief, it safeguards and enforces morality, it vouches for the efficiency of ritual and contains practical rules for the guidance of man. Myth is thus a vital ingredient of human civilization; it is not an idle tale, but a hard-worked active force.[24]

Some have argued that worldviews rooted in myth show an unsophisticated, "pre-logical" mentality, and that myths are, along with magic, simply clumsy attempts to explain reality—an early conceptual way of thinking.[25] Most interpreters now agree, however, that the central question answered by myth is not what is true, but "what societies, civilizations and communities have found necessary to point to and preserve as centrally valid to their existence."[26] In his investigation into aboriginal myths about the sacred, Claude Lévi-Strauss has convincingly shown that they represent *la pensée sauvage* or *indigène,* which has a logic of its own—a logic of seeing what is valid in terms of order in nature, even when it seems chaotic.[27] The sacred can thus be expressed as a pattern of order identified through a knowledge of the concrete (an appreciation of the sensory qualities of objects in nature) rather than through a knowledge based on ratiocination and theory. The structure of myths that exhibit this order also reveals an understanding of the divine and of society—but in a worldview obtained by intuition rather than empirical analysis and theoretical justification. By extension, all myths show similar attempts to express a specific kind of knowledge of what is important. Not surprisingly, they are often set down in the language of revelation, insight and transcendence.[28]

In the Little Tradition of Asia, such myths often lie at the center of religious consciousness, expressed in popular religious events and rituals. The aftermath or truths articulated by these myths and their ritualization, notes Clifford Geertz, "spread beyond their specifically metaphysical contexts to provide a framework of general ideas in terms of which a wide range of experience—intellectual, emotional, moral—can be given meaningful form."[29] In contemporary Islamic Java, for instance, old myths from

[24] Bronislaw Malinowski, *Magic, Science and Religion* (New York: Doubleday, 1954), 101.

[25] For example, Lucien Levy-Bruhl, *How Natives Think* (Salem: Ayer Press, 1979), and James Frazer, *The Golden Bough* (London: Macmillan, 1971). Frazer sees myth and animism in Buddhism as "a common savage dogma incorporated into the system of a historical religion" (147).

[26] K. W. Bolle, "Myth," in Eliade, ed., *Encyclopedia of Religion,* vol. 10, p. 262.

[27] Claude Lévi-Strauss, *The Savage Mind (La Pensée Sauvage)* (Chicago: University of Chicago Press, 1966); *Anthropologie Structurale* (Paris: Plon, 1958). These notions are examined as well in *Tristes Tòpiques* (New York: Atheneum, 1978), 76, and *Paroles Données* (Paris: Plon, 1984), 53.

[28] See Northrop Frye, *The Great Code* (Toronto: Academic Press, 1982), 31.

[29] Clifford Geertz, *The Interpretation of Culture* (New York: Harper Basic Books, 1973), 123.

the Hindu epics are still well-loved, adapted to a Javanese setting and portrayed through elaborate and well-attended village performances of shadow puppets *(wayang kulit)*. By contrast, in neighboring Bali, where Hinduism survives as the dominant religion (although long divorced from its Indian philosophical source), indigenous non-Hindu expressions are still common. A popular drama, for example, centers on the ritual combat between two strange mythological figures: Rangda, the "monstrous queen of witches, used-up whore, child-killer—unqualified evil," and Barong, a "benign, somewhat ludicrous deity, who looks and acts like a cross between a clumsy bear, a foolish puppy and a strutting Chinese dragon, a parodic representation of human strength and weakness."[30] Each has potent *mana*-like powers, sufficient always to guarantee a stalemate in their encounters. These confrontations provoke intense audience response, "with participants rushing to the defence of Barong and, when Rangda lopes off the stage undefeated, turning inwards among themselves in a rage of unfulfilled passion." Here, through ritualistic theater and dramatic audience engagement, is a form of myth as expressive as that found in the Little Tradition of Asia, overflowing into daily life with vigor and religious significance. In his analysis Geertz concludes that "the alarming sense of touch-and-go, with the diminishing band of the entranced desperately attempting to keep the situation minimally in hand, is altogether overwhelming, even for a mere observer. The razor-thin dimensions of the line dividing reason from unreason, eros from thanatos, or the divine from the domestic, could hardly be more dramatized."[31]

These several dimensions of the Little Tradition of Asia, ranging from animism, spirit cult, and even the ritualization of myth, are not found at the village level alone. Many of these features have been assimilated into the classical religions of the Great Tradition. They have been adapted and even transformed to fit a new theological setting. Thus where one tradition ends and another begins is not always apparent. But the Little Tradition is not simply the archaic survival of old superstitions somehow tolerated or "contained" by the religions associated with the sublime fathers of Asia's Great Tradition, such as Confucius and the Buddha. The two traditions more often than not complement each other to produce the rich, living religious mosaic that has come to be associated with Asia.

THE INDIAN RELIGIOUS TRADITION

South Asia or the Indian subcontinent has been the birthplace of two major religions—Hinduism and Buddhism—and of several smaller but significant religions—notably Jainism and Sikhism. They are all sufficiently related in history, culture and worldview to be properly called the Indian religious tradition, which indeed is the very foundation of Indian civilization. India's exuberant religions have in one way or another touched most of Asia. Hin-

---

[30] Clifford Geertz, " 'Internal Conversion' in Contemporary Bali," in Lessa and Vogt, eds., *Reader in Comparative Religion*, 449.
[31] Ibid., 449.

duism never had a lasting, physical presence beyond the subcontinent, although a thousand years ago many of its customs and its political theory were the basis of civilization in Southeast Asia or "Farther India," and some of its influence endures intact. Buddhism, however, became one of the great missionary religions of world history. It adapted itself over centuries to numerous cultures and social environments, from Sri Lanka to Japan. It carried diverse ingredients of its Indian heritage, especially a cosmology and a way of thinking reflected in the philosophical language from the Sanskrit legacy, like the notion of *shunyata,* or "emptiness," as a religious goal. Consequently, the Indian religious tradition, so varied and versatile, has an extraordinary relevance for Asia, both historically and in the present. Yet, remarkably, its center of gravity was, and continues to be, in India itself. As mother of this tradition, the Hindu religion must be understood first.

Hinduism

Hinduism is a collective term for several religions and ways of being religious. Like the word India, it is derived from the name of the Indus River. Hindu origins are twofold: the indigenous religious practices of the inhabitants of India, who enjoyed varying degrees of civilization and religious independence until about the third century B.C., and the religion of the Aryans who entered India about 1200 B.C. The Aryans (literally "noble" people) migrated from the Caucasus and central Asian plateau, bringing with them a well-developed oral tradition of myths and sky gods. They overran a sophisticated but slumbering society centered at Moenjo-Daro and Harappa on the Indus, and spread quickly down the Gangetic plain. A rough, nomadic people, the light-skinned Aryans were in some ways similar to the later Vikings of Europe. They imposed their language (sometimes identified as early Sanskrit) and worldview on the dark-skinned indigenous Indians, yet they also borrowed theological notions and deities that met their needs. This annexation may have included the central notion of *samsara,* or the cyclical nature of life, which some argue was native to the conquered Indus Valley civilization.

Aryan religion is best embodied by the Veda (divine "knowledge"), an oral tradition of great complexity that is still a major underpinning of the Hindu worldview. It consisted of hymns or verses (Rig) honoring the various deities *(devas)* thought to have cosmic significance. These included such reified natural forces as Surya (the sun), Rudra (the storm god), Varuna (lord of light and darkness), and Agni (fire). Other gods, like the bellicose Indra, were associated with battle and war. Charismatically endowed priests or shamans *(rishis)* sought visions of the power of these gods (sometimes induced by ingesting *soma,* a "divine" hallucinogenic plant extract and the focus of complex ritual). The Rig Veda ("Verses of Knowledge ") was a collection *(samhita)* of such visions. It contains the earliest expressions of Hinduism's understanding of the cosmos, of the divine and of human destiny. Even now the Rig Veda is an object of veneration, although there are few occasions when the great sacrifices ordained in the Rig are actually celebrated. The hymns and rituals were more than just agencies of praise, however. Through them, *rishis* aspired to gain access to divine strength and favor. More importantly, the very order of the cosmos was thought to depend on the power of the hymns and their accompanying rituals.

A complex order of priests evolved over several centuries, and with them three other Vedas (Yajur, Sama and Atharva), as well as a scholastic interpretation of ritual conduct (the Brahmanas). But by 700 B.C., the definition and range of ritual was extended to include mental (meditative or "yogic") as well as physical performance, established on the belief that ritual sounds and actions could be internalized, converted into thought. This marked a major turning point in the development of Hinduism and led to a philosophical interpretation of what the Veda meant. At least some priests (*brahmans*) adopted a new religious life-style as well, retreating into places of solitude as hermits (*sannyasins*). In such a context, the last two sections of the Hindu scriptural canon (*shruti*, "that which is heard") were set down: the Aranyakas ("treatises of the forest dwellers") and the Upanishads ("knowledge gained by sitting at the feet of a forest teacher").

By the end of the Vedic age (ca. 500 B.C.) representing so-called Brahmanic Hinduism, the Indian worldview was largely installed. Many of the key doctrines of modern Hinduism can be traced to this formative stage, but although the canon of scripture was closed, interpretation of its meaning continued vigorously. This gave rise to a fresh new genre of noncanonical but still respected religious literature (*smriti*—"that which is memorized"). It even included grammatical and legal treatises (*sutras* and *shastras*), such as the third century B.C. *Laws of Manu,* which codified caste laws only hinted at in the Veda. Likewise, myths and legends, some from the indigenous Little Tradition, were adapted to meet new interest in gods, especially Siva and Vishnu, who had no role (or a minor one) to play in the old Vedic pantheon. Stories (*puranas*) about these popular "new" deities had wide appeal. So did the Epics, the Mahabharata and the Ramayana, essentially lessons on appropriate human conduct set in semihistorical or mythological context.

These literary achievements, combined with important philosophical works (such as the *Brahma Sutra,* a first-century A.D. commentary on the Upanishads), coalesced to produce a Hinduism that allowed for several "ways of being religious," and a wide range of beliefs within the context of a common and inclusive worldview. Simply put, this worldview was, and continues to be, grounded on the idea that the universe is objectively real and orderly. Cosmologically, the universe is thought to move in great cycles (*kalpas,* one of which is 4,320,000 years), each divided into four periods (*yugas*) of diminishing length and decreasing virtue. It affirms that eventually the universe will collapse in upon itself and precipitate a new creation from the old as part of a process that has no beginning and no end. (Sometimes interpreters contrast this to a "linear" understanding of time associated with the worldview of the Judeo-Christian and Islamic religions, which envisions an "end" or *eschaton*.) All of life is involved in this flowing dynamism. This is *samsara*: the ordered regularity of natural change, of life and death and rebirth, established in a law (*rita*) of the universe that even the gods cannot alter. Individual lives, whether of the gods (they have fantastically long lives but are not immortal), of human beings, of animals, even of plants, are all subject to *samsara*'s relentless cycle.

There is a force, however (associated with the cosmic law of *rita*), that is both in *samsara* and exceeds it. This is Brahman,[32] the energy of the universe present in everything, which is at the same time beyond *samsara*, death and rebirth. Hinduism avers that every living thing has a pure Self *(atman)* that it identifies with Brahman. All finite entities, beings or forms participate in or share the same *atman*. Human beings alone are endowed with the potential of realizing this "divine within," however. Hinduism fashions a whole "way of being religious" through the search for this saving knowledge *(jnana)* of Brahman. This is best seen in the Upanishads, whose central teaching is to perceive unity in what appears to be a fragmented, multiform universe. In a celebrated passage from the Chandogya Upanishad (6.11), a father teaches his son, Svetaketu, that a pot of honey is a collection of juices from many plants that bees have reduced to one essence, that rivers become one in the ocean, that a piece of salt dissolved in a trough of water affects the taste from whatever end one drinks. In a final instruction the boy is directed to dissect a figure to its minutest parts until nothing can be seen with the eye. The father observes that although the "final essence" *(animan)* cannot be perceived, a huge tree derives from this same essence. "This finest essence the whole universe has as its Self *(atman)*. That *(tat)* is the Real, that is the Self, and that you are *(tat tvam asi)*, Svetaketu." This important refrain associates a pure inner Self, *atman* (as apart from the ordinary self or ego, *jiva*), with the "source" of the universe. It reiterates the doctrine that there never was any difference between Self and Brahman in the first place. Awareness of this oneness with the divine constitutes salvation *(moksha* or *nirvana)*. The aspirant in the here and now can "know" that this is so, and so be saved. Freed from an everyday but distorted understanding of reality as a fragmented spectacle of objects and changes, this person is liberated from delusion *(maya)* and self-centeredness. Assuming that the person also lives an ethical life, such a person consumes the effects of previous unwholesome acts. This is "human perfecting" *(sadhana)* or "becoming of Being" *(atmansiddhi)*. For such an individual, *samsara* is overcome; there is to be no more rebirth.

Admittedly this ineffable notion of salvation exceeds the reach of most Hindus, who identify its attainment with the life of a recluse or *sadhu*. For the majority, salvation is understood in a lesser but more tangible sense as a better rebirth, which a person prepares for by living according to the rules of one's caste. This path constitutes a second "way of being religious," then, one that focuses on duty and responsibility (dharma), with appropriate action (karma). In classical Hindu doctrine, what is "reborn" is karma. Derived from the verb "to act" or "to do," karma means any action, no matter how modest, and its consequences. Karma also reflects the sum total

---

[32] "Brahman" is derived from the root *bhri,* "to burgeon or bear." Many words are closely related to it, including the Vedic god Brahma, the Brahman caste and the Brahmanas or ritual texts.

of a life's actions, good and bad, in relation to social duty (dharma). The notion of dharma ("to bear" or "to carry") can be associated with the Veda or eternal law *(sanatana dharma)*, or again with the divine cosmic law *(rita)* that maintains order in the universe. But chiefly the term's application takes the form of *varna dharma,* caste law, sacralized by brief mention in the Rig Veda (10.90), then carefully defined in later tradition.

The theoretical framework of the Hindu caste system is based on a hereditary and inescapable hierarchical structure of society. At the apex are the Brahmans, preservers and dispensers of the Veda, who today continue to provide ritual services to society. Second are the Kshatriya, at one time warrior-protectors of the Brahmans but now more likely to be socially identified as landowning farmers. The third level are the Vaishya, traditionally providers to the above two castes, who now are often shopkeepers and merchants. Finally come the Sudra, servants or workers, who perform manual tasks, such as tailors or carpenters, that are not regarded as seriously polluted. Outside of the *varna* system are the "scheduled castes" *(achuta* or "outcastes," whom Mohandas Gandhi called Harijan, or "children of god"). Customarily they are burdened by impure tasks such as working with leather, cleaning toilets, or being undertakers.[33] Presently, although the classical castes still exist in theory, the real constituent organizations of Hindu society are the many subsets of each caste known as *jatis* ("births"), which reflect hundreds of specific occupations. The economic dimension of caste revealed in this division of labor is the *jajmani* system, characterized by Louis Dumont as "the village network of specialization and interdependence between different castes."[34] Much has been done in modern secular India to give the Harijans and lower *jatis* access to education and professional mobility. But Hinduism continues to support a restrictive social order governed by customs associated with norms of pollution, occupation and marriage. Oppressive and unenlightened as this may seem to outsiders, it is consistent with the Indian worldview, which acknowledges acceptance of life's conditions and responsibilities, no matter how lowly, as part of a greater social order and even of the cosmic order. One of the worst transgressions is to try to take up another's dharma.

The third Hindu "way of being religious" is loving devotion *(bhakti)* to one or more of the gods or to their female consorts *(shakti)*. Hinduism is essentially a polytheistic religion, which affirms the existence of many deities. At the same time it is also henotheistic, meaning that the devotee can focus attention on a single god, believed to be omnipotent. Modern Hindu theism is largely focused on two gods—Siva and Vishnu. In turn this focus gives rise to the main branches of devotional Hinduism, Saivism and Vaisnavism. Each god is the subject of a complex mythology and tradition and reveals himself in several ways. Thus, Siva represents the ascetic, meditat-

---

[33] The scheduled castes comprise 100 million of India's 665 million people (1981 census). See *India 1986 Reference Annual* (New Delhi: Government of India Ministry of Information, 1987), p. 15 (Table 1.7) and p. 192.

[34] Louis Dumont, *Homo Hierarchicus* (Chicago: University of Chicago Press, 1980), 36.

ing god who triumphs over life's disorder by self-discipline *(tapas)*. But he is also a potent symbol of fertility. He is, furthermore, the "lord of the dance" of life *(nataraja)*, who teaches people not to fear the truth about life and death, but to accept *samsara* and work fruitfully within its process. Siva's consort, Kali, represents the divine mother *(shakti)*, an important theme in Hinduism. *Shakti* energizes Siva, and Siva and Kali are sometimes portrayed in sexual embrace. In this regard, R. S. Ellwood notes:

> The Indian world-view is deeply biological, tending always in the end to see the cosmos as a great living organism: it is not brain but virile sexuality which sometimes plays the God-part in the map of this organic cosmos, for in India it is finally not ratiocination that leads us to God-realization or grasping the oneness of the organism, but flashes of intense joy so sharp, or prolonged calm so steady, that we forget time and self-consciousness.[35]

Once again, such matters are complicated; like Siva, *shakti* destroys as well as creates. Devotees of these unusual aspects of Siva and *shakti* argue that it would be foolish to think that the terrible aspects of nature are not just as much a part of divine activity as those that are pleasant.

Vishnu, on the other hand, is celebrated for his several incarnations *(avataras)*. Tradition says that he descends to earth at times when dharma or caste law is carelessly conducted or ignored, something dangerous for both cosmic and social harmony. Two of his incarnations, Rama and Krishna, are particularly popular and enjoyed. Rama is venerated because of his absolute devotion to his kingly dharma. This includes having to banish his innocent and faithful wife, Sita, whose chastity was the object of rumor after her abduction by Ravana, an evil king. Krishna is a more complicated deity. Adored by some as a childish but divine prankster (Gopala or Govinda), and by others as a paramour of yearning souls (portrayed by the *gopis* or cow-girls, especially Radha, in the idyllic forests of Vrindaban), he is perhaps best known for his role as revealer of dharma in the Bhagavad Gita. Here he persuades a quailing prince (Arjuna) on the battlefield to fulfill his caste responsibility as a warrior, but is obliged to do so by making himself manifest as the absolute divine power in the cosmos. The Hindu interpretation of this episode impels Hinduism closer to a monotheistic belief in one, ultimate god. For the *bhakti* devotee of Krishna, Brahman is irrelevant. The spiritual objective is to offer up one's soul (now thought by some to be individual and personal) to the loving embrace of Krishna.

The Hindu worldview and ways of being religious are subtly and richly interwoven with Indian culture and society, making it resistant to possible needed social change but also to revolution and disorder. Essentially a "motherly" religion, Hinduism above all teaches acceptance and patience, respect for all living things and acknowledgment of responsibility in act and deed. It is arguably the most fecund of Asia's religions. But at the same time, in its institutional dimension, Hinduism continues to remain largely confined to people of Indian cultural background and is rarely directly practiced by those of other ethnic origin.

[35] R. S. Ellwood, *Many Peoples, Many Faiths* (Englewood Cliffs: Prentice-Hall, 1982), 66.

Buddhism

Buddhism was established by Gautama Sakyamuni (ca. 500–483 B.C.), a north Indian prince of Hindu background.[36] For over a millennium the Buddhist faith was strong and popular in the land of its birth, at times receiving important political or court endorsement, especially under Ashoka (. 273–253 B.C.), who also sent the religion to Sri Lanka, initiating its great missionary outreach. Eventually Buddhism was all but eclipsed in India, partly by resurgent Hinduism and later by an imposed and aggressive Islam. Today it is found in three major forms or "vehicles" (yana), the Hinayana, Mahayana and Vajrayana. Each is divided into numerous subsects. Hinayana ("Lesser Vehicle," now usually referred to as Theravada, or "tradition of the elders") is the dominant religion of Sri Lanka and all the countries of mainland Southeast Asia except Vietnam. Mahayana is associated with central, northern and east Asia, particularly China, Korea and Japan, but also with Vietnam. Vajrayana is the Buddhism of Tibet, but it is likewise found in China and elsewhere. (Of the forms of Buddhism, Vajrayana has made the greatest inroads among Western seekers.)

Buddhism is a world religion in a way that Hinduism is not, if only because it has slipped beyond one dominant culture and found a way to accommodate itself into many different human environments. This outreach brings great diversity of interpretation, belief and custom. For example, the Mahayana introduces several other buddhas (all mythological), and the Vajrayana borrows heavily from Hindu iconography and theism, features eschewed by Theravada. Yet despite this diversity, Buddhists everywhere hold allegiance to the prince Gautama as the one historical Buddha, the enlightened one who established a new, saving dharma, or "law." The life story of Gautama is integral to these salient teachings.

Gautama was born at Lumbini in the old kingdom of Kapilavastu, and pious legends surround his infancy and youth. Tradition says that seers told Gautama's father, Suddhodana, and mother, Mahamaya, that his birth was of momentous consequence for the universe. Astrological signs and physical marks on his body indicated that he would be a "turner of the wheel of law," but whether of a royal or spiritual "law" was undetermined. Fearful that he might choose to become a religious leader (which automatically meant a life of poverty and solitude), Gautama's parents shielded him from all signs of disorder, sadness and decay. A comely wife, Yasodhara, was found for him, and Gautama lived in privileged circumstances until about age 30. Curious about the world beyond the palace, Gautama eventually persuaded his charioteer to escort him on a covert tour of a nearby town. This event is called the Four Encounters; Gautama met human situations he had never seen before: a sick person, an old person, a corpse being carried to the charnel field, and a mendicant (sannyasin). In Buddhist art, these are vividly portrayed; the sick person, for example, will be covered with oozing sores, a face streaming with tears. The first three encounters

---

[36] In the Pali language, Gautama is transliterated as Gotama. A derivative of Sanskrit, Pali is the canonical language of early Buddhism. This chapter uses mostly the Sanskrit spelling for names and terms, with the occasional exception.

represent corporeal change and the inevitability of sickness, aging and death. The fourth figure, however, although dressed in orange rags (undertakers wash the dead with saffron, and *sannyasins* deliberately adopt this "polluted" color to show their disdain for the mortal world), had a radiant face, free from strain and worry. Greatly moved by this, Gautama resolved to leave home for homelessness to confront and resolve the dilemma of human suffering. Abandoning wife and wealth was not difficult, but Gautama was grieved by departure from his son, whom he henceforth named Rahula ("the fetter," that which bound the father to this world). Nevertheless, in an act celebrated in Buddhist tradition as the Great Going Forth (Pabbaja), Gautama quietly vanished from the court. Cutting his hair and taking on the simple garment of the renunciant, he crossed a river marking the boundary of his father's principality (river is as well a symbol of *samsara*) and entered the forest wilderness on the other side. Buddhist scripture carefully records how seven years of asceticism and study of the Veda with fellow renunciants brought Gautama no closer to the understanding of reality he yearned for. At last, rejecting seclusion and asceticism, he chose a "middle way" *(madhyamika)* between indulgence and self-denial. Then, at a secluded spot (near present-day Patna), he sat beneath a large fig tree, resolved to discover for himself the meaning of existence. This is the "enlightenment," described as a momentous meditative struggle with the emotional and cosmic forces of disorder and disharmony. Gautama emerged from this experience enlightened *(budh,* making him a buddha) as to the causes of human suffering. Spurned by the other fiercely ascetic forest mendicants, he went to the holy city of Varanasi where, at the deer park of Isipatana, he "set in motion the wheel of law." Gautama's new law (dharma) repudiated much of the old Hindu dharma's emphasis on ritual and caste.[37] He taught a way to salvation based on simple, straightforward ethics and on coming to grips with painfulness. This was often expressed in plain, orderly terms that could be easily remembered, such as the Five Grasping Aggregates, the Three Signs of Existence and the Four Noble Truths. What outwardly appears uncomplicated, however, had profound layers of explanation beneath the surface, and the Buddha's teachings are among the most elegantly argued of any religious vision in history.

Of several formulas that might be used to set down the Buddhist worldview, that of the Four Noble Truths is the most well-known. These are, first, that much of life is painful *(duhkha)*. This is not to suggest that happiness in life is impossible, but that for the most part human beings

---

[37] The Buddha was not alone in this protest. A. L. Basham points out that sixth century B.C. India was a "time of economic and political upheaval, the result of which was a state of theological anarchy." *History and Doctrines of the Ajivikas* (London: Nuzac, 1951), 100. An important contemporary of the Buddha, and a similar heterodox protestor against the cultic dimension of Hinduism, was the Tirthankara ("ford-crosser") Vardhamana Mahavira. He established the great religion of Jainism (from *jina,* a "conqueror"), based on the principle of nonviolence *(ahimsa).* Strict prohibitions against travel confined this faith to India, but although today few in numbers (about 4 million adherents), Jain "passivity" has made a lasting impact on the history of Asian religions.

experience pain as a result of failing to accept the impermanent nature of existence. Buddhist scripture indicates three major classifications of pain (bodily pain, pain caused by psychological trauma, and pain caused by the changeable nature of things). It concludes that human beings invite pain into their lives. The world by itself is neither painful nor painless; one's relationship with the world through consciousness and attitude constitutes it one way or the other.

The second truth (*samudaya*, "arising") carefully develops the cause of pain in a celebrated formula that stands at the heart of the Buddhist doctrine. It is known as "the series of dependencies" *(pratityasamutpada)*. This traces 12 psycho-physical factors that give rise to painfulness, such as ignorance, unconscious volition, use of the senses, craving and birth itself. Craving (*trishna*, or *tanha* in Pali) is often singled out as particularly deleterious, but Buddhism does not reject all volition or condemn all desire. Its goal is to redirect craving away from harmful, selfish aims to purer, more affirmative objectives. Buddhism recognizes, however, that deep unconscious "cankers" *(asava)* disturb even the spiritually advanced and are only finally rooted out at the highest stages of meditation and self-discipline. The account of causality also points to the key Buddhist doctrine of "non-self" *(anatman)*. The Buddha maintained a distinction between two sorts of truth (the conventional and ultimate) as a way to respond to the ambiguities of "non-self." At one level, fleeting and constantly changing, the self exists as "name and form," as ego *(asmimana)*. By its acts and deeds it creates karma, and the Buddha acknowledges that this accumulates as an energy that causally proceeds in *samsara* to rebirth. This is shared with Hindu doctrine, but the Buddha rejects the Hindu notion of an absolute Brahman and its individualized appearance in each person as *atman*. To hold this view is to cling to an idea of permanency, and since this is in turn further based on frail human hope and willed ignorance, it would ultimately result in delusion and painfulness. Despite the fact that it was in direct opposition to human desires, the Buddha also taught that, at an ultimate level, there is no self. Such an entity exists conventionally, and only momentarily. Nothing in the psycho-physical organism has real permanency. Even hair, nails and teeth, the Buddha noted, have an ever-changing structure.

The third truth (*nirodha*, cessation) states that there is release from painfulness. This is nirvana (from the verb "to extinguish"). It can never be fully defined. Nirvana represents the Buddhist ideal that salvation is a private journey of discovery. Indeed, the Buddha's last words were "work out your own salvation with diligence."[38] Nirvana is interpreted in several ways. For the Theravada, nirvana is best described in psychological terms, as a condition of perfect equilibrium in which one seeks nothing, is disappointed in nothing and can lose nothing one will regret. On the other hand, for the Mahayana, nirvana is conceived of as an ideal metaphysical state. The Mahayana is skeptical about the realism of the Theravada, especially about the value of empirical or scientific knowledge *(tarka)* in estab-

---

[38] *Digha Nikaya* 2.156 *(Dialogues of the Buddha)*, Pali Text Society, Vol. 2, p. 173.

lishing the nature of nirvana. Theravada interest in causality is judged by the Mahayana to be rooted in the phenomenal world and in rational conceptualization (prapanca). Somewhat like the Hindu Upanishads, the Mahayana proffers a notion of the absolute, the "real" that stands behind the world of apparent multiplicity. This is sometimes referred to in the language of paradox, the via negativa of "emptiness" (shunyata—referring to a condition or state empty in terms of conventional description) or "suchness" (Tathata). It is "suchness" if and when one takes it "such as it is" without adding anything to it or subtracting anything from it. The real is open only to that wisdom with which it is identical, to a perspectiveless and suppositionless nondual intuition (prajna) free from egoistic conceptualization. The real is also the "Buddha nature," the Buddha's enlightened knowledge, the absolute body of the law (dharmakaya), perfect being, an indescribable one without a second (anirvacaniya). Further, the real as nirvana is not ontologically separate from samsara. The only difference between the two is epistemic, as the admired Madhyamika philosopher Nagarjuna (ca. A.D. 150) maintained when he wrote: "Having regard to causes or conditions we call this world a phenomenal world. This same world, when causes and conditions are disregarded, is called Absolute." [39] In other words, samsara and nirvana are the same for the aware and enlightened one.

The fourth truth (marga, "path" or "way") sets out eight ethical and meditative factors that, successfully pursued, lead to the cessation of painfulness. The object is to "see things as they really are" (yathabhutam). The path is practical, consistent with the Buddha's teaching that one should attend only to those things that have a real bearing on one's destiny—in this case, to overcome suffering. Moreover, there is no suggestion that the Four Noble Truths are the only way to attain this goal. The truths are means, a "raft" to cross the turbulent river of samsara. But it is not a raft that lasts forever. For that matter, neither does the Buddha. Both will ultimately be let go of by the one who attains nirvana. For this reason, while Gautama was still alive, people worshipped him as the embodiment of what has come to be known as Buddhist values, but demanded nothing from him and expected nothing. The Theravada school still upholds this, though at the village level and in the Mahayana and Vajrayana, Gautama has been accorded transcendental significance.

By the end of the 14th century, the advance of Buddhism from India into mainland Southeast Asia saw Theravada widely and popularly embraced. It has remained the dominant faith there ever since, guided by an order of monks, the sangha; there are now no more nuns, only a female novitiate. The sangha lives essentially on charity, with strict rules of poverty and an austere life-style. Monkish self-discipline and purity are greatly venerated. In countries such as Burma and Thailand, most males will become monks, if only briefly, for a taste of the holy life. To feed a monk and to participate in religious acts gain merit, and are taken to contribute to a better rebirth. Interestingly, monks are only peripherally involved in

[39] See T. R. V. Murti, *The Central Philosophy of Buddhism* (London: Allen and Unwin, 1968), 233.

rites of passage (marriages, funerals, etc.). Their real impact is found in their daily presence in society as exemplars of the possibility of human perfection. From time to time the *sangha* demands a role in political affairs, arguing that it safeguards the true identity of a Buddhist nation. In this way Buddhism becomes a potent force in everyday life, work and politics, giving it a dimension many find controversial and at odds with what the Buddha taught.

On the other hand, Mahayana Buddhism, which entered China through the silk routes as early as the third century A.D., filled a spiritual vacuum occasioned by the chaotic fall of the Han Dynasty. It reached its golden age in the T'ang (618–907), by which time it had spread to Korea and Japan. Mahayana is distinguished by several hallmarks, notably an acknowledgment of Gautama Buddha's omniscience, the conception of the *bodhisattva* and an emphasis on compassion *(karuna)*. No longer was Gautama regarded as merely a great teacher. The fact that he knows everything implies that he *is* everything. Other buddhas shared in this role, such as Amitabha (Amida in Japan) and Vairocana. In addition, a second level of saving figures, the *bodhisattva* ("enlightened beings") was introduced, such as Avalokiteshvara (who becomes the goddess Kuan Yin in China) and Maitreya (Mi Le Fo, or Miroku in Japan, "the Buddha yet to come," sometimes portrayed as an obese jolly figure who dispenses good karma from a large bag). New scriptures were introduced, for example the famous first-century A.D. *Lotus Sutra,* which describes the multitudinous Buddha worlds and their angelic hosts. Similarly, new customs complemented meditation, notably the *nienfo* (*nembutsu* in Japan), a powerful practice of reciting the Buddha's name. The 12th-century patriarch Honen taught that the *nembutsu,* accompanied by sincere faith, would guarantee rebirth in the "pure land" (paradise), with ultimate enlightenment.

Of the many Mahayana schools in the Orient, perhaps the most well-known is Ch'an, a phonetic transfer from the Pali *jhana,* "levels of consciousness," or "Zen" in Japan. Zen searches for what is in experience before its classification. This search for the raw experience of "being" is achieved through demanding meditation. One school (Rinzai) uses "nonsensical" problems *(koans)* to provoke the meditator into altered or transcendental states of consciousness. Enlightenment *(satori*—"acquiring a new point of view in our dealings with life and the world by an intuitive way of looking at the nature of things")[40] is thought to be sudden. Soto Zen, on the other hand, argues that enlightenment is gradual and not the resolution of such tension. Zen's indifference to cosmological details, and its utmost simplicity (visibly encountered in art and architecture) are in some ways more reminiscent of Theravada than Mahayana. It shows how the original message of seeking one's own salvation is preserved intact, despite centuries of adaptation and interpretation.

Dramatic social, political and economic changes in recent times have spawned new Buddhist sects in Japan, such as the Soka Gakkai. These are often charismatic, evangelical and somewhat politicized movements associ-

[40] D. T. Suzuki, *Zen Buddhism* (New York: Anchor, 1956), 83.

ated with nationalism. Once again they show Buddhism's versatility, its readiness to meet new conditions imaginatively. Both in China and Japan, Buddhism has been periodically attacked as an alien import from India. Many of its notions, however (like the concept of the *bodhisattva*), have been so popular that they have been absorbed or adapted into the indigenous religions of east Asia. In China and Japan's relatively syncretistic religious environment, Buddhism has never lost its importance alongside of Confucian, Taoist and Shinto devotion. In this way it is still the first among equals in the religious world of the Orient.

RELIGIONS OF CHINA AND JAPAN

As one of the oldest civilizations in the world, China has a vast religious history. Fascination with the universe and its energy produced a detailed cosmology by 1500 B.C. With it came practices in divination, which assumed that the world is a unity and each fragment of it must contain clues to what is or what will happen in other parts. Fluctuations in human history were considered manifestations of the same changes that could be observed at lower organic levels, like reading animal entrails or the pattern of cracks on specially prepared tortoise shells ("oracle bones"). Many centuries later, Tsou Yen (ca. 300 B.C.) and other "naturalists" codified these archaic theories. Of special importance was the cycle of five irreducible "elements": water, fire, wood, earth and metal. Each was understood to conquer its predecessor in recurring cycles. So, for example, burned wood creates ash from which metal eventually arises. Furthermore, each element regulated a dynastic cycle in history.

To the adept at reading signs in nature, human as well as natural history were predictable. The "naturalists" were also known as the Yin-Yang school because of their interest in the celebrated dual forces. *Yin* was associated with the moon, the earth, the female, and cognitive intuition. *Yang* was associated with the sun, fire, the male, and ratiocination. This was a contrastive but complementary dualism, each sustaining the other. It was incorporated into the *I Ching (Book of Changes)* and given a special status in the Chinese worldview. These early centuries also gave rise to animism, shamanism, ancestor veneration, dynastic gods and other aspects reminiscent of the Little Tradition. Many elements of these ancient religious beliefs were incorporated into the later religions of the Great Tradition— Confucianism, Taoism and even Buddhism.

Confucianism
Religion in China has always been eclectic, reflected in temples where representations of icons identified with other religions can be found alongside the central deity. It has sometimes been said that Chinese thought is best known for its essentially practical and humanistic worldview, that ethics and social philosophy are more prominent than speculative thought. This is an exaggeration. Religion in Chinese civilization is frequently theistic, superstitious and otherworldly, even at the level of the Great Tradition. Nonetheless, the famous figure of Confucius, the Master Kung fu-tzu (ca.

550–480 B.C.) and his teachings (*ju chia*—"school of gentle scholars") are rightly associated with the prudential, the this-worldly. Later, thoroughly un-Confucian values and practices were applied to the original *ju chia;* for example, harsh legalism to make it a more useful political instrument, and the metaphysics of medieval neo-Confucianism needed to combat rival Buddhist theories. Notwithstanding, the essence of what Confucius proffered has survived in the ubiquitous respect for tradition, family and authority in Chinese society anywhere and in the so-called Confucian work ethic.

Like Gautama in India, Confucius lived in an age embroiled in political and economic turmoil. Such changes as metallurgical technology and economic monopolies challenged the simple agrarian life-style that had sustained village and feudal society for centuries. It was a time of the "warring states" and, coincidentally, of the so-called One Hundred Schools, each of which offered a solution to the disorder and chaos. Confucius was the most enduring and influential teacher of this period, even though his own life was not considered professionally successful. He never made exclusivist claims and preferred to describe himself as a "transmitter" of the teachings of the sages. But in many ways Confucius was a paradigmatic revolutionary thinker. As Geoffrey Parrinder remarks, "It was the genius of Confucius to have converted much of the language of primitive religion into a vocabulary for ethics and to have transformed that religion into a moral system, as society passed from a concern with good and bad luck to a concern with right and wrong."[41] Although Confucius is taken to be the author of a canon of five "scriptures" and nine "books," only a few chapters in the *Analects (Lun Yu)* are now considered authentically his. In them, the central teaching declares that the natural order of the universe and the moral order of society constitute the great good. Order and harmony should thus be the goal of the human community. Confucius respected the rulers of old who were ideal examples of those who had perfected virtue *(te)*. Sometimes thought of as magical force, virtue is defined only in the ethical sense. Virtue alone will produce the desired order. As a teacher Confucius challenged students (usually, but not always, from the privileged classes) to discover the potential for virtue within themselves. Closely associated with the doctrine of virtue were the concepts of *li* (propriety, correctness of behavior) and *jen* (unselfishness, deference to others, humaneness). Confucius greatly developed the notion of *li,* which had come to mean customary rules of conduct, into that of a virtuous state of mind. Just as fine lines in a block of jade are imperative to the quality of that mineral, so *li* should be practiced as if it were one's second nature, something inherent in the human constitution.

Herbert Fingarette notes that for Confucius *li* was the basis for seeing life as a "Holy Rite," a "ceremony of living." He declares: "The substance of a vast area of human existence is ceremony. Promises, commitments, excuses, pleas, compliments, pacts. No word alone, independent of a ceremonial context, can be a promise."[42] Thus even the simple handshake should be seen as a sacred act. This is best summed up in *Analects* 5.3:

---

[41] Geoffrey Parrinder, *World Religions* (New York: Facts on File, 1971), 319.

[42] Herbert Fingarette, *Confucius: The Secular as Sacred* (New York: Harper Torch Book, 1972), 15.

Tzu-Kung asked: "What would you say about me as a person?"
The Master said: "You are a utensil."
Tzu-Kung asked again: "What sort of utensil?"
The Master replied: "A sacrificial vase of jade."

Here the vase is made sacred only because of its function in religious ritual. Otherwise it is merely a pot. This analogy is applied to human conduct, for the individual likewise gains and gives dignity by approaching others ritualistically as important in this life. The opposite of this is to humiliate another person, perhaps the greatest transgression in the Confucian sense of the order of things. *Jen* (humaneness) was also a term of action, focusing on service to the larger social whole rather than to oneself. The fundamental unit of living is the family, where parents deserve the "filial piety" *(hsiao)* of their children. *Jen* is also expressed in the classic "Five Relationships": prince and subject, father and son, older brother and younger brother, husband and wife, friend and friend. Hierarchical as this system is, it is nonetheless established on the principle that, regardless of one's level of social membership, others are of equal dignity and worth. One who lives by respectful participation in society becomes "man as he should be" *(chun tzu)*. "Becoming as one should be" requires no precise sequence of action. It simply occurs after what is difficult has been accomplished. This is the key to *ju chia:* personal effort alone yields virtue, which is in effect salvation. There is no interest expressed in gods or the spirit world, no mysticism and no clergy. Like Buddhism, Confucian teachings express the sacred in an immanentist rather than transcendental fashion.

Confucianism became the official doctrine of Chinese society and polity in the first century A.D. A system of examination for the state bureaucracy evolved, based on interpretation of Confucian texts and principles; it lasted until 1911. Further, Confucianism became a "temple religion," scholars and civic officials taking the place of clergy. Confucianism continues to have a ritualized, ceremonial dimension outside the People's Republic of China, especially in Taiwan and among Chinese expatriate communities. But its principal consequence is still not that of a cultic religion. Everywhere Confucianism continues to mean respect for authority, correct behavior and a work ethic. Once dynastic China was marked by rigid social stratification, with officials and nobility on the one hand and the masses on the other. This balance of bureaucracy and people, developed on Confucian lines centuries ago, persists in contemporary China in many ways: the state provides the "legitimate ideology"—its "mandate" to rule—and patriotism is defined as support for that ideology. There is little room for loyal opposition or political tolerance. Lucien Pye points out that this reflection of the Confucian ethos at the "mandarin" level continues to lead to a sense of moral superiority and state *hubris,* and is not particularly pragmatic.[43] Yet, generally, if paradoxically, wherever Chinese culture prevails the work ethic associated with Confucian teaching hallows many sensible, attractive values. These include frugality, self-discipline and a sense of commitment to one's family, for whom one must work hard and sacrifice. This makes Con-

[43] Lucien Pye, "On Chinese Pragmatism in the 1980's," *China Quarterly* 106 (June 1986), 210.

fucianism a powerful continuing force, and, as one interpreter has put it, this spirit of Confucius "will be better understood in the future than the system attached to his name over the centuries, so alien to him in many ways."[44]

Taoism

A second religion associated with the Great Tradition in China is Taoism. Tao, or "way," is a word used by Confucianism and Buddhism, but it is more frequently identified with the teachings of Lao-tzu, a possible contemporary of Confucius. It is necessary to distinguish between the philosophical and mystical Taoism of Lao-tzu and the "religious" (hsien) and ritualistic Taoism of later popular cults. Lao-tzu is the putative author of the classical Book of the Way of Virtue (Tao Te Ching), a series of short but profound chapters on Tao as the simple, formless, desireless essence underlying the laws of change. Even before creation, Tao existed as pure potential, the one primordial energy, neither negative nor positive. Later it was referred to as a treasure, a single pearl in the midst of a boundless ocean. From it all things evolved, as the Tao Te Ching 42 notes: "The Way gives birth to one; one gives birth to two [the complementary forces of yin and yang]; two gives birth to three [heaven, earth and man]; three gives birth to the ten thousand things."

To regulate one's life in conformity with Tao means to be utterly plain and, like Tao, unaggressive. Such an outlook suggests that one should cultivate "weakness" in a special sense, to be as an infant (sublime and without guile) or as water (yielding), or as the passive force of yin ("the ravine of the world," metaphor for the vaginal passage). In short, "reversal" is the movement of Tao, associated with the soft and the weak. The opposite are the stiff and the hard, the aggressive partners that are the companions of death. To regulate one's life in conformity with change, rather than to resist it, brings its own wisdom and tranquillity, as the Tao Te Ching 46 suggests when it claims: "There is no greater disaster than not knowing contentment with what one has."

Taoism is celebrated for its doctrine of wu wei or "doing nothing" that is unnatural or unspontaneous. This is not to be confused with idleness. To live harmoniously, one has to let go or let things happen in the path of natural change. "To hold and fill to overflowing is not as good as to stop in time. Sharpen a sword-edge to its very sharpest and the edge will not last. . . . Withdraw as soon as your work is done. Such is Heaven's way" (Tao Te Ching 9). Such an attitude toward life may appear quietist and vulnerable to manipulation by others. But to the Taoist, beneath the surface of receptiveness there is an enormous energy against which nothing can prevail. Lao-tzu observes that nothing is softer and weaker than water, and yet nothing is better for attacking hard and strong things. "Through this," he claims, "I know the advantage of taking no action" (wu wei).

Perhaps for these reasons philosophical Taoism has become, as an indi-

[44] K. J. Joblin, "Will Confucianism Survive?" in Chai-Shin Yu, ed., Korean and Asian Religious Tradition (Toronto: University of Toronto Press, 1977), p. 118.

vidual and personal way of being religious, the perfect opposite to the Confucian model, which emphasizes the primacy of family, community and state. Likewise, it suggests a life-style that is freer in spirit than Confucianism and more life-affirming than Buddhism. Further, it tends to recommend the everyday pastoral existence of the farmer or villager; they have a better chance to remain like "uncarved blocks of wood" (p'u) than those in a more complex urban environment.

Classical Taoism is overshadowed in history and current practice by a complex ritualistic cult. This form of Taoism evolved centuries ago as the notion of wu wei was linked with ritual action as distinct from everyday action. A priestly order emerged to conduct these rituals. Its function was to keep things right if they had not yet gone wrong, and to set them right if they had. The celebrant of these rituals needed a special virtue (te) that had increasingly become identified with potency, or magical power. Consistent with classical Taoism, it was argued that such a person "accomplishes without having to act." This became associated with the emperor as well; he was thought to need more than just the Confucian notion of virtue to rule effectively and, above all, to achieve a long life. Contemporary Taoist ritual is a rich constellation of liturgy, music, vestments, incense and altars in startling contrast to the stately simplicity advocated by Lao-tzu. There is no modern interest in inherited medieval Taoist practices like alchemy. But Taoist priests are required to know the structure of the universe and its cycles, and have the potency to make ritual effective. These rituals can be loosely categorized as those for the living (ch'i-jang chai— "fasts for requests and exorcisms") and those for the dead (k'ai-tu chai— "fasts for opening and crossing over" into heaven). The goal of the former is to invoke health, wealth and longevity, and for the latter to appease souls that may be resentful, especially souls of those who have died prematurely. Taoism has also always been more adept than Confucianism at assimilating and transforming local cults of the Little Tradition. For this reason it remains quintessentially representative of China's multifaceted religious history.

Shinto

Just as Taoism in China represents deep-rooted indigenous beliefs, so Shinto reflects cultural beliefs in Japan. Shinto (literally "way of the gods") had no name until it was obliged to distinguish itself from imported Confucianism and Buddhism in the seventh century. It was simply there, as a world-affirming way of life. In many ways it remains today what it always has been—a religion without dogma or scripture, with no precise ethical system, based on a profound admiration for the creative power, beauty, and natural rhythms of nature. Edwin O. Reischauer remarks that no other element has run so persistently through the whole history of the Japanese people.[45]

Not unexpectedly, Shinto mythology (set down in the seventh century

[45] Edwin O. Reischauer, Introduction in S. D. P. Picken, Shinto: Japan's Spiritual Roots (Tokyo: Kodansha, 1980).

Kojiki and *Nihonshoki)* is the basis of this unique and exclusively Japanese worldview. A creation story focuses on two primal spirits, the brother and sister Izangi and Izanami. Tradition says they generated Amaterasu Omikami, the sun goddess and symbol of purity and order, and her brother, Susanoo Mikoto, representative of impurity and disorder. Shinto belief maintains a link between Amaterasu and her great-great-grandson Jimmu (660 B.C.), the first emperor, who, by tradition, established the Japanese state. Jimmu is the direct forebear of all the Japanese emperors, and indirectly of the Japanese people themselves. Just as Amaterasu was venerated as the power of the sun, so other things thought to be wonderful in nature and in society were accepted as worthy of worship. These are the *kami* (spirits), numbering in the millions. Some of them represent the clan *(uji)* from which one descends; others represent great heroes of old (such as Admiral Togo, who sank the Russian fleet in 1904 in the Tsushima Strait); still others are associated with natural objects and places. The *kami* of the last category can be identified with something as simple as a rock of exquisite character in the garden, or with a waterfall or mountain thought to have special power. More than 100,000 shrines *(jinja)*, built only with natural materials, mark these divine locations. These are not temples where teaching and preaching might be conducted, but simply sites that emanate a feeling of the numinous and give the visitor a sense of renewal. Priests *(shinshoku)* and their unmarried female assistants *(miko)* conduct rituals there.

Shrines are important places of pilgrimage that express Japanese culture and fuse the Japanese people in a unique and forceful way. Most *kami* do not have shrines, however, and may be indicated (if at all) by a solitary *torii* (initially a gate of two posts linked by a rope, now also a formal entrance to a shrine) or by the presence of simple wooden votive tablets *(ema)*. All Shinto rituals are aimed to evoke a *kami*'s protection or to appease his possible irritation. At the personal level these have come to include certain rites of passage (thanksgiving for the birth of a child, marriage; however, death is left to the Buddhists to memorialize). They also involve rites of purification *(ohari)* by which impurities are removed, sometimes through the agency of a priest but often in a solitary fashion. A devotee might ritually bathe in seawater (thought to be particularly efficacious) or under the revitalizing freshness of a waterfall. Another might climb a sacred hill or embrace the tranquillity of a holy grove of trees. But, "just as the flow of life of the individual may be under the wing of the *kami,* so too may that of the community. This protection is acknowledged, invoked and appreciated in the *matsuri.*"[46]

Matsuri rituals signal important times of the year in the traditional Japanese calendar, and virtually all the colorful public festivals in contemporary Japan are of Shinto origin. Nonetheless, as in China, so in Japan personal religious loyalty commonly extends to more than one religion. Shinto focuses on this world and discovering a harmonious relationship with the natural environment. One may embrace this aim, but also acknowledge Buddhist teachings about life after death, as well as the appro-

[46] Ibid., 29.

priateness of the Confucian ethical system. At the center of Japanese cultural consciousness, however, Shinto retains its place as the quiet traditional heart of a complete Japanese worldview that seems incomparably well-equipped to meet the challenges of modernity and change.

ISLAM IN ASIA

Islam has spread to virtually every corner of Asia and constitutes the religion of the majority in the nations of Pakistan, Bangladesh, Brunei, Indonesia and Malaysia. Elsewhere, it may have a demographically small outreach (in India, 11 percent; China, 2 percent; Myanmar, 4 percent), but nonetheless is a visible and often important constituent of culture and society. Within this Islamic world, the many differences in religious practice, custom and interpretation render generalized transcultural observations unreliable. For instance, it has been pointed out that in Southeast Asia it is impossible to ascertain the minimal condition for being accepted as a Muslim.[47] The criteria of recognition stretch from simple willingness to participate in an Islamic festival to living by the full imperatives and design of Islamic life. Likewise, Islamic traditions and laws have for centuries fashioned various arrangements for coexistence with local models of jurisprudence and custom (adat).

So, in Indonesia, a rural or village level of religious practice (abangan) fuses Islam with elements of the Little Tradition—something that is not acceptable to the more orthodox perspective found among the middle class and in urban settings (santri). Given Islamic presence in Indonesia for 500 years, it is not surprising to find this disparity. As W. C. Smith notes, however, "to reduce what Islam is conceptually to what Islam has been or is in the process of becoming would be to fail to recognize its religious quality . . . for Islamic truth must necessarily transcend Islamic actuality."[48]

That "quality" is set forth in Islam's Great Tradition avowed by Muslims everywhere. "Islam" is a derivative of the Arabic root slm, from which several words come, like salima (to be safe), aslama (to submit) and muslimum (one who is safe or who submits, to God's will). It is the youngest of the world's principal religions, established by the Arab prophet Muhammad (ca. A.D. 570–632). Orphaned in childhood, he spent an uneventful youth in Mecca, a desert city modestly prominent as a center of trade and an ancient site of religious pilgrimage. It was a fragmented and culturally isolated tribal society. Links with the once agriculturally prosperous Arabia Felix to the south (Yemen) had collapsed with the decline of that kingdom in the fifth century. Tradition describes it as a period of "the great ignorance" (al-jahiliya). Although Judaism and variants of Christianity were vaguely known, Arabian religion was generally animist, polytheist, and

[47] R. F. Ellen, "Social Theory, Ethnography and the Understanding of Practical Islam in South-east Asia," in M. B. Hooker, ed., Islam in South-east Asia (Leiden: E. J. Brill, 1983), 83.
[48] Smith, Toward a World Theology, p. 30.

without doctrinal coherence. Muhammad's tribe, the Quraysh, controlled the most important shrine in Mecca, the Kaaba, which marked a black meteor (its presence in the desert had been considered sacred for centuries).

In his 39th year Muhammad initiated his momentous reform of these religious practices. By that time he had married a rich widow, Khadijah, and appeared content to manage her affairs. Tradition records, however, that Muhammad sought solitude, and at an unexpected moment he heard god (Allah) speak to him through an intermediary (the angel Gabriel) with the celebrated words: "Recite *(Iqra!):* in the name of Your Lord, the Creator, who created man from a clot of blood. Recite: Your Lord is the most bounteous one, who by the pen has taught the masses things they did not know" (Koran 96.1).

For the next 20 years these spoken but invisible prophetic encounters continued and were set down as the Koran, or recital. As revelation, the Koran is taken to be the will of God made into speech, the eternal, unchanging Word of the divine, unbegotten by and unmodified by Muhammad. Its sacred content was vouchsafed to Muhammad alone, and through him transmitted to humanity. It is argued that to Muslims, the Koran is not like the Hebrew or Christian Bible, a mere collection of holy writ. Its recitation and memorization are an "interiorizing" of the divine, a partaking of a holy "communion."[49] Read in translation, the Koran bears only a nominal relationship to what it represents when heard in Arabic. Certainly the Koran is not systematic theology. It can be contradictory in points of doctrine, and conveys nothing of Muhammad's biography. For his life story and the pious legends that came to be associated with him, Islam provides the *hadith.* Though of lesser significance than the Koran, these stories are an exemplary pattern of conduct for the community of believers, based on the life of the prophet.

Muhammad's reforming message of monotheism forced him to flee from the Quraysh and Mecca to Yathrib in 622. This celebrated event, the Hijrah, marks the actual commencement of Islam as a unique religion. Its plan of salvation and worldview gained rapid appeal and became the means of widespread unification. By 630, Muhammad had gained control of Mecca, purged the Kaaba of its 300 idols and set in motion a religious force that would spread to the limits of the then-known world within a century. Despite this success, Muhammad never wavered from his plain, almost ascetic life style. He returned to Yathrib (now Medina, "the city of the prophet") and died in simple but peaceful circumstances in 632. Leadership of his inspired faith passed first into the successful hands of the "four rightly-guided ones" *(al-rashidun),* followed by a cataclysmic split into the two great branches of the Sunni ("path of tradition") and the Shi'at Ali ("partisans of Ali") in 661.

The Sunni have always represented the overwhelming majority of Islam (85 percent). Their leaders (caliphs) went on to establish the great Umayyad Dynasty centered in Damascus (661–750), the Abbasid Dynasty of Bagh-

---

[49] See W. C. Smith, *Questions of Religious Truth* (New York: Scribners, 1967), chapter 2, "Is the Qur'an the Word of God?"

dad (750–1258), and later the Ottoman Dynasty in Asia Minor (1481– 1924). The Sunni theoretically acknowledged the primacy of community *(ummah)* and consensus *(ijma)* in matters of religious interpretation and authority. Important schools of jurisprudence also arose in conjunction with the flowering of Islamic law *(shariah)*, such as the liberal Hanafites and the more conservative Shafiites. The Sunni branch of Islam and these schools prevail over most of Asia today. Also of special significance were Arab and Indian "Sufi" Muslim mystics, who belonged to *tarikas,* or "brotherhoods," and who peacefully took Islam along the trade routes to Southeast Asia. There it slowly and gently established itself in the Malay peninsula and the Indonesian archipelago without directly opposing a decaying indigenous religious tradition. Most remarkably, this is just what did not happen in the Indian subcontinent, where Islam was introduced with force from the time of Tamerlane (r. 1363–1405), until the end of the reign of Aurangzeb (1658–1707), the last great Mughal emperor. This manner of appropriation must be acknowledged and appreciated to understand the version of Islam that has come to the East.

Common to Muslims everywhere is an Islamic way of life *(al-din)* based on "five pillars." The first is an attestation *(shahada)* of faith in monotheism, and in Muhammad as the prophet of God. The other pillars refer to religious and moral duties as "acts of worship" *(ibadat)*. Each requires right intention *(niyah)* to be efficacious. The second pillar is ritual prayer *(salat)* five times a day, preceded by purificatory ablutions. The call *(adhan)* to these prayers by the muezzin is common to the whole Muslim world, everywhere in the same passionate Arabic. When prayer takes place in the mosque *(masjid)*, especially on Fridays *(al-Jumah)*, it is led by an *imam* (a respected male in the community—there is no clergy). Prayer involves a precise sequence of genuflections *(rakah)*, and is always conducted facing Mecca. Women are segregated from men, but the custom of having a screen *(maqsurah)* divide them is now fading.

The third pillar, fasting *(saum)* from first to last light during the lunar month of Ramadan, commemorates Muhammad's disciplined life. It represents freedom from domination by human wants and celebrates spiritual life that exists beyond the everyday world.

The giving of alms *(zakat)* to the poor or to just causes that further the struggle *(jihad)* of Islam is the fourth pillar, considered both a vital social responsibility and a "loan" to Allah.

Finally, the fifth pillar is a pilgrimage *(hajj)* to Mecca, which, if possible, should be made by all Muslim men and women at least once in a lifetime. Of two weeks' duration in the tenth lunar month, it is a highly complex ritual composed of the lesser *(umra)* and the greater *(hajj)* pilgrimages. The former involves circumambulation of the Kaaba and a visit to the adjoining sacred well of Zamzan. These sites are hallowed by their association with the patriarch Abraham, the handmaid Hagar, and her son Ismail (Ishmael, from whom Arabs claim descent). The latter focuses on nearby Mt. Arafat, where Muhammad delivered his last sermon. Pilgrimage is fundamentally important to Islam as a means of transcending ethnic, linguistic, and class distinctions. It provides its own sacred words (such as

1791

"labakkya!" or "Lord, I am here!," the devotees' exultant cry as they approach the holy places) and symbols (such as the *kiswa,* the awesome and exquisite drapery that graces the monumental cube of the Kaaba, replaced each year at the end of the *hajj*). Above all, it is an outward, concrete expression of the unity of *dar al-Islam* (the house of Islam).

The resurgence of Islam in the late 20th century has deep consequences for Asia. As "revivalism," it is sometimes known as *dakwah* (literally, "to call"). Where Islam is the religion of the majority, this can be manifested by a marked tendency to politicize the faith. Theonomous politics can operate at several levels, such as decreeing Islam to be the state religion and introducing Koranic law (Pakistan), or supporting Islamic dress codes and building mosques with state money (Malaysia). Revivalism, however, can bring with it an edge of militancy and *hubris.* As Geertz notes, often the "scripturalism" involved is not "reformation" but "ideologization," representative of a movement towards a "schoolmaster's Islam."[50] This enables Islam to exercise absolute authority over the character of modernization, to direct new ways of thinking about nationalism and new approaches to social, economic and political development.

Some observers dispute the alleged impact Islam makes on modernization or the impact modernization makes on Islam. They rightly point out that modernization does not necessarily mean the sometimes-dreaded epithet, Westernization. In the case of Islam, however, Western or foreign influence appears to threaten in ways not necessarily associated with borrowed technology and models of economic progress. Thus Islamic revivalism is, at times, subtly fueled by other motivations, such as the perceived need to eradicate a still-lingering domination of a worldview associated with a one-time colonial power—now seen to retard a new sense of nationhood. In other instances, sheer envy of foreign wealth and dominance, whether from abroad or as represented in a minority community, stirs insecurity and backlash in the name of Islam.

Edward Shils and others have pointed out the obvious indispensability of religion and tradition to human society, and Islamic Asia cannot realistically be expected to foster entirely secular states and polities.[51] At the same time, more so than nations culturally enriched and supported by other religions, the Islamic states of Asia face the challenge of obtaining the right balance that will fuse the religious values of tradition with "the modern mainsprings of creative social action."[52] As Geertz concludes, "the predicament for Islam today is not so much what to believe as how to believe it."[53]

CHRISTIANITY IN ASIA

This survey would be incomplete and to a degree warped without reference to Christianity. Nestorian Christianity has been in Asia at least since the

[50] Geertz, *Islam Observed,* 70.
[51] Edward Shils, *Tradition* (Chicago: University of Chicago Press, 1981), 1–20.
[52] Soedjatmoko, "Memorandum," in R. N. Bellah, ed., *Religion and Progress in Modern Asia* (New York: Free Press, 1965), xv.
[53] Geertz, *Islam Observed,* 17, 59.

fourth century. So-called Thomas Christians in southwest India were loosely affiliated with the Patriarchate of Baghdad. Their influence spread through southern India and to Sri Lanka. In the north, Nestorians entered China by the seventh century, and rapidly established a self-sustaining indigenous church.

However, the real impact of Christianity came only with Western penetration into Asia during the age of exploration and conquest, beginning with Vasco da Gama in 1498. Christianity accompanied the Portuguese far into Southeast Asia, where it took root in places not yet touched by Islam (for example, Flores and Timor). In the same era, the Jesuit Francis Xavier (1506–52) launched his renowned mission to Asia, first in India (1542), then in China and Japan (1549). His efforts were multiplied by the brilliant work of Matteo Ricci (1552–1610), who spent 28 years in China. Ricci adopted traditional Chinese dress and maintained Chinese ceremonies and religious terms to explain and promote Christianity, but the hostility of rival religious orders to his far-seeing strategy eventually resulted in the proscription of Chinese rites and a long period of enmity to Christianity in China. By this time, as J. D. Spence notes, "global exploration, international trade and evangelization . . . flowed together in one mighty enterprise." [54] The form of Christianity preached and circulated became entirely Western, and any notion of an indigenous expression of the religion, such as Ricci proposed, vanished for four centuries.

Thus, when Spain colonized the Philippines in the mid-16th century as "an act of devotion" to make it "a showcase of faith," friars virtually became government officials. [55] A consequence of this zeal is that 93 percent of the population of the Philippines today is Roman Catholic. It is the only major Christian country in Asia. French and therefore Catholic influence was strong in Vietnam as well, but in China and Japan, Roman Catholicism entered into a parlous rhythm of periodic repression that would last until the mid-19th century. It was perceived as an alien and therefore potentially destabilizing cultural force.

Elsewhere, British and Dutch colonial initiatives gained hegemony over vast territories in South and Southeast Asia. Initially, Christian missionary outreach was not a priority for either power, but in the mid-19th century it suddenly expanded and became closely allied with colonial political objectives. For the British any early tolerance shown to the indigenous religions of India, Ceylon or Burma was challenged by ardent Christian societies, evangelicals and politicians. So, for example, Christian religious imperialists overturned Ceylon's 1815 Kandy Convention, which had guaranteed protection of Buddhism by the Crown. Actions of this sort aroused Buddhism and Hinduism to become agencies of political and nationalist ambition. Nonetheless, everywhere in colonial Asia a complex societal arrangement emerged linking Christianity to a new privileged native class. This was reinforced by Christianity's monopoly over quality education and

---

[54] Jonathan D. Spence, *The Memory Palace of Matteo Ricci* (New York: Penguin Books, 1985), 123.

[55] D. J. Steinberg, et al., *In Search of Southeast Asia* (Honolulu: University of Hawaii Press, Rev. ed. 1985), 45.

medical facilities. These features spread into China with the opening of the "treaty ports" and the interior in the late 19th century. On a reduced scale, and without the same religio-cultural assertiveness, Christian missionary work also rapidly expanded in late 19th-century Japan.

The indigenization of Christian leadership and theology in Asia is a mid-20th century phenomenon. For example, the Anglican church in South Asia became autonomous only in 1930, electing its own bishops and determining its mission strategy independent of the Church of England. Experiments in ecumenism or interdenominational union were first undertaken in Asia, for example the Church of South India in 1954. The churches of South Asia have also shown interest in developing a regional theology that uses the resources of the Indian worldview to "unwrap the mystery of Christ in Eastern terms."[56] Everywhere, however, Christianity has to contend with its old colonialist image and new political realities. Examples of Christian life in Buddhist, Muslim and communist Asia indicate the complexity of this issue.

In largely Buddhist Myanmar, Christianity has found itself essentially largely identified with minority tribal groups who are politically fractious. Active mission work is out of the question. In Islamic Malaysia, Christianity is confined almost entirely to the non-Malay minorities, and use of Bahasa Malaysia to describe sacred Christian notions (i.e., Allah for "God") is prohibited, leading to further sharpening of ethnic and communal differences. In neighboring Muslim Indonesia, Christianity is much freer to participate in community needs (such as the charitable work of the Full Gospel Businessmen's Association). But despite some denominational cooperation (the Persekuetuan Gereja Indonesia, or federation of Protestant and Roman Catholic congregations), the indigenization of the church in Indonesia has led to increasing fragmentation into dozens of subsects, whose consequences are highly problematic.

Finally, in communist China and Vietnam, different situations confront Christianity. In the People's Republic of China, Christianity has been encouraged to organize itself as the "Three-Self Patriotic Movement" (self-supporting, self-governing, self-propagating), and to be entirely free from external denominational links (viz. Rome). Less than 1 percent of China is Christian, but with somewhat more liberal conditions since 1975, many "crypto-Christians" have come forward and acknowledge both their patriotism and their faith.[57] In Vietnam, on the other hand, where 7 percent are Roman Catholic, the church has had to purge itself both of a distant colonial and recent anti-communist past. Houtart and Lemercinier have shown how the collective identity of Vietnamese Roman Catholics was seriously threatened by the Viet Minh's social and economic reforms of the 1950s.[58] Many fled south, where Christianity was identified with an anti-communist

[56] J. A. T. Robinson, *Truth Is Two-Eyed* (London: SCM, 1970), 132.
[57] D. B. Barrett, ed., *World Christian Encyclopedia* (New York: Oxford University Press, 1982), 231.
[58] François Houtart and Geneviève Lemercinier, *Hai Van: Life in a Vietnamese Commune* (London: Zed Books, 1986), 162.

polity. Despite the ultimate victory of the communists, Christianity was never directly scourged. A 1978 agreement between church and state now provides government control over religion in general. For instance, expensive cultic practices are prohibited, and the role of the priest has been depoliticized. Roman Catholicism is no longer an "exclusive source of concern for group identity." This marks a synthesis of religious and socialist values, something increasingly embraced by Catholics as they become aware of the possibility of survival under an ideologically estranged regime. But once again, this points up the remarkable adaptability of life and religion in Asia.

FURTHER READING

The Little Tradition:
Geertz, Clifford. *The Interpretation of Cultures: Selected Essays.* New York: Basic Books, 1973.
————. *The Religion of Java.* Glencoe, Illinois: Free Press, 1960.
Hinduism:
Kinsley, David R. *Hinduism.* Englewood Cliffs, New Jersey: Prentice-Hall, 1982.
Younger, Paul. *Introduction to Indian Religious Thought.* Philadelphia: Westminster Press, 1972.
Buddhism:
Dumoulin, Heinrich, ed. *Buddhism in the Modern World.* New York: Macmillan, 1976.
Swearer, Donald K. *Buddhism in Transition.* Philadelphia: Westminster Press, 1970.
Confucianism:
Fingarette, Herbert. *Confucius: The Secular as Sacred.* New York: Harper & Row, 1972.
Thompson, Laurence G., ed. *Chinese Religion: An Introduction.* 2nd ed. Encino, California: Dickenson, 1975.
Taoism:
Langerway, John. *Taoist Ritual in Chinese Society and History.* New York: Macmillan, 1987.
Shinto:
Picken, Stuart D. B. *Shinto.* Tokyo and New York: Kodansha International, 1980.
Varley, H. Paul. *Japanese Culture.* 3rd ed. Honolulu: University of Hawaii Press, 1984.
Islam:
Ruthven, Malise. *Islam in the World.* London and New York: Oxford University Press, 1984.
Esposito, John L., ed. *Islam in Asia.* London and New York: Oxford University Press, 1987.
Christianity:
Barrett, David B., ed. *World Christian Encyclopedia: A Comparative Study of Churches and Religions in the Modern World,* A.D. *1900–2000.* Nairobi and New York: Oxford University Press, 1982.

WOMEN IN ASIA TODAY

ELISABETH CROLL AND MARINA
THORBORG

INTRODUCTION

In the space of a short essay it is difficult to take adequate account of the variety in cultural values, the diversity of kinship patterns, the complexity of religions and other prescriptive codes, and the different socioeconomic and political forces that shape, differentiate and change societies in modern Asia and women's place within them. Additionally, and apart from the obvious difficulty of drawing general conclusions from the widely differing circumstances in which women find themselves in the nations of Asia—indeed, even among the various ethnic subgroups within nations—there are also the divisions among urban and rural women and the differences with respect to age, class, occupation and residence. This article can thus only survey briefly the roles and status of women in Asia today and identify the socioeconomic and political issues that affect the way in which Asian women perceive and experience their lives.

An Asian woman's chances in life and expectations are very much determined by and a reflection of cultural and religious prescriptions and a number of socioeconomic and political factors that define the value attached to her person, her socioeconomic and political roles, and the status ascribed to those roles. What immediately impresses most students of Asian life is the wide range in preferred, desirable and observable female behavior and attributes, ranging from women secluded or confined to the family courtyard by the custom of purdah to the highly visible women of the marketplace, and the educated, articulate professional women in the cities and active in the national political institutions. This diversity and range in women's expectations and experience reflects variations in the scale and scope of socioeconomic and political changes in women's role and status throughout Asia, involving location, religion, caste or class, and kinship patterns. What also impresses analysts is not only the variation in life-styles but also the plethora of prescriptions defining ideal female behavior and attributes, and gender relations.

New legal codes incorporating women's rights to work, property, political representation and equality are uneasily juxtaposed in Asian societies with older cultural and religious prescriptions also incorporated into traditional folk sayings that celebrate, to a greater or lesser degree, male superiority. Legislation exists in most Asian countries to provide for the equitable treatment of women, the establishment of educational facilities for girls, the acceptance of women's participation in political institutions, women's representation in the main professions and occupations, and the protection of women workers. Legislation in support of women's rights is common enough, but very often is either regarded as an achievement in and of itself or is taken to symbolize a new status for women regardless of the degree to which it is popularized and implemented. Frequently, also, women's rights are incorporated into new legal codes regardless of the socioeconomic conditions that directly impinge on legal provisions and directly impede their implementation. Moreover, directly countering any influence of the new legal codes are the various religious texts and codes, which commonly incorporate ideas of male superiority and dominance.

Hinduism—a general term denoting a collection of many diverse religions embracing a wide variety of sects, local cults and regional practices in India—attributes to women polluting qualities that not only threaten male ritual purity but also the general well-being of man, the superior being. In Islamic countries—Pakistan, Indonesia and Malaysia—the unchangeable decrees of Allah enshrined within the Koran posit the authority of man over woman, given that Allah had "made the one superior to the other." Similarly, the Confucian texts and codes of conduct that governed social relations in China, Japan and, to a lesser extent, Korea drew attention to the differences between men and women. According to Confucian texts, women were as secondary and compliant to men as earth was to heaven. In the Buddhist hierarchy in Sri Lanka and Burma (now Myanmar) women also had a low symbolic position, embodying as they did both irrational and undesirable attributes that mitigated against their participation in public occupations and institutions. It is also the case that within many Asian societies there were numerous animistic traditions coexistent with these religions that, according higher status to deviant women, permitted them a resource with which to challenge role and status prescriptions. The very deviance of these traditions, however, rendered them secondary to the dominant religions. Also, alongside the formal and official codes, and surviving them when they became outmoded, folklore and proverbs handed down orally from generation to generation continued to embody male superiority in sayings that characterized women as innately inferior and incapable of improvement.

However potent the great religions are in their continuing influence, they are only one of a number of factors, and are of varying importance in determining the scope of female roles and the real as opposed to ideal status of women. An Asian woman's life expectations and life experience are also very much determined by family structure and kinship system. Social scientists usually distinguish several different types of family structures or units that share a common residence, budget and cooking stove. These range in form from the smaller, simpler nuclear family, made up of parents and unmarried children, to the various forms of extended and complex families, made up of three or more generations and coresidential married children. In Asia these units are most commonly patrilocal, in that wives are recruited into their husbands' households—though in some parts of Malaysia and Indonesia brides continue to reside with their mothers. It is generally hypothesized that the smaller and simpler the household the less restricted are the roles of women and the higher their status. That is, the wife is less likely to be subjected to the authority of a woman of the older generation; her economic contribution is likely to be more necessary to the subsistence and welfare of the household; and the division of labor is likely to be more complementary, with the wife participating in the management and decision making of the household. On the other hand, the larger the family structure the more likely women's affairs are to be managed by the men of the family; divorce, if available at all, is more likely to be initiated by men; women rarely have property rights; and the guardianship of children rests with the father or male kinsmen. Smaller and simpler nuclear households are more commonly found in Southeast Asia—including Burma, Thailand, the Philippines, Malaysia and Indonesia—than in South or East Asia, in urban rather than in rural areas, and in lower-income rather than in higher-income households and families.

As important as family structure in determining the reciprocal status and respective roles of women and men is the larger kinship system incorporating the family unit. Most kinship reckoning in South and East Asia takes the patrilineal form, in that it emphasizes the male line, which may then be utilized as a framework for the formulation of larger corporate kin groupings. In patrilineal-descent groups, which have an overt and explicit interest in perpetuating the male line, daughters are less valued than sons; daughters leave the household upon marriage, property is kept intact for a son or sons, and women as daughters, brides, wives and widows are controlled and denied full property rights and the guardianship of their children in the interests of the kin group. In most of Southeast Asia, kinship is bilineal, which gives more equal weighting to female lines, to female inheritance, and to women's rights to property, children and divorce.

Although the rights and duties, and with them roles and status, of women and men are more equally balanced in Southeast Asia, other factors may also influence gender relations. For instance, the effect of Islam in Malaysia and Singapore and of the Spanish in the Philippines has been to introduce a greater degree of male bias. In Java and Laos, however, residence may be with or near the wife's parents and there is more of a female bias. In parts of Indonesia and Malaysia kinship is reckoned on the basis of matrilineal descent, but it can be argued that in these circumstances, although women may acquire a greater measure of independence, they are still subject to some control by male kinsmen, their status is not as high as their brothers and their roles are still relatively circumscribed. Matrilineal descent does not predominate in any of the Asian societies, and its incidence does not affect the general hypothesis that men and women are more likely to be equal in status and their respective roles less rigidly demarcated in the smaller and simpler rather than in the larger, elaborate family structures, and in societies that emphasize bilineal rather than unilineal reckoning of kin relations.

To a large extent, cultural and religious prescriptions as well as family and kinship systems set the structural and ideological framework for the range of women's socioeconomic and political activities. Among the most important factors affecting the economic value of daughters, wives and mothers are the type and range of economic activities to which they have access. Their opportunities to participate in different types of economic activity are not only affected by the cultural framework, but also to an increasing degree decided by the ranges of occupations available, which in turn are determined by levels and types of economic development. In contemporary Asia the majority of women are still to be found in some form of agriculture-based activities, whether they be directly involved in the fields or in processing foods within the seclusion of their homes, or are indirectly involved in home-based handicraft industries processing agricultural products. With economic development and expanding industrialization, women have also been increasingly drawn into manufacturing. The global trend toward the predominance of women in light industry also applies in Asia; and where countries choose to concentrate on the development of light industry, women consequently dominate the labor force. When this policy is carried to its extreme, as it is in established Asian export processing zones producing textiles, toys and electronics, then women make up over four-fifths of the labor force.

With increasing industrialization women have not only been incorporated into manufacturing, but they have also found new avenues for employment in the expanding service sectors, including tourism, and in the professions. These new employment opportunities are within both the formal and informal sectors, sometimes making visible services that were previously hidden and therefore accorded low value. Although visibility does not necessarily heighten the value accorded to these services it generally does so. Just as in the most advanced European economies, more and more women in Asia are to be found in the professions. Indeed, in modern Asian cities the concentration of large numbers of professional women is immediately impressive even to the most casual of observers; and it can be argued that it is the new range, types and values of economic activities available to Asian women that constitute the single most important determinant of female status.

It is, however, the interaction of cultural and religious prescriptions, family and kinship structures, and economic opportunities that, depending on the degree to which they either counterbalance or mutually reinforce each other, produces the striking variations in women's roles and status within Asia.

DEMOGRAPHIC TRENDS

An individual woman's life chances and expectancy are very much related to the value attached to girls and daughters; and indications of their value include sex ratio, infant mortality and life expectancy figures. Life expectancy, the sex ratio and the literacy rate are all counted as part of the physical quantity of life index.[1] On a global scale, 104 to 105 boys are born to every 100 girls; but female infants are less likely to survive birth accidents and are more likely to be the victims of infanticide, employed in many peasant societies as a means of reducing family size. The female infant survival rate is one of the hidden areas of history, one that is difficult to appraise and document. Indeed, the scale of female infanticide is almost impossible to ascertain because of the anomalies in birth registration: not all births, let alone deaths, of infants are registered. However, there is sufficient quantitative and qualitative evidence in South and East Asia, and most recently in China, to suggest that preference for sons is still a significant factor affecting sex ratios. Although son preference is commonly thought of as a remnant of traditional practices or a survival of a feudal past, there continue to be very plausible economic reasons for such a continued and marked preference. Daughters, for instance, do not continue the family line, do not have the same earning capacity as boys, are frequently lost to another household upon marriage, and are rarely in a position to provide the same support for elderly parents as their brothers. Nor is female infanticide necessarily confined to backward rural areas or poor countries, or to the period immediately after birth. In any society, the lower the status accorded to women in relation to men in the economic, legal, cultural and social spheres, the fewer women of each age-group survive in relation to men. Warfare may often deplete the number of males, but it can also hide otherwise even more disproportion between the sexes; according to Esther Boserup's authoritative study of women's roles, this can occur particularly in Muslim, Hindu and Confucian cultures.[2] The phenomenon can either be weakened or nullified through secularization, or worsened by revivalist religious movements in the cultures concerned.

The sex ratio most favorable to females exists in Southeast Asia (99 males to 100 females)—especially in Indonesia, with 97 men to 100 women; followed by Malaysia and Thailand, with 101 men each (see Table 1a). The sex ratio in Vietnam of 95 men to 100 women may be explained by more than two decades of war.[3] In East Asia, Japan's low ratio of 97 males to 100 females is counterbalanced by the high ratio in China. (In prerevolutionary China, female infanticide and the unique custom of foot binding took a heavy toll among infants and young girls, contributing to a sex ratio of more than 115 men to 100 women, with a higher proportion of women in the older age cohorts.) The sex ratio may have worsened as a result of strict official population policies—particularly on the local level in the countryside—in the 1970s, and as a result of the implementation of the one-child policy, which led to an upsurge in female infanticide in the 1980s. This phenomenon may have been widespread enough to influence the national 1982 census data of 106 men to 100 women, which was confirmed

[1] M. D. Morris, *Measuring the Cognition of the World's Poor: The Physical Quality of Life Index* (New York, 1979).

[2] Esther Boserup, *Women's Role in Economic Development* (London: Allen & Unwin, 1970).

[3] World Bank, *World Development Report 1988*.

again in 1985.[4] In 1972 Japan had a sex ratio of 103:100, although from 1906 to 1925 and again from 1932 until 1936 the sex ratio hovered between equality and 101:100. In 1947, when population enumerations were resumed after World War II—and because of the war—the sex ratio was down to 95:100.[5] In South Asia the sex ratio more uniformly favors males. It is interesting to note that in Sri Lanka, a predominantly Buddhist country, men have attained the highest survival rate in the region. Sri Lanka's sex ratio has become more balanced during the last century, with 114 men to 100 women in 1871, 111 men in 1953, 105 in 1971,[6] and 103 in 1985. (See references for Table 1a.)

Although infant mortality is not broken down by sex in Table 1a, small-scale and field studies suggest that the rates, already generally high in many societies because of unavailability of food, food taboos, and lack of health care and other resources, are particularly high for daughters. This is due to frequent active neglect expressed either directly or indirectly. East Asia uniformly, and particularly Japan, has managed to achieve the lowest infant mortality rate in Asia. That for Japan is on a par with the Scandinavian countries, where the lowest rates in the world can be found. Both Singapore and Hong Kong have rates below that of the U.S. rate of 10.6. Since 1949 China has managed to lower its infant mortality rate drastically, even if some account is taken of margins of error. Infant mortality data is among the hardest to come by, due to varying definitions and underdeveloped infrastructure, so that a newborn dead or eventually dying baby girl may never be registered. Even so, China's infant mortality rate of over 200 per 1,000 live births in the late 1940s has declined to 34 per 1,000, which is a lower rate than many countries in Southeast Asia. While levels of infant mortality fluctuate in Southeast Asia, they are uniformly lower than the figures for South Asia, with the obvious exception of Sri Lanka.

Overall, as Table 1b shows, the number of attended births is closely correlated to maternal as well as infant mortality. Maternal mortality is estimated to be an average of 346 per 10,000 live births for developing economies; 217 for exporters of manufactures; and 384 for highly indebted countries. For oil exporters it is 704 per 10,000 which demonstrates that even if resources are available they are not necessarily distributed to maintain a health infrastructure oriented toward serving women. Hence, maternal mortality may not only reflect a country's economic level of development, but also a cultural bias. South Asia, except Sri Lanka, displays the highest levels of maternal mortality together with Indonesia; conversely, the city-state of Singapore, followed by Japan, has the lowest rate of maternal mortality. One further factor affecting women's health and survival is the birth and contraception-usage rate.

[4] Marina Thorborg, "Befolkningspolitik i Kina fran Confucius vara Dagar" (Population Policy in China from Confucius Till Today), *Den Ny Verlden*, 20, no. 4 (1987): 35–58; People's Republic of China, State Statistical Bureau, *Statistical Yearbook of China 1986*.
[5] Japan Statistical Bureau, *Japan Statistical Yearbook 1987*, Table 2:1.
[6] Sri Lanka, Women's Bureau, *Women of Sri Lanka in Statistics* (Colombo: 1985).

Table 1a
SEX RATIO, LIFE EXPECTANCY AND INFANT
MORTALITY IN SELECTED COUNTRIES

Country	Sex ratio male:female 1985	Life expectancy at birth (years) 1986		Infant mortality (per 1,000) 1986
		male	female	
WORLD TOTAL*	101:100	—	—	—
SOUTH ASIA*	105:100	—	—	—
Bangladesh	105:100	51	50	121
India	106:100	57	56	86
Nepal	102:100	48	47	130
Pakistan	110:100	52	51	111
Sri Lanka	103:100	68	72	25
SOUTHEAST ASIA*	99:100	—	—	—
Indonesia	97:100	55	58	87
Malaysia	101:100	67	71	27
Philippines	102:100	62	65	46
Singapore	104:100	70	75	9
Thailand	101:100	62	66	41
Vietnam	95:100	63	68	47
EAST ASIA*	105:100	—	—	—
China	106:100	68	70	34
Japan	97:100	75	81	6
Republic of Korea	102:100	66	73	25

Note: Infant mortality rate is the number of infants who die before reaching one year of age, per 1,000 live births in a given year.
Sources: *U.N. Demographic Yearbook 1986 (1988). The rest from World Bank, World Development Report 1988, Annex, World Development Indicators, Table 33.

As Table 1c demonstrates, China's vigorous birth control policies have led to the highest usage of contraceptives in the region, on a par with Singapore and above that of far more industrialized countries such as the Republic of Korea and Japan. Thailand and Sri Lanka both demonstrate a higher usage of contraceptives than the remaining countries of Southeast Asia, while Malaysia shows the most rapid increase in contraceptive use between 1970 and 1985. Due to the lack of resources after decades of devastating war and because of the loss of lives, Vietnam, like South Asia as a whole, has a low use of contraceptives. Although in India during the

Table 1b
BIRTHS ATTENDED BY HEALTH STAFF, MATERNAL MORTALITY

Country	Births attended by health staff (percent) 1984	Maternal mortality per 10,000 live births 1980
SOUTH ASIA		
Bangladesh	—	600
India	33	500
Nepal	10	850
Pakistan	24	600
Sri Lanka	87	90
SOUTHEAST ASIA		
Indonesia	31	800
Malaysia	82	59
Philippines	—	80
Singapore	100	11
Thailand	33	270
Vietnam	100	110
EAST ASIA		
China	—	44
Japan	100	15
Republic of Korea	65	34

Source: World Bank, *World Development Report 1988,* Annex, World Development Indicators, Table 33.

last 15 years the number of women using contraceptives has tripled, still only one out of three women practices contraception.

The use of contraception in a country is dependent on levels of development, resources, policies, and attitudes toward family planning. Religion, as such, plays a less important role, in that past experience has shown that religious codes can be reinterpreted to accommodate a changed official line. When introducing contraception and birth control in a developing country, national goals have usually been of overriding importance, with little attention directed toward women's rights to self-determination or control over their own persons.

Together with infant and maternal mortality, life expectancy is another indicator and determinant of the value attached to the roles and status of women. As Table 1a shows, the life expectancy of women is particularly low in South Asian societies, with the exception of Sri Lanka. Within South Asia, Bhutan has a particularly low life expectancy for women: 45.1

Table 1c
PERCENTAGE OF MARRIED WOMEN
OF CHILDBEARING AGE
USING CONTRACEPTION

Country	Year 1970	1985
SOUTH ASIA		
Bangladesh	—	25
India	12	35
Nepal	—	15
Pakistan	6	11
Sri Lanka	—	62
SOUTHEAST ASIA		
Indonesia	—	40
Malaysia	7	51
Philippines	16	44
Singapore	45	74
Thailand	15	65
Vietnam	—	20
EAST ASIA		
China	—	74
Japan	53	64
Republic of Korea	32	70

Source: World Bank, *World Development Report 1988,* Table 28.

years.[7] Sri Lanka has a life expectancy of 72 years for women, on a par with that of the Republic of Korea and above that of Southeast Asia, except for Singapore. Women survive men by seven years in the Republic of Korea and by six years in Japan. Japan has the highest life expectancy for women in Asia, while the figures for China lie somewhere between those for South and Southeast Asia. In Southeast Asia women survive men by three to five years.

It has been argued that demographic indicators are directly linked both to levels of economic development and to cultural values that determine a woman's life course. Demographically, the women of South Asia, with the exception of Sri Lanka, are disadvantaged. Sri Lanka is an exception in South Asia; there the women live considerably longer (they also survive to a greater extent in relation to men), and experience a markedly lower rate of infant mortality and a decidedly lower birth rate. All the countries of South Asia are classified as low-income economies, hence it is less likely that economic factors explain Sri Lanka's more favorable demographic trends.

[7] *U.N. Demographic Yearbook 1984,* p. 158ff.

Sri Lanka contrasts with the rest of South Asia in that it is a predominantly Buddhist country, whereas in Pakistan, India and Bangladesh, Hindu and Islamic cultures predominate; and as one authoritative study has suggested, it is these latter cultures placing lower value on women that is one of the factors explaining the striking demographic differences. Countries within Southeast Asia uniformly show the most favorable demographic trends for women; the differences between individual countries can be correlated with economic, development and cultural factors and with state policies. East Asia is more mixed, with Japan showing demographic trends most favorable to women, and China—with the exception of infant mortality—showing similarities to South Asia or lying somewhere between that region and Southeast Asia. The demographic differences can also be accounted for by contrasting levels of economic development and state policies. These Asian-wide patterns are also duplicated in the 'data on access of women to education.

EDUCATION

It has been argued that above all it is perhaps in access to education that Asian women have suffered most discrimination. Although early Hindu, Islamic and Confucian texts all record renowned women scholars, analyses of Confucian, Muslim and Hindu cultures show them to be less favorably inclined toward women's education than other cultures. Nevertheless, in all Asian societies there has been a significant improvement in both the rates for female literacy and in female school enrollments in the past 20 years. Perhaps of some influence here has been the Karachi Plan, which, drawn up for developing countries of Asia and the Pacific in 1960, had as its goal the establishment, within a period of not more than 20 years (1969–89), of a system of universal, compulsory and free primary school education of seven years or more. While by 1988 no country had entirely achieved this goal, almost universal schooling at the primary and secondary levels, was at hand in East Asia, Southeast Asia and Sri Lanka. The Philippines, Sri Lanka and Thailand have the highest percentage of women in higher education, while Bangladesh has the lowest. Women make up about approximately 25 percent of the students in higher education in India, Pakistan, Indonesia, China, Japan and the Republic of Korea (see Table 2). The majority of those in Asia who do not attend school are girls; in some cases they make up 75 percent of all those not attending school. This is particularly the case in rural China and South Asia, with Sri Lanka being the exception.

Table 2 clearly illustrates differences in both literacy and female school enrollment between South, East and Southeast Asia. In East and Southeast Asia girls constitute upward of 44 percent of primary school enrollments; and with the exception of China and Indonesia upward of 60 percent of women are literate. Overall, Southeast Asia has the highest rates of female literacy and school enrollments. Within Southeast Asia, the Philippines and Thailand display the smallest differences in literacy rates between the sexes and have the highest proportion of women in higher education. In

Table 2
EDUCATION

| Country | Literacy rate* | | Female school enrollments** | | |
	Male	Female	Primary	Secondary	Tertiary
SOUTH ASIA	1981		1985		1981
Bangladesh	39.7	18.0	33.5	19.0	13.6
India	54.8	25.7	33.5	26.0	27.3
Nepal	29.6	10.3	20.5	15.0	—
Pakistan	36.0	15.2	23.5	17.0	25.6
Sri Lanka	91.3	82.0	48.3	51.9	43.6
SOUTHEAST ASIA	1980		1985		1980
Indonesia	77.5	57.7	46.0	36.5	25.0
Malaysia	79.6	59.7	47.0	49.0	36.3
Philippines	83.9	82.8	48.0	50.0	55.6
Singapore	91.6	74.0	44.5	51.0	38.0
Thailand	92.3	84.0	48.0[b]	47.0[b]	42.6
Vietnam	90.5[a]	78.3[a]	45.5	45.0	35.0
EAST ASIA	1980		1985		1980
China	79.2	51.1[c]	44.8	40.2	30.0
Japan	99.0	96.7	47.5	49.5	25.0
Republic of Korea	94.4[d]	81.0[d]	47.0	44.0	25.0[d]

*Of all persons 15 years and above.
**Percentage of total enrollment.
[a] 1979.
[b] 1980.
[c] 1982.
[d] 1970.

Sources: Unless otherwise indicated, the literacy rate data is calculated from *UNESCO Statistical Yearbook 1987*. Data for Japan, see Marina Thorborg, *Identification of Priority Research Issues on Women in Asia* (Stockholm, 1986). 1985 enrollment data calculated from World Bank, *World Development Report 1988*. For 1981 enrollment data, see Thorborg, op. cit. For Sri Lanka enrollments, see Sri Lanka, Ministry of Education and University Grants Commission, *School Census,* 1985. For Chinese enrollments, see People's Republic of China, State Statistical Bureau, *Statistical Yearbook of China 1986,* p. 640.

Singapore and Malaysia, too, although there is a wider gap in the literacy rates between the sexes, women also show a high involvement in tertiary education. East Asia shows the same mixed picture as for other indicators of female status. Japan has achieved the highest literacy rates in Asia for both men and women, although only one-quarter of those in tertiary education are women. China shows a slightly higher proportion in tertiary education, but there is a greater discrepancy in the literacy rates for men and women, and 70 percent of adult illiterates are known to be women.[8] The only country in South Asia to have high literacy rates and to have achieved more equitable proportions of male and female school enrollments is Sri Lanka. For the remaining countries of South Asia, 25 percent of women or less are estimated to be literate and one-third or less of the primary school enrollments are women. However, in India and Pakistan slightly over 25 percent of the tertiary educational enrollments are women, a percentage not too different from those of China, Korea, Japan and Indonesia. While women's literacy rates and levels of educational attainment contribute to and reflect levels of economic development, they also have an important effect on their own and their children's life expectations and employment.

WOMEN IN PRODUCTION

Measuring women's participation in production according to standard definitions has often been likened to evaluating the tip of the iceberg without taking adequate account of what is under water. Women have commonly worked from dawn to dusk, but depending on environment, class and biases their contributions to the overall economy have been differently accounted for. In Asian societies, as elsewhere, one important source of bias lies in the definition of "housework" to include activities such as processing food for sale in the market, raising domestic livestock and engaging in small handicraft operations. Thus, women undertaking these activities are commonly classified as housewives. In regions where women's work, and especially manual labor outside the confines of the family household, is demeaning to family status, few wish to define themselves or be defined as "workers." International classifications and categories based largely on Western industrialized experience take little account of extended family forms and family labor, migration patterns combining urban and rural residence, or base of occupation. Moreover, in most Asian economies, women work primarily in the informal sector, but so far there has been little systematic inquiry into the extent of their participation and contribution. Contrary to official statistics, there are women who work in brick kilns, and in construction and mining; others work at home on a piecework basis; and still others are street hawkers, subsidiary workers in family businesses and domestic servants. Thus, it is necessary to change definitions so as to include women in official statistics—not least in order to provide them with legislative protection.

A number of factors therefore lead to the underestimation of female laborers, and to problems in the development of indicators and classifications appropriate to the economic and social structures of Asian societies and for Asian-wide comparisons. One measure that is appropriate is the economic

[8] Marina Thorborg, *Identification of Priority Research Issues on Women in Asia: A Report on Research and Research Organisations with Bibliography,* part 1: Country Reports; part 2: Bibliography. 2d ed. (Stockholm: Sarec Dokumentation, 1986).

activity rate, which simultaneously indicates the occupational types and the scope of work definitions used, the degree of development a country has experienced, and the degree of men's and women's measurable economic activity. The activity rate of women measures their involvement in production, be it modern or customary in form, outside the confines of the household. The economic activity rate of women is measured by comparing those who are economically active with all women in a total population. In general, about half of any population is estimated to be of working age, the other half being either below or above that age. For example, an activity rate of 54 percent would mean that practically all able-bodied women of working age take part in productive activities, and/or that the scope of definition might be wider than in another country with an activity rate of 20 percent, and/or that the former country has a larger formal sector—i.e., is more industrialized (see Table 3).

The female economic activity rate is highest in East Asia, particularly in China, and in Southeast Asia in Thailand, Vietnam and Singapore. Overall, it is highest in Southeast Asia where the percentage of women in total manufacturing employment is also high. The highest female economic activity rate, and the only one above 50 percent, occurs in Thailand, which also has one of the highest rates of both female literacy and tertiary education.[9] Thailand displays less difference in economic activity rate between the sexes despite the fact that it is less economically developed than Japan and Singapore, both of which have considerably lower female activity rates of 15 percent and 40 percent, respectively. In China, state policy for the past 30 years has continuously encouraged the female population to enter the labor force. Vietnam, also a centrally planned economy and in addition still recovering from the effects of war and an uneven sex ratio, has also mobilized women to enter the labor force.[10] In contrast, the lowest female activity rates in Asia are in South Asia, with the rate dropping to a little over five percent in the case of Pakistan and Bangladesh.[11]

THE FEMALE LABOR FORCE

In Asia women commonly engage in agriculture or in processing, in manufacturing, and in service and related occupations. One feature of rural Asian life immediately observable in decades past was the numbers of women, and especially poor women, laboring in family agricultural and allied activities including field cultivation, the tending of domestic livestock, and small home-based processing and handicraft operations. Women played the dominant role in the rice-dominated rural economies of southern India and

[9] Barbara Ward, *Women in the New Asia: The Changing Social Roles of Men and Women in South and South-East Asia* (Paris: UNESCO, 1963); W. Weekes-Vagliani and B. Grossat, *Women in Development: At the Right Time for the Right Reason* (Paris: OECD Development Center, 1980).

[10] Marina Thorborg, "Women's Economic Position in Republican China 1911–1949," in "La Donna della Cina Imperiale i della Cina Republicana," ed. Lionello Lanciotto, *Civiltà Veneziana Studi* 36 (1980): 123–46.

[11] In ILO *Yearbook of Labor Statistics 1986*, Table 1.

Table 3
ECONOMIC ACTIVITY RATE[1] AND PAID EMPLOYMENT IN MANUFACTURING

Country	Year	Economic activity rate Male Female		Year	Paid employment in manufacturing (women in % of total manufacturing employment)
SOUTH ASIA					
Bangladesh	1984	53.5	5.4		
India	1981	52.7	19.8	1984	9.5
Pakistan	1985	51.7	5.8		
Sri Lanka	1981	64.7	23.1	1984	37.8
SOUTHEAST ASIA					
Indonesia	1985	50.0	27.9	1976	47.0
Malaysia[2]	1980	48.5	26.0	1979	44.6
Philippines	1980	60.1	28.0	1976	47.0
Singapore	1985	59.8	35.2	1986	46.8
Thailand	1984	55.9	50.1	1984	44.7
Vietnam	1980–82	n.a.	47.0	—	—
EAST ASIA					
China	1982	57.3	47.0	1985	36.4
Japan	1986	60.7	38.8	1986	35.4
Republic of Korea	1986	46.8	30.6	1986	39.0

[1] Activity rate = Total economically active population divided by total population, as a percentage.
[2] Refers to peninsular Malaysia only.
Sources: Unless otherwise indicated, the data is taken from *ILO Yearbook of Labour Statistics 1987*. Economic activity rate is calculated from Table 1; paid employment in manufacturing is calculated from Tables 5 a and b. Economic activity rate of Philippines, Vietnam, China, see Marina Thorborg, *Identification of Priority Research Issues on Women in Asia* (Stockholm, 1986). For Sri Lanka, see *Census of Population 1981*. For Japan, see *Statistical Handbook of Japan 1987*. For paid employment in manufacturing in China, see China, State Statistical Bureau, *Statistical Yearbook of China 1986;* for Japan, see *Statistical Handbook of Japan 1987*.

South China, and in Southeast Asia where women frequently held and owned land in their own names. They played a less important productive role in the dry, ploughed wheat and maize lands of northern India and North China; and they did not generally work in the fields at all in the Islamic regions of India and East Bengal. The common division of labor, whereby men cultivated cash crops and women farmed subsistence crops applied less

1809

to Asia than other continents, in that Asian women also cultivated cash crops.

The number of women employed in agriculture in Asia has declined over the past few decades, although it has been a more general trend that women remain in agriculture once alternative economic opportunities present themselves to their menfolk. Agriculture is then defined as the least attractive, the least productive and the least remunerative of occupations—in which women are trapped due to their lack of training and ability to be mobile, and because of their traditional family obligations.[12] In Southeast Asia, men began to move away from agriculture at the turn of the century; in Japan, during the 1950s; and in China, in the 1970s.[13] For example, in China (and particularly, close to urban areas) the feminization of agriculture is taking place at the present time, which explains the discrepancy in Table 3 between the high economic activity rate of women and their considerably lower participation rate in manufacturing—in comparison to men. In the Republic of Korea, Malaysia and the Philippines less than half of their female work force is in agriculture. Still, four-fifths of the women work on the land in India and China, while about two-thirds do the same in Bangladesh, Pakistan, Thailand and Vietnam. In Sri Lanka and Indonesia every second woman is an agricultural worker. (See Table 4.) Parallel to the feminization of agriculture has been the overall gradual decline in numbers of men and women remaining in agriculture. Thus, Japan not only has the smallest number of workers in agriculture in Asia but also the lowest percentage of women agricultural workers. Indeed, the population of women working in agriculture is frequently cited not only as a measure of women's status but also of a country's stage of industrialization indicating lower proportions employed in manufacturing industries and service occupations.

The modern economies of most Asian societies have been dominated by the expansion of light manufacturing, a development that has conventionally provided new employment opportunities for women. Where light industry dominates the modern economy it may be that more women than men are employed in the modern industrial sector. This was the case in Japan and China in the 1930s. In China female labor accounted for 50 percent of the workers engaged in manufacturing in 1930 and 57 percent in 1932.[14] Worldwide, between 1960 and 1984, the trend toward the development of light industry has meant that women in manufacturing have increased by some 104 percent compared to 70 percent for men. In South Asia, however, few women are employed in manufacturing indus-

---

[12] Boserup, *Women's Role.*

[13] Marina Thorborg, "Chinese Employment Policy in 1949–78 with Special Emphasis on Women in Rural Production," in *Chinese Economy, Post-Mao* (Washington, D.C.: U.S. Congress, Joint Economic Committee, November 1978); Thorborg, "Hemmafruar och Verkskvinnor i Maos Kina" (Housewives and Women in the Work Force in Mao's China), *Historisk Tidskrift*, no. 1 (1981); Thorborg, "Research on Women in the Chinese Economy" in *Theoretical and Methodological Problems in Research on Women in Developing Countries*, no. 5 (Copenhagen: Women's Research Center in Social Sciences, December 1982).

[14] Thorborg, "Women's Economic Position."

Table 4

FEMALE LABOR FORCE PARTICIPATION
BY MAJOR OCCUPATIONS
(in percentage)

Occupations	Sri Lanka 1981	India 1981	Pakistan 1985	Bangla- desh 1983	Thailand 1984	Malaysia* 1979	Singa- pore 1986	Indo- nesia 1985	Philip- pines 1985	Vietnam 1982	China 1982	Republic of Korea 1986	Japan 1986
Professional, technical and related workers	13.3	2.3	10.1	3.1	3.2	6.7	11.4	3.9	9.8		4.4	5.6	10.7
Administrative, executive and managerial workers	0.8	0.1	0.9	0.1	0.5	0.2	3.4	0.03	0.6		0.4	0.1	0.5
Clerical and related workers	6.7	0.8	3.4	1.6	2.6	9.8	29.2	1.9	5.9		0.7	10.7	25.2
Sales and related workers	2.7	1.1	10.1	5.3	10.2	8.3	12.2	20.9	23.5	40.0	1.9	18.1	14.2
Service workers	5.1	1.9	4.5	8.5	3.6	11.6	17.6	5.7	13.6		2.4	16.5	12.1
Production and transport workers	16.3	6.8	27.1	30.4	7.9	20.7	25.2	13.4	11.8		13.0	22.7	26.8
Agricultural workers	52.4	57.7	50.1	44.1	72.4	42.8	0.7	53.7	34.9	60.0	77.1	26.2	10.0
Not classified by occupation	2.9	30.0	0.3	2.7	0.0	0.0	0.2	0.3	0.03		0.1	—	0.3

Note: The distribution of the active female population by economic sectors usually excludes persons whose situation is not clearly defined or who are seeking work for the first time; in a few cases unemployed women workers are also excluded. For Sri Lanka unemployed workers are excluded.

* Refers to peninsular Malaysia.

Sources: Unless otherwise indicated, the data is calculated from ILO, *Yearbook of Labor Statistics 1987*, Tables 2 and 3C. For Bangladesh and Vietnam, see Marina Thorborg, *Identification of Priority Records Issues on Women in Asia* (Stockholm, 1986). For Sri Lanka, see Sri Lanka, Women's Bureau, Census Data, 1985, Table 69.

tries. In Nepal and Bangladesh there are as yet few manufacturing industries, and in India male and female paid employment in manufacturing increased by 15 percent and 11 percent, respectively, between 1977 and 1985. While in mining, quarrying and construction total male paid employment rose and female employment declined, in transport, storage and communications female employment increased by 81 percent compared to 76 percent for male employment. In China, rapidly industrializing on a large scale, there has been a more rapid growth for female (51 percent) than male (31 percent) paid employment in manufacturing between 1977 and 1986.

A most important development in the expansion of labor-intensive manufacturing has been the establishment of export processing zones in East and Southeast Asia in the 1960s. A substantial redeployment of labor-intensive industries from developed to developing countries has taken place, particularly in the export processing zones; and due to the nature of these industries—mostly textiles and electronics—more women than men are employed. The growth of export processing zones in Asia from the mid-1970s onward contributed more to female than to male industrial employment. Women's participation in industry in the developing countries worldwide increased from 21 percent of industrial employment in 1960 to 26.5 percent in 1980, and the sharpest rise took place in Asia.[15]

In 1965 the export processing zone of Kaohsiung on Taiwan was established, followed chronologically by different types of export processing zones in the Republic of Korea, India, the Philippines, Malaysia, Indonesia, Sri Lanka, China and Thailand. It is estimated that about 1.3 million people work in export processing zones in all the developing countries; and of this number about 0.8 million were working in Asia as of 1986. Most Asians employed in the different types of export processing zones are presently active in Singapore, the Republic of Korea, Hong Kong, Malaysia, Taiwan and Sri Lanka. Of total employment in export processing zones outside of the developed countries, those cited above in East and Southeast Asia comprise 40 percent.[16] The textile and electronics industries almost exclusively dominate manufacturing in the export processing zones; and as of 1975 about three-quarters of the zone workers were engaged in these branches. Since then no greater change has taken place.[17] Electronics industries employ almost half of the labor force in the export processing zones of Asia, accounting for over 300,000 workers. Worldwide, women usually make up more than two-thirds of the workers in export processing zones, while the rate for Asia is more than four-fifths. Three-quarters of this female labor force is very young—14 to 24 years old—and in most cases still unmarried.

[15] L. Paukert, *The Role of Women in Industrial Development.* UNIDO/18, 484, September 13, 1984 (study prepared as a contribution by UNIDO to the "World Survey on the Role of Women in Development", to be considered by the World Conference to Review and Appraise the Achievements of the United Nations Decade for Women, Nairobi, 1985).

[16] O. Kreyer, Jurgen Henrichs and Folker Frobel, *Export Processing Zones in Developing Countries: Results of a New Survey.* Working Paper no. 43 (Geneva: ILO, 1987).

[17] Ibid.

Altogether, it is estimated that over sixth-sevenths of the women employees in Asian export processing zones are less than 30 years of age, married without children, or single. In Malaysia, Taiwan and Sri Lanka the establishment of export processing zones has been responsible for the sharp rise in female employment in manufacturing; and in Sri Lanka, while employment in the manufacturing sector between 1978 and 1984 expanded by 21 percent for women, it contracted to 12 percent for men. The incorporation of women into the manufacturing industries located in the export processing zones is frequently of short duration. Although they may receive wages higher than those employed outside of the export processing zones, they are often made redundant after four to six years, during which time span the hard labor and long hours have frequently led to some deterioration in health. They leave work equipped with few replicable skills. Because of the divisions of the work process, those skills that the workers acquire are often minimal and fit only a few women for reemployment in other industries or sectors of the economy.[18]

The most developed economies in Asia have increasingly showed a trend away from light industry to capital-intensive heavy industries and to services, both of which areas tend to employ more male than female workers. A change of policy in the Republic of Korea led to the promotion of heavy industry and especially of industries such as shipbuilding in the 1970s. Although heavy industries, in comparison to light industries, usually generate less employment with respect to investment of capital, the number of male workers in industry between the years 1977 to 1986 increased by 36 percent, compared to increases of 12 percent in the number of women workers.[19] Japan, which today earns more from export licenses and technical knowledge than products, has a more rapidly growing service sector than a manufacturing sector. Thus, male employment in manufacturing increased by only 6.4 percent from 1976 to 1986, while female employment in the services increased by 15 percent.[20]

The feminization of office work is a continuing feature of the most industrialized countries of Asia.[21] In Japan and Singapore the greater part of the female work force is employed in clerical work rather than in sales or services. In Singapore the proportion of women working in sales and services combined is about equal to that in office work (see Tables 4, 5a, 5b and 5c). Sri Lanka and Japan are the only other countries in the region

---

[18] J. Currie, *Export Processing Zones in the 1980s.* The Economist Intelligence Unit Report No. 190; United Nations, *An Evaluation of Export Processing Zones in Selected Asian Countries.* ESCAP/UNCTC Publications Series B, no. 8 (1985); Marina Thorborg, "The Development of Special Economic Zones in Asia with Reference to the People's Republic of China, *Proceedings of the 31st International Congress of Human Sciences in Asia and North Africa* (Tokyo–Kyoto, Aug. 31–Sept. 7 1983) 2 (1984): 756; Thorborg, "New Ways to Industrialization in Asia with Special Reference to China and Sri Lanka," in *Southeast Asia between Autocracy and Democracy* (London: Routledge, 1986).
[19] ILO *Yearbook of Labor Statistics 1987* (calculated from Table 5a).
[20] Ibid.
[21] ILO *Yearbook of Labor Statistics 1986* (calculated from Table 5b).

Table 5a

PERCENTAGE SHARE OF OCCUPATIONAL
GROUPS: (1) PROFESSIONAL, TECHNICAL AND
RELATED WORKERS; (2) ADMINISTRATIVE
AND MANAGERIAL WORKERS—OUT OF
TOTAL WOMEN WORKERS IN ASIAN
COUNTRIES

Country	Year to which data correspond	Professional, technical and related workers			Administrative and managerial workers		
		1970s	1980s	1984	1970s	1980s	1984
Bangladesh	1974	2.5	—	—	—	—	—
Hong Kong	1971, 1984	6.5	—	6.8	1.6	—	1.3
India	1971, 1981	2.7	2.3	—	0.1	0.1	—
Indonesia	1977, 1985	2.2	3.9	—	0.04	0.3	—
Japan	1977, 1986	8.4	—	10.7	0.5	0.8	0.5
Republic of Korea	1977, 1986	2.3	3.3	4.6	0.2	—	0.1
Malaysia	1977, 1980	6.3	7.0	—	0.2	0.2	—
Nepal	1971	0.1	—	—	0.2	—	—
Philippines	1977, 1985	12.1	10.6	—	0.4	0.8	—
Singapore	1970, 1980	11.8	9.4	10.7	0.3	1.8	2.7
Sri Lanka	1970, 1980, 1981	6.3	8.2	—	0.1	0.2	—
Thailand	1970, 1982	1.5	3.0	—	—	0.7	—

Sources: ILO, *Yearbook of Labor Statistics*, various issues. Taken from A. V. Jose, "Employment Diversification of Women in Asian Countries: An Assessment," ILO/ARTEP.

Table 5b

PERCENTAGE SHARE OF OCCUPATIONAL GROUPS: (1) CLERICAL AND RELATED WORKERS; (2) PRODUCTION WORKERS, TRANSPORT EQUIPMENT OPERATORS AND LABORERS—OUT OF TOTAL WOMEN WORKERS IN ASIAN COUNTRIES

Country	Year to which data correspond	Clerical and related workers			Production workers, transport equipment operators and laborers		
		1970s	1980s	1984	1970s	1980s	1984
Bangladesh	1974	0.2	—	—	12.2	—	—
Hong Kong	1971, 1984	7.3	—	23.7	54.1	—	43.1
India	1971, 1981	0.7	0.8	—	4.9	6.8	—
Indonesia	1977, 1985	0.9	1.9	—	13.5	13.4	—
Japan	1977, 1986	22.0	23.2	25.2	27.4	24.2	26.8
Republic of Korea	1977, 1986	5.0	8.0	9.7	22.1	18.6	20.6
Malaysia	1977, 1979	8.3	9.1	—	20.9	14.5	—
Nepal	1971	0.1	—	—	0.6	—	—
Philippines	1977, 1985	6.3	6.0	—	14.9	13.3	—
Singapore	1970, 1980	13.9	25.7	30.5	25.1	34.0	27.1
Sri Lanka	1970, 1980, 1981	1.8	3.1	—	11.3	16.1	—
Thailand	1970, 1982	0.8	1.6	—	5.0	8.0	—

Sources: ILO, *Yearbook of Labor Statistics*, various issues. Taken from A. V. Jose, "Employment Diversification of Women in Asian Countries: An Assessment," ILO/ARTEP.

Table 5c
PERCENTAGE SHARE OF OCCUPATIONAL
GROUPS: (1) SALES WORKERS; (2) SERVICE
WORKERS—OUT OF TOTAL WOMEN
WORKERS IN ASIAN COUNTRIES

Country	Year to which data correspond	Sales workers			Service workers		
		1970s	1980s	1984	1970s	1980s	1984
Bangladesh	1974	1.3	—	—	10.2	—	—
Hong Kong	1971, 1984	6.1	8.1	—	14.9	—	15.3
India	1971, 1981	1.5	1.1	—	3.1	1.9	—
Indonesia	1977, 1985	18.9	20.9	—	5.4	5.7	—
Japan	1977, 1986	14.5	14.2	13.9	15.1	11.7	12.1
Republic of Korea	1977, 1986	13.7	10.8	17.5	9.8	9.2	16.0
Malaysia	1977, 1979	7.8	6.0	—	10.8	7.4	—
Nepal	1971	0.5	—	—	0.4	—	—
Philippines	1977, 1985	20.0	18.9	—	14.2	13.3	—
Singapore	1970, 1980	8.6	11.9	12.3	19.3	13.2	15.3
Sri Lanka	1970, 1980, 1981	1.5	3.6	—	4.0	4.5	—
Thailand	1970, 1982	5.8	11.5	—	3.0	3.1	—

Sources: ILO, *Yearbook of Labor Statistics*, various issues. Taken from A. V. Jose, "Employment Diversification of Women in Asian Countries: An Assessment," ILO/ARTEP.

having proportionally more women in clerical work than in either sales or services, but not to the degree of Japan and Singapore (see Tables 4, 5a, 5b and 5c). This might reflect the high educational attainment of the women of Sri Lanka compared to its general level of economic development. All other countries in the region have the reverse situation, with a higher proportion of women working in sales and services than in office work. The most industrialized countries, such as Japan and Singapore, tend to have less women working in transport and production than in clerical work (see Table 5b). In other countries of the region fewer women perform clerical work than are engaged in transport and production: with ratios of 19:1 in Bangladesh and China, India, Pakistan and Indonesia; 3:1 in Thailand and Sri Lanka; 2:1 in the Republic of Korea. The Philippines and Malaysia have a ratio of 2:1. (See Tables 4 and 5b.)

It is usually more difficult for women to be promoted to positions of status and authority in administration and management, and in all Asian societies the rate is less than 3.5 percent (see Table 4). Despite the high proportion of the population in the service sector in Japan and Korea, less than 0.5 percent of women has been recruited into executive or management positions. In Sri Lanka, where a relatively high 14.1 percent of women in 1984 were employed as professionals, technical and related workers— which again probably reflects their high rate of tertiary education—only 0.8 percent of these were in executive positions. Interestingly, in some societies with a high degree of segregation by sex in the workplace, women can rise to positions of management and authority that might be denied to them in less strictly segregated circumstances. This trend probably explains why in Pakistan there is a high proportion of professional women (see Table 4). In societies where secularizing trends may reduce sex segregation in the workplace, males frequently have moved into these positions of management and authority.

POWER, AUTHORITY AND STATUS

Within the domain of family and household, women in Asia, as in many other societies, may exercise more authority than in other socioeconomic and political institutions. Although it is difficult to obtain data on intrafamilial relations or to generalize, it does seem that within the smaller nuclear households of Asian societies, for example, it is frequently the women who manage and allocate family resources. In larger South Asian households women probably have the least influence, while in East Asia women's authority is more a matter for negotiation or bargaining and individual capacities. In kin groups reckoned by the male line, leadership and ceremonial roles are normally reserved for men; but outside of domestic and kin groups and where urban and rural communities are characterized by a degree of fluidity, informality and flexibility, political space less open to formal monopoly and manipulation may be provided. In this local political arena there may be scope for the appropriation of power and authority usually reserved for formal channels, thus allowing women informal opportunities to express their individual or collective needs and interests, be it through residential groups or women's cooperatives, of consumer, union or other local political organizations. However, the very fluidity and informality of these institutions is reflected in the dearth of figures for most types of community-level participation by women.

Women's participation in national political institutions and processes is extremely restricted, and despite variations between societies is very much limited to types of political structures and channels of general political participation available to the population at large. In countries with highly centralized and authoritarian forms of government, few channels for participation are open to those not holding formal government or official appointments. Alternatively, the state may have created channels of participation open to selected individuals, or some democratic forms of participation based on election and representation. Although these avenues of participation are in theory open to women and some are even specifically reserved for women, nowhere are women represented in the same proportions as men or in proportion to their numbers in education or production. Many outstanding women politicians in Asian societies have been daughters, wives or sisters of men who have taken a leading role and who have encouraged them to enter politics. Otherwise, while women may vote and be elected to office, the numbers of those in politics remain disproportionately low. Access to political processes, the costs of electioneering, the pressure of domestic duties and the traditional dominance of men in politics are all seen as obstacles to the active participation of women.

In East Asia—in Japan specifically—the voting rate of women has long exceeded that of men. Nevertheless, there are few women represented among the senators of the Upper and Lower House or in the prefectural assemblies. They are active, however, in women's organizations, in trade unions, and in associations to do with consumer rights, education, child care, pollution control and nuclear disarmament or peace. In China the number of women in political positions of responsibility has not risen as much as the government anticipated in 1949. The proportion of women on the Central Committee and in the National People's Congress has consistently hovered around 20 percent in the past two decades, although women's representatives have been coopted onto most local leadership committees. An important vehicle for women's political participation has been the Women's Federation, the national organization of women, which after primarily representing the interests of the party and government to women for several decades has recently much more directly articulated the interests of its female constituency to the party and government. In the Republic of Korea 10 years ago, one study of political participation concluded that "leadership from parliament to village level is male"[22] with a few, perhaps two to three women, elected by regional constituencies to the Korean National Assembly.

In Southeast Asia, despite the high numbers of educated and employed women, the numbers holding political office are not significantly higher than in East and South Asia. Vietnam may be an exception because of the

[22] Soon Young and S. Yoon, "The Role of Korean Women in National Development," in S. Mattiell, *Virtues in Conflict* (Seoul: Royal Asiatic Society) 157–67.

numbers of women engaged in anticolonial struggles and because of the war of independence, which thrust women into positions they may not otherwise have held and indeed may not continue to hold in the future. Even in 1980, although women constituted 80 percent of the less powerful National Assembly, only six of the 131 members of the more authoritative Central Committee of the party were women.[23] In Thailand, at the national level, less than three percent of the Thai House of Representatives are women, and in 1979 only three of the 225 senators were women; and at provincial, district and committee levels women are not well represented in formal decision-making areas.[24] In Malaysia, although participation in national policies is a postwar phenomenon for men as well as for women, the participation granted to women is much more limited, partly because the banning of women from a leading role in Islamic worship can render them ineligible for election in some regions. Thus, women are only permitted a total of one percent of seats in the decision-making body of the United Malays National Organization, even though they make up 50 percent of the membership. Nevertheless, women are represented in parliament and in the Senate by between four percent and 10 percent of their members.[25] In Indonesia less than 10 percent of the members of national and provincial legislatives are women, although the government took the unusual step in 1978 of appointing a woman as junior minister for economic affairs.[26]

In South Asia, despite the restrictions of Islam, purdah and segregation by sex, the number of women holding political office is not significantly lower than in other parts of Asia. In Pakistan and Bangladesh women are nominated to a very small number of reserved seats in the national assemblies, and although this may limit their channels of participation it is likely that fewer women would be elected than are at present nominated. In Pakistan a few well-known women, frequently educated abroad or the kin of male politicians, have played a greater part in national politics. The number of women in both central and state governments in India has been about five percent since independence,[27] with participation, as in most other Asian societies, largely confined to those from urban, educated and well-known political families. Indeed, many of the best-known women political leaders in the world are those who have risen to prominence in Asian societies, including Indira Gandhi, Sirimavo Bandaranaike, Benazir Bhutto, Jian Qing and Corazon Aquino. However, the status of individual role models remains somewhat nebulous, and it was said of India during the rule of Indira Gandhi that "the benefits which women as a group derive

[23] *Far Eastern Economic Review,* June 20, 1980.

[24] J. Nantanee, et al., *The Status of Thai Women in Two Rural Areas* (Bangkok: National Council of Women of Thailand, 1977).

[25] L. Manderson, "Women in Politics: Change of Continuation; The Case of Malay Women in Peninsular Malaysia." Paper presented before the 7th Conference of the International Association of Historians of Asia (Bangkok: 1977).

[26] Y. R. Noor, *Indonesian Women's Participation in Development* (Brussels: Centre d'Etude du Sud-Est Asiatique et l'Extrême Orient, 1976).

[27] M. F. Katzenstein, "Towards Equality? Cause and Consequence of the Political Prominence of Women in India," *Asian Survey* 78 (1979): 473–86.

from the prominence of a few women in leadership positions are not substantial"[28].

CONCLUSION

In terms of access to knowledge, power and resources, and their allocation, in Asia as elsewhere women are relegated to a secondary role and a dependent status whatever their importance in production and reproduction. Differences among women according to class, age and location decide to a large extent their access to power, knowledge and resources; in addition, broad differences can be traced between East, Southeast and South Asia. The strong and elaborate patriarchal family and kinship system, Hindu and Islamic religious ideals, and the almost total lack of economic activity outside the household have circumscribed the roles and depressed the status of women according to almost all indicators in India, Pakistan and Bangladesh. In Southeast Asia some of these influences have been counterbalanced by factors such as substantial economic roles and a bilineal kinship system. In East Asia circumscribing factors have been counterbalanced by strong state, political or economic interventions that have gone some way toward changing women's roles and status.

In Asia today what is impressive is the rapid spread and scale of modernization, which women have accommodated within their own life spans, contributed to and sometimes benefited from. Even in South Asia, where there has been less change than in East and Southeast Asia, increasing educational opportunities, new economic activities and family planning programs are presently and gradually affecting women's roles and status. Frequently, however, it is assumed that the multifarious factors redefining female roles and status are also uniformly affecting modernization and development with their concomitant resources and rights benefits for women. Leaving aside the complex question of the gender-specific benefits to be gained from the processes of modernization and development, what a survey of women in modern Asia societies illustrates so well is that the multifarious factors influencing women's roles and status range from those mutually supportive of improved status to those in direct conflict with such a goal.

While educational opportunities, new income-generating and employment opportunities, and improvements in diet and health may well redefine female roles and benefit women, women may equally well continue to be or even increasingly be discriminated against as a result of countering influences of religious revivalist movements—presently a trend in Islamic Asian societies. Similarly, it is not at all clear that any increase in the mobility and the employment of women as a result of further industrialization, urbanization or migration will permanently break down patriarchal kin and family groups and further the personal independence of women. However, if at present unusual extremes between tradition and modernity lie juxtaposed within the continent of Asia, it is likely that factors shaping women's

[28] Ibid.

lives, expectations and experiences will continue in the future to coexist—uneasily checked and balanced.

FURTHER READING

Bardis, Panos D., and Das, Man Singh, eds. *The Family in Asia.* New Delhi: Vikas, 1978; London: Allen & Unwin, 1979.

Chipp, Sylvia A., and Green, Justin J., eds. *Asian Women in Transition.* University Park: Pennsylvania State University Press, 1980.

Epstein, T. Scarlett, and Watts, Rosemary A., eds. *The Endless Day: Some Case Material on Asian Rural Women.* Oxford and New York: Pergamon Press, 1981.

Fan, Kok-Sim. *Women in Southeast Asia; A Bibliography,* Boston: G. K. Hall, 1982.

Jahan, R. and Papanek, H. *Women and Development: Perspectives from Southeast Asia.* Dacca: Bangladesh Institute of Law and International Affairs, 1979.

Papanek, H. "Women in South and Southeast Asia: Issues and Research." *Social Change* 7, no. 1 (1977).

Sun, M., et al. "Asian Women. Still One Step Behind." *Far Eastern Economic Review* 123, no. 1 (1984).

Thorborg, Marina, ed. *Identification of Priority Research Issues on Women in Asia: A Report on Research and Research Organisations with Bibliography.* Stockholm: Swedish Agency for Research Cooperation with Developing Countries, 1986.

Ward, Barbara. *Women in the New Asia: The Changing Social Roles of Men and Women in South and South-East Asia.* Paris: UNESCO, 1963.

Whyte, Robert O., and Whyte, Pauline. *The Women of Rural Asia.* Boulder, Colorado: Westview Press, 1982.

MINORITY GROUPS IN ASIA AND FURTHER EAST

EDMUND LEACH

ALL the countries of Asia and the Pacific that lie east of Arabia have political minorities that pose serious problems for the present-day governments. They were products of the colonial era. The colonies have mostly gone but the minorities remain. This essay considers why this should be the case.

Almost without exception the frontiers of the present-day sovereign states of South and Southeast Asia as shown in political atlases published in the Western world are the product of political bargains and administrative arrangements made by the European colonial powers during the 19th and early 20th centuries. Such frontiers pay scant regard to the ethnic peculiarities of the populations that they contain. At least 60 quite different languages are spoken by the inhabitants of modern Burma (now Myanmar), and some of these correspond to cultural differences quite as radical as those that separate an Englishman from a Turk. The frontiers on the map do not correspond to cultural frontiers on the ground, so people of essentially the same ethnic background are regularly found living on both sides of the border. The situation is further complicated by the fact that the European colonial powers seldom consulted the Chinese, who, because of their numbers, must ultimately make all the crucial decisions about where the political frontiers shall lie. Maps of western or southern China purchased in Beijing show the Chinese frontiers as in quite different positions from those recorded on international maps of European origin. Only recently a postcard received from Beijing was said to show "Jingpo girls. Most of the Jingpo live in the Dai and Jingpo Autonomous Prefecture of Dehong, Yunnan Province, southwestern China." In Burma these girls would be described as Jinghpaw (i.e., Kachin) with the gloss: "Most Jinghpaw live in the Kachin State in the regions bordering on Yunnan Province, southwestern China." The long term implications of such discrepancies are discouraging.

As the British experience shows, there is no readily predictable final outcome to the conflicts that such ethnic ambiguity entails. During the past three centuries the English have completely assimilated the Cornish and have arrived at a reasonably stable political synthesis with both the Welsh and the Scots, but they have failed altogether to come to terms with the inhabitants of Northern Ireland.

Similar puzzles present themselves all over Asia. A great variety of factors may be relevant, but the seemingly obvious is not necessarily the case. Thus it might be supposed that when the numerical size of the "minority" and the level of its economic and technical sophistication is high, as in the case of the conflict between Hindu Tamils and Sinhalese Buddhists in Sri Lanka, or that between immigrant Indians and indigenous Melanesians in Fiji, the issues must be of a quite different order from those posed by the numerically tiny tribal minorities of Burma, or by the tribal inhabitants of Nagaland and Mizoland in eastern Assam, or by the Buddhist Chakma in the Chittagong Hill tracts of Bangladesh. But that is not how things are. The "tribal minorities" maintain their existence by perpetuating civil war against the "authorities," and the larger-scale political factions based on ethnic difference such as are found in Sri Lanka and Fiji do much the same.

DISSIDENT MINORITIES

Three examples of dissident minorities that would not now be regarded as tribal minorities (though two of them have been so described in the past) will be briefly discussed: (1) the New Zealand Maori, (2) the Tamil/Sinhalese conflict in Sri Lanka, and (3) the recent conflict between local and immigrant populations in Fiji. I want to show that there are generalities in what I am saying but that if there is a division of type it is not the opposition of tribal/non-tribal that is significant. After these three examples are considered the concentration will be on *tribal* minorities.

The New Zealand Maori

In 1961 the official census reckoned that the total population of New Zealand was about 2.5 million, of whom 170,000 were rated as Maori; of these only about 35,000 were "full-blooded" Maori. The Maori population declined from 56,000 in 1857 to 42,000 in 1896 but thereafter increased rapidly. It is quite untrue to assert (as is sometimes done) that New Zealand has no race problem. The last 40 years of the 19th century saw open warfare between the indigenous Maori and the colonial Pakeha (whites). In many cases the behavior of the whites was abominable. But the fact that Maori/Pakeha intermarriage was common throughout the period and is now taken for granted [1] has blurred the edges of the Maori "identity." Furthermore, since World War II there has been a large amount of immigration from Polynesian dependencies of New Zealand (e.g., Cook Islands). These immigrants work in industry rather than on farms and are treated as inferiors by the local-born Maori, who have a monopoly of the sheep-shearing trade. The Pakeha seem to treat the Cook Islanders as inferior Maori. Any race problem that may erupt in New Zealand will probably emerge from

[1] John Harré, *Maori and Pakeha: A Study of Mixed Marriages in New Zealand* (Wellington: Reed, 1966).

the immigrant Cook Islanders and their descendants. The Maori "proper" have a future like that of Welsh-speaking Welshmen; the issue is not whether they are biologically "full-blooded" Maori or some alternative racial mixture but whether they choose to adopt a way of life that today passes for "traditional" Maori. Some will certainly do so; the majority will not.

Sri Lanka

At present the total population of Sri Lanka is about 15 million, of whom about 2.8 million are Tamil speakers. The Tamils represent 92% of the people of the Northern Province of Jaffna and about 38% of those of the Eastern Province around Batticaloa. Tambiah[2] points out that the simple polarization, Hindu Tamil versus Buddhist Sinhalese, as a description of the extreme ethnic diversity of the total population is an invention of the latter part of the 19th century that became hardened and greatly exaggerated during the 40 years of post-colonial independence. After 2,000 years of living together as members of a plural society in unstable but broadly amicable relations, the population of Sri Lanka has now become polarized into a wholly imaginary dichotomy: dark-skinned, Tamil-speaking Hindus on the one hand; fair-skinned, Sinhalese-speaking Buddhists on the other.

The dichotomy is imaginary by various criteria. The Buddhist inhabitants of Sri Lanka do not necessarily speak Sinhalese; the Sinhalese speakers are not necessarily Buddhist—many are Muslim or Hindu or Christian. There are many varieties of Sinhalese (e.g., Kandyans, "Low Country Sinhalese," Karava). Likewise, at least three kinds of Tamil are spoken in Sri Lanka—that of the Jaffna area, that of Batticaloa and that of the Indian tea garden laborers in the highlands. A great many other minorities are neither Sinhalese nor Tamil by any reckoning. The quarreling has been whipped up for political reasons by a variety of interested parties, but especially by the rival hierarchies of Buddhist monks. The quarreling is lethal; it is difficult to see how it can benefit anyone, but it is important to remember that the heartland of Tamil speakers is in South India, not in Sri Lanka. For this reason the hopelessness of the situation is not unlike that of Northern Ireland, where the existence of Irish nationalists both in Southern Ireland and in the United States makes it impossible that Irish nationalism in Northern Ireland will quietly fade away.

Fiji

The Fijian story is somewhat similar but less ancient and on a much smaller scale. Also, the two communities, Fijian and Indian, are more or less the same size, whereas both in New Zealand and in Sri Lanka the numerical dominance of the majority group is overwhelming. The similarity lies in the fact that at the beginning of the 19th century the culture of Fiji was extremely diverse. The territory includes over 300 islands; the inhabitants of some of them were formerly cannibals. The population is now about half a million, slightly more than half of whom are of quite recent Indian ori-

[2]S. J. Tambiah, *Sri Lanka: Ethnic Fratricide and the Dismantling of Democracy* (Chicago: University of Chicago Press, 1986).

1824

gin. The Indians first arrived as indentured laborers to work on (British) government sugar plantations. Immigration of this kind ceased in 1916, but in due course the Indians, through their hard work and efficiency, came to be permanent leaseholders of all the best land and to control the whole economy. But the indigenous Fijian chiefs control the small but highly efficient army and police. One of the terms of the treaty by which the British monarch became the supreme chief of Fiji stipulated that titular ownership of all land should remain permanently in Fijian hands. There is still virtually no intermarriage between the Indians and the local Fijians. The distrust engendered between the two communities by this fundamental cultural fact is what the recent coups have been all about. The best hope for the future is that the British Commonwealth powers will not try to impose by force their specialized one-person/one-vote ideas of what constitutes "democracy."

These cases indicate some principal variables that crop up in the "minority problems" that are likely to become newsworthy. In the first place, is the minority in fact a minority? In Fiji the rival parties are approximately the same size, and both are now increasing at much the same rate. In New Zealand the Maori have been a small and shrinking minority for over 150 years. They show signs of ultimately merging with the white majority. The Maori have no backup support outside New Zealand. In Sri Lanka the Tamils are a minority overall but locally (e.g., in Jaffna) they are in a majority. Sinhalese and Tamils have lived together peacefully in the past and would have continued to do so were it not for political manipulation. All arguments about the incompatibility of language, religion, and race are fictional. Even the caste groups are essentially the same though the names are different (e.g., Jaffna Tamil Vellala = Sinhalese Goigama). But Buddhist monks on the one hand and South Indian politicians on the other are eager to keep matters on the boil. The problems of Sri Lanka strongly resemble those of Northern Ireland and therefore are likely to persist.

These three cases do not include a case of outright genocide. In the next section two examples of this type will be considered: the Muslim Bangladeshi treatment of the Buddhist Chakma and the Muslim Indonesian treatment of the Christians of East Timor. Historically genocide has been the commonest mode of "solving" minority problems. In the 19th century the Tasmanians were eliminated in this way, and the Australian Aborigines have only just survived. But let us now consider minority groups that can genuinely be labeled "tribal."

TRIBAL MINORITIES

Considered one by one the significance of tribal minorities may seem small, but they exist in every Asian country and in many parts of the Pacific; they number many millions of individuals. They are thin on the ground, but in some countries, such as Burma, Thailand, Malaysia and Indonesia, the map area inhabited by the tribal peoples is substantially greater than that occupied by the more concentrated politically dominant group. Indeed, in several independent sovereign states in Oceania—Papua New Guinea being the largest—no ethnic group is clearly politically dominant and no national language is spoken other than English-derived pidgin; the whole population is made up of "tribal minorities." The polity is viable because of mineral resources. From some points of view this might be thought to be a desirable state of affairs, but it is clearly highly unstable.

That granted, two distinct types of tribal minority may usefully be distinguished. The first are populations that are wholly encompassed by more sophisticated neighbors. Bailey[3] describes such a case from Central India. The future of such people is predestined; in due course they will be absorbed culturally, linguistically and politically by their neighbors. The second type are populations that straddle a political frontier, which may be on land or sea. The destiny of this latter type of tribal minority is far less certain. Such people are often in a position to control trans-frontier trade and to levy taxes on the traders who, as likely as not, are smuggling illicit commodities. The profits and political influence resulting from such trade may be substantial.

In nearly all cases the number of distinguishable linguistic groups within the frontier tribal area is very large. Matisoff[4] provides a good account of just what this means in the far north of Thailand, though Matisoff, as a professional linguist, has a vested interest in emphasizing the complexity. Similarly, the end papers of ter Haar[5] show the complexity of the differences of *adat* (native law) in Indonesia. In this case the diversity reflects the "divide and rule" interests of an earlier generation of Dutch colonial administrators. If each such group, whether defined by language or by custom, were considered as a separate ethnic unit deserving special individual attention, then the administrative problems posed by the tribal minorities would prove insuperable. But outside the monographs of academic anthropologists the problem on the ground is today quite different.

In the borderlands of Burma and Assam and Thailand the minorities that matter are those that appear in news reports under such labels as Naga, Chin, Kachin and Karen. Originally these names were merely category terms invented by foreigners to lump together a mixture of very small superficially distinct groups; it is only the political accidents of the past 50 years that have molded the populations concerned into incipient nations. Fifty years ago no self-conscious ethnic community existed that thought of itself as "the Nagas"; there were only Angami, Ao, Rengma, Sema, Konyak, and so on, all busily engaged in perennial mutual hostilities. Today the inhabitants of the Naga Hills are aware of themselves as Nagas and

[3] F. G. Bailey, *Tribe, Caste and Nation* (Manchester: Manchester University Press, 1960).
[4] James A. Matisoff, "Linguistic Diversity and Language Contact" in John McKinnon and Wanat Bhruksasri, eds., *Highlanders of Thailand* (Kuala Lumpur: Oxford University Press, 1983), 56–87.
[5] B. ter Haar, *Adat Law in Indonesia* (New York: Institute of Pacific Relations, 1948).

therefore they constitute a genuine political force. The concern here is with tribal minorities of this somewhat enhanced scale.

At this level the common assumption that the adjective "tribal" is equivalent to "primitive" or "backward" needs to be treated with caution.

In general, the tribal peoples do occupy inaccessible parts of the country, and on that account they are, quite literally, "backwoodsmen." A certain primitiveness follows automatically from the lack of communications. These are people who exist on the margins of the world economic system: compared with that of even the least sophisticated townsman their standard of living is elementary. Suitably selected photographs and journalistic propaganda can readily depict the typical tribesman as a naked savage. Even so, it does not follow that such tribesmen are ill-qualified to take advantage of changing political and economic circumstances. The quality of the educated elite among the tribal peoples is often as good as or better than that on which the central government has to rely.

History is relevant here. When the European colonial regimes were first elaborated during the 19th century the tribal peoples of East Asia appeared preeminently primitive. Consequently they received a disproportionate amount of charitable aid. Most colonial governments paid exaggerated respect to local religious prejudices. But "religious" in this context referred only to the acknowledged major religions—Christianity, Hinduism, Buddhism, Islam. The religions of the tribal minorities were deemed to be mere superstition that deserved no protection. The great surge of 19th-century Christian missionary endeavor was therefore diverted toward the primitives. In the eyes of the administration the Christian conversion of a Buddhist or a Muslim might entail all sorts of unforeseeable political consequences, but surely the conversion of a cannibal or a headhunter could only be for the good? Maybe; yet in the long run this too had political consequences. The well-financed schools of the Christian missions often provided an education vastly superior to anything contained in the traditional system of the "civilized" major groups.

Today the leaders of the tribal minorities are almost invariably mission-trained Christians of considerable educational attainment. They frequently display an almost European contempt for the ignorant stupidity of their "heathen" political overlords. In consequence, the cultural gulf that now separates the tribal minorities from their nominal masters is much wider than it was in the original pre-missionary phase of colonial expansion. The prospect is lamentable. The opposition of Christian versus Buddhist or of Christian versus Muslim offers truly formidable obstacles to any attempted cultural synthesis or assimilation.

Another relevant historical detail is that in some (but not all) cases the colonial authorities systematically recruited military police from the "tribals" rather than from the majority population. In Burma, for example, before 1940 locally recruited military and military police were drawn from the Kachin, Chin and Karen tribal minorities, but very few from the majority Buddhist population of Burmese and Shans. Similarly in Indonesia, the bulk of the Dutch colonial army was recruited from the Eastern Islands in the vicinity of Amboina where most of the population are of Papuan extraction and converts to the Dutch Reformed Church. Government policy was plainly designed to range these dark-skinned Christians in opposition to the Indonesian Muslim population that is heavily concentrated in the island of Java.

QUESTIONS OF SOVEREIGNTY

Although the successor governments depend less on the loyalty of tribal soldiers, the military competence of tribal minorities still has wide political ramifications. For example, the paradox by which Indonesia pursued a chauvinistic policy toward Western New Guinea (now Irian Jaya) at a time when the government's control over Indonesia proper was only notional was certainly influenced by the potential threat that an otherwise unemployed Amboinese soldiery might offer to the internal security of the state. Or again there is the case of Burma. When the country was granted independence in 1948, the commander-in-chief of the army, Gen. Smith Dun, was a highly qualified and much respected Karen. During the very confused political developments of the next 15 years there was at least one point when a senior Kachin chief, Sima Sinwa Nawng, was designated as president of the Union of Burma. But this was a very temporary phase. Since 1962 the country has had a military dominated government led by men who trained under the Japanese, and members of minorities who benefited from British rule (Karen, Kachin, Chin and Shan) have been in varying degrees pursuing the insurrections that commenced in the late 1940s and 1950s.

Yet although education and military advantage often place the leaders of the tribal minority on a par with the leaders of the political majority, basic problems remain unresolved. These stem from a fixed belief that the tribal minorities are, in their very essence, both primitive and inferior.

Despite all the talk of Asian freedom and emancipation from the slave mentality of the colonial epoch, the central governments of countries such as India, Myanmar and Indonesia have tended to inherit the prejudices and administrative habits of their British and Dutch predecessors. Colonial administrators treated tribal peoples with ruthless severity. The military punitive expedition seldom achieved any useful purpose, but it was the stock response of all colonial governments to any form of trouble in tribal areas. The successor governments tend to react in an identical manner with equal lack of effect. Indeed, the indications are that, over the past few years, certain governments, that of India in particular, have been *more* prone than their colonial predecessors to resort to military sanctions against the tribal peoples of their border zones.

The issue of national frontiers is relevant here. The tribal peoples are frequently located in mountainous regions lying between the major states— the sub-Himalayan area between Assam and west China is a case in point. During the colonial period many such regions were left unadministered, that is, they were treated as buffer zones, a tacitly neutral no-man's-land that the great powers could conveniently leave alone. In such circumstances the tribal peoples enjoyed, in practice if not in theory, a large measure of independence. In contrast, the successor states are preoccupied, to an exaggerated degree, with questions of sovereignty. Because of this, the precise details of political frontiers have come to assume an ominous importance. The territorial claims of the Indian government in the North-East Frontier are no different from those of the previous British Raj, but whereas the British were often satisfied enough with a notional frontier on a notional map, the Indians have felt obliged to establish effective administration up to the very limits of their territory, to the clear detriment of the tribal peoples concerned. Elwin[6] shows how this worked out in the case of the inhabitants of the Assam North-East Frontier. The government was paternalistic toward the local inhabitants, but they entirely lost their former independence.

Closer administration brings benefits in the form of better communications, medical services, education, trade and so on, but this is true of all colonial enterprise. In any particular case these advantages have to be weighed against the countless difficulties that ensue from the intensification of ethnic solidarity. The Indian government may honestly plead that its attitude toward the tribal peoples is one of high moral purpose, that it aims to bring civilization and economic development to the primitive peoples of Eastern Assam. But this is an old story. The vices of paternalistic colonialism are not a peculiarity of white-skinned rulers, and nationalist consciousness pays no heed to good intentions.

The currently existing nations of Southern Asia have proudly achieved their statehood by throwing off the shackles of colonial domination. Yet, in respect to the tribal peoples, they have simply taken over the role of the former colonial powers. Vis-à-vis the tribal minorities, most of the central governments continue to act as if they themselves were colonial imperialists. Good works are imposed by force. Yet one may predict that where administrative policies of tutelage and apartheid depend on military sanction, in the long run political nemesis is certain. In any tribal situation a policy of military coercion has the automatic consequence of consolidating a nationalist opposition out of the confusion of preexisting tribal loyalties. In such circumstances (unless, as in the Soviet Union, the central authorities are prepared to be quite exceptionally ruthless), the long-term advantage seems to lie with the advocates of political independence even when economic factors seem to indicate precisely the opposite. That an independent Naga state would be an economic absurdity does not necessarily imply that such a state will never come into being.

The balkanization of Asia into a vast array of petty independent sovereignties seems undesirable from almost every point of view, yet the existence of the tribal minorities offers the constant threat of this kind of development. How far such balkanization proceeds will depend in part on how well the civilian politicians of the existing state manage to control their military. Every act of military suppression postpones still further the prospect of cultural assimilation. This comment needs to be considered against the background fact that in non-Communist Asia in 1988, Paki-

[6] Verrier Elwin, *A Philosophy of NEFA* (Shillong: Sachin Roy, 1959).

stan, Bangladesh, Myanmar, Indonesia, Thailand and Taiwan all had governments dominated by the military, while further east the Philippines and Fiji often seemed to be heading the same way.

If the tribal minorities are to play their part in a larger statehood they must be treated with respect. Military restraint is not enough; civil administrators of such regions must learn to behave as civil servants and cease to parade themselves as imitation European nabobs and pukka sahibs. The problem posed by the minorities would largely disappear if the central governments concerned devoted their energies to civilizing the administration instead of civilizing the population.

THE UNCERTAIN SCALE OF THE MINORITY PROBLEMS

Earlier versions of this essay have included estimates of the numbers of people and the areas of land involved. This no longer seems a useful exercise.

Ever since the days of the Roman Empire, the European colonial powers have been obsessional census takers. The bureaucrats needed to know just whom they could tax and how taxpayers should be classified. The resulting counting of heads amounted to a policy of divide and rule; the number of minorities was maximized. The governments of the successor states have mostly gone to the other extreme; they have counted heads but refused to classify the heads thus counted. The ethnic injustice that then results is sometimes very striking.

Thus, taken as a whole, Bangladesh is one of the most densely populated areas in the world. The language spoken by the majority is Bengali; their religion is Muslim. But the frontier region to the east of the country (the Chittagong Hill Tracts) is very thinly populated and was formerly inhabited by a Buddhist people called the Chakma who spoke their own language. It would seem that the government of Bangladesh does not recognize the Chakma as having any special rights to their ancestral land. Their territory is simply a thinly populated region which is suitable for colonization by Muslim Bengalis from the west who are short of lands. Thus no quantification of the "Chakma minority problem" is possible.

Many similar situations are found in Indonesia. Parts of that huge archipelago are much more densely populated than others. West Irian, which has a native Melanesian (black) population, is thinly populated; Java and Madura, with a brown-skinned Muslim population, are the most densely populated. The Indonesian authorities do not actually deny the existence of cultural minorities but they usually ride roughshod over any attempt by local culture groups to assert their independence. A striking example is provided by the eastern half of Timor. The area had been a Portuguese colony since 1586; it was annexed by Indonesia in the mid-1970s. The local inhabitants have engaged in civil war against the Jakarta authorities ever since. Officially this minority does not exist; the insurgents are bandits and rebels. But if they gave up the fight they would indeed cease to exist.

So also in the Myanmar/Thailand border area; there has been a continuous civil war between the Burmese government and some Karens for over

30 years, with the Karens usually in the ascendancy. All statements about these matters published in press releases, either in Yangon (Rangoon) or in Bangkok, should be viewed with the utmost skepticism, but the fact that this warfare goes on is clearly of the utmost importance for the people concerned. Yet in the substantial body of ethnographic literature concerning this part of the map that has appeared since this article was last revised in 1969,[7] we are told less rather than more about the key fact that the Karen are a transfrontier minority. Instead we are given a skewed picture as seen from the Thailand side of the official frontier.

Charles F. Keyes, the most able of the anthropologists concerned, comments as follows: "The vast majority for whom the term Karen is appropriate live in Burma, and it is from Burma that the first studies of the Karen come. Unfortunately, it has been next to impossible for anthropologists, linguists, historians and others to carry out any research among the Karen of Burma since before World War II. The war itself, followed by the Karen rebellion against the newly established Union of Burma, the persistence of rebellion in a number of Karen areas and the closing of Burma to outside scholars after the establishment of military rule in 1962 have prevented almost any research being undertaken among Karen populations."[8] As indicated, almost all the minorities discussed in this essay are in a precisely similar situation.

Minorities play an important part in the developing political scene in the whole region covered by this book. It is a paradox that they can only continue to exist if they show themselves to be successfully hostile to the internationally recognized governmental authority. It follows that information about them will be systematically suppressed by the governmental authorities concerned.

FURTHER READING

Bailey, F. G., *Tribe, Caste, and Nation: A Study of Political Activity and Political Change in Highland Orissa.* Manchester: Manchester University Press; Bombay: Oxford University Press, 1960.

Elwin, Verrier. *A Philosophy for NEFA.* 2nd rev. ed. Shillong: Sachin Roy on behalf of the North-East Frontier Agency, 1959.

Hamilton, J. W. *Pwo Karen: At the Edge of Mountain and Plain.* American Ethnographical Society Monograph No. 60. St. Paul, Minnesota: West Publishing, 1976.

Harré, John. *Maori and Pakeha: A Study of Mixed Marriages in New Zealand.* Wellington: A. H. and A. W. Reed; New York: Praeger for the Institute of Race Relations, London, 1966.

[7] See for example J. W. Hamilton, *Pwo Karen: At the Edge of Mountain and Plain,* American Ethnographical Society Monograph no. 60, (St. Paul, Minnesota: West Publishing Co., 1976); Charles F. Keyes, ed., *Ethnic Adaptation and Identity: The Karen on the Thai Frontier with Burma* (Philadelphia: ISHI, 1979); John McKinnon and Wanat Bhruksasri, eds., *Highlanders of Thailand* (Kuala Lumpur: Oxford University Press, 1983).

[8] Keyes, p. 8.

Keyes, Charles F., ed. *Ethnic Adaptation and Identity: The Karen on the Thai Frontier with Burma.* Philadelphia: Institute for the Study of Human Issues, 1979.

Kunstadter, Peter, ed. *Southeast Asian Tribes, Minorities and Nations.* Princeton, New Jersey: Princeton University Press, 1967.

Leach, Edmund. "The Frontiers of 'Burma.' " *Comparative Studies in Society and History* 3, no. 1 (1960).

————. "The Political Future of Burma." In de Jouvenel, B., ed. *Futuribles.* Geneva: Droz, 1963.

————. *Political Systems of Highland Burma: A Study of Kachin Social Structure.* London: G. Bell, 1954; London: Athlone Press, 1964 and 1977.

McKinnon, John, and Bhruksasri, Wanat, eds. *Highlanders of Thailand.* Kuala Lumpur and New York: Oxford University Press, 1983.

Tambiah, S. J. *Sri Lanka: Ethnic Fratricide and the Dismantling of Democracy.* Chicago: University of Chicago Press, 1986.

ter Haar, Barend. *Adat Law in Indonesia.* New York: Institute of Pacific Relations, 1948.

INDEX

A

Abe, Shintaro 139, 1230
ABIM—*See Angkatan Belia Islam Malaysia*
Aborigines
  population
    in Australia 435, 1614, 1639, 1707
    in Japan 566–567, 569, 575–578
    in New Zealand 250, 673, 676, 684
    in Siberia and Far East 767–768
    in Taiwan 347, 820, 824, 832
  religion
    and the Little Tradition 1767
Abortion
  and fertility rates 80, 1518–1519
Abraham, A. S. 1127
ABU—*See Asia-Pacific Broadcasting Union*
Acheson, Dean 941–942, 944–948, 950, 1082
Acupuncture 80, 1626
ADB—*See Asian Development Bank*
ADF—*See Asian Development Fund*
Advertising
  newspaper 1656–1657
  television
    in China, by Western companies 1696
    in Indonesia 1700–1701
Affluent Society, The (book) 1505
Afghanistan, Republic of 3–13, 421–431
  agriculture 3, 10
  army 424–428
  autocratic modernization 425–426
  bureaucracy 424–425, 428
  civil wars 424
  constitutional system 5–7, 426
  economy 9–11
  education 11–12
  employment 11
  foreign trade 10–11
  geography 3–4
  history 7–9, 421–422
  Islamic influence 423, 426–427, 430,
    1065–1066, 1285–1287
  Khalq regime 427–428
  kinship groups 422
  land reform 427
  languages 5, 423
  leftist revolution 427–428
  mass media 12, 426
  minerals 3–4, 10
  monarchy 423–424
  natural gas 10, 422
  political parties 6–7
  population distribution 4–5
  resistance movements 429–431

  road construction 422
  social services 11
  and the Soviet Union 4–5, 428–431, 1185,
    1193–1195
  tourist industry 10
  U.S. involvement 429–430
AFPFL—*See Anti-Fascist People's League*
Agency for International Development, U.S.
  (AID) 1638
Aging
  population 1528
Aglipayan Church (Iglesia Filipino In-
    dependiente) 308, 732, 1056, 1069
Agriculture
  ADB loans 1493
  and ASEAN 1348
  and Asian peasantry 1580–1584
  and China's Great Leap Forward 492
  and deforestation 1556–1557, 1569
  investment costs 1585–1586
  and land/labor usages 1579
  mechanization 1587–1588
  Oceanian exports 1444–1445
  tables 392, 395–396
  women's role in 1799, 1808–1810
  *See also specific country, commodity by
    name*
Agriculture Special Fund (ASF) 1475–1476
Aguinaldo, Emilio 311, 727
AIBD—*See Asian Institute of Broadcast De-
    velopment*
AID—*See Agency for International Develop-
    ment, U.S.*
AIJV (ASEAN Industrial Joint Venture)
  1109–1110, 1376–1377
Ainu (Ezo) people 566–567, 569, 575–576
Akhromeyev, Sergei 1257
Akihito, Emperor (Japan) 128, 132, 139
Akiner, Shirin v
  "Soviet Central Asia" 785–804
Alebua, Ezekiel 277
Alejandro, Leandro 738
Alesana, Tofilau Eti 283
Alkazi, Ebrahim 1718
Alliance Party (Malaysia) 630
All India Muslim League 1038
ALP—*See Australian Labour Party*
Aluminum production
  Australia 21
Alwei, Syed 1724
Amanullah, King (Afghanistan) 8, 422, 425,
  996
Ambedkar, B. R. 521

INDEX

Index

OK

S

(*continued from front flap*)

Contributors include such authorities as Bruce Cumings and Takashi Inoguchi on the history of postwar Asia, Haruhiro Fukui on political parties, Judith Nagata on religion and politics, Christopher Howe on Japan and the world economy, Andrew Nathan on Taiwan, Mohan Rao on peasants, Anthony Rowley on banking and investment, and Edmund Leach on Asian minority groups.

Robert H. Taylor is professor of politics in the University of London and head of the Department of Economic and Political Studies at the university's School of Oriental and African Studies. Born in Ohio, he received his doctorate from Cornell University and taught previously at the University of Sydney and Wilberforce University. He is the author of *The State in Burma* and coeditor of *Context, Meaning and Power in Southeast Asia* as well as a contributing author to *In Search of Southeast Asia: A Modern History* (2nd ed.).

**HANDBOOKS
TO THE MODERN WORLD**

Already published:

WESTERN EUROPE
edited by Richard Mayne

THE SOVIET UNION AND EASTERN
EUROPE
edited by George Schöpflin

THE MIDDLE EAST
edited by Michael Adams

AFRICA
edited by Sean Moroney

Forthcoming:

CANADA

THE UNITED STATES